First Conference on Machine Translation (WMT 2016)

Held at ACL 2016

Berlin, Germany
7 – 12 August 2016

ISBN: 978-1-5108-2772-1

ACL 2016

The 54th Annual Meeting of the
Association for Computational Linguistics

Proceedings of the First Conference on Machine Translation
(WMT)

August 7-12, 2016
Berlin, Germany

Production and Manufacturing by
Taberg Media Group AB
Box 94, 562 02 Taberg
Sweden

Introduction

The First Conference on Machine Translation (WMT 2016) took place on Thursday and Friday, August 11–12, 2016 in Berlin, Germany, immediately following the annual meeting of the Association for Computational Linguistics (ACL).

This is the first time WMT has been held as a conference, following 10 earlier editions where it was held as a workshop. WMT was held for the first time at HLT-NAACL 2006 in New York City, USA. In the following years the Workshop on Statistical Machine Translation was held at ACL 2007 in Prague, Czech Republic, ACL 2008, Columbus, Ohio, USA, EACL 2009 in Athens, Greece, ACL 2010 in Uppsala, Sweden, EMNLP 2011 in Edinburgh, Scotland, NAACL 2012 in Montreal, Canada, ACL 2013 in Sofia, Bulgaria, ACL 2014 in Baltimore, USA, and EMNLP 2015 in Lisbon, Portugal.

The focus of our conference was to use parallel corpora for machine translation. Recent experimentation has shown that the performance of SMT systems varies greatly with the source language. In this conference we encouraged researchers to investigate ways to improve the performance of SMT systems for diverse languages, including morphologically more complex languages, languages with partial free word order, and low-resource languages.

Prior to the conference, in addition to soliciting relevant papers for review and possible presentation, we conducted 10 shared tasks. This consisted of five translation tasks: Machine Translation of News, Machine Translation of IT domain, Biomedical Translation, Multimodal Machine Translation, and Cross-lingual Pronoun Prediction, three evaluation tasks: Metrics, Quality Estimation, and Tuning, as well as the Automatic Post-Editing and Bilingual Document Alignment tasks. Five of these tasks were run at WMT for the first time. The Machine Translation of IT domain and the Biomedical Translation tasks extend the general translation task by focusing on measuring translation quality for domain-specific applications. The Multimodal Machine Translation task includes image descriptions in multiple languages, as well as non-textual information in the form of image features to measure the quality of generating image descriptions in multiple languages. The Cross-lingual Pronoun Prediction focuses on the problem of generating the correct pronoun in translation. Finally, the Bilingual Document Alignment addresses the problem of automatically finding parallel documents in a large collection of documents to facilitate the creation of parallel corpora.

The results of all shared tasks were announced at the conference, and these proceedings also include overview papers for the shared tasks, summarizing the results, as well as providing information about the data used and any procedures that were followed in conducting or scoring the tasks. In addition, there are short papers from each participating team that describe their underlying system in greater detail.

Like in previous years, we have received a far larger number of submission than we could accept for presentation. This year we have received 42 full research paper submissions. In total, WMT 2016 featured 13 full paper oral presentations (31% acceptance rate) and 87 shared task poster presentations. The invited talk was given by Spence Green entitled "Interactive Machine Translation: From Research to Practice".

We would like to thank the members of the Program Committee for their timely reviews. We also would like to thank the participants of the shared task and all the other volunteers who helped with the evaluations.

Ondřej Bojar, Christian Buck, Rajen Chatterjee, Christian Federmann, Liane Guillou, Barry Haddow, Matthias Huck, Antonio Jimeno Yepes, Aurelie Neveol, Mariana Neves, Pavel Pecina, Martin Popel, Philipp Koehn, Christof Monz, Matteo Negri, Matt Post, Lucia Specia, Karin Verspoor, Joerg Tiedemann, and Marco Turchi

Co-Organizers

Organizers:

Ondřej Bojar (Charles University in Prague)
Christian Buck (University of Edinburgh)
Rajen Chatterjee (FBK)
Christian Federmann (MSR)
Liane Guillou (University of Edinburgh)
Barry Haddow (University of Edinburgh)
Matthias Huck (University of Edinburgh)
Antonio Jimeno Yepes (IBM Research Australia)
Aurelie Neveol (LIMSI, CNRS)
Mariana Neves (Hasso-Plattner Institute)
Pavel Pecina (Charles University in Prague)
Martin Popel (Charles University in Prague)
Philipp Koehn (University of Edinburgh / Johns Hopkins University)
Christof Monz (University of Amsterdam)
Matteo Negri (FBK)
Matt Post (Johns Hopkins University)
Lucia Specia (University of Sheffield)
Karin Verspoor (University of Melbourne)
Joerg Tiedemann (University of Helsinki)
Marco Turchi (FBK)

Invited Speaker:

Spence Green, Lilt

Program Committee:

Lars Ahrenberg (Linköping University)
Alexander Allauzen (Université Paris-Sud / LIMSI-CNRS)
Tim Anderson (Air Force Research Laboratory)
Daniel Beck (University of Sheffield)
Jose Miguel Benedi (Universitàt Politecnica de València)
Nicola Bertoldi (FBK)
Alexandra Birch (University of Edinburgh)
Arianna Bisazza (University of Amsterdam)
Graeme Blackwood (IBM Research)
Frédéric Blain (University of Sheffield)
Fabienne Braune (University of Stuttgart)
Chris Brockett (Microsoft Research)
José G. C. de Souza (eBay Inc.)
Michael Carl (Copenhagen Business School)
Marine Carpuat (University of Maryland)

Francisco Casacuberta (Universitàt Politecnica de València)
Daniel Cer (Google)
Mauro Cettolo (FBK)
Rajen Chatterjee (Fondazione Bruno Kessler)
Boxing Chen (NRC)
Colin Cherry (NRC)
David Chiang (University of Notre Dame)
Eunah Cho (Karlsruhe Institute of Technology)
Kyunghyun Cho (New York University)
Vishal Chowdhary (Microsoft)
Praveen Dakwale (University of Amsterdam)
Steve DeNeefe (SDL Language Weaver)
Michael Denkowski (Amazon.com)
Jacob Devlin (Microsoft Research)
Markus Dreyer (Amazon.com)
Nadir Durrani (QCRI)
Marc Dymetman (Xerox Research Centre Europe)
Minwei Feng (IBM Watson Group)
Andrew Finch (NICT)
Orhan Firat (Middle East Technical University)
Marina Fomicheva (Universitat Pompeu Fabra)
José A. R. Fonollosa (Universitat Politècnica de Catalunya)
Mikel Forcada (Universitat d'Alacant)
George Foster (NRC)
Alexander Fraser (Ludwig-Maximilians-Universität München)
Markus Freitag (IBM Research)
Michel Galley (Microsoft Research)
Ekaterina Garmash (University of Amsterdam)
Daniel Gildea (University of Rochester)
Kevin Gimpel (Toyota Technological Institute at Chicago)
Jesús González-Rubio (Universitat Politécnica de València)
Francisco Guzmán (Qatar Computing Research Institute)
Thanh-Le Ha (Karlsruhe Institute of Technology)
Nizar Habash (New York University Abu Dhabi)
Keith Hall (Google Research)
Greg Hanneman (Carnegie Mellon University)
Christian Hardmeier (Uppsala universitet)
Saša Hasan (Lilt Inc.)
Eva Hasler (University of Cambridge)
Yifan He (New York University)
Kenneth Heafield (University of Edinburgh)
Carmen Heger (Iconic)
John Henderson (MITRE)
Felix Hieber (Amazon Research)
Hieu Hoang (University of Edinburgh)
Stéphane Huet (Université d'Avignon)
Young-Sook Hwang (SKPlanet)

Gonzalo Iglesias (University of Cambridge)
Abe Ittycheriah (IBM)
Laura Jehl (Heidelberg University)
Doug Jones (MIT Lincoln Laboratory)
Marcin Junczys-Dowmunt (Adam Mickiewicz University, Poznań)
Roland Kuhn (National Research Council of Canada)
Shankar Kumar (Google)
Mathias Lambert (Amazon.com)
Phillippe Langlais (Université de Montréal)
William Lewis (Microsoft Research)
Lemao Liu (NICT)
Qun Liu (Dublin City University)
Shujie Liu (Microsoft Research Asia, Beijing, China)
Saab Mansour (ebay)
Daniel Marcu (ISI/USC)
Arne Mauser (Google, Inc)
Mohammed Mediani (Karlsruhe Institute of Technology)
Wolfgang Menzel (Hamburg University)
Abhijit Mishra (Indian Institute of Technology Bombay)
Yusuke Miyao (National Instutite of Informatics)
Maria Nadejde (University of Edinburgh)
Preslav Nakov (Qatar Computing Research Institute, HBKU)
Graham Neubig (Nara Institute of Science and Technology)
ThuyLinh Nguyen (Carnegie Mellon University)
Jan Niehues (Karlsruhe Institute of Technology)
Kemal Oflazer (Carnegie Mellon University - Qatar)
Tsuyoshi Okita (Ludwig-Maximilians-Universität München)
Noam Ordan (Univeristy of Haifa)
Daniel Ortiz-Martínez (Technical University of Valencia)
Pavel Pecina (Charles University in Prague)
Stephan Peitz (Apple)
Sergio Penkale (Lingo24)
Martin Popel (Charles University in Prague, Faculty of Mathematics and Physics, UFAL)
Maja Popović (Humboldt University of Berlin)
Stefan Riezler (Heidelberg University)
Johann Roturier (Symantec)
Baskaran Sankaran (IBM T.J. Watson Research Center)
Hassan Sawaf (eBay Inc.)
Rico Sennrich (University of Edinburgh)
Kashif Shah (University of Sheffield)
Michel Simard (NRC)
Patrick Simianer (Heidelberg University)
Linfeng Song (University of Rochester)
David Steele (The University of Sheffield)
Sara Stymne (Uppsala University)
Katsuhito Sudoh (NTT Communication Science Laboratories)
Aleš Tamchyna (Charles University in Prague, UFAL MFF)

Christoph Tillmann (IBM Research)
Ke M. Tran (University of Amsterdam)
Yulia Tsvetkov (Carnegie Mellon University)
Dan Tufiş (Research Institute for Artificial Intelligence, Romanian Academy)
Ferhan Ture (Comcast Labs)
Masao Utiyama (NICT)
Ashish Vaswani (University of Southern California Information Sciences Institute)
Yannick Versley (University of Heidelberg)
David Vilar (Nuance)
Martin Volk (University of Zurich)
Taro Watanabe (Google)
Bonnie Webber (University of Edinburgh)
Marion Weller-Di Marco (Universität Stuttgart)
Philip Williams (University of Edinburgh)
Hua Wu (Baidu)
Joern Wuebker (Lilt, Inc.)
Peng Xu (Google Inc.)
Wenduan Xu (Cambridge University)
François Yvon (LIMSI/CNRS)
Hao Zhang (Google)
Joy Ying Zhang (Carnegie Mellon University)
Hai Zhao (Shanghai Jiao Tong University)
Tiejun Zhao (Harbin Institute of Technology)

Table of Contents

Conference Program

Thursday, August 11, 2016

8:45–9:00   *Opening Remarks*

9:00–10:30   **Session 1: Shared Tasks Overview Presentations I**

9:00–9:20   *Shared Task: News Translation*

Findings of the 2016 Conference on Machine Translation
Ondřej Bojar, Rajen Chatterjee, Christian Federmann, Yvette Graham, Barry Haddow, Matthias Huck, Antonio Jimeno Yepes, Philipp Koehn, Varvara Logacheva, Christof Monz, Matteo Negri, Aurelie Neveol, Mariana Neves, Martin Popel, Matt Post, Raphael Rubino, Carolina Scarton, Lucia Specia, Marco Turchi, Karin Verspoor and Marcos Zampieri

9:20–9:35   *Shared Task: IT-Domain Translation*

9:35–9:50   *Shared Task: Biomedical Translation*

9:50–10:10   *Shared Task: Metrics*

Results of the WMT16 Metrics Shared Task
Ondřej Bojar, Yvette Graham, Amir Kamran and Miloš Stanojević

10:10–10:30   *Shared Task: Tuning*

Results of the WMT16 Tuning Shared Task
Bushra Jawaid, Amir Kamran, Miloš Stanojević and Ondřej Bojar

10:30-11:00   *Coffee Break*

11:00–12:30 Session 2: Shared Tasks Poster Session I

11:00–12:30 *Shared Task: News Translation*

LIMSI@WMT'16: Machine Translation of News
Alexandre Allauzen, Lauriane Aufrant, Franck Burlot, Ophélie Lacroix, Elena Knyazeva, Thomas Lavergne, Guillaume Wisniewski and François Yvon

TÜBİTAK SMT System Submission for WMT2016
Emre Bektaş, Ertugrul Yilmaz, Coskun Mermer and İlknur Durgar El-Kahlout

ParFDA for Instance Selection for Statistical Machine Translation
Ergun Bicici

Sheffield Systems for the English-Romanian WMT Translation Task
Frédéric Blain, Xingyi Song and Lucia Specia

MetaMind Neural Machine Translation System for WMT 2016
James Bradbury and Richard Socher

NYU-MILA Neural Machine Translation Systems for WMT'16
Junyoung Chung, Kyunghyun Cho and Yoshua Bengio

The JHU Machine Translation Systems for WMT 2016
Shuoyang Ding, Kevin Duh, Huda Khayrallah, Philipp Koehn and Matt Post

Yandex School of Data Analysis approach to English-Turkish translation at WMT16 News Translation Task
Anton Dvorkovich, Sergey Gubanov and Irina Galinskaya

Hybrid Morphological Segmentation for Phrase-Based Machine Translation
Stig-Arne Grönroos, Sami Virpioja and Mikko Kurimo

The AFRL-MITLL WMT16 News-Translation Task Systems
Jeremy Gwinnup, Tim Anderson, Grant Erdmann, Katherine Young, Michaeel Kazi, Elizabeth Salesky and Brian Thompson

The Karlsruhe Institute of Technology Systems for the News Translation Task in WMT 2016
Thanh-Le Ha, Eunah Cho, Jan Niehues, Mohammed Mediani, Matthias Sperber, Alexandre Allauzen and Alexander Waibel

PJAIT Systems for the WMT 2016
Krzysztof Wolk and Krzysztof Marasek

11:00–12:30 *Shared Task: IT-domain Translation*

DFKI's system for WMT16 IT-domain task, including analysis of systematic errors
Eleftherios Avramidis

ILLC-UvA Adaptation System (Scorpio) at WMT'16 IT-DOMAIN Task
Hoang Cuong, Stella Frank and Khalil Sima'an

Data Selection for IT Texts using Paragraph Vector
Mirela-Stefania Duma and Wolfgang Menzel

SMT and Hybrid systems of the QTLeap project in the WMT16 IT-task
Rosa Gaudio, Gorka Labaka, Eneko Agirre, Petya Osenova, Kiril Simov, Martin Popel, Dieke Oele, Gertjan van Noord, Luís Gomes, João António Rodrigues, Steven Neale, João Silva, Andreia Querido, Nuno Rendeiro and António Branco

JU-USAAR: A Domain Adaptive MT System
Koushik Pahari, Alapan Kuila, Santanu Pal, Sudip Kumar Naskar, Sivaji Bandyopadhyay and Josef van Genabith

Dictionary-based Domain Adaptation of MT Systems without Retraining
Rudolf Rosa, Roman Sudarikov, Michal Novák, Martin Popel and Ondřej Bojar

11:00–12:30 *Shared Task: Biomedical Translation*

English-Portuguese Biomedical Translation Task Using a Genuine Phrase-Based Statistical Machine Translation Approach
José Aires, Gabriel Lopes and Luís Gomes

The TALP–UPC Spanish–English WMT Biomedical Task: Bilingual Embeddings and Char-based Neural Language Model Rescoring in a Phrase-based System
Marta R. Costa-jussà, Cristina España-Bonet, Pranava Madhyastha, Carlos Escolano and José A. R. Fonollosa

LIMSI's Contribution to the WMT'16 Biomedical Translation Task
Julia Ive, Aurélien Max and François Yvon

IXA Biomedical Translation System at WMT16 Biomedical Translation Task
Olatz Perez-de-Viñaspre and Gorka Labaka

11:00–12:30   *Shared Task: Metrics*

CobaltF: A Fluent Metric for MT Evaluation
Marina Fomicheva, Núria Bel, Lucia Specia, Iria da Cunha and Anton Malinovskiy

DTED: Evaluation of Machine Translation Structure Using Dependency Parsing and Tree Edit Distance
Martin McCaffery and Mark-Jan Nederhof

chrF deconstructed: beta parameters and n-gram weights
Maja Popović

CharacTer: Translation Edit Rate on Character Level
Weiyue Wang, Jan-Thorsten Peter, Hendrik Rosendahl and Hermann Ney

Extract Domain-specific Paraphrase from Monolingual Corpus for Automatic Evaluation of Machine Translation
Lilin Zhang, Zhen Weng, Wenyan Xiao, Jianyi Wan, Zhiming Chen, Yiming Tan, Maoxi Li and Mingwen Wang

11:00–12:30   *Shared Task: Tuning*

Particle Swarm Optimization Submission for WMT16 Tuning Task
Viktor Kocur and Ondřej Bojar

12:30–14:00   *Lunch*

Friday, August 12, 2016

9:00–10:30   Session 5: Shared Tasks Overview Presentations II

9:00–9:20   *Shared Task: Cross-Lingual Pronoun Prediction*

Findings of the 2016 WMT Shared Task on Cross-lingual Pronoun Prediction
Liane Guillou, Christian Hardmeier, Preslav Nakov, Sara Stymne, Jörg Tiedemann,
Yannick Versley, Mauro Cettolo, Bonnie Webber and Andrei Popescu-Belis

9:20–9:45   *Shared Task: Multimodal Machine Translation and Cross-Lingual Image Description*

A Shared Task on Multimodal Machine Translation and Crosslingual Image Description
Lucia Specia, Stella Frank, Khalil Sima'an and Desmond Elliott

9:45–10:00   *Shared Task: Bilingual Document Alignment*

Findings of the WMT 2016 Bilingual Document Alignment Shared Task
Christian Buck and Philipp Koehn

10:00–10:15   *Shared Task: Automatic Post-Editing*

10:15–10:30   *Shared Task: Quality Estimation*

10:30-11:00   *Coffee Break*

11:00–12:30   Session 6: Shared Tasks Poster Session II

11:00–12:30   *Shared Task: Cross-Lingual Pronoun Prediction*

Cross-lingual Pronoun Prediction with Linguistically Informed Features
Rachel Bawden

The Kyoto University Cross-Lingual Pronoun Translation System
Raj Dabre, Yevgeniy Puzikov, Fabien Cromieres and Sadao Kurohashi

Pronoun Prediction with Latent Anaphora Resolution
Christian Hardmeier

It-disambiguation and source-aware language models for cross-lingual pronoun prediction
Sharid Loáiciga, Liane Guillou and Christian Hardmeier

Pronoun Language Model and Grammatical Heuristics for Aiding Pronoun Prediction
Ngoc Quang Luong and Andrei Popescu-Belis

Cross-Lingual Pronoun Prediction with Deep Recurrent Neural Networks
Juhani Luotolahti, Jenna Kanerva and Filip Ginter

Pronoun Prediction with Linguistic Features and Example Weighing
Michal Novák

Feature Exploration for Cross-Lingual Pronoun Prediction
Sara Stymne

A Linear Baseline Classifier for Cross-Lingual Pronoun Prediction
Jörg Tiedemann

Cross-lingual Pronoun Prediction for English, French and German with Maximum Entropy Classification
Dominikus Wetzel

11:00–12:30   *Shared Task: Multimodal Machine Translation and Cross-Lingual Image Description*

BAD LUC@WMT 2016: a Bilingual Document Alignment Platform Based on Lucene
Laurent Jakubina and Phillippe Langlais

Using Term Position Similarity and Language Modeling for Bilingual Document Alignment
Thanh Le, Hoa Trong Vu, Jonathan Oberländer and Ondřej Bojar

The ADAPT Bilingual Document Alignment system at WMT16
Pintu Lohar, Haithem Afli, Chao-Hong Liu and Andy Way

WMT2016: A Hybrid Approach to Bilingual Document Alignment
Sainik Mahata, Dipankar Das and Santanu Pal

English-French Document Alignment Based on Keywords and Statistical Translation
Marek Medved', Miloš Jakubícek and Vojtech Kovár

The ILSP/ARC submission to the WMT 2016 Bilingual Document Alignment Shared Task
Vassilis Papavassiliou, Prokopis Prokopidis and Stelios Piperidis

Word Clustering Approach to Bilingual Document Alignment (WMT 2016 Shared Task)
Vadim Shchukin, Dmitry Khristich and Irina Galinskaya

11:00–12:30 *Shared Task: Automatic Post-Editing*

The FBK Participation in the WMT 2016 Automatic Post-editing Shared Task
Rajen Chatterjee, José G. C. de Souza, Matteo Negri and Marco Turchi

Log-linear Combinations of Monolingual and Bilingual Neural Machine Translation Models for Automatic Post-Editing
Marcin Junczys-Dowmunt and Roman Grundkiewicz

USAAR: An Operation Sequential Model for Automatic Statistical Post-Editing
Santanu Pal, Marcos Zampieri and Josef van Genabith

11:00–12:30 *Shared Task: Quality Estimation*

Bilingual Embeddings and Word Alignments for Translation Quality Estimation
Amal Abdelsalam, Ondřej Bojar and Samhaa El-Beltagy

Cross-language Projection of Dependency Trees with Constrained Partial Parsing for Tree-to-Tree Machine Translation

Yu Shen[1], **Chenhui Chu**[2]*, **Fabien Cromieres**[2] and **Sadao Kurohashi**[1]
[1]Graduate School of Informatics, Kyoto University
[2]Japan Science and Technology Agency
{shen-yu,kuro}@nlp.ist.i.kyoto-u.ac.jp {chu,fabien}@pa.jst.jp

Abstract

Tree-to-tree machine translation (MT) that utilizes syntactic parse trees on both source and target sides suffers from the non-isomorphism of the parse trees due to parsing errors and the difference of annotation criterion between the two languages. In this paper, we present a method that projects dependency parse trees from the language side that has a high quality parser, to the side that has a low quality parser, to improve the isomorphism of the parse trees. We first project a part of the dependencies with high confidence to make a partial parse tree, and then complement the remaining dependencies with partial parsing constrained by the already projected dependencies. MT experiments verify the effectiveness of our proposed method.

1 Introduction

According to how syntactic parse trees are used in machine translation (MT), there are 4 types of MT approaches: string-to-string that does not use parse trees (Chiang, 2005; Koehn et al., 2007), string-to-tree that uses parse trees on the target side (Galley et al., 2006; Shen et al., 2008), tree-to-string that uses parse trees on the source side (Quirk et al., 2005; Liu et al., 2006; Mi and Huang, 2008), and tree-to-tree that uses parse trees on both sides (Zhang et al., 2008; Richardson et al., 2015). Intuitively, the tree-to-tree approach seems to be the most appropriate. The reason is that it could preserve the structure information on both sides, which leads to fluent and accurate translations.

In practice, however, good quality parsers on both the source and target sides are difficult to ac-

quire. In many cases, the parsing quality of one side is much higher than that of the other side, because the higher quality side has a well annotated treebank or is linguistically easier to parse. For example, in the case of Japanese-Chinese MT that we study in this paper, the head-final characteristic of Japanese (Isozaki et al., 2010) makes the dependency parsing for Japanese much easier than that of Chinese. Currently, the dependency parsing accuracy of Japanese is over 90% (Kawahara and Kurohashi, 2006), while the Chinese parsing accuracy is less than 80% (Shen et al., 2012). Another problem is the annotation criterion difference of the treebanks in different languages, which are used for training the parsers. For example, the dependency annotations of noun phrases and coordination could be different among different languages. For example, in Japanese, noun phrases and coordination are annotated as modifier-head dependencies (Kawahara and Kurohashi, 2006), while in Chinese they are annotated as sibling dependencies (Shen et al., 2012). These two problems lead to the parse difference between the source and target parse trees, which affects the translation rule extraction in tree-to-tree MT that requires the isomorphism of the parse trees. This extremely limits the translation quality of tree-to-tree MT.

In this paper, we present an approach that projects dependency trees from a high quality (HQ) parser to a low quality (LQ) parser using alignment information. The projection could reduce the parsing errors on the LQ side, and address the annotation criterion difference problem. This can make the LQ trees isomorphic to the HQ trees, which can benefit the translation rule extraction in tree-to-tree MT, and thus improve the MT performance. The idea of cross-language projection of parse trees has been proposed previously, e.g., (Ganchev et al., 2009; Jiang et al., 2010; Goto

---

*Corresponding author.

Proceedings of the First Conference on Machine Translation, Volume 1: Research Papers, pages 1–11,
Berlin, Germany, August 11-12, 2016. ©2016 Association for Computational Linguistics

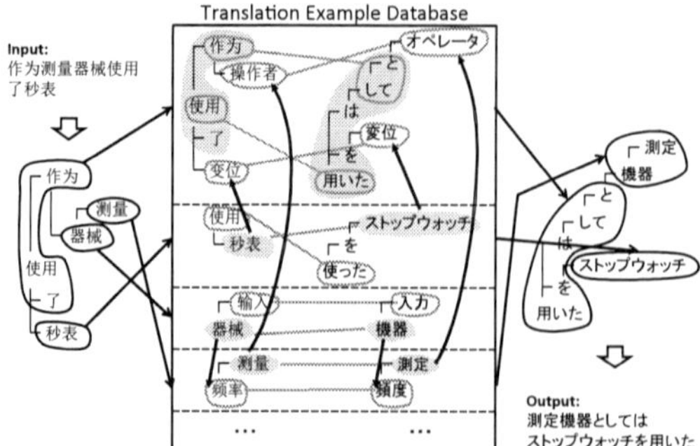

Fig. 1: An example of the KyotoEBMT system on Chinese-to-Japanese translation.

et al., 2015). However, few studies have been conducted in the context of dependency based tree-to-tree MT, which is the setting of this paper.

In addition, we propose a novel constrained partial parsing method to address the word alignment problems such as unaligned words and alignment errors in projection. In detail, we first apply a partial projection step to project a part of the dependencies with high confidence judged by the alignment information and a projectivity criterion. We thus obtain a projected "partial tree." We then find the missing dependencies from this partial tree by applying a "partial parsing" method: we apply a parser to find the missing dependencies subject to respecting the projected dependencies, so that we obtain a full dependency tree. Initially, the LQ parser is used for the partial parsing process. Once the entire projection process has been finished, we select a part of the projected trees based on the dependency projection ratio of the partial projection step, and re-train a parser for the LQ side. This re-trained parser tends to be more isomorphic to the HQ parser, and thus we again apply it for the partial parsing process.

We conduct experiments with an open source dependency based tree-to-tree MT system KyotoEBMT[1] (Richardson et al., 2015) on the Japanese-Chinese language pair. Because of the improvement of the isomorphism of the source and target parse trees by our proposed method, we achieve significant MT performance improvements on both Japanese-to-Chinese and Chinese-to-Japanese translation directions.

2 The Difficulties of Tree-to-Tree MT
2.1 Overview of the KyotoEBMT System

This study is conducted on the KyotoEBMT system (Richardson et al., 2015), which is a represen-

[1] http://nlp.ist.i.kyoto-u.ac.jp/EN/index.php?KyotoEBMT

tative dependency based tree-to-tree MT system. Figure 1 shows an overview of the KyotoEBMT system on Chinese-to-Japanese translation. The translation example database is automatically constructed from a parallel training corpus by means of a discriminative alignment model (Riesa et al., 2011). It contains "examples" that form the hypotheses to be combined during decoding. Note that both source and target sides of all the examples are stored in dependency trees. An input sentence is also parsed and transformed into a dependency tree. For all the subtrees in the input dependency tree, matching hypotheses are searched in the example database. This step is the most time consuming part, and a fast subtree retrieval method (Cromieres and Kurohashi, 2011) is used. There are many available hypotheses for one subtree, and also, there are many possible hypothesis combinations. The best combination is detected by a lattice-based decoder, which optimizes a log-linear model (Cromieres and Kurohashi, 2014). In the example in Figure 1, four hypotheses are used. They are combined and produce an output dependency tree, which is the final translation. For more details of the system, please refer to (Richardson et al., 2015).

2.2 The Translation Example Extraction Problem

One advantage of the KyotoEBMT system is that it can handle examples that are discontinuous as a word sequence but continuous structurally, because of the usage of both source and target parse trees. In Figure 2, for example, the translation example of "26-31:類似することを示唆する/4:表明 14:类似 (show the similarity)" and "0-2:このことは30-35:示唆するものと思われる/0-4:认为这一现象表明 (I think that this phenomenon shows)" can be extracted by the KyotoEBMT system, because they are continuous in the parse trees. However, in phrase based MT (Koehn et al., 2007), both of these two translation examples could not be extracted. The reason for this is that "4:表明 (show)" and "14:类似 (similarity)" are discontinuous in the Chinese sentence; similarly, "0-2:このことは (this phenomenon)" and "30-35:示唆するものと思われる (I think that shows)" are discontinuous in the Japanese sentence.

On the other hand, it also adds the constraint that a translation example has to share the same structure on the parse trees to guarantee the quality

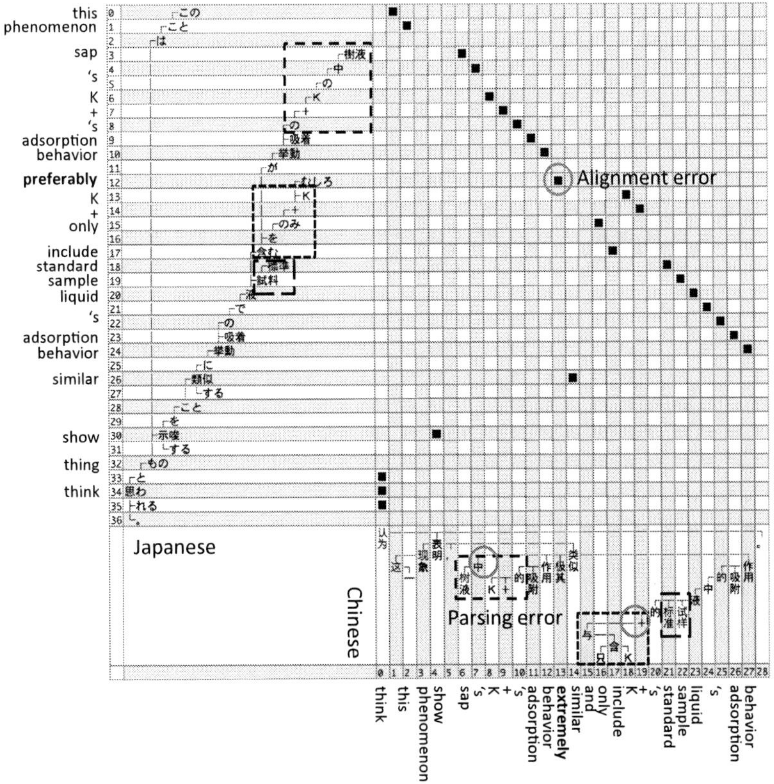

Fig. 2: A motivated example that shows a word aligned Japanese-Chinese parse tree pair, where the solid black boxes show the word alignments.

of the extracted examples. This could be a problem because of two reasons. The main reason is parsing error. In Figure 2, for example, because of the parsing errors in the Chinese parse tree, the translation examples of "3-8:樹液中のＫ＋の/6-10:树液中Ｋ＋的 (sap's K+)," and "13-17:Ｋ＋のみを含む/16-19:只含Ｋ＋ (only include K+)" could not be extracted. The other reason is the annotation criterion difference. In Figure 2, for example, the translation example of "18:標準 19:試料/21:标准 22:试样(standard sample)" could not be extracted, though both of the parses are correct. In Japanese this kind of noun phrase structure is annotated as the modifier-head, while in Chinese it is annotated as siblings depending on the last word.

One possible solution to address the above problem is to loosen the constraint for translation example extraction. For example, to extract the "18:標準 19:試料/21:标准 22:试样(standard sample)" example caused by the annotation criterion difference, we might allow the extraction of examples that are modifier-head and sibling subtrees on the source and target sides, respectively. However,

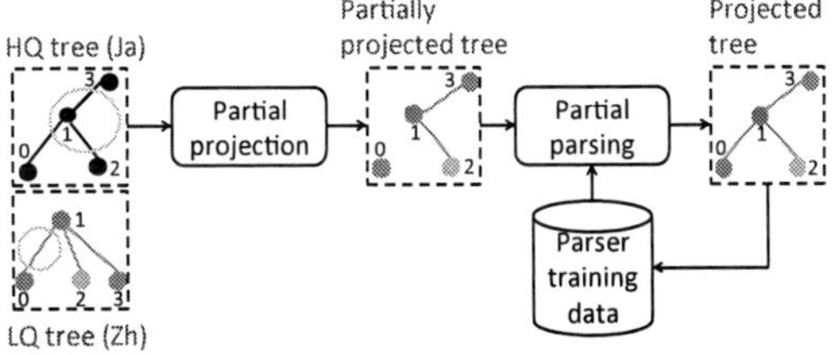

Fig. 3: An overview of our constrained partial parsing based projection method.

firstly, even the loosening in this degree could also lead to other noisy translation examples; secondly, what kind of loosening is required for the parse error case is unclear, because the types of parse errors are diverse. Therefore, instead of loosening the constraint, we choose the cross-lingual projection approach to address the problem.

3 Projection of Dependency Trees with Constrained Partial Parsing

Figure 3 is an overview of our proposed constrained partial parsing method. Firstly, we apply a partial projection process to project a part of the dependencies from the HQ tree using the HQ tree, word alignment information and a projectivity criterion. Note that the word alignment information is omitted in Figure 3 for simplification. In Figure 3, the circled part in the HQ tree is projected. Next, we apply partial parsing to complement the other dependencies in the partially projected tree using the LQ parser. In Figure 3, as the LQ parser could parse the circled part in the original LQ tree correctly, it also complements the dependencies for the partially projected tree correctly. Once we obtained the projected trees, we select a part of the highly confident projected trees as training data to re-train the LQ parser. Finally, we apply the re-trained LQ parser for the partial parsing process, which further improves the quality of projection.

In the remaining of this section, we describe the details of partial projection, partial parsing, and re-training of the LQ parser in Section 3.1, 3.2, and 3.3 respectively.

3.1 Partial Projection

3.1.1 Direct Mapping for Dependency Tree Projection

We first present a direct mapping method for dependency tree projection using word alignment, which can be formalized as below.

Given a parallel sentence pair (S, T), where $S = s_1...s_i...s_n$, and $T = t_1...t_j...t_m$ are sentences of the HQ and LQ sides, respectively; s_i and t_j denote the word index (which also denotes the node index in the dependency tree) in the corresponding sentences. We have a dependency tree for S denoted as $Tree_S = \{(s_i, s_k)...\}$ that is composed of a set of dependencies, where (s_i, s_k) means that the word s_i is dependent on the word s_k. We also have an alignment set $A = \{a(s_i, t_j)...\}$ from S to T, where $a(s_i, t_j)$ means that the HQ word s_i is aligned to the LQ word t_j. The new LQ parse tree $Tree_T^{new}$ is projected from $Tree_S$. We first perform the following preprocessing for the unaligned HQ words.

- *unaligned words (HQ side)*: If s_i is an unaligned word, link the dependencies around s_i. More specifically, if s_i is unaligned, and $(s_h, s_i) \in Tree_S$, $(s_i, s_k) \in Tree_S$, we add (s_h, s_k) to $Tree_S$, and discard (s_h, s_i) and (s_i, s_k) from $Tree_S$. This preprocess can make two distinct words separated by unaligned words be a modifier-head pair. For example, in Figure 2, because "32:もの

(thing)" is an unaligned word, we add (30:示唆 (show), 33:と (and)) to $Tree_S$.

We then process each source node s_i in $Tree_S$ in a top-down manner (from the root node to the leaf node) by applying the following rules divided by the alignment types.

- *one to one alignment*: If s_i aligns to a unique t_j, s_k aligns to a unique t_l, and $(s_i, s_k) \in Tree_S$, add (t_j, t_l) to $Tree_T^{new}$. For example, in Figure 2, the Japanese dependency (0:この (this), 1:こと (phenomenon)) is projected to the Chinese side as (1:这2:一 (this)) by applying this rule.

- *many to one alignment*: If $(s_i, s_k, ...)$ aligns to t_j, we take the head s_r (e.g., s_k) from $(s_i, s_k, ...)$ as the representative, and then perform the same process as in the one to one alignment case. For example, in Figure 2, a(33:と 34:思わ 35:れる (think), 0:认为(think)) is a many to one alignment, and we select the head "34:思わ" as the representative.

- *one to many alignment*: If s_i aligns to several words $(t_j, t_l, ...)$, similar to the many to one alignment case, we take the head t_r (e.g., t_j) from $(t_j, t_l, ...)$ based on the original LQ tree as the representative, and then perform the same process as in the one to one alignment case for s_i and t_r.

- *many to many alignment*: Reduce this to one-to-many and many-to-one cases, i.e., select the representatives for both sides, and then perform the same process as in the one to one alignment case.

3.1.2 Partial Projection with Direct Mapping

There are several cases that the direct mapping method could not deal with:

1. *the other nodes in the one to many alignment case*: For the nodes (e.g., t_l) (in $(t_j, t_l, ...)$ that align to one word s_i) other than the representative t_r, there are no clues to determine their dependencies during the projection.

2. *unaligned words (LQ side)*: If t_j is an unaligned word, there are also no clues for the projection. For example, in Figure 2, because the word Chinese "3:现象 (phenomenon)",

"15:与 (and)" and "20:的 ('s)" are unaligned words, we cannot determine their dependencies by projection.

3. *alignment errors*: Because the direct mapping method highly depends on word alignments, erroneous word alignments would lead to wrong projected dependency results. For example, in Figure 2, the Japanese word "12:むしろ (preferably)" is incorrectly aligned to the Chinese word "13:及其 (extremely)"; this erroneous alignment would project the Japanese dependency (12:むしろ (preferably), 14:+) to the Chinese side, leading to a projected dependency of (13:及其 (extremely), 19:+), which is obviously incorrect. Alignment errors could happen due to many factors, one of which is translation shift. The erroneous alignment in Figure 2 is caused by this.

Because of the existence of the above cases, we only apply the direct mapping method for partial projection. For the (1) and (2) cases, we leave the dependencies for these words as null. For the (3) case, we propose a projectivity criterion to detect the alignment error, and again leave the dependencies as null. Note that all of these three cases are processed during the top-down projection process.

3.1.3 Adding a Projectivity Criterion to the Projection Process

Projectivity is a property of dependency parsing, which informally means that there should not be crossing arcs in a dependency tree (Kubler et al., 2009). For example, $Tree_T^{new} = \{(0,2)(1,3)(2,3)(3,-1)\}$ (-1 denotes the root) is not projective, because the arc of modifier-head pair (0,2) and that of modifier-head pair (1,3) is crossed. We use the projectivity property to detect alignment errors during the top-down projection process. Suppose that by processing the HQ tree from the root, we already have a partially projected LQ subtree. Next, we want to project a new dependency in the HQ tree to the LQ side. If adding this newly projected dependency to the partially projected subtree leads to non-projectivity,[2] we give up this projection and leave the dependency as null.

Many alignment errors can be detected by the property of projectivity. For example, in Figure

---

[2] Note that not all non-projectivites are caused by alignment errors; a few of them are also due to translation shift.

2, if we use the erroneous alignment a(12:むしろ (preferably), 13:及其 (extremely)) to project the Japanese dependency (12:むしろ (preferably), 14:+) to the Chinese side, we obtain the dependency of (13:及其 (extremely), 19:+). Before the projection for the node "12:むしろ (preferably)", because the node "24: 挙動 (behavior)" is an ancestor of this node in the Japanese tree, it has been projected. The dependency (24: 挙動 (behavior), 26:類似 (similar)) has been projected to the Chinese side, leading the dependency of (27:作用 (behavior), 14:类似 (similar)). (13:及其 (extremely), 19:+) and (27:作用 (behavior), 14:类似 (similar)) lead to non-projectivity. Therefore, we leave the dependency for "13:及其 (extremely)" as null.

3.2 Partial Parsing

After the partial projection step, we obtain partial projected trees, with null dependencies discussed in Section 3.1.2. We then perform partial parsing to complement these null dependencies. Before the description of the partial parsing method, we first review the formalism of dependency parsing used in many previous studies such as (Kubler et al., 2009; Shen et al., 2012):

$$Y^* = argmax_{Y \in \Phi(X)} score(Y, X) \qquad (1)$$

where $X = x_1...x_i...x_n$ is the input sentence, Y is a candidate tree, $\Phi(X)$ is a set of all possible dependency trees over X. Y can be denoted as $Y = \{(m, h) : 0 \le m \le n, 0 \le h \le n\}$, where (m, h) is a dependency from the modifier x_m to the head x_h. The problem of dependency parsing is to search the best tree from $\Phi(X)$ that maximizes the score function $score(Y, X)$. The score function can be factorized as the summation of the scores of its factors (subtrees):

$$score(Y, X) = \sum_{F \in Y} score(F, X) \qquad (2)$$

The score function for each factor is denoted as the inner product of a feature and a weight vector:

$$score(F, X) = w \cdot f(F, X) \qquad (3)$$

The weight vector can be learnt by e.g., the averaged structured perceptron algorithm (Collins, 2002) on an annotated treebank. During parsing, the parser would utilize the learnt weight vector to determine the best parse tree.

In our partial parsing method, we aim to keep the dependencies in partial projected trees, while complement the null dependencies to construct a projective tree. To realize this, we set extremely high scores to the projected dependencies to maximize the $score(F, X)$ for these dependencies, while for the null dependencies we set relatively small scores. Doing so, the parser would search the best tree that respects the partial projected dependencies. In our experiments, we used the projective second order graph based dependency parser (Shen et al., 2012). We set the initial dependency scores for the projected dependencies to $1e12$, and 0 to the null dependencies.

3.3 Re-train a New Low Quality Side Parser

Re-training a new LQ parser on the projected trees is necessary for two reasons. Initially, we use the original LQ parser for the partial parsing process, because we do not have a better choice; due to the low accuracy and the annotation criterion difference problem of the LQ parser, we have the risk that it will produce unsatisfying parsing results, especially for the trees with a low ratio of dependencies being projected. Secondly, if we perform the LQ-to-HQ direction MT, we should make the parsed trees of the input sentences isomorphic to the projected trees. Re-training a new LQ parser on the projected trees could address both of these two problems. As the re-trained parser tend to be more isomorphic to the HQ parser, it could be more effective for the partial parsing process, and could be applied for parsing the input sentences for the LQ-to-HQ direction MT task.

Therefore, after the entire projection process, we select a part of the projected trees, and re-train a parser for the LQ side. How to select the projected trees for training the new LQ parser is an open question. The main question is how to take the balance of the quality and quantity of the projected trees. Currently, the selection criterion is empirical based on the ratio of dependencies projected by the partial projection process in a tree, defined by

$$ratio = \frac{\#projected\_dependencies}{\#all\_dependencies} \quad (4)$$

The motivation behind this is that the more dependencies projected by the partial projection in a tree, the more isomorphic would the projected tree be as the HQ tree, and the less affect would be introduced by the original LQ parser during the partial parsing process. We set a threshold, and use the trees with the ratio higher than the threshold for training the parser. We tried several thresholds in our preliminary experiments, and selected the best threshold of 0.78 (170k trees) based on the MT performance.[3]

4 Experiments

We conducted Japanese-Chinese MT experiments to verify the effectiveness of our constrained partial parsing based projection method.

4.1 Settings

We conducted experiments on the scientific domain MT task on the Japanese-Chinese paper excerpt corpus (ASPEC-JC),[4] which is one subtask of the workshop on Asian translation (WAT)[5] (Nakazawa et al., 2015). The ASPEC-JC task uses 672,315, 2,090, and 2,107 sentences for training, development, and testing, respectively. We used the tree-to-tree MT system KyotoEBMT[6] (Richardson et al., 2015) for all of our MT experiments. For Chinese, we used the Chinese analyzing tool KyotoMorph[7] proposed by Shen et al. (2014) for segmentation and part-of-speech (POS) tagging, and the SKP parser[8] (Shen et al., 2012) for parsing. As the baseline Chinese parser, we trained SKP with the Penn Chinese treebank version 5 (CTB5)[9] containing 18k sentences in news domain, and an in-house scientific domain treebank of 10k sentences. For Japanese, we used JUMAN[10] (Kurohashi et al., 1994) for morphological analyzing, and the KNP parser for parsing[11] (Kawahara and Kurohashi, 2006). We trained two 5-gram language models for Chinese and Japanese, respectively, on the training data of the ASPEC corpus using the KenLM toolkit[12] with interpolated Kneser-Ney discounting, and used them for all the experiments. In all of our experiments, we used the discriminative alignment model Nile[13] (Riesa et al., 2011) for word alignment; tuning was performed by the k-best batch

---

[3] The average partial projection ratio was 0.70.
[4] http://lotus.kuee.kyoto-u.ac.jp/ASPEC/
[5] http://orchid.kuee.kyoto-u.ac.jp/WAT/
[6] http://nlp.ist.i.kyoto-u.ac.jp/EN/index.php?KyotoEBMT)
[7] https://bitbucket.org/msmoshen/kyotomorph-beta
[8] https://bitbucket.org/msmoshen/skp-beta
[9] https://catalog.ldc.upenn.edu/LDC2005T01
[10] http://nlp.ist.i.kyoto-u.ac.jp/EN/index.php?JUMAN
[11] http://nlp.ist.i.kyoto-u.ac.jp/EN/index.php?KNP
[12] https://github.com/kpu/kenlm/
[13] https://github.com/neubig/nile

MIRA (Cherry and Foster, 2012) with 10 iterations, and it was re-run for every experiment.

Note that, in our task, Japanese is the HQ parser side, and Chinese is the LQ parser side, because of the parsing accuracy difference (90% v.s. 80%). Therefore, in our experiments, we projected the Japanese parse trees to Chinese. We compared the MT performance of our proposed projection method with the baseline Chinese parser. For Japanese-to-Chinese MT experiments, we compared the MT results of the Chinese training data parsed by the baseline parsed, to those of the projected trees. For Chinese-to-Japanese MT, we also re-parsed the development and test Chinese sentences using the SKP model trained on the projected Chinese trees, for the comparison.

4.2 MT Results

Table 1 shows the results, where KyotoEBMT is the baseline system that used the Chinese parser trained on CTB5; Baseline partial parsing denotes the projection systems that used the Chinese parser trained on CTB5 for the partial parsing process; Re-trained partial parsing denotes the systems that used the Chinese parser re-trained on the projected trees for the partial parsing process. For reference, we also show the MT performance of the phrase based, string-to-tree, and tree-to-string systems, which are based on the open-source GIZA++/Moses pipeline (Koehn et al., 2007). Note that in all of the Moses, string-to-tree, and tree-to-string settings, Japanese is always in the string format, and Chinese is parsed by the Berkeley parser[14] (Petrov and Klein, 2007).[15] The significance tests were performed using the bootstrap resampling method (Koehn, 2004).

We can see that, the Baseline KyotoEBMT system outperforms the Moses, string-to-tree, and tree-to-string systems, which verifies the effectiveness of the tree-to-tree approach. The performance difference of KyotoEBMT against the other three MT approaches on the Ja-to-Zh direction is much larger than those of the Zh-to-Ja direction. The reason for this is that KyotoEBMT is much more sensitive to the parsing accuracy on the source side, because the source tree is utilized in the ordering of the final translation. Therefore using Chinese as the source side limits the effectiveness

---

System	Ja-to-Zh	Zh-to-Ja
Moses phrase based	27.25	33.94
Moses string-to-tree	26.20	N/A
Moses tree-to-string	N/A	33.49
Baseline KyotoEBMT	29.33	34.73
Baseline partial parsing	30.12†	35.84†
Re-trained partial parsing	**30.28**†	**36.18**†‡

Tab. 1: BLEU scores for ASPEC Ja-to-Zh and Zh-to-Ja ("†," and "‡" indicate that the result is significantly better than "Baseline KyotoEBMT" and "Baseline partial parsing" at $p < 0.01$, respectively).

System	Ja-to-Zh	Zh-to-Ja
Baseline KyotoEBMT	13.13M	8.43M
Baseline partial parsing	15.69M	9.88M
Re-trained partial parsing	15.69M	9.90M

Tab. 2: Number of hypotheses for the test sentences.

of the KyotoEBMT system. Baseline partial parsing performs significantly better than the Baseline KyotoEBMT, and Re-trained partial parsing further improves the performance significantly. We also observe slightly more improvement on the Zh-to-Ja direction than the Ja-to-Zh direction. The reason is similar to the one above that in Zh-to-Ja task, we not only improve the translation example extraction, but also the quality of the input trees.

To further understand the reason for the MT improvement, we investigated the number of hypotheses for the test sentences. The number of hypotheses for a test sentence is the number all the matching hypotheses in the example database for all the subtrees in the input dependency structure of the test sentence (refer to Section 2.1). The entire number of hypotheses for all the test sentences of different systems are shown in table 2. We can see that the number of hypotheses for the partial parsing systems is greatly larger than the baseline KyotoEBMT system. The reason for this is that our projection method significantly increased the isomorphism of the source and target trees in the training corpus, making more translation examples being extractable. More hypotheses are potentially to improve the final MT performance.

In addition, we investigated the translation results of the Baseline KyotoEBMT and Re-trained partial parsing systems. We found that there are

---

[14] https://github.com/slavpetrov/berkeleyparser

[15] We show the MT performance of Moses that only parsed the Chinese data, because these were the baseline systems of WAT.

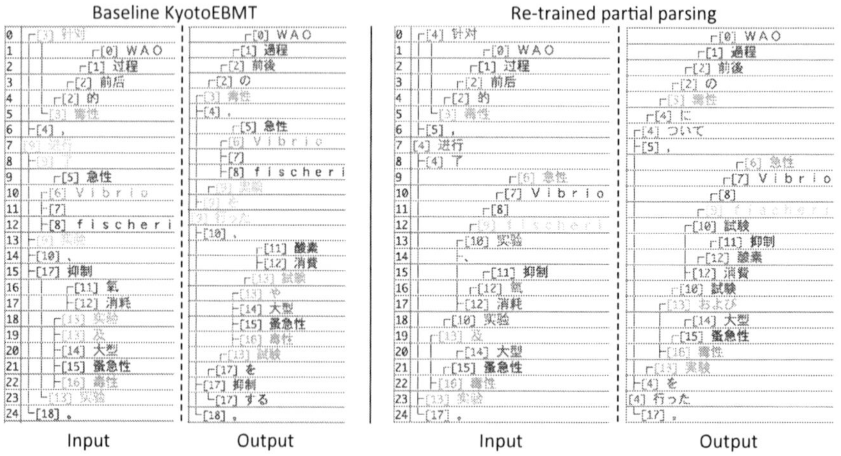

Fig. 4: An improved example of Zh-to-Ja translation (The subtrees in corresponding IDs/colors in the input and output dependency trees show the translation examples being used during translation).

three reasons that lead to the improvement. We explain these reasons through an improved example of Zh-to-Ja translation shown in Figure 4. The first reason is the improvement of the input parse tree. There is a crucial parsing error in the input tree of the Baseline KyotoEBMT system. The KyotoMorph incorrectly assigned a wrong POS tag "VV (verb)" for the word "15:抑制 (inhibition)", which should be "NN (noun)" in fact. This leads to this word be the head of the whole following noun phrase. Using this erroneous input parse tree, this word is also translated into the head of the entire noun phrase. Our Re-trained partial parsing correctly parsed the word "15:抑制 (inhibition)" as a part of the noun phrase "15-18:抑制氧消耗实验(inhibition of oxygen consumption test)", leading to the correct translation. Although the Re-trained partial parsing could not correct the wrong POS tag of the word, because we also used this kind of data to train the parser, it successfully parsed this sentence. The second reason is the increase of translation hypotheses. The number of hypotheses for the Baseline KyotoEBMT system is 2,447, while the number of hypotheses of the Re-trained partial parsing system is 3,311. The number of hypotheses for "0:针对...7:进行 8:了 (about...performed)" increased from 52 to 176 by the Re-trained partial parsing system, which improved the translation. The third reason is the isomorphism of the input and output target dependency trees. Note that the noun phrases "15-18: 抑制氧消耗实验(inhibition of oxygen consumption test)" and "20-23:大型蚤急性毒性实验(large-

scale flea acute toxicity test)" are parsed as siblings in the Baseline KyotoEBMT system, while in our Re-trained partial parsing model they are parsed as modifier-head dependencies, which are isomorphic to the Japanese parse tree. One unsatisfying point is that "21:蚤急性 (flea acute)" is an unknown word, which is a difficult technical term that could not be translated by both of the two systems.

5 Related Work

There are many previous studies that propose many methods to address the difficulties in projecting the parse trees from a resource rich language (e.g., English) to a low resource language, to improve the parsing accuracy of the low resource language. The difficulties in projection can be mainly divided into two categories: word alignment errors and annotation criterion difference (Ganchev et al., 2009).

To address the word alignment error problem, several studies have proposed to train a target parser on high confidence partially projected trees. Ganchev et al. (2009) presented a partial projection method with constraints such as language-specific annotation rules. They then trained a target parser using the partially projected trees. Spreyer and Kuhn (2009) proposed a similar method that trains both graph-based and transition-based dependency parsers on the partially projected trees. Rasooli and Collins (2015) proposed a method to train a target parser on "dense" projected trees. The "dense" projected trees might only contain a part of dependencies over a threshold. Our proposed method differs from the previous studies in several aspects: we propose the use of the projectivity criterion for partial projection; we utilize the original target parser and propose a constrained partial parsing algorithm; we re-train a target parser on the full trees generated by the partial parsing.

To address the annotation criterion difference problem in projection, Hwa et al. (2005) firstly projected the dependency parse trees, and then applied post projection transformations based on manually created rules. Jiang et al. (2011) presented a method that tolerates the syntactic non-isomorphism between languages. This allows the projected parse trees do not have to follow the annotation criterion of the source parse trees. Our proposed method does not adjust the annotation criterion difference between the source and the projected trees, because in our tree-to-tree MT task, we prefer isomorphic trees.

Only a few studies have been conducted to improve MT performance via projection. For string-to-string MT (Koehn et al., 2007), Goto et al. (2015) proposed a pre-ordering method that projects target side constituency trees to the source side, and then generates pre-ordering rules based on the projected trees. For tree-to-string MT, Jiang et al. (2010) combined projection and supervised constituency parsing by guiding the parsing procedure of the supervised parser with the projected parser. They showed that the guided parser achieved comparable MT results on a tree-to-string system (Liu et al., 2006), compared to a normal supervised parser trained on thousands of CTB trees. For tree-to-tree MT (Richardson et al., 2015), Shen et al. (2015) proposed a naive projection method. They complemented the remaining dependencies for a partially projected tree with a backtracking method. Namely, they reused the dependencies in the original target tree for the complement without considering the partially projected dependencies. In contrast, in this paper we propose partial parsing for the complement, in which we search for the best parse tree by taking account of the partially projected dependencies.

6   Conclusion

In this paper, we proposed a constrained partial parsing method for projection to address the non-isomorphic parse tree problem in a dependency based tree-to-tree MT system. Experiments verified the effectiveness of our proposed method. As future work, firstly, we plan to design a better way for selecting the projected trees for re-training the LQ parser. Secondly, we plan to perform the partial parsing in several iterations. Finally, we plan to conduct experiments on more language pairs to show the language-dependence of our proposed method.

Acknowledgments

We especially thank to Dr. Mo Shen for the insightful discussion of the constrained partial parsing method with us.

References

Colin Cherry and George Foster. 2012. Batch tuning strategies for statistical machine translation. In *Proceedings of the 2012 Conference of the North American Chapter of the Association for Computational Linguistics: Human Language Technologies*, pages 427–436, Montréal, Canada, June. Association for Computational Linguistics.

David Chiang. 2005. A hierarchical phrase-based model for statistical machine translation. In *Proceedings of the 43rd Annual Meeting of the Association for Computational Linguistics (ACL'05)*, pages 263–270, Ann Arbor, Michigan, June. Association for Computational Linguistics.

Michael Collins. 2002. Discriminative training methods for hidden markov models: Theory and experiments with perceptron algorithms. In *Proceedings of the 2002 Conference on Empirical Methods in Natural Language Processing*, pages 1–8. Association for Computational Linguistics, July.

Fabien Cromieres and Sadao Kurohashi. 2011. Efficient retrieval of tree translation examples for syntax-based machine translation. In *Proceedings of the 2011 Conference on Empirical Methods in Natural Language Processing*, pages 508–518, Edinburgh, Scotland, UK., July. Association for Computational Linguistics.

Fabien Cromieres and Sadao Kurohashi. 2014. Translation rules with right-hand side lattices. In *Proceedings of the 2014 Conference on Empirical Methods in Natural Language Processing (EMNLP)*, pages 577–588, Doha, Qatar, October. Association for Computational Linguistics.

Michel Galley, Jonathan Graehl, Kevin Knight, Daniel Marcu, Steve DeNeefe, Wei Wang, and Ignacio Thayer. 2006. Scalable inference and training of context-rich syntactic translation models. In *Proceedings of the 21st International Conference on*

Computational Linguistics and 44th Annual Meeting of the Association for Computational Linguistics, pages 961–968, Sydney, Australia, July. Association for Computational Linguistics.

Kuzman Ganchev, Jennifer Gillenwater, and Ben Taskar. 2009. Dependency grammar induction via bitext projection constraints. In *Proceedings of the Joint Conference of the 47th Annual Meeting of the ACL and the 4th International Joint Conference on Natural Language Processing of the AFNLP*, pages 369–377, Suntec, Singapore, August. Association for Computational Linguistics.

Isao Goto, Masao Utiyama, Eiichiro Sumita, and Sadao Kurohashi. 2015. Preordering using a target-language parser via cross-language syntactic projection for statistical machine translation. *ACM Trans. Asian Low-Resour. Lang. Inf. Process.*, 14(3):13:1–13:23, June.

Rebecca Hwa, Philip Resnik, Amy Weinberg, Clara Cabezas, and Okan Kolak. 2005. Bootstrapping parsers via syntactic projection across parallel texts. *Natural language engineering*, 11(03):311–325.

Hideki Isozaki, Katsuhito Sudoh, Hajime Tsukada, and Kevin Duh. 2010. Head finalization: A simple reordering rule for sov languages. In *Proceedings of the Joint Fifth Workshop on Statistical Machine Translation and MetricsMATR*, pages 244–251, Uppsala, Sweden, July. Association for Computational Linguistics.

Wenbin Jiang, Yajuan Lv, Yang Liu, and Qun Liu. 2010. Effective constituent projection across languages. In *Coling 2010: Posters*, pages 516–524, Beijing, China, August. Coling 2010 Organizing Committee.

Wenbin Jiang, Qun Liu, and Yajuan Lv. 2011. Relaxed cross-lingual projection of constituent syntax. In *Proceedings of the 2011 Conference on Empirical Methods in Natural Language Processing*, pages 1192–1201, Edinburgh, Scotland, UK., July. Association for Computational Linguistics.

Daisuke Kawahara and Sadao Kurohashi. 2006. A fully-lexicalized probabilistic model for japanese syntactic and case structure analysis. In *Proceedings of the Human Language Technology Conference of the NAACL, Main Conference*, pages 176–183, New York City, USA, June. Association for Computational Linguistics.

Philipp Koehn, Hieu Hoang, Alexandra Birch, Chris Callison-Burch, Marcello Federico, Nicola Bertoldi, Brooke Cowan, Wade Shen, Christine Moran, Richard Zens, Chris Dyer, Ondrej Bojar, Alexandra Constantin, and Evan Herbst. 2007. Moses: Open source toolkit for statistical machine translation. In *Proceedings of the 45th Annual Meeting of the Association for Computational Linguistics Companion Volume Proceedings of the Demo and Poster Sessions*, pages 177–180, Prague, Czech Republic, June. Association for Computational Linguistics.

Philipp Koehn. 2004. Statistical significance tests for machine translation evaluation. In Dekang Lin and Dekai Wu, editors, *Proceedings of EMNLP 2004*, pages 388–395, Barcelona, Spain, July. Association for Computational Linguistics.

Sandra Kubler, Ryan McDonald, Joakim Nivre, and Graeme Hirst. 2009. *Dependency Parsing*. Morgan and Claypool Publishers.

Sadao Kurohashi, Toshihisa Nakamura, Yuji Matsumoto, and Makoto Nagao. 1994. Improvements of Japanese morphological analyzer JUMAN. In *Proceedings of the International Workshop on Sharable Natural Language*, pages 22–28.

Yang (1) Liu, Qun Liu, and Shouxun Lin. 2006. Tree-to-string alignment template for statistical machine translation. In *Proceedings of the 21st International Conference on Computational Linguistics and 44th Annual Meeting of the Association for Computational Linguistics*, pages 609–616, Sydney, Australia, July. Association for Computational Linguistics.

Haitao Mi and Liang Huang. 2008. Forest-based translation rule extraction. In *Proceedings of the 2008 Conference on Empirical Methods in Natural Language Processing*, pages 206–214, Honolulu, Hawaii, October. Association for Computational Linguistics.

Toshiaki Nakazawa, Hideya Mino, Isao Goto, Graham Neubig, Sadao Kurohashi, and Eiichiro Sumita. 2015. Overview of the 2nd Workshop on Asian Translation. In *Proceedings of the 2nd Workshop on Asian Translation (WAT2015)*, pages 1–28, Kyoto, Japan, October.

Slav Petrov and Dan Klein. 2007. Improved inference for unlexicalized parsing. In *Human Language Technologies 2007: The Conference of the North American Chapter of the Association for Computational Linguistics; Proceedings of the Main Conference*, pages 404–411, Rochester, New York, April. Association for Computational Linguistics.

Chris Quirk, Arul Menezes, and Colin Cherry. 2005. Dependency treelet translation: Syntactically informed phrasal SMT. In *Proceedings of the 43rd Annual Meeting of the Association for Computational Linguistics (ACL'05)*, pages 271–279, Ann Arbor, Michigan, June. Association for Computational Linguistics.

Mohammad Sadegh Rasooli and Michael Collins. 2015. Density-driven cross-lingual transfer of dependency parsers. In *Proceedings of the 2015 Conference on Empirical Methods in Natural Language Processing*, pages 328–338, Lisbon, Portugal, September. Association for Computational Linguistics.

John Richardson, Raj Dabre, Chenhui Chu, Fabien Cromières, Toshiaki Nakazawa, and Sadao Kurohashi. 2015. KyotoEBMT System Description for the 2nd Workshop on Asian Translation. In *Proceedings of the 2nd Workshop on Asian Translation (WAT2015)*, pages 54–60, Kyoto, Japan, October.

Jason Riesa, Ann Irvine, and Daniel Marcu. 2011. Feature-rich language-independent syntax-based alignment for statistical machine translation. In *Proceedings of the 2011 Conference on Empirical Methods in Natural Language Processing*, pages 497–507, Edinburgh, Scotland, UK., July. Association for Computational Linguistics.

Libin Shen, Jinxi Xu, and Ralph Weischedel. 2008. A new string-to-dependency machine translation algorithm with a target dependency language model. In *Proceedings of ACL-08: HLT*, pages 577–585, Columbus, Ohio, June. Association for Computational Linguistics.

Mo Shen, Daisuke Kawahara, and Sadao Kurohashi. 2012. A reranking approach for dependency parsing with variable-sized subtree features. In *Proceedings of the 26th Pacific Asia Conference on Language, Information, and Computation*, pages 308–317, Bali,Indonesia, November. Faculty of Computer Science, Universitas Indonesia.

Mo Shen, Hongxiao Liu, Daisuke Kawahara, and Sadao Kurohashi. 2014. Chinese morphological analysis with character-level pos tagging. In *Proceedings of ACL*, pages 253–258.

Yu Shen, Chenhui Chu, Fabien Cromieres, and Sadao Kurohashi. 2015. Cross-language projection of dependency trees for tree-to-tree machine translation. In *Proceedings of the 29th Pacific Asia Conference on Language, Information and Computing (PACLIC2015)*, pages 80–88, Shanghai, China, 10.

Kathrin Spreyer and Jonas Kuhn. 2009. Data-driven dependency parsing of new languages using incomplete and noisy training data. In *Proceedings of the Thirteenth Conference on Computational Natural Language Learning (CoNLL-2009)*, pages 12–20, Boulder, Colorado, June. Association for Computational Linguistics.

Min Zhang, Hongfei Jiang, Aiti Aw, Haizhou Li, Chew Lim Tan, and Sheng Li. 2008. A tree sequence alignment-based tree-to-tree translation model. In *Proceedings of ACL-08: HLT*, pages 559–567, Columbus, Ohio, June. Association for Computational Linguistics.

Improving Pronoun Translation by Modeling Coreference Uncertainty

Ngoc Quang Luong and **Andrei Popescu-Belis**
Idiap Research Institute
Rue Marconi 19, CP 592
1920 Martigny, Switzerland
{nluong,apbelis}@idiap.ch

Abstract

Information about the antecedents of pronouns is considered essential to solve certain translation divergencies, such as those concerning the English pronoun *it* when translated into gendered languages, e.g. for French into *il*, *elle*, or several other options. However, no machine translation system using anaphora resolution has so far been able to outperform a phrase-based statistical MT baseline. We address here one of the reasons for this failure: the imperfection of automatic anaphora resolution algorithms. Using parallel data, we learn probabilistic correlations between target-side pronouns and the gender and number features of their (uncertain) antecedents, as hypothesized by the Stanford Coreference Resolution system on the source side. We embody these correlations into a secondary translation model, which we invoke upon decoding with the Moses statistical phrase-based MT system. This solution outperforms a deterministic pronoun post-editing system, as well as a statistical MT baseline, on automatic and human evaluation metrics.

1 Introduction

Pronoun translation remains a challenge for machine translation (MT), likely because solving certain translation divergencies between source and target pronouns requires non-local information, possibly from one or more sentences before the one that is being translated. In this paper, we focus on the divergencies that occur when translating the English neutral pronouns *it* and *they* into French. Depending on their functions (referential or pleonastic) and on their actual antecedents,

Source: *My cat brought home a mouse that he hunted, and it₁ was not dead but it₂ was mortally wounded. What is the best way to kill it₃ humanely?*
MT: *Mon chat a ramené à la maison une souris qui il a chassé, et il₁ était pas mort, mais il₂ a été mortellement blessé. Quelle est la meilleure façon de le₃ tuer humainement?*

Figure 1: Wrong translations of *it* into French (1–3) resulting in a serious misunderstanding.

there are almost twenty different lexical items that can serve as translations into French, e.g. for *it*: *il*, *elle*, *ce/c'*, *cela*, *ça*, *on*, *le*, and others.

For instance, in an example from an online discussion forum shown in Figure 1, two referents are mentioned, a cat and a mouse, which are translated in French by nouns with different genders: masculine for cat (*le chat*) vs. feminine for mouse (*la souris*). The three instances of *it*, referring to the mouse, should be translated into feminine French pronouns: respectively *elle*, *elle* and *la* (the latter is an object pronoun). However, the online MT system to which we submitted this example translated all of them with the masculine forms, making the readers think that the author intends to kill his/her cat.

The designers of MT systems have been aware of this problem and sometimes tried to address it, starting already from rule-based systems. However, it is only recently that specific strategies for translating pronouns have been proposed and evaluated (see Hardmeier (2014), Section 2.3.1). Most of the strategies have attempted to convey information from anaphora resolution systems to statistical MT ones, by constraining target pronouns based on features of their antecedents in the target language (Hardmeier and Federico,

Proceedings of the First Conference on Machine Translation, Volume 1: Research Papers, pages 12–20,
Berlin, Germany, August 11-12, 2016. ©2016 Association for Computational Linguistics

2010; Le Nagard and Koehn, 2010). Still, at the DiscoMT 2015 shared task on pronoun-focused EN/FR translation (Hardmeier et al., 2015), none of the submitted systems was able to outperform a well-trained phrase-based statistical MT baseline. Apart from the need for considering first the functions of pronouns and then their antecedents, if any (Guillou, 2016), one of the reasons that limit performance is the large number of errors made by co-reference or anaphora resolution systems.

In this paper, we attempt to model the uncertainty of an off-the-shelf coreference resolution system (Lee et al.'s (2011) Stanford system) with respect to its impact on MT. We propose to learn from parallel data the correlations between target side pronouns and the gender/number of their (uncertain) antecedents, as hypothesized by the coreference resolution system. These correlations are represented as an additional translation model, which we baptize 'coreference model' or CM. We use this model as an additional translation table in the Moses phrase-based statistical MT system (Koehn et al., 2007) along with a standard phrase-based translation table. While decoding, the antecedents are obtained from the Stanford system as well, and their target-side features are obtained through alignment and POS analysis. Through experiments based on the DiscoMT 2015 data (transcripts of TED talks), and automatic and human evaluation metrics, we show that our solution outperforms a deterministic pronoun post-editing system, as well as the DiscoMT 2015 statistical MT baseline.

Below, we first review previous work (Section 2) before explaining how the coreference model is constructed (Section 3). The integration of the model into the Moses SMT decoder is presented in Section 4. We report and discuss the results of our experiments in Section 5.

2   Related Work

Following considerable achievements during the early 1990s, many rule-based and statistical anaphora resolution systems have been designed in the past two decades (Mitkov, 2002; Ng, 2010). However, only recently were they exploited as a knowledge source for improving pronoun translation. Using rule-based or statistical methods for anaphora resolution, several studies have attempted to integrate anaphora resolution with statistical MT, as reviewed by Hardmeier (2014, Section 2.3.1). Le Nagard and Koehn (2010) trained an English-French translation model on an annotated corpus in which each occurrence of the English pronouns *it* and *they* was annotated with the gender of its antecedent on the target side. Their system correctly translated 40 pronouns out of the 59 that they examined, but was not able to outperform a baseline that was not aware of coreference, which correctly translated 41 pronouns. These results were likely due to the insufficient performance of anaphora resolution.

Integrating anaphora resolution with statistical MT, Guillou (2012) deployed pronoun-focused translation in English-Czech SMT, studying the imperfect coreference and alignment results. Hardmeier and Federico (2010) proposed to integrate a word dependency model into the SMT decoder as an additional feature function, which kept track of pairs of source words acting respectively as antecedent and anaphor in a coreference link. This model helped to improve slightly the English-German SMT performance (F-score customized for pronouns) on the WMT News Commentary 2008 and 2009 test sets, with relative gains of 0.9% and 0.7% respectively.

Following the same strategy, in a previous study (Luong et al., 2015), we combined linearly the score obtained from a coreference resolution system with the score from the search graph of the Moses decoder, to determine whether an English-French SMT pronoun translation should be changed into the opposite gender (e.g. *il* → *elle*). Our system thus combines knowledge from the coreference links and the MT search graph with several post-editing rules. Although our system performed best among the six participants in the pronoun-focused shared task at the 2015 DiscoMT workshop (Hardmeier et al., 2015), it still remained below the SMT baseline.

Several other studies attempted to automatically correct (post-edit) pronouns in SMT output, including as features the baseline translation of each pronoun. A considerable set of coreference features, used in a deep neural network architecture, was presented by Hardmeier (2014, Chapters 7–9), who observed significant improvements on TED talks and News Commentaries. Alternatively, to avoid extracting features from an anaphora resolution system, Callin et al. (2015) developed a classifier based on a feed-forward neural network, which considered as features the preceding nouns and determiners along with their parts-of-speech. Their predictor worked particularly well, with over 80% of F-score, on the *ce* and *ils* target pronouns for English-French MT. The predictor reached an overall macro F-score of 55.3% for all classes, thus outperforming the DiscoMT 2015 shared task systems and baseline after the submissions were closed.

Similarly to the approach proposed by Le Nagard and Koehn (2010), we employ the gender and number of the hypothesized antecedents to help with pronoun translation. However, instead of training an SMT system on the gender-marked datasets and then testing it on an annotated test set, in which coreference predictions are always used with absolute confidence, we model the probabilistic connection between a given pronoun and a given gender/number on a large-scale dataset, and integrate it into SMT decoder. This enables us to exploit the probabilistic scores of the translation and language models, and of the coreference model at the time of decoding, which leads to an improvement in the translation of pronouns.

3 Modeling Coreference Uncertainty from Parallel Data

The translation model used by an SMT decoder indicates how likely a source word or phrase is to be translated into a target one. However, in the phrase-based MT models, but also in hierarchical ones, the phrase table cannot constrain the generation of a target pronoun based on features of its antecedent. Moreover, such features cannot be reliably obtained from anaphora resolution systems, as they are quite error prone.

We propose to model the uncertainty of anaphora resolution and the acceptable variability of pronoun EN/FR translation by estimating the likelihood of observing a target language pronoun depending on the *gender* and *number* of its antecedent (noted respectively as 'G' and 'N'), as hypothesized by the Stanford coreference resolution system (Lee et al., 2011).

The construction of the model is represented in Figure 2, and explained in detail in the remainder of this section. In a nutshell, we extract pairs of pronouns and their antecedents from the source-side of a large bilingual corpus. Then, we obtain the gender and number of the translation of the antecedent through target-side POS tagging. Finally, we estimate the co-occurrence probability of each

target-side *(pronoun, G/N)* pair from these observations.

We build the model over transcripts and translations of TED talks from the IWSLT training data (Cettolo et al., 2012) with about 180,000 English-French sentence pairs, as presented in more detail in Section 5.1.

3.1 Extraction of Coreference Links

To build the coreference-aware translation model, we perform coreference resolution on the source side. From the available off-the-shelf coreference resolution systems, we examined the Stanford system (Lee et al., 2011) and BART (Versley et al., 2008). We conducted a manual evaluation on 202 instances of *it* and *they* extracted from the TED talks. The Stanford system correctly detected the antecedents of 121 of them (60% accuracy), while BART only solved correctly 93 (46%), a markedly lower score. We thus selected Stanford system, and used it to identify, on the source side, the antecedents of all instances of *it* and *they*.

We then project the noun phrase antecedents of *it* and *they* to the target side thanks to the alignment information.[1] If the target counterpart of the source antecedent contains multiple words, we keep only the first noun or pronoun that is detected, which is likely the headword. We determine the gender and number (G/N) of the antecedent through French part-of-speech analysis with Morfette (Chrupala et al., 2008). If the coreference system proposes a pronoun as the antecedent, we also use its G/N value. The antecedent identification is considered unsuccessful if the system generates no antecedent, or if either the source headword or the aligned target phrase are not nouns or pronouns; in such cases, the corresponding pairs are not retained.

If the co-reference resolution system could output a probability distribution over several potential antecedents for a given pronoun, which is currently not the case of the freely available Stanford system, then this could be added as a confidence score to each *(pronoun, G/N)* pair. Another possibility would be to estimate the confidence of each link as the average accuracy p of the system, computed over a set with ground-truth links. Here,

---

[1] For training, one could also, more directly, perform anaphora resolution on the target side of the parallel corpus. However, this cannot be done during decoding, since the correctness of the target pronoun, which is precisely the problem we address, is a key feature for anaphora resolution.

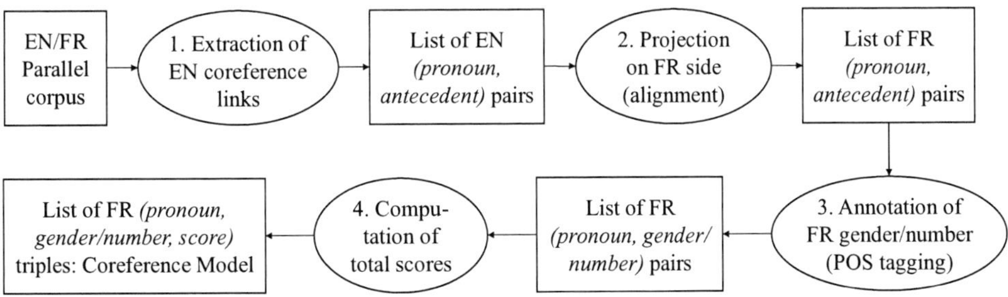

Figure 2: Data and processing steps for the construction of the EN/FR Coreference Model.

however, we assign a confidence score of 1 to the antecedent hypothesized by the Stanford system and implicitly a zero value to all other links to the pronouns. For instance, in the following French text: *"J'aime cette maison. Elle est jolie."*, if the anaphora resolver detects *maison* (a French feminine singular noun) as the referent of the target pronoun *elle*, then we extract the corresponding link: *(elle, feminine/singular, 1.0)* assign a zero value to the other three possibilities: *(elle, masculine/singular, 0.0)*, *(elle, masculine/plural, 0.0)* and *(elle, feminine/plural, 0.0)*. With a suitable coreference resolver, however, these values could be different from 0 and 1.

This stage results in a list of all extracted French pronouns, translations of *it* and *they*, along with the G/N features of their antecedents, and an associated score. Theoretically, if source-side anaphora resolution and source-target alignment were perfect, these features would be the ones predicted by the dictionaries: masculine/singular for *il*, feminine/singular for *elle*, and so on. However, the point of counting these pairs is to model the uncertainty of the anaphora resolution system over large corpora. In other words, we aim to learn, for instance, in which contexts a source-side *it*, with a target-side antecedent identified as masculine singular, is translated by *il* or could be translated by another pronoun, if other features from the translation model increase the likelihood of this translation, assuming in this case that the anaphora resolution system was mistaken. Our model thus also allows other possible translations of *it* such as *cela* or *ce*, which are less directly constrained by the gender of the antecedent.

3.2 Assignment of Co-occurrence Scores

Once a list containing all observed triples (*pronoun, G/N, confidence score*) is generated from the training corpus, we compute the co-occurrence

probability between each pronoun and G/N features. This value is obtained by summing up all the confidence scores of triples where the pronoun and this G/N value appear together, then normalizing by the sum of the scores of those containing this G/N value:

$$P(pronoun|\text{G/N}) = \frac{\sum score(\text{G/N}, pronoun)}{\sum score(\text{G/N})}$$

The new triples including G/N values, pronouns and their co-occurrence scores constitute our Coreference Model (CM). To simplify the model and avoid noise, all triples with a probability lower than 10^{-5} are removed, leading to a final model with 4,878 triples. This rather large number with respect to the number of French pronouns and possible G/N values is due to the alignment stage, as a source pronoun might be mapped to multiple target words, e.g. *they $\rightarrow$ ils ont*, or *it $\rightarrow$ qu' il*, or *it $\rightarrow$ coupez-le*. This generates a large number of spurious triples, but their co-occurrence scores, as defined above, remain quite low.

The Coreference Model does not simply convey the likelihood of translating a source pronoun into a specific target one, given the antecedent's G/N value, but, more importantly, it models the likelihood of translation options under uncertain co-reference hypotheses, as well as the legitimate variations of pronouns (e.g. *il/ce* or *ils/on*). As we will show, the CM provides helpful information to the SMT decoder, to improve pronoun choice when several translation options are available.

4 Coreference-Aware Decoder

The Moses phrase-based statistical MT decoder (Koehn et al., 2007) searches among hypotheses stored in the search graph for a candidate t^* that maximizes its objective function given the input s:

$$t^* = \arg\max_t \sum_{k=1}^{n_F} \lambda_k f_k(t, s)$$

```
[mapping]
0 T 0 # Translation options from Table 0
1 T 1 # Additional options from Table 1
[feature]
PhraseDictionaryMemory path=path_to_table
[decoding-graph-backoff]
0 #first table used for everything
1 #second table used for unknown single word
[weight]
TranslationModel0= 0.2 0.2 0.2 0.2 #default
TranslationModel1= 0.8 #weight of CM table
```

Figure 3: Options in 'moses.ini' for adding the CM backoff table to the translation models considered by Moses.

where $f_k(t, s)$ is one of the n_F feature functions, coming from various models (e.g. the language model, the translation model, the re-ordering model or the word penalty model) and λ_k is the weight of the function. Here, we add to the Moses decoder an additional back-off translation table, based directly on the Coreference Model. The goal is to use the Moses default phrase table for any source word other than *it* or *they*, and use the CM table for these pronouns. In order to process all occurrences of *it* and *they* with the back-off CM table, we turn them into unknown words for the default table, simply by substituting them by the G/N value of their antecedent, as hypothesized by the coreference system, as explained below. This decoder is called *coreference-aware decoder* (CAD), and finds the best translation as the one that maximizes the objective function above, with an additional term: the CM feature function $f_{\text{CM}}(t, s)$ corresponding to the CM table, with a weight λ_{CM}.

In implementation terms, in the Moses environment, we declare the new table in the [feature] section of the 'moses.ini' configuration file, and specify its role as a back-off table in the [decoding-graph-backoff] and [mapping] sections. The weight λ_{CM} of the added table is declared in the [weight] section, as shown in Figure 3. In our experiments, we assign a default weight of 0.8 to the CM model, which is identical to the sum of the four feature functions related to the default table. The optimization of this weight will be studied in future work.

Before using the Coreference-Aware Decoder, the document to be translated is pre-processed by the anaphora resolution system, thus marking all coreference links from either *it* or *they* back to their most likely antecedent noun phrases.[2] We distinguish the following two possibilities.

If the coreference link is inter-sentential, i.e. if the antecedent belongs to the preceding sentence, then we use the translation of this preceding sentence, and pass the extracted G/N value on to the current one. For instance, with the source text: *"I like this house. It has a nice view."*, the first sentence is translated into: *"J'aime cette maison."*, then the G/N value of the hypothesized antecedent *maison* (feminine/singular) is used to replace the pronoun *it* in the second sentence as follows: *"feminine/singular has a nice view"*.

If the coreference link is intra-sentential, i.e. if the antecedent and pronoun are in the same sentence, then we first translate the sentence to obtain the antecedent's G/N value, and afterward we replace the pronoun with this value and translate the sentence a second time. Therefore, unlike the first case, the cost of translation is doubled as a second pass is needed. Processing intra-sentential anaphora in one pass remains to be studied in the future.

5 Experiments and Results

5.1 Data and Evaluation Metrics

We built the phrase table on the following parallel datasets: aligned TED talks from the WIT[3] corpus (Cettolo et al., 2012), Europarl v. 7 (Koehn, 2005), News Commentary v. 9 and other news data from WMT 2007–2013 (Bojar et al., 2014). The language model was trained on the target side (French) of all above datasets. Then, the system was tuned on a development set of 887 sentences from IWSLT 2010 provided for the shared task on pronoun translation of the DiscoMT 2015 workshop (Hardmeier et al., 2015). The test set was also the one from the DiscoMT 2015 shared task, with 2,093 English sentences along with French gold-standard translations, extracted from 12 recent TED talks. The test set contains 809 occurrences of *it* and 307 of *they*.

We processed each talk separately, translating its sentences in order. As explained above, after translating each sentence, the G/N values of any target antecedents, if any, are passed to the current or following sentence containing the anaphoric

---

[2]Forward or cataphoric links have never been observed with this coreference resolution system.

pronoun. If the antecedent is unidentified or not nominal (due to errors of anaphora resolution or alignment), we let these pronouns be translated by the default phrase table. As a result, only 367 occurrences of *it* and 196 of *they* (i.e. 563 instances or about 50% of the total) are processed by the Coreference-Aware Decoder, and have the potential to improve over the SMT baseline. The accuracy of the new decoder will be therefore evaluated only over the pronouns that have actually been processed.

5.2 Results using Automatic Metrics

We report the performance first by automatically computing the following four scores, inspired by the ACT metric for evaluating the translation of discourse connectives (Hajlaoui and Popescu-Belis, 2013). These scores rely on the comparison of the system's pronouns (candidates) with the ones in the reference translation.

- C_1: Number of candidate pronouns which are identical to the reference ones.
- C_2: Number of candidate pronouns which are "similar" to the reference ones. Similarity allows for two equivalence classes of French pronouns, accounting for the variants of *"ce"* and *"ça"* with or without apostrophe, and for two different symbols used for the apostrophe: $\{ce, c', c'\}$ and $\{ça, ca, ç', ç'\}$.
- C_3: Number of candidate pronouns which are not identical or similar to the reference.
- C_4: Number of source pronouns which are untranslated in the candidate translation.

Although these scores, even taken together, are only an imperfect reflection of translation correctness, it is likely that increasing the first two scores (C_1 and C_2) indicates improved quality, as we will verify here using human metrics.[3] Below, we will also consider the number of "correct" translations, $C_1 + C_2$, as an indicator of quality.

We compare the performance obtained by our coreference-aware decoder (noted CM) against the two following systems:

---

[3]In theory, the target pronoun does not need to be identical to the reference one to be correct: it must only point to the same antecedent. Some variation is in reality acceptable such as among expletive pronouns (*it* → *ce / cela / il*), or due to different translations of an antecedent in the candidate and the reference, but this variation will not be tolerated by our metric. However, in the hundreds of sentences we rated for this study, we never observed such a variation of the antecedent's gender or number.

Sys.	C1	C2	C3	C4	C1+C2	Acc.
BL	194	38	284	47	232	.41
PE	185	38	292	48	223	.40
CM	**210**	**43**	241	69	**253**	.45

Table 1: Detailed scores of the three systems: BL, PE and CM. The accuracy is the proportion of good translations ($C_1 + C_2$) over the total number of pronouns (563). CM outperforms both PE and BL on all scores.

- **BL**: the baseline MT system provided by the DiscoMT 2015 workshop organizers for the pronoun-focused translation shared task, built using the Moses toolkit. This system was trained on the same datasets as CM, but was tuned on IWSLT 2010 development data and IWSLT 2011 test data (1,705 sentences).

- **PE**: our post-editing system for the translations of *it* and *they* generated by a baseline SMT system (Luong et al., 2015), which was the highest scoring system at the DiscoMT 2015 shared task on pronoun-focused translation. It was trained on the DiscoMT 2015 data and tuned on the IWSLT 2010 development data.

We translated the test set using the three systems, and computed the $C1, \ldots, C_4$ scores over the 563 pronouns. The results, shown in Table 1, reveal that CM outperforms both BL and PE, with gains in the numbers of exact translations (C_1) of 16 and 25 pronouns respectively. In terms of the number of correct translations ($C_1 + C_2$), CM is also the best-performing one, with 21 instances above BL and 30 above PE.

For the sake of completeness, we also compare the performance of three above mentioned systems in overall Precision, Recall and F-score for pronouns, as proposed by Hardmeier and Federico (2010) and used in DiscoMT 2015 among other metrics. We also compute the BLEU score to investigate the impact of pronoun improvement on the global translation quality. The results in Table 2 show that CM surpasses BL and PE by 0.022 and 0.025 in terms of F-score, which is very similar to the above $C_1 + C_2$ score. In terms of BLEU, CM outperforms BL and PE by respectively 0.35 and 0.06 BLEU points. The small magnitude of these differences is due to the sparseness of pronouns in the evaluated texts, but they tend to confirm the improvements brought by the CM.

Sys.	Prec.	Rec.	F-score	BLEU
BL	.337	.348	.342	35.81
PE	.334	.343	.339	35.52
CM	**.414**	**.324**	**.364**	35.87

Table 2: Overall precision, recall, F-score and BLEU score of BL, PE and CM.

Significance tests were conducted for CM vs. BL and CM vs. PE using McNemar's test, which compares binary pairwise data (correct or incorrect pronouns in our case) between two systems. We calculate the p-values for the two pairs of systems either when considering only exact matches (C_1) as positive results, or when allowing similar pronouns as well ($C_1 + C_2$). For CM vs. BL, the p-values are respectively 0.049 and 0.046, while for CM vs. PE they are respectively 0.007 and 0.012. As these values are all below 0.05, the improvements brought by CM over each of the two other systems are statistically significant at the 95% level.

5.3   Human Evaluation

The automatic metrics have demonstrated that the system using the Coreference Model is closer to the reference, in terms of pronouns, than the Baseline and the Post-editing systems. Our automatic metric is particularly strict in requiring identity to the reference, with only minimal variation accepted on the forms of *"ce"* and *"ça"*. However, in French, some variations of pronouns are acceptable. For instance, the indefinite pronoun *"on"* may replace the third person plural pronouns *"ils"* or *"elles"*; the pronouns *"il"* and *"ce"* may be substituted in some cases (e.g. as in *il est important* $\approx$ *c'est important*); and idiomatic translations are frequent (e.g. *on discute de ça* $\approx$ *on en discute*).

Therefore, in addition to automatic metrics, we performed a human evaluation of the translated pronouns. Two annotators with good knowledge of French and English evaluated the 329 sentences of the test set, containing 563 instances of *it* and *they*. For each sentence, the annotators were shown the English source sentence and the preceding one, followed by the outputs of the three systems for the source sentence, as well as the reference translation of this sentence and the preceding one, as exemplified in Table 3 on the next page. The positions in the source sentence of all pro-

System	Correct	Incorrect	Accuracy
Evaluation 1: two evaluators (adjudicated)			
BL	53	20	.73
PE	52	21	.71
CM	**57**	16	**.78**
Evaluation 2: one evaluator			
BL	360	203	.64
PE	344	219	.61
CM	**370**	193	**.66**

Table 4: Number of correctly vs. incorrectly translated pronouns by the three systems BL, PE and CM. In Evaluation 1, they are rated on 40 blocks by two human annotators after deliberation. In Evaluation 2, they are rated on the full set (329 blocks) by one annotator.

nouns to be evaluated were specified. The order of the three systems was randomly assigned in each such evaluation block and was hence unknown to annotators.

The annotators were instructed to judge pronouns according to their subjective impression of correction, based mainly on compatibility with the antecedent, and not on the identity to the reference translation, which was shown only to make sure that the source was correctly understood. The score of an evaluated pronoun is 1 if correct and 0 if not, and the system's score is the sum of the scores over all source pronouns.

Due to time limitations, one annotator completed the entire evaluation (329 blocks with 563 pronouns), whereas the other one completed 40 blocks which contained 73 occurrences of *it* and *they* in the source. Of the total of $73 \times 3 = 219$ instances of the 40 blocks rated by the two annotators, the annotators agreed on the rating (correct or incorrect) of 188 instances and disagreed on 31, corresponding to a Kappa score of 0.645, i.e. a moderate agreement. The annotators deliberated to analyze their differences and reached consensus over 26 additional instances, leading to an adjudicated Kappa score of 0.939.

The accuracy of the three systems computed against the adjudicated annotations of 73 source pronouns is shown in Table 4, as *Evaluation 1*, while accuracy over the full set of 563 source pronouns rated by only one annotator (hence with a smaller confidence) is shown as *Evaluation 2*. The results from *Evaluation 1* indicate that CM is the best performing system among the three, with rel-

SRC–1	when he was born , he was diagnosed with diastrophic dwarfism , a very disabling condition , [. . .]
SRC	and it was suggested to them that they leave him at the hospital so that he could die there quietly .
SYS1	et il a suggéré qu' ils le laisser à l' hôpital pour qu' il puisse y mourir paisiblement . it()= ||| they(7)= |||
SYS2	et il a suggéré qu' ils le laisser à l' hôpital pour qu' il puisse y mourir paisiblement . it()= ||| they(7)= |||
SYS3	et il a suggéré qu' elles le laisser à l' hôpital pour qu' il puisse y mourir paisiblement . it()= ||| they(7)= |||
REF	on leur a suggéré de le laisser à l' hôpital pour qu' il puisse y mourir en paix .
REF–1	lorsqu' il est né , on lui a diagnostiqué un nanisme diastrophique , une maladie très handicapante , [. . .]

Table 3: Example of a block for human evaluation: source sentence SRC (and the preceding one SRC–1) followed by the three system translations in random order, the reference translation REF and the preceding sentence.

ative improvements of 5.5% and 6.9% over BL and PE respectively. Although less reliable, results from *Evaluation 2* show that CM outperforms BL by 10 correct translations (ca. 1.8%), and PE by 26 correct translations (ca. 4.6%). These proportions are in the same order as those from *Evaluation 1*.

The results of *Evaluation 2* show a considerable increase of the accuracy of all systems compared to the scores from the automatic metrics, with relative gains slightly above 20%. As expected, in all three systems, a large number of pronouns judged as incorrect by the automated metric because they differed from the reference (C_3) have been judged as correct by the human evaluators. However, although they are higher, human scores are strongly correlated with automatic ones: Pearson's correlation coefficient between $C_1 + C_2$ and scores from *Evaluation 1* is 0.994, while for *Evaluation 2* it is 0.936.

Example 1
SRC: But it takes time , **it** takes money .
CM: Mais ça prend du temps , ça prend de l' argent .
REF: Mais ça prend du temps et [none] de l' argent .

Example 2
SRC: [. . .] we know what it is : **it** 's the wikipedia .
CM: [. . .] nous savons ce que c' est : wikipédia .
REF: [. . .] nous la connaissons maintenant : wikipedia .

Figure 4: Examples of pronouns that are considered as correct by human judges, although different from the reference.

Figure 4 shows two examples in which candidate pronouns were judged as correct by both annotators, although they differ from the reference. In Example 1, the second *it* in the source sentence was translated into *ça* by CM, but was not translated in the reference, as the human translator combined two identical source pronouns into a unique target one. Similarly, in Example 2, CM translated the first *it* into a French subject pronoun

(*c'*), while the reference used a third person object pronoun (*la*). A more flexible assessment than the strict automatic one thus increases the scores of the systems.

6 Conclusion and Perspectives

This paper proposed a Coreference Model, constructed from the gender and number information of each pronoun antecedent, to model the uncertainty of anaphora resolution for integration with SMT and improve pronoun translation from English to French. The proposed Coreference-Aware Decoder outperformed the phrase-based baseline SMT system, as well as one that uses anaphora information for post-editing without modeling its uncertainty, on the test set from the DiscoMT 2015 shared task. These significant improvements show that appropriate modeling of co-reference uncertainty is helpful, and will remain so as long as anaphora resolution is imperfect.

In the future, this work can be extended in several ways. Firstly, we intend to obtain probabilities of anaphor-antecedent links from a different coreference resolver, which would be better adapted to our needs than the ones we examined. Secondly, we will optimize the weight of our Coreference Model on a held-out development set. Thirdly, we will enrich the model with more types of features in addition to gender and number, for instance humanness, formality, or abstractness, which help to distinguish effectively between several translation options of *it* and *they*, and are also relevant to other language pairs. Finally, the complexity of pronoun translation evaluation, reflected in the differences between human and automatic assessments, requires further research as well.

Acknowledgments

We are grateful for their support to the Swiss National Science Foundation (SNSF) under the Sinergia MODERN project (www.idiap.ch/project/modern/, grant n. 147653) and to the European Union under the Horizon 2020 SUMMA project (www.summa-project.eu, grant n. 688139).

References

Ondrej Bojar, Christian Buck, Christian Federmann, Barry Haddow, Philipp Koehn, Johannes Leveling, Christof Monz, Pavel Pecina, Matt Post, Herve Saint-Amand, Radu Soricut, Lucia Specia, and Ales Tamchyna. 2014. Findings of the 2014 Workshop on Statistical Machine Translation. In *Proceedings of the Ninth Workshop on Statistical Machine Translation*, pages 12–58, Baltimore, MD, USA.

Jimmy Callin, Christian Hardmeier, and Jörg Tiedemann. 2015. Part-of-speech driven cross-lingual pronoun prediction with feed-forward neural networks. In *Proceedings of the Second Workshop on Discourse in Machine Translation*, pages 59–64, Lisbon, Portugal.

Mauro Cettolo, Christian Girardi, and Marcello Federico. 2012. Wit^3: Web inventory of transcribed and translated talks. In *Proceedings of the 16th Conference of the European Association for Machine Translation (EAMT)*, pages 261–268, Trento, Italy.

Grzegorz Chrupala, Georgiana Dinu, and Josef van Genabith. 2008. Learning morphology with Morfette. In *Proceedings of the 6th International Conference on Language Resources and Evaluation (LREC)*, Marrakech, Morocco.

Liane Guillou. 2012. Improving pronoun translation for statistical machine translation. In *Proceedings of EACL 2012 Student Research Workshop (13th Conference of the European Chapter of the ACL)*, pages 1–10, Avignon, France.

Liane Guillou. 2016. *Incorporating Pronoun Function into Statistical Machine Translation*. PhD thesis, University of Edinburgh, UK.

Najeh Hajlaoui and Andrei Popescu-Belis. 2013. Assessing the accuracy of discourse connective translations: Validation of an automatic metric. In *Proceedings of the 14th International Conference on Intelligent Text Processing and Computational Linguistics (CICLing)*, LNCS 7817, pages 236–247, Samos, Greece. Springer.

Christian Hardmeier and Marcello Federico. 2010. Modelling pronominal anaphora in statistical machine translation. In *Proceedings of International Workshop on Spoken Language Translation (IWSLT)*, Paris, France.

Christian Hardmeier, Preslav Nakov, Sara Stymne, Jörg Tiedemann, Yannick Versley, and Mauro Cettolo. 2015. Pronoun-focused MT and cross-lingual pronoun prediction: Findings of the 2015 DiscoMT shared task on pronoun translation. In *Proceedings of the Second Workshop on Discourse in Machine Translation*, pages 1–16, Lisbon, Portugal.

Christian Hardmeier. 2014. *Discourse in Statistical Machine Translation*. PhD thesis, Uppsala University, Sweden.

Philipp Koehn, Hieu Hoang, Alexandra Birch, Chris Callison-Burch, Marcello Federico, Nicola Bertoldi, Brooke Cowan, Wade Shen, Christine Moran, Richard Zens, Chris Dyer, Ondrej Bojar, Alexandra Constantin, and Evan Herbst. 2007. Moses: Open source toolkit for statistical machine translation. In *Proceedings of the 45th Annual Meeting of the Association for Computational Linguistics (ACL)*, pages 177–180, Prague, Czech Republic.

Philipp Koehn. 2005. Europarl: A parallel corpus for statistical machine translation. In *Proceedings of the 10th Machine Translation Summit*, pages 79–86, Phuket, Thailand.

Ronan Le Nagard and Philipp Koehn. 2010. Aiding pronoun translation with co-reference resolution. In *Proceedings of the Joint 5th Workshop on Statistical Machine Translation and Metrics (MATR)*, pages 258–267, Uppsala, Sweden.

Heeyoung Lee, Yves Peirsman, Angel Chang, Nathanael Chambers, Mihai Surdeanu, and Dan Jurafsky. 2011. Stanford's multi-pass sieve coreference resolution system at the CoNLL-2011 shared task. In *Proceedings of the Fifteenth Conference on Computational Natural Language Learning (CoNLL): Shared Task*, pages 28–34, Portland, OR.

Ngoc Quang Luong, Lesly Miculicich Werlen, and Andrei Popescu-Belis. 2015. Pronoun translation and prediction with or without coreference links. In *Proceedings of the Second Workshop on Discourse in Machine Translation*, pages 94–100, Lisbon, Portugal.

Ruslan Mitkov. 2002. *Anaphora Resolution*. Longman, London, UK.

Vincent Ng. 2010. Supervised noun phrase coreference research: The first fifteen years. In *Proceedings of the 48th Annual Meeting of the Association for Computational Linguistics (ACL)*, pages 1396–1411, Uppsala, Sweden.

Yannick Versley, Simone Paolo Ponzetto, Massimo Poesio, Vladimir Eidelman, Alan Jern, Jason Smith, Xiaofeng Yang, and Alessandro Moschitti. 2008. BART: A modular toolkit for coreference resolution. In *Proceedings of the 46th Annual Meeting of the Association for Computational Linguistics on Human Language Technologies: Demo Session*, HLT-Demonstrations '08, pages 9–12, Columbus, Ohio.

Modeling verbal inflection for English to German SMT

Anita Ramm
IMS
University of Stuttgart, Germany
ramm@ims-uni.stuttgart.de

Alexander Fraser
CIS
University of Munich, Germany
fraser@cis.uni-muenchen.de

Abstract

German verbal inflection is frequently wrong in standard statistical machine translation approaches. German verbs agree with subjects in person and number, and they bear information about mood and tense. For subject–verb agreement, we parse German MT output to identify subject–verb pairs and ensure that the verb agrees with the subject. We show that this approach improves subject-verb agreement. We model tense/mood translation from English to German by means of a statistical classification model. Although our model shows good results on well-formed data, it does not systematically improve tense and mood in MT output. Reasons include the need for discourse knowledge, dependency on the domain, and stylistic variety in how tense/mood is translated. We present a thorough analysis of these problems.

1 Introduction

Statistical machine translation of English into German faces two main problems involving verbs: (i) correct placement of the verbs, and (ii) generation of the appropriate inflection for the verb.

The position of verbs in German and English differs greatly and often large-range reorderings are needed to place the German verbs in the correct positions. Gojun and Fraser (2012) showed that the *preordering* approach applied on English–to–German SMT overcomes large problems with both missing and misplaced verbs.

Fraser et al. (2012) proposed an approach for handling inflectional problems in English to German SMT, focusing on the problems of sparsity caused by nominal inflection. However, they do not handle the verbs, ensuring neither that verbs appear in the correct position (which is a problem due to the highly divergent word order of English and German), nor that verbs are correctly inflected (problematic due to the richer system of verbal inflection in German). In many cases, verbs do not match their subjects (in person and number) which makes understanding of translations difficult. In addition to person and number, the German verbal inflection also includes information about tense and mood. If these are wrong (i.e. do not correspond to the tense/mood in the source), very important information, such as point of time and modality of an action/state expressed by the verb, is incorrect. This can lead to false understanding of the overall sentence.

In this paper, we reimplement the nominal inflection modeling for translation to German presented by Fraser et al. (2012) and combine it with the reordering of the source data (Gojun and Fraser, 2012). In a novel extension, we present a method for correction of the agreement errors, and an approach for modeling the translation of tense and mood from English into German. While the subject-verb agreement problems are dealt with successfully, modeling of tense/mood translation is problematic due to many reasons which we will analyze in detail.

In Section 2, we give an overview of the processing pipeline for handling verbal inflection. The method for handling subject–verb agreement errors is described in Section 3, while modeling of tense/mood translation is presented in Section 4. The impact of the proposed methods for modeling verbal inflection on the quality of the MT output is shown in Section 5. An extensive discussion of the problems related to modeling tense/mood is given in Section 6. Finally, future work is presented in Section 7.

Proceedings of the First Conference on Machine Translation, Volume 1: Research Papers, pages 21–31,
Berlin, Germany, August 11-12, 2016. ©2016 Association for Computational Linguistics

2 Overall architecture

2.1 Ensuring correct German verb placement

Different positions of verbs in English and German often require word movements over a large distance. This leads to two problems in German translations generated by SMT systems concerning the verbs: either the verbs are not generated at all, or they are placed incorrectly.

To ensure that our MT output contains the maximum number of (correctly placed) finite verbs, we reorder English prior to training and translation using a small set of reordering rules originally described by Gojun and Fraser (2012). The verbs in the English part of the training, tuning and testing data are moved to the positions typical for German which increases the syntactic similarity of English and German sentences. We train an SMT system on the reordered English and apply it to the reordered English test set.

This approach has good results in terms of the position of the verbs in German translations. However, the problem of incorrect verbal inflection is unresolved. In fact, the reordering makes the agreement problems even worse due to movements of verbs away from their subjects (cf. Section 3.1).

2.2 Inflection of the German SMT output

Fraser et al. (2012) proposed a method for handling nominal inflection for English to German SMT. They work with a *stemmed* representation of the German words in which certain morphological features such as case, number, etc. are omitted. After the translation step, for nominal stemmed words in the MT output, morphological features are predicted using a set of pre-trained classifiers and finally surface forms are generated resulting in fully-inflected German MT output.

In their approach, the verbs are neither stemmed nor inflected, but instead handled as normal words. Thus, in the translation step, the decoder (in interaction with the German language model) decides on the inflected verb forms in the final MT output.

2.3 Adding verbal inflection modeling

As a baseline SMT system, we use a system trained on the reordered English sentences (cf. Section 2.1) and stemmed German data with nominal inflection modeling as a post-processing step (cf. Section 2.2). In our system, we extend the

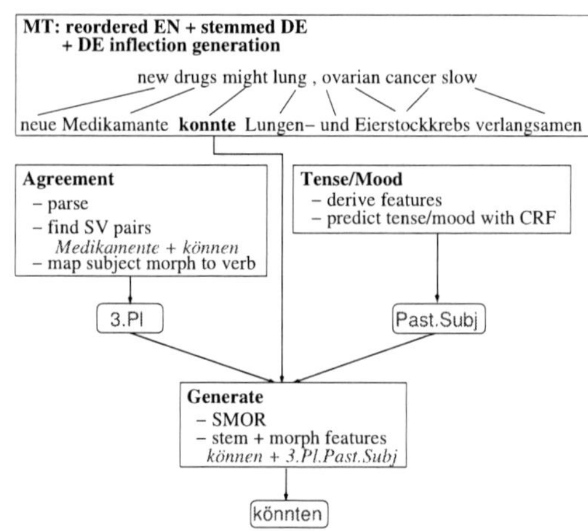

Figure 1: Processing pipeline. The verbal inflection modeling consists of two components: (i) a component for deriving agreement features person and number, and (ii) a component for predicting tense and mood. The inflected verbs are generated with SMOR (Schmid et al., 2004), a morphology generation tool for German.

baseline by identifying finite verbs in the baseline MT output, predicting their morphological features and finally producing the correct inflected output (see Figure 1).

Verbal morphological features include information about person/number, as well as tense and mood. Particularly the modeling of tense/mood translation is interesting: in this paper, we present a method to model the translation of English tense and mood into German considering all German tenses/moods in a single model. In addition, we present a detailed discussion which is, to our knowledge, the first deep analysis of this topic.

The processing pipeline is given in Figure 1. After translation of the reordered English input to a German stem-like representation, the nominal feature prediction is performed followed by our novel verbal feature prediction. Finally, the entire German MT output is inflected by combining the stems and the predicted features to produce surface forms (normal words).

3 Correction of the subject–verb agreement

3.1 Problem description

In many languages, the subject is located near the corresponding finite verb. However, in languages such as German, the subject might be very far from

Data	avg dist in words	>5 words
News	3.9	24%
Europarl	3.7	22%
Crawled	2.9	15%

Table 1: Subject–verb distances in German texts.

the verb. We extracted subject–verb pairs from German corpora and computed their distances. The results are summarized in Table 1.

News and *Europarl* are composed of more complex sentences than the corpus crawled from the internet. While in the crawled data, there are more sentences with smaller subject–verb distances, *News* and *Europarl* expose larger distances between subjects and finite verbs.

Although the average distance in words is rather small, there is a fair amount of subject–verb pairs with distance larger than 5 words (in Europarl 22%, in News 25%) which are problematic for training the translation system. Even for small distances, it is not guaranteed that the agreement is generated correctly due to the missing appropriate translation phrases. Moreover, the German language model trained on the same data would probably have problems to extract n-grams which ensure the correct subject–verb agreement for *all* possible subject–verb combinations.

Translating reordered English (cf. section 2.1) dramatically improves the problems of misplaced and missing verbs, but at the same time makes the extraction of translation phrases with subject–verb agreement even harder. Particularly problematic are movements of the verbs in subordinate clauses where the entire German VP is placed at the clause end, while the subject is normally placed in the 2nd position (after the complementizer). In our training data, 20% of the clauses are reordered in a way that the distance between the reordered finite verb and the subject is more than 5 words.

An example of a reordered English subordinate clause is given in Figure 2: the English verb *said* is ambiguous with respect to person and number. Translated independently from its subject, it is not guaranteed that the German translation will contain the correctly inflected finite verb since the German language model is very unlikely to have the exact 6-gram which could ensure the agreement between the subject *ich/I* and the inflected verb *habe/have*.

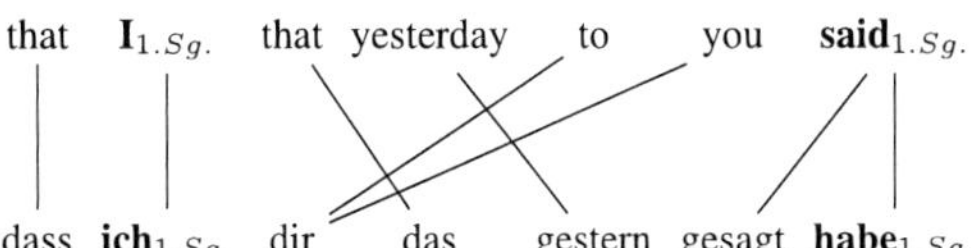

Figure 2: Example of a subject–verb distance caused by the reordering of the English clause *'that I said that yesterday to you'*.

3.2 Parsing for detection of subject–verb pairs

Agreement correction depends on correct identification of subject–verb pairs. Although we work with English parses where the subjects can be correctly identified in many cases, this information source seems not to be sufficient. Problematic are syntactic divergences where the English subject does not correspond to the German subject.

Initially, we aimed at predicting agreement features. However, we were not able to build a classifier with satisfying results due to the problems mentioned above. We thus applied a method implemented in *Depfix* (Rosa et al., 2012). They parse the MT output, extract subject–verb pairs from the trees and copy the agreement information of the subject to the corresponding verb. Although the idea of parsing MT output may not sound very promising, the results are surprisingly good.

We implement the agreement correction for English–German SMT as an automatic post-editing step applied on the fully inflected MT output. The MT output is first annotated with morphological information (Müller et al., 2013) and subsequently parsed (Björkelund and Nivre, 2015). The person and number of the subjects are then mapped from the subject to the finite verbs.

To generate the appropriate inflected verb, we use SMOR (Schmid et al., 2004), a morphology generation tool for German. Based on the stem of the verb, as well as its morphological features person, number, tense and mood (cf. section 4), the inflected verb form is generated. In case the tool produces multiple surface form possibilities (which is very rare for verbs) we use the frequency of the alternatives (derived from a large German corpus) as a filter: the most frequent alternative is chosen.

4 Modeling tense and mood

We define the modeling of tense and mood as a classification problem. In the following, we present the problem in more detail, motivate the machine learning features that we use and give a detailed evaluation of the classification model.[1]

4.1 Problem description

We distinguish between tense/mood of the finite verbs and tense/mood of the clauses. The German finite verbs can be present or past. As for the mood, they can be indicative, subjunctive and imperative.[2]

4.1.1 Tense

The tense of the finite verb does not necessarily match the clausal tense. For example, given the clausal tense *perfect*, the finite auxiliary is in present tense, while the main verb is a past participle: *[habe$_{Pres.Ind}$/have gesagt$_{ppart}$/said]$_{perfect}$*.

We model the translation of clausal tenses from English to German and than map the clausal tense to the corresponding tense of the finite verb.

German has six indicative clausal tenses (cf. Table 3). While in some languages, the use of tense underlies strict rules, the use of tenses in German often follows from the register (spoken vs. written) or even from the author's stylistic preferences (e.g. (Sammon, 2002), (Collins and Hollo, 2010)).

4.1.2 Mood

In addition to six indicative German tenses, we also distinguish two further tense/mood combinations: *Konjunktiv I* (present subjunctive) and *Konjunktiv II* (past subjunctive). While Konjunktiv II corresponds to English conditionals, Konjunktiv I is used in the context of indirect speech.

The use of subjunctives in German is not only quite complex, but also largely user- and register-dependent. For example, while Konjunktiv I occurs in *Europarl* and *News*, it is almost never used in the web-crawled corpus, as we will see in the following sections.

---

[1]Note that aspect is not encoded in the German verbal morphology. For expressing progressive aspect, adverbials (e.g. *gerade/at the moment*) or prepositional phrases (e.g. *Ich/I bin/am am/at Arbeiten/work 'I am working'*) are used (cf. e.g. (Heinold, 2015)). In this work, we do not explicitly model aspect.

[2]In this work, we ignore imperatives. Imperatives do not bear morphological information about tense and mood: they solely distinguish the person (singular/plural). We simply retain imperatives generated by the baseline system.

Info type	Example
STEMS	haben$_{VAFIN}$ sagen$_{VVPP}$
POS	VAFIN, VVPP
RFTagger	1.Sg.Past.Subj
RULE	if VP consists of an auxiliary (VAFIN) and a participle (VVPP) and if the finite verb is Past.Subj ⇒ konjunktivII (past subjunctive)'

Table 2: Information used to derive tense for the VP *hätte/would-have gesagt/said.*

4.2 Tense/mood prediction model

4.2.1 Model

For the classifier training, we use the toolkit *Wapiti* (Lavergne et al., 2010) which supports both multi-label maximum entropy classification and bigram linear-chain CRF classification.

We train a maximum entropy model, as well as a bigram linear-chain CRF model. The latter model captures intra-sentence tense/mood dependencies, i.e. between verbs within clauses of a single sentence: the prediction of tense/mood for the current clause considers the prediction made for the preceding clause.

Inter-sentence dependencies are however not modeled. The prediction for the first clause of the sentence under consideration does not take the last prediction made for the previous sentence into account.

4.2.2 Data

The training instances are extracted from Europarl, News Commentary and Crawled corpus. The English part of the corpus is parsed with the constituent parser of (Charniak and Johnson, 2005), while the German data is stemmed (cf. Section 2.2). We use the automatically computed word alignment (Och and Ney, 2003) in order to identify verb pairs in a given sentence pair.

We work with a set of 8 labels which includes six German tenses and the two subjunctive moods (see Table 3). In the training data, the labels are annotated by rule-based mapping of the German VPs. We use information about the verbs, their POS tags, as well as the morphological analysis of the finite verb to derive labels for each German VP (see Table 2 for an example mapping). The distribution of the labels in the corpora we use is given in Table 3.

For each finite verb, a training instance with features from English and German parallel sentence is extracted. Finite verbs of a sentence build

tense/mood	news	europarl	crawl	news+ euro+ crawl
present	54	63	71	62
perfect	11	14	12	12
imperfect	19	6	9	11
pluperfect	3	2	3	2.6
future I	1	3	1	1.6
future II	0.5	0.1	1	0.5
konjunktiv I	1	0.9	0.7	0.8
konjunktiv II	8	7	2	5.8

Table 3: Distribution of the tense/mood labels in the German corpora (given in percentage).

a sequence which allows for taking into account the tense/mood dependency between finite verbs within a sentence.

For the classifier training, we only use instances where the German verb is aligned with at least one English word. Furthermore, if the mapping of a VP to tense in one of the languages fails, the training instance is omitted as well. In total, we extract 5.2 million training instances.

4.2.3 Feature set

Each German finite verb gets features assigned from both English and German. The English features are extracted on the basis of the clauses. Given the alignment between the German finite verb and a specific word in English, the features are used which are extracted from the clause the English word is placed in. Since in the training, finite German verbs may be aligned with arbitrary English words (i.e. not only verbs), the clause-wide features allow to extract features also for these verbs.

Lexical features Lexical features give information about lexical choice of the verbs. To avoid sparsity problems, we abstract the English VP to a certain extent: we use information about (i) main (meaning-bearing) verbs, (ii) a sequence of auxiliaries without the main verb since the auxiliaries in English are used to form different tense/moods. By having access to the main verbs from both the current clause, as well as from the preceding clause, we account for the fact that the verbs (or their sequences) influence the use of tense/mood.

Contextual features Words preceding the German finite verb are useful for some specific contexts in which Konjunktiv is used.

Semantics/discourse The combination of clauses, i.e. clause types, has impact on the choice

Feature	English	German
finite verb	said	haben
finite verb align	–	said
VP	said	–
VP correct	yes	–
main verb	said	sagen
prev. clause main verb	–	denken
auxiliaries	VBD	–
main suffix	id	–
sentence main verb	think	–
word-1	–	gesagt
word-2	–	gestern
clause type	SBAR	–
preceding clause type	S-MAIN	–
following clause type	END	–
syntactical tense	past	–
logical tense	past	–
conditional context	no	–
composed sent	yes	–

Table 4: Full feature set for modeling tense/mood translation. The values are derived for the German finite verb *haben/have* from the clause pair given in Figure 2 assuming that the full English sentence is *'I think that I said that yesterday to you.'*

of tense/mood. Moreover, we use the information whether the sentence is composed (i.e. consists of more than one clause) to account for the fact that some tense/moods, e.g. Konjunktiv, are rarely used in simple sentences. The conditional context is derived by a simple check whether the conjunction in the subordinate clause is *if*.

The features are summarized in Table 4. Our model does not only use these features, but also a number of their combinations to strengthen contexts for specific tense/moods.

4.2.4 Classifier evaluation

Although both maximum entropy, as well as CRF models trained on the same data using the same feature set perform equally well, CRF performs better for certain labels as shown in Table 5.

We further evaluate the CRF model on test sets from different domains (cf. Table 6). Note that the test sets are well-formed sentences taken from the corpora we work with. We contrast evaluation results gained on well-formed test data to those obtained for noisy MT output. The evaluation on the well-formed data is given in F_1-scores while the MT output is evaluated with BLEU.

The row *mostFreqTense* is considered to be a baseline: the verbs are annotated with tense which is the most frequent German tense given a specific English tense (cf. Figure 3). It is interesting that

tense/mood	$F_{1_{CRF}}$	$F_{1_{me}}$
present	0.92	0.92
perfect	0.81	0.81
imperfect	0.85	0.85
pluperfect	**0.74**	0.73
future I	**0.84**	0.83
future II	0.50	0.50
konjunktiv I	**0.27**	0.17
konjunktiv II	0.83	0.83
overall	0.87	0.87

Table 5: Performance of a CRF vs. maximum entropy classifier gained for a test set containing 5,000 sentence from the news corpus.

the baseline performs equally well when applied on news and crawl, it however leads to lower F_1 for the europarl test set. This indicates that the tense usage in europarl deviates from that in news and crawled corpora.

Our model is considerably better than the baseline. It leads to better results on both well-formed test sets, as well as on the MT output.

tense/mood	$F_{1_{CRF}}$			BLEU
	news	europarl	crawl	MT-news
mostFreqTense	0.70	0.64	0.70	21.79
our model	0.87	0.90	0.88	21.95

Table 6: Classifier evaluation using different features and different test sets. Each of the clean data test sets contain 5,000 sentences. Clean data sets are evaluated in terms of F_1 scores, while the MT output is evaluated with BLEU.

The difference in performance gained on test sets from different domains (although small) raises the question whether the classifier is solely to be trained on in-domain data. Since we work with MT output of the news test set, we would have to train the classifier only on the news data. Due to the corpus size (272k sentences), we get into sparsity problems since many lexical features are used. A further reason for using additional (out-of-domain) training data are low-frequent labels which then get more training instances.

In summary, the evaluation indicates that a single classifier leads to different results when applied on data from different domains. Furthermore, the initial experiments showed that having better results on the clean data does not necessarily lead to better results for the noisy MT output.

5 Verbal morphology in MT output

5.1 Baseline system

Our baseline system is trained on reordered English sentences (cf. Section 2.1) and stemmed German data (cf. Section 2.2). It is trained on a corpus consisting of 4.5 M sentences from news, Europarl and crawled texts. It uses a 5-gram language model trained on 1.5 billion German words.

The baseline system translates reordered English into stemmed German in which the verbs are surface forms and enriched with POS tags.

5.2 Evaluation of the verbs in MT output

The baseline SMT system is applied on a news test set from WMT 2015.[3]

The baseline MT output we aim at correcting is surprisingly good. The stem- and surface-based comparison of the verbs in the baseline with the reference revealed that 82% of the verbs in the baseline are already correctly inflected. This quite high number though takes only 21% of the verbs in the baseline into account: nearly 80% of the verbs in the baseline do not match the reference, i.e. the lexical choice (the lemma) of the verbs differs from the reference.

Our verbal inflection correcting system changes 242 (6%) of the verbs output by the baseline SMT system. Given the strong baseline we work with, we would in fact do worse if we changed more (i.e. already correctly inflected) verbs.

Considering the fact that most of the finite verbs do not match the reference and are thus not considered with automatic metrics such es BLEU (cf. Section 5.2.1), we also carried out a human evaluation which is presented in Section 5.2.2.

5.2.1 Automatic evaluation

In Table 7, the BLEU scores (Papineni et al., 2002) of the MT output with predicted verbal inflection are presented.

	$BLEU_{ci}$
Surface	21.59
Baseline	22.00
Verbal inflection	22.05
Agreement	22.08
Tense/mood	21.95

Table 7: BLEU scores of MT outputs with corrected verbal inflection.

Verbal inflection denotes MT output for which all verbal features are derived/predicted and then used to generate the inflected verb forms. The translation quality does not increase (in terms of BLEU) significantly. Most of the improvement comes from the agreement correction (given in row *Agreement*) while the tense/mood prediction (row *Tense/mood*) lowers the BLEU score.

5.2.2 Manual evaluation of MT

70 sentence pairs consisting of the baseline MT output and MT output with corrected verbal inflection with respect to tense and mood were evaluated by four human evaluators. The evaluators annotated the better translation alternative with 1, the worse one with 2. For each of the translations, the *majority vote* (most frequent annotation) was computed. The counts of the human votes are given in Table 8.

MT	Grade			
	1	2	3	nA
Baseline	**29**	19	4	19
Verbal inflection	17	31	4	19

Table 8: Results of human evaluation. 1 = better, 2 = worse, 3 = don't know, nA = no majority vote.

Human evaluators prefer the choice of tense (expressed in verbal inflection) made by the baseline. Only a third of the alternatives with verbal inflection handling are considered to be better than the baseline. An interesting fact is that the annotator agreement in terms of Kappa was only 0.33 which means that the annotators often disagreed which translation alternative was better.

In Table 9, a few example MT outputs are shown in which the verbal inflection is correct, while the baseline is incorrect. The VI translation of SRC1 shows corrected agreement between the plural subject *Kläger/claimants* and the finite verb *legten/presented*. The translations of SCR2 and SRC3 show the corrected tense. In SRC2, the English verb in past tense is in VI also translated as past tense. In SRC3, the German translation of the subordinate clause should be past subjunctive as generated by VI.

VI correct	SRC1	the claimants presented proof of extortion
	BL	*legte$_{3.Sg}$ die Kläger Beweise von Erpressung
	VI	legten$_{3.Pl}$ die Kläger Beweise von Erpressung
	SRC2	then he put his finger on it
	BL	dann *legt$_{Pres.Ind}$ er seinen Finger auf sie
	VI	dann legte$_{Past.Ind}$ er seinen Finger auf sie
	SRC3	I fear I may need more surgery
	BL	ich fürchte, ich *kann$_{Pres.Ind}$ eine Operation nötig
	VI	ich fürchte, ich könnte$_{Past.Subj}$ eine Operation nötig
VI incorrect	SRC4	Maybe his father intended to be cruel
	BL	vielleicht soll$_{Pres.Ind}$ seine Vater grausam zu sein
	VI	vielleicht *sollte$_{Past.Subj}$ seine Vater grausam zu sein
	SRC5	" i have rung mr piffl and suggested that we get together "
	BL	"ich habe$_{Pres.Ind}$ geklingelt Herr piffl und schlug vor, dass wir gemeinsam"
	VI	"ich *hatte$_{Past.Ind}$ geklingelt Herr piffl und schlug vor, dass wir gemeinsam"
	SRC6	no word could get beyond the soundproofing
	BL	kein Wort konnte üer die Schalldämmung
	VI	kein Wort *könte über die Schalldämmung

Table 9: Example of MT outputs with improved (upper part) and incorrect verbal inflection (lower part). *SRC* denotes the source sentences, the baseline translations are indicated with *BL*, while the translations with verbal inflection handling are indicated with *VI*.

The VI translation of *intended* in SRC4 retains the tense in the source sentences. The human evaluators, however, prefer the baseline translation, which switches to present tense. German has two past tenses: the baseline translation of *have rung* in SRC5 is perfect (*habe geklingelt*), while the VI translation is pluperfect (*hatte geklingelt*). Even for a human, it is hard to decide which of the translations is *better*. The translation of SRC6 shows a problem with English modal verbs such as *could* which expose functional ambiguity. As subjunctive, *could* almost always translates into subjunctive German modal *könnte*. Thus the model always predicts konjunktiv II given English modals for which the past indicative form equals to the subjunctive form.

6 Discussion

6.1 Subject–verb agreement

Correction of the subject–verb agreement proposed by Rosa et al. (2012) and adapted in this work for English–German SMT, relies on how accurate the identification of the subject–verb rela-

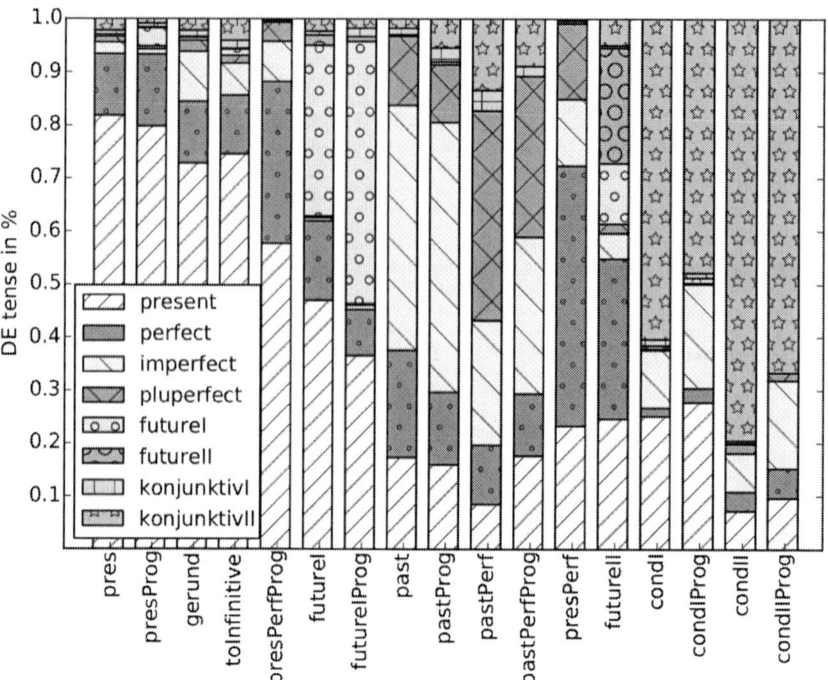

Figure 3: Distribution of tense translations derived from the training corpora (news, europarl, crawl). English tense/mood values are given on the x-axis, while the percentage of the German tense/moods for the corresponding EN tense/mood is given on the y-axis.

tions in noisy MT output is. The better the translation, the higher the probability of acquiring correct subject–verb pairs from the parse trees. However, the quality of the translations varies greatly, even within a single test set. Rosa et al. (2012) reported on different results achieved for different test sets. Another possibility is to use a classification model which predicts agreement features of the verbs using various contextual information as successfully applied on English–Spanish (Gispert and Mariño, 2008).

Our attempt to build such a model for German, led to disappointing results: on the one hand, a more accurate identification of the subjects in the English constituent parse trees is required: the use of the dependency trees combined with pronoun resolution (similar to a simple pronoun resolution described in (Avramidis and Koehn, 2008)) might reduce this problem. More correct subject identification in the source language is however not sufficient: due to syntactic divergences, the German subject may match other constituents in the source language (e.g. object or preposition phrase). A prediction model having access to information extracted from both English dependency trees, as

well as German MT parses (in combination with clues on the reliability of the extracted information) might give good results regarding the prediction of agreement features for German finite verbs.

6.2 Tense and mood

Register/domain Looking at Figure 3, it becomes obvious that a single English tense can translate into different German tenses. Always choosing the most frequent German tense for a given English tense does not lead to satisfying results (cf. Table 6). On the other hand, Schiehlen (1998), who presented one of the first studies on learning the tense translation from bilingual corpora, stated that this simple tense mapping already achieved the accuracy of 95%. We achieve 70%. This is probably due to register and domain difference: while Schiehlen (1998) worked with corpora related to appointment scheduling (spoken language), we work with news data (written language) which has important differences with respect to tense translation.

Tense usage The correct choice of tense in both human and automatic translation depends on factors which are beyond the scope of our approach (we model the lexical choice of the verbs and syntax). This is true even though some languages have strict tense usage rules. One factor may simply be a *rule* such as the one found in the EC guidelines for translation from English to German[4]: *"Protokolle oder Berichte von Sitzungen werden in der deutschsprachigen Fassung stets im Präsens verfasst..."* / "It is required to use present tense in the translation of protocols and reports, regardless of the tense in the source language." Such a rule does not apply to the translation of news articles. However, in news articles tense/moods are used, in particular subjunctive mood, in which the reporter does not present his own assessment of a situation, but what someone else said (Csipak, 2015), which are almost never used in texts found on the internet (see konjunktiv I + II in Table 3).

Language–pair specific features Ye et al. (2006) presented thoughts about the knowledge that human translators use. The aim was to use this knowledge to model tense translation for Chinese–English. For this specific language pair (and possibly for the corpus used), the knowledge about temporal ordering of the actions was the key information. On the other hand, for English–French, Meyer et al. (2013) found that a *narrativity* feature helps to translate the English past tense into one of the possible French tenses.

Tense switch We observed sentence pairs in which the English is written in past tense, while in German, present tense is used. Obviously, there are contexts in which tense switches are allowed. We assume that these sentences are headlines which allow for this kind of tense variation.

Tense interchangeability It seems that in numerous contexts, tense translation can sometimes even be a matter of taste. Sammon (2002) states that in German the imperfect and perfect are interchangeable in many contexts, the difference between the two tenses being largely stylistic. A similar example is reported speech where Konjunktiv I, Konjunktiv II and indicative tenses are often used interchangeably (Csipak, 2015).

Sequential problem It is also not very clear whether the tense/mood is to be dealt with as a

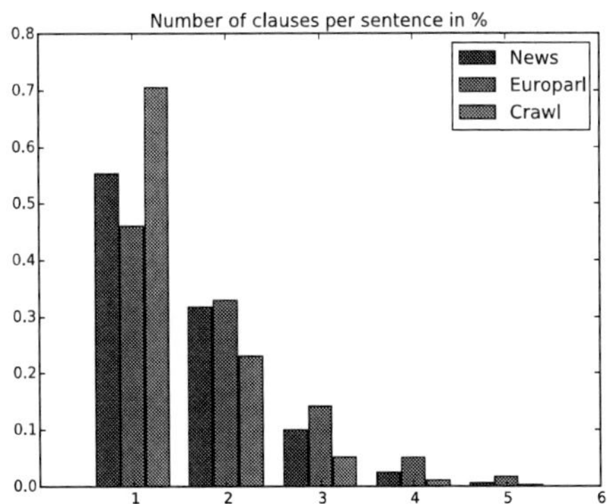

Figure 4: Percentage of sentences from different corpora containing different number of clauses.

sequential problem or not. On the one hand, in the monolingual context of correcting English tense, Tajiri et al. (2012) argues for a sequential tense model. On the other hand Ye et al. (2006) observed that sequential dependence of the tenses is not as strong as expected. In the bilingual context, there seems to be a strong dependence on the tense in the source language. Statistics about the number of clauses in the sentences shown in Figure 4, shows that our data mostly consists of simple sentences containing only one clause (i.e. one finite verb). In other words, for most of the sentences, an intra-sentence tense sequence is simply not given. Inter-sentence tense modeling, i.e., across sentence boundaries, could be more reasonable, as for example, presented by Gong et al. (2012) for Chinese to English SMT.

Evaluation of the verbs The final question we raise is how to evaluate translations with respect to information related to discourse such as tense and modality (or negation as discussed by Fancellu and Webber (2014)). Automatic evaluation such as BLEU is not appropriate since it compares the translation with the reference mainly on the *lexical* level. What about human evaluation? Our evaluators have a Kappa score of 0.33 which is rather low. The humans thus allow for a certain variance in tense/mood translation which metrics like BLEU cannot capture given only one reference translation. Ideally, we would have multiple references in which all possible tenses are given. Creating such an evaluation test set could be done by gap-filling method proposed by Hardmeier (2014) for evaluation of pronoun translation.

---

[4]Guidelines for translations into German used by the European Commission: `http://ec.europa.eu/translation/german/guidelines/documents/german_style_guide_en.pdf`

Summary For modeling mood translation, features such as reported speech, conditional context, polite form, etc. would more clearly describe the contexts in which a specific mood occurs. The information about tense ordering proposed by Ye et al. (2006) for Chinese–English would probably be helpful also for English–to–German translation. However, the extraction of such features is more complicated than simply using *surface* features such as words, POS tags, etc.

7 Future work

The verbal inflection handling that we present in this paper is implemented as a post-processing step to the translation. We use the words, i.e. verbs, generated by the SMT system and change them according to our inflection models. An interesting approach would, however, be to use a more abstract representation of German VPs which would allow for generation of all of the words in a VP as specified by the inflection model. For example, we could handle inserting/deleting verbs (auxiliaries), reflexives or even negation.

As for the modeling of tense and mood, we are going to explore possibilities to include discourse knowledge (which was discussed in the previous section) into the classification model. Such a model could also be used within the translation step, for example, to rerank translation alternatives.

Acknowledgments

This work was partially supported by Deutsche Forschungsgemeinschaft grant Models of Morphosyntax for Statistical Machine Translation (Phase 2). This work has received funding from the European Union's Horizon 2020 research and innovation programme under grant agreement No. 644402 (HimL) and from the European Research Council (ERC) under grant agreement No. 640550.

References

Eleftherios Avramidis and Philipp Koehn. 2008. Enriching morphologically poor languages for statistical machine translation. In *Proceedings of the Annual Meeting of the Association for Computational Linguistics (ACL-HLT)*, pages 763–770, Columbus, Ohio, June.

Anders Björkelund and Joakim Nivre. 2015. Non-deterministic oracles for unrestricted non-projective transition-based dependency parsing. In *Proceedings of the 14th International Conference on Parsing Technologies*, pages 76–86, Bilbao, Spain, July. Association for Computational Linguistics.

Eugene Charniak and Mark Johnson. 2005. Coarse-to-fine n-best parsing and MaxEnt discriminative reranking. In *Proceedings of the 43rd Annual Meeting on Association for Computational Linguistics (ACL)*, Ann Arbor, Michigan.

Peter Collins and Carmella Hollo. 2010. *English grammar. An introduction*. Palgrave macmillan, 2 edition.

Eva Csipak. 2015. *Free factive subjunctives in German*. Niedersächsische Staats- und Universitätsbibliothek Göttingen.

Federico Fancellu and Bonnie Webber. 2014. Applying the semantics of negation to SMT through n-best list re-ranking. In *Proceedings of the 14th Conference of the European Chapter of the Association for Computational Linguistics*, Gothenburg, Sweden, April.

Alexander Fraser, Marion Weller, Aoife Cahill, and Fabienne Cap. 2012. Modeling inflection and word-formation in SMT. In *Proceedings of the the the European Chapter of the Association for Computational Linguistics (EACL)*, Avignon, France.

Adrià de Gispert and Jose B. Mariño. 2008. On the impact of morphology in English to Spanish statistical MT. *Speech Communication*, 50(11-12):1034–1046.

Anita Gojun and Alexander Fraser. 2012. Determining the placement of German verbs in English-to-German SMT. In *Proceedings of the 13th Conference of the European Chapter of the Association for Computational Linguistics (EACL)*, pages 726–735, Avignon, France, April.

Zhengxian Gong, Min Zhang, Chewlim Tan, and Guodong Zhou. 2012. N-gram-based tense models for statistical machine translation. In *Proceedings of the 2012 Joint Conference on Empirical Methods in Natural Language Processing and Computational Natural Language Learning (EMNLP-CoNLL)*, pages 276–285, Jeju Island, Korea, July.

Christian Hardmeier. 2014. Discourse in statistical machine translation. In *Studia Linguistica Upsaliensia, vol. 14. Acta Universitatis Upsaliensis*, Uppsala, Sweden.

Simone Heinold. 2015. *Tempus, Modus und Aspekt im Deutschen. Ein Studienbuch*. narr studienbcher.

Thomas Lavergne, Olivier Cappé, and François Yvon. 2010. Practical very large scale CRFs. In *Proceedings the 48th Annual Meeting of the Association for Computational Linguistics (ACL)*, pages 504–513. Association for Computational Linguistics, July.

Thomas Meyer, Cristina Grisot, and Andrei Popescu-Belis. 2013. Detecting narrativity to improve English to French translation of simple past verbs. In *Proceedings of the 1st DiscoMT Workshop at 51st Annual Meeting of the Association for Computational Linguistics (ACL)*.

Thomas Müller, Helmut Schmid, and Hinrich Schütze. 2013. Efficient higher-order CRFs for morphological tagging. In *Proceedings of the 2013 Conference on Empirical Methods in Natural Language Processing*, pages 322–332, Seattle, Washington, USA, October. Association for Computational Linguistics.

Franz Josef Och and Hermann Ney. 2003. A systematic comparison of various statistical alignment models. *Computational Linguistics*, 29(1):19–51.

Kishore Papineni, Salim Roukos, Todd Ward, and Wei-Jing Zhu. 2002. Bleu: A method for automatic evaluation of machine translation. In *Proceedings of the 40th Annual Meeting on Association for Computational Linguistics*, pages 311–318, Stroudsburg, PA, USA. Association for Computational Linguistics.

Rudolf Rosa, David Mareček, and Ondřej Dušek. 2012. DEPFIX: a system for automatic correction of Czech MT outpus. In *Proceedings of the Seventh Workshop on Statistical Machine Translation*, pages 362–368, Montréal, Canada, June.

Geoff Sammon. 2002. *Exploring English grammar*. Cornelson Verlag.

Michael Schiehlen. 1998. Learning Tense Translation from Bilingual Corpora. In *COLING-ACL 1998 36th Annual Meeting of the Association for Computational Linguistics and 17th International Conference on Computational Linguistics*, pages 1183–1187, Montral, Quebec, Canada, August.

Helmut Schmid, Arne Fitschen, and Ulrich Heid. 2004. SMOR: A German computational morphology covering derivation, composition, and inflection. In *Proceedings of the 4th International Conference on Language Resources and Evaluation (LREC)*, Lisbon, Portugal.

Toshikazu Tajiri, Mamoru Komachi, and Yuji Matsumoto. 2012. Tense and aspect error correction for ESL learners using global context. In *Proceedings of the 50th Annual Meeting of the Association for Computational Linguistics (ACL): Short Papers - Volume 2*, pages 198–202, Jeju Island, Korea, July.

Yang Ye, Victoria Li Fossum, and Steven Abney. 2006. Latent features in automatic tense translation between Chinese and English. In *Proceedings of the Seventh SIGHAN Workshop on Chinese Language Processing*, Sidney, Australia, July.

Modeling Selectional Preferences of Verbs and Nouns in String-to-Tree
Machine Translation

Maria Nădejde
School of Informatics
University of Edinburgh
m.nadejde@sms.ed.ac.uk

Alexandra Birch
School of Informatics
University of Edinburgh
a.birch@ed.ac.uk

Philipp Koehn
Department of Computer Science
Johns Hopkins University
phi@jhu.edu

Abstract

We address the problem of mistranslated predicate-argument structures in syntax-based machine translation. This paper explores whether knowledge about semantic affinities between the target predicates and their argument fillers is useful for translating ambiguous predicates and arguments. We propose a selectional preference feature based on the selectional association measure of Resnik (1996) and integrate it in a string-to-tree decoder. The feature models selectional preferences of verbs for their core and prepositional arguments as well as selectional preferences of nouns for their prepositional arguments.

We compare our features with a variant of the neural relational dependency language model (RDLM) (Sennrich, 2015) and find that neither of the features improves automatic evaluation metrics. We conclude that mistranslated verbs, errors in the target syntactic trees produced by the decoder and underspecified syntactic relations are negatively impacting these features.

1 Introduction

Syntax-based machine translation systems have had some success when applied to language pairs with major structural differences such as German-English or Chinese-English. Modeling the target side syntactic structure is important in order to produce grammatical, fluent translations and could be an intermediate step on which to build a semantic representation of the target sentence. However these systems still suffer from errors such as scrambled or mis-translated predicate-argument structures. We give a few examples of such errors in Table 1. In example a) the baseline system MT1 mistranslates the verb *besichtigt* as *viewed*. The system MT2 which uses information about the semantic affinity between the verb and its argument produces the correct translation *visited*. The semantic affinity score , shown on the right, for the verb *viewed* and argument *trip* in the syntactic relation *prep_on* is indicating a stronger affinity than for the baseline translation. In example b) the baseline system MT1 mistranslates the noun *Aufnahmen* as *recordings* while the system MT2 produces the correct translation *images* which is a better fit for the prepositional modifier *from the telescope*.

Syntax-based MT systems handle long distance reordering with synchronous translation rules such as:

$$root \rightarrow \langle RB^{\sim 0} VBZ^{\sim 1} sich\ nsubj^{\sim 2} prep^{\sim 3},$$
$$RB^{\sim 0} nsubj^{\sim 2} VBZ^{\sim 1} prep^{\sim 3} \rangle$$

This rule is useful for reordering the verb and its arguments according to the target side word order. However the rule does not contain the lexical head for the verb, the subject and the prepositional modifier. Therefore the entire predicate argument structure is translated by subsequent independent rules. The language model context will capture at most the verb and one main argument. Due to the lack of a larger source or target context the resulting predicate-argument structures are often not semantically coherent.

This paper explores whether knowledge about semantic affinities between the target predicates and their argument fillers is useful for translating ambiguous predicates and arguments. We propose a selectional preference feature for string-to-tree statistical machine translation based on the information theoretic measure of Resnik (1996). The feature models selectional preferences of verbs for

32

Proceedings of the First Conference on Machine Translation, Volume 1: Research Papers, pages 32–42,
Berlin, Germany, August 11-12, 2016. ©2016 Association for Computational Linguistics

| | | | (relation, predicate, argument) | Affinity |

a)

	SRC	Bei nur einer Reise können nicht alle davon *besichtigt* werden.		
	REF	You won't be able to *visit* all of them on one trip .		
	MT1	Not all of them can be *viewed* on only one trip.	(prep_on, *viewed*, trip)	-0.154
	MT2	Not all of them can be *visited* on only one trip.	(prep_on, *visited*, trip)	1.042

b)

	SRC	Eine der schärfsten *Aufnahmen* des Hubble-Teleskops		
	REF	One of the sharpest *pictures* from the Hubble telescope		
	MT1	One of the strongest *recordings* of the Hubble telescope	(prep_of, *recordings*, telescope)	-0.0004
	MT2	One of the strongest *images* from the Hubble telescope	(prep_from, *images*, telescope)	0.3917

Table 1: Examples of errors in the predicate-argument structure produced by a syntax-based MT system. a) mistranslated verb b) mistranslated noun. Semantic affinity scores are shown on the right. Higher scores indicate a stronger affinity. Negative scores indicate a lack of affinity.

their core and prepositional arguments as well as selectional preferences of nouns for their prepositional arguments.

Previous work has addressed the selectional preferences of prepositions for noun classes (Weller et al., 2014) but not the semantic affinities between a predicate and its argument class. Another line of research on improving translation of predicate-argument structures includes modeling reordering and deletion of semantic roles (Wu and Fung, 2009; Liu and Gildea, 2010; Li et al., 2013). These models however do not encode information about the lexical semantic affinities between target predicates and their arguments. Sennrich (2015) proposes a relational dependency language model (RDLM) for string-to-tree machine translation. One component of RDLM predicts the head word of a dependent conditioned on a wide syntactic context. Our feature is different as it quantifies the amount of information that the predicate carries about the argument class filling a particular syntactic function.

For one variant of the proposed feature we found a slight improvement in automatic evaluation metrics when translating short sentences as well as an increase in precision for verb translation. However the features generally did not improve automatic evaluation metrics. We conclude that mistranslated verbs, errors in the target syntactic trees produced by the decoder and under-specified syntactic relations are negatively impacting these features.

The paper is structured as follows. Section 2 describes related work on improving translation of predicate-argument structures. Section 3 introduces the selectional preference feature. Section 4 describes the experimental setup and Section 5 presents the results of automatic evaluation as well as a qualitative analysis of the machine translated output.

2 Related work

From a syntactic perspective, a correct predicate-argument structure will have the sub-categorization frame of the predicate filled in. Weller et al. (2013) use sub-categorization information to improve case-prediction for noun phrases when translating into German. Case prediction for noun phrases is important in the German language as it indicates the grammatical function. Their approach however did not produce strong improvements over the baseline. From a large corpus annotated with dependency relations, they extract verb-noun tuples and their associated syntactic functions: direct object, indirect object, subject. They also extract triples of verb-preposition-noun in order to predict the case of noun-phrases within prepositional-phrases. The probabilities of such tuples and triples are computed using relative frequencies and then used as a feature for a CRF classifier that predicts the case of noun-phrases. Weller et al. (2013) apply the CRF classifier to the output of a word-to-stem phrased-based translation system as a post-processing step. In contrast, our model is used directly as a feature in the decoder. While Weller et al. (2013) identify the arguments of the verb and their grammatical function by projecting the information from the source sentence we use the dependency tree produced by the string-to-tree decoder. We also consider prepositional modifiers of nouns.

Weller et al. (2014) propose using noun class information to model selectional preferences of prepositions in a string-to-tree translation system. They use the noun class information to annotate PP translation rules in order to restrict their applicability to specific semantic classes. In our work we don't impose hard constraints on the translation rules, but rather soft constraints using our model as a feature in the decoder. While we use word embeddings to cluster arguments, Weller et al. (2014) experiment with a lexical semantic taxonomy and clustering words based on co-occurrences within a window or syntactic features extracted from dependency-parsed data.

Modeling reordering and deletion of semantic roles (Wu and Fung, 2009; Liu and Gildea, 2010; Li et al., 2013) has been another line of research on improving translation of predicate-argument structures. Liu and Gildea (2010) propose modeling reordering of a complete semantic frame while Li et al. (2013) propose finer grained features that distinguish between predicate-argument reordering and argument-argument reordering. Gao and Vogel (2011) and Bazrafshan and Gildea (2013) annotate target non-terminals with the semantic roles they cover in order to extract synchronous grammar rules that cover the entire predicate argument structure. These models however do not encode information about the lexical semantic affinities between target predicates and their arguments.

In this work we focus on using selectional preference over predicate and arguments in the target as this is a simple way of leveraging external knowledge in the translation framework.

3 Selectional Preference Feature

3.1 Learning Selectional Preferences

Selectional preferences describe the semantic affinities between predicates and their argument fillers. For example, the verb "drinks" has a strong preference for arguments in the conceptual class of "liquids". Therefore the word "wine" can be disambiguated when it appears in relation to the verb "drinks". A corpus driven approach to modeling selectional preferences usually involves extracting triples of (*syntactic relation, predicate, argument*) and computing co-occurrence statistics. The predicate and argument are represented by their head words and the triples are extracted from automatically parsed data. Another typical step is generalizing over seen arguments. Approaches to generalization include using an ontology such as Word-Net (Resnik, 1996), using distributional semantics

similarity (Erk et al., 2010; Séaghdha, 2010; Ritter et al., 2010), clustering (Sun and Korhonen, 2009), multi-modal datasets (Shutova et al., 2015), and neural networks (Cruys, 2014).

Our feature is based on the measure proposed by Resnik (1996). It uses unsupervised clusters to generalize over seen arguments. Resnik (1996) uses selectional preferences of predicates for word sense disambiguation. The information theoretic measure for selectional preference proposed by Resnik quantifies the difference between the posterior distribution of an argument class given the verb and the prior distribution of the class. For instance, "person" has a higher prior probability than "insect" to appear in the subject relation, but, knowing the verb is "fly", the posterior probability becomes higher for "insect".

Resnik's model defines *selectional preference strength* of a predicate as:

$$
\begin{aligned}
SelPref(p, r) &= KL(P(c|p, r) \parallel P(c|r)) \\
&= \sum_c P(c|p, r) log \frac{P(c|p, r)}{P(c|r)}
\end{aligned}
\tag{1}
$$

where KL is the Kullback - Leibler divergence, r is the relation type, p is the predicate and c is the conceptual class of the argument. Resnik uses WordNet to obtain the conceptual classes of arguments, therefore generalizing over seen arguments. The *selectional association* or semantic affinity between a predicate and an argument class is quantified as the relative contribution of the class towards the overall selectional strength of the predicate:

$$
SelAssoc(p, r, c) = \frac{P(c|p, r) log \frac{P(c|p, r)}{P(c|r)}}{SelStr(p, r)}
\tag{2}
$$

We give examples of the *selectional preference strength* and *selectional association* scores for different verbs and their arguments in Table 2. The verb *see* takes on many arguments as direct objects and therefore has a lower selectional preference strength for this syntactic relation. In contrast the predicate *hereditary* takes on fewer arguments for which it has a stronger selectional preference.

Several selectional preference models have been used as features in discriminative syntactic parsing systems. Cohen et al. (2012) observe

Verb	Relation	SelPref	Argument	SelAssoc
see	dobj	0.56	PRN	0.123
			movie	0.022
			episode	0.001
is–hereditary	nsubj	1.69	disease	0.267
			monarchy	0.148
			title	0.082
drink	dobj	3.90	water	0.144
			wine	0.061
			glass	0.027

Table 2: Example of *selectional preference* (SelPref) and *selectional association* (SelAssoc) scores for different verbs. PRN is the class of pronouns.

that when parsing out-of-domain data many attachment errors occur for the following syntactic configurations: head (V or N) – prep – obj and head (N) – adj. The authors proposed a class-based measure of selectional preferences for these syntactic configurations and learn the argument classes using Latent Dirichlet Allocation (LDA). Kiperwasser and Goldberg (2015) compare different measures of lexical association between head word and modifier word for improving dependency parsing. Their results show that the association measure based on pointwise mutual information (PMI) has similar generalization capabilities as a measure of distributional similarity between word embeddings. van Noord (2007) has shown that bilexical association scores computed using PMI for all types of dependency relations are a useful feature for improving dependency parsing in Dutch.

3.2 Adaptation of Selectional Preference Models for Syntax-Based Machine Translation.

We are interested in modeling selectional preferences of verbs for their core and prepositional arguments as well as selectional preferences of nouns for their prepositional arguments. We identify the relation between a predicate and its modifier from the dependency tree produced by a string-to-tree machine translation system. Since we are interested in using the feature during decoding, we need the model to be fast to query and have broad coverage.

Our selectional preference feature is a variant of the information theoretic measure of Resnik (1996) defined in Eq 2. While Resnik uses the WordNet classes of the arguments, this is not appropriate for a machine translation task where the vocabulary has millions of words and English is not the only targeted language. Therefore we adapt Resnik's selectional association measure in two ways.

In the first model *SelAssoc_L* we compute the co-occurrence statistics defined in Eq 2 over lemmas of the predicate and argument head words.

In the second model *SelAssoc_C* we replace the WordNet classes in Eq 2 with word clusters[1] . We obtain the word clusters by applying the k-means algorithm to the glovec word embeddings (Pennington et al., 2014).

Prepositional phrase attachment remains a frequent and challenging error for syntactic parsers (Kummerfeld et al., 2012) and translation of prepositions is a challenge for SMT (Weller et al., 2014). Therefore we decide to use two separate features: one for main arguments (*nsubj, nsubjpass, dobj, iobj*) and one for prepositional arguments.

3.3 Comparison with a Neural Relational Dependency Language Model.

Sennrich (2015) proposes a relational dependency language model (RDLM) for string-to-tree machine translation, which he trains using a feed-forward neural network. For a sentence S with symbols $w_1, w_2, ...w_n$ and dependency labels $l_1, l_2, ...l_n$ with l_i the label of the incoming arc at position i, RDLM is defined as:

---

[1] We have not done experiments with WordNet classes.

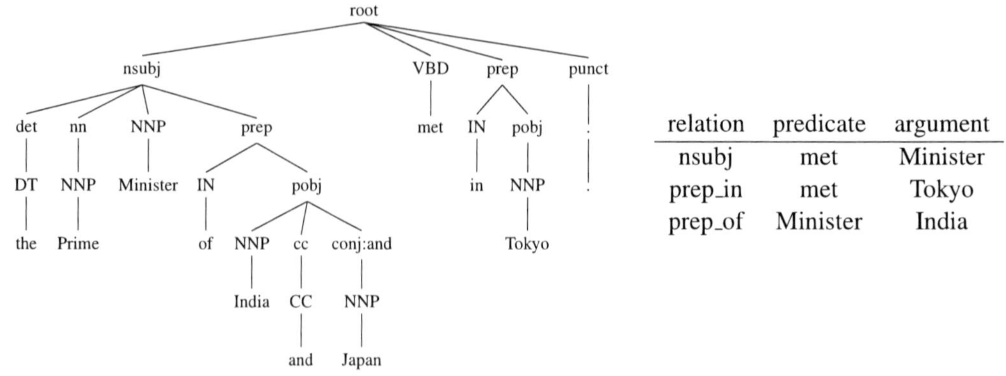

Figure 1: Example of a translation and its dependency tree in constituency representation produced by the string-to-tree SMT system. Triples extracted during decoding are shown on the right.

$$P(S, D) \approx \prod_{i=1}^{n} P_l(i) \times P_w(i)$$

$$P_l(i) = P(l_i \mid h_s(i)_1^q, l_s(i)_1^q, h_a(i)_1^r, l_a(i)_1^r)$$

$$P_w(i) = P(w_i \mid h_s(i)_1^q, l_s(i)_1^q, h_a(i)_1^r, l_a(i)_1^r, l_i)$$

$$(3)$$

where for each of q siblings and r ancestors of w_i, h_s and h_a are their head words and l_s and l_a their dependency labels. The $P_w(i)$ distribution models similar information as our proposed feature $SelAssoc$. However we use $h_a(i)_1, l_i$ as context and consider only a subset of dependency labels: *nsubj, nsubjpass, dobj, iobj, prep*. The reduced context alleviates problems of data sparsity and is more reliably extracted at decoding time. The subset of dependency relations identify arguments for which predicates might exhibit selectional preferences. Our feature is different from $RDLM - P_w$ as it quantifies the amount of information that the predicate carries about the argument class filling a particular syntactic function. We hypothesize that such information is useful when translating arguments that appear less frequently in the training data but are prototypical for certain predicates. For example the triples *(bus, drive, dobj)* and *(van, drive, dobj)* have the following log posterior probabilities and $SelAssoc$ scores: log P(bus | drive, dobj) = -5.44, log P(van | drive, dobj)= -5.58 and SelAssoc(bus, drive, dobj) = 0.0079, SelAssoc(van, drive, dobj) = 0.0103.

4   Experimental setup

Our baseline system for translating German into English is the Moses string-to-tree toolkit imple-

menting GHKM rule extraction (Galley et al., 2004, 2006; Williams and Koehn, 2012). The string-to-tree translation model is based on a synchronous context-free grammar (SCFG) that is extracted from word-aligned parallel data with target-side syntactic annotation. The system was trained on all available data provided at WMT15 [2] (Bojar et al., 2015). The number of sentences in the training, tuning and test sets are shown in Table 3. We use the following rule extraction parameters: *Rule Depth = 5, Node Count = 20, Rule Size = 5*. At decoding time we give a high penalty to glue rules and allow non-terminals to span a maximum of 50 words. We train a 5-gram language model on all available monolingual data [3] using the SRILM toolkit (Stolcke, 2002) with modified Kneser-Ney smoothing (Chen and Goodman, 1998) for training and KenLM (Heafield, 2011) for language model scoring during decoding.

Train	Tune	Test
4,472,694	2000	8172

Table 3: Number of sentences in the training, tuning and test sets. The test set consists of the WMT newstest2013, 2014 and 2015.

The English side of the parallel corpus is annotated with dependency relations using the Stanford dependency parser (Chen and Manning, 2014). The dependency structure is then converted to a constituency representation which is needed to run the GHKM rule extraction. We use the conversion

---

[2]http://www.statmt.org/wmt15/translation-task.html
[3]target side of the parallel corpus, the monolingual English News Crawl, Gigaword and news-commentary

algorithm and the head word extraction method described in Sennrich (2015).

For training the selectional preference features we extract triples of *(dependency relation, predicate, argument)* from parsed data, where the predicate and argument are identified by their head word. We use the english side of the parallel data and the Gigaword v.5 corpus parsed with Stanford typed dependencies (Napoles et al., 2012). We use Stanford dependencies in the collapsed version which resolves coordination [4] and collapses the prepositions. Figure 1 shows an example of a translated sentence, its dependency tree produced by the string-to-tree system and the triples extracted at decoding time. We consider the following main arguments: *nsubj, nsubjpass, dobj, iobj* and *prep* arguments attached to both verbs and nouns. Table 4 shows the number of extracted triples.

Type of relation	Number of triples
main	540,109,283
prep	810,118,653
nsubj	315,852,775
nsubjpass	32,111,962
dobj	188,412,178
iobj	3,732,368

Table 4: Number of relation triples extracted from parsed data. The data consists of the English side of the parallel data and Gigaword. *main* arguments include: nsubj, nsubjpass, dobj, iobj.

We integrate the feature in a bottom-up chart decoder. The feature has several scores:

- A counter for the dependency triples covered by the current hypothesis.

- A selectional association score aggregated over all main arguments: nsubj, nsubjpass, dobj, iobj.

- A selectional association score aggregated over all prepositional arguments with no distinction between noun and verb modifiers.

For both tuning and evaluation of all machine translation systems we use a combination of the cased BLEU score and head-word chain metric (HWCM) (Liu and Gildea, 2005). The HWCM metric implemented in the Moses toolkit computes

the harmonic mean of precision and recall over head-word chains of length 1 to 4. The head-word chains are extracted directly from the dependency tree produced by the string-to-tree decoder and from the parsed reference. Tuning is performed using batch MIRA (Cherry and Foster, 2012) on 1000-best lists. We report evaluation scores averaged over the newstest2013, newstest2014 and newstest2015 data sets provided by WMT15.

5 Evaluation

5.1 Error analysis

We wanted to get an idea about how often the verb and its arguments are mistranslated. For this purpose we manually annotated errors in sentences with more than 5 words and at most 15 words. With this criterion we avoided translations with scrambled predicate-argument structures. Each sentence had roughly one main verb.

To have a more reliable error annotation we first post-edited 100 translations from the baseline system. We then compared the translations with their post-editions and annotated error categories using the BLAST tool (Stymne, 2011). We considered a *sense* error category when there was a wrong lexical choice for the head of a main argument, a prepositional modifier or the main verb. We also annotated mistranslated prepositions.

Error Category	Error Count	Total
Preposition	18	143
Sense	53	388
Main argument	18	145
Prep modifier	9	143
Main verb	26	100

Table 5: Number of mistranslated words in 100 sentences manually annotated with error categories.

In Table 5 we can see that 26 percent of the verbs are mistranslated and about 10 percent of the arguments. Mistranslated verbs are problematic since the feature produces the selectional association scores for the wrong verb. Although the semantic affinity is mutual, the formulation of the score conditions on the verb. In the cases when both the verb and the argument are mistranslated the association score might be high although the translation is not faithful to the source.

---

[4] Coordination is not resolved at decoding time.

5.2 Evaluation of the Selectional Preference Feature

First, we determine the effectiveness of our selectional association features. We compare the two different selectional association features described in section 3.2: *SelAssoc_L* and *SelAssoc_C* . We report the results of automatic evaluation in Table 6.

Neither of the features improved the automatic evaluation scores. The *SelAssoc_L* suffers from data sparsity while the *SelAssoc_C* feature is overgeneralizing due to noisy clustering. Adding both features compensates for these issues, however we only see a slight improvement in BLEU scores for shorter sentences[5]: 25.59 compared to 25.40 for the baseline system. We further investigate whether sparse features are more informative.

System	BLEU -c	HWCM
Baseline	26.45	24.47
+ SelAssoc_L	$26.41_{-.04}$	$24.52_{+.05}$
+ SelAssoc_C	$26.48_{+.03}$	$24.54_{+.07}$
+ SelAssoc_L + SelAssoc_C	$26.48_{+.03}$	$24.47_{+.00}$
+ Bin (SelAssoc_L + SelAssoc_C)	$26.37_{-.08}$	$24.53_{+.06}$
+ RDLM–P_w (1, 0, 0)	$26.35_{-.10}$	$24.75_{+.28}$
+ RDLM–P_w (2, 1, 1)	$26.38_{-.07}$	$24.83_{+.36}$

Table 6: Results for string-to-tree systems with *SelAssoc* and RDLM–P_w features. The number of clusters used with *SelAssoc_C* is 500. The triples in parenthesis indicate the context size for ancestors, left siblings and right siblings respectively. The RDLM–P_w configuration (1, 0, 0) captures similar syntactic context as the selectional preference features.

We changed the format of the features in order to experiment with sparse features. By using sparse features we let the tuning algorithm discriminate between low and high values of the *SelAssoc* score. For each of the *SelAssoc* features we normalized the scores to have zero mean and standard deviation one and mapped them to their corresponding percentile. A sparse feature was created for each percentile, below and above the mean [6] resulting in a total of 20 sparse features. However this formulation of the feature also did

not improve the evaluation scores as shown in the fifth row of Table 6.

The lack of variance in automatic evaluation scores can be explained by: a) the feature touches only a few words in the translation and b) the relation between a predicate and its argument is identified at later stages of the bottom-up chart-based decoding when many lexical choices have already been pruned out. The *SelAssoc* scores, similar to mutual information scores, are sensitive to outlier events with low frequencies in the training data. In the next section we investigate whether a more robust model would mitigate some of these issues and experiment with a neural relational dependency language model (RDLM) (Sennrich, 2015).

5.3 Comparison with a Relational Dependency LM

The RDLM (Sennrich, 2015) is a feed-forward neural network which learns two probability distributions conditioned on a large syntactic context described in Eq 3: P_w predicts the head word of the dependent and P_l the dependency relation. We compare our feature with RDLM–P_w.

For training the RDLM–P_w we use the parameters for the feed-forward neural network described in Sennrich (2015): 150 dimensions for input layer, 750 dimensions for the hidden layer, a vocabulary of 500 000 words and 100 noise samples. We train the RDLM–P_w on the target side of the parallel data. Although we use less data than for training the *SelAssoc* features, the neural network is inherently good at learning generalizations and selecting the appropriate conditioning context.

We experiment with different configurations for RDLM–P_w by varying the number of ancestors as well as left and right siblings:

- ancestors = 1, left = 0, right = 0

- ancestors = 2, left = 1, right = 1

The first configuration captures similar syntactic context as the *SelAssoc* features. The only exception is the *prep* relation for which the head of *pobj*, the actual preposition, is a sibling of the argument. The results are shown in the last two lines of Table 6 and the configuration is marked between parentheses for the ancestors, left siblings and right siblings respectively.

The RDLM–P_w performs slightly better than the selectional preference feature in terms of the HWCM scores. An increase in HWCM is to be

---

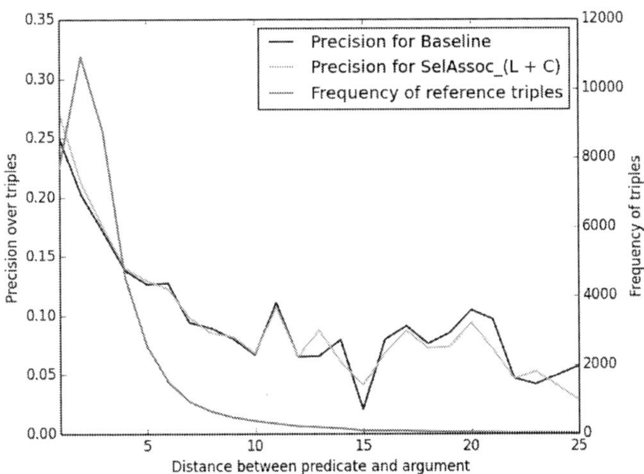

Figure 2: Frequency and translation precision of triples with respect to the distance between the predicate and its arguments. Frequency is computed for triples extracted from the reference sentences of the tests sets. Translation precision is computed over triples extracted from the output of the two translation systems: baseline system and the system with *SelAssoc_L* and *SelAssoc_C* features.

expected since the RDLM–P_w models all dependency relations. However there is not a significant contribution from having a larger syntactic context.

5.4 Analysis

In this section we investigate possible reasons for the low impact of our selectional preference features. We look at how frequently our features are triggered, and how precision is influenced by the distance between predicates and arguments.

Firstly we are interested in how often the feature triggers and how it influences the overall selectional association score of the test set. On average, 4.85 triples can be extracted per sentence produced by our system. Out of these, 4.35 triples get scored by the *SelAssoc_C* feature and 3.56 by the *SelAssoc_L* feature. The selectional association scores are higher on average for our system than for the baseline as shown in Table 7. The *SelAssoc_C* feature seems to overgeneralize for the *prep* relations as the scores are on average higher than for the reference triples. We therefore conclude that our feature is having an impact on the translation system.

Secondly we want to understand the interaction between the *SelAssoc* features and the language model. For this purpose we compute the frequency and translation precision of triples with respect to

	SelAssoc_L		SelAssoc_C	
System	main	prep	main	prep
Baseline	0.067	0.039	0.164	0.147
+ SelAssoc_L + SelAssoc_C	0.074	0.041	0.175	0.305
Reference	0.077	0.043	0.186	0.163

Table 7: Average selectional association scores for the test sets. Scores are aggregated over the *main* and *prep* argument types. *main* arguments include: nsubj, nsubjpass, dobj, iobj.

the distance between the predicate and its arguments. Figure 2 shows the frequency of triples extracted from the reference sentence as well as the translation precision of triples extracted from the output of the translation systems. For more reliable precision scores we lemmatized all predicates and arguments. Most arguments are within a 5 word window from the predicate. Therefore most triples are also scored by the language model. For these triples we see only a slight increase in precision for our system. This result indicates that for predicates and arguments that are close to each other, the feature is not adding much information. As the distance increases the precision decreases drastically for both systems. A longer distance between predicates and arguments also implies a

Source	Das 16-jährige Mädchen und der 19-jährige Mann **brachen** kurz nach Sonntagmittag in Govetts Leap in Blackheath **zu ihrer Tour auf**.
Reference	The 16-year old girl and the 19-year old man **went on their tour** shortly after Sunday lunch at Govetts Leap in Blackheath.
Baseline	The 16-year old girl and the 19-year old man **broke** shortly after Sunday lunch in Govetts Leap in Blackheath **on their tour**.

Figure 3: Examples of a complex sentence with multiple prepositional modifiers. Information about semantic roles is needed to identify the relevant prepositional modifier.

more complex syntactic structure which will negatively impact the quality of extracted triples and the selectional association scores.

5.5 Discussion

One reason for the small impact of both *SelAssoc* and RDLM–P_w features could be the poor quality of the syntactic trees produced by the decoder for longer sentences. In the cases where the relation between predicate and argument can be reliably extracted, such as the example in Fig 1, the features are not adding more information than is already covered by the language model.

In more complex sentences there are cases where the features score modifiers that are not important for disambiguating the verb. The example in Figure 3 has several prepositional modifiers but only *on tour* could help disambiguate the verb *brachen (went)*. In such cases identifying the semantic roles of the modifiers in the source and projecting them on the target might be useful for better estimation of semantic affinities.

The error analysis on short sentences showed that translation of verbs is problematic for syntax-based systems. This is confirmed by the low precision scores[7] for verb translation shown in Table 8. Although there is a slight improvement in precision, generally mistranslated verbs impact our features as the semantic affinity is scored for the wrong verb. A solution would be to add the source verbs in the conditioning context.

System	Precision
baseline	46.10
+ SelAssoc_L + SelAssoc_C	$46.26_{+.16}$
+ RDLM–P_w (2, 1, 1)	$46.31_{+.21}$

Table 8: Evaluation of verb translation in the test set. Precision scores are computed over verb lemmas against the reference translations.

[7]The precision scores were computed over verb lemmas extracted automatically from the test sets. In total 21633 source verbs were evaluated.

6 Conclusions

This paper explores whether knowledge about semantic affinities between the target predicates and their argument fillers is useful for translating ambiguous predicates and arguments. We propose three variants of a selectional preference feature for string-to-tree statistical machine translation based on the selectional association measure of Resnik (1996). We compare our features with a variant of the neural relational dependency language model (RDLM) (Sennrich, 2015) and find that neither of the features improves automatic evaluation metrics. We conclude that mistranslated verbs, errors in the target syntactic trees produced by the decoder and underspecified syntactic relations are negatively impacting these features. We propose to address these issues in future work by augmenting the feature with source side information such as the source verb and the semantic roles of its arguments.

Acknowledgments

We thank the anonymous reviewers as well as Rico Sennrich for his feedback and assistance with RDLM . This project has received funding from the European Union's Horizon 2020 research and innovation programme under grant agreements 644402 (HimL) and 645452 (QT21). We are also grateful for support by a Google Faculty Research Award.

References

Marzieh Bazrafshan and Daniel Gildea. 2013. Semantic roles for string to tree machine translation. In *Proceedings of the 51st Annual Meeting of the Association for Computational Linguistics*. Sofia, Bulgaria, ACL 2013, pages 419–423.

Ondřej Bojar, Rajen Chatterjee, Christian Federmann, Barry Haddow, Matthias Huck, Chris Hokamp, Philipp Koehn, Varvara Logacheva, Christof Monz, Matteo Negri, Matt Post, Carolina Scarton, Lucia Specia, and Marco Turchi.

2015. Findings of the 2015 workshop on statistical machine translation. In *Proceedings of the Tenth Workshop on Statistical Machine Translation*. Lisbon, Portugal, pages 1–46.

Danqi Chen and Christopher Manning. 2014. A fast and accurate dependency parser using neural networks. In *Proceedings of the 2014 Conference on Empirical Methods in Natural Language Processing (EMNLP)*. Association for Computational Linguistics, Doha, Qatar, pages 740–750.

Stanley F. Chen and Joshua Goodman. 1998. An empirical study of smoothing techniques for language modeling. Technical report, Harvard University.

Colin Cherry and George Foster. 2012. Batch tuning strategies for statistical machine translation. In *Proceedings of the 2012 Conference of the North American Chapter of the Association for Computational Linguistics: Human Language Technologies*. Montreal, Canada, NAACL HLT '12, pages 427–436.

Raphael Cohen, Yoav Goldberg, and Michael Elhadad. 2012. Domain adaptation of a dependency parser with a class-class selectional preference model. In *Proceedings of ACL 2012 Student Research Workshop*. ACL '12, pages 43–48.

Tim Van De Cruys. 2014. A neural network approach to selectional preference acquisition. In *Proceedings of the 2014 Conference on Empirical Methods in Natural Language Processing (EMNLP)*. ACL '14, pages 26–35.

Katrin Erk, Sebastian Padó, and Ulrike Padó. 2010. A flexible, corpus-driven model of regular and inverse selectional preferences. *Comput. Linguist.* 36(4):723–763.

Michel Galley, Jonathan Graehl, Kevin Knight, Daniel Marcu, Steve DeNeefe, Wei Wang, and Ignacio Thayer. 2006. Scalable inference and training of context-rich syntactic translation models. In *ACL-44: Proceedings of the 21st International Conference on Computational Linguistics and the 44th annual meeting of the Association for Computational Linguistics*. Morristown, NJ, USA, pages 961–968.

Michel Galley, Mark Hopkins, Kevin Knight, and Daniel Marcu. 2004. What's in a translation rule? In *Proceedings of Human Language Technologies: Conference of the North American Chapter of the Association of Computational Linguistics*. HLT-NAACL '04.

Qin Gao and Stephan Vogel. 2011. Utilizing target-side semantic role labels to assist hierarchical phrase-based machine translation. In *Proceedings of the Fifth Workshop on Syntax, Semantics and Structure in Statistical Translation*. Portland, Oregon, USA, pages 107–115.

Kenneth Heafield. 2011. Kenlm: Faster and smaller language model queries. In *Proceedings of the Sixth Workshop on Statistical Machine Translation*. Edinburgh, Scotland, WMT '11, pages 187–197.

Eliyahu Kiperwasser and Yoav Goldberg. 2015. Semi-supervised dependency parsing using bilexical contextual features from auto-parsed data. In *Proceedings of the 2015 Conference on Empirical Methods in Natural Language Processing*. pages 1348–1353.

Jonathan K. Kummerfeld, David Hall, James R. Curran, and Dan Klein. 2012. Parser showdown at the wall street corral: An empirical investigation of error types in parser output. In *Proceedings of the 2012 Joint Conference on Empirical Methods in Natural Language Processing and Computational Natural Language Learning*. EMNLP-CoNLL '12, pages 1048–1059.

Junhui Li, Philip Resnik, and Hal Daum. 2013. Modeling syntactic and semantic structures in hierarchical phrase-based translation. In *Proceedings of Human Language Technologies: Conference of the North American Chapter of the Association of Computational Linguistics,*. Atlanta, Georgia, USA, number June in NAACL-HLT 2013, pages 540–549.

Ding Liu and Daniel Gildea. 2005. Syntactic features for evaluation of machine translation. In *ACL 2005 Workshop on Intrinsic and Extrinsic Evaluation Measures for Machine Translation and/or Summarization*. Ann Arbor, MI, pages 25–32.

Ding Liu and Daniel Gildea. 2010. Semantic role features for machine translation. In *Proceedings of the 23rd International Conference on Computational Linguistics*. pages 716–724.

Courtney Napoles, Matthew Gormley, and Benjamin Van Durme. 2012. Annotated gigaword. In *Proceedings of the Joint Workshop on Automatic Knowledge Base Construction and Webscale Knowledge Extraction*. Association for

Computational Linguistics, Stroudsburg, PA, USA, AKBC-WEKEX '12, pages 95–100.

Jeffrey Pennington, Richard Socher, and Christopher D. Manning. 2014. Glove: Global vectors for word representation. In *Proceedings of the 2014 Conference on Empirical Methods in Natural Language Processing (EMNLP 2014)*. pages 1532–1543.

Philip Resnik. 1996. Selectional constraints: an information-theoretic model and its computational realization. *Cognition* 61:127–159.

Alan Ritter, Mausam, and Oren Etzioni. 2010. A latent dirichlet allocation method for selectional preferences. In *Proceedings of the 48th Annual Meeting of the Association for Computational Linguistics*. Stroudsburg, PA, USA, ACL '10, pages 424–434.

Diarmuid Ó. Séaghdha. 2010. Latent variable models of selectional preference. In *Proceedings of the 48th Annual Meeting of the Association for Computational Linguistics*. Stroudsburg, PA, USA, ACL '10, pages 435–444.

Rico Sennrich. 2015. Modelling and Optimizing on Syntactic N-Grams for Statistical Machine Translation. *Transactions of the Association for Computational Linguistics* 3:169–182.

Ekaterina Shutova, Niket Tandon, and Gerard de Melo. 2015. Perceptually grounded selectional preferences. In *Proceedings of the 53rd Annual Meeting of the Association for Computational Linguistics and the 7th International Joint Conference on Natural Language Processing*. ACL '15, pages 950–960.

Andreas Stolcke. 2002. SRILM – an Extensible Language Modeling Toolkit. In *Proc. of the Int. Conf. on Spoken Language Processing (ICSLP)*. volume 3.

Sara Stymne. 2011. Blast: A tool for error analysis of machine translation output. In *Proceedings of the 49th Annual Meeting of the Association for Computational Linguistics: Human Language Technologies: Systems Demonstrations*. Portland, Oregon, HLT '11, pages 56–61.

Lin Sun and Anna Korhonen. 2009. Improving verb clustering with automatically acquired selectional preferences. In *Proceedings of the 2009 Conference on Empirical Methods in Natural Language Processing: Volume 2 - Volume 2*. EMNLP '09, pages 638–647.

Gertjan van Noord. 2007. Using self-trained bilexical preferences to improve disambiguation accuracy. In *Proceedings of the 10th International Conference on Parsing Technologies*. IWPT '07, pages 1–10.

Marion Weller, Alexander Fraser, and Sabine Schulte im Walde. 2013. Using subcategorization knowledge to improve case prediction for translation to german. In *Proceedings of the 51st Annual Meeting of the Association for Computational Linguistics (Volume 1: Long Papers)*. Association for Computational Linguistics, Sofia, Bulgaria, pages 593–603.

Marion Weller, Sabine Schulte Im Walde, and Alexander Fraser. 2014. Using noun class information to model selectional preferences for translating prepositions in smt. In *Proceedings of the 11th Conference of the Association for Machine Translation in the Americas*. Vancouver, BC, AMTA '14, pages 275–287.

Philip Williams and Philipp Koehn. 2012. Ghkm rule extraction and scope-3 parsing in moses. In *Proceedings of the Seventh Workshop on Statistical Machine Translation*. pages 388–394.

Dekai Wu and Pascale Fung. 2009. Semantic roles for SMT: a hybrid two-pass model. In *Proceedings of Human Language Technologies: The 2009 Annual Conference of the North American Chapter of the Association for Computational Linguistics, Companion Volume: Short Papers*. pages 13–16.

Modeling Complement Types in Phrase-Based SMT

Marion Weller-Di Marco[1,2], Alexander Fraser[2], Sabine Schulte im Walde[1]

[1]Institut für Maschinelle Sprachverarbeitung, Universität Stuttgart
[2]Centrum für Informations- und Sprachverarbeitung,
Ludwig-Maximilians-Universität München
`{dimarco|schulte}@ims.uni-stuttgart.de    fraser@cis.lmu.de`

Abstract

We explore two approaches to model complement types (NPs and PPs) in an English-to-German SMT system: A simple abstract representation inserts pseudo-prepositions that mark the beginning of noun phrases, to improve the symmetry of source and target complement types, and to provide a flat structural information on phrase boundaries. An extension of this representation generates context-aware synthetic phrasetable entries conditioned on the source side, to model complement types in terms of grammatical case and preposition choice. Both the simple preposition-informed system and the context-aware system significantly improve over the baseline; and the context-aware system is slightly better than the system without context information.

1 Introduction

SMT output is often incomprehensible because it confuses complement types (noun phrases/NPs vs. prepositional phrases/PPs) by generating a wrong grammatical case, by choosing an incorrect preposition, or by arranging the complements in a meaningless way. However, the choice of complement types in a translation represents important information at the syntax-semantics interface: The case of an NP determines its syntactic function and its semantic role; similarly, the choice of preposition in a PP sets the semantic role of the prepositional phrase.

While the lexical content of a target-language phrase is defined by the source sentence, the exact choice of preposition and case strongly depends on the target context, and most specifically on the target verb. For example, the English verb phrase *to call for sth.* can be translated into German by *etw.*

erfordern (subcategorizing a direct-object NP but no preposition) or by *(nach) etw. verlangen* (subcategorizing either a direct-object NP or a PP headed by the preposition *nach*). Differences in grammatical case and syntactic functions between source and target side include phenomena like subject-object shifting: *[I]*$_{\text{SUBJ}}$ *like [the book]*$_{\text{OBJ}}$ vs. *[das Buch]*$_{\text{SUBJ}}$ *gefällt [mir]*$_{\text{OBJ}}$. Here, the English object corresponds to a German subject, whereas the English subject corresponds to the indirect object in the German sentence.

Selecting the wrong complement type or an incorrect preposition obviously has a major effect on the fluency of SMT output, and also has a strong impact on the perception of semantic roles. Consider the sentence *John looks for his book*. When the preposition *for* is translated literally by the preposition *für*, the meaning of the translated sentence *John sucht für sein Buch* shifts, such that *the book* is no longer the object that is searched, but rather a recipient of the search. To preserve the source meaning, the prepositional phrase headed by *for* must be translated as a direct object of the verb *suchen*, or as a PP headed by the preposition *nach*.

Since prepositions tend to be highly ambiguous, the choice of a preposition depends on various factors. Often, there is a predominant translation, such as *for → für*, which is appropriate in many contexts, but unsuitable in other contexts. Such translation options are often difficult to override, even when there are clues that the translation is wrong. Furthermore, even though prepositions are highly frequent words, there can be coverage problems if a preposition is not aligned with the specific preposition required by the context, due to structural mismatches.

This paper presents two novel approaches to improve the modeling of complement types. A simple approach introduces an abstract representation of "placeholder prepositions" at the beginning of

Proceedings of the First Conference on Machine Translation, Volume 1: Research Papers, pages 43–53,
Berlin, Germany, August 11-12, 2016. ©2016 Association for Computational Linguistics

noun phrases on the source and target sides. The insertion of these placeholder prepositions leads to a more symmetric structure and consequently to a better coverage of prepositions, as all NPs are effectively transformed into PPs, and prepositions in one language without a direct equivalent in the other language can be aligned. Furthermore, the placeholder prepositions function as explicit phrase boundaries and are annotated with grammatical case, so they provide flat structural information about the syntactic function of the phrase. The placeholder representation leads to a significant improvement over a baseline system without prepositional placeholders.

Our second approach enhances the abstract placeholder representation, and integrates source-side context into the phrase table of the SMT system to model different complement types. This is done by generating synthetic phrase-table entries containing contextually predicted prepositions. With this process, we aim to (i) improve the preposition choice conditioned on the source sentence, and to (ii) manipulate the scores in the generated entries to favour context-appropriate translations. Generating phrase-table entries allows to create prepositions in contexts not observed in the parallel training data. The resulting phrase-table entries are unique for each context and provide the best selection of translation options in terms of complement realization on token-level. This variant significantly outperforms the baseline, and is slightly better than the system with inserted placeholder prepositions.

2   Related Work

Our work is related to three research areas: using source-side information, previous approaches to model case and prepositions and the synthesis of phrase-table entries.

Source-side information has been applied to SMT before, often for the purpose of word sense disambiguation and improving lexical choice (Carpuat and Wu, 2007; Gimpel and Smith, 2008; Jeong et al., 2010; Tamchyna et al., 2014), but without a focus on synthesis or syntactic-semantic aspects such as subcategorization.

Prepositions are difficult to translate and responsible for many errors, as has been shown in many evaluations of machine translation. For example, Williams et al. (2015) presented a detailed error analysis of their shared task submissions, listing the number of missing/wrong content and function words. For the language pair English–German, the combined number of *missing/wrong/added prepositions* is one of the most observed error types. Agirre et al. (2009) were among the first to use rich linguistic information to model prepositions and grammatical case in Basque within a rule-based system, leading to an improved translation quality for prepositions. Their work is extended by Shilon et al. (2012) with a statistical component for ranking translations. Weller et al. (2013) use a combination of source-side and target-side features to predict grammatical case on the SMT output, but without taking into account different complement types (NP vs. PP). Weller et al. (2015) predict prepositions as a post-processing step to a translation system in which prepositions are reduced to placeholders. They find, however, that the reduced representation leads to a general loss in translation quality. Experiments with annotating abstract information to the placeholders indicated that grammatical case plays an important role during translation. We build on their observations, but in contrast with generating prepositions in a post-processing step, prepositions in our work are accessible to the system during decoding, and the phrase-table entries are optimized with regard to the source-sentence. Finnish is a highly inflective language with a very complex case and preposition system. Tiedemann et al. (2015) experimented with pseudo-tokens added to Finnish data to account for the fact that Finnish morphological markers (case) often correspond to a separate English word (typically a preposition). Due to the complexity of Finnish, only a subset of markers is considered. The pseudo-tokens are applied to a Finnish–English translation system, but a manual evaluation remains inconclusive about the effectiveness of their method. For the preposition-informed representation in our work, we adapt both source and target language to obtain more isomorphic parallel data. Also, we translate *into* the morphologically rich language, which requires morphological modeling with regard to, e.g., grammatical case and portmanteau prepositions (cf. section 3) to ensure morphologically correct output.

Synthetic phrases have been implemented by Chahuneau et al. (2013) to translate into morphologically rich languages. They use a discriminative model based on source-side features (dependency information and word clusters) to predict inflected target words based on which phrase-table entries

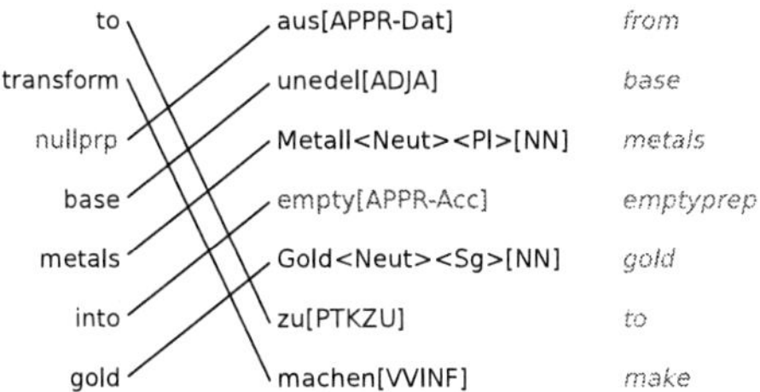

Figure 1: Example for preposition-informed representation with empty placeholders heading NPs.

are generated. They report an improvement in translation quality for several language pairs. In contrast, our approach concentrates on the generation of closed-class function words to obtain the most appropriate complement type given the source sentence. This includes generating word sequences not observed in the training data, i.e. adding/changing prepositions for a (different) PP or removing prepositions to form an NP. A task related to synthesizing prepositions is that of generating determiners, the translation of which is problematic when translating from a language like Russian that does not have definiteness morphemes. Tsvetkov et al. (2013) create synthetic translation options to augment the phrase-table. They use a classifier trained on local contextual features to predict whether to add or remove determiners for the target-side of translation rules. In contrast with determiners, which are local to their context, we model and generate function words with semantic content which are subject to complex interactions with verbs and other subcategorized elements throughout the sentence.

3 Inflection Prediction System

We work with an inflection prediction system which first translates into a stemmed representation with a component for inflecting the SMT output in a post-processing step. The stemmed representation contains markup (POS-tags and number/gender on nouns and case on prepositions, as can be seen in figure 1) which is used as input to the inflection component. Inflected forms are generated based on the morphological features *number*, *case*, *gender* and *strong/weak*, which are predicted on the SMT output using a sequence model and a morphological tool (cf. section 6.1). Modeling morphology is necessary when modifying German prepositions, as they determine grammatical case and changing a preposition might require to adapt the

inflection of the respective phrase, too. Portmanteau prepositions (contracted forms of preposition and determiner) are split during the synthesizing and translation process, and are merged after the inflection step. For more details about modeling complex morphology, see for example Toutanova et al. (2008), Fraser et al. (2012) or Chahuneau et al. (2013).

4 Preposition-Informed Representation

Our first approach introduces a simple abstract representation that inserts pseudo-preposition markers to indicate the beginning of noun phrases. This representation serves two purposes: to adjust the source and target sides for structural mismatches of different complement types, and to provide information about syntactic functions and semantic roles via the annotation of grammatical case.

Placeholders for empty prepositions are inserted at the beginning of noun phrases in both the source and target language. Figure 1 provides an example of the training data with two structural mismatches: the PP on the source side *into gold* corresponds to the NP Gold<Sg>[NN] on the target side, and the NP on the source side (*base metals*) corresponds to the PP aus unedel Metall on the target side. Without the placeholders at the beginning of noun phrases, the word alignment for these phrases contains either unaligned overt prepositions[1], or imprecise one-to-many alignments containing prepositions such as "*into gold* → Gold<Sg>[NN]", which are wrong in many contexts.

The placeholder prepositions lead to a cleaner word alignment: the inserted empty preposition on the source side (in *nullprp base metals*) is aligned to the overt preposition aus on the target side, whereas the overt source preposition in *into gold* can be aligned to an empty preposition on the target side. As a consequence of the improved word alignment, the resulting system has a better coverage of individual prepositions, and the amount of prepositions being lumped together with an adjacent word via alignment is reduced. In addition, the placeholder between Metall and Gold provides an explicit phrase boundary between a PP and a direct object NP. The annotation with grammatical case provides information about the syntactic function of a phrase, such as a subject (EMPTY-Nom) or a direct object (EMPTY-Acc). For PPs, the case repre-

---

[1] We use the term *overt prepositions* for actually present prepositions, as opposed to "empty" prepositions.

sentence 1: nullprp beginners look **for weapons** in different ways .

sentence 2: nullprp screenshot of the site that accepts nullprp orders **for weapons** .

	1 **NP/PP** **src**	2 **tag** **src**	3 **word** **src**	4 **func** **src**	5 **head** **src**	6 **head** **trg**	7 **parent** **src**	8 **parV** **src**	9 **parV** **trg**	10 **parN** **src**	11 **parN** **trg**	**best-5** **predicted**	
sentence 1	PP	IN	for	prep	weapon	Waffe	V	look	–	–	–	**nach-Dat** **empty-Acc** empty-Nom von-Dat für-Acc	0.349 0.224 0.206 0.067 0.064
sentence 2	PP	IN	for	prep	weapon	Waffe	N	–	–	order	–	**für-Acc** empty-Nom von-Dat nach-Dat empty-Acc	0.559 0.184 0.087 0.078 0.053

Table 1: Source and target side features for the prediction of placeholders in the phrase *for weapons* → `PREP Waffe<P1>[NN]` in two sentences, using the top-5 five predictions; appropriate prepositions are bold. The prediction model corresponds to model (2) in table 7.

sents an indicator whether a preposition is part of a directional (accusative) or a locational (dative) PP.

5 Synthetic Phrase-Table Entries

Our second, extended approach generates synthetic phrases from intermediate generic placeholders. We combine source-side and target-side features to synthesize phrase-table entries that are unique for the respective source-side context.

5.1 Motivation and Example

The preposition-informed representation presents a straightforward solution to handle different structures on the source and target side. However, there are two remaining issues: first, the distribution of translation probabilities might favour a complement realization that is invalid for the respective context; and second, the required preposition might not even occur in the parallel training data as a translation of the source phrase. As a solution to these problems, we explore the idea of synthesizing phrase-table entries, in order to adjust the translation options to token-level requirements in a way that allows to take into account relevant information from the entire source sentence.

As a basis for the prediction of synthetic phrase-table entries, all empty and overt prepositions are replaced with a generic placeholder `PREP`. In the prediction step, generic placeholders are transformed into an overt or an empty preposition. Every phrase can thus be inflected as either PP or NP, depending on the sentence context. The format of the synthesized phrases corresponds to that of the preposition-informed system, with one major difference: for each source phrase, a unique set of target-phrases (possibly with new word sequences) is generated to provide an optimal set of translation options on token level.

Table 1 illustrates the first step of the process: the two sentences above the table both contain the phrase *for weapons*, which occur in different contexts. The predominant literal translation of *for* is *für*, which is however only correct in the second sentence, modifying the noun *order*. In the context of the verb *look*, the preposition *nach* or the empty preposition are correct. Thus, for the underlying target phrase `PREP Waffe<P1>[NN]`, different prepositions need to be available for different contexts: for the first sentence, the intermediate placeholder entry should yield `nach Waffe<P1>[NN]` and `EMPTY-Acc Waffe<P1>[NN]`; for the second sentence, it should yield `für Waffe<P1>[NN]` (bold in table 1). In particular, it is possible to generate target entries that have not been observed in the training data in combination with the source phrase. This is, for example, the case for `EMPTY-Acc Waffe<P1>[NN]` which does not occur as a possible translation option of *for weapons* in the preposition-informed system.

5.2 Prediction Features

Table 1 shows the set of source-side and target-side features used to train a maximum entropy classifier for the prediction task. As phrase-table entries are often short, we rely heavily on source-side features centered around the placeholder preposition. Via dependency parses (Choi and Palmer, 2012), relevant information is gathered in the source sentence. Source information comes from the entire sentence, and may go beyond the phrase boundary, whereas

	Target	$p(e\mid f)$
Prep-Informed	für[Acc] Waffe<Fem><Pl>[NN]	0.333
	nach[Dat] Waffe<Fem><Pl>[NN]	0.148
	für[Acc] nuklear<Pos>[ADJA]	0.037
	für[Acc] militärisch<Pos>[ADJA]	0.037
	für[Acc] die<+ART>[ART]	0.037
Synthetic Phrases — sentence 1	nach[Dat] Waffe<Fem><Pl>[NN]	0.192 ✓
	empty[Acc] Waffe<Fem><Pl>[NN]	0.131 ✓
	empty[Nom] Waffe<Fem><Pl>[NN]	0.121
	für[Acc] Waffe<Fem><Pl>[NN]	0.094
	von[Dat] Waffe<Fem><Pl>[NN]	0.038
sentence 2	für[Acc] Waffe<Fem><Pl>[NN]	0.336 ✓
	empty[Nom] Waffe<Fem><Pl>[NN]	0.101
	von[Dat] Waffe<Fem><Pl>[NN]	0.045
	nach[Dat] Waffe<Fem><Pl>[NN]	0.041
	die<+ART>[ART] Waffe<Fem><Pl>[NN]	0.037

Table 2: The top-5 synthetic phrases according to $p(e\mid f)$ for the phrase *for weapons* based on the predictions from table 1. Phrases marked with ✓ are correct in the respective context.

the target-side context is restricted to the phrase.

The source-side features comprise the type of the aligned phrase (1), the tag (2) and the word (3), as well as the syntactic function of that phrase in the source sentence (4: subj, obj, prep), and the governed noun (5: *weapon*). Furthermore, the word (verb (8) or noun (10)) governing the aligned preposition is identified and used as a feature alongside with its tag information (7: V/N). The content words from the source side, head-src (5) and parent-V/N (9,11) are then projected to the target side, if present in the phrase. In addition, up to three words to the left or right of the placeholder provide target-side context, depending on the length of the target phrase. From these features, information about the verb and the syntactic role in the source sentence are probably most important. While the content of an NP (e.g., *to order weapons/cake/etc.*) is not necessarily relevant to determine the realization of a placeholder[2], the training also relies on *feature n-grams* such as noun-verb tuples or preposition-noun-verb triples, which contain important information about subcategorizational preferences.

As training data for this model, we use all extracted source/target/alignment triples containing a relevant preposition from the preposition-informed system; the preposition with case annotation is used as the label. We record which sentence was used to extract each phrase in order to obtain the token-level source-side context. For the prediction

---

[2]Our experiments indicated that using features (5) and (6) as individual features tends to be harmful, whereas in combination with other features they provide useful information.

task, the model is applied to phrase-table entries obtained on the placeholder representation: For each n-gram in the source sentence, the relevant phrase-table entries are identified and the respective features are extracted from the source sentence. Based on the top-5 predictions, along with the prediction scores, context-dependent phrase-table entries are generated. Since the complement realization also depends on lexical decisions in the target sentence (such as the verb), there are often several valid options and there is no possibility to decide for *one* particular realization without the actual target sentence context during the prediction step. We thus work with the set of n-best predictions to provide a *selection* of probable phrase-table entries given the source-sentence.

In this model, each preposition to be predicted is treated as one instance; this means that each preposition is predicted independently. In the case of several prepositions occurring in a single phrase, we consider all permutations of the respective n-best predictions.

5.3 Building the Phrase Table

To build the phrase-table with synthesized target phrases, we start by building a phrase table on data with generic placeholders, using the word alignments from the preposition-informed system. The entries are then separated into two groups: entries with and without placeholders. Entries without placeholders do not need any further processing, and are kept for the final phrase table, including translation probabilities and lexical weights. Phrase-table entries whose target side contains a placeholder are then selected to undergo the prediction step.

A prediction for all phrases is not feasible, so we restrict the table to the top-20 entries according to $p(e\mid f)$. This filtering is applied to the phrase table of the preposition-informed system; the phrase-table entries containing generic placeholders are then selected accordingly. With this process of phrase selection, the synthetic-phrase system and the preposition-informed system rely on the same set of underlying phrase-table entries.

5.4 Scores in Phrase and Reordering Table

A phrase table typically contains the translation probabilities $p(f\mid e)$ and $p(e\mid f)$, as well as the lexical probabilities $lex(f\mid e)$ and $lex(e\mid f)$. For the newly generated entries, new scores have to be computed: the lexical weight of a phrase can be calculated based on the lexical weights of the individual words. In contrast, the translation probability of a newly generated phrase cannot be calculated. We consider the translation probability from the placeholder representation table as an approximate translation probability independent of the actual preposition; the classifier (ME) score indicates how well a particular preposition fits into the target-phrase. We present three variants to estimate the translation probabilities and then explore several ways to use the scores as features to be optimized by MERT training.

SCORE-VARIANT 1: The placeholder translation probability and the ME scores are used as separate features. An indicator feature counts the predicted prepositions. Non-synthesized phrases get a pseudo ME-score of 1, and $exp(0)$ for the indicator feature. In the case of $n > 1$ prepositions, the ME scores are multiplied, and the indicator feature is set to $exp(n)$.

SCORE-VARIANT 2: Variant 1 is extended with the product of the placeholder translation probabilities and the ME score, to account for cases where lexically bad translation options received a high ME score and thus are boosted erroneously.

SCORE-VARIANT 3A: We consider the placeholder translation probability as the probability of a phrase to contain *some* preposition and use it as the basis to calculate a score for the phrase to contain the *predicted* preposition, using the ME score. Note, however, that the prediction score does not provide the probability of the target phrase representing a translation of the source phrase, but only how well the predicted preposition fits into the target phrase; this leads to potentially high ME scores for bad translation options. For this reason, we "dampen" the prediction score with the lexical probability as an indicator for the quality of the source-target pair, resulting in the following formula:

$$P_{prep}(e|f) = P_{PlaceHolder}(e|f) * (ME + lex(e|f))$$

where ME is the prediction score and $P_{PlaceHolder}$ is the translation probability based on the placeholder representation. lex is the lexical probability based on the phrase containing the generated prepositions. In a variant (3b), the resulting translation probability scores are then normalized such that they sum to 1 with the entries without prepositions, whose probability mass remains unchanged and corresponds to that in the preposition-informed system. This aims at obtaining a "real" probability distribution with context-dependent scores for phrases containing prepositions that is as close as possible to that in the preposition-informed system: probabilities of phrases without prepositions remain the same, whereas the scores for the generated phrases are normalized to share the remaining probability mass given a source phrase.

In variants 1 and 2, the ME-based scores are used as additional features to the lexical and placeholder translation probabilities, whereas in variant 3, new phrase-translation probabilities are computed based on the placeholder probabilities and the prediction scores to replace the placeholder probabilities. Table 2 shows the generated entries and the scores for $p(e|f)$ according to score variant 3b for the predictions from table 1; suitable translation options are marked with ✓. For sentence 1, the two possible variants *nach* and *empty* are top-ranked, whereas the top entry from the preposition-informed system, *für*, is unlikely to be selected in this context. For sentence 2, the top-ranked preposition *für* is even more likely than in the preposition-informed system. The entries for both sentence 1 and sentence 2 show that the previous two top-ranked candidates (`für Waffe<Pl>[NN]` and `nach Waffe<Pl>[NN]`) are now expanded and take up the top-5 positions for sentence 1 and the top-4 positions for sentence 2. As a result, the lexically invalid options on positions 3-5 from the preposition-informed system are disfavoured.

For the reordering table, we use the statistics from the placeholder representation. We assume that no changes in the reordering are caused by modifying the complement type or modifying prepositions; this assumption was verified experimentally (details are omitted).

6 Experiments and Results

We compare the preposition-informed system with the synthetic-phrases system where we explore different ways to integrate the synthetic phrases.

6.1 Experimental Setup

All systems were built using the Moses phrase-based framework. We used 4.592.139 parallel sentences aligned with GIZA++ for translation model training, and 45M sentences (News14+parallel data) to build a 5-gram language model. We used NewsTest13 (3000 sentences) for development and NewsTest14 (3003 sentences) as test set. These

System		BLEU
baseline-1	Surface forms	19.17
baseline-2	Stemmed	19.35
prep-informed system (P-1)	Stemmed + $\emptyset$-CASE	19.76
prep-informed system (P-2)	Stemmed + $\emptyset$-CASE-top-20	19.73

Table 3: Scores for baselines and preposition-informed system.

System	Features used for MERT tuning	BLEU
SP-1	SCORE-VARIANT-1	19.76
SP-2	SCORE-VARIANT-2	19.83
SP-3a	SCORE-VARIANT-3	19.80
SP-3b	SCORE-VARIANT-3, norm. $P_{prep}(e\|f)$	19.86*

Table 4: Variants of the synthetic-phrases system. * marks significant improvement over system P-2 (with pair-wise bootstrap resampling with sample size 1,000 and a p-value of 0.05)

datasets are from the WMT2015 shared task.

To predict the four morphological features number, gender, case and strong/weak for inflecting the stemmed output, we trained 4 CRF sequence models on the target-side of the parallel data. These features are predicted as a sequence of labels (i.e. case/number/etc of consecutive words in an NP/PP) at sentence level. For the prediction of the placeholder prepositions, we trained a maximum entropy model on the parallel training data. In contrast to the morphological features, each preposition in a phrase is predicted independently. For all models, we used the toolkit Wapiti (Lavergne et al., 2010). The German data was parsed with BitPar (Schmid, 2004) and German inflected forms were generated with the morphological resource SMOR (Schmid et al., 2004).

6.2 Baselines

We consider two baselines:

BASELINE-1: a standard phrase-based translation system trained on surface forms without any form of morphological modeling.

BASELINE-2: a system with morphological modeling, as described in section 3. Portmanteau prepositions are split into preposition and article prior to translation and merged in a post-processing step. Otherwise, prepositions are not modeled.

6.3 Results

The preposition-informed system contains overt prepositions and empty prepositions annotated with grammatical case at the beginning of noun phrases,

as described in section 4. Empty prepositions are simply deleted from the SMT output after translation before generating inflected forms. The introduction of empty prepositions into the training data leads to statistically significant improvements in BLEU over both the surface system (baseline-1) and the inflection prediction system (baseline-2), cf. Table 3. Furthermore, restricting the phrase-table to the top-20 entries according to $p(e\|f)$ (system P-2) does not decrease performance.

Table 4 shows the results for the variants of the synthetic-phrases systems, which all significantly outperform baseline-2. Even though the difference is small, the best system (SP-3b) is significantly better than system P-2, the preposition-informed system using the top-20 translation table entries. It is, however, not significantly better than system P-1, which uses all phrase-table entries. This is reasonable considering that SP-3b is built from placeholder entries based on the same phrase inventory as system P-2.

The system with the lowest score (SP-1) uses lexical and placeholder phrase probabilities combined with the ME prediction scores and the count feature. System SP-2, extended with the product of the phrase translation probability and the ME score, yields a slightly better result. For system SP-3, in which new phrase-translation probabilities replace the placeholder probabilities, we compare a version with and without normalized $p(e\|f)$ scores: the normalization leads to a best overall score; all synthetic-phrases systems score in a similar range, however.

7 Discussion

In this section, we summarize the results and in particular, discuss the use of newly generated phrases. We also attempt to analyze potential side-effects on the phrase table and present additional experiments to better handle these effects.

7.1 Summary of Results

The insertion of placeholder prepositions leads to an improvement over both baselines due to the cleaner alignment enabled by the more similar source and target sides. Furthermore, the empty prepositions can function as phrase boundaries and provide "flat structural" information in the form of annotated grammatical case.

The synthetic-phrases approach aims at generating a context-sensitive variant of the preposition-

	SP-1	SP-2	SP-3a	SP-3b
new	1489	1507	1391	1398
regular	38132	34541	35101	33571

Table 5: Number of newly generated and regular phrase-table entries used to translate the test set (3003 sentences).

informed system that is able to generate new entries if needed. We explored different score settings, either as separate features (variants 1/2) or combined into a translation probability score in (variant 3). While all variants perform similarly, the best system is significantly better than the preposition-informed system built on the top-20 phrase-table entries. This shows that the proposed method of synthetic phrases indeed improves translation quality. However, the difference is very small and only applies to one pair of system variants, which makes it difficult to draw a solid conclusion.

7.2 Use of Newly Generated Phrases

An important property in the presented method is the ability to generate new phrases. Table 5 shows the distribution of phrases used to translate the test set. For the 3003 sentences, roughly 1500 new phrases have been applied; on average, this corresponds to about one new phrase in one out of two sentences. Given that function words usually are thought to be well-covered in NLP training data, this number is substantial.

The following example illustrates how newly generated translation options can improve translations by closing coverage gaps. Table 6 shows the translations for an input sentence (EN) of the preposition-informed system P-2 and the synthetic-phrases system SP-2. The two outputs are identical and both correct, except for the wrong preposition *zur* in system P-2. To translate the sentence with the synthetic-phrases system, these new translation options[3] have been used:

the deutsche bahn → die Ø-Nom deutsche Bahn
to improve Ø the → **auf-Acc** eine Verbesserung Ø-Gen der
railway line in → Eisenbahnlinie in-Dat

In particular, the phrase pair "*to improve Ø the →* **auf-Acc** *eine Verbesserung Ø-Gen der*" enables a translation with the correct preposition. Due to the segmentation of the sentence, the English verb *hope* is translated as part of another phrase, which excludes a translation as one unit such as *hope*

EN	nullprp the deutsche bahn hopes to improve nullprp the kinzigtal railway line in the coming year.
P-2	die deutsche Bahn hofft **zur** Verbesserung der kinzigtal Eisenbahnlinie im kommenden Jahr.
SP-2	die deutsche Bahn hofft **auf eine** Verbesserung der kinzigtal Eisenbahnlinie im kommenden Jahr.

Table 6: Improved translation output by applying a newly generated translation option.

to → *hoffen auf*. Furthermore, there is a structural shift between the source side phrase "*hope to improve*$_{\text{VERB}}$", and the German sentence with the structure "*hofft* PREP *Verbesserung*$_{\text{NOUN}}$". The incorrect *zu* in the preposition-informed system would be a valid connection to a following verb, but cannot be used to introduce a PP in this context.

7.3 Side-Effects on the Phrase-Table

A recurring problem in the synthetic-phrases system are lexically wrong translations that are boosted due to unreasonably high ME scores in comparison to lexically more correct options. In particular, this is the case when infrequent words occur within a lexically wrong translation, which also happens to have lexical and phrase translation probabilities in a similar range as better translation candidates. When predicting prepositions for such phrases, the ME model is often overly confident and outputs comparatively high prediction scores based on an insufficient amount of training examples[4].

Consider as an example the English phrase *for bags* and two of its translation options: "PREP *Taschen*" ('bags') and "PREP *Müllsäcke*" ('garbage bags'), which have similar translation and lexical probabilities. In the ME training data, there are only very few occurrences of PREP *Müllsäcke*. As a result, the ME very confidently reproduces the seen training instances with a score around 0.9 for the top-ranked preposition. In comparison, the predictions for PREP *Taschen* are more balanced due to more occurrences of this word, with a score of around 0.55 for the top-ranked preposition. Thus, the incorrect *für Müllsäcke* option is boosted by its prediction score and consequently gets chosen by the synthetic-phrases system.

Lexical features, e.g., in verb-noun tuples, are important for the prediction power of our ME model. However, the example above illustrates how infrequent words can be harmful. We addressed

---

[3] Shown in inflected format for better readability.

[4] Note that the model must be trained on parallel data only as it makes use of source-side features.

	SP-1	SP-2	SP-3a	SP-3b
(1) no infreq nouns	19.59	19.85	19.71	19.94*
(2) reduced data	19.82	19.58	19.73	19.64

Table 7: Results when filtering out infrequent nouns in the ME training data (1) or reducing the amount of source-target-alignment triples used for ME training (2). * marks significant improvement over system P-2.

	prep-informed		synth-phrases	
	missing	wrong	missing	wrong
verbs	32	11	23	10
nouns	2	15	2	17
prepositions	6	6	3	8
gram. case	–	4	–	3

Table 8: Manual error analysis of 50 randomly selected sentences.

this problem by weighting down the prediction scores using lexical and/or phrase translation probabilities. In addition, we also experimented with replacing infrequent words with dummy tokens to still benefit from lexical information while excluding insufficiently represented words. The first line in table 7 shows the results for prediction models trained on data where infrequent nouns (*freq < 25*) occurring in the NP/PP (features 5 and 6 in table 1) are omitted when training the prediction ME. The general outcome is similar to the experiments reported in table 4, with variants SP-2 and SP-3b being slightly better. The result for system SP-3b is the overall best result. This suggests that a careful representation of infrequent lexical items in training data benefits the prediction quality.

In an attempt to reduce the training data to relevant entries, we restricted the source-target-alignment triples used to train the prediction ME to those occurring in the top-20 filtered table. Thus, all entries in the phrase-table are covered by the model, while infrequent and non-relevant training instances are mostly omitted. The results are listed in the second line in table 7; however, this model leads to generally worse results than the previous ones. We assume that removing a subset of training triples leads to a somewhat unbalanced training set.

7.4 Distribution in Phrase Table

Another, potentially negative, effect on the phrase distribution in the phrase table stems from integrating the n-best predictions per place-holder entry: an already dominant translation option can be further reinforced if it does not only represent the top-most translation option (as in the preposition-informed or place-holder table), but can be expanded to several entries. An equally valid, but less probable translation option is then less accessible if its prediction scores are in the same range, as this translation is then dispreferred by its translation scores and has to compete with several entries stemming from the original top translation option. Consider the example of the phrase "*expand nullprp their*": in the preposition-informed system, the lexically correct translation *erweitern* EMPTY-Acc *ihre* is ranked third according to $p(e|f)$, with two meaningless translations (only determiner or only preposition) as the two top-ranked translations, which is already a bad starting point for translation of the verb. In the synthetic-phrases system, "descendants" of the previously top-2 meaningless translations now are expanded and fill the positions 1-5, resulting in the correct translation option being ranked 6th.

This effect can also be positive by promoting lexically correct translation options (in cases where the leading translation is correct, but is closely followed by a less suited translation). For example, it can be seen in the example in table 2 where the lexically incorrect phrases are moved to lower positions. However, it might also happen that literal translations are preferred over less common senses in cases of word sense ambiguities. A small manual evaluation (cf. next section) showed that slightly more verbs are translated with the synthetic phrases system. Verbs in English-to-German translation are often omitted during translation; the effect of enhancing literal translations might be responsible for the observed tendency to translate more verbs.

The different score variants explored in the previous section aim to find a combination that considers these factors, but the results show that it is a difficult task to account for all possible interactions.

7.5 Manual Evaluation

We carried out a small manual evaluation for 50 sentences (length 10-20 words) randomly chosen from system SP-3b in table 7, the best overall system, in comparison to the preposition-informed system P-2. Two native speakers annotated errors concerning missing or incorrect verbs, nouns and prepositions, as well as incorrect grammatical case. Table 8 depicts the outcome: The number of errors found in the categories *preposition* and *grammatical case* are similar for both systems. A slight improvement

EN	this is mainly *due to the higher contribution* from the administrative budget ...
P-2	das ist hauptsächlich ***auf** die höheren Beiträge* aus dem Verwaltungshaushalt ...
SP-3b	das ist vor allem ***wegen** den höheren Beiträgen* aus dem Verwaltungshaushalt ...

Table 9: Example for unclear error categories.

is found, however, for the number of translated verbs, which are known to be generally difficult for the language pair English-to-German. We assume that this is due to a tendency to strengthen literal translations, from which verbs might benefit as they are generally less well represented in the phrase-table.

Note, however, that there are other relevant factors that this manual evaluation does not take into account, such as, e.g., the overall structure of the sentence. Furthermore, the evaluation of verbs and its subcategorized elements is often difficult as there might be several valid options for annotation, which is illustrated by the example in table 9. The translations of the two systems are nearly identical, except for the prepositions heading the translation for *due to the higher contribution* (and consequently the realization of grammatical case in the respective phrases, which is correct given the respective preposition). The sentence produced by the synthetic-phrases system is correct, preserving the structure of the English sentence by translating *due to* as *wegen+Dative* (*wegen+Genitive* would be correct, too.). Thus, replacing the preposition *auf* and adjusting the grammatical case in the sentence produced by the preposition-informed system would lead to the same, valid, translation. However, the preposition *auf* strongly triggers the reader to expect the verb *zurückführen (auf)* ('to attribute (to)') which also would lead to a valid translation. Such cases make the evaluation of prepositions and complement types difficult, as the error category (*missing verb* or *wrong preposition*) is not always clear.

8   Conclusion and Future Work

We compared two approaches for modeling complement types in English-to-German SMT. Our experiments showed that explicit information about different complement types (insertion of empty placeholders) leads to improved SMT quality. The results of the synthetic-phrases system are slightly better than those of the preposition-informed system, with two variants being significantly better.

As the differences are rather small and apply only to some system pairs, it is difficult to draw a clear conclusion concerning the effectiveness of the synthetic-phrases method. Our analysis showed, however, that newly generated phrases are indeed used within the systems and help to improve translation quality. We consider this a confirmation that the generation of synthetic phrases for handling subcategorization is a sound approach.

In future work, we plan to explore models that predict the complete target *phrase* given the source phrase and subcategorization-relevant features instead of predicting the *preposition* in a target phrase.

Acknowledgments

This project has received funding from the European Union's Horizon 2020 research and innovation programme under grant agreement No 644402 (HimL), from the European Research Council (ERC) under grant agreement No 640550, from the DFG grants *Distributional Approaches to Semantic Relatedness* and *Models of Morphosyntax for Statistical Machine Translation (Phase Two)* and from the DFG Heisenberg Fellowship SCHU-2580/1.

References

Eneko Agirre, Aitziber Atutxa, Gorka Labaka, Mikel Lersundi, Aingeru Mayor, and Kepa Sarasola. 2009. Use of Rich Linguistic Information to Translate Prepositions and Grammatical Cases to Basque. In *Proceedings of the 13th Annual Conference of the EAMT*, Barcelona, Spain.

Marine Carpuat and Dekai Wu. 2007. Improving Statistical Machine Translation using Word Sense Disambiguation. In *Proceedings of the 2007 Joint Conference on Empirical Methods in Natural Language Processing and Computational Natural Language Learning*, Prague, Czech Republic.

Victor Chahuneau, Eva Schlinger, Noah A. Smith, and Chris Dyer. 2013. Translating into Morphologically Rich Languages with Synthetic Phrases. In *Proceedings of the 2013 Conference on Empirical Methods in Natural Language Processing (EMNLP)*, Seattle, Washington.

Jinho D. Choi and Martha Palmer. 2012. Getting the Most out of Transition-Based Dependency Parsing. In *Proceedings of the 49th Annual Meeting of the Association for Computational Linguistics: Human Language Technologies*, Portland, Oregon.

Alexander Fraser, Marion Weller, Aoife Cahill, and Fabienne Cap. 2012. Modeling Inflection and Word-

Formation in SMT. In *Proceedings of the the European Chapter of the Association for Computational Linguistics (EACL)*, Avignon, France.

Kevin Gimpel and Noah A. Smith. 2008. Rich Source-Side Context for Statistical Machine Translation. In *Proceedings of the Third Workshop on Statistical Machine Translation*, Columbus, Ohio.

Minwoo Jeong, Kristina Toutanova, Hisami Suzuki, and Chris Quirk. 2010. A Discriminative Lexicon Model for Complex Morphology. In *In Proceedings of the Ninth Conference of the Association for Machine Translation in the Americas.*, Denver, Colorado.

Thomas Lavergne, Olivier Cappé, and François Yvon. 2010. Practical very large scale CRFs. In *Proceedings the 48th Annual Meeting of the Association for Computational Linguistics (ACL)*, Uppsala, Sweden.

Helmut Schmid, Arne Fitschen, and Ulrich Heid. 2004. SMOR: a German Computational Morphology Covering Derivation, Composition, and Inflection. In *Proceedings LREC 2004*, Lisbon, Portugal.

Helmut Schmid. 2004. Efficient Parsing of Highly Ambiguous Context-Free Grammars with Bit Vectors. In *Proceedings of the International Conference on Computational Linguistics.*

Reshef Shilon, Hanna Fadida, and Shuly Wintner. 2012. Incorporating Linguistic Knowledge in Statistical Machine Translation: Translating Prepositions. In *Proceedings of the Workshop on Innovative Hybrid Approaches to the Processing of Textual Data, EACL 2012*, Avignon, France.

Aleš Tamchyna, Fabienne Braune, Alexander Fraser, Marine Carpuat, Hal Daumé III, and Chris Quirk. 2014. Integrating a Discriminative Classifier into Phrase-based and Hierarchical Decoding. In *The Prague Bulletin of Mathematical Linguistics, Number 101*, pages 29–41.

Jörg Tiedemann, Filip Ginter, and Jenna Kanerva. 2015. Morphological Segmentation and OPUS for Finnish-English Machine Translation. In *Proceedings of the Tenth Workshop on Statistical Machine Translation*, Lisbon, Portugal.

Kristina Toutanova, Hisami Suzuki, and Achim Ruopp. 2008. Applying Morphology Generation Models to Machine Translation. In *Proceedings of ACL08-HLT*, Columbus, Ohio.

Julia Tsvetkov, Chris Dyer, Lori Levin, and Archna Bhatia. 2013. Generating English Determiners in Phrase-Based Translation with Synthetic Translation Options. In *Proceedings of the Eighth Workshop on Statistical Machine Translation*, Sofia, Bulgaria.

Marion Weller, Alexander Fraser, and Sabine Schulte im Walde. 2013. Using Subcategorization Knowledge to Improve Case Prediction for Translation to German. In *Proceedings of the Association for Computational Linguistics (ACL)*, Sofia, Bulgaria.

Marion Weller, Alexander Fraser, and Sabine Schulte im Walde. 2015. Target-Side Generation of Prepositions for SMT. In *Proceedings of EAMT 2015*, Antalya, Turkey.

Philip Williams, Rico Sennrich, Maria Nadejde, Matthias Huck, and Philpp Koehn. 2015. Edinburgh's Syntax-Based Systems at WMT 2015. In *Proceedings of the Tenth Workshop on Statistical Machine Translation*, Lisbon, Portugal.

Alignment-Based Neural Machine Translation

Tamer Alkhouli, Gabriel Bretschner,
Jan-Thorsten Peter, Mohammed Hethnawi, Andreas Guta and Hermann Ney
Human Language Technology and Pattern Recognition Group
RWTH Aachen University, Aachen, Germany
{surname}@cs.rwth-aachen.de

Abstract

Neural machine translation (NMT) has emerged recently as a promising statistical machine translation approach. In NMT, neural networks (NN) are directly used to produce translations, without relying on a pre-existing translation framework. In this work, we take a step towards bridging the gap between conventional word alignment models and NMT. We follow the hidden Markov model (HMM) approach that separates the alignment and lexical models. We propose a neural alignment model and combine it with a lexical neural model in a log-linear framework. The models are used in a standalone word-based decoder that explicitly hypothesizes alignments during search. We demonstrate that our system outperforms attention-based NMT on two tasks: IWSLT 2013 German→English and BOLT Chinese→English. We also show promising results for re-aligning the training data using neural models.

1 Introduction

Neural networks have been gaining a lot of attention recently in areas like speech recognition, image recognition and natural language processing. In machine translation, NNs are applied in two main ways: In N-best rescoring, the neural model is used to score the first-pass decoding output, limiting the model to a fixed set of hypotheses (Le et al., 2012; Sundermeyer et al., 2014a; Hu et al., 2014; Guta et al., 2015). The second approach integrates the NN into decoding, potentially allowing it to directly determine the search space.

There are two approaches to use neural models in decoding. The first integrates the mod-

els into phrase-based decoding, where the models are used to score phrasal candidates hypothesized by the decoder (Vaswani et al., 2013; Devlin et al., 2014; Alkhouli et al., 2015). The second approach is referred to as neural machine translation, where neural models are used to hypothesize translations, word by word, without relying on a pre-existing framework. In comparison to the former approach, NMT does not restrict NNs to predetermined translation candidates, and it does not depend on word alignment concepts that have been part of building state-of-the-art phrase-based systems. In such systems, the HMM and the IBM models developed more than two decades ago are used to produce Viterbi word alignments, which are used to build standard phrase-based systems. Existing NMT systems either disregard the notion of word alignments entirely (Sutskever et al., 2014), or rely on a probabilistic notion of alignments (Bahdanau et al., 2015) independent of the conventional alignment models.

Most recently, Cohn et al. (2016) designed neural models that incorporate concepts like fertility and Markov conditioning into their structure. In this work, we also focus on the question whether conventional word alignment concepts can be used for NMT. In particular, (1) We follow the HMM approach to separate the alignment and translation models, and use neural networks to model alignments and translation. (2) We introduce a lexicalized alignment model to capture source reordering information. (3) We bootstrap the NN training using Viterbi word alignments obtained from the HMM and IBM model training, and use the trained neural models to generate new alignments. The new alignments are then used to re-train the neural networks. (4) We design an alignment-based decoder that hypothesizes the alignment path along with the associated translation. We show competitive results in comparison to attention-based

Proceedings of the First Conference on Machine Translation, Volume 1: Research Papers, pages 54–65,
Berlin, Germany, August 11-12, 2016. ©2016 Association for Computational Linguistics

models on the IWSLT 2013 German→English and BOLT Chinese→English task.

1.1 Motivation

Attention-based NMT computes the translation probability depending on an intermediate computation of an alignment distribution. The alignment distribution is used to choose the positions in the source sentence that the decoder attends to during translation. Therefore, the alignment model can be considered as an implicit part of the translation model. On the other hand, separating the alignment model from the lexical model has its own advantages: First, this leads to more flexibility in modeling and training: not only can the models be trained separately, but they can also have different model types, e.g. neural models, count-based models, etc. Second, the separation avoids propagating errors from one model to the other. In attention-based systems, the translation score is based on the alignment distribution, which risks propagating errors from the alignment part to the translation part. Third, using separate models makes it possible to assign them different weights. We exploit this and use a log-linear framework to combine them. We still retain the possibility of joint training, which can be performed flexibly by alternating between model training and alignment generation. The latter can be performed using forced-decoding.

In contrast to the count-based models used in HMMs, we use neural models, which allow covering long context without having to explicitly address the smoothing problem that arises in count-based models.

2 Related Work

Most recently, NNs have been trained on large amounts of data, and applied to translate independent of the phrase-based framework. Sutskever et al. (2014) introduced the pure encoder-decoder approach, which avoids the concept of word alignments. Bahdanau et al. (2015) introduced an attention mechanism to the encoder-decoder approach, allowing the decoder to attend to certain source words. This method was refined in (Luong et al., 2015) to allow for local attention, which makes the decoder attend to representations of source words residing within a window. These translation models have shown competitive results, outperforming phrase-based systems when using ensembles on

tasks like IWSLT English→German 2015 (Luong and Manning, 2015).

In this work, we follow the same standalone neural translation approach. However, we have a different treatment of alignments. While the attention-based soft-alignment model computes an alignment distribution as an intermediate step within the neural model, we follow the hard alignment concept used in phrase extraction. We separate the alignment model from the lexical model, and train them independently. At translation time, the decoder hypothesizes and scores the alignment path in addition to the translation.

Cohn et al. (2016) introduce several modifications to the attention-based model inspired by traditional word alignment concepts. They modify the network architecture, adding a first-order dependence by making the attention vector computed for a target position directly dependent on that of the previous position. Our alignment model has a first-order dependence that takes place at the input and output of the model, rather than an architectural modification of the neural network.

Yang et al. (2013) use NN-based lexical and alignment models, but they give up the probabilistic interpretation and produce unnormalized scores instead. Furthermore, they model alignments using a simple distortion model that has no dependence on lexical context. The models are used to produce new alignments which are in turn used to train phrase systems. This leads to no significant difference in terms of translation performance. Tamura et al. (2014) propose a lexicalized RNN alignment model. The model still produces non-probabilistic scores, and is used to generate word alignments used to train phrase-based systems. In this work, we develop a feed-forward neural alignment model that computes probabilistic scores, and use it directly in standalone decoding, without constraining it to the phrase-based framework. In addition, we use the neural models to produce alignments that are used to re-train the same neural models.

Schwenk (2012) proposed a feed-forward network that computes phrase scores offline, and the scores were added to the phrase table of a phrase-based system. Offline phrase scoring was also done in (Alkhouli et al., 2014) using semantic phrase features obtained using simple neural networks. In comparison, our work does not rely on the phrase-based system, rather, the neural networks are used to hypothesize translation candidates directly, and the scores are computed online during decoding.

We use the feed-forward joint model introduced in (Devlin et al., 2014) as a lexical model, and introduce a lexicalized alignment model based on it. In addition, we modify the bidirectional joint model presented in (Sundermeyer et al., 2014a) and compare it to the feed-forward variant. These lexical models were applied in phrase-based systems. In this work, we apply them in a standalone NMT framework.

Forced alignment was applied to train phrase tables in (Wuebker et al., 2010; Peitz et al., 2012). We generate forced alignments using a neural decoder, and use them to re-train neural models.

Tackling the costly normalization of the output layer during decoding has been the focus of several papers (Vaswani et al., 2013; Devlin et al., 2014; Jean et al., 2015). We propose a simple method to speed up decoding using a class-factored output layer with almost no loss in translation quality.

3   Statistical Machine Translation

In statistical machine translation, the target word sequence $e_1^I = e_1, ..., e_I$ of length I is assigned a probability conditioned on the source word sequence $f_1^J = f_1, ..., f_J$ of length J. By introducing word alignments as hidden variables, the posterior probability $p(e_1^I|f_1^J)$ can be computed using a lexical and an alignment model as follows.

$$p(e_1^I|f_1^J)$$
$$= \sum_{b_1^I} p(e_1^I, b_1^I|f_1^J)$$
$$= \sum_{b_1^I} \prod_{i=1}^{I} p(e_i, b_i|b_1^{i-1}, e_1^{i-1}, f_1^J)$$
$$= \sum_{b_1^I} \prod_{i=1}^{I} \underbrace{p(e_i|b_1^i, e_1^{i-1}, f_1^J)}_{\text{lexical model}} \cdot \underbrace{p(b_i|b_1^{i-1}, e_1^{i-1}, f_1^J)}_{\text{alignment model}}$$

where $b_1^I = b_1, ..., b_I$ denotes the alignment path, such that b_i aligns the target word e_i to the source word f_{b_i}. In this general formulation, the lexical model predicts the target word e_i conditioned on the source sentence, the target history, and the alignment history. The alignment model is lexicalized using the source and target context as well. The sum over alignment paths is replaced by the maximum during decoding (cf. Section 5).

4   Neural Network Models

There are two common network architectures used in machine translation: feed-forward NNs (FFNN) and recurrent NNs (RNN). In this section we will discuss alignment-based feed-forward and recurrent neural networks. These networks are conditioned on the word alignment, in addition to the source and target words.

4.1   Feed-forward Joint Model

We adopt the feed-forward joint model (FFJM) proposed in (Devlin et al., 2014) as the lexical model. The authors demonstrate the model has a strong performance when applied in a phrase-based framework. In this work we explore its performance in standalone NMT. The model was introduced along with heuristics to resolve unaligned and multiply aligned words. We denote the heuristic-based source alignment point corresponding to the target position i by $\hat{b}_i$. The model is defined as

$$p(e_i|b_1^i, e_1^{i-1}, f_1^J) = p(e_i|e_{i-n}^{i-1}, f_{\hat{b}_i-m}^{\hat{b}_i+m}) \qquad (1)$$

and it computes the probability of a target word e_i at position i given the n-gram target history $e_{i-n}^{i-1} = e_{i-n}, ..., e_{i-1}$, and a window of $2m + 1$ source words $f_{\hat{b}_i-m}^{\hat{b}_i+m} = f_{\hat{b}_i-m}, ..., f_{\hat{b}_i+m}$ centered around the word $f_{\hat{b}_i}$.

As the heuristics have implications on our alignment-based decoder, we explain them by the examples shown in Figure 1. We mark the source and target context by rectangles on the x- and y-axis, respectively. The left figure shows a single source word 'Jungen' aligned to a single target word 'offspring', in which case, the original source position is used, i.e., $\hat{b}_i = b_i$. If the target word is aligned to multiple source words, as it is the case with the words 'Mutter Tiere' and 'Mothers' in the middle figure, then $\hat{b}_i$ is set to the middle alignment point. In this example, the left alignment point associated with 'Mutter' is selected. The right figure shows the case of the unaligned target word 'of'. $\hat{b}_i$ is set to the source position associated with the closest aligned target word 'full', preferring right to left. Note that this model does not have special handling of unaligned source words. While these words can be covered indirectly by source windows associated with aligned source words, the model does not explicitly score them.

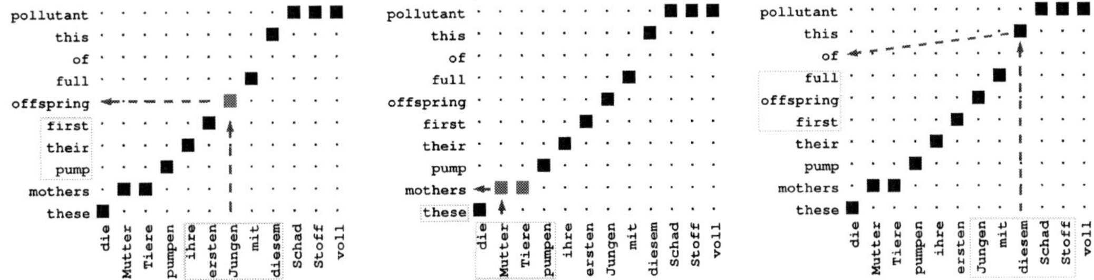

Figure 1: Examples on resolving word alignments to obtain word affiliations.

Computing normalized probabilities is done using the softmax function, which requires computing the full output layer first, and then computing the normalization factor by summing over the output scores of the full vocabulary. This is very costly for large vocabularies. To overcome this, we adopt the class-factored output layer consisting of a class layer and a word layer (Goodman, 2001; Morin and Bengio, 2005). The model in this case is defined as

$$p(e_i|e_{i-n}^{i-1}, f_{\hat{b}_i-m}^{\hat{b}_i+m}) =$$

$$p(e_i|c(e_i), e_{i-n}^{i-1}, f_{\hat{b}_i-m}^{\hat{b}_i+m}) \cdot p(c(e_i)|e_{i-n}^{i-1}, f_{\hat{b}_i-m}^{\hat{b}_i+m})$$

where c denotes a word mapping that assigns each target word to a single class, where the number of classes is chosen to be much smaller than the vocabulary size $|C| << |V|$. Even though the full class layer needs to be computed, only a subset of the significantly-larger word layer has to be considered, namely the words that share the same class $c(e_i)$ with the target word e_i. This helps speeding up training on large-vocabulary tasks.

4.2 Bidirectional Joint Model

The bidirectional RNN joint model (BJM) presented in (Sundermeyer et al., 2014a) is another lexical model. The BJM uses the full source sentence and the full target history for prediction, and it is computed by reordering the source sentence following the target order. This requires the complete alignment information to compute the model scores. Here, we introduce a variant of the model that is conditioned on the alignment history instead of the full alignment path. This is achieved by computing forward and backward representations of the source sentence in its original order, as done in (Bahdanau et al., 2015). The model is given by

$$p(e_i|b_1^i, e_1^{i-1}, f_1^J) = p(e_i|\hat{b}_1^i, e_1^{i-1}, f_1^J)$$

Note that we also use the same alignment heuristics presented in Section 4.1. As this variant does not require future alignment information, it can be applied in decoding. However, in this work we apply this model in rescoring and leave decoder integration to future work.

4.3 Feed-forward Alignment Model

We propose a neural alignment model to score alignment paths. Instead of predicting the absolute positions in the source sentence, we model the jumps from one source position to the next position to be translated. The jump at target position i is defined as $\Delta_i = \hat{b}_i - \hat{b}_{i-1}$, which captures the jump from the source position $\hat{b}_{i-1}$ to $\hat{b}_i$. We modify the FFNN lexical model to obtain a feed-forward alignment model. The feed-forward alignment model (FFAM) is given by

$$p(b_i|b_1^{i-1}, e_1^{i-1}, f_1^J) = p(\Delta_i|e_{i-n}^{i-1}, f_{\hat{b}_{i-1}-m}^{\hat{b}_{i-1}+m}) \quad (2)$$

This is a lexicalized alignment model conditioned on the n-gram target history and the $(2m + 1)$-gram source window. Note that, different from the FFJM, the source window of this model is centered around the source position $\hat{b}_{i-1}$. This is because the model needs to predict the jump to the next source position $\hat{b}_i$ to be translated. The alignment model architecture is shown in Figure 2.

In contrast to the lexical model, the output vocabulary of the alignment model is much smaller, and therefore we use a regular softmax output layer for this model without class-factorization.

4.4 Feed-forward vs. Recurrent Models

RNNs have been shown to outperform feed-forward variants in language and translation modeling. Nevertheless, feed-forward networks have their own advantages: First, they are typically

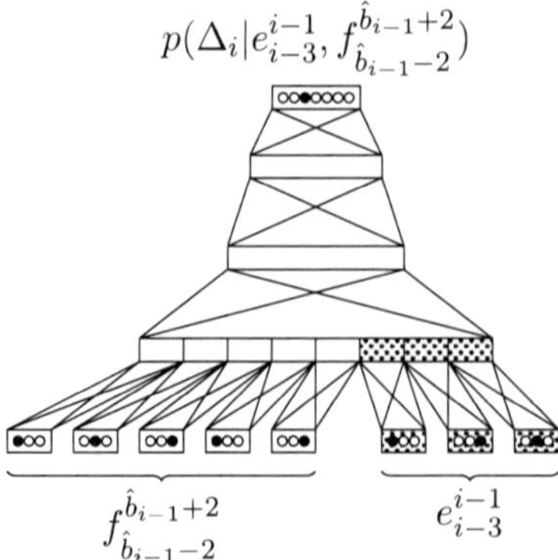

Figure 2: A feed-forward alignment NN, with 3 target history words, 5-gram source window, a projection layer, 2 hidden layers, and a small output layer to predict jumps.

faster to train due to their simple architecture, and second, they are more flexible to integrate into beam search decoders. This is because feed-forward networks only depend on a limited context. RNNs, on the other hand, are conditioned on an unbounded context. This means that the complete hypotheses during decoding have to be maintained without any state recombination. Since feed-forward networks allow the use of state recombination, they are potentially capable of exploring more candidates during beam search.

5 Alignment-based Decoder

In this section we present the alignment-based decoder. This is a beam-search word-based decoder that predicts one target word at a time. As the models we use are alignment-based, the decoder hypothesizes the alignment path. This is different from the NMT approaches present in the literature, which are based on models that either ignore word alignments or compute alignments as part of the attention-based model.

In the general case, a word can be aligned to a single word, multiple words, or it can be unaligned. However, we do not use the general word alignment notion, rather, the models are based on alignments derived using the heuristics discussed in Section 4. These heuristics simplify the task of the decoder, as they induce equivalence classes over the alignment paths, reducing the number of possible alignments the decoder has to hypothesize significantly. As a result of using these heuristics, the task of hypothesizing alignments is re-

---

Algorithm 1 Alignment-based Decoder

```
 1:  procedure TRANSLATE(f_1^J, beamSize)
 2:      hyps ← initHyp        ▷previous set of partial hypotheses
 3:      newHyps ← ∅           ▷current set of partial hypotheses
 4:      while GETBEST(hyps) not terminated do
 5:          ▷compute alignment distribution in batch mode
 6:          alignDists ← ALIGNMENTDISTRIBUTION(hyps)
 7:          ▷hypothesize source alignment points
 8:          for pos From 1 to J do
 9:              ▷compute lexical distributions of all
10:              ▷hypotheses in hyps in batch mode
11:              dists ← LEXICALDISTRIBUTION(hyps, pos)
12:              ▷expand each of the previous hypotheses
13:              for hyp in hyps do
14:                  jmpCost ← SCORE(alignDists, hyp, pos)
15:                  dist ← GETDISTRIBUTION(dists, hyp)
16:                  dist ← PARTIALSORT(dist, beamSize)
17:                  cnt ← 0
18:                  ▷hypothesize new target word
19:                  for word in dist do
20:                      if cnt > beamSize then
21:                          break
22:                      newHyp ← EXTEND(hyp, word, pos, jmpCost)
23:                      newHyps.INSERT(newHyp)
24:                      cnt ← cnt + 1
25:          PRUNE(newHyps, beamSize)
26:          hyps ← newHyps
27:
28:      ▷return the best scoring hypothesis
29:      return GETBEST(hyps)
```

---

duced to enumerating all J source positions a target word can be aligned to. The following is a list of the possible alignment scenarios and how the decoder covers them.

- Multiply-aligned target words: the heuristic chooses the middle link as an alignment point. Therefore, the decoder is able to cover these cases by hypothesizing J many source positions for each target word hypothesis.

- Unaligned target words: the heuristic aligns these words using the nearest aligned target word in training (cf. Figure 1, right). In decoding, these words are handled as aligned words.

- Multiply-aligned source words: covered by revisiting a source position that has already been translated.

- Unaligned source words: result if no target word is generated using a source window centered around the source word in question.

The decoder is shown in Algorithm 1. It involves hypothesizing alignments and translation words. Alignments are hypothesized in the loop starting at line 8. Once an alignment point is set to position *pos*, the lexical distribution over the full target vocabulary is computed using this position in line 11. The distribution is sorted and the best candidate translations lying within the beam are used to expand the partial hypotheses.

We batch the NN computations, calling the alignment and lexical networks for all partial hypotheses in a single call to speed up computations as shown in lines 6 and 11. We also exploit the beam and apply partial sorting in line 16, instead of completely sorting the list. Partial sorting has a linear complexity on average, and it returns a list whose first $beamSize$ words have better scores compared to the rest of the list.

We terminate translation if the best scoring partial hypothesis ends with the sentence end symbol. If a hypothesis terminates but it scores worse than other hypotheses, it is removed from the beam, but it still competes with non-terminated hypotheses. Note that we do not have any explicit coverage constraints. This means that a source position can be revisited many times, hence generating one-to-many alignment cases. This also allows having unaligned source words.

In the alignment-based decoder, an alignment distribution is computed, and word alignments are hypothesized and scored using this distribution, leading alignment decisions to become part of beam search. The search space is composed of both alignment and translation decisions. In contrast, the search space in attention-based decoding is composed of translation decisions only.

Class-Factored Output Layer in Decoding

The large output layer used in language and translation modeling is a major bottleneck in evaluating the network. Several papers discuss how to evaluate it efficiently during decoding using approximations. In this work, we exploit the class-factored output layer to speed up training. At decoding time, the network needs to hypothesize all target words, which means the full output layer should be evaluated. In the case of using a class-factored output layer, this results in an additional computational overhead from computing the class layer. In order to speed up decoding, we propose to use the class layer to choose the top scoring k classes, then we evaluate the word layer for each of these classes only. We show this leads to a significant speed up with minimal loss in translation quality.

Model Combination

We embed the models in a log-linear framework, which is commonly used in phrase-based systems. The goal of the decoder is to find the best scoring hypothesis as follows.

$$\hat{e}_1^{\hat{I}} = \arg\max_{I, e_1^I} \left\{ \max_{\hat{b}_1^I} \sum_{m=1}^{M} \lambda_m h_m(f_1^J, e_1^I, \hat{b}_1^I) \right\}$$

where λ_m is the model weight associated with the model h_m, and M is the total number of models. The model weights are automatically tuned using minimum error rate training (MERT) (Och, 2003). Our main system includes a lexical neural model, an alignment neural model, and a word penalty, which is the count of target words. The word penalty becomes important at the end of translation, where hypotheses in the beam might have different final lengths.

6 Forced-Alignment Training

Since the models we use require alignments for training, we initially use word alignments produced using HMM/IBM models using GIZA++ as initial alignments. At first, the FFJM and the FFAM are trained separately until convergence, then the models are used to generate new word alignments by force-decoding the training data as follows.

$$\tilde{b}_1^I(f_1^J, e_1^I) = \arg\max_{b_1^I} \prod_{i=1}^{I} p^{\lambda_1}(\Delta_i | e_{i-n}^{i-1}, f_{b_{i-1}-m}^{b_{i-1}+m})$$
$$\cdot p^{\lambda_2}(e_i | e_{i-n}^{i-1}, f_{b_i-m}^{b_i+m})$$

where λ_1 and λ_2 are the model weights. We modify the decoder to only compute the probabilities of the target words in the reference sentence. The for loop in line 19 of Algorithm 1 collapses to a single iteration. We use both the the feed-forward joint model (FFJM) and the feed-forward alignment model (FFAM) to perform force-decoding, and the new alignments are used to retrain the models, replacing the initial GIZA++ alignments.

Retraining the neural models using the forced-alignments has two benefits. First, since the alignments are produced using both of the lexical and alignment models, this can be viewed as joint training of the two models. Second, since the neural decoder generates these alignments, training neural models based on them yields models that are more consistent with the neural decoder. We verify this claim in the experiments section.

	IWSLT		BOLT	
	De	**En**	**Zh**	**En**
Sentences	4.32M		4.08M	
Run. Words	108M	109M	78M	86M
Vocab.	836K	792K	384K	817K
FFNN/BJM Vocab.	173K	149K	169K	128K
Attention Vocab.	30K	30K	30K	30K
FFJM params	177M		159M	
BJM params	170M		153M	
FFAM params	101M		94M	
Attention params	84M		84M	

Table 1: Corpora and NN statistics.

7 Experiments

We carry out experiments on two tasks: the IWSLT 2013 German→English shared translation task,[1] and the BOLT Chinese→English task. The corpora statistics are shown in Table 1. The IWSLT phrase-based baseline system is trained on all available bilingual data, and uses a 4-gram LM with modified Kneser-Ney smoothing (Kneser and Ney, 1995; Chen and Goodman, 1998), trained with the SRILM toolkit (Stolcke, 2002). As additional data sources for the LM, we selected parts of the Shuffled News and LDC English Gigaword corpora based on the cross-entropy difference (Moore and Lewis, 2010), resulting in a total of 1.7 billion running words for LM training. The phrase-based baseline is a standard phrase-based SMT system (Koehn et al., 2003) tuned with MERT (Och, 2003) and contains a hierarchical reordering model (Galley and Manning, 2008). The in-domain data consists of 137K sentences.

The BOLT Chinese→English task is evaluated on the "discussion forum" domain. We use a 5-gram LM trained on 2.9 billion running words in total. The in-domain data consists of a subset of 67.8K sentences. We used a set of 1845 sentences as a tune set. The evaluation set `test1` contains 1844 and `test2` contains 1124 sentences.

We use the FFNN architecture for the lexical and alignment models. Both models use a window of 9 source words, and 5 target history words. Both models use two hidden layers, the first has 1000 units and the second has 500 units. The lexical model uses a class-factored output layer, with 1000 singleton classes dedicated to the most frequent words, and 1000 classes shared among the rest of the words. The classes are trained using a separate tool to optimize the maximum likelihood

[1] http://www.iwslt2013.org

training criterion with the bigram assumption. The alignment model uses a small output layer of 201 nodes, determined by a maximum jump length of 100 (forward and backward). 300 nodes are used for word embeddings. Each of the FFNN models is trained on CPUs using 12 threads, which takes up to 3 days until convergence. We train with stochastic gradient descent using a batch size of 128. The learning rate is halved when the development perplexity increases.

Each BJM has 4 LSTM layers: two for the forward and backward states, one for the target state, and one after merging the source and target states. The size of the word embeddings and hidden layers is 350 nodes. The output layers are identical to those of the FFJM models.

We compare our system to an attention-based baseline similar to the networks described in (Bahdanau et al., 2015). All such systems use single models, rather than ensembles. The word embedding dimension is 620, each direction of the encoder and the decoder has a layer of 1000 gated recurrent units (Cho et al., 2014). Unknowns and numbers are carried out from the source side to the target side based on the largest attention weight.

To speed up decoding of long sentences, the decoder hypothesizes 21 and 41 source positions around the diagonal, for the IWSLT and the BOLT tasks, respectively. We choose these numbers such that the translation quality does not degrade. The beam size is set to 16 in all experiments. Larger beam sizes did not lead to improvements. We apply part-of-speech-based long-range verb reordering rules to the German side in a preprocessing step for all German→English systems (Popović and Ney, 2006), including the baselines. The Chinese→English systems use no such preordering. We use the GIZA++ word alignments to train the models. The networks are fine-tuned by training additional epochs on the in-domain data only (Luong and Manning, 2015). The LMs are only used in the phrase-based systems in both tasks, but not in the NMT systems.

All translation experiments are performed with the *Jane* toolkit (Vilar et al., 2010; Wuebker et al., 2012). The alignment-based NNs are trained using an extension of the *rwthlm* toolkit (Sundermeyer et al., 2014b). We use an implementation based on Blocks (van Merriënboer et al., 2015) and Theano (Bergstra et al., 2010; Bastien et al., 2012) for the attention-based experiments. All results are mea-

#	system	test 2010		eval 2011	
		BLEU	TER	BLEU	TER
1	phrase-based system	28.9	51.0	32.9	46.3
2	+ monolingual data	30.4	49.5	35.4	44.2
3	attention-based RNN	27.9	51.4	31.8	46.5
4	+fine-tuning	29.8	48.9	32.9	45.1
5	FFJM+dp+wp	21.6	56.9	24.7	53.8
6	FFJM+FFAM+wp	26.1	53..1	29.9	49.4
7	+fine-tuning	29.3	50.5	33.2	46.5
8	+BJM Rescoring	**30.0**	**48.7**	**33.8**	**44.8**
9	BJM+FFAM+wp+fine-tuning	29.8	49.5	33.7	45.8

Table 2: IWSLT 2013 German→English results in BLEU [%] and TER [%].

sured in case-insensitive BLEU [%] (Papineni et al., 2002) and TER [%] (Snover et al., 2006) on a single reference. We used the multeval toolkit (Clark et al., 2011) for evaluation.

7.1 IWSLT 2013 German→English

Table 2 shows the IWSLT German→English results. FFJM refers to feed-forward lexical model. We compare against the phrase-based system with an LM trained on the target side of the bilingual data (row #1), the phrase-based system with an LM trained on additional monolingual data (row #2), the attention-based system (row #3), and the attention-based system after fine-tuning towards the in-domain data (row #4). First, we experiment with a system using the FFJM as a lexical model and a linear distortion penalty (dp) to encourage monotone translation as the alignment model. We also include a word penalty (wp). This system is shown in row #5. In comparison, if the distortion penalty is replaced by the feed-forward alignment model (FFAM), we observe large improvements of 4.5% to 5.2% BLEU (row #5 vs. #6). This highlights the significant role of the alignment model in our system. Moreover, it indicates that the FFAM is able to model alignments beyond the simple monotone alignments preferred by the distortion penalty.

Fine-tuning the neural networks towards in-domain data improves the system by up to 3.3% BLEU and 2.9% TER (row #6 vs #7). The gain from fine-tuning is larger than the one observed for the attention-based system. This is likely due to the fact that our system has two neural models, and each of them is fine-tuned.

We apply the BJM in 1000-best list rescoring (row #8). Which gives another boost, leading our system to outperform the attention-based system by 0.9% BLEU on eval 2011, while a compa-

rable performance is achieved on test 2010. In order to highlight the difference between using the FFJM and the BJM, we replace the FFJM scores after obtaining the N-best lists with the BJM scores and apply rescoring (row #9). In comparison to row #7, we observe up to 0.5% BLEU and 1.0% TER improvement. This is expected as the BJM captures unbounded source and target context in comparison to the limited context of the FFJM. This calls for a direct integration of the BJM into decoding, which we intend to do in future work. Our best system (row #8) outperforms the phrase-based system (row #1) by up to 1.1% BLEU and 2.3% TER. While the phrase-based system can benefit from training the LM on additional monolingual data (row #1 vs. #2), exploiting monolingual data in NMT systems is still an open research question.

7.2 BOLT Chinese→English

The BOLT Chinese→English experiments are shown in Table 3. Again, we observe large improvements when including the FFAM in comparison to the distortion penalty (row #5 vs #6), and fine-tuning improves the results considerably. Including the BJM in rescoring improves the system by up to 0.4% BLEU. Our best system (row #8) outperforms the attention-based model by up to 0.4% BLEU and 2.8% TER. We observe that the length ratio of our system's output to the reference is 93.3-94.9%, while it is 99.1-102.6% for the attention-based system. In light of the BLEU and TER scores, the attention-based model does not benefit from matching the reference length. Our system (row #8) still lags behind the phrase-based system (row #1). Note, however, that in the WMT 2016 evaluation campaign,[2] it was demonstrated that NMT can outperform phrase-based systems on several tasks including German→English and English→German. Including monolingual data (Sennrich et al., 2016) in training neural translation models can boost performance, and this can be applied to our system.

7.3 Neural Alignments

Next, we experiment with re-aligning the training data using neural networks as described in Section 6. We use the fine-tuned FFJM and FFAM to realign the in-domain data of the IWSLT German→English task. These models are initially

---

[2] http://matrix.statmt.org/

#	system	test1 BLEU	test1 TER	test2 BLEU	test2 TER
1	phrase-based system	17.6	68.3	16.9	67.4
2	+ monolingual data	17.9	67.9	17.0	67.1
3	attention-based RNN	14.8	76.1	13.6	76.9
4	+fine-tuning	16.1	73.1	15.4	72.3
5	FFJM+dp+wp	10.1	77.2	9.8	75.8
6	FFJM+FFAM+wp	14.4	71.9	13.7	71.3
7	+fine-tuning	15.8	70.3	15.4	69.4
8	+BJM Rescoring	**16.0**	**70.3**	**15.8**	**69.5**
9	BJM+FFAM+wp+fine-tuning	**16.0**	70.4	15.7	69.7

Table 3: BOLT Chinese→English results in BLEU [%] and TER [%].

Alignment Source	test 2010 BLEU	test 2010 TER	eval 2011 BLEU	eval 2011 TER
GIZA++	25.6	53.6	29.3	49.7
Neural Forced decoding	25.9	52.4	29.5	49.4

Table 4: Re-alignment results in BLEU [%] and TER [%] on the IWSLT 2013 German→English in-domain data. Each system includes FFJM, FFAM and word penalty.

trained using GIZA++ alignments. We train new models using the re-aligned data and compare the translation quality before and after re-alignment. We use 0.7 and 0.3 as model weights for the FFJM and FFAM, respectively. These values are based on the model weights obtained using MERT. The results are shown in Table 4. Note that the baseline is worse than the one in Table 2 as the models are only trained on the in-domain data. We observe that re-aligning the data improves translation quality by up to 0.3% BLEU and 1.2% TER. The new alignments are generated using the neural decoder, and using them to train the neural networks results in training that is more consistent with decoding. As future work, we intend to re-align the full bilingual data and use it for neural training.

7.4 Class-Factored Output Layer

Figure 3 shows the trade-off between speed and performance when evaluating words belonging to the top classes only. Limiting the evaluation to words belonging to the top class incurs a performance loss of 0.4% BLEU only when compared to the full evaluation of the output layer. However, this corresponds to a large speed-up. The system is about 30 times faster, with a translation speed of 0.4 words/sec. In conclusion, not only does the class layer speed up training, but it can also be used to speed up decoding considerably. We use the top 3 classes throughout our experiments.

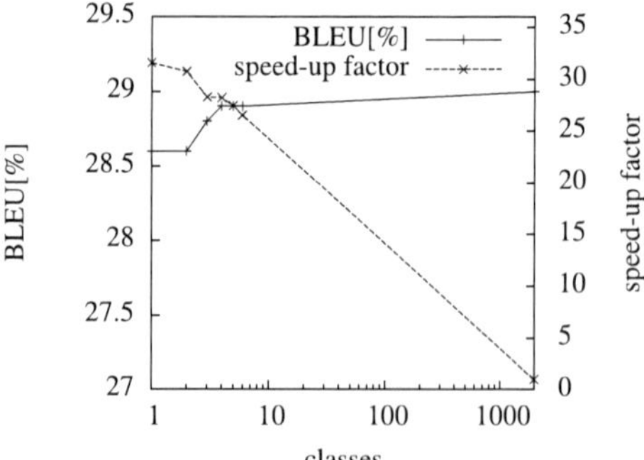

Figure 3: Decoding speed-up and translation quality using top scoring classes in a class-factored output layer. The results are computed for the IWSLT German→English dev dataset.

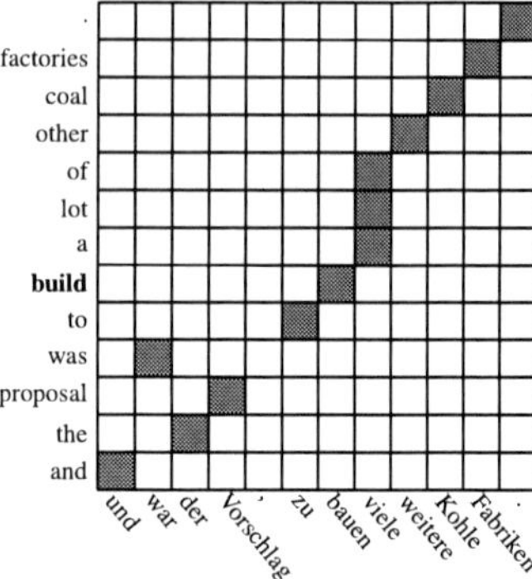

Figure 4: A translation example produced by our system. The shown German sentence is preordered.

8 Analysis

We show an example from the German→English task in Figure 4, along with the alignment path. The reference translation is 'and the proposal has been to build a lot more coal plants .'. Our system handles the local reordering of the word 'was', which is produced in the correct target order. An example on the one-to-many alignments is given by the correct translation of 'viele' to 'a lot of'.

As an example on handling multiply-aligned target words, we observe the translation of 'Nord Westen' to 'northwest' in our output. This is possible because the source window allows the FFNN to translate the word 'Westen' in context of the word 'Nord'.

Table 5 lists some translation examples produced by our system and the attention-based system, where maximum attention weights are used

1	source	sie würden verhungern nicht , und wissen Sie was ?
	reference	they wouldn 't *starve* , and you know what ?
	attention NMT	you wouldn 't interview , and guess what ?
	our system	they wouldn 't *starve* , and you know what ?
2	source	denn sie sind diejenigen , die sind auch Experten für Geschmack .
	reference	because they 're the ones that are *experts in flavor* , too .
	attention NMT	because they 're the ones who are also experts .
	our system	because they 're the ones who are also *experts in flavor* .
3	source	es ist ein Online Spiel , in dem Sie müssen überwinden eine Ölknappheit .
	reference	this is an online game in which you try to survive an *oil shortage* .
	attention NMT	it 's an online game where you need to get through a UNKOWN .
	our system	it 's an online game in which you have to overcome an astrolabe .
4	source	es liegt daran , dass gehen nicht Möglichkeiten auf diesem Planeten zurück, sie gehen vorwärts .
	reference	it 's because *possibilities* on this planet , they *don 't go back* , they go forward .
	attention NMT	it 's because there 's no way back on this planet , they 're going to move forward .
	our system	it 's because *opportunities don 't go* on this planet , they go forward .

Table 5: Sample translations from the IWSLT German→English `test` set using the attention-based system (Table 2, row #4) and our system (Table 2, row #7). We highlight the (pre-ordered) source words and their aligned target words. We underline the source words of interest, italicize *correct* translations, and use bold-face for incorrect translations.

as alignment. While we use larger vocabularies compared to the attention-based system, we observe incorrect translations of rare words. E.g., the German word Ölknappheit in sentence 3 occurs only 7 times in the training data among 108M words, and therefore it is an unknown word for the attention system. Our system has the word in the source vocabulary but fails to predict the right translation. Another problem occurs in sentence 4, where the German verb "zurückgehen" is split into "gehen ... zurück". Since the feed-forward model uses a source window of size 9, it cannot include both words when it is centered at any of them. Such insufficient context might be resolved when integrating the bidirectional RNN in decoding. Note that the attention-based model also fails to produce the correct translation here.

9   Conclusion

This work takes a step towards bridging the gap between conventional word alignment concepts and NMT. We use an HMM-inspired factorization of the lexical and alignment models, and employ the Viterbi alignments obtained using conventional HMM/IBM models to train neural models. An alignment-based decoder is introduced and a log-linear framework is used to combine the models. We use MERT to tune the model weights. Our system outperforms the attention-based system on the German→English task by up to 0.9% BLEU, and on Chinese→English by up to 2.8%

TER. We also demonstrate that re-aligning the training data using the neural decoder yields better translation quality.

As future work, we aim to integrate alignment-based RNNs such as the BJM into the alignment-based decoder. We also plan to develop a bidirectional RNN alignment model to make jump decisions based on unbounded context. In addition, we want to investigate the use of coverage constraints in alignment-based NMT. Furthermore, we consider the re-alignment experiment promising and plan to apply re-alignment on the full bilingual data of each task.

Acknowledgments

This paper has received funding from the European Union's Horizon 2020 research and innovation programme under grant agreement n° 645452 (QT21). Tamer Alkhouli was partly funded by the 2016 Google PhD Fellowship for North America, Europe and the Middle East.

References

Tamer Alkhouli, Andreas Guta, and Hermann Ney. 2014. Vector space models for phrase-based machine translation. In *EMNLP 2014 Eighth Workshop on Syntax, Semantics and Structure in Statistical Translation*, pages 1–10, Doha, Qatar, October.

Tamer Alkhouli, Felix Rietig, and Hermann Ney. 2015. Investigations on phrase-based decoding with recurrent neural network language and translation models. In *Proceedings of the EMNLP 2015 Tenth Workshop on Statistical Machine Translation*, pages 294–303, Lisbon, Portugal, September.

Dzmitry Bahdanau, Kyunghyun Cho, and Yoshua Bengio. 2015. Neural machine translation by jointly learning to align and translate. In *International Conference on Learning Representations*, San Diego, Calefornia, USA, May.

Frédéric Bastien, Pascal Lamblin, Razvan Pascanu, James Bergstra, Ian J. Goodfellow, Arnaud Bergeron, Nicolas Bouchard, and Yoshua Bengio. 2012. Theano: new features and speed improvements. December.

James Bergstra, Olivier Breuleux, Frédéric Bastien, Pascal Lamblin, Razvan Pascanu, Guillaume Desjardins, Joseph Turian, David Warde-Farley, and Yoshua Bengio. 2010. Theano: a CPU and GPU math expression compiler. In *Proceedings of the Python for Scientific Computing Conference*, Austin, TX, USA, June.

Stanley F. Chen and Joshua Goodman. 1998. An Empirical Study of Smoothing Techniques for Language Modeling. Technical Report TR-10-98, Computer Science Group, Harvard University, Cambridge, MA, August.

Kyunghyun Cho, Bart van Merrienboer, Caglar Gulcehre, Dzmitry Bahdanau, Fethi Bougares, Holger Schwenk, and Yoshua Bengio. 2014. Learning phrase representations using RNN encoder–decoder for statistical machine translation. In *Proceedings of the 2014 Conference on Empirical Methods in Natural Language Processing*, pages 1724–1734, Doha, Qatar, October.

Jonathan H. Clark, Chris Dyer, Alon Lavie, and Noah A. Smith. 2011. Better hypothesis testing for statistical machine translation: Controlling for optimizer instability. In *49th Annual Meeting of the Association for Computational Linguistics*, pages 176–181, Portland, Oregon, June.

Trevor Cohn, Cong Duy Vu Hoang, Ekaterina Vymolova, Kaisheng Yao, Chris Dyer, and Gholamreza Haffari. 2016. Incorporating structural alignment biases into an attentional neural translation model. In *Proceedings of the 2016 Conference of the North American Chapter of the Association for Computational Linguistics: Human Language Technologies*, pages 876–885, San Diego, California, June.

Jacob Devlin, Rabih Zbib, Zhongqiang Huang, Thomas Lamar, Richard Schwartz, and John Makhoul. 2014. Fast and Robust Neural Network Joint Models for Statistical Machine Translation. In *52nd Annual Meeting of the Association for Computational Linguistics*, pages 1370–1380, Baltimore, MD, USA, June.

Michel Galley and Christopher D. Manning. 2008. A simple and effective hierarchical phrase reordering model. In *Proceedings of the Conference on Empirical Methods in Natural Language Processing*, pages 848–856, Honolulu, Hawaii, USA, October.

Joshua Goodman. 2001. Classes for fast maximum entropy training. In *Proceedings of the IEEE International Conference on Acoustics, Speech, and Signal Processing*, volume 1, pages 561–564, Utah, USA, May.

Andreas Guta, Tamer Alkhouli, Jan-Thorsten Peter, Joern Wuebker, and Hermann Ney. 2015. A Comparison between Count and Neural Network Models Based on Joint Translation and Reordering Sequences. In *Conference on Empirical Methods on Natural Language Processing*, pages 1401–1411, Lisbon, Portugal, September.

Yuening Hu, Michael Auli, Qin Gao, and Jianfeng Gao. 2014. Minimum translation modeling with recurrent neural networks. In *Proceedings of the 14th Conference of the European Chapter of the Association for Computational Linguistics*, pages 20–29, Gothenburg, Sweden, April.

Sébastien Jean, Kyunghyun Cho, Roland Memisevic, and Yoshua Bengio. 2015. On using very large target vocabulary for neural machine translation. In *Proceedings of the Annual Meeting of the Association for Computational Linguistics*, pages 1–10, Beijing, China, July.

Reinhard Kneser and Hermann Ney. 1995. Improved backing-off for M-gram language modeling. In *Proceedings of the International Conference on Acoustics, Speech, and Signal Processing*, volume 1, pages 181–184, May.

Philipp Koehn, Franz J. Och, and Daniel Marcu. 2003. Statistical Phrase-Based Translation. In *Proceedings of the 2003 Meeting of the North American chapter of the Association for Computational Linguistics*, pages 127–133, Edmonton, Canada, May/June.

Hai Son Le, Alexandre Allauzen, and François Yvon. 2012. Continuous Space Translation Models with Neural Networks. In *Conference of the North American Chapter of the Association for Computational Linguistics: Human Language Technologies*, pages 39–48, Montreal, Canada, June.

Minh-Thang Luong and Christopher D. Manning. 2015. Stanford neural machine translation systems for spoken language domains. In *Proceedings of the International Workshop on Spoken Language Translation*, pages 76–79, Da Nag, Vietnam, December.

Minh-Thang Luong, Hieu Pham, and Christopher D. Manning. 2015. Effective approaches to attention-based neural machine translation. In *Conference on Empirical Methods in Natural Language Processing*, pages 1412–1421, Lisbon, Portugal, September.

R.C. Moore and W. Lewis. 2010. Intelligent Selection of Language Model Training Data. In *Proceedings of the 48th Annual Meeting of the Association for Computational Linguistics*, pages 220–224, Uppsala, Sweden, July.

Frederic Morin and Yoshua Bengio. 2005. Hierarchical probabilistic neural network language model. In *Proceedings of the international workshop on artificial intelligence and statistics*, pages 246–252, Barbados, January.

Franz Josef Och. 2003. Minimum Error Rate Training in Statistical Machine Translation. In *Proceedings of the 41th Annual Meeting of the Association for Computational Linguistics*, pages 160–167, Sapporo, Japan, July.

Kishore Papineni, Salim Roukos, Todd Ward, and Wei-Jing Zhu. 2002. Bleu: a Method for Automatic Evaluation of Machine Translation. In *Proceedings of the 41st Annual Meeting of the Association for Computational Linguistics*, pages 311–318, Philadelphia, Pennsylvania, USA, July.

Stephan Peitz, Arne Mauser, Joern Wuebker, and Hermann Ney. 2012. Forced derivations for hierarchical machine translation. In *International Conference on Computational Linguistics*, pages 933–942, Mumbai, India, December.

Maja Popović and Hermann Ney. 2006. POS-based word reorderings for statistical machine translation. In *Language Resources and Evaluation*, pages 1278–1283, Genoa, Italy, May.

Holger Schwenk. 2012. Continuous Space Translation Models for Phrase-Based Statistical Machine Translation. In *25th International Conference on Computational Linguistics*, pages 1071–1080, Mumbai, India, December.

Rico Sennrich, Barry Haddow, and Alexandra Birch. 2016. Improving neural machine translation models with monolingual data. In *Proceedings of 54th Annual Meeting of the Association for Computational Linguistics*, August.

Matthew Snover, Bonnie Dorr, Richard Schwartz, Linnea Micciulla, and John Makhoul. 2006. A Study of Translation Edit Rate with Targeted Human Annotation. In *Proceedings of the 7th Conference of the Association for Machine Translation in the Americas*, pages 223–231, Cambridge, Massachusetts, USA, August.

Andreas Stolcke. 2002. SRILM – An Extensible Language Modeling Toolkit. In *Proceedings of the International Conference on Speech and Language Processing*, volume 2, pages 901–904, Denver, CO, September.

Martin Sundermeyer, Tamer Alkhouli, Joern Wuebker, and Hermann Ney. 2014a. Translation Modeling with Bidirectional Recurrent Neural Networks. In *Conference on Empirical Methods on Natural Language Processing*, pages 14–25, Doha, Qatar, October.

Martin Sundermeyer, Ralf Schlüter, and Hermann Ney. 2014b. rwthlm - the RWTH Aachen university neural network language modeling toolkit. In *Interspeech*, pages 2093–2097, Singapore, September.

Ilya Sutskever, Oriol Vinyals, and Quoc V. V Le. 2014. Sequence to sequence learning with neural networks. In *Advances in Neural Information Processing Systems 27*, pages 3104–3112, Montréal, Canada, December.

Akihiro Tamura, Taro Watanabe, and Eiichiro Sumita. 2014. Recurrent neural networks for word alignment model. In *52nd Annual Meeting of the Association for Computational Linguistics*, pages 1470–1480, Baltimore, MD, USA.

Bart van Merriënboer, Dzmitry Bahdanau, Vincent Dumoulin, Dmitriy Serdyuk, David Warde-Farley, Jan Chorowski, and Yoshua Bengio. 2015. Blocks and fuel: Frameworks for deep learning. *CoRR*, abs/1506.00619.

Ashish Vaswani, Yinggong Zhao, Victoria Fossum, and David Chiang. 2013. Decoding with large-scale neural language models improves translation. In *Proceedings of the 2013 Conference on Empirical Methods in Natural Language Processing*, pages 1387–1392, Seattle, Washington, USA, October.

David Vilar, Daniel Stein, Matthias Huck, and Hermann Ney. 2010. Jane: Open source hierarchical translation, extended with reordering and lexicon models. In *ACL 2010 Joint Fifth Workshop on Statistical Machine Translation and Metrics MATR*, pages 262–270, Uppsala, Sweden, July.

Joern Wuebker, Arne Mauser, and Hermann Ney. 2010. Training phrase translation models with leaving-one-out. In *Proceedings of the Annual Meeting of the Association for Computational Linguistics*, pages 475–484, Uppsala, Sweden, July.

Joern Wuebker, Matthias Huck, Stephan Peitz, Malte Nuhn, Markus Freitag, Jan-Thorsten Peter, Saab Mansour, and Hermann Ney. 2012. Jane 2: Open source phrase-based and hierarchical statistical machine translation. In *International Conference on Computational Linguistics*, pages 483–491, Mumbai, India, December.

Nan Yang, Shujie Liu, Mu Li, Ming Zhou, and Nenghai Yu. 2013. Word alignment modeling with context dependent deep neural network. In *51st Annual Meeting of the Association for Computational Linguistics*, pages 166–175, Sofia, Bulgaria, August.

Neural Network-based Word Alignment through Score Aggregation

Joël Legrand[1,2,†] and **Michael Auli**[3] and **Ronan Collobert**[3]

[1] Idiap Research Institute, Martigny, Switzerland

[2] Ecole Polytechnique Fédérale de Lausanne (EPFL), Lausanne, Switzerland

[3] Facebook AI Research, Menlo Park

Abstract

We present a simple neural network for word alignment that builds source and target word window representations to compute alignment scores for sentence pairs. To enable unsupervised training, we use an aggregation operation that summarizes the alignment scores for a given target word. A soft-margin objective increases scores for true target words while decreasing scores for target words that are not present. Compared to the popular Fast Align model, our approach improves alignment accuracy by 7 AER on English-Czech, by 6 AER on Romanian-English and by 1.7 AER on English-French alignment.

1 Introduction

Word alignment is the task of finding the correspondence between source and target words in a pair of sentences that are translations of each other. Generative models for this task (Brown et al., 1990; Och and Ney, 2003; Vogel et al., 1996) still form the basis for many machine translation systems (Koehn et al., 2003; Chiang, 2007).

Recent neural approaches include Yang et al. (2013) who introduce a feed-forward network-based model trained on alignments that were generated by a traditional generative model. This treats potentially erroneous alignments as supervision. Tamura et al. (2014) sidesteps this issue by negative sampling to train a recurrent-neural network on unlabeled data. They optimize a global loss that requires an expensive beam search to approximate the sum over all alignments.

In this paper we introduce a word alignment model that is simpler in structure and which relies on a more tractable training procedure. Our model is a neural network that extracts context information from source and target sentences and then computes simple dot products to estimate alignment links. Our objective function is word-factored and does not require the expensive computation associated with global loss functions. The model can be easily trained on unlabeled data via a novel but simple *aggregation operation* which has been successfully applied in the computer vision literature (Pinheiro and Collobert, 2015). The aggregation combines the scores of all source words for a particular target word and promotes source words which are likely to be aligned with a given target word according to the knowledge the model has learned so far. At test time, the aggregation operation is removed and source words are aligned to target words by choosing the highest scoring candidates (§2, §3).

We evaluate several forms for our aggregation operation such as computing the sum, max and LogSumExp over alignment scores. Results on English-French, English-Romanian, and Czech-English alignment show that our model significantly outperforms Fast Align, a popular log-linear reparameterization of IBM Model 2 (Dyer et al., 2013; §4).

2 Aggregation Model

In the following, we consider a target-source sentence pair $(\mathbf{e}, \mathbf{f})$, with $\mathbf{e} = (e_1, \ldots, e_{|\mathbf{e}|})$ and $\mathbf{f} = (f_1, \ldots, f_{|\mathbf{f}|})$. Words are represented by f_j and e_i, which are indices in source and target dictionaries. For simplicity, we assume here that word indices are the only feature fed to our architecture. Given a source word f_j and a target word e_i, our architecture embeds a window (of size d^f_{win}

---

†This work was conducted while the first author did an internship at Facebook AI Research.

Proceedings of the First Conference on Machine Translation, Volume 1: Research Papers, pages 66–73,
Berlin, Germany, August 11-12, 2016. ©2016 Association for Computational Linguistics

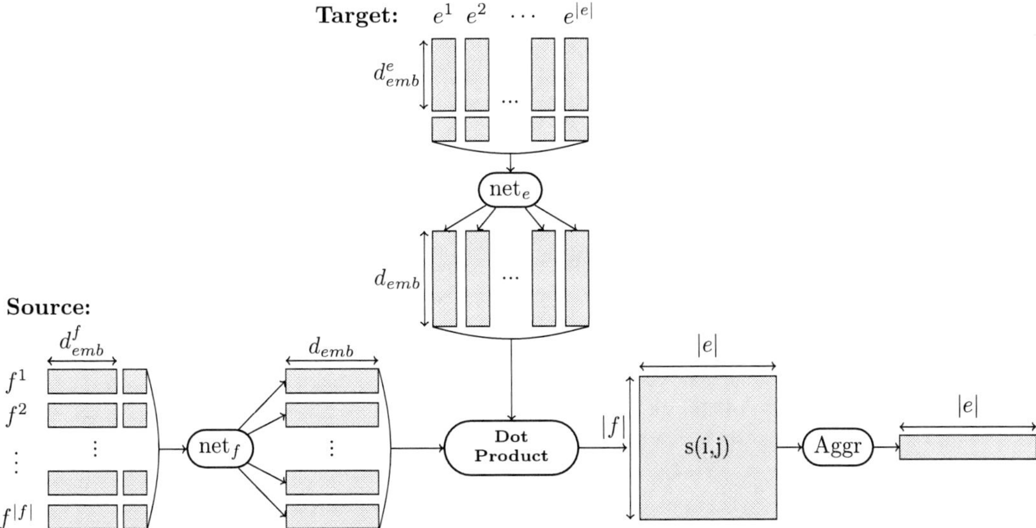

Figure 1: Illustration of the model. The two networks net_e and net_f compute representations for source and target words. The score of an alignment link is a simple dot product between those source and target word representations. The aggregation operation summarizes the alignment scores for each target word.

and d^e_{win}, respectively) centered around each of these words into a d_{emb}-dimensional vector space. The embedding operation is performed with two distinct neural networks:

$$\text{net}_e([\mathbf{e}]^{d^e_{win}}_i) \in \mathbb{R}^{d_{emb}}$$

and

$$\text{net}_f([\mathbf{f}]^{d^f_{win}}_j) \in \mathbb{R}^{d_{emb}},$$

where we denote the window operator as

$$[\mathbf{x}]^d_i = (x_{i-d/2}, \ldots, x_{i+d/2}).$$

The matching score between a source word f_j and a target word e_i is then given by the dot-product:

$$s(i, j) = \text{net}_e([\mathbf{e}]^{d^e_{win}}_i) \cdot \text{net}_f([\mathbf{f}]^{d^f_{win}}_j). \quad (1)$$

If e_i is aligned to f_{a_i}, the score $s(i, a_i)$ should be high, while scores $s(i, j)\ \forall j \neq a_i$ should be low.

2.1 Unsupervised Training

In this paper, we consider an unsupervised setup where the alignment is not known at training time. We thus cannot minimize or maximize matching scores (1) in a direct manner. Instead, given a target word e_i we consider the aggregated matching scores over the source sentence:

$$s_{aggr}(i, \mathbf{f}) = \underset{j=1}{\overset{|f|}{\text{Aggr}}}\, s(i, j), \quad (2)$$

where Aggr is an aggregation operator (§2.2). Consider a matching (positive) sentence pair $(\mathbf{e}^+, \mathbf{f})$ and a negative sentence pair $(\mathbf{e}^-, \mathbf{f})$. Given a word at index i^+ in the positive target sentence, we want to maximize the aggregated score $s_{aggr}(i^+, \mathbf{f})$ $(1 \leq i^+ \leq |\mathbf{e}^+|)$ because we know it should be aligned to at least one source word.[1] Conversely, given a word at index i^- in the negative target sentence, we want to minimize $s_{aggr}(i^-, \mathbf{f})$ $(1 \leq i^- \leq |\mathbf{e}^-|)$ because it is unlikely that the source sentence can explain the negative target word. Following these principles, we consider a simple soft-margin loss:

$$\mathcal{L}(\mathbf{e}^+, \mathbf{e}^-, \mathbf{f}) = \sum_{i^+=1}^{|\mathbf{e}^+|} \log(1 + e^{-s_{aggr}(i^+, \mathbf{f})})$$
$$+ \sum_{i^-=1}^{|\mathbf{e}^-|} \log(1 + e^{+s_{aggr}(i^-, \mathbf{f})}). \quad (3)$$

Training is achieved by minimizing (3) and by sampling over triplets $(\mathbf{e}^+, \mathbf{e}^-, \mathbf{f})$ from the training data.

---

[1]We discuss how we handle unaligned target words in §2.3. Also, depending on the decoding algorithm the model can be used to predict many-to-many alignments.

2.2 Choosing the Aggregation

The aggregation operation (2) is only present during training and acts as a filter which aims to explain a given target word e_i by one or more source words. If we had the word alignments, then we would sum over the source words f_j aligned with e_i. However, in our setup alignments are not available at training time, so we must rely on what the model has learned so far to filter the source words. We consider the following strategies:

- **Sum:** ignore the knowledge learned so far, and assign the same weight to all source words f_j to explain e_i.[2] In this case, we have

$$s_{aggr}(i, \mathbf{f}) = \sum_{j=1}^{|\mathbf{f}|} s(i, j).$$

- **Max:** encourage the best aligned source word f_j, according to what the model has learned so far. In this case, the aggregation is written as:

$$s_{aggr}(i, \mathbf{f}) = \max_{j=1}^{|\mathbf{f}|} s(i, j).$$

- **LSE:** give similar weights to source words with similar scores. This can be achieved with a LogSumExp aggregation operation (also called LogAdd), and is defined as:

$$s_{aggr}(i, \mathbf{f}) = \frac{1}{r} \log \left(\sum_{j=1}^{|\mathbf{f}|} e^{r\, s(i, j)} \right), \quad (4)$$

where r is a positive scalar (to be chosen) controlling the smoothness of the aggregation. For small r, the aggregation is equivalent to a sum, and for large r, the aggregation acts as a max.

2.3 Decoding

At test time, we align each target word e_i with the source word f_j for which the matching score $s(i, j)$ in (1) is highest.[3] However, not every target word is aligned, so we consider only alignments with a matching score above a threshold:

$$s(i, j) > \mu^-(e_i) + \alpha\, \sigma^-(e_i), \quad (5)$$

---

[2] This can be seen by observing that the gradients for all source words are the same.

[3] This may result in a source word being aligned to multiple target words.

where α is a tunable hyper-parameter, and

$$\mu^-(e_i) = \mathop{\mathbb{E}}_{\{\tilde{e}_k = e_i \in \tilde{\mathbf{e}},\, \tilde{f}_{j^-} \in \tilde{\mathbf{f}}^-\}} \left[s(k, j^-) \right]$$

is the expectation over all training sentences $\tilde{\mathbf{e}}$ containing the word e_i, and all words $\tilde{f}_j^-$ belonging to a corresponding negative source sentence $\tilde{\mathbf{f}}^-$, and $\sigma^-(e_i)$ is the respective variance.

3 Neural Network Architecture

Our model consists of two convolutional neural networks net_e and net_f as shown in (1). Both of them take the same form, so we detail only the target architecture.

3.1 Word embeddings

The discrete features $[\mathbf{e}]_i^{d_{win}^e}$ are embedded into a d_{emb}^e-dimensional vector space via a lookup-table operation as first introduced in Bengio et al. (2000):

$$
\begin{aligned}
x_i^e &= \mathrm{LT}_{W^e}([\mathbf{e}]_i^{d_{win}^e}) \\
&= \left(\mathrm{LT}_{W^e}(e_{i-d_{win}^e/2}), \ldots, \mathrm{LT}_{W^e}(e_{i+d_{win}^e/2}) \right),
\end{aligned}
$$

where the lookup-table operation applied at index k returns the kth column of the parameter matrix W^e:

$$\mathrm{LT}_{W^e}(k) = W^e_{\bullet,\, k}.$$

The matrix W^e is of size $|\mathcal{V}^e| \times d_{emb}^e$, where $\mathcal{V}^e$ is the target vocabulary, and d_{emb}^e is the word embedding size for the target words.

3.2 Convolutional layers

The word embeddings output by the lookup-table are concatenated and fed through two successive 1-D convolution layers. The convolutions use a step size of one and extract context features for each word. The kernel sizes k_1^e and k_2^e determine the size of the window $d_{win}^e = k_1^e + k_2^e - 1$ over which features will be extracted by net_e. In order to obtain windows centered around each word, we add $(k_1^e + k_2^e)/2 - 1$ padding words at the beginning and at the end of each sentence.

The first layer cnn^e applies the linear transformation $M^{e,1}$ exactly k_2^e times to consecutive spans of size k_1^e to the d_{win}^e words in a given window:

$$
cnn^e(x_i^e) = M^{e,1}
\begin{pmatrix}
\mathrm{LT}_{W^e}([\mathbf{e}]_{i-a}^{k_1^e}) \\
\vdots \\
\mathrm{LT}_{W^e}([\mathbf{e}]_{i+a}^{k_1^e})
\end{pmatrix},
$$

where $a = \lfloor \frac{k_1^e}{2} \rfloor$, $M^{e,1} \in \mathbb{R}^{d_{hu}^e \times (d_{emb}^e \, k_1^e)}$ is a matrix of parameters, and d_{hu}^e is the number of hidden units (hu). The outputs of the first layer cnn^e are concatenated to form a matrix of size $k_2^e \, d_{hu}^e$ which is fed to the second layer:

$$\mathrm{net}_e(x_i^e) = M^{e,2} \tanh(cnn^e(x_i^e)) \qquad (6)$$

where $M^{e,2} \in \mathbb{R}^{d_{emb} \times (k_2^e \, d_{hu}^e)}$ is a matrix of parameters, and the $tanh(\cdot)$ operation is applied element wise. The parameters W^e, $M^{e,1}$ and $M^{e,2}$ are trained by stochastic gradient descent to minimize the loss (3) introduced in §2.1.

3.3 Additional Features

In addition to the raw word indices, we consider two additional discrete features which were handled in the same way as word features by introducing an additional lookup-table for each of them. The output of all lookup-tables was concatenated, and fed to the two-layer neural network architecture (6).

Distance to the diagonal. This feature can be computed for a target word e_i and a source word f_j:

$$diag(i,j) = \left| \frac{i}{|\mathbf{e}|} - \frac{j}{|\mathbf{f}|} \right| ,$$

This feature allows the model to learn that aligned sentence pairs use roughly the same word order and that alignment links remain close to the diagonal. We use this feature only for the source network because it encodes relative position information which only needs to be encoded once. If we would use absolute position instead, then we would need to encode this information both on the source and the target side.

Part-of-speech Words pairs that are good translations of each other are likely to carry the same part of speech in both languages (Melamed, 1995). We therefore add the part-of-speech information to the model.

Char n-gram. We consider unigram character position features. Let K be the maximum size for a word in a dictionary. We denote the dictionary of characters as $\mathcal{C}$. Every character is represented by its index c (with $1 < c < |\mathcal{C}|$). We associate every character c at position k with a vector at position $((k-1) * |\mathcal{C}|) + c$ in a lookup-table. For a given word, we extract all unigram character position embeddings, and average them to obtain a character embedding for a given word.

4 Experiments

4.1 Datasets

We use the English-French Hansards corpus as distributed by the NAACL 2003 shared task (Mihalcea and Pedersen, 2003). This dataset contains 1.1M sentence pairs and the test and validation sets contain 447 and 37 examples respectively. We also evaluate on the Romanian-English dataset of the ACL 2005 shared task (Martin et al., 2005) comprising 48K sentence pairs for training, 248 for testing and 17 for validation. For English-Czech experiments, we use the WMT news commentary corpus for training (150K sentence pairs) and a set of 515 sentences for testing (Bojar and Prokopová, 2006).

4.2 Evaluation

Our models are evaluated in terms of precision, recall, F-measure and Alignment Error Rate (AER). We train models in each language direction and then symmetrize the resulting alignments using either the *intersection* or the *grow-diag-final-and* heuristic (Och and Ney, 2003; Koehn et al., 2003). We validated the choice of symmetrization heuristic on each language pair and chose the best one for each model considering the two aforementioned types as well as *grow-diag-final* and *grow-diag*.

Additionally, we train phrase-based machine translation models with our alignments using the popular Moses toolkit (Koehn et al., 2007). For English-French, we train on the news commentary corpus v10, for English-Czech we used news commentary corpus v11, and for Romanian-English we used the Europarl corpus v8. We tuned our models on the WMT2015 test set for English-Czech as well as for Romanian-English; for English-French we tuned on the WMT2014 test set. Final results are reported on the WMT2016 test set for English-Czech as well as Romanian-English, and for English-French we report results on the WMT2015 test set (as there is no track for this language-pair in 2016).

We compare our model to Fast Align, a popular log-linear reparameterization of IBM Model 2 (Dyer et al., 2013).

4.3 Setup

The kernel sizes of the target network $\mathrm{net}_e(\cdot)$ are set to $k_1^e = k_2^e = 3$ for all language pairs. The kernel sizes of the source network $\mathrm{net}_f(\cdot)$ are set to $k_1^f = k_2^f = 3$ for Romanian-English as well as English-Czech; and for English-French we used $k_1^f = k_2^f = 1$.

The number of hidden units are $d_{hu}^e = d_{hu}^f = 256$ and d_{emb} is set to 256, The source $\mathcal{V}_f$ and target $\mathcal{V}_e$ dictionaries consist of the 30K most common words for English, French and Romanian, and 80K for Czech. All other words are mapped to a unique *UNK* token. The word embedding sizes d_{emb}^e and d_{emb}^f, as well as the char-n-gram embedding size is 128. For LSE, we set $r = 1$ in (4).

We initialize the word embeddings with a simple PCA computed over the matrix of word co-occurrence counts (Lebret and Collobert, 2014). The co-occurrence counts were computed over the common crawl corpus provided by WMT16. For part of speech tagging we used the Stanford parser on English-French data, and MarMoT (Mueller et al., 2013) for Romanian-English as well as English-Czech.

We trained 4 systems for the ensembles, each using a different random seed to vary the weight initialization as well as the shuffling of the training set. We averaged the alignment scores predicted by each system before decoding. The alignment threshold variables $\mu^-(e_i)$ and $\sigma^-(e_i)$ for decoding (§2.3) were estimated on 1000 random training sentences, using 100 negative sentences for each of them. Words not appearing in this training subset were assigned $\mu^-(e_i) = \sigma^-(e_i) = 0$.

For systems where $d_{win}^e > 1$ and $d_{win}^f > 1$, we saw a tendency of aligning frequent words regardless on if they appeared in the center of the context window or not. For instance, a common mistake would be to align "the *cat* sat", with "PADDING *le* chat". To prevent such behavior, we occasionally replaced the center word in a target window by a random word during training. We do this for every second training example on average and we tuned this rate on the validation set.

4.4 Results

We first explore different choices for the aggregation operator (§2.2), followed by an ablation to investigate the impact of the different additional features (§3.3). Next we compare to the Fast Align baseline. Finally, we evaluate our alignments within a full translation system for all language pairs.

4.4.1 Aggregation operation

Table 1 shows that the LogSumExp (LSE) aggregator performs best on all datasets for every direction as well as in the symmetrized setting using the grow-diag-final heuristic. All results are based on a single model trained with the 'distance to the diagonal' feature detailed above.[4] We therefore use LSE for the remaining experiments.

	Max	Sum	LSE
En-Fr	18.1	23.0	**15.1**
Fr-En	20.7	26.9	**15.8**
symmetrized	14.8	24.1	**12.8**
Ro-En	42.2	42.0	**37.6**
En-Ro	40.4	40.2	**35.7**
symmetrized	36.4	35.6	**32.2**
En-Cz	27.9	35.6	**24.5**
Cz-En	26.5	33.6	**24.5**
symmetrized	21.8	32.7	**21.0**

Table 1: Alignment error rates for different aggregation operations in each language direction and with *grow-diag-final-and* symmetrization.

4.4.2 Additional features

Table 2 shows the effect of the different input features. Both POS and the distance to the diagonal feature significantly improve accuracy. Position information via the 'distance to the diagonal' feature is helpful for all language pairs, and POS information is more effective for Romanian-English and English-Czech which involve morphologically rich languages. We use the POS and 'distance to the diagonal feature' for the remaining experiments.

4.4.3 Comparison with the baseline

In the following results we label our model as NNSA (Neural network score aggregation). On English-French data (Table 3) our model outperforms the baseline (Dyer et al., 2013) in each individual language direction as well as for the symmetrized setting. With an ensemble of four models, we outperform the baseline by 1.7 AER (from 11.4 to 9.7), and with an individual model we outperform it by 1.2 AER (from 11.4 to 10.2). Note that the choice of symmetrization heuristic greatly

	English-French			Romanian-English			English-Czech		
	En-Fr	Fr-En	sym	Ro-En	En-Ro	sym	En-Cz	Cz-En	sym
words	22.2	24.2	15.7	47.0	45.5	40.3	36.9	36.3	29.5
+ POS	20.9	23.9	15.3	45.3	42.9	36.9	35.6	33.7	28.2
+ diag	15.1	15.8	12.8	37.6	35.7	32.2	24.8	24.5	21.0
+ POS + diag	**13.2**	**12.1**	**10.2**	**33.1**	**32.2**	**27.8**	**24.6**	**22.9**	**19.9**

Table 2: Alignment error rates using different input features in each language direction and with *grow-diag-final-and* symmetrization.

	P	R	F1	AER
English-French				
Baseline	49.6	89.8	63.9	16.7
NNSA	64.7	80.7	71.8	13.2
+ ensemble	61.5	85.8	71.6	**11.6**
French-English				
Baseline	52.9	88.4	66.2	16.2
NNSA	61.7	86.3	72.0	12.1
+ ensemble	62.6	86.7	72.7	**11.6**
symmetrized				
Baseline (inter)	69.6	84.0	76.1	11.4
NNSA (gdfa)	60.4	88.5	71.8	10.2
+ ensemble	59.3	89.9	71.4	**9.7**

Table 3: English-French results on the test set in terms of precision (P), recall (R), F-score (F1) and AER; ensemble denotes a combination of four systems and we use the *intersection* (inter) and *grow-diag-final-and* symmetrization (gdfa) heuristics.

	P	R	F1	AER
Romanian-English				
Baseline	70.0	61.0	65.2	34.8
NNSA	75.1	65.2	69.8	30.2
+ ensemble	75.8	62.8	68.7	**31.3**
English-Romanian				
Baseline	71.3	60.8	65.6	34.4
NNSA	78.1	61.7	69.0	31.1
+ ensemble	78.4	63.2	70.0	**30.0**
symmetrized				
Baseline (gdfa)	69.5	66.5	68.0	32.0
NNSA (gdfa)	74.1	71.8	73.0	27.0
+ ensemble	73.0	74.5	73.7	**26.0**

Table 4: Romanian-English results (cf. Table 3).

affects accuracy, both for the baseline and NNSA.

On Romanian-English (Table 4) our model outperforms the baseline in both directions as well. Adding ensembles further improves accuracy and leads to a significant improvement of 6 AER over the best symmetrized baseline result (from 32 to 26).

On English-Czech (Table 5) our model outperforms the baseline in both directions as well. We added the character feature to better deal with the morphologically rich nature of Czech and the feature reduced AER by 2.1 in the symmetrized setting. An ensemble improved accuracy further and led to a 7 AER improvement over the best symmetrized baseline result (from 22.8 to 15.8).

4.4.4 BLEU evaluation

Table 6 presents the BLEU evaluation of our alignments. For each language-pair, we select the best alignment model reported in Tables 3, 4 and 5, and align the training data. We use the alignments to run the standard phrase-based training pipeline using those alignments. Our BLEU results show the average BLEU score and standard deviation for five runs of minimum error rate training (MERT; Och 2003).

Our alignments achieve slightly better results for Romanian-English as well as English-Czech while performing on par with Fast Align on English-French translation.

5   Analysis

In this section, we analyze the word representations learned by our model. We first focus on the source representations: given a source window, we obtain its distributional representation and then compute the Euclidean distance to all other source windows in the training corpus. Table 7 shows the nearest windows for two source windows; the closest windows tend to have similar meanings.

---

[4]We use kernel sizes $k_1^e = k_2^e = 3$ and $k_1^f = k_2^f = 1$ for all language pairs in this experiment.

	P	R	F1	AER
English-Czech				
Baseline	68.4	73.3	70.7	26.6
NNSA	72.0	74.3	73.1	24.6
+ char n-gram	73.8	75.4	74.6	23.2
+ ensemble	78.8	77.2	78.0	**20.0**
Czech-English				
Baseline	68.6	74.0	71.2	25.7
NNSA	74.1	74.0	74.0	22.9
+ char n-gram	78.1	74.1	76.1	21.4
+ ensemble	79.1	77.7	78.4	**18.7**
symmetrized				
Baseline (inter)	88.1	66.6	76.0	22.8
NNSA (gdfa)	75.7	80.3	76.3	19.9
+ char n-gram	76.9	81.3	79.1	17.8
+ ensemble	78.9	83.2	81.0	**15.8**

Table 5: Czech-English results (cf. Table 3).

	Baseline	NNSA
French-English	25.4 ± 0.1	$\mathbf{25.5 \pm 0.1}$
Romanian-English	21.3 ± 0.1	$\mathbf{21.6 \pm 0.1}$
Czech-English	17.2 ± 0.1	$\mathbf{17.6 \pm 0.1}$

Table 6: Average BLEU score and standard deviation for five runs of MERT.

We then analyze the relation between source and target representations: given a source window we compute the alignment scores for all target sentences in the training corpus. Table 8 shows for two source windows which target words have the largest alignment scores. The example "in working together" is particularly interesting since the aligned target words *collabore, coordonés,* and *concertés* mean *collaborate, coordinated,* and *concerted,* which all carry the same meaning as the source window phrase.

6 Conclusion

In this paper, we present a simple neural network alignment model trained on unlabeled data. Our model computes alignment scores as dot products between representations of windows around source and target words. We apply an *aggregation operation* borrowed from the computer vision literature to make unsupervised training possible. The aggregation operation acts as a filter over alignment scores and allows us to determine which source words explain a given target word.

the voting process	in working together
the voting area	for working together
the voting power	with working together
the voting rules	from working together
the voting system	about working together
the voting patterns	by working together
the voting ballots	and working together
their voting patterns	while working together

Table 7: Analysis of source window representations. Each column shows a window over the source sentence followed by several close neighbors in terms of Euclidean distance (among the 30 nearest).

the voting process	in working together
vote	travaillé
voteraient	travailleront
votent	collaboration
voter	travaillant
votant	oeuvrant
scrutin	concerts
suffrage	coordonés
procédure	concert
investiture	collabore
élections	coopération

Table 8: Analysis of source and target representations. Each column shows a source window and the target words which are most aligned according to our model.

We improve over Fast Align, a popular log-linear reparameterization of IBM Model 2 (Dyer et al., 2013) by up to 6 AER on Romanian-English, 7 AER on English-Czech data and 1.7 AER on English-French alignment. Furthermore, we evaluated our model as part of a full machine translation pipeline and showed that our alignments are better or on par compared to Fast Align in terms of BLEU.

References

Yoshua Bengio, Réjean Ducharme, and Pascal Vincent. A Neural Probabilistic Language Model. In *NIPS*, 2000.

Ondřej Bojar and Magdalena Prokopová. Czech-English Word Alignment. In *Proceedings of the Fifth International Conference on Language Resources and Evaluation (LREC 2006)*, 2006.

Peter F. Brown, John Cocke, Stephen Della

Pietra, Vincent J. Della Pietra, Frederick Jelinek, John D. Lafferty, Robert L. Mercer, and Paul S. Roossin. A Statistical Approach to Machine Translation. *Computational Linguistics*, 1990.

David Chiang. Hierarchical Phrase-Based Translation. *Computational Linguistics*, 2007.

Chris Dyer, Victor Chahuneau, and Noah A. Smith. A simple, fast, and effective reparameterization of IBM Model 2. In *Proc. of NAACL*, 2013.

Philipp Koehn, Franz J. Och, and Daniel Marcu. Statistical Phrase-based Translation. In *Proc. of NAACL*, 2003.

Philipp Koehn, Hieu Hoang, Alexandra Birch, Chris Callison-Burch, Marcello Federico, Nicola Bertoldi, Brooke Cowan, Wade Shen, Christine Moran, Richard Zens, Chris Dyer, Ondřej Bojar, Alexandra Constantin, and Evan Herbst. Moses: Open source toolkit for statistical machine translation. In *Proceedings of the 45th Annual Meeting of the ACL on Interactive Poster and Demonstration Sessions*, ACL '07, 2007.

Rémi Lebret and Ronan Collobert. Word Embeddings through Hellinger PCA. In *Proc. of EACL*, 2014.

Joel Martin, Rada Mihalcea, and Ted Pedersen. Word Alignment For Languages With Scarce Resources. In *Proc. of WPT*, 2005.

Dan I. Melamed. Automatic evaluation and uniform filter cascades for inducing n-best translation lexicons. In *Third Workshop on Very Large Corpora*, 1995.

Rada Mihalcea and Ted Pedersen. An Evaluation Exercise for Word Alignment. In *Proc. of WPT*, 2003.

Thomas Mueller, Helmut Schmid, and Hinrich Schütze. Efficient higher-order CRFs for morphological tagging. In *Proceedings of the 2013 Conference on Empirical Methods in Natural Language Processing*, 2013.

Franz J. Och and Hermann Ney. A Systematic Comparison of Various Statistical Alignment Models. *Computational Linguistics*, 2003.

Franz Josef Och. Minimum error rate training in statistical machine translation. In *Proc of ACL*, 2003.

Pedro O. Pinheiro and Ronan Collobert. From Image-level to Pixel-level Labeling with Convolutional Networks. In *Proc. of CVPR*, 2015.

Akihiro Tamura, Taro Watanabe, and Eiichiro Sumita. Recurrent Neural Networks for Word Alignment Model. In *Proc. of ACL*, 2014.

Stephan Vogel, Hermann Ney, and Christoph Tillmann. HMM-Based Word Alignment in Statistical Translation. In *Proc. of COLING*, 1996.

Nan Yang, Shujie Liu, Mu Li, Ming Zhou, and Nenghai Yu. Word Alignment Modeling with Context Dependent Deep Neural Network. In *Proc. of ACL*, 2013.

Using Factored Word Representation
in Neural Network Language Models

Jan Niehues, Thanh-Le Ha, Eunah Cho and Alex Waibel
Institute for Anthropomatics
Karlsruhe Institute of Technology, Germany
`firstname.secondname@kit.edu`

Abstract

Neural network language and translation models have recently shown their great potentials in improving the performance of phrase-based machine translation. At the same time, word representations using different word factors have been translation quality and are part of many state-of-the-art machine translation systems. used in many state-of-the-art machine translation systems, in order to support better translation quality.

In this work, we combined these two ideas by investigating the combination of both techniques. By representing words in neural network language models using different factors, we were able to improve the models themselves as well as their impact on the overall machine translation performance. This is especially helpful for morphologically rich languages due to their large vocabulary size. Furthermore, it is easy to add additional knowledge, such as source side information, to the model.

Using this model we improved the translation quality of a state-of-the-art phrase-based machine translation system by 0.7 BLEU points. We performed experiments on three language pairs for the news translation task of the WMT 2016 evaluation.

1 Introduction

Recently, neural network models are deployed extensively for better translation quality of statistical machine translation (Le et al., 2011; Devlin et al., 2014). For the language model as well as for the translation model, neural network-based models showed improvements when used during decoding as well as when used in re-scoring.

In phrase-based machine translation (PBMT), word representation using different factors (Koehn and Hoang, 2007) are commonly used in state-of-the-art systems. Using Part-of-Speech (POS) information or automatic word clusters is especially important for morphologically rich languages which often have a large vocabulary size. Language models based on these factors are able to consider longer context and therefore improve the modelling of the overall structure. Furthermore, the POS information can be used to improve the modelling of word agreement, which is often a difficult task when handling morphologically rich languages.

Until now, word factors have been used relatively limited in neural network models. Automatic word classes have been used to structure the output layer (Le et al., 2011) and as input in feed forward neural network language models (Niehues and Waibel, 2012).

In this work, we propose a multi-factor recurrent neural network (RNN)-based language model that is able to facilitate all available information about the word in the input as well as in the output. We evaluated the technique using the surface form, POS-tag and automatic word clusters using different cluster sizes.

Using this model, it is also possible to integrate source side information into the model. By using the model as a bilingual model, the probability of the translation can be modelled and not only the one of target sentence. As for the target side, we use a factored representation for the words on the source side.

The remaining of the paper is structured as following: In the following section, we first review the related work. Afterwards, we will shortly describe the RNN-based language model used in our experiments. In Section 4, we will introduce the factored RNN-based language model. In the next

Proceedings of the First Conference on Machine Translation, Volume 1: Research Papers, pages 74–82,
Berlin, Germany, August 11-12, 2016. ©2016 Association for Computational Linguistics

section, we will describe the experiments on the WMT 2016 data. Finally, we will end the paper with a conclusion of the work.

2 Related Work

Additional information about words, encoded as word factors, e.g. the lemma of word, POS tags, etc., is employed in state-of-the-art phrase-based systems. (Koehn and Hoang, 2007) decomposes the translation of factored representations to smaller mapping steps, which are modelled by translation probabilities from input factor to output factor or by generating probabilities of additional output factors from existing output factors. Then those pre-computed probabilities are jointly combined in the decoding process as a standard translation feature scores. In addition, language models using these word factors have shown to be very helpful to improve the translation quality. In particular, the aligned-words, POS or word classes are used in the framework of modern language models (Mediani et al., 2011; Wuebker et al., 2013).

Recently, neural network language models have been considered to perform better than standard n-gram language models (Schwenk, 2007; Le et al., 2011). Especially the neural language models constructed in recurrent architectures have shown a great performance by allowing them to take a longer context into account (Mikolov et al., 2010; Sundermeyer et al., 2013).

In a different direction, there has been a great deal of research on bringing not only target words but also source words into the prediction process, instead of predicting the next target word based on the previous target words (Le et al., 2012; Devlin et al., 2014; Ha et al., 2014).

However, to the best of our knowledge, word factors have been exploited in a relatively limited scope of neural network research. (Le et al., 2011; Le et al., 2012) use word classes to reduce the output layer's complexity of such networks, both in language and translation models. In the work of (Niehues and Waibel, 2012), their Restricted Boltzmann Machines language models also encode word classes as an additional input feature in predicting the next target word. (Tran et al., 2014) use two separate feed forward networks to predict the target word and its corresponding suffixes with the source words and target stem as input features.

Our work exhibits several essential differences from theirs. Firstly, we leverage not only the target morphological information but also word factors from both source and target sides in our models. Furthermore, we could use as many types of word factors as we can provide. Thus, we are able to make the most of the information encoded in those factors for more accurate prediction.

3 Recurrent Neural Network-based Language Models

In contrast to feed forward neural network-based language models, recurrent neural network-based language models are able to store arbitrary long word sequences. Thereby, they are able to directly model $P(w|h)$ and no approximations by limiting the history size are necessary. Recently, several authors showed that RNN-based language models could perform very well in phrase-based machine translation. (Mikolov et al., 2010; Sundermeyer et al., 2013)

In this work, we used the torch7[1] implementation of an RNN-based language model (Léonard et al., 2015). First, the words were mapped to their word embeddings. We used an input embedding size of 100. Afterwards, we used two LSTM-based layers. The first has the size of the word embeddings and for the second we used a hidden size of 200. Finally, the word probabilities were calculated using a softmax layer.

The models were trained using stochastic gradient descent. The weights were updated using mini-batches with a batch size of 128. We used a maximum epoch size of 1 million examples and selected the model with the lowest perplexity on the development data.

4 Factored Language Model

When using factored representation of words, words are no longer represented as indices in the neural network. Instead, they are represented a tuples of indices $w = (f_1, \ldots, f_D)$, where D is the number of different factors used to describe the word. These factors can be the word itself, as well as the POS, automatic learned classes (Och, 1999) or other information about the word. Furthermore, we can use different types of factors for the input and the output of the neural network.

---

[1] http://torch.ch/

Figure 1: Factored RNN Layout

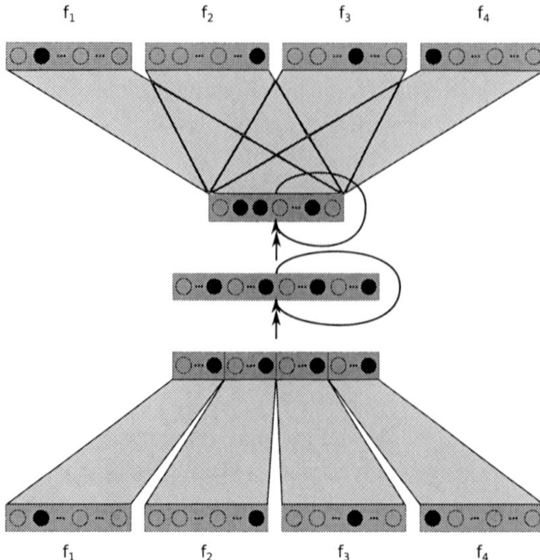

4.1 Input Representation

In a first step, we obtained a factored representation for the input of the neural network. In the experiments, we represented a word by its surface form, POS-tags and automatic word class, but the framework can be used for any number of word factors. Although there are factored approaches for n-gram based language models (Bilmes and Kirchhoff, 2003), most n-gram language models only use one factor. In contrast, in neural network based language models, it is very easy to add additional information as word factors. We can learn different embeddings for each factor and represent the word by concatenating the embeddings of several factors. As shown in the bottom of Figure 1, we first project the different factors to the continuous factor embeddings. Afterwards, we concatenate these embeddings into a word embedding.

The advantage of using several word factors is that we can use different knowledge sources to represent a word. When a word occurs very rarely, the learned embedding from its surface form might not be helpful. The additional POS information, however, is very helpful. While using POS-based language models in PBMT may lead to losing the information about high frequent words, in this approach we can have access to all information by concatenating the factor embeddings.

4.2 Output Representation

In addition to use different factors in the input of the neural network, we can also use different factors on the output. In phrase-based machine translation, n-gram language models based on POS-tags have been shown to be very successful for morphologically rich languages.

Porting this idea to neural network language models, we can not only train a model to predict the original word f_1 given the previous words in factor representation $h = (f_{1,1}, \ldots, f_{1,D}), \ldots, (f_{i,1}, \ldots, f_{i,D})$, but also train a model to predict he POS-tags (e.g. f_2) given the history h.

In a first step, we proposed to train individual models for all factors $1, \ldots, D$ generating probabilities $P_1, \ldots, P_D$ for every sentence. Then these probabilities can be used as features for example in re-scoring of the phrase-based MT system.

Considering that it can be helpful to consider all factors of the word in the input, it can be also helpful to jointly train the models for predicting the different output factors. This is motivated by the fact that multi-task learning has shown to be beneficial in several NLP tasks (Collobert et al., 2011). Predicting all output features jointly requires a modification of the output layer of the RNN model. As shown in Figure 1, we replace the single mapping from the LSTM-layer to the softmax layer, by D mappings. Each mapping then learns to project the LSTM-layer output to the factored output probabilities. In the last layer, we use D different softmax units. In a similar way as the conventional network, the error between the output of the network and the reference is calculated during training.

Using this network, we will no longer predict the probability of one word factor $P_d, d \in \{1, \ldots D\}$, but D different probability distributions $P_1, \ldots, P_D$. In order to integrate this model into the machine translation system we explored two different probabilities. First, we used only the joint probability $P = \prod_{d=1}^{D} P_d$ as a feature in the log-linear combination. In addition, we also used the joint probability as well as all individual probabilities P_d as features.

4.3 Bilingual Model

Using the model presented before, it is possible to add additional information to the model as well. One example we explored in this work is to use

Figure 2: Bilingual Model

Target word	w_i	w_{i+1}	w_{i+2}
Surface form	completed	a	pilot
POS	VVD	DT	NN
Word class	87	37	17
Source word	$s_{a(i+1)}$	$s_{a(i+2)}$	$s_{a(i)}$
Surface form	ein	Pilotproject	abgeschlossen
POS	ART	NN	VVPP

the model as a bilingual model (BM). Instead of using only monolingual information by considering the previous target factors as input, we used source factors additionally. Thereby, we can now model the probability of a word given the previous target words and information about the source sentence. So in this case we model the translation probability and no longer the language model probability.

When predicting the target word w_{i+1} with its factors $f_{i+1,1}, \ldots, f_{i+1,D}$, the input to the RNN is the previous target word $w_i = f_{i,1}, \ldots, f_{i,D}$. Using the alignment, we can find the source word $s_{a(i+1)}$, which is aligned to the target word w_{i+1}. When we add the features of source word

$$s_{a(i+1)} = (f^s_{a(i+1),1}, \ldots, f^s_{a(i+1),D_s})$$

to the ones of the target word w_i and create a new bilingual token

$$b_i = (f_{i+1,1}, \ldots, f_{i+1,D}, f^s_{a(i+1),1}, \ldots, f^s_{a(i+1),D_s})$$

, we now can predict the target word given the previous target word and the aligned source word.

In the example in Figure 2, we would insert (completed,VVD,87,ein,ART) to predict (a,DT,37).

In this case the number of input factors and output factors are no longer the same. In the input, we have $D + D_s$ input factors, while we have only D factors on the output of the network.

5 Experiments

We evaluated the factored RNNLM on three different language pairs of the WMT 2016 News Translation Task. In each language pair, we created an n-best list using our phrase-based MT system and used the factored RNNLM as an additional feature in rescoring. It is worth noting that the POS and word class information are already present during decoding of the baseline system by n-gram-based language models based on each of these factors. First, we performed a detailed analysis on the English-Romanian task. In addition, we used the model in a German-English and English-German translation system. In all tasks, we used the model in re-scoring of a PBMT system.

5.1 System Description

The baseline system is an in-house implementation of the phrase-based approach. The system used to generate n-best lists for the news tasks is trained on all the available training corpora of the WMT 2015 Shared Translation task. The system uses a pre-reordering technique (Rottmann and Vogel, 2007; Niehues and Kolss, 2009; Herrmann et al., 2013) and facilitates several translation and language models. As shown in Table 1, we use two to three word-based language models and one to two cluster-based models using 50, 100 or 1,000 clusters. The custers were trained as described in (Och, 1999). In addition, we used a POS-based language model in the English-Romainian system and a bilingual language model (Niehues et al., 2011) in English to German and German to English systems. The POS tags for English-Romanian were generated by the tagger described in (Ion et al., 2012) and the ones for German by RFTagger (Schmid and Laws, 2008).

Table 1: *Features*

	EN-RO	EN-DE	DE-EN
wordLM	2	3	3
POSLM	1	0	0
clusterLM	2	1	2
BiLM	0	1	1
#features	22-23	20	22

In addition, we used discriminative word lexica (Niehues and Waibel, 2013) during decoding and source discriminative word lexica in rescoring (Herrman et al., 2015).

A full system description can be found in (Ha et al., 2016).

The German to English baseline system uses 20 features and the English to German systems uses 22 features.

The English-Romanian system was optimized on the first part of news-dev2016 and the rescoring was optimized on this set and a subset of 2,000 sentences from the SETimes corpus. This part of the corpus was of course excluded for training the model. The system was tested on the second half of news-dev2016.

The English-German and German-English systems were optimized on news-test2014 and also the re-scoring was optimized on this data. We tested the system on news-test2015.

For English to Romanian and English to German we used an n-best List of 300 entries and for German to English we used an n-best list with 3,000 entries.

For decoding, for all language directions, the weights of the system were optimized using minimum error rate training (Och, 2003). The weights in the rescoring were optimized using the List-Net algorithm (Cao et al., 2007) as described in (Niehues et al., 2015).

The RNN-based language models for English to Romanian and German to English were trained on the target side of the parallel training data. For English to German, we trained the model and the Europarl corpus and the News commentary corpus.

5.2 English - Romanian

In the first experiment on the English to Romanian task, we only used the scores of the RNN language models. The baseline system has a BLEU score (Papineni et al., 2002) of 29.67. Using only the language model instead of the 22 features, of course, leads to a lower performance, but we can see clear difference between the different language models. All systems use a word vocabulary of 5K words and we used four different factors. We used the word surface form, the POS tags and word clusters using 100 and 1,000 classes.

The baseline model using words as input and words as output reaches a BLEU score of 27.88. If we instead represent the input words by factors, we select entries from the n-best list that generates a BLEU score of 28.46. As done with the n-gram language models, we can also predict the other factors instead of the words themselves. In all cases, we use all four factors as input factors. As shown in Table 2, all models except for the one with 100 classes perform similarly, reaching up between 28.46 and 28.49. The language model predicting only 100 classes only reaches a BLEU score of 28.23. It suggests that this number of classes is too low to disambiguate the entries in the n-best list.

Table 2: *English - Romanian Single Score*

Input	Prediction	Single
Word	Word	27.88
All factors	Word	28.46
All factors	POS	28.48
All factors	100 Cl.	28.23
All factors	1,000 Cl.	28.49
All factors	All factors	28.54

If we predict all factors together and use then the joint probability, we can reach the best BLEU score of 28.54 as shown in the last line of the table. This is 0.7 BLEU points better than the initial word based model.

After evaluating the model as the only knowledge source, we also performed experiments using the model in combination with the other models. We evaluated the baseline and the best model in three different configuration in Table 3 using only the joint probability. The three baseline configuration differ in the models used during decoding. Thereby, we are able to generate different n-best lists and test the models on different conditions.

Table 3: *English - Romanian Language Models*

Model	Conf1	Conf2	Conf3
Baseline	29.86	30.00	29.75
LM 5K	29.79	29.84	29.73
LM 50K	29.64	29.84	29.83
Factored LM 5K	29.94	30.01	30.01
Factored LM 50K	30.05	30.27	30.29

In Table 3, we tested the word-based and the factored language model using a vocabulary of 5K and 50K words. Features from each model are used in addition to the features of the baseline system. As shown in the table, the word-based RNN language models perform similarly, but both could not improve over the baseline system. One possible reason for this is that we already use several language models in the baseline model and they are partly trained on much larger data. While the RNN models are trained using only the target language model, one word-based language model is trained on the Romanian common crawl corpus. Furthermore, the POS-based and word cluster language models use a 9-gram history and therefore, can already model quite long dependencies.

But if we use a factored language model, we are

able to improve over the baseline system. Using the additional information of the other word factors, we are able to improve the bilingual model in all situations. The model using a surface word vocabulary of 5,000 words can improve by 0.1 to 0.3 BLEU points. The model using a 50K vocabulary can even improve by up to 0.6 BLEU points.

Table 4: *English - Romanian Bilingual Models*

Model	Dev	Test
Baseline	40.12	29.75
+ Factored LM 50K	40.87	30.17
+ Factored BM 5K	41.11	30.44
+ Factored BM 50K	41.16	30.57

After analyzing the different language models, we also evaluate how we can use the factored representation to include source side information. The results are summarized in Table 4. In these experiments, we used not only the the joint probability, but also the four individual probabilities as features. Therefore, we will add five scores for every model, since each model is added to its previous configuration in this experiment.

Exploiting all five probabilities of the language model brought us the similar improvement we achieved using the joint probability from the model. On the test set, the improvements are slightly worse. When adding the model using source side information based on a vocabulary of 5K and 50K words, however, we get additional improvements. Adopting the both bilingual models (BM) along with a factored LM, we improved the BLEU score further leading up to the best score of 30.57 for the test set.

5.3 English - German

In addition to the experiments on English to Romanian, we also evaluated the models on the task of translating English News to German. For the English to German system, we use three factors on the source side and four factors on the target side. In English, we used the surface forms as well as automatic word cluster based on 100 and 1,000 classes. On the target side, we used fine-graind POS-tags generated by the RFTagger (Schmid and Laws, 2008), in addition to the factors for the source side.

The experiments using only the scores of the model are summarized in Table 5. In this experiment, we analyzed a word based- and a factored

Table 5: *English - German Single Score*

Model	Single
LM 5K	20.92
Factored LM 5K	21.69
BM 5K	21.33
Factored BM 5K	21.92

language models as well as bilingual models. As described in section 4.3, the difference between the language model and the bilingual model is that the latter uses the source side information as additional factor.

Using only the word-based language model we achieved a BLEU score of 20.92. Deploying a factored language model instead, we can improve the BLEU score by 0.7 BLEU points to 21.69. While we achieved a score of 21.33 BLEU points by using a proposed bilingual model, we improved the score up to 21.92 BLEU points by adopting all factors for the bilingual model.

Table 6: *English-German Language Model*

Model	Conf1	Conf2
Baseline	23.25	23.40
Factored LM 5K	23.63	23.77
Factored BM 5K	23.43	23.48

In addition to the analysis on the single model, we also evaluated the model's influence by combining the model with the baseline features. We tested the language model as well as the bilingual model on two different configurations. Adopting the factored language model on top of the baseline features improved the translation quality by around 0.4 BLEU points for both configurations, as shown in Table 6. Although the bilingual model could also improve the translation quality, it could not outperform the factored language model. The combination of the two models, LM and BM, did not lead to further improvements. In summary, the factored language model improved the BLEU score by 0.4 points.

5.4 German - English

Similar experiments were conducted on the German to English translation task. For this language pair, we built models using a vocabulary size of 5,000 words. The models cover word surface forms and two automatic word clusters, which are based on 100 and 1,000 word classes respectively. First, we will evaluate the performance of the system using only this model in rescoring. The results are summarized in Table 7.

Table 7: *German - English Single Score*

Model	Single
LM 5K	26.11
Factored LM 5K	26.96
BM 5K	26.77
Factored BM 5K	26.81

The word based language model achieves a BLEU score 26.11. Extending the model to include factors improves the BLEU score by 0.8 BLEU points to 26.96. If we use a bilingual model, a word based model achieves a BLEU score of 26.77 and the factored one a BLEU score of 26.81. Although the factored model performed better than the word-based models, in this case the bilingual model cannot outperform the language model.

Table 8: *German - English Language Model*

Model	Single
Baseline	29.33
+ Factored BM 5K	29.51
+ Factored LM 5K	29.66

In a last series of experiments, we used the scores combined with the baseline scores. The results are shown in Table 8. In this language pair, we can improve over the baseline system by using both models. The final BLEU score is 0.3 BLEU points better than the initial system.

6 Conclusion

In this paper, we presented a new approach to integrate additional word information into a neural network language model. This model is especially promising for morphologically rich languages. Due to their large vocabulary size, additional information such as POS-tags are expected to model rare words effectively.

Representing words using factors has been successfully deployed in many phrase-based machine translation systems. Inspired by this, we represented each word in our neural network language model using factors, facilitating all available information of the word. We showed that using the factored neural network language models can improve the quality of a phrase-based machine translation system, which already uses several factored language models.

In addition, the presented framework allows an easy integration of source side information. By incorporating the alignment information to the source side, we were able to model the translation process. In this model, the source words as well as the target words can be represented by word factors.

Using these techniques, we are able to improve the translation system on three different language pairs of the WMT 2016 evaluation. We performed experiments on the English-Romanian, English-German and German-English translation task. The suggested technique yielded up to 0.7 BLEU points of improvement on all three tasks.

Acknowledgments

The project leading to this application has received funding from the European Union's Horizon 2020 research and innovation programme under grant agreement n° 645452. The research by Thanh-Le Ha was supported by Ministry of Science, Research and the Arts Baden-Württemberg.

References

Jeff A. Bilmes and Katrin Kirchhoff. 2003. Factored language models and generalized parallel backoff. In *Proceedings of the 2003 Conference of the North American Chapter of the Association for Computational Linguistics on Human Language Technology: Companion Volume of the Proceedings of HLT-NAACL 2003–short Papers - Volume 2*, NAACL-Short '03, pages 4–6, Stroudsburg, PA, USA. Association for Computational Linguistics.

Z. Cao, T. Qin, T.-Y. Liu, M.-F. Tsai, and H. Li. 2007. Learning to rank: from pairwise approach to listwise approach. In *Proceedings of the 24th international conference on Machine learning*, Icml â07, pages 129–136, New York, NY, USA. Acm.

Ronan Collobert, Jason Weston, Léon Bottou, Michael Karlen, Koray Kavukcuoglu, and Pavel P. Kuksa. 2011. Natural language processing (almost) from scratch. *CoRR*, abs/1103.0398.

J. Devlin, R. Zbib, Z. Huang, T. Lamar, R. Schwartz, and J. Makhoul. 2014. Fast and robust neural network joint models for statistical machine translation. In *Proceedings of the 52st Annual Meeting of the Association for Computational Linguistics (ACL 2014)*, volume 1, pages 1370–1380, Baltimore, Maryland, USA.

Thanh-Le Ha, Jan Niehues, and Alex Waibel. 2014. Lexical Translation Model Using a Deep Neural Network Architecture. In *Proceedings of the 11th International Workshop on Spoken Language Translation (IWSLT14)*, Lake Tahoe, CA, USA.

Thanh-Le Ha, Eunah Cho, Jan Niehues, Mohammed Mediani, Matthias Sperber, Alexandre Allauzen, and yAlex Waibel. 2016. The karlsruhe institute of technology systems for the news translation task in wmt 2016. In *Proceedings of the ACL 2016 First Conference on Machine Translation (WMT2016)*.

Teresa Herrman, Jan Niehues, and Alex Waibel. 2015. Source Discriminative Word Lexicon for Translation Disambiguation. In *Proceedings of the 12th International Workshop on Spoken Language Translation (IWSLT15)*, Danang, Vietnam.

Teresa Herrmann, Jan Niehues, and Alex Waibel. 2013. Combining Word Reordering Methods on different Linguistic Abstraction Levels for Statistical Machine Translation. In *Proceedings of the Seventh Workshop on Syntax, Semantics and Structure in Statistical Translation*, Altanta, Georgia, USA.

Radu Ion, Elena Irimia, Dan Stefanescu, and Dan Tufis. 2012. Rombac: The romanian balanced annotated corpus. In Nicoletta Calzolari (Conference Chair), Khalid Choukri, Thierry Declerck, Mehmet U?ur Do?an, Bente Maegaard, Joseph Mariani, Asuncion Moreno, Jan Odijk, and Stelios Piperidis, editors, *Proceedings of the Eight International Conference on Language Resources and Evaluation (LREC'12)*, Istanbul, Turkey, may. European Language Resources Association (ELRA).

Philipp Koehn and Hieu Hoang. 2007. Factored translation models. In *In Proceedings of the 2007 Joint Conference on Empirical Methods in Natural Language Processing and Computational Natural Language Learning (EMNLP-CoNLL*, pages 868–876.

Hai-Son Le, Ilya Oparin, Alexandre Allauzen, Jean-Luc Gauvain, and François Yvon. 2011. Structured output layer neural network language model. In *Proceedings of the International Conference on Audio, Speech and Signal Processing*, pages 5524–5527.

Hai-Son Le, Alexandre Allauzen, and François Yvon. 2012. Continuous Space Translation Models with Neural Networks. In *Proceedings of the 2012 conference of the north american chapter of the association for computational linguistics: Human language technologies (NAACL)*, pages 39–48. Association for Computational Linguistics.

Nicholas Léonard, Sagar Waghmare, Yang Wang, and Jin-Hwa Kim. 2015. rnn : Recurrent library for torch. *CoRR*, abs/1511.07889.

Mohammed Mediani, Eunah Cho, Jan Niehues, Teresa Herrmann, and Alex Waibel. 2011. The KIT english-french translation systems for IWSLT 2011.

In *2011 International Workshop on Spoken Language Translation, IWSLT 2011, San Francisco, CA, USA, December 8-9, 2011*, pages 73–78.

Tomas Mikolov, Martin Karafiát, Lukas Burget, Jan Cernockỳ, and Sanjeev Khudanpur. 2010. Recurrent neural network based language model. In *INTERSPEECH*, volume 2, page 3.

Jan Niehues and Muntsin Kolss. 2009. A POS-Based Model for Long-Range Reorderings in SMT. In *Proceedings of the Fourth Workshop on Statistical Machine Translation (WMT 2009)*, Athens, Greece.

J. Niehues and A. Waibel. 2012. Continuous space language models using restricted boltzmann machines. In *Proceedings of the Ninth International Workshop on Spoken Language Translation (IWSLT 2012)*, Hong Kong.

Jan Niehues and Alex Waibel. 2013. An MT Error-Driven Discriminative Word Lexicon using Sentence Structure Features. In *Proceedings of the Eighth Workshop on Statistical Machine Translation*, Sofia, Bulgaria.

Jan Niehues, Teresa Herrmann, Stephan Vogel, and Alex Waibel. 2011. Wider Context by Using Bilingual Language Models in Machine Translation. In *Sixth Workshop on Statistical Machine Translation (WMT 2011)*, Edinburgh, Scotland, United Kingdom.

Jan Niehues, Quoc Khanh Do, Alexandre Allauzen, and Alex Waibel. 2015. Listnet-based MT Rescoring. *EMNLP 2015*, page 248.

Franz Josef Och. 1999. An Efficient Method for Determining Bilingual Word Classes. In *Proceedings of the Ninth Conference of the European Chapter of the Association for Computational Linguistics (EACL 1999)*, Bergen, Norway.

F.J. Och. 2003. Minimum error rate training in statistical machine translation. In *Proceedings of the 41th Annual Meeting of the Association for Computational Linguistics (ACL 2003)*, Sapporo, Japa.

K. Papineni, S. Roukos, T. Ward, and W.-jing Zhu. 2002. Bleu: a method for automatic evaluation of machine translation. In *Proceedings of the 40th Annual Meeting of the Association for Computational Linguistics (ACL 2002)*, pages 311–318, Philadelphia, Pennsylvania.

Kay Rottmann and Stephan Vogel. 2007. Word Reordering in Statistical Machine Translation with a POS-Based Distortion Model. In *Proceedings of the 11th International Conference on Theoretical and Methodological Issues in Machine Translation (TMI 2007)*, Skövde, Sweden.

Helmut Schmid and Florian Laws. 2008. Estimation of Conditional Probabilities with Decision Trees and an Application to Fine-Grained POS Tagging. In *Proceedings of the 22nd International Conference on Computational Linguistics*, Manchester, United Kingdom.

Holger Schwenk. 2007. Continuous space language models. *Computer Speech & Language*, 21(3):492–518.

Martin Sundermeyer, Ilya Oparin, Jean-Luc Gauvain, Ben Freiberg, Ralf Schluter, and Hermann Ney. 2013. Comparison of feedforward and recurrent neural network language models. In *Acoustics, Speech and Signal Processing (ICASSP), 2013 IEEE International Conference on*, pages 8430–8434. IEEE.

Ke Tran, Arianna Bisazza, Christof Monz, et al. 2014. Word translation prediction for morphologically rich languages with bilingual neural networks. Association for Computational Linguistics.

Joern Wuebker, Stephan Peitz, Felix Rietig, and Hermann Ney. 2013. Improving statistical machine translation with word class models. In *Conference on Empirical Methods in Natural Language Processing*, pages 1377–1381, Seattle, WA, USA, October.

Linguistic Input Features Improve Neural Machine Translation

Rico Sennrich and **Barry Haddow**
School of Informatics, University of Edinburgh
`rico.sennrich@ed.ac.uk, bhaddow@inf.ed.ac.uk`

Abstract

Neural machine translation has recently achieved impressive results, while using little in the way of external linguistic information. In this paper we show that the strong learning capability of neural MT models does not make linguistic features redundant; they can be easily incorporated to provide further improvements in performance. We generalize the embedding layer of the encoder in the attentional encoder–decoder architecture to support the inclusion of arbitrary features, in addition to the baseline word feature. We add morphological features, part-of-speech tags, and syntactic dependency labels as input features to English↔German and English→Romanian neural machine translation systems. In experiments on WMT16 training and test sets, we find that linguistic input features improve model quality according to three metrics: perplexity, BLEU and CHRF3. An open-source implementation of our neural MT system is available[1], as are sample files and configurations[2].

1 Introduction

Neural machine translation has recently achieved impressive results (Bahdanau et al., 2015; Jean et al., 2015), while learning from raw, sentence-aligned parallel text and using little in the way of external linguistic information.[3] However, we hypothesize that various levels of linguistic annotation can be valuable for neural machine translation. Lemmatisation can reduce data sparse-ness, and allow inflectional variants of the same word to explicitly share a representation in the model. Other types of annotation, such as parts-of-speech (POS) or syntactic dependency labels, can help in disambiguation. In this paper we investigate whether linguistic information is beneficial to neural translation models, or whether their strong learning capability makes explicit linguistic features redundant.

Let us motivate the use of linguistic features using examples of actual translation errors by neural MT systems. In translation out of English, one problem is that the same surface word form may be shared between several word types, due to homonymy or word formation processes such as conversion. For instance, *close* can be a verb, adjective, or noun, and these different meanings often have distinct translations into other languages. Consider the following English→German example:

1. *We thought a win like this might be close.*

2. *Wir dachten, dass ein solcher Sieg nah sein könnte.*

3. **Wir dachten, ein Sieg wie dieser könnte schließen.*

For the English source sentence in Example 1 (our translation in Example 2), a neural MT system (our baseline system from Section 4) mistranslates *close* as a verb, and produces the German verb *schließen* (Example 3), even though *close* is an adjective in this sentence, which has the German translation *nah*. Intuitively, part-of-speech annotation of the English input could disambiguate between verb, noun, and adjective meanings of *close*.

As a second example, consider the following German→English example:

4. *Gefährlich ist die Route aber dennoch .*
   dangerous is the route but still .

---

[1] `https://github.com/rsennrich/nematus`
[2] `https://github.com/rsennrich/wmt16-scripts`
[3] Linguistic tools are most commonly used in preprocessing, e.g. for Turkish segmentation (Gülçehre et al., 2015).

Proceedings of the First Conference on Machine Translation, Volume 1: Research Papers, pages 83–91,
Berlin, Germany, August 11-12, 2016. ©2016 Association for Computational Linguistics

5. *However the route is dangerous .*

6. **Dangerous is the route , however .*

German main clauses have a verb-second (V2) word order, whereas English word order is generally SVO. The German sentence (Example 4; English reference in Example 5) topicalizes the predicate *gefährlich* 'dangerous', putting the subject *die Route* 'the route' after the verb. Our baseline system (Example 6) retains the original word order, which is highly unusual in English, especially for prose in the news domain. A syntactic annotation of the source sentence could support the attentional encoder-decoder in learning which words in the German source to attend (and translate) first.

We will investigate the usefulness of linguistic features for the language pair German↔English, considering the following linguistic features:

- lemmas

- subword tags (see Section 3.2)

- morphological features

- POS tags

- dependency labels

The inclusion of lemmas is motivated by the hope for a better generalization over inflectional variants of the same word form. The other linguistic features are motivated by disambiguation, as discussed in our introductory examples.

2   Neural Machine Translation

We follow the neural machine translation architecture by Bahdanau et al. (2015), which we will briefly summarize here.

The neural machine translation system is implemented as an attentional encoder-decoder network with recurrent neural networks.

The encoder is a bidirectional neural network with gated recurrent units (Cho et al., 2014) that reads an input sequence $x = (x_1, ..., x_m)$ and calculates a forward sequence of hidden states $(\overrightarrow{h}_1, ..., \overrightarrow{h}_m)$, and a backward sequence $(\overleftarrow{h}_1, ..., \overleftarrow{h}_m)$. The hidden states $\overrightarrow{h}_j$ and $\overleftarrow{h}_j$ are concatenated to obtain the annotation vector h_j.

The decoder is a recurrent neural network that predicts a target sequence $y = (y_1, ..., y_n)$. Each word y_i is predicted based on a recurrent hidden state s_i, the previously predicted word y_{i-1}, and

a context vector c_i. c_i is computed as a weighted sum of the annotations h_j. The weight of each annotation h_j is computed through an *alignment model* α_{ij}, which models the probability that y_i is aligned to x_j. The alignment model is a single-layer feedforward neural network that is learned jointly with the rest of the network through back-propagation.

A detailed description can be found in (Bahdanau et al., 2015), although our implementation is based on a slightly modified form of this architecture, released for the dl4mt tutorial[4]. Training is performed on a parallel corpus with stochastic gradient descent. For translation, a beam search with small beam size is employed.

2.1   Adding Input Features

Our main innovation over the standard encoder-decoder architecture is that we represent the encoder input as a combination of features (Alexandrescu and Kirchhoff, 2006).

We here show the equation for the forward states of the encoder (for the simple RNN case; consider (Bahdanau et al., 2015) for GRU):

$$\overrightarrow{h}_j = \tanh(\overrightarrow{W} E x_j + \overrightarrow{U} \overrightarrow{h}_{j-1}) \qquad (1)$$

where $E \in \mathbb{R}^{m \times K_x}$ is a word embedding matrix, $\overrightarrow{W} \in \mathbb{R}^{n \times m}$, $\overrightarrow{U} \in \mathbb{R}^{n \times n}$ are weight matrices, with m and n being the word embedding size and number of hidden units, respectively, and K_x being the vocabulary size of the source language.

We generalize this to an arbitrary number of features $|F|$:

$$\overrightarrow{h}_j = \tanh(\overrightarrow{W} (\overset{|F|}{\underset{k=1}{\|}} E_k x_{jk}) + \overrightarrow{U} \overrightarrow{h}_{j-1}) \qquad (2)$$

where $\|$ is the vector concatenation, $E_k \in \mathbb{R}^{m_k \times K_k}$ are the feature embedding matrices, with $\sum_{k=1}^{|F|} m_k = m$, and K_k is the vocabulary size of the kth feature. In other words, we look up separate embedding vectors for each feature, which are then concatenated. The length of the concatenated vector matches the total embedding size, and all other parts of the model remain unchanged.

---

[4]`https://github.com/nyu-dl/`
`dl4mt-tutorial`

3 Linguistic Input Features

Our generalized model of the previous section supports an arbitrary number of input features. In this paper, we will focus on a number of well-known linguistic features. Our main empirical question is if providing linguistic features to the encoder improves the translation quality of neural machine translation systems, or if the information emerges from training encoder-decoder models on raw text, making its inclusion via explicit features redundant. All linguistic features are predicted automatically; we use Stanford CoreNLP (Toutanova et al., 2003; Minnen et al., 2001; Chen and Manning, 2014) to annotate the English input for English→German, and ParZu (Sennrich et al., 2013) to annotate the German input for German→English. We here discuss the individual features in more detail.

3.1 Lemma

Using lemmas as input features guarantees sharing of information between word forms that share the same base form. In principle, neural models can learn that inflectional variants are semantically related, and represent them as similar points in the continuous vector space (Mikolov et al., 2013). However, while this has been demonstrated for high-frequency words, we expect that a lemmatized representation increases data efficiency; low-frequency variants may even be unknown to word-level models. With character- or subword-level models, it is unclear to what extent they can learn the similarity between low-frequency word forms that share a lemma, especially if the word forms are superficially dissimilar. Consider the following two German word forms, which share the lemma *liegen* 'lie':

- *liegt* 'lies' (3.p.sg. present)

- *läge* 'lay' (3.p.sg. subjunctive II)

The lemmatisers we use are based on finite-state methods, which ensures a large coverage, even for infrequent word forms. We use the Zmorge analyzer for German (Schmid et al., 2004; Sennrich and Kunz, 2014), and the lemmatiser in the Stanford CoreNLP toolkit for English (Minnen et al., 2001).

3.2 Subword Tags

In our experiments, we operate on the level of subwords to achieve open-vocabulary translation with a fixed symbol vocabulary, using a segmentation based on *byte-pair encoding* (BPE) (Sennrich et al., 2016c). We note that in BPE segmentation, some symbols are potentially ambiguous, and can either be a separate word, or a subword segment of a larger word. Also, text is represented as a sequence of subword units with no explicit word boundaries, but word boundaries are potentially helpful to learn which symbols to attend to, and when to forget information in the recurrent layers. We propose an annotation of subword structure similar to popular IOB format for chunking and named entity recognition, marking if a symbol in the text forms the beginning (B), inside (I), or end (E) of a word. A separate tag (O) is used if a symbol corresponds to the full word.

3.3 Morphological Features

For German→English, the parser annotates the German input with morphological features. Different word types have different sets of features – for instance, nouns have case, number and gender, while verbs have person, number, tense and aspect – and features may be underspecified. We treat the concatenation of all morphological features of a word, using a special symbol for underspecified features, as a string, and treat each such string as a separate feature value.

3.4 POS Tags and Dependency Labels

In our introductory examples, we motivated POS tags and dependency labels as possible disambiguators. Each word is associated with one POS tag, and one dependency label. The latter is the label of the edge connecting a word to its syntactic head, or 'ROOT' if the word has no syntactic head.

3.5 On Using Word-level Features in a Subword Model

We segment rare words into subword units using BPE. The subword tags encode the segmentation of words into subword units, and need no further modification. All other features are originally word-level features. To annotate the segmented source text with features, we copy the word's feature value to all its subword units. An example is shown in Figure 1.

4 Evaluation

We evaluate our systems on the WMT16 shared translation task English↔German. The parallel

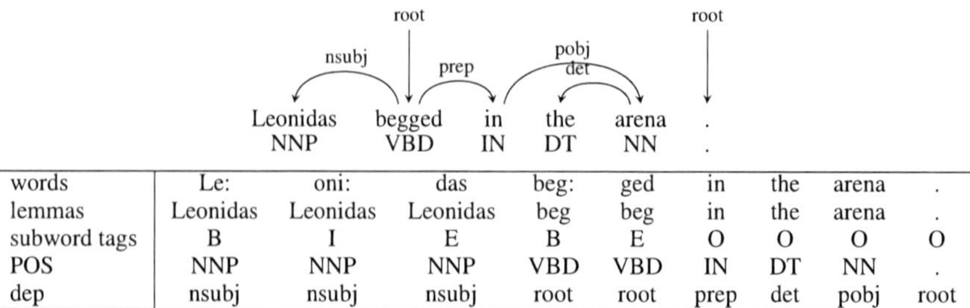

words	Le:	oni:	das	beg:	ged	in	the	arena	.
lemmas	Leonidas	Leonidas	Leonidas	beg	beg	in	the	arena	.
subword tags	B	I	E	B	E	O	O	O	O
POS	NNP	NNP	NNP	VBD	VBD	IN	DT	NN	.
dep	nsubj	nsubj	nsubj	root	root	prep	det	pobj	root

Figure 1: Original dependency tree for sentence *Leonidas begged in the arena* ., and our feature representation after BPE segmentation.

training data consists of about 4.2 million sentence pairs.

To enable open-vocabulary translation, we encode words via joint BPE[5] (Sennrich et al., 2016c), learning 89 500 merge operations on the concatenation of the source and target side of the parallel training data. We use minibatches of size 80, a maximum sentence length of 50, word embeddings of size 500, and hidden layers of size 1024. We clip the gradient norm to 1.0 (Pascanu et al., 2013). We train the models with Adadelta (Zeiler, 2012), reshuffling the training corpus between epochs. We validate the model every 10 000 minibatches via BLEU and perplexity on a validation set (newstest2013).

For neural MT, perplexity is a useful measure of how well the model can predict a reference translation given the source sentence. Perplexity is thus a good indicator of whether input features provide any benefit to the models, and we report the best validation set perplexity of each experiment. To evaluate whether the features also increase translation performance, we report case-sensitive BLEU scores with mteval-13b.perl on two test sets, newstest2015 and newstest2016. We also report CHRF3 (Popović, 2015), a character n-gram F_3 score which was found to correlate well with human judgments, especially for translations out of English (Stanojević et al., 2015).[6] The two metrics may occasionally disagree, partly because they are highly sensitive to the length of the output. BLEU is precision-based, whereas CHRF3 considers both precision and recall, with a bias for recall. For BLEU, we also report whether differences between systems are statistically significant

<hr>

[5]https://github.com/rsennrich/subword-nmt

[6]We use the re-implementation included with the subword code

	input vocabulary			embedding	
feature	EN	DE	model	all	single
subword tags	4	4	4	5	5
POS tags	46	54	54	10	10
morph. features	-	1400	1400	10	10
dependency labels	46	33	46	10	10
lemmas	800000	1500000	85000	115	167
words	78500	85000	85000	*	*

Table 1: Vocabulary size, and size of embedding layer of linguistic features, in system that includes all features, and contrastive experiments that add a single feature over the baseline. The embedding layer size of the word feature is set to bring the total size to 500.

according to a bootstrap resampling significance test (Riezler and Maxwell, 2005).

We train models for about a week, and report results for an ensemble of the 4 last saved models (with models saved every 12 hours). The ensemble serves to smooth the variance between single models.

Decoding is performed with beam search with a beam size of 12.

To ensure that performance improvements are not simply due to an increase in the number of model parameters, we keep the total size of the embedding layer fixed to 500. Table 1 lists the embedding size we use for linguistic features – the embedding layer size of the word-level feature varies, and is set to bring the total embedding layer size to 500. If we include the lemma feature, we roughly split the embedding vector one-to-two between the lemma feature and the word feature. The table also shows the network vocabulary size; for all features except lemmas, we can represent all feature values in the network vocabulary – in the case of words, this is due to BPE segmentation. For lemmas, we choose the same vocabulary size as for words, replacing rare lemmas with a special UNK symbol.

Sennrich et al. (2016b) report large gains from using monolingual in-domain training data, automatically back-translated into the source language to produce a synthetic parallel training corpus. We use the synthetic corpora produced in these experiments[7] (3.6–4.2 million sentence pairs), and we trained systems which include this data to compare against the state of the art. We note that our experiments with this data entail a syntactic annotation of automatically translated data, which may be a source of noise. For the systems with synthetic data, we double the training time to two weeks.

We also evaluate linguistic features for the lower-resourced translation direction English→Romanian, with 0.6 million sentence pairs of parallel training data, and 2.2 million sentence pairs of synthetic parallel data. We use the same linguistic features as for English→German. We follow Sennrich et al. (2016a) in the configuration, and use dropout for the English→Romanian systems. We drop out full words (both on the source and target side) with a probability of 0.1. For all other layers, the dropout probability is set to 0.2.

4.1 Results

Table 2 shows our main results for German→English, and English→German. The baseline system is a neural MT system with only one input feature, the (sub)words themselves. For both translation directions, linguistic features improve the best perplexity on the development data (47.3 → 46.2, and 54.9 → 52.9, respectively). For German→English, the linguistic features lead to an increase of 1.5 BLEU (31.4→32.9) and 0.5 CHRF3 (58.0 → 58.5), on the newstest2016 test set. For English→German, we observe improvements of 0.6 BLEU (27.8 → 28.4) and 1.2 CHRF3 (56.0 → 57.2).

To evaluate the effectiveness of different linguistic features in isolation, we performed contrastive experiments in which only a single feature was added to the baseline. Results are shown in Table 3. Unsurprisingly, the combination of all features (Table 2) gives the highest improvement, averaged over metrics and test sets, but most features are beneficial on their own. Subword tags give small improvements for English→German,

but not for German→English. All other features outperform the baseline in terms of perplexity, and yield significant improvements in BLEU on at least one test set. The gain from different features is not fully cumulative; we note that the information encoded in different features overlaps. For instance, both the dependency labels and the morphological features encode the distinction between German subjects and accusative objects, the former through different labels (*subj* and *obja*), the latter through grammatical case (*nominative* and *accusative*).

We also evaluated adding linguistic features to a stronger baseline, which includes synthetic parallel training data. In addition, we compare our neural systems against phrase-based (PBSMT) and syntax-based (SBSMT) systems by (Williams et al., 2016), all of which make use of linguistic annotation on the source and/or target side. Results are shown in Table 4. For German→English, we observe similar improvements in the best development perplexity (45.2 → 44.1), test set BLEU (37.5→38.5) and CHRF3 (62.2 → 62.8). Our test set BLEU is on par to the best submitted system to this year's WMT 16 shared translation task, which is similar to our baseline MT system, but which also uses a right-to-left decoder for reranking (Sennrich et al., 2016a). We expect that linguistic input features and bidirectional decoding are orthogonal, and that we could obtain further improvements by combining the two.

For English→German, improvements in development set perplexity carry over (49.7 → 48.4), but we see only small, non-significant differences in BLEU and CHRF3. While we cannot clearly account for the discrepancy between perplexity and translation metrics, factors that potentially lower the usefulness of linguistic features in this setting are the stronger baseline, trained on more data, and the low robustness of linguistic tools in the annotation of the noisy, synthetic data sets. Both our baseline neural MT systems and the systems with linguistic features substantially outperform phrase-based and syntax-based systems for both translation directions.

In the previous tables, we have reported the best perplexity. To address the question about the randomness in perplexity, and whether the best perplexity just happened to be lower for the systems with linguistic features, we show perplexity on our development set as a function of training time

---

[7]The corpora are available at `http://statmt.org/rsennrich/wmt16_backtranslations/`

system	German→English					English→German				
	ppl ↓	BLEU ↑		CHRF3 ↑		ppl ↓	BLEU ↑		CHRF3 ↑	
	dev	test15	test16	test15	test16	dev	test15	test16	test15	test16
baseline	47.3	27.9	31.4	54.0	58.0	54.9	23.0	27.8	52.6	56.0
all features	46.2	28.7*	32.9*	54.8	58.5	52.9	23.8*	28.4*	53.9	57.2

Table 2: German↔English translation results: best perplexity on dev (newstest2013), and BLEU and CHRF3 on test15 (newstest2015) and test16 (newstest2016). BLEU scores that are significantly different ($p < 0.05$) from respective baseline are marked with (*).

system	German→English					English→German				
	ppl ↓	BLEU ↑		CHRF3 ↑		ppl ↓	BLEU ↑		CHRF3 ↑	
	dev	test15	test16	test15	test16	dev	test15	test16	test15	test16
baseline	47.3	27.9	31.4	54.0	58.0	54.9	23.0	27.8	52.6	56.0
lemmas	47.1	28.4	32.3*	54.6	58.7	53.4	23.8*	28.5*	53.7	56.7
subword tags	47.3	27.7	31.5	54.0	58.1	54.7	23.6*	28.1	53.2	56.4
morph. features	47.1	28.2	32.4*	54.3	58.4	-	-	-	-	-
POS tags	46.9	28.1	32.4*	54.1	57.8	53.2	24.0*	28.9*	53.3	56.8
dependency labels	46.9	28.1	31.8*	54.2	58.3	54.0	23.4*	28.0	53.1	56.5

Table 3: Contrastive experiments with individual linguistic features: best perplexity on dev (newstest2013), and BLEU and CHRF3 on test15 (newstest2015) and test16 (newstest2016). BLEU scores that are significantly different ($p < 0.05$) from respective baseline are marked with (*).

system	German→English					English→German				
	ppl ↓	BLEU ↑		CHRF3 ↑		ppl ↓	BLEU ↑		CHRF3 ↑	
	dev	test15	test16	test15	test16	dev	test15	test16	test15	test16
PBSMT (Williams et al., 2016)	-	29.9	35.1	56.2	60.9	-	23.7	28.4	52.6	56.6
SBSMT (Williams et al., 2016)	-	29.5	34.4	56.0	61.0	-	24.5	30.6	55.3	59.9
baseline	45.2	31.5	37.5	57.0	62.2	49.7	27.5	33.1	56.3	60.5
all features	44.1	32.1*	38.5*	57.5	62.8	48.4	27.1	33.2	56.5	60.6

Table 4: German↔English translation results with additional, synthetic training data: best perplexity on dev (newstest2013), and BLEU and CHRF3 on test15 (newstest2015) and test16 (newstest2016). BLEU scores that are significantly different ($p < 0.05$) from respective baseline are marked with (*).

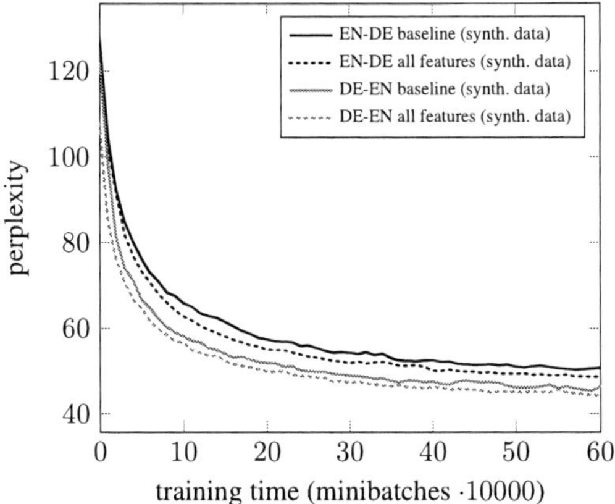

Figure 2: English→German (black) and German→English (red) development set perplexity as a function of training time (number of minibatches) with and without linguistic features.

system	ppl ↓	BLEU ↑	CHRF3 ↑
(Peter et al., 2016)	-	28.9	57.1
baseline	74.9	23.8	52.5
all features	72.7	24.8*	53.5
baseline (+synth. data)	50.9	28.2	56.1
all features (+synth. data)	50.1	29.2*	56.6

Table 5: English→Romanian translation results: best perplexity on newsdev2016, and BLEU and CHRF3 on newstest2016. BLEU scores that are significantly different ($p < 0.05$) from respective baseline are marked with (*).

for different systems (Figure 2). We can see that perplexity is consistently lower for the systems trained with linguistic features.

Table 5 shows results for a lower-resourced language pair, English→Romanian. With linguistic features, we observe improvements of 1.0 BLEU over the baseline, both for the systems trained on parallel data only (23.8→24.8), and the systems which use synthetic training data (28.2→29.2). According to BLEU, the best submission to WMT16 was a system combination by Peter et al. (2016). Our best system is competitive with this submission.

Table 6 shows translation examples of our baseline, and the system augmented with linguistic features. We see that the augmented neural MT systems, in contrast to the respective baselines, successfully resolve the reordering for the German→English example, and the disambiguation of *close* for the English→German example.

system	sentence
source	Gefährlich ist die **Route** aber dennoch.
reference	However **the route** is dangerous.
baseline	Dangerous is **the route**, however.
all features	However, **the route** is dangerous.
source	[We thought] a win like this might be **close**.
reference	[...] dass ein solcher Gewinn **nah** sein könnte.
baseline	[...] ein Sieg wie dieser könnte **schließen**.
all features	[...] ein Sieg wie dieser könnte **nah** sein.

Table 6: Translation examples illustrating the effect of adding linguistic input features.

5 Related Work

Linguistic features have been used in neural language modelling (Alexandrescu and Kirchhoff, 2006), and are also used in other tasks for which neural models have recently been employed, such as syntactic parsing (Chen and Manning, 2014). This paper addresses the question whether linguistic features on the source side are beneficial for neural machine translation. On the target side, linguistic features are harder to obtain for a generation task such as machine translation, since this would require incremental parsing of the hypotheses at test time, and this is possible future work.

Among others, our model incorporates information from a dependency annotation, but is still a sequence-to-sequence model. Eriguchi et al. (2016) propose a tree-to-sequence model whose encoder computes vector representations for each phrase in the source tree. Their focus is on exploiting the (unlabelled) structure of a syntactic annotation, whereas we are focused on the disambiguation power of the functional dependency labels.

Factored translation models are often used in phrase-based SMT (Koehn and Hoang, 2007) as a means to incorporate extra linguistic information. However, neural MT can provide a much more flexible mechanism for adding such information. Because phrase-based models cannot easily generalize to new feature combinations, the individual models either treat each feature combination as an atomic unit, resulting in data sparsity, or assume independence between features, for instance by having separate language models for words and POS tags. In contrast, we exploit the strong generalization ability of neural networks, and expect that even new feature combinations, e.g. a word that appears in a novel syntactic function, are handled gracefully.

One could consider the lemmatized representation of the input as a second source text, and perform multi-source translation (Zoph and Knight, 2016). The main technical difference is that in our approach, the encoder and attention layers are shared between features, which we deem appropriate for the types of features that we tested.

6 Conclusion

In this paper we investigate whether linguistic input features are beneficial to neural machine translation, and our empirical evidence suggests that this is the case.

We describe a generalization of the encoder in the popular attentional encoder-decoder architecture for neural machine translation that allows for the inclusion of an arbitrary number of input features. We empirically test the inclusion of various linguistic features, including lemmas, part-of-speech tags, syntactic dependency labels, and morphological features, into English↔German, and English→Romanian neural MT systems. Our experiments show that the linguistic features yield improvements over our baseline, resulting in improvements on newstest2016 of 1.5 BLEU for German→English, 0.6 BLEU for English→German, and 1.0 BLEU for English→Romanian.

In the future, we expect several developments that will shed more light on the usefulness of linguistic (or other) input features, and whether they will establish themselves as a core component of neural machine translation. On the one hand, the machine learning capability of neural architectures is likely to increase, decreasing the benefit provided by the features we tested. On the other hand, there is potential to explore the inclusion of novel features for neural MT, which might prove to be even more helpful than the ones we investigated, and the features we investigated may prove especially helpful for some translation settings, such as very low-resourced settings and/or translation settings with a highly inflected source language.

Acknowledgments

This project has received funding from the European Union's Horizon 2020 research and innovation programme under grant agreements 645452 (QT21), and 644402 (HimL).

References

Andrei Alexandrescu and Katrin Kirchhoff. 2006. Factored Neural Language Models. In *Proceedings of the Human Language Technology Conference of the NAACL, Companion Volume: Short Papers*, pages 1–4, New York City, USA. Association for Computational Linguistics.

Dzmitry Bahdanau, Kyunghyun Cho, and Yoshua Bengio. 2015. Neural Machine Translation by Jointly Learning to Align and Translate. In *Proceedings of the International Conference on Learning Representations (ICLR)*.

Danqi Chen and Christopher Manning. 2014. A Fast and Accurate Dependency Parser using Neural Networks. In *Proceedings of the 2014 Conference on Empirical Methods in Natural Language Processing (EMNLP)*, pages 740–750, Doha, Qatar. Association for Computational Linguistics.

Kyunghyun Cho, Bart van Merrienboer, Caglar Gulcehre, Dzmitry Bahdanau, Fethi Bougares, Holger Schwenk, and Yoshua Bengio. 2014. Learning Phrase Representations using RNN Encoder–Decoder for Statistical Machine Translation. In *Proceedings of the 2014 Conference on Empirical Methods in Natural Language Processing (EMNLP)*, pages 1724–1734, Doha, Qatar. Association for Computational Linguistics.

Akiko Eriguchi, Kazuma Hashimoto, and Yoshimasa Tsuruoka. 2016. Tree-to-Sequence Attentional Neural Machine Translation. *ArXiv e-prints*.

Çaglar Gülçehre, Orhan Firat, Kelvin Xu, Kyunghyun Cho, Loïc Barrault, Huei-Chi Lin, Fethi Bougares, Holger Schwenk, and Yoshua Bengio. 2015. On Using Monolingual Corpora in Neural Machine Translation. *CoRR*, abs/1503.03535.

Sébastien Jean, Orhan Firat, Kyunghyun Cho, Roland Memisevic, and Yoshua Bengio. 2015. Montreal Neural Machine Translation Systems for WMT'15 . In *Proceedings of the Tenth Workshop on Statistical Machine Translation*, pages 134–140, Lisbon, Portugal. Association for Computational Linguistics.

Philipp Koehn and Hieu Hoang. 2007. Factored Translation Models. In *Proceedings of the 2007 Joint Conference on Empirical Methods in Natural Language Processing and Computational Natural Language Learning (EMNLP-CoNLL)*, pages 868–876, Prague, Czech Republic. Association for Computational Linguistics.

Tomas Mikolov, Wen-tau Yih, and Geoffrey Zweig. 2013. Linguistic Regularities in Continuous Space Word Representations. In *HLT-NAACL*, pages 746–751. The Association for Computational Linguistics.

Guido Minnen, John A. Carroll, and Darren Pearce. 2001. Applied morphological processing of English. *Natural Language Engineering*, 7(3):207–223.

Razvan Pascanu, Tomas Mikolov, and Yoshua Bengio. 2013. On the difficulty of training recurrent neural networks. In *Proceedings of the 30th International Conference on Machine Learning, ICML 2013*, pages 1310–1318, Atlanta, USA.

Jan-Thorsten Peter, Tamer Alkhouli, Hermann Ney, Matthias Huck, Fabienne Braune, Alexander Fraser, Aleš Tamchyna, Ondřej Bojar, Barry Haddow, Rico Sennrich, Frédéric Blain, Lucia Specia, Jan Niehues, Alex Waibel, Alexandre Allauzen, Lauriane Aufrant, Franck Burlot, Elena Knyazeva, Thomas Lavergne, François Yvon, and Marcis Pinnis. 2016. The QT21/HimL Combined Machine Translation System. In *Proceedings of the First Conference on Machine Translation (WMT16)*, Berlin, Germany.

Maja Popović. 2015. chrF: character n-gram F-score for automatic MT evaluation. In *Proceedings of the Tenth Workshop on Statistical Machine Translation*, pages 392–395, Lisbon, Portugal. Association for Computational Linguistics.

Stefan Riezler and John T. Maxwell. 2005. On Some Pitfalls in Automatic Evaluation and Significance Testing for MT. In *Proceedings of the ACL Workshop on Intrinsic and Extrinsic Evaluation Measures for Machine Translation and/or Summarization*, pages 57–64, Ann Arbor, Michigan. Association for Computational Linguistics.

Helmut Schmid, Arne Fitschen, and Ulrich Heid. 2004. A German Computational Morphology Covering Derivation, Composition, and Inflection. In *Proceedings of the IVth International Conference on Language Resources and Evaluation (LREC 2004)*, pages 1263–1266.

Rico Sennrich and Beat Kunz. 2014. Zmorge: A German Morphological Lexicon Extracted from Wiktionary. In *Proceedings of the 9th International Conference on Language Resources and Evaluation (LREC 2014)*, Reykjavik, Iceland.

Rico Sennrich, Martin Volk, and Gerold Schneider. 2013. Exploiting Synergies Between Open Resources for German Dependency Parsing, POS-tagging, and Morphological Analysis. In *Proceedings of the International Conference Recent Advances in Natural Language Processing 2013*, pages 601–609, Hissar, Bulgaria.

Rico Sennrich, Barry Haddow, and Alexandra Birch. 2016a. Edinburgh Neural Machine Translation Systems for WMT 16. In *Proceedings of the First Conference on Machine Translation (WMT16)*, Berlin, Germany.

Rico Sennrich, Barry Haddow, and Alexandra Birch. 2016b. Improving Neural Machine Translation Models with Monolingual Data. In *Proceedings of the 54th Annual Meeting of the Association for Computational Linguistics (ACL 2016)*, Berlin, Germany.

Rico Sennrich, Barry Haddow, and Alexandra Birch. 2016c. Neural Machine Translation of Rare Words with Subword Units. In *Proceedings of the 54th Annual Meeting of the Association for Computational Linguistics (ACL 2016)*, Berlin, Germany.

Miloš Stanojević, Amir Kamran, Philipp Koehn, and Ondřej Bojar. 2015. Results of the WMT15 Metrics Shared Task. In *Proceedings of the Tenth Workshop on Statistical Machine Translation*, pages 256–273, Lisbon, Portugal. Association for Computational Linguistics.

Kristina Toutanova, Dan Klein, Christopher D. Manning, and Yoram Singer. 2003. Feature-Rich Part-of-Speech Tagging with a Cyclic Dependency Network. In *Proceedings of the 2003 Human Language Technology Conference of the North American Chapter of the Association for Computational Linguistics*.

Philip Williams, Rico Sennrich, Maria Nadejde, Matthias Huck, Barry Haddow, and Ondřej Bojar. 2016. Edinburgh's Statistical Machine Translation Systems for WMT16. In *Proceedings of the First Conference on Machine Translation (WMT16)*.

Matthew D. Zeiler. 2012. ADADELTA: An Adaptive Learning Rate Method. *CoRR*, abs/1212.5701.

Barret Zoph and Kevin Knight. 2016. Multi-Source Neural Translation. In *NAACL HLT 2016*.

A Framework for Discriminative Rule Selection in Hierarchical Moses

Fabienne Braune[1], Alexander Fraser[1], Hal Daumé III[2], and Aleš Tamchyna[3]

[1]Center for Information and Language Processing, University of Munich, Germany
[2]Computer Science and UMIACS, University of Maryland
[3]Charles University in Prague, Prague Czech Republic

Abstract

Training discriminative rule selection models is usually expensive because of the very large size of the hierarchical grammar. Previous approaches reduced the training costs either by (i) using models that are local to the source side of the rules or (ii) by heavily pruning out negative samples. Moreover, all previous evaluations were performed on small scale translation tasks, containing at most 250,000 sentence pairs. We propose two contributions to discriminative rule selection. First, we test previous approaches on two French-English translation tasks in domains for which only limited resources are available and show that they fail to improve translation quality. To improve on such tasks, we propose a rule selection model that is (i) global with rich label-dependent features (ii) trained with all available negative samples. Our global model yields significant improvements, up to 1 BLEU point, over previously proposed rule selection models. Second, we successfully scale rule selection models to large translation tasks but have so far failed to produce significant improvements in BLEU on these tasks.

1 Introduction

Hierarchical phrase-based machine translation (Chiang, 2005) performs non-local reordering in a formally syntax-based way. It allows flexible rule extraction and application by using a grammar without linguistic annotation. As a consequence, many hierarchical rules can be used to translate a given input segment even though only a subset of these yield a correct translation. For instance, rules r_1 to r_3 can be applied to translate the French sentence F_1 below although only r_1 yields the correct translation E.

(r_1) X $\rightarrow$ $\langle$ X_1 pratique X_2, practical X_1 X_2 $\rangle$
(r_2) X $\rightarrow$ $\langle$ X_1 pratique X_2, X_1 X_2 practice $\rangle$
(r_3) X $\rightarrow$ $\langle$ X_1 pratique X_2, X_2 X_1 process $\rangle$

F_1 Une étude de l' (intérêt)$_{X_1}$ **pratique** (de notre approche)$_{X_2}$.
  *A study on the (interest)$_{X_1}$ **practical** (of our approach)$_{X_2}$.*

E A study on the **practical** (interest)$_{X_1}$ (of our approach)$_{X_2}$.

The rule scoring heuristics defined by (Chiang, 2005) do not handle rule selection in a satisfactory way and many authors have come up with solutions. Models that use the syntactic structure of the source and target sentence have been proposed by (Marton and Resnik, 2008; Marton et al., 2012; Chiang et al., 2009; Chiang, 2010; Liu et al., 2011). These approaches exclusively take into account syntactic structure and do not model rule selection (see Section 6 for a detailed discussion). Following the work on phrase-sense disambiguation by (Carpuat and Wu, 2007), other authors improve rule selection by defining features on the structure of hierarchical rules and combining these with information about the source sentence (Chan et al., 2007; He et al., 2008; He et al., 2010; Cui et al., 2010). In these approaches, rule selection is the task of selecting the target side of a rule given its source side as well as contextual information about the source sentence. This task is modeled as a multiclass classification problem.

Because of the very large size of hierarchical grammars, the training procedure for discriminative rule selection models is typically very expensive: multiclass classification is performed over

Proceedings of the First Conference on Machine Translation, Volume 1: Research Papers, pages 92–101,
Berlin, Germany, August 11-12, 2016. ©2016 Association for Computational Linguistics

millions of classes (one for each possible target side of a hierarchical rule). To overcome this problem, previous approaches reduced the training costs by either (i) using models that are local to the source side of hierarchical rules or (ii) heavily pruning out negative samples from the training data. (Chan et al., 2007; He et al., 2008; He et al., 2010) train one (local) classifier for each source side or pattern of hierarchical rules instead of defining a (global) model over all rules. Cui et al. (2010) train global models but in addition to rule table pruning, they heavily prune out negative instances. Finally, in all previous approaches, a small amount of fixed features is used for training and prediction.

While previous approaches have been shown to work on a small[1] English-Chinese news translation task, we show (in Section 4) that on French-English tasks on domains for which only a limited amount of training data is available (which we call low resource tasks), they fail to improve over a hierarchical baseline. This failure is caused by the fact that the models proposed so far do not take advantage of all information available in the training data. Local models prevent feature sharing between rules with different source sides or patterns (see Section 2.3) while aggressive pruning removes important information from the training data (see Section 3.2). On low resource translation tasks, this loss hurts translation quality. Moreover, the small set of features used in previous work does not provide a representation of the training data that is as powerful as it could be for classification (see Section 2.2).

We improve on previous work in two ways. First, we define a global rule selection model with a rich set of feature combinations. Our global model enables feature sharing while the large amount of features we use offers a complete representation of the available training data. We train our model with all acquired training examples. The exhaustive training of a feature rich global model allows us to take full advantage of the training data. We show on two low-resource French-English translation tasks that local and pruned models often fail to improve over a hierarchical baseline while our global model with exhaustive training yields significant improvements on scientific and medical texts (see Section 4). In a second

contribution, we successfully scale rule selection models to large scale translation tasks but fail to produce significant improvements in BLEU over a hierarchical baseline on these tasks.

Because our approach needs scaling to a large amount of training examples, we need a classifier that is fast and supports online streaming. We use the high-speed classifier Vowpal Wabbit[2] (VW) which we fully integrate in the syntax component (Hoang et al., 2009) of the Moses machine translation toolkit (Koehn et al., 2007). To allow researchers to replicate our results and improve on our work, we make our implementation publicly available as part of Moses.

2 Global Rule Selection Model

The goal of rule selection is to choose the correct target side of a hierarchical rule, given a source side as well as other sources of information such as the shape of the rule or its context of application in the source sentence. The latter includes lexical features (e.g. the words surrounding the source span of an applied rule) or syntactic features (e.g. the position of an applied rule in the source parse tree). The rule selection task can be modeled as a multi-class classification problem where each target-side corresponding to a source side gets a label.

Contrary to (Chan et al., 2007; He et al., 2008; He et al., 2010), we solve the classification problem by building a single global discriminative model instead of using one maximum entropy classifier for each source side or pattern. We solve the rule selection problem through multi-class classification while (Cui et al., 2010) approximate the problem by using a binary classifier.

2.1 Model Definition

We denote SCFG rules by $X \rightarrow \langle \alpha, \gamma \rangle$, where α is a source and γ a target language string (Chiang, 2005). By $C(f, \alpha)$ we denote information of the source sentence f and the source side α. $R(\alpha, \gamma)$ represents features on hierarchical rules. Our discriminative model estimates $P(\gamma \mid \alpha, C(f, \alpha), R(\alpha, \gamma))$ and is normalized over the set G' of candidate target sides γ' for a given α. The function $GTO : \alpha \rightarrow G'$ generates, given the source side, the set G' of all corresponding target sides γ'. The estimated distribution can be written

[1]In (He et al., 2008; Cui et al., 2010), the size of the training data is about 240k parallel sentences.

[2]http://hunch.net/~vw/. Implemented by John Langford and many others.

as:

$$P(\gamma \mid \alpha, C(f, \alpha), R(\alpha, \gamma)) =$$
$$\frac{\exp(\sum_i \lambda_i h_i(\alpha, C(f, \alpha), R(\alpha, \gamma)))}{\sum_{\gamma' \in GTO(\alpha)} \exp(\sum_i \lambda_i h_i(\alpha, C(f, \alpha), R(\alpha, \gamma')))}$$

In the same fashion as for local models, our global model predicts the target side of a rule given its source side and contextual features, meaning that it still disambiguates between rules with the *same* source side using rich context information. However, because the global model trains a *single* classifier over all rules, it captures information that is shared among rules with different source sides (see Section 2.3 for more details).

2.2 Feature Templates

We now present the feature templates $R(\alpha, \gamma)$ and $C(f, \alpha)$ in the equation presented in Section 2.1. While in isolation the features composing the templates are similar to the features used in previous work (He et al., 2008; He et al., 2010; Cui et al., 2010), we create powerful representations by dividing our feature set into fixed and label-dependent features and taking the cross product of these.

We begin by presenting the features in our templates. To this aim suppose that rule r_4 has been extracted from sentence F_2. The 1-best parse tree of F_2 is given in Figure 1.

(r_4) X $\rightarrow \langle$ pratique X_1 X_2, X_2 X_1 process $\rangle$

F_2 Une étude de la **pratique** (de l'ingénérie)$_{X_1}$ (informatique)$_{X_2}$
  *A study on the **process** (of software)$_{X_1}$ (development)$_{X_2}$.*

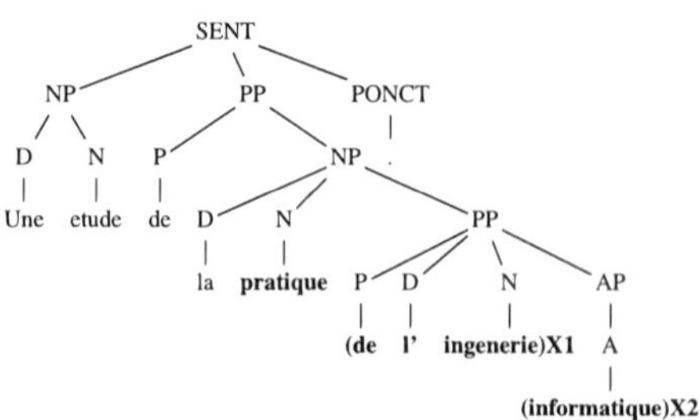

Figure 1: Parse tree of Sentence F_2

The rule internal features $R(\alpha, \gamma)$ are given in Figure 2. The source context features $C(f, \alpha)$ are divided into (i) lexical and (ii) syntactic features. Lexical features are given in Figure 3 where the term "factored form" denotes the surface form, POS tag and lemma of a word. Syntactic features are in Figure 4.

In order to create powerful representations, we combine the features above into more complex templates. To this aim, we distribute our features into two categories:

1. A set of fixed features S on the source sentence context and source side of the rule.
2. A set of features T which varies with the target side of the rule, which we call *label-dependent*.

The set S includes the lexical and syntactic features in Figures 3 and 4 as well as shape features on the source side α (2 first rows of Figure 2). The set T contains all shape features involving the target side of the rules (5 last rows of Figure 2). Our feature space consists of all source and target features S and T as well as the cross product $S \times T$.

The features resulting from the cross product $S \times T$ capture many aspects of rule selection that are lost when the features are considered in isolation. For instance, the cross product of (i) the lexical features (Figure 3) and source word shape features (Figure 2, row 2) with (ii) the target word shape features (Figure 2, row 4) create typical templates of a discriminative word lexicon. In the same fashion, the cross product of (i) the syntactic features (Figure 4) with (ii) the target alignment shape feature (Figure 2, row 6) creates the templates of a reordering model using syntactic features.

2.3 Feature Sharing

An advantage of global models over local ones is that they allow feature sharing between rules with different source sides. Through sharing, features that do not depend on the source side of rules but are nevertheless often seen across all rules can be captured. As an illustration, assume that rules r_5 and r_6 have been extracted from sentence F_3 below. The 1-best parse of F_3 is given in Figure 5.

(r_5) X $\rightarrow \langle$ modèles X_1 de bas X_2, X_1 X_2 models $\rangle$

(r_6) X $\rightarrow \langle$ modèles X_1 de X_2, X_1 X_2 models $\rangle$

F_3 Un article sur les **modèles** (statistiques)$_{X_1}$ de (bas niveau)$_{X_2}$.

94

Feature Template	Example
Source side α	*pratique_X1_X2* (one feature)
Words in α	*pratique X1 X2* (three features)
Target side γ	*X2_X1_process*
Words in γ	*X2 X1 process*
Aligned terminals in α and γ	*pratique↔process*
Aligned non-terminals in α and γ	*X1↔X2 X2↔X1* (two features)
Best baseline translation probability	*Most_Frequent*

Figure 2: Rule shape features

Feature Template	Example
first factored form left of α	*la, D, la*
second factored form left of α	*de, P, de*
first factored form right of α	*., PONCT, .*
second factored form right of α	*None, None, None*

Figure 3: Lexical features

Feature Template	Example
Does α match a constituent	*no_match*
Type of matched constituent	*None*
Parent of matched constituent	*None*
Lowest parent of unmatched constituent	*NP*
Span width covered by α	*5*

Figure 4: Syntactic features

*A paper on the **models** (statistical)$_{X_1}$ of (low-level)$_{X_2}$*

Although r_4, r_5 and r_6 have completely different source sides, they share many contextual features such as:

(i) The POS tags of the first and second words to the left of the segment where the rules are applied (which are P and D)

(ii) The syntactic structure of this segment (which is that (i) it is not a complete constituent and (ii) it has a NP as its lowest parent)

(iii) The rule span width (which is 5)

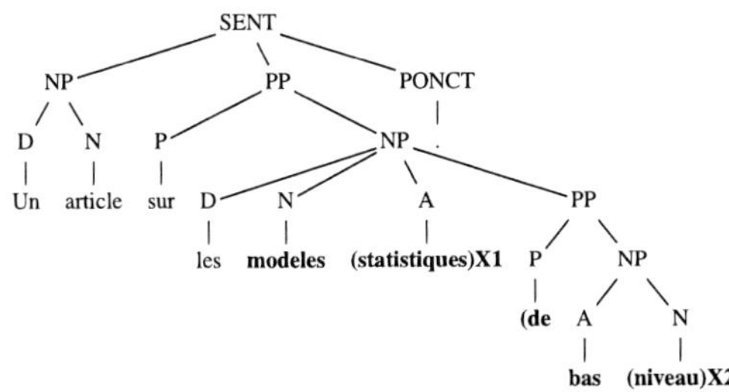

Figure 5: Parse tree of Sentence F_3

A global model would assign high weights to features (i) to (iii) while local models fail to capture this generalization.

3 Exhaustive Model Training

Training examples for our classifier are generated each time a hierarchical rule can be extracted from the parallel corpus (see Section 3.1). This procedure leads to a very large number of training examples. In contrast to (Cui et al., 2010), we do not prune out negative samples and use all available data to train our model.

3.1 Training procedure

We create training examples using the rule extraction procedure in (Chiang, 2005). We first extract a rule-table in the standard way. Then, each time a rule $a_1 : X \rightarrow \langle \alpha, \gamma \rangle$ can be extracted from the parallel corpus, we create a new training example. γ is the correct class and receives a cost of 0. We create incorrect classes using the rules $a_2, \ldots, a_n$ in the rule-table that have the same source side as a_1 but different target sides. As an example, suppose that rule r_1 introduced in Section 1 has been extracted from sentence F_1. The target side "practical X_1 X_2" is a correct class and gets a cost of 0. The target side of all other rules having the same source side, such as r_2 and r_3, are incorrect classes.

This process leads to a very large number of training examples, and for each of these we generally have multiple incorrect classes. The total number of training examples for our French-English data sets are displayed in Table 1. We do

Data	Science	Medical	News
Sentences	139,215	111,165	1,572,099
Examples	47,952,867	25,435,958	583,165,140
cost 0	50,718,190	26,458,411	597,575,905
cost 1	493,271,397	170,064,556	8,805,099,861
avg 1	10.28	6.68	15.09

Table 1: Number of training examples (Examp.) The last line shows the average amount of negative samples (avg 1) for each training example.

not prune out negative instances and use all acquired examples for model training. To scale to this amount of training samples, we use the high-speed classifier Vowpal Wabbit (VW). For model training, we use the cost-sensitive one-against-all-reduction (Beygelzimer et al., 2005) of VW. Specifically, the training algorithm which we use is the label dependent version of Cost Sensitive One Against All which uses classification.[3] Two features of VW which are useful for our work are feature hashing and quadratic feature expansion. The quadratic expansion allows us to take the cross-product of the simple source and target features without having to actually write this expansion to disk, which would be prohibitive. Feature hashing (Weinberger et al., 2009) is also important for scaling the classifier to the enormous number of features created by the cross-product expansion.

We avoid overfitting to training data by employing early stopping once classifier accuracy decreases on a held-out dataset.[4] Our model is integrated in the hierarchical framework as an additional feature of the log-linear model.

3.2 Training without Pruning of Negative Examples

By not pruning negative samples, we keep important information for model training. As an illustration, consider the example presented above (Section 3.1) where rule r_1 is a positive instance and r_2 and r_3 are negative samples. The negative instances indicate that in the context of sentence F_1, the internal features of r_2 and r_3 are not correct. For instance, a piece of information that could be paraphrased into I is lost.

I In the syntactic and lexical context of F_1 the terminal *pratique* should neither be translated into *practice* nor into *process*

Consider sentence F_4, which has a similar context to F_1 in terms of the lexical and syntactic features described in Section 2.2. To illustrate the syntactic features common to F_1 and F_4, we give the 1-best parse trees of these sentences in Figures 6 and 7.

F_4 Les avantages de l' (aspect)$_{X_1}$ **pratique** (de la robotique)$_{X_2}$.
*The advantages of the (aspect)$_{X_1}$ **practical** (of robotics)$_{X_2}$.*

In pruning-based approaches, if r_2 and r_3 appear infrequently in the training data, they are pruned out and information I is lost. If at decoding time candidate rules that share features with r_2 and r_3 are bad candidates to translate F_1 and F_4 then their application is not blocked by the discriminative model basing on I. For instance, if rules r_7 and r_8 have high scores in the hierarchical model but are bad candidates in the context of sentences F_1 and F_4 then a pruned model fails to block their application. In other words, the discriminative model does not learn that rules containing the lexical items *practice* and *process* on the target language side are bad candidates to translate F_1 and F_4. As a consequence, the application of r_7 and r_8 to F_4 generates the erroneous translations E_1^* and E_2^* below.

(r_7) X $\rightarrow$ $\langle$ X_1 pratique X_2, X_2 X_1 practice $\rangle$
(r_8) X $\rightarrow$ $\langle$ X_1 pratique X_2, X_1 X_2 process $\rangle$

E_1^* The advantages of the of robotics aspects practice
E_2^* The advantages of the aspects of robotics process

4 Experiments on small domains

In a first set of experiments, we evaluate our approach on two low resource French-English trans-

---

[3]The command line parameter to VW is "csoaa_ldf mc".

[4]We use the development set which is also used for tuning with MIRA, as we will discuss later in the paper.

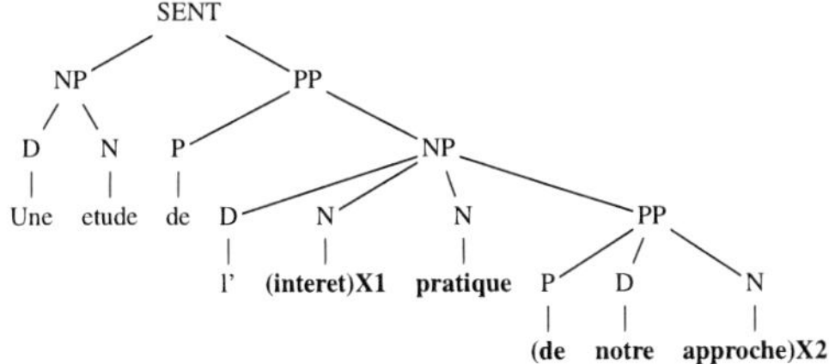

Figure 6: Parse tree of Sentence F_1

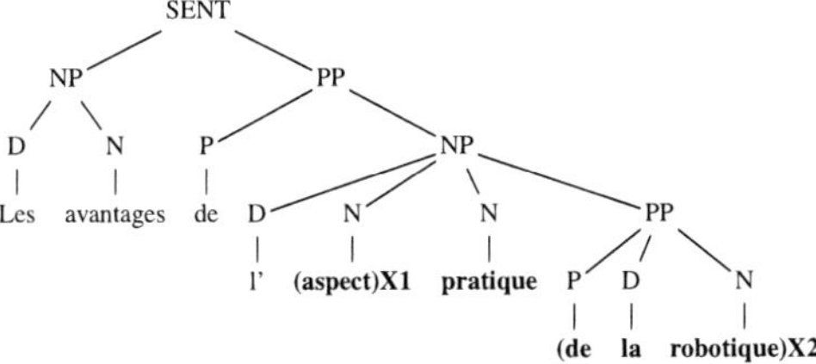

Figure 7: Parse tree of Sentence F_4

lation tasks: (i) a set of scientific articles and (ii) a set of biomedical texts. As these data sets cover small domains, they allow us to investigate the usefulness of our approach in this context. The goal of our experiments is to verify three hypotheses:

h_1 *Our approach beats a hierarchical baseline.*

h_2 *Our global model outperforms its local variants.*

h_3 *Our exhaustive training procedure beats systems trained with pruned data.*

4.1 Experimental Setup

Our scientific data consists of the scientific abstracts provided by Carpuat et al. (2013). The training data contains 139,215 French and English parallel sentences. The development and test sets both consist of 3916 parallel sentences. For the medical domain, we use the biomedical data from EMEA (Tiedemann, 2009). As training data, we used 472,231 sentence pairs from EMEA. We removed duplicate sentences and constructed development and test data by randomly selecting 4000 sentence-pairs. After removal of duplicate sentences, development and test data, we obtain 111,165 parallel sentences for training. For all data sets, we trained a 5-gram language model using the SRI Language Modeling Toolkit (Stolcke, 2002). The training data for the language model is the English side of the training corpus for each task.

We train the model in the standard way, using GIZA++. After training, we reduce the number of translation rules using significance testing (Johnson et al., 2007). For feature extraction, we parse the French part of our training data using the Berkeley parser (Petrov et al., 2006) and lemmatize and POS tag it using Morfette (Chrupała et al., 2008). We train the rule-selection model using VW. All systems are tuned using batch MIRA (Cherry and Foster, 2012). We measure the overall translation quality using 4-gram BLEU (Papineni et al., 2002), which is computed on tokenized and lowercased data for all systems. Statistical significance is computed with the pairwise bootstrap resampling technique of (Koehn, 2004).

4.2 Compared Systems

We investigate systems including a discriminative model in the three setups, given in Figure 4.2. For each setup, we train a global model using a single classifier. For instance, for the setup (Lex-Glob) we train a classifier with the lexical and rule shape features presented in Section 2.2 together with their cross product.

Description	Name
Rule shape and lexical features	LexGLob
Rule shape and syntactic features	SyntGlob
Rule shape, lexical and syntactic features	LexSyntGlob

Figure 8: Setups of evaluated discriminative models.

In order to verify our first hypothesis (h_1), we show that our approach yields significant improvements over the hierarchical model in (Chiang, 2005). The results of this experiment are given in Table 2.

To verify our second hypothesis (h_2), we show that global rule selection models significantly improve over their local variants. For this second evaluation, we train local models with the feature templates in Figure 4.2. Local models with rule shape and lexical features are used in (He et al., 2008). We further test the performance of local rule selection models by also including syntactic features and a combination of those with the lexical features. We report the results in Table 3 where the local systems are denoted by *LexLoc*, *SyntLoc* and *LexSyntLoc*.

For our third hypothesis (h_3), we show that pruning hurts translation quality. To this aim, we take our best performing global model, which uses syntactic and rule shape features and perform heavy pruning of negative examples in the data used for classifier training. To exactly reproduce the context-based target model in (Cui et al., 2010), we pruned as many negative examples as necessary to obtain approximately the same amount of positive and negative examples they report. We removed negative instances created from rules with target side frequency < 5000. In the next section, we denote this system by *SyntPrun* and compare it to the hierarchical baseline as well as to our global model in Table 4.

4.3 Results

The outcome of our experiments confirm hypotheses h_1 and h_3 on all data sets and h_2 on medical data only.

The results of our first evaluation (Table 2) show that on all data sets our global rule selection model outperforms the hierarchical baseline (h_1).

The results of our second evaluation (i.e. local vs. global models in Table 3) show that h_2 holds on the medical domain only. On scientific data, global rule selection models in all setups perform slightly better than their local versions but the difference is not statistically significant. Note that all rule selection models except *LexLoc* outperform the hierarchical baseline. The best performing system is a global model with syntactic features (*SyntGlob*). On medical texts, global models outperform their local variants for all feature templates. In each setup, the improvement of local models over the global ones is statistically significant. *SyntGlob* achieves the best performance and yields significant improvements over the baseline. The good performance of *SyntGlob* on scientific and especially medical data can be explained by the fact that syntactic features are less sparse than lexical features and hence generalize better. This is especially important within a global model that allows feature sharing between source sides of rules. Even a combination of lexical and syntactic features underperforms syntactic features on their own because of the sparse lexical features.

The results of our third evaluation are displayed in Table 4. These show that on all data sets our global model without pruning outperforms the same model with pruned training data (h_3). These results also show that the pruned model fails to outperform the hierarchical baseline. Note that this result is consistent with the results reported

System	Science	Medical
Hierarchical	31.22	48.67
LexGlob	**31.69**	48.94
LexSyntGlob	**31.89**	48.97
SyntGlob	**32.27**	**49.66**

Table 2: Evaluation of global models against hierarchical baseline. The results in bold are statistically significant improvements over the Baseline (at confidence $p < 0.05$).

System	Science	Medical
Hierarchical	31.22	48.67
LexLoc	31.50	48.43
LexSyntLoc	**31.74**	48.51
SyntLoc	**31.85**	48.76
LexGlob	**31.69**	48.94*
LexSyntGlob	**31.89**	48.97*
SyntGlob	**32.27**	**49.66***

Table 3: Evaluation of global models against local. We use * to mark global systems that yield statistically significant (at confidence $p < 0.05$) improvements over their local variants. The results in bold are statistically significant improvements over the hierarchical baseline.

in (Cui et al., 2010): their Context-based target model yields very low improvements when used in isolation.

5 Large scale Experiments

In a second set of experiments, we evaluate the usefulness of our approach on two large scale translation tasks: (i) a French-to-English news translation task trained on 1,500,000 parallel sentences and (ii) an English-to-Romanian news translation task trained on 600,000 parallel sentences. The training data for the first task consists of the French-English part of the Europarl-v4 corpus. Development and test sets are from the French-to-English news translation task of WMT 2009 (Callison-Burch et al., 2009). For the second task, we use the English-Romanian part of the Europarl-v8 corpus. Development and test sets are from the English-to-Romanian news translation task of WMT 2016. The setup of these experiments is the same as described in Section 4.1 except for the language model of the English-to-Romanian task, which was trained using lmplz

System	Science	Medical
Hierarchical	31.22	48.67
SyntGlob	**32.27**	**49.66**
SyntPrun	31.00	48.61

Table 4: Evaluation of global model against pruned. The results in bold are statistically significant improvements over the Baseline (at confidence $p < 0.05$).

System	Fr-En News	En-Ro News
Hierarchical	20.96	24.16
LexGlob	21.01	24.23
LexSyntGlob	21.04	24.19
SyntGlob	21.14	24.52

Table 5: Evaluation of large scale tasks. No significant difference in performance between the evaluated models.

(Heafield et al., 2013) on the Romanian part of the Common Crawl corpus.

Our goal is to verify if on large scale translation tasks our global rule selection model outperforms a hierarchical baseline (hypothesis h_1 above). The results, given in Table 5, show that on large scale tasks, rule selection models with syntactic features yield small improvements over the hierarchical baseline. However, none of these is statistically significant. Hence hypothesis h_1 does not hold on large domains.

6 Related Work

(Marton and Resnik, 2008; Marton et al., 2012) improve hierarchical machine translation by augmenting the translation model with fine-grained syntactic features of the source sentence. The used features reward rules that match syntactic constituents and punish non-matching rules. (Chiang et al., 2009) integrate these features into a translation model containing a large number of other features such as discount or insertion features. (Chiang, 2010) extends the approach in (Marton and Resnik, 2008) by also including syntactic information of the target sentence that is built during decoding while (Liu et al., 2011) define a discriminative model over source side constituent labels instead of rewarding matching constituents. The training data for their model is based on source

sentence derivations.[5] In contrast to this work, we define a rule selection model, i.e. a discriminative model on the target side of hierarchical rules. The training data for our model is based on the hierarchical rule extraction procedure: we acquire training instances by labeling candidate rules extracted from the same sentence pairs.

Similar to our work, (He et al., 2008) define a discriminative rule selection model including lexical features, similar to the ones we presented in Section 2.2. Their work bases on (Chan et al., 2007) which integrate a word sense disambiguation system into a hierarchical system. As opposed to (He et al., 2008), this work focuses on hierarchical rules containing only terminal symbols and having length 2. These approaches train rule selection models that are local to the source side of hierarchical rules. (He et al., 2010) generalize this work by defining a model that is local to source patterns instead of the source side of each rule. We extend these approaches by defining a global model that generalizes to all rules instead of rules with the same source side or source pattern. We also extend the feature set by defining models on syntactic features.

(Cui et al., 2010) propose a joint rule selection model over the source and target side of hierarchical rules. Our work is similar to their Context Based Target Model (CBTM) but it integrates much more information by not reducing the rule selection problem to a binary classification problem and by not pruning the set of negative examples. We show empirically that the exhaustive training of our model significantly improves over their CBTM.

Finally, several authors train local rule selection models for different types of syntax- and semantics- based systems. (Liu et al., 2008) train a local discriminative rule selection model for tree-to-string machine translation. (Zhai et al., 2013) propose a discriminative model to disambiguate predicate argument structures (PAS). In contrast, our rule selection model uses syntactic features on hierarchical rules and is a global model.

All[6] of the mentioned models are trained using the maximum entropy approach (Berger et al., 1996) which seems not to scale well as reported in

---

[5]The training instances are obtained by performing bilingual parsing on the training data and extracting the obtained rules from the derivation forest.

[6]All of the models except (Chan et al., 2007) which uses an SVM, which is also not efficient.

(Cui et al., 2010). By using a high-speed streaming classifier we are able to train a global model doing true multi-class classification without pruning of training examples.

7 Conclusion and Future Work

We have presented two contributions to previous work on rule selection. First, we improved translation quality on low resource translation tasks by defining a global discriminative rule selection model trained on all available training examples. In a second contribution, we successfully scaled our global rule selection model to large scale translation tasks and presented the first evaluation of discriminative rule selection on such tasks. However, we failed so far to produce significant improvements in BLEU over a hierarchical baseline on large scale French-to-English and English-to-Romanian translation tasks. To allow researchers to replicate our results and improve on our work, we make our implementation publicly available as part of Moses.

Acknowledgements

We thank all members of the DAMT team of the 2012 JHU Summer Workshop. This work was partially supported by Deutsche Forschungsgemeinschaft grant Models of Morphosyntax for Statistical Machine Translation (Phase 2). This work has received funding from the European Union's Horizon 2020 research and innovation programme under grant agreement No. 644402 (HimL) and from the European Research Council (ERC) under grant agreement No. 640550.

References

Adam L. Berger, Stephen A. Della Pietra, and Vincent J. Della Pietra. 1996. A maximum entropy approach to natural language processing. *Computational Linguistics*, 22(1):39–72, March.

Alina Beygelzimer, John Langford, and Bianca Zadrozny. 2005. Weighted one-against-all. In *AAAI*, pages 720–725.

Chris Callison-Burch, Philipp Koehn, Christof Monz, and Josh Schroeder. 2009. Findings of the 2009 Workshop on Statistical Machine Translation. In *Proc. 4th Workshop on Statistical Machine Translation*, pages 1–28.

Marine Carpuat and Dekai Wu. 2007. Improving statistical machine translation using word sense disambiguation. In *In The 2007 Joint Conference on Empirical Methods in Natural Language Processing and Computational Natural Language Learning (EMNLP-CoNLL 2007*, pages 61–72.

Marine Carpuat, Hal Daumé III, Katharine Henry, Ann Irvine, Jagadeesh Jagarlamudi, and Rachel Rudinger. 2013. SenseSpotting: Never let your parallel data tie you to an old domain. In *Proc. ACL*.

Yee Seng Chan, Hwee Tou Ng, and David Chiang. 2007. Word sense disambiguation improves statistical machine translation. In *Proceedings of the 45th Annual Meeting of the Association of Computational Linguistics*, pages 33–40, Prague, Czech Republic, June. Association for Computational Linguistics.

Colin Cherry and George Foster. 2012. Batch tuning strategies for statistical machine translation. In *NAACL 2012*.

David Chiang, Kevin Knight, and Wei Wang. 2009. 11,001 new features for statistical machine translation. In *Proc. NAACL*.

David Chiang. 2005. Hierarchical phrase-based translation. In *Proceedings of the 43th Annual Meeting of the Association of Computational Linguistics*, page 263270. Association for Computational Linguistics.

David Chiang. 2010. Learning to translate with source and target syntax. In *Proceedings of the 48th Annual Meeting of the Association of Computational Linguistics*, pages 1443–1452. The Association for Computer Linguistics.

Grzegorz Chrupała, Georgiana Dinu, and Josef Van Genabith. 2008. Learning morphology with morfette. In *LREC 2008*.

Lei Cui, Dongdong Zhang, Mu Li, Ming Zhou, and Tiejun Zhao. 2010. A joint rule selection model for hierarchical phrase-based translation. In *Proceedings of the ACL 2010 Conference*, pages 6–11. Association for Computational Linguistics.

Zhongjun He, Qun Liu, and Shouxun Lin. 2008. Improving statistical machine translation using lexicalized rule selection. In *COLING*, pages 321–328.

Zhongjun He, Yao Meng, and Hao Yu. 2010. Maximum entropy based phrase reordering for hierarchical phrase-based translation. In *Proceedings of the 2010 Conference on Empirical Methods in Natural Language Processing*, EMNLP '10.

Kenneth Heafield, Ivan Pouzyrevsky, Jonathan H. Clark, and Philipp Koehn. 2013. Scalable modified Kneser-Ney language model estimation. In *Proc. ACL*.

Hieu Hoang, Philipp Koehn, and Adam Lopez. 2009. A unified framework for phrase-based, hierarchical, and syntax-based statistical machine translation. In *In Proceedings of the International Workshop on Spoken Language Translation (IWSLT*, pages 152–159.

Howard Johnson, Joel Martin, George Foster, and Roland Kuhn. 2007. Improving Translation Quality by Discarding Most of the Phrasetable. In *Proc. of EMNLP-CoNLL 2007*.

Philipp Koehn, Hieu Hoang, Alexandra Birch, Chris Callison-Burch, Marcello Federico, Nicola Bertoldi, Brooke Cowan, Wade Shen, Christine Moran, Richard Zens, Chris Dyer, Ondřej Bojar, Alexandra Constantin, and Evan Herbst. 2007. Moses: Open Source Toolkit for Statistical Machine Translation. In *Proc. of ACL: Demo and Poster Sessions*, pages 177–180, Prague, Czech Republic, June. ACL.

Philipp Koehn. 2004. Statistical significance tests for machine translation evaluation. In *Proc. EMNLP*, pages 388–395.

Qun Liu, Zhongjun He, Yang Liu, and Shouxun Lin. 2008. Maximum entropy based rule selection model for syntax-based statistical machine translation. In *Proceedings of the Conference on Empirical Methods in Natural Language Processing*, EMNLP '08, pages 89–97. Association for Computational Linguistics.

Lemao Liu, Tiejun Zhao, Chao Wang, and Hailong Cao. 2011. A unified and discriminative soft syntactic constraint model for hierarchical phrase-based translation. In *Proceedings of the 13th Machine Translation Summit*, pages 253–261.

Yuval Marton and Philip Resnik. 2008. Soft syntactic constraints for hierarchical phrased-based translation. In *Proceedings of the 46th Annual Meeting of the Association of Computational Linguistics*, pages 1003–1011.

Yuval Marton, David Chiang, and Philip Resnik. 2012. Soft syntactic constraints for arabic—english hierarchical phrase-based translation. *Machine Translation*, 26(1-2):137–157, March.

Kishore Papineni, Salim Roukos, Todd Ward, and Wei jing Zhu. 2002. BLEU: a method for automatic evaluation of machine translation. In *Proc. 40th ACL*, pages 311–318.

Slav Petrov, Leon Barrett, Romain Thibaux, and Dan Klein. 2006. Learning accurate, compact, and interpretable tree annotation. In *Proceedings of the 21st International Conference on Computational Linguistics and the 44th Annual Meeting of the Association for Computational Linguistics*, pages 433–440. Association for Computational Linguistics.

Andreas Stolcke. 2002. Srilm - an extensible language modeling toolkit. In *Proceedings of the International Conference on Spoken language Processing*, pages 901–904.

Jörg Tiedemann. 2009. News from opus : A collection of multilingual parallel corpora with tools and interfaces. In *Recent Advances in Natural Language Processing V*, volume V, pages 237–248. John Benjamins.

Kilian Weinberger, Anirban Dasgupta, John Langford, Alex Smola, and Josh Attenberg. 2009. Feature hashing for large scale multitask learning. In *Proceedings of the 26th Annual International Conference on Machine Learning (ICML)*.

Feifei Zhai, Jiajun Zhang, Yu Zhou, and Chengqing Zong. 2013. Handling ambiguities of bilingual predicate-argument structures for statistical machine translation. In *Proceedings of the 51st Annual Meeting of the Association for Computational Linguistics*, pages 1127–1136, Sofia, Bulgaria, August. Association for Computational Linguistics.

Fast and highly parallelizable phrase table for statistical machine translation

Nikolay Bogoychev
The University of Edinburgh
11 Crichton St, Edinburgh EH8 9LE
United Kingdom
n.bogoych@ed.ac.uk

Hieu Hoang
Moses Machine Translation CIC
hieu@moses-mt.org

Abstract

Speed of access is a very important property for phrase tables in phrase based statistical machine translation as they are queried many times per sentence. In this paper we present a new standalone phrase table, optimized for query speed and memory locality. The phrase table is cache free and can optionally incorporate a reordering table within. We are able to achieve two times faster decoding by using our phrase table in the Moses decoder in place of the current state-of-the-art phrase table solution without sacrificing translation quality. Using a new, experimental version of Moses we are able to achieve 10 times faster decoding using our novel phrase table.

1 Introduction

Phrase tables are the most basic component of a statistical machine translation decoder, containing the parallel phrases necessary to perform phrase-based machine translation. Due to the noisy nature of phrase extraction and the large phrase vocabulary, phrase tables' size can reach hundreds of gigabytes in size. Lopez (2008) describes phrase tables of size of half of terabyte. A decade ago it was prohibitively expensive for a phrase table of this size to reside in memory, even if hardware supported it: a gigabyte of RAM back in 2006 costed about a 100 USD, compared to 5 USD in 2016. Because of that for a long time Machine Translation was considered a big data problem and the engineering efforts were focused on reducing the model size. This lead to the creation of several binary phrase table implementations that tackled the memory usage problem: Zens and Ney (2007) and Junczys-Dowmunt (2012b) developed memory mapped phrase tables which also reduce memory usage using specific datastructures. The former uses a trie (Fredkin, 1960) and the latter uses specific for the purpose phrasal rank encoding. Lopez (2007) and Germann (2015) developed suffix array based phrase tables, which work directly with the parallel corpora in order to enable easier addition of new data, avoid long binarization times and keep memory usage low, but traditional precomputed phrase tables offer better performance. RAM prices have dropped 20 times over the past 10 years and high performance server machines have hundreds of gigabytes of memory. For those machines it is no longer needed to sacrifice query performance in favour of compression techniques such as the one in Junczys-Dowmunt (2012a). Furthermore the machines nowadays are highly parallel and locking caches which didn't hurt performance in the past now prevent implementations from scaling. We have designed a new phrase table called **ProbingPT** based on linear probing hash (Heafield, 2011) for storage and lock-free querying, in order to deliver the best possible performance in modern use cases where memory is not an issue.

2 Implementation

First, we will give a brief overview of Junczys-Dowmunt's (2012b) CompactPT which is currently the state of the art phrase table in terms of both speed and space usage. It uses phrasal rank compression (Junczys-Dowmunt, 2012a) which can be viewed as a form of byte pair encoding (Gage, 1994). The method recursively encodes bigger strings as a composition of several smaller ones until only small units remain. Minimum perfect hashing (Nick Cercone, 1983) is used to hash phrases to their expansions and on top of that bit aligned Huffman encoding is used to fur-

Proceedings of the First Conference on Machine Translation, Volume 1: Research Papers, pages 102–109,
Berlin, Germany, August 11-12, 2016. ©2016 Association for Computational Linguistics

ther compress the phrases. This approach achieves the smallest model size but it has several drawbacks when it comes to lookup. First, minimum perfect hashing requires a secondary hash function called fingerprinting in order to avoid false positives which results in increased CPU usage. Second, while phrasal rank encoding is extremely space efficient, it is quite slow to compute, because of the multitude of random memory accesses necessary to reconstruct a single phrase. The reason is that when a request to read a portion of memory is submitted what is actually fetched is not only the bytes that were requested but also the surrounding bytes. This is because usually when one byte of memory is accessed, the surrounding bytes would also be necessary so memory has been designed to fetch things in small burst, called DRAM bursts. As such peak memory performance can only be achieved by accessing consecutive memory and random memory accesses reduce the total memory bandwidth, because some of fetched bytes are not used.

In order to speed up querying in CompactPT, extensive caching is used but it is not thread local and causes a lot of locking for higher thread count. In our experiments we found that more than 8 threads actually hurt CompactPT's performance. The phrase table also has a mode which disables phrasal rank encoding and caching. In this mode performance at higher thread count doesn't decrease but instead flattens out, however it is unable to achieve better performance than the phrase rank encoding version no matter the thread count.[1] Even if caches don't cause lock contention at higher thread count, they carry additional overhead during runtime. Our goal in design was to eliminate the necessity for cache by using high performance datastructures and eliminate random memory accesses to maximize the memory bandwidth.

2.1 ProbingPT

Our phrase table is based on an existing linear probing hash table implementation (Heafield, 2011). Linear probing hash provides $O(1)$ search time, has a very small overhead per entry stored and is shown to be very fast in practice (Heafield, 2011). The phrase table consists of two byte arrays: The first contains the probing hash table and the second one contains the payloads (phrase probabilities, word alignments and optionally lexically reordering scores) associated with each entry in the hash table. Hashes of the source phrases are used as keys. When the phrase table is queried, the source phrase is hashed and we try to find it in the probing hash table. If it is found inside the hash table we are given a start and end index corresponding to the location of the target phrases associated with the source phrase queried inside the payloads byte array. The payloads byte array stores consecutively in binary format each target phrase together with its scores and word alignment information. We have also provided the option to store lexical reordering information and sparse features. Unlike previous phrase tables implementations, this phrase table doesn't employ any compression method which allows for all target phrases associated with a single source phrase to be fetched in a single memory operation. In contrast, both Junczys-Dowmunt's (2012b) and Zens and Ney (2007) employ pointer chasing during querying in order to extract and reassemble the results. Their approaches are more space-efficient but incur higher memory cost due to increased number of random memory accesses. Furthermore our implementation doesn't require any scratch memory to decompress queries: they can be read directly from the payloads byte array which contributes to its speed and avoids extra memory operations (allocations/deallocations) or the need for caching. Storing lexical reordering information inside the phrase table reduces the memory usage, because we no longer need to store a key for every lexical reordering score, as we reuse the phrase table key. Extracting lexical reordering scores no longer carries an extra performance penalty as querying is tied to the phrase table query and all related scores would be fetched with the same DRAM burst, because they are stored consecutively in memory. To our knowledge, this is the first phrase table implementation that incorporates lexical reordering table.

The phrase table is part of upstream Moses[2] but it can also be used standalone.[3]

3 Experimental setup

For our performance evaluation we used French-English model trained on 2 million EUROPARL sentences. We used a KenLM (Heafield, 2011)

---

language model and cube pruning algorithm (Chiang, 2007) with a pop-limit of 400. We time the end to end translation of 200,000 sentences from the training set. All experiments were performed on a machine with two Xeon E5-2680 processors clocked at 2.7 Ghz with total of 16 cores and 16 hyperthreads and 290 GB of RAM. In all of our figures "32 cores" means 16 cores and 16 hyperthreads. Note that hyperthread do not provide additional computational power but merely permit better resource utilization by allowing more work to be scheduled for the CPU by the OS. This allows the CPU to already have scheduled work to do while a scheduled process is waiting for IO. Using hyperthreads will not necessarily increase performance and in cases with high lock contention it can be detrimental for performance.

3.1 Decoders

We use two different decoders for our experiments: The widely used moses machine translation decoder, available publically and *Moses2*, an experimental faster version of Moses.[4] We perform some benchmarks using Moses to show the speedup our implementation offers as a drop-in replacement to existing phrase tables in the widely used decoder. Unfortunately Moses has known multi-threading issues that come from the usage of several functions which call **std::locale** as part of their initiations, which carries a global lock.[1] As such it is not entirely adequate to use it to measure the performance of the phrase tables because it serves as a bottleneck that might hide performance issues. Thus we used the highly optimized *Moses2* to show the speed our phrase table can achieve when it is running on a fast decoder, optimized for multi-threading. Furthermore because of their intrusive nature, integrated lexical reordering tables are only implemented in *Moses2*. It is expected that when *Moses2* matures it will be merged back into Moses master.

3.2 PhraseTables

In our experiments we focus on comparing ProbingPT against CompactPT. There are currently two other phrase tables: PhraseDictionaryOnDisk, a multithreading enabled implementation of the Zens and Ney (2007) phrase table and PhraseDictionaryMemory, an in-memory phrase table which reads in the raw phrase table and puts it

inside a hash map. Junczys-Dowmunt (2012b) has shown that CompactPT is faster than PhraseDictionaryOnDisk under any condition, so we do not run experiments against it. PhraseDictionaryMemory comes with the downside that it needs to parse in the phrase table first, before decoding can commence, which leads to long loading times and huge memory usage. In our experimental setup, the in-memory phrase table took 20 minutes to load and consumed 86 GBs of memory, more than ten times more memory than any other phrase table. Even when disregarding loading time, we found out that it is consistently 1-5% slower than ProbingPT in various thread configurations. We decided not to include those results, as they do not show anything interesting and because of the aforementioned shortcomings, PhraseDictionaryMemory is seldom used in practice, unless the dataset involved is really tiny.

ProbingPT and CompactPT produced identical translations under the same decoder. In our tests 3 out of 200,000 sentences slightly differ in their translation. This is expected according to Junczys-Dowmunt (2012b) because CompactPT's fingerprinting leads to collisions and extracting the wrong phrase in few rare cases. We conclude that our implementation is correct and can be used as drop-in replacement for CompactPT. We have provided the complete set of conducted experiments on Figure 5 in the appendix. Those are useful if the reader wishes to compare system/user time usage between different configurations.

3.3 Model sizes

Phrase table	Size
ProbingPT	5.8 GB
ProbingPT + Reordering (RO)	8.2 GB
CompactPT	1.3 GB
CompactPT RO	0.6 GB

Table 1: Phrase table sizes

CompactPT which is designed to minimize model size has naturally lower model size compared to ProbingPT. However the extra RAM used is only 2% of the available on our test system which is insignificant. Using the extra memory is justified by the increased performance.

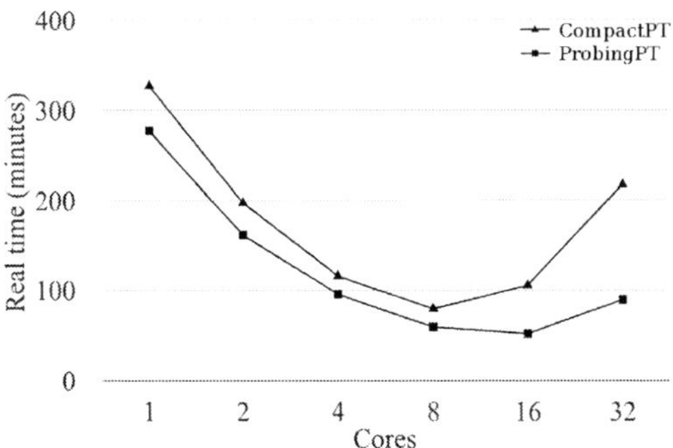

Figure 1: Real time comparison of Moses between ProbingPT and CompactPT together with reordering models based on CompactPT.

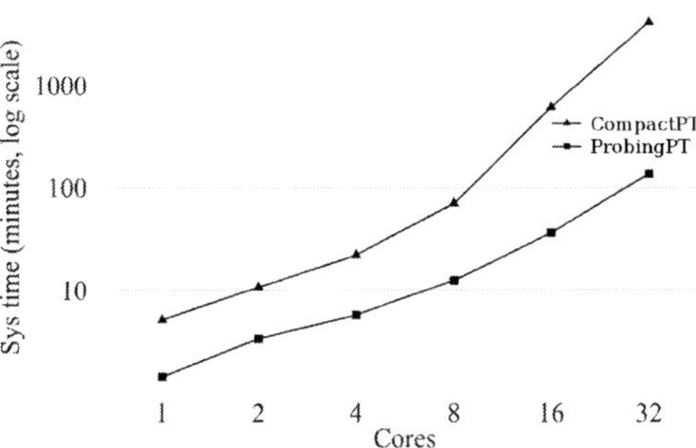

Figure 3: System time comparison of the systems on Figure 2. The comparison is in log scale.

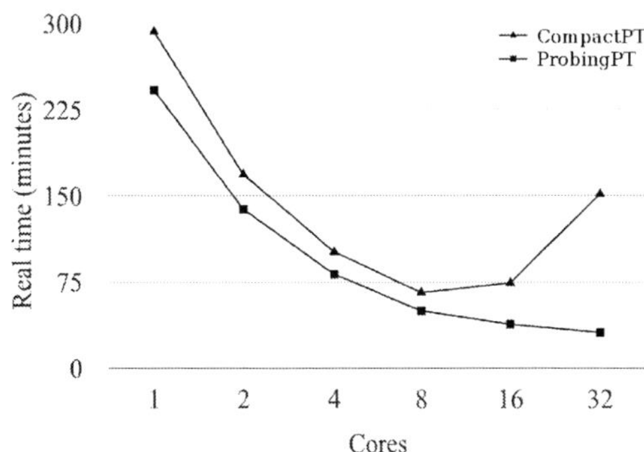

Figure 2: Real time comparison of Moses between ProbingPT and CompactPT

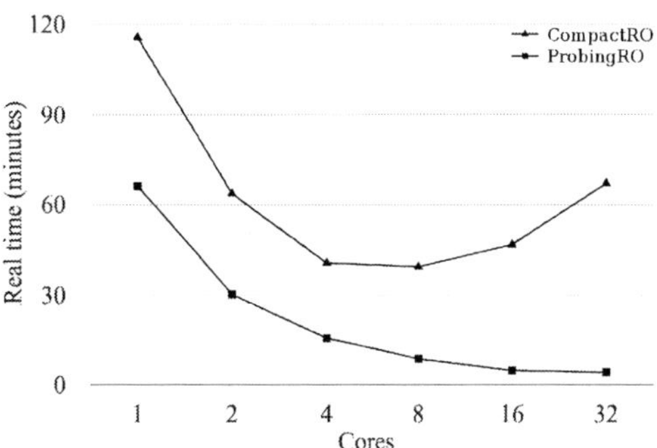

Figure 4: *Moses2* comparison between ProbingPT integrated reordering and CompactPT based reordering. Both systems use ProbingPT as a phrase table.

4 Evaluation

Figure 1 shows performance comparison of two systems with CompactPT based reordering tables that differ in the phrase table used. The best performing ProbingPT system here delivers about 30% better performance compared to the corresponding CompactPT system. We see that the CompactPT system doesn't improve its performance when using more than 8 threads, but the ProbingPT one continues to scale further until it starts using hyperthreads.

We find it likely that the performance of the ProbingPT system on Figure 1 is hampered by the inclusion of CompactPT based reordering. Moses doesn't support ProbingPT based reordering and in order to measure the head-to-head performance of the two phrase tables we conducted the same test using two systems that do not use reordering tables and only differ by the phrase table, as shown on Figure 2. We can see that ProbingPT

consistently outperforms CompactPT by 10-20% at lower thread count but the difference grows as much as 5 times in favour of ProbingPT at the maximum available thread count on the system. If we compare the best performance achieved from both system, ProbingPT is capable of delivering twice the performance of CompactPT. It is important to note that ProbingPT's performance always increases with the increase of the thread count, whereas CompactPT's performance doesn't improve past 8 threads. We can also see that the ProbingPT based system can even take advantage of hyperthreads, which is not possible with any system that uses CompactPT based table (Figure 1). On Table 2 we can observe that removing the reordering table from the CompactPT system has a much smaller effect than removing it from the ProbingPT system. This hints that lexicalized reordering only slows down the decoder because it is implemented in a inefficient manner. We can conclude that Moses can achieve faster translation times on highly parallel systems by using ProbingPT.

4.1 Why is CompactPT slower?

In the single-threaded case it likely that CompactPT's many random memory accesses cause it to be slower than ProbingPT, because consecutive memory accesses are much faster due to the DRAM burst effect. When the thread count grows, the performance gap between CompactPT and ProbingPT widens, because of the locking that goes on in the former's cache. This can be seen from Figure 3 which shows the system time used during the execution of the phrase table only test. System time shows how much time a process has spent inside kernel routines, which includes but is not limited to locking and memory allocation. The ProbingPT system uses orders of magnitude less system time compared to the CompactPT one. The system time used in the CompactPT system grows linearly until 8 threads and then the growth rate starts increasing at a faster rate widening the gap with ProbingPT. This is also the reason why CompactPT's performance severely degrades when using hyperthreads. The ProbingPT system on the other hand (Figure 3) increases its usage of system time at a linear rate even when using hyperthreads. We can conclude that the simpler design of ProbingPT scales very well with the increase of number of threads and is suitable for use in modern translation systems running on contemporary hardware.

4.2 Integrated reordering table

As integrated lexical reordering is only available in *Moses2* we conducted an experiment where we compare systems using CompactPT based reordering and ProbingPT integrated reordering (Figure 4). The best ProbingPT based system is able to translate all sentences in our test set in only 4 minutes, whereas the best CompactPT reordering system took 39 minutes (Table 3). We also observed limited scaling when using CompactPT based reordering: the best performance was achieved at 8 threads. For contrast with Moses (Table 2) we can see that lexicalized reordering has negligeble impact on performance if it is used within ProbingPT (We believe the reason we are getting slightly worse results when not using a reordering table are due to a bug in our implementation). We are not entirely certain which factor contributed

more to the increased performance: having a reordering table based on the faster ProbingPT or the reduced IO and computational resources that the integrated reordering table requires. As we do not currently have a standalone ProbingPT based reordering table we can not say for sure. Nevertheless we achieve 10x speedup by using our novel reordering table within *Moses2*.

4.3 Profiling the code

We were very surprised of the speedup our phrase table offered, particularly in *Moses2*, because in phrase based decoding, the number of phrase table queries increases linearly with the length of the sentence. They constitute a tiny fraction of the number of language model queries, which are about 1 million per sentence (Heafield, 2013). We decided to investigate our results using Google's profiler.[5] We profiled the pair of systems, displayed on Figure 4, because they showed the highest relative difference between each other. In the system which has ProbingPT based reordering, the language model is responsible for about 40% of the decoding runtime, compared with only 1% in the *Moses2* system with CompactPT based reordering. In the latter system the runtime is dominated by CompactPT search and **std::locale** locking due to the phrase table using string operations during its search.

In Moses the difference between using ProbingPT and CompactPT is not so apparent, before we go to higher thread count, because the decoder itself is very slow and hides the phrase table inefficiencies. It is clear that even though the phrase table queries are a small part of the full decoding process, they are enough to slow it down 10 times if no other bottlenecks exist. Using ProbingPT for both the phrase table and the reordering model makes for a compelling combination.

5 Future work

In the future we will add support for hierarchical phrase tables inside ProbingPT. In hierarchical machine translation the burden on the phrase table is a lot higher so the improved performance would be even more noticeable. Given the difference between the systems with and without ProbingPT based reordering in Table 3 we believe that adding that feature to Moses will allow us to get performance similar to that in the final column of

---

[5] https://github.com/gperftools/gperftools

Cores	CompactPT, RO	CompactPT, NoRO	ProbingPT, RO	ProbingPT, NoRO
1	327	300	277	242
2	197	167	161	138
4	116	101	96	82
8	80	66	60	50
16	106	74	52	39
32	218	151	90	31

Table 2: Time (in minutes) it took to translate our test set with Moses with different number of cores used. The systems differ by the type of phrase table used (ProbingPT or CompactPT) and whether they use a reordering table (based on CompactPT). The fastest translation time for each system is highligthed.

Cores	CompactRO	ProbingRO	NoRO
1	116	66	72
2	64	30	35
4	40	15	18
8	39	9	10
16	46	5	6
32	67	4	5

Table 3: Time (in minutes) it took to translate our test set with *Moses2* with different number of cores used. Since the only phrase table that is used is ProbingPT, the systems differ by the reordering table used. The fastest translation time for each system is highligthed.

Table 2, while maintaining the quality of the more complex model described in the first column of the same table.

6   Conclusion

As hardware evolves extremely fast, it may prove useful to revisit old problems which are considered solved. The new available technology compels us to reconsider our priorities and decisions we took in the past.

We designed a faster phrase table that is able to take full advantage of the modern highly parallel CPUs. It shows better performance than related work and also scales better with higher thread count and it helped us expose performance issues in Moses. We believe ProbingPT is useful to industry and researchers who use modern server machines with many cores and a lot of main memory. Enthusiast machine translation users would probably prefer to use CompactPT as it is most suitable when memory is limited and the thread count is low.

Acknowledgements

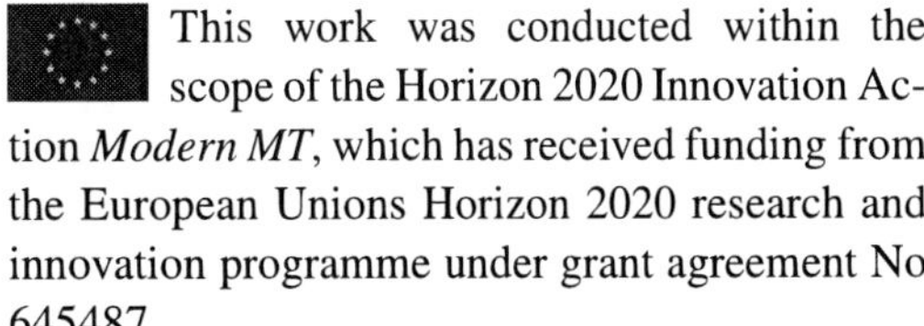 This work was conducted within the scope of the Horizon 2020 Innovation Action *Modern MT*, which has received funding from the European Unions Horizon 2020 research and innovation programme under grant agreement No 645487.

This work is sponsored by the Air Force Research Laboratory, prime contract FA8650-11-C-6160. The views and conclusions contained in this document are those of the authors and should not be interpreted as representative of the official policies, either expressed or implied, of the Air Force Research Laboratory or the U.S. Government.

We thank Adam Lopez, Kenneth Heafield, Ulrich Germann, Rico Sennrich, Marcin Junczys-Dowmunt, Nathan Schneider, Sorcha Gilroy, Clara Vania and the anonymous reviewers for productive discussion of this work and helpful comments on previous drafts of the paper. Any errors are our own.

References

David Chiang. 2007. Hierarchical phrase-based translation. *Comput. Linguist.*, 33(2):201–228, June.

Edward Fredkin. 1960. Trie memory. *Commun. ACM*, 3(9):490–499, sep.

Philip Gage. 1994. A new algorithm for data compression. *C Users J.*, 12(2):23–38, February.

Ulrich Germann. 2015. Sampling phrase tables for the moses statistical machine translation system. *Prague Bull. Math. Linguistics*, 104:39–50.

Kenneth Heafield. 2011. KenLM: faster and smaller language model queries. In *Proceedings of the EMNLP 2011 Sixth Workshop on Statistical Machine Translation*, pages 187–197, Edinburgh, Scotland, United Kingdom, July.

Kenneth Heafield. 2013. *Efficient Language Modeling Algorithms with Applications to Statistical Machine Translation*. Ph.D. thesis, Carnegie Mellon University, September.

Marcin Junczys-Dowmunt. 2012a. Phrasal rank-encoding: Exploiting phrase redundancy and translational relations for phrase table compression. *Prague Bull. Math. Linguistics*, 98:63–74.

Marcin Junczys-Dowmunt. 2012b. A space-efficient phrase table implementation using minimal perfect hash functions. In *Text, Speech and Dialogue - 15th International Conference, TSD 2012, Brno, Czech Republic, September 3-7, 2012. Proceedings*, pages 320–327.

Adam Lopez. 2007. Hierarchical phrase-based translation with suffix arrays. In *Proceedings of the 2007 Joint Conference on Empirical Methods in Natural Language Processing and Computational Natural Language Learning (EMNLP-CoNLL)*, pages 976–985, Prague, Czech Republic, June. Association for Computational Linguistics.

Adam Lopez, 2008. *Tera-Scale Translation Models via Pattern Matching*, pages 505–512. Coling 2008 Organizing Committee, 8.

John Boates Nick Cercone, Max Krause. 1983. Minimal and almost minimal perfect hash function search with application to natural language lexicon design. *CAMWA*, 9(1):215–231.

Richard Zens and Hermann Ney. 2007. Efficient phrase-table representation for machine translation with applications to online mt and speech translation. In *Human Language Technology Conf. / North American Chapter of the Assoc. for Computational Linguistics Annual Meeting*, pages 492–499, Rochester, NY, April.

A Experiments Matrix

Cores/Variant		Moses1 + compactpt + compactreord	moses1 + compactpt + no reord	moses1 + probing + compactreord	moses1 + probing + no reord	moses2 + probing + compactreord	moses2 + probing + integratedRO	moses2 + probing + no reord
	real	327m3.554s	292m44.73s	277m10.41s	241m51.16s	115m35.32s	66m2.933s	72m28.06s
	user	318m46.127s	287m36.13s	273m16.02s	240m23.27s	112m26.00s	63m18.006s	71m27.24s
1	sys	8m6.706s	5m6.16s	3m48.58s	1m26.12s	3m10.58s	2m33.317s	1m3.68s
	real	197m18.17s	168m36.05s	161m24.43s	138m8.04s	63m33.20s	30m9.780s	35m18.24s
	user	374m27.39s	325m28.96s	314m7.35s	272m17.22s	120m21.88s	59m27.849s	69m53.43s
2	sys	17m28.34s	10m43.95s	7m52.60s	3m21.41s	6m36.93s	0m48.234s	0m38.95s
	real	116m1.57s	101m4.74s	95m55.83s	81m43.00s	40m34.79s	15m24.667s	18m30.99s
	user	423m32.44s	378m36.98s	366m26.63s	319m20.53s	150m12.16s	61m5.165s	73m22.10s
4	sys	36m47.68s	22m9.95s	14m48.15s	5m42.96s	11m50.91s	0m25.914s	0m32.56s
	real	79m56.00s	66m0.99s	59m41.43s	50m14.49s	39m19.77s	8m35.280s	10m17.52s
	user	501m11.52s	449m3.61s	433m34.24s	383m49.20s	288m40.73s	67m57.790s	81m25.37s
8	sys	127m49.32s	70m31.53s	36m35.65s	12m32.91s	25m20.14s	0m26.249s	0m32.35s
	real	105m37.01s	74m10.77s	52m15.47s	38m25.06s	46m43.13s	4m42.100s	5m57.21s
	user	600m33.02s	562m59.64s	612m47.32s	557m28.61s	681m40.37s	74m3.060s	93m42.05s
16	sys	1072m12.89s	607m53.22s	205m19.05s	36m28.92s	64m17.28s	0m30.157s	0m42.36s
	real	217m58.10s	151m22.90s	89m46.79s	31m25.80s	66m54.80s	4m7.794s	5m12.37s
	user	779m59.18s	709m57.34s	668m15.93s	752m32.02s	233m23.18s	129m38.242s	163m29.34s
16 + 16 hyper	sys	6175m37.16s	4115m3.50s	2188m54.82s	135m58.88s	1903m43.26s	0m57.126s	1m21.11s

Figure 5: A matrix of all experiments conducted.

A Comparative Study on Vocabulary Reduction for Phrase Table Smoothing

Yunsu Kim, Andreas Guta, Joern Wuebker*, and **Hermann Ney**
Human Language Technology and Pattern Recognition Group
RWTH Aachen University, Aachen, Germany
{surname}@cs.rwth-aachen.de
*Lilt, Inc.
joern@lilt.com

Abstract

This work systematically analyzes the smoothing effect of vocabulary reduction for phrase translation models. We extensively compare various word-level vocabularies to show that the performance of smoothing is not significantly affected by the choice of vocabulary. This result provides empirical evidence that the standard phrase translation model is extremely sparse. Our experiments also reveal that vocabulary reduction is more effective for smoothing large-scale phrase tables.

1 Introduction

Phrase-based systems for statistical machine translation (SMT) (Zens et al., 2002; Koehn et al., 2003) have shown state-of-the-art performance over the last decade. However, due to the huge size of phrase vocabulary, it is difficult to collect robust statistics for lots of phrase pairs. The standard phrase translation model thus tends to be sparse (Koehn, 2010).

A fundamental solution to a sparsity problem in natural language processing is to reduce the vocabulary size. By mapping words onto a smaller label space, the models can be trained to have denser distributions (Brown et al., 1992; Miller et al., 2004; Koo et al., 2008). Examples of such labels are part-of-speech (POS) tags or lemmas.

In this work, we investigate the vocabulary reduction for phrase translation models with respect to various vocabulary choice. We evaluate two types of smoothing models for phrase translation probability using different kinds of word-level labels. In particular, we use automatically generated word classes (Brown et al., 1992) to obtain

label vocabularies with arbitrary sizes and structures. Our experiments reveal that the vocabulary of the smoothing model has no significant effect on the end-to-end translation quality. For example, a randomized label space also leads to a decent improvement of BLEU or TER scores by the presented smoothing models.

We also test vocabulary reduction in translation scenarios of different scales, showing that the smoothing works better with more parallel corpora.

2 Related Work

Koehn and Hoang (2007) propose integrating a label vocabulary as a factor into the phrase-based SMT pipeline, which consists of the following three steps: mapping from words to labels, label-to-label translation, and generation of words from labels. Rishøj and Søgaard (2011) verify the effectiveness of word classes as factors. Assuming probabilistic mappings between words and labels, the factorization implies a combinatorial expansion of the phrase table with regard to different vocabularies.

Wuebker et al. (2013) show a simplified case of the factored translation by adopting hard assignment from words to labels. In the end, they train the existing translation, language, and reordering models on word classes to build the corresponding smoothing models.

Other types of features are also trained on word-level labels, e.g. hierarchical reordering features (Cherry, 2013), an n-gram-based translation model (Durrani et al., 2014), and sparse word pair features (Haddow et al., 2015). The first and the third are trained with a large-scale discriminative training algorithm.

For all usages of word-level labels in SMT,

Proceedings of the First Conference on Machine Translation, Volume 1: Research Papers, pages 110–117,
Berlin, Germany, August 11-12, 2016. ©2016 Association for Computational Linguistics

a common and important question is which label vocabulary maximizes the translation quality. Bisazza and Monz (2014) compare class-based language models with diverse kinds of labels in terms of their performance in translation into morphologically rich languages. To the best of our knowledge, there is no published work on systematic comparison between different label vocabularies, model forms, and training data size for smoothing phrase translation models—the most basic component in state-of-the-art SMT systems. Our work fulfills these needs with extensive translation experiments (Section 5) and quantitative analysis (Section 6) in a standard phrase-based SMT framework.

3 Word Classes

In this work, we mainly use unsupervised word classes by Brown et al. (1992) as the reduced vocabulary. This section briefly reviews the principle and properties of word classes.

A word-class mapping c is estimated by a clustering algorithm that maximizes the following objective (Brown et al., 1992):

$$\mathcal{L} := \sum_{e_1^I} \sum_{i=1}^{I} p(c(e_i)|c(e_{i-1})) \cdot p(e_i|c(e_i)) \quad (1)$$

for a given monolingual corpus $\{e_1^I\}$, where each e_1^I is a sentence of length I in the corpus. The objective guides c to prefer certain collocations of class sequences, e.g. an auxiliary verb class should succeed a class of pronouns or person names. Consequently, the resulting c groups words according to their syntactic or semantic similarity.

Word classes have a big advantage for our comparative study: The structure and size of the class vocabulary can be arbitrarily adjusted by the clustering parameters. This makes it possible to prepare easily an abundant set of label vocabularies that differ in linguistic coherence and degree of generalization.

4 Smoothing Models

In the standard phrase translation model, the translation probability for each segmented phrase pair $(\tilde{f}, \tilde{e})$ is estimated by relative frequencies:

$$p_{\text{std}}(\tilde{f}|\tilde{e}) = \frac{N(\tilde{f}, \tilde{e})}{N(\tilde{e})} \quad (2)$$

where N is the count of a phrase or a phrase pair in the training data. These counts are very low for many phrases due to a limited amount of bilingual training data.

Using a smaller vocabulary, we can aggregate the low counts and make the distribution smoother. We now define two types of smoothing models for Equation 2 using a general word-label mapping c.

4.1 Mapping All Words at Once (map-all)

For the phrase translation model, the simplest formulation of vocabulary reduction is obtained by replacing all words in the source and target phrases with the corresponding labels in a smaller space. Namely, we employ the following probability instead of Equation 2:

$$p_{\text{all}}(\tilde{f}|\tilde{e}) = \frac{N(c(\tilde{f}), c(\tilde{e}))}{N(c(\tilde{e}))} \quad (3)$$

which we call *map-all*. This model resembles the word class translation model of Wuebker et al. (2013) except that we allow any kind of word-level labels.

This model generalizes all words of a phrase without distinction between them. Also, the same formulation is applied to word-based lexicon models.

4.2 Mapping Each Word at a Time (map-each)

More elaborate smoothing can be achieved by generalizing only a sub-part of the phrase pair. The idea is to replace one source word at a time with its respective label. For each source position j, we also replace the target words aligned to the source word f_j. For this purpose, we let $a_j \subseteq \{1, ..., |\tilde{e}|\}$ denote a set of target positions aligned to j. The resulting model takes a weighted average of the redefined translation probabilities over all source positions of $\tilde{f}$:

$$p_{\text{each}}(\tilde{f}|\tilde{e}) = \sum_{j=1}^{|\tilde{f}|} w_j \cdot \frac{N(c^{(j)}(\tilde{f}), c^{(a_j)}(\tilde{e}))}{N(c^{(a_j)}(\tilde{e}))} \quad (4)$$

where the superscripts of c indicate the positions that are mapped onto the label space. w_j is a weight for each source position, where $\sum_j w_j = 1$. We call this model *map-each*.

We illustrate this model with a pair of three-word phrases: $\tilde{f} = [f_1, f_2, f_3]$ and $\tilde{e} = [e_1, e_2, e_3]$ (see Figure 1 for the in-phrase word alignments). The map-each model score for this phrase pair is:

$$
\begin{array}{cccc}
e_1 & \cdot & \cdot & \blacksquare \\
e_2 & \cdot & \cdot & \blacksquare \\
e_3 & \blacksquare & \cdot & \cdot \\
& f_1 & f_2 & f_3
\end{array}
$$

Figure 1: Word alignments of a pair of three-word phrases.

$$
p_{\text{each}}(\,[f_1, f_2, f_3] \mid [e_1, e_2, e_3]\,) =
$$

$$
w_1 \cdot \frac{N([c(f_1), f_2, f_3], [c(e_1), e_2, e_3])}{N([c(e_1), e_2, e_3])}
$$

$$
+\, w_2 \cdot \frac{N([f_1, c(f_2), f_3], [e_1, e_2, e_3])}{N([e_1, e_2, e_3])}
$$

$$
+\, w_3 \cdot \frac{N([f_1, f_2, c(f_3)], [e_1, c(e_2), c(e_3)])}{N([e_1, c(e_2), c(e_3)])}
$$

where the alignments are depicted by line segments.

First of all, we replace f_1 and also e_1, which is aligned to f_1, with their corresponding labels. As f_2 has no alignment points, we do not replace any target word accordingly. f_3 triggers the class replacement of two target words at the same time. Note that the model implicitly encapsulates the alignment information.

We empirically found that the map-each model performs best with the following weight:

$$
w_j = \frac{N(c^{(j)}(\tilde{f}), c^{(a_j)}(\tilde{e}))}{\displaystyle\sum_{j'=1}^{|\tilde{f}|} N(c^{(j')}(\tilde{f}), c^{(a_{j'})}(\tilde{e}))} \tag{5}
$$

which is a normalized count of the generalized phrase pair itself. Here, the count is relatively large when f_j, the word to be backed off, is less frequent than other words in $\tilde{f}$. In contrast, if f_j is a very frequent word and one of the other words in $\tilde{f}$ is rare, the count becomes low due to that rare word. The same logic holds for target words in $\tilde{e}$. After all, Equation 5 carries more weight when a rare word is replaced with its label. The intuition is that a rare word is the main reason for unstable counts and should be backed off above all. We use this weight for all experiments in the next section.

In contrast, the map-all model merely replace all words at one time and ignore alignments within phrase pairs.

5 Experiments

5.1 Setup

We evaluate how much the translation quality is improved by the smoothing models in Section 4. The two smoothing models are trained in both source-to-target and target-to-source directions, and integrated as additional features in the log-linear combination of a standard phrase-based SMT system (Koehn et al., 2003). We also test linear interpolation between the standard and smoothing models, but the results are generally worse than log-linear interpolation. Note that vocabulary reduction models by themselves cannot replace the corresponding standard models, since this leads to a considerable drop in translation quality (Wuebker et al., 2013).

Our baseline systems include phrase translation models in both directions, word-based lexicon models in both directions, word/phrase penalties, a distortion penalty, a hierarchical lexicalized reordering model (Galley and Manning, 2008), a 4-gram language model, and a 7-gram word class language model (Wuebker et al., 2013). The model weights are trained with minimum error rate training (Och, 2003). All experiments are conducted with an open source phrase-based SMT toolkit Jane 2 (Wuebker et al., 2012).

To validate our experimental results, we measure the statistical significance using the paired bootstrap resampling method of Koehn (2004). Every result in this section is marked with ‡ if it is statistically significantly better than the baseline with 95% confidence, or with † for 90% confidence.

5.2 Comparison of Vocabularies

The presented smoothing models are dependent on the label vocabulary, which is defined by the word-label mapping c. Here, we train the models with various label vocabularies and compare their smoothing performance.

The experiments are done on the IWSLT 2012 German→English shared translation task. To rapidly perform repetitive experiments, we train the translation models with the in-domain TED portion of the dataset (roughly 2.5M running words for each side). We run the monolingual word clustering algorithm of (Botros et al., 2015) on each side of the parallel training data to obtain class label vocabularies (Section 3).

We carry out comparative experiments regarding the three factors of the clustering algorithm:

1) **Clustering iterations.** It is shown that the number of iterations is the most influential factor in clustering quality (Och, 1995). We now verify its effect on translation quality when the clustering is used for phrase table smoothing.

As we run the clustering algorithm, we extract an intermediate class mapping for each iteration and train the smoothing models with it. The model weights are tuned for each iteration separately. The BLEU scores of the tuned systems are given in Figure 2. We use 100 classes on both source and target sides.

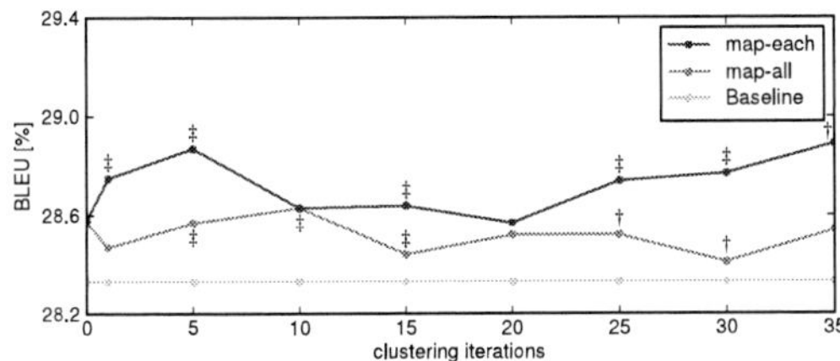

Figure 2: BLEU scores for clustering iterations when using individually tuned model weights for each iteration. Dots indicate those iterations in which the translation is performed.

The score does not consistently increase or decrease over the iterations; it is rather on a similar level ($\pm\,0.2\%$ BLEU) for all settings with slight fluctuations. This is an important clue that the whole process of word clustering has no meaning in smoothing phrase translation models.

To see this more clearly, we keep the model weights fixed over different systems and run the same set of experiments. In this way, we focus only on the change of label vocabulary, removing the impact of nondeterministic model weight optimization. The results are given in Figure 3.

This time, the curves are even flatter, resulting in only $\pm\,0.1\%$ BLEU difference over the iterations. More surprisingly, the models trained with the initial clustering, i.e. when the clustering algorithm has not even started yet, are on a par with those trained with more optimized classes in terms of translation quality.

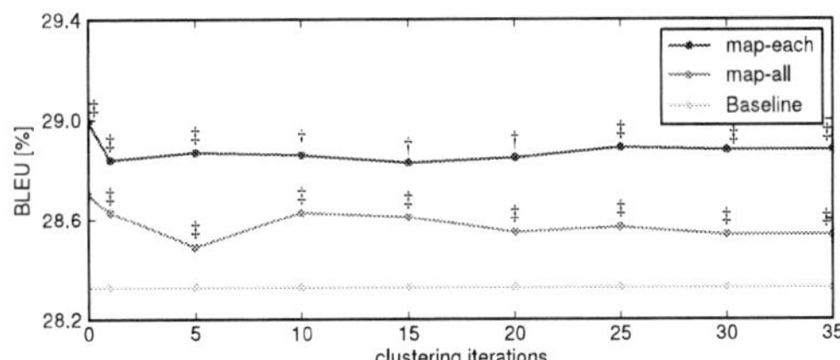

Figure 3: BLEU scores for clustering iterations when using a fixed set of model weights. The weights that produce the best results in Figure 2 are chosen.

2) **Initialization of the clustering.** Since the clustering process has no significant impact on the translation quality, we hypothesize that the initialization may dominate the clustering. We compare five different initial class mappings:

- random: randomly assign words to classes
- top-frequent (default): top-frequent words have their own classes, while all other words are in the last class
- same-countsum: each class has almost the same sum of word unigram counts
- same-#words: each class has almost the same number of words
- count-bins: each class represents a bin of the total count range

	Initialization	BLEU [%]	TER [%]
Baseline		28.3	52.2
+ map-each	random	28.9[‡]	51.7[‡]
	top-frequent	29.0[‡]	51.5[‡]
	same-countsum	28.8[‡]	51.7[‡]
	same-#words	28.9[‡]	51.6[‡]
	count-bins	29.0[‡]	51.4[‡]

Table 1: Translation results for various initializations of the clustering. 100 classes on both sides.

Table 1 shows the translation results with the map-each model trained with these initializations—without running the clustering algorithm. We use the same set of model weights used in Figure 3. We find that the initialization method also does not affect the translation performance. As an extreme case, random clustering is also a fine candidate for training the map-each model.

3) Number of classes. This determines the vocabulary size of a label space, which eventually adjusts the smoothing degree. Table 2 shows the translation performance of the map-each model with a varying number of classes. Similarly as before, there is no serious performance gap among different word classes, and POS tags and lemmas also comform to this trend.

However, we observe a slight but steady degradation of translation quality ($\approx$ -0.2% BLEU) when the vocabulary size is larger than a few hundreds. We also lose statistical significance for BLEU in these cases. The reason could be: If the label space becomes larger, it gets closer to the original vocabulary and therefore the smoothing model provides less additional information to add to the standard phrase translation model.

	#vocab (source)	BLEU [%]	TER [%]
Baseline		28.3	52.2
+ map-each	100	29.0‡	51.5‡
(word class)	200	28.9†	51.6‡
	500	28.7	51.8‡
	1000	28.7	51.8‡
	10000	28.7	51.9†
+ map-each (POS)	52	28.9†	51.5‡
+ map-each (lemma)	26744	28.8	51.7‡

Table 2: Translation results for different vocabulary sizes.

The series of experiments show that the map-each model performs very similar across vocabulary size and its structure. From our internal experiments, this argument also holds for the map-all model. The results do not change even when we use a different clustering algorithm, e.g. bilingual clustering (Och, 1999). For the translation performance, the more important factor is the log-linear model training to find an optimal set of weights for the smoothing models.

5.3 Comparison of Smoothing Models

Next, we compare the two smoothing models by their performance in four different trans-

lation tasks: IWSLT 2012 German→English, WMT 2015 Finnish→English, WMT 2014 English→German, and WMT 2015 English→Czech. We train 100 classes on each side with 30 clustering iterations starting from the default (top-frequent) initialization.

Table 3 provides the corpus statistics of all datasets used. Note that a morphologically rich language is on the source side for the first two tasks, and on the target side for the last two tasks. According to the results (Table 4), the map-each model, which encourages backing off infrequent words, performs consistently better (maximum +0.5% BLEU, -0.6% TER) than the map-all model in all cases.

5.4 Comparison of Training Data Size

Lastly, we analyze the smoothing performance for different training data sizes (Figure 4). The improvement of BLEU score over the baseline decreases drastically when the training data get smaller. We argue that this is because the smoothing models are only the additional scores for the phrases seen in the training data. For smaller training data, we have more out-of-vocabulary (OOV) words in the test set, which cannot be handled by the presented models.

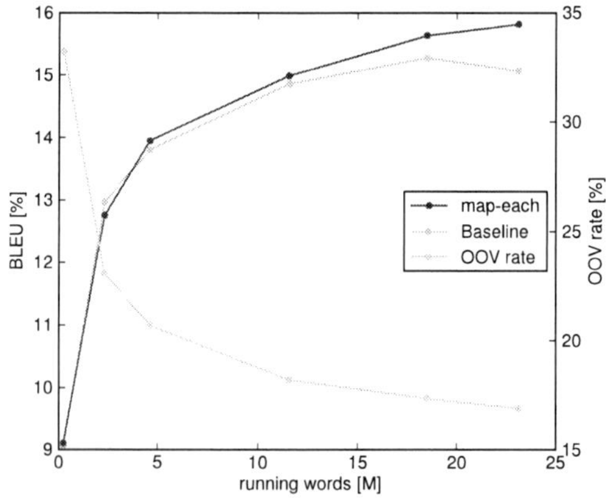

Figure 4: BLEU scores and OOV rates for the varying training data portion of WMT 2015 Finnish→English data.

6 Analysis

In Section 5.2, we have shown experimentally that more optimized or more fine-grained classes do not guarantee better smoothing performance. We now verify by examining translation outputs that

	IWSLT 2012		WMT 2015		WMT 2014		WMT 2015	
	German	English	Finnish	English	English	German	English	Czech
Sentences	130k		1.1M		4M		0.9M	
Running Words	2.5M	2.5M	23M	32M	104M	105M	23.9M	21M
Vocabulary	71k	49k	509k	88k	648k	659k	161k	345k

Table 3: Bilingual training data statistics for IWSLT 2012 German→English, WMT 2015 Finnish→English, WMT 2014 English→German, and WMT 2015 English→Czech tasks.

	de-en		fi-en		en-de		en-cs	
	BLEU [%]	TER [%]	BLEU [%]	TER [%]	BLEU [%]	TER [%]	BLEU [%]	TER [%]
Baseline	28.3	52.2	15.1	72.6	14.6	69.8	15.3	68.7
+ map-all	28.6‡	51.6‡	15.3‡	72.5	14.8‡	69.4‡	15.4‡	68.2‡
+ map-each	**29.0‡**	**51.4‡**	**15.8‡**	**72.0‡**	**15.1‡**	**69.0‡**	**15.8‡**	**67.6‡**

Table 4: Translation results for IWSLT 2012 German→English, WMT 2015 Finnish→English, WMT 2014 English→German, and WMT 2015 English→Czech tasks.

			Top 200 TER-improved Sentences	
Model	Classes	#vocab	Common Input [%]	Same Translation [%]
map-each	optimized	100	-	-
	non-optimized	100	89.5	89.9
	random	100	88.5	89.8
	lemma	26744	87.0	92.6
map-all	optimized	100	56.0	54.5

Table 5: Comparison of translation outputs for the smoothing models with different vocabularies. "optimized" denotes 30 iterations of the clustering algorithm, whereas "non-optimized" means the initial (default) clustering.

the same level of performance is not by chance but due to similar hypothesis scoring across different systems.

Given a test set, we compare its translations generated from different systems as follows. First, for each translated set, we sort the sentences by how much the sentence-level TER is improved over the baseline translation. Then, we select the top 200 sentences from this sorted list, which represent the main contribution to the decrease of TER. In Table 5, we compare the top 200 TER-improved translations of the map-each model setups with different vocabularies.

In the fourth column, we trace the input sentences that are translated by the top 200 lists, and count how many of those inputs are overlapped across given systems. Here, a large overlap indicates that two systems are particularly effective in a large common part of the test set, showing that they behaved analogously in the search process. The numbers in this column are computed against the map-each model setup trained with 100 optimized word classes (first row). For all map-each settings, the overlap is very large—around 90%.

To investigate further, we count how often the two translations of a single input are identical (the last column). This is normalized by the number of common input sentences in the top 200 lists between two systems. It is a straightforward measure to see if two systems discriminate translation hypotheses in a similar manner. Remarkably, all systems equipped with the map-each model produce exactly the same translations for the most part of the top 200 TER-improved sentences.

We can see from this analysis that, even though a smoothing model is trained with essentially different vocabularies, it helps the translation process in basically the same manner. For comparison, we also compute the measures for a map-all model, which are far behind the high similarity among the map-each models. Indeed, for smoothing phrase translation models, changing the model structure for vocabulary reduction exerts a strong influence in the hypothesis scoring, yet changing the vocabulary does not.

7 Conclusion

Reducing vocabulary using word-label mapping is a simple and effective way of smoothing phrase translation models. By mapping each word in a phrase at a time, the translation quality can be improved by up to +0.7% BLEU and -0.8% TER over a standard phrase-based SMT baseline, which is superior to Wuebker et al. (2013).

Our extensive comparison among various vocabularies shows that different word-label mappings are almost equally effective for smoothing phrase translation models. This allows us to use any type of word-level label, e.g. a randomized vocabulary, for the smoothing, which saves a considerable amount of effort in optimizing the structure and granularity of the label vocabulary. Our analysis on sentence-level TER demonstrates that the same level of performance stems from the analogous hypothesis scoring.

We claim that this result emphasizes the fundamental sparsity of the standard phrase translation model. Too many target phrase candidates are originally undervalued, so giving them any reasonable amount of extra probability mass, e.g. by smoothing with random classes, is enough to broaden the search space and improve translation quality. Even if we change a single parameter in estimating the label space, it does not have a significant effect on scoring hypotheses, where many other models than the smoothed translation model, e.g. language models, are involved with large weights. Nevertheless, an exact linguistic explanation is still to be discovered.

Our results on varying training data show that vocabulary reduction is more suitable for large-scale translation setups. This implies that OOV handling is more crucial than smoothing phrase translation models for low-resource translation tasks.

For future work, we plan to perform a similar set of comparative experiments on neural machine translation systems.

Acknowledgments

This paper has received funding from the European Union's Horizon 2020 research and innovation programme under grant agreement n° 645452 (QT21).

References

Arianna Bisazza and Christof Monz. 2014. Class-based language modeling for translating into morphologically rich languages. In *Proceedings of 25th International Conference on Computational Linguistics (COLING 2014)*, pages 1918–1927, Dublin, Ireland, August.

Rami Botros, Kazuki Irie, Martin Sundermeyer, and Hermann Ney. 2015. On efficient training of word classes and their application to recurrent neural network language models. In *Proceedings of 16th Annual Conference of the International Speech Communication Association (Interspeech 2015)*, pages 1443–1447, Dresden, Germany, September.

Peter F. Brown, Peter V. deSouza, Robert L. Mercer, Vincent J. Della Pietra, and Jenifer C. Lai. 1992. Class-based n-gram models of natural language. *Computational Linguistics*, 18(4):467–479, December.

Colin Cherry. 2013. Improved reordering for phrase-based translation using sparse features. In *Proceedings of 2013 Conference of the North American Chapter of the Association for Computational Linguistics: Human Language Technologies (NAACL-HLT 2013)*, pages 22–31, Atlanta, GA, USA, June.

Nadir Durrani, Philipp Koehn, Helmut Schmid, and Alexander Fraser. 2014. Investigating the usefulness of generalized word representations in smt. In *Proceedings of 25th Annual Conference on Computational Linguistics (COLING 2014)*, pages 421–432, Dublin, Ireland, August.

Michel Galley and Christopher D. Manning. 2008. A simple and effective hierarchical phrase reordering model. In *Proceedings of 2008 Conference on Empirical Methods in Natural Language Processing (EMNLP 2008)*, pages 848–856, Honolulu, HI, USA, October.

Barry Haddow, Matthias Huck, Alexandra Birch, Nikolay Bogoychev, and Philipp Koehn. 2015. The edinburgh/jhu phrase-based machine translation systems for wmt 2015. In *Proceedings of 2016 EMNLP 10th Workshop on Statistical Machine Translation (WMT 2016)*, pages 126–133, Lisbon, Portugal, September.

Philipp Koehn and Hieu Hoang. 2007. Factored translation models. In *Proceedings of 2007 Joint Conference on Empirical Methods in Natural Language Processing and Computational Natural Language Learning (EMNLP-CoNLL 2007)*, pages 868–876, Prague, Czech Republic, June.

Philipp Koehn, Franz Josef Och, and Daniel Marcu. 2003. Statistical phrase-based translation. In *Proceedings of 2003 Conference of the North American Chapter of the Association for Computational Linguistics on Human Language Technology (NAACL-HLT 2003)*, pages 48–54, Edmonton, Canada, May.

Philipp Koehn. 2004. Statistical significance tests for machine translation evaluation. In *Proceedings of 2004 Conference on Empirical Methods in Natural Language Processing (EMNLP 2004)*, pages 388–395, Barcelona, Spain, July.

Philipp Koehn. 2010. *Statistical Machine Translation.* Cambridge University Press, New York, NY, USA.

Terry Koo, Xavier Carreras, and Michael Collins. 2008. Simple semi-supervised dependency parsing. In *Proceedings of 46th Annual Meeting of the Association for Computational Linguistics (ACL 2008)*, pages 595–603, Columbus, OH, USA, June.

Scott Miller, Jethran Guinness, and Alex Zamanian. 2004. Name tagging with word clusters and discriminative training. In *Proceedings of 2004 Conference of the North American Chapter of the Association for Computational Linguistics: Human Language Technologies (NAACL-HLT 2004)*, pages 337–342, Boston, MA, USA, May.

Franz Josef Och. 1995. Maximum-likelihood-schätzung von wortkategorien mit verfahren der kombinatorischen optimierung. Studienarbeit, Friedrich-Alexander-Universität Erlangen-Nürnberg, Erlangen, Germany, May.

Franz Josef Och. 1999. An efficient method for determining bilingual word classes. In *Proceedings of 9th Conference on European Chapter of Association for Computational Linguistics (EACL 1999)*, pages 71–76, Bergen, Norway, June.

Franz Josef Och. 2003. Minimum error rate training in statistical machine translation. In *Proceedings of 41st Annual Meeting of the Association for Computational Linguistics (ACL 2003)*, pages 160–167, Sapporo, Japan, July.

Christian Rishøj and Anders Søgaard. 2011. Factored translation with unsupervised word clusters. In *Proceedings of 2011 EMNLP 6th Workshop on Statistical Machine Translation (WMT 2011)*, pages 447–451, Edinburgh, Scotland, July.

Joern Wuebker, Matthias Huck, Stephan Peitz, Malte Nuhn, Markus Freitag, Jan-Thorsten Peter, Saab Mansour, and Hermann Ney. 2012. Jane 2: Open source phrase-based and hierarchical statistical machine translation. In *Proceedings of 24th International Conference on Computational Linguistics (COLING 2012)*, pages 483–492, Mumbai, India, December.

Joern Wuebker, Stephan Peitz, Felix Rietig, and Hermann Ney. 2013. Improving statistical machine translation with word class models. In *Proceedings of 2013 Conference on Empirical Methods in Natural Language Processing (EMNLP 2013)*, pages 1377–1381, Seattle, USA, October.

Richard Zens, Franz Josef Och, and Hermann Ney. 2002. Phrase-based statistical machine translation. In Matthias Jarke, Jana Koehler, and Gerhard Lakemeyer, editors, *25th German Conference on Artificial Intelligence (KI2002)*, volume 2479 of *Lecture Notes in Artificial Intelligence (LNAI)*, pages 18–32, Aachen, Germany, September. Springer Verlag.

Examining the Relationship between Preordering and Word Order Freedom in Machine Translation

Joachim Daiber   **Miloš Stanojević**   **Wilker Aziz**   **Khalil Sima'an**

Institute for Logic, Language and Computation (ILLC)
University of Amsterdam
{initial.last}@uva.nl

Abstract

We study the relationship between word order freedom and preordering in statistical machine translation. To assess word order freedom, we first introduce a novel entropy measure which quantifies how difficult it is to predict word order given a source sentence and its syntactic analysis. We then address preordering for two target languages at the far ends of the word order freedom spectrum, German and Japanese, and argue that for languages with more word order freedom, attempting to predict a unique word order given source clues only is less justified. Subsequently, we examine lattices of n-best word order predictions as a unified representation for languages from across this broad spectrum and present an effective solution to a resulting technical issue, namely how to select a suitable source word order from the lattice during training. Our experiments show that lattices are crucial for good empirical performance for languages with freer word order (English–German) and can provide additional improvements for fixed word order languages (English–Japanese).

1 Introduction

Word order differences between a source and a target language are a major challenge for machine translation systems. For phrase-based models, the number of possible phrase permutations is so large that reordering must be constrained locally to make the search space for the best hypothesis feasible. However, constraining the space locally runs the risk that the optimal hypothesis is rendered out of reach. Preordering of the source sentence has been embraced as a way to ensure the reachability of certain target word order constellations for improved prediction of the target word order. Preordering aims at predicting a permutation of the source sentence which has minimal word order differences with the target sentence; the permuted source sentence is passed on to a backend translation system trained to translate target-order source sentences into target sentences. In essence, the preordering approach makes the assumption that it is feasible to predict target word order given only clues from the source sentence. In the vast majority of work on preordering, a single preordered source sentence is passed on to the backend system, thereby making the stronger assumption that it is feasible to predict a *unique* preferred target word order. But how reasonable are these assumptions and for which target languages?

Intuitively, the assumption of a *unique preordering* seems reasonable for translating into fixed word order languages such as Japanese, but for translation into languages with less strict word order such as German, this is unlikely to work. In such languages there are multiple comparably plausible target word orders per source sentence because the underlying predicate-argument structure can be expressed with mechanisms other than word order alone (e.g. morphological inflections or intonation). For these languages, it seems rather unlikely to be able to choose a unique word order given only source sentence clues. In this paper, we want to shed light on the relationship between the target language's word order freedom and the feasibility of preordering. We start out by contributing an information-theoretic measure to quantify the difficulty in predicting a preferred word order given the source sentence and its syntax. Our measure provides empirical support for the intuition that it is often not possible to predict a unique word order for free word order languages, whereas it is

Proceedings of the First Conference on Machine Translation, Volume 1: Research Papers, pages 118–130,
Berlin, Germany, August 11-12, 2016. ©2016 Association for Computational Linguistics

more feasible for fixed word order languages such as Japanese. Subsequently, we study the option of passing the n-best word order predictions, instead of 1-best, to the backend system as a lattice of possible word orders of the source sentence.

For the training of the backend system, the use of such permutation lattices raises a question: What should constitute the training corpus for a lattice-preordered translation system? In previous work using single word order predictions, the training data consists of pairs of source and target sentences where the source sentence is either in target order (i.e. order based on word alignments) or preordered (i.e. predicted order). In this work we contribute a novel approach for selecting training instances from the lattice of word order permutations: We select the permutation providing the best match with the target-order source sentence (we call this process "lattice silver training").

Our experiments show that for English–Japanese and English–German lattice preordering has a positive impact on the translation quality. Whereas lattices enable further improvement for preordering English into the strict word order language Japanese, lattices in conjunction with our proposed lattice silver training scheme turn out to be crucial to reach satisfactory empirical performance for English–German. This result highlights that when predicting word order of free word order languages given source clues only, it is important to ensure that the word order predictions and the backend system are suitably fitted together.

2   Related Work

Preordering has been explored from the perspective of the upper-bound achievable translation quality in several studies, including Khalilov and Sima'an (2012) and Herrmann et al. (2013), which compare various systems and provide oracle scores for syntax-based preordering models. Target-order source sentences, in which the word order is determined via automatic alignments, enable translation systems great jumps in translation quality and provide improvements in compactness and efficiency of downstream phrase-based translation models. Approaches have largely followed two directions: (1) predicting word order based on some form of source-syntactic representation and (2) approaches which do not depend on source syntax.

2.1   Source Syntax-Based Preordering

Many approaches to preordering have made use of syntactic representations of the source sentence, including Collins et al. (2005) who restructure the source phrase structure parse tree by applying a sequence of transformation rules. More recently, Jehl et al. (2014) learn to order sibling nodes in the source-side dependency parse tree. The space of possible permutations is explored via depth-first branch-and-bound search (Balas and Toth, 1983). In later work, the authors further improve this model by replacing the logistic regression classifier with a feed-forward neural network (de Gispert et al., 2015), which results in improved empirical results and eliminates the need for feature engineering. Lerner and Petrov (2013) train classifiers to predict the permutations of up to 6 tree nodes in the source dependency tree. The authors found that by only predicting the best 20 permutations of n nodes, they could cover a large majority of the reorderings in their data.

2.2   Preordering without Source Syntax

Tromble and Eisner (2009) learn to predict the orientation of any two words (straight or inverted order) using a perceptron. The search for the best reordering is performed with a $O(n^3)$ chart parsing algorithm. More basic approaches to syntax-less preordering include the application of multiple MT systems (Costa-jussà and Fonollosa, 2006), where a first system learns preordering and a second learns to translate the preordered sentence into the target sentence. Finally, there have been successful attempts at the automatic induction of parse trees from aligned data (DeNero and Uszkoreit, 2011) and the estimation of latent reordering grammars (Stanojević and Sima'an, 2015) based on permutation trees (Zhang and Gildea, 2007).

2.3   Lattice Translation

A lattice is an acyclic finite-state automaton defining a finite language. A more restricted class of lattices, namely, confusion networks (Bertoldi et al., 2007), has been extensively used to pack alternative input sequences for decoding.[1] However, applications mostly focused on speech translation (Ney, 1999; Bertoldi et al., 2007), or to account for lexical and/or segmentation ambiguity due to pre-processing (Xu et al., 2005; Dyer, 2007). In very

---

[1]A confusion network is a special case of a lattice where every path from start to final state goes through every node.

few occasions, lattice input has been used to determine the space of permutations of the input considered by the decoder (Knight and Al-Onaizan, 1998; Kumar and Byrne, 2003). The effectiveness of lattices of permutations was demonstrated by Zhang et al. (2007). However, except in the cases of n-gram based decoders (Khalilov et al., 2009) this approach is not a common practice.

Dyer et al. (2008) formalized lattice translation both for phrase-based and hierarchical phrase-based MT. The former requires a modification of the standard phrase-based decoding algorithm as to maintain a coverage vector over states, rather than input word positions. The latter requires intersecting a lattice and a context-free grammar, which can be seen as a generalized form of parsing (Klein and Manning, 2001). In this work, we focus on phrase-based models.

The space of translation options in standard phrase-based decoding with a distortion limit d grows with $O(\text{stack size} \times n \times 2^d)$ where n represents the input length, and the number of translation options is capped due to beam search (Koehn et al., 2003). With lattice input, the dependency on n is replaced by $|Q|$ where Q is the set of states of the lattice. The *stack size* makes the number of translation options explored by the decoder independent of the number of transitions in the lattice.

As in standard decoding, the states of a lattice can also be visited non-monotonically. However, two states in a lattice are not always connected by a path, and, in general, paths connecting two nodes might differ in length. Dyer et al. (2008) proposed to pick the shortest path between two nodes to be representative of the distance between them.[2] Just like in standard decoding, a *distortion limit* is imposed to keep the space of translations tractable.

In this work, we use lattice input to constrain the space of permutations of the source allowed within the decoder. Moreover, in most cases we completely disable the decoder's further reordering capabilities. Because our models can perform global permutation operations without ad hoc distortion limits, we can reach far more complex word orders. Crucially, our models are better predictors of word order than standard distortion-based reordering, thus we manage to decode with relatively small permutation lattices.

3 Quantifying Word Order Freedom

While varying degrees of word order freedom are a well-studied topic in linguistics, word order freedom has only recently been studied from a quantitative perspective. This has been enabled partly by the increasing availability of syntactic treebanks. Kuboň and Lopatková (2015) propose a measure of word order freedom based on a set of six common word order types (SVO, SOV, etc.). Futrell et al. (2015) define various entropy measures based on the prediction of word order given unordered dependency trees. Both approaches require a dependency treebank for each language.

In practical applications such as machine translation, it is difficult to quantify the influence of word order freedom. For an arbitrary language pair, our goal is to quantify a notion of the target language's word order freedom based only on parallel sentences and source syntax. In their head direction entropy measure, Futrell et al. (2015) approach the problem of quantifying word order freedom by measuring the difficulty of recovering the correct linear order from a sentence's unordered dependency tree. We approach the problem of quantifying a target language's word order freedom by measuring the difficulty of predicting target word order based on the source sentence's dependency tree. Hence, we ask questions such as: How difficult is it to predict French word order based on the syntax of the English source sentence?

3.1 Source Syntax and Target Word Order

We represent the target sentence's word order as a sequence of order decisions. Each order decision encodes for two source words, a and b, whether their translation equivalents are in the order (a, b) or (b, a). The source sentences are parsed with a dependency parser.[3] The target-language order of the words in the source dependency tree is then determined by comparing the target sentence positions of the words aligned to each source word. Figure 1 shows the percentage of dependent-head pairs in the source dependency tree whose target order can be correctly guessed by always choosing the more common decision.[4]

---

[2]This is achieved by running an all-pairs shortest path algorithm prior to decoding – see for example Chapter 25 of (Cormen et al., 2001). MOSES uses the Floyd-Warshall algorithm, which runs in time $O(|Q|^3)$.

[3]http://cs.cmu.edu/~ark/TurboParser/

[4]For English–Japanese, we use manual word alignments of 1,235 sentences from the *Kyoto Free Translation Task* (Neubig, 2011) and for English–German, we use a manually word-aligned subset of Europarl (Padó and Lapata, 2006) consisting of 987 sentences.

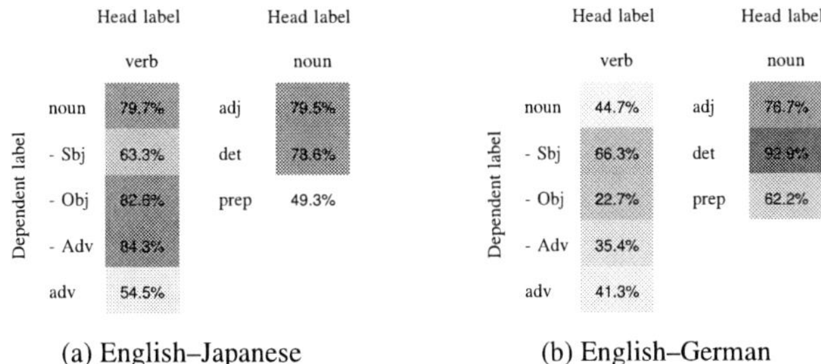

(a) English–Japanese   (b) English–German

Figure 1: Source word pairs whose target order can be predicted using only the words' labels.

German and Japanese Both language pairs differ significantly in how strictly the target language's word order is determined by the source language's syntax. English–German shows strict order constraints within phrases, such as that adjectives and determiners precede the noun they modify in the vast majority of cases (Figure 1b). However, English–German also shows more freedom on the clause level, where basic syntax-based predictions for the positions of nouns relative to the main verb are insufficient. For English–Japanese on the other hand, the position of the nouns relative to the main verb is more rigid, which is demonstrated by the high scores in Figure 1a. These results are in line with the linguistic descriptions of both target languages. From a technical point of view, they highlight that any treatment of English–German word order must take into account information beyond the basic syntactic level and must allow for a given amount of word order freedom.

3.2 Bilingual Head Direction Entropy

While such a qualitative comparison provides insight into the order differences of selected language pairs, it is not straight-forward to compare across many language pairs. From a linguistic perspective, Futrell et al. (2015) use entropy to compare word order freedom in dependency corpora across various languages. While the authors observed that artifacts of the data such as treebank annotation style can hamper comparability, they found that a simple entropy measure for the prediction of word order based on the dependency structure provided a good quantitative measure of word order freedom.

We follow Futrell et al. (2015) in basing our measure on conditional entropy, which provides a straight-forward way to quantify to which extent target word order is determined by source syntax.

$$H(Y|X) = -\sum_{x \in \mathcal{X}} p(x) \sum_{y \in \mathcal{Y}} p(y|x) \log p(y|x)$$

Conditional entropy measures the amount of information required to describe the outcome of a random variable Y given the value of a second random variable X. Given a dependent-head pair in the source dependency tree, X consists of the dependent's and the head's part of speech, as well as the dependency relation between them. Note that as in all of our experiments the source language is English, the space of outcomes of X is the same across all language pairs. Y in this case is the word pair's target-side word order in the form of a (a, b) or (b, a) decision. We estimate $H(Y|X)$ using the bootstrap estimator of DeDeo et al. (2013), which is less prone to sample bias than maximum likelihood estimation.[5]

Influence of word alignments Futrell et al. (2015) use human-annotated dependency trees for each language they consider. Our estimation only involves word-aligned bilingual sentence pairs with a source dependency tree. Manual alignments are available for a limited number of language pairs and often only for a diminishingly small number of sentences. Consequently the question arises, whether automatic word alignments are sufficient for this task. To answer this question, we apply our measure to a set of manually aligned as well as a larger set of automatically aligned sentence pairs. In addition to the German and Japanese alignments mentioned above, we use manual alignments for English–Italian (Farajian et al., 2014), English–French (Och and Ney, 2003), English–Spanish (Graça et al., 2008) and English–Portuguese (Graça et al., 2008).

---

[5]We observe an average of 1,033 values for X per language pair and perform 10,000 Monte-Carlo samples.

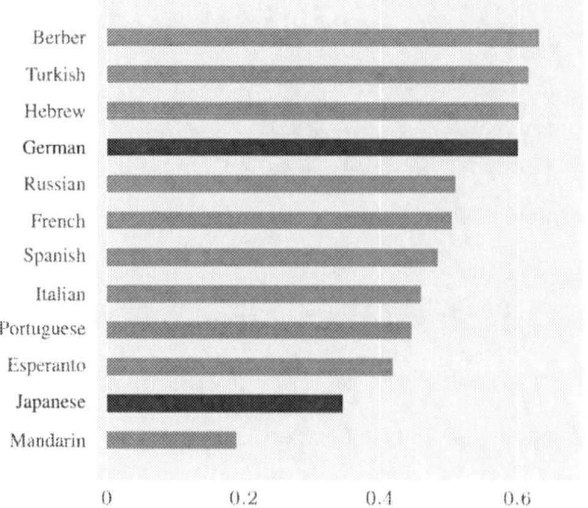

Figure 2: Bilingual head direction entropy with English source side.

Since a limited number of manually aligned sentences are available, it is important to avoid bias due to sample size. Hence, we randomly sample the same number of dependency relations from each language pair. Considering only those languages for which we have both manual and automatic alignments, we can determine how well their word order freedom rankings correlate. Even though the number of samples for the manually aligned sentences is limited to 500 due to the size of the smallest set of manual alignments, we find a high correlation of Spearman's $\rho = 0.77$ between the rankings of the 6 languages that occur in both sets (Zwillinger and Kokoska, 1999).

Influence of source syntax Another factor that may influence our estimated degree of word order freedom is the form and granularity of the source side's syntactic representation: More detailed representations may disambiguate cases that are difficult to predict with a more bare representation. As we are interested in the bilingual case and, specifically, in preordering, we content ourselves with using the same syntactic representation, i.e. dependency trees, that many preordering models use (e.g., Jehl et al. (2014), Lerner and Petrov (2013)).

Comparison to monolingual measures Our measure is similar to Futrell et al. (2015)'s head direction entropy; however, it also offers several advantages. While monolingual head direction entropy requires a dependency treebank for each language, our bilingual head direction entropy only requires dependency annotation for the source language (English in our case). One of

their caveats, the influence of the widely varying dependency annotation styles across treebanks, is also not present in our method, since a single dependency style is used for the source language. We have demonstrated that automatic alignments perform on a comparable level to manual alignments. Accordingly, the amount of data that can be used to estimate the measure is only limited by the availability of parallel sentences. Finally, while dependency treebanks rarely cover the same corpora or even domains, our method can utilize sentences from the same or similar corpora for each language, thus minimizing potential corpus biases.

Translation from English Figure 2 plots bilingual head direction entropy for an English source side and a set of typologically diverse languages on the target side. For each language pair, we use 18,000 sentence pairs and automatic alignments from the Tatoeba corpus (Tiedemann, 2012).[6]

Languages at the top of the plot in Figure 2 show a greater degree of word order freedom with respect to the English source syntax. Thus, predicting their word order from English source clues alone is likely to be difficult. We argue that in such cases it is crucial to pass on the ambiguity over the space of predictions to the translation model. By doing so, word order decisions can be influenced by translation decisions, while still shaping the space of reachable translations.

4 Preordering Free and Fixed Word Order Languages

The measure of word order freedom introduced in the previous section enables us to estimate how difficult it is to predict the target language's word order based on the source language. In this section, we introduce the two preordering models we use to predict the word order of German and Japanese. Experiments with these models will allow us to examine the relationship between preordering and word order freedom.

4.1 Neural Lattice Preordering

Based on their earlier work, which used logistic regression and graph search for preordering (Jehl et al., 2014), de Gispert et al. (2015) introduce a neural preordering model. In this model, a feed-forward neural network is trained to estimate the

---

[6]The alignments were produced using GIZA++ (Och and Ney, 2003) with *grow-diag-final-and* symmetrization.

swap probabilities of nodes in the source-side dependency tree. Search is performed via the depth-first branch-and-bound algorithm. The authors have found this model to be fast and to produce high quality word order predictions for a variety of languages.

Model estimation Training examples are extracted from all possible pairs of children of a dependency tree node, including the head itself. For each pair, the two nodes are swapped if swapping them reduces the number of crossing alignment links. The crossing score of two nodes a and b (a precedes b in linear order) and their aligned target indexes A_a and A_b is defined as follows:

$$\text{cs}(a, b) = |\, \{(i, j) \in A_a \times A_b : i > j\}\, |$$

Training instances generated in this manner are then used to estimate the swap probability $p(i, j)$ for two indexes i and j. For each node in the source dependency tree, the best possible permutation of its children (including the head) is determined via graph search. The score of a permutation of length k is defined as follows:

$$\text{score}(\pi) = \prod_{1 \leq i < j \leq k | \pi[i] > \pi[j]} p(i, j)$$
$$\cdot \prod_{1 \leq i < j \leq k | \pi[i] < \pi[j]} 1 - p(i, j)$$

We closely follow de Gispert et al. (2015) for the implementation of the estimator of $p(i, j)$. A feed-forward neural network (Bengio et al., 2003) is trained to predict the orientation of a and b based on a sequence of 20 features, such as the words, the words' POS tags, the dependency labels, etc.[7] The network consists of 50 nodes on the input layer, 2 on the output layer, and 50 and 100 on the two hidden layers. We use a learning rate of 0.01, batch size of 1000 and perform 20 training epochs.

Search Search in this model consists of finding the sequence of swaps leading to the best overall score according to the model. Let a partial permutation of k nodes be a sequence of length $k' < k$ containing each integer in $\{1, ..., k\}$ at most once. The score of a new permutation obtained by extending a partial permutation π' of length k' by

---

[7] Our implementation is based on `http://nlg.isi.edu/software/nplm/`.

one element can be computed efficiently as:

$$\text{score}(\pi' \cdot \langle i \rangle) = \text{score}(\pi')$$
$$\cdot \prod_{j \in V | i > j} p(i, j)$$
$$\cdot \prod_{j \in V | i < j} 1 - p(i, j)$$

k-**best search** Target languages such as German allow for a significant amount of word order freedom; hence, the depth-first branch-and-bound algorithm, which extracts the single best permutation, may not be the best choice in this case. In the context of the Traveling Salesman Problem, van der Poort et al. (1999) show that general branch-and-bound search can be extended to retrieve k-best results while keeping the same guarantees and computational complexity. Only minor changes are necessary to adapt the search for the best permutation to finding the k-best permutations: We keep a set $bestk$ of the best permutations and a single $bound$. If for a permutation π', $\text{score}(\pi') > bound$, instead of updating the bound to the single best permutation and remembering it, the following steps are performed:

1. If $|bestk| = k$:

    – Remove worst permutation from the set.

2. Add π' to $bestk$.

3. The new $bound$ will be the score of the worst permutation in $bestk$.

4.2 Reordering Grammar Induction

Reordering Grammar (RG) (Stanojević and Sima'an, 2015) is a recent approach for preordering that is hierarchical and fully unsupervised. It is based on inducing a probabilistic context-free grammar from aligned parallel data. This grammar can predict permutation trees (PETs) (Zhang and Gildea, 2007) — projective constituency trees that can fully describe any permutation. PETs are reminiscent of ITG (Wu, 1997) with the important distinction that PETs can handle any permutation, unlike ITG which can only handle binarizable ones. As in ITG, constituents in PETs are labeled with the permutation of their children.

Induction of RGs is performed by specifying a generative probabilistic model and then estimating its parameters using the EM algorithm. The reasoning behind using EM is that many latent variables are present in the model. Only the source sentence and its permutation are observed during training. The exact PET that generated this permutation is not observed and there could be (exponentially) many PETs that could have generated the observed permutation. Hence, the bracketings of potential PETs are treated as latent variables.

The second source of latent variables is state splitting of non-terminals (labels that indicate how to reorder the children) in a similar way as done in monolingual parsing (Matsuzaki et al., 2005; Petrov et al., 2006; Prescher, 2005). Each latent permutation tree has many latent derivations and the generative probabilistic model needs to account for them. The probability of the observed permutation π is defined in the following way:

$$P(\pi) = \sum_{\Delta \in \mathrm{PEF}(\pi)} \sum_{d \in \Delta} \prod_{r \in d} P(r)$$

where $\mathrm{PEF}(\pi)$ returns the Permutation Forest of π (i.e., the set of PETs that can generate the permutation π), Δ represents a permutation tree, d represents a derivation of a permutation tree and r represents a production rule. Efficient estimation for this model is done by using the standard Inside-Outside algorithm (Lari and Young, 1990).

At test time, the source sentence is parsed with the estimated grammar in order to find the derivation of a permutation tree with the lowest expected cost. More formally, the decoding task can be described as:

$$\hat{d} = \arg\min_{d \in \mathrm{Chart}(\mathbf{s})} \sum_{d' \in \mathrm{Chart}(\mathbf{s})} P(d')\, \mathrm{cost}(d, d')$$

where $P(d) = \prod_{r \in d} P(r)$ is the probability of a derivation, and $\mathrm{Chart}(\mathbf{s})$ is the space of all possible derivations of all possible permutation trees for source sentence $\mathbf{s}$. Two main modifications to this formula are made in order to make inference fast: First, Kendall τ is used as a cost function because it decomposes well,[8] which allows usage of efficient dynamic programming minimum Bayes-risk (MBR) computation (DeNero et al., 2009). Second, instead of computing the MBR derivation over the full chart, computation is done over 10,000 unbiased samples from the chart. To build the permutation lattice with this model we use the top n permutations which have the lowest expected Kendall τ cost.

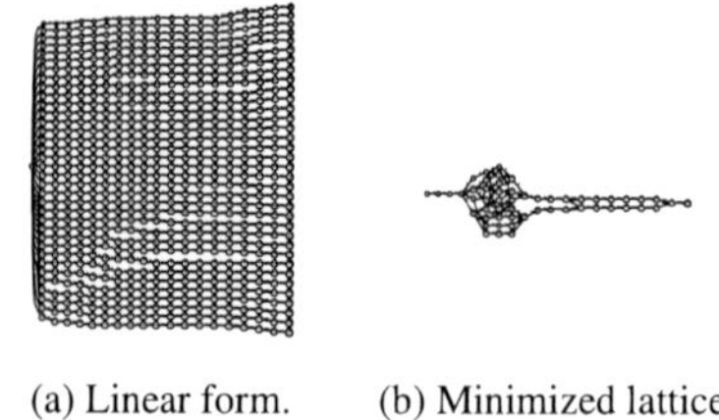

(a) Linear form.   (b) Minimized lattice.

Figure 3: Example permutation lattice.

5 Machine Translation with Permutation Lattices

5.1 Permutation Lattices

We call a *permutation lattice* for sentence $\mathbf{s} = \langle \mathbf{s}_1, \ldots, \mathbf{s}_n \rangle$ an acyclic finite-state automaton where every path from the initial state reaches an accepting state in exactly n uniquely labeled transitions. Transitions are labeled with pairs in $\{(i, \mathbf{s}_i)_{i=1}^n\}$ and each path represents an arbitrary permutation of the source's n tokens.

In a permutation lattice with states Q and transitions E, every path between any two states $u, v \in Q$ has exactly the same length. Let $\mathrm{out}^*(x)$ denote the transitive closure of $x \in Q$, that is, the set of states reachable from x. If two nodes are at all connected, $v \in \mathrm{out}^*(u)$, then the distance between them equals $d_v - d_u$, where d_x is x's distance from the initial state. This observation allows a speed up of non-monotone translation of a permutation lattice. Namely, to precompute shortest distances, necessary to impose a distortion limit, instead of running a fully fledged all-pairs shortest path algorithm $O(|Q|^3)$ (Cormen et al., 2001), we can compute transitive closure in time $O(|Q| \times |E|)$ (Simon, 1988) followed by single-source distance in time $O(|Q| + |E|)$ (Mohri, 2002).

We produce permutation lattices by compressing the n-best outputs from the reordering models into a minimal deterministic acceptor. Unweighted determinization and minimization are performed using OpenFST (Allauzen et al., 2007). The results of this process are very compact representations that can be decoded efficiently. As an illustration, Figure 3 shows an English sentence from WMT newstest 2014 preordered for translation into German before (3a) and after minimization (3b).[9] Table 1 shows the influence of the number of predicted permutations on the lattice sizes

---

[8]More precisely, we use the Kendall τ distance between the permutations that are yields of the derivations.

[9]Example sentence: *The Kluser lights protect cyclists, as well as those travelling by bus and the residents of Bergle.*

for English–German. Permutation quality is measured by Kendall τ distance to the gold permutation (best-out-of-n).

Permutations	Kendall τ	Lattice	
		States	Transitions
Monotone	83.78	23	22
5	84.69	24	52
10	85.23	33	69
100	86.20	72	138
1000	86.75	123	233

Table 1: Permutations and lattice size (En–De).

5.2 Lattice Silver Training

While for first-best word order predictions, there are two straight-forward options for how to select training instances for the MT system, it is less clear how to do this in the case of permutation lattices. In standard preordering, the word order of the source sentence in the training set is commonly determined by reordering the source sentence to minimize the number of crossing alignment links (we denote this as $\mathbf{s}'$). Alternatively, the trained preordering model can be applied to the source side of the training set, which we call $\hat{\mathbf{s}}'_1$. There is a trade-off between both methods: While $\mathbf{s}'$ will generally produce more compact and less noisy phrase tables, it may include phrases that are not reachable by the preordering model. The predicted order $\hat{\mathbf{s}}'_1$, on the other hand, may be too constrained to reach helpful hypotheses. For lattices, one option would be to extract all possible phrases from the lattice directly. Here, we consider a simpler alternative: Instead of selecting either the gold order $\mathbf{s}'$ or the predicted order $\hat{\mathbf{s}}'_1$, we select the order $\hat{\mathbf{s}}'$ which is closest to both the lattice predictions and the gold order $\mathbf{s}'$. Since this order is a mix of the lattice predictions and the gold order, we call this training scheme lattice silver training.

Let $(\mathbf{s}, \mathbf{t})$ be a training instance consisting of a source sentence $\mathbf{s}$ and a target sentence $\mathbf{t}$ and let $\mathbf{s}'$ be the target-order source sentence obtained via the word alignments. For each training instance, we select the preordered source $\hat{\mathbf{s}}'$ as follows:

$$\hat{\mathbf{s}}' = \underset{\hat{\mathbf{s}}'_L \in \pi_k(\mathbf{s})}{\arg\max} \ \mathrm{overlap}(\hat{\mathbf{s}}'_L, \mathbf{s}')$$

where $\pi_k(\mathbf{s})$ is the set of k-best permutations predicted by the preordering model. Each $\hat{\mathbf{s}}'_L \in \pi_k(\mathbf{s})$ represents a single path through the lattice. As

the cost function, we use n-gram overlap, as commonly used in string kernels (Lodhi et al., 2002):

$$\mathrm{overlap}(\hat{\mathbf{s}}'_L, \mathbf{s}') = \sum_{n=2}^{7} \left(\sum_{c \in C^n_{\mathbf{s}'}} \mathrm{count}_{\hat{\mathbf{s}}'_L}(c) \right)$$

where $C^n_{\mathbf{s}'}$ denotes all candidate n-grams of length n in $\mathbf{s}'$ and $\mathrm{count}_{\hat{\mathbf{s}}'_L}(c)$ denotes the number of occurrences of n-gram c in $\hat{\mathbf{s}}'_L$. Ties between permutations with the same overlap are broken using the permutations' scores from the preordering model.

6 Experiments

6.1 Experimental Setup

In our translation experiments, we use the following experimental setup, datasets and parameters.

Translation system Translation experiments are performed with a phrase-based machine translation system, a version of Moses (Koehn et al., 2007) with extended lattice support.[10] We use the basic Moses features and perform 15 iterations of batch MIRA (Cherry and Foster, 2012).

English–Japanese Our experiments are performed on the NTCIR-8 Patent Translation (PATMT) Task. Tuning is performed on the NTCIR-7 dev sets, and translation is evaluated on the test set from NTCIR-9. All data is tokenized (using the Moses tokenizer for English and KyTea 5 for Japanese (Neubig et al., 2011)) and filtered for sentences between 4 and 50 words. As a baseline we use a translation system with distortion limit 6 and a lexicalized reordering model (Galley and Manning, 2008). We use a 5-gram language model estimated using *lmplz* (Heafield et al., 2013) on the target side of the parallel corpus.

English–German For translation into German, we built a machine translation system based on the WMT 2016 news translation data.[11] The system is trained on all available parallel data, consisting of 4.5m sentence pairs from Europarl (Koehn, 2005), Common Crawl (Smith et al., 2013) and the News Commentary corpus. We removed all sentences longer than 80 words and tokenization and truecasing is performed using the standard Moses tokenizer and truecaser. We use a 5-gram Kneser-Ney language model, estimated using *lmplz* (Heafield

---

[10]Made available at `https://github.com/wilkeraziz/mosesdecoder`.

[11]`http://statmt.org/wmt16/`

et al., 2013). The language model is trained on 189m sentences from the target sides of Europarl and News Commentary, as well as the News Crawl 2007-2015 corpora. Word alignment is performed using MGIZA (*gdfa* with 6, 6, 3 and 3 iterations of IBM M1, HMM, IBM M3 and IBM M4). As a baseline we use a translation system with distortion limit 6 and a distortion-based reordering model. Tuning is performed on newstest 2014 and we evaluate on newstest 2015.

Preordering models For German, we use the neural lattice preordering model introduced in Section 4.1. The model is trained on the full parallel training data (4.5m sentences) based on the automatic word alignments used by the translation system. Source dependency trees are produced by TurboParser,[12] which was trained on the English version of HamleDT (Zeman et al., 2012) with content-head dependencies. For translation into Japanese, we train a Reordering Grammar model for 10 iterations of EM on a training set consisting of 786k sentence pairs with automatic alignments.

6.2 Translation Experiments

We report lowercased BLEU (Papineni et al., 2002) and Kendall τ calculated from the force-aligned hypothesis and reference. Statistical significance tests are performed for the translation scores using the bootstrap resampling method with p-value < 0.05 (Koehn, 2004). The standard preordering systems ("first-best" in Table 2 and 4) use an additional lexicalized reordering model (MSD), while the lattice systems use only lattice distortion. For training preordered translation models, we recreate word alignments from the original MGIZA alignments and the permutation for En–De and re-align preordered and target sentences for En–Ja using MGIZA.[13]

English–German Translation results for translation into German are shown in Table 2.

For this language pair, we found standard preordering to work poorly. This is despite the fact that the oracle order (i.e. the source words in the test set are preordered according to the word alignments) shows significant potential. A lattice packed with 1000 permutations on the other hand,

---

[12]http://cs.cmu.edu/~ark/TurboParser/

[13]Re-aligning the sentences with MGIZA generally improves results, which implies that we are likely underestimating the results for En–De.

	DL	Translation BLEU	Word order Kendall τ
Baseline	6	21.76	54.75
Oracle order	6	26.68	58.05
	0	26.41	57.92
First-best	6	21.21[A]	53.44
Lattice (silver)	0	21.88[B]	54.51

[A]Stat. significant against baseline. [B]Stat. significant against first-best.

Table 2: Translation results English–German.

performs better even when translating monotonically with a distortion limit of 0.

Lattice silver training To examine the utility of the lattice silver training scheme, we train systems which differ only in the way the training data is extracted. Table 3 shows that for English–German, lattice silver training is successful in bridging the gap between the preordering model and the alignment-based target word order, both for monotonic translation and when allowing the decoder to additionally reorder translations.

	Distortion limit 0	3
Gold training	21.44	21.60
Lattice silver training	21.88	21.88

Table 3: Lattice silver training (BLEU, En–De).

English–Japanese Results for translation into Japanese are shown in Table 4.

Discussion Although preordering with a single permutation already works well for the strict word order language Japanese, packing the word order ambiguity into a lattice allows the machine translation system to achieve even better translation monotonically than allowing a distortion of 6 and an additional lexicalized reordering model on top

	DL	Translation BLEU	Word order Kendall τ
Baseline	6	29.65	44.87
Oracle order	6	34.22	56.23
	0	30.55	53.98
First-best	6	32.14[A]	49.68
Lattice	0	32.50[AB]	50.79

[A]Stat. significant against baseline. [B]Stat. significant against first-best.

Table 4: Translation results English–Japanese.

of a single permutation. We noticed that lexicalized reordering helped the first-best systems and hence report this stronger baseline. In principle, lexicalized reordering can also be used with 0-distortion lattice translation, and we plan to investigate this option in the future. Linguistic intuition and the empirical results presented in Section 3 suggest that compared to Japanese, German shows more word order freedom. Consequently, we assumed that a first-best preordering model would not perform well on the language pair English–German, and indeed the results in Table 2 confirm this assumption. For both language pairs, translating a lattice of predicted permutations outperforms the baselines, thus reducing the gap between translation with predicted word order and oracle word order. However, permutation lattices turn out to be the key to enabling any improvement at all for the language pair English–German in the context of preordering. This language pair can benefit from the improved interaction between word order and translation decisions. These findings go in tandem with our analysis in Section 3 (see Figures 1 and 2), particularly, the prediction of our information-theoretic word order freedom metric that it should be more difficult to determine German word order from English clues. Our main focus in this paper was on the language pairs English–German and English–Japanese. Hence, while our results provide an empirical data point for the utility of permutation lattices for free word order languages, we plan to provide further empirical support by performing experiments with a broader range of language pairs in future work.

7 Conclusion

The world's languages differ widely in how they express meaning, relying on indicators such as word order, intonation or morphological markings. Consequently, some languages exhibit stricter word order than others. Our goal in this paper was to examine the effect of word order freedom on machine translation and preordering. We provided an empirical comparison of language pairs in terms of the difficulty of predicting the target language's word order based on the source language. Our metric's predictions agree both with the intuition provided by linguistic theory and the empirical support we present in the form of translation experiments. We show that addressing uncertainty in word order predictions, and in particular doing so with permutation lattices, can be an indispensable tool for dealing with word order in machine translation. The experiments we performed in this paper confirm this previous finding and we further build on it by introducing a new method for training machine translation systems for lattice-preordered input, which we call *lattice silver training*. Finally, we found that while lattices are indeed helpful for English–Japanese, for which standard preordering already works well, they are crucial for translation into the freer word order language German.

Acknowledgements

We thank the three anonymous reviewers for their constructive comments and suggestions. This work received funding from EXPERT (EU FP7 Marie Curie ITN nr. 317471), NWO VICI grant nr. 277-89-002 (Khalil Sima'an), DatAptor project STW grant nr. 12271 and QT21 project (H2020 nr. 645452).

References

Cyril Allauzen, Michael Riley, Johan Schalkwyk, Wojciech Skut, and Mehryar Mohri. 2007. OpenFst: A general and efficient weighted finite-state transducer library. In *Proceedings of the Ninth International Conference on Implementation and Application of Automata, (CIAA 2007)*, volume 4783 of *Lecture Notes in Computer Science*, pages 11–23. Springer. http://www.openfst.org.

Egon Balas and Paolo Toth. 1983. Branch and bound methods for the traveling salesman problem. Technical report, Carnegie-Mellon Univ. Pittsburgh PA Management Sciences Research Group.

Yoshua Bengio, Réjean Ducharme, Pascal Vincent, and Christian Janvin. 2003. A neural probabilistic language model. *J. Mach. Learn. Res.*, 3:1137–1155, March.

Nicola Bertoldi, Richard Zens, and Marcello Federico. 2007. Speech translation by confusion network decoding. In *IEEE International Conference on Acoustics, Speech and Signal Processing*, volume 4 of *ICASSP '07*, pages 1297–1300, Honolulu, HI, April. IEEE.

Colin Cherry and George Foster. 2012. Batch tuning strategies for statistical machine translation. In *Proceedings of the 2012 Conference of the North American Chapter of the Association for Computational Linguistics: Human Language Technologies*, pages 427–436, Montréal, Canada, June.

Michael Collins, Philipp Koehn, and Ivona Kucerova. 2005. Clause restructuring for statistical machine translation. In *Proceedings of the 43rd Annual Meeting of the Association for Computational Linguistics (ACL'05)*, pages 531–540, Ann Arbor, Michigan, June.

Thomas H. Cormen, Clifford Stein, Ronald L. Rivest, and Charles E. Leiserson. 2001. *Introduction to Algorithms*. McGraw-Hill Higher Education, 2nd edition.

Marta R. Costa-jussà and José A. R. Fonollosa. 2006. Statistical machine reordering. In *Proceedings of the 2006 Conference on Empirical Methods in Natural Language Processing*, pages 70–76, Sydney, Australia, July.

Adrià de Gispert, Gonzalo Iglesias, and Bill Byrne. 2015. Fast and accurate preordering for SMT using neural networks. In *Proceedings of the 2015 Conference of the North American Chapter of the Association for Computational Linguistics: Human Language Technologies*, pages 1012–1017, Denver, Colorado, May–June.

Simon DeDeo, Robert X. D. Hawkins, Sara Klingenstein, and Tim Hitchcock. 2013. Bootstrap methods for the empirical study of decision-making and information flows in social systems. *Entropy*, 15(6):2246–2276.

John DeNero and Jakob Uszkoreit. 2011. Inducing sentence structure from parallel corpora for reordering. In *Proceedings of the 2011 Conference on Empirical Methods in Natural Language Processing*, pages 193–203, Edinburgh, Scotland, UK., July.

John DeNero, David Chiang, and Kevin Knight. 2009. Fast consensus decoding over translation forests. In *Proceedings of the Joint Conference of the 47th Annual Meeting of the ACL and the 4th International Joint Conference on Natural Language Processing of the AFNLP: Volume 2 - Volume 2*, ACL '09, pages 567–575, Stroudsburg, PA, USA.

Christopher Dyer, Smaranda Muresan, and Philip Resnik. 2008. Generalizing word lattice translation. In *Proceedings of ACL-08: HLT*, pages 1012–1020, Columbus, Ohio, June.

Christopher J. Dyer. 2007. The "noisier channel": Translation from morphologically complex languages. In *Proceedings of the Second Workshop on Statistical Machine Translation*, pages 207–211, Prague, Czech Republic, June.

M. Amin Farajian, Nicola Bertoldi, and Marcello Federico. 2014. Online word alignment for online adaptive machine translation. In *Proceedings of the EACL 2014 Workshop on Humans and Computer-assisted Translation*, pages 84–92, Gothenburg, Sweden, April.

Richard Futrell, Kyle Mahowald, and Edward Gibson. 2015. Quantifying word order freedom in dependency corpora. In *Proceedings of the Third International Conference on Dependency Linguistics (Depling 2015)*, pages 91–100, Uppsala, Sweden, August. Uppsala University, Uppsala, Sweden.

Michel Galley and Christopher D. Manning. 2008. A simple and effective hierarchical phrase reordering model. In *Proceedings of the 2008 Conference on Empirical Methods in Natural Language Processing*, pages 848–856, Honolulu, Hawaii, October.

João Graça, Joana Paulo Pardal, and Luísa Coheur. 2008. Building a golden collection of parallel multi-language word alignments.

Kenneth Heafield, Ivan Pouzyrevsky, Jonathan H. Clark, and Philipp Koehn. 2013. Scalable modified Kneser-Ney language model estimation. In *Proceedings of the 51st Annual Meeting of the Association for Computational Linguistics*, pages 690–696, Sofia, Bulgaria, August.

Teresa Herrmann, Jochen Weiner, Jan Niehues, and Alex Waibel. 2013. Analyzing the potential of source sentence reordering in statistical machine translation. In *Proceedings of the International Workshop on Spoken Language Translation (IWSLT 2013)*.

Laura Jehl, Adrià de Gispert, Mark Hopkins, and Bill Byrne. 2014. Source-side preordering for translation using logistic regression and depth-first branch-and-bound search. In *Proceedings of the 14th Conference of the European Chapter of the Association for Computational Linguistics*, pages 239–248, Gothenburg, Sweden, April.

Maxim Khalilov and Khalil Sima'an. 2012. Statistical translation after source reordering: Oracles, context-aware models, and empirical analysis. *Natural Language Engineering*, 18:491–519, 10.

Maxim Khalilov, José A. R. Fonollosa, and Mark Dras. 2009. Coupling hierarchical word reordering and decoding in phrase-based statistical machine translation. In *Proceedings of the Third Workshop on Syntax and Structure in Statistical Translation*, SSST '09, pages 78–86, Stroudsburg, PA, USA.

Dan Klein and Christopher D. Manning. 2001. Parsing and hypergraphs. In *Seventh International Workshop on Parsing Technologies (IWPT- 2001)*, October.

Kevin Knight and Yaser Al-Onaizan. 1998. Translation with finite-state devices. In *Proceedings of the Association for Machine Translation in the Americas*, AMTA, pages 421–437, Langhorne, PA, USA.

Philipp Koehn, Franz Josef Och, and Daniel Marcu. 2003. Statistical phrase-based translation. In *Proceedings of the 2003 Conference of the North American Chapter of the Association for Computational Linguistics on Human Language Technology - Volume 1*, NAACL '03, pages 48–54, Stroudsburg, PA, USA.

Philipp Koehn, Hieu Hoang, Alexandra Birch, Chris Callison-Burch, Marcello Federico, Nicola Bertoldi, Brooke Cowan, Wade Shen, Christine Moran, Richard Zens, Chris Dyer, Ondřej Bojar, Alexandra Constantin, and Evan Herbst. 2007. Moses: Open source toolkit for statistical machine translation. In *Proceedings of the 45th Annual Meeting of the ACL on Interactive Poster and Demonstration Sessions*, ACL '07, pages 177–180, Stroudsburg, PA, USA.

Philipp Koehn. 2004. Statistical significance tests for machine translation evaluation. In *Proceedings of the 2004 Conference on Empirical Methods in Natural Language Processing*, pages 388–395.

Philipp Koehn. 2005. Europarl: A parallel corpus for statistical machine translation. In *Proceedings of Machine Translation Summit X*, volume 5, pages 79–86.

Vladislav Kuboň and Markéta Lopatková. 2015. Free or fixed word order: What can treebanks reveal? In Jakub Yaghob, editor, *ITAT 2015: Information Technologies Applications and Theory, Proceedings of the 15th conference ITAT 2015*, volume 1422 of *CEUR Workshop Proceedings*, pages 23–29, Praha, Czechia. Charles University in Prague, CreateSpace Independent Publishing Platform.

Shankar Kumar and William Byrne. 2003. A weighted finite state transducer implementation of the alignment template model for statistical machine translation. In *Proceedings of the 2003 Conference of the North American Chapter of the Association for Computational Linguistics on Human Language Technology - Volume 1*, NAACL '03, pages 63–70, Stroudsburg, PA, USA.

K. Lari and S. J. Young. 1990. The estimation of stochastic context-free grammars using the inside-outside algorithm. *Computer Speech and Language*, 4:35–56.

Uri Lerner and Slav Petrov. 2013. Source-side classifier preordering for machine translation. In *Proceedings of the 2013 Conference on Empirical Methods in Natural Language Processing*, pages 513–523, Seattle, Washington, USA, October.

Huma Lodhi, Craig Saunders, John Shawe-Taylor, Nello Cristianini, and Chris Watkins. 2002. Text classification using string kernels. *J. Mach. Learn. Res.*, 2:419–444, March.

Takuya Matsuzaki, Yusuke Miyao, and Jun'ichi Tsujii. 2005. Probabilistic CFG with latent annotations. In *Proceedings of the 43rd Annual Meeting of the Association for Computational Linguistics (ACL'05)*, pages 75–82, Ann Arbor, Michigan, June.

Mehryar Mohri. 2002. Semiring frameworks and algorithms for shortest-distance problems. *Journal of Automata, Languages and Combinatorics*, 7(3):321–350, January.

Graham Neubig, Yosuke Nakata, and Shinsuke Mori. 2011. Pointwise prediction for robust, adaptable japanese morphological analysis. In *Proceedings of the 49th Annual Meeting of the Association for Computational Linguistics: Human Language Technologies*, pages 529–533, Portland, Oregon, USA, June.

Graham Neubig. 2011. The Kyoto free translation task. http://www.phontron.com/kftt.

Hermann Ney. 1999. Speech translation: coupling of recognition and translation. In *IEEE International Conference on Acoustics, Speech, and Signal Processing*, volume 1, pages 517–520, Phoenix, AZ, March. IEEE.

Franz Josef Och and Hermann Ney. 2003. A systematic comparison of various statistical alignment models. *Computational Linguistics*, 29(1):19–51.

Sebastian Padó and Mirella Lapata. 2006. Optimal constituent alignment with edge covers for semantic projection. In *Proceedings of the 21st International Conference on Computational Linguistics and 44th Annual Meeting of the Association for Computational Linguistics*, pages 1161–1168, Sydney, Australia, July.

Kishore Papineni, Salim Roukos, Todd Ward, and Wei-Jing Zhu. 2002. BLEU: a method for automatic evaluation of machine translation. In *Proceedings of the 40th annual meeting on association for computational linguistics*, pages 311–318.

Slav Petrov, Leon Barrett, Romain Thibaux, and Dan Klein. 2006. Learning accurate, compact, and interpretable tree annotation. In *Proceedings of the 21st International Conference on Computational Linguistics and the 44th Annual Meeting of the Association for Computational Linguistics*, ACL-44, pages 433–440, Stroudsburg, PA, USA.

Detlef Prescher. 2005. Inducing head-driven pcfgs with latent heads: Refining a tree-bank grammar for parsing. In *In ECML05*.

K. Simon. 1988. An improved algorithm for transitive closure on acyclic digraphs. *Theor. Comput. Sci.*, 58(1-3):325–346, June.

Jason R. Smith, Herve Saint-Amand, Magdalena Plamada, Philipp Koehn, Chris Callison-Burch, and Adam Lopez. 2013. Dirt cheap web-scale parallel text from the common crawl. In *Proceedings of the 51st Annual Meeting of the Association for Computational Linguistics (Volume 1: Long Papers)*, pages 1374–1383, Sofia, Bulgaria, August.

Miloš Stanojević and Khalil Sima'an. 2015. Reordering grammar induction. In *Proceedings of the 2015 Conference on Empirical Methods in Natural Language Processing*, pages 44–54, Lisbon, Portugal, September.

Jörg Tiedemann. 2012. Parallel data, tools and interfaces in opus. In Nicoletta Calzolari (Conference Chair), Khalid Choukri, Thierry Declerck, Mehmet Ugur Dogan, Bente Maegaard, Joseph Mariani, Jan Odijk, and Stelios Piperidis, editors, *Proceedings of the Eight International Conference on Language Resources and Evaluation (LREC'12)*, Istanbul, Turkey, may.

Roy Tromble and Jason Eisner. 2009. Learning linear ordering problems for better translation. In *Proceedings of the 2009 Conference on Empirical Methods in Natural Language Processing*, pages 1007–1016, Singapore, August.

Edo S van der Poort, Marek Libura, Gerard Sierksma, and Jack A.A van der Veen. 1999. Solving the k-best traveling salesman problem. *Computers & Operations Research*, 26(4):409 – 425.

Dekai Wu. 1997. Stochastic inversion transduction grammars and bilingual parsing of parallel corpora. *Computational linguistics*, 23(3):377–403.

Jia Xu, Evgeny Matusov, Richard Zens, and Hermann Ney. 2005. Integrated chinese word segmentation in statistical machine translation. In *International Workshop on Spoken Language Translation*, Pittsburgh.

Daniel Zeman, David Mareček, Martin Popel, Loganathan Ramasamy, Jan Štěpánek, Zdeněk Žabokrtský, and Jan Hajič. 2012. Hamledt: To parse or not to parse? In *Proceedings of the Eight International Conference on Language Resources and Evaluation (LREC'12)*, Istanbul, Turkey, may. European Language Resources Association (ELRA).

Hao Zhang and Daniel Gildea. 2007. Factorization of synchronous context-free grammars in linear time. In *NAACL Workshop on Syntax and Structure in Statistical Translation (SSST)*, pages 25–32.

Yuqi Zhang, Richard Zens, and Hermann Ney. 2007. Chunk-level reordering of source language sentences with automatically learned rules for statistical machine translation. In *Proceedings of the NAACL-HLT 2007/AMTA Workshop on Syntax and Structure in Statistical Translation*, SSST '07, pages 1–8, Stroudsburg, PA, USA.

Daniel Zwillinger and Stephen Kokoska. 1999. *CRC Standard Probability and Statistics Tables and Formulae*. CRC Press.

Findings of the 2016 Conference on Machine Translation (WMT16)

Ondřej Bojar
Charles University

Rajen Chatterjee
FBK

Christian Federmann
Microsoft Research

Yvette Graham
Dublin City University

Barry Haddow
Univ. of Edinburgh

Matthias Huck
LMU Munich

Antonio Jimeno Yepes
IBM Research Australia

Philipp Koehn
JHU / Edinburgh

Varvara Logacheva
Univ. of Sheffield

Christof Monz
Univ. of Amsterdam

Matteo Negri
FBK

Aurélie Névéol
LIMSI-CNRS

Mariana Neves
HPI/Potsdam

Martin Popel
Charles University

Matt Post
Johns Hopkins Univ.

Raphael Rubino
Saarland University

Carolina Scarton
Univ. of Sheffield

Lucia Specia
Univ. of Sheffield

Marco Turchi
FBK

Karin Verspoor
Univ. of Melbourne

Marcos Zampieri
Saarland University

Abstract

This paper presents the results of the WMT16 shared tasks, which included five machine translation (MT) tasks (standard news, IT-domain, biomedical, multimodal, pronoun), three evaluation tasks (metrics, tuning, run-time estimation of MT quality), and an automatic post-editing task and bilingual document alignment task. This year, 102 MT systems from 24 institutions (plus 36 anonymized online systems) were submitted to the 12 translation directions in the news translation task. The IT-domain task received 31 submissions from 12 institutions in 7 directions and the Biomedical task received 15 submissions systems from 5 institutions. Evaluation was both automatic and manual (relative ranking and 100-point scale assessments).

The quality estimation task had three sub-tasks, with a total of 14 teams, submitting 39 entries. The automatic post-editing task had a total of 6 teams, submitting 11 entries.

1 Introduction

We present the results of the shared tasks of the First Conference on Statistical Machine Translation (WMT) held at ACL 2016. This conference builds on nine previous WMT workshops (Koehn and Monz, 2006; Callison-Burch et al., 2007, 2008, 2009, 2010, 2011, 2012; Bojar et al., 2013, 2014, 2015).

This year we conducted several official tasks. We report in this paper on five tasks:

- news translation (§2, §3)
- IT-domain translation (§4)
- biomedical translation (§5)
- quality estimation (§6)
- automatic post-editing (§7)

The conference featured additional shared tasks that are described in separate papers in these proceedings:

- tuning (Jawaid et al., 2016)
- metrics (Bojar et al., 2016b)
- cross-lingual pronoun prediction (Guillou et al., 2016)
- multimodal machine translation and crosslingual image description (Specia et al., 2016)
- bilingual document alignment (Buck and Koehn, 2016)

In the news translation task (§2), participants were asked to translate a shared test set, optionally restricting themselves to the provided training data. We held 12 translation tasks this year, between English and each of Czech, German, Finnish, Russian, Romanian, and Turkish. The Romanian and Turkish translation tasks were new this year, providing a lesser resourced data condition on challenging language pairs. The system outputs for each task were evaluated both automatically and manually.

The human evaluation (§3) involves asking human judges to rank sentences output by anonymized systems. We obtained large numbers of rankings from researchers who contributed

Proceedings of the First Conference on Machine Translation, Volume 2: Shared Task Papers, pages 131–198,
Berlin, Germany, August 11-12, 2016. ©2016 Association for Computational Linguistics

evaluations proportional to the number of tasks they entered. We made data collection more efficient and used TrueSkill as ranking method. We also explored a novel way of ranking machine translation systems by judgments of adequacy and fluency on a 100-point scale.

The IT translation task (§4) was introduced this year and focused on domain adaptation of MT to the IT (information technology) domain and translation of answers in a cross-lingual help-desk service, where hardware&software troubleshooting answers are translated from English to the users' languages: Bulgarian, Czech, German, Spanish, Basque, Dutch and Portuguese. Similarly as in the News translation task, training and test data were provided and the system outputs were evaluated both automatically and manually.

Another task newly introduced this year was the biomedical translation task (§5). Participants were asked to translate the titles and abstracts of scientific articles indexed in the Scielo database. Training and test data were provided for two subdomains, biological sciences and health sciences, and three language pairs, Portuguese/English, Spanish/English and French/English. This task therefore provided data for a language not previously covered in WMT, Portuguese. The system outputs for each language pair were evaluated both automatically and manually.

The quality estimation task (§6) this year included three subtasks: sentence-level prediction of post-editing effort scores, word and phrase-level prediction of good/bad labels, and document-level prediction of human post-editing scores. Datasets were released with English→German IT translations for sentence and word/phrase level, and English↔Spanish news translations for document level.

The automatic post-editing task (§7) examined automatic methods for correcting errors produced by an unknown machine translation system. Participants were provided with training triples containing source, target and human post-edits, and were asked to return automatic post-edits for unseen (source, target) pairs. In this second round, the task focused on correcting English→German translations in the IT domain.

The primary objectives of WMT are to evaluate the state of the art in machine translation, to disseminate common test sets and public training data with published performance numbers, and

to refine evaluation and estimation methodologies for machine translation. As before, all of the data, translations, and collected human judgments are publicly available.[1] We hope these datasets serve as a valuable resource for research into statistical machine translation and automatic evaluation or prediction of translation quality. News and IT translations are also available for interactive visualization and comparison of differences between systems at `http://wmt.ufal.cz` using MT-ComparEval (Sudarikov et al., 2016).

2   News Translation Task

The recurring WMT task examines translation between English and other languages in the news domain. As in the previous years, we include German, Czech, Russian, and Finnish. New languages this years are Romanian and Turkish.

We created a test set for each language pair by translating newspaper articles and provided training data.

2.1   Test data

The test data for this year's task was selected from online sources, as before. We took about 1500 English sentences and translated them into the other 5 languages, and then additional 1500 sentences from each of the other languages and translated them into English. This gave us test sets of about 3000 sentences for our English-X language pairs, which have been either originally written in English and translated into X, or vice versa. The composition of the test documents is shown in Table 1.

The stories were translated by professional translators, funded by the EU Horizon 2020 projects CRACKER and QT21 (German, Czech, Romanian), by Yandex[2], a Russian search engine company (Turkish, Russian), and by BAULT, a research community on building and using language technology funded by the University of Helsinki (Finnish). For Finnish, a second translation was provided as well, but not used in the evaluation. All of the translations were done directly, and not via an intermediate language.

For Turkish we also released an additional 500 sentence development set, and for Romanian a third of the test set were released as a development

---

[1] `http://statmt.org/wmt16/results.html`
[2] `http://www.yandex.com/`

set instead. For the other languages, test sets from previous years are available as development sets.

2.2 Training data

As in past years we provided parallel corpora to train translation models, monolingual corpora to train language models, and development sets to tune system parameters. Some training corpora were identical from last year (Europarl[3], United Nations, French-English 10^9 corpus, Common Crawl, Russian-English parallel data provided by Yandex, Wikipedia Headlines provided by CMU) and some were updated (CzEng v1.6pre (Bojar et al., 2016a), News Commentary v11, monolingual news data).

We added a few new corpora:

- Romanian Europarl (Koehn, 2002)
- SETIMES2 from OPUS for Romanian–English and Turkish–English (Tiedemann, 2009)
- Monolingual data sets from CommonCrawl (Buck et al., 2014)

Some statistics about the training materials are given in Figure 1.

2.3 Submitted systems

We received 102 submissions from 24 institutions. The participating institutions and their entry names are listed in Table 2; each system did not necessarily appear in all translation tasks. We also included 36 online statistical MT systems (originating from 4 services), which we anonymized as ONLINE-A,B,F,G.

For presentation of the results, systems are treated as either *constrained* or *unconstrained*, depending on whether their models were trained only on the provided data. Since we do not know how they were built, these online and commercial systems are treated as unconstrained during the automatic and human evaluations.

3 Human Evaluation

Each year, we conduct a human evaluation campaign to assess translation quality and determine the final ranking of candidate systems. This section describes how we prepared the evaluation data, collected human assessments, and computed the official results.

Over the past few years, our method of collecting and evaluating the manual translations has settled into the following pattern. We ask human annotators to rank the outputs of five systems. From these rankings, we produce pairwise translation comparisons, and then evaluate them with a version of the TrueSkill algorithm adapted to our task. We refer to this approach (described in Section 3.4) as the *relative ranking* approach (RR), so named because the pairwise comparisons denote only relative ability between a pair of systems, and cannot be used to infer their absolute quality. These results are used to produce the official ranking for the WMT 2016 tasks. However, work in evaluation over the past few years has provided fresh insight into ways to collect *direct assessments* (DA) of machine translation quality. In this setting, annotators are asked to provide an assessment of the direct quality of the output of a system relative to a reference translation. In order to evaluate the potential of this approach for future WMT evaluations, we conducted a direct assessment evaluation in parallel. This evaluation, together with a comparison of the official results, is described in Section 3.5.

3.1 Evaluation campaign overview

Following the trend from previous years, WMT16 ended up being the largest evaluation campaign to date. Similar to last year, we collected *researcher-based judgments* only (as opposed to crowd-sourcing annotations from a tool like Mechanical Turk). For the News translation task, a total of 150 individual annotator accounts were involved. Users came from 33 different research groups and contributed judgments on 10,833 HITs.

Each HIT comprises three 5-way ranking tasks for a total of 32,499 such tasks. Under ordinary circumstances, each of the tasks would correspond to ten individual pairwise system comparisons denoting whether a system A was judged better than, worse than, or equivalent to another system B. However, since many systems have produced the same outputs for a particular sentence, we are often able to produce more than ten comparisons (Section 3.2), ending up with a total of 569,287 pairwise annotations—a 75.2% increase over the expected baseline of 324,990 pairs. This is smaller than last year's gain of 87.1% as we have decided to preserve punctuation differences. Section 3.2 provides more details on our pre-processing.

---

[3]As of Fall 2011, the proceedings of the European Parliament are no longer translated into all official languages.

Europarl Parallel Corpus

	German ↔ English		Czech ↔ English		Finnish ↔ English		Romanian ↔ English	
Sentences	1,920,209		646,605		1,926,114		399,375	
Words	50,486,398	53,008,851	14,946,399	17,376,433	37,814,266	52,723,296	10,943,404	10,891,847
Distinct words	381,583	115,966	172,461	63,039	693,963	115,896	73,353	42,650

News Commentary Parallel Corpus

	German ↔ English		Czech ↔ English		Russian ↔ English	
Sentences	242,770		191,432		174,253	
Words	6,284,116	6,307,244	4,385,588	4,914,094	4,452,010	4,681,362
Distinct words	153,835	68,039	154,044	62,043	151,228	55,382

Common Crawl Parallel Corpus

	French ↔ English		German ↔ English		Czech ↔ English		Russian ↔ English	
Sentences	3,244,152		2,399,123		161,838		878,386	
Words	91,328,790	81,096,306	54,575,405	58,870,638	3,529,783	3,927,378	21,018,793	21,535,122
Distinct words	889,291	859,017	1,640,835	823,480	210,170	128,212	764,203	432,062

United Nations Parallel Corpus

	French ↔ English	
Sentences	12,886,831	
Words	411,916,781	360,341,450
Distinct words	565,553	666,077

Yandex 1M Parallel Corpus

	Russian ↔ English	
Sentences	1,000,000	
Words	24,121,459	26,107,293
Distinct words	701,809	387,646

10^9 Word Parallel Corpus

	French ↔ English	
Sentences	22,520,400	
Words	811,203,407	668,412,817
Distinct words	2,738,882	2,861,836

CzEng Parallel Corpus

	Czech ↔ English	
Sentences	51,424,584	
Words	592,890,104	699,087,647
Distinct words	3,073,115	1,727,574

Wiki Headlines Parallel Corpus

	Russian ↔ English		Finnish ↔ English	
Sentences	514,859		153,728	
Words	1,191,474	1,230,644	269,429	354,362
Distinct words	282,989	251,328	127,576	96,732

Europarl Language Model Data

	English	German	Czech	Finnish
Sentence	2,218,201	2,176,537	668,595	2,120,739
Words	59,848,044	53,534,167	14,946,399	39,511,068
Distinct words	123,059	394,781	172,461	711,868

News Language Model Data

	English	German	Czech	Russian	Finnish	Romanian
Sentence	145,573,876	187,008,695	53,383,346	56,371,276	6,740,879	2,280,642
Words	3,355,935,396	3,331,396,767	879,993,532	1,016,368,612	83,112,454	54,793,949
Distinct words	5,487,137	16,166,174	3,824,351	3,834,224	2,572,117	504,438

Common Crawl Language Model Data

	English	German	Czech	Russian	Finnish	Romanian	Turkish
Sent.	3,074,921,453	2,872,785,485	333,498,145	1,168,529,851	157,264,161	288,806,234	511,196,951
Words	65,128,419,540	65,154,042,103	6,694,811,063	23,313,060,950	2,935,402,545	8,140,378,873	11,882,126,872
Dist.	342,760,462	339,983,035	50,162,437	101,436,673	47,083,545	37,846,546	88,463,295

Test Set

	German ↔ EN		Czech ↔ EN		Russian ↔ EN		Finnish ↔ EN		Romanian ↔ EN		Turkish ↔ EN	
Sent.	2,999		2,999		2,998		3,000		1,999		2,998	
Words	64,379	65,647	57,097	66,457	62,840	71,068	48,839	64,611	50,603	48,531	54,420	67,468
Dist.	12,234	8,877	15,163	8,639	16,304	8,963	16,092	8,413	9,851	6,953	15,395	8,799

Figure 1: Statistics for the training and test sets used in the translation task. The number of words and the number of distinct words (case-insensitive) is based on the provided tokenizer.

Language	Sources (Number of Documents)
English	ABC News (5), BBC (5), Brisbane Times (2), CBS News (2), CNN (1), Christian Science Monitor (2), Daily Mail (4), Euronews (1), Fox News (2), Guardian (9), Independent (1), Los Angeles Times (3), Medical Daily (1), News.com Australia (4), New York Times (1), Reuters (3), Russia Today (2), Scotsman (2), Sky (1), Sydney Morning Herald (5), stv.tv (1), Telegraph (4), The Local (2), Time Magazine (1), UPI (3), Xinhua Net (1).
Czech	aktuálně.cz (2), blesk.cz (3), deník.cz (8), e15.cz (2), iDNES.cz (12), ihned.cz (4), lidovky.cz (7), Novinky.cz (1), tyden.cz (6), ZDN (1).
German	Wirtschaftsblatt (1), Abendzeitung München (1), Abendzeitung Nürnberg (1), Ärztezeitung (1), Aachener Nachrichten (4), Berliner Kurier (1), Borkener Zeitung (1), Come On (1), Die Presse (2), Dülmener Zeitung (2), Euronews (1), Frankfurter Rundschau (1), Göttinger Tageblatt (1), Hessische/Niedersächsische Allgemeine (1), In Franken (4), Kleine Zeitung (3), Kreisanzeiger (1), Kreiszeitung (1), Krone (2), Lampertheimer Zeitung (1), Lausitzer Rundschau (1), Merkur (2), Morgenweb (1), Mitteldeutsche Zeitung (1), NTV (2), Nachrichten.at (6), Neues Deutschland (2), Neue Presse Coburg (1), Neue Westfälische (1), Ostfriesenzeitung (2), Passauer Neue Presse (1), Rheinzeitung (1), Schwarzwälder Bote (1), Segeberger Zeitung (1), Stuttgarter Nachrichten (1), Südkurier (3), Tagesspiegel (1), Teckbote (1), Thueringer Allgemeine (1), Thüringische Landeszeitung (1), tz München (1), Usinger Anzeiger (6), Volksblatt (3), Westfälischer Anzeiger (1), Weser Kurier (1), Wiesbadener Kurier (2), Westfälische Nachrichten (4), Westdeutsche Zeitung (3), Willhelmshavener Zeitung (1), Yahoo (1).
Finnish	Aamulehti (4), Etelä-Saimaa (2), Etelä-Suomen Sanomat (1), Helsingin Sanomat (12), Ilkka (5), Iltalehti (10), Ilta-Sanomat (31), Kaleva (3), Karjalainen (7), Kouvolan Sanomat (2).
Russian	168.ru (1), aif (2), altapress.ru (2), argumenti.ru (1), BBC Russian (1), Euronews (2), Fakty (3), Russia Today (1), Izvestiya (3), Kommersant (13), Lenta (7), lgng (2), MK RU (1), New Look Media (1), Novaya Gazeta (3), Novinite (1), ogirk.ru (1), pnp.ru (2), rg.ru (1), Rosbalt (2), rusplit.ru (1), Sport Express (10), trud.ru (2), tumentoday.ru (1), Vedomosti (1), Versia (2), Vesti (11), VM News (1).
Romanian	National (1), HotNews (1), Info Press (1), Puterea (1), ziare.ro (29), Ziarul de Iași (17)
Turkish	hurriyet (37), Sabah (26), Zaman (23)

Table 1: Composition of the test set. For more details see the XML test files. The `docid` tag gives the source and the date for each document in the test set, and the `origlang` tag indicates the original source language.

In total, our human annotators spent nearly 39 days and 3 hours working in Appraise. This gives an average annotation time of 6.4 hours per user. The average annotation time per HIT amounts to 5 minutes and 12 seconds. This is a little slower than last year's average time of 4 minutes and 53 seconds. Similar to the previous campaign, several of the annotators passed the mark of more than 100 HITs annotated (the maximum number being 684) and, again, some worked for more than 24 hours (the most patient annotator contributing a little over 99 hours of annotation work).

The effort that goes into the manual evaluation campaign each year is impressive, and we are grateful to all participating individuals and teams. We believe that human annotation provides the best decision basis for evaluation of machine translation output and it is great to see continued contributions on this large scale.

3.2 Data collection

The system ranking is produced from a large set of pairwise judgments, each of which indicates the relative quality of the outputs of two systems' translations of the same input sentence. Annotations are collected in an evaluation campaign that enlists participants in the shared task to help. Each team is asked to contribute one hundred so-called "Human Intelligence Tasks" (HITs) per primary system submitted.

We continue to use the open-source Appraise[4] (Federmann, 2012) tool for our data collection. Last year, we had provided the following instructions at the top of each HIT page:

You are shown a source sentence followed by several candidate translations. Your task is to rank the translations from best to worst (ties are allowed).

This year, in order to optimize screen space we have streamlined the user interface, removing the instruction text (which instead was communicated to annotators outside of the HIT annotation interface) and trimming vertical spacing. A screenshot of the Appraise relative ranking interface is shown in Figure 2.

Annotators are asked to rank the outputs from 1 (best) to 5 (worst), with ties permitted. Note that a *lower* rank is better, and that this is clear from the interface design. Annotators can decide to skip a ranking task but are instructed to do this only as a last resort, e.g., if the translation candidates shown on screen are clearly misformatted or contain data

---

[4]https://github.com/cfedermann/Appraise

ID	Institution
AALTO	Aalto University (Grönroos et al., 2016)
ABUMATRAN-*	Abu-MaTran (Sánchez-Cartagena and Toral, 2016)
AFRL-MITLL	Air Force Research Laboratory / MIT Lincoln Lab (Gwinnup et al., 2016)
AMU-UEDIN	Adam Mickiewicz Uni. / Uni. Edinburgh (Junczys-Dowmunt et al., 2016)
CAMBRIDGE	University of Cambridge (Stahlberg et al., 2016)
CMU	Carnegie Mellon University
CU-MERGEDTREES	Charles University (Mareček, 2016)
CU-CHIMERA CU-TAMCHYNA	Charles University (Tamchyna et al., 2016)
CU-TECTOMT	Charles University (Dušek et al., 2015)
JHU-*	Johns Hopkins University (Ding et al., 2016)
KIT, KIT-LIMSI	Karlsruhe Institute of Technology (Ha et al., 2016)
LIMSI	University of Paris (Allauzen et al., 2016)
LMU-CUNI	University of Munich / Charles University (Tamchyna et al., 2016)
METAMIND	Salesforce Metamind (Bradbury and Socher, 2016)
NRC	National Research Council Canada (Lo et al., 2016)
NYU-MONTERAL	New York University / University of Montréal (Chung et al., 2016)
PARFDA	Ergun Bicici (Bicici, 2016a)
PJATK	Polish-Japanese Academy of Inf. Technology (Wołk and Marasek, 2016)
PROMT	PROMT Automated Translation Solutions (Molchanov and Bykov, 2016)
QT21-HIML	QT21 System Combination (Peter et al., 2016b)
RWTH	RWTH Aachen (Peter et al., 2016a)
TBTK	TÜBITAK (Bektaş et al., 2016)
UEDIN-NMT	University of Edinburgh (Sennrich et al., 2016)
UEDIN-PBMT UEDIN-SYNTAX	University of Edinburgh (Williams et al., 2016)
UEDIN-LMU	University of Edinburgh / University of Munich (Huck et al., 2016)
UH-*	University of Helsinki (Tiedemann et al., 2016)
USFD-RESCORING	University of Sheffield (Blain et al., 2016)
UUT	Uppsala University (Tiedemann et al., 2016)
YSDA	Yandex School of Data Analysis (Dvorkovich et al., 2016)
ONLINE-[A,B,F,G]	Four online statistical machine translation systems

Table 2: Participants in the shared translation task. Not all teams participated in all language pairs. The translations from the commercial and online systems were not submitted by their respective companies but were obtained by us, and are therefore anonymized in a fashion consistent with previous years of the workshop.

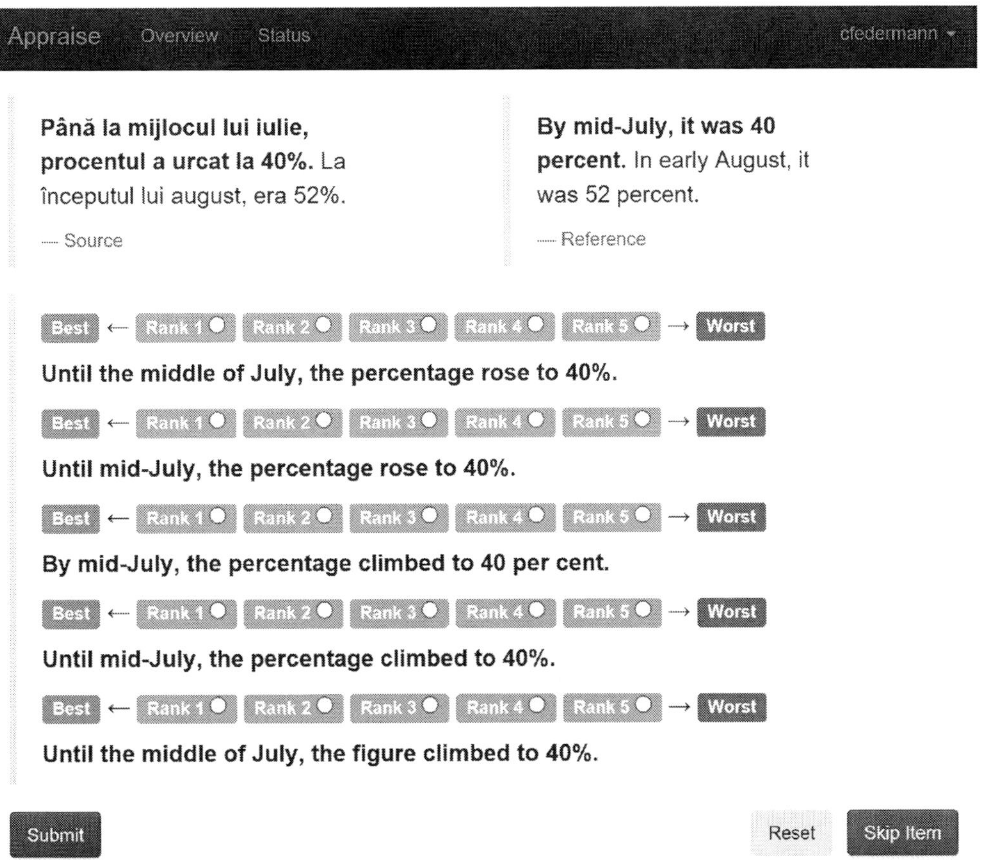

Figure 2: Screenshot of the Appraise interface used in the human evaluation campaign. The annotator is presented with a source segment, a reference translation, and up to five outputs from competing systems (anonymized and displayed in random order), and is asked to rank these according to their translation quality, with ties allowed.

issues (wrong language, encoding errors or other, obvious problems). Similar to last year, only a few ranking tasks have been skipped in WMT16.

Each HIT consists of three so-called *ranking tasks*. In a ranking task, an annotator is presented with a source segment, a human reference translation, and the outputs of up to five anonymized candidate systems, randomly selected from the set of participating systems, and displayed in random order. This year, as with last year, we perform a redundancy cleanup as an initial preprocessing step and create *multi-system outputs* to avoid confusing annotators with identical content: instead of selecting five systems and displaying their (identical) outputs, we select five *distinct* outputs, and then propagate the collected rankings to all the individual systems within each of the respective multi-system outputs. Last year, however, nearly-identical outputs were collapsed if they differed only on punctuation. Because punctuation is an important component of producing quality MT output, this year, we only collapse outputs that are exactly the same, apart from differences in nonzero whitespace.

To demonstrate how this works, we provide the following example. First, consider the case where we select system outputs directly, instead of the multi-system outputs described above. Here, we consider an annotation provided by a judge among the outputs of systems A, B, F, H, and J:

	1	2	3	4	5
F				•	
A				•	
B		•			
J					•
H		•			

The joint rankings provided by a ranking task are then expanded to a set of *pairwise rankings* produced by considering all $\binom{n}{2} \leq 10$ combinations of all $n \leq 5$ outputs in the respective ranking task.

Language Pair	Systems	Comparisons	Comparisons/Sys
Czech→English	12	125,788	10,482.3
English→Czech	20	192,487	9,624.3
Finnish→English	9	30,519	3,391.0
English→Finnish	13	38,254	2,942.6
German→English	10	20,937	2,093.7
English→German	15	50,989	3,399.2
Romanian→English	7	15,822	2,260.2
English→Romanian	12	11,352	946.0
Russian→English	10	27,353	2,735.3
English→Russian	12	34,414	2,867.8
Turkish→English	9	10,188	1,132.0
English→Turkish	9	11,184	1,242.6
Totals WMT16	138	569,287	4,125.2
WMT15	131	542,732	4,143.0
WMT14	110	328,830	2,989.3
WMT13	148	942,840	6,370.5
WMT12	103	101,969	999.6
WMT11	133	63,045	474.0

Table 3: Amount of data (pairwise comparisons after "de-collapsing" *multi-system outputs*) collected in the WMT16 manual evaluation campaign. The final five rows report summary information from previous years of the workshop. Note how many rankings we get for Czech language pairs; these include systems from the tuning shared task.

As the number of outputs n depends on the number of identical (and, hence, redundant) *multi-system outputs* in the original data, we end up getting varying numbers of corresponding binary judgments. Now, consider the case of *multi-system outputs*. If the outputs of system A and F from above are actually identical, the annotator this year would see an easier ranking task:[5]

	1	2	3	4	5
AF				•	
B		•			
J					•
H			•		

Both examples would be reduced to the following set of pairwise judgments:

$$A > B, A = F, A > H, A < J$$
$$B < F, B < H, B < J$$
$$F > H, F < J$$
$$H < J$$

Here, $A > B$ should be read is "A is ranked higher than (worse than) B". Note that by this procedure, the absolute value of ranks and the magnitude of their differences are discarded. In the case of multi-system outputs, this set of pairwise rankings would have been produced with less annotator effort. This productivity gain grows in the number of systems that produce identical output, and this situation is quite common, due in part to the fact that many systems are built on the same underlying technology. Table 3 has more details.

3.3 Annotator agreement

Each year we calculate annotator agreement scores for the human evaluation as a measure of the reliability of the rankings. We measured pairwise agreement among annotators using Cohen's kappa coefficient (κ) (Cohen, 1960). If $P(A)$ be the proportion of times that the annotators agree, and $P(E)$ is the proportion of time that they would agree by chance, then Cohen's kappa is:

$$\kappa = \frac{P(A) - P(E)}{1 - P(E)}$$

Note that κ is basically a normalized version of $P(A)$, one which takes into account how meaningful it is for annotators to agree with each other by incorporating $P(E)$. The values for κ range from 0 to 1, with zero indicating no agreement and 1 perfect agreement.

We calculate $P(A)$ by examining all pairs of

---

[5]Technically, another distinct output would have been inserted, if possible, so as to present the annotator with five, but we ignore that for illustration purposes.

Language Pair	WMT12	WMT13	WMT14	WMT15	WMT16
Czech→English	0.311	0.244	0.305	0.458	0.244
English→Czech	0.359	0.168	0.360	0.438	0.381
German→English	0.385	0.299	0.368	0.423	0.475
English→German	0.356	0.267	0.427	0.423	0.369
French→English	0.272	0.275	0.357	0.343	—
English→French	0.296	0.231	0.302	0.317	—
Russian→English	—	0.278	0.324	0.372	0.339
English→Russian	—	0.243	0.418	0.336	0.340
Finnish→English	—	—	—	0.388	0.293
English→Finnish	—	—	—	0.549	0.484
Romanian→English	—	—	—	—	0.379
English→Romanian	—	—	—	—	0.341
Turkish→English	—	—	—	—	0.322
English→Turkish	—	—	—	—	0.319
Mean	0.330	0.260	0.367	0.405	0.357

Table 4: κ scores measuring inter-annotator agreement for WMT16. See Table 5 for corresponding intra-annotator agreement scores. WMT14–WMT16 results are based on researchers' judgments only, whereas prior years mixed judgments of researchers and crowdsourcers.

outputs[6] which had been judged by two or more judges, and calculating the proportion of time that they agreed that $A < B$, $A = B$, or $A > B$. In other words, $P(A)$ is the empirical, observed rate at which annotators agree, in the context of pairwise comparisons.

As for $P(E)$, it captures the probability that two annotators would agree randomly. Therefore:

$$P(E) = P(A<B)^2 + P(A=B)^2 + P(A>B)^2$$

Note that each of the three probabilities in $P(E)$'s definition are squared to reflect the fact that we are considering the chance that *two* annotators would agree by chance. Each of these probabilities is computed empirically, by observing how often annotators actually rank two systems as being tied.

Table 4 shows final κ values for inter-annotator agreement for WMT11–WMT16 while Table 5 details intra-annotator agreement scores. The exact interpretation of the kappa coefficient is difficult, but according to Landis and Koch (1977), 0–0.2 is *slight*, 0.2–0.4 is *fair*, 0.4–0.6 is *moderate*, 0.6–0.8 is *substantial*, and 0.8–1.0 is *almost perfect*.

Compared to last year's results, inter-annotator agreement rates have decreased. Notably, for Czech→English, we see a drop from 0.458 to 0.244. English→Czech decreases from 0.438 to 0.381. Considering that the total number of data points collected as well as the number of annotators for these language pairs have increased substantially, the lower agreement score seems plausible.[7] We observe a small increase in agreement for German→English (from 0.423 to 0.475) and a drop for English→German (from 0.434 to 0.369). Scores for both Russian language pairs are similar to what had been measured in WMT15. For Finnish, we again see a decrease (from 0.388 to 0.293 for Finnish→English and from 0.549 to 0.484 for English→Finnish) and our new languages, Romanian and Turkish, end up with *fair* annotator agreement. The average inter-annotator agreement across all languages is 0.357, which is also *fair* and comparable to researchers' agreement over the last years. Intra-annotator agreement scores have mostly decreased compared to WMT15, except for both Russian language pairs. The new languages show *moderate* agreement except for English→Turkish which achieves a *fair* score. On average we observe an intra-annotator agreement which is comparable to researcher-based scores from WMT13–WMT15.

---

[6]Regardless if they correspond to an individual system or to a set of systems ("multi-system") producing identical translations. Thus, when computing annotator agreement scores, we effectively treat both individual and multi-systems in the same way, as "individual comparison units". By doing so, we avoid artificially inflating our agreement scores based on the automatically inferred $A = B$ ties from multi-systems.

[7]Both Czech→English and English→Czech contain tuning-task systems with very similar quality (according to both human evaluation and BLEU), which makes the annotation task more difficult.

Language Pair	WMT12	WMT13	WMT14	WMT15	WMT16
Czech→English	0.454	0.479	0.382	0.694	0.504
English→Czech	0.390	0.290	0.448	0.584	0.438
German→English	0.392	0.535	0.344	0.801	0.552
English→German	0.433	0.498	0.576	0.676	0.529
French→English	0.360	0.578	0.629	0.510	—
English→French	0.414	0.495	0.507	0.426	—
Russian→English	—	0.450	0.629	0.506	0.552
English→Russian	—	0.513	0.570	0.492	0.528
Finnish→English	—	—	—	0.562	0.549
English→Finnish	—	—	—	0.697	0.617
Romanian→English	—	—	—	—	0.621
English→Romanian	—	—	—	—	0.552
Turkish→English	—	—	—	—	0.559
English→Turkish	—	—	—	—	0.352
Mean	0.407	0.479	0.522	0.595	0.529

Table 5: κ scores measuring intra-annotator agreement, i.e., self-consistency of judges, across for the past few years of the human evaluation campaign. Scores are in line with results from WMT14 and WMT15.

3.4 Producing the human ranking

The collected pairwise rankings are used to produce the official human ranking of the systems. Since WMT14, we have used the TrueSkill method for producing the official ranking, in the following fashion. We produce 1,000 bootstrap-resampled datasets over all of the available data (i.e., datasets sampled uniformly with replacement from the complete dataset). We run TrueSkill over each dataset. We then compute a *rank range* for each system by collecting the absolute rank of each system in each fold, throwing out the top and bottom 2.5%, and then clustering systems into equivalence classes containing systems with over-lapping ranges, yielding a partial ordering over systems at the 95% confidence level.

The full list of the official human rankings for each task can be found in Table 6, which also reports all system scores, rank ranges, and clusters for all language pairs and all systems. The official interpretation of these results is that systems in the same cluster are considered tied. Given the large number of judgments that we collected, it was possible to group on average about two systems in a cluster, even though the systems in the middle are typically in larger clusters.

In Figure 3–5, we plotted the human evaluation result against everybody's favorite metric BLEU. Although these two metrics correlate generally well, the plots clearly suggest that a fair comparison of systems of different kinds cannot rely on automatic scores. Rule-based systems receive a much lower BLEU score than statistical systems (see for instance English–German, e.g., PROMT-RULE). The same is true to a lesser degree for statistical syntax-based systems (see English–German, UEDIN-SYNTAX vs. UEDIN-PBMT).

3.5 Direct Assessment Manual Evaluation

In addition to the standard relative ranking (RR) manual evaluation, this year a new method of human evaluation was also trialed in the main translation task: monolingual direct assessment (DA) of translation fluency (Graham et al., 2013) and adequacy (Graham et al., 2014, 2016).

Agreement between human assessors of translation quality is a known problem in evaluation of MT and DA therefore aims to simplify translation assessment, which conventionally takes the form of a bilingual evaluation, by restructuring the task into a monolingual assessment. Figure 6 provides a screen shot of DA adequacy assessment, where the task is structured as a monolingual similarity of meaning task.

Human assessors are asked to rate a given translation by how adequately it expresses the meaning of the corresponding reference translation on an analogue scale, which corresponds to an underlying absolute 0–100 rating. DA fluency assessment is similar with two exceptions, firstly no reference translation is displayed and secondly, assessors are asked to rate how much they agree that a given translation is fluent target language text. DA flu-

Czech–English

#	score	range	system
1	0.62	1	UEDIN-NMT
2	0.32	2	JHU-PBMT
3	0.21	3	ONLINE-B
4	0.11	4-6	TT-BLEU-MIRA
	0.10	4-7	TT-AFRL
	0.09	4-7	TT-NRC-NNBLEU
	0.07	5-8	TT-NRC-MEANT
	0.03	7-10	TT-BEER-PRO
	0.00	8-10	PJATK
	0.00	8-10	TT-BLEU-MERT
5	−0.07	11	ONLINE-A
6	−1.48	12	CU-MRGTREES

English–Czech

#	score	range	system
1	0.59	1	UEDIN-NMT
2	0.43	2	NYU-MONTREAL
3	0.34	3	JHU-PBMT
4	0.30	4-5	CU-CHIMERA
	0.30	4-5	CU-TAMCHYNA
5	0.22	6-7	UEDIN-CU-SYTX
	0.19	6-7	ONLINE-B
6	0.16	8-11	TT-BLEU-MIRA
	0.15	8-12	TT-BEER-PRO
	0.15	8-13	TT-BLEU-MERT
	0.14	9-14	TT-AFRL2
	0.14	9-14	TT-AFRL1
	0.13	9-14	TT-DCU
	0.13	11-14	TT-FJFI
7	0.08	15	ONLINE-A
8	−0.03	16	CU-TECTOMT
9	−0.43	17	TT-USAAR-HMM-MERT
10	−0.54	18	CU-MRGTREES
11	−1.13	19	TT-USAAR-HMM-MIRA
12	−1.33	20	TT-USAAR-HARM

Romanian–English

#	score	range	system
1	0.58	1-2	ONLINE-B
	0.38	1-2	UEDIN-NMT
2	0.10	3	UEDIN-PBMT
3	−0.09	4-5	UEDIN-SYNTAX
	−0.19	4-6	ONLINE-A
	−0.32	5-7	JHU-PBMT
	−0.46	6-7	LIMSI

English–Romanian

#	score	range	system
1	0.45	1-2	UEDIN-NMT
	0.43	1-2	QT21-HIML-COMB
2	0.20	3-7	KIT
	0.16	3-7	UEDIN-PBMT
	0.14	3-7	ONLINE-B
	0.14	3-7	UEDIN-LMU-HIERO
	0.12	3-7	RWTH-COMB
3	−0.15	8-10	LIMSI
	−0.23	8-10	LMU-CUNI
	−0.26	8-11	JHU-PBMT
	−0.43	10-12	USFD-RESCORING
	−0.57	11-12	ONLINE-A

German–English

#	score	range	system
1	0.82	1	UEDIN-NMT
2	0.25	2-5	ONLINE-B
	0.21	2-5	ONLINE-A
	0.19	2-5	UEDIN-SYNTAX
	0.18	2-6	KIT
	0.04	5-7	UEDIN-PBMT
	0.03	6-7	JHU-PBMT
3	−0.12	8	ONLINE-G
4	−0.67	9	JHU-SYNTAX
5	−0.93	10	ONLINE-F

Russian–English

#	score	range	system
1	0.45	1-2	AMU-UEDIN
	0.43	1-3	ONLINE-G
	0.33	2-4	NRC
	0.25	3-5	ONLINE-B
	0.16	4-5	UEDIN-NMT
2	0.04	6-7	ONLINE-A
	0.02	6-7	AFRL-MITLL-PHR
3	−0.11	8-9	AFRL-MITLL-CNTR
	−0.17	8-9	PROMT-RULE
4	−1.39	10	ONLINE-F

English–Russian

#	score	range	system
1	0.79	1	PROMT-RULE
2	0.30	2-4	AMU-UEDIN
	0.26	2-5	ONLINE-B
	0.26	2-5	UEDIN-NMT
	0.20	3-5	ONLINE-G
3	0.10	6	NYU-MONTREAL
4	−0.02	7-8	JHU-PBMT
	−0.07	7-10	LIMSI
	−0.10	8-10	ONLINE-A
	−0.15	9-10	AFRL-MITLL-PHR
5	−0.31	11	AFRL-MITLL-VERB
6	−1.26	12	ONLINE-F

Turkish–English

#	score	range	system
1	0.82	1-2	ONLINE-B
	0.65	1-3	ONLINE-G
	0.56	2-3	ONLINE-A
2	0.21	4-5	TBTK-SYSCOMB
	0.12	4-6	PROMT-SMT
	−0.00	5-6	YSDA
3	−0.67	7-8	JHU-SYNTAX
	−0.76	7-9	JHU-PBMT
	−0.94	8-9	PARFDA

English–German

#	score	range	system
1	0.49	1	UEDIN-NMT
2	0.40	2	METAMIND
3	0.29	3	UEDIN-SYNTAX
4	0.17	4	NYU-MONTREAL
5	−0.01	5-10	ONLINE-B
	−0.01	5-10	KIT-LIMSI
	−0.02	5-10	CAMBRIDGE
	−0.02	5-10	ONLINE-A
	−0.03	5-10	PROMT-RULE
	−0.05	6-10	KIT
6	−0.14	11-12	JHU-SYNTAX
	−0.15	11-12	JHU-PBMT
7	−0.26	13-14	UEDIN-PBMT
	−0.33	13-15	ONLINE-F
	−0.34	14-15	ONLINE-G

Finnish–English

#	score	range	system
1	0.42	1-4	UEDIN-PBMT
	0.40	1-4	ONLINE-G
	0.39	1-4	ONLINE-B
	0.34	1-4	UH-OPUS
2	0.01	5	PROMT-SMT
3	−0.11	6-7	UH-FACTORED
	−0.13	6-7	UEDIN-SYNTAX
4	−0.29	8	ONLINE-A
5	−1.03	9	JHU-PBMT

English–Finnish

#	score	range	system
1	0.36	1-3	ONLINE-G
	0.31	1-4	ABUMATRAN-NMT
	0.29	1-4	ONLINE-B
	0.23	3-5	ABUMATRAN-CMB
	0.16	4-5	UH-OPUS
2	−0.01	6-8	ABUMATRAN-PB
	−0.02	6-8	NYU-MONTREAL
	−0.02	6-8	ONLINE-A
3	−0.14	9-10	JHU-PBMT
	−0.23	9-12	UH-FACTORED
	−0.28	10-13	AALTO
	−0.30	10-13	JHU-HLTCOE
	−0.35	11-13	UUT

English–Turkish

#	score	range	system
1	0.76	1-2	ONLINE-G
	0.62	1-2	ONLINE-B
2	0.38	3	ONLINE-A
3	0.06	4	YSDA
4	−0.13	5-6	JHU-HLTCOE
	−0.19	5-7	TBTK-MORPH
	−0.29	6-7	CMU
5	−0.54	8-9	JHU-PBMT
	−0.66	8-9	PARFDA

Table 6: Official results for the WMT16 translation task. Systems are ordered by their inferred system means, though systems within a cluster are considered tied. Lines between systems indicate clusters according to bootstrap resampling at p-level $p \leq .05$. Systems with gray background indicate use of resources that fall outside the constraints provided for the shared task.

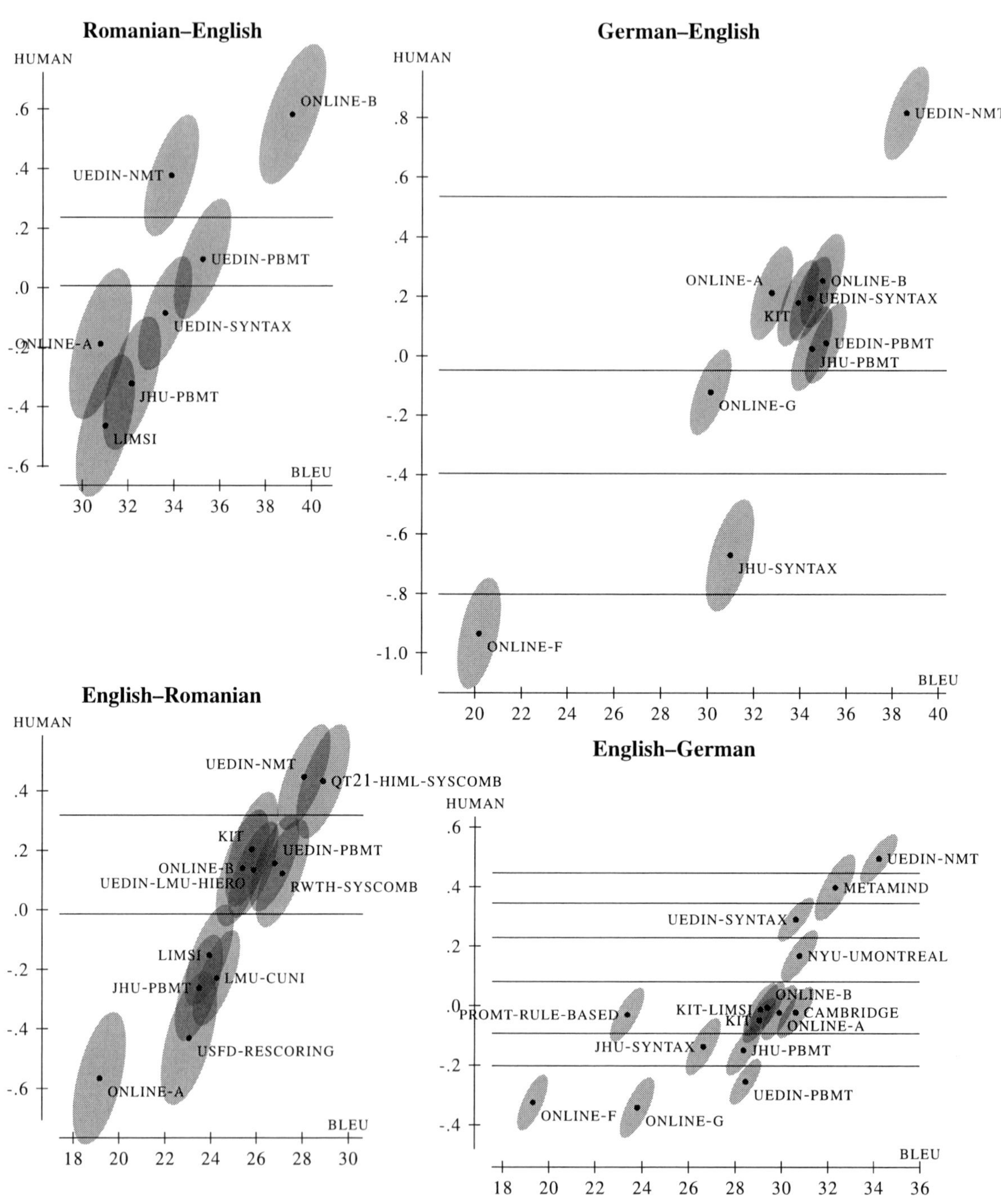

Figure 3: Human evaluation scores versus BLEU scores for the German–English and Romanian–English language pairs illustrate the need for human evaluation when comparing systems of different kind. Confidence intervals are indicated by the shaded ellipses. Rule-based systems and to a lesser degree syntax-based statistical systems receive a lower BLEU score than their human score would indicate. The big cluster in the Czech-English plot are tuning task submissions.

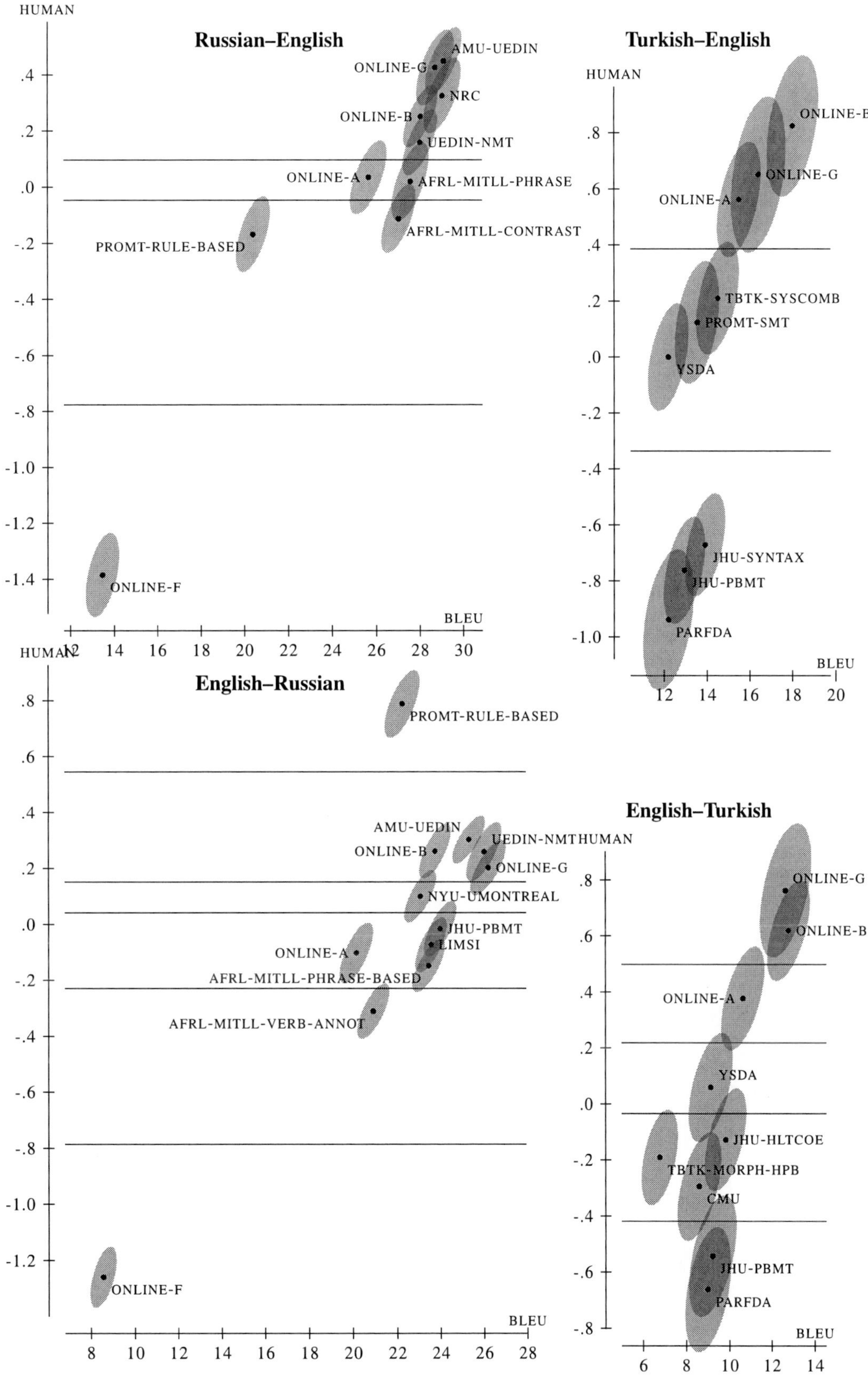

Figure 4: Human evaluation scores versus BLEU scores for the Russian–English and Turkish–English language pairs

143

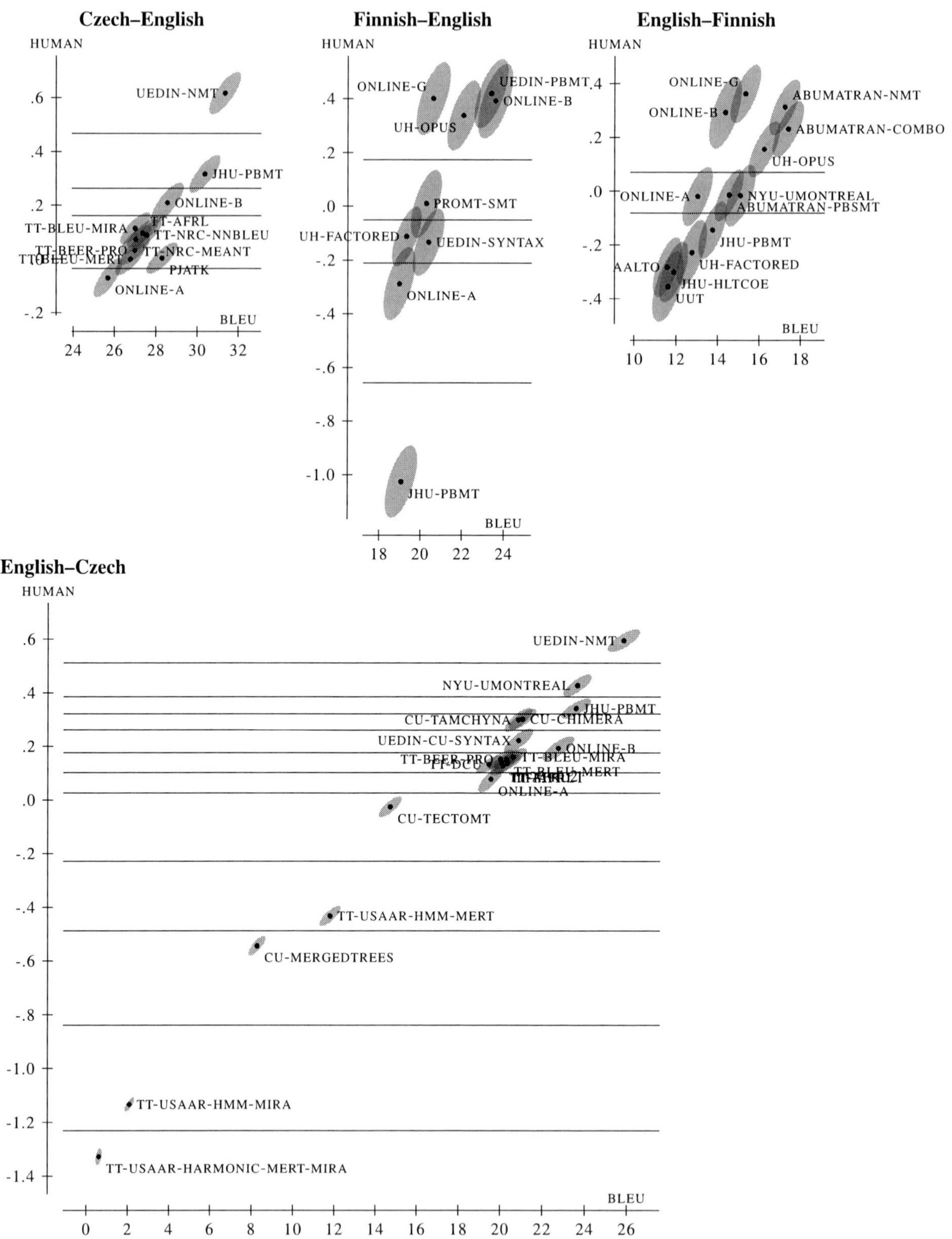

Figure 5: Human evaluation scores versus BLEU scores for the Czech–English and Finnish–English language pairs

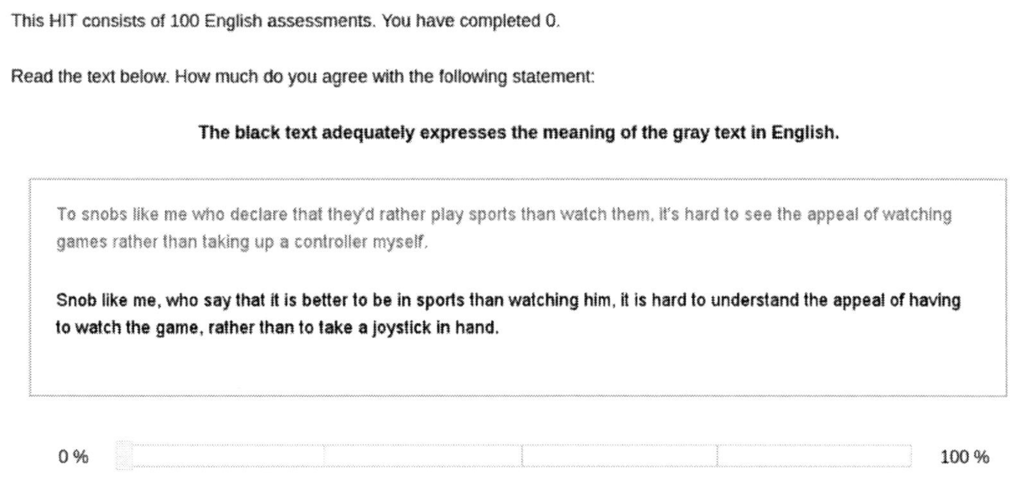

Figure 6: Direct Assessment of translation adequacy as carried out by workers on Mechanical Turk.

ency therefore provides a dimension of the assessment that cannot be biased by the presence of a reference translation. For both fluency and adequacy, the simpler monolingual assessment DA employs also allows the sentence length restriction to be removed.[8]

DA also aims to avoid the possible source of bias identified in Bojar et al. (2011), introduced by simultaneous assessment of several translations at once, where systems for which translations were more frequently compared to other low or high quality outputs resulted in either an unfair advantage or disadvantage for that system. We therefore elicit assessments of individual translations in isolation from the output of other systems, an important criteria when aiming for absolute quality judgments.

Large numbers of human assessments of translations for seven language pairs (cs-en, de-en, fi-en, ro-en, ru-en, tr-en and en-ru) were collected on Amazon's Mechanical Turk.[9] Table 7 shows overall numbers of translation assessments carried out.

Translations are arranged in sets of 100-translations per HIT to ensure sufficient repeat items per worker, before application of strict quality control measures to filter out assessments from poorly performing workers. When an analogue (or 100-points, in practice) scale is employed, agree-

ment cannot be measured using the conventional Kappa coefficient, ordinarily applied to evaluation of human assessment where judgments are discrete categories or preferences. Instead, we filter human assessors by how consistently they rate translations of known distinct quality.

A degraded version of a given original system output translation is automatically generated by substituting a sequence of words with a random phrase, itself selected from elsewhere in the reference document. Together with the original output, the degraded translation is known as a *bad reference* translation pair. Bad reference pairs are subsequently hidden within HITs, and provide a mechanism for filtering out workers who are simply not up to the task or those attempting to game the system. Assessments of workers who do not reliably score bad reference translations significantly lower than corresponding genuine system output translations are filtered out by comparison of scores they attribute to bad reference pairs within HITs. More specifically, we apply a paired Wilcoxon signed-rank test to score distributions of bad reference pairs, yielding a p-value for each worker we subsequently employ as a reliability estimate. Assessments of workers whose p-value lies above the conventional 0.05 threshold are omitted from the evaluation of systems.

Table 8 shows the number of unique workers who evaluated MT output on Mechanical Turk via DA for WMT16 for both fluency and adequacy, those who met our filtering requirement by show-

---

[8]The maximum sentence length with RR was 30 in WMT16.

[9]www.mturk.com

	Adequacy			Fluency		
	Pre Quality Control	Post Quality Control	Ave. per System	Pre Quality Control	Post Quality Control	Ave. per System
cs-en	30,000	16,800 (56.0%)	2,800	16,880	6,880 (40.8%)	1,146
de-en	68,800	33,760 (49.1%)	3,376	20,480	10,400 (50.8%)	1,040
fi-en	63,040	30,080 (47.7%)	3,342	21,760	9,680 (44.5%)	1,075
ro-en	27,920	16,000 (57.3%)	2,285	18,960	8,000 (42.2%)	1,142
ru-en	64,960	37,040 (57.0%)	3,704	24,640	11,520 (46.8%)	1,152
tr-en	48,640	18,400 (37.8%)	2,044	28,000	10,640 (38.0%)	1,182
en-ru	38,160	15,920 (41.7%)	1,326	-	-	-
Overall	341,520	168,000 (49.2%)	2,666	130,720	57,120 (43.7%)	1,120

DA Manual Evaluation Assessments

Table 7: Numbers of system output translations evaluated on Mechanical Turk for direct assessment (DA) in WMT16, numbers exclude quality control items.

	All	(A) Sig. Diff. Bad Ref.	(A) & No Sig. Diff. Exact Rep.
Adequacy	1307	735	717 (98%)
Fluency	864	380	372 (98%)

DA Workers

Table 8: Number of unique human assessors for DA adequacy and fluency on Mechanical Turk in WMT16, (A) those whose scores for bad reference pairs were significantly different and numbers of unique human assessors in (A) whose scores for exact repeat items also showed no significant difference, paired Wilcoxon signed-rank significance test was applied in both cases.

ing a significantly lower score for bad reference items, and the proportion of those workers who simultaneously showed no significant difference between scores they attributed in repeat assessment of an identical previous translation.

In order to iron out differences in scoring strategies of distinct workers, human assessment scores for translations are standardized according to each individual worker's overall mean and standard deviation score. Subsequently, the overall score of a given MT system participating in the shared task simply comprises the mean (standardized) score of its translations.

Table 9 includes mean DA fluency and adequacy scores for all to-English systems participating in WMT16 translation task, while Table 10 includes results for the single out-of-English language pair for which DA was run this year, English to Russian. Mean standardized scores for systems not significantly lower than that of any other participating system, according to Wilcoxon signed-rank test, for a given language pair, are highlighted in bold. Although we also evaluated the fluency of

translations, mean standardized adequacy scores should provide the primary mechanism for ranking competing systems, since it is entirely possible to achieve a high fluency score without conveying the meaning of the source input. Fluency can be employed as a secondary mechanism to break systems tied for adequacy or for diagnostic purposes. Figures 7, 8 and 9 show results of combining significance test conclusions for DA adequacy and fluency, where any ties between systems tied for adequacy are broken if that system outperformed the other with respect to fluency. It should be noted that RR provide official task results, while DA results are investigatory and do not indicate official translation task winners.

Finally, we compare scores of the official ranking to mean standardized adequacy scores for systems evaluated with DA. Table 11 shows the Pearson correlation between Trueskill scores for systems evaluated by researchers with relative preference judgments (official results) and DA mean scores collected via crowd-sourcing, showing high levels of agreement reached overall for all language pairs as correlations range from 0.92 to 0.997.

		DA Adequacy		**DA** Fluency	
		mean z	mean raw (%)	mean z	mean raw (%)
cs-en	UEDIN-NMT	**0.207**	75.4	**0.499**	78.7
	JHU-PBMT	0.101	72.6	0.194	69.3
	ONLINE-B	0.051	70.8	0.052	64.6
	ONLINE-A	0.000	69.5	−0.057	61.2
	PJATK	−0.024	69.0	−0.014	62.8
	CU-MERGEDTREES	−0.503	55.8	−0.754	41.1
de-en	UEDIN-NMT	**0.204**	75.8	**0.339**	77.5
	ONLINE-A	0.095	72.7	0.094	70.1
	ONLINE-B	0.086	72.2	0.015	68.4
	UEDIN-SYNTAX	0.065	71.5	0.141	71.8
	KIT	0.062	71.4	0.192	72.7
	UEDIN-PBMT	0.042	70.9	0.004	68.6
	JHU-PBMT	0.019	70.5	0.084	70.5
	ONLINE-G	0.009	70.2	−0.067	65.3
	ONLINE-F	−0.204	64.0	−0.348	57.8
	JHU-SYNTAX	−0.261	62.4	−0.237	62.5
fi-en	ONLINE-B	**0.095**	66.9	**0.100**	65.4
	UEDIN-PBMT	**0.087**	66.3	**0.149**	66.6
	ONLINE-G	**0.084**	66.4	0.009	62.3
	UH-OPUS	**0.065**	65.9	**0.105**	65.3
	PROMT-SMT	−0.037	62.9	−0.093	58.8
	UEDIN-SYNTAX	−0.090	61.5	−0.041	60.9
	UH-FACTORED	−0.098	61.2	−0.020	61.1
	ONLINE-A	−0.126	60.6	−0.094	58.5
	JHU-PBMT	−0.391	52.7	−0.320	53.1
ro-en	ONLINE-B	**0.129**	73.9	0.051	66.7
	UEDIN-NMT	0.044	71.2	**0.258**	71.9
	UEDIN-PBMT	0.025	71.0	0.028	65.6
	UEDIN-SYNTAX	0.000	69.9	−0.020	64.6
	ONLINE-A	−0.012	69.7	−0.015	64.3
	LIMSI	−0.123	66.7	−0.071	62.8
	JHU-PBMT	−0.160	65.7	−0.187	60.2
ru-en	ONLINE-G	**0.115**	74.2	0.100	69.9
	AMU-UEDIN	**0.103**	73.3	0.178	72.2
	ONLINE-B	0.083	72.8	0.030	67.8
	NRC	0.060	72.7	0.092	69.9
	PROMT-RULE-BASED	0.044	72.1	−0.102	63.8
	UEDIN-NMT	0.011	71.1	**0.245**	74.3
	ONLINE-A	−0.007	70.8	0.020	66.7
	AFRL-MITLL-PHRASE	−0.040	70.1	0.047	68.4
	AFRL-MITLL-CONTRAST	−0.071	69.3	−0.020	66.5
	ONLINE-F	−0.322	61.8	−0.472	54.7
tr-en	ONLINE-B	**0.163**	57.1	**0.250**	60.0
	ONLINE-G	0.109	55.0	0.166	58.7
	ONLINE-A	0.002	52.2	0.130	57.8
	TBTK-SYSCOMB	−0.077	49.6	0.009	53.2
	PROMT-SMT	−0.079	49.2	−0.057	51.4
	YSDA	−0.088	49.5	−0.036	52.6
	JHU-PBMT	−0.355	41.0	−0.416	43.1
	JHU-SYNTAX	−0.364	40.8	−0.307	46.4
	PARFDA	−0.367	40.5	−0.406	42.3

DA to-English Translation Task

Table 9: DA mean scores for WMT16 translation task participating systems for translation into English.

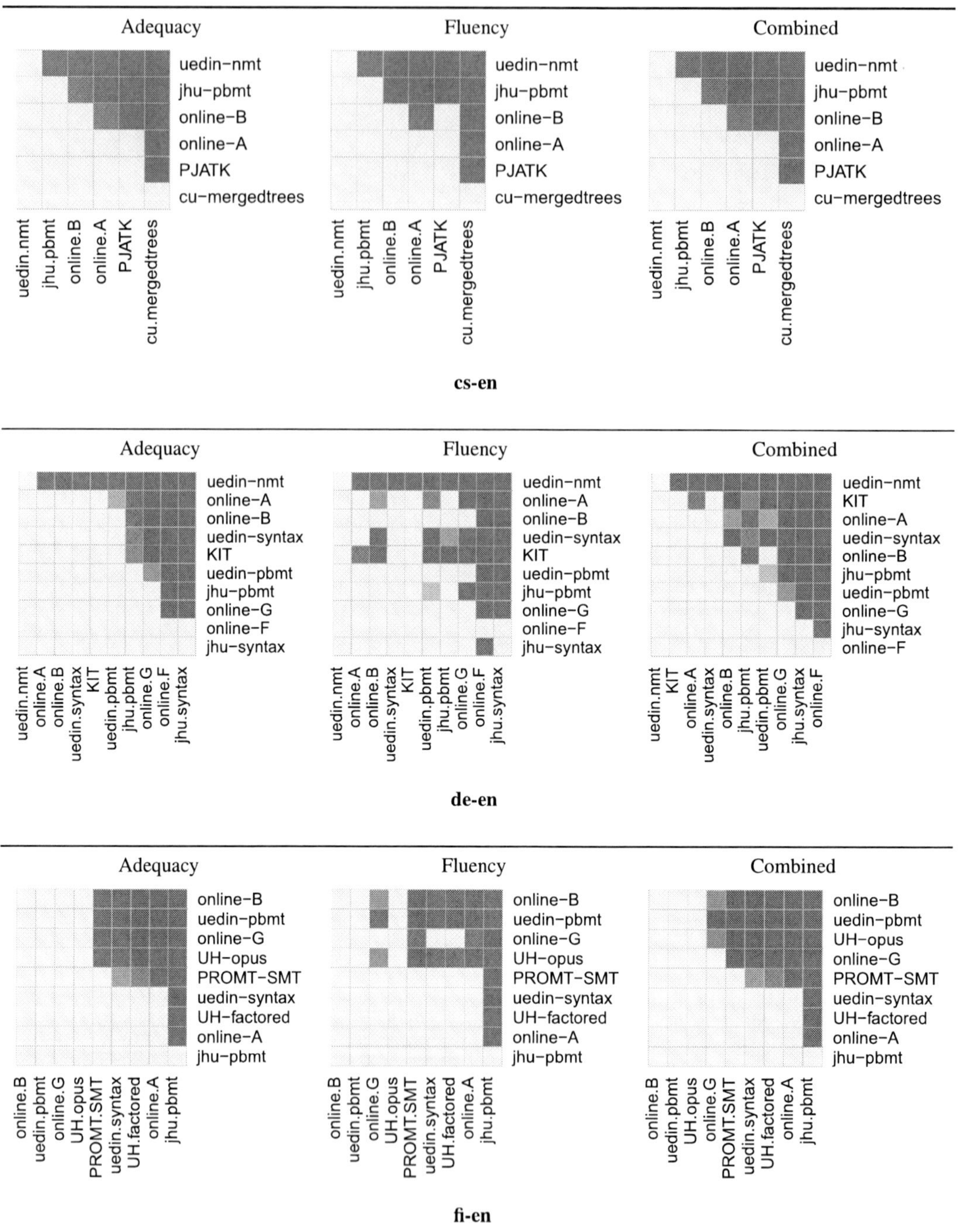

Figure 7: Significance test results for pairs of systems competing in the news domain translation task (cs-en, de-en, fi-en), where a green cell denotes a significantly higher DA adequacy or fluency score for the system in a given row over the system in a given column, "Combined" results show overall conclusions when adequacy is primarily used to rank systems with fluency used to break ties between systems tied with respect to adequacy.

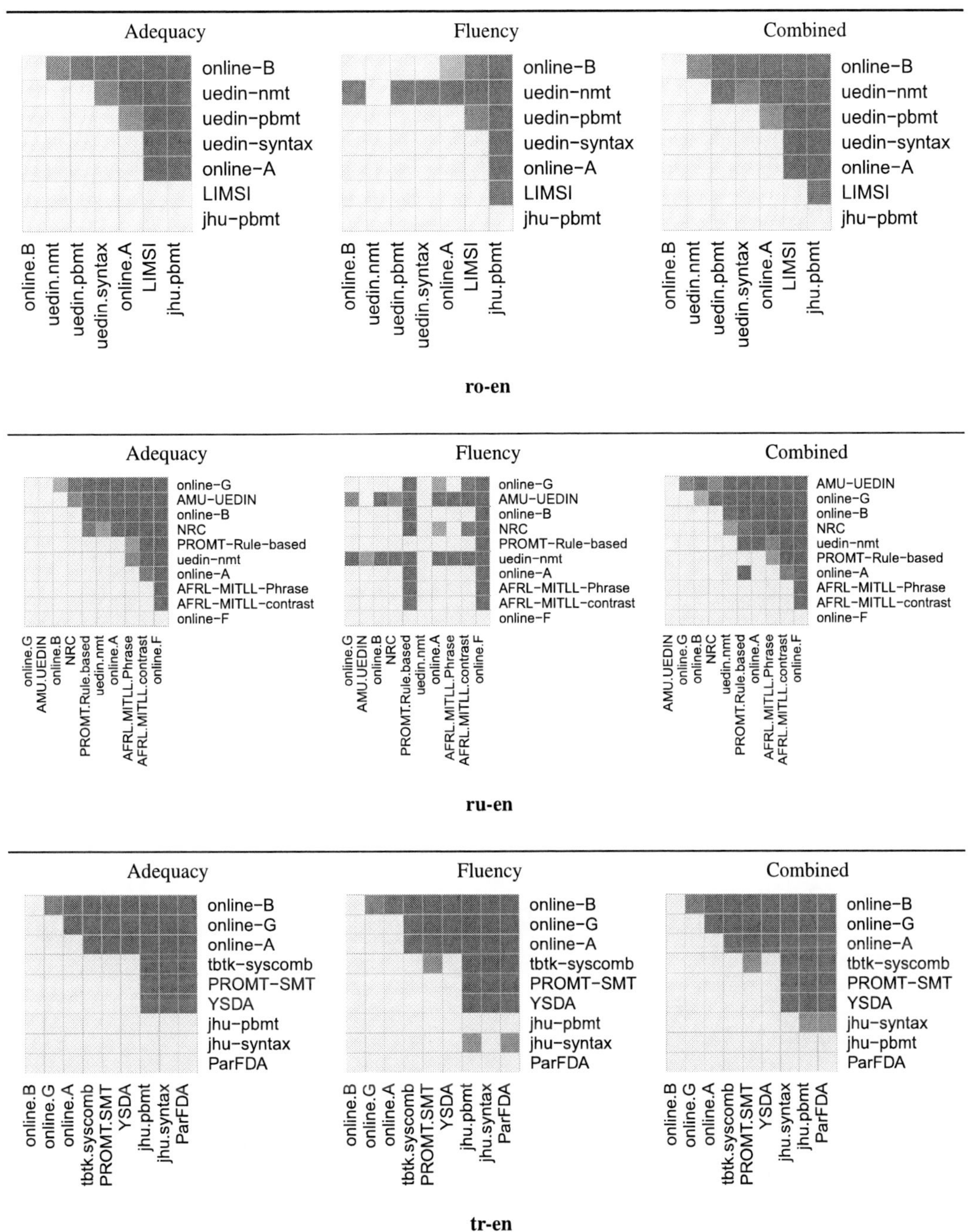

Figure 8: Significance test results for pairs of systems competing in the news domain translation task (ro-en, ru-en, tr-en), where a green cell denotes a significantly higher DA adequacy or fluency score for the system in a given row over the system in a given column, "Combined" results show overall conclusions when adequacy is primarily used to rank systems with fluency used to break ties between systems tied with respect to adequacy.

	Adequacy	
	mean z	mean raw (%)
PROMT-RULE-BASED	**0.258**	69.0
ONLINE-G	0.101	63.8
ONLINE-B	0.092	62.5
AMU-UEDIN	0.084	63.4
UEDIN-NMT	0.062	63.2
ONLINE-A	−0.008	60.8
JHU-PBMT	−0.023	58.6
NYU-UMONTREAL	−0.042	58.3
LIMSI	−0.072	58.9
AFRL-MITLL-PHRASE	−0.077	58.3
AFRL-MITLL-VERB-ANN	−0.093	57.8
ONLINE-F	−0.489	43.7

DA English to Russian

Table 10: DA mean scores for WMT16 translation task participating systems for translation from English into Russian.

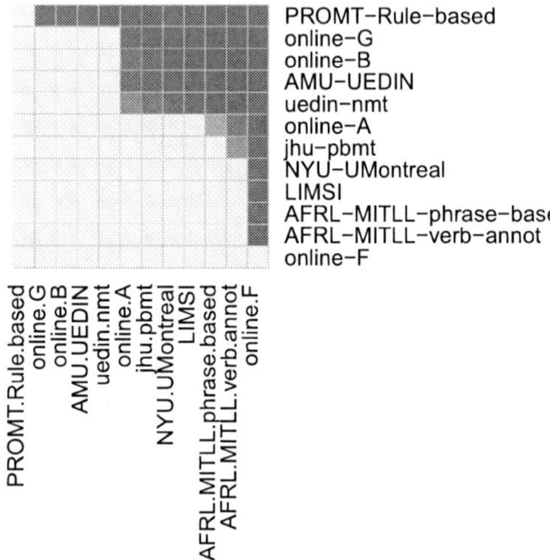

Figure 9: Significance test results for pairs of systems competing in the news domain translation task (en-ru), where a green cell denotes a significantly higher DA adequacy score for the system in a given row over the system in a given column.

cs-en	0.997
fi-en	0.996
tr-en	0.988
de-en	0.964
ru-en	0.961
ro-en	0.920
en-ru	0.975

DA Correlation with **RR**

Table 11: Correlation between overall DA standardized mean adequacy scores and RR Trueskill scores.

4 IT Translation Task

The IT-domain translation task introduced this year brought several novelties to WMT:

- 4 out of the 7 languages of the IT task are new in WMT (Bulgarian, Basque, Dutch and Portuguese),

- adaptation to the IT domain with its specifics such as frequent named entities (mostly menu items, names of products and companies) and technical jargon,

- adaptation to translation of answers in help-desk service setting (many of the sentences are instructions with imperative verbs, which is very rare in the News translation task and may require adaptation of the whole translation pipeline, including e.g. part-of-speech taggers).

4.1 Data

The test set consisted of 1000 answers from the Batch 3 of the QTLeap Corpus.[10] The in-domain training data contained 2000 answers from the Batches 1 and 2 and also localization files from several open-source projects (LibreOffice, KDE, VLC) and bilingual dictionaries of IT-related terms extracted from Wikipedia. The out-of-domain training data contained all the corpora from the News Task (see Figure 1), plus PaCo2-EuEn Basque-English corpus and SETimes with Bulgarian-English parallel sentences.

"Constrained" systems were restricted to use only these training data provided by the organizers. Linguistic tools such as morphological analyzers, taggers, parsers, word-sense disambiguation or named entity recognizer were allowed in the constrained condition. The split of Batches 1 and 2 into the training set and development test set was left to the participants.

4.2 Submitted systems

31 systems were submitted in total for the 7 language pairs.

Avramidis (2016) describes all English→German QTL-* systems (DFKI). Rosa et al. (2016) describe QTL-CHIMERA (Charles University). Gaudio et al. (2016) describe the remaining QTL-* systems (partners

---

[10]http://metashare.metanet4u.eu/go2/qtleapcorpus

from the QTLeap project: HF&FCUL for Portuguese, UPV/EHU for Spanish and Basque, IICT-BAS for Bulgarian, CUNI for Czech and UG for Dutch). Duma and Menzel (2016) describe UHDS-DOC2VEC and UHBS-LMI (University of Hamburg). Pahari et al. (2016) describe JU-USAAR (Jadavpur University & Saarland University). Cuong et al. (2016) describe ILLC-UVA-SCORPIO (University of Amsterdam). IILC-UVA-DS is based on Hoang and Sima'an (2014). PROMT-RULE-BASED and PROMT-HYBRID systems were submitted by the PROMT LLC company and they are not described in any paper.

QTL-MOSES is the standard Moses setup (MERT-tuned on the in-domain training data, but otherwise without any domain-adaptation) and serves as a baseline.

4.3 Human evaluation

The main results are presented in Table 12. The PROMT-* systems won all three language pairs, for which they were submitted, but they were trained using additional training data not available to other participants, so they are considered unconstrained and not comparable to the constrained systems. In all language pairs except for English→Bulgarian, the baseline (QTL-MOSES) was outperformed by all other systems.

Table 13 reports the amount of pairwise comparisons collected and inter- and intra-annotator agreement of the human evaluation, which is in a similar range as in the News task (cf. Tables 4 and 5).

5 Biomedical Translation Task

This is the first time that we have run the Biomedical Translation task at WMT. This task aims to evaluate systems for the translation of biomedical titles and abstracts from scientific publications. In this first edition of the challenge, we have focused on three language pairs (considering both translation directions), namely, English/Portuguese (EN/PT), English/Spanish (EN/ES) and English/French (EN/FR), and documents in the two sub-domains of biological sciences and health sciences.

5.1 Task description

The participants were provided with training data and were required to submit automatic translations

English→Bulgarian

#	score	range	system
1	5.26	1	QTL-MOSES
2	−5.26	2	QTL-DEEPFMOSES

English→Czech

#	score	range	system
1	0.53	1–2	QTL-CHIMERA-PURE
	0.43	1–2	ILLC-UVA-DS
2	0.13	3	QTL-TECTOMT
3	−0.47	4–5	QTL-CHIMERA-PLUS
	−0.62	4–5	QTL-MOSES

English→German

#	score	range	system
1	1.61	1	PROMT-RULE-BASED
2	−0.04	2–5	UHBS-LMI
	−0.06	2–6	UHDS-DOC2VEC
	−0.06	2–6	QTL-RBMT-SMTMENUS
	−0.09	3–6	RBMT
	−0.10	3–6	QTL-RBMT-MENUS
3	−0.19	7–8	DFKI-SYNTAX
	−0.19	7–8	JU-USAAR
4	−0.38	9	QTL-SELECTION
5	−0.49	10	QTL-MOSES

English→Spanish

#	score	range	system
1	3.53	1	PROMT-HYBRID
2	−0.80	2–3	QTL-CHIMERA
	−0.81	2–3	QTL-TECTOMT
3	−1.93	4	QTL-MOSES

English→Basque

#	score	range	system
1	1.57	1	QTL-TECTOMT
2	−1.57	2	QTL-MOSES

English→Dutch

#	score	range	system
1	1.95	1	ILLC-UVA-SCORPIO
2	0.36	2	QTL-CHIMERA
3	0.15	3	QTL-TECTOMT
4	−2.46	4	QTL-MOSES

English→Portuguese

#	score	range	system
1	4.61	1	PROMT-HYBRID
2	−1.06	2	QTL-TECTOMT
3	−1.27	3	QTL-CHIMERA
4	−2.28	4	QTL-MOSES

Table 12: Official results for the WMT16 IT translation task. Systems are ordered by their inferred system means, though systems within a cluster are considered tied. Lines between systems indicate clusters according to bootstrap resampling at p-level $p \leq .05$. Systems with gray background indicate use of resources that fall outside the constraints provided for the shared task.

Language pair	Systems	Comparisons	Comparisons/sys	Inter-κ	Intra-κ
English→Bulgarian	2	1,769	884.5	0.447	0.627
English→Czech	5	16,870	3,374.0	0.330	0.463
English→German	10	38,733	3,873.3	0.385	0.492
English→Spanish	4	8,538	2,134.5	0.351	0.398
English→Basque	2	1,485	742.5	0.483	0.610
English→Dutch	4	7,278	1,819.5	0.258	0.249
English→Portuguese	4	7,794	1,948.5	0.594	0.705
Sum	31	82,467			
Mean			2,660.2	0.407	0.506

Table 13: Amount of manual-evaluation pairwise comparisons (after "de-collapsing" *multi-system outputs*) collected and κ scores measuring inter- and intra-annotator agreement in the IT task. Cf. Tables 3, 4 and 5 for the respective News task statistics.

for each document in the test set. Details on the data, baseline system, automatic evaluation and manual validation are described below.

Data

We provided the participants with training data of parallel documents for the three language pairs as well as monolingual documents for each of the four languages, as summarized in Table 14. We did not provide any development data and the participants were free to split the training data into a training and a development datasets.

The training data consisted mainly of the Scielo corpus (Neves et al., 2016), a parallel collection of scientific publications composed of either titles, abstracts or title and abstracts which were retrieved from the Scielo database. For the Scielo corpus, we compiled parallel documents for all language pairs in the two sub-domains, except for the EN/FR, where only health was considered, as there were inadequate parallel documents available for biology in that pair. In previous work (Neves et al., 2016), the training data was aligned using the GMA alignment tool. The quality of the alignment was found to be satisfactory so that aligned training data could be made available to the participants.

The test set consisted of 500 documents (title and abstract) for each of the two directions of each language pair, i.e., English to Portuguese (en-pt), Portuguese to English (pt-en), English to Spanish (en-es), Spanish to English (es-en), English to French (en-fr) and French to English (fr-en). None of the test documents was included in the training data and there is no overlap of documents between the test sets for any language pair, translation direction and sub-domain.

Additionally, we prepared a corpus of parallel titles from MEDLINE® for all three language pairs. Finally, we also provided monolingual documents for the four languages, i.e., English, French, Spanish and Portuguese, retrieved from the Scielo database. These consist of documents in the Scielo database which have no corresponding document in another language.

Evaluation metric

We computed the BLEU score for each of the runs in comparison to the reference translation, i.e., the original text made available in the Scielo database, as provided by the authors of the publications.

Baseline

Our baseline system was described in previous work (Neves et al., 2016). It consists of the statistical MT system Moses [11] trained on both the Scielo corpus and on the parallel collection of Medline titles. We did not make use of the monolingual collection as we did not train a language model.

Manual validation

We carried out a manual evaluation for 100 random sentences for some selected pairs in the test data. We used the 3-way ranking task in the Appraise tool [12] which typically shows the source and the reference translation, and allows the pairwise comparison of two translations (A and B).

However, to distance the manual evaluation from the automatic BLEU evaluation which compares automatic runs to the reference translation, we treated the reference translation as one of the systems and therefore suppressed the reference translation in the interface. Evaluators were only presented with the source sentence, and two translations to rank. Evaluators were blind to the nature of the sentences they were evaluating: automatic system A vs. system B, reference translation vs. system, or system vs. reference translation.

When comparing two translations in the 3-way ranking task in Appraise, evaluators were presented with four options: (1) A>B, translation A is better than translation B; (2) A=B, the quality of the two candidate translations is similar; (3) A<B, translation B is better than translation A; and (4) Flag Error, to indicate that one of the translations did not seem to refer to the same source sentence or there is some other misalignment. The latter situation could happen when the original sentence pairs were not perfectly aligned. This may be due to the fact that the reference translations are created by the article authors independently of the WMT challenge goals. These authors are not professional writers or professional translators, so that some of the content may only be present in one of the languages, i.e., not every sentence in one language has a directly corresponding sentence in the other language. Thus, when selecting the corresponding sentences in the reference translation, we do it based on the automatic alignment provided by the GMA tool, which performs with at least 80% accuracy for our training data (Neves

---

[11]http://www.statmt.org/moses/
[12]https://github.com/cfedermann/Appraise

Table 14: Statistics on training and test collections for the Biomedical Translation Task. "T" corresponds to percentage of titles and "A" to percentage of abstracts, separated by a slash. "Docs" to total number of documents, "Lang" identifies the language, "Sents" to total number of sentences and "Tokens" to total number of tokens.

Dataset	Train	Docs	T/A	Lang	Sents	Tokens
Biological	EN/ES	17,672	49.4/97.7	EN	138,073	3,819,190
				ES	128,894	3,887,818
	EN/PT	18,180	31.1/96.1	EN	128,357	3,807,296
				PT	125,717	3,598,618
Health	EN/ES	75,856	55.6/99.5	EN	628,966	15,978,198
				ES	606,231	17,168,994
	EN/PT	65,659	74.0/92.8	EN	541,272	14,457,939
				PT	525,721	14,447,017
	EN/FR	1,135	64.5/99.7	EN	9,393	250,907
				FR	9,501	320,132

Dataset	Test	Docs	T/A	Lang	Sents	Tokens
Biological	en-es	500	100/100	EN	4,344	116,388
				ES	4,070	125,491
	es-en	500	100/100	ES	4,113	124,343
				EN	4,405	115,045
	en-pt	500	100/100	EN	4,333	114,705
				PT	4,205	120,591
	pt-en	500	100/100	PT	4,029	114,970
				EN	4,164	108,120
Health	en-fr	500	100/100	EN	5,093	137,321
				FR	5,782	208,795
	fr-en	500	100/100	FR	5,784	206,559
				EN	5,178	137,638
	en-es	500	100/100	EN	5,111	127,112
				ES	5,027	141,473
	es-en	500	100/100	ES	5,198	144,666
				EN	5,276	128,742
	en-pt	500	100/100	EN	3,858	99,001
				PT	3,776	101,991
	pt-en	500	100/100	PT	3,826	106,735
				EN	3,930	102,813

et al., 2016).

Regarding assigning the second option, i.e., A=B, we considered situations in which both translations were equally bad or good. In some cases, both candidate translations exhibited either lexical or grammatical issues, but the evaluator could not rank one candidate as definitely better or worse than the other. Sometimes, both candidates were correct and were acceptable translations of the source sentence, even if not identical. Currently, this distinction is not captured in the statistics computed by Appraise.

5.2 Participants

Five teams participated in the Biomedical Translation task, submitting a total of 40 runs. Participants are listed in Table 15; a short description of their systems is provided below.

Istrionbox The Istrionbox team utilized a non-log-linear model based on a weighted average of the translation and language models. They aligned the training documents on the phrase level using an aligner based on a lexicon which contains more than 930,000 terms derived from many parallel corpora for English/Portuguese. The language model was based on phrases, instead of words, as well as the translation model. For the various runs that the team submitted, they experimented with assigning equal or different weights for the distinct models trained on the biological or the health corpora, and they also considered a bilingual lexicon and named entities.

IXA The IXA team adapted a general-domain statistical machine translation system to the biomedical domain. Three approaches were developed for English-Spanish and Spanish-English language pairs, using Moses and three corpora (News corpora, Scielo Health and Scielo Biological, both the bilingual and monolingual documents). In the system used for the first submission, the medical vocabulary SNOMED-CT is used to extend the vocabulary to address the problem of out-of-vocabulary (OOV) words. In the system used for the second submission, OOV words are

Team ID	Participating team
Istrionbox	Istrionbox, Portugal (Aires et al., 2016)
IXA	University of the Basque Country UPV/EHU, Spain (Perez-de Viñaspre and Labaka, 2016)
LIMSI-TLP	LIMSI, France (Ive et al., 2016)
TALP-UPC	Universitat Politècnica de Catalunya, Spain (Costa-jussà et al., 2016)
uedin	University of Edinburgh, UK (Williams et al., 2016)

Table 15: Participants in the WMT16 Biomedical Translation task.

addressed by expanding generated phase tables with morphological variants and transliterations of the remaining words. In the system used for the third submission, the IXA team used the test set provided by the organizers to optimize the method used in the second submission.

TALP The TALP team's system is a standard phrase-based system based on Moses and MERT and enhanced with vocabulary expansion using bilingual word embeddings and a character-based neural language model with rescoring. The former focuses on resolving out-of-vocabulary words, while the latter enhances the fluency of the system.

LIMSI-TLP The LIMSI-TLP system is a MOSES-based statistical machine translation system, rescored with Structured Output Layer neural network models. It relied on additional in-domain data, including data from the WMT'14 medical translation task (English-French) and a set of English-French Cochrane systematic review abstracts. They also experiment with a confusion network system combination which combines the outputs of Phrase Based SMT systems trained either to translate entire source sentences or specific syntactic constructs extracted from those sentences. The approach is implemented using Confusion Network decoding.

uedin The University of Edinburgh team used the phrase-based statistical model from Moses including hierarchical lexicalized reordering model with four orientations in both directions. The translation model was trained on data from the WMT13, the Scielo training data as well as the EMEA corpus. The language model was based on the interpolation of various language models trained separately on monoligual English corpora, such as the WMT14 medical, Scielo, EMEA and English LDC GigaWord corpus.

5.3 Results

The five participating teams submitted a total of 40 runs. However, only the Spanish–English and English–Spanish language pairs attracted submissions from more than one team. In addition, one language pair (fr-en) did not receive any submission. Table 16 presents the BLEU score for each run as well as for our baseline system.

All runs obtained a much higher BLEU score than the baseline system, except for the en-pt and pt-en submissions, with BLEU scores just slightly superior to the baseline. The LIMSI run showed the best improvement over the baseline (246% absolute improvement, from 9.24 to 22.75). Overall, however, the BLEU scores for all language pairs remain quite moderate. Regarding comparison of the various runs and teams for each language pair, we did not observe considerable differences between them, except for the the runs of the "uedin" system, which obtained around two BLEU points more than other runs.

We rank the systems as follows according to their BLEU scores, with B=biology and H=health, and bl=baseline:

- en-pt(B): Istrionbox>bl;

- en-pt(H): Istrionbox>bl;

- pt-en(B): Istrionbox>bl;

- pt-en(H): Istrionbox>bl;

- en-es(B): TALP>IXA>bl;

- en-es(H): TALP>IXA>bl;

- es-en(B): uedin>IXA>TALP>bl;

- es-en(H): uedin>IXA>TALP>bl;

- en-fr(H): LIMSI>bl;

Languages	Team ID	Run ID	BLEU score	
			Biological	Health
en-pt	Istrionbox	1	17.55	19.01
		2	16.47	18.33
		3	16.45	18.37
	Baseline	-	15.38	17.22
pt-en	Istrionbox	1	20.88	21.50
		2	20.17	20.17
		3	20.14	20.62
	Baseline	-	17.59	18.48
en-es	IXA	1	31.57	28.09
		2	31.32	28.06
		3	29.61	28.13
	TALP	1	31.18	28.11
		2	31.17	27.85
		3	33.22	29.47
	Baseline	-	17.82	16.88
es-en	IXA	1	30.66	27.96
		2	30.59	27.97
		3	29.51	28.12
	TALP	1	29.68	27.42
		2	29.41	26.74
		3	29.83	27.27
	uedin	1	31.49	29.05
	Baseline	-	18.78	16.92
en-fr	LIMSI	1	-	22.52
		2	-	22.75
	Baseline	-	-	9.24

Table 16: Official BLEU scores for the WMT16 Biomedical Translation task.

For the pairwise manual validation of sentences, and given the high number of runs for some language pairs, e.g., Spanish–English and English–Spanish, we did not perform a pairwise evaluation for every pair of two systems. Instead, we considered only one run from each participant for each language pair and dataset: the one that achieved the best BLEU score in the automatic evaluation. An exception was made for the English–French and English-Portuguese tasks for which we had only one participating team: we considered all combinations of runs and reference translations for English–French and combinations of the reference translation and both the run with best BLEU score and the one that the participant (Istrionbox) reported as their best run. The results of the manual validation are presented in Table 17.

Only one run (IXA run 3, English–Spanish, health dataset) was comparable to the reference translation: 30 vs. 26 for A>B and A<B, respec-

tively. For all other cases, the reference translation was assigned to be better than the other translation at least twice as many times.

Regarding comparison between teams and runs, i.e., ES2PT (biological and health) and English–French, we did not observe much difference when comparing distinct runs of the same team. When comparing runs from distinct teams, IXA clearly outperformed TALP in two comparisons: Spanish–English biological (57 vs. 24) and Spanish–English health (48 vs. 22). On the other hand, TALP slightly outperformed IXA in one dataset: English–Spanish biological (16 vs. 7). Finally, the uedin system was clearly superior to TALP in the Spanish–English biological dataset (60 vs. 20) and to both TALP and IXA in the Spanish–English health dataset (54 vs. 19 and 41 vs. 15, respectively).

We rank the systems as follows according to our manual validation (ref=reference):

Datasets	Pairs	Runs	Total	A>B	A=B	A<B
Biological	en-es	TALP run3 vs. reference	97	18	20	59
		IXA run1 vs. TALP run3	70	7	47	16
		reference vs. IXA run1	96	50	30	16
	es-en	IXA run1 vs. reference	76	17	19	40
		reference vs. uedin run1	75	43	14	18
		TALP run3 vs. IXA run1	100	24	19	57
		reference vs. TALP run3	68	52	6	10
		IXA run1 vs. uedin run1	100	30	31	39
		uedin run1 vs. TALP run3	100	60	20	20
	en-es	reference vs. Istrionbox run1	80	54	20	6
		Istrionbox run3 vs. Istrionbox run1	99	22	52	25
		Istrionbox run3 vs. reference	80	4	14	62
	pt-en	reference vs. Istrionbox run3	78	67	7	4
Health	en-fr	reference vs. LIMSI-TLP run2	91	71	5	15
		LIMSI-TLP run1 vs. LIMSI-TLP run2	88	26	40	22
		LIMSI-TLP run1 vs. reference	85	8	12	65
	en-es	reference vs. IXA run3	93	30	37	26
		IXA run3 vs. TALP run3	82	23	40	19
		TALP run3 vs. reference	94	21	28	45
	es-en	reference vs. IXA run3	82	41	29	12
		IXA run3 vs. TALP run1	100	48	30	22
		TALP run1 vs. reference	75	8	20	47
		IXA run3 vs. uedin run1	100	15	44	41
		reference vs. uedin run1	79	44	20	15
		TALP run1 vs. uedin run1	100	19	27	54
	en-pt	Istrionbox run3 vs. Istrionbox run1	100	29	42	29
		Istrionbox run1 vs. reference	80	4	15	61
		reference vs. Istrionbox run3	82	62	17	3
	pt-en	Istrionbox run1 vs. reference	89	6	1	82

Table 17: Results for the manual validation carried out in Appraise for the Biomedical Translation task.

- en-pt (B): ref>Istrionbox;

- en-pt (H): ref>Istrionbox;

- pt-en (B): ref>Istrionbox;

- pt-en (H): ref>Istrionbox;

- en-es (B): ref>TALP> IXA;

- en-es (H): {IXA,ref}>TALP;

- es-en (B): ref>uedin>IXA>TALP;

- es-en (H): ref>uedin> IXA>TALP;

- en-fr (H): ref>LIMSI;

5.4 Discussion

In this section we analyze the errors we observed in the translations submitted by teams, the lessons we learned in this first edition of the task and our plans for future work.

Error analysis. During our manual analysis of a sample of the translations that were submitted for the test data, we noticed that their quality is still poor in comparison to the reference translations. We identified numerous problems, as summarized below:

- many missing words or words in the source language mixed in with the target language, probably due to words or concepts in the source language that could not be translated to the target language;

- incorrect ordering of adjectives and nouns, given that, in contrast to English, nouns typically precede adjectives in Portuguese, Spanish and French;

- incorrect agreement of nouns, verbs and adjectives with respect to gender and number;

- incorrect punctuation, e.g., periods placed in the middle of a sentence;

- incorrect casing for words, e.g., common words which were capitalized or in upper case;

- missing translations for acronyms, i.e., the acronym in the source language was used instead.

We note that some of these issues were ignored during the manual evaluation, for instance, incorrect capitalization was not penalized if the translation was otherwise better or comparable to the other translation.

Lessons learned. We performed a comparison of the systems based only on the overall results on the complete test set and on the samples of sets that we randomly selected for manual validation. For this first edition of the Biomedical Translation task, we aimed at providing an evaluation platform for the automatic translation of scientific publications, in particular for titles and abstracts in the biomedical domain.

In this first edition of the task, the training and test data was obtained from the parallel publications available in Scielo. We did not perform manual translation of the documents for either the training or the test data, but rather used the original text available in Scielo for all languages under consideration here. In practice, this means that the reference translations were produced by the article authors independently of the WMT challenge goals. These authors are not professional writers or professional translators, and some of them may have limited proficiency in the languages they are required to use for publication. This situation has an impact on the quality of the reference translations, compared to other WMT tasks. It is reflected in the manual evaluation which indicates that for some language pairs (notably English–Spanish health), participant runs were rated overall as better or equal to the reference translation. Our experience with this first edition of the task indicates that the Scielo corpus is a valuable resource for biomedical WMT, however more work is needed in terms of quality assurance to ensure that meaningful evaluation results can be obtained.

Plan for future editions. In next editions, we plan to build on the established pipeline to collect and pre-process Scielo data to prepare a new test dataset. More importantly, we plan to work towards improved data and evaluation quality.

While we initially focused on characterizing the quality of the alignment in the parallel Scielo corpus, we are planning to craft a higher quality dataset by removing any sentence pairs with alignment issues. Furthermore, the data set will also be pruned for sentences exhibiting lexical, grammatical or fluency issues. These steps will contribute to improve the significance of the evaluation results, especially in terms of BLEU scores.

Furthermore, we believe that the nature of scientific texts and biomedical texts in particular calls for specific evaluation metrics. One of the intended uses of translation systems in the biomedi-cal domain is to provide health professionals with access to the latest research results that are published in a language other than their native language. Consequently, health professionals may use the translated information to make clinical decisions impacting patients care. It is vital that translation systems do not contribute to the dissemination of incorrect clinical information. Therefore, the evaluation of biomedical translation systems should include an assessment at the document level indicating whether a translation conveyed erroneous clinical information.

6 Quality Estimation

The fifth edition of the WMT shared task on quality estimation (QE) of machine translation (MT) builds on the previous editions of the task (Callison-Burch et al., 2012; Bojar et al., 2013, 2014, 2015), with "traditional" tasks at sentence and word levels, a new task for entire documents quality prediction, and a variant of the word-level task: phrase-level estimation.

The goals of this year's shared task were:

- To advance work on sentence and word-level quality estimation by providing domain-specific, larger and professionally annotated datasets.

- To analyse the effectiveness of different types of quality labels provided by humans for longer texts in document-level prediction.

- To investigate quality estimation at a new level of granularity: phrases.

These goals are addressed through three groups of tasks: Task 1 at sentence level (Section 6.3), Task 2 at word and phrase levels (Section 6.4), and Task 3 at document level (Section 6.6). Tasks 1 and 2 provide the same dataset with English-German translations generated by a statistical machine translation (SMT) system, while Task 3 provides an English-Spanish dataset of translations taken from all participating systems in WMT08-WMT13. These datasets were annotated with different labels for quality: for Tasks 1 and 2, the labels were automatically derived from the post-editing of the machine translation output, while for Task 3, scores were computed based on a two-stage post-editing process. Any external resource, including additional quality estimation training data, could be used by participants (no distinction between *constrained* and *unconstrained* tracks was made). As presented in Section 6.1, participants were also provided with a baseline set of features for each task, and a software package to extract these and other quality estimation features and perform model learning, with suggested methods for all levels of prediction. Participants, described in Section 6.2, could submit up to two systems for each task.

Data used to build MT systems or internal system information (such as model scores or n-best lists) were made available on request for Tasks 1 and 2.

6.1 Baseline systems

Sentence-level baseline system: For Task 1, QuEst++[13] (Specia et al., 2015) was used to extract 17 features from the SMT source/target language training corpus:

- Number of tokens in source & target sentences.

- Average source token length.

- Average number of occurrences of the target word within the target sentence.

- Number of punctuation marks in source and target sentences.

- Language model probability of source and target sentences based on models built from the SMT training corpus.

- Average number of translations per source word in the sentence as given by IBM Model 1 extracted from the SMT training corpus.

- Percentage of unigrams, bigrams and trigrams in frequency quartiles 1 (lower frequency words) and 4 (higher frequency words) in the source language extracted from the source SMT training corpus.

- Percentage of unigrams in the source sentence seen in the source SMT training corpus.

These features were used to train a Support Vector Regression (SVR) algorithm using a Radial Basis Function (RBF) kernel within the scikit-learn toolkit (Pedregosa et al., 2011).[14]

---

[13]https://github.com/ghpaetzold/
questplusplus

[14]http://scikit-learn.org/

The γ, ϵ and C parameters were optimised via grid search with 5-fold cross validation on the training set.

Word-level baseline system: For Tasks 2 and $2p$, the baseline features were extracted with the Marmot tool (Logacheva et al., 2016b).

For the baseline system we used a number of features that have been found the most informative in previous research on word-level QE. Our baseline set of features is loosely based on the one described in (Luong et al., 2014). It contains the following 22 features:

- Word count in the source and target sentences, source and target token count ratio. Although these features are sentence-level (i.e. their values will be the same for all words in a sentence), the length of a sentence might influence the probability of a word being wrong.

- Target token, its left and right contexts of one word.

- Source word aligned to the target token, its left and right contexts of one word. The alignments were taken from the SMT system that produced the automatic translations.

- Binary dictionary features: whether target token is a stopword, a punctuation mark, a proper noun, a number.

- Target language model features:
  - The order of the highest order ngram which starts and end with the target token.
  - Backoff behaviour of the ngrams (t_{i-2}, t_{i-1}, t_i), (t_{i-1}, t_i, t_{i+1}), (t_i, t_{i+1}, t_{i+2}), where t_i is the target token (the backoff behaviour was computed as described in (Raybaud et al., 2011)).

- The order of the highest order ngram which starts and ends with the source token.

- The Part-of-speech tags of the target and source tokens.

This set of baseline features is similar to the one used at WMT15 QE shared task (Bojar et al., 2015). We excluded three features used the last year: pseudo-reference features and number of WordNet senses for the source and target tokens.

We model the task as a sequence prediction problem, and train our baseline system using the Linear-Chain Conditional Random Fields (CRF) algorithm with the `CRFSuite` tool (Okazaki, 2007). The model was trained using the passive-aggressive optimisation algorithm.

Phrase-level baseline system: The phrase-level features were also extracted with `Marmot`, but they are different from the word-level features. The baseline set of phrase-level features is based on a list of features which were used for sentence-level QE in `QuEst++` toolkit. These so-called "black-box" features do not use the internal information from the MT system. We use the following feature set consisting of 72 features, using the SMT source/target language training corpus:

- Source phrase frequency features:

    - average frequency of ngrams (unigrams, bigrams, trigrams) from different quartiles of frequency (from the low frequency to high frequency ngrams);
    - percentage of distinct source ngrams (unigrams, bigrams, trigrams) seen in a corpus of the source language.

- Translation probability features:

    - average number of translations per source word in the sentence (with different translation probability thresholds: 0.01, 0.05, 0.1, 0.2, 0.5);
    - average number of translations per source word in the sentence (with different translation probability thresholds: 0.01, 0.05, 0.1, 0.2, 0.5) weighted by the frequency of each word in the source corpus.

- Punctuation features:

    - difference between numbers of various punctuation marks (periods, commas, colons, semicolons, question and exclamation marks) in the source and the target phrases;
    - difference between numbers of various punctuation marks normalised by the length of the target phrase;
    - percentage of punctuation marks in the target and the source.

- Language model features:

    - log probability of the source and the target phrases;
    - perplexity of the source and the target phrases.

- Phrase statistics:

    - lengths of the source and target phrases;
    - ratio of the source and the target phrase lengths;
    - average length of tokens in source and target phrases;
    - average occurrence of target word within the phrase.

- Alignment features:

    - Number of unaligned target words;
    - Number of target words aligned to more than one word;
    - Average number of alignments per word in the target phrase.

- Part-of-speech features:

    - percentage of content words in the source and target phrases;
    - percentage of words of a particular part-of-speech (verb, noun, pronoun) in the source and the target phrases;
    - ratio of numbers of words of a particular part-of-speech (verb, noun, pronoun) in the source and the target phrases;
    - percentage of numbers and alphanumeric tokens in the source and the target phrases;
    - ratio of the percentage of numbers and alphanumeric tokens in the source and the target phrases;

This feature set was originally designed for sentences. We expect that since phrases are sequences of words of varied length, they can be treated analogously for QE. However, unlike sentences, which are translated independently, phrases are related to their neighbouring phrases in a sentence, and in this respect they are similar to words in the context of QE. Therefore, as in the baseline word-level system, we treat phrase-level QE as a sequence labelling task and model it using Conditional Random Fields. The phrase-level baseline system is trained with `CRFSuite` using the passive-aggressive optimisation algorithm.

Document-level baseline system: For Task 3, 17 baseline features equivalent to those for sentence level were extracted at document level using QuEst++. These features are aggregations of sentence-level baseline features. Some sentence-level features were summed (number of tokens in the source and target sentences and number of punctuation marks in source and target sentences), while all remaining were averaged.

The model was trained with a SVR algorithm with RBF kernel using the scikit-learn toolkit. The γ, ϵ and C parameters were optimised via grid search with 5-fold cross validation on the training set.

6.2 Participants

Table 18 lists all participating teams submitting systems to any of the tasks. Each team was allowed up to two submissions for each task. In the descriptions below, participation in specific tasks is denoted by a task identifier.

CDACM (Task 2): The CDACM team participated in Task 2 for the word and phrase-level QE. They use a Recurrent Neural Network Language Model (RNN-LM) architecture for word-level QE. To estimate the phrase-level quality, they use the output of the word-level QE system. For this task, they use a modified RNN-LM with other RNN variants like Long Short Term Memory (LSTM), deep LSTM and Gated Recurring Units (GRU). The modified system predicts a label (OK/BAD) rather than predicting the word as in the case of standard RNN-LM. The input to the system is a word sequence, similar to the standard RNN-LM. They also tried bilingual models with RNN-LM and found that they perform better than monolingual models. In the training data, the distribution of labels (OK/BAD) is skewed, with significantly more OK labels. To handle this issue, they use strategies to replace the OK label with sub-labels to balance the distribution. The sub-labels are OK_B, OK_I, OK_E, depending on the location of the token in the sentence.

POSTECH (Task 1, Task 2): POSTECH's submissions (SENT/RNN for Task 1, WORD/RNN for Task 2 and PHR/RNN for Task 2p) are RNN-based QE systems consisting of two component: two bidirectional RNNs on the source and target sentences in the first component and other RNNs for predicting the final quality in the second component. The first component is an RNN-based modified neural MT model which generates quality vectors. Quality vectors indicate a sequence of vectors about target words' translation quality. The second component using other RNNs predicts the quality at sentence level (Task 1), word level (Task 2), and phrase level (Task 2p). POSTECH's RNN-based systems are entirely neural approaches for QE. Due to the small amount of data to train the prediction models, each component of the systems is trained separately by using different training data. To train the first component of the systems, the Europarl v7 English-German parallel corpus was used. To train the second component of the systems, WMT16 QE task English-German datasets were used.

RTM (Task 1, Task 2, Task 3): Referential translation machines (RTMs) (Biçici and Way, 2015) are a language-independent approach for predicting translation quality, as well as for addressing other text similarity tasks. They eliminate the need to access any task or domain specific information or resource. SVR and regression trees are used in combination with feature selection and partial least squares for the document and sentence-level prediction tasks and global linear models with dynamic learning were used for the word and phrase-level prediction tasks.

SHEF (Task 1): The SHEF systems exploit RNNs and the principle of compositionality to offer a resource-light solution to sentence-level QE. They use only one side of the translation, the source (SRC) or the target (TGT). They split the sentence in ngrams and train a model that predicts the quality of ngrams. To calculate the quality of an entire sentence translation, they split its source/target side in ngrams, estimate their quality individually, then average their quality scores. They use word embedding models trained over 7 billion words as external resource (English and German) using word2vec.

SHEF-LIUM (Task 1): The two joint submissions from the University of Sheffield and LIUM use (i) a Continuous Space Language Model (CSLM) to extract sentence embeddings and cross-entropy scores, (ii) a neural network MT (NMT) model, (iii) a set of QuEst++ features (iv) a combination of features produced by QuEst++ and the features produced with CSLM and NMT. When added to QuEst++ standard feature sets for Task 1, the CSLM sentence embed-

ID	Participating team
CDACM	Centre for Development of Advanced Computing, India (Patel and M, 2016)
POSTECH	Pohang University of Science and Technology, Republic of Korea (Kim and Lee, 2016)
RTM	Referential Translation Machines, Turkey (Bicici, 2016b)
SHEF	University of Sheffield, UK (Paetzold and Specia, 2016)
SHEF-LIUM	University of Sheffield, UK and Laboratoire d'Informatique de l'Université du Maine, France (Shah et al., 2016)
SHEF-MIME	University of Sheffield, UK (Beck et al., 2016)
UAlacant	University of Alicante, Spain (Esplà-Gomis et al., 2016)
UFAL	Nile University, Egypt & Charles University, Czech Republic (Abdel-salam et al., 2016)
UGENT	Ghent University, Belgium (Tezcan et al., 2016)
UNBABEL	Unbabel, Portugal (Martins et al., 2016)
USFD	University of Sheffield, UK (Logacheva et al., 2016a)
USHEF	University of Sheffield, UK (Scarton et al., 2016)
UU	Uppsala University, Sweden (Sagemo and Stymne, 2016)
YSDA	Yandex School of Data Analysis, Russia (Kozlova et al., 2016)

Table 18: Participants in the WMT16 Quality Estimation shared task.

ding features along with the cross entropy and NMT likelihood led to large improvements in prediction, and achieved third place in the scoring and second place in the ranking task variants according to the official evaluation metrics. Neural network features alone also performed very well. This is a very encouraging finding since for many language pairs it is sometime hard to find appropriate resources to build hand-crafted features, while the neural network features used only require (sufficient) monolingual data to train models, which is available in abundance for many languages.

SHEF-MIME (Task 2): The University of Sheffield's submission to the word-level QE task is based on imitation learning, an approach that treats structured prediction as a sequence of actions taken by a binary classifier. This approach allows the use of arbitrary information from previous tag predictions and has the ability to train the classifier using non-decomposable loss functions over the predicted structure. The submitted system uses the baseline features provided by the shared task organisers plus additional features relying on the predicted structure, such as previous tag ngrams and the total number of BAD predictions. It employs an online learning algorithm as the underlying classifier and uses a loss function based on the official shared task evaluation metric. No external data or resources were used for this submission.

UALacant (Task 2): The submissions of the Universitat d'Alacant team focus for Task 2 were obtained by applying the approach by Esplà-Gomis et al. (2015), which uses any source of bilingual information available online in order to spot sub-segment correspondences between the source segment and the translation hypothesis. These sub-segment correspondences are used to extract a collection of features that are then used by a multilayer perceptron to determine the final word-level QE labels. The probabilities provided by this classifier for every word in a phrase are then used as new features for a second multilayer perceptron that is able to obtain quality estimates at the phrase level. Three sources of bilingual information available online were used by the UAlacant submissions: two online MT systems, Lucy LT KWIK[15] and Google Translate,[16] and the bilingual concordancer Reverso Context.[17] Two systems were submitted, both for word-level and phrase-level QE tasks: one using only features based on external sources of bilingual information, and another combining them with the baseline features provided by the task organisers.

---

[15]http://www.lucysoftware.com/catala/traduccio-automatica/kwik-translator-/
[16]http://translate.google.com
[17]http://context.reverso.net/translation/

UFAL (Task 1): The submission is based on word alignments and bilingual distributed representations to introduce a new set of features for the sentence-Level QE task. The features extracted include three alignment-based features, three bilingual embedding-based features, two embedding-based features constrained on alignment links, as well as a set of 74 bigrams used as boolean features. The set of bigrams represents the most frequent bigrams in translations that have changed after the post-edition, and they are compiled by aligning translations to their post-editions provided in the WMT QE datasets. To produce these features, GIZA++ (Och and Ney, 2003) was used for word alignment and `Multivec` (Berard et al., 2016) was used for the bilingual model, which jointly learns distributed representations for source and target languages using a parallel corpus. To build the bilingual model, domain-specific data compiled from the resources made available for the WMT 16 IT-Domain shared task was used. As prediction model, a Linear Regression model using `scikit-learn` was built using a combination of `QuEst++` baseline features and the new features proposed.

UGENT-LT3 (Task 1, Task 2): The submissions for the word-level task use 41 features in combination with the baseline feature set to train binary classifiers. The 41 additional features attempt to capture accuracy errors (concerned with the meaning transfer from the source to target sentences) using word and phrase alignment probabilities, fluency errors (concerned with the well-formedness of target sentence) using language models trained on word surface forms and on part-of-speech tags, and terminology errors (concerned with the domain-specific terminology) using a bilingual terminology list. Based on the combined feature set, SCATE-RF uses random forests for binary classification, which combines decision trees into an ensemble. SCATE-ENS uses the same feature set and combines different algorithms into an ensemble by applying the majority voting scheme. For the sentence-level task, SCATE-SVM1 adds 18 features to the baseline feature set to train SVR models using an RBF kernel. SCATE-SVM2 additionally utilises an extra feature, which is based on the percentage of words that are labelled as BAD by the best word-level QE system (SCATE RF). External language resources from the IT domain are used to extract the additional features for both tasks.

UNBABEL (Task 2): Two systems were submitted for the word-level task. UNBABEL_2_linear is a feature-based linear sequential model. It uses the baseline features provided by the shared task organisers (with slight changes) conjoined with individual labels and pairs of consecutive labels. It also uses various syntactic dependency-based features (dependency relations, heads, and second-order structures like siblings and grandparents). The syntactic dependencies are predicted with `TurboParser` trained on the TIGER German treebank. UNBABEL_2_ensemble uses a stacked architecture, inspired by the last year's QUETCH+ system (Kreutzer et al., 2015), which combines three neural systems: one feedforward and two recurrent ones. The predictions of these systems are added as additional features in the linear system above. The following external resources were used: part-of-speech tags and extra syntactic dependency information obtained with `TurboTagger` and `TurboParser` (Martins et al., 2013), trained on the Penn Treebank (for English) and on the version of the German TIGER corpus used in the SPMRL shared task (Seddah et al., 2014) for German. For the neural models, pretrained word embeddings from `Polyglot` (Al-Rfou et al., 2013) and those produced with a neural MT system (Bahdanau et al., 2014) were used.

USFD (Task 2): USFD's submissions tested two different approaches for phrase-level QE. The first one (CONTEXT submission) is an enhancement of the baseline feature set provided with the context features. The additional features consist of the source and target tokens which precede and follow the phrase under consideration, part-of-speech tags of these tokens, and language model scores for ngrams at the borders of the phrase. The second approach (W&SLP4PT submission) learns phrase-level labels from predictions at other levels. The models are trained on a set of seven features that are based on (i) the phrase segmentation itself (length and ratio to the sentence), (ii) word-level predictions (number of predicted OK/BAD words in the current phrase and in the sentence), and (iii) the predicted quality of the sentence. `CRFsuite` is used to train the prediction models in both cases.

USHEF (Task 3): Two different systems were submitted for Task 3. The first system (BASE-EMB-GP) combines the 17 baseline features with word embeddings from the source documents (English) using a Gaussian Process (GP) model. The word embeddings were learned by using the Continuous Bag-of-Words (CBOW) model (Mikolov et al., 2013), trained on the Google's billion-word corpus,[18] with a vocabulary size of 527K words. Document embeddings are extracted by averaging word embeddings in the document. The GP model was trained with two Rational Quadratic kernels (Rasmussen and Williams, 2006): one for the 17 baseline features and another for the 500 features from the embeddings. Since each kernel has its own set of hyperparameters, the full model can leverage the contributions from the two different sets. The second system (GRAPH-DISC) combines the baseline features with discourse-aware features. The discourse aware features are the same as the ones used by Scarton et al. (2015a) plus Latent Semantic Analysis (LSA) cohesion features (Scarton and Specia, 2014), number of subtrees and height of the Rhetorical Structure Theory (RST) tree and entity graph-based coherence scores (Sim Smith et al., 2016). Discourse-aware and RST tree features were extracted only for English (tools are only available for this language), LSA features were extracted for both languages, and entity graph-based coherence scores were extracted for the target language only (Spanish), as the source documents are expected to be coherent. This QE model was trained with an SVR algorithm.

UU (Task 1): The UU system uses SVR to predict HTER scores based on features extracted with QuEst++ plus additional features. The feature vector consists of a combination of the 17 baseline features and top performing new features proposed by UU. These new features are related to reordering and noun translation, grammatical correspondence and structural integrity, based on parse trees and part-of-speech tags. The system submitted uses Kendall Tau distances in alignments between source and target for measuring reordering, noun group ratio, verb ratio and probabilistic context free grammars probabilities.

YSDA (Task 1): The YSDA submission is based on a simple idea that the more complex the sentence is the more difficult it is to translate. For this purpose, it uses information provided by syntactic parsing (information from parsing trees, some specific language constructions, etc). Additionally, it uses features based on pseudo-references, back-translation, web-scale language model, word alignments (as given by the data for Task 2), and combinations of several features. A regression model was training to predict BLEU as target metric instead HTER. The machine learning pipeline uses an SVR with RBF kernel to predict BLEU scores, followed by a linear SVR to predict HTER scores from BLEU scores. As external resources, the system uses a syntactic parser, pseudo-references and back-translation from web-scale MT system, and a web-scale language model.

6.3 Task 1: Predicting sentence-level quality

This task consists in scoring (and ranking) translation sentences according to the percentage of their words that need to be fixed. HTER (Snover et al., 2006) is used as quality score, i.e. the minimum edit distance between the machine translation and its manually post-edited version in [0,1].

As in previous years, two variants of the results could be submitted:

- **Scoring**: An absolute HTER score for each sentence translation, to be interpreted as an error metric: lower scores mean better translations.

- **Ranking**: A ranking of sentence translations for all source sentences from best to worst. For this variant, it does not matter how the ranking is produced (from HTER predictions or by other means). The reference ranking is defined based on the true HTER scores.

Data The data is the same as that used for the WMT16 Automatic Post-editing task, collected By the QT21 Project[19] in the Information Technology (IT) domain.[20] Source segments are English sentences and target segments are German translations produced by a strong SMT system built within the QT21 Project. The human post-editions

---

[18]https://github.com/ciprian-chelba/
1-billion-word-language-modeling-benchmark

[19]http://www.qt21.eu/
[20]The source sentences and reference translations were provided by TAUS (https://www.taus.net/) and come from a unique IT vendor.

are a manual revision of the target, done by professional translators using the PET post-editing tool (Aziz et al., 2012). HTER labels were computed using the TERCOM tool[21] with default settings (tokenised, case insensitive, exact matching only), and scores capped to 1.

As training and development data, we provided English-German datasets with 12,000 and 1,000 source sentences, their machine translations, post-editions and HTER scores. As test data, we provided an additional set of 2,000 English-German source-translations pairs produced by the same SMT system used for the training data.

Evaluation Evaluation was performed against the true HTER label and/or ranking, using the following metrics:

- Scoring: Pearson's r correlation score (primary metric, official score for ranking submissions), Mean Average Error (MAE) and Root Mean Squared Error (RMSE).

- Ranking: Spearman's ρ rank correlation and DeltaAvg.

Statistical significance on Pearson r and Spearman rho was computed using the William's test, following the approach suggested in (Graham, 2015).

Results Table 19 summarises the results for Task 1, ranking participating systems best to worst using Pearson's r correlation as primary key. Spearman's ρ correlation scores should be used to rank systems according to the ranking variant. We note that three systems have not submitted results ranking evaluation variant.

6.4 Task 2: Predicting word-level quality

The goal of this task is to evaluate the extent to which we can detect word-level errors in MT output. Various classes of errors can be found in translations, but for this task we consider all error types together, aiming at making a binary distinction between OK and BAD tokens. The decision to bucket all error types together was made because of the lack of sufficient training data that could allow consideration of more fine-grained error tags.

Data This year's word-level task uses the same dataset as Task 1, for a single language pair: English-German. Each instance of the training, development and test sets consists of the following elements:

- Source sentence (English).

- Automatic translation (German).

- Manual post-edition of the automatic translation.

- Word-level binary (OK/BAD) labelling of the automatic translation.

The binary labels for the datasets were acquired automatically with the TERCOM tool. The tool identifies four types of errors: *substitution* of a word with another word, *deletion* of a word (word was omitted by the translation system), *insertion* of a word (a spurious word was added by the translation system), and word or sequence of words *shift* (word order error). Every word in the machine-translated sentence is tagged with one of these error types or not tagged if it matches a word from the reference.

All the untagged (correct) words were tagged with OK, while the words tagged with substitution and insertion errors were assigned the tag BAD. The deletion errors are not associated with any word in the automatic translation, so we could not consider them. We also disabled the shift errors by running TERCOM with the option '-d 0'. The reason for that is the fact that searching for shifts introduces significant noise in the annotation. The tool cannot discriminate between cases where a word was really shifted and where a word (especially common words such as prepositions, articles and pronouns) was deleted in one part of the sentence and then independently inserted in another part of this sentence, i.e. to correct an unrelated error. The statistics of the datasets are outlined in Table 20.

Evaluation This year's evaluation procedure is different from the one used in previous QE tasks. Previously, the submissions were evaluated in terms of F_1-score for the BAD class. However, this metric was criticised for being biased towards "pessimistic" labellings. It tends to rate higher the outputs of systems which labelled most of words as BAD, e.g. a trivial "all-BAD" baseline outperforms many real systems in terms of F_1-BAD score (Bojar et al., 2013).

Therefore, this year we used a different metric: the multiplication of F_1-scores of the BAD and OK classes (herein referred to as $\mathbf{F_1}$-**mult**). As it

---

[21]`http://www.cs.umd.edu/~snover/tercom/`

System ID	Pearson's r ↑	MAE ↓	RMSE ↓	Spearman's ρ ↑	DeltaAvg ↑
English-German					
• YSDA/SNTX+BLEU+SVM	0.525	12.30	16.41	–	–
POSTECH/SENT-RNN-QV2	0.460	13.58	18.60	0.483	7.663
SHEF-LIUM/SVM-NN-emb-QuEst	0.451	12.88	17.03	0.474	8.129
POSTECH/SENT-RNN-QV3	0.447	13.52	18.38	0.466	7.527
SHEF-LIUM/SVM-NN-both-emb	0.430	12.97	17.33	0.452	7.886
UGENT-LT3/SCATE-SVM2	0.412	19.57	24.11	0.418	7.615
UFAL/MULTIVEC	0.377	13.60	17.64	0.410	7.114
RTM/RTM-FS-SVR	0.376	13.46	17.81	0.400	6.655
UU/UU-SVM	0.370	13.43	18.15	0.405	6.519
UGENT-LT3/SCATE-SVM1	0.363	20.01	24.63	0.375	7.008
RTM/RTM-SVR	0.358	13.59	18.06	0.384	6.379
BASELINE	0.351	13.53	18.39	0.390	6.300
SHEF/SimpleNets-SRC	0.320	13.92	18.23	–	–
SHEF/SimpleNets-TGT	0.283	14.35	18.22	–	–

Table 19: Official results for the scoring ad ranking variants of the WMT16 Quality Estimation Task 1. The systems are ranked according to the Pearson r metric and significance results are also computed for this metric. The winning submissions are indicated by a •. These are the top-scoring submission and those that are not significantly worse according to Williams test with 95% confidence intervals. The systems in the grey area are not different from the baseline system at a statistically significant level according to the same test.

	Sentences	Words	% of BAD words
Training	12,000	210,958	21.4
Development	1,000	19,487	19.54
Test	2,000	34,531	19.31

Table 20: Datasets for Task 2.

was shown in (Logacheva et al., 2016c), this metric is not biased neither towards "pessimistic" nor to "optimistic" labellings, and is good at discriminating between different systems.

We tested the significance of the results using randomisation tests (Yeh, 2000) with Bonferroni correction (Abdi, 2007).

Results The results for Task 2 are summarised in Table 21. We show the performance of all participating systems as well as the baseline model. The results are ordered by the F_1-mult metric. The top three submissions are statistically significantly different from any other system. However, we cannot unambiguously depict other significance groups in the table. Therefore, we only show the systems which are not significantly different from the baseline (grey area). The models above and below the grey area are significantly better and worse than the baseline system, respectively.

In order to show and analyse the groups of significantly different systems we plot the results of significance test as a heatmap (see Table 22). Here, a cell at the crossing of a row and a column corresponding to different submissions contains the information about the significance of the difference in their results: the darker the cell is, the lower is the significance in the difference for the pair of systems. The coloured frames denote groups of submissions which are not significantly different.

We should also note that in order to adequately evaluate the significance for multiple experiments we used Bonferroni correction. The essence of this method is that in cases when multiple results are compared (i.e. multiple comparisons are performed) the final significance level is computed as the initial significance level over the number of comparisons. In our case we had 91 comparisons which gave us $\alpha_B = \frac{\alpha}{91} = 0.0005$ for the significance level of 0.05. Bonferroni correction is quite a conservative method, so the number of significance groups may vary when using a different correction technique.

Overall, there are 10 groups of significantly different results: three of them contain one submission (the three best-performing models), other seven contain two to five models each (these are the groups denoted by frames of different colours).

6.5 Task 2p: predicting phrase-level quality

As an extension of the word-level task, we introduced a new task: phrase-level prediction. For this task, given a "phrase" (segmentation as given by the SMT decoder), participants are asked to label it as 'OK' or 'BAD'. Errors made by MT engines are interdependent and one incorrectly chosen word can cause more errors, especially in its local context. Phrases as produced by SMT decoders can be seen as a representation of this local context and in this task we ask participants to consider them as atomic units, using phrase-specific information to

System ID	F_1-**mult** $\uparrow$	F_1-BAD	F_1-OK
English-German			
• UNBABEL/ensemble	0.495	0.560	0.885
UNBABEL/linear	0.463	0.529	0.875
UGENT-LT3/SCATE-RF	0.411	0.492	0.836
UGENT-LT3/SCATE-ENS	0.381	0.464	0.821
POSTECH/WORD-RNN-QV3	0.380	0.447	0.850
POSTECH/WORD-RNN-QV2	0.376	0.454	0.828
UAlacant/SBI-Online-baseline	0.367	0.456	0.805
CDACM/RNN	0.353	0.419	0.842
SHEF/SHEF-MIME-1	0.338	0.403	0.839
SHEF/SHEF-MIME-0.3	0.330	0.391	0.845
BASELINE	0.324	0.368	0.880
RTM/s5-RTM-GLMd	0.308	0.349	0.882
UAlacant/SBI-Online	0.290	0.406	0.715
RTM/s4-RTM-GLMd	0.273	0.307	0.888

Table 21: Official results for the WMT16 Quality Estimation Task 2. The winning submissions are indicated by a •. These are the top-scoring submission and those that are not significantly worse according to approximate randomisation tests with 95% confidence intervals. The grey area indicates the submissions whose results are not statistically different from the baseline according to the same test.

improve upon the results of the word-level task.

Data The data to be used is exactly the same as for Task 1 and the word-level task. The labelling of this data was adapted from word-level labelling by assigning the 'BAD' tag to any phrase that contains at least one 'BAD' word. The phrase segmentation used in this dataset is the original segmentation of sentences produced by the SMT decoder during translation.

The dataset statistics are outlined in Table 23 (this is similar to Table 20, but shows the percentage of incorrect phrases instead of words).

Evaluation Although the QE was produced at the level of phrases, we used word-level metrics to evaluate the performance of participating systems. This choice was motivated by the fact that the length of phrases can vary significantly, and an incorrectly labelled phrase can actually mean 1 to 5 incorrectly labelled words, while phrase-level metrics do not weigh incorrect labels by the length of the phrases. We decided to use word-level evaluation to make the results of this task more intuitive. We used the same metric as the one used in task 2: multiplication of word-level F_1-OK and word-level F_1-BAD (F_1-mult). However, the test set was re-labelled in order to agree with phrase boundaries: if a phrase had at least one BAD word, all its labels were replaced with BAD.

Thus, the sequence

OK || BAD OK OK || OK || BAD OK || OK OK

was converted to:

OK || BAD BAD BAD || OK || BAD BAD || OK OK

As in Task 2, statistical significance was computed using randomisation tests with Bonferroni correction.

Results The results of the phrase-level task are represented in Table 24. Here, unlike the word-level task, we cannot find a single winner: although the F_1-mult scores of the top five systems vary from 0.379 to 0.364, this difference is not significant. However, all the winning submissions outperform the baseline.

Analogously to the previous task, we provide the F_1-BAD and F_1-OK scores in order to better understand the differences between the models. We can see that some models have very close F_1-mult scores, although their per class components scores can differ. For example, the F_1-mult scores of two submissions by the USFD team are very close (0.367 and 0.364). However, if we decompose these scores, we will see that both F_1-BAD and F_1-OK scores of the two models have around 2% of absolute difference: the W&SLP4PT model is more "pessimistic" (i.e. it is better at labelling BAD words), while the CONTEXT model identifies the correct words more accurately. However, the combinations of these scores lead to very similar F_1-mult. The situation is the same with all top five submissions: the differences in F_1-BAD are levelled off by the F_1-OK component, and the values of the F_1-mult are closer than those of F_1-BAD.

This suggests that the F_1-mult score might not be an best metric for the phrase-level task. While in the phrase-level models phrases of different length are treated in the same way, the word-level metric unfolds each phrase-level label to a set of

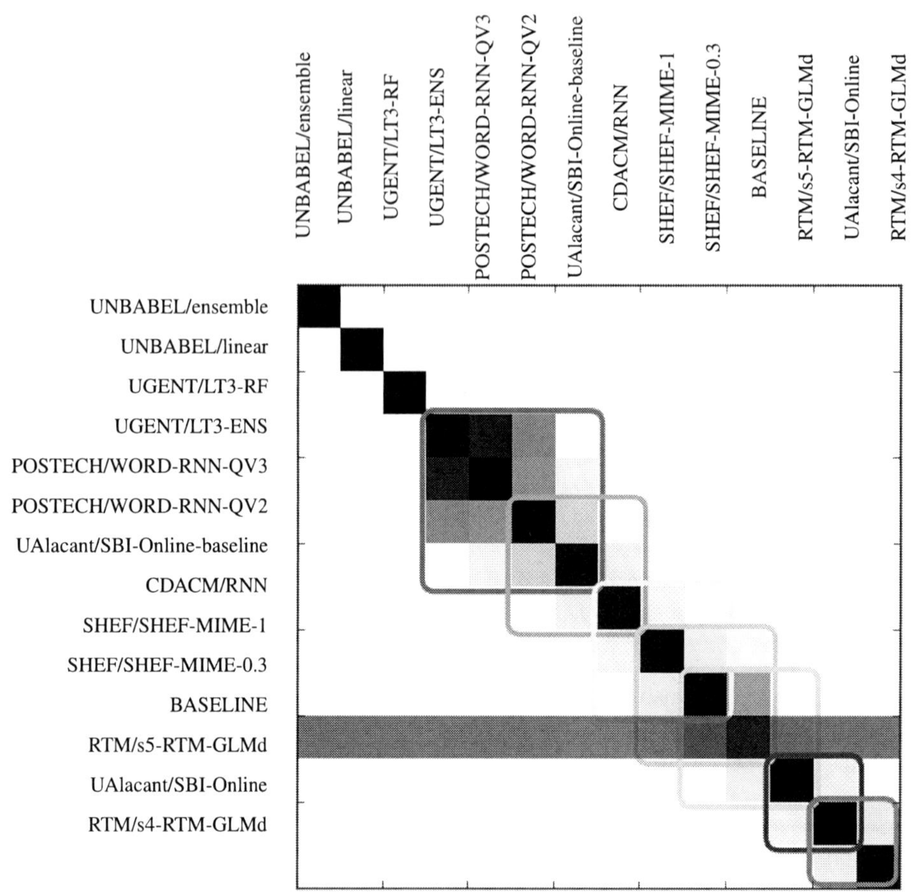

Table 22: Randomised significance test for the word-level task with Bonfferroni correction. The darker the cell, the lower the significance level of the difference between the scores of the corresponding systems. The coloured frames denote groups of submissions which are not significantly different. The blue row shows the baseline system.

	Sentences	Words	% of BAD words
Training	12,000	210,958	29.84
Development	1,000	19,487	30.21
Test	2,000	34,531	29.53

Table 23: Datasets for Task 2p.

word-level labels, thus giving different importance to phrases of different lengths. In order to find a more suitable metric we tested another evaluation strategy. We evaluated the submissions in terms of phrase-level F_1-scores: here all phrases were considered as uniform atomic units regardless of their lengths, and F_1-BAD and F_1-OK were computed as harmonic means of precision and recall for phrase-level of OK and BAD labels.

Table 25 shows the performance of phrase-level QE models measured in terms of multiplication of phrase-level F_1-scores. Except for some changes in the order of models, this ranking is very similar to the official one represented in Table 24. Here, the order of submissions by the POSTECH and CDACM teams is different from the ranking produced with the primary metric, but they are still not significantly different. On the other hand, the USFD team models are no longer best-performing under the phrase-level F_1-score. This evaluation shows that phrase-level F_1-mult is slightly better at discriminating between models, although they are still considered too close and no single best-performing approach can be identified.

6.6 Task 3: Predicting document-level quality

The document-level QE task consists in scoring and ranking documents according to their predicted quality. Knowing the quality of entire documents is useful for scenarios where fully automated approaches are used. An example is *gisting*, mainly if the user of the system does not know the source language. Another example are scenarios where post-editing is not an option or cannot be performed for the entire data.

Different from last year's task, in this second edition we use entire documents and a document-oriented quality score. The quality scores are achieved by a two-stage post-editing method (Scarton et al., 2015b), with post-editing done by professional translators. In the first stage, sentences are shuffled and post-edited without context (PE1). In the second stage, the post-edited sentences (from the first stage) are put together in the document context and post-edited again (PE2) by the same translator. This approach aims to isolate problems that can only be solved with document-level information.

Although the annotation task is considerably simple to perform, generating reliable quality labels from the data is not a trivial task. Average (AVG) and Standard Deviation (STDEV) of HTER between PE1 and MT ($PE_1 \times MT$), PE2 and MT ($PE_2 \times MT$) and PE2 and PE1 ($PE_2 \times PE_1$) are presented in Table 26.[22]

As shown in Table 26, $PE_1 \times MT$ and $PE_2 \times MT$ show low variation. As discussed last year (Bojar et al., 2015), we hypothesise that the low variation in the scores means that quality labels are not not able to distinguish documents reliably. $PE_2 \times PE_1$ values, on the other hand, show a high variation, indicating that the documents vary more when only document-wide errors are considered. However, taking only $PE_2 \times PE_1$ as quality label is not ideal as it disregards problems at word and sentence levels, which certainly also influence the quality of the document as whole. Our solution is to combine the scores such as to maintain a high enough variation in the data, while considering all issue levels. More specifically, we use a linear combination of $PE_1 \times MT$ and $PE_2 \times PE_1$ (Equation 1).

$$f = w_1 \cdot PE_1 \times MT + w_2 \cdot PE_2 \times PE_1, \qquad (1)$$

where w_1 and w_2 are empirically defined weights. w_1 was fixed to 1, while w_2 was optimised aiming at finding how much relevance we should give to each component in order to meet two criteria. First, the final label (f) should lead to significant data variation (in terms of standard deviation on the mean). Second, the difference between the MAE of the mean baseline[23] and the MAE of the official baseline QE system should be large enough.[24] The quality labels were defined by Equation 1 with $w_1 = 1$ and $w_2 = 13$.

---

[22]HTER was calculated by using the `Asiya` toolkit implementation of TER (non-tokenised and case insensitive) (Giménez and Màrquez, 2010).

[23]This baseline is calculated by assuming the mean of the training set as the predicted value of all instances in the test set.

[24]In our experiments, for variance we defined that the ratio between the standard deviation and mean should be at least 0.5 and for MAE difference, we defined it to be at least 0.1. w_2 was increased by 1 at each iteration and the optimisation process stopped when any of the requirements was met.

System ID	F_1-**mult** $\uparrow$	F_1-BAD	F_1-OK
English-German			
• CDACM/RNN	0.380	0.503	0.755
• POSTECH/PHR-RNN-QV3	0.378	0.495	0.764
• POSTECH/PHR-RNN-QV2	0.369	0.478	0.772
• USFD2/W&SLP4PT	0.368	0.486	0.757
• USFD2/CONTEXT	0.365	0.470	0.777
RTM/s5_RTM-GLMd	0.327	0.408	0.802
BASELINE	0.321	0.401	0.800
RTM/s4_RTM-GLMd	0.307	0.377	0.814
Ualacant/SBI-Online-baseline	0.259	0.493	0.526
UAlacant/SBI-Online	0.098	0.459	0.213

Table 24: Official results for the WMT16 Quality Estimation Task 2p. The winning submissions are indicated by a •. These are the top-scoring submission and those that are not significantly worse according to approximate randomisation tests with 95% confidence intervals. The grey area indicates the submissions whose results are not statistically different from the baseline.

System ID	F_1-**mult** $\uparrow$	F_1-BAD	F_1-OK
English-German			
• POSTECH/PHR-RNN-QV3	0.393	0.518	0.759
• POSTECH/PHR-RNN-QV2	0.388	0.504	0.771
• CDACM/RNN	0.378	0.500	0.756
USFD/CONTEXT	0.364	0.467	0.780
USFD/W&SLP4PT	0.363	0.475	0.764
RTM/s5-RTM-GLMd	0.331	0.413	0.802
BASELINE	0.311	0.389	0.799
RTM/s4-RTM-GLMd	0.306	0.376	0.815
UAlacant/SBI-Online-baseline	0.275	0.502	0.547
UAlacant/SBI-Online	0.146	0.456	0.320

Table 25: Results for the WMT16 Quality Estimation Task 2p computed in terms of phrase-level F_1-scores. The winning submissions are indicated by a •. These are the top-scoring submission and those that are not significantly worse according to approximate randomisation tests with 95% confidence intervals. The grey area indicates the submissions whose results are not statistically different from the baseline.

	$PE_1 \times MT$	$PE_2 \times MT$	$PE_2 \times PE_1$
AVG	0.346	0.381	0.042
STDEV	0.108	0.091	0.034
Ratio	0.312	0.239	0.810

Table 26: AVG and STDEV of the post-edited data.

Data The documents were extracted from the WMT translation task test data from 2008 to 2013, using submissions from all participating MT systems. Source documents were randomly chosen. For each source document, a translation was taken from a different MT system. We considered EN-ES as language pair, extracting 208 documents. All documents were post-edited as previously explained. 146 documents were used for training and 62 for test.

Evaluation The evaluation of the document-level task was the same as that for the sentence-level task. Pearson's r, MAE and RMSE are reported as evaluation metrics for the scoring task, with Pearson's r as official metric for the ranking of systems. For the ranking task, Spearman's ρ correlation and DeltaAvg are reported, with Spearman's rho as main metric. The significance of the results is evaluated by applying the Williams test on Pearson's r scores.

Results The results of both the scoring and ranking variants of the task are given in Table 27, sorted from best to worst by using the Pearson's r scores as primary key. USHEF/BASE-EMB-GP and RTM/RTM-FS+PLS-TREE showed the best scores, with no significant difference between them. The other two systems are not statistically significantly different from the baseline.

The two winning submissions are very different. The BASE-EMB-GP system combines word embeddings with the official baseline features in a GP model with two-kernels, while RTM-FS+PLS-TREE is an RTM implementation that explores more sophisticated features from the source and target texts. For ranking variant, however, RTM-FS+PLS-TREE showed better results. Moreover, this is the only system with higher scores than the baseline that is also significantly better than the baseline.

6.7 Discussion

In what follows, we discuss the main findings of this year's shared task based on the goals we had

System ID	**Pearson's r** $\uparrow$	MAE $\downarrow$	RMSE $\downarrow$	Spearman's ρ $\uparrow$	DeltaAvg $\uparrow$
English-Spanish					
• USHEF/BASE-EMB-GP	0.391	0.295	0.128	0.393	0.111
• RTM/RTM-FS+PLS-TREE	0.356	0.253	0.118	0.476	0.123
RTM/RTM-FS-SVR	0.293	0.268	0.125	0.360	0.119
BASELINE	0.286	0.278	0.139	0.354	0.093
USHEF/GRAPH-DISC	0.256	0.285	0.144	0.285	0.061

Table 27: Official results for the scoring ad ranking variants of the WMT16 Quality Estimation Task 3. The systems are ranked according to the Pearson r metric and significance results are also computed for this metric. The winning submissions are indicated by a •. These are the top-scoring submission and those that are not significantly worse according to Williams test with 95% confidence intervals. The systems in the grey area are not different from the baseline system at a statistically significant level according to the same test.

previously identified for it.

Domain specific, professionally done post-editions

Last year we used the largest dataset of all editions of the shared task to date (for sentence and phrase-level QE): $\sim$14K segment pairs altogether. However, the findings were somewhat inconclusive as the quality of the dataset was dubious (crowd-sourced post-editions). This year we were able to collect a dataset of comparable size (15K) but in a completely controlled way, and with professional (paid) translators to ensure the quality of the data. Another critical difference in this year's main dataset is its domain: IT, as opposed to the rather general, "news" domain that had been used so far. Finally, we had access to the SMT system that produced the translations, which was very important for the new task introduced this year – phrase-level QE. For phrase-level QE, the segmentation of the sentences in phrases was necessary. Having a more repetitive text domain was deemed particularly relevant for the word and phrase-level tasks, where data sparsity is a major issue.

In practice, we found that this year's main dataset is similar to last year's in terms of error distribution at the word-level: about 20% of the words are labelled as BAD. One thing to notice, however, is that with the new data systems did not seem to benefit from filtering data out. Last year, various systems reported improvements from filtering out significant portions of the "all/mostly GOOD" sentences, which could have meant that these sentences may not have been correct, but did not get post-edited by the crowdworkers.

In terms of progress with respect to last year for comparable tasks, although direct comparisons are not possible, we observed that:

- For sentence-level, the Pearson correlation of the winning submission last year was 0.39 (against 0.14 of the baseline system). This year, the winning submission reached 0.52 Pearson correlation, with many other systems above 0.4 (against 0.35 of the same baseline system as last year). One can speculate that the task was made somewhat "easier" by using high quality data, but the delta in Pearson correlation between the baseline and winning submission is still very substantial.

- For word-level, the main metric used this year (F_1-mult) is different from the one used last year (F_1-BAD), and this may have been the metric most systems optimised against, so looking at the F_1-BAD results for both years is not entirely fair to this year's systems, but nevertheless this year's systems performed much better: 0.56 against 0.43 last year. The baseline system used last year was much simpler, and therefore comparisons against the baseline cannot be made.

Effectiveness of new quality label provided by humans for document-level prediction

Participation in the document-level task was again disappointingly low, with only four systems. Document-level QE is still a relative new area and engaging the community is therefore still a challenge.

The main changes in this year's task were the fact that entire documents are used (potentially resulting in the need for more discourse/document-wide features), and the the fact that the quality labels are computed based on human post-editing. We start by analysing the new quality label against automatic metrics (such as BLEU) used in previous work. Our hypothesis is that automatic metrics are not reliable labels for document-level evaluation (as discussed in (Scarton et al., 2015b)). Therefore, we expect that our new label would perform differently from these metrics. We use correlation to measure whether or not the new label shows different behaviour. Table 28 shows Pearson r correlation scores for automatic metrics versus the new label, as well as between HTER and all labels. The HTER score was calculated considering the last version of the two-stage post-editing method ($PE_2 \times MT$).

	NEW ($\downarrow$)	BLEU($\uparrow$)	TER($\downarrow$)	METEOR($\uparrow$)
BLEU	-0.168	-	-	-
TER	$+0.195$	-0.928	-	-
METEOR	-0.186	$+0.954$	-0.961	-
HTER($\downarrow$)	$\mathbf{+0.516}$	-0.462	$+0.449$	-0.452

Table 28: Pearson r correlation between automatic metrics, our new label (NEW) and HTER. All correlation scores are significant with 95% of confidence.

Although the new label showed some correlation to BLEU, TER and METEOR, the best correlation is showed with HTER. On the other hand, the automatic metrics showed higher correlation among themselves than against HTER scores, which is expected since such metrics are similar in many ways.

An important observation is that the automatic metrics are calculated against a human translation and HTER is calculated against a post-edited version. The effect of this is that BLEU, TER and METEOR compare the MT output to a human translation that can be completely different from the MT output, without necessarily meaning that the machine translation is bad. HTER, conversely, compares the MT output to its post-edited version.

It is also worth noticing that although HTER did not show a high variation (0.091 for mean 0.381 - third column of Table 26), similar to the automatic metrics, it still did not show very high correlation with BLEU, TER and METEOR. Conversely, the new label showed high correlation with HTER, but much lower correlation with BLEU, TER and METEOR than HTER itself. This seems to indicate that the new label captures different information than BLEU, TER and METEOR. Therefore, we believe that the new label and standard evaluation metrics provide complementary information on translation quality.

In terms of features, most are similar to those used by the systems submitted last year, which are aggregations of sentence-level feature values. Therefore, our hypothesis that discourse/document-aware features would show better results on evaluating full document was not proved. Systems using discourse-aware features (USHEF/GRAPH-DISC) did not show improvements relative to the baseline system. This could be an indication of the limitations of the features or of the labels themselves.

QE at the phrase level

One of the main motivations for switching from the word level to phrase level is the fact that MT errors are often context-dependent, and the wrong choice of a word might be explained by an error in its context. A good example of such errors are adjectives that take the gender of the noun they depend on, and become erroneous if this noun is replaced with another noun of a different gender.

This motivation suggests that the phrases to be used as atomic units in a phrase-level QE system should be syntactically motivated. However, there can be other approaches. For example, the very popular SMT systems manipulate sequences of words as opposed to single words. These sequences – referred to as "phrases" – are not linguistically motivated phrases. During decoding these phrases are selected or rejected as atomic units (regardless of the quality of the individual words they consist of), and thus it may be useful to estimate the quality of the entire phrase.

Overall, there is no single answer to what should be considered as a "phrase" in a phrase-level QE system. A fully-fledged phrase-level QE system should be able to handle both the segmentation of a sentence into phrases and the labelling of each phrase for quality. However, each of these two steps is a complex problem on itself. Therefore, for the first edition of the task we decided to simplify it and provide the phrase segmentation. Following Logacheva et al. (2015), we considered a "phrase" the final segmentation produced by the SMT decoder by an MT decoder that generated the automatic translations in the dataset. This segmentation is useful for decoding-time QE.

The baseline phrase-level QE system uses a set of features which were originally designed for sentences and later adapted for smaller sequences. These features were used to train a CRF model. Participants chose many different techniques to model the task. The best performing ones are deep neural networks: the Recurrent Neural Network from the POSTECH team which predicts the phrase-level label and the CDACM Recurrent Neural Network whose word-level predictions were successfully applied to the phrase-level task. Two of the submitted models make use of the baseline feature set: the USFD team enhanced it with context information, while the UAlacante team combined it with features based on pseudo-reference translations coming from a number of sources.

Several teams attempted to take into account the predictions for other the task at other levels. The phrase-level submission from CDACM simply labels the phrase-level test set using word-level predictions; while the UAlacant submission uses the probability of each word in a phrase being labelled as BAD along with other external features. Similarly, USFD uses information on word labels within a phrase as well as the information on sentence-level quality.

Comparison of word-level and phrase-level models The word-level and phrase-level systems that participated in Tasks 2 and 2p are not directly comparable. Although they are evaluated on the same test sentences, and the labels for the test set come from the same post-editions, they are not identical. The labels for the phrase-level test set were modified in order to comply with the phrase-level training data. We established a pessimistic approache where a phrase is considered BAD if any of its words is BAD. We changed the word-level labels so that all labels within a BAD phrase are also BAD. This is analogous to replacing some OK labels with BAD labels for words.

Nevertheless, we can still try to compare the word-level and phrase-level submissions if we change the word-level submissions appropriately. Let us consider that a word-level QE model was used to label phrases for quality. Following the rules mentioned above we will label a phrase as BAD if our QE model labelled any of words of this phrase as BAD. After performing this transformation we can use the Task 2p test set to evaluate both phrase-level and (modified) word-level submissions.

While this comparison is an approximation as the submitted word-level models were not trained to predict the quality of phrases, it still allows a rough comparison between word-level and phrase-level QE models. One of the purposes of the phrase-level task was to understand if the subsentence-level QE can benefit from joint labelling of groups of words, and this cross-task comparison is a means to try to answer that question.

Table 29 contains the joint results of Tasks 2 and 2p. The best-performing system is the winning word-level submission. Moreover, the word-level systems tend to perform better in this task in general: the top seven positions in this joint table are occupied by the word-level systems. Some of the phrase-level systems which performed well turn out not to be better than the word-level baseline system. Presumably, this result means that defining the quality for individual words yields better results in general.

Another observation we can make from this table is the change in the significance level of the results: some of the word-level submissions which were significantly different from the word-level baseline model in the original (word-level) task are no longer different in the phrase-level version. This can shed some light on the difficulties we had with defining the single best phrase-level system: perhaps the lack of significance in the differences between the labellings is derived from the phrase-level task itself. Alternatively, as it was discussed in Section 6.5, it could be explained by the fact that F_1-mult score is not a suitable metric for phrase-level QE.

In order to examine how the phrase-level task relates to the word-level one more closely we performed a different comparison. Some of the teams presented their results for both variants of Task 2, and the majority of them have similar models for both levels: they tried to adapt their original word-level system for the phrase-level task. We can compare these pairs of systems to see if the adaptation was successful. This is not a direct comparison, because the models, although similar, cannot be identical due to differences between words and phrases. This comparison was only done for analysis, as it can give us more insights on the future perspectives for the phrase-level task. Table 30 outlines the results of this comparison.[25]

Here, in order to enable the direct comparison, we adapted the word-level systems to phrase-level test set the same way as we did for Table 29. It can be clearly seen that the performance of word-level systems is better than that of the analogous phrase-level systems. There are multiple possible reasons for that, for example, wrong choice of phrase-level features, limitations of models originally designed for word-level QE in dealing effectively with word

---

[25]The submission by the CDACM team was not included in the table because their phrase-level submission is an adaptation of word-level predictions to phrase level. It was performed analogously to our word-level submissions adaptation, therefore it should be no different.

	System ID	F_1-**mult** ↑
	English-German	
• **word**	UNBABEL/ensemble	0.517
word	UNBABEL/linear	0.487
word	UGENT-LT3/SCATE-RF	0.426
word	POSTECH/WORD-RNN-QV3	0.399
word	UGENT-LT3/SCATE-ENS	0.395
word	POSTECH/WORD-RNN-QV2	0.388
word	CDACM/RNN	0.381
phrase	CDACM/RNN	0.379
phrase	POSTECH/PHR-RNN-QV3	0.378
phrase	POSTECH/PHR-RNN-QV2	0.369
word	UAlacant/SBI-Online-baseline	0.369
phrase	USFD/W&SLP4PT	0.367
word	SHEF/SHEF-MIME-0.3	0.367
word	SHEF/SHEF-MIME-1	0.367
phrase	USFD/CONTEXT	0.364
word	BASELINE	0.360
word	RTM/s5-RTM-GLMd	0.344
phrase	RTM/s5-RTM-GLMd	0.327
phrase	BASELINE	0.321
word	RTM/s4-RTM-GLMd	0.313
phrase	RTM/s4-RTM-GLMd	0.307
word	UAlacant/SBI-Online	0.290
phrase	UAlacant/SBI-Online-baseline	0.259
phrase	UAlacant/SBI-Online	0.097

Table 29: Comparison of submissions for Tasks 2 and 2p in terms of word-level F_1-mult scores computed on the test set used for the Task 2p. Word-level systems (Task 2) are indicated by "**word**", while phrase-level systems (Task 2p), by "**phrase**". The winning submission is indicated with •. The grey area indicates the models which are not significantly different from the word-level baseline system, the cyan area indicates the models which are not significantly different from the phrase-level baseline.

System ID	Word-level	Phrase-level
English-German		
POSTECH/RNN-QV3	0.399	0.378
POSTECH/RNN-QV2	0.388	0.369
RTM/s5-RTM-GLMd	0.344	0.327
RTM/s4-RTM-GLMd	0.313	0.307
Ualacant/SBI-Online-baseline	0.369	0.259
Ualacant/SBI-Online	0.290	0.097

Table 30: Comparison of systems' performance in Task 2 (word-level) and 2p (phrase-level). Performance is evaluated in terms of word-level F_1-mult scores computed on the test set used for the Task 2p. The submissions to the word-level task are modified in order to comply with the phrase-level task.

sequences.

Nevertheless, it is worth noticing the phrase-level QE systems introduced a number of interesting strategies that allowed them to outperform a strong baseline phrase-level model. Finally, we recall that the evaluation metric – word-level F_1-mult – has difficulties to distinguish phrase-level systems. This suggests that we may need to find a different metric for evaluation of the phrase-level task, with phrase-level F_1-mult one of the candidates.

7 Automatic Post-editing Task

This year WMT hosted the second round of the shared task on MT automatic post-editing (APE), which consists in automatically correcting the errors present in a machine translated text. As pointed out by Chatterjee et al. (2015b), from the application point of view the task is motivated by its possible uses to:

- Improve MT output by exploiting information unavailable to the decoder, or by performing deeper text analysis that is too expensive at the decoding stage;

- Cope with systematic errors of an MT system whose decoding process is not accessible;

- Provide professional translators with improved MT output quality to reduce (human) post-editing effort;

- Adapt the output of a general-purpose MT system to the lexicon/style requested in a specific application domain.

Also this year, the general framework consisted in a "black box" scenario in which the MT system that produced the translations is unknown to the participants and cannot be modified. However, building on the lessons learned in the first pilot round (Bojar et al., 2015), some changes have been made.

The major differences concern the domain and the origin of the data. First, we moved from the general `news` domain to the more specific `information technology` (IT) domain. This novelty is motivated by the difficulties observed in the pilot round, in which the baseline (the simple *do-nothing* APE system that leaves all the test sentences unmodified) remained unbeaten. Indeed, the scarce repetitiveness of the `news` domain prevented participants to learn from the training data effective correction patterns that are also applicable to the test set. Second, concerning the origin of the data, we moved from post-edits obtained from non-professional crowdsourced workforce to material collected from professional translators. Data collected from trained professionals represents first of all a more standard scenario for the translation industry. Besides this, they are considered to guarantee higher translation coherence, feature higher repetitiveness and, eventually, make the APE task more feasible by automatic systems.

Other changes concern the language combination and the evaluation mode. As regards the languages, we moved from English-Spanish to English-German, which is one of the language pairs covered by the QT21 Project[26] that supported data collection and post-editing. Concerning the evaluation, we changed from TER scores computed both in case-sensitive and case-insensitive mode to a single ranking based on case sensitive measurements.

Besides these changes the new round of the APE task included some extensions in the evaluation. BLEU (Papineni et al., 2002) has been introduced as a secondary evaluation metric to measure the improvements over the rough MT output. In addition, to gain further insights on final output quality, a subset of the outputs of the submitted systems has also been manually evaluated.

Based on these changes and extensions, the goals of this year's shared task were to: *i)* improve and stabilize the evaluation framework in view of future rounds, *ii)* analyze the effect on task

[26] http://www.qt21.eu/

feasibility of data coming from a narrow domain, *iii)* analyze the effect of post-edits collected from professional translators, *iv)* analyze how humans perceive TER/BLEU performance differences between different systems, *v)* measure the progress made during one year of research on the APE task.

Although the changes made with respect to the first pilot round prevent from fair and informative result comparisons, we believe that these objectives were successfully achieved. Most noticeably, the higher feasibility of the task brought by domain-specific data and professional post-edits resulted in significant baseline improvements (up to 3.2 TER and 5.5 BLEU points), which are also evident to human evaluation. These positive results, together with the increase in the number of participants with respect to the pilot round (from four to six), represent a good starting point for future rounds of the APE task.

7.1 Task description

Similar to last year, participants were provided with training and development data consisting of (*source, target, human post-edit*) triplets, and were asked to return automatic post-edits for a test set of unseen (*source, target*) pairs.

7.1.1 Data

One of the findings of the first pilot task was that the origin and the domain of the data pose specific challenges to the participating systems. In particular, our analysis highlighted the strong dependence of system results on data repetitiveness, which tends to be higher within restricted domains and with coherent post-edits. On one side, restricted domains are more likely to feature smaller vocabularies and to be more repetitive (or, in other terms, less sparse). This situation, in turn, will likely determine a higher applicability of the learned error correction patterns. On the other side, coherent post-edits (like those produced within controlled professional environments) will result in a lower variability in the correction of specific errors and, in turn, in favorable conditions to learn and gather reliable statistics. These considerations motivate some of the major changes of this year's round of the APE task, namely those concerning the domain (a specific one as opposed to `news`) and the origin of the post-edits (from professional translators instead of crowdsourced).

The data used this year was released by the QT21 Project. This material was obtained by randomly sampling from a collection of English-German (*source, target, human post-edit*) triplets drawn from the Information Technology (IT) domain.[27] Also this year, the main reason for random sampling was to induce a higher data homogeneity and, in turn, to increase the chances that correction patterns learned from the training set can be applied also to the test set. The downside of losing information yielded by text coherence (an aspect that some APE systems might take into consideration) has hence been accepted in exchange for a higher error repetitiveness across the three data sets.

The training and development sets respectively consist of $12,000$ and $1,000$ instances. In each instance:

- The source (SRC) is a tokenized English sentence whose length ranges between 3 and 30 tokens;

- The target (TGT) is a tokenized German translation of the source. Translations were obtained with a statistical MT system.[28] This information, however, was unknown to participants, for which the MT system was a black-box.

- The human post-edit (PE) is a manually-revised version of the target, done by professional translators.[29]

Test data ($2,000$ instances) consists of (*source, target*) pairs having similar characteristics of those in the training set. Human post-edits of the test target instances were left apart to measure system performance.

Table 31 provides some basic statistics about the data. As discussed in Section 7.3, the differences in the domain and the origin of this year's data can contribute to explain the large improvements over the baseline, which in the first pilot round unfortunately remained unbeaten. These differences are highlighted by the Repetition Rate

(RR[30]) scores reported in Table 32. Values are indeed very close to those observed in the IT-related corpus (the Autodesk Post-Editing Data corpus[31]) that was used last year as a term of comparison to motivate the high difficulty of dealing with news data.

7.1.2 Evaluation metric

System performance was evaluated by computing the distance between *automatic* and *human* post-edits of the machine-translated sentences present in the test set (i.e. for each of the $2,000$ target test sentences). Differently from the first edition of the task, in which this distance was only measured in terms of Translation Error Rate (TER) (Snover et al., 2006), this year the BLEU (Papineni et al., 2002) score was also used. TER is an evaluation metric commonly used in MT-related tasks (e.g. in quality estimation) to measure the minimum edit distance between an automatic translation and a reference translation.[32] BLEU is the reference metric for MT evaluation and is based on modified n-gram precision to find how many of the n-grams in the candidate translation are present in the reference translation over the entire test set. The main difference between the two metrics is that TER works at word level, while BLEU takes advantage of words and n-grams with n from 2 to 4. Systems were ranked based on the average TER calculated on the test set by using the TERcom[33] software: lower average TER scores correspond to higher ranks. BLEU was computed using the multi-bleu.perl package[34] available in MOSES.

Differently from the pilot round, in which TER was computed both in case-sensitive and case-insensitive mode, this year we opted for only one mode. Working with German, for which case errors are of crucial importance, participants' submissions were evaluated with the more strict case-sensitive mode.

---

[27]The source sentences (together with their reference translations which were not used for the task) were provided by TAUS (https://www.taus.net/) and originally come from a unique IT vendor.

[28]It consists of a phrase-based machine translation system leveraging generic and in-domain parallel training data and using a pre-reordering technique (Herrmann et al., 2013). It takes also advantages of POS and word class-based language models.

[29]German native speakers working at Text&Form https://www.textform.com/.

[30]Repetition rate measures the repetitiveness inside a text by looking at the rate of non-singleton n-gram types (n=1...4) and combining them using the geometric mean. Larger value means more repetitions in the text.

[31]https://autodesk.app.box.com/Autodesk-PostEditing

[32]Edit distance is calculated as the number of edits (word insertions, deletions, substitutions, and shifts) divided by the number of words in the reference. Lower TER values indicate lower distance from the reference as a proxy for higher MT quality.

[33]http://www.cs.umd.edu/~snover/tercom/

[34]https://github.com/moses-smt/mosesdecoder/blob/master/scripts/generic/multi-bleu.perl

	Tokens			Types			Lemmas		
	SRC	TGT	PE	SRC	TGT	PE	SRC	TGT	PE
Train (12,000)	201,505	210,573	214,720	9,328	14,185	16,388	5,628	11,418	13,244
Dev (1,000)	17,827	19,355	19,763	2,931	3,333	3,506	1,922	2,686	2,806
Test (2,000)	31,477	34,332	35,276	3,908	4,695	5,047	2,479	3,753	4,050

Table 31: Data statistics.

	APE@WMT15 (EN-ES, news, crowd)	APE@WMT16 (EN-DE, IT, prof.)
SRC	2.905	6.616
TGT	3.312	8.845
PE	3.085	8.245

Table 32: Repetition Rate (RR) of the WMT15 (English-Spanish, news domain, crowdsourced post-edits) and WMT16 (English-German, IT domain, professional post-editors) APE Task data.

7.1.3 Baseline

The official baseline results are the TER and BLEU scores calculated by comparing the raw MT output with the human post-edits. In practice, the baseline APE system is a system that leaves all the test targets unmodified.[35] Baseline results are reported in Table 34.

Monolingual translation as another term of comparison. To get some insights about the progress with respect to the first pilot task, participating systems were also evaluated against a re-implementation of the approach firstly proposed by Simard et al. (2007).[36] Last year, in fact, this statistical post-editing approach represented the common backbone of all submissions (this is also reflected by the close results achieved by participants in the pilot task). For this purpose, a phrase-based SMT system based on Moses (Koehn et al., 2007) was used. Translation and reordering models were estimated following the Moses protocol with default setup using MGIZA++ (Gao and Vogel, 2008) for word alignment. For language modeling we used the KenLM toolkit (Heafield, 2011) for standard n-gram modeling with an n-gram length of 5. Finally, the APE system was tuned on

the development set, optimizing TER/BLEU with Minimum Error Rate Training (Och, 2003). The results of this additional term of comparison are also reported in Table 34.

For each submitted run, the statistical significance of performance differences with respect to the baselines and the re-implementation of Simard et al. (2007) was calculated with the bootstrap test (Koehn, 2004).

7.2 Participants

This year, six teams (two more than in the pilot round) participated in the APE task by submitting a total of eleven runs. Participants are listed in Table 33; a short description of their systems is provided in the following.

Adam Mickiewicz University. This system is among the very first ones exploring the application of neural translation models to the APE task. In particular, it investigates the following aspects: *i)* the use of artificially-created post-edited data to train the neural models, *ii)* the log-linear combination of monolingual and bilingual models in an ensemble-like manner, *iii)* the addition of task-specific features in the log-linear model to control the final output quality. Concerning the data, in addition to the official training and development material, the system exploits the English-German bilingual training material released for the IT-domain and news translation shared tasks. The German monolingual common crawl corpus admissible for these two tasks is also exploited. This data is used by a "round-trip translation" approach aimed to artificially create the huge amount of triples needed to train the neural models. Such models are attentional encoder-decoder models (Bahdanau et al., 2014) trained with subword units (Sennrich et al., 2015) in order to deal with the limited ability of neural translation models to handle out-of-vocabulary words. They include both monolingual models trained to translate from TGT to PE, and cross-lingual models trained to translate from SRC to PE. An ensemble is obtained through their log-linear combination with empirically-set weights (higher for the

---

[35]In the case of TER, the baseline is computed by averaging the distances between each machine-translated sentence and its human-revised version. The actual evaluation metric is the human-targeted TER (HTER). For the sake of clarity, since TER and HTER compute edit distance in the same way (the only difference is in the origin of the correct sentence used for comparison), henceforth we will use TER to refer to both metrics.

[36]This is done based on the description provided in (Simard et al., 2007). Our re-implementation, however, is not meant to officially represent such approach. Discrepancies with the actual method are indeed possible due to our misinterpretation or to wrong guesses about details that are missing in the paper.

ID	Participating team
AMU	Adam Mickiewicz University, Poland (Junczys-Dowmunt and Grundkiewicz, 2016)
CUNI	Univerzita Karlova v Praze, Czech Republic (Libovický et al., 2016)
DCU	Dublin City University, Ireland
FBK	Fondazione Bruno Kessler, Italy (Chatterjee et al., 2016)
JUSAAR	Jadavpur University, India & Saarland University, Germany
USAAR	Saarland University, Germany (Pal et al., 2016)

Table 33: Participants in the WMT16 Automatic Post-editing task.

TGT-to-PE model). Finally, a task-specific feature based on string matching is added to the log-linear combination to control the faithfulness of the APE results with regard to the input. This is done by penalizing words in the output that do not appear in the input to be corrected.

Univerzita Karlova v Praze. Also this system is based on the neural translation model with attention proposed by Bahdanau et al. (2014) and extends it to include multiple encoders able to manage different input representations. Each encoder is a bidirectional RNN that takes in input a one-hot vector for each representation of a word. The decoder is an RNN which receives an embedding of the previously produced word as an input in every time step together with the hidden state from the previous time step. The RNNs output is then used to compute the attention and the next word distribution. The attention is computed over each of the encoders separately. The initial state of the decoder is obtained by a weighted combination of the encoders final states. To improve the capability of the network to focus on the edits made by the post-editors, the target sentence is converted in the minimum-length sequence of edit operations performed on the machine-translated sentence. For this purpose, the network vocabulary is extended adding two more tokens (keep and delete) and the new representation is made of a sequence of keep, delete and insert operations, where the insert operation is defined by placing the word itself. The different inputs used for the APE task submission are the source sentence and its translation into the target language and the sequence of edits. The network is trained using only the task data. To better handle the complexity of the German target language, different language-dependent pre- and post-processing are used, in particular, splitting the contracted prepositions and articles and separating some pronouns from their case ending.

Dublin City University. This system is designed as an automatic rule learning system. It considers four types of editings, i.e. replacement, deletion, insertion and reordering, as generalized replacement (GR) editings. GR editings are learned from aligning words in source and target sentences and records replacement pairs and their corresponding contexts for each source and target sentence pair. When the source word is empty, it is of an insertion editing; similarly, when the target word is empty, it is of a deletion editing. When the source words and target words in a GR editing both comprise the same set of words but with different orderings, it is of a reordering editing. The word-based GR editings and their generalization which uses POSs to replace their context words, comprise the whole rule set of GR editings. There is no linguistic knowledge incorporated in the system, which therefore can be applied to any language for post-editing purposes. Three things are learned from the training set, 1) the GR rules, 2) the precedence ordering of these rules, and 3) the maximum number of rules to be applied to a sentence. For each set of GR rules, the precedence ordering can be ranked based on the counts of replacement words, the counts of their context words, the lengths of GR editings, the number of occurrences of GR editings observed in training set and/or their combinations. In the training phase, given a set of GR rules, the system will apply the rules to the training set using different settings of precedence ordering and maximum number of rules to be applied for each sentence. The system is trained when one setting is selected if the system yields the best overall post-edited results by applying that setting. In the test phase, the GR rules will be applied to each sentence in the test set using the trained precedence ordering and stop when the maximum number of rules to be applied is met for that sentence.

Fondazione Bruno Kessler. This system combines the monolingual statistical approaches previously exploited in Chatterjee et al. (2015a) with a factored machine translation model that is able to leverage benefits from both. One is the monolingual statistical translation approach proposed by Simard et al. (2007). The other is the context-aware variant proposed by Béchara et al. (2011). The former is more robust and it better generalizes the learned post-editing rules. The latter is prone to data sparsity, word alignment and tuning problems due to its richer representation of the terms. Nevertheless, by integrating knowledge about the source context in the learned rules, its precision is a good complement to the higher recall of (Simard et al., 2007). By enabling a straightforward integration of additional annotation (factors) at the word-level, factored translation models (Koehn and Hoang, 2007) are used to leverage such complementarity. In the FBK system they include part-of-speech-tag and class-based neural language models (LM) along with statistical word-based LM to improve the fluency of the post-edits. These models are built upon a data augmentation technique (i.e. the extension of the monolingual parallel corpus with the post-edits available in the training data), which helps to mitigate the problem of over-correction in phrase-based APE systems. One of the submitted runs incorporates a quality estimation model (C. de Souza et al., 2013, 2014), which aims to select the best translation between the MT output and the automatic post-edit.

Jadavpur University & Saarland University. This system contains three basic components: statistical APE, word deletion model and word surface form correction model. The final generated translation is the product of a multi-engine re-ranking system. The statistical APE component is based on the phrase-based APE approach of Pal et al. (2015). MT outputs generally contain four types of errors: presence of unwarranted words, wrong word surface form, absence of some relevant words, and wrong word order. The system tries to address the first two types of errors. The word deletion model is based on source language context modelling and target language word deletion frequency in the training data. The surface form correction model tries to fix the morphological errors by generating all possible surface forms for each root word present in the MT output and

to select the most likely sequence of word surface forms by applying a language model. The word deletion model and the word surface form correction model are applied to all the APE outputs. Finally, the generated translation candidates are ranked using a ranking algorithm based on language model information and a length-based heuristic. The top ranked output is chosen as the final APE output.

Saarland University. This system combines the Operation Sequence Model (OSM) (Durrani et al., 2011) with the classic phrase-based statistical MT (PB-SMT) approach. The OSM-APE method represents the post-edited translation process as a linear sequence of operations such as lexical generation of post-edited translation and their orderings. The translation and reordering decisions are conditioned on n previous translation and reordering decisions. This technique is able to model both local and long-range reorderings that are quite useful when dealing with the German language. To improve the capability of choosing the correct edit to process, eight new features are added to the log-linear model. These features capture the cost of deleting a phrase and different information on possible gaps in reordering operations. The monolingual alignments between the MT outputs and their post-edits are computed using different methods based on TER, METEOR (Snover et al., 2006) and Berkeley Aligner (Liang et al., 2006). Only the task data is used for these submissions.

7.3 TER/BLEU results

The official TER and BLEU results achieved by participants are reported in Table 34. The submitted runs are sorted based on the average (case-sensitive) TER measured on test data, which was this year's primary evaluation metric.

Looking at the performance of the two baselines, i.e. the raw MT output (Baseline) and the basic statistical APE approach of Simard et al. (2007), the latter outperforms the former with both metrics. This indicates that, under this year's evaluation conditions, the MT outputs could be improved by learning from human post-editors' work.

Differently from the pilot task (Bojar et al., 2015), in which none of the runs was able to beat the baselines, this year half of the participants achieved this goal by producing automatic post-edited sentences that result in lower TER (with a

ID	Avg. TER	BLEU
AMU Primary	21.52	67.65
AMU Contrastive	23.06	66.09
FBK Contrastive	23.92	64.75
FBK Primary	23.94	64.75
USAAR Primary	24.14	64.10
USAAR Constrastive	24.14	64.00
CUNI Primary	24.31	63.32
(Simard et al., 2007)	24.64	63.47
Baseline	24.76	62.11
DCU Contrastive	26.79	58.60
JUSAAR Primary	26.92	59.44
JUSAAR Contrastive	26.97	59.18
DCU Primary	28.97	55.19

Table 34: Official results for the WMT16 Automatic Post-editing task – average TER ($\downarrow$), BLEU score ($\uparrow$).

maximum of -3.24 points) and higher BLEU score (up to +5.54 points). All differences with respect to such baselines are statistically significant. This suggests that the correction patterns learned from the data were reliable enough to allow most systems to effectively correct the original MT output.

The obvious question is whether the improvements observed this year are due to the new data set (i.e. domain-specific texts and professional post-edits) or to a real technology jump (i.e. the use of neural end-to-end APE systems, factored or operational sequential models). A partial answer is given by the performance of the approach of Simard et al. (2007), which we run on the data of both rounds of the APE task with the same implementation. Although its results on the two test sets are difficult to compare (also due to the different language setting), the overall TER scores and the relative distances with respect to the other submitted runs can give us some indications.

First of all, on the pilot test set, the basic statistical APE method damaged the original MT output quality, with a TER reduction of about 1 point. On this year's data it achieves a small improvement (though statistically significant only in terms of BLEU). This suggests that, as hypothesized in Section 7.1.1, the higher repetitiveness featured by the selected data can facilitate the work of the APE systems. The new scenario, with repetition rates for SRC, TGT and PE that are more than twice the values measured last year (see Table 32), makes them able to learn from the training data a larger number of reliable and re-applicable correction patterns. However, the large improvements ob-

tained this year by the top runs can only be reached by moving from the basic statistical MT backbone shared by all last year's participants to new and more reliable APE solutions. Indeed, its distance from the top-ranked systems has increased from 0.6 up to 3.12 TER points. While on one side it is true that the new data made the task easier, on the other side the deployed solutions and the increased results' distance over the basic statistical APE approach indicate a significant step forward.

In terms of TER and BLEU evaluations, there are minor differences (only for the lower ranked systems) between the two rankings. This confirms that both metrics capture similar linguistic phenomena and the use of n-grams does not show particular advantages.

7.4 System/performance analysis

Differently from the pilot round, in which TER results were more concentrated (the difference between the top and the lowest ranked system was about 1.5 points), this year systems' performance is distributed within an interval of about 7.5 points. Indeed, the two rankings of Table 34 can be seen as composed of three blocks: the best system, the systems scoring around the baselines and the lower performing systems. Trying to go beyond rough TER/BLEU measurements and to shed light on such performance differences, in this section we focus on a more fine-grained analysis of systems' behaviour and the corresponding errors.

7.4.1 System behaviour

A first interesting aspect to analyse is systems' behaviour which, compared to last year, reflects the larger variety of approaches explored. *Does this variety result in major differences in the correction strategies/operations?* To answer this question, we first analysed the submitted runs taking into consideration the changes made by each system to the test instances. Table 35 shows the number of modified, improved and deteriorated sentences. It's worth noting that, as observed last year, for all the systems the number of modified sentences is higher than the sum of the improved and the deteriorated ones. This difference is represented by modified sentences for which the corrections do not yield TER variations. This grey area, for which quality improvement/degradation can not be automatically assessed, contributes to motivate the human evaluation discussed in Section 7.5

	Modified	Improved	Deteriorated
AMU Primary	1,613	935	374
AMU Contrastive	1475	776	386
FBK Contrastive	640	377	148
FBK Primary	654	384	153
USAAR Primary	421	290	74
USAAR Contrastive	499	314	105
CUNI Primary	498	284	138
(Simard et al., 2007)	700	320	253
DCU Contrastive	407	48	314
JUSAAR Primary	1,521	320	835
JUSAAR Contrastive	1,540	326	837
DCU Primary	797	54	651

Table 35: Number of test sentences modified, improved and deteriorated by each submitted run.

Looking at the numbers in Table 35, it becomes evident that the overall number of modified sentences is considerably larger than in the pilot task. On average, the best run submitted by each team modified 42.5% sentences. This amount is much larger than last year, when the percentage was 18.0%, probably due to the higher repetitiveness of the data which makes possible to learn more reliable and applicable correction rules. The same holds for the average number of improved sentences, which this year is significantly larger (18.7% vs. 11% in the pilot). This trend is confirmed by the performance of our re-implementation of Simard et al. (2007), which modified 35% of the sentences (vs. 26% in the pilot), improving 45% (vs. 11% last year) and deteriorating 36% of them (vs. 61%).

These figures, however, vary considerably across the submitted runs. Among the systems that improve over the basic statistical APE approach, the top-ranked one modified an impressive number of test sentences (80%), which is more than twice the amount of items changed by the other submissions. For the same system, the improved and the deteriorated ones are respectively about 58% and 23% of the total, which is in line with the other participants that improved the baseline. An interesting general conclusion that we can draw is that the neural approach adopted by the top-ranked system allowed it to better cope with the data sparsity issues that affect the other methods (despite the higher repetitiveness of this year's data). More thorough investigations that are beyond the scope of this overview should verify the hypothesis that learning and generalising rules from a relatively small amount of human post-edits is easier with

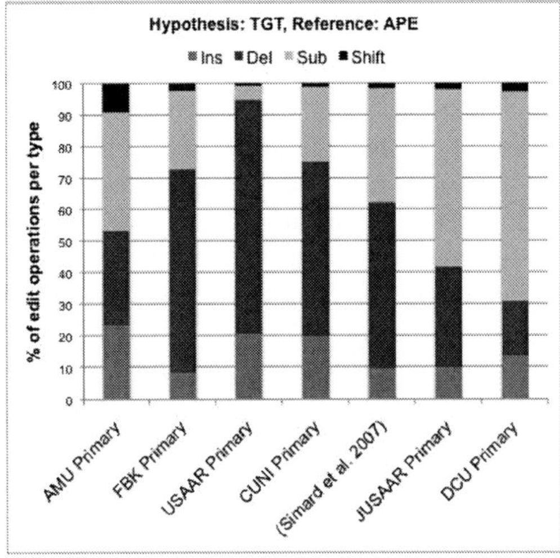

Figure 10: System Behaviour – TER(MT, APE)

neural models than with pure statistical solutions. Another aspect that should be checked is whether the neural solution performs better *per se* or thanks to the much larger amount of training data needed for its deployment.

Further insights about systems' behaviour can be drawn from the analysis of Figure 10. It plots the distribution of the edit operations done by each system (insertions, deletions, substitutions, shifts) obtained by computing the TER between the original MT output and the output of each system as reference (only for the primary submissions).

The figure evidences some interesting trends, starting from the much larger proportion of shifts made by the top-ranked neural approach. More than 450 shift operations (9.2% of the total), in fact, represent the major difference between the behaviour of the winning system and all the

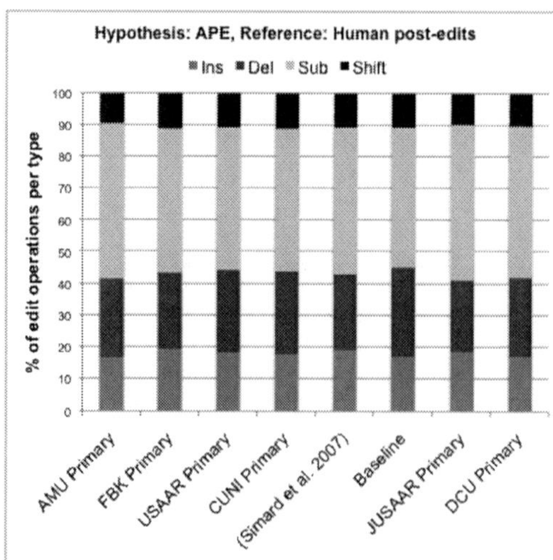

Figure 11: System Error – TER(APE, human post-edits)

other submissions (the second-ranked one performs only 26 shifts, 2.5% of the total). It is likely, but this should be verified, that the available training data featured correction patterns that the neural method was able to model and re-apply better than the other solutions. Overall, the behaviour of the best system is the most balanced with respect the three other operations. In total, insertions, deletions and substitutions (respectively 1,132, 1,465 and 1,807) are considerably more that those made by the other systems and they are more evenly distributed (23%, 30% and 37% respectively). As a term of comparison, the second-ranked primary submission performed much less operations (83 insertions, 652 deletions and 248 substitutions), with a clear predominance (65%) of deletions that is common also to other submissions. As a general remark, best results seem to be associated with a rather homogeneous distribution of the types of correction patterns learned by the system.

7.4.2 System error

Another interesting aspect to analyse is the effect of the different methods on the types of errors made by each system. *Does the variety in the approaches result in major differences in the types of errors made?* To answer this question, Figure 11 plots the distribution of the edit operations needed to transform the output of each system into the human post-edits available for each test sentence. Such distribution of systems' errors is obtained by computing the TER between their output and the human post-edits of the original translations as reference.

The figure does not show visible trends that can provide us with useful hints. In terms of error distribution, the task baseline, our re-implementation of Simard et al. (2007), and the submitted primary runs show almost identical ratios. Insertions range between 17% and 20% of the total, deletions range between 23% and 28%, substitutions range between 44% and 49%. The highest percentage of substitution errors suggests that the major problem for all systems is the lexical choice. Half of the errors in the APE output belong to this error category, indicating that learning the appropriate lexical replacements from human post-edits is still one of the main challenges. Comparing the error distribution in the MT baseline (our ground truth in terms of what has to be corrected) with the actions actually made by each system as shown in Figure 10, it is interesting to emphasise the higher similarity with the distributions of the operations made by the top-performing system. "AMU Primary", indeed, seems to perform a slightly larger amount of insertions compared to the total insertions actually needed, while the other operations are substantially in line with the expected amount. Based on TER information, nothing can be said about which of them are actually correct/wrong. The only conclusions we can draw at this stage are: *i)* a good amount of MT errors is corrected (the global TER decreases), *ii)* the actions of the top-performing system are quite evenly distributed, *iii)* such distribution is the closest to the distribution of ground truth operations but *iv)* errors (missing corrections and/or wrong corrections) still remain in all classes.

In light of these considerations, we performed further analysis by evaluating this years' APE submissions also from another point of view. To this aim, in the next section we try to understand the relation between the participants' performance and the human perception of translation quality.

7.5 Human Evaluation

To assess the quality of APE systems and produce a ranking based on human judgement, as well as analyze how humans perceive TER/BLEU performance differences between the submitted systems, two runs of human evaluations were conducted. The whole evaluation took approximately a month and was performed mainly by student translators who annotated the APE systems' outputs. This subsection describes the human evaluation procedure, gives details about the annotators' backgrounds and profiles, and finally presents the results of the evaluation.

7.5.1 Evaluation Procedure

The two runs of human evaluation were conducted using the Appraise[37] (Federmann, 2012) open-source annotation platform through the *ranking task* interface. A ranking task consists of a source segment and the outputs of up to 5 anonymized APE systems randomly selected from the set of participants and displayed in random order to human evaluators. The main difference between the two evaluation runs is the following: for the first run, the annotators were presented with a translation reference consisting of the manual post-edit of the machine-translated source segment, while for the second run no translation reference was presented to the human evaluator. For both evaluation runs, the non-post-edited MT output was included among the systems to evaluate. For the second evaluation run, the human post-edited version of the MT output was included among the systems to evaluate.

A total of 200 randomly extracted source segments taken from the test set presented in Table 31 with their corresponding systems' outputs were considered for the first evaluation run, while 100 source segments went through the second run. The decision to consider a larger set of segments for the first evaluation run is based on the previous editions of WMT, where human evaluations conducted for the translation tasks included a translation reference. The smaller scale evaluation for the second run can be seen as a pilot study, where no translation reference is given to the annotators and where the human post-edit is presented as part of the anonymized systems. The latter setup allows us to see if APE systems can reach human post-editing in terms of quality while avoiding evaluation bias towards a reference.

We carried out six annotation sessions in a controlled environment of approximately 45 to 60 minutes each, divided in two blocks of equal duration with a small break in between. Prior to the human evaluation task, we provided annotators with a pilot study in order to be introduced to the ranking task and be familiarized with the annotation interface. For each source sentence, five systems' outputs were randomly selected among the partic-

ipants and the non-post-edited MT output. For the second evaluation run, the human post-edit was included in the random selection of target sentences to annotate. The human annotators then ranked the outputs from 1 to 5 (1 being the best) with ties allowed. All source segments were evaluated by at least 3 annotators. The annotations were then used with the TrueSkill[38] adaptive ranking system to produce a score for each system based on their inferred means (Sakaguchi et al., 2014). This score was used to sort and cluster the systems submitted by the participants, as well as the MT output and the human post-edit, and produce the final ranking presented in Section 7.5.3

7.5.2 Annotators Background

A total of 37 annotators participated in the manual evaluation of APE systems, including 30 5th semester B.A. students in the *Comparative Linguistics, Literature, and Translation* program taught in Saarland University.[39] The remaining 7 evaluators are expert translators and lecturers at Saarland University in the *Applied Linguistics, Translation and Interpreting* department.[40] Among the annotators, 34 are native German speakers with strong English skills and have completed introductory courses such as translation theory and translation studies, machine translation, CAT tools, and MT evaluation and post-editing. The remaining 3 annotators have strong German skills and have been living in Germany for several years.

7.5.3 Results

The first and second runs of human evaluation results are respectively presented in Table 36 and Table 37.

The first run shows a preference for the AMU Primary system compared to the other submissions (Table 36). These results confirm those obtained with the automatic metrics as shown in Table 34 and we can see that two systems are above the Baseline (the raw MT output). The CUNI Primary and USAAR Primary systems are in the same cluster with the Baseline, which indicates a non-significant difference with $p \leq 0.05$. Two systems are in a single cluster below the baseline, namely JUSAAR Primary and DCU Primary, being on par with the results obtained using au-

---

[37]https://github.com/cfedermann/Appraise

[38]https://github.com/keisks/wmt-trueskill
[39]http://fr46.uni-saarland.de/?id=2393
[40]http://fr46.uni-saarland.de

#	Score	Range	ID
1	1.967	1	AMU Primary
2	0.033	2	FBK Primary
3	-0.108	3-4	CUNI Primary
	-0.191	3-5	USAAR Primary
	-0.211	3-5	Baseline
4	-0.712	6-7	JUSAAR Primary
	-0.778	6-7	DCU Primary

Table 36: Results of the first run of human evaluation including human post-edited MT output as translation reference. Scores and ranges are obtained with TrueSkill (Sakaguchi et al., 2014). Lines between systems indicate clusters according to bootstrap resampling at p-level $p \leq 0.05$ based on $1,000$ runs. Systems within a cluster are considered tied.

#	Score	Range	ID
1	2.058	1	Human Post-edit
2	0.867	2	AMU Primary
3	-0.213	3-4	CUNI Primary
	-0.348	3-6	FBK Primary
	-0.374	3-6	USAAR Primary
	-0.499	5-7	Baseline
	-0.675	6-8	JUSAAR Primary
	-0.816	7-8	DCU Primary

Table 37: Results of the second run of human evaluation without translation reference provided to annotators. Scores and ranges are obtained with TrueSkill (Sakaguchi et al., 2014). Lines between systems indicate clusters according to bootstrap resampling at p-level $p \leq 0.05$ based on $1,000$ runs. Systems within a cluster are considered tied.

tomatic metrics. The correlation between automatic metrics and the first manual evaluation run indicates the reliability of popular MT metrics for the evaluation of APE systems. On average, annotators needed 53 seconds to perform one ranking task, while the fastest ranking was performed in 18.3 seconds and the slowest one took more than 4 minutes and 30 seconds (averaged over at least 3 annotators for the same source segment). The agreement between annotators on the first run of evaluation is $k = 0.481$ according to Fleiss' Kappa (Fleiss, 1971).

The results of the second run of manual evaluation (Table 37) show that the human post-editing of MT output is preferred by human annotators when compared to the other systems' outputs, reaching the first position. It indicates that, in spite of the significant improvements over the original MT output, none of the submitted APE systems managed to reach the translation quality achieved by human post-editing. The second position in the ranking is reached by the AMU Primary sys-

tem, while a single cluster is ranked third and contains all the remaining systems as well as the Baseline. This smaller amount of clusters can be due to the limited scale of the second run of manual evaluation involving 100 source segments only, compared with the 200 segments for the first run. However, this second run shows that the AMU Primary system is again preferred by human evaluators compared to the other systems without necessarily being closer to the human post-edited MT output, which is not included as a translation reference, and thus without biasing human judgements. The agreement between annotators for the second run of evaluation is slightly lower compared to the first run, with a Fleiss' Kappa of $k = 0.466$. For both runs, the inter-annotator agreement is considered moderate. On average, the annotators needed 60 seconds per ranking task, while the fastest ranked outputs was completed in 21.7 seconds and the slowest one in 3 minutes.

7.6 Lessons learned and outlook

The objectives of this pilot APE task were to: *i)* improve and stabilize the evaluation framework in view of future rounds, *ii)* analyze the effect on task feasibility of data coming from a narrow domain, *iii)* analyze the effect of post-edits collected from professional translators, *iv)* analyze how humans perceive TER/BLEU performance differences between different systems, *v)* measure the progress made during one year of research on the APE task.

Concerning the first point, no specific issues emerged this year calling for major changes. The overall format, starting from the baselines and the evaluation metrics adopted, will likely be kept also for the next round.

As regards points *ii)* and *iii)* the positive effect of domain-specific data and professional-quality post-edits is evident. Most likely, these favorable conditions for automatic post-editing will be kept as well, also because they represent a more standard translation scenario compared to the generic news domain.

Regarding point *iv)*, an interesting finding of the manual evaluation is a correlation between human judgements and the results obtained with automatic metrics. This confirms the reliability of popular MT metrics, namely BLEU and TER, for APE systems evaluation. Despite the baseline improvements and the significant overall TER/BLEU gains, the feedback from human evaluators regarding the quality of the APE MT segments is not fully positive yet, showing that there is still room for improvement. One explanation for this is probably related to the domain specificity of the data set used for this year's APE shared task. Many segments contain sets of instructions and commands that are used in user manuals of the IT domain and were given to annotators without context. The annotators also pointed out that they considered difficult to rank very similar segments, as most APE systems do not make substantial modifications of the MT output, which results in similar outputs in terms of quality and leads to challenging comparisons for humans. This aspect is emphasized when no translation reference is given to the annotators. In this case, only the top-ranked system emerges as a source of corrections that are significantly better than the baseline (in spite of the impressive TER and BLEU gains, respectively up to -3.24 and +5.54 points).

In terms of progress over the last year, this was a successful follow-up. More participants, some of which new, resulted in a larger variety in the submitted systems. Those pursuing the phrase-based approach that dominated the pilot round managed to improve over this common backbone in different ways. Other teams introduced interesting novelties, bringing also into the APE framework the popularity of neural approaches. The tangible result is represented by the large improvements over the (last year unbeaten) baseline achieved by most of the systems. Such gains indicate the good potential of APE systems to improve MT output in black-box conditions and motivate further research and developments.

Acknowledgments

This work was supported in parts by the MosesCore, QT21, QTLeap, EXPERT and CRACKER projects funded by the European Commission (7th Framework Programme and H2020).

The APE task organizers would also like to thank Jan Niehues for training the KIT system used to produce the MT output, Text&Form for producing the manual post-edits, and the annotators involved in the manual evaluation.

References

Abdelsalam, A., Bojar, O., and El-Beltagy, S. (2016). Bilingual Embeddings and Word Alignments for Translation Quality Estimation. In *Proceedings of the First Conference on Machine Translation*, Berlin, Germany. Association for Computational Linguistics.

Abdi, H. (2007). The bonferroni and šidák corrections for multiple comparisons. *Encyclopedia of measurement and statistics*, 3:103–107.

Aires, J., Lopes, G., and Gomes, L. (2016). English-Portuguese Biomedical Translation Task Using a Genuine Phrase-Based Statistical Machine Translation Approach. In *Proceedings of the First Conference on Machine Translation*, Berlin, Germany. Association for Computational Linguistics.

Al-Rfou, R., Perozzi, B., and Skiena, S. (2013). Polyglot: Distributed Word Representations for Multilingual NLP. In *Proceedings of the 17th Conference on Computational Natural Language Learning*, pages 183–192, Sofia, Bulgaria.

Allauzen, A., Aufrant, L., Burlot, F., Lacroix, O., Knyazeva, E., Lavergne, T., Wisniewski, G., and Yvon, F. (2016). LIMSI@WMT16: Machine Translation of News. In *Proceedings of the First Conference on Machine Translation*, Berlin, Germany. Association for Computational Linguistics.

Avramidis, E. (2016). DFKI's system for WMT16 IT-domain task, including analysis of systematic errors. In *Proceedings of the First Conference on Machine Translation*, Berlin, Germany. Association for Computational Linguistics.

Aziz, W., de Sousa, S. C. M., and Specia, L. (2012). Pet: a tool for post-editing and assessing machine translation. In *Eighth International Conference on Language Resources and Evaluation*, LREC, pages 3982–3987, Instanbul, Turkey.

Bahdanau, D., Cho, K., and Bengio, Y. (2014). Neural machine translation by jointly learning to align and translate. *arXiv preprint arXiv:1409.0473*.

Béchara, H., Ma, Y., and van Genabith, J. (2011). Statistical Post-Editing for a Statistical MT System. In *Proceedings of the 13th Machine Translation Summit*, pages 308–315, Xiamen, China.

Beck, D., Vlachos, A., Paetzold, G., and Specia, L. (2016). SHEF-MIME: Word-level Quality

Estimation Using Imitation Learning. In *Proceedings of the First Conference on Machine Translation*, Berlin, Germany. Association for Computational Linguistics.

Bektaş, E., Yilmaz, E., Mermer, C., and Durgar El-Kahlout, . (2016). TÜBTAK SMT System Submission for WMT2016. In *Proceedings of the First Conference on Machine Translation*, Berlin, Germany. Association for Computational Linguistics.

Berard, A., Servan, C., Pietquin, O., and Besacier, L. (2016). MultiVec: a Multilingual and Multilevel Representation Learning Toolkit for NLP. In *Proceedings of the Tenth International Conference on Language Resources and Evaluation (LREC 2016)*.

Biçici, E. and Way, A. (2015). Referential translation machines for predicting semantic similarity. *Language Resources and Evaluation*, pages 1–27.

Bicici, E. (2016a). ParFDA for Instance Selection for Statistical Machine Translation. In *Proceedings of the First Conference on Machine Translation*, Berlin, Germany. Association for Computational Linguistics.

Bicici, E. (2016b). Referential Translation Machines for Predicting Translation Performance. In *Proceedings of the First Conference on Machine Translation*, Berlin, Germany. Association for Computational Linguistics.

Blain, F., Song, X., and Specia, L. (2016). Sheffield Systems for the English-Romanian WMT Translation Task. In *Proceedings of the First Conference on Machine Translation*, Berlin, Germany. Association for Computational Linguistics.

Bojar, O., Buck, C., Callison-Burch, C., Federmann, C., Haddow, B., Koehn, P., Monz, C., Post, M., Soricut, R., and Specia, L. (2013). Findings of the 2013 Workshop on Statistical Machine Translation. In *Proceedings of the Eighth Workshop on Statistical Machine Translation*, pages 1–44, Sofia, Bulgaria. Association for Computational Linguistics.

Bojar, O., Buck, C., Federmann, C., Haddow, B., Koehn, P., Leveling, J., Monz, C., Pecina, P., Post, M., Saint-Amand, H., Soricut, R., Specia, L., and Tamchyna, A. (2014). Findings of the 2014 workshop on statistical machine translation. In *Proceedings of the Ninth Workshop on Statistical Machine Translation*, pages 12–58, Baltimore, Maryland, USA. Association for Computational Linguistics.

Bojar, O., Chatterjee, R., Federmann, C., Haddow, B., Huck, M., Hokamp, C., Koehn, P., Logacheva, V., Monz, C., Negri, M., Post, M., Scarton, C., Specia, L., and Turchi, M. (2015). Findings of the 2015 workshop on statistical machine translation. In *Proceedings of the Tenth Workshop on Statistical Machine Translation*, pages 1–46, Lisbon, Portugal. Association for Computational Linguistics.

Bojar, O., Dušek, O., Kocmi, T., Libovický, J., Novák, M., Popel, M., Sudarikov, R., and Variš, D. (2016a). CzEng 1.6: Enlarged Czech-English Parallel Corpus with Processing Tools Dockered. In *Text, Speech and Dialogue: 19th International Conference, TSD 2016, Brno, Czech Republic, September 12-16, 2016, Proceedings*. Springer Verlag. In press.

Bojar, O., Ercegovčević, M., Popel, M., and Zaidan, O. (2011). A grain of salt for the wmt manual evaluation. In *Proceedings of the Sixth Workshop on Statistical Machine Translation*, pages 1–11, Edinburgh, Scotland. Association for Computational Linguistics.

Bojar, O., Graham, Y., , and Stanojević, A. K. M. (2016b). Results of the WMT16 Metrics Shared Task . In *Proceedings of the First Conference on Machine Translation*, Berlin, Germany. Association for Computational Linguistics.

Bradbury, J. and Socher, R. (2016). MetaMind Neural Machine Translation System for WMT 2016. In *Proceedings of the First Conference on Machine Translation*, Berlin, Germany. Association for Computational Linguistics.

Buck, C., Heafield, K., and Van Ooyen, B. (2014). N-gram counts and language models from the common crawl. *LREC*, 2:4.

Buck, C. and Koehn, P. (2016). Findings of the WMT 2016 Bilingual Document Alignment Shared Task. In *Proceedings of the First Conference on Machine Translation*, Berlin, Germany. Association for Computational Linguistics.

C. de Souza, J. G., Buck, C., Turchi, M., and Negri, M. (2013). FBK-UEdin participation to the WMT13 Quality Estimation shared-task. In *Proceedings of the Eighth Workshop on Statistical Machine Translation*, pages 352–358.

C. de Souza, J. G., González-Rubio, J., Buck, C., Turchi, M., and Negri, M. (2014). FBK-UPV-UEdin participation in the WMT14 Quality Estimation shared-task. In *Proceedings of the Ninth Workshop on Statistical Machine Translation*, Baltimore, MD, USA.

Callison-Burch, C., Fordyce, C. S., Koehn, P., Monz, C., and Schroeder, J. (2007). (Meta-) evaluation of machine translation. In *Proceedings of the Second Workshop on Statistical Machine Translation*, pages 136–158, Prague, Czech Republic. Association for Computational Linguistics.

Callison-Burch, C., Fordyce, C. S., Koehn, P., Monz, C., and Schroeder, J. (2008). Further meta-evaluation of machine translation. In *Proceedings of the Third Workshop on Statistical Machine Translation*, pages 70–106, Columbus, Ohio. Association for Computational Linguistics.

Callison-Burch, C., Koehn, P., Monz, C., Peterson, K., Przybocki, M., and Zaidan, O. (2010). Findings of the 2010 joint workshop on statistical machine translation and metrics for machine translation. In *Proceedings of the Joint Fifth Workshop on Statistical Machine Translation and MetricsMATR*, pages 17–53, Uppsala, Sweden. Association for Computational Linguistics.

Callison-Burch, C., Koehn, P., Monz, C., Post, M., Soricut, R., and Specia, L. (2012). Findings of the 2012 workshop on statistical machine translation. In *Proceedings of the Seventh Workshop on Statistical Machine Translation*, pages 10–48, Montreal, Canada. Association for Computational Linguistics.

Callison-Burch, C., Koehn, P., Monz, C., and Schroeder, J. (2009). Findings of the 2009 Workshop on Statistical Machine Translation. In *Proceedings of the Fourth Workshop on Statistical Machine Translation*, pages 1–28, Athens, Greece. Association for Computational Linguistics.

Callison-Burch, C., Koehn, P., Monz, C., and Zaidan, O. (2011). Findings of the 2011 workshop on statistical machine translation. In *Proceedings of the Sixth Workshop on Statistical Machine Translation*, pages 22–64, Edinburgh, Scotland. Association for Computational Linguistics.

Chatterjee, R., C. de Souza, J. G., Negri, M., and Turchi, M. (2016). The FBK Participation in the WMT 2016 Automatic Post-editing Shared Task. In *Proceedings of the First Conference on Machine Translation*, Berlin, Germany. Association for Computational Linguistics.

Chatterjee, R., Turchi, T., and Negri, M. (2015a). The FBK Participation in the WMT15 Automatic Post-editing Shared Task. In *Proceedings of the 10th Workshop on Statistical Machine Translation (WMT)*.

Chatterjee, R., Weller, M., Negri, M., and Turchi, M. (2015b). Exploring the Planet of the APEs: a Comparative Study of State-of-the-art Methods for MT Automatic Post-Editing. In *Proceedings of the 53rd Annual Meeting of the Association for Computational Linguistics)*, Beijing, China.

Chung, J., Cho, K., and Bengio, Y. (2016). NYU-MILA Neural Machine Translation Systems for WMT16. In *Proceedings of the First Conference on Machine Translation*, Berlin, Germany. Association for Computational Linguistics.

Cohen, J. (1960). A Coefficient of Agreement for Nominal Scales. *Educational and Psychological Measurement*, 20(1):37–46.

Costa-jussà, M. R., España Bonet, C., Madhyastha, P., Escolano, C., and Fonollosa, J. A. R. (2016). The TALP–UPC Spanish–English WMT Biomedical Task: Bilingual Embeddings and Char-based Neural Language Model Rescoring in a Phrase-based System. In *Proceedings of the First Conference on Machine Translation*, Berlin, Germany. Association for Computational Linguistics.

Cuong, H., Frank, S., and Sima'an, K. (2016). ILLC-UvA Adaptation System (Scorpio) at WMT'16 IT-DOMAIN Task. In *Proceedings of the First Conference on Machine Translation*, Berlin, Germany. Association for Computational Linguistics.

Ding, S., Duh, K., Khayrallah, H., Koehn, P., and Post, M. (2016). The JHU Machine Translation Systems for WMT 2016. In *Proceedings of the First Conference on Machine Translation*, Berlin, Germany. Association for Computational Linguistics.

Duma, M.-S. and Menzel, W. (2016). Data Selection for IT Texts using Paragraph Vector. In *Proceedings of the First Conference on Machine*

Translation, Berlin, Germany. Association for Computational Linguistics.

Durrani, N., Schmid, H., and Fraser, A. (2011). A joint sequence translation model with integrated reordering. In *Proceedings of the 49th Annual Meeting of the Association for Computational Linguistics: Human Language Technologies-Volume 1*, pages 1045–1054. Association for Computational Linguistics.

Dušek, O., Gomes, L., Novák, M., Popel, M., and Rosa, R. (2015). New Language Pairs in TectoMT. In *Proceedings of the Tenth Workshop on Statistical Machine Translation*, pages 98–104, Lisbon, Portugal. Association for Computational Linguistics.

Dvorkovich, A., Gubanov, S., and Galinskaya, I. (2016). Yandex School of Data Analysis approach to English-Turkish translation at WMT16 News Translation Task. In *Proceedings of the First Conference on Machine Translation*, Berlin, Germany. Association for Computational Linguistics.

Esplà-Gomis, M., Sánchez-Martínez, F., and Forcada, M. (2015). UAlacant word-level machine translation quality estimation system at WMT 2015. In *Proceedings of the Tenth Workshop on Statistical Machine Translation*, pages 309–315, Lisbon, Portugal.

Esplà-Gomis, M., Sánchez-Martínez, F., and Forcada, M. (2016). UAlacant word-level and phrase-level machine translation quality estimation systems at WMT 2016. In *Proceedings of the First Conference on Machine Translation*, Berlin, Germany. Association for Computational Linguistics.

Federmann, C. (2012). Appraise: an open-source toolkit for manual evaluation of mt output. *The Prague Bulletin of Mathematical Linguistics*, 98:25–35.

Fleiss, J. L. (1971). Measuring nominal scale agreement among many raters. *Psychological bulletin*, 76(5):378.

Gao, Q. and Vogel, S. (2008). Parallel Implementations of Word Alignment Tool. In *Proceedings of the ACL 2008 Software Engineering, Testing, and Quality Assurance Workshop*, pages 49–57, Columbus, Ohio.

Gaudio, R., Labaka, G., Agirre, E., Osenova, P., Simov, K., Popel, M., Oele, D., van Noord, G., Gomes, L., António Rodrigues, J. a., Neale, S., Silva, J. a., Querido, A., Rendeiro, N., and Branco, A. (2016). SMT and Hybrid systems of the QTLeap project in the WMT16 IT-task. In *Proceedings of the First Conference on Machine Translation*, Berlin, Germany. Association for Computational Linguistics.

Giménez, J. and Màrquez, L. (2010). Asiya: An Open Toolkit for Automatic Machine Translation (Meta-)Evaluation. *The Prague Bulletin of Mathematical Linguistics*, (94):77–86.

Graham, Y. (2015). Improving Evaluation of Machine Translation Quality Estimation. In *53rd Annual Meeting of the Association for Computational Linguistics and Seventh International Joint Conference on Natural Language Processing of the Asian Federation of Natural Language Processing*, pages 1804–1813, Beijing, China.

Graham, Y., Baldwin, T., Moffat, A., and Zobel, J. (2013). Continuous Measurement Scales in Human Evaluation of Machine Translation. In *Proceedings of the 7th Linguistic Annotation Workshop & Interoperability with Discourse*, pages 33–41, Sofia, Bulgaria. Association for Computational Linguistics.

Graham, Y., Baldwin, T., Moffat, A., and Zobel, J. (2014). Is machine translation getting better over time? In *Proceedings of the 14th Conference of the European Chapter of the Association for Computational Linguistics*, pages 443–451, Gothenburg, Sweden. Association for Computational Linguistics.

Graham, Y., Baldwin, T., Moffat, A., and Zobel, J. (2016). Can machine translation systems be evaluated by the crowd alone. *Natural Language Engineering*, pages 1–28.

Grönroos, S.-A., Virpioja, S., and Kurimo, M. (2016). Hybrid Morphological Segmentation for Phrase-Based Machine Translation. In *Proceedings of the First Conference on Machine Translation*, Berlin, Germany. Association for Computational Linguistics.

Guillou, L., Hardmeier, C., Nakov, P., Stymne, S., Tiedemann, J., Versley, Y., Cettolo, M., Webber, B., and Popescu-Belis, A. (2016). Findings of the 2016 WMT Shared Task on Cross-lingual Pronoun Prediction. In *Proceedings of the First Conference on Machine Transla-*

tion, Berlin, Germany. Association for Computational Linguistics.

Gwinnup, J., Anderson, T., Erdmann, G., Young, K., Kazi, M., Salesky, E., and Thompson, B. (2016). The AFRL-MITLL WMT16 News-Translation Task Systems. In *Proceedings of the First Conference on Machine Translation*, Berlin, Germany. Association for Computational Linguistics.

Ha, T.-L., Cho, E., Niehues, J., Mediani, M., Sperber, M., Allauzen, A., and Waibel, A. (2016). The Karlsruhe Institute of Technology Systems for the News Translation Task in WMT 2016. In *Proceedings of the First Conference on Machine Translation*, Berlin, Germany. Association for Computational Linguistics.

Heafield, K. (2011). KenLM: Faster and Smaller Language Model Queries. In *Proceedings of the EMNLP 2011 Sixth Workshop on Statistical Machine Translation*, pages 187–197, Edinburgh, Scotland, United Kingdom.

Herrmann, T., Niehues, J., and Waibel, A. (2013). Combining Word Reordering Methods on different Linguistic Abstraction Levels for Statistical Machine Translation. In *Proceedings of the Seventh Workshop on Syntax, Semantics and Structure in Statistical Translation*, Altanta, Georgia, USA.

Hoang, C. and Sima'an, K. (2014). Latent domain translation models in mix-of-domains haystack. In *Proceedings of COLING 2014, the 25th International Conference on Computational Linguistics: Technical Papers*, pages 1928–1939, Dublin, Ireland. Dublin City University and Association for Computational Linguistics.

Huck, M., Fraser, A., and Haddow, B. (2016). The Edinburgh/LMU Hierarchical Machine Translation System for WMT 2016. In *Proceedings of the First Conference on Machine Translation*, Berlin, Germany. Association for Computational Linguistics.

Ive, J., Max, A., and Yvon, F. (2016). LIMSI's Contribution to the WMT'16 Biomedical Translation Task. In *Proceedings of the First Conference on Machine Translation*, Berlin, Germany. Association for Computational Linguistics.

Jawaid, B., Kamran, A., Stanojević, M., and ojar, O. (2016). Results of the WMT16 Tuning Shared Task. In *Proceedings of the First Conference on Machine Translation*, Berlin, Germany. Association for Computational Linguistics.

Junczys-Dowmunt, M., Dwojak, T., and Sennrich, R. (2016). The AMU-UEDIN Submission to the WMT16 News Translation Task: Attention-based NMT Models as Feature Functions in Phrase-based SMT. In *Proceedings of the First Conference on Machine Translation*, Berlin, Germany. Association for Computational Linguistics.

Junczys-Dowmunt, M. and Grundkiewicz, R. (2016). Log-linear Combinations of Monolingual and Bilingual Neural Machine Translation Models for Automatic Post-Editing. In *Proceedings of the First Conference on Machine Translation*. Association for Computational Linguistics.

Kim, H. and Lee, J.-H. (2016). Recurrent Neural Network based Translation Quality Estimation. In *Proceedings of the First Conference on Machine Translation*, Berlin, Germany. Association for Computational Linguistics.

Koehn, P. (2002). Europarl: A multilingual corpus for evaluation of machine translation. Unpublished, http://www.isi.edu/~koehn/europarl/.

Koehn, P. (2004). Statistical Significance Tests for Machine Translation Evaluation. In *Proceedings of EMNLP 2004*, pages 388–395, Barcelona, Spain.

Koehn, P. and Hoang, H. (2007). Factored Translation Models. In *EMNLP-CoNLL 2007, Proceedings of the 2007 Joint Conference on Empirical Methods in Natural Language Processing and Computational Natural Language Learning*, pages 868–876, Prague, Czech Republic.

Koehn, P., Hoang, H., Birch, A., Callison-Burch, C., Federico, M., Bertoldi, N., Cowan, B., Shen, W., Moran, C., Zens, R., Dyer, C., Bojar, O., Constantin, A., and Herbst, E. (2007). Moses: Open Source Toolkit for Statistical Machine Translation. In *Proceedings of the 45th Annual Meeting of the Association for Computational Linguistics Companion Volume Proceedings of the Demo and Poster Sessions*, pages 177–180, Prague, Czech Republic.

Koehn, P. and Monz, C. (2006). Manual and automatic evaluation of machine translation between european languages. In *Proceedings on the Workshop on Statistical Machine Translation*, pages 102–121, New York City. Association for Computational Linguistics.

Kozlova, A., Shmatova, M., and Frolov, A. (2016). YSDA Participation in the WMT'16 Quality Estimation Shared Task. In *Proceedings of the First Conference on Machine Translation*, Berlin, Germany. Association for Computational Linguistics.

Kreutzer, J., Schamoni, S., and Riezler, S. (2015). QUality Estimation from ScraTCH (QUETCH): Deep Learning for Word-level Translation Quality Estimation. In *Proceedings of the Tenth Workshop on Statistical Machine Translation*, pages 297–303, Lisboa, Portugal. Association for Computational Linguistics.

Landis, J. R. and Koch, G. G. (1977). The Measurement of Observer Agreement for Categorical Data. *Biometrics*, 33:159–174.

Liang, P., Taskar, B., and Klein, D. (2006). Alignment by agreement. In *Proceedings of the main conference on Human Language Technology Conference of the North American Chapter of the Association of Computational Linguistics*, pages 104–111. Association for Computational Linguistics.

Libovický, J., Helcl, J., Tlustý, M., Bojar, O., and Pecina, P. (2016). CUNI at Post-editing and Multimodal Translation Tasks. In *Proceedings of the First Conference on Machine Translation*. Association for Computational Linguistics.

Lo, C.-k., Cherry, C., Foster, G., Stewart, D., Islam, R., Kazantseva, A., and Kuhn, R. (2016). NRC Russian-English Machine Translation System for WMT 2016. In *Proceedings of the First Conference on Machine Translation*, Berlin, Germany. Association for Computational Linguistics.

Logacheva, V., , and Specia, L. (2015). Phrase-level Quality Estimation for Machine Translation. In *Proceedings of the 12th International Workshop on Spoken Language Translation*, Da Nang, Vietnam.

Logacheva, V., Blain, F., and Specia, L. (2016a). USFD Phrase-level Quality Estimation Systems. In *Proceedings of the First Conference on Machine Translation*, Berlin, Germany. Association for Computational Linguistics.

Logacheva, V., Hokamp, C., and Specia, L. (2016b). MARMOT: A Toolkit for Translation Quality Estimation at the Word Level. In *Proceedings of the 10th edition of the Language Resources and Evaluation Conference*, Portorož, Slovenia.

Logacheva, V., Lukasik, M., and Specia, L. (2016c). Metrics for Evaluation of Word-Level Machine Translation Quality Estimation. In *Proceedings of the 54th Annual Meeting of the Association for Computational Linguistics*, Berlin, Germany.

Luong, N. Q., Besacier, L., and Lecouteux, B. (2014). Lig system for word level qe task at wmt14. In *Proceedings of the Ninth Workshop on Statistical Machine Translation*, pages 335–341, Baltimore, Maryland, USA. Association for Computational Linguistics.

Mareček, D. (2016). Merged bilingual trees based on Universal Dependencies in Machine Translation. In *Proceedings of the First Conference on Machine Translation*, Berlin, Germany. Association for Computational Linguistics.

Martins, A., Almeida, M., and Smith, N. (2013). Turning on the turbo: Fast third-order non-projective turbo parsers. In *Proceedings of the 51st Annual Meeting of the Association for Computational Linguistics*, pages 617–622, Sofia, Bulgaria.

Martins, A. F. T., Astudillo, R., Hokamp, C., and Kepler, F. (2016). Unbabel's Participation in the WMT16 Word-Level Translation Quality Estimation Shared Task. In *Proceedings of the First Conference on Machine Translation*, Berlin, Germany. Association for Computational Linguistics.

Mikolov, T., Yih, W.-t., and Zweig, G. (2013). Linguistic regularities in continuous space word representations. In *Proceedings of NAACL 2013*.

Molchanov, A. and Bykov, F. (2016). PROMT Translation Systems for WMT 2016 Translation Tasks. In *Proceedings of the First Conference on Machine Translation*, Berlin, Germany. Association for Computational Linguistics.

Neves, M., Yepes, A. J., and Névéol, A. (2016). The Scielo Corpus: a Parallel Corpus of Scientific Publications for Biomedicine. In *Proceedings of the Tenth International Conference on Language Resources and Evaluation (LREC 2016)*, Paris, France. European Language Resources Association (ELRA).

Och, F. J. (2003). Minimum Error Rate Training in Statistical Machine Translation. In *Proceedings of the 41st Annual Meeting on Association for Computational Linguistics - Volume 1*, ACL '03, pages 160–167, Sapporo, Japan.

Och, F. J. and Ney, H. (2003). A Systematic Comparison of Various Statistical Alignment Models. *Comput. Linguist.*, 29(1):19–51.

Okazaki, N. (2007). CRFsuite: a fast implementation of Conditional Random Fields.

Paetzold, G. and Specia, L. (2016). SimpleNets: Quality Estimation with Resource-Light Neural Networks. In *Proceedings of the First Conference on Machine Translation*, Berlin, Germany. Association for Computational Linguistics.

Pahari, K., Kuila, A., Pal, S., Naskar, S. K., Bandyopadhyay, S., and van Genabith, J. (2016). JU-USAAR: A Domain Adaptive MT System. In *Proceedings of the First Conference on Machine Translation*, Berlin, Germany. Association for Computational Linguistics.

Pal, S., Mihaela, V., Naskar, S. K., and van Genabith, J. (2015). USAAR-SAPE: An English–Spanish Statistical Automatic Post-Editing System. In *Proceedings of the 10th Workshop on Statistical Machine Translation (WMT)*, pages 216–221.

Pal, S., Zampieri, M., and van Genabith, J. (2016). USAAR: An Operation Sequential Model for Automatic Statistical Post-Editing. In *Proceedings of the First Conference on Machine Translation*. Association for Computational Linguistics.

Papineni, K., Roukos, S., Ward, T., and Zhu, W.-J. (2002). BLEU: A Method for Automatic Evaluation of Machine Translation. In *Proceedings of the 40th Annual Meeting on Association for Computational Linguistics*, ACL '02, pages 311–318.

Patel, R. N. and M, S. (2016). Translation Quality Estimation using Recurrent Neural Network. In *Proceedings of the First Conference on Machine Translation*, Berlin, Germany. Association for Computational Linguistics.

Pedregosa, F., Varoquaux, G., Gramfort, A., Michel, V., Thirion, B., Grisel, O., Blondel, M., Prettenhofer, P., Weiss, R., Dubourg, V., Vanderplas, J., Passos, A., Cournapeau, D., Brucher, M., Perrot, M., and Duchesnay, E. (2011). Scikit-learn: Machine learning in Python. *Journal of Machine Learning Research*, 12:2825–2830.

Perez-de Viñaspre, O. and Labaka, G. (2016). IXA Biomedical Translation System at WMT16 Biomedical Translation Task. In *Proceedings of the First Conference on Machine Translation*, Berlin, Germany. Association for Computational Linguistics.

Peter, J.-T., Alkhouli, T., Guta, A., and Ney, H. (2016a). The RWTH Aachen University English-Romanian Machine Translation System for WMT 2016. In *Proceedings of the First Conference on Machine Translation*, Berlin, Germany. Association for Computational Linguistics.

Peter, J.-T., Alkhouli, T., Ney, H., Huck, M., Braune, F., Fraser, A., Tamchyna, A., Bojar, O., Haddow, B., Sennrich, R., Blain, F., Specia, L., Niehues, J., Waibel, A., Allauzen, A., Aufrant, L., Burlot, F., knyazeva, e., Lavergne, T., Yvon, F., Daiber, J., and Pinnis, M. (2016b). The QT21/HimL Combined Machine Translation System. In *Proceedings of the First Conference on Machine Translation*, Berlin, Germany. Association for Computational Linguistics.

Rasmussen, C. E. and Williams, C. K. I. (2006). *Gaussian Processes for Machine Learning*. MIT Press, Cambridge, Massachusetts.

Raybaud, S., Langlois, D., and Smali, K. (2011). this sentence is wrong. detecting errors in machine-translated sentences. *Machine Translation*, 25(1):1–34.

Rosa, R., Sudarikov, R., Novák, M., Popel, M., and Bojar, O. (2016). Dictionary-based Domain Adaptation of MT Systems without Retraining. In *Proceedings of the First Conference on Machine Translation*, Berlin, Germany. Association for Computational Linguistics.

Sagemo, O. and Stymne, S. (2016). The UU Submission to the Machine Translation Quality Estimation Task. In *Proceedings of the First Conference on Machine Translation*, Berlin, Germany. Association for Computational Linguistics.

Sakaguchi, K., Post, M., and Van Durme, B. (2014). Efficient elicitation of annotations for human evaluation of machine translation. In *Proceedings of the Ninth Workshop on Statistical Machine Translation*, pages 1–11, Baltimore, Maryland, USA. Association for Computational Linguistics.

Sánchez-Cartagena, V. M. and Toral, A. (2016). Abu-MaTran at WMT 2016 Translation Task: Deep Learning, Morphological Segmentation and Tuning on Character Sequences. In *Proceedings of the First Conference on Machine Translation*, Berlin, Germany. Association for Computational Linguistics.

Scarton, C., Beck, D., Shah, K., Sim Smith, K., and Specia, L. (2016). Word embeddings and discourse information for Quality Estimation. In *Proceedings of the First Conference on Machine Translation*, Berlin, Germany. Association for Computational Linguistics.

Scarton, C. and Specia, L. (2014). Document-level translation quality estimation: exploring discourse and pseudo-references. In *Proceedings of the 17th Annual Conference of the European Association for Machine Translation*, pages 101–108, Dubrovnik, Croatia.

Scarton, C., Tan, L., and Specia, L. (2015a). USHEF and USAAR-USHEF participation in the WMT15 QE shared task. In *Proceedings of the Tenth Workshop on Statistical Machine Translation*, pages 317–322, Lisboa, Portugal. Association for Computational Linguistics.

Scarton, C., Zampieri, M., Vela, M., van Genabith, J., and Specia, L. (2015b). Searching for Context: a Study on Document-Level Labels for Translation Quality Estimation. In *Proceedings of the 18th Annual Conference of the European Association for Machine Translation*, pages 121–128, Antalya, Turkey.

Seddah, D., Kübler, S., and Tsarfaty, R. (2014). Introducing the SPMRL 2014 Shared Task on Parsing Morphologically-rich Languages. In *Proceedings of the First Joint Workshop on Statistical Parsing of Morphologically Rich Languages and Syntactic Analysis of Non-Canonical Languages*, pages 103–109, Dublin, Ireland.

Sennrich, R., Haddow, B., and Birch, A. (2015). Neural machine translation of rare words with subword units. *arXiv preprint arXiv:1508.07909*.

Sennrich, R., Haddow, B., and Birch, A. (2016). Edinburgh Neural Machine Translation Systems for WMT 16. In *Proceedings of the First Conference on Machine Translation*, Berlin, Germany. Association for Computational Linguistics.

Shah, K., Bougares, F., Barrault, L., and Specia, L. (2016). SHEF-LIUM-NN: Sentence level Quality Estimation with Neural Network Features. In *Proceedings of the First Conference on Machine Translation*, Berlin, Germany. Association for Computational Linguistics.

Sim Smith, K., Aziz, W., and Specia, L. (2016). Cohere: A Toolkit for Local Coherence. In *Proceedings of the 10th International Conference on Language Resources and Evaluation*, Portorož, Slovenia.

Simard, M., Goutte, C., and Isabelle, P. (2007). Statistical phrase-based post-editing. In *Human Language Technologies 2007: The Conference of the North American Chapter of the Association for Computational Linguistics; Proceedings of the Main Conference*, pages 508–515, Rochester, New York. Association for Computational Linguistics.

Snover, M., Dorr, B., Schwartz, R., Micciulla, L., and Makhoul, J. (2006). A Study of Translation Edit Rate with Targeted Human Annotation. In *Proceedings of Association for Machine Translation in the Americas*, pages 223–231, Cambridge, Massachusetts, USA.

Specia, L., Frank, S., Sima'an, K., and Elliott, D. (2016). A Shared Task on Multimodal Machine Translation and Crosslingual Image Description. In *Proceedings of the First Conference on Machine Translation*, Berlin, Germany. Association for Computational Linguistics.

Specia, L., Paetzold, G., and Scarton, C. (2015). Multi-level Translation Quality Prediction with QuEst++. In *53rd Annual Meeting of the Association for Computational Linguistics and Seventh International Joint Conference on Natural Language Processing of the Asian Federation of Natural Language Processing: System Demonstrations*, pages 115–120, Beijing, China.

Stahlberg, F., Hasler, E., and Byrne, B. (2016). The Edit Distance Transducer in Action: The University of Cambridge English-German System at WMT16. In *Proceedings of the First Conference on Machine Translation*, Berlin,

Germany. Association for Computational Linguistics.

Sudarikov, R., Popel, M., Bojar, O., Burchardt, A., and Klejch, O. (2016). Using MT-ComparEval. In *Translation Evaluation: From Fragmented Tools and Data Sets to an Integrated Ecosystem*, pages 76–82.

Tamchyna, A., Sudarikov, R., Bojar, O., and Fraser, A. (2016). CUNI-LMU Submissions in WMT2016: Chimera Constrained and Beaten. In *Proceedings of the First Conference on Machine Translation*, Berlin, Germany. Association for Computational Linguistics.

Tezcan, A., Hoste, V., and Macken, L. (2016). UGENT-LT3 SCATE Submission for WMT16 Shared Task on Quality Estimation. In *Proceedings of the First Conference on Machine Translation*, Berlin, Germany. Association for Computational Linguistics.

Tiedemann, J. (2009). News from OPUS - a collection of multilingual parallel corpora with tools and interfaces. In *Proceedings of the Conference on Recent Advances in Natural Language Processing*, pages 237–248. John Benjamins.

Tiedemann, J., Cap, F., Kanerva, J., Ginter, F., Stymne, S., Östling, R., and Weller-Di Marco, M. (2016). Phrase-Based SMT for Finnish with More Data, Better Models and Alternative Alignment and Translation Tools. In *Proceedings of the First Conference on Machine Translation*, Berlin, Germany. Association for Computational Linguistics.

Williams, P., Sennrich, R., Nadejde, M., Huck, M., Haddow, B., and Bojar, O. (2016). Edinburgh's Statistical Machine Translation Systems for WMT16. In *Proceedings of the First Conference on Machine Translation*, Berlin, Germany. Association for Computational Linguistics.

Wołk, K. and Marasek, K. (2016). PJAIT Systems for the WMT 2016. In *Proceedings of the First Conference on Machine Translation*, Berlin, Germany. Association for Computational Linguistics.

Yeh, A. (2000). More Accurate Tests for the Statistical Significance of Result Differences. In *Coling-2000: the 18th Conference on Computational Linguistics*, pages 947–953, Saarbrücken, Germany.

A Pairwise System Comparisons by Human Judges

Tables 40–46 show pairwise comparisons between systems for each language pair. The numbers in each of the tables' cells indicate the percentage of times that the system in that column was judged to be better than the system in that row, ignoring ties. Bolding indicates the winner of the two systems.

Because there were so many systems and data conditions the significance of each pairwise comparison needs to be quantified. We applied the Sign Test to measure which comparisons indicate genuine differences (rather than differences that are attributable to chance). In the following tables ⋆ indicates statistical significance at $p \leq 0.10$, † indicates statistical significance at $p \leq 0.05$, and ‡ indicates statistical significance at $p \leq 0.01$, according to the Sign Test.

Each table contains final rows showing how likely a system would win when paired against a randomly selected system (the expected win ratio score) and the rank range according bootstrap resampling ($p \leq 0.05$). Gray lines separate clusters based on non-overlapping rank ranges.

	ONLINE-B	UEDIN-NMT	UEDIN-PBMT	UEDIN-SYNTAX	ONLINE-A	JHU-PBMT	LIMSI
ONLINE-B	–	.47⋆	.43‡	.39‡	.39‡	.38‡	.36‡
UEDIN-NMT	**.53**⋆	–	.45‡	.43‡	.41‡	.40‡	.39‡
UEDIN-PBMT	**.57**‡	**.55**‡	–	.46†	.45‡	.39‡	.41‡
UEDIN-SYNTAX	**.61**‡	**.57**‡	**.54**†	–	.49	.44‡	.44‡
ONLINE-A	**.61**‡	**.59**‡	**.55**‡	**.51**	–	.47⋆	.47⋆
JHU-PBMT	**.62**‡	**.60**‡	**.61**‡	**.56**†	**.53**⋆	–	.46†
LIMSI	**.64**‡	**.61**‡	**.59**‡	**.56**†	**.53**⋆	**.54**†	–
score	.58	.37	.09	-.08	-.18	-.32	-.46
rank	1-2	1-2	3	4-5	4-6	5-7	6-7

Table 38: Head to head comparison, ignoring ties, for Romanian-English systems

	UEDIN-NMT	QT21-HimL-SysComb	KIT	UEDIN-PBMT	ONLINE-B	UEDIN-LMU-HIERO	RWTH-SYSCOMB	LIMSI	LMU-CUNI	JHU-PBMT	USFD-RESCORING	ONLINE-A
UEDIN-NMT	–	.48	.43⋆	.40†	.36‡	.42†	.38‡	.31‡	.37‡	.34‡	.28‡	.25‡
QT21-HimL-SysComb	.52	–	.44	.41†	.44	.40†	.41†	.30‡	.25‡	.28‡	.22‡	.22‡
KIT	**.57**⋆	**.56**	–	.52	.44	.47	.43⋆	.36‡	.35‡	.41†	.33‡	.34‡
UEDIN-PBMT	**.60**†	**.59**†	.48	–	.49	.47	**.57**⋆	.39‡	.36‡	.32‡	.32‡	.34‡
ONLINE-B	**.64**‡	**.56**	**.56**	**.51**	–	.49	.49	.41†	.37‡	.35‡	.28‡	.36‡
UEDIN-LMU-HIERO	**.58**†	**.60**†	**.53**	**.53**	**.51**	–	.50	.43⋆	.37‡	.38‡	.30‡	.29‡
RWTH-SYSCOMB	**.62**‡	**.59**†	**.57**⋆	**.43**⋆	**.51**	.50	–	.42⋆	.38‡	.42⋆	.34‡	.31‡
LIMSI	**.69**‡	**.70**‡	**.64**‡	**.61**‡	**.59**†	**.57**⋆	**.58**⋆	–	.48	.43⋆	.47	.35‡
LMU-CUNI	**.63**‡	**.75**‡	**.65**‡	**.64**‡	**.63**‡	**.63**‡	**.62**‡	**.52**	–	**.52**	.42†	.40†
JHU-PBMT	**.66**‡	**.72**‡	**.59**†	**.68**‡	**.65**‡	**.62**‡	**.58**⋆	**.57**⋆	.48	–	.50	.42†
USFD-RESCORING	**.72**‡	**.78**‡	**.67**‡	**.68**‡	**.72**‡	**.70**‡	**.66**‡	.53	**.58**†	.50	–	.39‡
ONLINE-A	**.75**‡	**.78**‡	**.66**‡	**.66**‡	**.64**‡	**.71**‡	**.69**‡	**.65**‡	**.60**†	**.58**†	**.61**‡	–
score	.44	.43	.20	.15	.14	.13	.12	-.15	-.22	-.26	-.43	-.56
rank	1-2	1-2	3-7	3-7	3-7	3-7	3-7	8-10	8-10	8-11	10-12	11-12

Table 39: Head to head comparison, ignoring ties, for English-Romanian systems

	UEDIN-NMT	JHU-PBMT	ONLINE-B	TT-BLEU-MIRA	TT-AFRL	TT-NRC-NNBLEU	TT-NRC-MEANT	TT-BEER-PRO	PJATK	TT-BLEU-MERT	ONLINE-A	CU-MERGEDTREES
UEDIN-NMT	–	.42‡	.41‡	.36‡	.36‡	.37‡	.35‡	.35‡	.35‡	.36‡	.33‡	.14‡
JHU-PBMT	**.58‡**	–	.45‡	.45‡	.43‡	.44‡	.42‡	.40‡	.41‡	.40‡	.38‡	.13‡
ONLINE-B	**.59‡**	**.55‡**	–	.47★	.46†	.46‡	.45‡	.45‡	.44‡	.42‡	.43‡	.16‡
TT-BLEU-MIRA	**.64‡**	**.55‡**	**.53★**	–	.49	.47†	.47†	.45‡	.45‡	.42‡	.45‡	.15‡
TT-AFRL	**.64‡**	**.57‡**	**.54†**	**.51**	–	.49	.47†	.43‡	.46‡	.45‡	.44‡	.16‡
TT-NRC-NNBLEU	**.63‡**	**.56‡**	**.54‡**	**.53†**	**.51**	–	.50	.46‡	.47‡	.43‡	.46†	.16‡
TT-NRC-MEANT	**.65‡**	**.58‡**	**.55‡**	**.53†**	**.53†**	.50	–	.46†	.48†	.47‡	.45‡	.15‡
TT-BEER-PRO	**.65‡**	**.60‡**	**.55‡**	**.55‡**	**.57‡**	**.54‡**	**.54†**	–	.49	.49	.47★	.17‡
PJATK	**.65‡**	**.59‡**	**.56‡**	**.55‡**	**.54‡**	**.53‡**	**.52†**	**.51**	–	.50	.47★	.18‡
TT-BLEU-MERT	**.64‡**	**.60‡**	**.58‡**	**.58‡**	**.55‡**	**.57‡**	**.53‡**	**.51**	.50	–	.48	.19‡
ONLINE-A	**.67‡**	**.62‡**	**.57‡**	**.55‡**	**.56‡**	**.54†**	**.55‡**	**.53★**	**.53★**	**.52**	–	.19‡
CU-MERGEDTREES	**.86‡**	**.87‡**	**.84‡**	**.85‡**	**.84‡**	**.84‡**	**.85‡**	**.83‡**	**.82‡**	**.81‡**	**.81‡**	–
score	.61	.31	.20	.11	.09	.09	.07	.03	.00	.00	-.07	-.148
rank	1	2	3	4-6	4-7	4-7	5-8	7-10	8-10	8-10	11	12

Table 40: Head to head comparison, ignoring ties, for Czech-English systems

	UEDIN-NMT	NYU-UMONTREAL	JHU-PBMT	CU-CHIMERA	CU-TAMCHYNA	UEDIN-CU-SYNTAX	ONLINE-B	TT-BLEU-MIRA	TT-BEER-PRO	TT-BLEU-MERT	TT-AFRL2	TT-AFRL1	TT-DCU	TT-FJFI	ONLINE-A	CU-TECToMT	TT-USAAR-HMM-MERT	CU-MERGEDTREES	TT-USAAR-HMM-MIRA	TT-USAAR-HARMONIC
UEDIN-NMT	–	.38‡	.31‡	.33‡	.33‡	.35‡	.31‡	.26‡	.25‡	.27‡	.22‡	.25‡	.28‡	.26‡	.21‡	.20‡	.11‡	.07‡	.00‡	.01‡
NYU-MONTREAL	**.62‡**	–	.43‡	.42‡	.41‡	.37‡	.33‡	.38‡	.36‡	.37‡	.34‡	.36‡	.31‡	.37‡	.30‡	.21‡	.14‡	.09‡	.01‡	.00‡
JHU-PBMT	**.69‡**	**.57‡**	–	.45‡	.47†	.47	.38‡	.37‡	.37‡	.38‡	.36‡	.35‡	.35‡	.36‡	.35‡	.28‡	.10‡	.12‡	.01‡	.00‡
CU-CHIMERA	**.67‡**	**.58‡**	**.55‡**	–	.49	.46★	.43‡	.40‡	.39‡	.40‡	.39‡	.39‡	.40‡	.39‡	.39‡	.30‡	.12‡	.10‡	.01‡	.00‡
CU-TAMCHYNA	**.67‡**	**.59‡**	**.53†**	**.51**	–	.45†	.42‡	.41‡	.41‡	.40‡	.40‡	.39‡	.39‡	.38‡	.39‡	.29‡	.16‡	.11‡	.01‡	.00‡
UEDIN-CU-SNTX	**.65‡**	**.63‡**	**.53**	**.54★**	**.54†**	–	.49	.48	.47	.47★	.49	.45†	.46†	.44‡	.40‡	.37‡	.16‡	.14‡	.01‡	.00‡
ONLINE-B	**.69‡**	**.67‡**	**.62‡**	**.57‡**	**.58‡**	.51	–	.48★	.46‡	.48†	.44‡	.44‡	.48★	.46‡	.41‡	.38‡	.15‡	.12‡	.01‡	.00‡
TT-BLEU-MIRA	**.74‡**	**.62‡**	**.63‡**	**.60‡**	**.59‡**	.52	.52★	–	.49	.46★	.46†	.46†	.43‡	.47★	.43‡	.39‡	.12‡	.13‡	.01‡	.00‡
TT-BEER-PRO	**.75‡**	**.64‡**	**.63‡**	**.61‡**	**.59‡**	.53	.54‡	**.51**	–	**.51**	.47	.47★	.46†	.47†	.46★	.40‡	.14‡	.11‡	.01‡	.00‡
TT-BLEU-MERT	**.73‡**	**.63‡**	**.62‡**	**.60‡**	**.60‡**	.53★	.52†	.54★	.49	–	.48	.48	.48	.48	.44‡	.39‡	.11‡	.14‡	.01‡	.00‡
TT-AFRL2	**.78‡**	**.66‡**	**.64‡**	**.61‡**	**.60‡**	.51	.56‡	.54†	.53	.52	–	.47	.48★	.48	.43‡	.42‡	.14‡	.11‡	.00‡	.00‡
TT-AFRL1	**.75‡**	**.64‡**	**.65‡**	**.61‡**	**.61‡**	.55†	.56‡	.54†	.53★	.52	.53	–	.48	.49	.45†	.42‡	.14‡	.10‡	.00‡	.00‡
TT-DCU	**.72‡**	**.69‡**	**.65‡**	**.60‡**	**.61‡**	.54†	.52★	.57‡	.54†	.52	.52★	.52	–	**.51**	.42‡	.44‡	.12‡	.14‡	.01‡	.00‡
TT-FJFI	**.74‡**	**.63‡**	**.64‡**	**.61‡**	**.62‡**	.56‡	.54‡	.53★	.53†	.52	.52	.51	.49	–	.47	.44‡	.13‡	.15‡	.01‡	.00‡
ONLINE-A	**.79‡**	**.70‡**	**.65‡**	**.61‡**	**.61‡**	.60‡	.59‡	.57‡	.54★	.56‡	.57‡	.55†	.58‡	.53	–	.42‡	.20‡	.15‡	.03‡	.00‡
CU-TECToMT	**.80‡**	**.79‡**	**.72‡**	**.70‡**	**.71‡**	.63‡	.62‡	.61‡	.60‡	.61‡	.58‡	.58‡	.56‡	.56‡	.58‡	–	.29‡	.23‡	.02‡	.00‡
TT-US'R-'-MERT	**.89‡**	**.86‡**	**.90‡**	**.88‡**	**.84‡**	.84‡	.85‡	.88‡	.86‡	.89‡	.86‡	.86‡	.88‡	.87‡	.80‡	.71‡	–	.49	.05‡	.01‡
CU-MTREES	**.93‡**	**.91‡**	**.88‡**	**.90‡**	**.89‡**	.86‡	.88‡	.87‡	.89‡	.86‡	.89‡	.90‡	.86‡	.85‡	.85‡	.77‡	.51	–	.04‡	.00‡
TT-US'R-MIRA	**.100‡**	**.99‡**	**.99‡**	**.99‡**	**.99‡**	.99‡	.99‡	.99‡	.99‡	.99‡	.100‡	.100‡	.99‡	.99‡	.97‡	.98‡	.95‡	.96‡	–	.07‡
TT-US'R-HARM	**.99‡**	**.100‡**	**.100‡**	**.100‡**	**.100‡**	.100‡	.100‡	.100‡	.100‡	.100‡	.100‡	.100‡	.100‡	.100‡	.100‡	.100‡	.99‡	.100‡	.93‡	–
score	.59	.42	.34	.30	.30	.22	.19	.16	.15	.15	.13	.13	.13	.12	.07	-.02	-.43	-.54	-.113	-.132
rank	1	2	3	4-5	4-5	6-7	6-7	8-11	8-12	8-13	9-14	9-14	9-14	11-14	15	16	17	18	19	20

Table 41: Head to head comparison, ignoring ties, for English-Czech systems

	UEDIN-NMT	ONLINE-B	ONLINE-A	UEDIN-SYNTAX	KIT	UEDIN-PBMT	JHU-PBMT	ONLINE-G	JHU-SYNTAX	ONLINE-F
UEDIN-NMT	–	.38‡	.34‡	.36‡	.34‡	.34‡	.32‡	.31‡	.19‡	.21‡
ONLINE-B	**.62‡**	–	.50	.48	.49	.44†	.43‡	.40‡	.30‡	.28‡
ONLINE-A	**.66‡**	.50	–	**.52**	.48	.44†	.44†	.44‡	.32‡	.25‡
UEDIN-SYNTAX	**.64‡**	**.52**	.48	–	.50	.46★	.47	.40‡	.29‡	.29‡
KIT	**.66‡**	**.51**	**.52**	.50	–	.45†	.47	.43‡	.31‡	.27‡
UEDIN-PBMT	**.66‡**	**.56†**	**.56†**	**.54★**	**.55†**	–	.48	.44‡	.33‡	.31‡
JHU-PBMT	**.68‡**	**.57‡**	**.56†**	**.53**	**.53**	**.52**	–	.47	.31‡	.29‡
ONLINE-G	**.69‡**	**.60‡**	**.56‡**	**.60‡**	**.57‡**	**.56‡**	**.53**	–	.37‡	.34‡
JHU-SYNTAX	**.81‡**	**.70‡**	**.68‡**	**.71‡**	**.69‡**	**.67‡**	**.69‡**	**.63‡**	–	.50
ONLINE-F	**.79‡**	**.72‡**	**.75‡**	**.71‡**	**.73‡**	**.69‡**	**.71‡**	**.66‡**	.50	–
score	.81	.25	.21	.19	.17	.04	.02	-.12	-.67	-.93
rank	1	2-5	2-5	2-5	2-6	5-7	6-7	8	9	10

Table 42: Head to head comparison, ignoring ties, for German-English systems

	UEDIN-NMT	METAMIND	UEDIN-SYNTAX	NYU-UMONTREAL	ONLINE-B	KIT-LIMSI	CAMBRIDGE	ONLINE-A	PROMT-RULE-BASED	KIT	JHU-SYNTAX	JHU-PBMT	UEDIN-PBMT	ONLINE-F	ONLINE-G
UEDIN-NMT	–	.46	.34‡	.41‡	.31‡	.31‡	.31‡	.29‡	.32‡	.27‡	.27‡	.31‡	.28‡	.25‡	.22‡
METAMIND	.54	–	.41‡	.40‡	.33‡	.36‡	.35‡	.35‡	.34‡	.33‡	.29‡	.34‡	.30‡	.29‡	.30‡
UEDIN-SYNTAX	.66‡	.59‡	–	.44†	.35‡	.39‡	.35‡	.33‡	.41‡	.38‡	.27‡	.36‡	.25‡	.27‡	.27‡
NYU-UMontreal	.59‡	.60‡	.56†	–	.39‡	.48	.41‡	.45⋆	.41‡	.44†	.37‡	.39‡	.38‡	.35‡	.34‡
ONLINE-B	.69‡	.67‡	.65‡	.61‡	–	.49	.51	.49	.49	.48	.46†	.42‡	.38‡	.38‡	.32‡
KIT-LIMSI	.69‡	.64‡	.61‡	.52	.51	–	.53	.48	.50	.45	.47	.42‡	.39‡	.42‡	.43†
CAMBRIDGE	.69‡	.65‡	.65‡	.59‡	.49	.47	–	.47	.53⋆	.46⋆	.42‡	.48	.39‡	.43‡	.42‡
ONLINE-A	.71‡	.65‡	.67‡	.55⋆	.51	.52	.53	–	.47	.49	.47⋆	.44‡	.38‡	.37‡	.36‡
PROMT-Rule-based	.68‡	.66‡	.59‡	.59‡	.51	.50	.47⋆	.53	–	.48	.46†	.47⋆	.42‡	.39‡	.41‡
KIT	.73‡	.67‡	.62‡	.56†	.52	.55	.54⋆	.51	.52	–	.46†	.44‡	.40‡	.42‡	.41‡
JHU-SYNTAX	.73‡	.71‡	.73‡	.63‡	.54†	.53	.58‡	.53⋆	.54†	.54†	–	.48	.42‡	.46⋆	.42‡
JHU-PBMT	.69‡	.66‡	.64‡	.61‡	.58‡	.58‡	.52	.56‡	.53⋆	.56‡	.52	–	.43‡	.47	.47
UEDIN-PBMT	.72‡	.70‡	.75‡	.62‡	.62‡	.61‡	.61‡	.62‡	.58‡	.60‡	.58‡	.57‡	–	.45⋆	.48
ONLINE-F	.75‡	.71‡	.73‡	.65‡	.62‡	.58‡	.57‡	.63‡	.61‡	.58‡	.54⋆	.53	.55⋆	–	.48
ONLINE-G	.78‡	.70‡	.73‡	.66‡	.68‡	.57†	.58‡	.64‡	.59‡	.59‡	.58‡	.53	.52	.52	–
score	.49	.39	.28	.16	-.00	-.01	-.02	-.02	-.03	-.04	-.13	-.15	-.25	-.32	-.34
rank	1	2	3	4	5-10	5-10	5-10	5-10	5-10	6-10	11-12	11-12	13-14	13-15	14-15

Table 43: Head to head comparison, ignoring ties, for English-German systems

	UEDIN-PBMT	ONLINE-G	ONLINE-B	UH-OPUS	PROMT-SMT	UH-FACTORED	UEDIN-SYNTAX	ONLINE-A	JHU-PBMT
UEDIN-PBMT	–	.50	.48	.49	.40‡	.36‡	.38‡	.32‡	.21‡
ONLINE-G	.50	–	.51	.47⋆	.39‡	.41‡	.38‡	.30‡	.23‡
ONLINE-B	.52	.49	–	.50	.39‡	.36‡	.34‡	.35‡	.22‡
UH-OPUS	.51	.53⋆	.50	–	.42‡	.38‡	.38‡	.34‡	.24‡
PROMT-SMT	.60‡	.61‡	.61‡	.58‡	–	.46†	.46†	.42‡	.28‡
UH-FACTORED	.64‡	.59‡	.64‡	.62‡	.54†	–	.50	.47	.28‡
UEDIN-SYNTAX	.62‡	.62‡	.66‡	.62‡	.54†	.50	–	.46†	.29‡
ONLINE-A	.68‡	.70‡	.65‡	.66‡	.58‡	.53	.54†	–	.34‡
JHU-PBMT	.79‡	.77‡	.78‡	.76‡	.72‡	.72‡	.71‡	.66‡	–
score	.42	.40	.39	.33	.01	-.11	-.13	-.28	-.102
rank	1-4	1-4	1-4	1-4	5	6-7	6-7	8	9

Table 44: Head to head comparison, ignoring ties, for Finnish-English systems

	ONLINE-G	ABUMATRAN-NMT	ONLINE-B	ABUMATRAN-COMBO	UH-OPUS	ABUMATRAN-PBSMT	NYU-UMONTREAL	ONLINE-A	JHU-PBMT	UH-FACTORED	AALTO	JHU-HLTCOE	UUT
ONLINE-G	–	.50	.49	.47⋆	.46⋆	.38‡	.43‡	.39‡	.33‡	.34‡	.32‡	.30‡	.33‡
ABUMATRAN-NMT	.50	–	.48	.43⋆	.46⋆	.41‡	.43‡	.35‡	.37‡	.38‡	.35‡	.36‡	.34‡
ONLINE-B	**.51**	**.52**	–	.50	.46⋆	.41‡	.40‡	.41‡	.38‡	.35‡	.38‡	.33‡	.31‡
ABUMATRAN-COMBO	**.53**⋆	**.57**⋆	.50	–	.48	.38‡	.45†	.40‡	.38‡	.38‡	.37‡	.37‡	.37‡
UH-OPUS	**.54**⋆	**.54**⋆	**.54**⋆	**.52**	–	.45†	.47	.45†	.42‡	.38‡	.39‡	.39‡	.37‡
ABUMATRAN-PBSMT	**.62**‡	**.59**‡	**.59**‡	**.62**‡	**.55**†	–	.47	**.51**	.47	.42‡	.41‡	.42‡	.41‡
NYU-UMONTREAL	**.57**‡	**.57**‡	**.60**‡	**.55**†	**.53**	**.53**	–	.50	.46⋆	.44‡	.44‡	.45†	.41‡
ONLINE-A	**.61**‡	**.65**‡	**.59**‡	**.60**‡	**.55**†	.49	.50	–	.47	.42‡	.40‡	.37‡	.43‡
JHU-PBMT	**.67**‡	**.63**‡	**.62**‡	**.62**‡	**.58**‡	**.53**	**.54**⋆	**.53**	–	.47	.46⋆	.43‡	.43‡
UH-FACTORED	**.66**‡	**.62**‡	**.65**‡	**.62**‡	**.62**‡	**.58**‡	**.56**‡	**.58**‡	**.53**	–	.49	.46⋆	.47
AALTO	**.68**‡	**.65**‡	**.62**‡	**.63**‡	**.61**‡	**.59**‡	**.56**‡	**.60**‡	**.54**⋆	**.51**	–	**.51**	.46⋆
JHU-HLTCOE	**.70**‡	**.64**‡	**.67**‡	**.63**‡	**.61**‡	**.58**‡	**.55**†	**.62**‡	**.57**‡	**.54**⋆	.49	–	.47⋆
UUT	**.67**‡	**.66**‡	**.69**‡	**.63**‡	**.63**‡	**.59**‡	**.59**‡	**.57**‡	**.57**‡	**.53**	**.54**⋆	**.53**⋆	–
score	.36	.31	.29	.23	.15	-.01	-.01	-.01	-.14	-.22	-.28	-.30	-.35
rank	1-3	1-4	1-4	3-5	4-5	6-8	6-8	6-8	9-10	9-12	10-13	10-13	11-13

Table 45: Head to head comparison, ignoring ties, for English-Finnish systems

	PROMT-RULE-BASED	AMU-UEDIN	ONLINE-B	UEDIN-NMT	ONLINE-G	NYU-UMONTREAL	JHU-PBMT	LIMSI	ONLINE-A	AFRL-MITLL-PHRASE	AFRL-MITLL-VERB-A	ONLINE-F
PROMT-RULE-BASED	–	.38‡	.34‡	.33‡	.33‡	.31‡	.26‡	.31‡	.20‡	.26‡	.21‡	.07‡
AMU-UEDIN	**.62**‡	–	.44†	**.51**	.46⋆	.45⋆	.33‡	.35‡	.32‡	.31‡	.28‡	.14‡
ONLINE-B	**.66**‡	**.56**†	–	.50	.46	.46	.33‡	.37‡	.36‡	.36‡	.26‡	.11‡
UEDIN-NMT	**.67**‡	.49	.50	–	.50	.43‡	.40‡	.36‡	.35‡	.35‡	.30‡	.14‡
ONLINE-G	**.67**‡	**.54**⋆	**.54**	.50	–	.46⋆	.40‡	.41‡	.39‡	.38‡	.33‡	.13‡
NYU-UMONTREAL	**.69**‡	**.55**⋆	**.54**	**.57**‡	**.54**⋆	–	.50	.42‡	.43‡	.43‡	.38‡	.16‡
JHU-PBMT	**.74**‡	**.67**‡	**.67**‡	**.60**‡	**.60**‡	.50	–	.43†	.46⋆	.40‡	.37‡	.20‡
LIMSI	**.69**‡	**.65**‡	**.63**‡	**.64**‡	**.59**‡	**.58**‡	**.57**†	–	**.51**	.45⋆	.40‡	.20‡
ONLINE-A	**.80**‡	**.68**‡	**.64**‡	**.65**‡	**.61**‡	**.57**‡	**.54**⋆	.49	–	.47	.42‡	.17‡
AFRL-MITLL-PHRASE	**.74**‡	**.69**‡	**.64**‡	**.65**‡	**.62**‡	**.57**‡	**.60**‡	**.55**⋆	**.53**	–	.41‡	.20‡
AFRL-MITLL-VERB-A	**.79**‡	**.72**‡	**.74**‡	**.70**‡	**.67**‡	**.62**‡	**.63**‡	**.60**‡	**.58**‡	**.59**‡	–	.25‡
ONLINE-F	**.93**‡	**.86**‡	**.89**‡	**.86**‡	**.87**‡	**.84**‡	**.80**‡	**.80**‡	**.83**‡	**.80**‡	**.75**‡	–
score	.78	.30	.26	.25	.20	.10	-.01	-.07	-.10	-.14	-.31	-.126
rank	1	2-4	2-5	2-5	3-5	6	7-8	7-10	8-10	9-10	11	12

Table 46: Head to head comparison, ignoring ties, for English-Russian systems

	AMU-UEDIN	ONLINE-G	NRC	ONLINE-B	UEDIN-NMT	ONLINE-A	AFRL-MITLL-PHRASE	AFRL-MITLL-CONTRA	PROMT-RULE-BASED	ONLINE-F
AMU-UEDIN	–	**.51**	.44†	.47	.41‡	.37‡	.38‡	.34‡	.35‡	.16‡
ONLINE-G	.49	–	.47	.44†	.41‡	.38‡	.41‡	.35‡	.36‡	.18‡
NRC	**.56**†	**.53**	–	.47	.45†	.40‡	.39‡	.38‡	.34‡	.19‡
ONLINE-B	**.53**	**.56**†	**.53**	–	.49	.44†	.42‡	.41‡	.36‡	.22‡
UEDIN-NMT	**.59**‡	**.59**‡	**.55**†	**.51**	–	.45†	.46⋆	.40‡	.44‡	.23‡
ONLINE-A	**.63**‡	**.62**‡	**.60**‡	**.56**†	**.55**†	–	.48	.47	.45†	.22‡
AFRL-MITLL-PHRASE	**.62**‡	**.59**‡	**.61**‡	**.58**‡	**.54**⋆	**.52**	–	.45†	.46†	.25‡
AFRL-MITLL-CONTRA	**.66**‡	**.65**‡	**.62**‡	**.59**‡	**.60**‡	**.53**	**.55**†	–	.50	.29‡
PROMT-RULE-BASED	**.65**‡	**.64**‡	**.66**‡	**.64**‡	**.56**‡	**.55**†	**.54**†	.50	–	.23‡
ONLINE-F	**.84**‡	**.82**‡	**.81**‡	**.78**‡	**.77**‡	**.78**‡	**.75**‡	**.71**‡	**.77**‡	–
score	.44	.42	.32	.25	.15	.03	.02	-.11	-.16	-.138
rank	1-2	1-3	2-4	3-5	4-5	6-7	6-7	8-9	8-9	10

Table 47: Head to head comparison, ignoring ties, for Russian-English systems

	ONLINE-B	ONLINE-G	ONLINE-A	TBTK-SYSCOMB	PROMT-SMT	YSDA	JHU-SYNTAX	JHU-PBMT	PARFDA
ONLINE-B	–	.44†	.45⋆	.35‡	.32‡	.31‡	.21‡	.20‡	.17‡
ONLINE-G	**.56**†	–	.47	.38‡	.36‡	.31‡	.19‡	.19‡	.19‡
ONLINE-A	**.55**⋆	**.53**	–	.41‡	.40‡	.35‡	.24‡	.15‡	.16‡
TBTK-SYSCOMB	**.65**‡	**.62**‡	**.59**‡	–	.47	.46	.26‡	.23‡	.23‡
PROMT-SMT	**.68**‡	**.64**‡	**.60**‡	**.53**	–	.46	.30‡	.29‡	.21‡
YSDA	**.69**‡	**.69**‡	**.65**‡	**.54**	**.54**	–	.32‡	.27‡	.26‡
JHU-SYNTAX	**.79**‡	**.81**‡	**.76**‡	**.74**‡	**.70**‡	**.68**‡	–	.47	.42⋆
JHU-PBMT	**.80**‡	**.81**‡	**.85**‡	**.77**‡	**.71**‡	**.73**‡	**.53**	–	.44
PARFDA	**.83**‡	**.81**‡	**.84**‡	**.77**‡	**.79**‡	**.74**‡	**.58**⋆	**.56**	–
score	.82	.65	.56	.21	.12	.00	-.67	-.76	-.93
rank	1-2	1-3	2-3	4-5	4-6	5-6	7-8	7-9	8-9

Table 48: Head to head comparison, ignoring ties, for Turkish-English systems

	ONLINE-G	ONLINE-B	ONLINE-A	YSDA	JHU-HLTCOE	TBTK-MORPH-HPB	CMU	JHU-PBMT	PARFDA
ONLINE-G	–	.45	.41†	.31‡	.26‡	.30‡	.25‡	.23‡	.16‡
ONLINE-B	**.55**	–	.46	.34‡	.29‡	.29‡	.30‡	.22‡	.18‡
ONLINE-A	**.59**†	**.54**	–	.42†	.38‡	.40‡	.29‡	.25‡	.25‡
YSDA	**.69**‡	**.66**‡	**.58**†	–	.43†	.44†	.40‡	.34‡	.31‡
JHU-HLTCOE	**.74**‡	**.71**‡	**.62**‡	**.57**†	–	.46	.45	.35‡	.35‡
TBTK-MORPH-HPB	**.70**‡	**.71**‡	**.60**‡	**.56**†	**.54**	–	.45⋆	.44†	.41‡
CMU	**.75**‡	**.70**‡	**.71**‡	**.60**‡	**.55**	**.55**⋆	–	.38‡	.42†
JHU-PBMT	**.77**‡	**.78**‡	**.75**‡	**.66**‡	**.65**‡	**.56**†	**.62**‡	–	.41†
PARFDA	**.84**‡	**.82**‡	**.75**‡	**.69**‡	**.65**‡	**.59**‡	**.58**†	**.59**†	–
score	.76	.61	.37	.05	-.12	-.19	-.29	-.54	-.66
rank	1-2	1-2	3	4	5-6	5-7	6-7	8-9	8-9

Table 49: Head to head comparison, ignoring ties, for English-Turkish systems

Results of the WMT16 Metrics Shared Task

Ondřej Bojar
Charles Univ. in Prague
MFF ÚFAL

Yvette Graham
Dublin City Univ.
ADAPT

Amir Kamran and **Miloš Stanojević**
Univ. of Amsterdam
ILLC

bojar@ufal.mff.cuni.cz   graham.yvette@gmail.com   {a.kamran,m.stanojevic}@uva.nl

Abstract

This paper presents the results of the WMT16 Metrics Shared Task. We asked participants of this task to score the outputs of the MT systems involved in the WMT16 Shared Translation Task. We collected scores of 16 metrics from 9 research groups. In addition to that, we computed scores of 9 standard metrics (BLEU, SentBLEU, NIST, WER, PER, TER and CDER) as baselines. The collected scores were evaluated in terms of system-level correlation (how well each metric's scores correlate with WMT16 official manual ranking of systems) and in terms of segment level correlation (how often a metric agrees with humans in comparing two translations of a particular sentence).

This year there are several additions to the setup: large number of language pairs (18 in total), datasets from different domains (news, IT and medical), and different kinds of judgments: relative ranking (RR), direct assessment (DA) and HUME manual semantic judgments. Finally, generation of large number of *hybrid systems* was trialed for provision of more conclusive system-level metric rankings.

1 Introduction

Automatic evaluation of machine translation quality is essential in the development and selection of machine translation systems. Many different automatic MT quality metrics are available and the Metrics Shared Task[1] is held annually at WMT to assess their quality, starting with Koehn and Monz (2006) and following up to Stanojević et al. (2015).

Metrics participating in the metrics task rely on the existence of reference translations with which MT outputs are compared, and the metrics task itself then needs manual judgments of translation quality in order to check the extent to which the automatic metrics can approximate the judgment. A related WMT task on quality estimation assesses the performance of methods where no reference translations are needed, requiring only the manual quality judgments (Bojar et al., 2016b).

This year, we keep the two main types of metric evaluation: *system-level*, where a metric is expected to provide a quality score for the whole translated document, and *segment-level*, where the score is needed for every individual sentence.

We experiment with several novelties. Specifically, test sets this year come from three domains: *news*, *IT* and *medical/health-related* texts.

The added domains bring in an extended set of languages. In sum, the metrics task this year includes 18 language pairs, English paired with Basque, Bulgarian, Czech, Dutch, Finnish, German, Polish, Portuguese, Romanian, Russian, Spanish, and Turkish, in one or both directions.

On the evaluation side, we rely on three golden truths of manual judgment:

- *Relative Ranking (RR)* of up to 5 different translation candidates at a time, as collected in WMT in the past,

- *Direct Assessment (DA)* evaluating the adequacy of a translation candidate on an absolute scale in isolation from other translations,

- *HUME*, a composite segment-level score aggregated over manual judgments of translation quality of semantic units of the source sentence.

Additional changes to the task evaluation include a change in the way we compute confidence

---

[1] http://www.statmt.org/wmt16/metrics-task/

Proceedings of the First Conference on Machine Translation, Volume 2: Shared Task Papers, pages 199–231,
Berlin, Germany, August 11-12, 2016. ©2016 Association for Computational Linguistics

Track	Test set	News Task	Tuning Task	IT Task	HimL Year 1	Hybrid	cs	de	ro	fi	ru	tr	cs	de	ro	fi	ru	tr	bg	es	eu	nl	pl	pt
		Systems					into-English						English into											
RRsysNews	newstest2016	✓	✓			✓	•	•	•	•	•	•	•	•	•	•	•	•						
RRsysIT	it-test2016			✓		✓							•	•						•	•	•	•		•
DAsysNews	newstest2016	✓	✓			✓	•	•	•	•	•	•	·	·	·	·	•	·						
RRsegNews	newstest2016	✓	✓				•	•	•	•	•	•	•	•	•	•	•	•						
DAsegNews	newstest2016	✓					•	•	•	•	•	•					•							
HUMEseg	himl2015				✓								•	•	•								•	

Table 1: Overview of "tracks" of the WMT16 metrics task. "•" indicates language pairs covered in the evaluation, "·" are language pairs planned but abandoned due to difficulties in obtaining human judgments.

intervals for metric correlations with human assessment, resulting in more reliable conclusions as to which metrics outperform others.

The official method of evaluation remains unchanged, relying on RR in both the system-level (TrueSkill) and segment-level (Kendall's τ) metrics, see below for details and references.

Our datasets are described in Section 2. This includes the test sets, system outputs, human judgments of translation quality as well as participating metrics across the tasks. Results of system-level metric evaluation are provided in Section 3.1 and Section 3.2, the results of the segment-level evaluation are provided in Section 3.3.

2 Data

Table 1 provides the complete picture of the golden truths, test sets, translation systems and language pairs involved in the metrics task this year. For simplicity, we called each of these setups a "track", indicating the underlying type of golden truth (RR/DA/HUME), system- or segment-level evaluation (sys/seg) and the particular test set.

While the set of setups is much larger this year, the participants of the task were affected rather minimally. Participants were only required to run metrics on the additional test sets and with an additional large set of hybrid systems in the system-level evaluation. As in the previous years, participants were allowed take part in any subset of language pairs and setups.

2.1 Test Sets

We use the following test sets:

newstest2016 is the main test set. It is the test set used in WMT16 News Translation Task (Bojar et al., 2016b), with approximately 3,000 sentences for each translation direction (with the exception of Romanian which only has

1,999 sentences). The set includes a single reference translation for each direction, except English→Finnish with two reference translations.

it-test2016 is the set of 1,000 sentences translated from English into seven other European languages. The IT test sentences typically contain instructions for operating commonly used software like web browsers, mail clients or image editors, e.g.: "In message box click on More > Archived."

himl2015 is part of the official test set created by the EU project HimL.[2] These are health-related texts from Cochrane summaries and NHS 24 online content. The texts originated in English and the target languages consist of Czech, German, Polish and Romanian versions created by post-edition of phrase-based MT output. From the full set of about 3,000 sentences, 800 were given as input to the participants of the metrics task and in the end about 340 sentences per language pair were used for evaluation, as those sentences have manual score suitable to employ as the golden truth for metric evaluation.

The sentences of NHS 24 tend to be shorter and simpler translations, e.g. "Choose lower fat options such as semi-skimmed milk and low fat yogurt.", while Cochrane summaries are longer and often contain specific terminology, e.g. "The purpose of this research was to determine how good the TEG and ROTEM assessments are at diagnosing TIC in adult trauma patients who are bleeding."

2.2 Translation Systems

Characteristics of the particular underlying translation task MT systems is likely an important fac-

---

[2]http://www.himl.eu/test-sets

tor affecting the difficulty of the metrics task. For instance, if all of the systems perform similarly, it will be more difficult, even for the humans, to distinguish between the quality of translations. If the task includes a wide range of systems of varying quality, however, or systems quite different in nature, this could in some way could make the task easier for metrics, with metrics that are more sensitive to certain aspects of MT output performing better.

The MT systems included in evaluation of metrics are as follows:

News Task Systems are all MT systems participating in the WMT16 News Translation Task (Bojar et al., 2016b). These systems differ widely in nature (standard phrase-based, syntax-based, transfer-based or even rule-based systems, also with a large number of neural MT systems), with the precise set of systems and system types also depending on specific language pair.

Tuning Task Systems are all Moses phrase-based systems run by the organizers of the WMT16 Tuning Task (Jawaid et al., 2016). All of these systems share the same phrase tables and language models, they are trained on relatively large volumes of data, and differ only in the model weights as provided by the participants of the tuning task. Tuning task was limited to Czech↔English language pairs.

IT Task Systems are participants of the WMT16 IT-domain Translation Task (Bojar et al., 2016b), translating only from English to seven other European languages. This is generally a smaller set of systems and the number of covered system architectures here is also smaller. As far as we know, no neural system was involved in the task.

HimL Year 1 Systems are MT systems released in the first year of the EU project HimL[3]. They are all Moses-based and trained on available data in the medical or health-related domain.

Hybrid Systems were created by combining the output of two newstest2016 translation task systems, with the aim of providing a larger

---

[3]http://www.himl.eu/

set of systems against which to evaluate metrics, as described further in Section 3.1. In short, we create 10K hybrid MT systems for each language pair.

Excluding the hybrid systems, we ended up with 171 system outputs across 18 language pairs and 3 test sets.

2.3 Manual MT Quality Judgments

There are three distinct "golden truths" employed to evaluate metrics this year: Relative Ranking (RR, as in previous year), Direct Assessment (DA) and HUME, a semantic-based manual metric.

The details of the methods are provided in this section, separately for system-level evaluation (Section 2.3.1, using RR and DA) and segment-level evaluation (Section 2.3.2, using RR, DA and HUME).

The RR manual judgments were provided by MT researchers taking part in WMT tasks, as in recent years of the campaign, after it was empirically established that judgments of RR collected through crowd-sourcing platforms were not reliable (Bojar et al., 2013). DA judgments are more robust in this respect and while the original plan was to collect DA from both researchers and crowd-sourced non-experts, only the latter ultimately took place due to time constraints.

2.3.1 System-level Manual Quality Judgments

In system-level evaluation, the goal is to assess the quality of translation of an MT system for the whole document. Both our manual scoring methods RR and DA nevertheless proceed sentence by sentence, aggregating the final score in some way.

Relative Ranking (RR) As in previous WMT shared tasks, human assessors of MT output (only researchers this year) were presented with the source language input, target language reference translation and the output of five distinct MT output translations. Human assessors were required to rank the five translations from best to worse, with ties allowed. As introduced in WMT15, identical translations from distinct systems were collapsed into a single translation before running the human evaluation to increase the overall efficiency of RR human assessment.

Each five-tuple relative ranking was employed to produce 10 pairwise assessments, later combined into a score for each MT system that reflects the frequency by which the output of that system was preferred to the output of other systems. Several methods have been tested in the past for the exact score calculation and WMT16 has again adopted TrueSkill as the official ranking approach. Please see the WMT16 overview paper for details on how this score is computed.

To increase annotator efficiency, a maximum sentence length of 30 words was applied to RR human assessment.

Direct Assessment (DA) In addition to the standard relative ranking (RR) manual evaluation employed to yield official system rankings in WMT16 translation task, this year the translation task also trialed a new method of human evaluation, monolingual direct assessment (DA) of translation fluency (Graham et al., 2013) and adequacy (Graham et al., 2014; Graham et al., 2016). For investigatory purposes, therefore, we also include evaluation of metrics with reference to the newly trialed human assessment method.

Since sufficient levels of agreement in human assessment of translation quality are difficult to achieve, the DA setup simplifies the task of translation assessment (conventionally a bilingual task) into a simpler monolingual assessment for both fluency and adequacy. Furthermore, DA avoids bias that has been problematic in previous evaluations introduced by simultaneous assessment of several alternate translations of a given single source language input, where scores of systems for which translations were often compared to high or low quality translations resulted in an unfair advantage or disadvantage (Bojar et al., 2011). DA achieves this by assessment of individual translations in isolation from other outputs of the same source input.

Translation adequacy is structured as a monolingual assessment of similarity of meaning where the target language reference translation and the MT output are displayed to the human assessor. Human assessors rate a given translation by how adequately it expresses the meaning of the reference translation on an analogue scale corresponding to an underlying 0-100 rating scale.[4] Fluency assessment is similar to adequacy except that no reference is displayed and assessors are asked to rate how much they agree that a given translation

is fluent target language text.

Large numbers of DA human assessments of translations for seven language pairs (targeting English and Russian) were collected on Amazon's Mechanical Turk,[5] via sets of 100-translation hits to ensure sufficient repeat items per worker, before application of strict quality control measures to filter out assessments from poorly performing workers.

In order to iron out differences in scoring strategies attributed to distinct workers, human assessment scores for translations were standardized according to an individual worker's overall mean and standard deviation score. Mean standardized scores for translation task participating systems were computed by firstly taking the average of scores for individual translations in the test set (since some were assessed more than once), before combining all scores for translations attributed to a given MT system into its overall adequacy or fluency score.

Although the WMT16 Translation Task included both fluency and adequacy DA human assessment, the metrics task this year employed only DA adequacy scores. We hope to incorporate DA fluency into future metric evaluations, however.

Finally, although it is common to apply a sentence length restriction in WMT human evaluation, the simplified DA setup does not require restriction of the evaluation in this respect and no sentence length restriction was applied in DA WMT16.

2.3.2 Segment-level Manual Quality Judgments

Segment-level metrics have been evaluated against the pairwise judgments implied by the 5-way relative ranking annotation. This year, we add two new variants of human assessment: segment-level DA and HUME.

Segment-level DA Adequacy assessments were collected for translations sampled from the output of systems participating in WMT16 translation task for seven language pairs (Graham et al., 2015).[6] Since the actual MT system is not important for segment-level assessment, we sampled 500 translations per language pair at random.

---

[4]The only numbering displayed on the rating scale are extreme points 0 and 100%, and three ticks indicate the levels of 25, 50 and 75 %.

[5]http://www.mturk.com/

[6]Translations produced by ONLINEA were unfortunately omitted from segment-level DA due to submission and data collection timing constraints.

Metric	Participant
BEER	ILLC – University of Amsterdam (Stanojević and Sima'an, 2015)
CHARACTER	RWTH Aachen University (Wang et al., 2016)
CHRF1,2,3, WORDF1,2,3	Humboldt University of Berlin (Popović, 2016)
DEPCHECK	Charles University, no corresponding paper
DPMFCOMB-WITHOUT-RED	Chinese Academy of Sciences and Dublin City University (Yu et al., 2015)
MPEDA	Jiangxi Normal University (Zhang et al., 2016)
UoW.REVAL	University of Wolverhampton (Gupta et al., 2015b)
UPF-COBALT, COBALTF, METRICSF	Universitat Pompeu Fabra (Fomicheva et al., 2016)
DTED	University of St Andrews, (McCaffery and Nederhof, 2016)

Table 2: Participants of WMT16 Metrics Shared Task

Segment-level DA adequacy scores were collected as in system-level DA, described in Section 2.3.1, again with strict quality control and score standardization applied. To achieve accurate segment-level scores for translations, a human assessment of each translation was collected from 15 distinct human assessors before combination into a mean adequacy score for each individual translation. Although in general agreement in human assessment of MT has been difficult to achieve, segment-level DA scores employing a minimum of 15 repeat assessments have been shown to be almost perfectly replicable. In repeat experiments, for all tested language pairs, a correlation of above 0.9 between (a) segment-level DA scores for translations collected in an initial experiment run and (b) the same collected in a repeat evaluation of the same translations, by combining assessments of a minimum of 15 human assessors (Graham et al., 2015).

A distinction between DA and RR is that while RR works off a single set of human assessments for evaluation of both system-level and segment-level metrics, DA additionally includes a variant of its methodology designed specifically for evaluation of segment-level metrics.

HUME The HUME metric (Birch et al., 2016) is a novel human evaluation measure that decomposes over the UCCA semantic units. UCCA (Abend and Rappoport, 2013) is an appealing candidate for semantic analysis, due to its cross-linguistic applicability, support for rapid annotation, and coverage of many fundamental semantic phenomena, such as verbal, nominal and adjectival argument structures and their interrelations. HUME operates by aggregating human assessments of the translation quality of individual semantic units in the source sentence. We thus avoid the semantic annotation of machine-generated text, which is often garbled or semantically unclear. This also allows the re-use of the source semantic annotation for measuring the quality of different translations of the same source sentence, and avoids reliance on possibly suboptimal reference translations. HUME shows good inter-annotator agreement, and reasonable correlation with Direct Assessment (Graham et al., 2015).

2.4 Participants of the Metrics Shared Task

Table 2 lists the participants of the WMT16 Shared Metrics Task, along with their metrics. We have collected 16 metrics from a total of 9 research groups.

The following subsections provide a brief summary of all the metrics that participated. The list is concluded by our baseline metrics in Section 2.4.10.

2.4.1 BEER

BEER (Stanojević and Sima'an, 2015) is a trained evaluation metric with a linear model that combines features capturing character n-grams and permutation trees. BEER has participated in previous years of the evaluation task. This year the learning algorithm is improved (linear SVM instead of logistic regression) and some features that are relatively slow to compute are removed (paraphrasing, syntax and permutation trees) which resulted in a very large speed-up. BEER is usually trained for ranking but in this case there was a compromise: the initial model is trained for ranking (RR) with ranking SVM and then the output from SVM is scaled using trained regression model to approximate absolute judgment (DA).

2.4.2 CHARACTER

CHARACTER (Wang et al., 2016) is a novel character-level metric inspired by the commonly applied translation edit rate (TER). It is defined as the minimum number of character edits required to adjust a hypothesis, until it completely matches the reference, normalized by the length of the hypothesis sentence. CHARACTER calculates the character-level edit distance while performing the shift edit on word level. Unlike the strict matching criterion in TER, a hypothesis word is considered to match a reference word and could be shifted, if the edit distance between them is below a threshold value. The Levenshtein distance between the reference and the shifted hypothesis sequence is computed on the character level. In addition, the lengths of hypothesis sequences instead of reference sequences are used for normalizing the edit distance, which effectively counters the issue that shorter translations normally achieve lower TER.

2.4.3 CHRF and WORDF

WORDF1,2,3 (Popović, 2016) calculate a simple F-score combination of the precision and recall of word n-grams of maximal length 4 with different setting for the β parameter ($\beta = 1$, 2, or 3). Precision and recall that are used in computation of the F-score are arithmetic averages of precisions and recalls, respectively, for the different n-gram orders. CHRF1,2,3 calculate the F-score of character n-grams of maximal length 6. β parameter gives β times weight to recall: $\beta = 1$ implies equal weights for precision and recall.

2.4.4 DEPCHECK

DEPCHECK is based on the automatic post-editing tool Depfix (Rosa, 2014). For each sentence, DEPCHECK computes the percentage of nodes postedited by Depfix, obtaining a "relative depcheck error rate" (RDER). The value of the DEPCHECK metric is then defined as $1 - \text{RDER}$. DEPCHECK does not distinguish the error types or whether there was more than one Depfix rule applied to a node. It is suggested for a future version of DEPCHECK to assign a weight (either by hand, or training from some golden data) to each rule that was applied to the MT output.

2.4.5 DPMFCOMB-WITHOUT-RED

The authors of DPMFCOMB-WITHOUT-RED follow the work on last year's metric DPMFCOMB (Yu et al., 2015), but modify it with two main differences. Firstly, they use the 'case insensitive' instead of 'case sensitive' option when using Asiya. Secondly, REDP are not used. Thus, DPMFCOMB-WITHOUT-RED is a combined metric including 57 single metrics. Weights of the individual metrics are trained with SVM-

rank, using training data from the English-targeted language pairs from WMT12 to WMT14. In the results DPMFCOMB-WITHOUT-RED is represented as DPMFCOMB for brevity.

2.4.6 DTED

DTED (McCaffery and Nederhof, 2016) is based on Tree Edit Distance. The scoring is done over the dependency parse tree of the output where the number of edit operations (insert, delete or substitute) needed to convert it to the correct (reference) dependency tree is used as an indicator of the translation quality. Unlike the majority of metrics which evaluate many aspects of translation, DTED evaluates only the word order.

2.4.7 MPEDA

MPEDA (Zhang et al., 2016) is developed on the basis of the METEOR metric. In order to accurately match words or phrases with the same or similar meaning, it extracts a domain-specific paraphrase table from the monolingual corpus and applies that paraphrase table to the METEOR metric to replace the general one. Unlike traditional paraphrase extraction approaches, it first filters out a domain-specific sub-corpus from a large general monolingual corpus and then extracts domain-specific paraphrase table from the sub-corpus by Markov Network model. Since the proposed paraphrase extraction approach can be used in all languages, MPEDA is language-independent.

2.4.8 UOW.REVAL

UOW.REVAL (Gupta et al., 2015b) uses dependency-tree Long Short Term Memory (LSTM) network to represent both the hypothesis and the reference with a dense vector. Training is performed using the judgements from WMT13 (Bojar et al., 2013) converted to similarity scores. The final score at the system level is obtained by averaging the segment level scores obtained from a neural network which takes into account both distance and Hadamard product of the two representations.

UOW.REVAL is the same as UOW_LSTM (Gupta et al., 2015a) that participated in the WMT15 task except that LSTM vector dimension is 150 for UoW.ReVal instead of 300.

into-English

Track	cs	de	ro	fi	ru	tr
RRsysNews	T4,F3,T6	T4,F1	T4,F1	T4,F1	T4,F2	T4,F2
RRsysIT						
DAsysNews	T4,F3,T7	T4,F1,T7	T4,F1,T7	T4,F1,T7	T4,F2,T7	T4,F2,T7
RRsegNews	T9	T9	T9	T9	T9	T9
DAsegNews	T9,F8	T9,F8	T9,F8	T9,F8	T9,F8	T9,F8
HUMEseg						

English into

Track	cs	de	ro	fi	ru	tr	bg	es	eu	nl	pl	pt
RRsysNews	T5,F4,T6	T5,F5	T5,F6	T5,F6	T5,F2	T5,F6						
RRsysIT	T8,F4	T8,F5					T8	T8,F7	T8	T8,F7		T8,F7
DAsysNews					T5,F2,T7							
RRsegNews	T10	T10	T10	T10	T10	T10						
DAsegNews					T10,F9							
HUMEseg	T11,F10	T11,F10	T11,F10								T11,F10	

Table 3: Overview of tables (T) and figures (F) reporting results of the individual "tracks" and language pairs.

2.4.9 UPF-COBALT, COBALTF and METRICSF

UPF-COBALT (Fomicheva et al., 2016) is an alignment-based metric that examines the syntactic contexts of lexically similar candidate and reference words in order to distinguish meaning-preserving variations from the differences indicative of MT errors. This year the metric was improved by explicitly addressing MT fluency. The new version of the metric, COBALTF, combines various components of UPF-COBALT with a number of fine-grained features intended to capture the number and scale of disfluent fragments contained in MT sentences. METRICSF is a combination of three evaluation systems, BLEU, METEOR and UPF-COBALT, with the fluency-oriented features.

2.4.10 Baseline Metrics

As mentioned by Bojar et al. (2016a), metrics task occasionally suffers from "loss of knowledge" when successful metrics participate only in one year.

We attempt to avoid this by regularly evaluating also a range of "baseline metrics":

- **Mteval.** The metrics MTEVALBLEU (Papineni et al., 2002) and MTEVAL-NIST (Doddington, 2002) were computed using the script `mteval-v13a.pl`[7] which is used in the OpenMT Evaluation Campaign and includes its own tokenization. We run `mteval` with the flag `--international-tokenization` since it performs slightly better (Macháček and Bojar, 2013).

- **Moses Scorer.** The metrics MOSES-BLEU, MOSESTER (Snover et al., 2006), MOSESWER, MOSESPER and MOSECDER (Leusch et al., 2006) were produced by the Moses scorer which is used in Moses model optimization. To tokenize the sentences, we used the standard tokenizer script as available in Moses toolkit. Since Moses scorer is versioned on Github, we strongly encourage authors of high-performing metrics to add them to Moses scorer, as this will ensure that their metric can be included in future tasks.

As for segment-level baselines, we employ the following modified version of BLEU:

- **SentBLEU.** The metric SENTBLEU is computed using the script sentence-bleu, part of the Moses toolkit. It is a smoothed version of BLEU that correlates better with human judgments for segment-level.

For computing system-level scores, the same script was employed as in last year's metric task. New scripts have been added for system-level hybrids and segment-level evaluation.

3 Results

Table 3 provides an overview of all the tables and figures in the rest of the paper. We discuss system-level results for news task systems (including tuning task systems) in Section 3.1. The system-level results for the IT domain are discussed in Section 3.2. The segment-level results are in Section 3.3. We end with discussion in Section 3.4.

3.1 System-Level Results for News Task

As in previous years, we employ the Pearson correlation (r) as the main evaluation measure for system-level metrics, as follows:

$$r = \frac{\sum_{i=1}^{n}(H_i - \overline{H})(M_i - \overline{M})}{\sqrt{\sum_{i=1}^{n}(H_i - \overline{H})^2}\sqrt{\sum_{i=1}^{n}(M_i - \overline{M})^2}} \quad (1)$$

where H are human assessment scores of all systems in a given translation direction, M are corresponding scores as predicted by a given metric. $\overline{H}$ and $\overline{M}$ are their means respectively.

---

[7] `http://www.itl.nist.gov/iad/mig/tools/`

Since some metrics, such as BLEU, for example, aim to achieve a strong positive correlation with human assessment, while error metrics, such as TER aim for a strong negative correlation, after computation of r for metrics, we compare metrics via the absolute value of a given metric's correlation with human assessment.

Table 4 includes results for system-level into-English metrics for evaluation of systems participating in the main translation task (newstest2016), evaluated against RR and DA human assessment variants, while Table 5 includes the same for the newstest2016 out-of-English language pairs (only Russian has the DA judgments). Tuning systems were excluded from Tables 4 and 5 and they are covered by Table 6 that shows correlations achieved by metrics with RR when the set of systems additionally includes tuning task systems.

In previous years, we reported empirical confidence intervals of system-level correlations obtained by bootstrap resampling human assessments data and computing confidence intervals for individual correlations with human assessment. Such confidence intervals reflect the variance due to particular sentences and assessors involved in the evaluation but lead to over-estimation of significant differences if employed to conclude which metrics outperform others. This year, as recommended by Graham and Baldwin (2014), instead we employ Williams significance test (Williams, 1959). Williams test is a test of significance of a difference in dependent correlations and therefore suitable for evaluation of metrics. Correlations not significantly outperformed by any other are highlighted in bold in Tables 4 and 5. Since RR is the official method of evaluation for this year's metrics task, bolded correlations under RR comprise official winners of the news domain portion of the system-level metrics task. DA results are included for comparison and are investigatory only.

With regard to which individual metric may or may not outperform other metrics, such as the important comparison as to which metrics significantly outperform the most widely employed metric BLEU (in its mteval or Moses scorer implementation), Figures 1, 2, 3, 4, 5, and 6 include significance test results for every competing pair of metrics including our baseline metrics. In heatmaps in Figures 1, 2, 3, 4, 5, and 6, the column labelled "MTEVALBLEU" or "MOSESBLEU" can be used to quickly observe which metrics achieve

	cs-en	en-cs
Human	RR + TT	RR + TT
Systems	12	20
WORDF2	.988	**.990**
WORDF1	.989	**.990**
MOSESBLEU	.989	**.987**
WORDF3	.988	**.989**
MTEVALBLEU	.985	**.986**
MOSESCDER	**.991**	.976
BEER	**.995**	.972
MPEDA	.988	.977
CHRF1	.990	.965
MTEVALNIST	.976	**.979**
CHRF2	.990	.952
CHRF3	.989	.935
CHARACTER	**.997**	.779
MOSESPER	.970	.803
MOSESTER	.974	.758
MOSESWER	.964	.755
UOW.REVAL	.982	-
newstest2016		

Table 6: Absolute Pearson correlation of cs-en and en-cs system-level metric scores with human assessment variant RR + TT, i.e. standard WMT relative ranking including tuning task systems.

a significant increase in correlation with human assessment over that of BLEU, where a green cell in the column denotes outperformance of BLEU by the metric in that row.

For investigatory purposes only, we also include hybrid-supersample (Graham and Liu, 2016) results for system-level metrics. 10K hybrid systems were created per language pair, with corresponding DA human assessment scores, by sampling pairs of systems from WMT16 translation task and creating a hybrid system by combining translations from each system to create new hybrid output test set documents, each with a corresponding DA human assessment score. Not all metrics participating in the system-level metrics shared task submitted metric scores for the large set of hybrid systems, possibly due to the increased time required to run metrics on the large set of 10K systems. In this respect, DA hybrid may provide some indication of which metrics are likely to be more feasible to employ for tuning purposes in MT systems out-of-the-box. Due to time constraints, this year it was only possible to include hybrid-supersampling results for language pairs evaluated by the DA human assessment variant.

Correlations of metric scores with human assessment of the large set of hybrid systems are

	cs-en		de-en		fi-en		ro-en		ru-en		tr-en	
Human	RR	DA	RR	DA	RR	DA	RR	DA	RR	DA	RR	DA
Systems	6	6	10	10	9	9	7	7	10	10	8	8
MPEDA	**.996**	**.993**	**.956**	.937	**.967**	**.976**	**.938**	**.932**	**.986**	.929	**.972**	**.982**
UoW.ReVal	**.993**	**.986**	**.949**	**.985**	**.958**	**.970**	**.919**	**.957**	**.990**	**.976**	**.977**	.958
BEER	**.996**	**.990**	.949	.879	**.964**	**.972**	**.908**	.852	**.986**	.901	**.981**	**.982**
CHRF1	.993	.986	.934	.868	**.974**	**.980**	.903	.865	**.984**	.898	**.973**	.961
CHRF2	**.992**	.989	.952	.893	**.957**	**.967**	.913	.886	**.985**	.918	.937	.933
CHRF3	.991	.989	**.958**	.902	.946	.958	.915	**.892**	**.981**	.923	.918	.917
CharacTer	**.997**	**.995**	**.985**	.929	.921	.927	**.970**	**.883**	.955	**.930**	.799	.827
MTEVALNIST	.988	.978	.887	.801	.924	.929	.834	.807	.966	.854	**.952**	**.938**
MTEVALBLEU	**.992**	**.989**	.905	.808	.858	.864	.899	.840	.962	.837	.899	.895
MOSESCDER	**.995**	**.988**	.927	.827	.846	.860	.925	.800	.968	.855	.836	.826
MOSESTER	**.983**	**.969**	.926	.834	.852	.846	.900	.793	.962	.847	.805	.788
WORDF2	**.991**	**.985**	.897	.786	.790	.806	.905	.815	.955	.831	.807	.787
WORDF3	**.991**	**.985**	.898	.787	.786	.803	.909	.818	.955	.833	.803	.786
WORDF1	**.992**	**.984**	.894	.780	.796	.808	.890	.804	.954	.825	.806	.776
MOSESPER	.981	.970	.843	.730	.770	.767	.791	.748	**.974**	.887	**.947**	.940
MOSESBLEU	**.991**	**.983**	.880	.757	.752	.759	.878	.793	.950	.817	.765	.739
MOSESWER	**.982**	**.967**	.926	.822	.773	.768	.895	.762	.958	.837	.680	.651
					newstest2016							

Table 4: Absolute Pearson correlation of to-English system-level metric scores with human assessment variants: RR = standard WMT relative ranking; DA = direct assessment of translation adequacy.

	en-cs		en-de		en-fi		en-ro		en-ru		en-tr	
Human	RR	DA	RR	DA	RR	DA	RR	DA	RR	DA	RR	DA
Systems	10		15		13		12		12	12	8	
CharacTer	**.947**	-	**.915**	-	**.933**	-	**.959**	-	**.954**	.966	**.930**	-
BEER	**.973**	-	.732	-	.940	-	**.947**	-	.906	.922	**.956**	-
CHRF2	.954	-	.725	-	**.974**	-	.828	-	.930	**.955**	**.940**	-
CHRF3	.954	-	.745	-	**.974**	-	.818	-	**.936**	**.960**	**.916**	-
MOSESCDER	**.968**	-	.779	-	.910	-	**.952**	-	.874	.874	.791	-
CHRF1	.955	-	.645	-	.931	-	.858	-	.901	.928	**.938**	-
WORDF3	**.964**	-	.768	-	.901	-	**.931**	-	.836	.840	.714	-
WORDF2	**.964**	-	.766	-	.899	-	**.933**	-	.836	.840	.715	-
WORDF1	**.964**	-	.756	-	.888	-	**.937**	-	.836	.839	.711	-
MPEDA	**.964**	-	.684	-	**.944**	-	.786	-	.856	.866	.860	-
MOSESBLEU	**.968**	-	.784	-	.857	-	**.944**	-	.820	.820	.693	-
MTEVALBLEU	**.968**	-	.752	-	.868	-	.897	-	.835	.838	.745	-
MTEVALNIST	**.975**	-	.625	-	.886	-	.882	-	.890	.897	.788	-
MOSESTER	.940	-	.742	-	.863	-	.906	-	.882	.879	.644	-
MOSESWER	.935	-	.771	-	.855	-	**.912**	-	.882	.876	.570	-
MOSESPER	**.974**	-	.681	-	.700	-	**.944**	-	.857	.854	.641	-
CHRF3.2REF	-	-	-	-	**.973**	-	-	-	-	-	-	-
CHRF2.2REF	-	-	-	-	**.970**	-	-	-	-	-	-	-
CHRF1.2REF	-	-	-	-	.923	-	-	-	-	-	-	-
WORDF3.2REF	-	-	-	-	.890	-	-	-	-	-	-	-
WORDF2.2REF	-	-	-	-	.887	-	-	-	-	-	-	-
WORDF1.2REF	-	-	-	-	.876	-	-	-	-	-	-	-
					newstest2016							

Table 5: Absolute Pearson correlation of out-of-English system-level metric scores with human assessment variants: RR = standard WMT relative ranking; DA = direct assessment of translation adequacy.

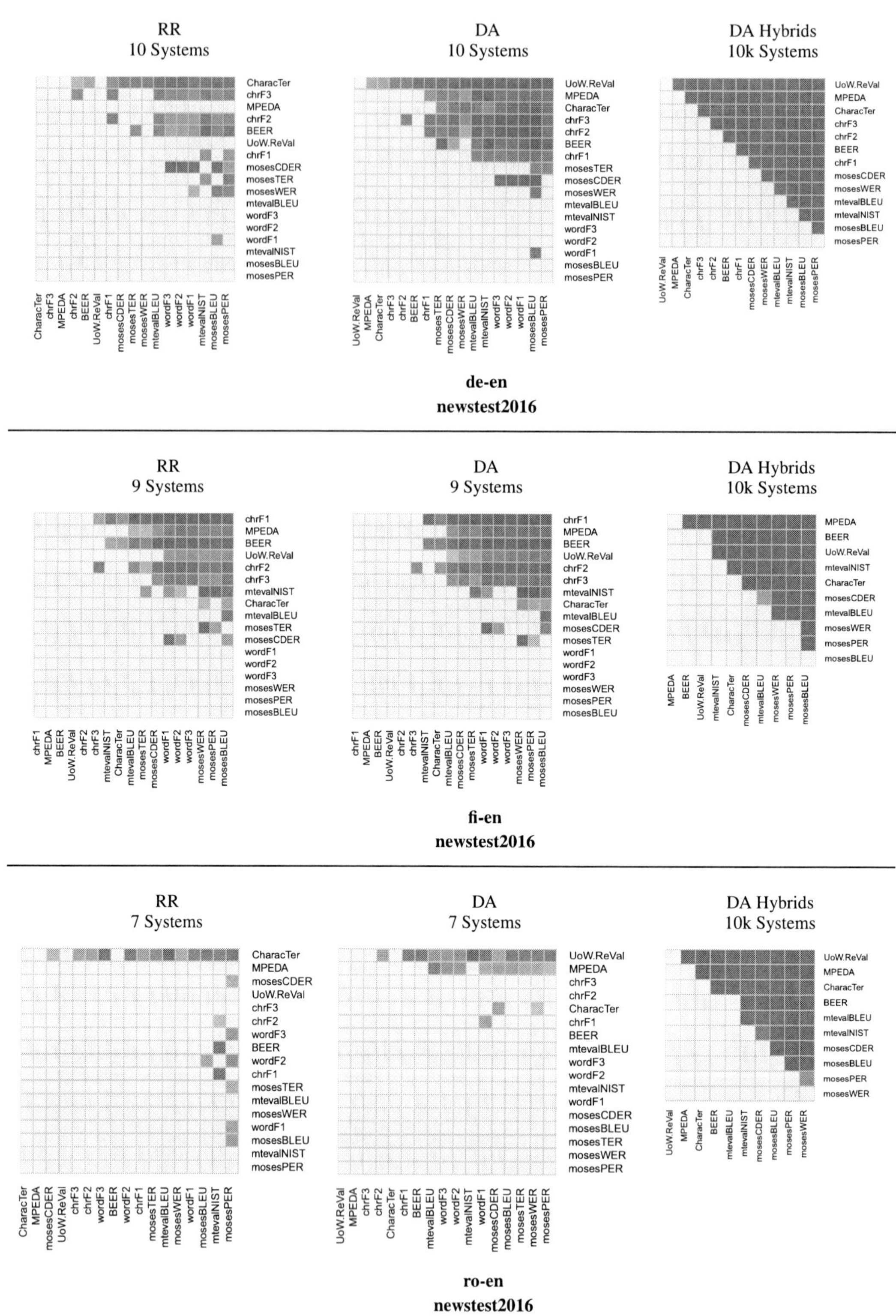

Figure 1: German-to-English (de-en), Finnish-to-English (fi-en) and Romanian-to-English (ro-en) system-level metric significance test results for human assessment variants; green cells denote a significant increase in correlation with human assessment for the metric in a given row over the metric in a given column according to Williams test; RR = standard WMT relative ranking for translation task systems only; DA = direct assessment of translation adequacy; DA Hybrids = direct assessment with hybrid super-sampling.

208

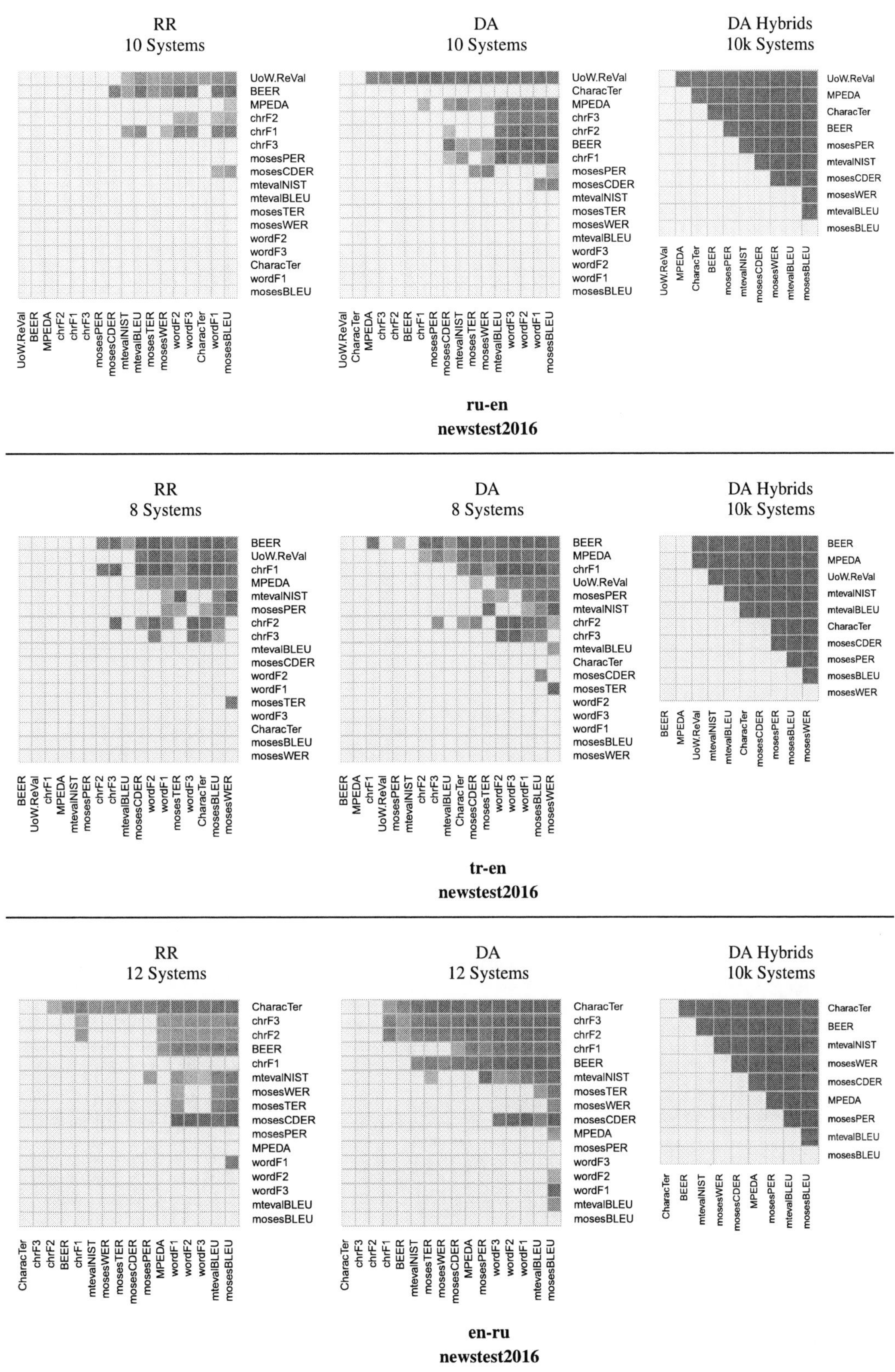

Figure 2: Russian-to-English (ru-en), Turkish-to-English (tr-en) and English-to-Russian (en-ru) system-level metric significance test results for human assessment variants; green cells denote a significant increase in correlation for the metric in a given row over the metric in a given column according to Williams test; RR = standard WMT relative ranking for translation task systems only; DA = direct assessment of translation adequacy; DA Hybrids = direct assessment with hybrid super-sampling.

209

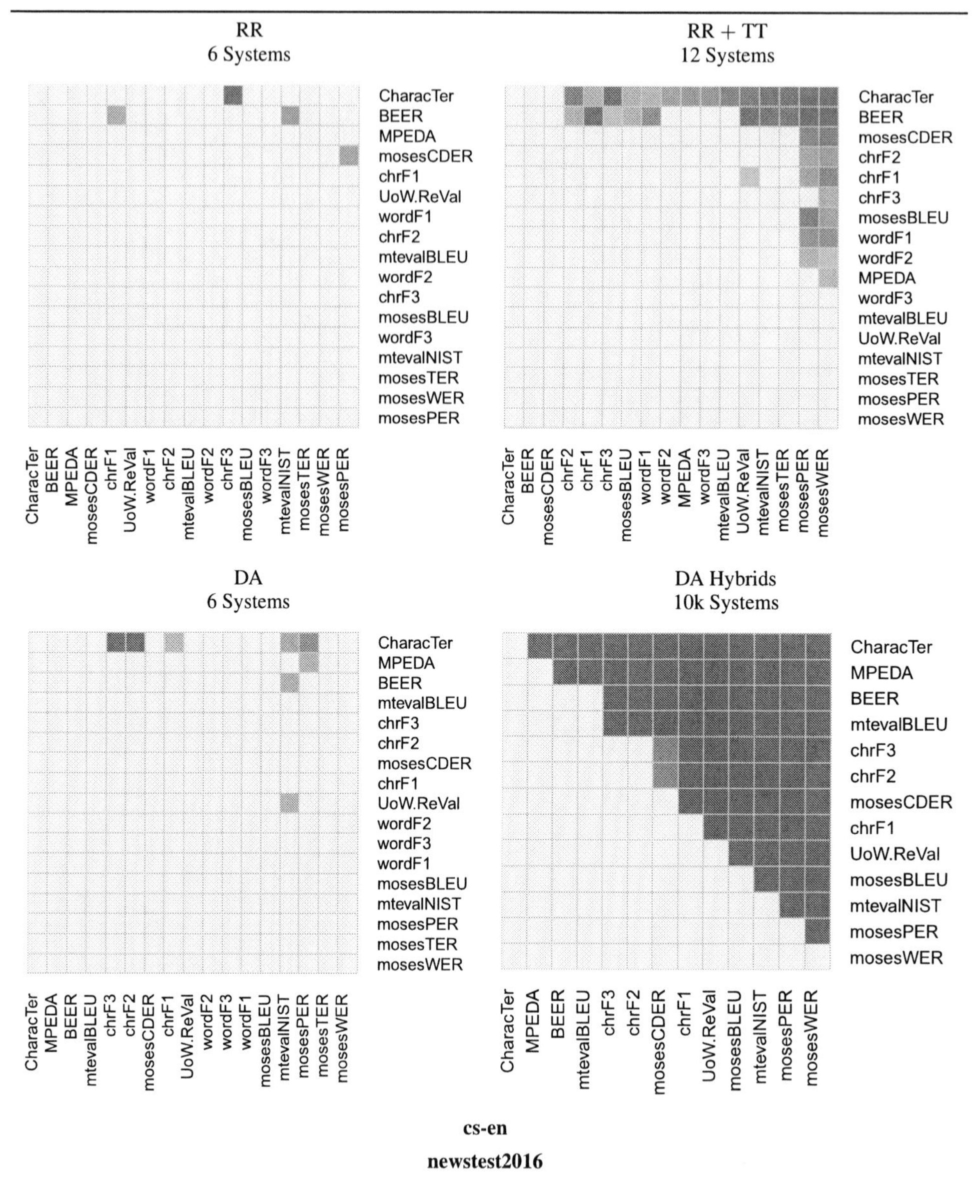

Figure 3: Czech-to-English (cs-en) system-level metric significance test results for human assessment variants; a green cell corresponds to a significant increase in correlation for the metric in a given row over the metric in a given column according to Williams test; RR = standard WMT relative ranking for translation task systems only; RR + TT = standard WMT relative ranking for all cs-en newstest2016 systems; DA = direct assessment of translation adequacy; DA Hybrids = direct assessment with hybrid super-sampling.

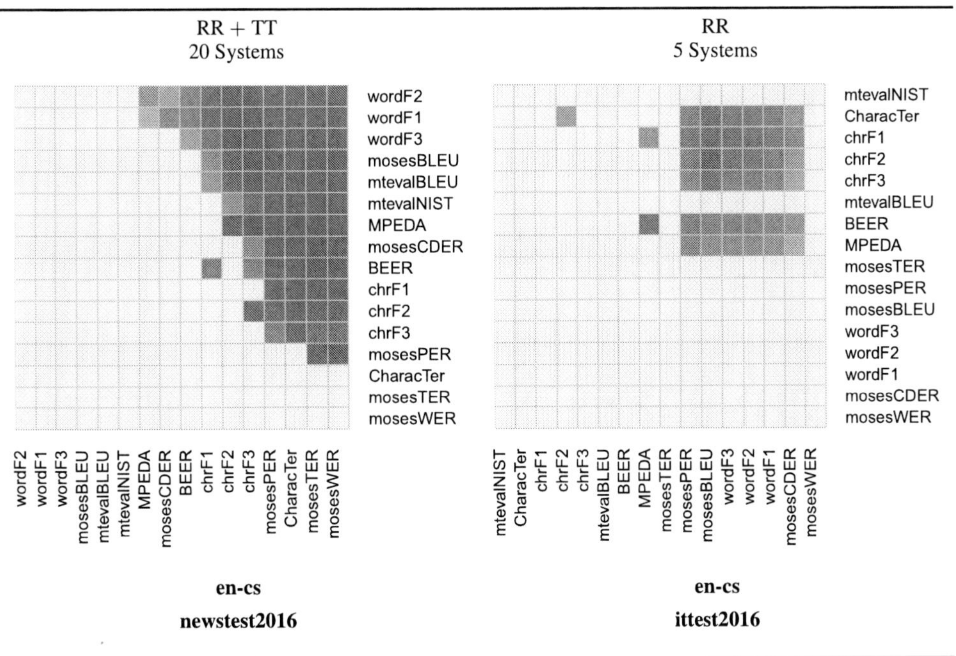

Figure 4: English-to-Czech (en-cs) system-level metric significance test results; a green cell corresponds to a significant increase in correlation for the metric in a given row over the metric in a given column according to Williams test; RR = standard WMT relative ranking; RR + TT = standard WMT relative ranking for translation and tuning task systems.

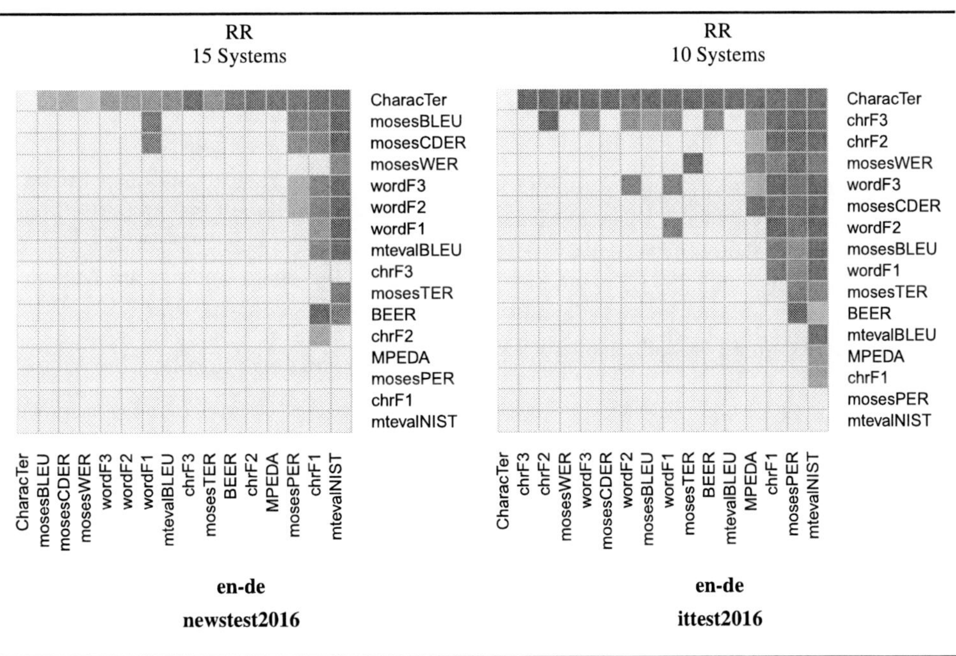

Figure 5: English-to-German (en-de) system-level metric significance test results; a green cell corresponds to a significant increase in correlation for the metric in a given row over the metric in a given column according to Williams test; RR = standard WMT relative ranking.

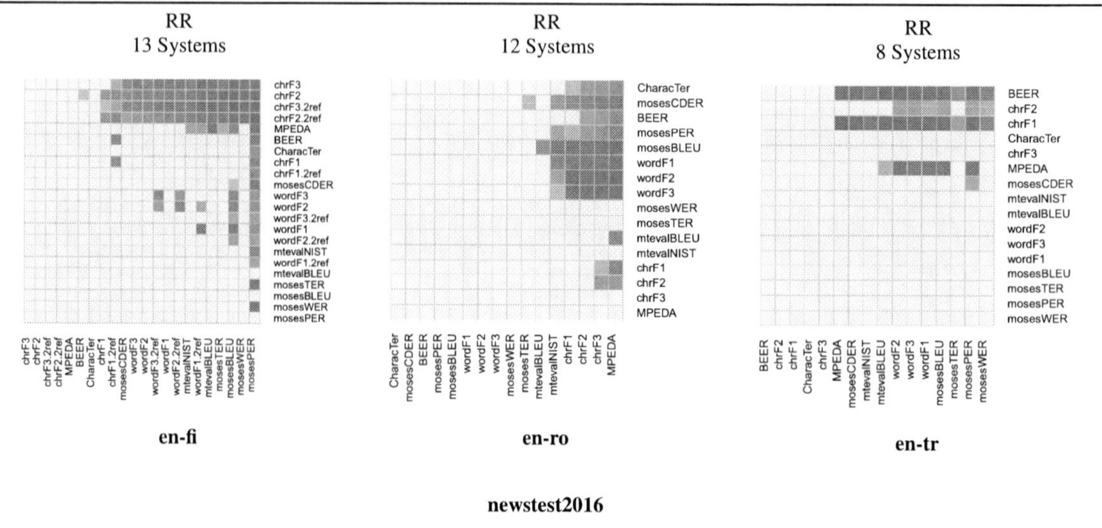

Figure 6: English-to-Finnish (en-fi), English-to-Romanian (en-ro) and English-to-Turkish (en-tr) system-level metric significance test results; a green cell corresponds to a significant increase in correlation for the metric in a given row over the metric in a given column according to Williams test; RR = standard WMT relative ranking.

shown in Table 7, where again metrics not significantly outperformed by any other are highlighted in bold. Results are for investigatory purposes only and do not indicate official winners, however. Figures 1, 2 and 3 also include significance test results for hybrid super-sampled correlations for all pairs of competing metrics for a given language pair.

In Appendix A, correlation plots for each language pair are also provided. The left-hand plot visualizes the correlation of MTEVALBLEU and manual judgements, while the right-hand plot shows the correlation for the best performing metrics for that pair according to both standard RR and DA, as per Tables 4, 5 and 7.

3.2 System-Level Results for IT Task

Since systems participating in the IT domain translation task were manually evaluated with RR, we include evaluation of metrics for translation of this specific domain. Results of all metrics evaluated on the IT domain MT systems are shown in Table 8, where official winning metrics for this domain are identified as those not significantly outperformed by any other metric according to Williams test, correlations for which are high-

lighted in bold.[8]

Full pairwise significance test results for every pair of competing metrics evaluated on IT domain systems for Spanish, Dutch and Portuguese are shown in Figure 7, German in Figure 5 and Czech in Figure 4. No significance tests are provided for IT domain Bulgarian and Basque, as all metrics achieved equal correlations.

We see from Table 8 and also Figure 7 that MOSESBLEU does not belong to the winners for several target languages (Czech, German, Dutch), but across the board, metrics are hard to distinguish on this specific test set.

3.3 Segment-Level Results

In WMT16, the official method for segment-level metric evaluation remains unchanged: a Kendall's Tau-like formulation of a given metric's agreement with pairwise human assessment of translations, collected through 5-way relative ranking (RR). However, we also trial evaluation of segment-level metrics with reference to segment-level DA human assessment (for the main translation task data set) and a semantic-based manual judgments HUME (for himl2015 data set).

---

[8]Bulgarian and Basque IT translation tasks included only two participating systems and all metrics were able to order them correctly, all resulting in a correlation of 1.0.

	cs-en	de-en	fi-en	ro-en	ru-en	tr-en	en-ru
Human	DA	DA	DA	DA	DA	DA	DA
Systems	10K	10K	10K	10K	10K	10K	10K
MPEDA	.988	.923	**.971**	.905	.923	**.975**	.860
BEER	.985	.871	.964	.828	.894	**.975**	.914
CHARACTER	**.989**	.918	.915	.850	.919	.822	**.954**
MTEVALNIST	.971	.790	.919	.784	.853	.919	.890
MTEVALBLEU	.985	.802	.849	.828	.833	.868	.831
MOSESCDER	.984	.819	.851	.777	.850	.822	.868
UOW.REVAL	.981	**.976**	.964	**.930**	**.967**	.951	-
MOSESPER	.970	.728	.758	.745	.877	.798	.846
MOSESWER	.962	.814	.758	.741	.834	.642	.870
MOSESBLEU	.979	.753	.747	.772	.819	.708	.813
CHRF3	.984	.892	-	-	-	-	-
CHRF2	.984	.882	-	-	-	-	-
CHRF1	.982	.856	-	-	-	-	-
				newstest2016			

Table 7: Absolute Pearson correlation of system-level metric scores with 10K hybrid systems: DA Hybrid = direct assessment of translation adequacy of 10K hybrid MT systems.

	en-bg	en-cs	en-de	en-es	en-eu	en-nl	en-pt
Human	RR	RR	RR	RR	RR	RR	RR
Systems	2	5	10	4	2	4	4
CHARACTER	**1.000**	**0.901**	**0.930**	**0.963**	**1.000**	**0.927**	0.976
CHRF3	**1.000**	**0.831**	0.700	**0.938**	**1.000**	**0.961**	0.990
CHRF2	**1.000**	0.837	0.672	0.933	**1.000**	**0.959**	0.986
BEER	**1.000**	**0.744**	0.621	0.931	**1.000**	**0.983**	**0.989**
CHRF1	**1.000**	**0.845**	0.588	0.915	**1.000**	**0.951**	0.967
MTEVALNIST	**1.000**	**0.905**	0.524	0.926	**1.000**	0.722	**0.993**
MPEDA	**1.000**	0.620	0.599	**0.951**	**1.000**	0.856	**0.989**
MOSESTER	**1.000**	**0.616**	0.628	**0.908**	**1.000**	0.835	**0.994**
MTEVALBLEU	**1.000**	**0.750**	0.621	**0.976**	**1.000**	0.596	**0.997**
MOSESWER	**1.000**	**0.009**	0.656	0.916	**1.000**	**0.903**	0.991
MOSESCDER	**1.000**	0.181	0.652	**0.932**	**1.000**	**0.914**	**0.997**
WORDF1	**1.000**	0.240	0.644	**0.959**	**1.000**	**0.911**	**0.997**
WORDF2	**1.000**	0.266	0.652	**0.965**	**1.000**	**0.900**	**0.997**
WORDF3	**1.000**	0.274	0.655	**0.966**	**1.000**	0.897	**0.996**
MOSESBLEU	**1.000**	0.296	0.650	**0.974**	**1.000**	0.886	**0.992**
MOSESPER	**1.000**	0.307	0.548	0.911	**1.000**	**0.938**	**0.998**
				ittest2016			

Table 8: System-level metric results (ittest2016): Pearson correlation of system-level metric scores with human assessment computed over standard WMT relative ranking (RR) human assessments; absolute values of correlation coefficients reported for all metrics.

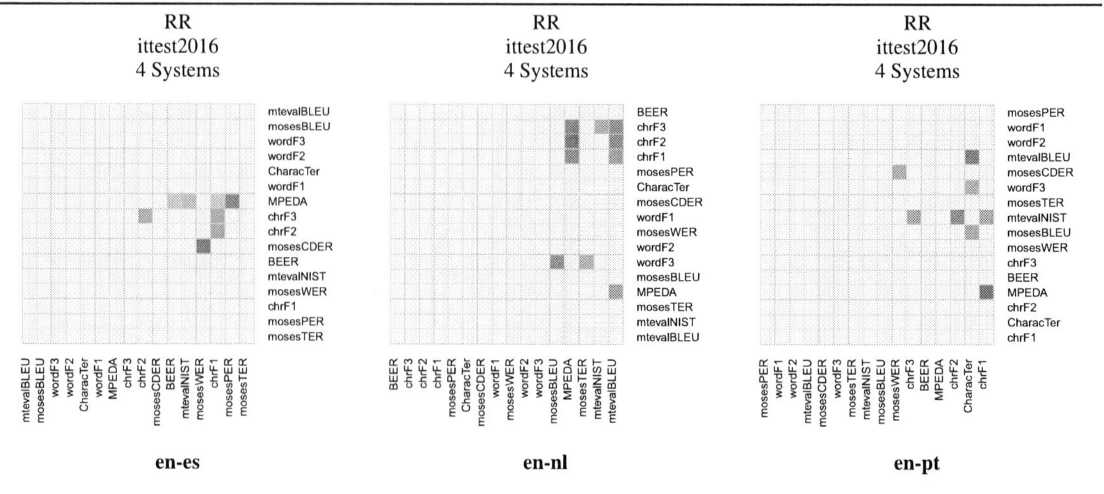

Figure 7: System-level metric ittest2016 significance test results for differences in metric correlation with human assessment for remaining out-of-English language pairs evaluated with relative ranking (RR) human assessment.

Segment-level DA Evaluation Segment-level DA adequacy scores, as described in Section 2.3.2, are employed as gold standard human scores for translations. Since DA segment-level scores are absolute judgments, in their raw (non-standardized) form corresponding simply to a percentage of the absolute adequacy of a given translation, evaluation of metrics simply takes the form of the computation of a Pearson correlation coefficient between metric and DA scores for translations. Significance of differences in metric performance, as in system-level DA metric evaluation, takes the form of Williams test for the significance of a difference in dependent correlations (Williams, 1959; Graham et al., 2015).

Segment-level HUME evaluation The evaluation of segment-level metrics with reference to HUME scores operates in a similar way to DA, by computing the Pearson correlation of HUME evaluation scores for individual translations with metric scores. Williams test is also applied to test for significant differences in metric performance.

Kendall's Tau-like Formulation We measure the quality of metrics' segment-level scores using a Kendall's Tau-like formulation, which is an adaptation of the conventional Kendall's Tau coefficient. Since we do not have a total order ranking of all translations we use to evaluate metrics, it is not possible to apply conventional

Kendall's Tau given the current RR human evaluation setup (Graham et al., 2015). Vazquez-Alvarez and Huckvale (2002) also note that a genuine pairwise comparison is likely to lead to more stable results for segment-level metric evaluation.

Our Kendall's Tau-like formulation, τ, for segment-level evaluation is as follows:

$$\tau = \frac{|Concordant| - |Discordant|}{|Concordant| + |Discordant|} \quad (2)$$

where $Concordant$ is the set of all human comparisons for which a given metric suggests the same order and $Discordant$ is the set of all human comparisons for which a given metric disagrees. The formula is not specific with respect to ties, i.e. cases where the annotation says that the two outputs are equally good.

The way in which ties (both in human and metric judgment) were incorporated in computing Kendall τ has changed across the years of WMT metrics tasks. Here we adopt the version from WMT14 and WMT15. For a detailed discussion on other options, see Macháček and Bojar (2014).

The method is formally described using the following matrix:

Given such a matrix $C_{h,m}$ where $h, m \in \{<, =, >\}$[9] and a metric, we compute the Kendall's τ for the metric the following way:

---

[9]Here the relation $<$ always means "is better than" even for metrics where the better system receives a higher score.

	Metric		
	$<$	$=$	$>$
Human $<$	1	0	-1
$=$	X	X	X
$>$	-1	0	1

$$\tau = \frac{\sum\limits_{\substack{h,m\in\{<,=,>\} \\ C_{h,m}\neq X}} C_{h,m}|S_{h,m}|}{\sum\limits_{\substack{h,m\in\{<,=,>\} \\ C_{h,m}\neq X}} |S_{h,m}|} \qquad (3)$$

We insert each extracted human pairwise comparison into exactly one of the nine sets $S_{h,m}$ according to human and metric ranks. For example the set $S_{<,>}$ contains all comparisons where the left-hand system was ranked better than right-hand system by humans and it was ranked the other way round by the metric in question.

To compute the numerator of our Kendall's τ formulation, we take the coefficients from the matrix $C_{h,m}$, use them to multiply the sizes of the corresponding sets $S_{h,m}$ and then sum them up. We do not include sets for which the value of $C_{h,m}$ is X. To compute the denominator, we simply sum the sizes of all the sets $S_{h,m}$ except those where $C_{h,m} = X$.

To summarize, the WMT16 matrix specifies to:

- exclude all human ties,

- count metric's ties only for the denominator (thus giving no credit for giving a tie),

- all cases of disagreement between human and metric judgments are counted as *Discordant*,

- all cases of agreement between human and metric judgments are counted as *Concordant*.

In previous years, we reported confidence intervals for the Kendall's Tau formulation, see Bojar et al. (2015) for details. However, since the formulation of Kendall's Tau is not computed in the standard way (we do not have a single overall ranking of translations, but rather rankings of sets of 5 translations), the accuracy of confidence intervals computed in this way is difficult to verify. To avoid the risk of drawing incorrect conclusions of significant differences in metric performance, we

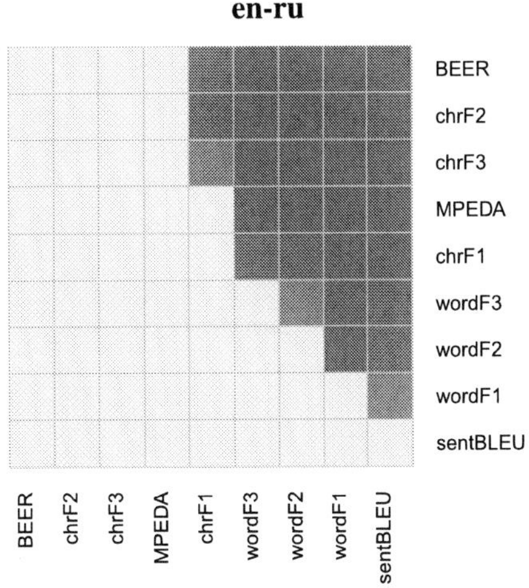

Figure 9: Direct Assessment (DA) segment-level metric significance test results for English to Russian (newstest2016): Green cells denote a significant win for the metric in a given row over the metric in a given column according to Williams test for difference in dependent correlation.

do not include confidence intervals with this year's Kendall's Tau formulation results.

Results of the segment-level human evaluation for translations sampled from the main translation task are shown in Tables 9 and 10, where metric correlations (for DA human assessment variant only) not significantly outperformed by any other metric are highlighted in bold. Since Kendall's Tau are traditionally employed to conclude task winners, while at the same time we currently lack a known reliable method of identifying significant differences between metrics, we postpone announcement of official winning segment-level metrics until further research has been carried out to establish a reliable method in this respect.

DA human assessment pairwise significance test results for differences in metric performance are included for investigatory purposes only in Figures 8 and 9.

Results of segment-level metrics task evaluated with HUME on the himl2015 data set are shown in Table 11, where metrics not significantly outperformed by any other in a given language pair are highlighted in bold, and these metrics are official winners of the himl2015 segment-level metric evaluation. Full pairwise significance test results for all metrics are shown in Figure 10.

Direction	cs-en		de-en		fi-en		ro-en		ru-en		tr-en	
Human Gold	RR	DA	RR	DA	RR	DA	RR	DA	RR	DA	RR	DA
# Assessments	70k	12k	15k	12k	19k	14k	11k	12k	18k	13k	7k	13k
# Translations	8.6k	560	2.4k	560	4.6k	560	2.2k	560	4.7k	560	2.2k	560
Correlation	τ	r	τ	r	τ	r	τ	r	τ	r	τ	r
DPMFcomb	.388	**.713**	.420	**.584**	.481	**.598**	.383	.627	.420	**.615**	.401	**.663**
METRICS-F	.345	**.696**	.421	**.601**	.447	.557	.388	**.662**	.412	**.618**	.424	**.649**
COBALT-F.	.336	.671	.415	**.591**	.433	.554	.361	.639	.397	**.618**	.423	.627
UPF-COBA.	.359	.652	.387	.550	.436	.490	.356	.616	.394	.556	.379	.626
BEER	.342	.661	.371	.462	.416	.471	.331	.551	.376	.533	.372	.545
MPEDA	.331	.644	.375	.538	.425	.513	.339	.587	.387	.545	.335	.616
CHRF2	.341	.658	.358	.457	.418	.469	.344	.581	.383	.534	.346	.556
CHRF3	.343	.660	.351	.455	.421	.472	.341	.582	.382	.535	.345	.555
CHRF1	.323	.644	.372	.454	.410	.452	.339	.570	.379	.522	.345	.551
UoW-ReVal	.261	.577	.329	.528	.376	.471	.313	.547	.314	.528	.342	.531
WORDF3	.299	.599	.293	.447	.377	.473	.304	.525	.343	.504	.287	.536
WORDF2	.297	.596	.296	.445	.378	.471	.300	.522	.341	.503	.283	.537
WORDF1	.290	.585	.293	.435	.369	.464	.293	.508	.336	.497	.275	.535
SENTBLEU	.284	.557	.265	.448	.368	.484	.272	.499	.330	.502	.245	.532
DTED	.201	.394	.130	.254	.209	.361	.144	.329	.201	.375	.142	.267

newstest-2016

Table 9: Segment-level metric results for to-English language pairs (newstest2016): Correlation of segment-level metric scores with human assessment variants, where τ are official results computed similar to Kendall's τ and over standard WMT relative ranking (RR) human assessments; r are Pearson correlation coefficients of metric scores with direct assessment (DA) of absolute translation adequacy; absolute value of correlation coefficients reported for all metrics.

Direction	en-cs		en-de		en-fi		en-ro		en-ru		en-tr	
Human Gold	RR	DA	RR	DA	RR	DA	RR	DA	RR	DA	RR	DA
# Assessments	118k	-	35k	-	31k	-	7k	-	21k	20k	7k	-
# Translations	12.9k	-	6.2k	-	4.1k	-	1.9k	-	6.0k	-	3.0k	-
Correlation	τ	r	τ	r	τ	r	τ	r	τ	r	τ	r
BEER	.422	-	.333	-	.364	-	.307	-	.405	**.666**	.337	-
CHRF2	.420	-	.329	-	.374	-	.304	-	.406	**.661**	.330	-
CHRF3	.421	-	.327	-	.380	-	.304	-	.400	**.661**	.326	-
CHRF1	.402	-	.320	-	.350	-	.305	-	.389	.642	.320	-
MPEDA	.393	-	.274	-	.342	-	.238	-	.372	**.645**	.255	-
WORDF2	.373	-	.247	-	.313	-	.250	-	.358	.580	.218	-
WORDF3	.373	-	.247	-	.314	-	.245	-	.359	.582	.216	-
WORDF1	.369	-	.245	-	.311	-	.248	-	.351	.573	.209	-
SENTBLEU	.359	-	.236	-	.306	-	.233	-	.328	.550	.222	-
CHRF3-2R.	-	-	.334	-	-	-	-	-	-	-	-	-
CHRF2-2R.	-	-	.331	-	-	-	-	-	-	-	-	-
CHRF1-2R.	-	-	.324	-	-	-	-	-	-	-	-	-
WORDF3-2.	-	-	.251	-	-	-	-	-	-	-	-	-
WORDF2-2.	-	-	.251	-	-	-	-	-	-	-	-	-
WORDF1-2.	-	-	.250	-	-	-	-	-	-	-	-	-
DEPCHECK	.109	-	-	-	-	-	-	-	-	-	-	-

newstest-2016

Table 10: Segment-level metric results for out-of-English language pairs (newstest2016): Absolute correlation of segment-level metric scores with human assessment variants, where τ are official results computed similar to Kendall's τ and over standard WMT relative ranking (RR) human assessments; r are Pearson correlation coefficients of metric scores with direct assessment (DA) of absolute translation adequacy; absolute value of correlation coefficients reported for all metrics.

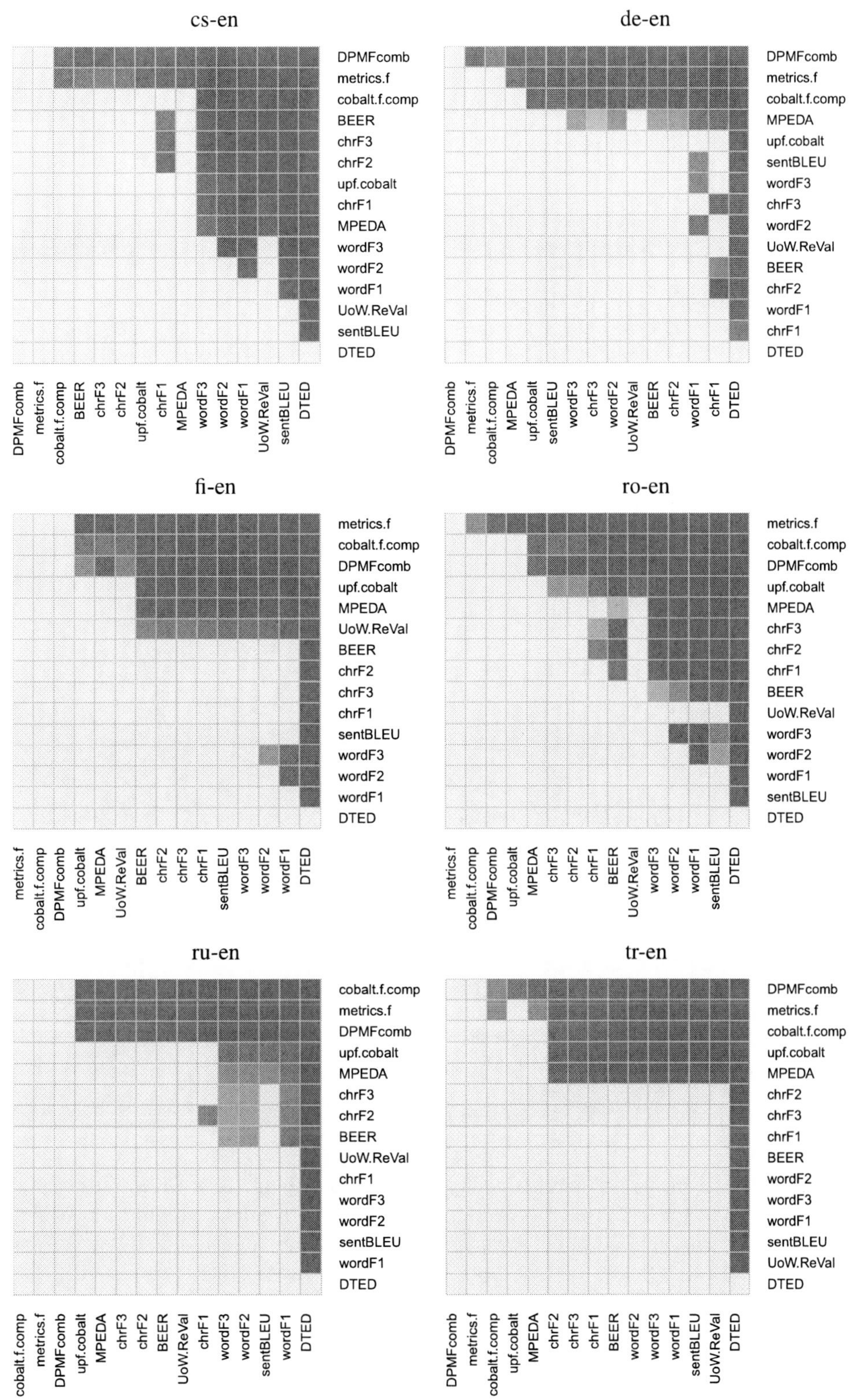

Figure 8: Direct Assessment (DA) segment-level metric significance test results for to-English language pairs (newstest2016): Green cells denote a significant win for the metric in a given row over the metric in a given column according to Williams test for difference in dependent correlation.

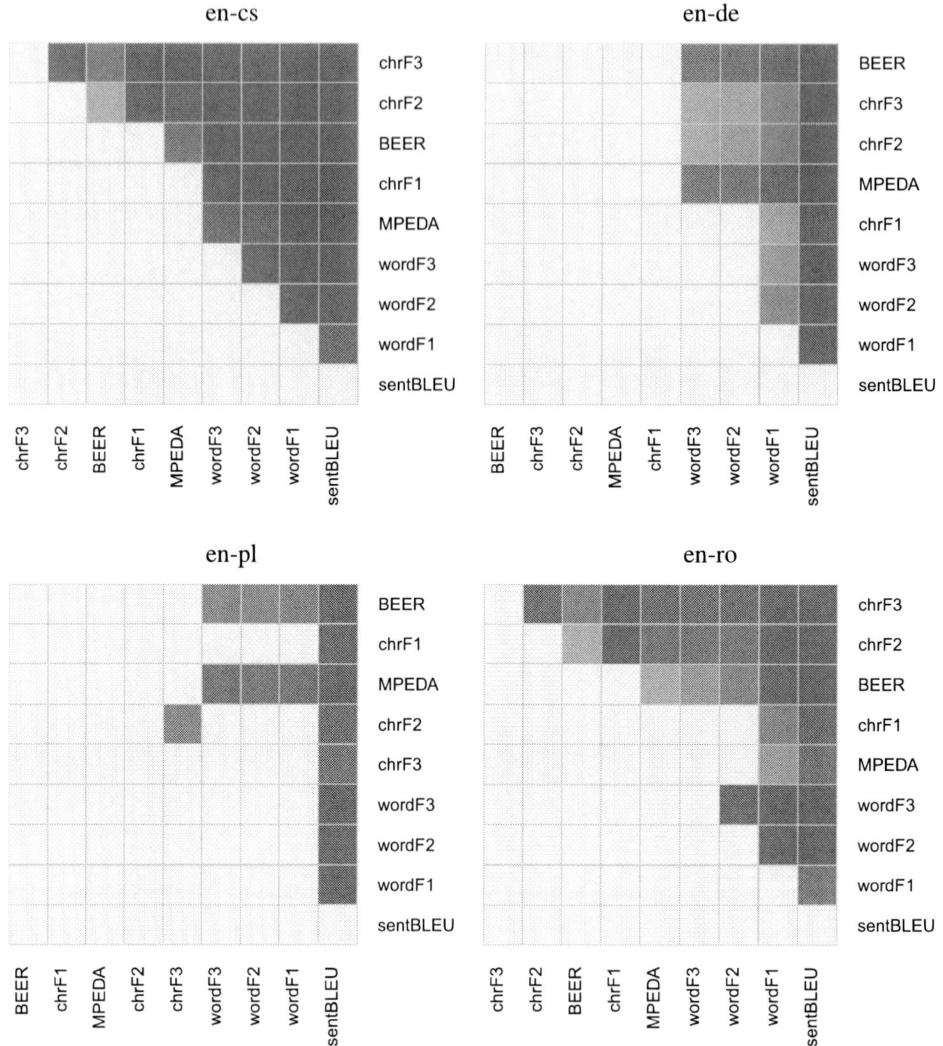

Figure 10: HUME segment-level metric significance test results (himl2015): Green cells denote a significant win for the metric in a given row over the metric in a given column according to Williams test for difference in dependent correlation; Winning metrics are those not significantly outperformed by any other (en-cs: CHRF3; en-de: BEER, CHRF3, CHRF2, MPEDA, CHRF1; en-pl: BEER, CHRF1, MPEDA, CHRF2; en-ro: CHRF3).

Direction	en-cs	en-de	en-ro	en-pl
Human Gold	HUME	HUME	HUME	HUME
n	339	330	349	345
Correlation	r	r	r	r
CHRF3	**.544**	**.480**	**.639**	.413
CHRF2	.537	**.479**	.634	**.417**
BEER	.516	**.480**	.620	**.435**
CHRF1	.506	**.467**	.611	**.427**
MPEDA	.468	**.478**	.595	**.425**
WORDF3	.413	.425	.587	.383
WORDF2	.408	.424	.583	.383
WORDF1	.392	.415	.569	.381
SENTBLEU	.349	.377	.550	.328
		himl-2015		

Table 11: Pearson correlation of segment-level metric scores with HUME human assessment variant.

3.4 Discussion

During the task, the DA evaluation, other than being more principled and discerning, has proved more reliable for crowd-sourcing human evaluation of MT.

It should be noted that DA requires distinct DA human evaluation variants for system and segment-level evaluation, but we may not see this as a negative but rather that DA provides a new method of human evaluation devised specifically for accurate evaluation of segment-level metrics.

Although this year DA was carried out through crowd-sourcing, while RR was completed by researchers, DA is not restricted to crowd-sourcing and could be carried out as-is by researchers or by slight modification by removal of the overhead of translation assessments included in DA for quality control. With any method of human evaluation, if we aim at crowd-sourcing, we must keep in mind that some languages are difficult to obtain workers for, observed in the fact that this year's WMT only collected crowd-sourced assessment for English and Russian as a target language. Although we employed a minimum of 15 human assessors for segment-level evaluation of metrics per segment, it might be worth noting that preliminary empirical evaluation has shown that the 15 human assessments we acquire do not need to be from distinct workers and when repeat assessments are allowed from the same worker, this also yields a correlation of above 0.9 with assessments of translations collected from strictly distinct workers. In other words, DA should be technically viable for all language pairs, if we employ researchers as opposed to crowd-sourced assessors (who may not be available for the language) and if we allow repeated assessments of the same segment by the same person.

Hybrid supersampling is a novel way of doing meta-evaluation of metric performance and it provided more conclusive results. Although we carried out hybrid supersampling for DA human evaluation only, the method is not DA specific, and it would be interesting to trial it with RR the future.

Character-level metrics again gave very good results on both system and segment level. The trend that started on WMT14 with BEER, then continued on WMT15 with BEER and CHRF, now happens with BEER, CHRF and CHARACTER. This growing number of character-level metrics suggests that community (at least the one that develops metrics) had started to adopt character-level matching as an important component of evaluation.

Just like in previous years, metrics that train their parameters get very high correlation with human judgment as exemplified with BEER and UOW.REVAL. This year's edition of the metrics task introduced different types of golden truths that opens the question towards which golden truth should metrics be trained. Should it be for RR by using some learning-to-rank algorithms, or for DA by using regression algorithms or some combination of the two.

The results this year again include surprises. For instance, evaluation of English-to-Czech this year suggests that WORDF, BLEU and NIST outperform CHRF under evaluation against RR both with and without tuning systems (Figure 4) on the news domain, whereas we have seen the exact opposite last year. The IT domain for English-to-Czech stays in line with last year's observations.

BLEU (and especially its Moses implementation) has been clearly outperformed by many metrics. That again highlights the question in MT as to why almost all systems remain to be optimized for BLEU. Optimization towards BLEU has driven system development and certainly achieved results in the past, but the relatively low correlation with human judgment is a sign that some alternative metrics should be considered. For this reason, we encourage metrics developers to add their metric to Moses scorer so that the MT community can more easily experiment with employing them as optimization objective functions. An additional motivation should also be so that valuable development work on metrics is not lost in the future. If added to Moses scorer, future metrics tasks could run easily these metrics as baselines, even if their authors are not participating in the task that year. That way, good performing metrics will live on and the results of the metrics task will be more comparable across years.

4 Conclusion

In this paper, we summarized the results of the WMT16 Metrics Shared Task, which assesses the quality of various automatic machine translation metrics. As in previous years, human judgments collected in WMT16 serve as the golden truth and we check how well the metrics predict the judgments at the level of individual sentences as well as at the level of the whole test set (system-level).

The more extensive meta-evaluation in this years task that involved large number of language pairs, different types of judgments and better measurements of the significance would hopefully shed some more light on the qualities of different metrics.

The patterns that can be observed in the results are that character-level metrics perform really well and that the number of them is growing over the years. Also, the trained metrics on average are performing better than non-trained metrics, especially for into-English language pairs.

Acknowledgments

We wouldn't be able to put this experiment together without tight collaboration with Matt Post and Christian Federmann who were running the core of WMT Shared Translation Task. This project has received funding from the European Union's Horizon 2020 research and innovation programme under grant agreements n° 645452 (QT21) and n° 644402 (HimL). The work on this project was also supported by the Dutch organization for scientific research STW grant nr. 12271.

References

Omri Abend and Ari Rappoport. 2013. Universal Conceptual Cognitive Annotation (UCCA). In *Proceedings of the 51st Annual Meeting of the Association for Computational Linguistics (Volume 1: Long Papers)*, pages 228–238, Sofia, Bulgaria, August. Association for Computational Linguistics.

Alexandra Birch, Barry Haddow, Ondřej Bojar, and Omri Abend. 2016. Hume: Human ucca-based evaluation of machine translation. *arXiv preprint arXiv:1607.00030*.

Ondřej Bojar, Miloš Ercegovčević, Martin Popel, and Omar Zaidan. 2011. A Grain of Salt for the WMT Manual Evaluation. In *Proceedings of the Sixth Workshop on Statistical Machine Translation*, pages 1–11, Edinburgh, Scotland, July. Association for Computational Linguistics.

Ondřej Bojar, Christian Buck, Chris Callison-Burch, Christian Federmann, Barry Haddow, Philipp Koehn, Christof Monz, Matt Post, Radu Soricut, and Lucia Specia. 2013. Findings of the 2013 Workshop on Statistical Machine Translation. In *Proceedings of the Eighth Workshop on Statistical Machine Translation*, pages 1–44, Sofia, Bulgaria, August. Association for Computational Linguistics.

Ondřej Bojar, Rajen Chatterjee, Christian Federmann, Barry Haddow, Matthias Huck, Chris Hokamp, Philipp Koehn, Varvara Logacheva, Christof Monz, Matteo Negri, Matt Post, Carolina Scarton, Lucia Specia, and Marco Turchi. 2015. Findings of the 2015 Workshop on Statistical Machine Translation. In *Proceedings of the Tenth Workshop on Statistical Machine Translation*, Lisboa, Portugal, September. Association for Computational Linguistics.

Ondřej Bojar, Christian Federmann, Barry Haddow, Philipp Koehn, Matt Post, and Lucia Specia. 2016a. Ten Years of WMT Evaluation Campaigns: Lessons Learnt. In *Proceedings of the LREC 2016 Workshop Translation Evaluation From Fragmented Tools and Data Sets to an Integrated Ecosystem*, pages 27–34, Portorose, Slovenia, 5.

Ondřej Bojar, Rajen Chatterjee, Christian Federmann, Yvette Graham, Barry Haddow, Matthias Huck, Antonio Jimeno Yepes, Philipp Koehn, Varvara Logacheva, Christof Monz, Matteo Negri, Aurelie Neveol, Mariana Neves, Martin Popel, Matt Post, Raphael Rubino, Carolina Scarton, Lucia Specia, Marco Turchi, Karin Verspoor, and Marcos Zampieri. 2016b. Findings of the 2016 Conference on Machine Translation. In *Proceedings of the First Conference on Machine Translation*, Berlin, Germany, August. Association for Computational Linguistics.

George Doddington. 2002. Automatic Evaluation of Machine Translation Quality Using N-gram Co-occurrence Statistics. In *Proceedings of the Second International Conference on Human Language Technology Research*, HLT '02, pages 138–145, San Francisco, CA, USA. Morgan Kaufmann Publishers Inc.

Marina Fomicheva, Núria Bel, Lucia Specia, Iria da Cunha, and Anton Malinovskiy. 2016. CobaltF: A Fluent Metric for MT Evaluation. In *Proceedings of the First Conference on Machine Translation*, Berlin, Germany, August. Association for Computational Linguistics.

Yvette Graham and Timothy Baldwin. 2014. Testing for Significance of Increased Correlation with Human Judgment. In *Proceedings of the 2014 Conference on Empirical Methods in Natural Language Processing (EMNLP)*, pages 172–176, Doha, Qatar, October. Association for Computational Linguistics.

Yvette Graham and Qun Liu. 2016. Achieving Accurate Conclusions in Evaluation of Automatic Machine Translation Metrics. In *Proceedings of the 15th Annual Conference of the North American Chapter of the Association for Computational Linguistics: Human Language Technologies*, San Diego, CA. Association for Computational Linguistics.

Yvette Graham, Timothy Baldwin, Alistair Moffat, and Justin Zobel. 2013. Continuous Measurement Scales in Human Evaluation of Machine Translation. In *Proceedings of the 7th Linguistic Annotation Workshop & Interoperability with Discourse*, pages 33–41, Sofia, Bulgaria. Association for Computational Linguistics.

Yvette Graham, Timothy Baldwin, Alistair Moffat, and Justin Zobel. 2014. Is Machine Translation Getting Better over Time? In *Proceedings of the 14th Conference of the European Chapter of the Association for Computational Linguistics*, pages 443–451, Gothenburg, Sweden, April. Association for Computational Linguistics.

Yvette Graham, Nitika Mathur, and Timothy Baldwin. 2015. Accurate Evaluation of Segment-level Machine Translation Metrics. In *Proceedings of the 2015 Conference of the North American Chapter of the Association for Computational Linguistics Human Language Technologies*, Denver, Colorado.

Yvette Graham, Timothy Baldwin, Alistair Moffat, and Justin Zobel. 2016. Can machine translation systems be evaluated by the crowd alone. *Natural Language Engineering*, FirstView:1–28, 1.

Rohit Gupta, Constantin Orasan, and Josef van Genabith. 2015a. Machine Translation Evaluation using Recurrent Neural Networks. In *Proceedings of the Tenth Workshop on Statistical Machine Translation*, Lisboa, Portugal, September. Association for Computational Linguistics.

Rohit Gupta, Constantin Orăsan, and Josef van Genabith. 2015b. ReVal: A Simple and Effective Machine Translation Evaluation Metric Based on Recurrent Neural Networks. In *Proceedings of the 2015 Conference on Empirical Methods in Natural Language Processing (EMNLP)*, Lisbon, Portugal.

Bushra Jawaid, Amir Kamran, Miloš Stanojević, and Ondřej ojar. 2016. Results of the WMT16 Tuning Shared Task. In *Proceedings of the First Conference on Machine Translation*, Berlin, Germany, August. Association for Computational Linguistics.

Philipp Koehn and Christof Monz. 2006. Manual and Automatic Evaluation of Machine Translation Between European Languages. In *Proceedings of the Workshop on Statistical Machine Translation*, StatMT '06, pages 102–121, Stroudsburg, PA, USA. Association for Computational Linguistics.

Gregor Leusch, Nicola Ueffing, and Hermann Ney. 2006. CDER: Efficient MT Evaluation Using Block Movements. In *In Proceedings of EACL*, pages 241–248.

Matouš Macháček and Ondřej Bojar. 2014. Results of the WMT14 metrics shared task. In *Proceedings of the Ninth Workshop on Statistical Machine Translation*, pages 293–301, Baltimore, MD, USA. Association for Computational Linguistics.

Matouš Macháček and Ondřej Bojar. 2013. Results of the WMT13 Metrics Shared Task. In *Proceedings of the Eighth Workshop on Statistical Machine Translation*, pages 45–51, Sofia, Bulgaria, August. Association for Computational Linguistics.

Martin McCaffery and Mark-Jan Nederhof. 2016. DTED: Evaluation of Machine Translation Structure Using Dependency Parsing and Tree Edit Distance. In *Proceedings of the First Conference on Machine Translation*, Berlin, Germany, August. Association for Computational Linguistics.

Kishore Papineni, Salim Roukos, Todd Ward, and Wei-Jing Zhu. 2002. BLEU: A Method for Automatic Evaluation of Machine Translation. In *Proceedings of the 40th Annual Meeting on Association for Computational Linguistics*, ACL '02, pages 311–318.

Maja Popović. 2016. chrF deconstructed: beta parameters and n-gram weights. In *Proceedings of the First Conference on Machine Translation*, Berlin, Germany, August. Association for Computational Linguistics.

Rudolf Rosa. 2014. Depfix, a tool for automatic rule-based post-editing of SMT. *The Prague Bulletin of Mathematical Linguistics*, 102:47–56.

Matthew Snover, Bonnie Dorr, Richard Schwartz, Linnea Micciulla, and John Makhoul. 2006. A study of translation edit rate with targeted human annotation. In *In Proceedings of Association for Machine Translation in the Americas*, pages 223–231.

Miloš Stanojević and Khalil Sima'an. 2015. BEER 1.1: ILLC UvA submission to metrics and tuning task. In *Proceedings of the Tenth Workshop on Statistical Machine Translation*, Lisboa, Portugal, September. Association for Computational Linguistics.

Miloš Stanojević, Amir Kamran, Philipp Koehn, and Ondřej Bojar. 2015. Results of the WMT15 Metrics Shared Task. In *Proceedings of the Tenth Workshop on Statistical Machine Translation*, Lisboa, Portugal, September. Association for Computational Linguistics.

Yolanda Vazquez-Alvarez and Mark Huckvale. 2002. The reliability of the ITU-t p.85 standard for the evaluation of text-to-speech systems. In *Proc. of ICSLP - INTERSPEECH*.

Weiyue Wang, Jan-Thorsten Peter, Hendrik Rosendahl, and Hermann Ney. 2016. CharacTer: Translation Edit Rate on Character Level. In *Proceedings of the First Conference on Machine Translation*, Berlin, Germany, August. Association for Computational Linguistics.

Evan James Williams. 1959. *Regression analysis*, volume 14. Wiley New York.

Hui Yu, Qingsong Ma, Xiaofeng Wu, and Qun Liu. 2015. CASICT-DCU Participation in WMT2015 Metrics Task. In *Proceedings of the Tenth Workshop on Statistical Machine Translation*, Lisboa, Portugal, September. Association for Computational Linguistics.

Lilin Zhang, Zhen Weng, Wenyan Xiao, Jianyi Wan, Zhiming Chen, Yiming Tan, Maoxi Li, and Mingwen Wang. 2016. Extract Domain-specific Paraphrase from Monolingual Corpus for Automatic Evaluation of Machine Translation. In *Proceedings of the First Conference on Machine Translation*, Berlin, Germany, August. Association for Computational Linguistics.

A System-Level Correlation Plots

The following figures plot the system-level results of MTEVALBLEU (left-hand plots) and the best performing (according to RR and DA, see Tables 4, 5 and 7) metrics for the given language pair (right-hand plots) against manual score.

Czech-English

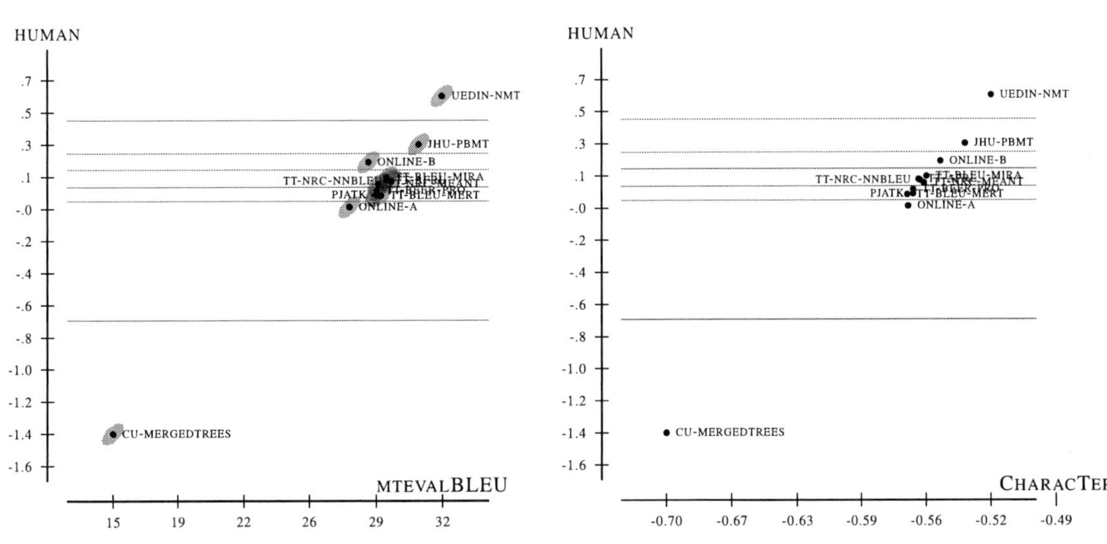

English-Czech

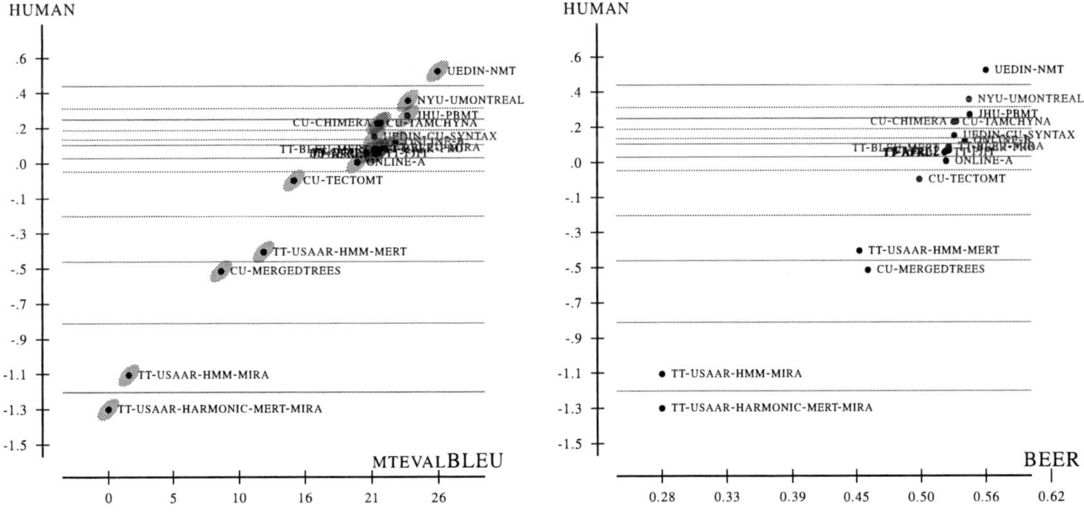

German-English

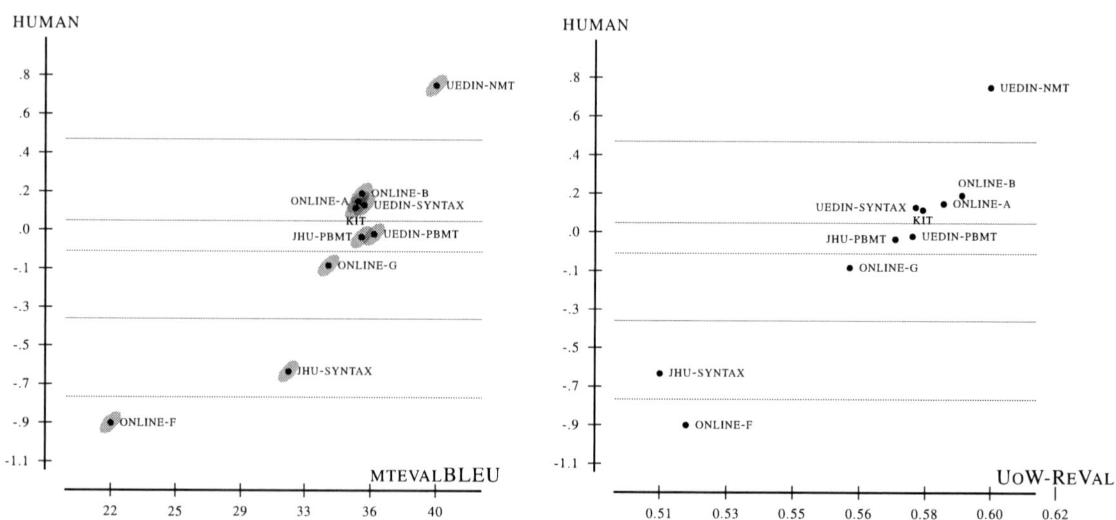

German-English

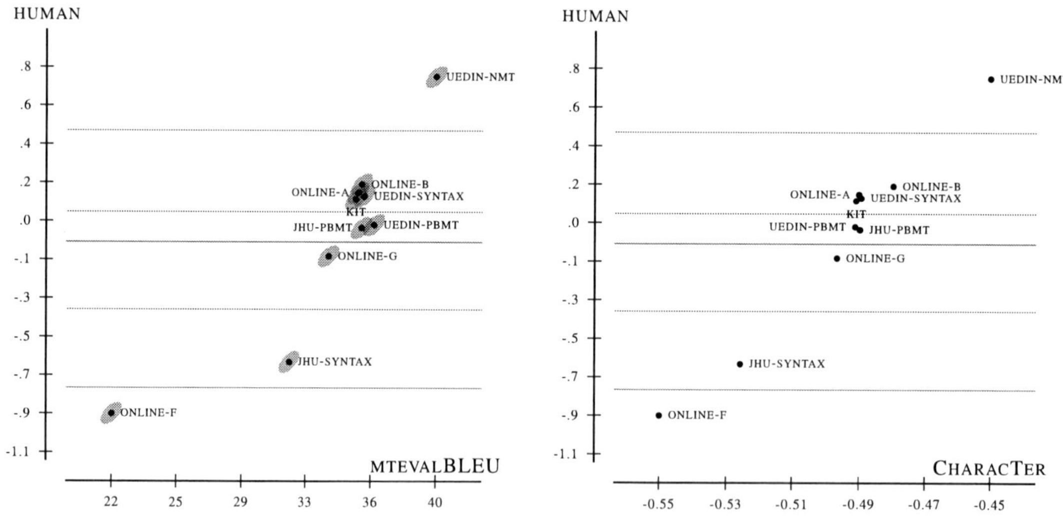

English-German

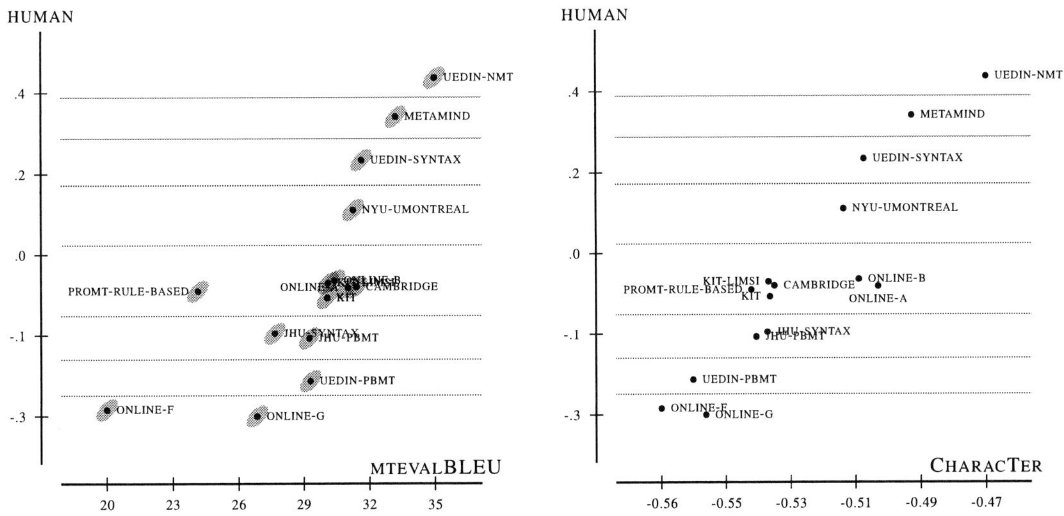

Finnish-English

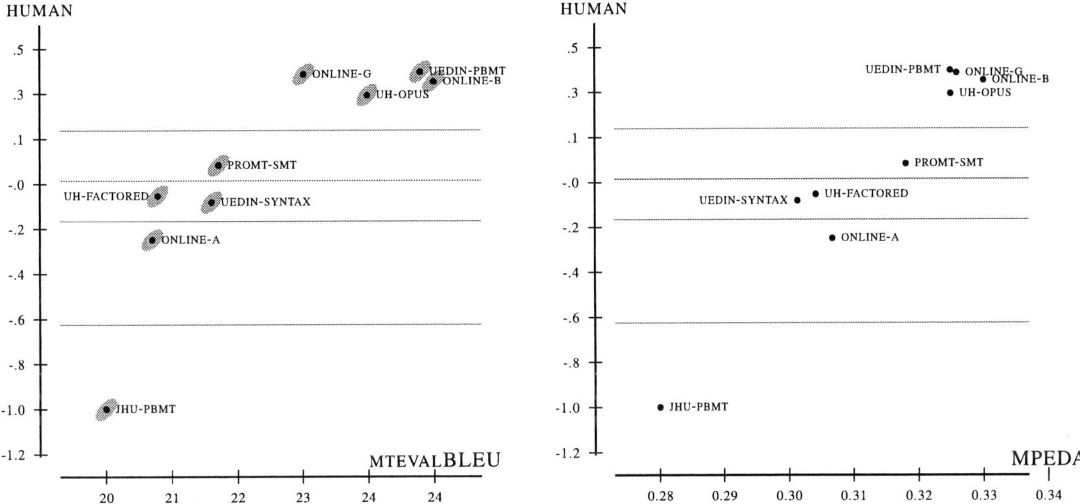

Finnish-English

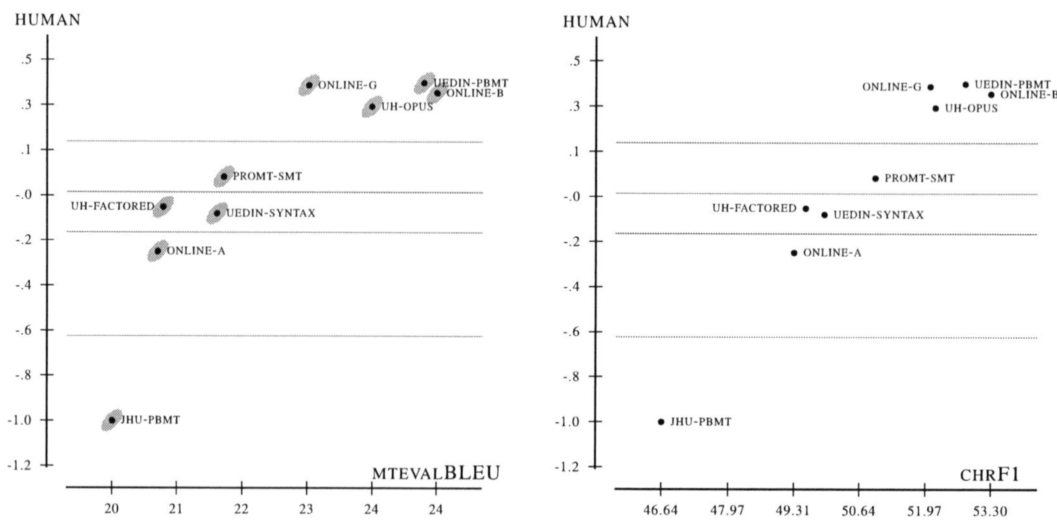

English-Finnish

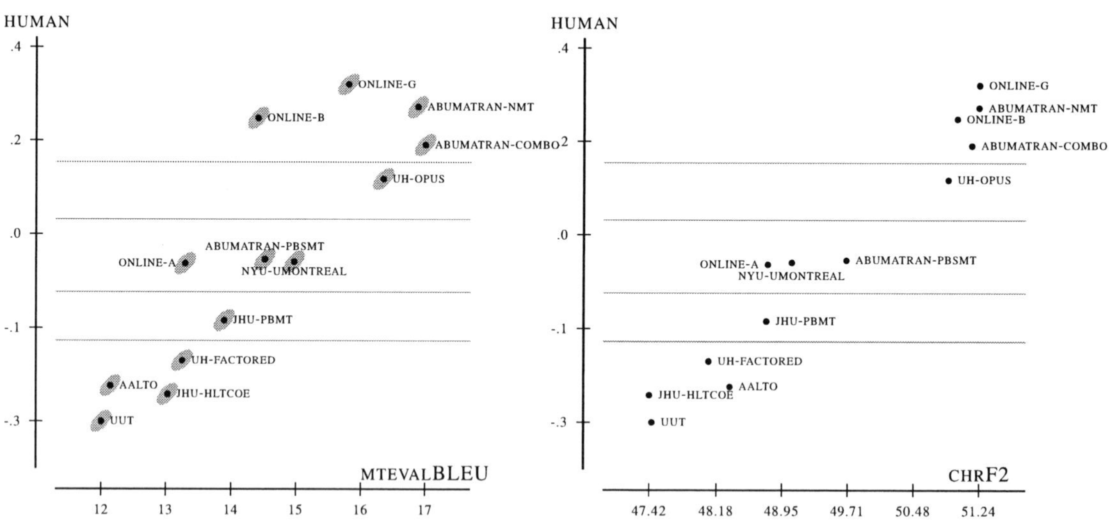

English-Finnish

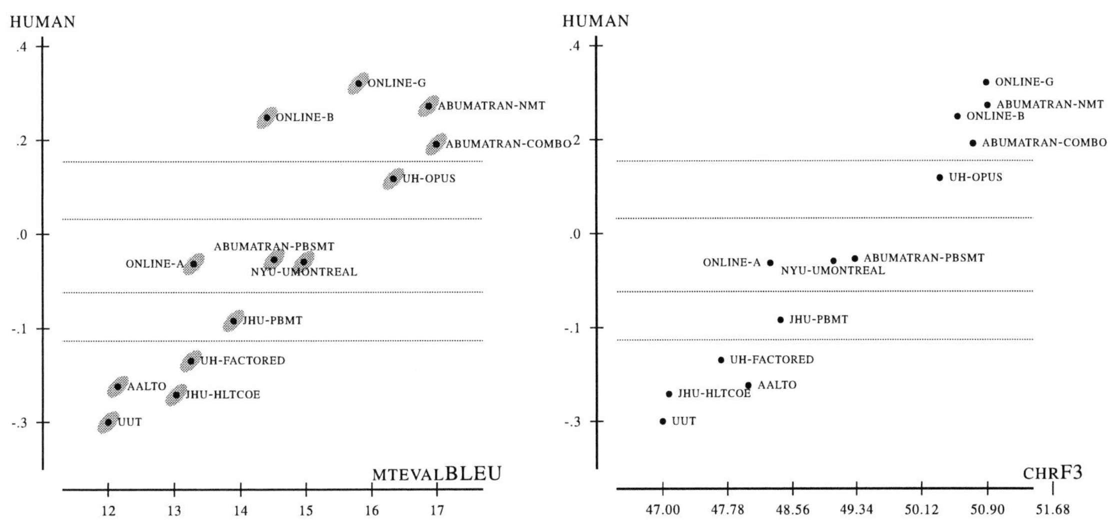

Romanian-English

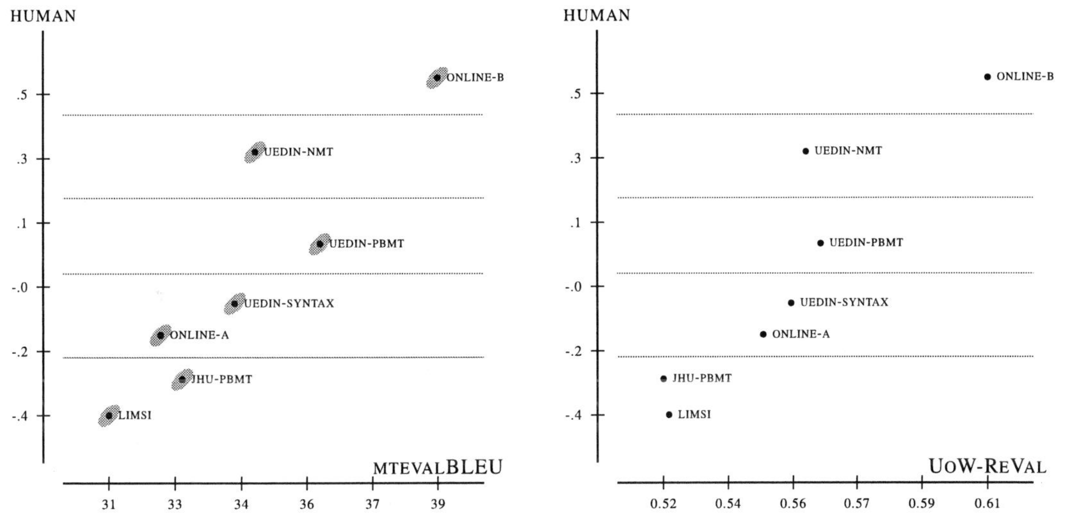

Romanian-English

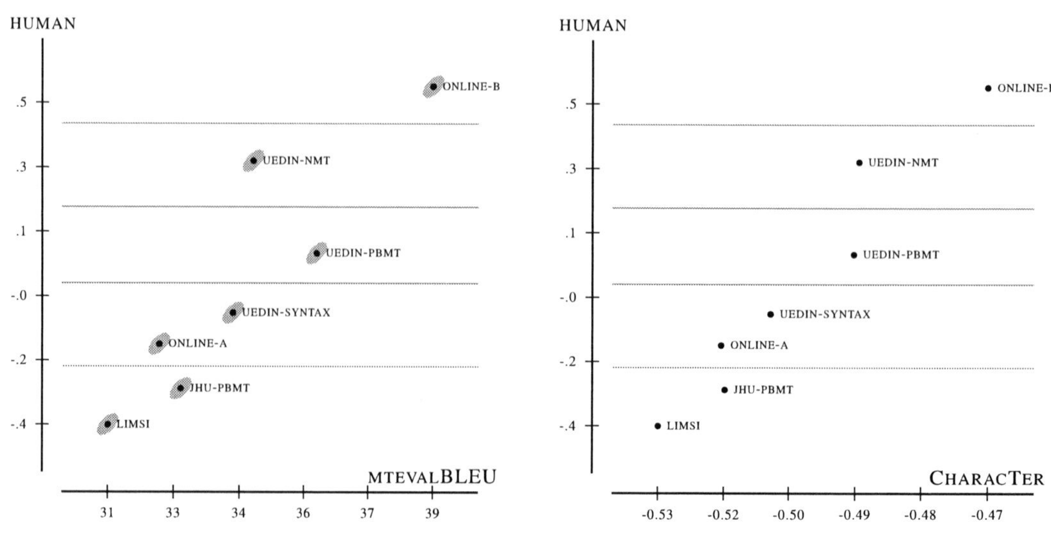

English-Romanian

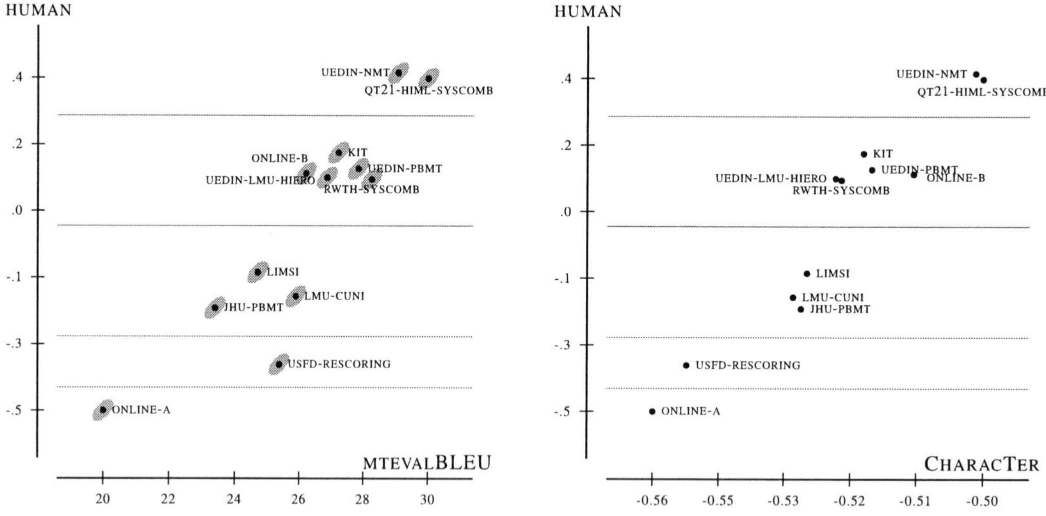

Russian-English

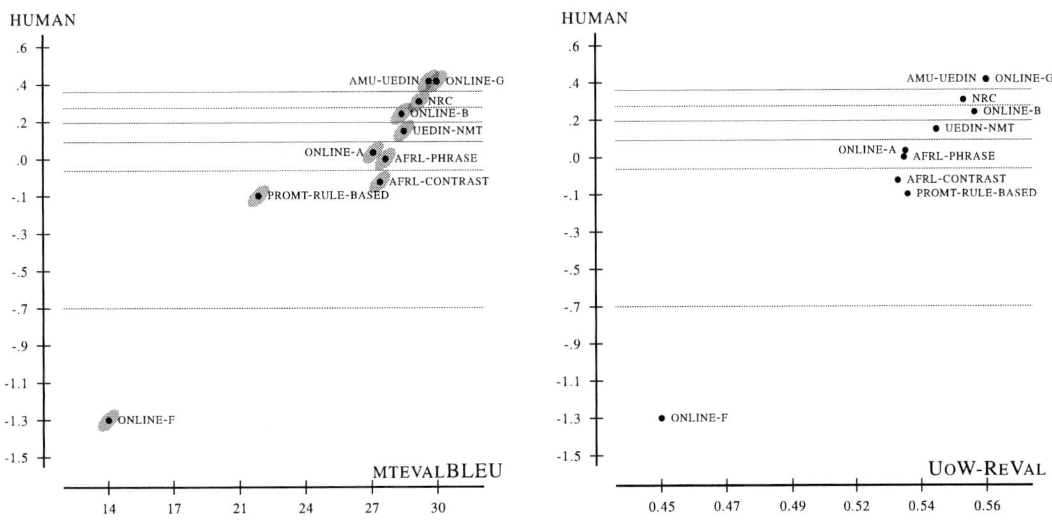

English-Russian

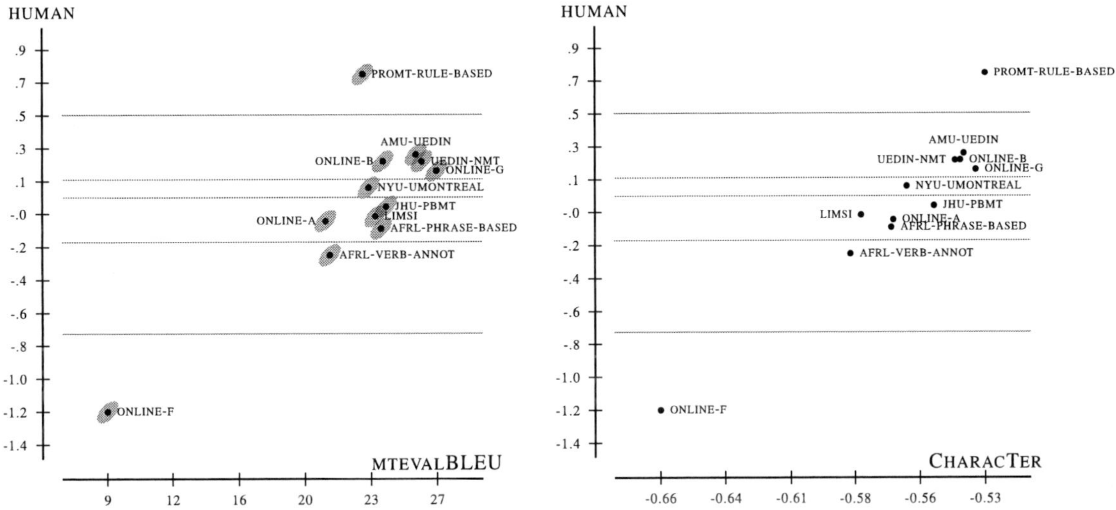

Turkish-English

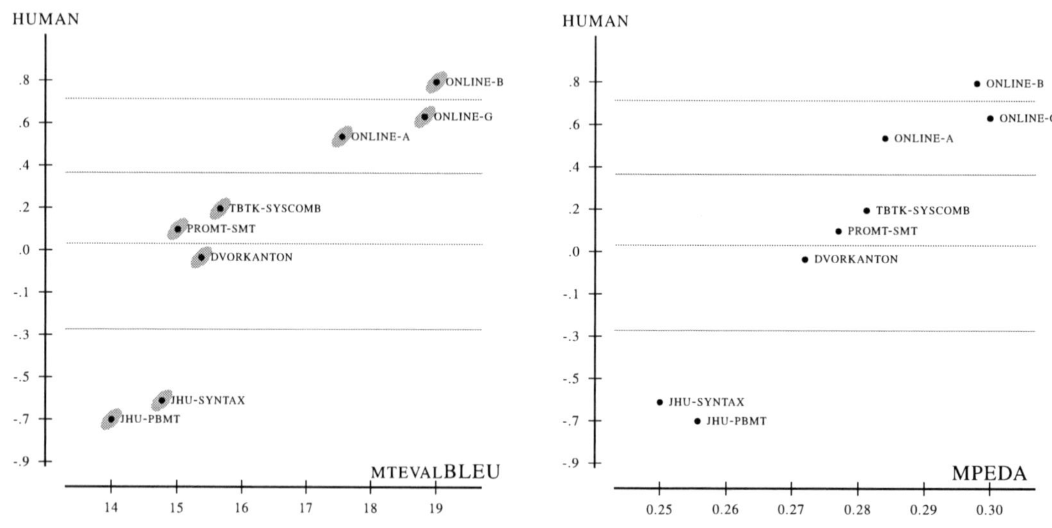

Turkish-English

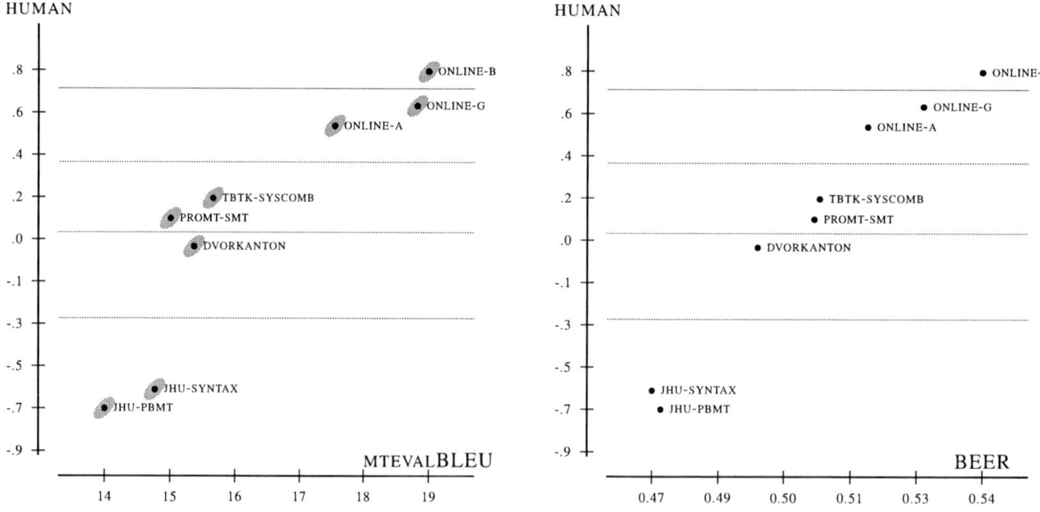

English-Turkish

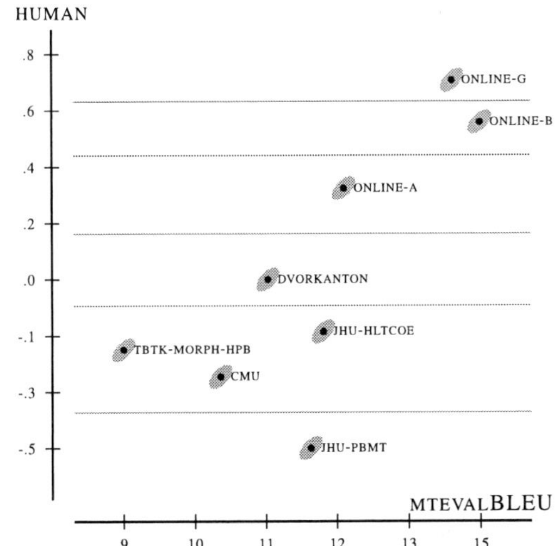

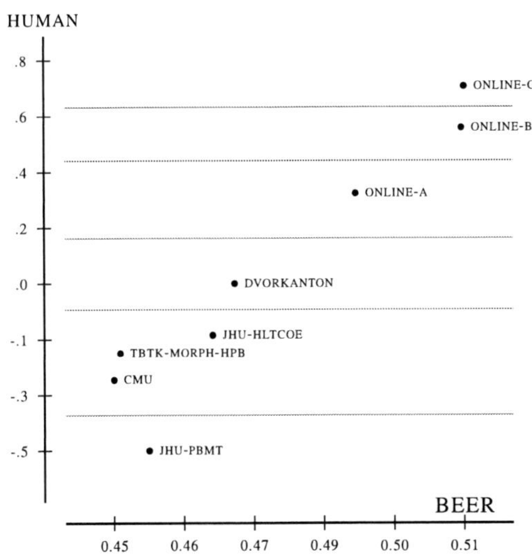

Results of the WMT16 Tuning Shared Task

Bushra Jawaid, Amir Kamran, Miloš Stanojević
University of Amsterdam
ILLC
`{initial.last}@uva.nl`

Ondřej Bojar
Charles University in Prague
MFF ÚFAL
`bojar@ufal.mff.cuni.cz`

Abstract

This paper presents the results of the WMT16 Tuning Shared Task. We provided the participants of this task with a complete machine translation system and asked them to tune its internal parameters (feature weights). The tuned systems were used to translate the test set and the outputs were manually ranked for translation quality. We received 4 submissions in the Czech-English and 8 in the English-Czech translation direction. In addition, we ran 2 baseline setups, tuning the parameters with standard optimizers for BLEU score. In contrast to previous years, the tuned systems in 2016 rely on large data.

1 New Introduction

The standard phrase based and hierarchical statistical machine translation (SMT) systems rely on several models that predict the hypothesis quality. Some of them are taking care that the translations are lexically correct (translation models), some that it is fluent (language models), some that it is not too long (word and phrase penalty) etc. The list of features can go from a dozen to a more than million of sparse features.

Clearly, not all of these features are equally important. For this reason they are combined in a linear model in which each one of the features is assigned a weight that scales its contribution to the total score of the hypothesis.

Estimating these weights has been an important part of MT research for many years. Different learning algorithms have been published, some helpful features proposed and many evaluation metrics considered as alternative objectives for optimization. In search for the best combination of proposed components of weight estimation, we organize this task in which the potential solutions can compete in a controlled setting: a fixed

system to be optimized and a fixed tuning and test set. Everything else is up to the participants.

This way of evaluation of the tuning algorithms and objectives can settle some of the dilemmas that existed in the community. For example, is KBMIRA better than MERT? The choice is usually based on recommendations between researchers or by their comparison on BLEU score which is not always the best way to compare two systems. In this task, we compare the systems based on how humans judge the output of these systems.

Another very common design choice is which objective to optimize. The evaluation metrics are usually designed to correlate well with human judgments of translation quality, see Bojar et al. (2016c) and the previous papers summarizing WMT metrics tasks. However, a metric that correlates well with humans on final output quality may not be usable in weight optimization for various technical reasons. Many metrics that have very high correlation with human judgment achieve that by using complex models that are very slow so they might present a bottle-neck in the tuning process when the chosen evaluation metric needs to evaluate a huge number of translations in the n-best lists.

BLEU (Papineni et al., 2002) was shown to be very hard to surpass (Cer et al., 2010) as a tuning metric and this is also confirmed by the previous WMT15 Tuning Task results (Stanojević et al., 2015) and by the results of the invitation-only WMT11 Tunable Metrics Task (Callison-Burch et al., 2010)[1]. Note however, that some metrics have been successfully used for system tuning (Liu et al., 2011; Beloucif et al., 2014).

The aim of the WMT16 Tuning Task[2] is (just like in WMT15 Tuning Task) to attract attention

---

[1] `http://www.statmt.org/wmt11/tunable-metrics-task.html`

[2] `http://www.statmt.org/wmt16/tuning-task/`

Proceedings of the First Conference on Machine Translation, Volume 2: Shared Task Papers, pages 232–238,
Berlin, Germany, August 11-12, 2016. ©2016 Association for Computational Linguistics

	Source	Sentences		Tokens		Types	
		cs	en	cs	en	cs	en
LM corpora	Europarl v7, News Commentary v11, News Crawl (2007-15), News Discussion v1	54M	206M	900M	4409M	2.1M	3.2M
TM corpora	CzEng 1.6pre for WMT16	44M		501M	587M	1.8M	1.2M
Dev set	newstest2015	2656		46K	54K	12.9K	7.7K
Test set	newstest2016	2999		56.9K	65.3K	15.1K	8.8K

Table 1: Data used in the WMT16 tuning task.

	Dev		Test	
Direction	Token	Type	Token	Type
en-cs	391	314	644	486
cs-en	289	199	507	331

Table 2: Out of vocabulary word counts

to the exploration of all the three aspects of model optimization: (1) the set of features in the model, (2) optimization algorithm, and (3) MT quality metric used in optimization.

For (1), we provide a fixed set of "dense" features and also allow participants to add additional "sparse" features. For (2), the optimization algorithm, task participants are free to use one of the available algorithms for direct loss optimization (Och, 2003; Zhao and Chen, 2009), which are usually capable of optimizing only a dozen of features, or one of the optimizers handling also very large sets of features (Cherry and Foster, 2012; Hopkins and May, 2011), or a custom algorithm. And finally for (3), participants can use any established evaluation metric or a custom one.

1.1 Tuning Task Assignment

The way the tuning task is organized is the same as in the previous WMT15 tuning task (Stanojević et al., 2015). Tuning task participants were given a complete model for the phrase-based variant of the machine translation system Moses (Koehn et al., 2007) and the development set (newstest2015), i.e. the source and reference translations. No "dev test" set was provided, since we expected that participants will internally evaluate various variants of their method by manually judging MT outputs. In fact, we offered to evaluate a certain number of translations into Czech for free to ease the participation for teams without any access to speakers of Czech.

A complete model consists of a phrase table extracted from the parallel corpus, two lexicalized reordering tables and the two language model extracted from the monolingual data. As such, this defines a fixed set of dense features which is big-

ger than last year both in the number of additional models and in the size of the models themselves (language models are trained on much bigger datasets). The participants were allowed to add any sparse features implemented in Moses Release 3.0 (corresponds to Github commit 2d6f616) and/or to use any optimization algorithm and evaluation metric.

Each submission in the tuning task consisted of the configuration of the MT system, i.e. the additional sparse features (if any) and the values of all the feature weights.

2 Details of Systems Tuned

The systems that were distributed for tuning are based on Moses (Koehn et al., 2007) implementation of phrase-based model. The language models were 5-gram models built using KenLM (Heafield et al., 2013) with modified Kneser-Ney smoothing (James, 2000) without pruning. For word alignments, we used fast-align toolkit (Dyer et al., 2013). Alignments are computed in both directions and symmetrized using *grow-diag-final-and* heuristic.

We use CzEng 1.6pre[3] (Bojar et al., 2016b) parallel data for the extraction of translation models. We train two language models for each translation direction: the first model is trained on CzEng 1.6pre target data and the second model is trained on concatenation of Europarl v7, News Commentary data (`parallel-nc-v11`), news data (2007-2013, 2014-v2, 2015) and additionally news discussion v1 (for English language model only), as released for WMT16[4]. We excluded CommonCrawl data because we wanted to avoid data without a clear match with the news domain.

Besides the translation tables and language models we also provided two lexicalised reordering models for each direction. Both reordering

---

[3]`http://ufal.mff.cuni.cz/czeng/`
`czeng16pre`
[4]`http://www.statmt.org/wmt16/`
`translation-task.html`

System	Participant
BLEU-MIRA, BLEU-MERT	baselines
AFRL	United States Air Force Research Laboratory (Gwinnup et al., 2016)
DCU	Dublin City University (Li et al., 2015)
FJFI-PSO	Czech Technical University in Prague (Kocur and Bojar, 2016)
ILLC-UvA-BEER	ILLC – University of Amsterdam (Stanojević and Sima'an, 2015)
NRC-MEANT, NRC-NNBLEU	National Research Council Canada (Lo et al., 2015)
USAAR	Saarland University (Liling Tan; no corresponding paper)

Table 3: Participants of WMT16 Tuning Shared Task

models were extracted using code readily available in Moses. One of the models is word-based (Koehn et al., 2005) and the other is hierarchical (Galley and Manning, 2008). Both reordering models use *msd* orientation in both forward and backward direction, with model conditioned on both the source and target languages (msd-bidirectional-fe).

Before any further processing, the data was pre-tokenized and tokenized (using standard Moses scripts) and lowercased. We also removed parallel sentences longer than 60 words or shorter than 4 words, no data cleaning was performed for monolingual data. Table 1 summarizes the final dataset sizes and Table 2 provides details on out-of-vocabulary items.

Aside from the dev set provided, the participants were free to use any other data for tuning (making their submission "unconstrained"), but no participant decided to do that. All tuning task submissions are therefore also constraint in terms of the WMT16 Translation Task (Bojar et al., 2016a).

We leave all decoder settings (n-best list size, pruning limits etc.) at their default values. While the participants may have used different limits during tuning, the final test run was performed at our site with the default values. It is indeed only the feature weights that differ.

3 Tuning Task Participants

The list of participants and the names of the submitted systems are shown in Table 3.

We provide a brief summary of each evaluated optimization method in the rest of this section, concluding with baseline approaches (Section 3.7).

3.1 ILLC-UvA-BEER

ILLC-UvA-BEER (Stanojević and Sima'an, 2015) was tuned using PRO (Hopkins and May, 2011) learning algorithm with new version of BEER evaluation metric. The authors claim that

common trained evaluation metrics learn to give too much importance to recall and thus lead to overly long translations in tuning. For that reason, they modify the training of BEER to value recall and precision equally. This modified version of BEER is used to train the MT system.

3.2 NRC-MEANT and NRC-NNBLEU

NRC-MEANT is a system tuned against MEANT (Lo et al., 2015) using batch MIRA with an additional length penalty to avoid semantic parsing unreasonably long MT output. Due to the additional huge language model in this year's baseline, the MT system would generate unreasonably long MT output in the second iteration of the tuning cycle. This severely affects the running time of MEANT because running automatic semantic parser on long sentences is costly. Therefore, a length penalty is implemented in MEANT: for MT output that is 2 times or 15 word tokens longer than the reference, MEANT does not run SRL on it and falls back to the backoff bag-of-word phrasal similarity. This could be one of the reasons why MEANT-tuned system is not performing as competitive as last year.

NRC-NNBLEU is a system tuned against a new metric that replaces the n-gram exact match in BLEU with n-gram word embeddings cosine similarity.

3.3 DCU

DCU (Li et al., 2015) is tuned with RED, an evaluation metric based on matching of dependency n-grams. As tuning algorithm the authors have used KBMIRA.

3.4 AFRL1 and AFRL2

As in the previous year's submissions (Erdmann and Gwinnup, 2015), the AFRL systems used Drem, which is a derivative-free optimization algorithm that interpolates n-best lists returned by the decoder. Methodology for the current tuning task is nearly identical, since recent changes to Drem mostly relate to improving treatment of n-best list rescoring techniques (Gwinnup et al., 2016). The objective function used within Drem is the same for cs-en AFRL and en-cs system AFRL1:

$$0.045 \cdot \text{NIST} + 0.45 \cdot \text{Meteor} + 0.1 \cdot \text{Kendall's } \tau.$$

The en-cs system AFRL2 uses the following objective, which tests the sensitivity of the result to the metric and the suitability of the metric chrF3 (Popović, 2015) as a tuning metric:

$$0.045 \cdot \text{NIST} + 0.45 \cdot \text{chrF3} + 0.1 \cdot \text{Kendall's } \tau.$$

The practice of regularizing each metric by using expected (i.e., soft-max) sufficient statistics is maintained as before (Erdmann and Gwinnup, 2015).

3.5 USAAR-*

USAAR submissions are similar to the ones from last year. They use both KBMIRA and MERT for tuning and combine them in different ways. USAAR-HMM trains with KBMIRA and MERT independently and then combines the weights of the final iterations by using harmonic mean. USAAR-HMM-MIRA is the same as USAAR-HMM except that after the harmonic mean is computed, the tuning is continued with KBMIRA for additional 25 iterations. USAAR-HMM-MERT is the same as USAAR-HMM-MIRA except that MERT is used instead of KBMIRA for continuing the training after harmonic averaging.

3.6 FJFI-PSO

FJFI-PSO (Kocur and Bojar, 2016) replaces the "inner optimization loop" in Moses MERT with Particle Swarm Optimization, an algorithm that lends itself easily to parallelization. Everything else in Moses MERT is unchanged and FJFI-PSO optimizes to the default BLEU.

3.7 Baseline Methods

In addition to the systems submitted, we provided three baselines:

- BLEU-MERT-DENSE – MERT tuning with BLEU without additional features

- BLEU-MIRA-DENSE – KBMIRA tuning with BLEU without additional features

Since all the submissions including the baselines were subject to manual evaluation, we did not run the MERT or MIRA optimizations more than once (as is the common practice for estimating variance due to optimizer instability). We simply used the default settings and stopping criteria and picked the weights that performed best on the dev set according to BLEU.

4 Results

We used the submitted `moses.ini` and (optionally) sparse `weights` files to translate the test set. The test set was not available to the participants at the time of their submission (not even the source side). We used the Moses recaser trained on the target side of the parallel corpus to recase the outputs of all the models.

Finally, the recased outputs were manually evaluated, jointly with regular translation task submissions of WMT (Bojar et al., 2016a). Monitoring the results of the tuning task already during the manual evaluation period, we observed that tuning systems perform very similarly. When most of the evaluated language pairs collected sufficient number of manual judgements, we asked the organizers of the translation task evaluation to reopen annotation interface for tuning systems, hoping for better separation of the submissions. The WMT16 evaluation data thus contain a number of annotation items where all ranked translation correspond to output of a tuning system. This subset of annotations may be of special interest, e.g. to analyze the behaviour of annotators when all candidate translations are very similar.

The resulting human rankings were used to compute the overall manual score using the TrueSkill method, same as for the main translation task (Bojar et al., 2016a).[5]

Tables 4 and 5 contain the results of the submitted systems sorted by their manual scores.

The horizontal lines represent separation between clusters of systems that perform similarly. Cluster boundaries are established by the same method as for the main translation task.

---

[5]As in previous year, we also checked TrueSkill scores when only tuning systems would be considered. Since this non-standard evaluation leads to the same clusters of similarly-performing systems as the official TrueSkill does, we do not report it here.

System Name	TrueSkill Score	BLEU
BLEU-MIRA	0.114	22.73
AFRL	0.095	22.90
NRC-NNBLEU	0.090	23.10
NRC-MEANT	0.073	22.60
ILLC-UvA-BEER	0.032	22.46
BLEU-MERT	0.000	22.51

Table 4: Results on Czech-English tuning

System Name	TrueSkill Score	BLEU
BLEU-MIRA	0.160	15.12
ILLC-UvA-BEER	0.152	14.69
BLEU-MERT	0.151	14.93
AFRL2	0.139	14.84
AFRL1	0.136	15.02
DCU	0.134	14.34
FJFI-PSO	0.127	14.68
USAAR-HMM-MERT	-0.433	7.95
USAAR-HMM-MIRA	-1.133	0.82
USAAR-HMM	-1.327	0.20

Table 5: Results on English-Czech tuning

5 Discussion

We see that manual evaluation of tuning systems can draw only very few clear division lines. Czech-to-English has only two clusters of significantly differing quality and English-to-Czech is even less discerning: all except USAAR-* systems fall into the same cluster. The low number of clusters was obtained also last year, but this year, we believe that the situation is worsened by the large-scale setup of the tuned systems.

There are a few observations that can be made about the baseline results.

Just like last year, KBMIRA turns out to consistently be better than MERT even for the system with small number of features. The difference is especially big for Czech-English where system tuned with MERT ended up as the worst and system tuned with KBMIRA as the best.

In fact, KBMIRA tuning for BLEU is not only better than MERT but better than any other tuning system for both language pairs. This baseline is a clear winner of this task. Some systems that did well last year did not repeat their success this year. For example, the last year's winner for English-Czech DCU was unfortunately worse than both baselines and three other systems.

Except for the winning baseline, the results do not generalize much over translation direction. ILLC-UvA-BEER is second best in English-Czech but second worst in Czech-English. Its success on English-Czech can probably be explained by character-level scoring that is important for morphologically rich language such as Czech.

The submitted systems used different combinations of tuning algorithms (MERT, KBMIRA, PRO, Drem or combinations of MERT and KBMIRA) and different metrics (BEER, BLEU, RED, MEANT and combinations of chrF, NIST, METEOR and Kendall τ) so it is difficult to see which aspect of the system contributed most to its results. Systems that we can compare directly are for example AFRL1 and AFRL2 where the main difference was that AFRL2 uses chrF3 in its mixture of metrics instead of METEOR. This particular variation has contributed to slight improvement in human score, but it degraded the BLEU score.

Optimizing for BLEU does not seem to be always beneficial. Even though the systems tuned for BLEU did well in the task, the systems that got the best BLEU scores are not the winning systems. For Czech-English, NRC-NNBLEU got the best BLEU score result, but it ended up third. Also, tuning for BEER with PRO consistently outperforms tuning for BLEU with MERT. It is difficult to say whether this is because PRO is a better learning algorithm or because BEER is a better metric. However, if we use KBMIRA instead of MERT then evaluation with BLEU seems to be sufficient to outperform all the other systems.

6 Conclusion

We presented the results of WMT16 Tuning Task, a shared task in optimizing parameters of a given phrase-based system when translating from English to Czech and vice versa.

This year, the tuned system was a large-scale one, trained on almost all of the available data in the constrained translation task. All the tuning task submissions were thus on the scale of a standard WMT system, validating the applicability of proposed methods from practical point of view. Given that the number of submitted systems was very similar to last year, we conclude that the participants succeeded in this challenge.

Overall, six teams took part in one or both directions, sticking to the constrained setting.

The submitted configurations were manually evaluated jointly with the systems of the main WMT translation task.

The results confirm that KBMIRA with the standard (dense) features optimized towards BLEU should be preferred over MERT. The clear winner of the task was KBMIRA system tuned for BLEU score, although the quality of most submitted systems is hard to distinguish manually.

Acknowledgments

We would like to thank to Christian Federmann for support during manual evaluation and to Matt Post for providing us with various types of outputs from the manual WMT ranking. This project has received funding from the European Union's Horizon 2020 research and innovation programme under grant agreements n° 645452 (QT21) and n° 644402 (HimL). The work on this project was also supported by the Dutch organisation for scientific research STW grant nr. 12271.

References

Meriem Beloucif, Chi-kiu Lo, and Dekai Wu. 2014. Improving MEANT Based Semantically Tuned SMT. In *Proc. of 11th International Workshop on Spoken Language Translation (IWSLT 2014)*, pages 34–41, Lake Tahoe, California.

Ondřej Bojar, Rajen Chatterjee, Christian Federmann, Yvette Graham, Barry Haddow, Matthias Huck, Antonio Jimeno Yepes, Philipp Koehn, Varvara Logacheva, Christof Monz, Matteo Negri, Aurelie Neveol, Mariana Neves, Martin Popel, Matt Post, Raphael Rubino, Carolina Scarton, Lucia Specia, Marco Turchi, Karin Verspoor, and Marcos Zampieri. 2016a. Findings of the 2016 Conference on Machine Translation. In *Proceedings of the First Conference on Machine Translation*, Berlin, Germany, August. Association for Computational Linguistics.

Ondřej Bojar, Ondřej Dušek, Tom Kocmi, Jindřich Libovický, Michal Novák, Martin Popel, Roman Sudarikov, and Dušan Variš. 2016b. CzEng 1.6: Enlarged Czech-English Parallel Corpus with Processing Tools Dockered. In *Text, Speech and Dialogue: 19th International Conference, TSD 2016, Brno, Czech Republic, September 12-16, 2016, Proceedings*. Springer Verlag, September 12-16. In press.

Ondřej Bojar, Yvette Graham, , and Amir Kamran Miloš Stanojević. 2016c. Results of the WMT16 Metrics Shared Task . In *Proceedings of the First Conference on Machine Translation*, Berlin, Germany, August. Association for Computational Linguistics.

Chris Callison-Burch, Philipp Koehn, Christof Monz, Kay Peterson, Mark Przybocki, and Omar Zaidan. 2010. Findings of the 2010 Joint Workshop on Statistical Machine Translation and Metrics for Machine Translation. In *Proceedings of the Joint Fifth Workshop on Statistical Machine Translation and MetricsMATR*, pages 17–53, Uppsala, Sweden, July.

Association for Computational Linguistics. Revised August 2010.

Daniel Cer, Christopher D. Manning, and Daniel Jurafsky. 2010. The Best Lexical Metric for Phrasebased Statistical MT System Optimization. In *Human Language Technologies: The 2010 Annual Conference of the North American Chapter of the Association for Computational Linguistics*, HLT '10, pages 555–563, Stroudsburg, PA, USA. Association for Computational Linguistics.

Colin Cherry and George Foster. 2012. Batch Tuning Strategies for Statistical Machine Translation. In *Proceedings of the 2012 Conference of the North American Chapter of the Association for Computational Linguistics: Human Language Technologies*, NAACL HLT '12, pages 427–436, Stroudsburg, PA, USA. Association for Computational Linguistics.

Chris Dyer, Victor Chahuneau, and Noah A. Smith. 2013. A Simple, Fast, and Effective Reparameterization of IBM Model 2. In *Proceedings of the 2013 Conference of the North American Chapter of the Association for Computational Linguistics: Human Language Technologies*, pages 644–648, Atlanta, Georgia, June. Association for Computational Linguistics.

Grant Erdmann and Jeremy Gwinnup. 2015. Drem: The AFRL Submission to the WMT15 Tuning Task. In *Proceedings of the Tenth Workshop on Statistical Machine Translation*, Lisboa, Portugal, September. Association for Computational Linguistics.

Michel Galley and Christopher D. Manning. 2008. A Simple and Effective Hierarchical Phrase Reordering Model. In *Proceedings of the Conference on Empirical Methods in Natural Language Processing*, EMNLP '08, pages 848–856, Stroudsburg, PA, USA. Association for Computational Linguistics.

Jeremy Gwinnup, Tim Anderson, Grant Erdmann, Katherine Young, Michaeel Kazi, Elizabeth Salesky, and Brian Thompson. 2016. The AFRL-MITLL WMT16 News-Translation Task Systems. In *Proceedings of the First Conference on Machine Translation*, Berlin, Germany, August. Association for Computational Linguistics.

Kenneth Heafield, Ivan Pouzyrevsky, Jonathan H. Clark, and Philipp Koehn. 2013. Scalable Modified Kneser-Ney Language Model Estimation. In *Proceedings of the 51st Annual Meeting of the Association for Computational Linguistics*, pages 690–696, Sofia, Bulgaria, August.

Mark Hopkins and Jonathan May. 2011. Tuning As Ranking. In *Proceedings of the Conference on Empirical Methods in Natural Language Processing*, EMNLP '11, pages 1352–1362, Stroudsburg, PA, USA. Association for Computational Linguistics.

Frankie James. 2000. Modified Kneser-Ney Smoothing of N-gram Models. Technical report.

Viktor Kocur and Ondřej Bojar. 2016. Particle Swarm Optimization Submission for WMT16 Tuning Task. In *Proceedings of the First Conference on Machine Translation*, Berlin, Germany, August. Association for Computational Linguistics.

Philipp Koehn, Amittai Axelrod, Alexandra B. Mayne, Chris Callison-Burch, Miles Osborne, and David Talbot. 2005. Edinburgh System Description for the 2005 IWSLT Speech Translation Evaluation. In *Proceedings of International Workshop on Spoken Language Translation*.

Philipp Koehn, Hieu Hoang, Alexandra Birch, Chris Callison-Burch, Marcello Federico, Nicola Bertoldi, Brooke Cowan, Wade Shen, Christine Moran, Richard Zens, Chris Dyer, Ondřej Bojar, Alexandra Constantin, and Evan Herbst. 2007. Moses: Open Source Toolkit for Statistical Machine Translation. In *Proceedings of the 45th Annual Meeting of the ACL on Interactive Poster and Demonstration Sessions*, ACL '07, pages 177–180, Stroudsburg, PA, USA. Association for Computational Linguistics.

Liangyou Li, Hui Yu, and Qun Liu. 2015. MT Tuning on RED: A Dependency-Based Evaluation Metric. In *Proceedings of the Tenth Workshop on Statistical Machine Translation*, Lisboa, Portugal, September. Association for Computational Linguistics.

Chang Liu, Daniel Dahlmeier, and Hwee Tou Ng. 2011. Better Evaluation Metrics Lead to Better Machine Translation. In *Proceedings of the Conference on Empirical Methods in Natural Language Processing*, EMNLP '11, pages 375–384, Stroudsburg, PA, USA. Association for Computational Linguistics.

Chi-kiu Lo, Philipp Dowling, and Dekai Wu. 2015. Improving evaluation and optimization of MT systems against MEANT. In *Proceedings of the Tenth Workshop on Statistical Machine Translation*, Lisboa, Portugal, September. Association for Computational Linguistics.

Franz Josef Och. 2003. Minimum Error Rate Training in Statistical Machine Translation. In *Proceedings of the 41st Annual Meeting on Association for Computational Linguistics - Volume 1*, ACL '03, pages 160–167, Stroudsburg, PA, USA. Association for Computational Linguistics.

Kishore Papineni, Salim Roukos, Todd Ward, and Wei-Jing Zhu. 2002. BLEU: A Method for Automatic Evaluation of Machine Translation. In *Proceedings of the 40th Annual Meeting on Association for Computational Linguistics*, ACL '02, pages 311–318.

Maja Popović. 2015. chrF: character n-gram F-score for automatic MT evaluation. In *Proceedings of the Tenth Workshop on Statistical Machine Translation*, Lisboa, Portugal, September. Association for Computational Linguistics.

Miloš Stanojević and Khalil Sima'an. 2015. BEER 1.1: ILLC UvA submission to metrics and tuning task. In *Proceedings of the Tenth Workshop on Statistical Machine Translation*, Lisboa, Portugal, September. Association for Computational Linguistics.

Miloš Stanojević, Amir Kamran, and Ondřej Bojar. 2015. Results of the WMT15 Tuning Shared Task. In *Proceedings of the Tenth Workshop on Statistical Machine Translation*, Lisboa, Portugal, September. Association for Computational Linguistics.

Bing Zhao and Shengyuan Chen. 2009. A Simplex Armijo Downhill Algorithm for Optimizing Statistical Machine Translation Decoding Parameters. In *HLT-NAACL (Short Papers)*, pages 21–24. The Association for Computational Linguistics.

LIMSI@WMT'16: Machine Translation of News

Alexandre Allauzen[1], Lauriane Aufrant[1,2], Franck Burlot[1], Elena Knyazeva[1],
Ophélie Lacroix[1], Thomas Lavergne[1], Guillaume Wisniewski[1], François Yvon[1]
[1]LIMSI, CNRS, Univ. Paris-Sud, Université Paris Saclay, 91 403 Orsay, France
[2] DGA, 60 boulevard du Général Martial Valin, 75 509 Paris, France
`firstname.lastname@limsi.fr`

Abstract

This paper describes LIMSI's submissions to the shared WMT'16 task "Translation of News". We report results for Romanian-English in both directions, for English to Russian, as well as preliminary experiments on reordering to translate from English into German. Our submissions use mainly NCODE and MOSES along with continuous space models in a post-processing step. The main novelties of this year's participation are the following: for the translation into Russian and Romanian, we have attempted to extend the output of the decoder with morphological variations and to use a CRF model to rescore this new search space; as for the translation into German, we have been experimenting with source-side pre-ordering based on a dependency structure allowing permutations in order to reproduce the target word order.

1 Introduction

This paper documents LIMSI's participation to the shared task of machine translation of news for three language pairs: English to Russian, Romanian-English in both directions and English to German. The reported experiments are mainly related to two challenging domains: inflection prediction and word order in morphologically rich languages.

In our systems translating from English into Romanian and Russian, we have attempted to address the difficulties that go along with translating into morphologically reach languages. First, a baseline system outputs sentences in which we reconsider the choices previously made for inflected words by generating their full paradigm. Second, a CRF model is expected to make better choices than the translation system.

For English to German, experiments are reported on the pre-ordering of the source sentence. Using the dependency structure of the sentence, the model predicts permutations of source words that lead to an order that is as close as possible to the right order in the target language.

2 System Overview

Our experiments mainly use NCODE,[1] an open source implementation of the n-gram approach, as well as MOSES[2] for some contrastive experiments. For more details about these toolkits, the reader can refer to (Koehn et al., 2007) for MOSES and to (Crego et al., 2011) for NCODE.

2.1 Data pre-processing and word alignments

All the English and Russian data have been cleaned by normalizing character encoding.

Tokenization for English text relies on in-house text processing tools (Déchelotte et al., 2008). For the Russian corpora, we used the `TreeTagger` tokenizer. For Romanian, we developed and used `tokro`, a rule-based tokenizer. After normalization of diacritics, it repeatedly applies 3 rules: (a) word splitting on slashes, except for url addresses, (b) isolation of punctuation characters from a pre-defined set (including quotes, parentheses and ellipses as triple dots) adjoined at the beginning or end of words (considering a few exceptions like 'Dr.' or 'etc.') and (c) clitic tokenization on hyphens, notably for 'nu', 'dă', 'și' and unstressed personal pronouns. The hyphen is kept on the clitic token. Multi-word expressions are not joined into a single token.

---

[1]`http://ncode.limsi.fr`
[2]`http://www.statmt.org/moses/`

Proceedings of the First Conference on Machine Translation, Volume 2: Shared Task Papers, pages 239–245,
Berlin, Germany, August 11-12, 2016. ©2016 Association for Computational Linguistics

The parallel corpora were tagged and lemmatized using `TreeTagger` (Schmid, 1994) for English and Russian (Sharoff and Nivre, 2011). The same pre-processing was obtained for Romanian with the TTL tagger and lemmatizer (Tufiş et al., 2008). Having noticed many sentence alignment errors and out-of-domain parts in the Russian common-crawl parallel corpus, we have used a bilingual sentence aligner[3] and proceeded to a domain adaptation filtering using the same procedure as for monolingual data (see section 2.2). As a result, one third of the initial corpus has been removed. Apart from the russian wiki-headlines corpus, the systems presented below used all the parallel data provided by the shared task.

Word alignments were trained according to IBM model 4, using MGIZA.

2.2 Language modelling and domain adaptation

Various English, Romanian and Russian language models (LM) were trained on the in-domain monolingual corpora, a subset of the common-crawl corpora and the relevant side of the parallel corpora (for English, the English side of the Czech-English parallel data was used). We trained 4-gram LMs, pruning all singletons with `lmplz` (Heafield, 2011).

In addition to in-domain monolingual data, a considerable amount of out-of-domain data was provided this year, gathered in the common-crawl corpora. Instead of directly training an LM on these corpora, we extracted from them in-domain sentences using the Moore-Lewis (Moore and Lewis, 2010) filtering method, more specifically its implementation in `XenC` (Rousseau, 2013). As a result, the common-crawl sub-corpora we have used contained about 200M sentences for Romanian and 300M for Russian and English. Finally, we perform a linear interpolation of these models, using the SRILM toolkit (Stolcke, 2002).

2.3 NCODE

NCODE implements the bilingual n-gram approach to SMT (Casacuberta and Vidal, 2004; Crego and Mariño, 2006b; Mariño et al., 2006) that is closely related to the standard phrase-based approach (Zens et al., 2002). In this framework, the translation is divided into two steps. To translate a source sentence **f** into a target sentence **e**, the source sentence is first reordered according to a set of rewriting rules so as to reproduce the target word order. This generates a word lattice containing the most promising source permutations, which is then translated. Since the translation step is monotonic, the peculiarity of this approach is to rely on the n-gram assumption to decompose the joint probability of a sentence pair in a sequence of bilingual units called tuples.

$$e^* = \arg\max_{\mathbf{e},\mathbf{a}} \sum_{k=1}^{K} \lambda_k f_k(\mathbf{f}, \mathbf{e}, \mathbf{a})$$

where K feature functions (f_k) are weighted by a set of coefficients (λ_k) and **a** denotes the set of hidden variables corresponding to the reordering and segmentation of the source sentence. Along with the n-gram translation models and target n-gram language models, 13 conventional features are combined: 4 *lexicon models* similar to the ones used in standard phrase-based systems; 6 *lexicalized reordering models* (Tillmann, 2004; Crego et al., 2011) aimed at predicting the orientation of the next translation unit; a "weak" distance-based *distortion model*; and finally a *word-bonus model* and a *tuple-bonus model* which compensate for the system preference for short translations. Features are estimated during the training phase. Training source sentences are first reordered so as to match the target word order by unfolding the word alignments (Crego and Mariño, 2006a). Tuples are then extracted in such a way that a unique segmentation of the bilingual corpus is achieved (Mariño et al., 2006) and n-gram translation models are then estimated over the training corpus composed of tuple sequences made of surface forms or POS tags. Reordering rules are automatically learned during the unfolding procedure and are built using part-of-speech (POS), rather than surface word forms, to increase their generalization power (Crego and Mariño, 2006a).

2.4 Continuous-space models

Neural networks, working on top of conventional n-gram back-off language models, have been introduced in (Bengio et al., 2003; Schwenk et al., 2006) as a potential means to improve conventional language models. More recently, these techniques have been applied to statistical machine translation in order to estimate continuous-space translation models (CTMs) (Schwenk et al., 2007; Le et al., 2012a; Devlin et al., 2014).

---

[3] *Bilingual Sentence Aligner*, available at `http://research.microsoft.com/apps/catalog/`

As in our previous participations (Le et al., 2012b; Allauzen et al., 2013; Pécheux et al., 2014; Marie et al., 2015), we take advantage of the proposal of (Le et al., 2012a). Using a specific neural network architecture, the *Structured OUtput Layer* (SOUL), it becomes possible to estimate n-gram models that use large output vocabulary, thereby making the training of large neural network language models feasible both for target language models (Le et al., 2011) and translation models (Le et al., 2012a). Moreover, the peculiar parameterization of continuous models allows us to consider longer dependencies than the one used by conventional n-gram models (e.g. $n = 10$ instead of $n = 4$). Initialization is an important issue when optimizing neural networks. For CTMs, a solution consists in pre-training monolingual n-gram models. Their parameters are then used to initialize bilingual models.

Given the computational cost of computing n-gram probabilities with neural network models, a solution is to resort to a two-pass approach: the first pass uses a conventional system to produce a k-best list (the k most likely hypotheses); in the second pass, probabilities are computed by continuous-space models for each hypothesis and added as new features. For this year evaluation, we used the following models: one continuous target language model and four CTMs as described in (Le et al., 2012a).

For English to Russian and Romanian to English, the models have the same architecture:

- words are projected into a 500-dimensional vector space;

- the feed-forward architecture includes two hidden layers of size 1000 and 500;

- the non-linearity is a sigmoid function;

All models are trained for 20 epochs, then the selection relies on the perplexity measured on a validation set. For CTMs, the validation sets are sampled from the parallel training data.

3   Experiments

For all our experiments, the MT systems are tuned using the `kb-mira` algorithm (Cherry and Foster, 2012) implemented in MOSES, including the reranking step. POS tagging is performed using the `TreeTagger` (Schmid, 1994) for English and Russian (Sharoff and Nivre, 2011), and TTL (Tufiş et al., 2008) for Romanian.

3.1   Development and test sets

Since only one development set was provided for Romanian, we split the given development set into two equal parts: newsdev-2016/1 and newsdev-2016/2. The first part was used as development set while the second part was our internal test set.

The Russian development and test sets we have used consisted in shuffled sentences from newstest 2012, 2013 and 2014. Tests were also performed on newstest-2015.

3.2   Hidden-CRF for inflection prediction

In morphologically rich languages, each single lemma corresponds to a large number of word forms that are not all observed in the training data. A traditional statistical translation system can not generate a non-observed form. On the other hand, even if a form has been seen at training time, it might be hard to use it in a relevant way if its frequency is low, which is a common phenomena, since the number of singletons in Romanian and Russian corpora is a lot higher than in English corpora. In such a situation, surface heuristics are less reliable.

In order to address this limitation, we tried to extend the output of the decoder with morphological variations of nouns, pronouns and adjectives. Therefore, for each word in the output baring one of these PoS-tags, we introduced all forms in the paradigm as possible alternatives. The paradigm generation was performed for Russian using pymorphy, a dictionary implemented as a Python module.[4] For Romanian, we used the crawled (thus sparse) lexicon introduced in (Aufrant et al., 2016).

Once the outputs were extended, we used a CRF model to rescore this new search space. The CRF can use the features of the MT decoder, but can also include morphological or syntactic features in order to estimate output scores, even for words that were not observed in the training data.

In the Russian experiment, oracle scores show that a maximum gain of 6.3 BLEU points can be obtained if the extension is performed on the full search space and 2.3 BLEU points on 300-best output of the NCODE decoder. The full search space, while being more promising, proved to be too large to be handled by the CRF, so the following experiments were performed on the 300-best output.

---

[4] `http://pymorphy.readthedocs.io/`

In order to train this model, we split the parallel data in two parts. The first (largest) part was used to train the translation system baseline. The second part was used for the training of the hidden CRF. First, the source side was translated with the baseline system, then the resulting output was extended (paradigm generation). References were obtained by searching for oracle translations in the augmented output. Models were trained using in-house implementation of hidden CRF (Lavergne et al., 2013) and used features from the decoder as well as additional ones: unigram and bigram of words and POS-tags; number, gender and case of the forms and of the surrounding ones; and information about nearest prepositions and verbs.

3.3 Experimental results

The experimental results were not conclusive, as, in the best configuration for Russian our model achieved the same results as the baseline and slightly worsened the NCODE+SOUL system (see Table 1).

System	MOSES	NCODE
Baseline	22.91	23.05
Baseline + SOUL		23.75
Baseline + Hidden-CRF		23.03
Baseline + SOUL + Hidden-CRF		23.46

Table 1: Results (BLEU) for English-Russian with NCODE and MOSES on the official test.

	System	MOSES	NCODE
En-Ro	Baseline	23.98	24.15
	Baseline + Hidden-CRF		23.68
Ro-En	Baseline	30.41	29.90
	Baseline + SOUL		30.60

Table 2: Results (BLEU) for English:Romanian with NCODE and MOSES on the official test.

As for Romanian (Table 2), our model performed worse than for Russian. We assume that this must be partly due to the sparsity of the lexicon used for Romanian, with which we only generated partial paradigms, as opposed to full paradigms for Russian.

3.4 Reordering experiments for English to German

NCODE translates a sentence by first re-ordering the source sentence and then monotonically decoding it. Reorderings of the source sentence are compactly encoded in a permutation lattice generated by iteratively applying POS-based reordering rules extracted from the parallel data.

In this year's WMT evaluation campaign we investigated ways to improve the re-ordering step by re-implementing the approach proposed by (Lerner and Petrov, 2013). This approach aims at taking advantage of the dependency structure of the source sentence to predict a permutation of the source words that is as close as possible to a correct syntactic word order in the target language: starting from the root of the dependency tree a classifier is used to recursively predict the order of a node and all its children. More precisely, for a family[5] of size n, a multiclass classifier is used to select the best ordering of this family among its $n!$ permutations. A different classifier is trained for each possible family size.

Predicting the best re-ordering These experiments were only performed for English to German translation. The source sentences were PoS-tagged and dependency parsed using the MATEPARSER (Bohnet and Nivre, 2012) trained on the UDT v2.0. The parallel source and target sentences were aligned in both directions with FASTALIGN (Dyer et al., 2013) and these alignments were merged with the intersection heuristic.[6]

The training set used to learn the classifiers is generated as follows: during a depth-first traversal of each source sentence, an example is extracted from a node if each child of this node is aligned with exactly one word in the target sentence. In this case, it is possible, by following the alignment links, to extract the order of the family members in the target language. An example is therefore a permutation of n members (1 head and its $n - 1$ children).

In practice, we did not extract training examples from families having more than 8 members[7] and train 7 classifiers (one binary classifier for the family made of a head and a single dependent and 6 multi-class classifiers able to discriminate between up to 5 040 classes). Our experiments used

---

[5]Following (Lerner and Petrov, 2013), we call family a head in a dependency tree and all its children.

[6]Preliminary experiments with the gdfa heuristic showed that the symmetrization heuristic has no impact on the quality of the predicted pre-ordering.

[7]Families with more than 8 members account for less than 0.5% of the extracted examples.

VOWPAL WABBIT, a very efficient implementation of the logistic regression capable to handle a large number of output classes.[8] The features used for training are the same as those proposed by (Lerner and Petrov, 2013): word forms, PoS-tags, relative positions of the head, children, their siblings and the gaps between them, etc.

Building permutation lattices In order to mitigate the impact of errouneously predicted word preorderings, we propose to build lattices of permutations rather than using just one reordering of the source sentence. This lattice includes the two best predicted permutations *at each node*.

It is built as follows: starting from an automaton with a single arc between the initial state and the final state labeled with the ROOT token, each arc is successively substituted by two automata describing two possible re-orderings of the token t corresponding to this arc label and its children in the dependency tree. Each of these automata has $n + 1$ arcs corresponding to the n children of t in the dependency tree and t itself that appear in the predicted order. The weight of the first arc is defined as the probability predicted by the classifier; all other arcs have a weight of 0.

MT experiments We report preliminary results for pre-ordering. All the source side of training data is reordered using the method described above. Then, the reordered source side, along with the target side, are considered as the new parallel training data on which a new NCODE system is trained (including new word alignment, tuple extraction, ...). For tuning and test steps, the learned classifiers are used to generate a permutation lattice that will be decoded.

In the following experiments, we use only news-commentary and Europarl datasets as parallel training data; the development and test sets are, respectively, newstest-2014 and newstest-2015.

These preliminary experiments show a significant decrease in BLEU score which deserves closer investigations. This performance drop is more important when more reordering paths ("2-best" in Table 3) are proposed to the MT system. A similar trend was also observed when using a dependency-based model only to predict the reordering lattices for a system trained on raw data and without the pre-ordering step.

As shown in Table 4, in a large majority of cases

Baseline system		
	dev	test
rule-based	19.4	18.5
Dependency-based pre-ordering		
	dev	test
1-best	18.5	17.7
2-best	18.2	17.2

Table 3: Translation results for pre-ordering on the English to German translation task

the members of a family have the same order in the source and in the target languages, a trend that is probably amplified by our instance extraction strategy. Dealing with skewed classes is a challenging problem in machine learning and it is not surprising that the performance of the classifier is rather low for the minority classes (see results in Table 4). It is interesting to note that the standard rule-based approach does not suffer from the class imbalance problem as all re-orderings observed in the training data are considered without taking into account their probability.

4 Discussion and Conclusion

This paper described LIMSI's submission to the shared WMT'16 task "Translation of News". We reported results for English-Romanian in both directions and for English into Russian, as well as English into German for which we have investigated pre-ordering of the source sentence. Our submissions used NCODE and MOSES along with continuous space translation models in a post-processing step. Most of our efforts this year were dedicated to the main difficulties of morphologically rich languages: word order and inflection prediction.

For the translation from English into Romanian and Russian, the generation of the paradigm of inflectional words and choice of the right word form using a CRF did not give any improvement over the baseline in our experimental conditions. The reason may be due to the fact that we did not only expect that the CRF would make a better choice than the baseline system regarding word inflection, we also assumed that these morphological predictions would help to make right decisions regarding lexical choices and word order. This was our motivation to run such a decoding extension

---

size	% mono.	prec.	prec. mono.	prec. non-mono.
2	85.6	88.2	97.6	31.5
3	71.3	79.0	95.5	37.6
4	62.0	74.3	95.9	38.8
5	51.8	68.4	91.8	43.2
6	41.9	53.4	81.8	32.8
7	46.2	14.7	18.3	11.6
8	25.0	7.5	12.1	6.0

Table 4: % of family that have the same order in English and German (% mono.), overall prediction performance (prec.) as well as precision for monotonic and non-monotonic reordering.

over the n-best hypotheses made by the baseline system: the CRF is then supposed to make decisions that go beyond word inflection, since it returns a single best translation. Presumably, the resulting search space turned out to be too complex for our CRF model to make relevant choices. We plan in the nearest future to address this issue by exploring a way to rely on the CRF for inflection prediction only.

We finally reiterate our past observations that continuous space translation models used in a post-processing step always yielded significant improvements across the board.

5   Acknowledgments

We would like to thank the anonymous reviewers for their helpful comments and suggestions. This work has been partly funded by the European Union's Horizon 2020 research and innovation programme under grant agreement No. 645452 (QT21).

References

Alexandre Allauzen, Nicolas Pécheux, Quoc Khanh Do, Marco Dinarelli, Thomas Lavergne, Aurélien Max, Hai-son Le, and François Yvon. 2013. LIMSI @ WMT13. In *Proceedings of WMT*, Sofia, Bulgaria.

Lauriane Aufrant, Guillaume Wisniewski, and François Yvon. 2016. Cross-lingual and supervised models for morphosyntactic annotation: a comparison on Romanian. In *Proceedings of the Tenth International Conference on Language Resources and Evaluation (LREC'16)*, Portorož, Slovenia, May. European Language Resources Association (ELRA).

Yoshua Bengio, Réjean Ducharme, Pascal Vincent, and Christian Jauvin. 2003. A neural probabilistic language model. *Journal of Machine Learning Research*.

Bernd Bohnet and Joakim Nivre. 2012. A transition-based system for joint part-of-speech tagging and labeled non-projective dependency parsing. In *Proceedings of the 2012 Joint Conference on Empirical Methods in Natural Language Processing and Computational Natural Language Learning*, pages 1455–1465, Jeju Island, Korea, July. Association for Computational Linguistics.

Francesco Casacuberta and Enrique Vidal. 2004. Machine translation with inferred stochastic finite-state transducers. *Computational Linguistics*, 30(3):205–225.

Colin Cherry and George Foster. 2012. Batch tuning strategies for statistical machine translation. In *Proceedings of NAACL-HLT*, Montréal, Canada.

Josep M. Crego and José B. Mariño. 2006a. Improving statistical MT by coupling reordering and decoding. *Machine Translation*, 20.

Joseph M. Crego and José B. Mariño. 2006b. Improving statistical mt by coupling reordering and decoding. *Machine translation*, 20(3):199–215, Jul.

Josep M. Crego, François Yvon, and José B. Mariño. 2011. N-code: an open-source bilingual N-gram SMT toolkit. *Prague Bulletin of Mathematical Linguistics*, 96.

Daniel Déchelotte, Gilles Adda, Alexandre Allauzen, Olivier Galibert, Jean-Luc Gauvain, Hélène Maynard, and François Yvon. 2008. LIMSI's statistical translation systems for WMT'08. In *Proceedings of NAACL-HTL Statistical Machine Translation Workshop*, Columbus, Ohio.

Jacob Devlin, Rabih Zbib, Zhongqiang Huang, Thomas Lamar, Richard Schwartz, and John Makhoul. 2014. Fast and robust neural network joint models for statistical machine translation. In *Proceedings of the 52nd Annual Meeting of the Association for Computational Linguistics (Volume 1: Long Papers)*, pages 1370–1380, Baltimore, Maryland, June. Association for Computational Linguistics.

Chris Dyer, Victor Chahuneau, and Noah A. Smith. 2013. A simple, fast, and effective reparameterization of ibm model 2. In *Proceedings of NAACL*, Atlanta, Georgia.

Kenneth Heafield. 2011. KenLM: Faster and Smaller Language Model Queries. In *Proceedings of WMT*, Edinburgh, Scotland.

Philipp Koehn, Hieu Hoang, Alexandra Birch, Chris Callison-Burch, Marcello Federico, Nicola Bertoldi, Brooke Cowan, Wade Shen, Christine Moran, Richard Zens, Chris Dyer, Ondrej Bojar, Alexandra Constantin, and Evan Herbst. 2007. Moses: Open source toolkit for statistical machine translation. In *Proceedings of the ACL Demo*, Prague, Czech Republic.

Thomas Lavergne, Alexandre Allauzen, and François Yvon. 2013. A fully discriminative training framework for statistical machine translation (un cadre d'apprentissage intégralement discriminant pour la traduction statistique) [in french]). In *Proceedings of TALN 2013 (Volume 1: Long Papers)*, pages 450–463, Les Sables d'Olonne, France, June. ATALA.

Hai-Son Le, Ilya Oparin, Alexandre Allauzen, Jean-Luc Gauvain, and François Yvon. 2011. Structured output layer neural network language model. In *Proceedings of ICASSP*, Prague, Czech Republic.

Hai-Son Le, Alexandre Allauzen, and François Yvon. 2012a. Continuous space translation models with neural networks. In *Proceedings of NAACL-HLT*, Montréal, Canada.

Hai-Son Le, Thomas Lavergne, Alexandre Allauzen, Marianna Apidianaki, Li Gong, Aurélien Max, Artem Sokolov, Guillaume Wisniewski, and François Yvon. 2012b. LIMSI @ WMT12. In *Proceedings of WMT*, Montréal, Canada.

Uri Lerner and Slav Petrov. 2013. Source-side classifier preordering for machine translation. In *Proceedings of the 2013 Conference on Empirical Methods in Natural Language Processing*, pages 513–523, Seattle, Washington, USA, October. Association for Computational Linguistics.

Benjamin Marie, Alexandre Allauzen, Franck Burlot, Quoc-Khanh Do, Julia Ive, elena knyazeva, Matthieu Labeau, Thomas Lavergne, Kevin Löser, Nicolas Pécheux, and François Yvon. 2015. LIMSI@WMT'15 : Translation task. In *Proceedings of the Tenth Workshop on Statistical Machine Translation*, pages 145–151, Lisbon, Portugal, September. Association for Computational Linguistics.

José B. Mariño, Rafael E. Banchs, Josep M. Crego, Adrià de Gispert, Patrik Lambert, José A. R. Fonollosa, and Marta R. Costa-jussà. 2006. N-gram-based machine translation. *Comput. Linguist.*, 32(4):527–549, December.

Robert C. Moore and William Lewis. 2010. Intelligent selection of language model training data. In *Proceedings of the ACL 2010 Conference Short Papers*, ACLShort '10, pages 220–224, Stroudsburg, PA, USA. Association for Computational Linguistics.

Nicolas Pécheux, Li Gong, Quoc Khanh Do, Benjamin Marie, Yulia Ivanishcheva, Alexandre Allauzen, Thomas Lavergne, Jan Niehues, Aurélien Max, and François Yvon. 2014. LIMSI @ WMT14 Medical Translation Task. In *Proceedings of WMT*, Baltimore, Maryland.

Anthony Rousseau. 2013. Xenc: An open-source tool for data selection in natural language processing. *The Prague Bulletin of Mathematical Linguistics*, (100):73–82.

Helmut Schmid. 1994. Probabilistic part-of-speech tagging using decision trees. In *Proceedings of ICNMLP*, Manchester, England.

Holger Schwenk, Daniel Déchelotte, and Jean-Luc Gauvain. 2006. Continuous space language models for statistical machine translation. In *Proceedings of the COLING/ACL*, Morristown, US.

Holger Schwenk, Marta R. Costa-jussa, and Jose A. R. Fonollosa. 2007. Smooth bilingual n-gram translation. In *Proceedings of the Conference on Empirical Methods in Natural Language Processing (EMNLP)*, pages 430–438, Prague, Czech Republic, June. Association for Computational Linguistics.

Serge Sharoff and Joakim Nivre. 2011. The proper place of men and machines in language technology processing russian without any linguistic knowledge. In *Russian Conference on Computational Linguistics*.

Andreas Stolcke. 2002. SRILM – An Extensible Language Modeling Toolkit. In *Proc. of the Int. Conf. on Speech and Language Processing (ICSLP)*, volume 2, pages 901–904, Denver, CO, September.

Christoph Tillmann. 2004. A unigram orientation model for statistical machine translation. In *Proceedings of HLT-NAACL 2004: Short Papers*, HLT-NAACL-Short '04, pages 101–104, Stroudsburg, PA, USA. Association for Computational Linguistics.

Dan Tufiş, Radu Ion, Ru Ceauşu, and Dan Ştefănescu. 2008. Racai's linguistic web services. In *Proceedings of the Sixth International Conference on Language Resources and Evaluation (LREC'08)*, Marrakech, Morocco, May. European Language Resources Association (ELRA).

Richard Zens, Franz Josef Och, and Hermann Ney. 2002. Phrase-Based Statistical Machine Translation. In *25th German Conf. on Artificial Intelligence (KI2002)*, pages 18–32, Aachen, Germany, September. Springer Verlag.

TÜBİTAK SMT System Submissions for WMT 2016

Emre Bektaş, Ertuğrul Yılmaz, Coşkun Mermer, İlknur Durgar El-Kahlout
TÜBİTAK-BİLGEM
Gebze 41470, Kocaeli, Turkey
{emre.bektas,yilmaz.ertugrul,coskun.mermer,ilknur.durgar}@tubitak.gov.tr

Abstract

We describe the TÜBİTAK Turkish-English machine translation systems submissions in both directions for the WMT 2016: News Translation Task. We experiment with phrase-based and hierarchical phrase-based systems for both directions using word-level and morpheme-level representations for the Turkish side. Finally we perform system combination which results in 0.5 BLEU increase for Turkish-to-English and 0.3 BLEU increase for English-to-Turkish.

1 Introduction

This paper presents TÜBİTAK's submissions for the news translation task of the First Conference on Machine Translation (WMT16) held at ACL 2016. Overview of the systems can be described as follows: We use both word-level and morphological feature-based representation of Turkish for both directions. We experiment with both phrase-based and hierarchical phrase-based systems. A large 5-gram language model is trained with data extracted from the common crawl corpus provided in Turkish and a 4-gram gigaword language model is used for English. Augmenting the training data with its content words (add a new parallel corpora to training consisting of only the content words for both languages) and using reversed training data on the source side in order to achieve better alignments at the root-word level and surface forms, are amongst the methods we employ. Finally system combination of systems with different paradigms is performed.

This paper is organized as follows: Section 2 introduces the challenges of practicing SMT for the Turkish-English language pair and summarizes the previous work. Section 3 provides background on the base SMT approaches we experiment with. Section 4 provides the experimental specifications and reports on the results in both directions. We conclude with section 5.

2 Turkish-English Statistical Machine Translation

Development of statistical machine translation (SMT) systems of typologically different languages have traditionally been quite challenging. The morphological complexity of Turkish compared to English as well as the constituency order difference between these languages makes the SMT practices especially challenging. English language structurally conforms to the Subject-Verb-Object (SVO) constituent order unlike Turkish which has a very flexible constituent order of mostly Subject-Object-Verb (SOV).

Turkish is an agglutinative language wherein words are created by concatenating morphemes (stems and affixes). These combinations are conditioned by certain morphological rules such as vowel harmony and consonant assimilation which are set to preserve the overall gentleness of the language. This means a morpheme can change its form while preserving its meaning in order to suit these rules. After a number of derivations word forms can become quite complex which results in a larger vocabulary. Such complex Turkish words typically align with whole phrases on the English side when sentence pairs are aligned at the word level. Such a morphologically complex language proves to be quite challenging from an SMT point of view.

To reduce the large vocabulary size and to force more one-to-one word alignments, researchers prefer a sub-word representation of the morphologically richer foreign language while translating to/from English.

Proceedings of the First Conference on Machine Translation, Volume 2: Shared Task Papers, pages 246–251,
Berlin, Germany, August 11-12, 2016. ©2016 Association for Computational Linguistics

Mapping the rich morphology of Turkish to the limited morphology of English has been addressed by several researchers. El-Kahlout et al. (2012) and Oflazer (2008) used morphological analysis to separate some Turkish inflectional morphemes that have counterparts on the English side in English-to-Turkish SMT. Along the same direction, Yeniterzi and Oflazer (2010) applied syntactic transformations such as joining function words on the English side to the related content words.

On the other hand Mermer and Akin (2010) used an unsupervised learning algorithm to find the segmentations automatically from parallel data. A series of segmentation schemes has been presented (Ruiz et al., 2012) to explore the optimal segmentation for statistical machine translation of Turkish to English. In addition, an important amount of effort was spent by several research groups on Turkish-to-English SMT in the IWSLT'09 (Paul, 2009) and IWSLT'10 (Paul et al., 2010) BTEC tasks, IWSLT'12 (Federico et al., 2012) and IWSLT'13 (Cettolo et al., 2013) TED tasks.

Several components such as the morphological analyzer and the Turkish word generator that were used in this submission were adopted from the experiments that had been conducted for IWSLT'13 TED tasks by Yilmaz et al. (2013).

3 Phrase-Based vs. Hierarchical Phrase-Based Systems

Although phrase-to-phrase translation (Koehn et al., 2003) overcomes many problems of word-to-word translation (Brown et al., 1993) and has been successful for some language pairs during the last decade, the continuity of phrases is its main shortcoming. In general, this is a problem for language pairs with very different word orders such as Chinese-English. For such language pairs, in order to generate the target phrase, we may need sub-phrases from different parts of the source sentence which are distant from each other. To overcome the limitations of the phrase-based model, Chiang (2007) has introduced a hierarchical phrase-based model that uses bilingual phrase pairs to generate hierarchical phrases that allow gaps and enable longer distance reorderings.

Previous work (El-Kahlout et al., 2012; Ruiz et al., 2012) showed that hierarchical phrase-based (HPB) systems outperform phrase-based (PB) sys-

tems for Turkish-English.

4 Experiments

4.1 Overview

In the experiments the SETIMES parallel corpora provided were used as training data. The systems were tuned with newsdev2016 consisting of 1000 sentences and tested with the test set newstest2016 of 3000 sentences. GIZA++ toolkit (Och and Ney, 2003) for the word alignment and Moses' base decoders for both HPB and PB systems were utilized. For the PB decoders lexicalized reordering was turned on, the distortion limit was set to 6 (dl = 6) unless no distortion limit (dl = -1) was explicitly indicated. For the HPB decoder cube pruning pop limit was set to 5000.

4.2 Word Representation vs. Full Segmentation

We implemented both the word-level representation and feature based representation of Turkish as baseline systems. As mentioned in Section 2, incorporating morphology when working with morphologically rich(er) languages in SMT is expected to perform better than the word-level approach.

Data Set	Sentences	# of Tokens
Turkish(Word)	208k	3.6M
Turkish(Feature)	208k	7.4M
English	208k	4.4M

Table 1: SETIMES parallel training data statistics.

Table 1 shows the training data statistics before and after morphological analysis. As it was commonplace for sentences to become quite a bit longer due to the morphological segmentation, in our experiments we used a maximum sentence length of 100.

4.3 Pre-processing

We normalized all the data used in the experiments. This includes removing extra spaces, dealing with unicode punctuation, normalizing quotation marks and commas. The word-level representation of Turkish and English were produced using the default Moses tokenizer.

A morphological analyzer (Oflazer, 1994) was used to produce the feature-based representation of the Turkish language. Each word is passed through the analyzer which outputs all the possible interpretations of that word containing the stem and the morphological features. Then morphological disambiguation is performed on the morphological analyses (Sak et al., 2007).

Once the contextually salient morphological interpretation is selected, we removed the redundant morphological features that do not correspond to a surface morpheme such as part-of-speech features (Noun, Verb etc.), 3rd singular agreement feature (A3sg), and positiveness feature (Pos) and so on. There only remained features that correspond to lexical morphemes making up a word such as dative (Dat), accusative (Acc), past participle (PastPart) and so on. We segmented the morphologically-analyzed Turkish sentences at every feature boundary, denoted by the (_) symbol. A typical sentence pair with Turkish word representation and full segmentation is as follows:

- **Word representation:** Kosova'nın özelleştirme süreci büyüteç altında.

- **Feature representation:** Kosova _Gen özel _Become _Caus _Inf2 süreç _P3sg büyüteç alt_P3sg _Loc.

- **Reference:** Kosova's privatisation process is under scrutiny.

4.4 Language Models

The language models were trained using SRILM (Stolcke, 2002) toolkit. For Turkish to English we used a 4-gram Gigaword language model. For English to Turkish experiments we used the monolingual Common Crawl Corpus hosted by Amazon Web Services as a public data set. While being quite large, the crawl data consisted of mostly out of domain grammatically and semantically broken sentences. Even though the provided data was supposed to be de-duplicated we encountered duplicates of sub-sentences embedded within a single sentence which may have been missed by the de-duplication script. We encountered sentences that include only a word, bad UTF-8 characters, sentences containing Turkish characters that were replaced with a UTF-8 place-holder character which were irreversible since all the non-Latin characters were mapped to the same place-holder.

Therefore we processed the monolingual data to train a stronger language model. Firstly we employed the same normalization process as was done on the training, tuning and the test corpus described in Section 4.3. We lowercased the sentences that included fully upper-cased words and phrases. Then we removed the parts in which some characters were irreversibly swapped by UTF-8 place-holder, empty lines, the sentences that consisted of only numbers or characters, URL's and dates.

In addition to the language models trained from the crawl data, two 5-gram language models were trained using the parallel corpora which were then interpolated with the aforementioned language models using SRILM.

Data Set	Lines	Total Words
TR-CC-lm	28M	796M

Table 2: Filtered crawl-data language model statistics.

4.5 Methods

In our experiments we used both HPB and PB decoders for both directions. For Turkish-to-English we observed that the HPB systems outperformed the PB systems and for English-to-Turkish PB systems outperformed the HPB ones. For both directions we augmented the training data with its content words in order to increase the alignments at root-word level. For the English side this was achieved by using TreeTagger (Schmid, 1994) to tag the sentences and remove all the non-content words (the remaining part-of-speech tags and conjunctions etc.) (Yilmaz et al., 2013). For the Turkish side the morphological analyzer we described in section 4.3 was used to strip the corpus of any non-content words, in this case part-of-speech features. Finally the Turkish and English corpora that consisted of only the content words were then added to the original parallel corpora effectively doubling its size and enlarging their vocabularies.

For another experiment, reversed corpora for the source side for each direction were used in hopes of achieving a more accurate word alignment.

Table 3 shows the experimental results of the official test set for the Turkish-to-English direction. We observed that removing the distortion limit (dl = -1) on re-ordering improves the performance of the PB system. Later the strength of the diverse systems were combined using the open-source system combination tool MEMT (Heafield

Experiment	newstest2016
1. HPB Word Rep.	12.78
2. HPB Feature rep.	14.68
3. 2 + GW_LM	15.46
4. 3 + Content Corpus	14.94
5. 3 + Reverse Corpus	13.42
6. 1 with PB	11.20
7. 2 with PB	13.36
8. 7 without dl	15.06

Table 3: BLEU scores of individual systems for Turkish-to-English.

and Lavie, 2010).

Experiment	newstest2016
1. PB Word Rep.	8.34
2. PB Feature Rep.	8.25
3. 1 + CC_LM	8.59
4. 3 + Content Corpus	8.00
5. 3 + Reverse Corpus	7.96
6. 1 with HPB	7.65
7. 2 with HPB	7.57

Table 4: BLEU scores of individual systems for English-to-Turkish.

Table 4 shows the experimental results of the official test set for the English-to-Turkish direction. We observe that the PB system with a word-level representation gives us the best result.

4.6 Post-processing

4.6.1 Turkish Word Generation

When using a feature-based translation model, a word generation step is required to generate the correct Turkish word from the outputs of systems which contain words represented with stems and sequence of morphemes. We used an in-house morphological generation tool that, given a text with words in a format where each morpheme is concatenated to the previous morpheme or stem, transforms these representations to the correct single-word form. This generation tool has been trained on a large Turkish corpus and works by simply creating a reverse-map through morphological segmentation of the corpus. This map contains stem+morpheme sequences as keys and their corresponding single-word forms as values. While creating this map, the disambiguation step of morphological segmentation is omitted to increase the coverage, as keeping multiple resolutions for a single-word form increases the number of keys for the reverse-map. We augmented the map to further increase the coverage.

The following are the working steps of the generation tool:

1. The system outputs and the combined map of "stem+morphemes to surface form" is taken as input.

2. Iterating through tokens, if an encountered token is:

   (a) a stem; simply output the token.
   (b) a "stem+morphemes" that is in the map; output its value.
   (c) otherwise; drop the trailing morpheme, and go to 2a.

An example of word generation is as follows:

- **Stem + Morpheme:** git_Aor_A1sg
- **Output Surface Form:** giderim
- **English:** I go

4.6.2 System Combination

System combination attempts to improve the quality of machine translation output by combining the outputs of different translation systems which usually are based on different paradigms such as phrase-based, hierarchical, etc. aiming to exploit and combine strengths of each system. The outputs of some of our translation systems, which are based on different methods as explained in the previous sections, were put into a combination task. We combined the outputs of some of the best performing (best tuning run in terms of BLEU score) hierarchical phrase-based systems using the open-source system combination tool, MEMT. We trained the system combination decoder over different development sets and selected the best ones as our primary submissions to the WMT 2016.

5 Conclusions

This paper described TÜBİTAK's submissions to the WMT'16 news translation task for the Turkish-English language pair. We used Moses in our submissions as well as other open source tools such as MEMT and TreeTagger. For the English-Turkish direction the crawl-data provided was processed and used to generate a 5-gram language model.

Experiment	newstest2016
1. HPB Feature Rep.	15.46
2. 1 + Content Corpus	14.94
3. PB Word Rep.	11.20
4. PB Feature Rep. dl -1	15.06
5. sys-comb	16.01

Table 5: BLEU scores of system combinations for Turkish-to-English.

Experiment	newstest2016
1. PB Feature Rep.	8.25
2. PB Word Rep.	8.59
3. HPB Word Rep.	7.65
4. 2 + Content Corpus	8.00
5. sys-comb	8.90

Table 6: BLEU scores of system combinations for English-to-Turkish.

A 4-gram gigaword language model for English was used. Due to the morphological discrepancy between the two languages, a morphological analyzer was used to apply full segmentation to the Turkish side. A word-generation tool was used to generate back the word forms of the Turkish sentences from its morphologically analysed counter-parts for English-to-Turkish. We observed that morphological-analysis performed quite well for the Turkish-to-English direction. We experimented with training data with its source side in reverse order and with its content words added to it. Employing system combination of different SMT paradigms resulted in 0.5 BLEU increase for Turkish-to-English and 0.3 BLEU increase for English-to-Turkish.

References

Peter F. Brown, Stephen A. Della Pietra, Vincent J. Della Pietra, and Robert L. Mercer. 1993. The mathematics of statistical machine translation: Parameter estimation. *Computational Linguistics*, 19:263–311.

Mauro Cettolo, Jan Niehues, Sebastian Stüker, Luisa Bentivogli, and Marcello Federico. 2013. Report on the 10th IWSLT evaluation campaign. *The 10th International Workshop on Spoken Language Translation, Heidelberg, Germany*.

David Chiang. 2007. Hierarchical phrase-based translation. *Computational Linguistics*, 33(2):201–228.

Ilknur Durgar El-Kahlout, Coskun Mermer, and Mehmet U. Dogan. 2012. *Recent Improvements In Statistical Machine Translation Between Turkish and English*. Cambridge Scholars Publishing.

Marcello Federico, Mauro Cettolo, Luisa Bentivogli, Michael Paul, and Sebastian Stüker. 2012. Overview of the IWSLT 2012 evaluation campaign. *Proceedings of the International Workshop on Spoken Language Translation, Hong Kong, HK*.

Kenneth Heafield and Alon Lavie. 2010. Combining machine translation output with open source: The Carnegie Mellon multi-engine machine translation scheme. *The Prague Bulletin of Mathematical Linguistics*, 93:27–36.

Phillip Koehn, Franz J. Och, and Daniel Marcu. 2003. Statistical phrasebased translation. *Proceedings of the Human Language Technology Conference and the North American Chapter of the Association for Computational Linguistics (HLT/NAACL)*, pages 127–133.

Coskun Mermer and Ahmet A. Akin. 2010. Unsupervised search for the optimal segmentation for statistical machine translation. *Proceedings of the ACL 2010 Student Research Workshop*, pages 31–36.

Franz J. Och and Hermann Ney. 2003. A systematic comparison of various statistical alignment models. *Computational Linguistics*, 29(1):19–51.

Kemal Oflazer. 1994. Two-level description of Turkish morphology. *Literary and Linguistic Computing*, 9:137–148.

Kemal Oflazer. 2008. Statistical machine translation into a morphologically complex language. *Computational Linguistics and Intelligent Text Processing, 9th International Conference, CICLing*, 4919:376–387.

Michael Paul, Mauro Federico, and Sebastian Stüker. 2010. Overview of the IWSLT 2010 evaluation campaign. *International Workshop on Spoken Language Translation (IWSLT 2010), Paris - France*.

Michael Paul. 2009. Overview of the IWSLT 2009 evaluation campaign. *Proceedings of IWSLT 2009, Tokyo - Japan*.

Nicholas Ruiz, Arianna Bisazza, Roldano Cattoni, and Marcello Federico. 2012. FBK's machine translation systems for IWSLT 2012's TED lectures. *Proceedings of the seventh International Workshop on Spoken Language Translation (IWSLT)*, pages 61–68.

Hasim Sak, Tunga Gungor, and Murat Saraclar. 2007. Morphological disambiguation of Turkish text with perception algorithm. *Proceedings of CICLING*, pages 107–118.

Helmut Schmid. 1994. Probabilistic part-of-speech tagging using decision trees. *Proceedings of the International Conference on New Methods in Language Modeling.*

Andreas Stolcke. 2002. SRILM an extensible language modeling toolkit. *Proceedings of ICSLP.*

Reyyan Yeniterzi and Kemal Oflazer. 2010. Statistical phrasebased translation. *Syntax-to-morphology mapping in factored phrase-based statistical machine translation from English to Turkish," in Proceedings of the 48th Annual Meeting of the Association for Computational Linguistics, ACL '10. Stroudsburg, PA, USA*, pages 454–464.

Ertugrul Yilmaz, Ilknur Durgar El-Kahlout, Zisan S. Ozil, and Coskun Mermer. 2013. Tubitak Turkish-English submissions for IWSLT 2013. *Proceedings of the 10th International Workshop on Spoken Language Translation*, pages 152–159.

ParFDA for Instance Selection for Statistical Machine Translation

Ergun Biçici

ergunbicici@yahoo.com

bicici.github.com

Abstract

We build parallel feature decay algorithms (ParFDA) Moses statistical machine translation (SMT) systems for all language pairs in the translation task at the first conference on statistical machine translation (Bojar et al., 2016a) (WMT16). ParFDA obtains results close to the top constrained phrase-based SMT with an average of 2.52 BLEU points difference using significantly less computation for building SMT systems than the computation that would be spent using all available corpora. We obtain BLEU bounds based on target coverage and show that ParFDA results can be improved by 12.6 BLEU points on average. Similar bounds show that top constrained SMT results at WMT16 can be improved by 8 BLEU points on average while German to English and Romanian to English translations results are already close to the bounds.

1 ParFDA

ParFDA (Biçici et al., 2015) is a parallel implementation of feature decay algorithms (FDA), a class of instance selection algorithms that use feature decay, developed for fast deployment of accurate SMT systems. We use ParFDA for selecting parallel training data and language model (LM) data for building SMT systems. ParFDA runs separate FDA5 (Biçici and Yuret, 2015) models on randomized subsets of the available data and combines the selections afterwards. ParFDA allows rapid prototyping of SMT systems for a given target domain or task. FDA pseudocode is in Figure 1. This year, we have kept record of which 1-gram or 2-grams of the test set have already been

foreach $S \in \mathcal{U}$ **do**
    $\mathrm{score}(S) \leftarrow \frac{1}{z} \sum_{f \in \mathrm{features}(S)} \mathrm{fval}(f)$
    $\mathrm{enqueue}(\mathcal{Q}, S, \mathrm{score}(S))$
while $|\mathcal{L}| < N$ **do**
    $S \leftarrow \mathrm{dequeue}(\mathcal{Q})$
    $\mathrm{score}(S) \leftarrow \frac{1}{z} \sum_{f \in \mathrm{features}(S)} \mathrm{fval}(f)$
    if $\mathrm{score}(S) \geq \mathrm{topval}(\mathcal{Q})$ **then**
        $\mathcal{L} \leftarrow \mathcal{L} \cup \{S\}$
        foreach $f \in \mathrm{features}(S)$ **do**
            $\mathrm{fval}(f) \leftarrow \mathrm{decay}(f, \mathcal{U}, \mathcal{L})$
    else
        $\mathrm{enqueue}(\mathcal{Q}, S, \mathrm{score}(S))$

Figure 1: The Feature Decay Algorithm: inputs are a sentence pool $\mathcal{U}$, test set features $\mathcal{F}$, and number of instances to select N and a priority queue $\mathcal{Q}$ stores sentence, S, scores score that sums feature values fval.

included to include an instance if otherwise found and we also use numeric expression identification using regular expressions to replace them with a label (Biçici, 2016) before instance selection.

We run ParFDA SMT experiments using Moses (Koehn et al., 2007) for all language pairs in both directions in the WMT16 translation task (Bojar et al., 2016a), which include English-Czech (en-cs), English-German (en-de), English-Finnish (en-fi), English-Romanian (en-ro), English-Russian (en-ru), and English-Turkish (en-tr).

2 ParFDA Moses SMT Experiments

The importance of ParFDA increases with the proliferation of training resources available for building SMT systems. Compared with WMT15 (Bojar et al., 2015), WMT16 observed significant increase in monolingual and parallel training data made available. Table 1 presents the statistics of the available training and LM corpora for the

Proceedings of the First Conference on Machine Translation, Volume 2: Shared Task Papers, pages 252–258,
Berlin, Germany, August 11-12, 2016. ©2016 Association for Computational Linguistics

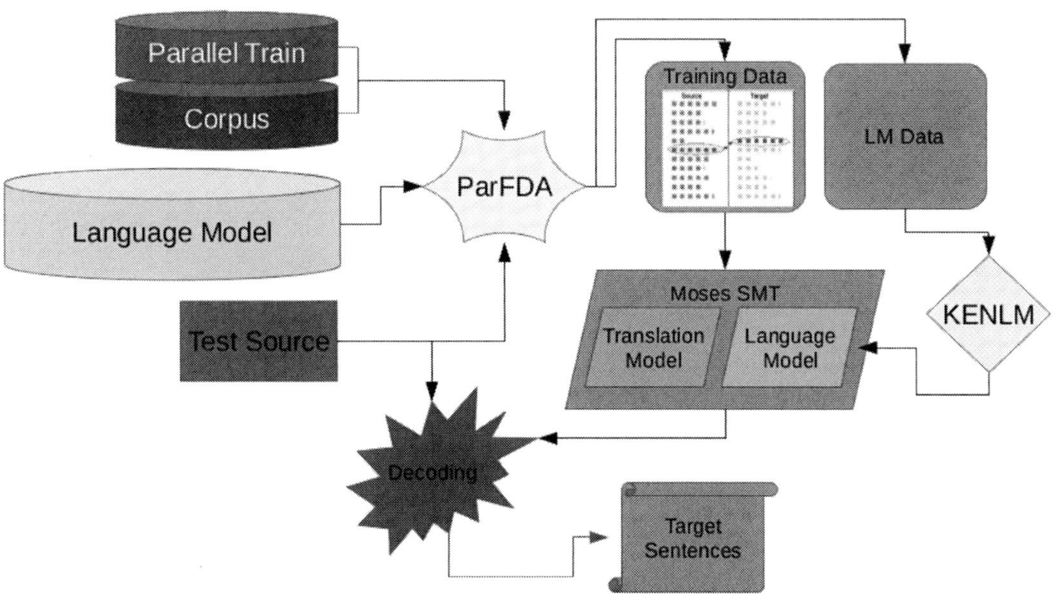

Figure 2: ParFDA Moses SMT workflow.

constrained (C) systems in WMT16 (Bojar et al., 2016a) as well as the statistics of the ParFDA selected subset training and LM data from C. TCOV lists the target coverage in terms of the 2-grams of the test set. Compared with last year, this year we do not use Common Crawl parallel corpus except for en-ru. We use Common Crawl monolingual corpus fi, ro, and tr datasets and we extended the LM corpora with previous years' corpora. We also use CzEng16pre (Bojar et al., 2016b) for en-cs.

We have increased the size of the training data selected to about 1.6 million instances to help with the reduction of out-of-vocabulary items. Except for translation directions involving Romanian and Turkish, this corresponds to increased training set size compared with ParFDA experiments in 2015, where we were able to obtain the top translation error rate (TER) performance in French to English translation using 1.261 million training sentences (Biçici et al., 2015). Due to the presence of peaks in SMT performance with increasing training set size (Biçici and Yuret, 2015), increasing the training set size need not improve the performance. We select about 15 million sentences for each LM not including the selected training set, which is added later. Table 1 shows the significant size differences between the constrained dataset (C) and the ParFDA selected data. We use 3-grams for selecting training data and 2-grams for LM corpus selection. Task specific data selection also improves the LM perplexity and the performance of the selected LM can be observed in Table 4.

We truecase all of the corpora, set the maximum sentence length to 126, use 150-best lists during tuning, set the LM order to 6 for all language pairs, and train the LM using KENLM (Heafield et al., 2013). For word alignment, we use mgiza (Gao and Vogel, 2008) where GIZA++ (Och and Ney, 2003) parameters set max-fertility to 10, the number of iterations to 7,3,5,5,7 for IBM models 1,2,3,4, and the HMM model, and learn 50 word classes in three iterations with the mkcls tool during training. The development set contains up to 5000 sentences randomly sampled from previous years' development sets (2011-2015) and remaining come from the development set for WMT16. ParFDA Moses SMT workflow is depicted in Figure 2.

ParFDA Moses SMT results for each translation direction at WMT16 are in Table 2 using BLEU over cased text, and F_1 (Biçici, 2011). We compare ParFDA results with the top constrained submissions at WMT16 in Table 3. [1] The average difference to the top constrained (TopC) submission in WMT16 is 5.26 BLEU points whereas the difference was 3.2 BLEU points in WMT15 (Biçici et al., 2015). Performance compared with the TopC phrase-based SMT improved over WMT15 results with 2.52 BLEU points difference on av-

---

[1] We use the results from matrix.statmt.org.

253

$S \to T$	Data	Training Data				LM Data	
		#word S (M)	#word T (M)	#sent (K)	TCOV	#word (M)	TCOV
en-cs	C	55.0	55.0	55025	0.544	1375.4	0.638
en-cs	ParFDA	1.9	1.9	1904	0.468	18.1	0.586
cs-en	C	55.0	55.0	55025	0.648	4859.0	0.743
cs-en	ParFDA	1.9	1.9	1906	0.588	18.2	0.695
en-de	C	4.5	4.5	4513	0.516	2393.0	0.669
en-de	ParFDA	1.7	1.7	1701	0.498	18.0	0.618
de-en	C	4.5	4.5	4513	0.602	4859.0	0.753
de-en	ParFDA	1.7	1.7	1692	0.584	18.0	0.701
en-fi	C	2.0	2.0	2026	0.275	2971.1	0.543
en-fi	ParFDA	1.6	1.6	1637	0.273	17.8	0.467
fi-en	C	2.0	2.0	2026	0.511	4859.0	0.746
fi-en	ParFDA	1.6	1.6	1626	0.508	17.8	0.693
en-ro	C	0.6	0.6	597	0.462	8065.6	0.736
en-ro	ParFDA	0.6	0.6	597	0.462	16.8	0.677
ro-en	C	0.6	0.6	597	0.508	4859.0	0.738
ro-en	ParFDA	0.6	0.6	597	0.508	16.8	0.693
en-ru	C	2.6	2.6	2570	0.455	1038.7	0.613
en-ru	ParFDA	1.7	1.7	1654	0.451	17.7	0.577
ru-en	C	2.6	2.6	2570	0.578	4859.0	0.728
ru-en	ParFDA	1.6	1.6	1643	0.574	17.9	0.682
en-tr	C	0.2	0.2	206	0.233	11671.0	0.642
en-tr	ParFDA	0.2	0.2	205	0.233	16.4	0.528
tr-en	C	0.2	0.2	206	0.423	4859.0	0.738
tr-en	ParFDA	0.2	0.2	205	0.423	16.4	0.685

Table 1: Data statistics for the available training and LM corpora in the constrained (C) setting compared with the ParFDA selected training and LM data. #words is in millions (M) and #sents in thousands (K). TCOV is target 2-gram coverage.

	$S \to en$						$en \to T$					
	cs-en	de-en	fi-en	ro-en	ru-en	tr-en	en-cs	en-de	en-fi	en-ro	en-ru	en-tr
BLEU	0.2641	0.3014	0.1744	0.2904	0.2525	0.1222	0.1942	0.2391	0.1248	0.2097	0.2193	0.0901
F_1	0.2718	0.3067	0.2077	0.289	0.2674	0.1641	0.2169	0.2592	0.1665	0.2258	0.2363	0.1346

Table 2: ParFDA results at WMT16.

erage, which is likely due to selecting increased number of training data.

We observe that various systems in TopC used character-level split and merge operations (referred as BPE or byte pair encoding) combined with neural networks (Sennrich et al., 2016). [2] We also compare ParFDA results with the TopC BPE and the average difference is 5.86 BLEU points. [3] WMT15 did not contain any submission with BPE. Average difference between TopC BPE and TopC phrase hints that majority of the in-creased performance difference is due to improvements obtained by BPE in TopC BPE results.

Table 4 compares the perplexity of the ParFDA selected LM with a LM trained on the ParFDA selected training data and a LM trained using all of the available training corpora and shows reductions in the number of OOV tokens reaching up to 45% and the perplexity up to 45%. Table 4 also presents the average log probability of tokens and the log probability of token <unk> returned by KENLM to token <unk>. The increase in the ratio between them in the last column shows that OOV in ParFDA LM are not just less but also less likely at the same time.

[2] For instance within en-de translation results: `matrix.statmt.org/matrix/systems_list/1840`.
[3] Some translation directions did not contain BPE results.

BLEU	cs-en	de-en	fi-en	ro-en	ru-en	tr-en	en-cs	en-de	en-fi	en-ro	en-ru	en-tr
ParFDA	0.2641	0.3014	0.1744	0.2904	0.2525	0.1222	0.1942	0.2391	0.1248	0.2097	0.2193	0.0901
TopC	0.314	0.386	0.204	0.352	0.291	0.145	0.258	0.342	0.174	0.289	0.26	0.098
- ParFDA	0.0499	0.0846	0.0296	0.0616	0.0385	0.0228	0.0638	0.1029	0.0492	0.0793	0.0407	0.0079
avg diff	0.0526											
TopC BPE	0.314	0.386		0.339	0.291		0.258	0.342	0.151	0.282	0.26	
- ParFDA	0.0499	0.0846		0.0486	0.0385		0.0638	0.1029	0.0262	0.0723	0.0407	
avg diff	0.0586											
TopC phrase	0.304	0.345	0.191	0.322	0.27	0.129	0.236	0.283	0.138	0.235	0.24	0.092
- ParFDA	0.0399	0.0436	0.0166	0.0316	0.0175	0.0068	0.0418	0.0439	0.0132	0.0253	0.0207	0.0019
avg diff	0.0252											
BPE - phrase	0.01	0.041		0.017	0.021		0.022	0.059	0.013	0.047	0.02	
avg diff	0.0278											

Table 3: ParFDA results compared with the top constrained results in WMT16 (TopC, from `matrix.statmt.org`) and their difference.

| | OOV Rate | | | | perplexity | | | | avg log prob. | | | <unk> log prob. | | | $\frac{\text{<unk>}}{\text{avg}}$ |
| | C | FDA5 | FDA5 | | C | FDA5 | FDA5 | | C | FDA5 | FDA5 | C | FDA5 | FDA5 | |
$S \to T$	train	train	LM	%red	train	train	LM	%red	train	train	LM	train	train	LM	%inc
en-cs	0.259	0.299	0.256	0.01	14946	11609	9428	0.37	-4.61	-4.57	-4.39	-7.8	-7.11	-7.77	0.05
en-de	0.361	0.372	0.28	0.22	7075	6217	4297	0.39	-4.28	-4.23	-3.94	-7.31	-7.08	-7.77	0.16
en-fi	0.409	0.412	0.237	0.42	45087	49807	27698	0.39	-5.67	-5.73	-4.96	-7.04	-7.0	-8.15	0.32
en-ro	0.389	0.389	0.239	0.39	3043	3043	2150	0.29	-3.92	-3.92	-3.58	-6.35	-6.35	-7.87	0.36
en-ru	0.317	0.319	0.288	0.09	10245	10787	8555	0.16	-4.55	-4.58	-4.41	-7.16	-7.09	-7.74	0.12
en-tr	0.416	0.416	0.229	0.45	18988	18988	15805	0.17	-5.14	-5.14	-4.63	-6.18	-6.18	-8.09	0.45
cs-en	0.285	0.336	0.27	0.05	2647	2095	1549	0.41	-3.64	-3.58	-3.38	-7.54	-6.88	-7.58	0.08
de-en	0.352	0.37	0.279	0.21	2521	2263	1426	0.43	-3.69	-3.65	-3.36	-7.1	-6.87	-7.58	0.17
fi-en	0.41	0.419	0.274	0.33	2753	2972	1509	0.45	-3.77	-3.81	-3.38	-6.57	-6.49	-7.55	0.28
ro-en	0.418	0.418	0.282	0.33	2017	2017	1422	0.29	-3.66	-3.66	-3.37	-6.24	-6.24	-7.54	0.31
ru-en	0.352	0.358	0.291	0.17	1907	1974	1532	0.2	-3.55	-3.57	-3.4	-6.98	-6.89	-7.58	0.13
tr-en	0.466	0.466	0.297	0.36	2250	2250	1584	0.3	-3.73	-3.73	-3.42	-5.98	-5.98	-7.54	0.38

Table 4: Perplexity comparison of the LM built from the training corpus (train), ParFDA selected training data (FDA5 train), and the ParFDA selected LM data (FDA5 LM). %red is proportion of reduction and prob. is used for probability.

3 Translation Upper Bounds with TCOV

In this section, we obtain upper bounds on the translation performance based on the target coverage (TCOV) of n-grams of the test set found in the selected ParFDA training data. We obtain translations based on TCOV by randomly replacing some number of tokens from a given sentence with a fixed OOV label proportional to TCOV starting from 1-grams. After OOVs for 1-grams are identified, OOV tokens for n-grams up to 5-grams are identified and BLEU is calculated with respect to the original. If the overall number of OOVs obtained before i-grams are enough to obtain the i-gram TCOV, then OOV identification for i-grams is skipped. Number of OOV tokens is identified by two possible functions for a given sentence T':

$$OOV_r = \text{round}((1 - \text{TCOV}) * |T'|) \quad (1)$$
$$OOV_f = \lfloor (1 - \text{TCOV}) * |T'| \rfloor \quad (2)$$

where $|T'|$ denotes the length of the sentence in the number of tokens.

We obtain each bound using 10000 such instances and repeat for 10 times. This TCOV BLEU bound is optimistic since it does not consider reorderings in the translation or differences in sentence length. Each plot in Tables 6 and 7 locates TCOV BLEU bound obtained from each n-gram and from n-grams combined up to and including n and ■ locates the ParFDA Moses SMT performance.

Table 5 compares TCOV BLEU bounds with ParFDA results and TopC from Table 3 and shows potential improvements in the translation performance for all translation directions at WMT16 and overall on average. Results in **bold** are close to OOV_r TCOV BLEU bound, which indicates that TopC translation results for de-en and ro-en directions are able to obtain results close to this bound.

4 Conclusion

We use ParFDA for selecting instances for building SMT systems using less computation over-

BLEU	cs-en	de-en	fi-en	ro-en	ru-en	tr-en	en-cs	en-de	en-fi	en-ro	en-ru	en-tr
OOV_r ParFDA bound	0.4501	0.3846	0.3516	0.3391	0.3968	0.3053	0.3292	0.3575	0.2415	0.3275	0.3383	0.1723
- ParFDA	0.186	0.0832	0.1772	0.0487	0.1443	0.1831	0.135	0.1184	0.1167	0.1178	0.119	0.0822
avg diff	0.126											
C BLEU bound	0.4908	**0.3864**	0.3518	**0.3392**	0.3969	0.3054	0.3679	0.3572	0.2416	0.3274	0.3381	0.1719
- TopC	0.1768	**0.0004**	0.1478	**-0.0128**	0.1059	0.1604	0.1099	0.0152	0.0676	0.0384	0.0781	0.0739
avg diff	0.0801											
OOV_f ParFDA bound	0.4766	0.4143	0.3729	0.3842	0.4337	0.3072	0.3792	0.3704	0.2382	0.3416	0.3768	0.2283
- ParFDA	0.2125	0.1129	0.1985	0.0938	0.1812	0.185	0.185	0.1313	0.1134	0.1319	0.1575	0.1382
avg diff	0.1534											
C BLEU bound	0.5344	0.4156	0.3719	0.3718	0.4337	0.3068	0.3945	0.3847	0.2384	0.3411	0.3769	0.2005
- TopC	0.2204	0.0296	0.1679	0.0198	0.1427	0.1618	0.1365	0.0427	0.0644	0.0521	0.1169	0.1025
avg diff	0.1048											

Table 5: 1,2,3,4,5-gram TCOV BLEU bounds compared with WMT16 results. **bold** are close to a bound.

all than the computation that would be spent using all available corpora while still achieve SMT performance that is close to the top performing phrase-based SMT systems. ParFDA results at WMT16 provides new results using the current phrase-based SMT technology towards rapid SMT system development in budgeted training scenarios. ParFDA works towards the development of task or data adaptive SMT solutions using specially moulded data rather than general purpose SMT systems built with a patchwork approach combining various sources of information and several processing steps.

We obtain BLEU bounds based on target coverage and show that top constrained results can be improved by 8 BLEU points on average and obtain results close to the bound for de-en and ro-en translation directions. Similar bounds show that ParFDA results can be improved by 12.6 BLEU points on average.

Acknowledgments

We thank the reviewers for providing constructive comments.

References

Ergun Biçici and Deniz Yuret. 2015. Optimizing instance selection for statistical machine translation with feature decay algorithms. *IEEE/ACM Transactions On Audio, Speech, and Language Processing (TASLP)*, 23:339–350.

Ergun Biçici, Qun Liu, and Andy Way. 2015. ParFDA for fast deployment of accurate statistical machine translation systems, benchmarks, and statistics. In *Proc. of the EMNLP 2015 Tenth Workshop on Statistical Machine Translation*, Lisbon, Portugal, 9. Association for Computational Linguistics.

Ergun Biçici. 2011. *The Regression Model of Machine Translation*. Ph.D. thesis, Koç University. Supervisor: Deniz Yuret.

Ergun Biçici. 2016. RTM at SemEval-2016 task 1: Predicting semantic similarity with referential translation machines and related statistics. In *SemEval-2016: Semantic Evaluation Exercises - International Workshop on Semantic Evaluation*, San Diego, USA, 6.

Ondrej Bojar, Rajan Chatterjee, Christian Federmann, Barry Haddow, Chris Hokamp, Matthias Huck, Pavel Pecina, Philipp Koehn, Christof Monz, Matteo Negri, Matt Post, Carolina Scarton, Lucia Specia, and Marco Turchi. 2015. Findings of the 2015 workshop on statistical machine translation. In *Proc. of the Tenth Workshop on Statistical Machine Translation*, Lisbon, Portugal, September.

Ondrej Bojar, Christian Buck, Rajan Chatterjee, Christian Federmann, Liane Guillou, Barry Haddow, Matthias Huck, Antonio Jimeno Yepes, Aurlie Nvol, Mariana Neves, Pavel Pacina, Martin Poppel, Philipp Koehn, Christof Monz, Matteo Negri, Matt Post, Lucia Specia, Karin Verspoor, Jrg Tiedemann, and Marco Turchi. 2016a. Proc. of the 2016 conference on statistical machine translation. In *Proc. of the First Conference on Statistical Machine Translation (WMT16)*, Berlin, Germany, August.

Ondřej Bojar, Ondřej Dušek, Tom Kocmi, Jindřich Libovický, Michal Novák, Martin Popel, Roman Sudarikov, and Dušan Variš. 2016b. CzEng 1.6: Enlarged Czech-English Parallel Corpus with Processing Tools Dockered. In *Text, Speech and Dialogue: 19th International Conference, TSD 2016, Brno, Czech Republic, September 12-16, 2016, Proceedings*. Springer Verlag, September 12-16. In press.

Qin Gao and Stephan Vogel, 2008. *Software Engineering, Testing, and Quality Assurance for Natural Language Processing*, chapter Parallel Implementations of Word Alignment Tool, pages 49–57. Association for Computational Linguistics.

Kenneth Heafield, Ivan Pouzyrevsky, Jonathan H. Clark, and Philipp Koehn. 2013. Scalable modified Kneser-Ney language model estimation. In *Proc. of*

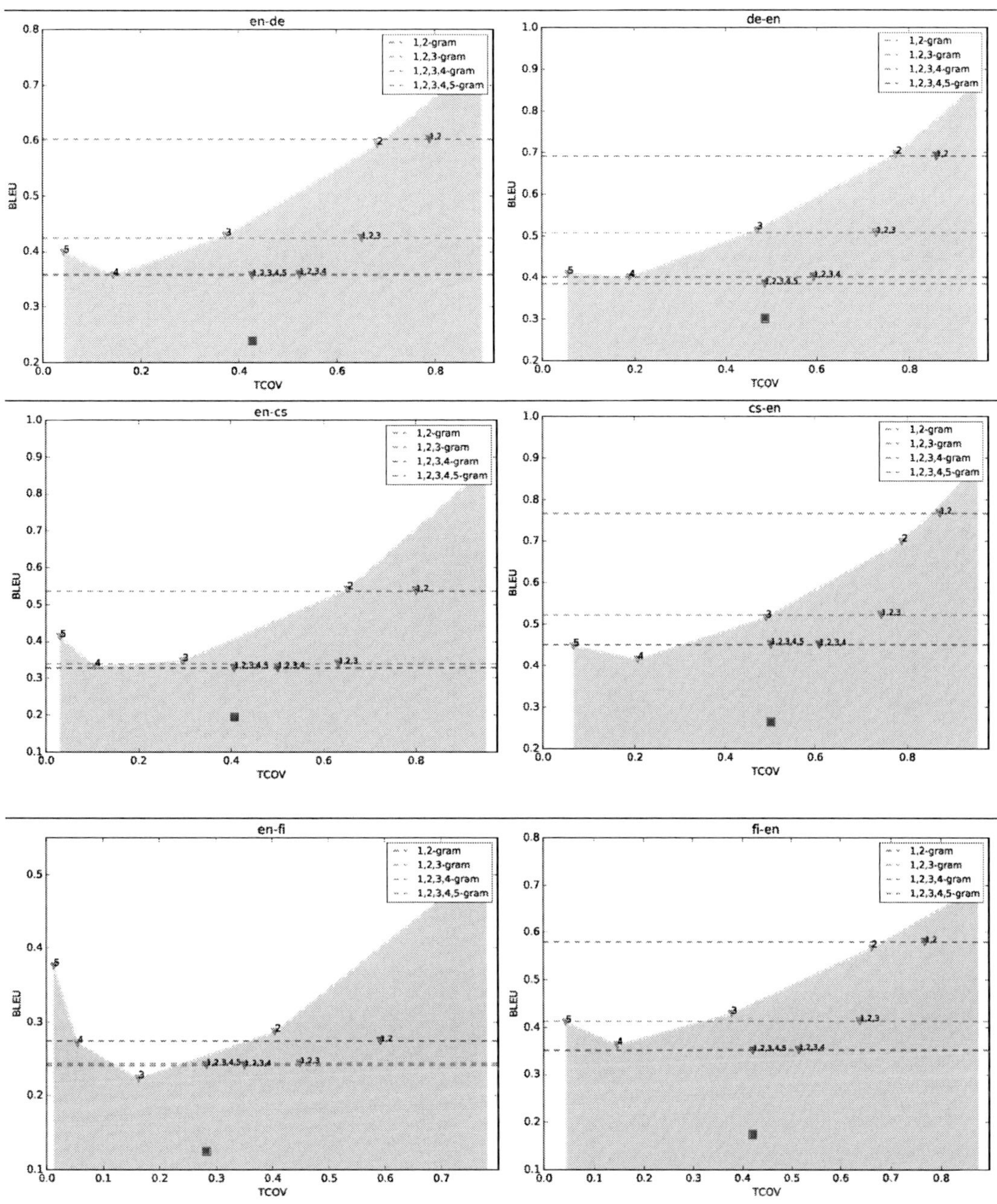

Table 6: ParFDA results (■) and OOV_r TCOV BLEU upper bounds for cs, de, and fi.

the 51st Annual Meeting of the Association for Computational Linguistics, pages 690–696, Sofia, Bulgaria, August.

Philipp Koehn, Hieu Hoang, Alexandra Birch, Chris Callison-Burch, Marcello Federico, Nicola Bertoldi, Brooke Cowan, Wade Shen, Christine Moran, Richard Zens, Chris Dyer, Ondrej Bojar, Alexandra Constantin, and Evan Herbst. 2007. Moses: Open source toolkit for statistical machine translation. In *Proc. of the 45th Annual Meeting of the Association*

for *Computational Linguistics Companion Volume Proc. of the Demo and Poster Sessions*, pages 177–180. Association for Computational Linguistics.

Franz Josef Och and Hermann Ney. 2003. A systematic comparison of various statistical alignment models. *Computational Linguistics*, 29(1):19–51.

Rico Sennrich, Barry Haddow, and Alexandra Birch. 2016. Edinburgh neural machine translation systems for wmt 16. In *Proc. of the ACL 2016*

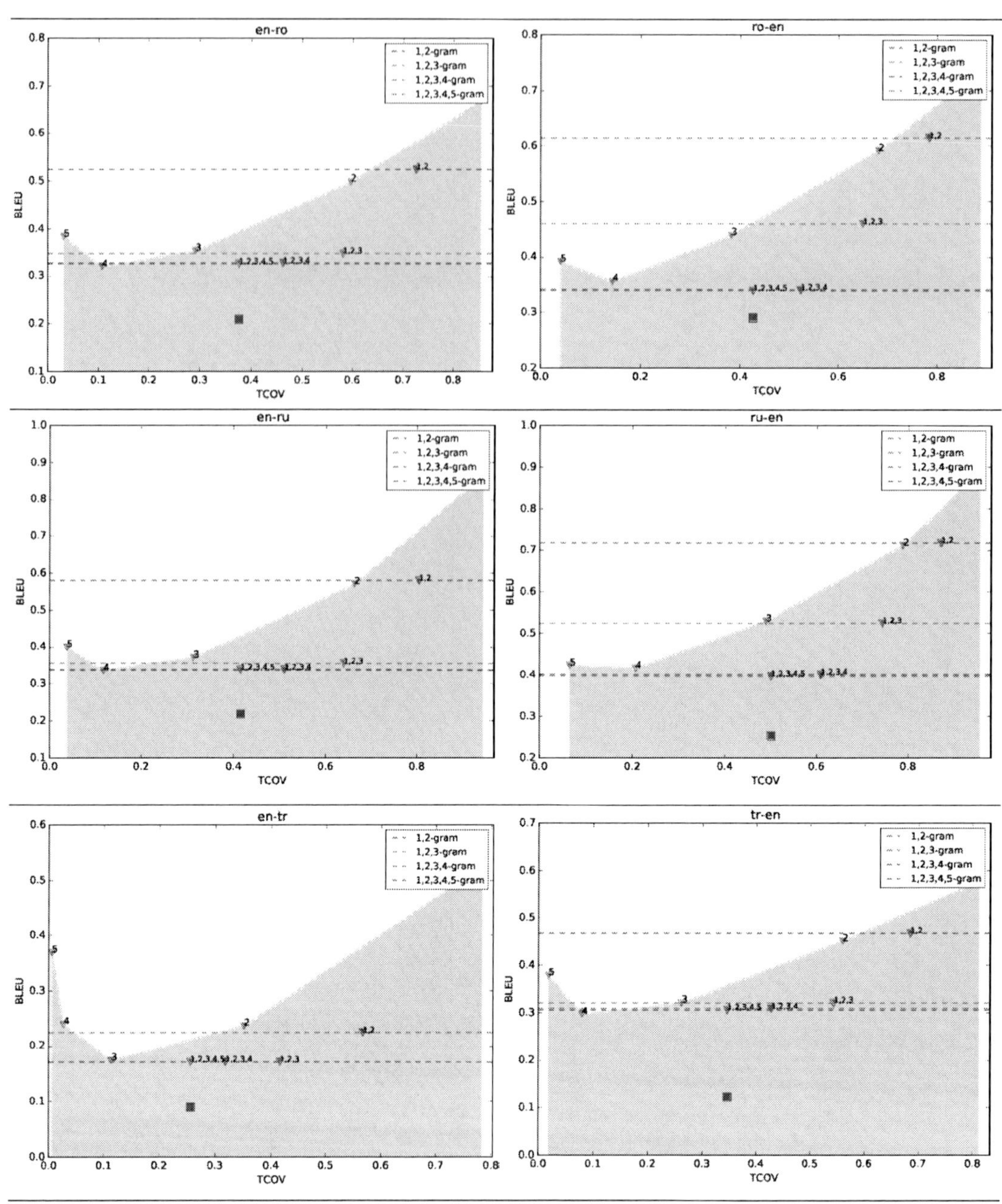

Table 7: ParFDA results (■) and OOV_r TCOV BLEU upper bounds for ro, ru, and tr.

Eleventh Workshop on Statistical Machine Translation, Berlin, Germany, 8. Association for Computational Linguistics.

Sheffield Systems for the English-Romanian Translation Task

Frédéric Blain   **Xingyi Song**   **Lucia Specia**
Department of Computer Science
The University of Sheffield
United Kingdom
{f.blain,xsong2,l.specia}@sheffield.ac.uk

Abstract

This paper provides an overview of the submissions the University of Sheffield for the English-Romanian Translation Task of the ACL 2016 First Conference on Machine Translation (WMT16). The submitted translations were produced with a phrase-based system trained using the Moses toolkit, in two variants: (i) n-best rescoring using additional features from Quality Estimation (primary submission), and (ii) a novel weighted ranking optimisation approach (secondary submission).

1 Introduction

This paper presents the submissions the University of Sheffield for the shared translation task, which is part of the ACL 2016 First Conference on Machine Translation (WMT16). We participated in the English-Romanian language pair.

Our primary submission investigates the use of additional features from Quality Estimation (QE) to better discriminate translation hypothesis within an n-best list produced by a phrase-based MT system built with the Moses toolkit (Koehn et al., 2007). The idea is to expand the n-best list feature set with additional features coming not from the MT system, but from external resources. Our expectation is that external, potentially richer features could help guide the decoder to produce better quality translations.

In addition to our primary system, we investigate the use of a different optimisation algorithm to tune the parameters of our phrase-based SMT system: the Weighted Ranking Optimisation (WRO) algorithm. Derived from the Pairwise Ranking Optimisation (PRO) algorithm (Hopkins and May, 2011), WRO addresses various limitations of PRO, as we discuss in Section 4.

In the following section we describe the settings of our phrase-based MT system. The two versions of our phrase-based system are presented in Section 3 and 4, respectively. We report our results on the newstest2016 test set in Section 5.

2 USFD Phrase-based System

We only used the data that was made officially available for the English-Romanian task (constrained submission). Statistics of the available training resources for the task are given in table 1.

As pre-processing, the English part of the data was tokenised using the Moses tokenisation script, while the Romanian part was tokenised using Tokro[1] (Allauzen et al., 2016), a rule-based tokeniser that normalises diacritics and splits punctuation and clitics.

Our phrase-based model was trained following the standard "baseline" settings of the Moses toolkit with MGIZA (Gao and Vogel, 2008) for word alignment and KenLM (Heafield, 2011) for language modelling. The phrase length was limited to 5. Lexicalised reordering models were trained using the same data.

We built a 5-gram Romanian language model (LM) from the linear interpolation of four individual LMs. The two first were built on the target side of the in-domain parallel corpora (Europarl7, SETimes2). For the two last, we use subsets of both the News Commentary (93%) and the Common Crawl (13%), selected using XenC-v2.1[2] (Rousseau, 2013) in mode 2[3] with the parallel corpora (Europarl7, SETimes2) as in-domain data.

---

[1] https://perso.limsi.fr/aufrant/software/tokro
[2] https://github.com/rousseau-lium/XenC/
[3] Implementation of the Moore-Lewis cross-entropy filtering method

Proceedings of the First Conference on Machine Translation, Volume 2: Shared Task Papers, pages 259–263,
Berlin, Germany, August 11-12, 2016. ©2016 Association for Computational Linguistics

	English		**Romanian**	
	# seg	# word	# seg	# word
Parallel data				
Europarl7	394k	10.4M	394k	10.4M
SETimes2	211k	5.03M	211k	5.36M
Monolingual data for language modelling				
News Commentary			2.28M	55.1M
– selected with XenC: 93%			2.1M	52.2M
Common Crawl			289M	7.93G
– selected with XenC: 13%			23.7M	577M
Development data				
newsdev_1	1k	24.7k	1k	26.7k
newsdev_2	1k	25.2k	1k	25.6k
setimes2	2k	47.8k	2k	50.9k

Table 1: Statistics of the available data for the English-Romanian Machine Translation Task (constrained submission). For our language modelling we only used 93% and 13% of the News Commentary and the Common Crawl corpus, respectively, after data selection.

The optimisation of the parameters was achieved using a 100-best Minimum Error Rate Training (MERT) (Och, 2003) towards the BLEU metric (Papineni et al., 2002).

3 N-best Rescoring with QE Features

Quality Estimation (QE) aims at measuring the quality of the Machine Translation (MT) output without reference translations. Generally, QE is addressed with various features indicating fluency, adequacy and complexity of the source-translation text pair. We hypothesise that these could help discriminate translation hypothesis in an n-best list.

In our scenario, we first generate 1000 distinct n-best translation candidates using the phrase-based system described in Section 2. For each translation candidate, we extend its feature set by adding 17 new features corresponding to the baseline `black-box` QE features[4] extracted with the QuEst++ toolkit[5] (Specia et al., 2015).

The baseline `black-box` feature extraction process does not require to train a complete QE system. For that, QuEst++ only requires some resources: both source and target language models, source-target lexical table, and n-gram counts. In

our case we use the same data as for our phrase-base SMT system in order to generate these resources.

Given the updated n-best with the decoder and QE features, we use the rescoring scripts available within the Moses toolkit[6] to learn new feature weights on a development set using the k-best MIRA algorithm (Cherry and Foster, 2012). Finally, the 1000-best list with distinct translations generated from the test set are rescored, re-ranked and the 1-best translation is used as final translation candidate.

4 Weighted Ranking Optimisation

The Weighted Ranking Optimisation algorithm is based on PRO. PRO estimates weights by classifying translation candidate pairs in the n-best list into "correctly ordered" and "incorrectly ordered" according an automatic evaluation metric. However, enumerating all possible pairs in the n-best is impractical, even with a small 100-best list the number of pairs still makes it impractical. PRO uses a sampling strategy to avoid this problem. The sampling strategy first randomly selects a Γ number of candidate pairs, and further select Ξ pairs of candidate with the largest metric difference. The model weights are then trained using the MegaM (Daume, 2004) classifier with the selected samples.

WRO uses same procedure as PRO, but with a different sampling strategy. Also, it uses a different weighting scheme for the training samples. In a nutshell, WRO aims to address the following limitations of PRO:

1. PRO's random sampling is not the optimum way for selecting samples since the target is not clear. As we only select a small sample from the entire sample space, a clearer target should give better training quality. We refer to these targets as `oracles`, as they are the translation output we want the system to produce, often the reference translation. In WRO, the oracles are the top 10% candidates (sorted by BLEU score) in the n-best list;

2. In PRO all sampled sentences are considered equally important. Although we select the same number of samples for each training

---

[4] `www.quest.dcs.shef.ac.uk/quest_files/`
`features_blackbox_baseline_17`
[5] `www.quest.dcs.shef.ac.uk`

[6] `http://github.com/moses-smt/`
`mosesdecoder/tree/master/scripts/`
`nbest-rescore`

sentence, these sentences may be very different. For example, reachable sentences[7] can be more important than unreachable ones. Unreachable translations are very common in SMT. They may be caused by words in the reference translation that do not appear in the system's phrase table, i.e. that have not been seen (enough) in the training corpus. This could also happen because the reference translation is inherently wrong, which is common in crowd-sourced corpora. In both cases, unreachable translations cannot be correctly scored by automatic evaluation metrics. Therefore, we cannot learn useful information from unreachable translations to discriminate between good and bad translations, and this often harms training performance.

3. PRO uses BLEU to assess the quality of translation candidates. However, BLEU was originally designed for document-level evaluation, and as such is less accurate for sentence-level evaluation.

The WRO procedure is described in Algorithm 1 with SIMPBLEU_RECALL (Song et al., 2013) used as the scoring function for the evaluation of translation candidates. In previous WMT editions (Callison-Burch et al., 2012; Macháček and Bojar, 2013), SIMPBLEU has been shown to have better correlation than BLEU for the assessment of translation quality at sentence-level.

Similar to PRO, we use n-best list Nb as one of our candidate pools for sample selection. We also create another list called oracle list, Nb_{oracle}. We select the top 10 percent of all candidates in the n-best list with the highest metric score as oracles and store them in the oracle list.

The sampling procedure includes two steps: first, a Γ number of candidate pairs $\{e_s, e'_s\}$ are randomly selected from the two lists, where e_s and e'_s are represented by their corresponding feature values $h(e_s)$ and $h(e'_s)$. Contrary to PRO, WRO focuses on ranking the oracle translations in the correct order among all candidates. In this case, we define the candidate e_s as an oracle that is randomly selected from the oracle list Nb_{oracle}, and

e'_s is the non-oracle that is randomly selected from the n-best list Nb. We select e'_s from entire n-best list (if e'_s is also included in the top 10% candidates with highest metric score, then the candidate with the better metric score is considered the oracle). The selected candidates are then evaluated by an automatic evaluation metric m. Sampled pairs with a metric difference (i.e. $m(e_s) - m(e'_s)$) below a threshold will be discarded. After the first step, we choose additional Ξ pairs with the greatest metric difference to generate our training instances.

The training instances and their label generation is the same as for PRO, except that we also add a global weight (w_G) to each training instance to indicate its importance. In this case, our training instances are:

$$\{+, w_G, h(e_s) - h(e'_s)\} \text{ if } m(e) - m(e') > 0$$
$$\{-, w_G, h(e_s) - h(e'_s)\} \text{ if } m(e) - m(e') < 0$$
$$(1)$$

We use w_G to penalise training samples generated from unreachable sentences. For the dataset in our experiments, empirical results have shown that a translation dataset with a SIMPBLEU score of 0.4 has acceptable translation quality. Therefore, we downweight a training sentence exponentially if the oracle candidate BLEU score is below 0.4. The w_G parameter is defined as:

$$w_G = \begin{cases} 1 & \text{if } BLEU_{Top} \geq 0.4 \\ e^{BLEU_{Top}-0.4} & \text{if } BLEU_{Top} < 0.4 \end{cases}$$
$$(2)$$

where the $BLEU_{Top}$ is the BLEU score of the oracle candidate.

After the sampling and training instance generation, we optimise the weights by any off-the-shelf binary classifier that supports weighted training instances. In our experiment, we use the MegaM (Daume, 2004) classifier, the same classifier as in PRO.

5 Results

For our primary submission, we used the two parts of the newsdev2016 development set in two ways: the first half (named newsdev_1) was used to tune our phrase-based SMT system, while the second half (named newsdev_2) was used as an internal test set. The results on the official newstest2016 corpus are presented in Table 2.

---

[7]A reachable sentence is a sentence for which the model can produce exactly the reference. However, exactly reproducing the reference is not always possible. Therefore in this paper we define a reachable sentence as the best translation hypothesis of a given sentence to reach a certain score.

Algorithm 1 Weighted Ranking Optimisation

Require: Development corpus $D = (f^t, r^t)_{s=1}^S$,
   Initial random weights Λ_0, $\Gamma = 5000$, $\Xi = 50$

1: **for** $i = 1$ to I iterations **do**
2:     MegaM Training instances $R = \{\}$
3:     **for each** (f, e) in D **do**
4:         Calculate w_G acc. Eq. 2
5:         $r_s = \{\}$
6:         $Nb = \text{DecodeNbest}(\Lambda_i, f)$
7:         $Nb_{top} = 10\%$ best SIMPBLEU(Nb)
8:         **while** length$(r_s) < \Gamma$ **do**
9:             select e_s from Nb_{top}
10:            select e_s' from Nb
11:            **if** $|m(e_s,) - m(e_s',)| > \text{threshold}$ **then**
12:                Generate samples x acc. Eq. 1
13:                $r_s \leftarrow r_s + x$
14:            **end if**
15:         **end while**
16:         Sort s according to $|m(e_s,) - m(e_s',)|$
17:         $R \leftarrow \Xi$ samples with the largest BLEU difference in r_s
18:     **end for**
19:     $\Lambda_{i+1} \leftarrow \text{MegaM}(R)$
20: **end for**
21: **return** (Λ_{i+1}, R)

	BLEU	BLEU-c	TER
MERT	24.17	**23.63**	80.13
+ rescored n-best	**24.49**	23.25	**78**
Oracle	34.56	32.81	69.54

Table 2: BLEU, BLEU-Cased and Translation Error Rate (TER) scores on newstest2016 of our phrase-based SMT submission with and without the use of n-best rescoring. The third line shows the upper bound of our system with the n-best entries scored and sorted against the reference translations using Meteor. The improvement in BLEU for our n-best rescoring over the baseline MERT is statistically significant with $p \leq 0.05$.

We can observe that n-best rescoring with additional features from QE can help identify better hypotheses within the pool of translation candidates. However, as we can see in last the row, we are still far from selecting the best possible hypothesis among those in the n-best list. This "oracle" selection corresponds to the upper bound performance using the current n-best list, based on Meteor (Denkowski and Lavie, 2011) scores measured for each translation candidate against its reference translation. This allows us to compare the actual rank of a translation hypothesis after the rescoring process with the rank it should theoretically have, if our rescoring method were perfect. We also noticed that most of the weights associated with the QE features are set to 0 after the training of the rescoring weights, and therefore most of these features do not get used.

Table 3 shows the performances of our phrase-based system tuned with either PRO or WRO, instead of MERT. We ran these two tuning algorithms on two different development sets: first on newsdev_2, similarly to our rescoring system, second using all the three development sets available for the task combined. We observe that with a smaller development set WRO performs similarly to our system tuned with PRO. However, when the size of the tuning corpus increases, PRO is able to benefit more from the latter, while the system tuned with WRO does not improve its performance.

6   Conclusions

We presented our phrase-based MT system built using Moses and two variants of this system that were submitted to the WMT16 English-Romanian translation task. As a primary system, we used n-best rescoring with QE features in an attempt to help identify the best translation hypothesis within a 1000 distinct n-best list. We observed some improvements from rescoring, but also the fact that some of the QE features had weights set to zero, and therefore were not used. In future work, we will experiment with a larger QE feature set, which could help us identify more useful features.

As a secondary system, we submitted the phrase-based system trained with WRO, an optimisation algorithm based on PRO which targets weaknesses of PRO in sampling translation candidates. The two algorithms performed similarly on the task, with PRO obtaining better results from using larger development sets.

Acknowledgments

This work was supported by the QT21 (H2020 No. 645452) project.

Algorithm	BLEU	BLEU-c	TER
Dev set: newsdev_2			
WRO	**24.64***	**23.35***	**76.29**
PRO	24.58	23.30	76.30
Dev set: newdev_1 + newsdev_2 + setimes2			
WRO	24.63	23.36	77.20
PRO	**24.76**	**23.49**	**77.05**

Table 3: BLEU, BLEU-Cased and Translation Error Rate (TER) scores of our phrase-based SMT submission on newstest2016 and tuned either with WRO or PRO. In the first row, we only used newsdev_2 as dev set, while in the second row we concatenated all the three dev sets together. The * indicates that the observed improvement of WRO over PRO are statistically significant with $p \leq 0.05$.

References

Alexandre Allauzen, Lauriane Aufrant, Franck Burlot, Elena Knyazeva, Thomas Lavergne, and François Yvon. 2016. LIMSI@WMT'16 : Machine translation of news. Berlin, Germany, August.

Chris Callison-Burch, Philipp Koehn, Christof Monz, Matt Post, Radu Soricut, and Lucia Specia. 2012. Findings of the 2012 workshop on statistical machine translation. In *Proceedings of the Seventh Workshop on Statistical Machine Translation*, pages 10–51, Montréal, Canada, June. Association for Computational Linguistics.

Colin Cherry and George Foster. 2012. Batch tuning strategies for statistical machine translation. In *Proceedings of the 2012 Conference of the North American Chapter of the Association for Computational Linguistics: Human Language Technologies*, pages 427–436. Association for Computational Linguistics.

Hal Daume. 2004. Notes on cg and lm-bfgs optimization of logistic regression. *Unpublished.*

Michael Denkowski and Alon Lavie. 2011. Meteor 1.3: Automatic metric for reliable optimization and evaluation of machine translation systems. In *Proceedings of the Sixth Workshop on Statistical Machine Translation*, pages 85–91. Association for Computational Linguistics.

Qin Gao and Stephan Vogel. 2008. Parallel implementations of word alignment tool. In *Software Engineering, Testing, and Quality Assurance for Natural Language Processing*, pages 49–57. Association for Computational Linguistics.

Kenneth Heafield. 2011. KenLM: Faster and Smaller Language Model Queries. In *Proceedings of the EMNLP 2011 Sixth Workshop on Statistical Machine Translation*, pages 187–197, Edinburgh, Scotland, United Kingdom, July.

Mark Hopkins and Jonathan May. 2011. Tuning as ranking. In *Proceedings of the 2011 Conference on Empirical Methods in Natural Language Processing*, pages 1352–1362, Edinburgh, Scotland, UK., July. Association for Computational Linguistics.

Philipp Koehn, Hieu Hoang, Alexandra Birch, Chris Callison-Burch, Marcello Federico, Nicola Bertoldi, Brooke Cowan, Wade Shen, Christine Moran, Richard Zens, Chris Dyer, Ondřej Bojar, Alexandra Constantine, and Evan Herbst. 2007. Moses: Open Source Toolkit for Statistical Machine Translation. pages 177–180, Prague, Czech Republic, June.

Matouš Macháček and Ondřej Bojar. 2013. Results of the WMT13 metrics shared task. In *Proceedings of the Eighth Workshop on Statistical Machine Translation*, pages 45–51, Sofia, Bulgaria, August. Association for Computational Linguistics.

Franz Josef Och. 2003. Minimum Error Rate Training in Statistical Machine Translation. pages 160–167, Sapporo, Japan, July.

Kishore Papineni, Salim Roukos, Todd Ward, and Wei-Jing Zhu. 2002. Bleu: a Method for Automatic Evaluation of Machine Translation. In *Proceedings of the 41st Annual Meeting of the Association for Computational Linguistics*, pages 311–318, Philadelphia, Pennsylvania, USA, July.

Anthony Rousseau. 2013. Xenc: An open-source tool for data selection in natural language processing. *The Prague Bulletin of Mathematical Linguistics*, (100):73–82.

Xingyi Song, Trevor Cohn, and Lucia Specia. 2013. Bleu deconstructed: Designing a better mt evaluation metric. In *CICLING*.

Lucia Specia, Gustavo Paetzold, and Carolina Scarton. 2015. Multi-level translation quality prediction with quest++. In *Proceedings of ACL-IJCNLP 2015 System Demonstrations*, pages 115–120, Beijing, China, July. Association for Computational Linguistics and The Asian Federation of Natural Language Processing.

MetaMind Neural Machine Translation System for WMT 2016

James Bradbury
MetaMind - A Salesforce Company
Palo Alto, CA
james.bradbury@salesforce.com

Richard Socher
MetaMind - A Salesforce Company
Palo Alto, CA
rsocher@salesforce.com

Abstract

Neural Machine Translation (NMT) systems, introduced only in 2013, have achieved state of the art results in many MT tasks. MetaMind's submissions to WMT '16 seek to push the state of the art in one such task, English→German news-domain translation. We integrate promising recent developments in NMT, including subword splitting and back-translation for monolingual data augmentation, and introduce the Y-LSTM, a novel neural translation architecture.

1 Introduction

The field of Neural Machine Translation (NMT), which seeks to use end-to-end neural networks to translate natural language text, has existed for only three years. In that time, researchers have explored architectures ranging from convolutional neural networks (Kalchbrenner and Blunsom, 2013) to recurrent neural networks (Chung et al., 2014) to attentional models (Bahdanau et al., 2015; Luong et al., 2015) and achieved better performance than traditional statistical or syntax-based MT techniques on many language pairs. NMT models first achieved state-of-the-art performance on the WMT English→German news-domain task in 2015 (Luong et al., 2015) and subsequent improvements have been reported since then (Sennrich et al., 2015a; Li and Jurafsky, 2016).

The problem of machine translation is fundamentally a sequence-to-sequence transduction task, and most approaches have been based on an encoder-decoder architecture (Sutskever et al., 2014; Cho et al., 2014). This entails coupled neural networks that encode the input sentence into a vector or set of vectors and decode that vector representation into an output sentence in a differ-

ent language respectively. Recently, a third component has been added to many of these models: an attention mechanism, whereby the decoder can attend directly to localized information from the input sentence during the output generation process (Bahdanau et al., 2015; Luong et al., 2015). The encoder and decoder in these models typically consist of one-layer (Cho et al., 2014) or multi-layer recurrent neural networks (RNNs); we use four- and five-layer long short-term memory (LSTM) RNNs. The attention mechanism in our four-layer model is what Luong (2015) describes as "Global attention (dot)"; the mechanism in our five-layer Y-LSTM model is described in Section 2.1.

Every NMT system must contend with the problem of unbounded output vocabulary: systems that restrict possible output words to the most common 50,000 or 100,000 that can fit comfortably in a softmax classifier will perform poorly due to large numbers of "out-of-vocabulary" or "unknown" outputs. Even models that can produce every word found in the training corpus for the target language (Jean et al., 2015) may be unable to output words found only in the test corpus. There are three main techniques for achieving fully open-ended decoder output. Models may use computed alignments between source and target sentences to directly copy or transform a word from the input sentence whose corresponding translation is not present in the vocabulary (Luong et al., 2015) or they may conduct sentence tokenization at the level of individual characters (Ling et al., 2015) or subword units such as morphemes (Sennrich et al., 2015b). The latter techniques allow the decoder to construct words it has not previously encountered out of known characters or morphemes; we apply the subword splitting strategy using Morfessor 2.0, an unsupervised morpheme segmentation model (Virpioja et

Proceedings of the First Conference on Machine Translation, Volume 2: Shared Task Papers, pages 264–267,
Berlin, Germany, August 11-12, 2016. ©2016 Association for Computational Linguistics

al., 2013).

Another focus of recent research has been ways of using monolingual corpus data, available in much larger quantities, to augment the limited parallel corpora used to train translation models. One way to accomplish this is to train a separate monolingual language model on a large corpus of the target language, then use this language model as an additional input to the decoder or for re-ranking output translations (Gülçehre et al., 2015). More recently, Sennrich (2015b) introduced the concept of augmentation through back-translation, where an entirely separate translation model is trained on a parallel corpus from the target language to the source language. This backwards translation model is then used to machine-translate a monolingual corpus from the target language into the source language, producing a pseudo-parallel corpus to augment the original parallel training corpus. We extend this back-translation method by translating a very large monolingual German corpus into English, then concatenating a unique subset of this augmentation corpus to the original parallel corpus for each training epoch.

2 Model Description

The model identified as `metamind-single` is based on the attention-based encoder-decoder framework described in Luong (2015), using the attention mechanism referred to as "Global attention (dot)." The encoder is a four-layer stacked LSTM recurrent neural network whose inputs (at the bottom layer) are vectors w_t^{in} corresponding to the subword units in the input sentence and which saves the topmost output state at each timestep e_t as the variable-length encoding matrix E. The decoder also contains a four-layer stacked LSTM whose states (c_0 and h_0 for each layer) are initialized to the last states for each layer of the encoder. At the first timestep, the decoder LSTM receives as input an initialization word vector w_0^{out}; its topmost output state h_t is concatenated with an encoder context vector κ_t computed as:

$$\text{score}(h_t, e_s) = h_t e_s^{\top}$$
$$\alpha_{st} = \text{softmax}_{\text{all } s}(\text{score}(h_t, e_s))$$
$$\kappa_t = \sum_s \alpha_{st} e_s$$

This concatenated output is then fed through an additional neural network layer to produce a final attentional output vector $\tilde{h}$, which serves as input to the output softmax:

$$\tilde{h} = \tanh(W_{\text{att}}[h_t; \kappa_t])$$
$$\text{output probabilities} = \text{softmax}(W_{\text{out}}\tilde{h})$$

For subsequent timesteps, the decoder LSTM receives as input the previous word vector w_{t-1}^{out} concatenated with the previous output vector $\tilde{h}$.

Decoding is performed using beam search, with beam width 16. The beam search decoder differs slightly from Luong (2015) in that we normalize output sentence probabilities by length, following Cho (2014), rather than performing ad-hoc adjustments to correct for short output sentences.

2.1 Y-LSTM Model

The model identified as `metamind-ylstm` uses a novel attentional framework we call the Y-LSTM. The encoder is a five-layer stacked LSTM recurrent neural network language model (RNN-LM) with subword-vector inputs w_t^{in}, whose topmost output state h_t^{top} is used as input to a softmax layer which predicts the next input token. The middle ($l = 3$) layer of this encoder RNN-LM is connected recurrently to a single-layer LSTM called the "tracker;" a_t denotes the set of inputs to a given LSTM layer:

$$a_t^{l \neq 3} = [h_t^{l-1}; h_{t-1}^l]$$
$$a_t^{l=3} = [h_t^{l-1}; h_{t-1}^l; h_{t-1}^{\text{tracker}}]$$
$$a_t^{\text{tracker}} = [h_{t-1}^{\text{tracker}}; h_t^3]$$

The hidden and memory states c_t^{tracker} and h_t^{tracker} of the tracker LSTM are saved at each timestep as the variable-length encoding matrices C and H. The decoder is an analogous RNN-LM with a tracker LSTM, identical except that the hidden and memory states of the decoder's tracker ($\tilde{c}_t^{\text{tracker}}$ and $\tilde{h}_t^{\text{tracker}}$) are replaced at each timestep with an attentional sum of the encoder's saved tracker states:

$$\text{score}(\tilde{h}_t, h_s) = \tilde{h}_t h_s^{\top}$$
$$\alpha_{st} = \text{softmax}_{\text{all } s}(\text{score}(\tilde{h}_t^{\text{tracker}}, h_s^{\text{tracker}}))$$
$$\tilde{c}_t^{\text{tracker}} = \sum_s \alpha_{st} c_s^{\text{tracker}}$$
$$\tilde{h}_t^{\text{tracker}} = \sum_s \alpha_{st} h_s^{\text{tracker}}$$

System	BLEU-c on `newstest2016`
Best phrase-based system (`uedin-syntax`)	30.6
Other NMT systems – single model	
NYU/U. Montreal character-based	30.8
U. Edinburgh subword-based (`uedin-nmt-single`)	31.6
Other NMT systems – ensemble or model combination	
U. Edinburgh ensemble of 4 (`uedin-nmt-ensemble`)	34.2
Our systems – single model	
`metamind-single`	31.6
`metamind-ylstm`	29.3
Our systems – ensemble	
`metamind-ensemble`	32.3
Ensemble of four checkpoints without Y-LSTM	32.1

Table 1: BLEU results on the official WMT 2016 test set. Only our main ensemble was entered into the human ranking process, coming in second place behind U. Edinburgh.

The overall network loss is the sum of the language model (negative log-likelihood over the output softmax) losses for the encoder and decoder.

3   Experiment Description

Initial tokenization and preprocessing of the WMT 2016 English→German news translation dataset was performed using the standard scripts provided with Moses (Koehn et al., 2007). Two further processing steps were used to create the subword-based training dataset. First, capitalized characters were replaced with a sequence of a capitalization control character (a Unicode private-use character) and the corresponding lowercase character, in order to allow the subword splitting algorithm to treat capitalized words as either inherently capitalized or capitalized versions of lowercase words. Without this step, much of the limited output softmax capacity is taken up with capitalized variants of common lowercase words; performing this transformation also allows us to forego "truecasing," which removes sentence-initial capitalization in a lossy and sometimes unhelpful way. Second, the capitalization-transformed training corpus for each language is ingested by a Morfessor 2.0 instance configured to use a balance between corpus and vocabulary entropy that produces a vocabulary of approximately 50,000 subword units.

For all experiments, we used using plain stochastic gradient descent with learning rate 0.7, gradient clipping at magnitude 5.0, dropout of 0.2, and learning rate decay of 50% per epoch after 8 epochs.

Following Sennrich (2015b), we first trained a non-Y-LSTM model in the reverse direction (German→English) on the full WMT '16 training corpus (4.4 million sentences). This model was then used simultaneously on 8 GPUs (with a beam search width of 4 for speed purposes) to translate 45 million sentences of the 2014 monolingual German news crawl into English. A full copy of the original training corpus was then concatenated with a unique subset of this augmentation corpus to create a new training corpus for each epoch from 1 to 10; the corpus for epoch 1 was then repeated as epoch 11 *et cetera*.

For `metamind-single`, we trained a non-Y-LSTM model using these augmented corpora, with data-parallel synchronous SGD across four GPUs enabling a batch size of 384 and training speed of about 2,500 subword units per second. The run submitted as `metamind-single` uses a single snapshot of this model after 12 total training epochs.

For `metamind-ylstm`, we trained a Y-LSTM model using the same corpora, with data-parallel synchronous SGD across four GPUs enabling a batch size of 320 and training speed of about 1,500 subword units per second. The run submitted as `metamind-ylstm` uses a single snapshot of this model after 9 total training epochs.

The run submitted as `metamind-ensemble` uses an equally-weighted ensemble of three snapshots of the `metamind-single` model (after 10, 11, and 12 epochs) and a single snapshot of the `metamind-ylstm` model after 9 total training epochs.

4 Results

Results for all three runs described above are presented in Table 1. Only the ensemble was submitted to the human evaluation process, with a final ranking of second place (behind U. Edinburgh's ensemble of four independently initialized models). Our best single model matches the performance of the best model from U. Edinburgh, which applies a similar attentional framework, subword splitting, and back-translated augmentation.

The Y-LSTM model underperformed relative to the model based on Luong (2015), but provided a small additional boost to the ensemble. The primary contribution of this model is to demonstrate that *purely* attentional NMT is possible: the only inputs to the decoder are through the attention mechanism. This may be helpful for using translation to build general attentional sentence encoding models, since the representation of the input sentence is entirely in the attentional encoding, not split between an attentional encoding vector and a vector representing the last timestep of the multi-layer encoder hidden state.

Acknowledgements

We would like to thank the developers of Chainer (Tokui et al.,), which we used for all models and experiments reported here. We also thank Stephen Merity, Kai Sheng Tai, and Caiming Xiong for their helpful feedback, and all participants in the manual evaluation campaign. We thank the Salesforce acquisition and IT teams for keeping the MetaMind compute cluster up and running throughout the acquisition process.

References

D. Bahdanau, K. Cho, and Y. Bengio. 2015. Neural machine translation by jointly learning to align and translate. In *ICLR*.

K. Cho, B. van Merrienboer, D. Bahdanau, and Y. Bengio. 2014. On the properties of neural machine translation: Encoder-decoder approaches. *CoRR*, abs/1409.1259.

J. Chung, C. Gulcehre, K. Cho, and Y. Bengio. 2014. Empirical evaluation of gated recurrent neural networks on sequence modeling. *arXiv preprint arXiv:1412.3555*.

Çaglar Gülçehre, Orhan Firat, Kelvin Xu, Kyunghyun Cho, Loïc Barrault, Huei-Chi Lin, Fethi Bougares, Holger Schwenk, and Yoshua Bengio. 2015. On using monolingual corpora in neural machine translation. *CoRR*, abs/1503.03535.

Sébastien Jean, Kyunghyun Cho, Roland Memisevic, and Yoshua Bengio. 2015. On using very large target vocabulary for neural machine translation. In *ACL*.

Nal Kalchbrenner and Phil Blunsom. 2013. Recurrent continuous translation models. In *EMNLP*.

Philipp Koehn, Hieu Hoang, Alexandra Birch, Chris Callison-Burch, Marcello Federico, Nicola Bertoldi, Brooke Cowan, Wade Shen, Christine Moran, Richard Zens, et al. 2007. Moses: Open source toolkit for statistical machine translation. In *Proceedings of the 45th annual meeting of the ACL on interactive poster and demonstration sessions*, pages 177–180. Association for Computational Linguistics.

Jiwei Li and Daniel Jurafsky. 2016. Mutual information and diverse decoding improve neural machine translation. *CoRR*, abs/1601.00372.

Wang Ling, Isabel Trancoso, Chris Dyer, and Alan W. Black. 2015. Character-based neural machine translation. *CoRR*, abs/1511.04586.

M. T. Luong, H. Pham, and C. D. Manning. 2015. Effective approaches to attention-based neural machine translation. In *EMNLP*.

Rico Sennrich, Barry Haddow, and Alexandra Birch. 2015a. Improving neural machine translation models with monolingual data. *CoRR*, abs/1511.06709.

Rico Sennrich, Barry Haddow, and Alexandra Birch. 2015b. Neural machine translation of rare words with subword units. *CoRR*, abs/1508.07909.

I. Sutskever, O. Vinyals, and Q. V. Le. 2014. Sequence to sequence learning with neural networks. In *NIPS*.

Seiya Tokui, Kenta Oono, and Shohei Hido. Chainer: a next-generation open source framework for deep learning.

Sami Virpioja, Peter Smit, Stig-Arne Grönroos, Mikko Kurimo, et al. 2013. Morfessor 2.0: Python implementation and extensions for morfessor baseline.

NYU-MILA Neural Machine Translation Systems for WMT'16

Junyoung Chung
Université de Montréal
junyoung.chung@umontreal.ca

Kyunghyun Cho
New York University

Yoshua Bengio
Université de Montréal
CIFAR Senior Fellow

Abstract

We describe the neural machine translation system of New York University (NYU) and University of Montreal (MILA) for the translation tasks of WMT'16. The main goal of NYU-MILA submission to WMT'16 is to evaluate a new character-level decoding approach in neural machine translation on various language pairs. The proposed neural machine translation system is an attention-based encoder–decoder with a subword-level encoder and a character-level decoder. The decoder of the neural machine translation system does not require explicit segmentation, when characters are used as tokens. The character-level decoding approach provides benefits especially when translating a source language into other morphologically rich languages.

1 Introduction

Word-level modelling with explicit segmentation has been a standard approach in statistical machine translation systems. This is mainly due to the issue of data sparsity, caused by the, exponential growth of the state space as the length of sequences grows larger. This becomes much more severe when a sequence is represented with characters. In addition to the data sparsity issue, in linguistics, words or their segmented-out lexemes are usually considered as basic units of meaning, which makes words to be more suitable when solving natural language processing tasks.

There are however two pressing issues here. The first issue is the absence of a perfect segmentation algorithm for any single language. A perfect segmentation algorithm should be able to segment given unsegmented sentence into a sequence of lexemes and morphemes. The other issue, which is specific to neural network approaches, is that neural machine translation systems suffers from increased complexity due to the large vocabulary size (Jean et al., 2015; Luong et al., 2015), which does not happen with character-level modelling.

Most issues of word-level modelling can be addressed to certain extent by switching into finer tokens, e.g., characters. In fact, to neural networks, each and every token in the vocabulary is treated as an independent entity, and the semantics of tokens are simply learned to maximize the objective function (Chung et al., 2016). This property allows a lot of freedom to the neural machine translation system in the choice of tokens.

The NYU-MILA neural machine translation system is built on the idea of directly generating characters, instead of words, that can possibly unlink a machine translation system from the need of explicit segmentation as a preprocessing step, which is often suboptimal in solving translation tasks. We focus on representing the target sentence as a sequence of characters, and the source sentence as a sequence of subwords (Sennrich et al., 2015).

2 System Description

In this section, we describe the details of the NYU-MILA neural machine translation system. In our system, we closely follow the neural machine translation model proposed by Bahdanau et al. (2015). A neural machine translation model (Forcada and Ñeco, 1997; Kalchbrenner and Blunsom, 2013; Cho et al., 2014; Sutskever et al., 2014) aims at building an end-to-end neural network that takes as input a source sentence $X = (x_1, \ldots, x_{T_x})$ and outputs its translation $Y = (y_1, \ldots, y_{T_y})$, where

---

This system description paper summarizes and details the experimental procedure described in Chung et al. (2016)

Proceedings of the First Conference on Machine Translation, Volume 2: Shared Task Papers, pages 268–271,
Berlin, Germany, August 11-12, 2016. ©2016 Association for Computational Linguistics

x_t and $y_{t'}$ are respectively source and target tokens. The neural network is constructed as a composite of an encoder network and a decoder network.

The encoder maps the input sentence X into its continuous representation. A bidirectional recurrent neural network, which consists of two recurrent neural networks (RNNs), is used to give more representational power to the encoder. The forward network reads the input sentence in a forward direction: $\overrightarrow{\mathbf{z}}_t = \overrightarrow{\phi}(e_x(x_t), \overrightarrow{\mathbf{z}}_{t-1})$, where $e_x(x_t)$ is a continuous embedding of the t-th input symbol, and ϕ is a recurrent activation function. Similarly, the reverse network reads the sentence in a reverse direction (right to left): $\overleftarrow{\mathbf{z}}_t = \overleftarrow{\phi}(e_x(x_t), \overleftarrow{\mathbf{z}}_{t+1})$. At each location in the input sentence, we concatenate the hidden states from the forward and reverse RNNs to form a context set: $C = \{\mathbf{z}_1, \ldots, \mathbf{z}_{T_x}\}$, where $\mathbf{z}_t = [\overrightarrow{\mathbf{z}}_t; \overleftarrow{\mathbf{z}}_t]$.

Then the decoder computes the conditional distribution over all possible translations based on this context set. This is done by first rewriting the conditional probability of a translation: $\log p(Y \mid X) = \sum_{t'=1}^{T_y} \log p(y_{t'} \mid y_{<t'}, X)$. For each conditional term in the summation, the decoder RNN updates its hidden state by

$$\mathbf{h}_{t'} = \phi(e_y(y_{t'-1}), \mathbf{h}_{t'-1}, \mathbf{c}_{t'}), \qquad (1)$$

where e_y is the continuous embedding of a target symbol. $\mathbf{c}_{t'}$ is a context vector computed by a soft-alignment mechanism:

$$\mathbf{c}_{t'} = f_{\text{align}}(e_y(y_{t'-1}), \mathbf{h}_{t'-1}, C)). \qquad (2)$$

The soft-alignment mechanism f_{align} weights each vector in the context set C according to its relevance given what has been translated. The weight of each vector $\mathbf{z}_t$ is computed by

$$\alpha_{t,t'} = \frac{1}{Z} e^{f_{\text{score}}(e_y(y_{t'-1}), \mathbf{h}_{t'-1}, \mathbf{z}_t)}, \qquad (3)$$

where f_{score} is a parametric function returning an unnormalized score for $\mathbf{z}_t$ given $\mathbf{h}_{t'-1}$ and $y_{t'-1}$. We use a feedforward network with a single hidden layer in this paper. Z is a normalization constant: $Z = \sum_{k=1}^{T_x} e^{f_{\text{score}}(e_y(y_{t'-1}), \mathbf{h}_{t'-1}, \mathbf{z}_k)}$. This procedure can be understood as computing the alignment probability between the t'-th target symbol and t-th source symbol.

The hidden state $\mathbf{h}_{t'}$, together with the previous target symbol $y_{t'-1}$ and the context vector $\mathbf{c}_{t'}$, is fed into a feedforward neural network to result in the conditional distribution:

$$p(y_{t'} \mid y_{<t'}, X) \propto e^{f_{\text{out}}^{y_{t'}}(e_y(y_{t'-1}), \mathbf{h}_{t'}, \mathbf{c}_{t'})}. \qquad (4)$$

The whole network, consisting of the encoder, decoder and soft-alignment mechanism, is then tuned end-to-end to minimize the negative log-likelihood using stochastic gradient descent. In our system, the source sentence X is a sequence of subword tokens extracted by byte-pair-encoding (BPE) (Sennrich et al., 2015), and the target sentence Y is represented as a sequence of characters.

3 Experimental Settings

In this section, we describe the details of the experimental settings for our system.

Corpora and Preprocessing We use all available training parallel corpora for four language pairs from WMT'16: En-Cs, En-De, En-Ru and En-Fi. They consist of 63.5M, 4.5M, 2.3M and 2M sentence pairs, respectively. We do not use any monolingual corpus. We only use the sentence pairs, when the source side is up to 50 subword symbols long and the target side is up to 500 characters. For all the pairs other than En-Fi, we use newstest-2013 as a development set, and for En-Fi, we use newsdev-2015 as a development set.

All of the source corpora were preprocessed using BPE (Sennrich et al., 2015), and for the target corpora, no additional preprocessing step is required. For the target vocabulary, we use 300 characters and two additional tokens reserved for $\langle$EOS$\rangle$ and $\langle$UNK$\rangle$. For the source vocabulary we constrain the size of BPE symbols up to $30,000$.

Models and Training We use gated recurrent units (Cho et al., 2014) (GRUs) for the recurrent neural networks. The encoder has 512 hidden units for each direction (forward and reverse), and the decoder has two hidden layer with 1024 units each. The embedding layers of both source and target sides have dimensionality of 512 without any non-linearity. Both f_{out} and f_{score} are feedforward neural networks with an intermediate hidden layer with 512 tanh units.

We train the model using stochastic gradient descent with Adam (Kingma and Ba, 2014) using the default parameters introduced in the paper. Each update is computed using a minibatch of 128 sentence pairs. The norm of the gradient is rescaled with a threshold set to 1 (Pascanu et al., 2013). We set the initial learning rate of 0.0001.

Language Pair	BLEU-c	TER	Ranking		
			BLEU-c cons.	BLEU-c uncons.	Human
En-Cs	23.6	0.639	2/12	2/12	2/8
En-De	30.8	0.583	3/12	3/12	4/11
En-Fi	15.1	0.771	3/12	4/13	4/11
En-Ru	23.1	0.677	6/7	6/8	4/8

Table 1: Empirical results of the NYU-MILA systems on WMT'16 test sets. All of our submitted systems are constrained. For ranking by BLEU-c scores, when there are multiple submissions from a single system, we count it as one system. Some of the systems that showed in BLEU-c case do not show in the human evaluation, hence the total number of systems does not match. We present the ranking in both constrained setting (cons.) and unconstrained setting (uncons.) on the table.

Decoding and Evaluation We use beamsearch to approximately find the most likely translation given a source sentence. We use a beam width of 15 to find the model with best translation quality. The translation quality is evaluated by using BLEU.[1] For the WMT'16 test sets, we use the same beam width.

Ensembles We build an ensemble model using eight independent neural machine translation models initialized with different parameters. We decode from an ensemble by taking the average of the output probabilities at each step.

Decoding Speed of the Character-Level Decoder We evaluate the decoding speed of the character-level decoder and compare with a subword-level decoder on newstest-2013 corpus (En-De) with a single Titan X GPU. The subword-level decoder generates 31.9 words per second, and the character-level decoder generates 27.5 words per second. Note that this is evaluated in an online setting, where only one sentence is translated at a time, and translating in a batch setting could differ from these results.

4 Experimental Results

The results of the NYU-MILA system is presented in Table 1. The character-level decoding works well on most of the languages that are tested, achieving comparable BLEU-c scores to other approaches using words or subwords (BPE) as tokens. Note that our system does not incorporate extra monolingual training corpus, and does not include any kind of postprocessing e.g., reranking.

5 Conclusion

We present the NYU-MILA neural machine translation system for WMT'16, which has a character-level decoder on the target side. Our results show that a character-level decoder can perform comparable to state-of-the-art systems. The NYU-MILA neural machine translation system achieved second rank in En-Cs and En-Fi (constrained only) and third rank in En-De. To the best of our knowledge the NYU-MILA system may be the only submitted system that directly generates characters instead of words or subwords. The biggest advantage of the character-level decoding approach is that the machine translation system no longer requires any preprocessing step, such as segmentation.

Acknowledgments

The authors would like to thank the developers of Theano (Team et al., 2016). We acknowledge the support of the following agencies for research funding and computing support: NSERC, Calcul Québec, Compute Canada, the Canada Research Chairs, CIFAR and Samsung. KC thanks the support by Facebook, Google (Google Faculty Award 2016) and NVIDIA (GPU Center of Excellence 2015-2016). JC thanks Orhan Firat for his constructive feedbacks.

References

Dzmitry Bahdanau, Kyunghyun Cho, and Yoshua Bengio. 2015. Neural machine translation by jointly learning to align and translate. In *Proceedings of the International Conference on Learning Representations (ICLR)*.

Kyunghyun Cho, Bart van Merrienboer, Caglar Gulcehre, Dzmitry Bahdanau, Fethi Bougares, Holger

---

[1] We used the multi-bleu.perl script from Moses during training and internal evaluation.

Schwenk, and Yoshua Bengio. 2014. Learning phrase representations using rnn encoder–decoder for statistical machine translation. In *Proceedings of the 2014 Conference on Empirical Methods in Natural Language Processing (EMNLP)*, pages 1724–1734.

Junyoung Chung, Kyunghyun Cho, and Yoshua Bengio. 2016. A character-level decoder without explicit segmentation for neural machine translation. *arXiv preprint arXiv:1603.06147*.

Mikel L Forcada and Ramón P Ñeco. 1997. Recursive hetero-associative memories for translation. In *International Work-Conference on Artificial Neural Networks*, pages 453–462. Springer.

Sébastien Jean, Kyunghyun Cho, Roland Memisevic, and Yoshua Bengio. 2015. On using very large target vocabulary for neural machine translation. In *Proceedings of the 53rd Annual Meeting of the Association for Computational Linguistics: Short Papers-Volume 2*.

Nal Kalchbrenner and Phil Blunsom. 2013. Recurrent continuous translation models. In *EMNLP*, volume 3, page 413.

Diederik Kingma and Jimmy Ba. 2014. Adam: A method for stochastic optimization. *arXiv preprint arXiv:1412.6980*.

Minh-Thang Luong, Ilya Sutskever, Quoc V Le, Oriol Vinyals, and Wojciech Zaremba. 2015. Addressing the rare word problem in neural machine translation. *arXiv preprint arXiv:1410.8206*.

Razvan Pascanu, Caglar Gulcehre, Kyunghyun Cho, and Yoshua Bengio. 2013. How to construct deep recurrent neural networks. *arXiv preprint arXiv:1312.6026*.

Rico Sennrich, Barry Haddow, and Alexandra Birch. 2015. Neural machine translation of rare words with subword units. *arXiv preprint arXiv:1508.07909*.

Ilya Sutskever, Oriol Vinyals, and Quoc V Le. 2014. Sequence to sequence learning with neural networks. In *Advances in Neural Information Processing Systems*, pages 3104–3112.

The Theano Development Team, Rami Al-Rfou, Guillaume Alain, Amjad Almahairi, Christof Angermueller, Dzmitry Bahdanau, Nicolas Ballas, Frédéric Bastien, Justin Bayer, Anatoly Belikov, et al. 2016. Theano: A python framework for fast computation of mathematical expressions. *arXiv preprint arXiv:1605.02688*.

The JHU Machine Translation Systems for WMT 2016

Shuoyang Ding, Kevin Duh, Huda Khayrallah, Philipp Koehn, and Matt Post
Center for Language and Speech Processing
Human Language Technology Center of Excellence
Department of Computer Science
Johns Hopkins University, Baltimore, MD
{dings,kevinduh,huda,phi,post}@jhu.edu

Abstract

This paper describes the submission of Johns Hopkins University for the shared translation task of ACL 2016 First Conference on Machine Translation (WMT 2016). We set up phrase-based, hierarchical phrase-based and syntax-based systems for all 12 language pairs of this year's evaluation campaign. Novel research directions we investigated include: neural probabilistic language models, bilingual neural network language models, morphological segmentation, and the attention-based neural machine translation model as reranking feature.

1 Introduction

The JHU 2016 WMT submission consists of phrase-based systems, hierarchical phrase-based systems, and syntax-based systems. In this paper we discuss features that we integrated into our system submissions. We also discuss the experiments we did with morphological pre-processing and neural reranking.

The JHU phrase-based translation systems for our participation in the WMT 2016 shared translation task[1] are based on the open source Moses toolkit (Koehn et al., 2007). We built upon strong baselines of the Edinburgh-JHU joint WMT submissions from the last year (Haddow et al., 2015), the Edinburgh syntax-based system submissions from the last year (Williams et al., 2015) as well as recent research in the field (Vaswani et al., 2013; Devlin et al., 2014). We also used the Apache Joshua translation toolkit (Post et al., 2015) to build hierarchical systems for two language tasks.

[1] http://www.statmt.org/wmt16

2 Moses Phrase-Based Systems

The phrase based system builds on the joint JHU-Edinburgh system from last year (Haddow et al., 2015). This year, we included Och clusters in various feature functions in the official submission. In addition, we included a large language model based on the CommonCrawl monolingual data and a neural network joint model.

2.1 Basic Configuration

We trained our systems with the following settings: a maximum sentence length of 80, grow-diag-final-and symmetrization of GIZA++ alignments, an interpolated Kneser-Ney smoothed 5-gram language model with KenLM (Heafield, 2011) used at runtime, hierarchical lexicalized reordering (Galley and Manning, 2008), a lexically-driven 5-gram operation sequence model (OSM) (Durrani et al., 2013) with 4 count-based supportive features, sparse domain indicator, phrase length, and count bin features (Blunsom and Osborne, 2008; Chiang et al., 2009), a distortion limit of 6, maximum phrase-length of 5, 100-best translation options, compact phrase table (Junczys-Dowmunt, 2012) minimum Bayes risk decoding (Kumar and Byrne, 2004), cube pruning (Huang and Chiang, 2007), with a stack-size of 1000 during tuning and 5000 during test and the no-reordering-over-punctuation heuristic (Koehn and Haddow, 2009). We optimize feature function weights with k-best MIRA (Cherry and Foster, 2012).

We used POS and morphological tags as additional factors in phrase translation models (Koehn and Hoang, 2007) for the German-English language pairs. We also trained target sequence models on the in-domain subset of the parallel corpus using Kneser-Ney smoothed 7-gram models. We used syntactic preordering (Collins et al., 2005)

272

Proceedings of the First Conference on Machine Translation, Volume 2: Shared Task Papers, pages 272–280,
Berlin, Germany, August 11-12, 2016. ©2016 Association for Computational Linguistics

Language Pair	Sentences
German–English	19,074
Czech–English	19,074
Finnish–English	1,500
Romanian–English	943
Russian-English	9,006
Turkish–English	500

Table 1: Tuning set sizes for phrase-based system

Language	Tokens	LM Size
Czech	6.7 billion	13GB
German	65.2 billion	107GB
English	65.1 billion	89GB
Finnish	2.9 billion	8GB
Romanian	8.1 billion	13GB
Russian	23.3 billion	41GB
Turkish	11.9 billion	23GB

Table 2: Sizes of the language model trained on the monomlingual corpora extracted from Common Crawl.

and compound splitting (Koehn and Knight, 2003) for the German-to-English systems. We did no language-specific processing for any other language.

The systems were tuned on a very large tuning set consisting of the test sets from 2008-2014, with a total of 19,074 sentences (see Table 1). We used news-test 2015 as development test set. Significantly less tuning data was available for Finnish, Romanian, and Turkish.

2.2 Och Clusters

As in last year's system, we use word classes in four feature functions: (i) the language model, (ii) the operation sequence model, (iii) the reordering model, and the (iv) sparse word translation features.

We generated Och clusters (Och, 1999) — a variant of Brown clusters — using mkcls. We have to choose a hyper parameter: the number of clusters. Our experiments and also prior work (Stewart et al., 2014) suggest that instead of committing to a single value, it is beneficial to use multiple numbers and use them in multiple feature functions concurrently. We used 50, 200, 600, and 2000 clusters, hence having 4 additional interpolated language models, 4 additional operation sequence models, 4 additional lexicalized reordering models, and 4 additional sets of sparse features.

The feature functions for word classes were trained exactly the same way as the corresponding feature functions for words. For instance, this means that the word class language model required training of individual models on the subcorpora, and then interpolation.

The computationally most expensive use of word clusters is in the language model, and to some degree the operation sequence model, both in terms of RAM and decoding speed. However, last year's experiments also showed that they are most effective there.

2.3 Huge Language Model

This year, large corpora of monolingual data were extracted from Common Crawl (Buck et al., 2014). We used this data to train 5-gram Kneser-Ney smoothed language models, pruning out 3–5 gram singletons. We trained these models with lmplz, as we did all other language models. We compressed the language models with KenLM with 4-bit quantization and use of the trie data structure.

The resulting size of the language model is listed in Table 2. The largest language model is the German model at 107GB, trained on 65.2 billion tokens, about an order of magnitude larger than previous data.

2.4 Neural Network Joint Model

The bilingual neural network language model, or neural network joint model for machine translation (NNJM), was first proposed in (Devlin et al., 2014). The basic idea is to construct neural language model as in (Vaswani et al., 2013), but include both the source and target side of the parallel corpus into the modeling context. Specifically, for a target word t_i within context $\mathcal{T}$ and $\mathcal{S}$, a (n + 2m + 1)-gram NNJM will model: $P(t_i \mid \mathcal{T}, \mathcal{S})$ where $\mathcal{T} = t_{i-n}, ..., t_{i-1}$, and $\mathcal{S} = s_{a_i-m}, ..., s_{a_i}, ..., s_{a_i+m}$ (a_i is the index of the word that is aligned to target word t_i).

We used the NPLM toolkit to build NNJMs for German-English, Romanian-English and Russian-English in both directions. We set the target side context window size to 5 and source side window size to 4. For all the NNJMs we built, the learning rate was set to 1.0 and we trained the models for 10 epochs. We kept all the other parameter values to their defaults.

2.5 Domain-Weighted Neural Network Probablistic Language Model

The neural probablistic language model (NPLM) was proposed by Bengio et al. (2003), but was not used inside the machine translation decoder until Vaswani et al. (2013) resolved the efficiency issues. It tries to approximate the same distribution as traditional language models with a feed forward neural network. Since discrete words are converted into continuous representations known as word embeddings, it has the potential to handle longer contexts without having to worry about issues with smoothing.

We used the NPLM toolkit[2] to build neural language models. Because of time and computation constraints we did not include these models in our final submission, but we experimented with different parameters for the relatively small Romanian monolingual data. We also tried different approaches to fine-tune the neural language model against the target side of English-Romanian tuning data, which will be discussed in this section.

The traditional way to handle domain relevance is to build language models for different domains of monolingual data separately, and then interpolate them by maximizing the probablity of a tuning set. This is because (1) the parallel data does not necessarily fit the domain of the monolingual data, and (2) querying several different language models would incur too much computation. But for NPLM, the non-linear layers make effective interpolation of different models less trivial.

To avoid interpolation and still accommodate domain adapation, we explored two solutions:

- consolidate all the monolingual data and train a large NPLM on the consolidated data
- fine-tune NPLM against the tuning corpus

The next natural question to ask is: how should the fine-tuning be done? We hereby propose three methods that we tried in our experiments:

1. Initialize with the weights obtained from training, go through the tuning corpus like training and back-propagate through all the weights in the network;
2. Like method 1, but only back-propagate through the last layer of the network. This could alleviate the problem of overfitting to the tuning data;

System	newsdev2016b
baseline	23.1
w/o untuned nplm on all data	23.5 (+.4)
w/o untuned nplm on setimes2	23.2 (+.1)
w/o all data nplm + method 1	23.4 (+.3)
w/o all data nplm + method 2	23.8 (+.7)
w/o all data nplm + method 3	24.0 (+.9)

Table 3: Comparison of English-Romanian translation results of baseline system and systems with tuned/untuned NPLMs

3. Take the interpolation weights $w_1, w_2, ..., w_n$ of the traditional language model trained on the same division of monolingual data with word count $c_1, c_2, ..., c_n$. Compute the normalized interpolation weights as follows:

$$\tilde{w}_i = \frac{w_i}{c_i}$$

   In place of weighting and combining multiple language models, we will weight the training data and train a single language model on the weighted data. For example, if language model trained on corpus 1 has weight 1.0 and language model trained on corpus 2 has weight 1.5, we will repeat corpus 1 twice and corpus 2 three times. We then train the NPLM on this repeated and consolidated corpus.

   Note that this method only used tuning data implicitly during the process of obtaining interpolation weights for the traditional language model.

Table 3 showed our English-Romanian translation results with NPLM trained on Romanian monolingual data. For method 3, we obtained the interpolation weights by first building language model on Europarl and setimes data using KenLM, and then interpolate the two language model against newsdev2016a data using SRILM. According to the interpolation weights obtained, we repeated setimes2 data for 108 times and did not repeat Europarl data before consolidation. Both the training and tuning were run for 5 epochs with a learning rate[3] of 0.25.

---

[3]The original NPLM paper used learning rate of 1. But in our experiments any learning rate more than 0.25 would cause inf values in the final parameters.

Language Pair	Best 2015	Baseline	w/ clusters	w/ CC LM	w/ both	w/ NNJM	w/ all & ttl100
English-Turkish	-	7.8	8.2 +0.3	9.4 +1.6	8.9 +1.1		
Turkish-English	-	14.0	14.3 +0.3	13.9 –0.1	14.1 +0.1		
English-Finnish	15.5	11.9	12.6 +0.7	12.2 +0.3	12.9 +1.0		
Finnish-English	19.7	16.5	16.9 +0.4	16.4 –0.1	16.9 +0.4		
English-Romanian	-	23.4	24.6 +1.2	23.4 +0.0	23.5 +0.1	23.7 +0.4	23.5 +0.1
Romanian-English	-	32.0	32.5 +0.5	32.5 +0.5	32.8 +0.8	32.0 +0.0	32.8 +0.8
English-Russian	24.3	23.9	25.0 +1.1	23.9 +0.0	24.9 +1.0	24.4 +0.5	25.2 +1.3
Russian-English	27.9	27.5	28.3 +0.7	28.1 +0.6	28.2 +0.7	27.8 +0.3	28.7 +1.2
English-Czech	18.8	18.2	19.2 +1.0	18.8 +0.6	19.6 +1.4		
Czech-English	26.2	27.0	27.7 +0.6	27.7 +0.7	28.1 +1.1		
English-German	24.9	22.7	23.0 +0.3	22.5 –0.2	22.7 +0.0	22.6 –0.1	22.9 +0.2
German-English	29.3	29.0	29.6 +0.6	29.6 +0.6	29.9 +0.9	29.6 +0.6	30.0 +1.0

Table 4: Phrase-Based Systems

NPLM generally improves the translation performance, but tuning method 1 does not help compared to the untuned version of the NPLM. Both method 2 and method 3 improve the performance even further. What's also interesting is that although we repeated setimes2 data so many times, solely building NPLM on setimes2 does not give a comparable performance, hence the coverage advantage as introduced by adding more datasets still makes a difference.

2.6 Results

Table 4 summarizes the impact of the contributions described in the preceeding sections. On their own, the use of Och clusters helped for all language pairs, the huge language model for almost all language pairs, and the neural network joint model for almost all language pairs. The gains are partially additive.

The biggest consistent gains are observed on Czech and Russian, in both directions, and for German–English — but not English–German. In the past we noted that the baseline English–German system, which includes a part-of-speech language model, is not helped much by the Och clusters. However, we are surprised by the lack of support from the huge language model.

For the other language pairs, the smaller tuning sets and hence higher variance in test scores make the results harder to interpret. The use of the huge language model gives mixed results, and gains are often not only not additive, but having more features hurts. See especially English–Romanian and Turkish–English where the best system does not include the huge language model, and Turkish–English where the best system only uses the huge language model.

Still, for all language pairs, the use of all fea-tures (and a translation table limit of 100) allowed us to outperform the strong baseline by +.1 to +1.3, for most language pairs around +1 BLEU.

3 Morphological Decomposition

We explored various methods for handling complex morphology. While we only apply these methods to Turkish, the methods are language independent. All of these methods were used and evaluated in the context of a Moses phrase-based system, as described in section 2.1.

We experimented with three segmentation algorithms: Morfessor (Virpioja et al., 2013), Chip-Munk (Cotterell et al., 2015), and Byte-Pair encoding (Sennrich et al., 2015). .

Morfessor implements a set of segmentation algorithms designed for languages with concatenative morphology (where additional morphemes are added to convey meaning, but the stem and existing morphemes are not typically altered). Turkish falls in this category.

We focus on the Morfessor baseline algorithm, and use it without supervised word segmentations. While the segmentation may resemble linguistic segmentation, this is not guaranteed.

ChipMunk is an algorithm for segmenting words into morphemes and labeling those segments. It jointly models segmentation and labeling of the segments. While we do not use the label information, the labeling of segments is designed to reduce certain segmentation errors. For example, it prevents a prefix from directly attaching to a suffix, which prevents the segmentation of reed into re-ed. Since we choose not to rely on linguistic knowledge of Turkish, we use the pre-trained model with the tag level parameter set to 2.

Byte Pair Encoding (Gage, 1994) is a compression algorithm that recursively replaces frequent

Language	Threshold	Token count
Turkish	none	8806
Turkish	0	9606
Turkish	2	9935
Turkish	5	10169
Turkish	10	10416
Turkish	20	10720
English	none	11514

Table 5: Token counts for different thresholds for Morfessor segmentation

Method	Processing	Thresh.	BLEU
baseline	-	-	13.9
Byte-Pair	preprocessing	-	13.7
Chipmunk	replace-rare	2	14.3
Chipmunk	replace-rare	10	14.9
Chipmunk	replace-rare	20	**15.4**
Chipmunk	replace-rare	20	14.7
Morfessor	replace-rare	0	13.5
Morfessor	replace-rare	2	13.7
Morfessor	replace-rare	5	14.0
Morfessor	replace-rare	10	**14.1**
Morfessor	replace-rare	20	14.2

Table 6: Turkish - English morphology results on newsdev2016b

consecutive bytes with a symbol that does not occur elsewhere. Each such replacement is called a merge, and the number of merges is a tunable parameter. The original text can be recovered using a lookup-table. Sennrich et al. (2015) applied this to word segmentation, and demonstrate its success at solving the large vocabulary problem in neural machine translation.

To create our training data for the Morfessor and ChipMunk experiments, we augment the original training data with a second copy that has been segmented. For the tuning and test data, we only segment words that occur infrequently. This allows frequent words to be translated directly, but also allows the system to learn from the subword units of all words, including frequent ones.

The number and type of subword units in each word segmented by byte pair encoding is dependent on the number of merges performed. Since byte pair encoding segments words into the largest unit found in the table, and common words will occur in the table, this means that no subword information is extracted from common words. We set the number of merges to 50,000, and report the result, but did not explore it further. Perhaps a smaller number of merges would force the segmentation of more frequent words.

Table 5 shows the number of tokens using Morfessor and different segmentation strategies, as well as the number of tokens in the English parallel text. We show the number of tokens here because a common rationale for segmenting morphological rich languages is to balance the number of tokens.

BLEU scores for different amounts of segmentation are in Table 6. We report cased score on the development test set described in section 2.1. We see the best improvements with the ChipMunk segmentation and a rare word replacement thresh-

old of 20. We also see gains with the fully unsupervised Morfessor segmentation.

None of these results completed in time for our official submission, which used unsegmented text.

4 Neural Sequence Model Reranking

We also experimented with N-best reranking using a neural sequence model. The motivation is to exploit the efficiency of standard phrase-based models for generating N-best hypotheses, combined with the modeling power of neural methods for scoring. This hybrid approach demonstrated positive results in, e.g. (Cohn et al., 2016).

First, we train neural attention models (Bahdanau et al., 2015) on our training bitext in both forward and reverse directions. For example, in the Russian-English task we would obtain a forward model $p(en|ru)$ that scores English hypotheses given Russian input, and a reverse model $p(ru|en)$ that scores the Russian input given an English hypothesis. We used the TensorFlow implementation (Abadi et al., 2015), with 2-layers of LSTMs and 1024 hidden units each; other hyperparameters use default settings. The training bitext is preprocessed so that top 10k vocabulary in terms of frequency are kept as is, frequency 1 singletons are mapped to an unknown word token (UNK), and all remaining mid-frequency words are mapped to one of 600 Brown clusters. Note that our vocabulary list of 10,601 is considerably less than those used in existing neural MT literature (e.g. 30k in (Bahdanau et al., 2015)). This is a trade-off between modeling power vs. training time, and we felt that a smaller vocabulary may be sufficient since our model only scores existing translations and do not need to generate.

Second, we generate distinct 50-best lists on our tuning set using a baseline Moses phrase-based system in Table 4. Each hypothesis is scored by the forward and reverse neural models, and together with the original Moses decoder score and word penalty features (for a total of 4 features), we reran MERT training and obtained optimal linear weights. This is the reranker system used for reranking test N-best lists.

Preliminary results with this approach were inconclusive. For example, on the Russian-English newstest2015, the BLEU score is 27.27 for 1-best vs. 27.31 for reranking. On German-English newstest2015, the BLEU score is 28.12 for 1-best and 28.22 for reranking. (Note, these results did not include a post-processing step and are thus not comparable to the numbers in Table 4). Analysis of the output showed that our rerankers appear conservative and do not frequently chooses hypotheses different from the 1-best. We believe more experimentation with different neural model hyperparameters is necessary. Future work also includes experimentation on larger N-best lists and comparison with direct 1-pass translation using neural models. This reranker was not included in the final submission.

5 Moses Syntax-based Systems

In this section we discuss our setup for the three string-to-tree syntax-based systems we submitted for German-English, English-German, and Turkish-English. Unless metioned in this section, we use the same setup as the baseline Moses phrase-based systems described in Section 2.

5.1 Preprocessing

Since we are building string-to-tree syntax-based models, we need to parse the target side of the parallel corpus before training. For our syntax-based models we used the Berkeley parser to parse the English side of the German-English and Turkish-English parallel corpus, and ParZu (Sennrich et al., 2009) to parse the German side of the English-German parallel corpus. For the Berkeley parser we used the default English grammar `eng_sm6.gr`. For ParZu we used clevertagger[4] as the POS-tagger,

SMOR[5] as the morphological analyzer, and used `zmorge-20140521-smor_newlemma.ca` as the model for morphological analysis. We pass the all corpus for syntax-based models through `deescape-special-chars.perl` before parsing to avoid formatting problems.

In addition to parsing, for English-German syntax-based model, we also used `hybrid_compound_splitter.py` to split the compound words in German, as in Edinburgh's WMT 2015 submission (Williams et al., 2015)[6]. We used the same morphological analyzer model as used for ParZu.

5.2 Feature Scores

The most significant difference between the syntax-based model and the phrase-based model is that the translation model score is calculated by SCFG translation rule scores instead of phrase pair scores. Specifically, a SCFG translation rule r is denoted as:

$$\mathcal{L} \to\, < \mathcal{S}, \mathcal{T}, \mathcal{A} >$$

where $\mathcal{L}$ is the left-hand side label as shared by both sides of the translation, $\mathcal{S}$ and $\mathcal{T}$ is a sequence of terminal and non-terminal nodes on the source and target side, respectively. $\mathcal{A}$ denotes the alignment between the source and target nodes. Given a derivation $\mathcal{D}$ that generates the sentence pair, the forward and inverse translation model score is:

$$fwd = \prod_{\mathcal{L} \to < \mathcal{S}, \mathcal{T}, \mathcal{A} > \in \mathcal{D}} P(\mathcal{L}, \mathcal{T} \mid \mathcal{S}, \mathcal{A})$$

$$inv = \prod_{\mathcal{L} \to < \mathcal{S}, \mathcal{T}, \mathcal{A} > \in \mathcal{D}} P(\mathcal{S} \mid \mathcal{L}, \mathcal{T}, \mathcal{A})$$

Apart from these two scores, we also added unknown word soft matching features and glue rule penalties. We also kept the lexical translation scores, word penalties and phrase penalties etc. as in the phrase-based translation models.

5.3 Configurations

To avoid problems during syntax-based rule extraction and decoding, we removed all the factors such as lemma and POS-tags and only use word during the training phase.

We used the GHKM rule extractor implemented in Moses to extract SCFG rules from the parallel

---

[4] https://github.com/rsennrich/clevertagger

[5] http://kitt.ifi.uzh.ch/kitt/zmorge/
[6] https://github.com/rsennrich/wmt2014-scripts

corpus. We set the maximum number of nodes (except target words) in the rules (`MaxNodes`) to 20, maximum rule depth (`MaxRuleDepth`) to 5, and the number of non-part-of-speech, non-leaf constituent labels (`MaxRuleSize`) to 5, and we allowed unary rules to appear in the extracted phrases. We also limited the maximum number of lexical items in a rule to 5.

To avoid excessive use of glue rules, we fixed the feature weight for glue rules as -99 during tuning step.

6   Joshua Systems

We also used the Apache Joshua translation toolkit[7] to build Hiero systems for two languages: English–Finnish and English–Turkish. The default settings were used for the Thrax grammar extractor: Hiero rules were extracted from spans as large as 10 words, and applied at decoding time to spans as long as 20 words. We used all of the provided bitext for both language tasks. All systems used three language models: one built on the target side of the bitext, another built on all available common-crawl monolingual data, and a third, class-based 9-gram language model built on the target side of the bitext after applying Brown clustering (k=2,000). Each of these received a separate weight. We tuned with k-best batch MIRA (Cherry and Foster, 2012).

Case is important for the human evaluation, and its proper handling has received some attention. Instead of applying a method such as true-casing (Lita et al., 2003), we use the following heuristic for these languages. First, we convert all data to lowercase at training time, so the models are learned in lowercase. At test time, input words are lowercased and marked with a tag denoting whether each source word was (a) lowercase, (b) Capitalized, or (c) ALL UPPERCASE. These case markings are then projected to the target words through the word-level alignments stored with grammar rules. This worked well for the language pairs under consideration, though it would obviously not work for all language pairs.

We also employed one small trick with Turkish punctuation: after removing whitespace inside balanced single-quotes, we remove the space from both sides of remaining single-quotes. This captured a common pattern and resulted in a small BLEU score gain that helped propel the system

---

[7] http://joshua.incubator.apache.org/

Language Pair	Phrase	Syntax	Joshua
English-Turkish	9.2	-	**9.8**
Turkish-English	12.9	**13.9**	-
English-Finnish	**13.8**	-	11.9
Finnish-English	19.1	-	-
English-Romanian	23.5	-	-
Romanian-English	32.2	-	-
English-Russian	24.0	-	-
Russian-English	27.9	-	-
English-Czech	23.6	-	-
Czech-English	30.4	-	-
English-German	**28.3**	27.3	-
German-English	**34.5**	32.3	-

Table 7: Official scores of all submission on newstest2016 (cased BLEU).

into first place (by cased BLEU). Although the English–Turkish system had the highest BLEU score, however, it was in the fifth cluster in the manual evaluation. The English–Finish system did not perform well by either metric.

7   Conclusion

Our submissions are summarized in Table 7. We submitted phrase-based systems for all 12 language pairs, syntax-based systems for 3 and Joshua hierarchical systems for 2 language pairs. For the low resource Turkish–English language pairs, the latter systems outperformed the phrase-based submission.

Compared to submissions from other groups, our performance is solid. In terms of neural machine translation components, we have seen gains from the use of the NNJM (Devlin et al., 2014) as a feature function but not in re-ranking with a sequence to sequence model. Given the success of these components in other systems, we will target their use in the future.

References

Martín Abadi, Ashish Agarwal, Paul Barham, Eugene Brevdo, Zhifeng Chen, Craig Citro, Greg S. Corrado, Andy Davis, Jeffrey Dean, Matthieu Devin, Sanjay Ghemawat, Ian Goodfellow, Andrew Harp, Geoffrey Irving, Michael Isard, Yangqing Jia, Rafal Jozefowicz, Lukasz Kaiser, Manjunath Kudlur, Josh Levenberg, Dan Mané, Rajat Monga, Sherry Moore, Derek Murray, Chris Olah, Mike Schuster, Jonathon Shlens, Benoit Steiner, Ilya Sutskever, Kunal Talwar, Paul Tucker, Vincent Vanhoucke, Vijay Vasudevan, Fernanda Viégas, Oriol Vinyals, Pete Warden,

Martin Wattenberg, Martin Wicke, Yuan Yu, and Xiaoqiang Zheng. 2015. TensorFlow: Large-scale machine learning on heterogeneous systems. Software available from tensorflow.org.

Dzmitry Bahdanau, Kyunghyun Cho, and Yoshua Bengio. 2015. Neural machine translation by jointly learning to align and translate. In *Proceedings of the International Conference on Learning Representations (ICLR)*.

Yoshua Bengio, Réjean Ducharme, Pascal Vincent, and Christian Jauvin. 2003. A neural probabilistic language model. *Journal of Machine Learning Research*, (3):1137–1155.

Phil Blunsom and Miles Osborne. 2008. Probabilistic inference for machine translation. In *Proceedings of the 2008 Conference on Empirical Methods in Natural Language Processing*, pages 215–223, Honolulu, Hawaii, October. Association for Computational Linguistics.

Christian Buck, Kenneth Heafield, and Bas Van Ooyen. 2014. N-gram counts and language models from the common crawl. *LREC*, 2:4.

Colin Cherry and George Foster. 2012. Batch tuning strategies for statistical machine translation. In *Proceedings of the 2012 Conference of the North American Chapter of the Association for Computational Linguistics: Human Language Technologies*, pages 427–436, Montréal, Canada, June. Association for Computational Linguistics.

David Chiang, Kevin Knight, and Wei Wang. 2009. 11,001 New Features for Statistical Machine Translation. In *Proceedings of Human Language Technologies: The 2009 Annual Conference of the North American Chapter of the Association for Computational Linguistics*, pages 218–226, Boulder, Colorado, June. Association for Computational Linguistics.

Trevor Cohn, Cong Duy Vu Hoang, Ekaterina Vymolova, Kaisheng Yao, Chris Dyer, and Gholamreza Haffari. 2016. Incorporating structural alignment biases into an attentional neural translation model. In *Proceedings of NAACL-16*.

Michael Collins, Philipp Koehn, and Ivona Kucerova. 2005. Clause restructuring for statistical machine translation. In *Proceedings of the 43rd Annual Meeting of the Association for Computational Linguistics (ACL'05)*, pages 531–540, Ann Arbor, Michigan, June. Association for Computational Linguistics.

Ryan Cotterell, Thomas Müller, Alexander Fraser, and Hinrich Schütze. 2015. Labeled morphological segmentation with semi-markov models. In *Proceedings of the Nineteenth Conference on Computational Natural Language Learning*, pages 164–174, Beijing, China, July. Association for Computational Linguistics.

Jacob Devlin, Rabih Zbib, Zhongqiang Huang, Thomas Lamar, Richard M Schwartz, and John Makhoul. 2014. Fast and Robust Neural Network Joint Models for Statistical Machine Translation. In *ACL*, pages 1370–1380.

Nadir Durrani, Alexander Fraser, Helmut Schmid, Hieu Hoang, and Philipp Koehn. 2013. Can markov models over minimal translation units help phrase-based SMT? In *Proceedings of the 51st Annual Meeting of the Association for Computational Linguistics*, Sofia, Bulgaria, August. Association for Computational Linguistics.

Philip Gage. 1994. A new algorithm for data compression. *C Users J.*, 12(2):23–38, February.

Michel Galley and Christopher D. Manning. 2008. A simple and effective hierarchical phrase reordering model. In *Proceedings of the 2008 Conference on Empirical Methods in Natural Language Processing*, pages 848–856, Honolulu, Hawaii, October.

B Haddow, M Huck, A Birch, and N Bogoychev. 2015. The Edinburgh/JHU Phrase-based Machine Translation Systems for WMT 2015. In *WMT*.

Kenneth Heafield. 2011. Kenlm: Faster and smaller language model queries. In *Proceedings of the Sixth Workshop on Statistical Machine Translation*, pages 187–197, Edinburgh, Scotland, United Kingdom, July.

Liang Huang and David Chiang. 2007. Forest rescoring: Faster decoding with integrated language models. In *Proceedings of the 45th Annual Meeting of the Association of Computational Linguistics*, pages 144–151, Prague, Czech Republic, June. Association for Computational Linguistics.

M. Junczys-Dowmunt. 2012. A phrase table without phrases: Rank encoding for better phrase table compression. In Mauro Cettolo, Marcello Federico, Lucia Specia, and Andy Way, editors, *Proceedings of th 16th International Conference of the European Association for Machine Translation (EAMT)*, pages 245–252.

Philipp Koehn and Barry Haddow. 2009. Edinburgh's Submission to all Tracks of the WMT 2009 Shared Task with Reordering and Speed Improvements to Moses. In *Proceedings of the Fourth Workshop on Statistical Machine Translation*, pages 160–164, Athens, Greece, March. Association for Computational Linguistics.

Philipp Koehn and Hieu Hoang. 2007. Factored translation models. In *Proceedings of the 2007 Joint Conference on Empirical Methods in Natural Language Processing and Computational Natural Language Learning (EMNLP-CoNLL)*, pages 868–876, Prague, Czech Republic, June. Association for Computational Linguistics.

Philipp Koehn and Kevin Knight. 2003. Empirical methods for compound splitting. In *Proceedings of Meeting of the European Chapter of the Association of Computational Linguistics (EACL)*.

Philipp Koehn, Hieu Hoang, Alexandra Birch, Chris Callison-Burch, Marcello Federico, Nicola Bertoldi, Brooke Cowan, Wade Shen, Christine Moran, Richard Zens, Chris Dyer, Ondrej Bojar, Alexandra Constantin, and Evan Herbst. 2007. Moses: open source toolkit for statistical machine translation. In *ACL*. Association for Computational Linguistics.

Shankar Kumar and William J. Byrne. 2004. Minimum bayes-risk decoding for statistical machine translation. In *HLT-NAACL*, pages 169–176.

Lucian Vlad Lita, Abe Ittycheriah, Salim Roukos, and Nanda Kambhatla. 2003. Truecasing. In *Proceedings of the 41st Annual Meeting on Association for Computational Linguistics-Volume 1*, pages 152–159. Association for Computational Linguistics.

Franz Josef Och. 1999. An Efficient Method for Determining Bilingual Word Classes. In *Proceedings of the 9th Conference of the European Chapter of the Association for Computational Linguistics (EACL)*, pages 71–76.

Matt Post, Yuan Cao, and Gaurav Kumar. 2015. Joshua 6: A phrase-based and hierarchical statistical machine translation system. *The Prague Bulletin of Mathematical Linguistics*.

Rico Sennrich, Gerold Schneider, Martin Volk, and Martin Warin. 2009. A new hybrid dependency parser for german. *Proceedings of the German Society for Computational Linguistics and Language Technology*, pages 115–124.

Rico Sennrich, Barry Haddow, and Alexandra Birch. 2015. Neural machine translation of rare words with subword units. *CoRR*, abs/1508.07909.

Darlene Stewart, Roland Kuhn, Eric Joanis, and George Foster. 2014. Coarse split and lump bilingual language models for richer source information in SMT. In *Proceedings of the Eleventh Conference of the Association for Machine Translation in the Americas (AMTA)*, volume 1, pages 28–41.

Ashish Vaswani, Yinggong Zhao, Victoria Fossum, and David Chiang. 2013. Decoding with Large-Scale Neural Language Models Improves Translation. In *EMNLP*, pages 1387–1392. EMNLP, October.

Sami Virpioja, Peter Smit, Stig-Arne Grönroos, Mikko Kurimo, et al. 2013. Morfessor 2.0: Python implementation and extensions for morfessor baseline.

Philip Williams, Rico Sennrich, Maria Nadejde, Matthias Huck, and Philipp Koehn. 2015. Edinburgh's Syntax-Based Systems at WMT 2015. In *WMT*, September.

Yandex School of Data Analysis approach to English-Turkish translation at WMT16 News Translation Task

Anton Dvorkovich[1,2]**, Sergey Gubanov**[2]**, and Irina Galinskaya**[2]
`{dvorkanton,esgv,galinskaya}@yandex-team.ru`

[1] Yandex School of Data Analysis, 11/2 Timura Frunze St., Moscow 119021, Russia
[2] Yandex, 16 Leo Tolstoy St., Moscow 119021, Russia

Abstract

We describe the English-Turkish and Turkish-English translation systems submitted by Yandex School of Data Analysis team to WMT16 news translation task. We successfully applied hand-crafted morphological (de-)segmentation of Turkish, syntax-based pre-ordering of English in English-Turkish and post-ordering of English in Turkish-English. We perform desegmentation using SMT and propose a simple yet efficient modification of post-ordering. We also show that Turkish morphology and word order can be handled in a fully-automatic manner with only a small loss of BLEU.

1 Introduction

Yandex School of Data Analysis participated in WMT16 shared task "Machine Translation of News" in Turkish-English language pair.

Machine translation between English and Turkish is a challenging task, due to the strong differences between languages. In particular, Turkish has rich *agglutinative morphology*, and the *word order* differs between languages (SOV in Turkish, SVO in English).

To deal with these dissimilarities, we preprocess both source and target parts of the parallel corpus before training: we perform morphological segmentation of Turkish and reordering of English into Turkish word order, aiming to achieve a monotonous one-to-one correspondence between tokens to aid SMT.

Since we changed the target side of the parallel corpus, at runtime we had to do post-processing: desegmentation of Turkish for EN-TR and post-ordering of English words for TR-EN. We employ additional SMT decoders to solve both tasks, which results in two-stage translation.

For morphological segmentation and English-to-Turkish reordering we tried both rule-based/supervised and fully unsupervised approaches.

2 Data & common system components

In our two systems (Turkish-English and English-Turkish) we used several common components described below.

The specific application of these tools varies for Turkish-English and English-Turkish systems, so we discuss it separately in Sections 4 and 3.

2.1 Phrase-based translator

We used an in-house implementation of phrase-based MT (Koehn et al., 2003) with Berkeley Aligner (Liang et al., 2006) and MERT tuning (Och, 2003).

2.2 English syntactic parser

We used an in-house transition-based English dependency parser similar to (Zhang and Nivre, 2011).

2.3 English-to-Turkish reorderers

We used two different reorderers that put English words in Turkish order. Both reorderers need an English dependency parse tree as input.

Rule-based reorderer modifies parse trees using rules similar to Tregex (Levy and Andrew, 2006), adapted to dependency trees[1]. We used a set of about 70 hand-crafted rules, an example of a rule is given in Figure 1.

```
w1 role 'PMOD'
    and .--> (w2 not role 'CONJ')
::
move group w1 before node w2;
```

Figure 1: Sample dependency tree reordering rule

---

[1] Our dependency tree reordering tool is available here: `https://github.com/yandex/dep_tregex`

Proceedings of the First Conference on Machine Translation, Volume 2: Shared Task Papers, pages 281–288,
Berlin, Germany, August 11-12, 2016. ©2016 Association for Computational Linguistics

Automatic reorderer uses word alignments on a parallel corpus to construct reference reorderings, and then trains a feedforward neural-network classifier which makes node-swapping decisions (de Gispert et al., 2015).

2.4 Turkish morphological analyzers

We used an in-house finite state transducer similar to (Oflazer, 1994) for Turkish morphological tagging, and structured perceptron similar to (Sak et al., 2007) for morphological disambiguation.

As an alternative, we trained our implementation of unsupervised morphology model, following (Soricut and Och, 2015), with a single distinctive feature: in each connected component C of the morphological graph, we select the lemma as $\mathrm{argmax}_C\left(\log f(w) - \alpha \cdot l(w)\right)$, where $l(w)$ is word length and $f(w)$ is word frequency[2]. This is a heuristic, justified by the facts, that (1) lemma tends to be shorter than other surface forms of a word, and (2) $\log f(w)$ is proportional to $l(w)$ (Strauss et al., 2007). We also make use of morphology induction for unseen words, as described in the original paper. The automatic method requires no disambiguation and yields no part-of-speech tags or morphological features.

2.5 Turkish morphological segmenter

We used three strategies for segmenting Turkish words into less-sparse units. The "simple" strategy splits a word into lemma and chain of affixes. The latter is chosen as suffix of the surface form, starting from $(l + 1)$-th letter, where l is lemma's length.

The "rule-based" strategy uses hand-crafted rules similar to (Oflazer and El-Kahlout, 2007), (Yeniterzi and Oflazer, 2010) or (Bisazza and Federico, 2009) to split word into lemma and groups of morphological features, some of which might be attached to lemma. Rules are designed to achieve a better correspondence between Turkish and English words. This strategy requires morphological analyzer to output features as well as lemma.

The "aggressive rule-based" strategy, in addition, forcefully splits all features attached to the lemma into a separate group.

2.6 NMT reranker

Finally, we used a sequence-to-sequence neural network with attention (Bahdanau et al., 2014) as a feature for 100-best reranking. We used hidden layer and embedding sizes of 100, and vocabulary sizes of 40000 (the Turkish side was morphologically segmented).

2.7 Data

For training translation model, language models, and NMT reranker, we used only the provided constrained data (SETIMES 2 parallel Turkish-English corpus, and monolingual Turkish and English Common Crawl corpora).

Throughout our experiments, we used the BLEU (Papineni et al., 2002) on provided devset (news-dev2016) to estimate the performance of our systems, tuning MERT on a random sample of 1000 sentences from the SETIMES corpus (these sentences, to which we refer as "the SETIMES subsample", were excluded from training data). For the final submissions, we tuned MERT directly on news-dev2016.

Due to our setup, we provide BLEU scores on news-dev2016 for our intermediate experiments and on news-test2016 for our final systems.

3 Turkish-English system

3.1 Baseline

For a baseline, we trained a standard phrase-based system: Berkeley Aligner (IBM Model 1 and HMM, both for 5 iterations); phrase table with up to 5 tokens per phrase, 40-best translation options per source phrase, and Good-Turing smoothing; 5-gram lowercased LM with stupid backoff and pruning of singleton n-grams due to memory constraints; MERT on the SETIMES subsample; simple reordering model, penalized only by movement distance, with distortion limit set to 16.

We lowercased both the training and development corpora, taking into account Turkish specifics: $I \rightarrow \imath$, $\dot{I} \rightarrow i$.

Baseline system achieves 10.84 uncased BLEU on news-dev2016 (here and on, we ignore case in BLEU computation).

---

[2]We used $\alpha = 0.6$ throughout our experiments.

#	System description	BLEU (uncased), dev[3]	BLEU (uncased), test[3]
1	Baseline, phrase-based	11.68	11.50
2	(1) + automatic morph., simple seg.	12.16	-
3	(1) + FST/perceptron morph., simple seg.	11.75	-
4	(1) + FST/perceptron morph., rule-based seg.	12.93	-
5	(1) + FST/perceptron morph., aggressive rule-based seg.	14.06	-
6	(5) + "reordered" post-ordering, rule-based reorderer	14.24	-
7	(5) + "translated" post-ordering, rule-based reorderer	15.13	-
8	(2) + "translated" post-ordering, automatic reorderer	13.43	13.39
9	(7) + NMT reranking in first stage	15.49	**15.12**

Table 1: Our TR-EN setups on news-dev2016 and news-test2016 (submitted system in bold)

3.2 Morphological segmentation

In Turkish-to-English translator we directly applied Turkish morphological segmenters (see Section 2.5) as an initial step in the pipeline (Oflazer and El-Kahlout, 2007; Bisazza and Federico, 2009).

The effect of different morphological tagging and segmentation methods is shown in Table 1.

FST/perceptron analyzer with aggressive rule-based segmentation (run #5) turned out to be the most successful method, bringing +2.60 BLEU.

Our segmenters split Turkish words into lemmas and auxiliary tokens like $ini or +a3sg. To account for the increased number of tokens on Turkish side, we increased the length of a target phrase from 5 to 10 (but still allowing only up to 5 non-auxiliary tokens in a phrase). In order to further decrease sparsity we also removed all diacritics from the intermediate segmented Turkish. Possible ambiguity in translations, caused by this, is handled by English LM.

For a rule-based segmentation we note that it is beneficial to aggressively separate away lemma and morphological features that would normally be attached to it (that is, if we acted according to the rules). We think the reason for this is the presence of errors and non-optimal decisions in our segmentation rules, but we still consider the extra split helpful:

- If we do the extra split, a wordform is segmented into a lemma and several auxiliary tokens, so if we have seen just the lemma, we might still translate the unseen wordform correctly.

- An excessive segmentation does not really hurt a phrase-based system, as shown by (Chang et al., 2008).

3.3 Post-ordering

It is not possible to directly apply English-to-Turkish reorderer as a preprocessing step in this translation direction, and we also counld not construct a Turkish-to-English reorderer (due to the absence of Turkish parser).

Instead, we reordered the target side of the parallel corpus on the training phase using the rule-based reorderer described in Section 2.3, and employed a second-stage translator to restore English word order at runtime, following (Sudoh et al., 2011).

As shown in Figure 2, the first, "monotonous translation" stage is trained to translate from Turkish to English that was reordered to the Turkish order[4], and the second, "reordering" stage is trained to translate from reordered English to normal English, relying on the LM and baseline reordering inside the phrase-based decoder.

---

[3] We tune on the SETIMES subsample for "dev" column, and on news-dev2016 for "test" column. So the same line lists the results for two sets of MERT coefficients.

[4] This does not mean we completely disable the baseline reordering mechanism in the decoder on this stage; that would have made sense only if (a) our English-to-Turkish reorderer was perfect and (b) if the two languages could be perfectly aligned using just word reordering. Obviously, neither of those is the case.

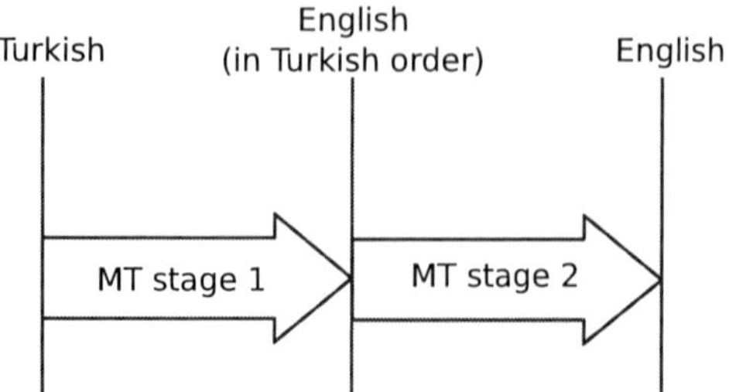

Figure 2: Two-stage post-ordering

Figures 3 and 4 illustrate the training of two-stage postordering systems. We explore two options for the training of the second, "reordering" stage: as the source-side, we can either use (a) the reordered English sentences, or (b) Turkish sentences translated to reordered English with first-stage translator.

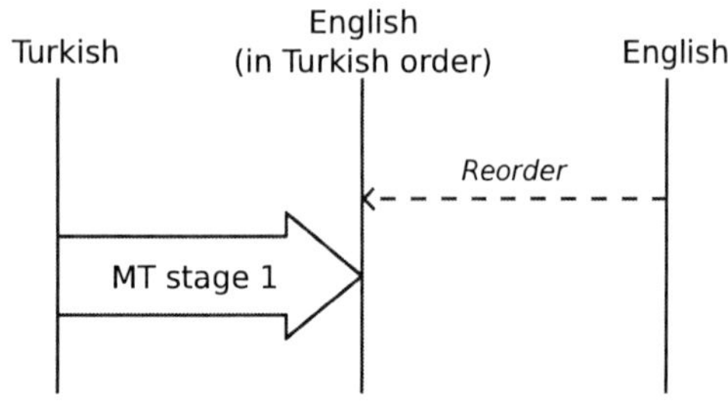

Figure 3: Training the "monotonous translation" stage of post-ordering system

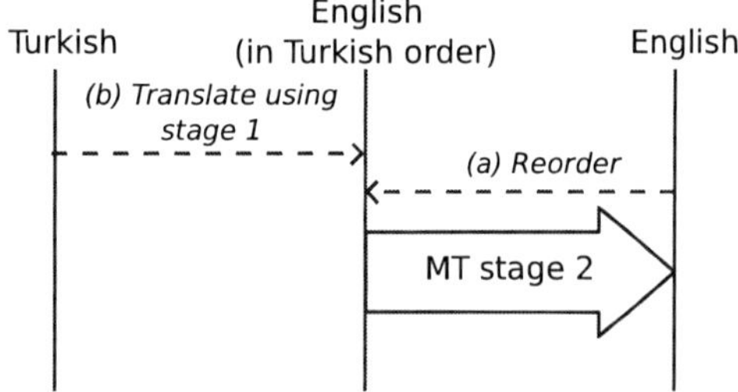

Figure 4: Two options for training the "reordering" stage of post-ordering system

The two decoders have two sets of MERT coefficients. We tune them jointly and iteratively: first, we tune the first-stage decoder (with second-stage coefficients fixed), optimizing BLEU of the whole-system output, then we tune the second-stage decoder (with first-stage coefficients fixed), again optimizing the whole-system BLEU, and so on.

As shown in Table 1, the best results are achieved using "translated Turkish" for training the second-stage translator, yielding an additional +1.60 BLEU.

3.4 NMT reranking

Finally, we enhanced the first-stage translator with a 100-best reranking which uses decoder features and a neural sequence-to-sequence network described in Section 2.6. To train the network, we used the same corpus used to train the first-stage PBMT translator (incorporating Turkish segmentation and English reordering).

NMT reranking yields an additional +0.47 BLEU score.

3.5 Final system

The complete pipeline of our submitted system is shown in Figure 5.

We selected the setup that performed best during experiments (#9 in Table 1), and re-tuned it on the development set; for contrastive runs we also re-tuned baseline and "fully automatic" systems (#1 and #8 respectively). See Table 1 for results.

Our best setup reaches 15.17 BLEU, which is a +3.17 BLEU improvement over the baseline.

The system without the hand-crafted rules achieves a lower improvement of +1.89 BLEU, which is a nice gain nevertheless. Comparing runs #2 and #3, we see that the decrease in BLEU is not due to the quality of morphological analysis; comparing runs #3 and #5, we see that the difference in quality is purely due to the segmentation scheme.

4 English-Turkish system

4.1 Baseline

As a baseline, we trained the same phrase-based system as in Section 3.1 (except we did not prune singleton n-grams in the Turkish language model).

Baseline system achieves 8.51 uncased BLEU on news-dev2016.

4.2 Pre-ordering

We directly apply English-to-Turkish reorderers described in Section 2.3 as a pre-processing step in the phrase-based MT pipeline, like e.g. (Xia and McCord, 2004; Collins et al., 2005). Results are shown in Table 2

The rule-based reorderer earns +1.65 BLEU against the baseline (run #2), so we selected it as a

#	System description	BLEU (uncased), dev[3]	BLEU (uncased), test[3]
1	Baseline, phrase-based	8.51	9.26
2	(1) + rule-based preordering	10.16	-
3	(1) + automatic preordering	9.79	-
4	(2) + deseg. from FST/perceptron morph. & rule-based seg.	11.32	**11.10**
5	(3) + deseg. from automatic morph. & simple seg.	10.41	11.03

Table 2: Our EN-TR setups on news-dev2016 and news-test2016 (submitted system in bold)

base for further improvements. The automatic reorderer performs almost as well as the rule-based (-0.37 BLEU).

4.3 Desegmentation

We decided to battle data sparsity on target side using morphological desegmentation: translate from English to segmented Turkish, then desegment the output.

After experiments in Section 3.2 we decided to use an aggressive rule-based segmenter. First-stage translator makes mistakes, sometimes producing wrong morphemes and/or morphemes in an incorrect order. To manage that, we decided to make desegmentation using machine translation (conceptually similar to post-ordering).

For training MT desegmenter we need only a monolingual corpus, so we can use more data than we used for training the first-stage translator. We concatenated the Turkish part of SETIMES parallel corpus with a random sample of 2 million sentences from Common Crawl monolingual Turkish corpus for training the MT desegmenter.

Like for segmentation, we increased the phrase length on the segmented Turkish side for both translation stages (see Section 3.2). We also removed diacritics from the segmented Turkish; natural Turkish language model employed on the desegmentation stage works like a context-aware restorer of diacritics. Like for post-ordering, we tune MERT coefficients of our two-stage translator jointly (see Secion 3.3).

Our desegmentation scheme yielded +1.16 BLEU (run #4).

4.4 Final system

The complete pipeline of our submitted system is shown in Figure 6.

For the submission, we re-tuned our best run #4 on news-dev2016; for contrastive runs we also re-tuned baseline and "fully-automatic" systems (#1 and #5 respectively). See Table 2 for results.

Our best setup reaches 11.10 BLEU on the testset, which is a +1.84 BLEU improvement over the baseline.

An almost equal BLEU improvement of +1.77 can still be achieved even if we do not use handcrafted rules for reordering or segmentation.

5 Conclusions

We successfully applied data preprocessing for improving MT quality, which resulted in +1.84 BLEU improvement on English-Turkish and +3.17 BLEU on Turkish-English. Handling Turkish morphology via segmentation/desegmentation and handling Turkish SOV word order via preordering/post-ordering both yield improvements of comparable importance.

We were able to avoid the manual construction of a desegmenter. We also proposed an efficient modification of post-ordering: to train the "post-ordering" stage by using the translations of the first stage. We believe that is benefitial due to a better between-stage consistency: what second-stage translator sees during training, it sees at run-time.

We also show that unsupervised methods for segmentation and reordering yield a comparable gain of +1.77 BLEU on English-Turkish and a lower gain +1.89 BLEU on Turkish-English. We believe that the lower gain on Turkish-English is due to the simpler segmentation scheme (not due to the lower quality of unsupervised morphology), but a further analysis is needed to understand why such scheme is sufficient for translating in reverse direction.

Our system turned out to be a quite long segmentation/translation/reordering pipeline. That suggests 3 different directions for the future work:

- Further improve the components of the pipeline.
- Replace "translation" components of the pipeline with another kind of decoder (e.g. NMT).
- Abandon the pipeline and consider joint methods, in order to beat error propagation.

6 Acknowledgements

We thank Valentin Goussev and Mariya Shmatova for the linguistic expertise. We also thank Alexey Baytin for the helpful advice.

References

Dzmitry Bahdanau, Kyunghyun Cho, and Yoshua Bengio. 2014. Neural machine translation by jointly learning to align and translate. *arXiv preprint arXiv:1409.0473*.

Arianna Bisazza and Marcello Federico. 2009. Morphological pre-processing for Turkish to English statistical machine translation. In *IWSLT*, pages 129–135.

Pi-Chuan Chang, Michel Galley, and Christopher D Manning. 2008. Optimizing Chinese word segmentation for machine translation performance. In *Proceedings of the third workshop on statistical machine translation*, pages 224–232. Association for Computational Linguistics.

Michael Collins, Philipp Koehn, and Ivona Kučerová. 2005. Clause restructuring for statistical machine translation. In *Proceedings of the 43rd annual meeting on association for computational linguistics*, pages 531–540. Association for Computational Linguistics.

Adrià de Gispert, Gonzalo Iglesias, and Bill Byrne. 2015. Fast and Accurate Preordering for SMT using Neural Networks. In *Proceedings of the 2015 Conference of the North American Chapter of the Association for Computational Linguistics: Human Language Technologies*, pages 1012–1017.

Philipp Koehn, Franz Josef Och, and Daniel Marcu. 2003. Statistical phrase-based translation. In *Proceedings of the 2003 Conference of the North American Chapter of the Association for Computational Linguistics on Human Language Technology-Volume 1*, pages 48–54. Association for Computational Linguistics.

Roger Levy and Galen Andrew. 2006. Tregex and Tsurgeon: tools for querying and manipulating tree data structures. In *Proceedings of the fifth international conference on Language Resources and Evaluation*, pages 2231–2234. Citeseer.

Percy Liang, Ben Taskar, and Dan Klein. 2006. Alignment by agreement. In *Proceedings of the main conference on Human Language Technology Conference of the North American Chapter of the Association of Computational Linguistics*, pages 104–111. Association for Computational Linguistics.

Franz Josef Och. 2003. Minimum error rate training in statistical machine translation. In *Proceedings of the 41st Annual Meeting on Association for Computational Linguistics-Volume 1*, pages 160–167. Association for Computational Linguistics.

Kemal Oflazer and Ilknur Durgar El-Kahlout. 2007. Exploring different representational units in English-to-Turkish statistical machine translation. In *Proceedings of the Second Workshop on Statistical Machine Translation*, pages 25–32. Association for Computational Linguistics.

Kemal Oflazer. 1994. Two-level description of Turkish morphology. *Literary and linguistic computing*, 9(2):137–148.

Kishore Papineni, Salim Roukos, Todd Ward, and Wei-Jing Zhu. 2002. BLEU: a method for automatic evaluation of machine translation. In *Proceedings of the 40th annual meeting on association for computational linguistics*, pages 311–318. Association for Computational Linguistics.

Haşim Sak, Tunga Güngör, and Murat Saraçlar. 2007. Morphological disambiguation of Turkish text with perceptron algorithm. In *Computational Linguistics and Intelligent Text Processing*, pages 107–118. Springer.

Radu Soricut and Franz Och. 2015. Unsupervised morphology induction using word embeddings. In *Proc. NAACL*.

Udo Strauss, Peter Grzybek, and Gabriel Altmann. 2007. Word length and word frequency. In *Contributions to the science of text and language*, pages 277–294. Springer.

Katsuhito Sudoh, Xianchao Wu, Kevin Duh, Hajime Tsukada, and Masaaki Nagata. 2011. Post-ordering in statistical machine translation. In *Proc. MT Summit*.

Fei Xia and Michael McCord. 2004. Improving a statistical MT system with automatically learned rewrite patterns. In *Proceedings of the 20th international conference on Computational Linguistics*, page 508. Association for Computational Linguistics.

Reyyan Yeniterzi and Kemal Oflazer. 2010. Syntax-to-morphology mapping in factored phrase-based statistical machine translation from English to Turkish. In *Proceedings of the 48th Annual Meeting of the Association for Computational Linguistics*, pages 454–464. Association for Computational Linguistics.

Yue Zhang and Joakim Nivre. 2011. Transition-based dependency parsing with rich non-local features. In *Proceedings of the 49th Annual Meeting of the Association for Computational Linguistics: Human Language Technologies: short papers-Volume 2*, pages 188–193. Association for Computational Linguistics.

A   Pipelines of the submitted systems

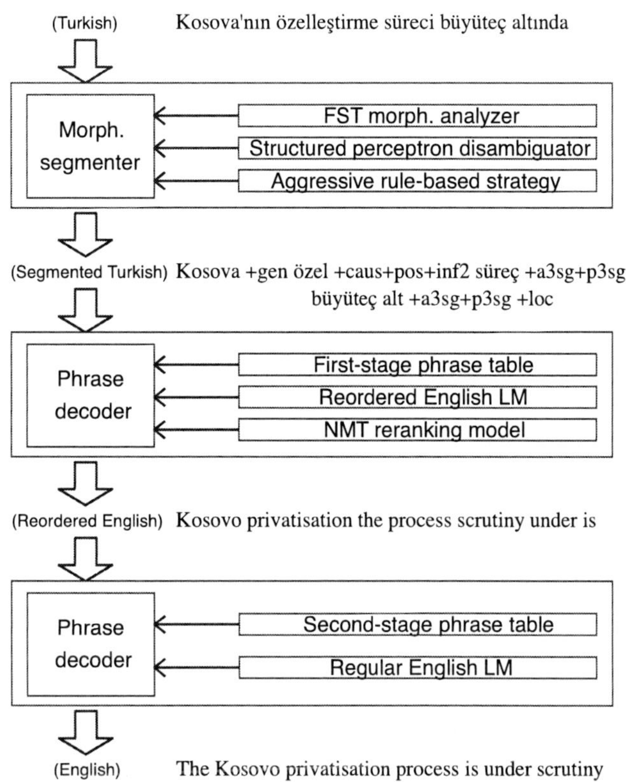

Figure 5: Pipeline of the submitted Turkish-English system

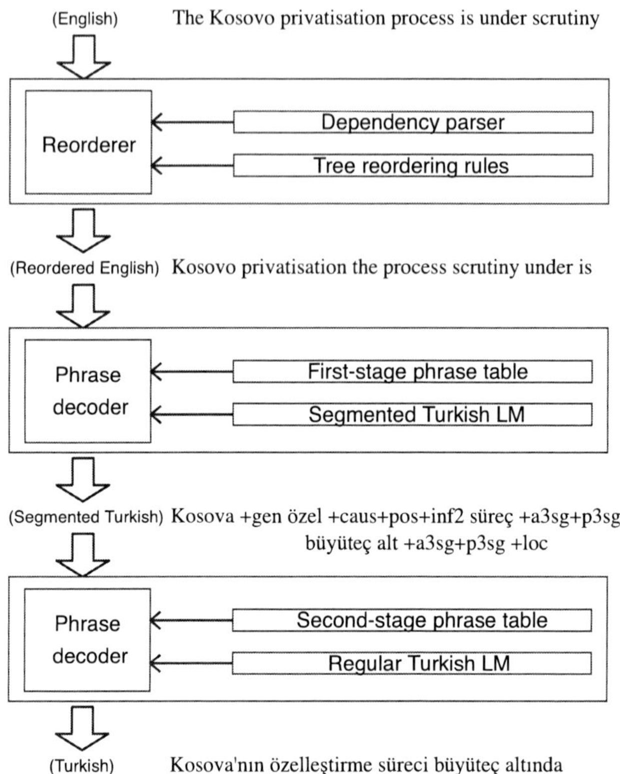

Figure 6: Pipeline of the submitted English-Turkish system

Hybrid Morphological Segmentation for Phrase-Based Machine Translation

Stig-Arne Grönroos
Department of Signal Processing and Acoustics
Aalto University, Finland
stig-arne.gronroos@aalto.fi

Sami Virpioja
Department of Computer Science
Aalto University, Finland
sami.virpioja@aalto.fi

Mikko Kurimo
Department of Signal Processing and Acoustics
Aalto University, Finland
mikko.kurimo@aalto.fi

Abstract

This article describes the Aalto University entry to the English-to-Finnish news translation shared task in WMT 2016. Our segmentation method combines the strengths of rule-based and unsupervised morphology. We also attempt to correct errors in the boundary markings by post-processing with a neural morph boundary predictor.

1 Introduction

Using words as translation tokens is problematic for synthetic languages with rich inflection, derivation or compounding. Such languages have very large vocabularies, leading to sparse statistics and many out-of-vocabulary words. Differences in morphological complexity between source and target languages also complicate alignment.

A common method for alleviating these problems is to segment the morphologically richer side as a pre-processing step. Over-segmentation is detrimental, however, as longer windows of history need to be used, and useful phrases become more difficult to extract. It is therefore important to find a balance in the amount of segmentation.

We consider the case that there are linguistic gold standard segmentations available for the morphologically complex target language. Even if there is no rule-based morphological analyzer for the language, a limited set of gold standard segmentations can be used for training a reasonably accurate statistical segmentation model in a supervised or semi-supervised manner (Ruokolainen et al., 2014; Cotterell et al., 2015).

While using a linguistically accurate morphological segmentation in a phrase-based SMT system may sound like a good idea, there is evidence that shows otherwise. In general, over-segmentation seems to be a larger problem for

NLP applications than under-segmentation (Virpioja et al., 2011). In the case of SMT, linguistic morphs may provide too high granularity compared to the second language, and deteriorate alignment (Habash and Sadat, 2006; Chung and Gildea, 2009; Clifton and Sarkar, 2011). Moreover, longer sequences of units are needed in the language model and the translation phrases to cover the same span of text.

An unsupervised morphological segmentation may alleviate these problems. A method based on optimizing the training data likelihood, such as Morfessor (Creutz and Lagus, 2002; Creutz and Lagus, 2007; Virpioja et al., 2013), ensures that common phenomena are modeled more accurately, for example by using full forms for highly-frequent words even if they consist of multiple morphemes. Data-driven methods also allow tuning the segmentation granularity, for example based on symmetry between the languages in a parallel corpus (Grönroos et al., 2015).

To combine the advantages of linguistic segmentation and data-driven segmentation, we propose a hybrid approach for morphological segmentation. We optimize the segmentation in a data-driven manner, aiming for a similar granularity as the second language of the language pair, but restricting the possible set of segmentation boundaries to those between linguistic morphs. That is, the segmentation method may decide to join any of the linguistic morphs, but it cannot add new segmentation boundaries to known linguistic morphs.

We show that it is possible to improve on the linguistically accurate segmentation by reducing the amount of segmentation in an unsupervised manner.

1.1 Related work

Rule-based and statistical segmentation for SMT have been extensively studied in isolation (Virpi-

Proceedings of the First Conference on Machine Translation, Volume 2: Shared Task Papers, pages 289–295,
Berlin, Germany, August 11-12, 2016. ©2016 Association for Computational Linguistics

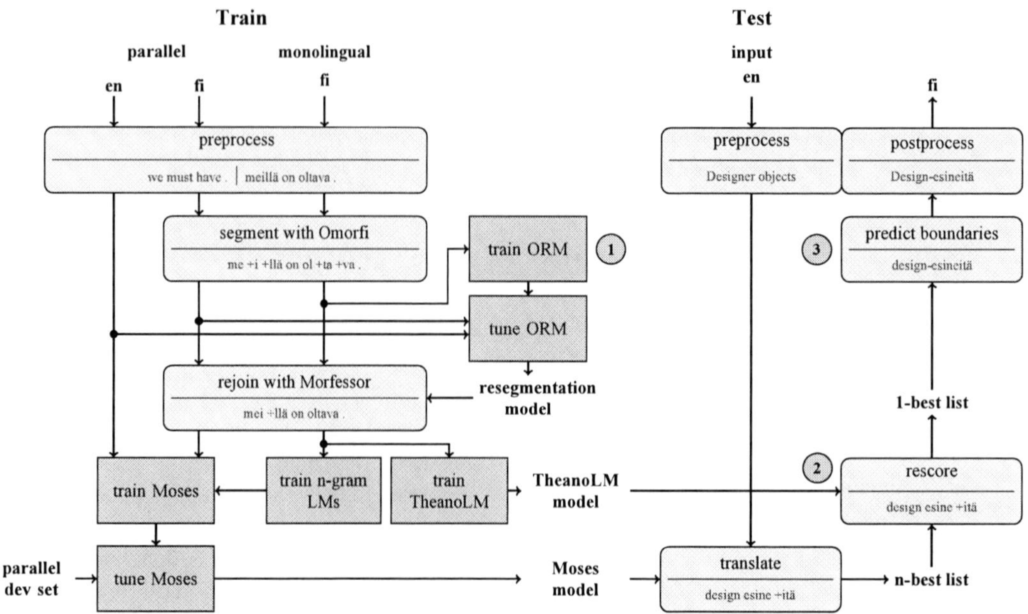

Figure 1: A pipeline overview of training of the system and using it for translation. Main contributions are hilighted with numbers 1-3. ORM is short for Omorfi-restricted Morfessor.

oja et al., 2007; Fishel and Kirik, 2010; Luong et al., 2010), and also the use of system combination to combine their strengths has been examined (De Gispert et al., 2009; Rubino et al., 2015; Pirinen et al., 2016).

Prediction of morph boundary types has been used in conjunction with compound splitting. Stymne and Cancedda (2011) apply rule-based compound splitting in the pre-processing stage, and a conditional random field with rich linguistic features for generating novel compounds in post-processing. Coalescence of compound parts in the translation output is promoted using POS-tag features. Cap et al. (2014) extend the post-predictor to also inflect the compound modifiers e.g. to add a linking morpheme.

Stymne et al. (2013) investigate several methods for splitting and merging compounds when translating into Germanic languages, and provide an extensive reading list on the topic.

2 System overview

An overview of the system is shown in Figure 1. The three main contributions of this work are indicated by numbered circles:

1. Combining rule-based morphological segmentation (Omorfi) to data-driven morphological segmentation (Morfessor).

2. Rescoring n-best lists with TheanoLM (Enarvi and Kurimo, 2016).

3. Correcting boundary markings with post-processing predictor.

Our system extends the phrase-based SMT system Moses (Koehn et al., 2007) to perform segmented translation, by adding pre-processing and post-processing steps, with no changes to the decoder.

The standard pre-processing steps not specified in Figure 1 consist of normalization of punctuation, tokenization, and statistical truecasing. All of these were performed with the tools included in Moses. The pre-processing steps are followed by morphological segmentation.

In addition, the parallel data was cleaned and duplicate sentences were removed. Cleaning was performed after morphological segmentation, as the segmentation can increase the length in tokens of a sentence.

The post-processing steps include rescoring of the n-best list, boundary prediction and desegmentation. These are followed by the standard post-processing steps, reversing the pre-processing steps: detruecasing and detokenization.

System	Tokens	Segmentation		
Words	3	hyötyajoneuvojen	tekniset	tienvarsitarkastukset
		[commercial vehicles']	*[technical]*	*[roadside inspections]*
Omorfi	11	hyöty@ ajo@ neuvo +j +en	teknise +t	tien@ varsi@ tarkastukse +t
		[utility] [drive] [counsel] [+Pl] [+Gen]	*[technical] [+Pl]*	*[road] [side] [inspection] [+Pl]*
ORM	5	hyötyajoneuvo +jen	tekniset	tienvarsi@ tarkastukset
		[commercial vehicle] [+Pl +Gen]	*[technical]*	*[roadside] [inspections]*
Source	6	technical roadside inspection of commercial vehicles		

Table 1: Worked example of two-stage morphological segmentation, beginning with rule-based Omorfi segmentation and followed by Omorfi-restricted Morfessor (ORM). The glosses below the segmentations show approximate meaning of the segments (Pl = plural suffix, Gen = genitive suffix).

2.1 Morphological segmentation

An example of the morphological segmentation is shown in Table 1.

2.1.1 Omorfi segmentation

We begin the morphological segmentation by applying the segmentation tool from Omorfi (Pirinen, 2015). Hyphens removed by Omorfi are reintroduced.

Omorfi outputs 5 types of intra-word boundaries, which we mark in different ways. Compound modifiers, identified by the WB or wB boundary type, are marked with a reserved symbol '@' at the right edge of the morph. Suffixes, identified by a leading morph boundary MB or derivation boundary DB, are marked with a '+' at the left edge. Boundaries of the type STUB (other stemmer-type boundary) are removed. This marking scheme leaves the compound head, or last stem of the word, unmarked. E.g. "yli{WB}voimai{STUB}s{MB}i{MB}a" is marked as "yli@ voimais +i +a".

Words not identified by Omorfi are collected in a separate vocabulary, and treated as unsegmentable.

2.1.2 Restricted Morfessor Baseline

In order to force the Morfessor method to follow the linguistic morphs produced by Omorfi, we added some new features to the Morfessor Baseline implementation by Virpioja et al. (2013). The new extension, Restricted Morfessor Baseline, is able to remove any of the given intra-word boundaries, but cannot introduce any new ones.

The standard training algorithm of Morfessor iterates over the word forms, testing whether to split the corresponding string to two parts or leave it as it is. If the string is split, the testing descends recursively to the substrings. The segmentation decisions are stored in a binary tree structure, where each node corresponds to a string. The root nodes are full word forms and leaf nodes are morphs.

The middle nodes are substrings shared by several word forms, which means that if two word forms have different restrictions on the same substring, some of the restrictions may be violated. While the amount of violations was in practice very small, we ensured that no restrictions were violated in the end by applying the recursive algorithm only for the two first epochs, and then switching to Viterbi training.

In Viterbi training, each word is re-segmented to the most likely segmentation given the current model parameters using an extension of the Viterbi algorithm. We modified the implementation of Virpioja et al. (2013) to remove the previous segments of the word from the parameters before re-analyzing the word, and re-adding the segments of the new optimal segmentation afterwards. Additive smoothing with smoothing constant 1.0 was applied in the Viterbi search.

Prior to the Viterbi training, we flattened the tree structure so that the root nodes (word forms) link directly to the leaf nodes (morphs), thus removing any shared substrings nodes that are not actual morphs. This way all word forms are segmented independently and all the restrictions are followed.

2.1.3 Tuning the amount of segmentation

Omorfi-restricted Morfessor was tuned following Grönroos et al. (2015) to bring the number of tokens on the Finnish target side as close as possible to the English source side. The corpus weight hyper-parameter α was chosen by minimizing the sentence-level difference in token counts between the English and the segmented Finnish sides of the parallel corpus.

2.2 Rescoring n-best lists

Segmentation of the word forms increases the distances spanned by dependencies that should be modeled by the language model. To compensate for this, we apply a strong recurrent neural language model, TheanoLM. A recurrent language model is able to use arbitrarily long contexts without suffering from data sparsity, as opposed to n-gram language models, which are limited to a short context window. The additional language model is used in a separate rescoring step, to speed up translation, and for ease of implementation.

The TheanoLM model was trained on morphologically segmented data. Morphs occurring less than 1000 times in the full monolingual data were removed from the vocabulary, and replaced with the tag <UNK>. To create a class vocabulary, the morphs were embedded in a 300-dimensional space using word2vec (Mikolov et al., 2013). The embeddings were clustered into 2000 classes, using agglomerative clustering with cosine distance. Due to TheanoLM limitations, only the Europarl and News data (but not Common Crawl) were used for training.

The TheanoLM parameters were: 100 nodes in the projection layer, 300 LSTM nodes in the hidden layer, dropout rate 0.25, adam optimization with initial learning rate 0.01, and minibatch 16.

2.3 Morph boundary correction

One benefit of segmented translation is the ability to generate new compounds and inflections, that were not seen in the training data. However, the ability can also lead to errors, e.g when an English word frequently aligned to a compound modifier is translated using such a morph, even though there is no compound head to modify. The "dangling" morph boundary marker will then cause the space to be omitted, forming an incorrect compound with whatever word happens to follow.

For example, the Finnish pronoun *moni* (many) is also a frequent prefix, as in *monitoimi-* (multipurpose) or *monikulttuurinen* (multicultural). This resulted in an erroneous novel compound in *moniliberaalien keskuudessa* ("among the multiliberals"), which was corrected by introducing a space between *moni* and *liberaalien*, leading to a correct translation ("many among the liberals").

In the opposite type of error, compounds may be translated as separate words, or hyphenated compounds translated with the hyphen omitted.

We trained a neural network predictor to correct such errors by predicting the boundary type {space, empty, hyphen} as an additional postprocessing step before joining the tokens.

The neural network takes as input both a token level representation, in the form of the same word2vec embeddings as used in rescoring, and a character level representation windowed to 4 characters before and after the boundary. The tokens are encoded by a bidirectional network of Gated Recurrent Units (Cho et al., 2014), while the characters are encoded by a feed-forward network.

Even though the boundary markers in the translation output are unreliable, they are a strong clue. Our predictor has access to the translated markers. During training markers were randomly corrupted to avoid relying too much on them.

2.4 Moses configuration

We used GIZA++ alignment. As decoding LMs, we used two SRILM n-gram models with modified-KN smoothing: a 3-gram and 5-gram model, trained from different data. Many Moses settings were left at their default values: phrase length 10, grow-diag-final-and alignment symmetrization, msd-bidirectional-fe reordering, and distortion limit 6.

The feature weights were tuned using MERT (Och, 2003), with BLEU (Papineni et al., 2002) of the post-processed hypothesis against a development set as the metric. 20 random restarts per MERT iteration were used, with iterations repeated until convergence.

The rescoring weights were tuned with a newly included script in Moses, which uses kb-MIRA instead of MERT.

3 Data

Our system participates in the constrained condition of the shared task. As parallel data, we used the Europarl-v8 and Wikititles corpora, resulting in 1 846 609 sentences after applying the Omorfi-restricted Morfessor segmentation and cleaning.

As monolingual data, we used the Finnish side of Europarl-v8, news.2014.fi.shuffled.v2, news.2015.fi.shuffled and Common Crawl. The total size of monolingual data after cleaning was 133 848 615 sentences, 2 135 919 860 morph tokens, and 11 771 367 morph types. Setting the frequency threshold to 1000 occurrences for the

Configuration	%BLEU, newstest 2015	2016	Example sentence Other applications could focus on muscle cells and insulin-producing cells, he added.
Omorfi-restricted Morfessor	10.77	11.27	Muissa sovelluksissa voi keskittyä lihas solujen ja insuliinia tuottavien solujen, hän lisäsi.
+boundary correction	10.83	11.27	Muissa sovelluksissa voi keskittyä lihassolujen ja insuliinia tuottavien solujen, hän lisäsi.
+rescoring	11.17	**11.73**	Muut sovellukset voivat keskittyä lihas soluja ja insuliinia tuottavia soluja, hän lisäsi.
+rescoring +boundary corr.	**11.21**	11.72	Muut sovellukset voivat keskittyä lihassoluja ja insuliinia tuottavia soluja, hän lisäsi.
Omorfi	10.00	10.59	Muut sovellukset voisi keskittyä lihassolujen ja insuliinia tuottavien soluja, hän lisäsi.
+boundary correction	10.07	10.61	Muut sovellukset voisi keskittyä lihassolujen ja insuliinia tuottavien soluja, hän lisäsi.
+rescoring	10.70	11.11	Muut sovellukset voivat keskittyä lihassoluja ja insuliinia tuottavien soluja, hän lisäsi.
+rescoring +boundary corr.	10.78	11.11	Muut sovellukset voivat keskittyä lihassoluja ja insuliinia tuottavien soluja, hän lisäsi.
Word baseline	10.48	10.65	Muut sovellukset voisivat keskittyä lihaksia ja insuliinia tuottavien solujen-, hän lisäsi.
Reference translation			Muut sovelluskohteet voisivat keskittyä lihassoluihin ja insuliinia tuottaviin soluihin, hän lisäsi.

Table 2: Results of automatic evaluation, in BLEU percentage points.

TheanoLM morph lexicon reduced the number of morph types to 121 735.

The complete monolingual data including the Common Crawl was only used for creating the morph lexicon and for training the 3-gram LM. For the 5-gram LM, the TheanoLM and the boundary predictor, the Common Crawl was omitted.

Because hyphenated compounds are much less frequent than non-hyphenated words, we enriched the training data for the boundary predictor by adding the list of words compounds containing a single hyphen and occurring more than 10 times in the full monolingual corpus.

4 Results

Results are summarized in Table 2, together with example translations produced by the different system configurations.

The Omorfi-restricted Morfessor segmentation leads consistently to an improvement over directly using the Omorfi segmentation. For all configurations on the newstest2016 set, and for newstest2015 without rescoring, the improvement is over +0.6 BLEU. On newstest2015 with rescoring, the improvement is slightly smaller, +0.47 BLEU.

Adding the TheanoLM rescoring increases BLEU between +0.4 and +0.7 BLEU. The increase is larger for the more aggressively segmented Omorfi system, supporting the conclusion that a strong language model is needed to compensate for the longer sequences.

In total, our best system results in a +1 BLEU improvement over the word baseline.

Boundary prediction gave a modest improvement of under +0.1 BLEU on the newstest2015 set, the effect on the newstest2016 set was neutral. While the predictor works reliably for the correct Finnish text it was trained on, manual inspection shows that the performance is erratic for disfluent translation output. Even while the minor cosmetic improvements are more common than errors, the benefit is hard to quantify.

Due to a mistake during data pre-processing, one of the n-gram language models penalizes the use of numbers. The problem affects all the evaluated systems and lowers the overall scores. However, it does not affect the increase in BLEU from the use of Omorfi-restricted Morfessor or rescoring. We verified this using BLEU of the test set with all source sentences containing numbers removed.

5 Conclusions

We propose a new morphological segmentation method, combining the strengths of rule-based and unsupervised morphology. We optimize the segmentation in a data-driven manner, aiming to balance granularity between the two languages, while restricting segmentation to a subset of the linguistic morph boundaries. Using this segmentation, we improve SMT quality over the linguistically accurate segmentation.

Using a neural morph boundary predictor to correct errors in the boundary markings does not lead to an improvement in BLEU.

In total, our best system results in a +1 BLEU improvement over the word baseline.

Acknowledgments

This research has been supported by the Academy of Finland under the Finnish Centre of Excellence Program 2012–2017 (grant n°251170), and LASTU Programme (grants n°256887 and 259934). Computer resources within the Aalto

University School of Science "Science-IT" project
were used.

References

Fabienne Cap, Alexander M Fraser, Marion Weller, and
Aoife Cahill. 2014. How to produce unseen teddy
bears: Improved morphological processing of compounds in SMT. In *14th Conference of the European
Chapter of the Association for Computational Linguistics (EACL)*, Gothenburg, Sweden. Association
for Computational Linguistics.

Kyunghyun Cho, Bart Van Merriënboer, Caglar Gulcehre, Dzmitry Bahdanau, Fethi Bougares, Holger
Schwenk, and Yoshua Bengio. 2014. Learning
phrase representations using RNN encoder-decoder
for statistical machine translation. In *Empirical
Methods in Natural Language Processing (EMNLP)*,
Doha, Qatar.

Tagyoung Chung and Daniel Gildea. 2009. Unsupervised tokenization for machine translation. In
*Empirical Methods in Natural Language Process-
ing (EMNLP)*, Singapore. Association for Computational Linguistics.

Ann Clifton and Anoop Sarkar. 2011. Combining morpheme-based machine translation with post-
processing morpheme prediction. In *ACL: HLT*,
Portland, Oregon, USA, June. Association for Computational Linguistics.

Ryan Cotterell, Thomas Müller, Alexander Fraser, and
Hinrich Schütze. 2015. Labeled morphological segmentation with semi-markov models. In *CONLL*,
Beijing, China. Association for Computational Linguistics.

Mathias Creutz and Krista Lagus. 2002. Unsupervised discovery of morphemes. In *ACL-02 Workshop on Morphological and Phonological Learning*,
Philadelphia, PA, USA, July. Association for Computational Linguistics.

Mathias Creutz and Krista Lagus. 2007. Unsupervised models for morpheme segmentation and morphology learning. *ACM Transactions on Speech and
Language Processing*, 4(1), January.

Adrià De Gispert, Sami Virpioja, Mikko Kurimo, and
William Byrne. 2009. Minimum Bayes risk com-
bination of translation hypotheses from alternative
morphological decompositions. In *Proceedings of
HLT-NAACL 2009: Short Papers*, Boulder, CO,
USA. Association for Computational Linguistics.

Seppo Enarvi and Mikko Kurimo. 2016. TheanoLM -
An Extensible Toolkit for Neural Network Language
Modeling. *ArXiv e-prints*, May. http://arxiv.
org/abs/1605.00942.

Mark Fishel and Harri Kirik. 2010. Linguistically
motivated unsupervised segmentation for machine
translation. In *Language Resources and Evaluation
(LREC)*, Valletta, Malta.

Stig-Arne Grönroos, Sami Virpioja, and Mikko Kurimo. 2015. Tuning phrase-based segmented translation for a morphologically complex target language. In *Tenth Workshop on Statistical Machine
Translation*, Lisbon, Portugal, September. Association for Computational Linguistics.

Nizar Habash and Fatiha Sadat. 2006. Arabic prepro-
cessing schemes for statistical machine translation.
In *Proceedings of HLT-NAACL*, New York, USA.
Association for Computational Linguistics.

Philipp Koehn, Hieu Hoang, Alexandra Birch, Chris
Callison-Burch, Marcello Federico, Nicola Bertoldi,
Brooke Cowan, Wade Shen, Christine Moran,
Richard Zens, et al. 2007. Moses: Open source
toolkit for statistical machine translation. In *45th
annual meeting of the ACL on interactive poster
and demonstration sessions*, Prague, Czech Republic. Association for Computational Linguistics.

Minh-Thang Luong, Preslav Nakov, and Min-Yen Kan.
2010. A hybrid morpheme-word representation
for machine translation of morphologically rich languages. In *Empirical Methods in Natural Language
Processing (EMNLP)*, Cambridge, MA, USA. Association for Computational Linguistics.

Tomas Mikolov, Ilya Sutskever, Kai Chen, Greg S Corrado, and Jeff Dean. 2013. Distributed representations of words and phrases and their compositionality. In *Advances in neural information processing
systems (NIPS)*, Lake Tahoe, NV, USA.

Franz Josef Och. 2003. Minimum error rate training in statistical machine translation. In *41st Annual
Meeting on Association for Computational Linguistics*, Sapporo, Japan. Association for Computational
Linguistics.

Kishore Papineni, Salim Roukos, Todd Ward, and Wei-
Jing Zhu. 2002. BLEU: a method for automatic
evaluation of machine translation. In *40th annual
meeting of the association for computational linguistics*, Philadelphia, PA, USA. Association for Computational Linguistics.

Tommi A Pirinen, Antonio Toral, and Raphael Rubino.
2016. Rule-based and statistical morph segments
in English-to-Finnish SMT. In *2nd International
Workshop on Computational Linguistics for Uralic
Languages*, Szeged, Hungary, Jan.

Tommi A Pirinen. 2015. Omorfi—Free and open
source morphological lexical database for Finnish.
In *20th Nordic Conference on Computational Linguistics (NODALIDA)*, Vilnius, Lithuania.

Raphael Rubino, Tommi Pirinen, Miquel Esplà-
Gomis, Nikola Ljubešić, Sergio Ortiz Rojas, Vassilis Papavassiliou, Prokopis Prokopidis, and Antonio Toral. 2015. Abu-MaTran at WMT 2015 translation task: Morphological segmentation and web

crawling. In *Tenth Workshop on Statistical Machine Translation*, Lisbon, Portugal, September. Association for Computational Linguistics.

Teemu Ruokolainen, Oskar Kohonen, Sami Virpioja, and Mikko Kurimo. 2014. Painless semi-supervised morphological segmentation using conditional random fields. In *European Chapter of the Association for Computational Linguistics (EACL)*, Gothenburg, Sweden, April. Association for Computational Linguistics.

Sara Stymne and Nicola Cancedda. 2011. Productive generation of compound words in statistical machine translation. In *Proceedings of the Sixth Workshop on Statistical Machine Translation*, Edinburgh, UK. Association for Computational Linguistics.

Sara Stymne, Nicola Cancedda, and Lars Ahrenberg. 2013. Generation of compound words in statistical machine translation into compounding languages. *Computational Linguistics*, 39(4).

Sami Virpioja, Jaakko J Väyrynen, Mathias Creutz, and Markus Sadeniemi. 2007. Morphology-aware statistical machine translation based on morphs induced in an unsupervised manner. *Machine Translation Summit XI*, 2007.

Sami Virpioja, Ville T. Turunen, Sebastian Spiegler, Oskar Kohonen, and Mikko Kurimo. 2011. Empirical comparison of evaluation methods for unsupervised learning of morphology. *Traitement Automatique des Langues*, 52(2).

Sami Virpioja, Peter Smit, Stig-Arne Grönroos, and Mikko Kurimo. 2013. Morfessor 2.0: Python implementation and extensions for Morfessor Baseline. Report 25/2013 in Aalto University publication series SCIENCE + TECHNOLOGY, Department of Signal Processing and Acoustics, Aalto University, Helsinki, Finland.

The AFRL-MITLL WMT16 News-Translation Task Systems

**Jeremy Gwinnup, Timothy Anderson,
Grant Erdmann, Katherine Young**
Air Force Research Laboratory
{jeremy.gwinnup.1,timothy.anderson.20,
grant.erdmann,katherine.young.1.ctr}@us.af.mil

**Michaeel Kazi, Elizabeth Salesky,
Brian Thompson**
MIT Lincoln Laboratory
{michaeel.kazi,elizabeth.salesky,
brian.thompson}@ll.mit.edu

Abstract

This paper describes the AFRL-MITLL statistical machine translation systems and the improvements that were developed during the WMT16 evaluation campaign. New techniques applied this year include Neural Machine Translation, a unique selection process for language modelling data, additional out-of-vocabulary transliteration techniques, and morphology generation.

1 Introduction

As part of the 2016 Conference on Machine Translation (WMT16) news-translation shared task, the MITLL and AFRL human language techology teams participated in the Russian–English and English–Russian news translation tasks. Our machine translation (MT) systems represent improvements to both our systems from IWSLT2015 (Kazi et al., 2015) and WMT15 (Gwinnup et al., 2015), the introduction of Neural Machine Translation rescoring, neural-net based recasing, unsupervised transliteration of out-of-vocabulary (OOV) words (Durrani et al., 2014), and an unique selection process for language modelling data. For the English–Russian translation task we experimented with techniques to improve morphology generation.

2 System Description

We submitted systems for the Russian–English and English–Russian news-domain machine translation shared tasks. For all submissions, we used the phrase-based variant of the Moses decoder (Koehn et al., 2007). As in previous years, our submitted systems used only the constrained data supplied when training.

2.1 Data Usage

In training our systems we drew on all the available data, filtering the new English Common Crawl monolingual data as described in §2.4 and §3.1. The Wikipedia Headlines corpus[1] was reserved to train a neural network based transliteration system described in §2.8.1.

2.2 Data Preprocessing

We processed the training data similarly to our WMT15 system (Gwinnup et al., 2015). We examined irregular behaviors in Moses's punctuation normalization script[2]. We ran a script that examines the source and target side of the parallel training data and removes lines that are identical in both the source and target in order to prevent the effects of wrong-language phrases "polluting" the phrase and rule tables.

2.3 Phrase Table Generation

We used the standard Moses method of extracting and creating phrase tables. Phrase tables were binarized using either the Compact Phrase Table (Junczys-Dowmunt, 2012) or ProbingPT (Bogoychev and Hoang, 2016) methods.

2.4 Language Model Data Selection

Using definitions below, we select as a language modelling set a subset S from the Common Crawl set C to maximize its similarity to a target set T, using a coverage metric $g(S, T)$. Defining $c_i(X)$ as the count of feature i's occurrence in corpus X,

$$g(S, T) = \frac{\sum_{i \in \mathcal{I}} f(\min(c_i(S), c_i(T)))}{\sum_{i \in \mathcal{I}} f(c_i(T)) + p_i(S, T)}$$

This work is sponsored by the Air Force Research Laboratory under Air Force contracts FA-8721-05-C-0002 and FA-8650-09-D-6939-029.

[1] http://statmt.org/wmt15/wiki-titles.tgz
[2] normalize-punctuation.perl

296

where the oversaturation penalty $p_i(S, T)$ is

$$\max(0, c_i(S) - c_i(T)) \left[f(c_i(T) + 1) - f(c_i(T)) \right].$$

We use $f(x) = \log(1 + x)$ as the submodular function to weight counts, and the feature set $\mathcal{I}$ is the set of all unigrams and bigrams. The target set T is made of the news test sets from 2013–2015.

The optimization problem, $\max_{S \subset C} g(S, T)$, is solved via greedy optimization, iteratively adding the segment to S that provides the largest increase in g. The set S is reviewed after each addition, removing any older segment in S that decreases g.

The Common Crawl corpus C is broken into easily-processed chunks of ten thousand segments, selecting five hundred segments from each chunk. This selection was repeated until we saw diminishing returns from adding further chunks, resulting in a language modelling subset of six million lines. These six million lines represent 0.17% of the 3.6 billion lines of data in the English portion of the Common Crawl.

2.5 Tuning Improvements

Improvements were made to our tuner, Drem (Erdmann and Gwinnup, 2015), since our last submission. Enforcement of minimum and maximum distance of the tuning result from prior decodes (i.e., tabu and fear constraints) is now implicitly enforced via L_1 penalty functions, making the process more robust to densely-packed decodes. Rescoring weights are now not penalized in the n-best list interpolation scheme, since they do not directly affect n-best lists. This new feature provides faster convergence of our NMT-rescored systems. Another improvement to Drem is that the metric chrF3 (Popović, 2015) is now available as a tuning objective function.

2.6 Neural Network Recaser

We noticed a substantial gap between uncased and cased BLEU scores on our systems. Addressing the problem in post-processing, it became apparent that recasing can only do so much on monolingual data. We therefore built a classifier that uses both the source-side and the target-side of the translations. The inputs to the classifier are:

- t_i, the word to be recased, as well as t_{i-1} and t_{i-2}
- $s_{a(i)}$, the source word aligned to t_i, plus $s_{a(i) \pm 1}$. Alignments were taken from Moses

output, and missing alignments were computed using the NNJM affiliation heuristic (Devlin et al., 2014).

- The status of the source word as lowercase, capitalized, or OTHER.

The exact classifier used could be anything; we chose a neural network because it is simple to create and robust. Our architecture is as follows:

1. Vocabulary of all words, excluding 25% of singletons
2. Input: Word vectors for these words, plus nine binary inputs ($s_{i-1} = lc, s_{i-1} = Uc, s_{i-1} = OTHER, s_i = lc \ldots$), all concatenated together into a single vector
3. Two hidden layers, default size 100
4. One softmax output, 3 output classes

The resulting recaser consistently yields +0.2-0.25 case-sensitive BLEU over a standard language model recaser.

2.7 Inflection Generation

English-Russian systems have the added challenge of generating morphologically rich word-forms. In addition to an English-Russian baseline, we trained two methods to generate inflected forms. First, we created a system with a separate inflection prediction component (Toutanova et al. 2008, Fraser et al. 2012). We trained an MT system from English to lemmatized Russian, using the Mystem[3] Russian morphological analyzer to lemmatize all available parallel data, and then trained a MT system from lemmatized Russian to Russian. Scoring against lemmatized references, the first step yielded 27.70 case-insensitive BLEU on `newstest2016`. However, while the lemru-ru system was successful with one-to-one lemmatized training data, it couldn't recover from mistakes in the MT output of the first step and the system overall did not perform as well as our baseline (17.19 cased BLEU).

We also attempted to address inflection generation during training using verb annotation, following the approach of Kirchhoff et al. (2015) for Arabic verb inflection. We use dependency parsing to identify the subject of the verb in the English sentence and then annotate the verb with the person and number of the subject. With a pronominal subject *he* or *she*, the verb is also annotated for gender.

---

[3] `https://api.yandex.ru/mystem`

Original: Woud n't you know it ?
Annotated: Would n't you know-2p it ?
Dependency Parse:

Index	Word	POS	Head	Relation
1	Would	MD	4	aux
2	n't	RB	4	neg
3	you	PRP	4	nsubj
4	know	VB	0	root
5	it	PRP	4	dobj
6	?	.	4	punct

Figure 1: Annotation via Dependency Parse

This provides the potential for the system to match annotated English verbs to the correctly inflected Russian verbs during training. Figure 1 shows an annotated sentence and the underlying dependency parse.

We use the Stanford parser (Klein and Manning, 2003) and conversion utility to generate the dependency parses, adjusting the tokenization of the input to match the Stanford treatment of contractions. We apply annotation to verbs with subjects listed as *nsubj* or *xsubj* in the dependency parse. Person, number, and gender are derived from the subject's POS tag and from the specific lexical item for pronouns. Coordinate subjects are counted as plural.

An unannotated MT system has a good chance of associating the correct verb form with the subject if the subject and verb are adjacent and can be extracted as a phrase, while more distant pairs are less likely to be found in the phrase table, leaving the verb open to translation in the wrong inflected form. Since annotation can increase data sparsity, it is better to apply it only when necessary.

Kirchhoff et al. (2015) address the data sparsity issue by only applying their annotation-trained model when their baseline model translates the subject and verb via separate phrases. In some of our systems, we simulated the use of a back-off model by restricting our annotation to subjects and verbs that occur with a minimum separation distance.

Figure 2 shows the potential effect of specifying a minimum separation distance. In the first sentence, the subject and verb are adjacent; any separation requirement greater than zero prevents annotation of the verb. The other sentences show a greater separation, and annotation will be main-

Would n't **you know**-2p it ?
The **country** was gradually **recovering**-3p-sg ..
The **interests** of people **take**-3p-pl precedence ..

Figure 2: Annotation at different separation distances.

tained if the separation requirement is less than 3.

In order to avoid the data sparsity problem, we ultimately created a factored version of the verb annotation system. The annotations were specified as factors on the verb, with a null factor on the unannotated words, e.g. `would|NONE n't|NONE you|NONE know|2p it|NONE ?|NONE`

In system 2 of our English-Russian systems (shown in Table 8), we used this factored input with no separation limit.

2.7.1 Discussion

We examined the effect of verb annotation on inflection choice using an enhanced version of the Hjerson (Popović, 2011) error analysis program, in conjunction with the Mystem Russian morphological analyzer. Factored verb annotation as described above failed to reduce the number of inflectional errors (shown in Table 1.)

Technique	Inf. Errors	Pct. Hyp. Words
Baseline	5823	9.349%
Annotated	5994	9.351%

Table 1: Hjerson performance

The verb annotation technique aims to increase the information available for the generation of verb inflections. Errors in verb inflection amount to just a small proportion of overall errors in our baseline system, so the room for improvement in translation quality is small (shown in Table 2.)

Error Type	Instances	Pct. Hyp. Words
Word Choice	30031	48.21%
Reordering	4479	7.19%
Inflection	5823	9.35%

Table 2: Hjerson classification of Error Types in Baseline System

Only about 18% of these 5823 baseline inflectional errors involve verbs; other errors involve nouns and pronouns (about 58%) or adjectives (about 24%). Meanwhile, the use of annotated data had unintended consequences for the other elements in the sentence. While our annotations were only applied to verbs in the training data, changes in inflection were observed for nouns and pronouns as well.

We used Mystem to provide a morphological analysis of the inflectional errors. We found that similar errors were made in both the baseline system and the annotated system. Looking at the error types by part of speech, we saw that verb errors for both systems primarily involved either number or gender, as opposed to tense or person. Pronoun errors for both systems showed a tendency for oblique cases in place of nominative.

For example, both systems displayed errors in which будут (third person plural) "they will" was generated instead of the reference form, будет (third person singular) "he will". The baseline system had 8 instances of this error, while the annotated system had 10 instances. The most frequent error was the substitution of the dative/locative first person singular pronoun мне "to me" for the nominative pronoun я "I". The baseline system had 16 instances of this error, compared to 20 instances for the annotated system.

The verb-annotated system performed worse than our baseline when evaluated with the BLEU metric. We hope to gain more insight from the human ranking of the two systems.

2.8 Transliteration

We employed two methods to address transliteration of remaining out-of-vocabulary (OOV) words: an unsupervised statistical transliteration approach and a novel character-based neural-network transliteration approach.

2.8.1 Neural Network Transliteration

We created a list of 54k Named Entity (NE) pairs from the Common Crawl using transliteration mining; we also derived NE pairs from the Wikipedia Headlines Corpus (Gwinnup et al., 2015). We employed these lists in building a neural network based transliterator. We trained an encoder-decoder LSTM network to produce characters in a target language given characters from a word in the source language. The network configuration was nearly the same as that in our NMT experiments, except the network was significantly smaller (hidden sizes of 100 and 200, with 1, 2, and 3 hidden layers) and had a beam of 5. A small (5k) sub-

set of the data was held out for evaluation/tuning. Since Russian nouns use case inflections, multiple Russian word forms may map to a single English spelling. For this reason, we tried rescoring with a unigram language model trained on the monolingual data to help weight the correct English spelling of words that may have been seen in the language modelling data but were not in the phrase table. The LM's unknown word probability was optimized on the validation set.

System	Exact matches
Baseline [0 edit distance]	23.1%
Single enc-dec	34.7%
Ensemble (6)	38.7%
Single enc-dec + LM rescore	42.5%
Ensemble (6) + LM rescore	45.8%

Table 3: Fraction of transliterations that match exactly, on validation set (subset of newstest2014)

We integrated this process into our SMT pipeline through different backoff phrase tables. Unknown words from the dev and test sets were transliterated via beam search (beam and stack size of 5) using the final system in Table 3 to create phrase table entries. The results are in Table 4. Gains may seem modest, however, there are not that many OOV words in newstest2015 − only 817 total unknowns, 515 of which we attempted to transliterate (ASCII entries and Capitalized words). Despite this, gains are consistent.

System	Cased BLEU
1. drop unknowns	28.07
2. pass-through unknowns	27.85
3. ASCII entries in backoff PT	27.86
4. 3 + cased words LM match	28.20
5. 3 + all cased Cyrillic words	28.16

Table 4: Neural Transliteration via Backoff PTs

2.8.2 Unsupervised Statistical Transliteration

As a contrast to our neural network transliteration approach, we also experimented with using the unsupervised statistical transliteration method (Durrani et al., 2014) included in Moses. System 2 in Table 7 and both systems in Table 8 employ this strategy as a post-decode step.

2.9 Neural MT

We describe a Neural Machine Translation system we developed and our strategies to integrate this system into our machine translation framework.

2.9.1 System

We trained a neural encoder-decoder network (Sutskever et al., 2014; Bahdanau et al., 2014; Luong et al., 2015) using the attention model from (Vinyals et al., 2015) to perform neural machine translation (NMT). We trained the model using Adagrad (Duchi et al., 2011) and found it improved performance over the learning rate schedule proposed in (Luong et al., 2015). We also found it advantageous to use a larger source vocabulary (200k-500k words worked well). Each instance of the system was comprised of two 1000-dim hidden layers, with beam and stack of 5. Our NMT results are shown in Table 5. They did not perform competitively with our SMT systems by themselves, however they were very useful in rescoring as others have noted (Auli et al., 2013).

System	Cased BLEU
1. Single model	21.00
2. Ensemble of 2	21.46

Table 5: Russian–English Neural MT Systems decoding `newstest2015`

2.9.2 Reranking

We compared two different ways of using the NMT system to augment our phrase-based system.

1. **Single set of weights** We augment the Moses n-best list with NMT scores for each sentence, and then tune the decode weights using Drem. We repeat this process 10 times, using the last weights to decode the test set and one-best calculation.

2. **Decode + rerank weights** We tune the decode weights using Drem, without the NMT scores. After 10 iterations, we merge the n-best lists together and compute NMT scores over the result. Then, we compute a second set of weights. To decode the test set, we pass the decode weights to Moses, augment the n-best list with NMT scores, and finally apply the one-best dot product using the second set of weights.

Features	Cased BLEU tst15
pb + BigLM	27.09
+ nmt	27.92
+ cc LM data	28.07
+ translit	28.20

Table 6: Score breakdown for en–ru submission system 1, average of 6 runs on `newstest2015`.

The first process produced scores of 27.22, and the second 27.92 (mteval, case+punc, `newstest2015`, average of 6).

3 Results

We submitted 2 Russian–English and 2 English–Russian systems for evaluation, each employing a different decoding strategy. Each system is described below. Automatically scored results reported in BLEU (Papineni et al., 2002) for our submission systems can be found in Table 7 for Russian–English and Table 8 for English–Russian.

Finally, as part of WMT16, the results of our submission systems were ranked by monolingual human judges against the machine translation output of other WMT16 participants. These judgments are reported in WMT (2016).

3.1 Russian–English

For both Russian–English system submissions, we reused the BigLM15 concept from our WMT15 submissions to build a monolithic language model from the following sources: Yandex[4], Commoncrawl (Smith et al., 2013), LDC Gigaword English v5 (Parker et al., 2011) and News Commentary. Submission system 1 included the data selected from the large Commoncrawl corpus as outlined in §2.4, while submission system 2 used this data to build a separate, complementary language model.

For submission system 1, we used a standard phrase based approach with the following parameters/features: distortion-limit of 8, no reordering over punctuation, hierarchical mslr reordering model (Galley and Manning, 2008), order 7 operational sequence model (Durrani et al., 2011), and a factored language model over the NYT Gigaword corpus with 600 word classes. We incorporated our Tensorflow Neural MT system in via reranking, and applied transliteration as backoff phrase tables during decoding. Lowercased out-

---

[4]`https://translate.yandex.ru/corpus?lang=en`

System	Cased BLEU	Unc. BLEU
1. pb + NMT rescore + BigLM(inc. CC data) + Neural translit	27.6	28.8
2. pb (clean data) + NMT rescore + CC subsel LM + Neural translit + Moses translit	27.0	28.4

Table 7: Russian–English MT Submission Systems decoding `newstest2016`

put was recased via neural network. A breakdown of scores for submission system one is indicated in Table 6.

For submission system 2, we used the same approach as system 1, removing the class-factored language model and utilizing both the BigLM used in our WMT15 systems and a secondary language model built from data selected from the monolingual CommonCrawl corpus as outlined in §2.4. While this system did use the same transliteration backoff phrase tables to handle OOVs, due to different preprocessing methodologies, some OOVs still remained in the output. The Moses unsupervised statistical transliterator was applied as a postprocess. Finally, the Moses statistical recaser was employed to recase the data before scoring.

3.2 English–Russian

Both English–Russian submission systems used a language model interpolated from individual models built from all available Russian data.

Submission system 1 is a standard baseline system employing hierarchical lexicalized reordering and an order 5 operation sequence model.

For submission system 2, we applied factored verb annotation on the training data to guide inflection choice, as outlined in §2.7. This system also employed hierarchical lexicalized reordering and an order 5 operation sequence model. While this system did not perform as well as system 1, we are interested to see the effect of this verb-annotation approach on the human-ranking portion of the evaluation.

Due to time and processing constraints we did not employ Neural Machine Translation rescoring

System	Cased BLEU	Unc. BLEU
1. enru-pb	23.42	23.52
2. enru-pb-facvban0	20.90	21.00

Table 8: English–Russian MT Submission Systems decoding `newstest2016`

in our English–Russian submission systems.

4 Conclusion

We present a series of improvements to our Russian–English and English–Russian machine translation systems. These include general improvements in working with large data sets (language model selection, Drem optimization, neural model rescoring) as well as improvements in language-specific processing (inflection selection/generation, NE transliteration, and neural network recasing). While these innovations show promise in addressing relevant issues in Russian–English and English–Russian MT, the overall MT results show that more work is needed to integrate these methods.

Acknowledgements

We wish to thank the anonymous reviewers for their comments and insight.

References

Michael Auli, Michel Galley, Chris Quirk, and Geoffrey Zweig. 2013. Joint language and translation modeling with recurrent neural networks. In *EMNLP*, volume 3, page 0.

Dzmitry Bahdanau, Kyunghyun Cho, and Yoshua Bengio. 2014. Neural machine translation by jointly learning to align and translate. *CoRR*, abs/1409.0473.

Nikolay Bogoychev and Hieu Hoang. 2016. Fast and highly parallelizable phrase table for statistical machine translation. In *Proc. of the First Conference on Statistical Machine Translation (WMT '16)*, Berlin, Germany, August.

Jacob Devlin, Rabih Zbib, Zhongqiang Huang, Thomas Lamar, Richard Schwartz, and John Makhoul. 2014. Fast and robust neural network joint models for statistical machine translation. In *Proc. of the 52nd Annual Meeting of the Association for Computational*

Opinions, interpretations, conclusions and recommendations are those of the authors and are not necessarily endorsed by the United States Government. Cleared for public release on 28 Apr 2016. Originator reference number RH-16-115466. Case number 88ABW-2016-2186.

Linguistics (Volume 1: Long Papers), Proc. of the ACL, Long Papers, pages 1370–1380, Baltimore, MD, USA.

John Duchi, Elad Hazan, and Yoram Singer. 2011. Adaptive subgradient methods for online learning and stochastic optimization. *The Journal of Machine Learning Research*, 12:2121–2159.

Nadir Durrani, Helmut Schmid, and Alexander Fraser. 2011. A joint sequence translation model with integrated reordering. In *Proc. of the 49th Annual Meeting of the Association for Computational Linguistics (ACL '11)*, pages 1045–1054, Portland, Oregon, June.

Nadir Durrani, Hassan Sajjad, Hieu Hoang, and Philipp Koehn. 2014. Integrating an unsupervised transliteration model into statistical machine translation. In *Proc. of the 14th Conference of the European Chapter of the Association for Computational Linguistics, volume 2: Short Papers*, pages 148–153, Gothenburg, Sweden, April. Association for Computational Linguistics.

Grant Erdmann and Jeremy Gwinnup. 2015. Drem: The AFRL submission to the WMT15 tuning task. In *Proc. of the Tenth Workshop on Statistical Machine Translation*, pages 422–427, Lisbon, Portugal, September.

Michel Galley and Christopher D. Manning. 2008. A simple and effective hierarchical phrase reordering model. In *Proc. of the Conference on Empirical Methods in Natural Language Processing*, EMNLP '08, pages 848–856.

Jeremy Gwinnup, Tim Anderson, Grant Erdmann, Katherine Young, Christina May, Michaeel Kazi, Elizabeth Salesky, and Brian Thompson. 2015. The AFRL-MITLL WMT15 system: There's more than one way to decode it! In *Proc. of the Tenth Workshop on Statistical Machine Translation*, pages 112–119, Lisbon, Portugal, September.

Marcin Junczys-Dowmunt. 2012. Phrasal rank-encoding: Exploiting phrase redundancy and translational relations for phrase table compression. *Prague Bulletin of Mathematical Linguistics*, 98:63–74.

Michaeel Kazi, Brian Thompson, Elizabeth Salesky, Tim Anderson, Grant Erdmann, Eric Hansen, Brian Ore, Katherine Young, Jeremy Gwinnup, Michael Hutt, and Christina May. 2015. The MITLL-AFRL IWSLT-2015 systems. In *Proc. of the 11th International Workshop on Spoken Language Translation (IWSLT'15)*, Da Nang, Vietnam, December.

Katrin Kirchhoff, Yik-Cheung Tam, Colleen Richey, and Wen Wang. 2015. Morphological modeling for machine translation of english-iraqi arabic spoken dialogs. In *Proc. of the 2015 Conference of the North American Chapter of the Association for Computational Linguistics: Human Language Technologies*, pages 995–1000, Denver, Colorado, May–June.

Dan Klein and Christopher D. Manning. 2003. Accurate unlexicalized parsing. In *Proc. of the 41st Annual Meeting of the Association for Computational Linguistics*, pages 423–430, Sapporo, Japan, July.

Philipp Koehn, Hieu Hoang, Alexandra Birch, Chris Callison-Burch, Marcello Federico, Nicola Bertoldi, Brooke Cowan, Wade Shen, Christine Moran, Richard Zens, Chris Dyer, Ondřej Bojar, Alexandra Constantin, and Evan Herbst. 2007. Moses: Open source toolkit for statistical machine translation. In *Proc. of the 45th Annual Meeting of the ACL on Interactive Poster and Demonstration Sessions*, ACL '07, pages 177–180.

Minh-Thang Luong, Hieu Pham, and Christopher D Manning. 2015. Effective approaches to attention-based neural machine translation. *arXiv preprint arXiv:1508.04025*.

Kishore Papineni, Salim Roukos, Todd Ward, and Wei-Jing Zhu. 2002. BLEU: A method for automatic evaluation of machine translation. In *Proc. of the 40th Annual Meeting of the Association for Computational Linguistics (ACL '02)*, pages 311–318, Philadelphia, Pennsylvania, July.

Robert Parker, David Graff, Junbo Kong, Ke Chen, and Kazuaki Maeda. 2011. English Gigaword Fifth Edition LDC2011T07. *Philadelphia: Linguistic Data Consortium*.

Maja Popović. 2011. Hjerson: An open source tool for automatic error classification of machine translation output. *The Prague Bulletin of Mathematical Linguistics (PBML)*, 96:59–68, 10.

Maja Popović. 2015. chrF: character n-gram F-score for automatic MT evaluation. In *Proc. of the Tenth Workshop on Statistical Machine Translation*, pages 392–395, Lisbon, Portugal, September.

Jason R. Smith, Herve Saint-Amand, Magdalena Plamada, Philipp Koehn, Chris Callison-Burch, and Adam Lopez. 2013. Dirt cheap web-scale parallel text from the common crawl. In *Proc. of the 51st Annual Meeting of the Association for Computational Linguistics (ACL '13)*, pages 1374–1383, Sofia, Bulgaria, August.

Ilya Sutskever, Oriol Vinyals, and Quoc V Le. 2014. Sequence to sequence learning with neural networks. In *Advances in neural information processing systems*, pages 3104–3112.

Oriol Vinyals, Łukasz Kaiser, Terry Koo, Slav Petrov, Ilya Sutskever, and Geoffrey Hinton. 2015. Grammar as a foreign language. In *Advances in Neural Information Processing Systems*, pages 2755–2763.

WMT. 2016. Findings of the 2016 Conference on Statistical Machine Translation. In *Proc. of the First Conference on Statistical Machine Translation (WMT '16)*, Berlin, Germany, August.

The Karlsruhe Institute of Technology Systems
for the News Translation Task in WMT 2016

†Thanh-Le Ha, †Eunah Cho, †Jan Niehues, †Mohammed Mediani,
†Matthias Sperber, *Alexandre Allauzen and †Alexandre Waibel
†Karlsruhe Institute of Technology, Karlsruhe, Germany
*LIMSI-CNRS, Orsay, France
†firstname.surname@kit.edu *surname@limsi.fr

Abstract

In this paper, we present the KIT translation systems as well as the KIT-LIMSI systems for the ACL 2016 First Conference on Machine Translation. We participated in the shared task Machine Translation of News and submitted translation systems for three different directions: English→German, German→English and English→Romanian.

We used a phrase-based machine translation system and investigated several models to rescore the system. We used neural network language and translation models. Using these models, we could improve the translation performance in all language pairs we participated.

1 Introduction

Following the research we have been conducted over previous years, in this paper, we describe our phase-based translation systems submitted to the First Conference on Machine Translation with the highlights on our new models.

In this evaluation, we mainly focused on using neural models in rescoring of a phrase-based machine translation system. We used three different types of neural models: a factored neural model, the continuous space translation models developed by LIMSI and a recurrent encoder-decoder model.

The paper is organized as follows: the next section gives a detailed description of our systems including the hightlighted models. The translation results for all directions are presented afterwards and we then close with a conclusion.

2 System Description

In this section, we first describe our common models we used in our baseline systems. Then specific models and new methods applied in this evaluation will be described.

2.1 Baseline Systems

For training our systems, we used all the data provided by the organizers.

In all of our translation systems, the preprocessing step was conducted prior to training. For English→Romanian, we used the preprocessing described in (Allauzen et al., 2016). For the systems involving German and English, it includes removing very long sentences and the sentence pairs which are length-mismatched, normalizing special symbols and smart-casing the first word of each sentence. In the direction of German→English, compound splitting (Koehn and Knight, 2003) was applied on the German side of the corpus. To improve the quality of the Common Crawl corpus being used in training, we filtered out noisy sentence pairs using an SVM classifier as described in (Mediani et al., 2011).

All of our translation systems are basically phrase-based. An in-house phrase-based decoder (Vogel, 2003) was used to generate all translation candidates from the word lattice and then the weights for the models were optimized following the Minimum Error Rate Training (MERT) method (Venugopal et al., 2005).

The word alignments were produced from the parallel corpora using the GIZA++ Toolkit (Och and Ney, 2003) for both directions. Afterwards, the alignments were combined using the *grow-diag-final-and* heuristic to form the phrase table. It was done by running the phrase extraction scripts from Moses toolkit (Koehn et al., 2007).

Unless stated otherwise, we used 4-gram language models (LM) with modified Kneser-Ney smoothing, trained with the SRILM toolkit (Stolcke, 2002). In the decoding phase, the LMs were scored by KenLM toolkit (Heafield, 2011). In

Proceedings of the First Conference on Machine Translation, Volume 2: Shared Task Papers, pages 303–310,
Berlin, Germany, August 11-12, 2016. ©2016 Association for Computational Linguistics

addition to word-based language models, we employed various types of non-word language models in our translation systems. They included bilingual LMs, cluster LMs and the LMs based on POS sequences. For cluster and POS-based LMs, we used an n-gram size of nine tokens. During decoding, these language models were used as additional models in the log-linear combination.

A family of lexical translation models, which we called discriminative word lexicon (DWL), were also utilized in our translation systems. A discriminative word lexicon, first introduced by (Mauser et al., 2009), is a lexical translation model which calculates the probability of a target word given the words of the source sentence. (Niehues and Waibel, 2013) proposed an extension of DWL where they use n consecutive source words as one feature, thus they could incorporate better the order information of the source sentences into classification. In addition to this DWL, we integrated a DWL in the reverse direction in rescoring. We will refer to this model as source DWL (SDWL). This model predicts the target word for a given source word using numbers of context features as described in details in (Herrmann et al., 2015).

To deal with the differences in word order between source and target languages, our systems employed various reordering strategies, which are described in the next section.

2.2 Reordering Models

In all translation directions, the reordering models based on POS tags were applied to change the word positions of the source sentence according to the target word order. In order to train such reordering models, probabilistic rules were extracted automatically from the POS-tagged training corpus and the alignments. The rules cover short-range reorderings (Rottmann and Vogel, 2007) as well as long-range reorderings (Niehues and Kolss, 2009). The POS tags were generated using the TreeTagger (Schmid and Laws, 2008).

Besides the POS-based reordering models, a tree-based reordering model, as described in (Herrmann et al., 2013), was also applied to better address the differences in sentence structure between German and English in our systems. We used the Stanford Parser (Rafferty and Manning, 2008; Klein and Manning, 2003) to generate syntactic parse trees for the source sentences in the training data. Then the tree-based reordering rules

were learnt based on the word alignments between source and target sentences, showing how to reorder the source constituents to match the word order of the corresponding target side.

The POS-based and tree-based reordering rules were applied to each input sentence to generate all reordered variants of the sentence. Then a word lattice was produced, encoding the original sentence order as well as those variants. The lattice was then used as the input to the decoder.

In addition, we utilized a lexicalized reordering model (Koehn et al., 2005), which encodes possible reordering orientations (monotone, swap or discontinuous) of each word and its original position in the phrase pair. Hence, it can be learnt directly from the phrase table, and the reordering probability for each phrase pair were then integrated into our log–linear framework as an additional score.

3 N-best list rescoring

In order to easily integrate more complex models, we used n-best list rescoring in our submission. We evaluated a neural network language model using a factored representation of the words. Using this framework, we were also able to easily extend the model to a bilingual model. Furthermore, we investigated the use of an encoder-decoder model in rescoring. Finally, in cooperation with LIMSI, we used the continuous space translation models in rescoring. We used the ListNet approach as described in Section 3.4 to estimate the weights of different models in our systems.

3.1   Factored Neural Network Models

Recently, the use of neural network models in rescoring of phrase-based machine translation has shown to lead to significant improvements (Le et al., 2012; Ha et al., 2015). In addition, phrase-based machine translation can profit from factored word representations (Hoang, 2007). Using POS-tags or automatic word classes often helps to model long-range dependencies (Rottmann and Vogel, 2007; Niehues and Kolss, 2009).

In this evaluation, we evaluated a combination of both. We used RNN-based language models that use a factored representation. We hoped to improve the modeling of rare words by richer word representations. In the experiments we used up to four different word factors: the word surface form, the POS tags as well as two cluster based word fac-

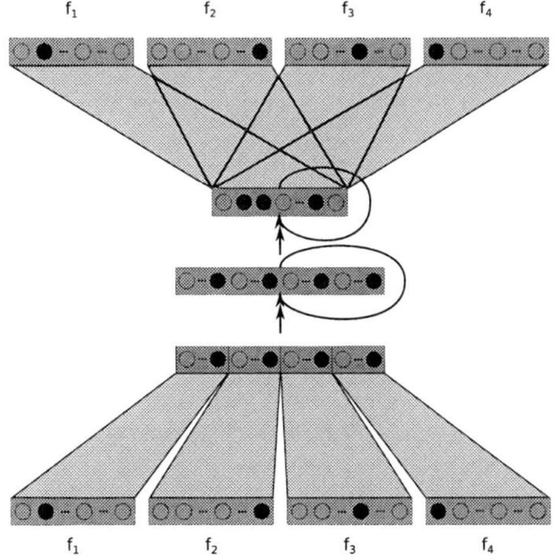

Figure 1: Factored RNN Layout

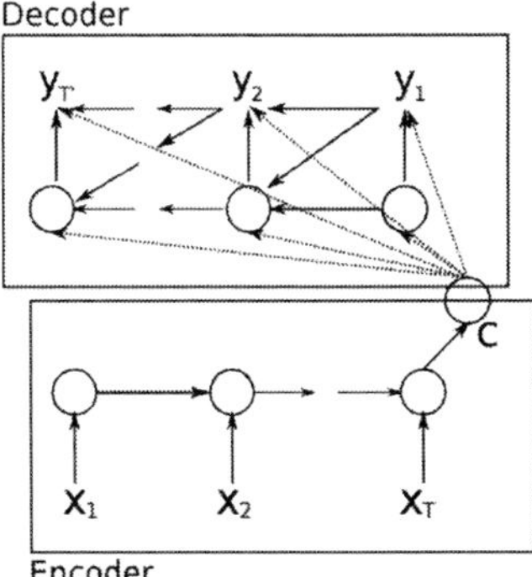

Figure 2: The recurrent encoder-decoder architecture for MT proposed by (Cho et al., 2014)

tors using 100 and 1,000 classes. The structure of the network is shown in Figure 1.

We used these word representations in the input and learnt word embeddings by using the concatenation of all word factor embeddings. On the target side, we also predicted different types of word factors.

We integrated the model into our systems by using the joint probability of all word factors as well as the individual factored probabilities as features.

Using this framework, it is straight-forward to extend it to a bilingual model which can also model translation probabilities. We achieved this by adding the word factored of the source word $s_{a(i+1)}$, that is aligned to the $i+1$ target word, to the representation of the i target word. Then we used the joint factors of the i target word and this source word to predict the $i+1$ target word. The bilingual model is referred as FactoredBM, and the language model-based is referred as FactoredLM in the evaluation section.

3.2 Recurrent Encoder-Decoder Models

The encoder-decoder architecture (Prat et al., 2001; Sutskever et al., 2014; Cho et al., 2014) has the ability of compressing all necessary information of a sequence of texts into fixed-length vectors and using this to produce an output sequence reflecting the transformation between those two sequences. Applied to machine translation, where we need to "transform" a sentence in source language to its translation in target language, the architecture has shown its usefulness. Recently, extensions of the recurrent units and the introduction

of attention mechanism allow us to train the networks to be capable of remembering longer contexts and putting decent word alignments between two sentences (Bahdanau et al., 2015; Luong et al., 2015).

Instead of using the architecture in an end-to-end fashion, which often called Neural MT (Bahdanau et al., 2015), in order to leverage other translation models that the phrase-based system produces, we opted to use it in our rescoring scheme (see 3.4).

We adapted the Neural MT framework[1] from (Luong et al., 2015) to be able to compute the conditional probability $p(f, e_i)$ in which f is the source sentence and e_i is the ith translation candidate of f produced by our phrase-based decoder.

Due to the limited time, this recurrent encoder-decoder-based (ReEnDe) feature was only employed in the direction of English→German. It helped to improve considerably our translation system. We trained several ReEnDe models on the parallel EPPC and NC data, then chose the model which performed best on our development set to be used in rescoring. This model consists of 4 layers of 1000 LTSM units with the local attention and learning rate decaying mechanism similar to what the authors of the Neural MT framework were using to achieve their best single system (Luong et al., 2015).

3.3 Continuous Space Translation Models

Neural networks, working on top of conventional n-gram back-off language models (BOLMs), have been introduced in (Bengio et al., 2003; Schwenk,

---

[1] https://github.com/lmthang/nmt.matlab

2007) as a potential mean to improve discrete language models. More recently, these techniques have been applied to statistical machine translation in order to estimate continuous-space translation models (CTMs) (Schwenk et al., 2007; Le et al., 2012; Devlin et al., 2014). As in previous submissions, we investigated the integration of n-gram CTMs. Introduced in (Casacuberta and Vidal, 2004), and extended in (Mariño et al., 2006; Crego and Mariño, 2006), an n-gram translation model is constructed based on a specific factorization of the joint probability of parallel sentence pairs, where the source sentence has been reordered beforehand. A sentence pair is decomposed into a sequence of bilingual units called *tuples* defining a joint segmentation. The joint probability of a *synchronized* and *segmented* sentence pair can be estimated using the n-gram assumption. During training, the segmentation is obtained as a by-product of source reordering. During the inference step, the SMT decoder is assumed to output for each source sentence a set of hypotheses along with their derivations, which allow CTMs to score the generated sentence pairs.

Note that conventional n-gram translation models manipulates bilingual tuples. The data sparsity issues for this model are thus particularly severe. Effective workarounds consist in factorizing the conditional probabitily of tuples into terms involving smaller units: the resulting model thus splits bilingual phrases in two sequences of respectively source and target words, synchronised by the tuple segmentation. Such bilingual word-based n-gram models were initially described in (Le et al., 2012).

However, in such models, the size of output vocabulary is a bottleneck when normalized distributions are needed (Bengio et al., 2003; Schwenk et al., 2007). Various workarounds have been proposed, relying for instance on a structured output layer using word-classes (Mnih and Hinton, 2008; Le et al., 2011). We assume in this work the same decomposition and architecture as in (Le et al., 2012) except for the output structures.

The model is trained using the *Noise Contrastive Estimation* or *NCE* for short (Gutmann and Hyvärinen, 2010; Mnih and Teh, 2012), which only delivers *quasi-normalized*. This technique is readily applicable for CTMs. Therefore, *NCE* models deliver a positive score, by applying the exponential function to the output layer activities, instead of the more costly softmax function.

Initialization is an important issue when optimizing neural networks. For CTMs, a solution consists in pre-training monolingual n-gram models. Their parameters are then used to initialize bilingual models.

Given the computational cost of computing n-gram probabilities with neural network models, a solution is to resort to a two-pass approach: the first pass uses a conventional system to produce a k-best list (the k most likely hypotheses); in the second pass, probabilities are computed by the CTMs for each hypothesis and added as new features. For this year evaluation, we used the following models: one continuous target language model and three CTMs as described in (Le et al., 2012). We also trained two versions of these four models by varying learning rate and the data resampling. We end up with 8 scores added to the k-best lists.

3.4 ListNet-based Rescoring

In order to facilitate more complex models like neural network translation models, we performed n-best list rescoring. In our experiments we generated 300-best lists for the development and test data respectively. In German→English system, we generate 3000-best list instead. We used the same data to train the rescoring that we have used for optimizing the translation system.

We trained the weights for the log-linear combination used during rescoring using the ListNet algorithm (Cao et al., 2007; Niehues et al., 2015). This technique defines a probability distribution on the permutations of the list based on the scores of the log-linear model and another one based on a reference metric. In our experiments we used the BLEU+1 score introduced by (Liang et al., 2006). Then we used the cross entropy between both distributions as the loss function for our training.

Using this loss function, we can compute the gradient and use stochastic gradient descent. We used batch updates with ten samples and tuned the learning rate on the development data.

The range of the scores of the different models may greatly differ and many of these values are negative numbers with high absolute value since they are computed as the logarithm of relatively small probabilities. Therefore, we rescaled all scores observed on the development data to the range of $[-1, 1]$ prior to rescoring.

4   Results

In this section, we present a summary of our experiments in the evaluation campaign. Individual components that lead to improvements in the translation performance are described step by step. The scores are reported in case-sensitive BLEU (Papineni et al., 2002).

In the rescoring scheme of our systems, the BLEU scores on the development set are normally smaller than those in the decoding phase because they are tuned by different optimization algorithms (ListNet and MERT). The rescoring configurations are mentioned in the tables in *italic texts*. The test scores from which we choose to be the submitted systems are mentioned in the tables in **bold numbers**.

4.1   English-German

Table 1 shows the results of our system for English→German translation task.

The baseline system consists of a phrase table extracted from all the parallel data, the word-based language models learned from all provided monolingual corpora including the large Common Crawl data. It also includes a 5-gram bilingual language model and 4-gram cluster language model trained on the monolingual part of all parallel corpora with additional information from the word alignments and 50 word classes described in Section 2.1. POS-based long-range reordering rules were applied. We used the performance in terms of BLEU on our development set to choose our combinations of features. The BLEU score of the baseline system over the test set was 22.91.

The system gained around 0.4 points on the test set in BLEU when adding lexicalized reorderings and the source-context DWLs. Both the DWLs and lexicalized reordering were trained only on EPPS and NC.

SDWL and recurrent encoder-decoder scores added into that system via the ListNet-based rescoring scheme brought considerable improvements of almost 0.9 BLEU points and this system was submitted to the conference's evaluation campaign.

On the other hands, another set of features was used in the rescoring process and helped to improve the translation performance by another 0.9 BLEU points. It included LIMSI's continuous space translation models, the factored neural network (both FactoredLM and FactoredBM) and the recurrent encoder-decoder scores. It was submitted as the joint KIT-LIMSI submission system.

System	Dev	Test
Baseline	21.81	22.91
+ DWL + Lex. Reorderings	22.44	23.34
+ ReEnDe	20.76	24.08
+ SDWL + ReEnDe	20.79	**24.21**
+ Factored + ReEnDe + CTMs	20.78	**24.24**

Table 1: Experiments for English→German

4.2   German-English

Table 2 shows the development steps of the German→English translation system.

The baseline system used EPPS, NC, and filtered web-crawled data for training the translation model. The phrase table was built using GIZA++ word alignment and lattice phrase extraction.

Altogether three language models were used in the baseline system, including a word-based language model, bilingual language model, and a language model built using 10M of selected data from monolingual data, based on cross entropy as described in Section 2.1. All language models were 4-gram. The word lattices are generated using short and long-range reordering rules, as well as tree-based reordering rules. A lexicalized reordering model is also included in the baseline system. We then enhanced our tree-based reordering using recursive rules. This successfully improved the translation by 0.7 BLEU points.

In this direction, we applied stemming for the German side of the corpus, inspired by (Slawik et al., 2015). Applied to the words which are *not* most frequently used $50,000$ words in the training corpus, the stemming yielded the improvement of 0.14 BLEU points.

As described in Section 2.1, we built a cluster language model using the MKCLS algorithm. Words from EPPS, NC, and the filtered crawl data were clustered into 100 different classes.

A DWL with source context increased the score on the test set slightly.

Using the additionally available monolingual data this year, we build an extra language model on words. Incorporating a big size of its training corpus, it boosts the translation performance by 0.4 BLEU points.

We then used the ListNet-based rescoring with additional models such as SDWL and Factored

LM. The rescoring is applied for $3,000$ N-best lists. The factored LM is trained for 5K of vocabulary. Finally, adding a factored BM gave another small improvement. This system was used to generate the translation submitted to the evaluation.

System	Dev	Test
Baseline	28.31	27.73
+ Resursive	28.83	28.84
+ Stem	28.83	28.98
+ MKCLS 100	28.90	29.08
+ DWL.SC	28.99	29.11
+ bigLM	28.97	29.51
+ *FactoredLM 5K + SDWL*	28.27	29.59
+ *FactoredBM 5K*	28.47	**29.66**

Table 2: Experiments for German→English

4.3 English-Romanian

The English→Romanian system was trained on all available parallel data and adapted to the SETimes corpus. We used pre-reordering and five language models, where two language models were word-based, two other language models were based on automatic word classes and another one was a POS-based language model. Finally, we used the DWL for this translation direction as well. The phrase-based MT system was optimized using MERT on the first half of the development set and then we generated 300-best lists.

The rescoring was optimized on the first half of the development set and on 2000 sentences from the SETimes corpus not used in training. We reported test scores on the second half of the development data.

First, we added the SDWL model in rescoring. This leads to some improvement on the development data and small improvements on the test data. Using also a factored language model and translation model could improve the translation performance by 0.7 BLEU points. We utilized a factored language model using a vocabulary of 50K words and two bilingual translation models: one with 50K word vocabulary and one with 5K words. All models used two word clusters with 100 and 1000 classes and on the Romanian side a POS factor.

5 Conclusion

In this paper, we have described the systems developed for our participation in the News Translation

System	Dev	Test
Baseline	39.74	29.69
+ *SDWL*	40.12	29.75
+ *FactoredRNN*	41.16	**30.57**

Table 3: Experiments for English→Romanian

shared tasks of the First Conference on Statistical Machine Translation evaluation. Our systems include English→German, German→English and English→Romanian translations. All translation candidates were generated using strong baseline phrase-based systems and then rescored in combination with our new neural network-based features. We could show that the usage of neural models in rescoring significantly improved the translation.

Acknowledgments

The project leading to this application has received funding from the European Union's Horizon 2020 research and innovation programme under grant agreement n° 645452.

References

Alexandre Allauzen, Lauriane Aufrant, Franck Burlot, Elena Knyazeva, Thomas Lavergne, and François Yvon. 2016. LIMSI@WMT'16 : Machine translation of news. In *Proceedings of the ACL 2016 First Conference on Machine Translation (WMT2016)*, August.

Dzmitry Bahdanau, Kyunghyun Cho, and Yoshua Bengio. 2015. Neural machine translation by jointly learning to align and translate. *ICLR 2015*.

Yoshua Bengio, Réjean Ducharme, Pascal Vincent, and Christian Janvin. 2003. A neural probabilistic language model. *Journal of Machine Learning Research*, 3:1137–1155.

Zhe Cao, Tao Qin, Tie yan Liu, Ming-Feng Tsai, and Hang Li. 2007. Learning to Rank: From Pairwise Approach to Listwise Approach. In *Proceedings of the 24th International Conference on Machine Learning*, pages 129–136, Corvallis, OR, USA.

Francesco Casacuberta and Enrique Vidal. 2004. Machine translation with inferred stochastic finite-state transducers. *Computational Linguistics*, 30(3):205–225.

Kyunghyun Cho, Bart Van Merriënboer, Çalar Gülçehre, Dzmitry Bahdanau, Fethi Bougares, Holger Schwenk, and Yoshua Bengio. 2014. Learning phrase representations using RNN encoder–decoder for statistical machine translation. In *Proceedings of the 2014 Conference on Empirical Methods in Natural Language Processing (EMNLP)*, pages 1724–1734, Doha, Qatar, October. Association for Computational Linguistics.

Josep Maria Crego and José B Mariño. 2006. Improving statistical mt by coupling reordering and decoding. *Machine Translation*, 20(3):199–215.

Jacob Devlin, Rabih Zbib, Zhongqiang Huang, Thomas Lamar, Richard Schwartz, and John Makhoul. 2014. Fast and robust neural network joint models for statistical machine translation. In *Proceedings of the 52nd Annual Meeting of the Association for Computational Linguistics (Volume 1: Long Papers)*, pages 1370–1380, Baltimore, Maryland.

Michael Gutmann and Aapo Hyvärinen. 2010. Noise-contrastive estimation: A new estimation principle for unnormalized statistical models. In Yeh Whye Teh and Mike Titterington, editors, *Proceedings of th International Conference on Artificial Intelligence and Statistics (AISTATS)*, volume 9, pages 297–304.

Thanh-Le Ha, Quoc-Khanh Do, Eunah Cho, Jan Niehues, Alexandre Allauzen, François Yvon, and Alex Waibel. 2015. The kit-limsi translation system for wmt 2015. *EMNLP 2015*, page 120.

Kenneth Heafield. 2011. KenLM: faster and smaller language model queries. In *Proceedings of the 6th Workshop on Statistical Machine Translation*, Edinburgh, United Kingdom.

Teresa Herrmann, Jan Niehues, and Alex Waibel. 2013. Combining Word Reordering Methods on different Linguistic Abstraction Levels for Statistical Machine Translation. In *Proceedings of the 7th Workshop on Syntax, Semantics and Structure in Statistical Translation*, Altanta, GA, USA.

Teresa Herrmann, Jan Niehues, and Alex Waibel. 2015. Source Discriminative Word Lexicon for Translation Disambiguation. In *Proceedings of the 12th International Workshop on Spoken Language Translation (IWSLT15)*, Danang, Vietnam.

Hieu Hoang. 2007. Factored translation models. In *In Proceedings of the 2007 Joint Conference on Empirical Methods in Natural Language Processing and Computational Natural Language Learning (EMNLP-CoNLL*, pages 868–876.

Dan Klein and Christopher D. Manning. 2003. Accurate Unlexicalized Parsing. In *Proceedings of the 41st Annual Meeting of the Association for Computational Linguistics*, Sapporo, Japan.

Philipp Koehn and Kevin Knight. 2003. Empirical Methods for Compound Splitting. In *Proceedings of the 10th Conference of the European Chapter of the Association for Computational Linguistics*, Budapest, Hungary.

Philipp Koehn, Amittai Axelrod, Alexandra B. Mayne, Chris Callison-Burch, Miles Osborne, and David Talbot. 2005. Edinburgh System Description for the 2005 IWSLT Speech Translation Evaluation. In *Proceedings of the 2nd International Workshop on Spoken Language Translation*, Pittsburgh, PA, USA.

Philipp Koehn, Hieu Hoang, Alexandra Birch, Chris Callison-Burch, Marcello Federico, Nicola Bertoldi, Brooke Cowan, Wade Shen, Christine Moran, Richard Zens, Chris Dyer, Ondrej Bojar, Alexandra Constantin, and Evan Herbst. 2007. Moses: Open Source Toolkit for Statistical Machine Translation. In *Proceedings of the 45th Annual Meeting of the Association for Computational Linguistics*, Prague, Czech Republic.

Hai-Son Le, Ilya Oparin, Alexandre Allauzen, Jean-Luc Gauvain, and François Yvon. 2011. Structured output layer neural network language model. In *Proceedings of ICASSP*, pages 5524–5527.

Hai-Son Le, Alexandre Allauzen, and François Yvon. 2012. Continuous space translation models with neural networks. pages 39–48, Montréal, Canada, June. Association for Computational Linguistics.

P. Liang, A. Bouchard-Côté, D. Klein, and B. Taskar. 2006. An End-to-end Discriminative Approach to Machine Translation. In *Proceedings of the 44th Annual Meeting of the Association for Computational Linguistics (ACL 2006)*, pages 761–768, Sydney, Australia.

Minh-Thang Luong, Hieu Pham, and Christopher D Manning. 2015. Effective approaches to attention-based neural machine translation. *Proceedings of the 2015 Conference on Empirical Methods in Natural Language Processing*.

José B. Mariño, Rafael E. Banchs, Josep M. Crego, Adrià de Gispert, Patrick Lambert, José A.R. Fonollosa, and Marta R. Costa-Jussà. 2006. N-gram-based machine translation. *Computational Linguistics*, 32(4):527–549.

Arne Mauser, Saša Hasan, and Hermann Ney. 2009. Extending Statistical Machine Translation with Discriminative and Trigger-based Lexicon Models. In *Proceedings of the 2009 Conference on Empirical Methods in Natural Language Processing: Volume 1 - Volume 1*, EMNLP '09, Singapore.

Mohammed Mediani, Eunah Cho, Jan Niehues, Teresa Herrmann, and Alex Waibel. 2011. The KIT English-French Translation systems for IWSLT 2011. In *Proceedings of the 8th International Workshop on Spoken Language Translation*, San Francisco, CA, USA.

Andriy Mnih and Geoffrey E Hinton. 2008. A scalable hierarchical distributed language model. In D. Koller, D. Schuurmans, Y. Bengio, and L. Bottou, editors, *Advances in Neural Information Processing Systems 21*, volume 21, pages 1081–1088.

Andriy Mnih and Yeh Whye Teh. 2012. A fast and simple algorithm for training neural probabilistic language models.

Jan Niehues and Muntsin Kolss. 2009. A POS-Based Model for Long-Range Reorderings in SMT. In *Proceedings of the 4th Workshop on Statistical Machine Translation*, Athens, Greece.

Jan Niehues and Alex Waibel. 2013. An MT Error-Driven Discriminative Word Lexicon using Sentence Structure Features. In *Proceedings of the 8th Workshop on Statistical Machine Translation*, Sofia, Bulgaria.

Jan Niehues, Quoc Khanh Do, Alexandre Allauzen, and Alex Waibel. 2015. Listnet-based MT Rescoring. *Proceedings of the 2015 Conference on Empirical Methods in Natural Language Processing*, page 248.

Franz Josef Och and Hermann Ney. 2003. A Systematic Comparison of Various Statistical Alignment Models. *Computational Linguistics*, 29(1).

K. Papineni, S. Roukos, T. Ward, and W.-jing Zhu. 2002. Bleu: a method for automatic evaluation of machine translation. In *Proceedings of the 40th Annual Meeting of the Association for Computational Linguistics (ACL 2002)*, pages 311–318, Philadelphia, Pennsylvania.

Federico Prat, Francisco Casacuberta, and María José Castro. 2001. Machine translation with grammar association: Combining neural networks and finite state models. In *Proceedings of the Second Workshop on Natural Language Processing and Neural Networks*, pages 53–60.

Anna N. Rafferty and Christopher D. Manning. 2008. Parsing Three German Treebanks: Lexicalized and Unlexicalized Baselines. In *Proceedings of the Workshop on Parsing German*.

Kay Rottmann and Stephan Vogel. 2007. Word Reordering in Statistical Machine Translation with a POS-Based Distortion Model. In *Proceedings of the 11th International Conference on Theoretical and Methodological Issues in Machine Translation*, Skövde, Sweden.

Helmut Schmid and Florian Laws. 2008. Estimation of Conditional Probabilities with Decision Trees and an Application to Fine-Grained POS Tagging. In *Proceedings of the 22nd International Conference on Computational Linguistics*, Manchester, United Kingdom.

Holger Schwenk, Marta R. Costa-jussa, and Jose A. R. Fonollosa. 2007. Smooth bilingual n-gram translation. pages 430–438, Prague, Czech Republic.

Holger Schwenk. 2007. Continuous space language models. *Computer Speech and Language*, 21(3):492–518, July.

Isabel Slawik, Jan Niehues, and Alex Waibel. 2015. Stripping adjectives: Integration techniques for selective stemming in smt systems. *Proceedings of the 18th Annual Conference of the European Association for Machine Translation (EAMT 2015)*.

Andreas Stolcke. 2002. SRILM – An Extensible Language Modeling Toolkit. In *Proceedings of the International Conference on Spoken Language Processing*, Denver, CO, USA.

Ilya Sutskever, Oriol Vinyals, and Quoc V Le. 2014. Sequence to sequence learning with neural networks. In *Advances in neural information processing systems*, pages 3104–3112.

Ashish Venugopal, Andreas Zollman, and Alex Waibel. 2005. Training and Evaluation Error Minimization Rules for Statistical Machine Translation. In *Proceedings of the ACL Workshop on Building and Using Parallel Texts*, Ann Arbor, MI, USA.

Stephan Vogel. 2003. SMT Decoder Dissected: Word Reordering. In *Proceedings of the International Conference on Natural Language Processing and Knowledge Engineering*, Beijing, China.

The Edinburgh/LMU Hierarchical Machine Translation System for WMT 2016

Matthias Huck[1], Alexander Fraser[1], Barry Haddow[2]
[1]Center for Information and Language Processing, LMU Munich
[2]School of Informatics, University of Edinburgh
mhuck@cis.lmu.de fraser@cis.lmu.de bhaddow@inf.ed.ac.uk

Abstract

This paper describes the hierarchical phrase-based machine translation system built jointly by the University of Edinburgh and the University of Munich (LMU) for the shared translation task at the ACL 2016 First Conference on Machine Translation (WMT16). The WMT16 Edinburgh/LMU system was trained for translation of news domain texts from English into Romanian. We participated in the shared task for machine translation of news under "constrained" conditions, i.e. using the provided training data only.

1 Introduction

While translation between English and many other European languages (such as Czech and German) has a long tradition in the shared tasks at the series of WMT workshops preceding the ACL 2016 First Conference on Machine Translation, English–Romanian has only been introduced this year as a new language pair.[1] The English–Romanian language pair has received less attention by the machine translation scientific community to date. The availability of a novel standardized evaluation scenario for English–Romanian in the framework of WMT facilitates research on that specific language pair.

In this work, we utilize the corpora that have been provided by the shared task organizers to engineer a competitive system for statistical machine translation (SMT) from English into Romanian. We specifically focus on studying machine translation into Romanian (rather than the inverse translation direction: from Romanian into English), thus aiming at making documents originally written in English available to a large community of speakers in their native language, Romanian. Applications are for instance in the health care sector, where, as part of the *Health in my Language* project (*HimL*), several project partners intend to make public health information available in a wider variety of languages.[2] The WMT task provides an interesting test bed for English→Romanian machine translation, though adaptation towards the specific domain (consumer health for *HimL*, rather than news) is also an important aspect that has to be considered in practice (Huck et al., 2015).

We investigate the effectiveness of *hierarchical phrase-based translation* (Chiang, 2005) for English→Romanian, a statistical machine translation paradigm that is closely related to phrase-based translation, but allows for phrases with gaps. Conceptionally, the translation model is formalized as a synchronous context-free grammar. We integrate several non-standard enhancements into our hierarchical phrase-based system and empirically evaluate their impact on translation quality.

Our system is furthermore one component in a combination of systems by members of the *HimL* project and another EU-funded project, *QT21*.[3] Measured in BLEU (Papineni et al., 2002), the *QT21/HimL* submission yields top translation quality amongst the shared task submissions.[4] The *QT21/HimL* submission highlights the continued success of system combinations based on the Jane machine translation toolkit (Freitag et al., 2014a) in open evaluation campaigns (Freitag et al., 2013; Freitag et al., 2014b; Freitag et al., 2014c). A description of the *QT21/HimL* combined submission is given by Peter et al. (2016).

---

[1]http://www.statmt.org/wmt16/
translation-task.html

[2]http://www.himl.eu

[3]http://www.qt21.eu

[4]http://matrix.statmt.org/matrix/
systems_list/1843

Proceedings of the First Conference on Machine Translation, Volume 2: Shared Task Papers, pages 311–318,
Berlin, Germany, August 11-12, 2016. ©2016 Association for Computational Linguistics

We proceed by presenting the particularities of our hierarchical phrase-based system, with a focus of interest on exploring non-standard enhancements and non-default configuration settings such as:

- Individual language models as features, rather than a single linearly interpolated language model; and another background language model estimated over concatenated corpora.
- Large CommonCrawl language model training data.
- Unpruned language models.
- More hierarchical rules than in default systems, by means of imposing less strict extraction constraints.
- A phrase orientation model for hierarchical translation (Huck et al., 2013).
- Lightly-supervised training (Schwenk, 2008; Schwenk and Senellart, 2009; Huck et al., 2011).
- Larger development data for tuning.

All our experiments are run with the open source `Moses` implementation (Hoang et al., 2009) of the hierarchical phrase-based translation paradigm.

2 System Overview

2.1 Hierarchical Phrase-Based Translation

In hierarchical phrase-based translation, a probabilistic synchronous context-free grammar is induced from bilingual training corpora. In addition to continuous *lexical* phrases as in standard phrase-based translation, *hierarchical* phrases with (usually) up to two non-terminals are extracted from the word-aligned parallel training data.

The non-terminal set of a standard hierarchical grammar comprises two symbols which are shared by source and target: the initial symbol S and one generic non-terminal symbol X. The initial symbol S is the start symbol of the grammar. The generic non-terminal X is used as a placeholder for the gaps within the right-hand side of hierarchical translation rules as well as on all left-hand sides of the translation rules that are extracted from the parallel training corpus.

Extracted rules of a standard hierarchical grammar are of the form $X \to \langle \alpha, \beta, \sim \rangle$ where $\langle \alpha, \beta \rangle$

is a bilingual phrase pair that may contain X, i.e. $\alpha \in (\{X\} \cup V_F)^+$ and $\beta \in (\{X\} \cup V_E)^+$, where V_F and V_E are the source and target vocabulary, respectively. The non-terminals on the source side and on the target side of hierarchical rules are linked in a one-to-one correspondence. The $\sim$ relation defines this one-to-one correspondence.

In addition to the extracted rules, a non-lexicalized *glue rule*

$$S \to \langle S^{\sim 0} X^{\sim 1}, S^{\sim 0} X^{\sim 1} \rangle \tag{1}$$

is incorporated into the hierarchical grammar that the system can use for serial concatenation of phrases as in monotonic phrase-based translation.

In the `Moses` implementation, the decoder internally adds a *sentence start* terminal symbol <s> and a *sentence end* terminal symbol </s> to the input before and after each sentence, respectively. Therefore, two more special rules

$$\begin{aligned} S &\to \langle \text{<s>}, \text{<s>} \rangle \\ S &\to \langle S^{\sim 0}\text{</s>}, S^{\sim 0}\text{</s>} \rangle \end{aligned} \tag{2}$$

are included which allow the decoder to finalize its translations.

Hierarchical search is conducted with a customized version of the CYK+ parsing algorithm (Chappelier and Rajman, 1998) and cube pruning (Chiang, 2007). A hypergraph which represents the whole parsing space is built employing CYK+. Cube pruning operates in bottom-up topological order on this hypergraph and expands at most k derivations at each hypernode.

2.2 Data and Preprocessing

Our system is trained using only permissible Romanian monolingual and English–Romanian parallel corpora provided by the organizers of the WMT16 shared task for machine translation of news: Europarl (Koehn, 2005), SETimes2 (Tyers and Alperen, 2010), News Crawl articles from 2015 (denoted as news2015 hereafter), and CommonCrawl (Buck et al., 2014).

The target side of the data is preprocessed with `tokro`, LIMSI's tokenizer for Romanian (Allauzen et al., 2016).[5] The English source side is tokenized using the `tokenizer.perl` script from the `Moses` toolkit. Romanian and English sentences are both frequent-cased (with `Moses`' `truecase.perl`).

---

[5] `https://perso.limsi.fr/aufrant/software/tokro`

We split the development set newsdev2016 into two halves (newsdev2016_1 with the first 1000 sentences and newsdev2016_2 with the last 999 sentences). During the system building process, we measure progress by evaluating on newsdev2016_2 as our internal unseen test set, while only newsdev2016_1 is utilized for tuning.

2.3 Training and Tuning

We create word alignments by aligning the bilingual data in both directions with MGIZA++ (Gao and Vogel, 2008). We use a sequence of IBM word alignment models (Brown et al., 1993) with five iterations of EM training (Dempster et al., 1977) of Model 1, three iterations of Model 3, and three iterations of Model 4. After EM, we obtain a symmetrized alignment by applying the grow-diag-final-and heuristic (Och and Ney, 2003; Koehn et al., 2003) to the two trained alignments. We extract synchronous context-free grammar rules that are consistent with the symmetrized word alignment from the parallel training data.

We train 5-gram language models (LMs) with modified Kneser-Ney smoothing (Kneser and Ney, 1995; Chen and Goodman, 1998). KenLM (Heafield, 2011) is employed for LM training and scoring, and SRILM (Stolcke, 2002) for linear LM interpolation.

Our translation model incorporates a number of different features in a log-linear combination (Och and Ney, 2002). We tune the feature weights with batch k-best MIRA (Cherry and Foster, 2012) to maximize BLEU (Papineni et al., 2002) on a development set. We run MIRA for 25 iterations on 200-best lists.

2.4 Baseline Setup

The features of our plain hierarchical phrase-based baseline are:

- Rule translation log-probabilities in both target-to-source and source-to-target direction, smoothed with Good-Turing discounting (Foster et al., 2006).
- Lexical translation log-probabilities in both target-to-source and source-to-target direction.
- Seven binary features indicating absolute occurrence count classes of translation rules (with count classes 1, 2, 3, 4, 5-6, 7-10, >10).

- An indicator feature that fires on applications of the glue rule.
- Word penalty.
- Rule penalty.
- A 5-gram language model.

We discard rules with non-terminals on their right-hand side if they are singletons in the training data. The baseline language model is a linear interpolation of three 5-gram LMs trained over the Romanian news2015, Europarl, and SETimes2 training data, respectively, with pruning of singleton n-grams of order three and higher.[6] We run the Moses chart-based decoder with cube pruning, configured at a maximum chart span of 25 and otherwise default settings.

2.5 Enhancements

We now describe modifications that we apply on top of the baseline. The results of the empirical evaluation will be given in Section 3.

Linear LM interpolation vs. individual LMs as features in the log-linear combination. Rather than employing a linearly interpolated LM, we integrate the individual LMs trained over the separate corpora (news2015, Europarl, SETimes2) directly into the log-linear feature combination of the system and let MIRA optimize their weights along with all other features in tuning.

Background LM. We add one more language model, which we denote as *background LM*. The background LM is estimated from a concatenation of the Romanian news2015, Europarl, and SETimes2 training data. The background LM does not replace the individual LMs in the log-linear combination, but acts as another feature with an associated weight.

CommonCrawl LM training data. A large Romanian CommonCrawl corpus has been released for the constrained track of the WMT16 shared task for machine translation of news. In our system, we utilize this corpus by adding it to the training data of the background LM. We append it to the concatenation of news2015, Europarl, and SETimes2 data and estimate a bigger background LM.

---

[6]Pruned individual LMs are trained with KenLM's `--prune '0 0 1'` parameters. Weights for linear LM interpolation are optimized on newsdev2016_1.

Pruned vs. unpruned LMs. We compare pruned and unpruned language models. In the pruned versions of the models, singleton n-grams of order three and higher are discarded, whereas all n-grams are kept in the unpruned versions.

More hierarchical rules. The baseline synchronous context-free grammar rules in the phrase table are extracted from the parallel training data with `Moses`' default settings: a maximum of five symbols on the source side, a maximum span of ten words, and no right-hand side non-terminal at gaps that cover only a single word on the source side. We allow for extraction of more hierarchical rules by applying less strict rule extraction constraints: a maximum of ten symbols on the source side, a maximum span of twenty words, and no lower limit to the amount of words covered by non-terminals at extraction time.

Phrase orientation model. We implemented a feature in `Moses` that resembles the phrase orientation model for hierarchical machine translation as described by Huck et al. (2013). The Huck et al. (2013) implementation had been released as part of the `Jane` toolkit (Vilar et al., 2010; Vilar et al., 2012; Huck et al., 2012). Our new `Moses` implementation technically operates in almost the same manner, except for minor implementation differences. Similarly to the type of lexicalized reordering models that are in common use in phrase-based systems (Galley and Manning, 2008), our model estimates the probabilities of orientation classes for each phrase (or: rule) from the training data. We use three orientation classes: *monotone*, *swap*, and *discontinuous*.[7]

Lightly-supervised training. We automatically translated parts (1.2 M sentences) of the monolingual Romanian news2015 corpus to English with a Romanian→English phrase-based statistical machine translation system (Williams et al., 2016). The resulting synthetic parallel corpus of the original Romanian news texts paired with machine-translated English counterparts is utilized for lightly-supervised training (Schwenk, 2008) of our English→Romanian hierarchical system.

We follow the approach outlined by Huck et al. (2011) to augment the system with the synthetic parallel data. A foreground phrase table extracted from the human-generated parallel data is filled up with entries from a background phrase table extracted from the synthetic parallel data. An entry from the background table is only added if the foreground table does not already contain a similar entry (Bisazza et al., 2011). A binary feature distinguishes background phrases from foreground phrases. For the background phrase table, we extract only lexical phrases (i.e., phrases without non-terminals on their right-hand side) from the synthetic parallel data, no hierarchical phrases. The phrase length for entries of the background table is restricted to a maximum number of five terminal symbols on the source side. Lexical scores over the phrases extracted from synthetic data are calculated with a lexicon model learned from the human-generated parallel data, as proposed by Huck and Ney (2012).

Larger development data. Since no dedicated unseen test set was available during system building, newsdev2016 was split into its first half (newsdev2016_1) and its second half (newsdev2016_2) so that we could tune on the first half and keep the second half untouched for evaluating progress in translation quality with the various enhancements. For the final system (our primary submission), we took the best configuration built in this manner and tuned it on both halves, i.e. all of newsdev2016. 1000 sentences (as in newsdev2016_1) are a relatively small size for a development set, and we suspected that the optimized feature weights could become more reliable with twice the amount of development data.[8] Good results when tuning on newsdev2016_1 and testing on newsdev2016_2 made us feel confident about keeping the overall system configuration fixed and re-tuning the feature weights on all of newsdev2016. We calculated the BLEU scores on newsdev2016_1 and newsdev2016_2 (both being part of the development set now) as a sanity check and then submitted a hypothesis translation for the evaluation set, newstest2016, without further internal validation on a test set.

---

[7]Using `Moses`' Experiment Management System (EMS) (Koehn, 2010), the phrase orientation model for hierarchical machine translation can be activated by simply adding a line `phrase-orientation = true` to the `[TRAINING]` section of the EMS configuration file.

[8]Whenever available, we typically attempt to use large development sets (in the order of a few thousand sentences), e.g. for Edinburgh's phrase-based systems for the German–English language pair (Haddow et al., 2015).

en→ro	newsdev2016_1	newsdev2016_2	newstest2016
baseline with interpolated LM over news2015, Europarl, SETimes2	22.1	26.6	23.0
+ three individual LMs (replacing the interpolated LM)	21.6	26.6	22.9
+ background LM over concatenation of news2015, Europarl, SETimes2	22.2	27.1	23.3
+ CommonCrawl LM training data in background LM	23.1	28.3	24.4
+ all LMs unpruned	23.4	28.6	24.4
+ more hierarchical rules	23.1	29.0	24.7
+ phrase orientation model	24.4	29.5	25.5
+ lightly-supervised training (*contrastive submission system*)	24.8	30.2	25.5
+ tuning on full newsdev2016 (*primary submission system*)	24.5	30.9	25.9

Table 1: Incremental improvements over a plain hierarchical phrase-based baseline for English→Romanian (case-sensitive BLEU scores). Feature weights are tuned on newsdev2016_1 in all experiments except the one in the bottom line, where both newsdev2016_1 and newsdev2016_2 are employed for tuning.

3 Experiments

Table 1 presents the results achieved with the plain hierarchical phrase-based baseline, and the gains when incrementally applying modifications as described in Section 2.5. The decoder output is postprocessed with the `detruecase.perl` script from the `Moses` toolkit for recasing and `tokro` with its `-r` command line switch for detokenization. We evaluate case-sensitive with `mteval-v13a.pl -c`.

3.1 Discussion

Replacing the baseline's linearly interpolated LM with three individual LMs as features in the log-linear combination deteriorates the BLEU score on the development set by half a point, but has barely any impact on translation quality on the test sets (±0.0 BLEU on newsdev2016_2, −0.1 BLEU on newstest2016). By also adding a background LM over the concatenated news2015, Europarl, and SETimes2 corpora, we attain a similar BLEU score on the development set as with the baseline's linearly interpolated LM, but a gain of +0.3 to +0.5 BLEU on the test sets, compared to the baseline.

Utilizing a larger amount of target-side monolingual resources by appending the Common-Crawl corpus to the background LM's training data is very beneficial and increases the BLEU scores by around one point. Not pruning the LMs, i.e. not discarding singleton *n*-grams of order three and higher, has a positive effect on newsdev2016_1 and newsdev2016_2 (+0.3 BLEU), but makes no difference on newstest2016. If we allow for extraction of more hierarchical rules, we slightly harm the result on the development set

again, but the model seems to generalize better, with +0.4 BLEU on newsdev2016_2 and +0.3 BLEU on newstest2016.

The phrase orientation model performs particularly well on newstest2016, with a gain of another +0.8 BLEU. Lightly-supervised training, on the other hand, does not boost translation quality on newstest2016 at all, though we see a decent improvement on newsdev2016_2, our internal test set. (+0.7 BLEU).

In our very last experiment, when we tune on the concatenation of newsdev2016_1 and newsdev2016_2, we find that employing the larger development data is of benefit to the system (+0.4 BLEU on newstest2016).

Overall, the two individual system enhancements that give us the largest improvements on newstest2016 are the large Romanian Common-Crawl corpus (+1.1 BLEU) and the phrase orientation model (+0.8 BLEU).

4 Summary

We built a hierarchical phrase-based system for translation of news texts from English into Romanian. By enhancing the system with non-standard components, we have been able to achieve an overall improvement over a plain hierarchical baseline of +2.9 BLEU points on the newstest2016 set.

Our `Moses` reimplementation of the phrase orientation model for hierarchical machine translation (Huck et al., 2013) has been released as part of `Moses` on GitHub.[9]

---

[9]`https://github.com/moses-smt/mosesdecoder`

Acknowledgments

This project has received funding from the European Union's Horizon 2020 research and innovation programme under grant agreement № 644402 (*HimL*).

We thank Franck Burlot and Lauriane Aufrant from LIMSI-CNRS in Orsay, France, for providing preprocessed corpora and sharing their Romanian tokenizer in the framework of a QT21/HimL cross-project collaboration.

References

Alexandre Allauzen, Lauriane Aufrant, Franck Burlot, Elena Knyazeva, Thomas Lavergne, and François Yvon. 2016. LIMSI@WMT'16: Machine Translation of News. In *Proc. of the ACL 2016 First Conf. on Machine Translation (WMT16)*, Berlin, Germany, August.

Arianna Bisazza, Nick Ruiz, and Marcello Federico. 2011. Fill-up versus Interpolation Methods for Phrase-based SMT Adaptation. In *Proc. of the Int. Workshop on Spoken Language Translation (IWSLT)*, pages 136–143, San Francisco, CA, USA, December.

Peter F. Brown, Stephen A. Della Pietra, Vincent J. Della Pietra, and Robert L. Mercer. 1993. The Mathematics of Statistical Machine Translation: Parameter Estimation. *Computational Linguistics*, 19(2):263–311, June.

Christian Buck, Kenneth Heafield, and Bas van Ooyen. 2014. N-gram Counts and Language Models from the Common Crawl. In *Proc. of the Language Resources and Evaluation Conference*, Reykjavík, Iceland, May.

Jean-Cédric Chappelier and Martin Rajman. 1998. A Generalized CYK Algorithm for Parsing Stochastic CFG. In *Proc. of the First Workshop on Tabulation in Parsing and Deduction*, pages 133–137, Paris, France, April.

Stanley F. Chen and Joshua Goodman. 1998. An Empirical Study of Smoothing Techniques for Language Modeling. Technical Report TR-10-98, Computer Science Group, Harvard University, Cambridge, MA, USA, August.

Colin Cherry and George Foster. 2012. Batch Tuning Strategies for Statistical Machine Translation. In *Proc. of the Conf. of the North American Chapter of the Assoc. for Computational Linguistics: Human Language Technologies (NAACL-HLT)*, pages 427–436, Montréal, Canada, June.

David Chiang. 2005. A Hierarchical Phrase-Based Model for Statistical Machine Translation. In *Proc.*
of the Annual Meeting of the Assoc. for Computational Linguistics (ACL), pages 263–270, Ann Arbor, MI, USA, June.

David Chiang. 2007. Hierarchical Phrase-Based Translation. *Computational Linguistics*, 33(2):201–228, June.

Arthur P. Dempster, Nan M. Laird, and Donald B. Rubin. 1977. Maximum Likelihood from Incomplete Data via the EM Algorithm. *J. Royal Statist. Soc. Ser. B*, 39(1):1–22.

George Foster, Roland Kuhn, and Howard Johnson. 2006. Phrasetable Smoothing for Statistical Machine Translation. In *Proc. of the Conf. on Empirical Methods for Natural Language Processing (EMNLP)*, pages 53–61, Sydney, Australia, July.

Markus Freitag, Stephan Peitz, Joern Wuebker, Hermann Ney, Nadir Durrani, Matthias Huck, Philipp Koehn, Thanh-Le Ha, Jan Niehues, Mohammed Mediani, Teresa Herrmann, Alex Waibel, Nicola Bertoldi, Mauro Cettolo, and Marcello Federico. 2013. EU-BRIDGE MT: Text Translation of Talks in the EU-BRIDGE Project. In *Proc. of the Int. Workshop on Spoken Language Translation (IWSLT)*, pages 128–135, Heidelberg, Germany, December.

Markus Freitag, Matthias Huck, and Hermann Ney. 2014a. Jane: Open Source Machine Translation System Combination. In *Proc. of the Conf. of the Europ. Chapter of the Assoc. for Computational Linguistics (EACL)*, pages 29–32, Gothenburg, Sweden, April.

Markus Freitag, Stephan Peitz, Joern Wuebker, Hermann Ney, Matthias Huck, Rico Sennrich, Nadir Durrani, Maria Nadejde, Philip Williams, Philipp Koehn, Teresa Herrmann, Eunah Cho, and Alex Waibel. 2014b. EU-BRIDGE MT: Combined Machine Translation. In *Proc. of the Workshop on Statistical Machine Translation (WMT)*, pages 105–113, Baltimore, MD, USA, June.

Markus Freitag, Joern Wuebker, Stephan Peitz, Hermann Ney, Matthias Huck, Alexandra Birch, Nadir Durrani, Philipp Koehn, Mohammed Mediani, Isabel Slawik, Jan Niehues, Eunah Cho, Alex Waibel, Nicola Bertoldi, Mauro Cettolo, and Marcello Federico. 2014c. Combined Spoken Language Translation. In *Proc. of the Int. Workshop on Spoken Language Translation (IWSLT)*, pages 57–64, Lake Tahoe, CA, USA, December.

Michel Galley and Christopher D. Manning. 2008. A Simple and Effective Hierarchical Phrase Reordering Model. In *Proc. of the Conf. on Empirical Methods for Natural Language Processing (EMNLP)*, pages 847–855, Honolulu, HI, USA, October.

Qin Gao and Stephan Vogel. 2008. Parallel Implementations of Word Alignment Tool. In *Software Engineering, Testing, and Quality Assurance for Natural*

Language Processing, SETQA-NLP '08, pages 49–57, Columbus, OH, USA, June.

Barry Haddow, Matthias Huck, Alexandra Birch, Nikolay Bogoychev, and Philipp Koehn. 2015. The Edinburgh/JHU Phrase-based Machine Translation Systems for WMT 2015. In *Proc. of the Workshop on Statistical Machine Translation (WMT)*, pages 126–133, Lisbon, Portugal, September.

Kenneth Heafield. 2011. KenLM: Faster and Smaller Language Model Queries. In *Proc. of the Workshop on Statistical Machine Translation (WMT)*, pages 187–197, Edinburgh, Scotland, UK, July.

Hieu Hoang, Philipp Koehn, and Adam Lopez. 2009. A Unified Framework for Phrase-Based, Hierarchical, and Syntax-Based Statistical Machine Translation. In *Proc. of the Int. Workshop on Spoken Language Translation (IWSLT)*, pages 152–159, Tokyo, Japan, December.

Matthias Huck and Hermann Ney. 2012. Pivot Lightly-Supervised Training for Statistical Machine Translation. In *Proc. of the Conf. of the Assoc. for Machine Translation in the Americas (AMTA)*, San Diego, CA, USA, October.

Matthias Huck, David Vilar, Daniel Stein, and Hermann Ney. 2011. Lightly-Supervised Training for Hierarchical Phrase-Based Machine Translation. In *Proc. of the EMNLP 2011 Workshop on Unsupervised Learning in NLP*, pages 91–96, Edinburgh, Scotland, UK, July.

Matthias Huck, Jan-Thorsten Peter, Markus Freitag, Stephan Peitz, and Hermann Ney. 2012. Hierarchical Phrase-Based Translation with Jane 2. *The Prague Bulletin of Mathematical Linguistics (PBML)*, 98:37–50, October.

Matthias Huck, Joern Wuebker, Felix Rietig, and Hermann Ney. 2013. A Phrase Orientation Model for Hierarchical Machine Translation. In *Proc. of the Workshop on Statistical Machine Translation (WMT)*, pages 452–463, Sofia, Bulgaria, August.

Matthias Huck, Alexandra Birch, and Barry Haddow. 2015. Mixed-Domain vs. Multi-Domain Statistical Machine Translation. In *Proc. of MT Summit XV, vol.1: MT Researchers' Track*, pages 240–255, Miami, FL, USA, October.

Reinhard Kneser and Hermann Ney. 1995. Improved Backing-Off for M-gram Language Modeling. In *Proceedings of the Int. Conf. on Acoustics, Speech, and Signal Processing*, volume 1, pages 181–184, Detroit, MI, USA, May.

Philipp Koehn, Franz Joseph Och, and Daniel Marcu. 2003. Statistical Phrase-Based Translation. In *Proc. of the Conf. of the North American Chapter of the Assoc. for Computational Linguistics: Human Language Technologies (NAACL-HLT)*, pages 127–133, Edmonton, Canada, May/June.

Philipp Koehn. 2005. Europarl: A Parallel Corpus for Statistical Machine Translation. In *Proc. of the MT Summit X*, Phuket, Thailand, September.

Philipp Koehn. 2010. An Experimental Management System. *The Prague Bulletin of Mathematical Linguistics (PBML)*, 94:87–96, September.

Franz Josef Och and Hermann Ney. 2002. Discriminative Training and Maximum Entropy Models for Statistical Machine Translation. In *Proc. of the Annual Meeting of the Assoc. for Computational Linguistics (ACL)*, pages 295–302, Philadelphia, PA, USA, July.

Franz Josef Och and Hermann Ney. 2003. A Systematic Comparison of Various Statistical Alignment Models. *Computational Linguistics*, 29(1):19–51, March.

Kishore Papineni, Salim Roukos, Todd Ward, and Wei-Jing Zhu. 2002. Bleu: a Method for Automatic Evaluation of Machine Translation. In *Proc. of the Annual Meeting of the Assoc. for Computational Linguistics (ACL)*, pages 311–318, Philadelphia, PA, USA, July.

Jan-Thorsten Peter, Tamer Alkhouli, Hermann Ney, Matthias Huck, Fabienne Braune, Alexander Fraser, Aleš Tamchyna, Ondřej Bojar, Barry Haddow, Rico Sennrich, Frédéric Blain, Lucia Specia, Jan Niehues, Alex Waibel, Alexandre Allauzen, Lauriane Aufrant, Franck Burlot, Elena Knyazeva, Thomas Lavergne, François Yvon, Stella Frank, and Mārcis Pinnis. 2016. The QT21/HimL Combined Machine Translation System. In *Proc. of the ACL 2016 First Conf. on Machine Translation (WMT16)*, Berlin, Germany, August.

Holger Schwenk and Jean Senellart. 2009. Translation Model Adaptation for an Arabic/French News Translation System by Lightly-Supervised Training. In *Proc. of the MT Summit XII*, Ottawa, Canada, August.

Holger Schwenk. 2008. Investigations on Large-Scale Lightly-Supervised Training for Statistical Machine Translation. In *Proc. of the Int. Workshop on Spoken Language Translation (IWSLT)*, pages 182–189, Waikiki, HI, USA, October.

Andreas Stolcke. 2002. SRILM – an Extensible Language Modeling Toolkit. In *Proc. of the Int. Conf. on Spoken Language Processing (ICSLP)*, volume 3, Denver, CO, USA, September.

Francis M. Tyers and Murat Serdar Alperen. 2010. South-East European Times: A parallel corpus of Balkan languages. In *Proc. of the LREC Workshop on Exploitation of Multilingual Resources and Tools for Central and (South-) Eastern European Languages*, pages 49–53, Malta, May.

David Vilar, Daniel Stein, Matthias Huck, and Hermann Ney. 2010. Jane: Open Source Hierarchical Translation, Extended with Reordering and Lexicon

Models. In *Proc. of the Workshop on Statistical Machine Translation (WMT)*, pages 262–270, Uppsala, Sweden, July.

David Vilar, Daniel Stein, Matthias Huck, and Hermann Ney. 2012. Jane: an advanced freely available hierarchical machine translation toolkit. *Machine Translation*, 26(3):197–216, September.

Philip Williams, Rico Sennrich, Maria Nădejde, Matthias Huck, Barry Haddow, and Ondřej Bojar. 2016. Edinburgh's Statistical Machine Translation Systems for WMT16. In *Proc. of the ACL 2016 First Conf. on Machine Translation (WMT16)*, Berlin, Germany, August.

The AMU-UEDIN Submission to the WMT16 News Translation Task: Attention-based NMT Models as Feature Functions in Phrase-based SMT

Marcin Junczys-Dowmunt[1,2], Tomasz Dwojak[1], Rico Sennrich[2]
[1]Faculty of Mathematics and Computer Science, Adam Mickiewicz University in Poznań
[2]School of Informatics, University of Edinburgh
`junczys@amu.edu.pl t.dwojak@amu.edu.pl`
`rico.sennrich@ed.ac.uk`

Abstract

This paper describes the AMU-UEDIN submissions to the WMT 2016 shared task on news translation. We explore methods of decode-time integration of attention-based neural translation models with phrase-based statistical machine translation. Efficient batch-algorithms for GPU-querying are proposed and implemented. For English-Russian, our system stays behind the state-of-the-art pure neural models in terms of BLEU. Among restricted systems, manual evaluation places it in the first cluster tied with the pure neural model. For the Russian-English task, our submission achieves the top BLEU result, outperforming the best pure neural system by 1.1 BLEU points and our own phrase-based baseline by 1.6 BLEU. After manual evaluation, this system is the best restricted system in its own cluster. In follow-up experiments we improve results by additional 0.8 BLEU.

1 Introduction

This paper describes the AMU-UEDIN submissions to the WMT 2016 shared task on news translation. We explore methods of decode-time integration of attention-based neural translation models with phrase-based decoding. Experiments have been conducted for the English-Russian language pair in both translation directions.

For these experiments we re-implemented the inference step of the models described in Bahdanau et al. (2015) (more exactly the DL4MT[1] variant also present in Nematus[2]) in efficient

C++/CUDA code that can be directly compiled as a Moses feature function. The GPU-based computations come with their own peculiarities which we reconcile with the two most popular phrase-based decoding algorithms — stack-decoding and cube-pruning.

While it seems at first that for English-Russian our phrase-based system is holding back the neural models in terms of BLEU, the manual evaluation reveals that our systems is tied with the pure neural systems, occupying the same top cluster for restricted systems with an even slightly higher TrueSkill score. We achieve the top BLEU result for the Russian-English task, outperforming the best pure neural system by 1.1 BLEU points and our own phrase-based baseline by 1.6 BLEU. After manual evaluation, this system is the best restricted system in its own cluster.

Our implementation is available as a Moses fork from `https://github.com/emjotde/ mosesdecoder_nmt`

2 Preprocessing

As we reuse the neural systems from Sennrich et al. (2016), we follow their preprocessing scheme for the phrase-based systems as well. All data is tokenized with the Moses tokenizer, for English the Penn-format tokenization scheme has been used. Tokenized text is true-cased.

Sennrich et al. (2016) use byte-pair-encoding (BPE) to achieve open-vocabulary translation with a fixed vocabulary of subword symbols (Sennrich et al., 2015b). For English, the vocabulary size is limited to 50,000 units, for Russian to 100,000. This has the interesting consequence of using subword units for phrase-based SMT. Although SMT seems to be better equipped to handle large vocabularies, the case of Russian still poses problems which are usually solved with transliteration

---

[1]`https://github.com/nyu-dl/ dl4mt-tutorial`
[2]`https://github.com/rsennrich/nematus`

Proceedings of the First Conference on Machine Translation, Volume 2: Shared Task Papers, pages 319–325,
Berlin, Germany, August 11-12, 2016. ©2016 Association for Computational Linguistics

mechanisms (Durrani et al., 2014). Resorting to subword units eliminates the need for these.[3]

3   Neural translation systems

As mentioned before, we reuse the English-Russian and Russian-English NMT models from Sennrich et al. (2016) and refer the reader to that paper for a more detailed description of these systems. In this section we give a short summarization for the sake of completeness.

The neural machine translation system is an attentional encoder-decoder (Bahdanau et al., 2015), which has been trained with Nematus. Additional parallel training data has been produced by automatically translating a random sample (2 million sentences) of the monolingual Russian News Crawl 2015 corpus into English (Sennrich et al., 2015a), which has been combined with the original parallel data in a 1-to-1 ratio.[4] The same has been done for the other direction. We used mini-batches of size 80, a maximum sentence length of 50, word embeddings of size 500, and hidden layers of size 1024. We clip the gradient norm to 1.0 (Pascanu et al., 2013). Models were trained with Adadelta (Zeiler, 2012), reshuffling the training corpus between epochs. The models have been trained model for approximately 2 weeks, saving every 30000 mini-batches.

For our experiments with PB-SMT integration, we chose the same four models that constituted the best-scoring ensemble from Sennrich et al. (2016). If less than four models were used, we chose the models with the highest BLEU scores among these four models as measured on a development set.

4   Phrase-Based baseline systems

We base our set-up on a Moses system (Koehn et al., 2007) with a number of additional feature functions. Apart from the default configuration with a lexical reordering model, we add a 5-gram operation sequence model (Durrani et al., 2013).

We perform no language-specific adaptations or modifications. The two systems differ only

with respect to translation direction and the available (monolingual) training data. For domain-adaptation, we rely solely on parameter tuning with Batch-Mira (Cherry and Foster, 2012) and on-line log-linear interpolation. Binary domain-indicators for each separate parallel corpus are introduced to the phrase-tables (four indicators) and a separate language model per parallel and monolingual resource is trained (en:16 and ru:12). All language models are 5-gram models with Modified Kneser-Ney smoothing and without pruning thresholds (Heafield et al., 2013). We treat different years of the News Crawl data as different domains to take advantage of possible recency-based effects. During parameter tuning on the newstest-2014 test set, we can unsurprisingly observe that weights for the last three LMs (2013, 2014, 2015) are much higher than for the remaining years.

After concatenating all resources, a large 5-gram background language model is trained, with 3-grams or higher n-gram orders being pruned if they occur only once. The same concatenated files and pruning settings are used to create a 9-gram word-class language model with 200 word-classes produced by word2vec (Mikolov et al., 2013).

5   NMT as Moses feature functions

As mentioned in the introduction, we implemented a C++/CUDA version of the inference step for the neural models trained with DL4MT or Nematus, which can be used directly with our code. One or multiple models can be added to the Moses log-linear model as different instances of the same feature, which during tuning can be separately weighted. Adding multiple models as separate features becomes thus similar to ensemble translation with pure neural models.

In this section we give algorithmic details about integrating GPU-based soft-attention neural translation models into Moses as part of the feature function framework. Our work differs from Alkhouli et al. (2015) in the following aspects:

1. While Alkhouli et al. (2015) integrate RNN-based translation models in phrase-based decoding, this work is to our knowledge the first to integrate soft-attention models.

2. Our implementation is GPU-based and our algorithms being tailored towards GPU computations require very different caching strategies from those proposed in Alkhouli et

---

[3]In experiments not described in this paper, we tried BPE encoding for the English-German language pair and found subword units to cope well with German compound nouns when used for phrase-based SMT.

[4]This artificial data has not been used for the creation of the phrase-based system, but it might be worthwhile to explore this possibility in the future. It might enable the phrase-based system to produce translation that are more similar to the neural output.

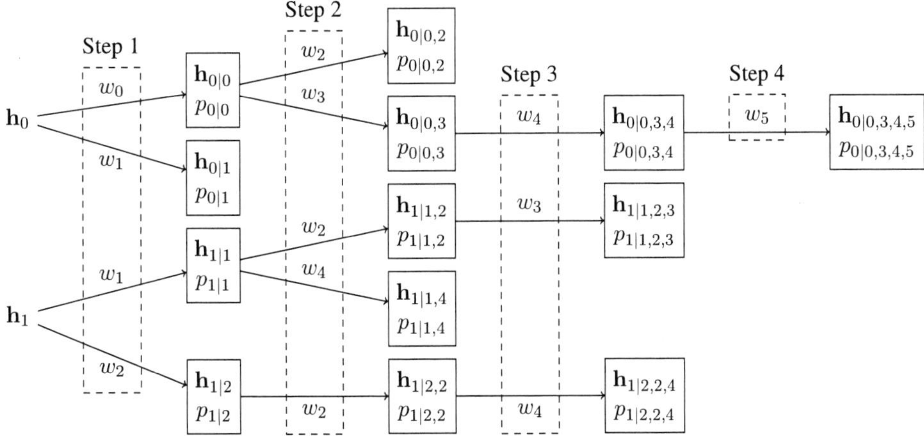

Figure 1: SCOREBATCH procedure for a forest consisting of two per-hypothesis prefix trees. Words are collected at the same tree depths across all trees in the forest.

al. (2015). Our implementation seems to be about 10 times faster on one GPU, 30 times faster when three GPUs are used.

5.1 Scoring hypotheses and their expansions

We assume through-out this section that the neural model has already been initialized with the source sentence and that the source sentence context is available at all time.

In phrase-based machine translation, a pair consisting of a translation hypothesis and a chosen possible target phrase that expands this hypothesis to form a new hypothesis can be seen as the smallest unit of computation. In the typical case they are processed independently from other hypothesis-expansion pairs until they are put on a stack and potentially recombined. Our aim is to run the computations on one or more GPUs. This makes the calculation of scores per hypothesis-expansion pair (as done for instance during n-gram language model querying) unfeasible as repeated GPU-access with very small units of computation comes with a very high overhead.

In neural machine translation, we treat neural states to be equivalent to hypotheses, but they are extended only by single words, not phrases, by performing computations over the whole target vocabulary. In this section, we present a batching and querying scheme that aims at taking advantage of the capabilities of GPUs to perform batched calculations efficiently, by combining the approaches from phrase-based and neural decoding.

Given is a set of pairs (h, t) where h is a decoding hypothesis and t a target phrase expanding the

1: **procedure** SCOREBATCH(L, NMT)
2:     Create forest of per-hypothesis prefix trees from all hypotheses and expansions in L
3:     **for** i **from** 1 **to** maximum tree depth **do**
4:         Construct embedding matrix E_i from all edge labels at depth i
5:         Construct row-wise corresponding state matrix H_{i-1} from source nodes
6:         Compute forward step:
$$(H_i, P_i) \leftarrow \text{NMT}(H_{i-1}, E_i)$$
7:         Cache state pointers and probabilities at target nodes

Figure 2: Scoring of hypothesis expansion pairs

hypothesis. In a naive approach (corresponding to unmodified stack decoding) the number of queries to the GPU would be equal to the total number of words in all expansions. A better algorithm might take advantage of common target phrase prefixes per hypothesis. The number of queries would be reduced to the number of collapsed edges in the per-hypothesis prefix-tree forest.

By explicitly constructing this forest of prefix trees where a single prefix tree encodes all target phrases that expand the same hypothesis, we can actually reduce the number of queries to the neural model to the maximum depth of any of the trees (i.e. the maximum target phrase length) as illustrated in Figures 1 and 2.

Target phrases t are treated as sequences of words w. Rectangles at tree nodes should be imagined to be empty before the preceding step has been performed. The first embedding matrix E_1 is constructed by concatenating embedding vectors $\mathbf{e}_i \leftarrow \text{LOOKUP}(w_i)$ as rows of the matrix, for all w_i marked in the first dashed rectangle. The initial state matrix H_0 is a row-wise concatenation of the neural hypothesis states, repeated for each outgoing edge. Thus, the embedding matrix and state matrix have the same number of corresponding rows. Example matrices for the first step take the following form:

$$
E_1 = \begin{bmatrix} \mathbf{e}_0 \\ \mathbf{e}_1 \\ \mathbf{e}_1 \\ \mathbf{e}_2 \end{bmatrix} \quad H_0 = \begin{bmatrix} \mathbf{h}_0 \\ \mathbf{h}_0 \\ \mathbf{h}_1 \\ \mathbf{h}_1 \end{bmatrix}
$$

Given the precomputed source context state, we can now perform one forward step in the neural network which yields a matrix of output states and a matrix of probabilities, both corresponding row-wise to the input state matrix and embedding matrix we constructed earlier. The target nodes for each edge pointed to after the first step are filled. Probabilities will be queried later during phrase-based scoring, neural hypothesis states are reused to construct the state matrix of the next step and potentially as initial states when scoring another batch of hypotheses at later time.

5.2 Two-pass stack decoding

Standard stack decoding still scores hypotheses one-by-one. In order to limit the number of modifications of Moses to a minimum, we propose two-pass stack decoding where the first pass is a hypothesis and expansions collection step and the second pass is the original expansion and scoring step. Between the two steps we pre-calculate per-hypothesis scores with the procedure described above. The data structure introduced in Figure 1 is then reused for probability look-up during the scoring phrase of stack decoding as if individual hypotheses where scored on-the-fly.

Figure 3 contains our complete proposal for two-pass stack decoding, a modification of the original stack decoding algorithm described in Koehn (2010). We dissect stack decoding into smaller reusable pieces that can be passed functors to perform different tasks for the same sets of hypotheses. The main reason for this is the small word "applicable" in line 12, which hides a complicated set of target phrase choices based on re-ordering limits and coverage vectors which should

```
1:  procedure TWOPASSSTACKDECODING
2:      Place empty hypothesis h_0 into stack S_0
3:      for stack S in stacks do
4:          L ← ∅
5:          PROCESSSTACK(S, GATHER{L})
6:          C ← SCOREBATCH(L, NMT)
7:          PROCESSSTACK(S, EXPAND{C})
8:
9:  procedure PROCESSSTACK(S, f)
10:      for hypothesis h in S do
11:          for target phrase t do
12:              if applicable then
13:                  Apply functor f(h, t)
14:
15:  procedure GATHER(h, t)
16:      L ← L ∪ {(h, t)}
17:
18:  procedure EXPAND(h, t)
19:      Look-up p for (h, t) in C
20:      Create new hypothesis ĥ from (h, t, p)
21:      Place ĥ on appropriate stack s
22:      if possible then
23:          Recombine hypothesis ĥ with other
                 hypotheses on stack s
24:      if stack s too big then
25:          Prune stack s
```

Figure 3: Two-pass stack decoding

not be discussed here. This allows our algorithm to collect exactly the set of hypotheses and expansions for score pre-calculation that will be used during the second expansion step.

As already mentioned, the number of forward steps for the NMT network per stack is equal to the greatest phrase length among all expansions. The total number of GPU queries increases therefore linearly with respect to the sentence length. Branching factors or stack sizes affect the matrix sizes, not the number of steps.[5]

For this method we do not provide results due to a lack of time. We confirmed for other experiments that improvements are smaller than for the next method. A comparison will be provided in an extended version of this work.

5.3 Stack rescoring

The previous approach cannot be used with lazy decoding algorithms — like cube pruning —

---

[5]Large matrix sizes, however, do slow-down translation speed significantly.

1: **procedure** STACKRESCORING
2:    Place empty hypothesis h_0 into stack S_0
3:    **for** stack S **in** stacks **do**
4:       $L \leftarrow \emptyset$
5:       **for** hypothesis h **in** S **do**
6:          Extract predecessors $(\bar{h}, \bar{t})$ from h
7:          $L \leftarrow L \cup \{(\bar{h}, \bar{t})\}$
8:       $C \leftarrow$ SCOREBATCH(L, NMT)
9:       **for** hypothesis h **in** S **do**
10:         Extract predecessors $(\bar{h}, \bar{t})$ from h
11:         Look-up p for $(\bar{h}, \bar{t})$ in C
12:         Recalculate score of h using p
13:      Create cache C_0 with 0-probabilities
14:      PROCESSSTACK(S, EXPAND$\{C_0\}$)

Figure 4: Stack decoding with stack rescoring

which has also been implemented in Moses. Apart from that, due to the large number of expansions even small stack sizes of around 30 or 50 quickly result in large matrices in the middle steps of BATCHSCORE where the prefix trees have the greatest number of edges at the same depth level. In the worst case, matrix size will increase by a factor b^d, where b is the branching factor and d is the current depth. In practice, however, the maximum is reached at the third or fourth step, as only few target phrases contain five or more words.

To address both shortcomings we propose a second algorithm: stack rescoring. This algorithm (Figure 4) relies on two ideas:

1. During hypothesis expansion the NMT feature is being ignored, only probabilities of 0 are assigned for this feature to all newly created hypotheses. Hypothesis recombination and pruning take place without NMT scores for the current expansions (NMT scores for all previous expansions are included). Any stack-based decoding algorithm, also cube-pruning, can be used in this step.

2. The BATCHSCORE procedure is applied to all direct predecessors of hypotheses on the currently expanded stack. Predecessors consist of the parent hypothesis and the expansion that resulted in the current hypothesis. The previously assigned 0-probabilities are replaced with the actual NMT scores.

This procedure results in a number of changes when compared to standard stack decoding approaches and the previous method:

- The maximum matrix row count is equal to the stack size, and often much smaller due to prefix collapsing. Branching factors are irrelevant and stack sizes of 2,000 or greater are possible. By contrast, for two-pass stack decoding stack sizes of around 50 could already result in row counts of 7,000 and more.

- With cube pruning, by setting cube pruning pop-limits much larger than the stack size many more hypotheses can be scored with all remaining feature functions before the survivors are passed to BATCHSCORE.

- Scoring with the NMT-feature is delayed until the next stack is processed. This may result in missing good translations due to recombination. However, the much larger stack sizes may counter this effect.

- N-best list extraction is more difficult, as hypotheses that have been recombined do not display correct cumulative sums for the NMT-feature scores. The one-best translation is always correctly scored as it has never been discarded during recombination, so there is no problem at test time. For tuning, where a correctly scored n-best list is required, we simply rescore the final n-best list with the same neural feature functions as during decoding. The resulting scores are the same as if they were produced at decode-time. Final n-best list rescoring can thus be seen as an integral part of stack-rescoring.

6 Experiments and results

For decoding, we use the cube-pruning algorithm with stack size of 1,000 and cube-pruning pop limit of 2,000 during tuning. At test time, a stack-size of 1,000 is kept, but the cube-pruning pop limit is increased to 5,000. We set a distortion limit of 12. We run 10 iterations of Batch-Mira (Cherry and Foster, 2012) and choose the best set of weights based on the development set. Our development set is a subset of 2,000 sentences from the newstest-2014 test set. Sentences have been selected to be shorter than 40 words to avoid GPU-memory problems. Our GPUs are three Nvidia GeForce GTX-970 cards with 4GB RAM each.

In this paper, similar as Alkhouli et al. (2015), we ignore the implications of the infinite neural state and hypothesis recombination in the face of

System	2015	2016
Phrase-Based (PB)	23.7	22.8
Pure neural:		
NMT-2	26.4	25.3
NMT-4 (Sennrich et al., 2016)	27.0	26.0
Stack rescoring:		
PB+NMT-2 (subm.)	—	**25.3**
Follow-up:		
NMT-4-Avg	26.7	25.5
PB+NMT-4-Avg	27.3	25.9

(a) BLEU scores English-Russian

System	2015	2016
Phrase-Based (PB)	27.4	27.5
Pure neural:		
NMT-3	28.3	27.8
NMT-4 (Sennrich et al., 2016)	28.3	28.0
Stack rescoring:		
PB+NMT-3 (subm.)	**29.5**	**29.1**
Follow-up:		
NMT-10-Avg	28.3	28.1
PB+NMT-10-Avg	**30.2**	**29.9**

(b) BLEU scores Russian-English

Table 1: Systems marked with **subm.** are our final WMT 2016 submissions.

	words/s
Alkhouli et al. (2015) (1 thread?)	0.19
Phrase-based PB (24 threads)	40.30
PB-NMT-10-Avg (3 GPUs)	4.83

Table 2: Translation speed for different configurations in words per second.

infinite state. We rely on the hypothesis recombination controlled by the states of the other feature functions. It is worth mentioning again that our phrase-based baseline features a 9-gram word-class language model which should be rather prohibitive of recombinations. If recombination was only allowed for hypotheses with the same partial translations, results were considerably worse.

6.1 Speed

Translation speed is difficult to compare across systems (Table 2). Even with three GPUs our system is ten times slower than than a pure PB-SMT system running with 24 CPU-threads. It is however unclear at this moment if the large stack sizes we use are really necessary. Significant speed-up might be achieved for smaller stacks.

6.2 Submitted results

Table 1 summarizes the results for our experiments. BLEU scores are reported for the newstest-2015 and newstest-2016 test sets.

Our baseline phrase-based systems (PB) are quite competitive when comparing to the best results of last year's WMT (24.4 and 27.9 for English-Russian and Russian-English, respec-

tively). NMT-4 is the best pure neural ensemble from Sennrich et al. (2016) for both translation directions. Due to memory restrictions, we were not able to use all four models as separate feature functions and limit ourselves to the best two models for English-Russian and best three for Russian-English. The pure neural ensembles are NMT-2 (en-ru) and NMT-3 (ru-en), respectively.

For English-Russian, our results stay behind the pure-neural 4-ensemble NMT-4 in terms of BLEU. In a direct comparison between ensembles of 2 models (PB+NMT-2 and NMT-2), we actually reach similar BLEU scores. However, in the manual evaluation our system is best restricted system, tied with the neural system. Absolute TrueSkill scores are even slightly higher for our system.

For Russian-English the best-performing pure neural system NMT-4 and the phrase-based baseline are only 0.5% BLEU apart. Adding three NMT models as feature functions to Moses results in a 1.1% BLEU improvement over the neural model and 1.6% over the phrase-based system. The systems PB-NMT-2 (en-ru) and PB-NMT-3 (ru-en) are our submissions to the WMT-2016 news translation task. PB-NMT-3 scores the top BLEU results for Russian-English. In the manual evaluation, our system is the best restricted system in its own cluster.

6.3 Follow-up experiments

Frustrated by the limited memory of our GPU cards and against better knowledge[6], we computed

---

[6]The neural network lore seems to suggest that this should not work, as neural networks are non-linear models. We only found one paper with evidence to the contrary: Utans (1996)

the element-wise average of all model weights in the NMT ensembles and saved the resulting model. Interestingly, the performance of these new models (NMT-4-Avg) is not much worse than the actual ensemble (NMT-4), while being four times smaller and four times faster at decode-time. The average models outperforms any single model or the smaller 2-ensembles. All models taking part in the average are parameter dumps saved at different points in time during the same training run. This seem to be an interesting results for model compression and deployment settings. We can also average more models: for the Russian-English direction we experiment with the parameter-wise average of ten models (NMT-10-Avg) which even slightly outperforms the real four-model ensemble NMT-4.

With this smaller model it is easier to tune and deploy our feature function. The performance of our combined setup improves for both translation directions. For English-Russian, however, the pure NMT system (NMT-4) remains ahead of our WMT 2016 submission. For Russian-English we get another improvement of 0.8 BLEU, which sets the new state-of-the-art for this direction.

Acknowledgments

This project has received funding from the European Union's Horizon 2020 research and innovation programme under grant agreements 644333 (TraMOOC) and 688139 (SUMMA) and was partially funded by the Amazon Academic Research Awards programme.

References

Tamer Alkhouli, Felix Rietig, and Hermann Ney. 2015. Investigations on phrase-based decoding with recurrent neural network language and translation models. In *Proceedings of the Tenth Workshop on Statistical Machine Translation*, pages 294–303, Lisbon, Portugal, September. Association for Computational Linguistics.

Dzmitry Bahdanau, Kyunghyun Cho, and Yoshua Bengio. 2015. Neural Machine Translation by Jointly Learning to Align and Translate. In *Proceedings of the International Conference on Learning Representations (ICLR)*.

Colin Cherry and George Foster. 2012. Batch tuning strategies for statistical machine translation. In *Proceedings of the 2012 Conference of the North American Chapter of the Association for Computational Linguistics: Human Language Technologies*, NAACL HLT '12, pages 427–436, Stroudsburg, PA, USA. Association for Computational Linguistics.

Nadir Durrani, Alexander Fraser, Helmut Schmid, Hieu Hoang, and Philipp Koehn. 2013. Can Markov models over minimal translation units help phrase-based SMT? In *ACL*, pages 399–405. The Association for Computer Linguistics.

Nadir Durrani, Hassan Sajjad, Hieu Hoang, and Philipp Koehn. 2014. Integrating an unsupervised transliteration model into statistical machine translation. In *Proceedings of the 14th Conference of the European Chapter of the Association for Computational Linguistics, EACL 2014, April 26-30, 2014, Gothenburg, Sweden*, pages 148–153.

Kenneth Heafield, Ivan Pouzyrevsky, Jonathan H. Clark, and Philipp Koehn. 2013. Scalable modified Kneser-Ney language model estimation. In *Proceedings of the 51st Annual Meeting of the ACL*, pages 690–696.

Philipp Koehn, Hieu Hoang, Alexandra Birch, Chris Callison-Burch, Marcello Federico, Nicola Bertoldi, Brooke Cowan, Wade Shen, Christine Moran, Richard Zens, Chris Dyer, Ondřej Bojar, Alexandra Constantin, and Evan Herbst. 2007. Moses: Open source toolkit for statistical machine translation. In *Proceedings of the 45th Annual Meeting of the ACL*, pages 177–180. ACL.

Philipp Koehn. 2010. *Statistical Machine Translation*. Cambridge University Press, New York, NY, USA, 1st edition.

Tomas Mikolov, Kai Chen, Greg Corrado, and Jeffrey Dean. 2013. Efficient estimation of word representations in vector space. *CoRR*, abs/1301.3781.

Razvan Pascanu, Tomas Mikolov, and Yoshua Bengio. 2013. On the difficulty of training recurrent neural networks. In *Proceedings of the 30th International Conference on Machine Learning, ICML 2013*, pages 1310–1318, , Atlanta, GA, USA.

Rico Sennrich, Barry Haddow, and Alexandra Birch. 2015a. Improving Neural Machine Translation Models with Monolingual Data. *ArXiv e-prints*, November.

Rico Sennrich, Barry Haddow, and Alexandra Birch. 2015b. Neural Machine Translation of Rare Words with Subword Units. *CoRR*, abs/1508.07909.

Rico Sennrich, Barry Haddow, and Alexandra Birch. 2016. Edinburgh Neural Machine Translation Systems for WMT 16. In *Proc. of the Conference on Machine Translation (WMT)*, Berlin, Germany.

Joachim Utans. 1996. Weight averaging for neural networks and local resampling schemes. In *Proc. AAAI-96 Workshop on Integrating Multiple Learned Models*, pages 133–138. AAAI Press.

Matthew D. Zeiler. 2012. ADADELTA: An Adaptive Learning Rate Method. *CoRR*, abs/1212.5701.

NRC Russian-English Machine Translation System for WMT 2016

Chi-kiu Lo Colin Cherry George Foster Darlene Stewart Rabib Islam
Anna Kazantseva Roland Kuhn

National Research Council Canada
1200 Montreal Road, Ottawa, Ontario K1A 0R6, Canada
FirstName.LastName@nrc.ca

Abstract

We describe the statistical machine translation system developed at the National Research Council of Canada (NRC) for the Russian-English news translation task of the First Conference on Machine Translation (WMT 2016). Our submission is a phrase-based SMT system that tackles the morphological complexity of Russian through comprehensive use of lemmatization. The core of our lemmatization strategy is to use different views of Russian for different SMT components: word alignment and bilingual neural network language models use lemmas, while sparse features and reordering models use fully inflected forms. Some components, such as the phrase table, use both views of the source. Russian words that remain out-of-vocabulary (OOV) after lemmatization are transliterated into English using a statistical model trained on examples mined from the parallel training corpus. The NRC Russian-English MT system achieved the highest uncased BLEU and the lowest TER scores among the eight participants in WMT 2016.

1 Introduction

We present NRC's submission to the Russian-English news translation task of WMT 2016. Russian-English is a challenging language pair for statistical machine translation because Russian is a highly inflectional and free word order language. Case information is encoded by modifying the Russian words, which makes the number of word types present in the Russian side of a Russian-English parallel corpus much higher than in the English side, introducing a data sparsity problem.

Lemmatization is one of the possible solutions for handling data sparsity when translating highly inflectional languages. However, Russian is a free word order language, meaning that case information conveyed through inflection plays an important role in disambiguating the meaning of a sentence. The MT system would be unable to recover this case information if we were to blindly lemmatize all the Russian words to their root form.

Instead, we rely most heavily on lemmatization only when the missing inflections are unlikely to cause ambiguity. For example, in automatic word alignment, the missing case information should not confuse the system as competing inflections are unlikely to appear in the same sentence (El Kholy and Habash, 2012). Therefore, we build automatic word alignments with lemmatized Russian, but then restore the Russian lemmas to their inflected forms before estimating our other model parameters. The end result is a system with higher-quality word alignments, but which can still use case information to drive its translation and reordering models. Similarly, our bilingual language models have large source context windows that allow them to resolve ambiguities introduced by lemmatization, so we build these based on lemmatized versions of the source by default. These include neural network joint models (NNJMs) and lexical translation models (NNLTMs) (Devlin et al., 2014).

We have found that blind lemmatization of phrase tables is actually quite harmful to translation, but Russian morphology still causes a significant increase in the number of OOVs. Therefore, we built a fallback Russian lemma phrase table for the OOVs in the Russian input, implemented as an interpolated phrase table. For any remaining Russian OOVs, we use a semi-supervised transliteration system to translate the word orthographically. This character-level subsystem is trained

Proceedings of the First Conference on Machine Translation, Volume 2: Shared Task Papers, pages 326–332,
Berlin, Germany, August 11-12, 2016. ©2016 Association for Computational Linguistics

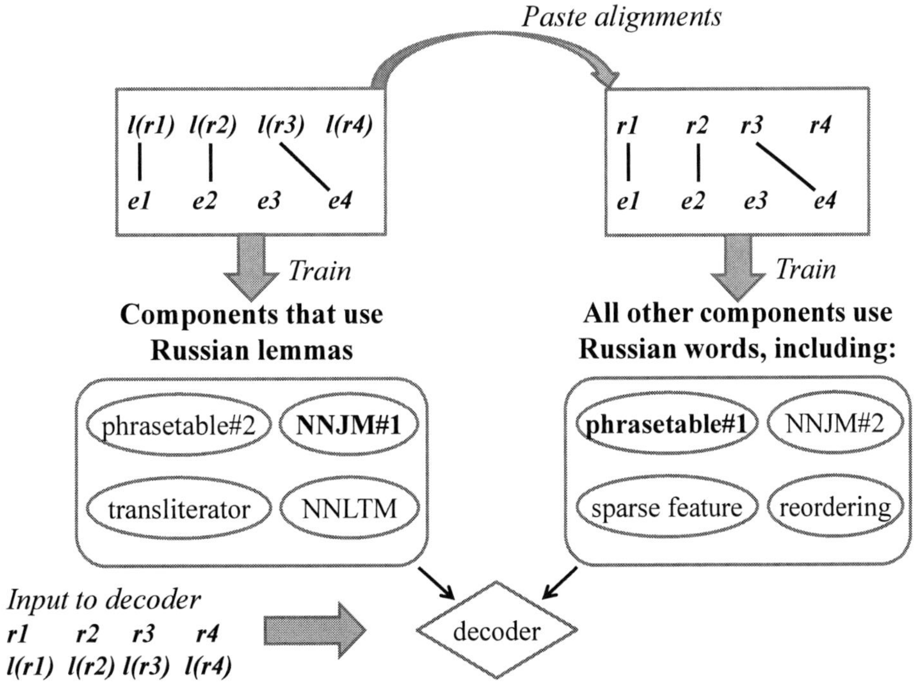

Figure 1: System diagram for the NRC Russian-English submission, highlighting our use of two different views of the Russian source. In this figure, Russian words in their inflected surface form are denoted as $r1, r2, \ldots$, while their automatically lemmatized root forms are denoted $l(r1), l(r2), \ldots$

on a transliteration corpus mined from our parallel training corpus, where the mining process is seeded by the name-pair corpora provided by the competition.

Figure 1 summarizes our lemmatization strategy. In this figure, phrasetable#1 corresponds to the phrase table given the highest weight in our interpolation (see Section 3.2), while NNJM#1 simply denotes that NNJM we found empirically to be the most informative. We did not have time to try duplicating all the models in this way; for instance, it might have been interesting to try lemma-based reordering models and an NNLTM based on Russian words rather than Russian lemmas, but we will leave this for future work.

The NRC submission achieved the highest uncased BLEU, the second highest cased BLEU and the lowest TER scores among the eight participants in the task, and ranked third out of ten systems in the human evaluation.

2 Portage - the NRC PBMT system

The core of the NRC MT system is *Portage* (Larkin et al., 2010). Portage is a conventional log-linear phrase-based SMT system. We describe the basic features of Portage in this section and the new features first tested on our Russian-English submission in the next section.

2.1 Data and preprocessing

We used all the Russian-English parallel corpora available for the constrained news translation task. They include the CommonCrawl corpus, the NewsCommentary v11 corpus, the Yandex corpus and the Wikipedia headlines corpus. We also added the WMT 12 and WMT 13 Russian-English news translation test set to the parallel training data. In total, 2.6 million parallel Russian-English sentences are used to train the translation model. For monolingual English corpora, we used the Gigaword corpus (191 million sentences) and the monolingual English corpus available for the constrained news translation task, which is a combination of the Europarl v7 corpus, the NewsCommentary v11 monolingual corpus and the NewsCrawl 2015 (206 million sentences in total). Due to resource limits, we have not used the newly released 3 billion sentence CommonCrawl monolingual English corpus. Our submitted system was tuned on the WMT 2014 test set. Both the Russian and English text in the parallel and monolingual corpora in the training/development/test corpora were lower cased and tokenized.

2.2 Translation model

We obtain the word alignment by first lemmatizing the Russian side of the parallel training data using Yandex `MyStem` (Segalovich, 2003). Word alignments are built for the lemmatized Russian using IBM2, HMM and IBM4 models. The Russian is then restored to its fully inflected surface form, and phrase-pairs are extracted for each of our three alignment methods. Counts from all three alignments are then combined into a single phrase table, with a maximum phrase length of 7 tokens. Phrase pairs were filtered so that the top 30 translations for each source phrase were retained.

Our internal development experiments indicated that using lemma alignments improved the translation quality of a baseline phrase-based system by roughly 0.2 BLEU, and also benefited the perplexity of the bilingual neural language models described in Section 2.5 and 3.1.

2.3 Language models

Our system consists of three n-gram language models (LMs) and two word class language models (Stewart et al., 2014). Each is included as a distinct feature in the decoder's log-linear model.

- A 4-gram LM trained on the target side of all the WMT parallel training corpora.

- A 6-gram LM trained on the Gigaword corpus.

- A 6-gram LM trained on the WMT monolingual English training corpus.

- A 6-gram, 200-word-class coarse LM trained on a concatenation of the target side of all the WMT parallel training corpora and the WMT monolingual English training corpus.

- A 6-gram, 800-word-class coarse LM trained on the same corpus as the 200-word-class model.

Word classes are built using `mkcls` (Och, 1999).

2.4 Distortion and sparse feature models

Similar to the translation model, our hierarchical distortion model and sparse feature model are based on Russian words but are built on the lemmatized alignment. The sparse feature model consists of the standard sparse features proposed in

Hopkins and May (2011) and sparse hierarchical distortion model features proposed in Cherry (2013).

2.5 Neural network joint model

We employ two neural network joint models, or NNJMs (Vaswani et al., 2013; Devlin et al., 2014). The NNJM is a feed-forward neural network language model that assumes access to a source sentence f and an aligned source index a_i, which points to the most influential source word for the translation of the target word e_i. The NNJM calculates the language modeling probability $p(e_i | e_{i-n+1}^{i-1}, f_{a_i-m}^{a_i+m})$, which accounts for the $n-1$ preceding target words, and for $2m+1$ words of source context, centered around f_{a_i}. Following Devlin et al. (2014), we use $n = 4$ and $m = 5$, resulting in 3 words of target context and 11 words of source context, effectively a 15-gram language model.

Our two models differ only in the rendering of their source strings, with one using lemmas, and the other using words. The lemma-to-word system achieved a development perplexity of 6.04, while the word-to-word system reached 6.78. Since our decoder's input is Russian words, the decoder needed to map words to lemmas before calculating lemma-based NNJM probabilities. This was done by running Yandex `MyStem` on the Russian source at test time, in order to build sentence-specific position-to-lemma mappings. For both models, the source link a_i is derived from IBM4 Russian-lemma to English-word alignments.

NNJM training data is pre-processed to limit vocabularies to 96K types for source or target inputs, and 32K types for target outputs. We build 400 deterministic word clusters for each corpus using `mkcls`. Any word not among the 96K / 32K most frequent words is replaced with its cluster. For our feed-forward network architecture, we used 192 units for source embeddings and 512 units for the single hidden layer. We train our models with mini-batch stochastic gradient descent, with a batch size of 128 words, and an initial learning rate of 0.3. We check our training objective on the development set every 20K batches, and if it fails to improve for two consecutive checks, the learning rate is halved. Training stops after 5 consecutive failed checks or after 90 checks. To enable efficient decoding, our models are self-normalized with a squared penalty on the log partition function, weighted with $\alpha = 0.1$ (Devlin et al., 2014).

2.6 Tuning and decoding

The parameters of the log-linear model were tuned by optimizing BLEU on the development set using the batch variant of MIRA (Cherry and Foster, 2012). Decoding uses the cube-pruning algorithm of (Huang and Chiang, 2007) with a 7-word distortion limit.

2.7 Rescoring

We rescored 1000-best lists output from the decoder using a rescoring model (Och et al., 2004; Foster et al., 2009) consisting of 82 features: 27 decoder features and 55 additional rescoring features. The rescoring model was tuned using n-best MIRA. Of the rescoring features, 51 consisted of various IBM features for word- and lemma-aligned IBM1, IBM2, IBM4 and HMM models, as well as various other standard length, n-gram, and n-best features.

The final four features used NNJMs for rescoring, two Russian-word NNJM rescoring features and two Russian-lemma ones. Following Devlin et al. (2014), one NNJM feature rescored the 1000-best list using a English-to-Russian NNJM, where the roles of the source and target languages are reversed, while the other used a right-to-left and English-to-Russian NNJM, where the Russian target side is traversed in reverse order. These NNJM variants were trained and self-normalized using the same parameters as the NNJMs used for decoding described above in Section 2.5, the only difference being to swap source and target and reverse target word order as described above. During development, rescoring improved our uncased BLEU score by 0.4 on newstest2015.

2.8 Truecasing

The decoder was used to translate the lowercased, rescored output to mixed case using a target side LM and a truecase map. The 3-gram truecasing LM was trained on the target side of all the WMT parallel training data as well as the WMT monolingual English corpus described in Section 2.1. Beginning of sentence case was normalized before training the LM. In addition, casing information was transferred heuristically from the source to the target for OOVs and title/upper cased multi-word sequences. Beginning-of-sentence case was also restored. There were no OOVs because of

transliteration (Section 3.3), so case for transliterated words was restored via a post-processing script. As a final step, the output was detokenized with rule-based methods.

3 New features

Our success in using Russian lemmas to improve word alignment and NNJMs to improve the overall system performance has inspired us to further develop new components to leverage these ideas. In this section, we describe the new features integrated with Portage in our submitted system: a neural network lexical translation model (NNLTM), a fallback Russian lemma phrase table, and a semi-supervised transliteration model.

3.1 Neural network lexical translation model

In addition to the NNJM feature described above, we also implemented the neural network lexical translation model (NNLTM) from (Devlin et al., 2014). The NNLTM is identical in structure to the NNJM except that it does not use target context. It is complementary to the NNJM because it accounts for all source words: for each source word f_j in the current sentence, it models $p(\bar{e}_{a_j} | f_{j-m}^{j+m})$, where $\bar{e}_{a_j}$ is the sequence of zero or more words aligned to f_j. Following Devlin et al. (2014), we set $m = 5$, and used 192 units for source embeddings and 512 units for the hidden layer.

We used a single NNLTM trained on source lemmas with source and target vocabulary sizes of 128K and 64K, and backoff to source classes as described above for the NNJM. On the target side, sequences of words $\bar{e}_{a_j}$ that were not among the most frequent 64K sequences were mapped to classes that depended on the `mkcls` class of their first word and their length, up to a maximum length of 2. For example, unknown word sequences A, A_B, and A_B_C get mapped to classes `mkcls`(A):1, `mkcls`(A):2, and `mkcls`(A):2 respectively.

Training and self-normalization details were identical to those for the NNJM. Perpexity on the development set was 10.41.

3.2 Fallback Russian lemma phrase table

To augment source coverage, we used an additional phrase table trained on source lemmas in a similar fashion to the regular phrase table described in Section 2.2. We combined the two tables statically prior to decoding, into a single table with non-lemmatized source phrases. For a given source text and its lemmatized version, we first create an expansion phrase table with an entry for each source phrase in the text whose lemmatized form is present in the lemmatized phrase table. The target phrase and scores for the entry are obtained from the lemmatized table; that is, entries for different surface forms of the same lemma will have identical scores in the expansion table. We then linearly interpolate the regular and expansion tables, using epsilon probabilities for missing entries, and a weight of 0.9 on the regular table.[1] The combined table is used in a standard way during decoding.

3.3 Transliteration

We transliterated the lemmatized forms of all Russian words whose surface forms are out-of-vocabulary, regardless of whether their lemmatized forms occurred in either the standard or the lemmatized phrase tables. Transliterations were encoded as translation rules with multiple scored alternatives, similar to the approach found to be optimal by Durrani et al. (2014). We experimented with letting transliterations compete with translations of lemmatized forms from the phrase table when available, but found that using only the transliteration rules for OOVs resulted in slightly higher BLEU scores.

Transliterations were produced by two versions of our Portage PBMT system trained to map Cyrillic character sequences into Latin ones. Words containing more than 2 characters, all of which were either alphabetic or hyphens, and at least one of which was non-ASCII, were transliterated with a standard system; others (about 20% of OOVs) were transliterated using a backoff system.

The standard transliteration system was trained on parallel corpora consisting of the *wiki-guessed-names* and *wiki-guessed-patronymic-names* corpora,[2] with first and last names split into separate entries; and additionally on 200K transliterated word pairs mined from the parallel corpora as described below. Two character 6-gram language models were trained on all word types from the English side of the parallel corpora, and from the English Gigaword. The standard system used KN smoothing for phrase probabilities and an indica-

System	5 runs ave.		best run
	dev	test	
word-aligned baseline	35.3	28.0	28.1
lemma-aligned baseline	35.3	28.2	28.3
+ lemma NNJM	36.1	28.7	28.8
+ word NNJM	36.3	28.8	28.8
+ NNLTM	36.3	28.8	28.9
+ fallback lemma table	36.8	29.1	29.2
+ transliteration	37.0	29.2	29.3
+ rescoring	–	–	29.7

Table 1: Selected results from our development experiments.

tor feature on phrase pairs from the mined corpus.

The backoff system was intended to enforce a more literal style of transliteration appropriate for non-words. It was trained only on the *guessed-*names* corpora, with a phrase length limit of 3 and a restriction to monotonic translation.

We used a semi-supervised approach to mine transliterated word pairs from the parallel corpora, loosely modeled on the work of Sajjad et al. (2012). We first extracted candidate pairs from one-to-one word alignments where both words were longer than 2 characters and contained only alphabetic characters. Next we scored each candidate pair e, f using the formula $\log p(e|f) + \log p(f|e) - \log p_n(e, f)$, where $p(e|f)$ and $p(f|e)$ are probabilities from (character-wise) HMM models trained on the *guessed-*names* corpora, and $p_n(e, f) = p_n(e)p_n(f)$ is a character unigram model. Finally, we ranked all candidates by descending score and retained the top 200K.

4 Development Experiments

We carried out a large number of development experiments throughout the design of this system, using the data conditions described in Section 2.1, with the WMT 2014 test set as our tuning set (dev), and the WMT 2015 test set as our test set. We monitored uncased BLEU on a system-tokenized version of the test set, reporting the average and the best of 5 random tuning replications.

Table 1 provides some selected results from these experiments and table 2 shows an example of how the different components improve the translation quality. The word baseline reflects a system with standard phrase-based features, reordering models, sparse features, monolingual language models and an uninterpolated phrase table. The

---

[1] We experimented with log-linear and backoff combinations, but these did not perform as well.

[2] Both corpora are provided as part of the official WMT 2016 Russia-to-English training data.

input	полиция карраты предъявила 20-летнему мужчине обвинение в отказе остановиться и опасном вождении .
reference	karratha police have charged a 20-year-old man with failing to stop and reckless driving .
word-aligned baseline	police charge man in 20-years punching карраты refusing to stop and dangerous driving .
lemma-aligned baseline	police charged карраты 20-years man indicted in refusing to stop and dangerous driving .
+ neural components	police charged карраты 20-years man charged with refusing to stop and dangerous driving .
+ OOV handling	karratha police charged a 20-year-old man accused of refusing to stop and dangerous driving .
+ rescoring	karratha police have charged a 20-year-old man accused of refusing to stop and dangerous driving .

Table 2: Example that shows significant improvements by using lemma alignments, adding neural components (i.e. 2NNJMs and NNLTM), adding OOV handling (i.e. fallback lemma table and transliteration) and rescoring.

alignment for all components in this word baseline is based on the surface form of the Russian word. We then replace the word alignment for all components with lemma alignment to form the lemma baseline. We then add the neural components, the fallback lemma table and the transliteration component. The rescoring step is only done on the best model as the final step before recasing and detokenizing.

Given such a strong lemma baseline, the biggest impact comes from the addition of the first NNJM. The next largest jump comes from the fallback Russian lemma phrase table, which also improved our OOV rate considerably. We were pleasantly surprised to see the transliteration component helping to the extent that it does. These sorts of point-wise vocabulary improvements do not always have a visible impact on BLEU. We are optimistic that its impact will be even more pronounced in the human evaluation.

5 Conclusion

We have presented the NRC submission to the WMT 2016 Russian-English news translation task. The key contributions of our system include 1) using Russian lemmas to improve word alignment while using the original Russian words to preserve case information in different models; 2) the incorporation of NNJMs and NNLTM; 3) a fallback Russian lemma phrase table for Russian OOVs and 4) a semi-supervised transliteration model built on a seed corpus mined from

the standard parallel training data. Our system achieved the highest uncased BLEU, the second highest cased BLEU and the lowest TER scores among the eight participants in WMT 2016, and ranked third out of ten systems in the human evaluation.

References

Colin Cherry and George Foster. 2012. Batch Tuning Strategies for Statistical Machine Translation. In *Proc. 2012 Conf. of the N. American Chapter of the Association for Computational Linguistics: Human Language Technologies*, pages 427–436, Montréal, Canada.

Colin Cherry. 2013. Improved reordering for phrase-based translation using sparse features. In *Proceedings of NAACL HLT 2013*.

Jacob Devlin, Rabih Zbib, Zhongqiang Huang, Thomas Lamar, Richard Schwartz, and John Makhoul. 2014. Fast and robust neural network joint models for statistical machine translation. In *Proceedings of the Annual Meeting of the Association for Computational Linguistics*, pages 1370–1380, Baltimore, Maryland, June.

Nadir Durrani, Hassan Sajjad, Hieu Hoang, and Philipp Koehn. 2014. Integrating an unsupervised transliteration model into statistical machine translation. In *EACL*, pages 148–153.

Ahmed El Kholy and Nizar Habash. 2012. Orthographic and morphological processing for english–arabic statistical machine translation. *Machine Translation*, 26(1):25–45.

George Foster, Boxing Chen, Eric Joanis, Howard Johnson, Roland Kuhn, and Samuel Larkin. 2009. PORTAGE in the NIST 2009 MT Evaluation. *Technical report, NRC-CNRC.*

Mark Hopkins and Jonathan May. 2011. Tuning as ranking. In *Proceedings of the Conference on Empirical Methods in Natural Language Processing*, pages 1352–1362. Association for Computational Linguistics.

Liang Huang and David Chiang. 2007. Forest Rescoring: Faster Decoding with Integrated Language Models. In *Proc. 45th Annual Meeting of the Assoc. for Comp. Linguistics*, pages 144–151, Prague, Czech Republic.

Samuel Larkin, Boxing Chen, George Foster, Uli Germann, Eric Joanis, J. Howard Johnson, and Roland Kuhn. 2010. Lessons from NRC's portage system at WMT 2010. In *5th Workshop on Statistical Machine Translation.*

Franz Josef Och, Daniel Gildea, Sanjeev Khudanpur, Anoop Sarkar, Kenji Yamada, Alexander M Fraser, Shankar Kumar, Libin Shen, David Smith, Katherine Eng, Viren Jain, Zhen Jin, and Radev Dragomir. 2004. A smorgasbord of features for statistical machine translation. In *Proceedings of the Human Language Technology Conference of the North American Chapter of the Association for Computational Linguistics: HLT-NAACL 2004*, pages 161–168.

Franz Josef Och. 1999. An efficient method for determining bilingual word classes. In *Proceedings of the Conference of the European Chapter of the Association for Computational Linguistics (EACL).*

Hassan Sajjad, Alexander Fraser, and Helmut Schmid. 2012. A statistical model for unsupervised and semi-supervised transliteration mining. In *Proceedings of the 50th Annual Meeting of the Association for Computational Linguistics: Long Papers-Volume 1*, pages 469–477. Association for Computational Linguistics.

Ilya Segalovich. 2003. A fast morphological algorithm with unknown word guessing induced by a dictionary for a web search engine. In *Proc. of MLMTA-2003*, Las Vegas, US.

Darlene Stewart, Roland Kuhn, Eric Joanis, and George Foster. 2014. Coarse "split and lump" bilingual language models for richer source information in SMT. In *Proceedings of the Eleventh Conference of the Association for Machine Translation in the Americas (AMTA)*, volume 1, pages 28–41.

Ashish Vaswani, Yinggong Zhao, Victoria Fossum, and David Chiang. 2013. Decoding with large-scale neural language models improves translation. In *Proceedings of the 2013 Conference on Empirical Methods in Natural Language Processing (EMNLP 2013)*, pages 1387–1392.

Merged bilingual trees based on Universal Dependencies in Machine Translation

David Mareček

Institute of Formal and Applied Linguistics
Faculty of Mathematics and Physics, Charles University in Prague
Malostranské náměstí 25, 118 00 Prague, Czech Republic
`marecek@ufal.mff.cuni.cz`

Abstract

In this paper, we present our new experimental system of merging dependency representations of two parallel sentences into one dependency tree. All the inner nodes in dependency tree represent source-target pairs of words, the extra words are in form of leaf nodes. We use Universal Dependencies annotation style, in which the function words, whose usage often differs between languages, are annotated as leaves. The parallel treebank is parsed in minimally supervised way. Unaligned words are there automatically pushed to leaves. We present a simple translation system trained on such merged trees and evaluate it in WMT 2016 English-to-Czech and Czech-to-English translation task. Even though the model is so far very simple and no language model and word-reordering model were used, the Czech-to-English variant reached similar BLEU score as another established tree-based system.

1 Introduction

Tree-based machine translation systems (Chiang et al., 2005; Dušek et al., 2012; Sennrich and Haddow, 2015) are alternatives to the leading phrase-based MT systems (Koehn et al., 2007) and newly very progressive neural MT systems (Bahdanau et al., 2015). Our approach aims to produce bilingual dependency trees, in which both source and target sentences are encoded together. We adapt the Universal Dependencies annotation style (Nivre et al., 2016), in which the functional words[1] are in

---

[1] Functional words are determiners, prepositions, conjunctions, auxiliary verbs, particles, etc.

the leaf nodes and therefore the grammatical differences between the languages does not much affect the common dependency structure. We were partially inspired by the Stochastic inversion transduction grammars (Wu, 1997).

Our *merged dependency trees* are defined in Section 2. The data we use and necessary preprocessing is in Section 3. The merging algorithm itself, which merges two parallel sentences into one, is described in Section 4. Section 5 presents the minimally supervised parsing of the merged sentences. The experimental translation system using the merged trees is described in Section 6. Finally, we present our results (Section 7) and conclusions (Section 8).

2 Merged trees

We introduce "merged trees", where parallel sentences from two languages are represented by a single dependency tree. Each node of the tree consists of two word-forms and two POS tags. An example of such merged dependency tree is in Figure 3. If two words are translations of each other (1-1 alignment), they share one node labeled by both of them. Words that do not have their counterparts in the other sentence (1-0 or 0-1 alignment) are also represented by nodes and the missing counterpart is marked by label <empty>. All such nodes representing a single word without any counterpart are leaf nodes. This ensures that the merged tree structure can be simply divided into two monolingual trees, not including empty nodes. The two separated trees are also "internally" isomorfic, the only differences are in leaves.

The annotation style of Universal Dependencies is suitable for the merged tree structures, since majority of function words are annotated as leaves there. Function words are the ones which often cannot be translated as one-to-one. For example,

Proceedings of the First Conference on Machine Translation, Volume 2: Shared Task Papers, pages 333–338,
Berlin, Germany, August 11-12, 2016. ©2016 Association for Computational Linguistics

ADJ	adjective	PART	particle
ADP	adposition	PRON	pronoun
ADV	adverb	PROPN	proper noun
AUX	auxiliary verb	PUNCT	punctuation
CONJ	coord. conj.	SCONJ	subord. conj.
DET	determiner	SYM	symbol
INTJ	interjection	VERB	verb
NOUN	noun	X	other
NUM	numeral		

Table 1: List of part-of-speech tags used in Universal Dependencies annotation style.

prepositions in one languages can be translated as different noun suffixes in another one. Some languages use determiners, some not. Auxiliary verbs are also used differently across languages.

3 Data

The parallel data we use in the experiments is the training part of the Czech-English parallel corpus CzEng 1.0 (Bojar et al., 2012). It consists of more than 15 million sentences, 206 million tokens on the Czech side and 232 million tokens on the English side. We extract the parallel sentences with original tokenization from the CzEng export-format together with the part-of-speech (POS) tags and the word alignment.

The original CzEng POS tags, Prague Dependency Treebank tags (Hajič et al., 2006) for Czech and Penn Treebank tags (Marcus et al., 1993) for English, are mapped to the universal POS tagset developed for Universal Dependencies (Nivre et al., 2016). The simple 1-to-1 mapping was taken from the GitHub repository.[2] The POS tags used in Universal Dependencies POS are listed in Table 1.

4 Merging algorithm

Parallel sentences tagged by the universal POS tags are then merged together using the algorithm in Figure 1. We describe the algorithm for the English-to-Czech translation, even though the procedure is generally language universal.

The algorithm uses two unidirectional alignments, which we call *en2csAlign* and *cs2enAlign*. For each English word, the *en2csAlign* defines its counterpart in the Czech sentence. The *cs2enAlign* defined the English counterpart for each Czech

Input: enF, enT, csF, csT: arrays of forms and tags of the English and Czech sentence
Input: $en2csAlign, cs2enAlign$: unidirectional alignment links between English and Czech
Output: $mrgF, mrgT$: arrays of form and tags of the merged sentence

$k = 0$;
foreach $i \in \{1, \cdots, |enF|\}$ **do**
    $used = 0$;
    foreach $j \in \{1, \cdots, |csF|\}$ **do**
        if $cs2enAlign[i] \neq j$ **then continue**;
        k++;
        if $en2csAlign[j] = i$ **then**
            $mrgF[k] = enF[i] + \text{'\_'} + csF[j]$;
            $mrgT[k] = enT[i] + \text{'\_'} + csT[j]$;
            $used = 1$;
        else
            $mrgF[k] = \text{'<empty>\_'} + csF[j]$;
            $mrgT[k] = \text{'<empty>\_'} + csT[j]$;
        end
    end
    if $used = 0$ **then**
        k++;
        $mrgF[k] = enF[i] + \text{'\_<empty>'}$;
        $mrgT[k] = enT[i] + \text{'\_<empty>'}$;
    end
end
return $mrgF, mrgT$;

Figure 1: Merging algorithm pseudocode.

word.[3] These alignment links are direct outputs from GIZA++ word-alignment tool (Och and Ney, 2003) before symmetrization.

The algorithm traverses through the source sentence and for each word, it collects all its target counterparts using the *cs2enAlign*[4] The Czech word, where the *cs2enAlign* and *en2csAlign* intersect, creates the word pair with the English one. The other Czech words stay alone and are completed with the $<empty>$ label. If there is no intersection counterpart for the English word, it is also completed with the $<empty>$ label.

Figure 2 shows one example of merging. The pairs of words connected by both *cs2enAlign*

---

[2] https://github.com/UniversalDependencies

[3] In CzEng corpus export format, these alignments are called *ali_there* and *ali_back*, sometimes they are also called *left* and *right* alignments.

[4] Since we search for all the Czech words that are aligned to the English one, we need the *cs2enAlign*.

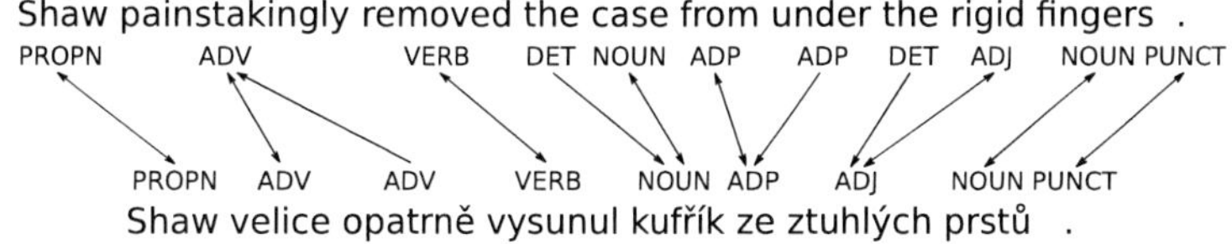

Figure 2: Example of merging English and Czech sentence together with the Universal Dependencies POS tags. Alignment links are depicted by arrows. Bidirectional arrows represent the intersection connections.

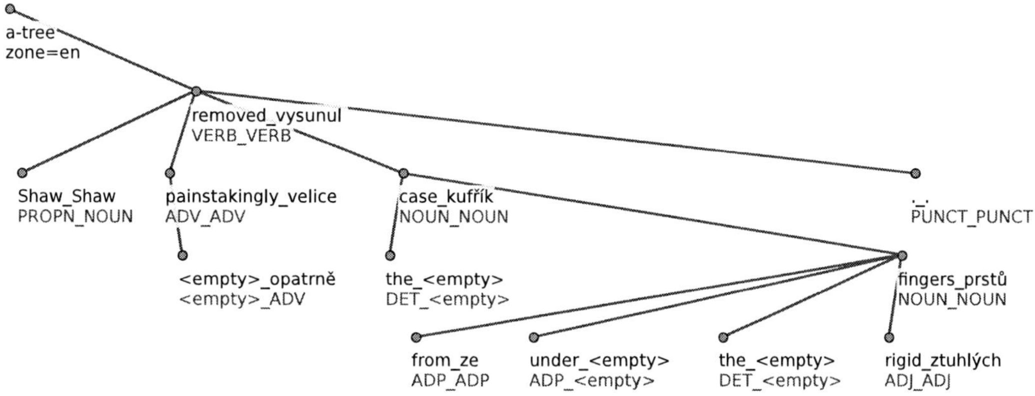

Figure 3: Example of English-Czech merged tree. The same sentence as in Figure 2 is shown.

and *en2csAlign* links are paired together into one word, their POS tags are paired in the same way. The words without intersection counterparts are paired with <empty> words or <empty> POS tags respectively. The tokens in the merged sentence are ordered primarily according to the English sentence. The Czech words with <empty> counterparts are together with Czech words aligned with the same English word. Globally, the Czech word order cannot be preserved due to crossing intersection alignment links, which is a quite common phenomenon.

5   Minimally Supervised Parallel Parsing

For parsing the merged sentences, we use the Unsupervised Dependency Parser (UDP) implemented by Mareček and Straka (2013). The source code is freely available,[5] and it includes a mech-

anism how to import external probabilities. The UDP is based on Dependency Model with Valence, a generative model which consists of two sub-models:

- Stop model $p_{stop}(\cdot|t_g, dir)$ represents probability of not generating another dependent in direction dir to a node with POS tag t_g. The direction dir can be left or right. If $p_{stop} = 1$, the node with the tag t_g cannot have any dependent in direction dir. If it is 1 in both directions, the node is a leaf.

- Attach model $p_{attach}(t_d|t_g, dir)$ represents probability that the dependent of the node with POS tag t_g in direction dir is labeled with POS tag t_d.

In other words, the *stop* model generates edges, while the *attach* model generates POS tags for the

---

[5] http://ufal.mff.cuni.cz/udp

ADP, ADV, AUX, CONJ, DET, PART, PRON, PUNCT, SCONJ, <empty>	1.0
ADJ, INTJ, SYM	0.7
NOUN, PROPN, NUM, X	0.4
else	0.1

Table 2: Stop probabilities priors set for individual POS tags.

new nodes. The inference is done using blocked Gibbs sampling (Gilks et al., 1996).

During the inference, the *attach* and the *stop* probabilities can be combined linearly with external prior probabilities p^{ext}:

$$p_{stop}^{final} = (1 - \lambda_{stop}) \cdot p_{stop} + \lambda_{stop} \cdot p_{stop}^{ext},$$

$$p_{attach}^{final} = (1 - \lambda_{atach}) \cdot p_{attach} + \lambda_{attach} \cdot p_{attach}^{ext},$$

where the parameters λ define their weights. In the original paper (Mareček and Straka, 2013), the external priors p_{stop}^{ext} were computed based on the reducibility principle on big raw corpora.

We use the external prior probabilities to define grammatical rules for POS tags based on UD annotation style. Our rules simply describe how likely a node with a particular POS is a leaf. In case of the merged trees there is a pair of POS tags in each node. We manually set the p_{stop}^{ext} for the POS tags pairs as listed in Table 2. In case the two POS tags in one node have different p_{stop}^{ext}, we take the higher one. For example, for the pair ADP_VERB, we set its prior stop probability to 1.0 (as to the tag ADP), even though the tag VERB should get 0.1.

It is possible to define different left and right p_{stop}^{ext} priors, however, we decided to set it equally for both the directions, since it is linguistically more language independent.

Example of a merged dependency tree is shown in Figure 3.

6 Our Simple Machine Translation System

Our simple translation system based on the merged-trees has the following 3 steps:

- **training:** We go through the training merged trees and compute so called *tree-n-gram* counts. The *tree-n-grams* are n-grams with added parent and children words into context.

- **parsing:** We parse the input data using a parser trained on the source parts of the merged-trees.

- **decoding:** We use the tree-n-gram counts to predict the most probable translation of each source tree.

In the training phase, we traverse the training merged-trees and collect the tree-n-gram counts. Besides looking on the previous and following words, we look also on the parent words. In the training and decoding phase, we work only with word forms, not with the POS tags. We denote w_i the i-th node in the merged tree and p_i its parent. The previous and following word are w_{i-1} and w_{i+1} respectively. We collect only the source words tree-n-gram counts. Their types are listed in Table 3.

1.	$count(w_{i-1}, w_i, w_{i+1})$
2.	$count(w_i, p_i, w_i + 1)$
3.	$count(w_i, p_i, w_{i-1})$
4.	$count(w_i, w_{i+1})$
5.	$count(w_i, w_{i-1})$
6.	$count(w_i, p_i)$
7.	$count(w_i)$

Table 3: Tree-n-gram types collected.

For each node, we also define full target translation, which consist of the target (in our case Czech) form of the node together with target forms of all child nodes with <empty> source (English) form. For example, in Figure 3, the full Czech translation of the node "*painstakingly_velice*" is not only the word "*velice*", but two words "*velice opatrně*".

The parsing phase is necessary to get monolingual tree for sentences we need to translate. Since the merged trees preserves the word ordering of the source sentences (English), we can be simply separate single English dependency trees from the merged trees. We train the MST parser (McDonald et al., 2005) on the separated source (English) trees. The parser is then used to parse the input sentences for translation.

In the decoding step, we translate the parsed source (English) tree into target (Czech) sentence. For each the source node, we go through the tree-n-gram list, from the largest n-gram to the single unigram (according to Table 3) and see, whether it

language pair	BLEU	BLEU cased
English-to-Czech	9.5	8.3
Czech-to-English	15.6	13.2

Table 4: Our system BLEU scores.

appears in the training data more than once[6]. If it is there, we translate the node by the most frequent Czech translation found in the training data. If not, we continue to the next type of n-gram until we find n-gram which appear in the training data more than once. If we end up with single unigram, it is enough if it appears once in the training data and we use its translation. In case the English word is out-of-vocabulary, we do not translate it and use the same form for Czech translation.

Note, that the Czech translation of a node can be more words or no word (in case the English word appears most frequently with the <empty> label).

When the whole dependency tree is translated, we simply project the tree into linear sentence by depth-first algorithm.

7 Results

We tested our translation system in WMT2016 News translation task on English-to-Czech and Czech-to-English language pairs. The BLEU scores (Papineni et al., 2002) are shown in Table 4. Both scores are quite low compared to the best translation systems reaching more 25 or 30 BLEU points respectively. However, for the Czech-to-English direction, the results are comparable with the established tree-based system TectoMT (Mareček et al., 2010; Dušek et al., 2012), which has 14.6 BLEU points and 13.6 BLEU points for the cased variant.

Our system is still under development. This is the first attempt to employ the merged trees in machine translation. So far, it does not use any language modelling or word reordering. The fact that not-aligned words are treated as function words can cause shorter translations with missing content words. All such shortcomings are planned to be solved in future work.

8 Conclusions

We presented the *merged trees*, bilingual dependency trees in Universal Dependencies style

---

[6]We do not use n-grams whose appear only once in the training data. We translate the node using a smaller n-gram instead

parsed by minimally supervised way. The main purpose of such trees is to help in machine translation. We showed very simple translation system and evaluated it WMT 2016 News translation task.

In future work, we will work on improving the system. We plan to employ machine learning, beam-search and language modelling to approach the better MT systems.

Acknowledgments

This work was supported by the grant 14-06548P of the Czech Science Foundation and the 7th Framework Programme of the EU grant QTLeap (No. 610516).

References

Dzmitry Bahdanau, Kyunghyun Cho, and Yoshua Bengio. 2015. Neural machine translation by jointly learning to align and translate. In *Proceedings of ICLR*.

Ondřej Bojar, Zdeněk Žabokrtský, Ondřej Dušek, Petra Galuščáková, Martin Majliš, David Mareček, Jiří Maršík, Michal Novák, Martin Popel, and Aleš Tamchyna. 2012. The Joy of Parallelism with CzEng 1.0. In *Proceedings of LREC2012*, Istanbul, Turkey, May. ELRA, European Language Resources Association.

David Chiang, Adam Lopez, Nitin Madnani, Christof Monz, Philip Resnik, and Michael Subotin. 2005. The Hiero Machine Translation System: Extensions, Evaluation, and Analysis. In *Proceedings of the Conference on Human Language Technology and Empirical Methods in Natural Language Processing*, HLT '05, pages 779–786, Stroudsburg, PA, USA. Association for Computational Linguistics.

Ondřej Dušek, Zdeněk Žabokrtský, Martin Popel, Martin Majliš, Michal Novák, and David Mareček. 2012. Formemes in English-Czech Deep Syntactic MT. In *Proceedings of the Seventh Workshop on Statistical Machine Translation*, WMT '12, pages 267–274, Stroudsburg, PA, USA. Association for Computational Linguistics.

Walter R. Gilks, S. Richardson, and David J. Spiegelhalter. 1996. *Markov chain Monte Carlo in practice*. Interdisciplinary statistics. Chapman & Hall.

Jan Hajič, Eva Hajičová, Jarmila Panevová, Petr Sgall, Petr Pajas, Jan Štěpánek, Jiří Havelka, and Marie Mikulová. 2006. Prague Dependency Treebank 2.0. CD-ROM, Linguistic Data Consortium, LDC Catalog No.: LDC2006T01, Philadelphia.

Philipp Koehn, Hieu Hoang, Alexandra Birch, Chris Callison-Burch, Marcello Federico, Nicola Bertoldi, Brooke Cowan, Wade Shen, Christine Moran,

Richard Zens, Chris Dyer, Ondřej Bojar, Alexandra Constantin, and Evan Herbst. 2007. Moses: Open Source Toolkit for Statistical Machine Translation. In *ACL 2007, Proceedings of the 45th Annual Meeting of the Association for Computational Linguistics Companion Volume Proceedings of the Demo and Poster Sessions*, pages 177–180, Prague, Czech Republic, June. Association for Computational Linguistics.

Mitchell P. Marcus, Mary Ann Marcinkiewicz, and Beatrice Santorini. 1993. Building a Large Annotated Corpus of English: The Penn Treebank. *Comput. Linguist.*, 19(2):313–330.

D. Mareček, M. Popel, and Z. Žabokrtský. 2010. Maximum entropy translation model in dependency-based MT framework. In *Proceedings of the Joint Fifth Workshop on Statistical Machine Translation and Metrics (MATR)*, pages 201–206. Association for Computational Linguistics.

David Mareček and Milan Straka. 2013. Stop-probability estimates computed on a large corpus improve Unsupervised Dependency Parsing. In *Proceedings of the 51st Annual Meeting of the Association for Computational Linguistics (Volume 1: Long Papers)*, pages 281–290, Sofia, Bulgaria, August. Association for Computational Linguistics.

Ryan McDonald, Fernando Pereira, Kiril Ribarov, and Jan Hajič. 2005. Non-Projective Dependency Parsing using Spanning Tree Algorithms. In *Proceedings of Human Langauge Technology Conference and Conference on Empirical Methods in Natural Language Processing (HTL/EMNLP)*, pages 523–530, Vancouver, BC, Canada.

Joakim Nivre, Marie-Catherine de Marneffe, Filip Ginter, Yoav Goldberg, Jan Hajič, Christopher Manning, Ryan McDonald, Slav Petrov, Sampo Pyysalo, Natalia Silveira, Reut Tsarfaty, and Daniel Zeman. 2016. Universal Dependencies v1: A Multilingual Treebank Collection. In *Proceedings of the 10th International Conference on Language Resources and Evaluation (LREC 2016)*, Portorož, Slovenia. European Language Resources Association.

Franz Josef Och and Hermann Ney. 2003. A Systematic Comparison of Various Statistical Alignment Models. *Computational Linguistics*, 29(1):19–51.

Kishore Papineni, Salim Roukos, Todd Ward, and Wei-Jing Zhu. 2002. BLEU: A Method for Automatic Evaluation of Machine Translation. In *Proceedings of the 40th Annual Meeting on Association for Computational Linguistics*, ACL '02, pages 311–318, Stroudsburg, PA, USA. Association for Computational Linguistics.

Rico Sennrich and Barry Haddow. 2015. A Joint Dependency Model of Morphological and Syntactic Structure for Statistical Machine Translation. In *Proceedings of the 2015 Conference on Empirical Methods in Natural Language Processing*, pages 2081–2087, Lisbon, Portugal, September. Association for Computational Linguistics.

Dekai Wu. 1997. Stochastic Inversion Transduction Grammars and Bilingual Parsing of Parallel Corpora. *Computational Linguistics*, 23(3):377–403.

PROMT Translation Systems for WMT 2016 Translation Tasks

Alexander Molchanov, Fedor Bykov
PROMT LLC
17E Uralskaya str. building 3, 199155,
St. Petersburg, Russia
`firstname.lastname@promt.ru`

Abstract

This paper provides an overview of the
PROMT submissions for the WMT16
Shared Translation Tasks. We participated
in seven language pairs with three different system configurations (rule-based, statistical and hybrid). We describe the architecture of the three configurations. We
show that fast and accurate customization
of the rule-based system can increase the
BLEU scores significantly.

1 Introduction

This paper presents the PROMT systems submitted for the Shared Translation Task of WMT16.
We participated in seven language pairs with
three different types of systems: English-
Russian, Russian-English, English-German (Rule-
based systems); Finnish-English, Turkish-English
(Statistical systems); English-Spanish, English-
Portuguese (Hybrid systems). The paper is organized as follows. In Section 1, we briefly outline
the three types of our systems and their features.
In Section 2, we describe the experimental setups
and the training data and present the results. Finally, Section 3 concludes the paper.

2 Systems Overview

2.1 RBMT System

The PROMT rule-based machine translation
(RBMT) System is a mature machine translation
system with huge linguistic structured databases
containing morphological, lexical and syntactic
features for the English, German, French, Spanish, Italian, Portuguese and Russian languages.

2.2 SMT System

Basic components

The PROMT SMT system is based on the Moses
open-source toolkit (Koehn et al., 2007). We use
MGIZA (Gao and Vogel, 2008) to generate word
alignments. We build the phrase tables and lexical reordering tables using the Moses toolkit. The
IRSTLM toolkit (Federico et al., 2008) is used
to build language models, which are scored using
KenLM (Heafield, 2011) in the decoding process.
We use ZMERT (Zaidan, 2009) for weights optimization. We use a complex recaser combining
a Moses-based recasing model and in-house rule-
based algorithms based on source text information
and word alignments.

Text preprocessing

We have a standard procedure for preprocessing
and filtering parallel data, which includes removing too long sentences, discarding sentence pairs
with significant length ratios etc. Text data is tokenized with in-house tokenizers and lowercased
before generating word alignments.

Processing Named Entities

The in-house Named Entities (NEs) Recognition
module allows to extract and process multiple
types of entities including personal and company
names, phone numbers, e-mails, dates etc. The
numeric elements of NEs are replaced with placeholders in training data. We use XML markup for
NEs and preserve the original values for numeric
elements during decoding.

2.3 Hybrid System

The PROMT Hybrid system is based on three
components: the RBMT module, the RBMT post-
processor and the statistical post-editing (SPE)
module. Text translation is performed as follows.
First, the RBMT module translates the source text

Proceedings of the First Conference on Machine Translation, Volume 2: Shared Task Papers, pages 339–343,
Berlin, Germany, August 11-12, 2016. ©2016 Association for Computational Linguistics

and outputs a complex structure containing the translation and its linguistic features (morphological and syntactic information, extracted named entities etc.). Second, the RBMT postprocessor generates XML based on the output of the RBMT module. Finally, the XML is fed to the SPE module which generates the output translation. The SPE module is basically a SMT system built on a parallel corpus of RBMT translations and their human references as described in (Simard et al., 2007). The SPE technique allows us to 1) handle systematic RBMT errors which are hard to deal with algorithmically; 2) fast and effectively adapt a translation system to a specific domain.

3 Experimental settings and results

In this section, we describe the experimental settings and report the results.

3.1 RBMT System

In this Section, we describe the RBMT submissions for English-Russian-English (News Task) and for English-German (News and IT Tasks).

Data

We used the News Commentary v11 and the Wiki Headlines parallel corpora to tune the system for the News Task. The batch 1 and batch2 sets from WMT16 training data were used for the English-German system for the IT Task.

RBMT system tuning

We have a semi-supervised technique for tuning the RBMT system. The technique is based on using the PROMT parsers. We use the following pipeline. We extract and build frequency lists of various types of NEs, out-of-vocabulary words (OOVs) and syntactic constructions. We analyze the most frequent units using human linguistic expertise. We modify the system by adding, removing or changing the values for the linguistic features of the system database elements. As a result, we obtain a system tuned for a specific text domain.

Results

Table 1 shows the BLEU scores (Papineni et al., 2002) for the baseline and the tuned RBMT systems for different language pairs measured on the newstest2016 test set and the batch3 test set for the IT Task. The huge difference between the base-

Language pair	Baseline	Tuned
en-ru	19,9	22,6
ru-en	20,29	21,21
en-de (News)	19,57	22,62
en-de (IT)	30,62	40,3

Table 1: Results for the RBMT submissions.

line and the tuned configuration for the English-German system (IT Task) is explained mostly by the fact that we use specific in-domain databases for IT.

3.2 SMT System

In this Section, we describe the SMT submissions for Turkish-English (News Task) and Finish-English (News Task).

Turkish-English

Data We used all Opus (Tiedemann, 2012) data and company private parallel data (which consists mostly of crawled and aligned texts from different news web-sites). The Subtitles were preprocessed as follows: 1) we built a list of unique source sentences with all corresponding target sentences, for each source sentence we selected the most frequent target sentence (this helped us to get rid of most noisy data); 2) the selected data was filtered using in-house language recognition tool; 3) target data was filtered using a language model built on 2014, 2015 news texts corpora from statmt.org. Table 2 shows the statistics regarding the parallel training data (note that statistics for OPUS do not include Subtitles as they are presented separately).

Corpus	#word S (M)	#word T (M)
Opus	47,2	36,9
Subtitles	291,9	274,8
Private data	2,9	2,7
Overall	342	314,4

Table 2: Parallel data statistics for the Turkish-English system for the source (S) and the target (T) sides. #words is in millions (M).

A 3-gram language model was built on 2014, 2015 news texts corpora from statmt.org. We used randomly selected sentence pairs from Tatoeba and TED corpora (4000 sentence pairs) and the whole newsdev2016 development set for tuning.

Morphological preprocessing Turkish is a highly agglutinative language with complex morphology. A common technique to reduce data sparseness and produce better word alignments is morphological segmentation of the Turkish side of parallel data (Bisazza and Federico, 2009). We apply this technique to our training data using the Nuve[1] morphological analyzer . We split off 32 types of affixes (one of them is removed from source text as it is not expected to have English counterparts). The source vocabulary size reduced substantially (2.3 to 1.8 million units). We do not yet perform the disambiguation, so we split words in every case when we have an analysis variant which contains affixes described in our segmentation rules.

OOVs We use the Nuve built-in stemmer to process OOVs. The technique is quite simple. The SMT model uses two phrase-tables: the primary table and the back-off table used to translate OOVs. The back-off table consists of the primary table vocabulary stems with several translations selected by a certain direct probability threshold. An OOV is stemmed and retranslated during decoding.

Finnish-English

Data The 2016 system is based on the existing PROMT 2015 system. The 2015 system uses OPUS data (except IT documentation corpora and Subtitles) and company private parallel data (which consists mostly of crawled and aligned texts from different news web-sites). We added the Subtitles corpus to the training data for the 2016 system. The subtitles were preprocessed in the same way as for the Turkish-English system except that we used a higher threshold when filtering the texts with the news language model. Table 3 shows the statistics regarding the parallel training data.

Corpus	#word S (M)	#word T (M)
Opus	274,1	192
Subtitles	100,2	95,6
Private data	2,8	3,3
Overall	377,1	290,9

Table 3: Parallel data statistics for the Finnish-English system for the source (S) and the target (T) sides. #words is in millions (M).

---

[1] https://github.com/hrzafer/nuve

We used the language model built for the Turkish-English system. The newsdev2015 and newstest2015 sets were used for tuning.

OOVs We use the NLTK (Loper and Bird, 2002) implementation of the Snowball stemming algorithm (Porter, 1980) and the in-house splitter for compound words based on the algorithm described in (Koehn and Knight, 2003). The procedure for processing OOVs is pretty much the same as for the Turkish-English system, but with the additional step of splitting compound words which are not present in the back-off phrase-table.

Results

The BLEU scores for the Finnish-English and the Turkish-English experiments are reported in Tables 4 and 5 respectively.

System	BLEU
2015 system	19,88
2016 system	21,05
2016 system+UNK	21,21

Table 4: Results for the Finnish-English SMT submissions. UNK stands for using the unknown words processing technique.

System	BLEU
baseline	14,69
baseline+morph. segmentation	14,77
baseline+morph. segmentation+UNK	14,85

Table 5: Results for the Turkish-English SMT submissions.

We did not perform the significance tests for the scores difference between system configurations. However, the difference between the Turkish-English models with and without morphological segmentation seems to be insignificant. This may be due to the absence of a disambiguation algorithm (our splitting technique may be improving and worsening the translation at the same time). We will see to that in future.

3.3 Hybrid System

In this Section, we describe the Hybryd submissions for English-Spanish (IT Task) and English-Portuguese (IT Task).

Data

We built two systems for each language pair: the baseline (built only on WMT16 IT Task data) and the improved system (WMT16 IT Task data with in-house IT documentation data). For the baseline system, we used the data as is. The target side of the private data for the improved system was filtered using a language model built on batch1 and batch2 development sets. 5% and 6.5% of the data were discarded for the English-Spanish and the English-Portuguese systems respectively. The discarded data is mostly some junk with residual html formatting. We also normalized the target data for English-Portuguese by converting the orthography for 50 most common words from Brazilian to Portuguese language variety. The filtered private data used for training amounts to 51,4 million tokens for Spanish and 29,7 million tokens for Portuguese. The language models for the systems were built on all target data. The batch1 and batch2 development sets were used for tuning the SPE module.

Results

The BLEU scores for both experiments are reported in Table 6. It is worthy to mention the sub-

Language pair	System		
	rbmt	hybrid (baseline)	hybrid (improved)
en-sp	32,0	37,6	42,7
en-pt	27,2	32,0	32,7

Table 6: Results for the hybrid submissions.

stantial difference between the English-Spanish and English-Portuguese results when comparing the baseline and improved hybrid systems. The difference between the training data size is not drastically significant whereas the difference in BLEU scores is. This may be due to the quality of our Portuguese data. We will examine this question in future.

4 Conclusions and future work

We have described the different approaches that we used for our participation in the WMT16 Shared Translation Task. Using different approaches to machine translation allows us to perform competitively in all language pairs. We describe the fast semi-supervised RBMT system customization technique which is effective in terms of BLEU. We plan to research the disambiguation impact on our morphological segmentation technique for Turkish and a more careful way of han-

dling OOVs for our SMT systems.

References

Arianna Bisazza and Marcello Federico. 2009. Morphological pre-processing for turkish to english statistical machine translation. In *Proceedings of IWSLT 2009*, Tokyo, Japan.

Marcello Federico, Nicola Bertoldi, and Mauro Cettolo. 2008. Irstlm: an open source toolkit for handling large scale language models. In *Proceedings of Interspeech*, Brisbane, Australia.

Qin Gao and Stephan Vogel. 2008. Parallel implementations of word alignment tool. In *Software Engineering, Testing, and Quality Assurance for Natural Language Processing, SETQA-NLP 08*, pages 49 – 57, Stroudsburg, PA, USA.

Kenneth Heafield. 2011. Kenlm : Faster and smaller language model queries. In *Proceedings of the Sixth Workshop on Statistical Machine Translation*, number 2009, pages 187 – 197, Edinburgh, Scotland, July. Association for Computational Linguistics.

Philipp Koehn and Kevin Knight. 2003. Empirical methods for compound splitting. In *Proceedings of the Eleventh Conference of the European Chapter of the Association for Computational Linguistics (EACL 2003)*, Budapest, Hungary.

Philipp Koehn, Hieu Hoang, Alexandra Birch, Chris Callison-Burch, Marcello Federico, Nicola Bertoldi, Brooke Cowan, Wade Shen, Christine Moran, Richard Zens, Chris Dyer, Ondrej Bojar, Alexandra Constantin, and Evan Herbst. 2007. Moses: open source toolkit for statistical machine translation. In *Proceedings of the 45th Annual Meeting of the ACL on Interactive Poster and Demonstration Sessions, ACL 07*, pages 177 – 180, Stroudsburg, PA, USA. Association for Computational Linguistics.

Edward Loper and Steven Bird. 2002. Nltk: the natural language toolkit. In *Proceedings of the ACL-02 Workshop on Effective tools and methodologies for teaching natural language processing and computational linguistics (ACL 02)*, volume 1, pages 63 – 70, Philadelphia, PA, July.

Kishore Papineni, Salim Roukos, Todd Ward, and Wei-Jing Zhu. 2002. Bleu: a method for automatic evaluation of machine translation. In *Proceedings of the 40th Annual Meeting of the Association for Computational Linguistics (ACL 02)*, pages 311 – 318, Philadelphia, PA, July.

Martin Porter. 1980. An algorithm for suffix stripping. In *Program: electronic library and information systems*, number 14(3), pages 130 – 137.

Michel Simard, Cyril Goutte, and Pierre Isabelle. 2007. Statistical phrase-based post-editing. In *Proceedings of The North American Chapter of the*

Association for Computational Linguistics Confer-ence (NAACL-07), pages 508 – 515, Rochester, NY, April.

Jorg Tiedemann. 2012. Parallel data, tools and inter-faces in opus. In *Proceedings of the Eight Interna-tional Conference on Language Resources and Eval-uation (LREC'12)*, Istanbul, Turkey, May. European Language Resources Association (ELRA).

Omar F. Zaidan. 2009. Z-mert: A fully configurable open source tool for minimum error rate training of machine translation systems. In *The Prague Bulletin of Mathematical Linguistics*, number 91, pages 79 – 88.

The QT21/HimL Combined Machine Translation System

Jan-Thorsten Peter[1], Tamer Alkhouli[1], Hermann Ney[1], Matthias Huck[2],
Fabienne Braune[2], Alexander Fraser[2], Aleš Tamchyna[2,3], Ondřej Bojar[3],
Barry Haddow[4], Rico Sennrich[4], Frédéric Blain[5], Lucia Specia[5],
Jan Niehues[6], Alex Waibel[6], Alexandre Allauzen[7], Lauriane Aufrant[7,8],
Franck Burlot[7], Elena Knyazeva[7], Thomas Lavergne[7], François Yvon[7],
Stella Frank[9], Mārcis Pinnis[10]

[1]RWTH Aachen University, Aachen, Germany
[2]LMU Munich, Munich, Germany
[3]Charles University in Prague, Prague, Czech Republic
[4]University of Edinburgh, Edinburgh, UK
[5]University of Sheffield, Sheffield, UK
[6]Karlsruhe Institute of Technology, Karlsruhe, Germany
[7]LIMSI, CNRS, Université Paris Saclay, Orsay, France
[8]DGA, Paris, France
[9]ILLC, University of Amsterdam, Amsterdam, The Netherlands
[10]Tilde, Riga, Latvia

```
[1]{peter,alkhouli,ney}@cs.rwth-aachen.de
[2]{mhuck,braune,fraser}@cis.lmu.de
[3]{tamchyna,bojar}@ufal.mff.cuni.cz
[4]bhaddow@inf.ed.ac.uk rico.sennrich@ed.ac.uk
[5]{f.blain,l.specia}@sheffield.ac.uk
[6]{jan.niehues,alex.waibel}@kit.edu
[7]{allauzen,aufrant,burlot,knyazeva,lavergne,yvon}@limsi.fr
[9]s.c.frank@uva.nl
[10]marcis.pinnis@tilde.lv
```


Abstract

This paper describes the joint submission of the QT21 and HimL projects for the English→Romanian translation task of the *ACL 2016 First Conference on Machine Translation* (WMT 2016). The submission is a system combination which combines twelve different statistical machine translation systems provided by the different groups (RWTH Aachen University, LMU Munich, Charles University in Prague, University of Edinburgh, University of Sheffield, Karlsruhe Institute of Technology, LIMSI, University of Amsterdam, Tilde). The systems are combined using RWTH's system combination approach. The final submission shows an improvement of 1.0 BLEU compared to the best single system on newstest2016.

1 Introduction

Quality Translation 21 (QT21) is a European machine translation research project with the aim of substantially improving statistical and machine learning based translation models for challenging languages and low-resource scenarios.

Health in my Language (HimL) aims to make public health information available in a wider variety of languages, using fully automatic machine translation that combines the statistical paradigm with deep linguistic techniques.

In order to achieve high-quality machine translation from English into Romanian, members of the QT21 and HimL projects have jointly built a combined statistical machine translation system. We participated with the QT21/HimL combined machine translation system in the WMT 2016 shared task for machine translation of news.[1] Core components of the QT21/HimL combined system are twelve individual English→Romanian translation engines which have been set up by different QT21 or HimL project partners. The outputs of all these individual engines are combined using the system combination approach as imple-

---

[1]http://www.statmt.org/wmt16/
translation-task.html

Proceedings of the First Conference on Machine Translation, Volume 2: Shared Task Papers, pages 344–355,
Berlin, Germany, August 11-12, 2016. ©2016 Association for Computational Linguistics

mented in Jane, RWTH's open source statistical machine translation toolkit (Freitag et al., 2014a). The Jane system combination is a mature implementation which previously has been successfully employed in other collaborative projects and for different language pairs (Freitag et al., 2013; Freitag et al., 2014b; Freitag et al., 2014c).

In the remainder of the paper, we present the technical details of the QT21/HimL combined machine translation system and the experimental results obtained with it. The paper is structured as follows: We describe the common preprocessing used for most of the individual engines in Section 2. Section 3 covers the characteristics of the different individual engines, followed by a brief overview of our system combination approach (Section 4). We then summarize our empirical results in Section 5, showing that we achieve better translation quality than with any individual engine. Finally, in Section 6, we provide a statistical analysis of certain linguistic phenomena, specifically the prediction precision on morphological attributes. We conclude the paper with Section 7.

2 Preprocessing

The data provided for the task was preprocessed once, by LIMSI, and shared with all the participants, in order to ensure consistency between systems. On the English side, preprocessing consists of tokenizing and truecasing using the Moses toolkit (Koehn et al., 2007).

On the Romanian side, the data is tokenized using LIMSI's tokro (Allauzen et al., 2016), a rule-based tokenizer that mainly normalizes diacritics and splits punctuation and clitics. This data is truecased in the same way as the English side. In addition, the Romanian sentences are also tagged, lemmatized, and chunked using the TTL tagger (Tufiş et al., 2008).

3 Translation Systems

Each group contributed one or more systems. In this section the systems are presented in alphabetic order.

3.1 KIT

The KIT system consists of a phrase-based machine translation system using additional models in rescoring. The phrase-based system is trained on all available parallel training data. The phrase

table is adapted to the SETimes2 corpus (Niehues and Waibel, 2012). The system uses a pre-reordering technique (Rottmann and Vogel, 2007) in combination with lexical reordering. It uses two word-based n-gram language models and three additional non-word language models. Two of them are automatic word class-based (Och, 1999) language models, using 100 and 1,000 word classes. In addition, we use a POS-based language model. During decoding, we use a discriminative word lexicon (Niehues and Waibel, 2013) as well.

We rescore the system output using a 300-best list. The weights are optimized on the concatenation of the development data and the SETimes2 dev set using the ListNet algorithm (Niehues et al., 2015). In rescoring, we add the source discriminative word lexica (Herrmann et al., 2015) as well as neural network language and translation models. These models use a factored word representation of the source and the target. On the source side we use the word surface form and two automatic word classes using 100 and 1,000 classes. On the Romanian side, we add the POS information as an additional word factor.

3.2 LIMSI

The LIMSI system uses NCODE (Crego et al., 2011), which implements the bilingual n-gram approach to SMT (Casacuberta and Vidal, 2004; Crego and Mariño, 2006; Mariño et al., 2006) that is closely related to the standard phrase-based approach (Zens et al., 2002). In this framework, translation is divided into two steps. To translate a source sentence into a target sentence, the source sentence is first reordered according to a set of rewriting rules so as to reproduce the target word order. This generates a word lattice containing the most promising source permutations, which is then translated. Since the translation step is monotonic, this approach is able to rely on the n-gram assumption to decompose the joint probability of a sentence pair into a sequence of bilingual units called tuples.

We train three Romanian 4-gram language models, pruning all singletons with KenLM (Heafield, 2011). We use the in-domain monolingual corpus, the Romanian side of the parallel corpora and a subset of the (out-of-domain) Common Crawl corpus as training data. We select in-domain sentences from the latter using the Moore-Lewis (Moore and Lewis, 2010) filtering method, more specifically its implementation in XenC (Rousseau, 2013). As a result, one third of the initial corpus is removed. Finally, we make a linear interpolation of these models, using the SRILM toolkit (Stolcke, 2002).

3.3 LMU-CUNI

The LMU-CUNI contribution is a constrained Moses phrase-based system. It uses a simple factored setting: our phrase table produces not only the target surface form but also its lemma and morphological tag. On the input, we include lemmas, POS tags and information from dependency parses (lemma of the parent node and syntactic relation), all encoded as additional factors.

The main difference from a standard phrase-based setup is the addition of a feature-rich discriminative translation model which is conditioned on both source- and target-side context (Tamchyna et al., 2016). The motivation for using this model is to better condition lexical choices by using the source context and to improve morphological and topical coherence by modeling the (limited left-hand side) target context.

We also take advantage of the target factors by using a 7-gram language model trained on sequences of Romanian morphological tags. Finally, our system also uses a standard lexicalized reordering model.

3.4 LMU

The LMU system integrates a discriminative rule selection model into a hierarchical SMT system, as described in (Tamchyna et al., 2014). The rule selection model is implemented using the high-speed classifier Vowpal Wabbit[2] which is fully integrated in Moses' hierarchical decoder. During decoding, the rule selection model is called at each rule application with syntactic context information as feature templates. The features are the same as used by Braune et al. (2015) in their string-to-tree system, including both lexical and soft source syntax features. The translation model features comprise the standard hierarchical features (Chiang, 2005) with an additional feature for the rule selection model (Braune et al., 2016).

Before training, we reduce the number of translation rules using significance testing (Johnson et al., 2007). To extract the features of the rule selection model, we parse the English part of our

---

[2] `http://hunch.net/~vw/` (VW). Implemented by John Langford and many others.

training data using the Berkeley parser (Petrov et al., 2006). For model prediction during tuning and decoding, we use parsed versions of the development and test sets. We train the rule selection model using VW and tune the weights of the translation model using batch MIRA (Cherry and Foster, 2012). The 5-gram language model is trained using KenLM (Heafield et al., 2013) on the Romanian part of the Common Crawl corpus concatenated with the Romanian part of the training data.

3.5 RWTH Aachen University: Hierarchical Phrase-based System

The RWTH hierarchical setup uses the open source translation toolkit Jane 2.3 (Vilar et al., 2010). Hierarchical phrase-based translation (HPBT) (Chiang, 2007) induces a weighted synchronous context-free grammar from parallel text. In addition to the contiguous lexical phrases, as used in phrase-based translation (PBT), hierarchical phrases with up to two gaps are also extracted. Our baseline model contains models with phrase translation probabilities and lexical smoothing probabilities in both translation directions, word and phrase penalty, and enhanced low frequency features (Chen et al., 2011). It also contains binary features to distinguish between hierarchical and non-hierarchical phrases, the glue rule, and rules with non-terminals at the boundaries. We use the cube pruning algorithm (Huang and Chiang, 2007) for decoding.

The system uses three backoff language models (LM) that are estimated with the KenLM toolkit (Heafield et al., 2013) and are integrated into the decoder as separate models in the log-linear combination: a full 4-gram LM (trained on all data), a limited 5-gram LM (trained only on in-domain data), and a 7-gram word class language model (wcLM) (Wuebker et al., 2013) trained on all data and with a output vocabulary of 143K words.

The system produces 1000-best lists which are reranked using a LSTM-based (Hochreiter and Schmidhuber, 1997; Gers et al., 2000; Gers et al., 2003) language model (Sundermeyer et al., 2012) and a LSTM-based bidirectional joined model (BJM) (Sundermeyer et al., 2014a). The models have a class-factored output layer (Goodman, 2001; Morin and Bengio, 2005) to speed up training and evaluation. The language model uses 3 stacked LSTM layers, with 350 nodes each. The BJM has a projection layer, and computes a forward recurrent state encoding the source and target history, a backward recurrent state encoding the source future, and a third LSTM layer to combine them. All layers have 350 nodes. The neural networks are implemented using an extension of the RWTHLM toolkit (Sundermeyer et al., 2014b). The parameter weights are optimized with MERT (Och, 2003) towards the BLEU metric.

3.6 RWTH Neural System

The second system provided by the RWTH is an attention-based recurrent neural network similar to (Bahdanau et al., 2015). The implementation is based on Blocks (van Merriënboer et al., 2015) and Theano (Bergstra et al., 2010; Bastien et al., 2012).

The network uses the 30K most frequent words on the source and target side as input vocabulary. The decoder and encoder word embeddings are of size 620. The encoder uses a bidirectional layer with 1024 GRUs (Cho et al., 2014) to encode the source side, while the decoder uses 1024 GRU layer.

The network is trained for up to 300K updates with a minibatch size of 80 using Adadelta (Zeiler, 2012). The network is evaluated every 10000 updates on BLEU and the best network on the news-dev2016/1 dev set is selected as the final network.

The monolingual News Crawl 2015 corpus is translated into English with a simple phrase-based translation system to create additional parallel training data. The new data is weighted by using the News Crawl 2015 corpus (2.3M sentences) once, the Europarl corpus (0.4M sentences) twice and the SETimes2 corpus (0.2M sentences) three times. The final system is an ensemble of 4 networks, all with the same configuration and training settings.

3.7 Tilde

The Tilde system is a phrase-based machine translation system built on LetsMT infrastructure (Vasijevs et al., 2012) that features language-specific data filtering and cleaning modules. Tilde's system was trained on all available parallel data. Two language models are trained using KenLM (Heafield, 2011): 1) a 5-gram model using the Europarl and SETimes2 corpora, and 2) a 3-gram model using the Common Crawl corpus. We also apply a custom tokenization tool that takes into account specifics of the Romanian language and handles non-translatable entities (e.g., file paths, URLs, e-mail addresses, etc.). During translation a rule-based localisation feature is applied.

3.8 Edinburgh/LMU Hierarchical System

The UEDIN-LMU HPBT system is a hierarchical phrase-based machine translation system (Chiang, 2005) built jointly by the University of Edinburgh and LMU Munich. The system is based on the open source Moses implementation of the hierarchical phrase-based paradigm (Hoang et al., 2009). In addition to a set of standard features in a log-linear combination, a number of non-standard enhancements are employed to achieve improved translation quality.

Specifically, we integrate individual language models trained over the separate corpora (News Crawl 2015, Europarl, SETimes2) directly into the log-linear combination of the system and let MIRA (Cherry and Foster, 2012) optimize their weights along with all other features in tuning, rather than relying on a single linearly interpolated language model. We add another background language model estimated over a concatenation of all Romanian corpora including Common Crawl. All language models are unpruned.

For hierarchical rule extraction, we impose less strict extraction constraints than the Moses defaults. We extract more hierarchical rules by allowing for a maximum of ten symbols on the source side, a maximum span of twenty words, and no lower limit to the amount of words covered by right-hand side non-terminals at extraction time. We discard rules with non-terminals on their right-hand side if they are singletons in the training data.

In order to promote better reordering decisions, we implemented a feature in Moses that resembles the phrase orientation model for hierarchical machine translation as described by Huck et al. (2013) and extend our system with it. The model scores orientation classes (*monotone*, *swap*, *discontinuous*) for each rule application in decoding.

We finally follow the approach outlined by Huck et al. (2011) for lightly-supervised training of hierarchical systems. We automatically translate parts (1.2M sentences) of the monolingual Romanian News Crawl 2015 corpus to English with a Romanian→English phrase-based statistical machine translation system (Williams et al., 2016). The foreground phrase table extracted from the human-generated parallel data is filled up with entries from a background phrase table extracted from the automatically produced News Crawl 2015 parallel data.

Huck et al. (2016) give a more in-depth description of the Edinburgh/LMU hierarchical machine translation system, along with detailed experimental results.

3.9 Edinburgh Neural System

Edinburgh's neural machine translation system is an attentional encoder-decoder (Bahdanau et al., 2015), which we train with nematus.[3] We use byte-pair-encoding (BPE) to achieve open-vocabulary translation with a fixed vocabulary of subword symbols (Sennrich et al., 2016c). We produce additional parallel training data by automatically translating the monolingual Romanian News Crawl 2015 corpus into English (Sennrich et al., 2016b), which we combine with the original parallel data in a 1-to-1 ratio. We use minibatches of size 80, a maximum sentence length of 50, word embeddings of size 500, and hidden layers of size 1024. We apply dropout to all layers (Gal, 2015), with dropout probability 0.2, and also drop out full words with probability 0.1. We clip the gradient norm to 1.0 (Pascanu et al., 2013). We train the models with Adadelta (Zeiler, 2012), reshuffling the training corpus between epochs. We validate the model every 10 000 minibatches via BLEU on a validation set, and perform early stopping on BLEU. Decoding is performed with beam search with a beam size of 12.

A more detailed description of the system, and more experimental results, can be found in (Sennrich et al., 2016a).

3.10 Edinburgh Phrase-based System

Edinburgh's phrase-based system is built using the Moses toolkit, with fast_align (Dyer et al., 2013) for word alignment, and KenLM (Heafield et al., 2013) for language model training. In our Moses setup, we use hierarchical lexicalized reordering (Galley and Manning, 2008), operation sequence model (Durrani et al., 2013), domain indicator features, and binned phrase count features. We use all available parallel data for the translation model, and all available Romanian text for the language model. We use two different 5-gram language models; one built from all the monolingual target text concatenated, without pruning, and one

built from only News Crawl 2015, with singleton 3-grams and above pruned out. The weights of all these features and models are tuned with k-best MIRA (Cherry and Foster, 2012) on first the half of newsdev2016. In decoding, we use MBR (Kumar and Byrne, 2004), cube-pruning (Huang and Chiang, 2007) with a pop-limit of 5000, and the Moses "monotone at punctuation" switch (to prevent reordering across punctuation) (Koehn and Haddow, 2009).

3.11 USFD Phrase-based System

USFD's phrase-based system is built using the Moses toolkit, with MGIZA (Gao and Vogel, 2008) for word alignment and KenLM (Heafield et al., 2013) for language model training. We use all available parallel data for the translation model. A single 5-gram language model is built using all the target side of the parallel data and a subpart of the monolingual Romanian corpora selected with Xenc-v2 (Rousseau, 2013). For the latter we use all the parallel data as in-domain data and the first half of newsdev2016 as development set. The feature weights are tuned with MERT (Och, 2003) on the first half of newsdev2016.

The system produces distinct 1000-best lists, for which we extend the feature set with the 17 baseline *black-box* features from sentence-level Quality Estimation (QE) produced with Quest++[4] (Specia et al., 2015). The 1000-best lists are then reranked and the top-best hypothesis extracted using the nbest rescorer available within the Moses toolkit.

3.12 UvA

We use a phrase-based machine translation system (Moses) with a distortion limit of 6 and lexicalized reordering. Before translation, the English source side is preordered using the neural preordering model of (de Gispert et al., 2015). The preordering model is trained for 30 iterations on the full MGIZA-aligned training data. We use two language models, built using KenLM. The first is a 5-gram language model trained on all available data. Words in the Common Crawl dataset that appear fewer than 500 times were replaced by UNK, and all singleton ngrams of order 3 or higher were pruned. We also use a 7-gram class-based language model, trained on the same data. 512 word

---

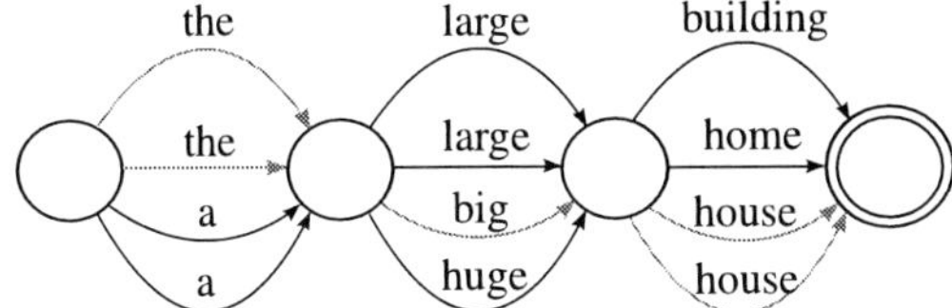

Figure 1: System A: *the large building*; System B: *the large home*; System C: *a big house*; System D: *a huge house*; Reference: *the big house*.

classes were generated using the method of Green et al. (2014).

4 System Combination

System combination produces consensus translations from multiple hypotheses which are obtained from different translation approaches, i.e., the systems described in the previous section. A system combination implementation developed at RWTH Aachen University (Freitag et al., 2014a) is used to combine the outputs of the different engines. The consensus translations outperform the individual hypotheses in terms of translation quality.

The first step in system combination is the generation of confusion networks (CN) from I input translation hypotheses. We need pairwise alignments between the input hypotheses, which are obtained from METEOR (Banerjee and Lavie, 2005). The hypotheses are then reordered to match a selected skeleton hypothesis in terms of word ordering. We generate I different CNs, each having one of the input systems as the skeleton hypothesis, and the final lattice is the union of all I generated CNs. In Figure 1 an example of a confusion network with $I = 4$ input translations is depicted. Decoding of a confusion network finds the best path in the network. Each arc is assigned a score of a linear model combination of M different models, which includes word penalty, 3-gram language model trained on the input hypotheses, a binary primary system feature that marks the primary hypothesis, and a binary voting feature for each system. The binary voting feature for a system is 1 if and only if the decoded word is from that system, and 0 otherwise. The different model weights for system combination are trained with MERT (Och, 2003).

5 Experimental Evaluation

Since only one development set was provided we split the given development set into two parts:

newsdev2016/1 and newsdev2016/2. The first part was used as development set while the second part was our internal test set. Additionally we extracted 2000 sentences from the Europarl and SETimes2 data to create two additional development and test sets. Most single systems are optimized for newsdev2016/1 and/or the SETimes2 test set. The system combination was optimized on the newsdev2016/1 set.

The single system scores in Table 1 show clearly that the UEDIN NMT system is the strongest single system by a large margin. The other standalone attention-based neural network contribution, RWTH NMT, follows, with only a small margin before the phrase-based contributions. The combination of all systems improved the strongest system by another 1.9 BLEU points on our internal test set, newsdev2016/2, and by 1 BLEU point on the official test set, newstest2016.

Removing the strongest system from our system combination shows a large degradation of the results. The combination is still slightly stronger then the UEDIN NMT system on newsdev2016/2, but lags behind on newstest2016. Removing the by itself weakest system shows a slight degradation on newsdev2016/2 and newstest2016, hinting that it still provides valuable information.

Table 2 shows a comparison between all systems by scoring the translation output against each other in TER and BLEU. We see that the neural networks outputs differ the most from all the other systems.

6 Morphology Prediction Precision

In order to assess how well the different system outputs predict the right morphology, we compute a precision rate for each Romanian morphological attribute that occurs with nouns, pronouns, adjectives, determiners, and verbs (Table 3). For this purpose, we use the METEOR toolkit (Banerjee and Lavie, 2005) to obtain word alignments between each system translation and the reference translation for newstest2016. The reference and hypotheses are tagged with TTL (Tufiş et al., 2008).[5] Each word in the reference that is assigned a POS tag of interest (noun, pronoun, adjective, determiner, or verb) is then compared to the word it is aligned to in the system output. When, for

---

[5]The hypotheses were tagged despite the risks that go along with tagging automatically generated sentences. A dictionary would have been a solution, but unfortunately we had no such resource for Romanian.

Individual Systems	newsdev2016/1		newsdev2016/2		newstest2016	
	BLEU	TER	BLEU	TER	BLEU	TER
KIT	25.2	57.5	29.9	51.8	26.3	55.9
LIMSI	23.3	59.5	27.2	55.0	23.9	59.2
LMU-CUNI	23.4	60.4	28.4	53.5	24.7	58.1
LMU	23.3	60.5	28.6	53.8	24.5	58.5
RWTH HPBT	25.4	58.7	29.3	53.3	25.9	57.6
RWTH NMT	25.1	57.4	30.6	49.6	26.5	55.4
Tilde	21.3	62.7	25.8	56.3	23.2	60.2
UEDIN-LMU HPBT	24.8	58.7	30.1	52.3	25.4	57.7
UEDIN PBT	24.7	59.3	29.1	53.2	25.2	58.1
UEDIN NMT	26.8	56.1	31.4	50.3	27.9	54.5
USFD	22.9	60.4	27.8	54.0	24.4	58.5
UvA	22.1	61.0	27.7	54.2	24.1	58.7
System Combination	28.7	55.5	33.3	49.0	28.9	54.2
- without UEDIN NMT	27.4	56.6	31.6	50.9	27.5	55.4
- without Tilde	28.8	55.5	33.0	49.5	28.7	54.5

Table 1: Results of the individual systems for the English→Romanian task. BLEU [%] and TER [%] scores are case-sensitive.

	KIT	LIMSI	LMU-CUNI	LMU	RWTH HPBT	RWTH NMT	Tilde	UEDIN-LMU HPBT	UEDIN PBT	UEDIN NMT	USFD	UvA	Average
KIT	-	55.0	55.9	51.7	56.2	48.2	50.3	54.6	55.1	42.8	56.6	54.1	52.8
LIMSI	29.3	-	54.3	52.1	51.8	43.0	49.8	55.3	56.2	38.2	57.3	52.1	51.4
LMU-CUNI	28.5	30.8	-	52.4	53.3	43.8	55.4	56.0	56.6	39.3	58.6	56.6	52.9
LMU	31.2	32.0	31.7	-	53.6	43.1	49.1	59.4	58.6	37.8	56.1	55.8	51.8
RWTH HPBT	28.5	32.4	31.2	30.8	-	47.5	50.1	54.9	55.6	41.8	53.9	55.3	52.2
RWTH NMT	33.7	37.9	37.3	37.5	34.8	-	40.8	44.3	45.3	46.0	43.8	43.6	44.5
Tilde	32.2	33.7	29.6	33.8	33.4	39.6	-	53.4	58.5	36.5	55.5	52.0	50.1
UEDIN-LMU HPBT	29.5	29.9	29.4	27.3	29.8	36.9	30.9	-	62.8	38.9	59.6	56.2	54.1
UEDIN PBT	28.4	28.9	28.5	27.0	29.3	35.4	27.0	24.2	-	39.4	60.2	58.6	55.2
UEDIN NMT	38.6	42.6	42.0	43.0	40.1	35.5	44.0	42.1	41.1	-	38.2	38.2	39.7
USFD	27.6	28.8	27.4	28.8	30.4	37.0	29.1	26.5	25.7	42.6	-	58.8	54.4
UvA	29.9	32.0	28.6	29.2	29.6	37.5	31.5	29.0	26.5	43.2	26.9	-	52.9
Average	30.7	32.6	31.4	32.0	31.8	36.6	33.2	30.5	29.3	41.3	30.0	31.3	-

Table 2: Comparison of system outputs against each other, generated by computing BLEU and TER on the system translations for newstest2016. One system in a pair is used as the reference, the other as candidate translation; we report the average over both directions. The upper-right half lists BLEU [%] scores, the lower-left half TER [%] scores.

Attribute	KIT	LIMSI	LMU-CUNI	LMU	RWTH HPBT	RWTH NMT	Tilde	UEDIN-LMU HPBT	UEDIN PBT	UEDIN NMT	USFD	UvA	Combination
Case	46.7%	46.0%	46.3%	45.7%	47.7%	48.0%	44.4%	46.3%	47.4%	49.8%	45.4%	45.4%	**50.8%**
Definite	50.5%	49.1%	50.0%	49.2%	50.5%	50.1%	47.2%	50.0%	50.5%	51.0%	49.2%	48.9%	**53.3%**
Gender	51.9%	51.0%	51.9%	51.3%	52.6%	52.1%	49.6%	51.9%	52.7%	53.0%	51.2%	50.9%	**54.9%**
Number	53.2%	51.7%	52.6%	52.3%	53.6%	53.7%	50.6%	52.9%	53.6%	54.9%	52.1%	51.8%	**56.3%**
Person	52.8%	51.3%	52.0%	52.0%	53.5%	55.0%	50.6%	52.6%	53.4%	**57.2%**	52.4%	51.6%	57.1%
Tense	45.8%	44.1%	44.7%	44.8%	45.7%	45.5%	42.3%	45.2%	45.1%	46.6%	44.9%	44.8%	**48.0%**
Verb form	45.9%	44.4%	45.5%	44.9%	46.6%	47.0%	43.9%	46.1%	46.5%	47.2%	45.5%	43.3%	**48.7%**
Reference words with alignment	57.7%	56.7%	57.3%	57.3%	58.3%	57.6%	55.7%	58.0%	58.5%	58.3%	57.3%	56.8%	**60.4%**

Table 3: Precision of each system on morphological attribute prediction computed over the reference translation using METEOR alignments. The last row shows the ratio of reference words for which METEOR managed to find an alignment in the hypothesis.

a given morphological attribute, the output and the reference have the same value (e.g. *Number=Singular*), we consider the prediction correct. The prediction is considered wrong in every other case.

The last row in Table 3 shows the ratio of reference words for which METEOR found an alignment in the hypothesis. We observe a high correlation between this ratio and the quality of the morphological predictions, showing that the accuracy is highly dependent on the alignments. We nevertheless observe that the predictions made by UEDIN NMT are strictly all better than UEDIN PBT, although the latter has slightly more alignments to the reference. The system combination makes the most accurate predictions for almost every attribute. The difference in precision with the best single system (UEDIN NMT) can be significant (2.3% for definite and 1.4% for tense) showing that the combination managed to effectively identify the strong points of each translation system.

7 Conclusion

Our combined effort shows that even with an extremely strong single best system, we still manage to improve the final result by one BLEU point by combining it with the other systems of all participating research groups.

The joint submission for English→Romanian is the best submission measured in terms of BLEU, as presented on the WMT submission page.[6]

---

[6] http://matrix.statmt.org/

Acknowledgments

This project has received funding from the European Union's Horizon 2020 research and innovation programme under grant agreements № 645452 (*QT21*) and 644402 (*HimL*).

References

Alexandre Allauzen, Lauriane Aufrant, Franck Burlot, Elena Knyazeva, Thomas Lavergne, and François Yvon. 2016. LIMSI@WMT'16 : Machine translation of news. In *Proc. of the ACL 2016 First Conf. on Machine Translation (WMT16)*, Berlin, Germany, August.

Dzmitry Bahdanau, Kyunghyun Cho, and Yoshua Bengio. 2015. Neural Machine Translation by Jointly Learning to Align and Translate. In *Proceedings of the International Conference on Learning Representations (ICLR)*.

Satanjeev Banerjee and Alon Lavie. 2005. METEOR: An Automatic Metric for MT Evaluation with Improved Correlation with Human Judgments. In *43rd Annual Meeting of the Assoc. for Computational Linguistics: Proc. Workshop on Intrinsic and Extrinsic Evaluation Measures for MT and/or Summarization*, pages 65–72, Ann Arbor, MI, USA, June.

Frédéric Bastien, Pascal Lamblin, Razvan Pascanu, James Bergstra, Ian J. Goodfellow, Arnaud Bergeron, Nicolas Bouchard, and Yoshua Bengio. 2012. Theano: new features and speed improvements. Deep Learning and Unsupervised Feature Learning NIPS 2012 Workshop.

James Bergstra, Olivier Breuleux, Frédéric Bastien, Pascal Lamblin, Razvan Pascanu, Guillaume Desjardins, Joseph Turian, David Warde-Farley, and Yoshua Bengio. 2010. Theano: a CPU and GPU math expression compiler. In *Proceedings of the Python for Scientific Computing Conference (SciPy)*, June. Oral Presentation.

Fabienne Braune, Nina Seemann, and Alexander Fraser. 2015. Rule Selection with Soft Syntactic Features for String-to-Tree Statistical Machine Translation. In *Proc. of the Conf. on Empirical Methods for Natural Language Processing (EMNLP)*.

Fabienne Braune, Alexander Fraser, Hal Daumé III, and Aleš Tamchyna. 2016. A Framework for Discriminative Rule Selection in Hierarchical Moses. In *Proc. of the ACL 2016 First Conf. on Machine Translation (WMT16)*, Berlin, Germany, August.

Francesco Casacuberta and Enrique Vidal. 2004. Machine translation with inferred stochastic finite-state transducers. *Computational Linguistics*, 30(3):205–225.

Boxing Chen, Roland Kuhn, George Foster, and Howard Johnson. 2011. Unpacking and Transforming Feature Functions: New Ways to Smooth Phrase Tables. In *MT Summit XIII*, pages 269–275, Xiamen, China, September.

Colin Cherry and George Foster. 2012. Batch Tuning Strategies for Statistical Machine Translation. In *Proc. of the Conf. of the North American Chapter of the Assoc. for Computational Linguistics: Human Language Technologies (NAACL-HLT)*, pages 427–436, Montréal, Canada, June.

David Chiang. 2005. A Hierarchical Phrase-Based Model for Statistical Machine Translation. In *Proc. of the 43rd Annual Meeting of the Association for Computational Linguistics (ACL)*, pages 263–270, Ann Arbor, Michigan, June.

David Chiang. 2007. Hierarchical Phrase-Based Translation. *Computational Linguistics*, 33(2):201–228.

Kyunghyun Cho, Bart van Merrienboer, Caglar Gulcehre, Dzmitry Bahdanau, Fethi Bougares, Holger Schwenk, and Yoshua Bengio. 2014. Learning Phrase Representations using RNN Encoder–Decoder for Statistical Machine Translation. In *Proceedings of the 2014 Conference on Empirical Methods in Natural Language Processing (EMNLP)*, pages 1724–1734, Doha, Qatar, October. Association for Computational Linguistics.

Joseph M. Crego and José B. Mariño. 2006. Improving statistical MT by coupling reordering and decoding. *Machine translation*, 20(3):199–215, Jul.

Josep Maria Crego, Franois Yvon, and José B. Mariño. 2011. N-code: an open-source Bilingual N-gram SMT Toolkit. *Prague Bulletin of Mathematical Linguistics*, 96:49–58.

Adrià de Gispert, Gonzalo Iglesias, and Bill Byrne. 2015. Fast and accurate preordering for SMT using neural networks. In *Proceedings of the 2015 Conference of the North American Chapter of the Association for Computational Linguistics: Human Language Technologies*, pages 1012–1017, Denver, Colorado, May–June.

Nadir Durrani, Alexander Fraser, Helmut Schmid, Hieu Hoang, and Philipp Koehn. 2013. Can Markov Models Over Minimal Translation Units Help Phrase-Based SMT? In *Proceedings of the 51st Annual Meeting of the Association for Computational Linguistics (Volume 2: Short Papers)*, pages 399–405, Sofia, Bulgaria, August.

Chris Dyer, Victor Chahuneau, and Noah A. Smith. 2013. A Simple, Fast, and Effective Reparameterization of IBM Model 2. In *Proceedings of NAACL-HLT*, pages 644–648, Atlanta, Georgia, June.

Markus Freitag, Stephan Peitz, Joern Wuebker, Hermann Ney, Nadir Durrani, Matthias Huck, Philipp Koehn, Thanh-Le Ha, Jan Niehues, Mohammed Mediani, Teresa Herrmann, Alex Waibel, Nicola Bertoldi, Mauro Cettolo, and Marcello Federico. 2013. EU-BRIDGE MT: Text Translation of Talks in the EU-BRIDGE Project. In *Proc. of the Int. Workshop on Spoken Language Translation (IWSLT)*, pages 128–135, Heidelberg, Germany, December.

Markus Freitag, Matthias Huck, and Hermann Ney. 2014a. Jane: Open Source Machine Translation System Combination. In *Proc. of the Conf. of the European Chapter of the Assoc. for Computational Linguistics (EACL)*, pages 29–32, Gothenberg, Sweden, April.

Markus Freitag, Stephan Peitz, Joern Wuebker, Hermann Ney, Matthias Huck, Rico Sennrich, Nadir Durrani, Maria Nadejde, Philip Williams, Philipp Koehn, Teresa Herrmann, Eunah Cho, and Alex Waibel. 2014b. EU-BRIDGE MT: Combined Machine Translation. In *Proc. of the Workshop on Statistical Machine Translation (WMT)*, pages 105–113, Baltimore, MD, USA, June.

Markus Freitag, Joern Wuebker, Stephan Peitz, Hermann Ney, Matthias Huck, Alexandra Birch, Nadir Durrani, Philipp Koehn, Mohammed Mediani, Isabel Slawik, Jan Niehues, Eunah Cho, Alex Waibel, Nicola Bertoldi, Mauro Cettolo, and Marcello Federico. 2014c. Combined Spoken Language Translation. In *Proc. of the Int. Workshop on Spoken Language Translation (IWSLT)*, pages 57–64, Lake Tahoe, CA, USA, December.

Yarin Gal. 2015. A Theoretically Grounded Application of Dropout in Recurrent Neural Networks. *ArXiv e-prints*.

Michel Galley and Christopher D. Manning. 2008. A simple and effective hierarchical phrase reordering model. In *Proceedings of the Conference on Empirical Methods in Natural Language Processing*, pages 848–856, Stroudsburg, PA, USA. Association for Computational Linguistics.

Qin Gao and Stephan Vogel. 2008. Parallel implementations of word alignment tool. In *Software Engineering, Testing, and Quality Assurance for Natural Language Processing*, pages 49–57. Association for Computational Linguistics.

Felix A. Gers, Jürgen Schmidhuber, and Fred Cummins. 2000. Learning to forget: Continual prediction with LSTM. *Neural computation*, 12(10):2451–2471.

Felix A. Gers, Nicol N. Schraudolph, and Jürgen Schmidhuber. 2003. Learning precise timing with lstm recurrent networks. *The Journal of Machine Learning Research*, 3:115–143.

Joshua Goodman. 2001. Classes for fast maximum entropy training. *CoRR*, cs.CL/0108006.

Spence Green, Daniel Cer, and Christopher D. Manning. 2014. An empirical comparison of features and tuning for phrase-based machine translation. In *In Procedings of the Ninth Workshop on Statistical Machine Translation*.

Kenneth Heafield, Ivan Pouzyrevsky, Jonathan H. Clark, and Philipp Koehn. 2013. Scalable Modified Kneser-Ney Language Model Estimation. pages 690–696, Sofia, Bulgaria, August.

Kenneth Heafield. 2011. KenLM: Faster and Smaller Language Model Queries. In *Proceedings of the EMNLP 2011 Sixth Workshop on Statistical Machine Translation*, pages 187–197, Edinburgh, Scotland, United Kingdom, July.

Teresa Herrmann, Jan Niehues, and Alex Waibel. 2015. Source Discriminative Word Lexicon for Translation Disambiguation. In *Proceedings of the 12th International Workshop on Spoken Language Translation (IWSLT15)*, Danang, Vietnam.

Hieu Hoang, Philipp Koehn, and Adam Lopez. 2009. A Unified Framework for Phrase-Based, Hierarchical, and Syntax-Based Statistical Machine Translation. In *Proc. of the Int. Workshop on Spoken Language Translation (IWSLT)*, pages 152–159, Tokyo, Japan, December.

Sepp Hochreiter and Jürgen Schmidhuber. 1997. Long short-term memory. *Neural computation*, 9(8):1735–1780.

Liang Huang and David Chiang. 2007. Forest Rescoring: Faster Decoding with Integrated Language Models. In *Proceedings of the 45th Annual Meeting of the Association for Computational Linguistics*, pages 144–151, Prague, Czech Republic, June.

Matthias Huck, David Vilar, Daniel Stein, and Hermann Ney. 2011. Lightly-Supervised Training for Hierarchical Phrase-Based Machine Translation. In *Proc. of the EMNLP 2011 Workshop on Unsupervised Learning in NLP*, pages 91–96, Edinburgh, Scotland, UK, July.

Matthias Huck, Joern Wuebker, Felix Rietig, and Hermann Ney. 2013. A Phrase Orientation Model for Hierarchical Machine Translation. In *Proc. of the Workshop on Statistical Machine Translation (WMT)*, pages 452–463, Sofia, Bulgaria, August.

Matthias Huck, Alexander Fraser, and Barry Haddow. 2016. The Edinburgh/LMU Hierarchical Machine Translation System for WMT 2016. In *Proc. of the ACL 2016 First Conf. on Machine Translation (WMT16)*, Berlin, Germany, August.

Howard Johnson, Joel Martin, George Foster, and Roland Kuhn. 2007. Improving Translation Quality by Discarding Most of the Phrasetable. In *Proc. of EMNLP-CoNLL 2007*.

Philipp Koehn and Barry Haddow. 2009. Edinburgh's Submission to all Tracks of the WMT 2009 Shared Task with Reordering and Speed Improvements to Moses. In *Proceedings of the Fourth Workshop on Statistical Machine Translation*, pages 160–164, Athens, Greece.

Philipp Koehn, Hieu Hoang, Alexandra Birch, Chris Callison-Burch, Marcello Federico, Nicola Bertoldi, Brooke Cowan, Wade Shen, Christine Moran, Richard Zens, Chris Dyer, Ondřej Bojar, Alexandra Constantine, and Evan Herbst. 2007. Moses: Open Source Toolkit for Statistical Machine Translation. pages 177–180, Prague, Czech Republic, June.

Shankar Kumar and William Byrne. 2004. Minimum Bayes-Risk Decoding for Statistical Machine Translation. In *HLT 2004 - Human Language Technology Conference*, Boston, MA, May.

José B. Mariño, Rafael E. Banchs, Josep M. Crego, Adrià de Gispert, Patrik Lambert, José A. R. Fonollosa, and Marta R. Costa-jussà. 2006. N-gram-based machine translation. *Comput. Linguist.*, 32(4):527–549, December.

R.C. Moore and W. Lewis. 2010. Intelligent Selection of Language Model Training Data. In *ACL (Short Papers)*, pages 220–224, Uppsala, Sweden, July.

Frederic Morin and Yoshua Bengio. 2005. Hierarchical probabilistic neural network language model. In Robert G. Cowell and Zoubin Ghahramani, editors, *Proceedings of the Tenth International Workshop on Artificial Intelligence and Statistics*, pages 246–252. Society for Artificial Intelligence and Statistics.

J. Niehues and A. Waibel. 2012. Detailed Analysis of Different Strategies for Phrase Table Adaptation in SMT. In *Proceedings of the 10th Conference of the Association for Machine Translation in the Americas*, San Diego, CA, USA.

Jan Niehues and Alex Waibel. 2013. An MT Error-Driven Discriminative Word Lexicon using Sentence Structure Features. In *Proceedings of the 8th Workshop on Statistical Machine Translation*, Sofia, Bulgaria.

Jan Niehues, Quoc Khanh Do, Alexandre Allauzen, and Alex Waibel. 2015. Listnet-based MT Rescoring. *EMNLP 2015*, page 248.

Franz Josef Och. 1999. An Efficient Method for Determining Bilingual Word Classes. In *Proceedings of the 9th Conference of the European Chapter of the Association for Computational Linguistics*, Bergen, Norway.

Franz Josef Och. 2003. Minimum Error Rate Training in Statistical Machine Translation. In *Proc. of the 41th Annual Meeting of the Association for Computational Linguistics (ACL)*, pages 160–167, Sapporo, Japan, July.

Razvan Pascanu, Tomas Mikolov, and Yoshua Bengio. 2013. On the difficulty of training recurrent neural networks. In *Proceedings of the 30th International Conference on Machine Learning, ICML 2013*, pages 1310–1318, , Atlanta, GA, USA.

Slav Petrov, Leon Barrett, Romain Thibaux, and Dan Klein. 2006. Learning Accurate, Compact, and Interpretable Tree Annotation. In *Proc. of the 21st Int. Conf. on Computational Linguistics and the 44th Annual Meeting of the Assoc. for Computational Linguistics*, pages 433–440.

Kay Rottmann and Stephan Vogel. 2007. Word Reordering in Statistical Machine Translation with a POS-Based Distortion Model. In *Proceedings of the 11th International Conference on Theoretical and Methodological Issues in Machine Translation*, Skövde, Sweden.

Anthony Rousseau. 2013. Xenc: An open-source tool for data selection in natural language processing. *The Prague Bulletin of Mathematical Linguistics*, (100):73–82.

Rico Sennrich, Barry Haddow, and Alexandra Birch. 2016a. Edinburgh Neural Machine Translation Systems for WMT 16. In *Proceedings of the First Conference on Machine Translation (WMT16)*, Berlin, Germany.

Rico Sennrich, Barry Haddow, and Alexandra Birch. 2016b. Improving Neural Machine Translation Models with Monolingual Data. In *Proceedings of the 54th Annual Meeting of the Association for Computational Linguistics (ACL 2016)*, Berlin, Germany.

Rico Sennrich, Barry Haddow, and Alexandra Birch. 2016c. Neural Machine Translation of Rare Words with Subword Units. In *Proceedings of the 54th Annual Meeting of the Association for Computational Linguistics (ACL 2016)*, Berlin, Germany.

Lucia Specia, Gustavo Paetzold, and Carolina Scarton. 2015. Multi-level translation quality prediction with quest++. In *Proceedings of ACL-IJCNLP 2015 System Demonstrations*, pages 115–120, Beijing, China, July. Association for Computational Linguistics and The Asian Federation of Natural Language Processing.

Andreas Stolcke. 2002. SRILM – An Extensible Language Modeling Toolkit. In *Proc. of the Int. Conf. on Speech and Language Processing (ICSLP)*, volume 2, pages 901–904, Denver, CO, September.

Martin Sundermeyer, Ralf Schlüter, and Hermann Ney. 2012. LSTM Neural Networks for Language Modeling. In *Interspeech*, Portland, OR, USA, September.

Martin Sundermeyer, Tamer Alkhouli, Joern Wuebker, and Hermann Ney. 2014a. Translation Modeling with Bidirectional Recurrent Neural Networks. In *Conference on Empirical Methods in Natural Language Processing*, pages 14–25, Doha, Qatar, October.

Martin Sundermeyer, Ralf Schlüter, and Hermann Ney. 2014b. rwthlm - The RWTH Aachen University Neural Network Language Modeling Toolkit . In *Interspeech*, pages 2093–2097, Singapore, September.

Aleš Tamchyna, Fabienne Braune, Alexander M. Fraser, Marine Carpuat, Hal Daumé III, and Chris Quirk. 2014. Integrating a Discriminative Classifier into Phrase-based and Hierarchical Decoding. *The Prague Bulletin of Mathematical Linguistics (PBML)*, 101:29–42.

Aleš Tamchyna, Alexander Fraser, Ondřej Bojar, and Marcin Junczsys-Dowmunt. 2016. Target-Side Context for Discriminative Models in Statistical Machine Translation. In *Proc. of ACL*, Berlin, Germany, August. Association for Computational Linguistics.

Dan Tufiş, Radu Ion, Ru Ceauşu, and Dan Ştefănescu. 2008. RACAI's Linguistic Web Services. In *Proceedings of the Sixth International Language Resources and Evaluation (LREC'08)*, Marrakech, Morocco, May. European Language Resources Association (ELRA).

Bart van Merriënboer, Dzmitry Bahdanau, Vincent Dumoulin, Dmitriy Serdyuk, David Warde-Farley, Jan Chorowski, and Yoshua Bengio. 2015. Blocks and Fuel: Frameworks for deep learning. *CoRR*, abs/1506.00619.

Andrejs Vasijevs, Raivis Skadiš, and Jörg Tiedemann. 2012. LetsMT!: A Cloud-Based Platform for Do-It-Yourself Machine Translation. In Min Zhang, editor, *Proceedings of the ACL 2012 System Demonstrations*, number July, pages 43–48, Jeju Island, Korea. Association for Computational Linguistics.

David Vilar, Daniel Stein, Matthias Huck, and Hermann Ney. 2010. Jane: Open source hierarchical translation, extended with reordering and lexicon models. In *ACL 2010 Joint Fifth Workshop on Statistical Machine Translation and Metrics MATR*, pages 262–270, Uppsala, Sweden, July.

Philip Williams, Rico Sennrich, Maria Nădejde, Matthias Huck, Barry Haddow, and Ondřej Bojar. 2016. Edinburgh's Statistical Machine Translation

Systems for WMT16. In *Proc. of the ACL 2016 First Conf. on Machine Translation (WMT16)*, Berlin, Germany, August.

Joern Wuebker, Stephan Peitz, Felix Rietig, and Hermann Ney. 2013. Improving statistical machine translation with word class models. In *Conference on Empirical Methods in Natural Language Processing*, pages 1377–1381, Seattle, WA, USA, October.

Matthew D. Zeiler. 2012. ADADELTA: An Adaptive Learning Rate Method. *CoRR*, abs/1212.5701.

Richard Zens, Franz Josef Och, and Hermann Ney. 2002. Phrase-Based Statistical Machine Translation. In *25th German Conf. on Artificial Intelligence (KI2002)*, pages 18–32, Aachen, Germany, September. Springer Verlag.

The RWTH Aachen University English-Romanian Machine Translation System for WMT 2016

Jan-Thorsten Peter, Tamer Alkhouli, Andreas Guta and Hermann Ney
Human Language Technology and Pattern Recognition Group
Computer Science Department
RWTH Aachen University
D-52056 Aachen, Germany
`<surname>@cs.rwth-aachen.de`

Abstract

This paper describes the statistical machine translation system developed at RWTH Aachen University for the English→Romanian translation task of the *ACL 2016 First Conference on Machine Translation* (WMT 2016).

We combined three different state-of-the-art systems in a system combination: A phrase-based system, a hierarchical phrase-based system and an attention-based neural machine translation system. The phrase-based and the hierarchical phrase-based systems make use of a language model trained on all available data, a language model trained on the bilingual data and a word class language model. In addition, we utilized a recurrent neural network language model and a bidirectional recurrent neural network translation model for reranking the output of both systems. The attention-based neural machine translation system was trained using all bilingual data together with the back-translated data from the News Crawl 2015 corpora.

1 Introduction

We describe the statistical machine translation (SMT) systems developed by RWTH Aachen University for English→Romanian language pair for the evaluation campaign of WMT 2016. Combining several single machine translation engines has proven to be highly effective in previous submissions, e.g. (Freitag et al., 2013; Freitag et al., 2014a; Peter et al., 2015). We therefore used a similar approach for this evaluation. We trained individual systems using state-of-the-art phrase-based, hierarchical phrase-based translation en-

gines, and attention-based recurrent neural networks ensemble. Each single system was optimized and the best systems were used in a system combination.

This paper is organized as follows. In Sections 2.2 through 2.5 we describe our translation software and baseline setups. Sections 2.6 describes the neural network models used in our translation systems. The attention based recurrent neural network ensemble is described in Section 2.7. Sections 2.8 explains the system combination pipeline applied on the individual systems for obtaining the combined system. Our experiments for each track are summarized in Section 3 and we conclude with Section 4.

2 SMT Systems

For the WMT 2016 evaluation campaign, the RWTH utilizes three different state-of-the-art translation systems:

- phrase-based
- hierarchical phrase-based
- attention based neural network ensemble

The phrase-based system is based on word alignments obtained with GIZA++ (Och and Ney, 2003). We use mteval from the Moses toolkit (Koehn et al., 2007) an TERCom to evaluate our systems on the BLEU (Papineni et al., 2002) and TER (Snover et al., 2006) measures. All reported scores are case-sensitive and normalized.

2.1 Preprocessing

The preprocessing of the data was provided by LIMISI. The Romanian side was tokenized using their tokro toolkit (Allauzen et al., 2016 to appear). The English side was tokenized using the Moses toolkit (Koehn et al., 2007). Both sides were true cased with Moses.

Proceedings of the First Conference on Machine Translation, Volume 2: Shared Task Papers, pages 356–361,
Berlin, Germany, August 11-12, 2016. ©2016 Association for Computational Linguistics

2.2 Phrase-based Systems

Our phrase-based decoder (PBT) is the implementation of the *source cardinality synchronous search* (SCSS) procedure described in (Zens and Ney, 2008). It is freely available for non-commercial use in RWTH's open-source SMT toolkit, Jane 2.3[1] (Wuebker et al., 2012). Our baseline contains the following models: Phrase translation probabilities and lexical smoothing in both directions, word and phrase penalty, distance-based reordering model, n-gram target language models and enhanced low frequency feature (Chen et al., 2011), a hierarchical reordering model (HRM) (Galley and Manning, 2008), and a high-order word class language model (wcLM) (Wuebker et al., 2013) trained on all monolingual data. The phrase table is trained on all bilingual data. Additionally we add synthetic parallel data as described in Section 2.4. Two different neural network models (cf. Sections 2.6) are applied in reranking. The parameter weights are optimized with MERT (Och, 2003) towards the BLEU metric.

2.3 Hierarchical Phrase-based System

The open source translation toolkit Jane 2.3 (Vilar et al., 2010) is also used for our hierarchical setup. Hierarchical phrase-based translation (HPBT) (Chiang, 2007) induces a weighted synchronous context-free grammar from parallel text. Additional to the contiguous *lexical* phrases, as used in PBT, *hierarchical* phrases with up to two gaps are extracted. Our baseline model contains models with phrase translation probabilities and lexical smoothing probabilities in both translation directions, word and phrase penalty. It also contains binary features to distinguish between hierarchical on non-hierarchical phrases, the glue rule, and rules with non-terminals at the boundaries. The enhanced low frequency feature (Chen et al., 2011) and the same n-gram language models as described in our PBT system are also used. We utilize the cube pruning algorithm (Huang and Chiang, 2007) for decoding. Neural networks are applied in reranking similar to the PBT system and the parameter weights are also optimized with MERT (Och, 2003) towards the BLEU metric.

---

[1] http://www-i6.informatik.rwth-aachen.de/jane/

2.4 Synthetic Source Sentences

The training data contains around 600k bilingual sentence pairs. To increase the amount of usable training data for the phrase-based and the neural machine translation systems we translated part of the monolingual training data back to English in a similar way as described by (Bertoldi and Federico, 2009) and (Sennrich et al., 2016 to appear).

We created a simple baseline phrase-based system for this task. All bilingual data is used to extract the phrase table and the system contains one language model which uses the English side of the bilingual data combined with the English News Crawl 2007-2015, News Commentary and News Discussion data.

This provides us with nearly 2.3M additional parallel sentences for training. The phrase-based system as well as the attention-based neural network system are trained with this additional data.

2.5 Backoff Language Models

Both phrase-based and hierarchical translation systems use three backoff language models (LM) that are estimated with the KenLM toolkit (Heafield et al., 2013) and are integrated into the decoder as separate models in the log-linear combination: A full 4-gram LM (trained on all data), a limited 5-gram LM (trained only on indomain data), and a 7-gram word class language model (wcLM). All of them use interpolated Kneser-Ney smoothing. For the word class LM, we train 200 classes on the target side of the bilingual training data using an in-house tool similar to `mkcls`. With these class definitions, we apply the technique described in (Wuebker et al., 2013) to compute the wcLM on the same data as the large LM.

2.6 Recurrent Neural Network Models

Our systems apply reranking on 1000-best lists using recurrent language and translation models. We use the long short-term memory (LSTM) architecture for recurrent layers (Hochreiter and Schmidhuber, 1997; Gers et al., 2000; Gers et al., 2003). The models have a class-factored output layer (Goodman, 2001; Morin and Bengio, 2005) to speed up training and evaluation. The class layer consists of 2000 word classes. The LSTM recurrent neural network language model (RNN-LM) (Sundermeyer et al., 2012) uses a vocabulary of 143K words. It is trained on the concatenation of the English side of the parallel data and the News

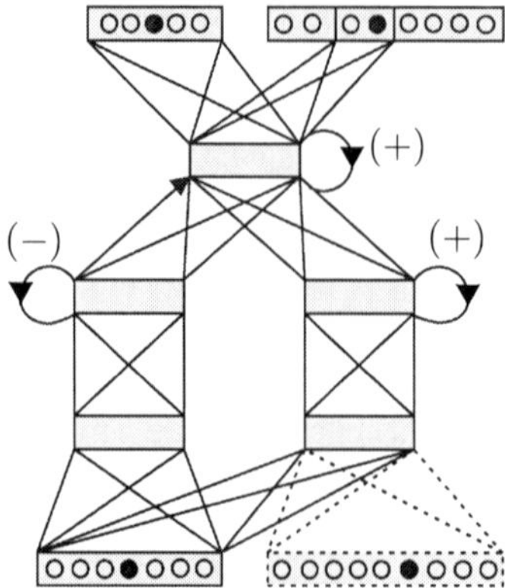

Figure 1: The architecture of the deep bidirectional joint model. By $(+)$ and $(-)$, we indicate a processing in forward and backward time directions, respectively. The dashed part indicates the target input. The model has a class-factored output layer.

Crawl 2015 corpus, amounting to 2.9M sentences (70.7M running words). We use one projection layer, and 3 stacked LSTM layers, with 350 nodes each.

In addition to the RNN-LM, we apply the deep bidirectional joint model (BJM) described in (Sundermeyer et al., 2014a) in 1000-best reranking. As the model depends on the complete alignment path, this variant cannot be applied directly in decoding (Alkhouli et al., 2015). The model assumes a one-to-one alignment between the source and target sentences. This is generated by assigning unaligned source and target words to $\epsilon_{unaligned}$ tokens that are added to the source and target vocabularies. In addition the source and target vocabularies are extended to include $\epsilon_{aligned}$ tokens, which are used to break down multiply-aligned source and target words using the IBM-1 translation tables. For more details we refer the reader to (Sundermeyer et al., 2014a).

The BJM has a projection layer, and computes a forward recurrent state encoding the source and target history, a backward recurrent state encoding the source future, and a third LSTM layer to combine them. The architecture is shown in Figure 1. All layers have 350 nodes. The model was trained on 604K sentence pairs, having 15.4M and 15.7M source and target words respectively. The has respectively 33K and 55K source and target vocabulary.

The neural networks were implemented using

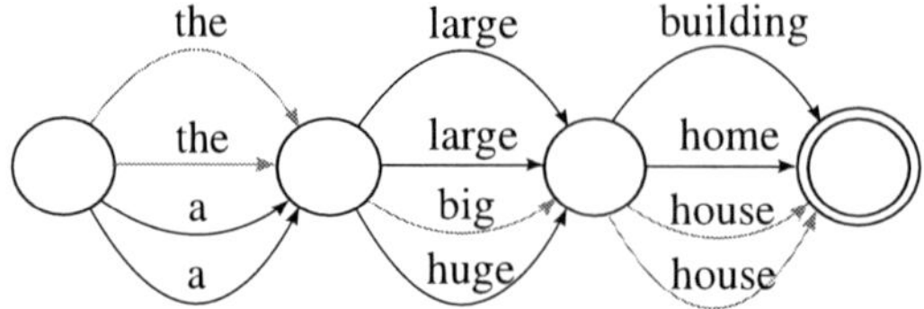

Figure 2: System A: *the large building*; System B: *the large home*; System C: *a big house*; System D: *a huge house*; Reference: *the big house*.

an extension of the RWTHLM toolkit (Sundermeyer et al., 2014b).

2.7 Attention Based Recurrent Neural Network

The second system provided by the RWTH is an attention-based recurrent neural network (NMT) similar to (Bahdanau et al., 2015). We use an implementation based on Blocks (van Merriënboer et al., 2015) and Theano (Bergstra et al., 2010; Bastien et al., 2012).

The network uses the 30K most frequent words on the source and target side as input vocabulary. The decoder and encoder word embeddings are of size 620, the encoder uses a bidirectional layer with 1024 GRUs (Cho et al., 2014) to encode the source side. A layer with 1024 GRUs is used by the decoder.

The network is trained for up to 300K iterations with a batch size of 80. The network was evaluated every 10000 iterations and the best network on the newsdev2016/1 dev set was selected.

The synthetic training data is used as described in Section 2.4 to create additional parallel training data. The new data is weighted by using the News Crawl 2015 corpus (2.3M sentences) once, the Europarl corpus (0.4M sentences) twice and the SETimes2 corpus (0.2M sentences) three times. We use an ensemble of 4 networks, all with the same configuration and training settings. If the neural network creates unknown word the source word where the strongest attention weight points to is copied to the target side. We did not use any regularization as dropout or Gaussian noise.

2.8 System Combination

System combination is applied to produce consensus translations from multiple hypotheses which are obtained from different translation approaches. The consensus translations outperform the individual hypotheses in terms of translation quality.

Table 1: Results of the individual systems for the English→Romanian task. BLEU and TER scores are case-sensitive and given in %.

Individual Systems	newsdev2016/1		newsdev2016/2		newstest2016	
	BLEU	TER	BLEU	TER	BLEU	TER
Phrase-Based	23.7	60.3	27.8	54.7	24.4	58.9
+ additional parallel data	24.3	59.4	29.2	53.0	25.0	58.2
+ NNs	26.0	55.9	31.4	50.7	26.0	56.0
Hierarchical	23.8	60.6	27.9	54.7	24.5	59.0
+ NNs	26.1	56.4	29.7	52.4	25.5	57.1
Attention Network	20.9	63.1	22.7	58.7	21.2	61.5
+ additional parallel data	23.4	59.4	27.6	52.7	24.0	58.0
+ ensemble	25.6	55.0	30.7	48.8	26.1	54.9
System Combination	27.6	55.0	31.7	50.3	26.9	55.4

A system combination implementation which has been developed at RWTH Aachen University (Freitag et al., 2014b) is used to combine the outputs of different engines.

The first step in system combination is generation of confusion networks (CN) from I input translation hypotheses. We need pairwise alignments between the input hypotheses, and the alignments are obtained by METEOR (Banerjee and Lavie, 2005). The hypotheses are then reordered to match a selected skeleton hypothesis in terms of word ordering. We generate I different CNs, each having one of the input systems as the skeleton hypothesis, and the final lattice will be the union of all I generated CNs. In Figure 2 an example of a confusion network with $I = 4$ input translations is depicted. The decoding of a confusion network is finding the shortest path in the network. Each arc is assigned a score of a linear model combination of M different models, which include word penalty, 3-gram language model trained on the input hypotheses, a binary primary system feature that marks the primary hypothesis, and a binary voting feature for each system. The binary voting feature for a system is 1 iff the decoded word is from that system, and 0 otherwise. The different model weights for system combination are trained with MERT.

3 Experimental Evaluation

All three systems use the same preprocessing as described in Section 2.1. The phrase-based system in its baseline configuration was improved by 0.6 BLEU and 0.7 TER points on newstest2016 by adding the synthetic data as described in Section 2.4. The neural networks (Section 2.6 improve the

Table 2: Comparing the systems against each other by computing the BLEU and TER score on the newstest2016. Each system is used as reference once, the reported value is the average between both which makes these value symmetrical. The upper half lists BLEU scores, the lower half TER scores. All values are given in %.

	PBT	HPBT	NMT	Average
PBT	-	62.6	51.1	56.9
HPBT	24.9	-	47.5	55.1
NMT	31.8	34.8	-	49.3
Average	28.3	29.8	33.3	

network by another 1.0 BLEU and 2.2 TER.

The neural networks also improve the hierarchical phrase-based system by 1.0 BLEU and 2.9 TER. We did not try to add the synthetic data to the hierarchical system.

Adding the synthetic data to the NMT system improve the baseline system by 3.8 BLEU and 3.5 TER. An ensemble of four similarly trained networks gives an additional improvement of 2.1 BLEU and in 3.1 TER.

The final step was to combine all three systems using the system combination (Section 2.8) which added another 0.8 BLEU points on top of the neural network system, but caused a small degradation in TER by 0.5 points.

The lower BLEU and higher TER score in Table 2 for the NMT system show that the translations created by it differ more from the PBT and HPBT system then there translation between each other.

4 Conclusion

RWTH participated with a system combination on the English→Romanian WMT 2016 evaluation campaign. The system combination included three different state-of-the-art systems: A phrase-based, a hierarchical phrase-based and a stand alone attention-based neural network system. The phrase-based and the hierarchical phrase-based systems where both supported by a neural network LM and BJM. Synthetic data was used to improve the amount of parallel data for the PBT and the NMT system.

We achieve a performance of 26.9 BLEU and 55.4 TER on the newstest2016 test set.

Acknowledgments

This paper has received funding from the European Union's Horizon 2020 research and innovation programme under grant agreement n° 645452 (QT21).

References

Tamer Alkhouli, Felix Rietig, and Hermann Ney. 2015. Investigations on phrase-based decoding with recurrent neural network language and translation models. In *EMNLP 2015 Tenth Workshop on Statistical Machine Translation*, pages 294–303, Lisbon, Portugal, September.

Alexandre Allauzen, Lauriane Aufrant, Franck Burlot, Elena Knyazeva, Thomas Lavergne, and François Yvon. 2016, to appear. LIMSI@WMT'16 : Machine translation of news. In *Proceedings of the Eleventh Workshop on Statistical Machine Translation*, Berlin, Germany, August. Association for Computational Linguistics.

Dzmitry Bahdanau, Kyunghyun Cho, and Yoshua Bengio. 2015. Neural Machine Translation by Jointly Learning to Align and Translate. In *Proceedings of the International Conference on Learning Representations (ICLR)*, San Diego, May.

Satanjeev Banerjee and Alon Lavie. 2005. METEOR: An Automatic Metric for MT Evaluation with Improved Correlation with Human Judgments. In *43rd Annual Meeting of the Assoc. for Computational Linguistics: Proc. Workshop on Intrinsic and Extrinsic Evaluation Measures for MT and/or Summarization*, pages 65–72, Ann Arbor, MI, June.

Frédéric Bastien, Pascal Lamblin, Razvan Pascanu, James Bergstra, Ian J. Goodfellow, Arnaud Bergeron, Nicolas Bouchard, and Yoshua Bengio. 2012. Theano: new features and speed improvements. Deep Learning and Unsupervised Feature Learning NIPS 2012 Workshop.

James Bergstra, Olivier Breuleux, Frédéric Bastien, Pascal Lamblin, Razvan Pascanu, Guillaume Desjardins, Joseph Turian, David Warde-Farley, and Yoshua Bengio. 2010. Theano: a CPU and GPU math expression compiler. In *Proceedings of the Python for Scientific Computing Conference (SciPy)*, June. Oral Presentation.

Nicola Bertoldi and Marcello Federico. 2009. Domain adaptation for statistical machine translation with monolingual resources. In *Proceedings of the Fourth Workshop on Statistical Machine Translation*, StatMT '09, pages 182–189, Stroudsburg, PA, USA. Association for Computational Linguistics.

Boxing Chen, Roland Kuhn, George Foster, and Howard Johnson. 2011. Unpacking and Transforming Feature Functions: New Ways to Smooth Phrase Tables. In *MT Summit XIII*, pages 269–275, Xiamen, China, September.

D. Chiang. 2007. Hierarchical Phrase-Based Translation. *Computational Linguistics*, 33(2):201–228.

Kyunghyun Cho, Bart van Merrienboer, Caglar Gulcehre, Dzmitry Bahdanau, Fethi Bougares, Holger Schwenk, and Yoshua Bengio. 2014. Learning Phrase Representations using RNN Encoder–Decoder for Statistical Machine Translation. In *Proceedings of the 2014 Conference on Empirical Methods in Natural Language Processing (EMNLP)*, pages 1724–1734, Doha, Qatar, October. Association for Computational Linguistics.

M. Freitag, S. Peitz, J. Wuebker, H. Ney, N. Durrani, M. Huck, P. Koehn, T.-L. Ha, J. Niehues, M. Mediani, T. Herrmann, A. Waibel, N. Bertoldi, M. Cetolo, and M. Federico. 2013. EU-BRIDGE MT: Text Translation of Talks in the EU-BRIDGE Project. In *Proc. of the Int. Workshop on Spoken Language Translation (IWSLT)*, pages 128–135, Heidelberg, Germany, December.

M. Freitag, S. Peitz, J. Wuebker, H. Ney, M. Huck, R. Sennrich, N. Durrani, M. Nadejde, P. Williams, P. Koehn, T. Herrmann, E. Cho, and A. Waibel. 2014a. EU-BRIDGE MT: Combined Machine Translation. In *Proc. of the Workshop on Statistical Machine Translation (WMT)*, pages 105–113, Baltimore, MD, USA, June.

Markus Freitag, Matthias Huck, and Hermann Ney. 2014b. Jane: Open Source Machine Translation System Combination. In *Proc. of the Conf. of the European Chapter of the Assoc. for Computational Linguistics (EACL)*, pages 29–32, Gothenberg, Sweden, April.

Michel Galley and Christopher D. Manning. 2008. A simple and effective hierarchical phrase reordering model. In *Proceedings of the Conference on Empirical Methods in Natural Language Processing*, pages 848–856, Stroudsburg, PA, USA. Association for Computational Linguistics.

Felix A. Gers, Jürgen Schmidhuber, and Fred Cummins. 2000. Learning to forget: Continual prediction with LSTM. *Neural computation*, 12(10):2451–2471.

Felix A. Gers, Nicol N. Schraudolph, and Jürgen Schmidhuber. 2003. Learning precise timing with lstm recurrent networks. *The Journal of Machine Learning Research*, 3:115–143.

Joshua Goodman. 2001. Classes for fast maximum entropy training. *CoRR*, cs.CL/0108006.

Kenneth Heafield, Ivan Pouzyrevsky, Jonathan H. Clark, and Philipp Koehn. 2013. Scalable modified Kneser-Ney language model estimation. In *Proceedings of the 51st Annual Meeting of the Association for Computational Linguistics*, pages 690–696, Sofia, Bulgaria, August.

Sepp Hochreiter and Jürgen Schmidhuber. 1997. Long short-term memory. *Neural computation*, 9(8):1735–1780.

Liang Huang and David Chiang. 2007. Forest Rescoring: Faster Decoding with Integrated Language Models. In *Proceedings of the 45th Annual Meeting of the Association for Computational Linguistics*, pages 144–151, Prague, Czech Republic, June.

Philipp Koehn, Hieu Hoang, Alexandra Birch, Chris Callison-Burch, Marcello Federico, Nicola Bertoldi, Brooke Cowan, Wade Shen, Christine Moran, Richard Zens, Chris Dyer, Ondřej Bojar, Alexandra Constantine, and Evan Herbst. 2007. Moses: Open Source Toolkit for Statistical Machine Translation. pages 177–180, Prague, Czech Republic, June.

Frederic Morin and Yoshua Bengio. 2005. Hierarchical probabilistic neural network language model. In Robert G. Cowell and Zoubin Ghahramani, editors, *Proceedings of the Tenth International Workshop on Artificial Intelligence and Statistics*, pages 246–252. Society for Artificial Intelligence and Statistics.

Franz Josef Och and Hermann Ney. 2003. A Systematic Comparison of Various Statistical Alignment Models. *Computational Linguistics*, 29(1):19–51, March.

Franz Josef Och. 2003. Minimum Error Rate Training in Statistical Machine Translation. In *Proc. of the 41th Annual Meeting of the Association for Computational Linguistics (ACL)*, pages 160–167, Sapporo, Japan, July.

Kishore Papineni, Salim Roukos, Todd Ward, and Wei-Jing Zhu. 2002. Bleu: a Method for Automatic Evaluation of Machine Translation. In *Proceedings of the 41st Annual Meeting of the Association for Computational Linguistics*, pages 311–318, Philadelphia, Pennsylvania, USA, July.

Jan-Thorsten Peter, Farzad Toutounchi, Stephan Peitz, Parnia Bahar, Andreas Guta, and Hermann Ney. 2015. The rwth aachen german to english mt system for iwslt 2015. In *International Workshop on Spoken Language Translation*, pages 15–22, Da Nang, Vietnam, December.

Rico Sennrich, Barry Haddow, and Alexandra Birch. 2016, to appear. Improving neural machine translation models with monolingual data. August.

Matthew Snover, Bonnie Dorr, Richard Schwartz, Linnea Micciulla, and John Makhoul. 2006. A Study of Translation Edit Rate with Targeted Human Annotation. In *Proceedings of the 7th Conference of the Association for Machine Translation in the Americas*, pages 223–231, Cambridge, Massachusetts, USA, August.

Martin Sundermeyer, Ralf Schlüter, and Hermann Ney. 2012. LSTM Neural Networks for Language Modeling. In *Interspeech*, Portland, OR, USA, September.

Martin Sundermeyer, Tamer Alkhouli, Joern Wuebker, and Hermann Ney. 2014a. Translation Modeling with Bidirectional Recurrent Neural Networks. In *Conference on Empirical Methods in Natural Language Processing*, pages 14–25, Doha, Qatar, October.

Martin Sundermeyer, Ralf Schlüter, and Hermann Ney. 2014b. rwthlm - the rwth aachen university neural network language modeling toolkit. In *Interspeech*, pages 2093–2097, Singapore, September.

Bart van Merriënboer, Dzmitry Bahdanau, Vincent Dumoulin, Dmitriy Serdyuk, David Warde-Farley, Jan Chorowski, and Yoshua Bengio. 2015. Blocks and fuel: Frameworks for deep learning. *CoRR*, abs/1506.00619.

David Vilar, Daniel Stein, Matthias Huck, and Hermann Ney. 2010. Jane: Open source hierarchical translation, extended with reordering and lexicon models. In *ACL 2010 Joint Fifth Workshop on Statistical Machine Translation and Metrics MATR*, pages 262–270, Uppsala, Sweden, July.

Joern Wuebker, Matthias Huck, Stephan Peitz, Malte Nuhn, Markus Freitag, Jan-Thorsten Peter, Saab Mansour, and Hermann Ney. 2012. Jane 2: Open source phrase-based and hierarchical statistical machine translation. In *International Conference on Computational Linguistics*, pages 483–491, Mumbai, India, December.

Joern Wuebker, Stephan Peitz, Felix Rietig, and Hermann Ney. 2013. Improving statistical machine translation with word class models. In *Conference on Empirical Methods in Natural Language Processing*, pages 1377–1381, Seattle, WA, USA, October.

Richard Zens and Hermann Ney. 2008. Improvements in Dynamic Programming Beam Search for Phrase-based Statistical Machine Translation. In *International Workshop on Spoken Language Translation*, pages 195–205, Honolulu, Hawaii, October.

Abu-MaTran at WMT 2016 Translation Task: Deep Learning, Morphological Segmentation and Tuning on Character Sequences

Víctor M. Sánchez-Cartagena
Prompsit Language Engineering
Av. Universitat s/n. Edifici Quorum III
E-03202 Elx, Spain
vmsanchez@prompsit.com

Antonio Toral
ADAPT Centre
School of Computing
Dublin City University, Ireland
antonio.toral@dcu.ie

Abstract

This paper presents the systems submitted by the Abu-MaTran project to the English-to-Finnish language pair at the WMT 2016 news translation task. We applied morphological segmentation and deep learning in order to address (i) the data scarcity problem caused by the lack of in-domain parallel data in the constrained task and (ii) the complex morphology of Finnish. We submitted a neural machine translation system, a statistical machine translation system reranked with a neural language model and the combination of their outputs tuned on character sequences. The combination and the neural system were ranked first and second respectively according to automatic evaluation metrics and tied for the first place in the human evaluation.

1 Introduction

This paper presents the machine translation (MT) systems submitted by the Abu-MaTran project to the WMT 2016 news translation task. We participated in the English-to-Finnish constrained task.

English-to-Finnish is a particularly challenging language pair for corpus-based MT because of the lack of in-domain parallel data (the only available parallel corpus in the shared task is *Europarl*) and the complex morphology of Finnish. The fact that the same root can be inflected in many different ways and that nouns can be joined together in order to build compound words exacerbates the aforementioned lack of parallel data problem.

As in our last year's submission (Rubino et al., 2015), we used morphological segmentation (Pirinen, 2015) on the Finnish side in order to deal with data scarcity and reduce the size of the Finnish vocabulary. We also used character-level evaluation

metrics during the development of our systems, which correlate better than word-based ones with human judgements according to the results of last year's metrics shared task (Stanojević et al., 2015) for English-to-Finnish.

When a Finnish sentence is morphologically segmented, it becomes much longer (number of tokens) than its English counterpart. This results in the distance between the Finnish tokens that depend on each other to produce a correct translation increasing too.[1] We addressed this potential issue by introducing deep learning in our systems: we submitted a neural MT (NMT) system and a phrase-based statistical MT (SMT) system enhanced with a neural language model (LM). In the latter, we reduced the length of the Finnish segmented sentences by joining the most frequent sequences of morphs. We also submitted a system that combines the outputs of our best NMT and SMT systems and is tuned on character sequences.

The paper is organised as follows: the data and tools used are described in Section 2, while our NMT, SMT and combined submissions are presented respectively in sections 3, 4 and 5. The paper ends with some concluding remarks.

2 Datasets and Tools

We preprocessed the training corpora with scripts included in the Moses toolkit (Koehn et al., 2007). We performed the following operations: punctuation normalisation, tokenisation, true-casing and escaping of problematic characters. The true-caser is lexicon-based and it was trained on all the monolingual data. In addition, we removed sentence pairs from the parallel corpora where either side is longer than 80 tokens.

---

[1] For instance, the distance between the morph that represents the case of an adjective and the morph that represents the case of the noun being modified by the adjective is increased. Morphs are the segments in which a word is split after applying morphological segmentation (see Section 3.1).

Proceedings of the First Conference on Machine Translation, Volume 2: Shared Task Papers, pages 362–370,
Berlin, Germany, August 11-12, 2016. ©2016 Association for Computational Linguistics

Corpus	Sentences (k)	Words (M)
Europarl v8	2 121	39.5
Common Crawl	113 995	2 416.7
News Crawl 2014–15	6 741	83.1

Table 1: Finnish monolingual data, after preprocessing, used to train the LMs of our SMT submission.

Corpus	Sentences (k)	Words (M)
Europarl v7	2 218	59.9
News Commentary v11	391	9.8
News Crawl 2007–15	117 446	2 713.2
News Discussions	57 804	983.2

Table 2: English monolingual data, after preprocessing, used to train the LM of the Finnish-to-English SMT system we used to backtranslate the Finnish *News Crawl* monolingual corpora into English (see Section 3).

Since the *Common Crawl* Finnish monolingual corpus was obtained by crawling websites, we applied a set of additional preprocessing steps in order to remove as much noisy data as possible: (i) detecting sentences with an incorrect character encoding and re-encoding them with the right one; (ii) replacing XML entities with the characters they represent; (iii) removing sentences with a low proportion of alphabetic characters (less than 50%); (iv) removing short sentences (less than 3 alphabetic tokens); and (v) removing sentences whose first 18 tokens are equal to those in another sentence. The last filtering is necessary because it is relatively common in the corpus to find the same sentence with some segment missing at the end. If these lines were kept, n-gram counts from which LM probabilities are estimated would be less reliable. As a result of these preprocessing steps, around 43 million sentences were removed.

Table 1 shows the Finnish monolingual corpora we used together with their size and Table 3 shows the same information for the parallel corpora. We used an additional synthetic parallel corpus to train our NMT system, which was obtained by backtranslating the Finnish *News Crawl* corpora into English with an SMT system (see Section 3).[2] The monolingual corpora used for training its LM are listed in Table 2.

Throughout the paper we evaluate the systems we build in terms on three automatic evaluation metrics: BLEU (Papineni et al., 2002),

| | | Words (M) | |
Corpus	Sentences (k)	English	Finnish
Europarl v8 backtranslated	1 901	50.9	36.6
News Crawl 2014–15 (only for NMT)	6 674	106.6	82.3

Table 3: Parallel data, after preprocessing, used to train our SMT and NMT systems.

TER (Snover et al., 2006) and chrF1 (Popović, 2015). As the performance obtained in the development (*newsdev2015*) and validation (*newstest2015*) sets guides our decisions, we believe it is sensible to use three metrics with different underlying methodologies and that work on different elements (words and characters). Statistical significance of the difference between systems is computed with paired bootstrap resampling (Koehn, 2004) ($p \leq 0.05$, 1 000 iterations).

3 Neural Machine Translation

NMT systems have been reported to outperform SMT systems for different language pairs (Sennrich et al., 2015a; Luong et al., 2015; Costa-Jussà and Fonollosa, 2016; Chung et al., 2016a). Unlike SMT, in which different models are trained independently and their weights are tuned jointly, in NMT all the components are jointly trained to maximise translation quality. NMT systems have a strong generalisation power because they encode words as real-valued vectors (similar words are close to each other in that vector space) and they are able to model long-distance phenomena thanks to the use of LSTM (Hochreiter and Schmidhuber, 1997) or GRU (Chung et al., 2014) units. We followed the encoder-decoder architecture with attention proposed by Bahdanau et al. (2015).[3]

NMT models are trained only from a parallel corpus, that is, they are not designed to make use of additional target-language (TL) monolingual corpora. Given the lack of in-domain parallel corpora available for English–Finnish, we trained our system on the concatenation of *Europarl* and a synthetic corpus obtained by backtranslating the in-domain monolingual Finnish corpora (*News Crawl*) from Finnish to English. Backtranslation has been reported to be a successful way of integrating TL monolingual corpora into an NMT system (Sennrich et al., 2015a). It was performed by means of a Finnish-to-English SMT system that

---

[2]The number of sentences in *News Crawl* displayed in tables 1 and 3 do not match because, due to time constraints, we did not backtranslate a few tens of thousands of sentences.

[3]We used the code available at: `https://github.com/sebastien-j/LV_groundhog/tree/master/experiments/nmt`

followed the set-up of the rule-based morphologically segmented system from our last year's constrained submission (Rubino et al., 2015). It was trained on *Europarl* and the concatenation of the English monolingual corpora listed in Table 2.

Most of the NMT architectures in the literature can only operate with a fixed TL vocabulary (that ranges from 30 000 to 80 000 words, according to Jean et al. (2015)), since training and decoding computational complexity grows with its size. Although Jean et al. (2015) proposed an to reduce that complexity and hence use larger vocabularies, Sennrich et al. (2015b) showed that segmenting words into smaller units can also reduce complexity, increase effective vocabulary size and even improve translation quality. We followed the latter strategy. The evaluation of character-based NMT approaches (Ling et al., 2015; Costa-Jussà and Fonollosa, 2016; Chung et al., 2016b) was left as future work.

In the remainder of this section, we present the segmentation approach we followed together with the alternatives we evaluated and we describe the training and decoding set-up of our NMT system, including the strategy followed to translate out-of-vocabulary words (OOVs).

3.1 Word Segmentation

Existing word segmentation approaches for NMT (Sennrich et al., 2015b) rely on frequencies of sequences of characters in the training corpus. We studied whether using linguistic information to segment the training corpus allows the neural network to generalise better: we applied the rule-based morphological segmentation provided by `Omorfi` (Pirinen, 2015) for Finnish. It splits words into morphs, that is, minimal segments carrying semantic or syntactic meaning.

We evaluated the segmentation schemes listed below.[4] Table 4 depicts an example of the effect they produce on a Finnish sentence.

- No segmentation at all.

- Byte pair encoding (BPE) on both the source language (SL) and the TL. This is one of the best performing strategies proposed by Sennrich et al. (2015b). It consists of initially segmenting each word in characters, and iteratively joining the most frequent pair of segments in the training corpus. We applied it independently to the SL and TL sides of the parallel corpus. We performed 60 000 join operations on each language.

- BPE only on the TL side of the parallel corpus, since Finnish is morphologically more complex than English.

- Morphological segmentation with `Omorfi` on the TL.

- BPE on the TL using the morphs produced by `Omorfi` as the starting point. We evaluated the effect of performing 1 000, 10 000, 25 000 and 50 000 join operations. Morphological segmentation produces an average sentence length significantly higher than that of the English side of the parallel corpus. After performing 1 000 operations, average sentence lengths are similar: we reduce vocabulary size without significantly increasing sentence length. As the number of operations increases, average sentence length is closer to that of the unsegmented approach.

For each of these segmentation schemes, we trained an NMT system on *Europarl* during 5 days (a model was saved every 3 hours of training), we chose the model that achieved the highest translation quality on *newsdev2015*[5] and evaluated it on *newstest2015*. The remainder of the training and decoding parameters were the same ones we used in our submission (described in Section 3.2).

Table 5 depicts the results of the evaluation together with the vocabulary size of the NMT system[6] and the proportion of tokens in the training corpus that belong to the vocabulary. Results show that, despite the fact that the BPE-based systems have full coverage of the training corpus, their performance is below that of the unsegmented alternative. These results are probably related to the fact that domains of the training and testing corpora do not match, and words in the test set that do not contain subsegments observed in the training

---

[4]We did not include unsupervised morphological segmentation (Virpioja et al., 2013; Grönroos et al., 2014) in our evaluation since the results in our last year's submission (Rubino et al., 2015, Table 4) showed that it was outperformed by rule-based morphological segmentation.

[5]Translation quality was measured by chrF1 in the segmentation alternatives that included BPE, since segments were joined before performing the evaluation and this metric is reported to correlate better than BLEU with human judgements. For the evaluation of the segmentation scheme based solely on `Omorfi`, we chose the best model according to BLEU, as the evaluation was performed before joining the morphs (the TL side of the development corpus was also segmented with `Omorfi`).

[6]This size may represent words or subword units, depending on whether word segmentation was performed.

Segmentation	Sentence
None	haluaisimme , ett oppisimme tst yhden perusasian
BPE: 60k ops	haluaisimme , ett opp→ ←isimme tst yhden perusasi→ ←an
`Omorfi`	halua→ ←isi→ ←mme , ett opp→ ←isi→ ←mme tst yhde→ ←n perus→ ←asia→ ←n
`Omorfi` + BPE: 1k ops.	halua→ ←isimme , ett opp→ ←isimme tst yhden perus→ ←asian
`Omorfi` + BPE: 50k ops.	haluaisimme , ett opp→ ←isimme tst yhden perus→ ←asian
English	*there is one basic lesson I would like us to learn from this*

Table 4: Example of the application of the different segmentation schemes described in Section 3.1 to a Finnish sentence. Arrows represent boundaries between the morphs in which a word is split. Note how the compound word *perusasian* is segmented by the different schemes: `Omorfi` splits it into *perus* ("basic"), *asia* ("thing, affair") and the case marker *-n*, while the application of BPE over it joins the marker to the second noun. The pure BPE scheme, however, fails to segment *perusasian* correctly.

corpus are segmented into very long sequences. The `Omorfi`-based approach, which is domain agnostic, is close to the unsegmented alternative in terms of BLEU and TER (there is no statistically significant difference between them) and clearly outperforms it in terms of the character-level metric chrF1. This shows the effect of segmentation: the system is probably producing a better translation for some parts of compound words and/or producing lemmas that can be found in the reference, but inflected in a different way. Finally, the combination of BPE with morphological segmentation does not bring a clear improvement. In view of the results, we decided to segment the TL side of the training corpus with `Omorfi` in our submission.

3.2 Training and Decoding Details

We generally followed the training set-up by Sennrich et al. (2015b). We defined a hidden layer size of 1 000 and an embedding layer size of 620. We used Adadelta (Zeiler, 2012) with a minibatch size of 80, and reshuffled the training set between epochs. We applied gradient clipping (Pascanu et al., 2013) with a cutoff of 1.0. The vocabulary contained the 50 000 most frequent SL tokens and the 50 000 most frequent TL tokens in the training corpus.

We trained our system during 8 days (a model was saved every 3 hours).[7] We chose the 4 models that produced the highest BLEU score on *news-dev2015*. The training of these 4 models continued for 12 hours without changing the values of the embedding layers. After that, we translated the test set with an ensemble of these 4 models.[8]

3.3 Dealing with Unknown Words

In order to translate OOVs,[9] we followed an enhanced version of the approach by Jean et al. (2015, Sec. 3.3). OOVs in the training corpus were replaced with the special token UNK, as were those in the SL sentences to be translated by the NMT system. As a result, the output contained some UNK tokens.

In order to replace the UNK tokens generated by the model, we identified the most likely SL word to which the unknown TL word was aligned. If the SL word started with an uppercase letter, we copied it to the output. Otherwise, we replaced the UNK token with its translation according to a bilingual dictionary obtained from the parallel corpus with `fast align` (Dyer et al., 2013).

For each UNK token, Jean et al. (2015) selected the SL word with the highest alignment probablity according to the attention mechanism, while our enhanced approach combines the attention mechanism and a heuristic that aims at preserving the named entities in the SL sentence. We considered the top 5 SL words with the highest attention alignment probability for each UNK token,[10] and, for each sentence, we chose the set of SL words that ensured that the maximum number of words that start with an uppercase letter in the SL sentence were included in the translation.[11] Ta-

---

[7]Training was performed on a NVIDIA Tesla K20 GPU.

[8]We used a beam size of 12 for beam search and normalised the probability by sentence length.

[9]We define OOVs as those words either not present in the training corpus or present but not frequent enough to be part of the NMT system vocabulary.

[10]We ignored those SL words whose probability was 4 times lower than that of the most probable SL word.

[11]We relied on the capitalisation of the first character to detect a named entity. We carried out a small study in order to test the accuracy of this approach: from 100 capitalized words (after truecasing) randomly chosen from the English side of *newstest2016*, 76 were named entities that do not need to be translated into Finnish (person names, place names, etc.) and 24 needed to be translated (days of the week, country names, demonyms, etc.). However, when we analyzed only those capitalized SL words that were not part of the vocabulary of the NMT system (and hence they were likely to produce an UNK symbol), the accuracy increased: 23 out of 24

| | voc. size | | coverage | | | | |
Segmentation	SL	TL	SL	TL	BLEU	TER	chrF1
None	50 000	50 000	99.80%	94.01%	**0.1090**	**0.8460**	41.6519
BPE: 60k ops. on SL; 60k ops. on TL	60 000	60 000	100%	100%	0.0838 ↓	0.9219 ↓	40.4590 ↓
BPE: 60k ops. only on TL	50 000	60 000	99.80%	100%	0.0844 ↓	0.9306 ↓	40.2059 ↓
`Omorfi` **on TL**	50 000	50 000	99.80%	99.30%	0.1085	0.8509	43.3688 ↑
`Omorfi` + BPE: 1k ops. on TL	50 000	50 000	99.80%	99.29%	0.1073	0.8837 ↓	42.6609 ↑
`Omorfi` + BPE: 10k ops. on TL	50 000	50 000	99.80%	98.98%	0.1009 ↓	0.8937 ↓	**43.6689** ↑
`Omorfi` + BPE: 25k ops. on TL	50 000	50 000	99.80%	98.39%	0.1034	0.8925 ↓	43.5525 ↑
`Omorfi` + BPE: 50k ops. on TL	50 000	50 000	99.80%	96.60%	0.0963 ↓	0.9500 ↓	43.1849 ↑

Table 5: Results of the evaluation of different word segmentation schemes on an NMT system trained on *Europarl*. The vocabulary size of the NMT system is depicted, as well as the proportion of tokens covered in the training copus. Scores displayed correspond to the evaluation on *newstest2015*. The best score for each metric is shown in bold. An arrow pointing upwards (↑) means that the corresponding system outperforms the system without segmentation by a statistically significant margin, while an arrow pointing downwards (↓) means the opposite: the system without segmentation wins.

System	BLEU	TER	chrF1
best individual model (most probable SL word)	0.1568	0.7714	49.52
ensemble (most probable SL word)	0.1819 ↑	**0.7409** ↑	52.21 ↑
ensemble (preserve named entities)	**0.1830** ↑	0.7411	**52.43** ↑

Table 6: Results of the evaluation on *newstest2016* of our NMT submission (in bold), the simpler strategy for translating unknown words by Jean et al. (2015, Sec. 3.3) (labelled as *most probable SL word*) and our best individual NMT model. The best score for each metric is shown in bold. An arrow pointing upwards (↑) means that the corresponding system outperforms the system in the previous row by a statistically significant margin.

ble 6 shows the results of the automatic evaluation of our submitted NMT system (in bold; as described in the previous section, it is an ensemble of 4 models) on *newstest2016*. We also evaluated the simpler OOV translation strategy by Jean et al. (2015), and the best NMT individual model according to BLEU on the development set. Our enhanced strategy for OOV translation resulted in a statistically significant improvement in terms of BLEU and chrF1. Note also the huge impact of model ensembling.

4 Statistical Machine Translation

Our work on SMT systems built upon our last year's best constrained individual system (Rubino et al., 2015). This was a phrase-based SMT system where the Finnish data was segmented to morphs with `Omorfi` (Pirinen, 2015). It also used two additional models: an Operation Sequence

Model (Durrani et al., 2011) and a Bilingual Neural Language Model (Devlin et al., 2014), as well as three reordering models: word- and phrase-based and hierarchical (Koehn et al., 2005; Galley and Manning, 2008).

This year's SMT systems used the same models and datasets, except for the LMs, which this time were log-linearly interpolated and used the additional corpus available (*Common Crawl*, cf. Table 1). We built three SMT systems, which share the same models and data, with the only difference being the segmentation used in the Finnish data:

- No segmentation.

- Segmentation on morphs (`Omorfi`).

- Segmentation on morphs followed by joining the most frequent sequences (`Omorfi` + BPE).

In the latter we joined the most frequent sequences (1 000 operations) so that the length of the Finnish side (measured in number of tokens) becomes similar to that of the English side. As previously mentioned in Section 3.1, this is a trade-off to avoid both having a big vocabulary (as is the case without segmentation), and having to deal with long-distance phenomena (as is the case with `Omorfi`).

Table 7 shows the results of these three SMT systems. We corroborate the results found out last year, i.e. morphological segmentation outperforms the unsegmented system by a statistically signifcant margin across all the automatic metrics. We also observe that joining the most frequent morphs results in a further improvement on BLEU (2.3% relative), and small changes in TER (−0.5%) and chrF1 (−0.3%).

words were named entities that do not need to be translated).

System	BLEU	TER	chrF1
No segmentation	0.1444	0.7775	49.63
`Omorfi`	0.1501 ↑	0.7717 ↑	**51.13** ↑
`Omorfi` + BPE	**0.1536** ↑	**0.7679** ↑	50.99 ↑

Table 7: Results of the evaluation on *newstest2016* of the SMT systems built. The best score for each metric is shown in bold. An arrow pointing upwards (↑) means that the corresponding system outperforms the system without segmentation by a statistically significant margin.

4.1 Reranking

We reranked the n-best list (top 500 distinct translations) produced by our best SMT system (`Omorfi` + BPE) using two neural LMs: left-to-right (i.e. trained in the same direction as the LMs included in the SMT system) and right-to-left (i.e. reverse direction). We hypothesise that the latter LM might bring a higher improvement as the sequences this LM is trained on have not been used by the SMT decoder.[12]

Both neural LMs were trained on in-domain data (a subset of 4 million sentences[13] randomly selected from *News Crawl*) with the `rwthlm` toolkit (Sundermeyer et al., 2014). The main parameters we used are as follows: vocabulary limited to the 50 000 most frequent tokens, 2 layers (linear and LSTM), both of size 200 and 1 000 word classes, generated with `mkcls`.

Table 8 shows the results of reranking using left-to-right and right-to-left neural LMs on their own and jointly (row bidirectional). Reranking with left-to-right or the right-to-left LMs on their own does not result in a substantial improvement. However, when both LMs are used jointly we observe better scores for all the metrics: 1.7% relative improvement for BLEU, -0.5% for TER and 0.1% for chrF1.

5 System Combination

As we have seen in the previous two sections, our best NMT system outperforms by a wide margin our best SMT system. These two systems are typologically different, and thus, despite the gap in performance, we might expect them to have complementary strengths. We therefore explored combining both systems in order to answer the following question: whether SMT, despite the gap in performance, can still be useful, used jointly with

System	BLEU	TER	chrF1
Without reranking	0.1536	0.7679	50.99
Left-to-right	0.1536	0.7671	50.96
Right-to-left	0.1536	0.7707	50.94
Bidirectional	**0.1562** ↑	**0.7644** ↑	**51.04**

Table 8: Results of the different reranking strategies applied to the best SMT system (`Omorfi` + BPE) on *newstest2016*. The best score for each metric is shown in bold, as is the system submitted. An arrow pointing upwards (↑) means that the corresponding system outperforms the system without reranking by a statistically significant margin.

NMT, to improve upon NMT on its own.

We combined the outputs produced by the best NMT and SMT systems with `MEMT` (Heafield and Lavie, 2010). We used default settings, except for radius (5), following empirical results obtained on *newsdev2015*. The LM used in the combination was built on the concatenation of all the Finnish monolingual corpora available, cf. Table 1.

As the systems combined use different segmentations (`Omorfi` in NMT and `Omorfi` followed by BPE in SMT), we joined the morphs before combining them. Therefore the tuning of the system combination was performed without segmentation. Since chrF1 was found to correlate well with human evaluation for Finnish last year (Stanojević et al., 2015), we explored tuning on this metric, alongside tuning on BLEU.

Finally, we reranked the n-best list of the system combination (top 500 translations) with the same procedure used to rerank the best SMT system (cf. Section 4.1). While the best SMT system was reranked on segmented data (`Omorfi` + BPE), the output of the system combination is not segmented. Therefore, similarly to what we did for system combination, we explored tuning the reranking on chrF1.

Table 9 shows the results of system combination and its rerankings. In system combination, we observe that tuning on character sequences results in considerably better scores compared to tuning on BLEU. That said, the output produced by the best system combination system without reranking (i.e. tuned on chrF1) is still worse than the one produced by the NMT system alone according the automatic metrics (-3.4% relative on BLEU and -0.1% on chrF1) except for TER (2.3% relative improvement).

Overall, reranking the system combination[14]

---

[12]Because of the way SMT decoders work they can use left-to-right LMs but not reverse LMs.

[13]Due to time constraints.

[14]We reranked the system combination that performed

System	BLEU	TER	chrF1
Best SMT	0.1562	0.7644	51.04
Best NMT	0.1830	0.7411	52.43
Combo (BLEU)	0.1638	0.7298 ↑	51.75
Combo (chrF1)	0.1767	**0.7241** ↑	52.37
Reranked (BLEU)	0.1791	0.7257 ↑	52.38
Reranked (chrF1)	**0.1845**	0.7290 ↑	**52.65** ↑

Table 9: Results of the system combination experiments on *newstest2016*. The best score for each metric is shown in bold, as is the system submitted. An arrow pointing upwards (↑) means that the corresponding system outperforms the best NMT system by a statistically significant margin.

yields better scores, tuning both on BLEU and chrF1, with the latter leading to the best results across all metrics (except TER). This system outperforms the NMT system in terms of TER and chrF1 and it is the system combination output that we submitted.

6 Conclusions

Our participation in WMT 2016 news translation shared task focused on tackling data scarcity in English-to-Finnish translation with the help of morphological segmentation and deep learning.

Our experiments showed that rule-based morphological segmentation improves translation quality when applied to both NMT and SMT. In the latter, we had to adapt the segmentation strategy to avoid generating a training corpus with very different SL and TL sentence lengths. On the contrary, difference in sentence length was not a relevant factor in NMT.

The use of deep learning approaches to MT allowed us to obtain a remarkable improvement over SMT. Our best NMT system outperforms our best SMT system by a huge margin and their combination is only slightly better than the NMT system according to automatic evaluation. Our best SMT system also includes a neural LM but our results suggest that pure neural MT approaches constitute an important breakthrough.

Tuning on character sequences (chrF1 metric),[15] used for system combination, resulted in better performance than tuning on the *de facto* standard BLEU, corroborating the results seen in human evaluation, i.e. better correlation.

Our combined and NMT submissions were

ranked first and second respectively (both in terms of BLEU and TER) in the English-to-Finnish news translation task automatic evaluation[16] and they tied for the first place in the human evaluation.

Acknowledgments

The research leading to these results has received funding from the European Union Seventh Framework Programme FP7/2007-2013 under grant agreement PIAP-GA-2012-324414 (Abu-MaTran). We would like to thank the Irish Centre for High-End Computing (www.ichec.ie) for providing computational infrastructure and Kazuki Irie for his help to our questions re RWTHLM.

References

Dzmitry Bahdanau, Kyunghyun Cho, and Yoshua Bengio. 2015. Neural Machine Translation by Jointly Learning to Align and Translate. *arXiv preprint arXiv:1409.0473* .

Junyoung Chung, Kyunghyun Cho, and Yoshua Bengio. 2016a. A character-level decoder without explicit segmentation for neural machine translation. *arXiv preprint arXiv:1603.06147* .

Junyoung Chung, Kyunghyun Cho, and Yoshua Bengio. 2016b. A character-level decoder without explicit segmentation for neural machine translation. *arXiv preprint arXiv:1603.06147* .

Junyoung Chung, Çaglar Gülçehre, KyungHyun Cho, and Yoshua Bengio. 2014. Empirical evaluation of gated recurrent neural networks on sequence modeling. *arXiv preprint arXiv:1412.3555* .

Marta R. Costa-Jussà and José A. R. Fonollosa. 2016. Character-based neural machine translation. *arXiv preprint arXiv:1603.00810* .

Jacob Devlin, Rabih Zbib, Zhongqiang Huang, Thomas Lamar, Richard Schwartz, and John Makhoul. 2014. Fast and Robust Neural Network Joint Models for Statistical Machine Translation. In *Proceedings of the 52nd Annual Meeting of the Association for Computational Linguistics (Volume 1: Long Papers)*. Baltimore, Maryland, pages 1370–1380.

Nadir Durrani, Helmut Schmid, and Alexander Fraser. 2011. A Joint Sequence Translation

---

best, i.e. the one tuned on chrF1.

[15]The code has been made available as part of Joshua and can be found at `https://github.com/apache/incubator-joshua/pull/27`

[16]The automatic evaluation scores reported in this paper do not always match those at `http://matrix.statmt.org` because we normalised the punctuation of the TL side of the test sets before computing them.

Model with Integrated Reordering. In *Proceedings of the 49th Annual Meeting of the Association for Computational Linguistics: Human Language Technologies*. Portland, Oregon, USA, pages 1045–1054.

Chris Dyer, Victor Chahuneau, and Noah A. Smith. 2013. A Simple, Fast, and Effective Reparameterization of IBM Model 2. In *Proceedings of the 2013 Conference of the North American Chapter of the Association for Computational Linguistics: Human Language Technologies*. Atlanta, Georgia, pages 644–648.

Michel Galley and Christopher D. Manning. 2008. A simple and effective hierarchical phrase reordering model. In *Proceedings of the Conference on Empirical Methods in Natural Language Processing*. Honolulu, Hawaii, pages 848–856.

Stig-Arne Grönroos, Sami Virpioja, Peter Smit, and Mikko Kurimo. 2014. Morfessor flatcat: An hmm-based method for unsupervised and semi-supervised learning of morphology. In *Proceedings of COLING 2014, the 25th International Conference on Computational Linguistics: Technical Papers*. Dublin City University and Association for Computational Linguistics, Dublin, Ireland, pages 1177–1185.

Kenneth Heafield and Alon Lavie. 2010. Combining Machine Translation Output with Open Source: The Carnegie Mellon Multi-Engine Machine Translation Scheme. *The Prague Bulletin of Mathematical Linguistics* 93:27–36.

Sepp Hochreiter and Jürgen Schmidhuber. 1997. Long short-term memory. *Neural computation* 9(8):1735–1780.

Sébastien Jean, Kyunghyun Cho, Roland Memisevic, and Yoshua Bengio. 2015. On using very large target vocabulary for neural machine translation. In *Proceedings of the 53rd Annual Meeting of the Association for Computational Linguistics and the 7th International Joint Conference on Natural Language Processing (Volume 1: Long Papers)*. Beijing, China, pages 1–10.

Philipp Koehn. 2004. Statistical significance tests for machine translation evaluation. In *Proceedings of the Conference on Empirical Methods in Natural Language Processing*. Barcelona, Spain, volume 4, pages 388–395.

Philipp Koehn, Amittai Axelrod, Alexandra Birch, Chris Callison-Burch, Miles Osborne, David Talbot, and Michael White. 2005. Edinburgh system description for the 2005 IWSLT speech translation evaluation. In *Proceesings of the International Workshop on Spoken Language Translation*. pages 68–75.

Philipp Koehn, Hieu Hoang, Alexandra Birch, Chris Callison-Burch, Marcello Federico, Nicola Bertoldi, Brooke Cowan, Wade Shen, Christine Moran, Richard Zens, Chris Dyer, Ondřej Bojar, Alexandra Constantin, and Evan Herbst. 2007. Moses: Open source toolkit for statistical machine translation. In *Proceedings of the 45th Annual Meeting of the ACL on Interactive Poster and Demonstration Sessions*. Prague, Czech Republic, pages 177–180.

Wang Ling, Isabel Trancoso, Chris Dyer, and Alan W Black. 2015. Character-based neural machine translation. *arXiv preprint arXiv:1511.04586* .

Minh-Thang Luong, Hieu Pham, and Christopher D. Manning. 2015. Effective approaches to attention-based neural machine translation. In *Proceedings of the 2015 Conference on Empirical Methods in Natural Language Processing*. Lisbon, Portugal, pages 1412–1421.

Kishore Papineni, Salim Roukos, Todd Ward, and Wei-Jing Zhu. 2002. Bleu: a method for automatic evaluation of machine translation. In *Proceedings of 40th Annual Meeting of the Association for Computational Linguistics*. Philadelphia, Pennsylvania, USA, pages 311–318.

Razvan Pascanu, Tomas Mikolov, and Yoshua Bengio. 2013. On the difficulty of training recurrent neural networks. In Sanjoy Dasgupta and David Mcallester, editors, *Proceedings of the 30th International Conference on Machine Learning (ICML-13)*. JMLR Workshop and Conference Proceedings, volume 28, pages 1310–1318.

Tommi A. Pirinen. 2015. Omorfi —free and open source morphological lexical database for finnish. In *Proceedings of the 20th Nordic Conference of Computational Linguistics (NODALIDA 2015)*. Vilnius, Lithuania, pages 313–315.

Maja Popović. 2015. chrF: character n-gram F-score for automatic MT evaluation. In *Proceedings of the Tenth Workshop on Statistical Machine Translation*. Lisbon, Portugal, pages 392–395.

Raphael Rubino, Tommi Pirinen, Miquel Esplà-Gomis, Nikola Ljubešić, Sergio Ortiz Rojas,

Vassilis Papavassiliou, Prokopis Prokopidis, and Antonio Toral. 2015. Abu-matran at wmt 2015 translation task: Morphological segmentation and web crawling. In *Proceedings of the Tenth Workshop on Statistical Machine Translation*. Lisbon, Portugal, pages 184–191.

Rico Sennrich, Barry Haddow, and Alexandra Birch. 2015a. Improving Neural Machine Translation Models with Monolingual Data. *arXiv preprint arXiv:1511.06709* .

Rico Sennrich, Barry Haddow, and Alexandra Birch. 2015b. Neural machine translation of rare words with subword units. *arXiv preprint arXiv:1508.07909* .

Matthew Snover, Bonnie Dorr, Richard Schwartz, Linnea Micciulla, and John Makhoul. 2006. A study of translation edit rate with targeted human annotation. In *Proceedings of the 7th biennial conference of the Association for Machine Translation in the Americas*. Cambridge, USA, pages 223–231.

Miloš Stanojević, Amir Kamran, Philipp Koehn, and Ondřej Bojar. 2015. Results of the WMT15 Metrics Shared Task. In *Proceedings of the Tenth Workshop on Statistical Machine Translation*. Lisbon, Portugal, pages 256–273.

Martin Sundermeyer, Ralf Schlüter, and Hermann Ney. 2014. rwthlm – the RWTH Aachen university neural network language modeling toolkit. In *Proceedings of the 15th Annual Conference of the International Speech Communication Association*. Singapore, pages 2093–2097.

Sami Virpioja, Peter Smit, Stig-Arne Grönroos, and Mikko Kurimo. 2013. Morfessor 2.0: Python implementation and extensions for morfessor baseline.

Matthew D Zeiler. 2012. Adadelta: An adaptive learning rate method. *arXiv preprint arXiv:1212.5701* .

Edinburgh Neural Machine Translation Systems for WMT 16

Rico Sennrich and **Barry Haddow** and **Alexandra Birch**
School of Informatics, University of Edinburgh
`{rico.sennrich,a.birch}@ed.ac.uk, bhaddow@inf.ed.ac.uk`

Abstract

We participated in the WMT 2016 shared news translation task by building neural translation systems for four language pairs, each trained in both directions: English↔Czech, English↔German, English↔Romanian and English↔Russian. Our systems are based on an attentional encoder-decoder, using BPE subword segmentation for open-vocabulary translation with a fixed vocabulary. We experimented with using automatic back-translations of the monolingual News corpus as additional training data, pervasive dropout, and target-bidirectional models. All reported methods give substantial improvements, and we see improvements of 4.3–11.2 BLEU over our baseline systems. In the human evaluation, our systems were the (tied) best constrained system for 7 out of 8 translation directions in which we participated.[1][2]

1 Introduction

We participated in the WMT 2016 shared news translation task by building neural translation systems for four language pairs: English↔Czech, English↔German, English↔Romanian and English↔Russian. Our systems are based on an attentional encoder-decoder (Bahdanau et al., 2015), using BPE subword segmentation for open-vocabulary translation with a fixed vocabulary (Sennrich et al., 2016b). We experimented with using automatic back-translations of the

monolingual News corpus as additional training data (Sennrich et al., 2016a), pervasive dropout (Gal, 2015), and target-bidirectional models.

2 Baseline System

Our systems are attentional encoder-decoder networks (Bahdanau et al., 2015). We base our implementation on the dl4mt-tutorial[3], which we enhanced with new features such as ensemble decoding and pervasive dropout.

We use minibatches of size 80, a maximum sentence length of 50, word embeddings of size 500, and hidden layers of size 1024. We clip the gradient norm to 1.0 (Pascanu et al., 2013). We train the models with Adadelta (Zeiler, 2012), reshuffling the training corpus between epochs. We validate the model every 10 000 minibatches via BLEU on a validation set (newstest2013, newstest2014, or half of newsdev2016 for EN↔RO). We perform early stopping for single models, and use the 4 last saved models (with models saved every 30 000 minibatches) for the ensemble results. Note that ensemble scores are the result of a single training run. Due to resource limitations, we did not train ensemble components independently, which could result in more diverse models and better ensembles.

Decoding is performed with beam search with a beam size of 12. For some language pairs, we used the AmuNMT C++ decoder[4] as a more efficient alternative to the theano implementation of the dl4mt tutorial.

2.1 Byte-pair encoding (BPE)

To enable open-vocabulary translation, we segment words via byte-pair encoding (BPE)[5] (Sen-

---

[1]We have released the implementation that we used for the experiments as an open source toolkit: `https://github.com/rsennrich/nematus`

[2]We have released scripts, sample configs, synthetic training data and trained models: `https://github.com/rsennrich/wmt16-scripts`

[3]`https://github.com/nyu-dl/dl4mt-tutorial`

[4]`https://github.com/emjotde/amunmt`

[5]`https://github.com/rsennrich/subword-nmt`

Proceedings of the First Conference on Machine Translation, Volume 2: Shared Task Papers, pages 371–376,
Berlin, Germany, August 11-12, 2016. ©2016 Association for Computational Linguistics

nrich et al., 2016b). BPE, originally devised as a compression algorithm (Gage, 1994), is adapted to word segmentation as follows:

First, each word in the training vocabulary is represented as a sequence of characters, plus an end-of-word symbol. All characters are added to the symbol vocabulary. Then, the most frequent symbol pair is identified, and all its occurrences are merged, producing a new symbol that is added to the vocabulary. The previous step is repeated until a set number of merge operations have been learned.

BPE starts from a character-level segmentation, but as we increase the number of merge operations, it becomes more and more different from a pure character-level model in that frequent character sequences, and even full words, are encoded as a single symbol. This allows for a trade-off between the size of the model vocabulary and the length of training sequences. The ordered list of merge operations, learned on the training set, can be applied to any text to segment words into subword units that are in-vocabulary in respect to the training set (except for unseen characters).

To increase consistency in the segmentation of the source and target text, we combine the source and target side of the training set for learning BPE. For each language pair, we learn 89 500 merge operations.

3 Experimental Features

3.1 Synthetic Training Data

WMT provides task participants with large amounts of monolingual data, both in-domain and out-of-domain. We exploit this monolingual data for training as described in (Sennrich et al., 2016a). Specifically, we sample a subset of the available target-side monolingual corpora, translate it automatically into the source side of the respective language pair, and then use this synthetic parallel data for training. For example, for EN→RO, the back-translation is performed with a RO→EN system, and vice-versa.

Sennrich et al. (2016a) motivate the use of monolingual data with domain adaptation, reducing overfitting, and better modelling of fluency. We sample monolingual data from the News Crawl corpora[6], which is in-domain with respect

type	DE	CS	RO	RU
parallel	4.2	52.0	0.6	2.1
synthetic ($* \rightarrow$EN)	4.2	10.0	2.0	2.0
synthetic (EN$\rightarrow *$)	3.6	8.2	2.3	2.0

Table 1: Amount of parallel and synthetic training data (number of sentences, in millions) for EN-* language pairs. For synthetic data, we separate the data according to whether the original monolingual language is English or not.

to the test set.

The amount of monolingual data backtranslated for each translation direction ranges from 2 million to 10 million sentences. Statistics about the amount of parallel and synthetic training data are shown in Table 1. With dl4mt, we observed a translation speed of about 200 000 sentences per day (on a single Titan X GPU).

3.2 Pervasive Dropout

For English↔Romanian, we observed poor performance because of overfitting. To mitigate this, we apply dropout to all layers in the network, including recurrent ones.

Previous work dropped out different units at each time step. When applied to recurrent connections, this has the downside that it impedes the information flow over long distances, and Pham et al. (2014) propose to only apply dropout to nonrecurrent connections.

Instead, we follow the approach suggested by Gal (2015), and use the same dropout mask at each time step. Our implementation differs from the recommendations by Gal (2015) in one respect: we also drop words at random, but we do so on a token level, not on a type level. In other words, if a word occurs multiple times in a sentence, we may drop out any number of its occurrences, and not just none or all.

In our English↔Romanian experiments, we drop out full words (both on the source and target side) with a probability of 0.1. For all other layers, the dropout probability is set to 0.2.

3.3 Target-bidirectional Translation

We found that during decoding, the model would occasionally assign a high probability to words based on the target context alone, ignoring the

---

[6]Due to recency effects, we expect last year's corpus to be most relevant, and sampled from News Crawl 2015 for EN-RO, EN-RU and EN-CS; for EN-DE, we re-used data from

(Sennrich et al., 2016a), which was randomly sampled from News Crawl 2007–2014.

system	EN→DE		DE→EN	
	dev	test	dev	test
baseline	22.4	26.8	26.4	28.5
+synthetic	25.8	31.6	29.9	36.2
+ensemble	27.5	33.1	31.5	37.5
+r2l reranking	**28.1**	**34.2**	**32.1**	**38.6**

Table 2: English↔German translation results (BLEU) on dev (newstest2015) and test (newstest2016). Submitted system in bold.

source sentence. We speculate that this is an instance of the label bias problem (Lafferty et al., 2001).

To mitigate this problem, we experiment with training separate models that produce the target text from right-to-left (r2l), and re-scoring the n-best lists that are produced by the main (left-to-right) models with these r2l models. Since the right-to-left model will see a complementary target context at each time step, we expect that the averaged probabilities will be more robust. In parallel to our experiments, this idea was published by Liu et al. (2016).

We increase the size of the n-best-list to 50 for the reranking experiments.

A possible criticism of the l-r/r-l reranking approach is that the gains actually come from adding diversity to the ensemble, since we are now using two independent runs. However experiments in (Liu et al., 2016) show that a l-r/r-l reranking systems is stronger than an ensemble created from two independent l-r runs.

4 Results

4.1 English↔German

Table 2 shows results for English↔German. We observe improvements of 3.4–5.7 BLEU from training with a mix of parallel and synthetic data, compared to the baseline that is only trained on parallel data. Using an ensemble of the last 4 checkpoints gives further improvements (1.3–1.7 BLEU). Our submitted system includes reranking of the 50-best output of the left-to-right model with a right-to-left model – again an ensemble of the last 4 checkpoints – with uniform weights. This yields an improvements of 0.6–1.1 BLEU.

4.2 English↔Czech

For English→Czech, we trained our baseline model on the complete WMT16 parallel training set (including CzEng 1.6pre (Bojar et al., 2016)), until we observed convergence on our heldout set (newstest2014). This took approximately 1M minibatches, or 3 weeks. Then we continued training the model on a new parallel corpus, comprising 8.2M sentences back-translated from the Czech monolingual news2015, 5 copies of news-commentary v11, and 9M sentences sampled from Czeng 1.6pre. The model used for back-translation was a neural MT model from earlier experiments, trained on WMT15 data. The training on this synthetic mix continued for a further 400,000 minibatches.

The right-left model was trained using a similar process, but with the target side of the parallel corpus reversed prior to training. The resulting model had a slightly lower BLEU score on the dev data than the standard left-right model. We can see in Table 3 that back-translation improves performance by 2.2–2.8 BLEU, and that the final system (+r2l reranking) improves by 0.7–1.0 BLEU on the ensemble of 4, and 4.3–4.9 on the baseline.

For Czech→English the training process was similar to the above, except that we created the synthetic training data (back-translated from samples of news2015 monolingual English) in batches of 2.5M, and so were able to observe the effect of increasing the amount of synthetic data. After training a baseline model on all the WMT16 parallel set, we continued training with a parallel corpus consisting of 2 copies of the 2.5M sentences of back-translated data, 5 copies of news-commentary v11, and a matching quantity of data sampled from Czeng 1.6pre. After training this to convergence, we restarted training from the baseline model using 5M sentences of back-translated data, 5 copies of news-commentary v11, and a matching quantity of data sampled from Czeng 1.6pre. We repeated this with 7.5M sentences from news2015 monolingual, and then with 10M sentences of news2015. The back-translations were, as for English→Czech, created with an earlier NMT model trained on WMT15 data. Our final Czech→English was an ensemble of 8 systems – the last 4 save-points of the 10M synthetic data run, and the last 4 save-points of the 7.5M run. We show this as ensemble8 in Table 3, and the +synthetic results are on the last (i.e. 10M) synthetic data run.

We also show in Table 4 how increasing the amount of back-translated data affects the results.

system	EN→CS		CS→EN	
	dev	test	dev	test
baseline	18.5	20.9	23.8	25.3
+synthetic	20.7	23.7	27.2	30.1
+ensemble	22.1	24.8	28.6	31.0
+ensemble8	–	–	**29.0**	**31.4**
+r2l reranking	**22.8**	**25.8**	–	–

Table 3: English↔Czech translation results (BLEU) on dev (newstest2015) and test (newstest2016). Submitted system in bold.

system	best single		ensemble4	
	dev	test	dev	test
baseline	23.8	25.3	25.5	26.8
+2.5M synthetic	26.7	29.4	27.7	30.4
+5M synthetic	27.2	29.3	28.2	30.4
+7.5M synthetic	27.2	29.7	28.4	30.8
+10M synthetic	27.2	30.1	28.6	31.0

Table 4: Czech→English translation results (BLEU) on dev (newstest2015) and test (newstest2016), after continued training with increasing amounts of back-translated synthetic data. For each row, training was continued from the baseline model until convergence.

We see that most of the gain from back-translation comes with the first batch, but increasing the amount of back-translated data does gradually improve performance.

4.3 English↔Romanian

The results of our English↔Romanian experiments are shown in Table 5. This language pair has the smallest amount of parallel training data, and we found dropout to be very effective, yielding improvements of 4–5 BLEU.[7]

We found that the use of diacritics was inconsistent in the Romanian training (and development) data, so for Romanian→English we removed diacritics from the Romanian source side, obtaining improvements of 1.3–1.4 BLEU.

Synthetic training data gives improvements of 4.1–5.1 BLEU. for English→Romanian, we found that the best single system outperformed the ensemble of the last 4 checkpoints on dev, and we thus submitted the best single system as primary

---

^{7}We also tested dropout for EN→DE with 8 million sentence pairs of training data, but found no improvement after 10 days of training. We speculate that dropout could still be helpful for datasets of this size with longer training times and/or larger networks.

system	EN→RO		RO→EN	
	dev	test	dev	test
baseline	20.2	19.2	23.6	22.7
+dropout	24.2	23.9	28.7	27.8
+remove diacritics	-	-	30.0	29.2
+synthetic	**29.3**	**28.1**	34.8	33.3
+ensemble	29.0	28.2	**35.3**	**33.9**

Table 5: English↔Romanian translation results (BLEU) on dev (newsdev2016), and test (newstest2016). Submitted system in bold.

system	EN→RU		RU→EN	
	dev	test	dev	test
baseline	21.3	20.3	22.7	22.5
+synthetic	25.8	24.3	27.1	26.9
+ensemble	**27.0**	**26.0**	**28.3**	**28.0**

Table 6: English↔Russian translation results (BLEU) on dev (newstest2015) and test (newstest2016). Submitted system in bold.

system.

4.4 English↔Russian

For English↔Russian, we cannot effectively learn BPE on the joint vocabulary because alphabets differ. We thus follow the approach described in (Sennrich et al., 2016b), first mapping the Russian text into Latin characters via ISO-9 transliteration, then learning the BPE operations on the concatenation of the English and latinized Russian training data, then mapping the BPE operations back into Cyrillic alphabet. We apply the Latin BPE operations to the English data (training data and input), and both the Cyrillic and Latin BPE operations to the Russian data.

Translation results are shown in Table 6. As for the other language pairs, we observe strong improvements from synthetic training data (4–4.4 BLEU). Ensembles yield another 1.1–1.7 BLEU.

5 Shared Task Results

Table 7 shows the ranking of our submitted systems at the WMT16 shared news translation task. Our submissions are ranked (tied) first for 5 out of 8 translation directions in which we participated: EN↔CS, EN↔DE, and EN→RO. They are also the (tied) best constrained system for EN→RU and RO→EN, or 7 out of 8 translation directions in total.

direction	BLEU rank	human rank
EN→CS	1 of 9	1 of 20
EN→DE	1 of 11	1 of 15
EN→RO	2 of 10	1–2 of 12
EN→RU	1 of 8	2–5 of 12
CS→EN	1 of 4	1 of 12
DE→EN	1 of 6	1 of 10
RO→EN	2 of 5	2 of 7
RU→EN	3 of 6	5 of 10

Table 7: Automatic (BLEU) and human ranking of our submitted systems (uedin-nmt) at WMT16 shared news translation task. Automatic rankings are taken from `http://matrix.statmt.org`, only considering primary systems. Human rankings include anonymous online systems, and for EN↔CS, systems from the tuning task.

Our models are also used in QT21-HimL-SysComb (Peter et al., 2016), ranked 1–2 for EN→RO, and in AMU-UEDIN (Junczys-Dowmunt et al., 2016), ranked 2–3 for EN→RU, and 1–2 for RU→EN.

6 Conclusion

We describe Edinburgh's neural machine translation systems for the WMT16 shared news translation task. For all translation directions, we observe large improvements in translation quality from using synthetic parallel training data, obtained by back-translating in-domain monolingual target-side data. Pervasive dropout on all layers was used for English↔Romanian, and gave substantial improvements. For English↔German and English→Czech, we trained a right-to-left model with reversed target side, and we found reranking the system output with these reversed models helpful.

Acknowledgments

This project has received funding from the European Union's Horizon 2020 research and innovation programme under grant agreements 645452 (QT21), 644333 (TraMOOC) and 644402 (HimL).

References

Dzmitry Bahdanau, Kyunghyun Cho, and Yoshua Bengio. 2015. Neural Machine Translation by Jointly Learning to Align and Translate. In *Proceedings of the International Conference on Learning Representations (ICLR)*.

Ondřej Bojar, Ondřej Dušek, Tom Kocmi, Jindřich Libovický, Michal Novák, Martin Popel, Roman Sudarikov, and Dušan Variš. 2016. CzEng 1.6: Enlarged Czech-English Parallel Corpus with Processing Tools Dockered. In *Text, Speech and Dialogue: 19th International Conference, TSD 2016, Brno, Czech Republic, September 12-16, 2016, Proceedings*. Springer Verlag, September 12-16. In press.

Philip Gage. 1994. A New Algorithm for Data Compression. *C Users J.*, 12(2):23–38, February.

Yarin Gal. 2015. A Theoretically Grounded Application of Dropout in Recurrent Neural Networks. *ArXiv e-prints*.

Marcin Junczys-Dowmunt, Tomasz Dwojak, and Rico Sennrich. 2016. The AMU-UEDIN Submission to the WMT16 News Translation Task: Attention-based NMT Models as Feature Functions in Phrase-based SMT. In *Proceedings of the First Conference on Machine Translation (WMT16)*, Berlin, Germany.

John D. Lafferty, Andrew McCallum, and Fernando C. N. Pereira. 2001. Conditional Random Fields: Probabilistic Models for Segmenting and Labeling Sequence Data. In *Proceedings of the Eighteenth International Conference on Machine Learning*, pages 282–289, San Francisco, CA, USA. Morgan Kaufmann Publishers Inc.

Lemao Liu, Masao Utiyama, Andrew Finch, and Eiichiro Sumita. 2016. Agreement on Target-bidirectional Neural Machine Translation . In *NAACL HLT 16*, San Diego, CA.

Razvan Pascanu, Tomas Mikolov, and Yoshua Bengio. 2013. On the difficulty of training recurrent neural networks. In *Proceedings of the 30th International Conference on Machine Learning, ICML 2013*, pages 1310–1318, , Atlanta, GA, USA.

Jan-Thorsten Peter, Tamer Alkhouli, Hermann Ney, Matthias Huck, Fabienne Braune, Alexander Fraser, Aleš Tamchyna, Ondřej Bojar, Barry Haddow, Rico Sennrich, Frédéric Blain, Lucia Specia, Jan Niehues, Alex Waibel, Alexandre Allauzen, Lauriane Aufrant, Franck Burlot, Elena Knyazeva, Thomas Lavergne, François Yvon, and Marcis Pinnis. 2016. The QT21/HimL Combined Machine Translation System. In *Proceedings of the First Conference on Machine Translation (WMT16)*, Berlin, Germany.

Vu Pham, Théodore Bluche, Christopher Kermorvant, and Jérôme Louradour. 2014. Dropout Improves Recurrent Neural Networks for Handwriting Recognition. In *14th International Conference on Frontiers in Handwriting Recognition, ICFHR 2014, Crete, Greece, September 1-4, 2014*, pages 285–290.

Rico Sennrich, Barry Haddow, and Alexandra Birch. 2016a. Improving Neural Machine Translation Models with Monolingual Data. In *Proceedings of the 54th Annual Meeting of the Association for Computational Linguistics (ACL 2016)*, Berlin, Germany.

Rico Sennrich, Barry Haddow, and Alexandra Birch. 2016b. Neural Machine Translation of Rare Words with Subword Units. In *Proceedings of the 54th Annual Meeting of the Association for Computational Linguistics (ACL 2016)*, Berlin, Germany.

Matthew D. Zeiler. 2012. ADADELTA: An Adaptive Learning Rate Method. *CoRR*, abs/1212.5701.

The Edit Distance Transducer in Action: The University of Cambridge English-German System at WMT16

Felix Stahlberg and **Eva Hasler** and **Bill Byrne**

Department of Engineering
University of Cambridge
Cambridge, UK

Abstract

This paper presents the University of Cambridge submission to WMT16. Motivated by the complementary nature of syntactical machine translation and neural machine translation (NMT), we exploit the synergies of Hiero and NMT in different combination schemes. Starting out with a simple neural lattice rescoring approach, we show that the Hiero lattices are often too narrow for NMT ensembles. Therefore, instead of a hard restriction of the NMT search space to the lattice, we propose to loosely couple NMT and Hiero by composition with a modified version of the edit distance transducer. The loose combination outperforms lattice rescoring, especially when using multiple NMT systems in an ensemble.

1 Introduction

Previous work suggests that syntactic machine translation such as Hiero (Chiang, 2007) and Neural Machine Translation (NMT) (Kalchbrenner and Blunsom, 2013; Sutskever et al., 2014; Cho et al., 2014; Bahdanau et al., 2015) are very different and have complementary strengths and weaknesses (Neubig et al., 2015; Stahlberg et al., 2016). Recent attempts to combine syntactic SMT and NMT report large gains over both baselines. Authors in (Neubig et al., 2015) used NMT to rescore n-best lists which were generated with a syntax-based system. They report that even with 1000-best lists, the gains of using the NMT rescorer often do not saturate. Syntactically Guided NMT (Stahlberg et al., 2016, SGNMT) constrains the NMT search space to Hiero translation lattices which contain significantly more hypotheses than n-best lists. In SGNMT, an NMT beam decoder with a relatively small beam can explore spaces much larger than n-best lists, yielding BLEU score improvements with far fewer expensive NMT evaluations.

However, these rescoring approaches enforce an exact match between the NMT and syntactic decoders. In general, this kind of hard restriction is best avoided when combining diverse systems (Liu et al., 2009; Frederking et al., 1994). For example, in speech recognition, ROVER (Fiscus, 1997) is a system combination approach based on a soft voting scheme. In machine translation, minimum Bayes-risk (MBR) decoding (Kumar and Byrne, 2004) can be used to combine multiple systems (de Gispert et al., 2009). MBR also does not enforce exact agreement between systems as it distinguishes between the *hypothesis space* and the *evidence space* (Goel and Byrne, 2000; Tromble et al., 2008).

We find that Hiero lattices generated by grammars extracted with the usual heuristics (Chiang, 2007) do not provide enough variety to explore the full potential of neural models, especially when using NMT ensembles. Therefore, we present a "soft" lattice-based combination scheme which uses standard operations on finite state transducers such as composition. Our method replaces the hard combination in previous methods with a similarity measure based on the edit distance, and gives the NMT decoder more freedom to diverge from the Hiero translations. We find that this loose coupling scheme is especially useful when using NMT ensembles.

2 Combining Hiero and NMT via Edit Distance Transducer

In contrast to the strict coupling in SGNMT, we propose to loosely couple Hiero and NMT via an edit distance transducer and shortest distance

Proceedings of the First Conference on Machine Translation, Volume 2: Shared Task Papers, pages 377–384,
Berlin, Germany, August 11-12, 2016. ©2016 Association for Computational Linguistics

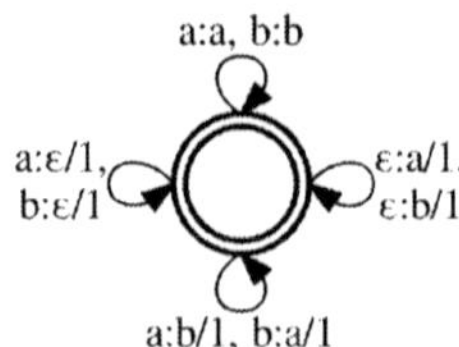

(a) Standard edit distance transducer.

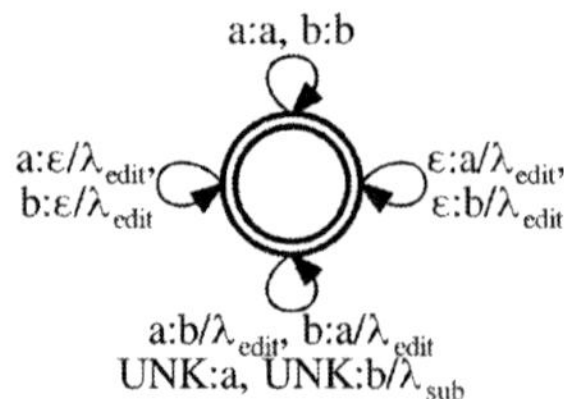

(b) Modified edit distance transducer E. 'a' is an NMT OOV.

Figure 1: "Flower automata" for calculating edit distances over the alphabet $\{a, b, \text{UNK}\}$.

search. With loose coupling, the NMT decoder is not restricted to the Hiero lattice as in previous work, but runs independently to produce translation lattices on its own, which are then combined with the Hiero lattices. The combination does not require an exact match. Instead, we will describe a procedure for combining NMT and Hiero that captures similarity under the edit distance and both the NMT and Hiero translation system scores. This scheme is implemented efficiently using standard FST operations (Allauzen et al., 2007). First, we introduce the FST composition operation and the edit distance transducer. We will describe the whole pipeline in Sec. 2.3.

2.1 Composition of Finite State Transducers

The composition of two weighted transducers T_1, T_2 (denoted as $T_1 \circ T_2$) over a semiring $(\mathbb{K}, \oplus, \otimes)$ is defined following (Mohri, 2004)

$$[T_1 \circ T_2](x, y) = \bigoplus_z T_1(x, z) \otimes T_2(z, y). \quad (1)$$

We will make extensive use of this operation as tool for building complex automata which make use of both the NMT and Hiero translation lattices.

2.2 The Edit Distance Transducer

Composition can be used together with a "flower automaton" to calculate the edit distance between two sequences (Mohri, 2003). The edit distance transducer shown in Fig. 1(a) transduces a sequence x to another sequence y over the alphabet $\{a, b\}$ and accumulates the number of edit operations via the transitions with cost 1. In our case, x corresponds to an NMT hypothesis which is to be combined with a Hiero hypothesis y. In contrast to SGNMT, where we require an exact match between NMT and Hiero (up to UNKs), our edit-distance-based scheme allows different hypotheses to be combined. We replaced the standard

definition of the edit distance transducer (Mohri, 2003) by a finer-grained model designed to work well for combining NMT and Hiero. Instead of uniform costs, we lower the cost for UNK substitutions as we want to encourage substituting NMT UNKs by words in the Hiero translation. We distinguish between three types of edit operations.

- **Type I**: Substituting UNK with a word outside the NMT vocabulary is free.

- **Type II**: For substitutions of UNK with a word inside the NMT vocabulary we add the cost λ_{sub}.

- **Type III**: All other edit operations are penalized with cost λ_{edit} (and $\lambda_{edit} > \lambda_{sub}$).

We will refer to the modified edit distance transducer as E. Fig. 1(b) shows E over the alphabet $\{a, b, \text{UNK}\}$, with 'a' being an NMT OOV.

2.3 Loose Coupling of Hiero and NMT

Our edit-distance-based scheme combines an NMT translation lattice N with a Hiero translation lattice H. Weights in N and H are scaled by λ_{nmt} and λ_{hiero}, respectively. The similarity measure between NMT and Hiero translations is parametrized with λ_{ins}, λ_{edit}, and λ_{sub}. We keep the various costs separated by using transducers with tropical sparse tuple vector semirings (Iglesias et al., 2015). Instead of single real-valued arc weights, this semiring uses vectors which can hold multiple features. The inner product of these vectors with a constant parameter vector determines the final weights on the arcs[1]. The sparse tuple vector semiring enables us to optimize the λ-parameters with LMERT (Macherey et al., 2008) on a development set.

---

[1] The ucam-smt tutorial contains details to the tropical sparse tuple vector semiring: http://ucam-smt.github.io/tutorial/basictrans.html#lmert_veclats_tst

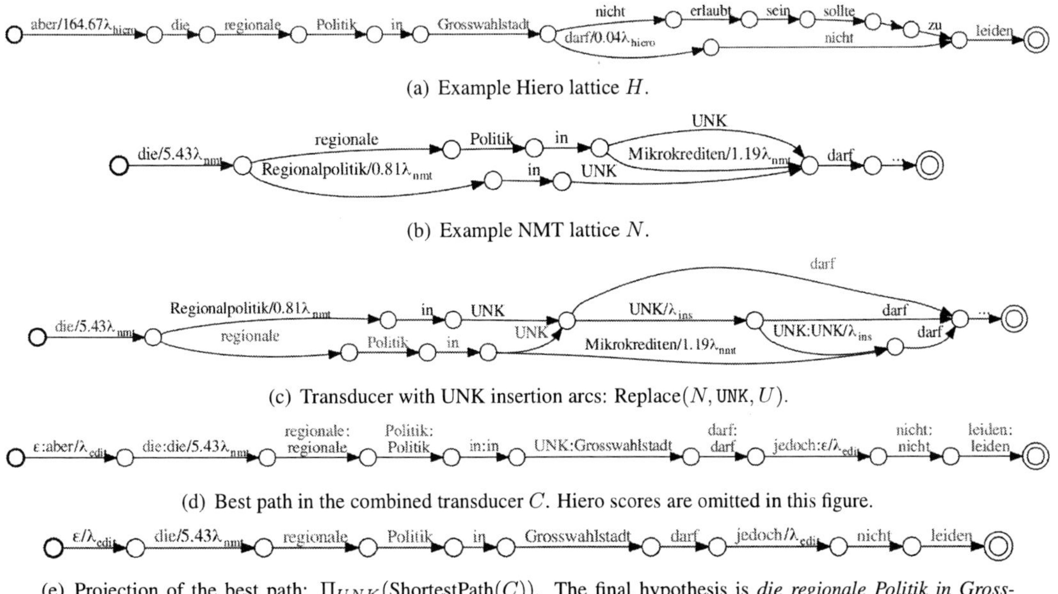

(a) Example Hiero lattice H.

(b) Example NMT lattice N.

(c) Transducer with UNK insertion arcs: Replace(N, UNK, U).

(d) Best path in the combined transducer C. Hiero scores are omitted in this figure.

(e) Projection of the best path: $\Pi_{UNK}(\text{ShortestPath}(C))$. The final hypothesis is *die regionale Politik in Grosswahlstadt darf jedoch nicht leiden*.

Figure 2: Combining Hiero and NMT via edit distance transducer.

Examples for H and N are shown in Fig. 2(a) and Fig. 2(b). The shortest path in H containing the string *nicht erlaubt sein sollte zu* has grammatical and stylistic flaws but is complete, whereas there is a better path in N with an UNK. Our goal is to merge these two hypotheses by using the NMT translation in N with the UNK replaced by a word from the Hiero lattice H.

1. **Adding UNK insertions**. We found that often NMT produces an isolated UNK token, even if multiple tokens are required. Therefore, we allow extending a single UNK token to a sequence of up to three UNK tokens. This is realized by replacing UNK arcs in N with the transducer U shown in Fig. 3 using OpenFST's `Replace` operation. Fig. 2(c) shows the result of the replace operation when applied to the example lattice N in Fig. 2(b). We denote this operation as follows:

$$\text{Replace}(N, \text{UNK}, U) \qquad (2)$$

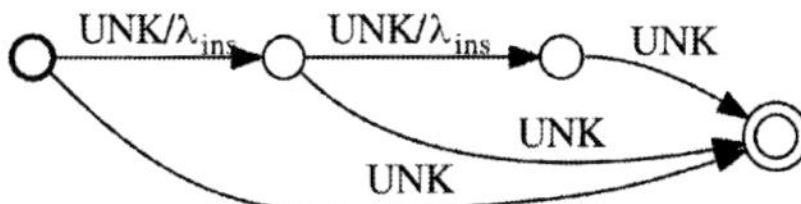

Figure 3: UNK extension transducer U.

2. **Composition with the edit distance transducer**. The next step finds the edit distances to the Hiero hypotheses as described in Sec. 2.2.

$$C := \text{Replace}(N, \text{UNK}, U) \circ E \circ H \qquad (3)$$

3. **Shortest path**. The above operation generates very large lattices, and dumping all of them is not feasible. We could use disambiguation (Iglesias et al., 2015; Mohri and Riley, 2015) on the combined transducer C to find the best alignment for each unique NMT hypothesis. However, we only need the single shortest path in order to generate the combined translation.

$$\text{ShortestPath}(C) \qquad (4)$$

4. **Projection**. A complete path in the transducer C has an NMT hypothesis on the input labels (marked green in Fig. 2(d)) and a Hiero hypothesis on the output labels (marked blue in Fig. 2(d)). Therefore, we can generate different translations from the best path in C. If we project the input labels on the output labels with OpenFST's `Project`, we obtain a hypothesis $\hat{t}_{NMT}$ in the NMT lattice N.

$$\hat{t}_{NMT} = \Pi_1(\text{ShortestPath}(C)) \qquad (5)$$

However, $\widehat{t}_{NMT}$ still contains UNKs. If we project on the input labels, we end up with the aligned Hiero hypothesis without UNKs (blue labels in Fig. 2(d))

$$\widehat{t}_{Hiero} = \Pi_2(\text{ShortestPath}(C)) \qquad (6)$$

but we do not use the NMT translation directly. Therefore, we introduce a new projection function Π_{UNK} which switches between preserving symbols on the input and output tapes: if the input label on an arc is UNK, we write the output label over the input label. Otherwise, we write the input label over the output label. This is equivalent to projecting the output labels to the input labels only if the input label is UNK, and then projecting the input labels to the output labels. As shown in Fig. 2(e), we obtain the NMT hypothesis, but the UNK is replaced by the matching word *Grosswahlstadt* from the Hiero lattice. Thus, the final combined translation is described by the following term:

$$\widehat{t}_{comb} = \Pi_{UNK}(\text{ShortestPath}(C)) \qquad (7)$$

In general, the final hypothesis $\widehat{t}_{comb}$ is a mix of an NMT and a Hiero hypothesis. We do not search for $\widehat{t}_{comb}$ directly but for pairs of NMT and Hiero translations which optimize the individual model scores as well as the distance between them. Stated more formally, the shortest path in C yields a pair $(\widehat{t}_{NMT}, \widehat{t}_{Hiero})$ for which holds

$$\widehat{t}_{NMT}, \widehat{t}_{Hiero} = \operatorname*{argmin}_{(t_N, t_H) \in N \times H} \Big(d_{edit}(t_N, t_H)$$
$$+ \lambda_{nmt} \cdot S_N(t_N|s) + \lambda_{hiero} \cdot S_H(t_H|s) \Big) \qquad (8)$$

where $d_{edit}(t_N, t_H)$ is the modified edit distance between t_N and t_H (according E and U), and $S_N(t_N|s)$ and $S_H(t_H|s)$ are the scores NMT and Hiero assign to the translations given source sentence s. If we interpret these scores as negative log-likelihoods, we arrive at a probabilistic interpretation of Eq. 8.

$$\widehat{t}_{NMT}, \widehat{t}_{Hiero} = \operatorname*{argmax}_{(t_N, t_H) \in N \times H} \Big($$
$$e^{-d_{edit}(t_N, t_H)} \cdot P(t_N, t_H|s) \Big) \qquad (9)$$

with (assuming independence)

$$P(t_N, t_H|s) := P_N(t_N|s)^{\lambda_{nmt}} \cdot P_H(t_H|s)^{\lambda_{hiero}}.$$

Eq. 9 suggests that we maximize the product of two quantities – the similarity between Hiero and NMT hypotheses and their joint probability. The FST operations allow to optimize over the set $N \times H$ efficiently. Note that the NMT lattice N is rather small in our case ($|N| \leq 20$) due to the small beam size used in NMT decoding. This makes it possible to solve Eq. 8 almost always without pruning [2].

3 Experimental Setup

The parallel training data includes *Europarl v7*, *Common Crawl*, and *News Commentary v10*. Sentence pairs with sentences longer than 80 words or length ratios exceeding 2.4:1 were deleted, as were *Common Crawl* sentences from other languages (Shuyo, 2010). We use *news-test2014* (the filtered version) as a development set, and keep *news-test2015* and *news-test2016* as test sets.

The NMT systems are built using the Blocks framework (van Merriënboer et al., 2015) based on the Theano library (Bastien et al., 2012) with the network architecture and hyper-parameters as in (Bahdanau et al., 2015): the encoder and decoder networks consist of 1000 gated recurrent units (Cho et al., 2014). The decoder uses a single maxout (Goodfellow et al., 2013) output layer with the feed-forward attention model described in (Bahdanau et al., 2015). In our final ensemble, we use 8 independently trained NMT systems with vocabulary sizes between 30,000 and 60,000.

Rules for our En-De Hiero system were extracted as described in (de Gispert et al., 2010). A 5-gram language model for the Hiero system was trained on WMT16 parallel and monolingual data (Heafield et al., 2013).

We apply gentle post-processing to the German output for fixing small number and currency formatting issues. The English source sentences in the training corpus are lower-cased. During decoding, we lower case only in-vocabulary words, and pass through OOVs with correct casing. We apply a simple heuristic for recognizing surnames to avoid literal translation of them into German[3].

Setup		news-test2014	news-test2015	news-test2016
Best in competition[4]		20.6	25.2	34.8
Hiero baseline		18.9	21.2	26.0
Single NMT	Pure NMT	17.5	19.6	23.2
	SGNMT (lattice rescoring)	21.2	23.5	28.7
	Edit distance transducer based combination	21.7	24.1	28.6
Ensemble NMT	Pure NMT	19.4	21.7	25.4
	SGNMT (lattice rescoring)	21.9	24.6	29.7
	Edit distance transducer based combination	**22.9**	**25.7**	**31.3**

Table 1: English-German lower-cased BLEU scores calculated with Moses `mteval-v13a.pl`.

Method	BLEU
NMT baseline: ShortestPath(N)	25.4
Hiero baseline: ShortestPath(H)	26.4
NMT hypothesis used for combination: $\widehat{t}_{NMT}$	26.7
Hiero hypothesis used for combination: $\widehat{t}_{Hiero}$	30.4
Combined translation: $\widehat{t}_{comb}$	31.3

Table 2: Projection methods on *news-test2016* with NMT 8-ensemble.

4   Results

Tab. 1 reports performance on *news-test2014*, *news-test2015*, and *news-test2016*[5]. Similarly to previous work (Stahlberg et al., 2016), we observe that rescoring Hiero lattices with NMT (SGNMT) outperforms both NMT and Hiero baselines significantly on all test sets. For SGNMT, we see further improvements of between +0.7 BLEU (*news-test2014*) and +1.1 BLEU (*news-test2015*) by using NMT ensembles rather than single NMT. However, these gains are rather small considering the improvements from using ensembles for the (pure) NMT baseline (between +1.9 BLEU and +2.2 BLEU). Our combination scheme makes better use of the ensembles. We report 31.3 BLEU on *news-test2016*, which in the English-German WMT'16 evaluation is among the best systems (within 0.1 BLEU) which do not use back-translation (Sennrich et al., 2016a). Back-translation is a technique for making use of monolingual data in NMT training, and we expect our system could benefit from back-translation, although we leave this analysis to future work.

The combination procedure we propose is non-trivial. It is not immediately clear how the gains arise as the final scores are mixtures between edit distance costs, NMT scores, and Hiero scores. In the remainder we will try to provide some insight. Unless stated otherwise, we report investigations

into the Hiero + NMT 8-system ensemble which yields the best results in Tab. 1.

First, we focus on the projection function $\Pi_{UNK}(\cdot)$ which switches between preserving the input and output label at the UNK symbol to produce the combined translation $\widehat{t}_{comb}$ (Eq. 7). As explained in Sec. 2.3, we can use OpenFST's `Project` operation to fetch the NMT and Hiero hypotheses $\widehat{t}_{NMT}$ and $\widehat{t}_{Hiero}$ which have been used to produce the combined translation (Eq. 5 and 6). Tab. 2 shows that the hypotheses that are aligned in the final transducer are often not the 1-best translations of any of the baseline systems. Remarkably, using the $\widehat{t}_{Hiero}$ translations results in 30.4 BLEU, which is a very substantial improvement over the baseline Hiero system (26.0 BLEU). Note that this BLEU score is achieved with hypotheses from the original Hiero lattice H but weighted in combination with the NMT scores and the edit distance. However, these selected paths are often given very low scores by Hiero: in only 8.6% of the sentences is the Hiero hypothesis left unchanged. If we look for $\widehat{t}_{Hiero}$ in the Hiero n-best list, we find that even very deep 20,000-best lists contain only 63.5% of the Hiero hypotheses which were selected by the combination scheme (Fig. 4). This indicates the benefit in using lattice-

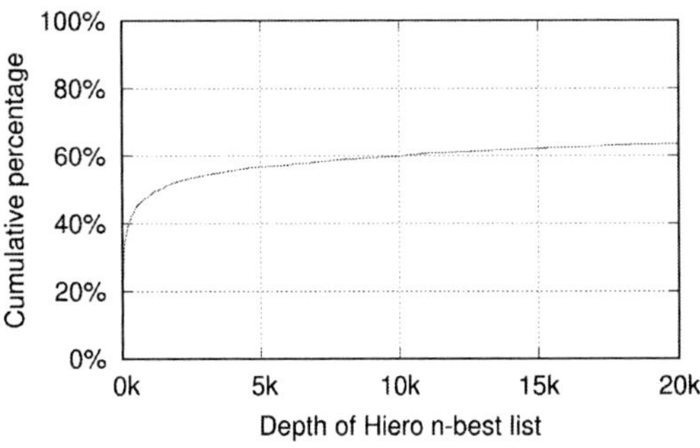

Figure 4: Percentage of $\widehat{t}_{Hiero}$ hypotheses found in the baseline Hiero n-best list.

[4]http://matrix.statmt.org/
[5]The code we used for SGNMT and ensembling is available at http://ucam-smt.github.io/sgnmt/html/.

Distance measure component	Avg. number per sentence	Percentage of affected sentences
UNK insertions (U)	0.16	12.9%
UNK→non-OOV substitutions (Type II)	1.34	55.9%
Other edit operations (Type III)	1.74	61.7%

Table 3: Breakdown of the distances measured between NMT and Hiero along the shortest path in C on *news-test2016*.

based approaches over n-best lists.

Next, we investigate the distance measure between NMT and Hiero translations, which is realized with the UNK insertion transducer U and the modified edit distance transducer E (Sec. 2.3). Tab. 3 shows that UNK insertions are relatively rare compared to the edit operations of types II and III allowed by E (Sec. 2.3). The average edit distance between NMT and Hiero disregarding UNKs on the best path (type III) is 1.74. In 61.7% of the cases the input and output labels differ not only at UNK – i.e. in only 38.3% of the sentences do we have an exact match between NMT and Hiero. We note that UNK is often replaced with an NMT in-vocabulary word (55.9% of the sentences). It seems that NMT often produces an UNK even if a better word is in the NMT vocabulary. This could be due to the over-representation of UNK in the NMT training corpus.

To study the effectiveness of our edit distance transducer based combination scheme in correcting NMT UNKs, we trained individual NMT systems with vocabulary sizes between 10,000 and 60,000. Tab. 4 shows that nearly one in six tokens (16.3%) produced by our pure NMT system with a vocabulary size of 30,000 are UNKs. Increasing the NMT vocabulary to 50k or 60k does improve pure NMT very significantly, but results show that these improvements are already captured by the combination scheme with Hiero. As in the literature, we see large variation in performance over individual NMT systems even with the same vocabulary size (Sennrich et al., 2016b), which could explain the small performance drop when increasing the vocabulary size from 50k to 60k.

One important practical issue for system building is the number of systems to be ensembled as training each individual NMT system takes a significant amount of time. Fig. 5 indicates that even for 8-ensembles the gains for pure NMT do not seem to saturate. The combination with Hiero via edit distance transducer also greatly benefits from using ensembles, but most of the gains are gotten with fewer systems.

Vocabulary size	Pure NMT		NMT+Hiero
	BLEU	# of UNKs	BLEU
10,000	18.9	18.0%	28.1
30,000	21.6	16.3%	28.8
50,000	23.2	9.1%	28.6
60,000	22.9	9.9%	28.5

Table 4: BLEU scores on *news-test2016* for different vocabulary sizes (single NMT). Each individual NMT system is combined with Hiero as described in Sec. 2.3.

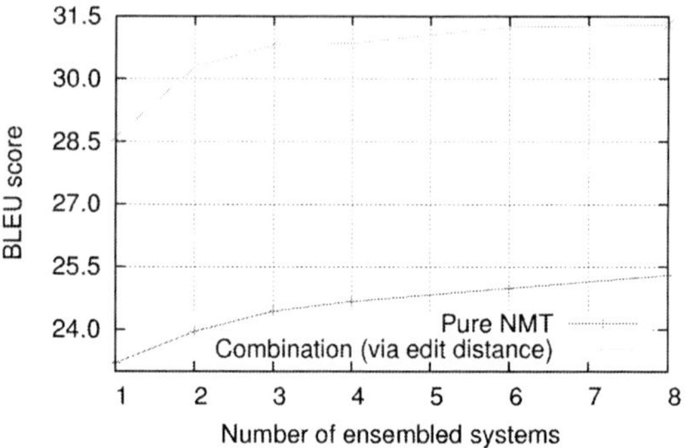

Figure 5: BLEU score over the number of systems in the ensemble on *news-test2016*.

5   Conclusion and Future Work

We have presented a method based on the edit distance that is effective in combining Hiero SMT systems with NMT ensembles. Our approach makes use of standard WFST operations, and we showed the effectiveness of the approach with a successful WMT'16 submission for English-German. In the future, we are planning to add back-translation (Sennrich et al., 2016a) and investigate the use of character- or subword-based NMT (Sennrich et al., 2016b; Chitnis and DeNero, 2015; Ling et al., 2015; Chung et al., 2016; Luong and Manning, 2016) within our combination framework.

Acknowledgements

This work was supported by the U.K. Engineering and Physical Sciences Research Council (EPSRC grant EP/L027623/1).

References

Cyril Allauzen, Michael Riley, Johan Schalkwyk, Wojciech Skut, and Mehryar Mohri. 2007. OpenFst: A general and efficient weighted finite-state transducer library. In *Implementation and Application of Automata*, pages 11–23. Springer.

Dzmitry Bahdanau, Kyunghyun Cho, and Yoshua Bengio. 2015. Neural machine translation by jointly learning to align and translate. In *ICLR*.

Frédéric Bastien, Pascal Lamblin, Razvan Pascanu, James Bergstra, Ian Goodfellow, Arnaud Bergeron, Nicolas Bouchard, David Warde-Farley, and Yoshua Bengio. 2012. Theano: new features and speed improvements. In *NIPS*.

David Chiang. 2007. Hierarchical phrase-based translation. *Computational Linguistics*, 33(2):201–228.

Rohan Chitnis and John DeNero. 2015. Variable-length word encodings for neural translation models. In *EMNLP*, pages 2088–2093.

Kyunghyun Cho, Bart van Merrienboer, Caglar Gulcehre, Fethi Bougares, Holger Schwenk, and Yoshua Bengio. 2014. Learning phrase representations using RNN encoder-decoder for statistical machine translation. In *EMNLP*.

Junyoung Chung, Kyunghyun Cho, and Yoshua Bengio. 2016. A character-level decoder without explicit segmentation for neural machine translation. In *ACL*.

Adrià de Gispert, Sami Virpioja, Mikko Kurimo, and William Byrne. 2009. Minimum Bayes risk combination of translation hypotheses from alternative morphological decompositions. In *NAACL*, pages 73–76.

Adrià de Gispert, Gonzalo Iglesias, Graeme Blackwood, Eduardo R Banga, and William Byrne. 2010. Hierarchical phrase-based translation with weighted finite-state transducers and shallow-n grammars. *Computational Linguistics*, 36(3):505–533.

Jonathan G Fiscus. 1997. A post-processing system to yield reduced word error rates: Recognizer output voting error reduction (ROVER). In *ASRU*, pages 347–354.

Robert Frederking, Sergei Nirenburg, David Farwell, Stephen Helmreich, Eduard Hovy, Kevin Knight, Stephen Beale, Constantine Domashnev, Donalee Attardo, Dean Grannes, et al. 1994. Integrating translations from multiple sources within the Pangloss Mark III machine translation system. In *AMTA*, pages 73–80.

Vaibhava Goel and William J Byrne. 2000. Minimum Bayes-risk automatic speech recognition. *Computer Speech & Language*, 14(2):115–135.

Ian Goodfellow, David Warde-farley, Mehdi Mirza, Aaron Courville, and Yoshua Bengio. 2013. Maxout networks. In *ICML*, pages 1319–1327.

Kenneth Heafield, Ivan Pouzyrevsky, Jonathan H. Clark, and Philipp Koehn. 2013. Scalable modified Kneser-Ney language model estimation. In *ACL*, pages 690–696.

Gonzalo Iglesias, Adrià de Gispert, and William Byrne. 2015. Transducer disambiguation with sparse topological features. In *EMNLP 2015*, pages 2275–2280.

Nal Kalchbrenner and Phil Blunsom. 2013. Recurrent continuous translation models. In *EMNLP*, page 413.

Shankar Kumar and William Byrne. 2004. Minimum Bayes-risk decoding for statistical machine translation. Technical report, DTIC Document.

Wang Ling, Isabel Trancoso, Chris Dyer, and Alan W Black. 2015. Character-based neural machine translation. *arXiv preprint arXiv:1511.04586*.

Yang Liu, Haitao Mi, Yang Feng, and Qun Liu. 2009. Joint decoding with multiple translation models. In *ACL*, pages 576–584.

Minh-Thang Luong and Christopher D Manning. 2016. Achieving open vocabulary neural machine translation with hybrid word-character models. In *ACL*.

Wolfgang Macherey, Franz Josef Och, Ignacio Thayer, and Jakob Uszkoreit. 2008. Lattice-based minimum error rate training for statistical machine translation. In *EMNLP*, pages 725–734.

Mehryar Mohri and Michael D Riley. 2015. On the disambiguation of weighted automata. In *Implementation and Application of Automata*, pages 263–278. Springer.

Mehryar Mohri. 2003. Edit-distance of weighted automata: General definitions and algorithms. *International Journal of Foundations of Computer Science*, 14(06):957–982.

Mehryar Mohri. 2004. Weighted finite-state transducer algorithms. An overview. In *Formal Languages and Applications*, pages 551–563. Springer.

Graham Neubig, Makoto Morishita, and Satoshi Nakamura. 2015. Neural reranking improves subjective quality of machine translation: NAIST at WAT2015. *arXiv preprint arXiv:1510.05203*.

Rico Sennrich, Barry Haddow, and Alexandra Birch. 2016a. Improving neural machine translation models with monolingual data. In *ACL*.

Rico Sennrich, Barry Haddow, and Alexandra Birch. 2016b. Neural machine translation of rare words with subword units. In *ACL*.

Nakatani Shuyo. 2010. Language detection library for Java. `http://code.google.com/p/language-detection/`. [Online; accessed 1-June-2016].

Felix Stahlberg, Eva Hasler, Aurelien Waite, and Bill Byrne. 2016. Syntactically guided neural machine translation. In *ACL*.

Ilya Sutskever, Oriol Vinyals, and Quoc V Le. 2014. Sequence to sequence learning with neural networks. In *Advances in Neural Information Processing Systems*, pages 3104–3112.

Roy W Tromble, Shankar Kumar, Franz Och, and Wolfgang Macherey. 2008. Lattice minimum Bayes-risk decoding for statistical machine translation. In *EMNLP*, pages 620–629.

Bart van Merriënboer, Dzmitry Bahdanau, Vincent Dumoulin, Dmitriy Serdyuk, David Warde-Farley, Jan Chorowski, and Yoshua Bengio. 2015. Blocks and fuel: Frameworks for deep learning. *arXiv preprint arXiv:1506.00619*.

CUNI-LMU Submissions in WMT2016:
Chimera Constrained and Beaten

Aleš Tamchyna[1,2]   **Roman Sudarikov**[1]   **Ondřej Bojar**[1]   **Alexander Fraser**[2]

[1]Charles University in Prague, Prague, Czech Republic
[2]LMU Munich, Munich, Germany
`surname@ufal.mff.cuni.cz`   `fraser@cis.uni-muenchen.de`

Abstract

This paper describes the phrase-based systems jointly submitted by CUNI and LMU to English-Czech and English-Romanian News translation tasks of WMT16. In contrast to previous years, we strictly limited our training data to the constraint datasets, to allow for a reliable comparison with other research systems. We experiment with using several additional models in our system, including a feature-rich discriminative model of phrasal translation.

1 Introduction

We have a long-term experience with English-to-Czech machine translation and over the years, our systems have grown together from rather diverse set of system types to a single system combination called CHIMERA (Bojar et al., 2013).

This system has been successful in the previous three years of WMT (Bojar et al., 2013; Tamchyna et al., 2014; Bojar and Tamchyna, 2015) and we follow a similar design this year. Unlike previous years, we only use constrained data in system training, to allow for a more meaningful comparison with the competing systems. The gains thanks to the additional data in contrast to the gains thanks the system combination have been evaluated in terms of BLEU in Bojar and Tamchyna (2015). The details of our English-to-Czech system are in Section 2.

In this work, we also present our system submission for English-Romanian translation. This system uses a factored setting similar to CHIMERA but lacks its two key components: the deep-syntactic translation system TectoMT and the rule-based post-processing component Depfix. All details are in Section 3.

2 English-Czech System

Our "baseline" setup is fairly complex, following Bojar et al. (2013). The key components of CHIMERA are:

- Moses, a phrase-based factored system (Koehn et al., 2007).

- TectoMT, a deep-syntactic transfer-based system (Popel and Žabokrtský, 2010).

- Depfix, a rule-based post-processing system (Rosa et al., 2012).

The core of the system is Moses. We combine it with TectoMT in a simple way which we refer to as "poor man's" system combination: we translate our development and test data with TectoMT first and then add the source sentences and their translations as additional (synthetic) parallel data to the Moses system. This new corpus is used to train a separate phrase table. At test time, we run Moses which uses both phrase tables and we correct its output using Depfix. The system is described in detail in Bojar et al. (2013).

Our subsequent analysis in Tamchyna and Bojar (2015) shows that the contribution of TectoMT is essential for the performance of CHIMERA. In particular, TectoMT provides new translations which are otherwise not available to the phrase-based system and it also improves the morphological and syntactic coherence of translations.

2.1 Translation Models

Similarly to previous years, we build two phrase tables – one from parallel data and another from TectoMT translations of the development and test sets. Here we describe the first phrase table.

Our main system uses CzEng16pre (Bojar et al., 2016) as parallel data. We train a factored TM

Proceedings of the First Conference on Machine Translation, Volume 2: Shared Task Papers, pages 385–390,
Berlin, Germany, August 11-12, 2016. ©2016 Association for Computational Linguistics

which uses surface forms on the source and produces target form, lemma and tag. Similarly to previous years, we find that increasing the phrase table limit (the maximum number of possible translations per source phrase) is necessary to obtain good performance.

Our input is also factored (though the phrase tables do not condition on these additional factors) and contains the form, lemma and morphological tag. We use these factors to extract rich features for our discriminative context model.

Linearly interpolated translation models. There is some evidence that when dealing with heterogeneous domains, it might be beneficial to construct the final TM as a linear, uniform interpolation of many small phrase tables (Carpuat et al., 2014). We experiment with splitting the data into 20 parts (without any domain selection, simply a random shuffle) and using linear interpolation to combine the partial models. The added benefit is that phrase extraction for all these parts can run in parallel (2h25m per part on average). The merging of these parts took 16h12m, which is still substantially faster than the single extraction (53h7m).

2.2 Language Models

Our LM configuration is based on the successful setting from previous years, however all LMs are trained using the constrained data; this is a major difference from our previous submissions which used several gigawords of monolingual text for language modeling.

We train an 7-gram LM on surface forms from all monolingual news data available for WMT. This LM is linearly interpolated (each year is a separate model) to optimize perplexity on a held-out set (WMT newstest2012). The individual LMs were pruned: we discarded all singleton n-grams (apart from unigrams).

All other LMs are trained on simple concatenation of the news part of CzEng16pre and all WMT monolingual news sets. We train 4-gram LMs on forms and lemmas (with a different pruning scheme: we discard 2- and 3-grams which appear fewer than 2 or 3 times, respectively).

We have two LMs over morphological tags to help maintain morphological coherence of translation outputs. The first LM is a 10-gram model and the second one is a 15-gram model, aimed at overall sentence structure. We prune all singleton n-grams (again, with the exception of unigrams).

2.3 Discriminative Translation Model

We add a feature-rich, discriminative model of phrasal translation to our system (Tamchyna et al., 2016). This classifier produces a single phrase translation probability which is additionally conditioned on the full source sentence and limited left-hand-side target context. The probability is added as an additional feature to Moses' log-linear model. The motivation for adding the context model is to improve lexical choice (which can be better inferred thanks to full source-context information) and morphological coherence.

The model uses a rich feature set on both sides: In the source, the model has access to the full input sentence and uses surface forms, lemmas and tags. On the target side, the model has access to limited context (similarly to an LM) and uses target surface forms, lemmas and tags. However, our English-Czech submission to WMT16 does not use target-context information due to time constraints.

2.4 Lexicalized Reordering and OSM

We experiment with using a lexicalized reordering model (Koehn et al., 2005) in the common setting: model monotone/swap/discontinuous reordering, word-based extraction, bidirectional, conditioned both on the source and target language.

We also train an operation sequence model (OSM, Durrani et al., 2013), which is a generative model that sees the translation process as a linear sequence of operations which generate a source and target sentence in parallel. The probability of a sequence of operations is defined according to an n-gram model, that is, the probability of an operation depends on the $n - 1$ preceding operations. We have trained our 5-gram model on surface forms, using the CzEng16pre corpus.

2.5 Hard POS for Short Words

In addition to the more principled attempts at improving our model, mainly Section 2.3, we also manually checked the output and added an ad-hoc solution for the single most disturbing error: the abbreviated form "'s" was often translated as the verb "to be" even in the clearly possessive uses.

The ambiguity of "'s" is apparently easy to resolve, our tagger does not have problems distinguishing and tagging the abbreviation as POS (possesive), VBZ (present tense) and other situations. While the POS information is readily available to the discriminative model, the model might not be able to pick it up due to its wide focus on many phenomena. As an alternative, we simply modify the input token and append the POS tag to it for all tokens under three characters.

This hack clearly helps with "'s": in a small manual analysis of 52 occurrences of "'s", the discriminative model still translated 7 possessive meanings as present tense, while the hacked model avoided these errors. It would be best to combine these two approaches, but we did not have the time to run this setting for the WMT evaluation.

2.6 Results

We evaluate all system variants on the WMT15 test set and report all BLEU scores in Table 1 prior to applying the last component, Depfix.

The reordering model achieved mixed results in our initial experiments and we opt not to include it in our final submission, relying instead only on the standard distortion penalty feature.

As in previous years, the addition of TectoMT to the main phrase table extracted from the parallel corpus (denoted "CzEng" in Table 1) is highly beneficial, improving the BLEU score by roughly 1.2 points. The addition of OSM also helps, adding about 0.7 points.

The source-context discriminative model does not improve translation quality according to BLEU. We suspect that the space for its contribution is diminished by the addition of TectoMT and possibly also the OSM and the strong LMs. This system (labelled with ∗) was submitted as a primary system CU-TAMCHYNA. After the deadline, we also ran an experiment which included target-context features in the model and obtained BLEU of 20.96.

Experiments with the interpolated TM ("CzEng$_{20\ parts}$" in the table) and POS appended to words under three characters show a lower BLEU score (20.70, denoted •) but we also carried out a small manual evaluation where the system output seemed to be better than the baseline (20.91). We therefore submitted this system as our primary CU-CHIMERA.

In the official WMT16 manual evaluation, both our systems end up in the same cluster, ranking #4 and #5 among all systems for this language pair. The hacked system • seems negligibly better (0.302 TrueSkill) than the one with the discriminative model (∗, reaching 0.299 TrueSkill).

As a contrastive result, CHIMERA, ranking #1 last year, achieves a BLEU score of 20.46 on newstest2015 (also prior to the application of Depfix). This suggests that even though we limited our training data this year, we did not lose anything in terms of translation quality.

TMs	OSM	Disc.	POS	BLEU
CzEng	-	-	-	19.08±0.62
CzEng+TectoMT	-	-	-	20.23±0.64
	✓	-	-	20.91±0.67
	✓	✓	-	20.89±0.69 ∗
CzEng$_{20\ parts}$+TectoMT	✓	-	✓	20.70±0.66 •
Chimera in WMT15	✓	-	-	20.46

Table 1: Different experiment configurations for CHIMERA. We report BLEU scores on newstest2015. The system denoted ∗ corresponds to our WMT16 submission `cu-tamchyna` and the system denoted • corresponds to `cu-chimera`.

3 English-Romanian System

We also submitted a constrained phrase-based system for English→Romanian translation which is loosely inspired by the basic components of CHIMERA. Additionally, our submission uses the source- and target-context discriminative translation model as well.

3.1 Data and Pre-Processing

We use all the data available to constrained submissions: Europarl v8 (Koehn, 2005) and SE-TIMES2 (Tiedemann, 2009) parallel corpora and News 2015 and Common Crawl monolingual corpora.[1] We split the official development set into two halves; we use the first part for system tuning and the second part serves as our test set.

Data pre-processing differs between English and Romanian. For English, we use Treex (Popel and Žabokrtský, 2010) to obtain morphological tags, lemmas and dependency parses of the sentences. For Romanian, we use the online tagger by Tufiş et al. (2008) as run by our colleagues at LIMSI-CNRS for the joint QT21 Romanian system (Peter et al., 2016).

3.2 Factored Translation

Similarly to CHIMERA, we train a factored phrase table which translates source surface forms to tuples (form, lemma, tag). Our input is factored and contains the form, lemma, morphological tag,

---

[1] `http://commoncrawl.org/`

lemma of dependency parent and analytical function ("surface" syntactic role, e.g. *Subj* for subjects). These additional source-side factors are again not used by the phrase table and serve only as information for the discriminative model.

3.3 Language Models

Our full system contains three separate language models (LMs). The first is a 5-gram LM over surface forms, trained on the target side of the parallel data and monolingual news 2015.

The second LM only uses 4-grams but additionally contains the full Common Crawl corpus. We prune this second LM by discarding 2-, 3- and 4-grams which appear fewer than 2, 3, 4 times, respectively.

Finally, we also include a 7-gram LM over morphological tags. We only use target parallel data for estimating the model.

3.4 Reordering Model

Similarly to our experiments with CHIMERA, we utilize a lexicalized reordering model (Koehn et al., 2005). Again, we model monotone/swap/discontinuous reordering, word-based extraction, bidirectional, conditioned both on the source and target language.

3.5 Discriminative Translation Model

We utilize the same discriminative model as for CHIMERA. For English-Romanian, we also use dependency parses of the source sentences and target-side context features as additional source of information in our official submission.

3.6 Results

Table 2 lists BLEU scores of various system settings. Each BLEU score is an average over 5 runs of system tuning (MERT, Och, 2003). The table shows how BLEU score develops as we add the individual components to the system: the 7-gram morphological LM ("tagLM"), the 4-gram LM from Common Crawl ("ccrawl"), the lexicalized reordering ("RR") and finally the discriminative translation model ("discTM").

We test for statistical significance using MultEval (Clark et al., 2011); we test each new component against the system without it (i.e., +tagLM is compared to baseline, +ccrawl is tested against +tagLM etc.). When the p-value is lower than 0.05, we mark the result in bold.

Setting	BLEU
baseline	26.2
+tagLM	**26.6**
+ccrawl	**28.0**
+RM	28.1
+discTM	**28.3**

Table 2: BLEU scores of system variants for English-Romanian translation.

We observe a relatively steady additive effect of the individual components: the addition of each model (apart from lexicalized reordering) leads to a statistically significant improvement in translation quality.

Our discriminative model further improves the system, despite only being trained on the parallel data (roughly 0.6 M sentence pairs) and building upon the strong language models which use orders-of-magnitude larger monolingual data (almost 300 M sentences). This variant (BLEU 28.3) corresponds to our submission LMU-CUNI.

4 Conclusion

We have described our English-Czech and English-Romanian submissions to WMT16: CU-CHIMERA, CU-TAMCHYNA and LMU-CUNI.

For English-Czech, our work is an incremental improvement of the previously successful CHIMERA system. This time, our submission is constrained and additionally uses interpolated TMs, an OSM and a discriminative phrasal translation model.

For English-Romanian, we have built a system somewhat similar to the statistical component of CHIMERA. We have added the discriminative model which conditions both on the source and target context to the system and obtained a small but significant improvement in BLEU.

5 Acknowledgement

This work has received funding from the European Union's Horizon 2020 research and innovation programme under grant agreements no. 644402 (HimL) and no. 645452 (QT21). This work has been using language resources stored and distributed by the LINDAT/CLARIN project of the Ministry of Education, Youth and Sports of the Czech Republic (project LM2015071). This work was partially supported by SVV project number 260 333.

References

Ondřej Bojar, Ondřej Dušek, Tom Kocmi, Jindřich Libovický, Michal Novák, Martin Popel, Roman Sudarikov, and Dušan Variš. 2016. CzEng 1.6: Enlarged Czech-English Parallel Corpus with Processing Tools Dockered. In *Text, Speech and Dialogue: 19th International Conference, TSD 2016, Brno, Czech Republic, September 12-16, 2016, Proceedings*. Springer Verlag. In press.

Ondřej Bojar, Rudolf Rosa, and Aleš Tamchyna. 2013. Chimera – Three Heads for English-to-Czech Translation. In *Proceedings of the Eighth Workshop on Statistical Machine Translation*. Association for Computational Linguistics, Sofia, Bulgaria, pages 92–98.

Ondřej Bojar and Aleš Tamchyna. 2015. CUNI in WMT15: Chimera Strikes Again. In *Proceedings of the Tenth Workshop on Statistical Machine Translation*. Association for Computational Linguistics, Lisboa, Portugal, pages 79–83.

Marine Carpuat, Cyril Goutte, and George Foster. 2014. Linear mixture models for robust machine translation. In *Proceedings of the Ninth Workshop on Statistical Machine Translation*. Association for Computational Linguistics, Baltimore, Maryland, USA, pages 499–509.

Jonathan H. Clark, Chris Dyer, Alon Lavie, and Noah A. Smith. 2011. Better hypothesis testing for statistical machine translation: Controlling for optimizer instability. In *Proceedings of the 49th Annual Meeting of the Association for Computational Linguistics: Human Language Technologies: Short Papers - Volume 2*. Association for Computational Linguistics, Stroudsburg, PA, USA, HLT '11, pages 176–181.

Nadir Durrani, Alexander M Fraser, Helmut Schmid, Hieu Hoang, and Philipp Koehn. 2013. Can markov models over minimal translation units help phrase-based smt? In *ACL (2)*. pages 399–405.

Philipp Koehn. 2005. Europarl: A Parallel Corpus for Statistical Machine Translation. In *Conference Proceedings: the tenth Machine Translation Summit*. AAMT, AAMT, Phuket, Thailand, pages 79–86.

Philipp Koehn, Amittai Axelrod, Alexandra Birch, Chris Callison-Burch, Miles Osborne, David Talbot, and Michael White. 2005. Edinburgh system description for the 2005 IWSLT speech translation evaluation. In *Proceedings of International Workshop on Spoken Language Translation*.

Philipp Koehn, Hieu Hoang, Alexandra Birch, Chris Callison-Burch, Marcello Federico, Nicola Bertoldi, Brooke Cowan, Wade Shen, Christine Moran, Richard Zens, Chris Dyer, Ondřej Bojar, Alexandra Constantin, and Evan Herbst. 2007. Moses: Open Source Toolkit for Statistical Machine Translation. In *ACL 2007, Proceedings of the 45th Annual Meeting of the Association for Computational Linguistics Companion Volume Proceedings of the Demo and Poster Sessions*. Association for Computational Linguistics, Prague, Czech Republic, pages 177–180.

Franz Josef Och. 2003. Minimum Error Rate Training in Statistical Machine Translation. In *Proc. of the Association for Computational Linguistics*. Sapporo, Japan.

Jan-Thorsten Peter, Tamer Alkhouli, Matthias Huck Hermann Ney, Fabienne Braune, Alexander Fraser, Aleš Tamchyna, Ondřej Bojar, Barry Haddow, Rico Sennrich, Frédéric Blain, Lucia Specia, Jan Niehues, Alex Waibel, Alexandre Allauzen, Lauriane Aufrant, Franck Burlot, Elena Knyazeva, Thomas Lavergne, François Yvon, Stella Frank, and Mārcis Pinnis. 2016. The QT21/HimL Combined Machine Translation System. In *Proceedings of the Tenth Workshop on Statistical Machine Translation*. Association for Computational Linguistics, Berlin, Germany. In print.

Martin Popel and Zdeněk Žabokrtský. 2010. TectoMT: Modular NLP Framework. In Hrafn Loftsson, Eirikur Rögnvaldsson, and Sigrun Helgadottir, editors, *IceTAL 2010*. Iceland Centre for Language Technology (ICLT), Springer, volume 6233 of *Lecture Notes in Computer Science*, pages 293–304.

Rudolf Rosa, David Mareček, and Ondej Dušek. 2012. DEPFIX: A System for Automatic Correction of Czech MT Outputs. In *Proceedings of the Seventh Workshop on Statistical Machine Translation*. Association for Computational Linguistics, Montréal, Canada, pages 362–368.

Aleš Tamchyna, Alexander Fraser, Ondřej Bojar, and Marcin Junczsys-Dowmunt. 2016. Target-Side Context for Discriminative Models in Statistical Machine Translation. In *Proc. of ACL*. Association for Computational Linguistics, Berlin, Germany. In print.

Aleš Tamchyna and Ondřej Bojar. 2015. What a Transfer-Based System Brings to the Combination with PBMT. In Bogdan Babych, Kurt Eberle, Patrik Lambert, Reinhard Rapp, Rafael Banchs, and Marta Costa-Jussà, editors, *Proceedings of the Fourth Workshop on Hybrid Approaches to Translation (HyTra)*. Association for Computational Linguistics, Association for Computational Linguistics, Stroudsburg, PA, USA, pages 11–20.

Aleš Tamchyna, Martin Popel, Rudolf Rosa, and Ondřej Bojar. 2014. CUNI in WMT14: Chimera Still Awaits Bellerophon . In *Proceedings of the Ninth Workshop on Statistical Machine Translation*. Association for Computational Linguistics, Baltimore, MD, USA, pages 195–200.

Jörg Tiedemann. 2009. News from OPUS - A collection of multilingual parallel corpora with tools and interfaces. In N. Nicolov, K. Bontcheva, G. Angelova, and R. Mitkov, editors, *Recent Advances in Natural Language Processing*, John Benjamins, Amsterdam/Philadelphia, Borovets, Bulgaria, volume V, pages 237–248.

Dan Tufis, Radu Ion, Alexandru Ceausu, and Dan Stefanescu. 2008. Racai's linguistic web services. In *Proceedings of the International Conference on Language Resources and Evaluation, LREC 2008, 26 May - 1 June 2008, Marrakech, Morocco*.

Phrase-Based SMT for Finnish with More Data, Better Models and Alternative Alignment and Translation Tools

Jörg Tiedemann
University of Helsinki

Fabienne Cap
Uppsala University

Jenna Kanerva and **Filip Ginter**
University of Turku

Sara Stymne
Uppsala University

Robert Östling
University of Helsinki

Marion Di Marco
University of Stuttgart

Abstract

This paper summarises the contributions of the teams at the University of Helsinki, Uppsala University and the University of Turku to the news translation tasks for translating from and to Finnish. Our models address the problem of treating morphology and data coverage in various ways. We introduce a new efficient tool for word alignment and discuss factorisations, gappy language models and re-inflection techniques for generating proper Finnish output. The results demonstrate once again that training data is the most effective way to increase translation performance.

1 Introduction

In this paper we revisit phrase-based models with and without factors to translate from and into a morphologically-rich language, Finnish. We discuss the impact of training data, the use of factored models and ideas of re-inflection as post-processing. We also introduce the framework of gappy language models within document-level machine translation (without much success in the given task). Our efforts prove the importance of training data once again and demonstrate the use of noisy and out-of-domain data sets as well as the possibility of integrating synthetic training data based on back-translation in phrase-based SMT.

2 Data and Tools

This section discusses data sets and tools that we applied in our models. We focus on non-standard resources but also summarise the basic setup of our training procedures.

Training Data: Our submissions include constrained and unconstrained systems. The constrained systems apply all the data provided by WMT and also the English Giga-Word corpus that is distributed by the LDC. Our best systems include additional parallel data sets coming from OPUS (Tiedemann, 2012) and syntactically analysed monolingual data from the Finnish Internet Parsebank (Luotolahti et al., 2015). Additional to the parallel data we used in our submission last year (Tiedemann et al., 2015a), we include the new version of the OpenSubtitle corpus (Lison and Tiedemann, 2016) with its 18.6 million aligned translation units in English and Finnish. Furthermore, we make use of alternative subtitle translations that have been aligned monolingually in the same collection (Tiedemann, 2016). Expanding the parallel corpus with alternative translations extends the subtitle corpus by roughly 350,000 translation units with about 6.8 million tokens (counting both languages together). The contribution is quite small compared to the original corpus with its 107 million Finnish tokens and 167 million English tokens, but, nevertheless, it contributes to the overall collection especially by providing additional variation of the translation examples, which is very valuable for the resulting system. The final training corpus contains 27.7 million translation units comprising 353 million English tokens and 244 million tokens in the Finnish part.

For Finnish, we also increased the coverage of our language model by further 4.9 billion tokens compared to our last year submission. The data comes from an extensive web-crawl and amounts to 9.5 billion tokens of text, deduplicated on document level. Five-gram language models are trained using KenLM (Heafield et al., 2013). The English language model based on the provided Common Crawl data is limited to trigrams.

Pre-Processing Tools: For processing Finnish, we apply the Finnish parsing pipeline developed at the University of Turku (Haverinen et

391

Proceedings of the First Conference on Machine Translation, Volume 2: Shared Task Papers, pages 391–398,
Berlin, Germany, August 11-12, 2016. ©2016 Association for Computational Linguistics

al., 2013). It integrates all the necessary pre-processing steps including tokenisation, morphological analyses and part-of-speech tagging, and produces dependency analyses according to the Universal Dependencies scheme.[1] The morphological component relies on OMorFi - an open-source finite-state toolkit with a large-coverage morphology for modern Finnish (Lindén et al., 2009). The readings given by OMorFi are combined with predictions of the *MarMoT* CRF-based tagger (Mueller et al., 2013), and the data is subsequently parsed using the *mate-tools* data-driven dependency parser (Bohnet, 2010). The labeled attachment score of the parsing pipeline is 82.7% and the pipeline is robust and reliable even for large data sets and long sentences (Pyysalo et al., 2015).

We also apply various pre-processing tools provided by the Moses toolbox. In particular, we make use of tokenisers (especially for English), punctuation and Unicode normalisers.

For the factored models of English, we built our own pre-processing pipeline mainly adapted from the Finnish pipeline but adjusted for processing English. They include tools for handling long sentences and keeping track of sentence alignment points when parsing parallel data sets. We use the English models for sentence boundary detection and tokenisation provided by OpenNLP,[2] which is compatible with the Penn Treebank style of tokenisation. This is important for the subsequent tagging and parsing steps, which we trained on the Universal Dependencies treebank for English using MarMoT and mate-tools.

MT Tools: Most of our systems are based on Moses (Koehn et al., 2007) and common components for training and tuning models. We apply KenLM (Heafield et al., 2013) and SRILM (Stolcke, 2002) for estimating language model parameters and MERT (Och, 2003) and batch-MIRA (Cherry and Foster, 2012) for parameter tuning. Most of our models are based on lowercased training data. All language models use order five with modified Kneser-Ney smoothing if not stated otherwise. All MT systems apply the phrase-based paradigm, some of them with factored representations and generation models if necessary.

For word alignment we experiment with different tools. We apply standard tools like GIZA++ (Och and Ney, 2003) and fast_align (Dyer et al., 2013) but also the recently proposed Bayesian word aligner **efmaral** (Östling, 2015). Efmaral is an efficient implementation of a Markov-Chain aligner using Gibbs sampling with a Bayesian extension of the IBM alignment models. It is both fast and accurate and works as a straightforward plug-in replacement for standard tools in the SMT training pipeline. The aligner is faster than fast_align but more accurate in terms of alignment error rate in various benchmark tests. The advantage of using Gibbs sampling rather than the Expectation-Maximisation algorithm (as do both fast_align and GIZA++) is that inference remains quadratic with respect to sentence length even when word order and fertility models are added, which enables the efficient use of higher-order models. This is the first time that the performance of this tool is reported in the setting of statistical machine translation.

Besides Moses, we also apply another phrase-based machine translation decoder, **Docent** (Hardmeier et al., 2013), which implements a stochastic local search decoder that is able to incorporate features with long-distance dependencies even across sentence boundaries. Docent emphasises document-level decoding but includes standard local features that make the decoder comparable with standard phrase-based SMT. The decoding algorithm applies randomly selected state-change operations to complete translation hypotheses (covering the whole document) that may be accepted by a strict hill-climbing procedure or a simulated annealing schedule. The main motivation for using Docent in our setup is to introduce non-local dependencies that may improve, for example, agreement problems in morphologically-rich languages such as Finnish. However, the experiments are very initial and, unfortunately, do not show the desired effect yet.

3 Translating English into Finnish

Our main efforts went into the development of translation models for the direction from English to Finnish. Four types of experiments were conducted: (1) Changing word alignment and data sets; (2) Factored models with morphological features; (3) Re-inflection models with robust generation from underspecified representations; and (4) Gappy language models for long-distance dependencies.

---

[1] http://universaldependencies.org
[2] https://opennlp.apache.org

3.1 Changing Alignment and Adding Data

Our first series of experiments considered three different word alignment tools that can be used in the training pipeline of standard phrase-based SMT. We use the well-known IBM alignment models (up to model 4) implemented in GIZA++, the modified IBM model 2 implemented in fast_align and the above introduced Bayesian word aligner based on fertility-enhanced HMM models implemented in efmaral. Table 1 summarises the results when applied in the constrained setup and tested on the news test set from WMT 2015. The three models use the same feature weights and the same symmetrisation and phrase extraction/scoring parameters to make the scores comparable with each other. The results indicate that efmaral is comparable and even better than GIZA++ in this setup even though it is magnitudes faster than the IBM model 4 training and Viterbi alignment. Efmaral is also considerably faster than fast_align, which makes it a valuable drop-in replacement of these standard tools. The processing times in Table 1 illustrate the significant gains when using efmaral making it possible to quickly align large amounts of bitexts. The advantage over fast_align can mainly be seen in CPU time with a speed-up of almost a factor of 10. fast_align, however, has the advantage to naturally run multithreaded over many cores whereas the collapsed Gibbs sampler of efmaral is not as easily parallelised. This can also be seen in our experiments which we ran on a 16 core machine with alignment in both directions in parallel. GIZA++ is by far the slowest option and does not lead to better translations either. The figure also excludes word clustering which is another time-consuming process that is necessary for running IBM model 4.

Part of the experiment is also the inclusion of additional training data. All those runs use efmaral, demonstrating that the software is capable to cope with large data sets. Note, however, that memory requirements grows with the size of the data ($\sum_{e,f}(|e| \times |f|)$) making it possible to run efficiently. The results of our experiments show that the additional data is useful even though it is coming from inappropriate domains. Especially striking is the gain by including alternative subtitle translations – a rather small part of the data. Apparently, those examples introduce necessary variations to push the quality of the models. Another impressive improvement can be seen with the in-

newstest 2015	BLEU	time for word align	
		real	CPU
GIZA++	13.65	38,514s	–
fast_align	13.56	682s	8,344s
efmaral	14.10	370s	895s
+ OPUS	14.81	–	–
+ alternatives	15.55	2,630s	6,599s
+ WWW-LM	16.98	–	–
retuned	18.11	–	–
back-translated	14.78	954s	2,606s
+ OPUS, ...	18.22	2,758s	7,187s

Table 1: Lower-cased BLEU scores for standard-phrase based SMT on development test data (newstest 2015). The first three and the second-to-last rows represent constrained settings whereas the other rows refer to systems with additional resources. Efmaral is used in all cases except for the two models at the top. The last two systems include back-translated news data. Running time is given for some aligners in terms of walltime (real) and CPU time (user+sys).

troduction of the large language model based on a diverse set of data. This Finnish language model is estimated on the Finnish Internet Parsebank (Luotolahti et al., 2015), totaling 9.5 billion tokens of text. The data is obtained from a large-scale Internet crawl, seeded from all Finnish pages in CommonCrawl.[3] However, actual CommonCrawl data is only a small fraction of the total, roughly 1.5B tokens, the remainder originating from an independent crawl. The data is heavily filtered, only preserving clean, parseable text comprising of complete sentences.

Even the models with additional data use the same feature weights and only replace the indicated component to enable comparisons between them. The system denoted by "retuned", however, shows the importance of proper tuning when replacing system components.

The final part of Table 1 shows additional results with back-translated news data in the constrained and unconstrained setup. We used our Finnish-English model to translate approximately 1.25 million sentences of the Finnish shuffled monolingual news data from 2014 and 2015 to enhance the parallel training data. The result in terms of BLEU significantly improves when these noisy data sets are included in the standard train-

[3]www.commoncrawl.org

ing pipeline. Note that the models are retuned from scratch in both cases.

3.2 Factored Models

The factored models we developed use features extracted from dependency trees coming out of the Finnish and English pre-processing pipelines. We include separate translation models for translating between English surface word forms and Finnish lemmas and for translating morphosyntactic features between the two languages. The latter includes dependency relations besides part-of-speech labels (on both sides) and detailed morphological information (in Finnish only). Table 2 summarises the results of these models.

newstest 2015	BLEU
(a) surface form	14.10
(b) morph	5.45
(c) constructions	10.89
combined (a) + (c)	14.17
+back-translated	14.70

Table 2: Lower-cased BLEU scores for factored SMT models on development test data (newstest 2015). System (a) is the same as the constrained model in Table 1. System (b) uses a factored model that translates surface words to target lemmas and morphosyntactic features separately. System (c) keeps closed-class words in the translation table of morphosyntactic features. (b) and (c) include a generation model trained on large monolingual parsed training data to generate surface word forms from lemmas and morphosyntactic features.

The morphologically enhanced factored model underperforms significantly when used in isolation. Therefore, we used a variant of the setup that replaces morphosyntactic features with surface words for all closed-class words in the training corpus. The assumption is that there is sufficient evidence for those word types even in morphologically-rich languages such as Finnish. Using this type of lexicalisation helps to find construction-like mappings between the two languages which seems to be beneficial for the system according to the scores in our experiments (system (c) in Table 2). In combination with the surface-oriented translation model this also leads to a slight improvement over the non-factored model (without back-translated news), which is also evident in the final scores of our submitted systems at least in the constrained setup (see Table 4).

3.3 Re-inflection Models

Furthermore, we also investigated re-inflection models. These experiments require a different representation of the training data for each variant and are, therefore, not directly comparable with the other systems. The underlying idea of what we call re-inflection models in our submission is that we reduce all Finnish training data to an underspecified representation, where words are reduced to their lemmas and noun and adjective compounds are split into their component parts. Then, we train models and translate from English into this underspecified representation of Finnish and in a post-processing step we then merge compounds and predict morphological features for Finnish. This approach has been successfully applied to Russian and Arabic (Toutanova et al., 2008) and to German (Fraser et al. (2012), Cap et al. (2014)). Note however, that for example Fraser et al. (2012) relied on German prepositions to predict case-markers on underspecified German SMT output. In contrast to many other languages, Finnish only has a limited number of stand-alone pre- and postpositions. Instead, the prepositional meaning is encoded by case-marking. We thus adapt an approach by Tiedemann et al. (2015b) and introduce *place-holder prepositions* in the Finnish training data, which are likely to correspond to the prepositions used on the English side and thus improve word alignment quality.

Place-holder Prepositions: In contrast to Tiedemann et al. (2015b), we do not apply factored models (with both, lemmatised and surface forms) here but strip the case-markers from those words and only keep the underspecified representation. Moreover, we apply the approach in the opposite translation direction, which requires a generation component. The place-holder prepositions will not only lead to improved word alignments, but we will also use them to predict case-markers after translation. Overall, we follow the processing pipeline of (Cap et al., 2014): we use a rule-based morphological analyser (Pirinen, 2015) to split compounds (using the Finnish parsing pipeline to disambiguate multiple analyses) and lemmatise all Finnish training data. Compound modifiers are reduced to their lemmas and marked with a symbol that distinguishes them from other words. Similar to Tiedemann et al. (2015b), we introduce place-holder prepositions at the beginning of noun phrases bearing the corresponding case-marker in order to support word alignment.

Prediction of Case-Markers After translation, we apply CRF models to predict the case markers of Finnish. Besides the occurrences of place-holder prepositions, these take some more local context, both on lemma and POS level into account. Clean-data experiments have shown that our CRF models for re-inflection are very accurate. We reduce all compounds of the CRF training data to their heads and train the models on this representation. As we are using the words and lemmas as features for the CRFs, the reduction of compounds to their heads reduces data sparsity and allows the model to better generalise over all occurrences. For the translation output we remove all compound modifiers before case prediction.

Morphological Generation The predicted case-markers are then fed into the morphological generation automaton (Pirinen, 2015) in order to get fully inflected forms. In cases where this generation failed, we used a supervised machine learning approach as a backoff (Durrett and DeNero, 2013).

Compound Processing In a final step, we merge compounds using a POS-matching strategy (Stymne et al., 2008). We merge the marked compound modifiers with the following word if it is a noun or adjective, and add hyphens for modifiers in coordinated compounds. Compounding forms of modifiers are restored based on corpus frequencies. Like Stymne et al. (2008) and Cap et al. (2014), we also merge compounds in every iteration of the tuning process before the translations are scored against the reference.

All re-inflection systems are constrained systems. We used Europarl and Wikipedia as parallel resources and all of the Finnish data available from WMT to train five-gram language models with SRILM (Stolcke, 2002) and KENLM (Heafield, 2011). No particular cleaning or pre-processing of the data has happened. This makes the re-inflection systems differ from all other systems in this paper. Otherwise, we trained a conventional phrase-based Moses system with default settings, tuned weights using batch-MIRA with "safe-hope" (Cherry and Foster, 2012) and used an underspecified representation of the tuning reference set to derive BLEU scores. The final result of our system is listed in Table 4.

3.4 Gappy Language Models

Tiedemann (2015) introduces the use of language models over selected words in the framework of document-level SMT using Docent applied to the pronoun-aware translation task of DiscoMT (Hardmeier et al., 2015). We extended this idea by developing a general framework for what we call *gappy language models* that refer to monolingual or bilingual n-gram language models over selected words and their alignments. We can use different factors attached to the source and target language tokens to filter for word sequences that we would like to consider. Given word alignments are used to establish the link between source and target tokens. Gappy language models may cross sentence-boundaries but may also stop at those borders. Regular expressions can be used to make the selection more flexible. Multi-word alignments can be concatenated into single tokens and empty alignments can be represented as a special token to avoid the length-penalising effect of N-gram models. Word selection based on the source language also helps as this is given and fixed. However, word alignment is noisy and may negatively influence the use of the extracted target item sequence. Therefore, the selection can also be done on target language properties only and an additional penalty feature is then used to control the length of the generated strings. Bilingual models add both source and aligned target tokens whereas monolingual models only use target language tokens. Items are always sorted in the order of the target language.

We experimented with various selections and bilingual models to see the effect of these additional features functions. Five-gram Language model parameters are estimated using KenLM (Heafield et al., 2013). Our main selection criteria are part-of-speech patterns (matching coarse universal POS labels) and dependency relations:

- nouns and their alignments (sentence-internal only and even document-wide)
- verbs and their alignments (sentence-internal only and even document-wide)
- subject-predicate sequences (including negation particles) and their alignments
- closed-class words and their alignments

Gappy language models are fully integrated in Docent but one unsolved problem is the tuning of their weights. Currently, we do not have a stable

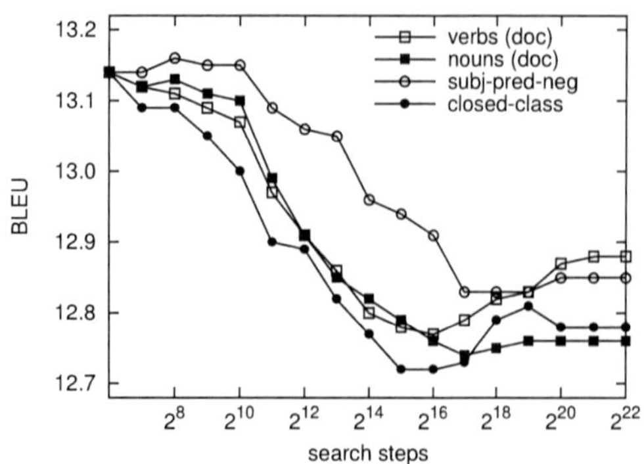

Figure 1: Adding gappy LM features and testing on development test data (newstest 2015).

framework for finding appropriate values for them and, hence, we needed to set them to a quite arbitrary value (0.1 in our case). The disappointing results of our extended models are shown in Figure 1. In general all of them seem to hurt performance in the current setup.

4 Translating Finnish into English

The Finnish–English models re-use the factored setup with pseudo-tokens that we introduced last year (Tiedemann et al., 2015a). The main differences to the previous systems are (i) the use of completely parsed bitexts even with the extended data sets (last year we only parsed Europarl from the constrained data), (ii) the large language model coming from the provided common crawl data (trigram model), and, (iii) improved compound splitting of surface words based on the morphological analyses and the analysed lemma information. For the latter, we use additional string matching heuristics to properly split compounds even if modifying components are inflected and cannot be matched with the lemmatised analyses in a straightforward way. Furthermore, we also add morphological information to the modifying compound components by looking up the most frequent analyses of the given form in a large analysed monolingual corpus. The scores for our factored models in the constrained and unconstrained settings are listed in Table 3.

Again, we can see the substantial impact of additional out-of-domain training data. Alternative subtitle translations contribute marginally in this translation direction. The common crawl data is useful but slows down decoding quite significantly.

newstest 2015	BLEU
basic	19.02
+ OPUS	21.42
+ alternatives	21.46
+ CC LM	22.09
basic + CC LM	19.33

Table 3: Lower-cased BLEU scores for factored SMT models for Finnish-to-English on development test data (newstest 2015).

5 Final Results and Discussions

Table 4 summarises the final scores when applying our models to the news test set from this year's evaluation campaign. A major, but not very surprising effect is the reduction of unknown words when adding more data. The factored model leads to slight improvements in the constrained setting but this does not carry over to the unconstrained setup. A significant difference is the number of unknown tokens which is much higher in the factored model. This may look surprising but when inspecting the data, we could identify the reason for this difference, which is due to the tokenisation applied in the factored setup. The models applied in this approach make different decisions, for example, when keeping numeric and monetary expressions together. This increases the number of unknown units without causing much harm in most cases. Other cases are clearly tokenisation errors. Some examples are listed below:

```
200k|ADJ|JJ|dep
228.89|NUM|CD|num
$22million|NOUN|NN|adpobj
2.5bn|NUM|CD|num
"wrestle|VERB|VB|xcomp
(yet|NOUN|NN|dobj
```

Note that the re-inflection model uses different data pre-processing pipelines and, therefore, the scores are not comparable with the others. In a contrastive run we could see modest improvements over the baseline models without re-inflection. Finally, we can also see that Finnish-English suffers more from unknown tokens even though we apply proper morphological analyses and compound splitting. This is something that we need to address in future work.

References

Bernd Bohnet. 2010. Very high accuracy and fast dependency parsing is not a contradiction. In *Proceed-

English – Finnish	BLEU lower	BLEU cased	TER	unknown words #tokens	#types
constrained - basic	13.3	12.7	0.782	1,582	862
constrained - factored	13.5	12.8	0.784	1,659	1,233
constrained - basic + back-translated	14.2	13.6	0.770	**1,024**	**649**
constrained + factored + back-translated	**14.3**	**13.6**	**0.765**	1,103	890
constrained - re-inflection	12.2	11.6	0.793		
unconstrained - basic	17.0	16.2	0.746	**124**	**60**
unconstrained - factored	16.6	15.7	**0.744**	804	593
unconstrained - basic + back-translated	**17.1**	**16.4**	0.752	544	305

Finnish – English	BLEU lower	BLEU cased	TER	unknown words #tokens	#types
constrained - factored	20.5	19.3	0.706	2,655	2,004
unconstrained - factored	**23.3**	**22.1**	**0.670**	**1,128**	**842**

Table 4: Official results for the WMT 2016 news test set. The systems including the back-translated news data were submitted after the deadline and will not be listed as official submissions. The system in *italics* are marked for manual evaluation at WMT.

ings of the 23rd International Conference on Computational Linguistics, COLING '10, pages 89–97. Association for Computational Linguistics.

Fabienne Cap, Alexander Fraser, Marion Weller, and Aoife Cahill. 2014. How to Produce Unseen Teddy Bears: Improved Morphological Processing of Compounds in SMT. In *EACL'14: Proceedings of the 14th Conference of the European Chapter of the Association for Computational Linguistics*, pages 579–587.

Colin Cherry and George Foster. 2012. Batch tuning strategies for statistical machine translation. In *HLT-NAACL'12: Proceedings of the Human Language Technology Conference of the North American Chapter of the Association for Computational Linguistics*, volume 12, pages 34–35. Association for Computational Linguistics.

Greg Durrett and John DeNero. 2013. Supervised learning of complete morphological paradigms. In *HLT-NAACL*, pages 1185–1195.

Chris Dyer, Victor Chahuneau, and Noah A. Smith. 2013. A simple, fast, and effective reparameterization of IBM Model 2. In *Proceedings of NAACL*, pages 644–648.

Alexander Fraser, Marion Weller, Aoife Cahill, and Fabienne Cap. 2012. Modeling inflection and word formation in SMT. In *EACL'12: Proceedings of the 13th Conference of the European Chapter of the Association for Computational Linguistics*, pages 664–674. Association for Computational Linguistics.

Christian Hardmeier, Sara Stymne, Jörg Tiedemann, and Joakim Nivre. 2013. Docent: A document-level decoder for phrase-based statistical machine translation. In *Proceedings of the 51st Annual Meeting of the Association for Computational Linguistics: System Demonstrations*, pages 193–198, Sofia, Bulgaria, August. Association for Computational Linguistics.

Christian Hardmeier, Preslav Nakov, Sara Stymne, Jörg Tiedemann, Yannick Versley, and Mauro Cettolo. 2015. Pronoun-focused MT and cross-lingual pronoun prediction: Findings of the 2015 DiscoMT shared task on pronoun translation. In *Proceedings of the Second Workshop on Discourse in Machine Translation*, pages 1–16, Lisbon, Portugal, September. Association for Computational Linguistics.

Katri Haverinen, Jenna Nyblom, Timo Viljanen, Veronika Laippala, Samuel Kohonen, Anna Missilä, Stina Ojala, Tapio Salakoski, and Filip Ginter. 2013. Building the essential resources for Finnish: The Turku Dependency Treebank. *Language Resources and Evaluation*, pages 1–39. In press. Available online.

Kenneth Heafield, Ivan Pouzyrevsky, Jonathan H. Clark, and Philipp Koehn. 2013. Scalable modified Kneser-Ney language model estimation. In *Proceedings of ACL*, pages 690–696.

Kenneth Heafield. 2011. KenLM: Faster and smaller language model queries. In *Proceedings of the Sixth Workshop on Statistical Machine Translation*, Edinburgh, UK, July. Association for Computational Linguistics.

Philipp Koehn, Hieu Hoang, Alexandra Birch, Chris Callison-Burch, Marcello Federico, Nicola Bertoldi, Brooke Cowan, Wade Shen, Christine Moran, Richard Zens, Christopher J. Dyer, Ondřej Bojar, Alexandra Constantin, and Evan Herbst. 2007. Moses: Open Source Toolkit for Statistical Machine Translation. In *Proceedings of ACL*, pages 177–180.

Krister Lindén, Miikka Silfverberg, and Tommi Pirinen. 2009. HFST tools for morphology — an efficient open-source package for construction of morphological analyzers. In *State of the Art in Computational Morphology*, volume 41 of *Communications in Computer and Information Science*, pages 28–47. Springer.

Pierre Lison and Jörg Tiedemann. 2016. OpenSubtitles2015: Extracting large parallel corpora from movie and TV subtitles. In *Proceedings of the 10th International Conference on Language Resources and Evaluation (LREC-2016)*, Portorož, Slovenia.

Juhani Luotolahti, Jenna Kanerva, Veronika Laippala, Sampo Pyysalo, and Filip Ginter. 2015. Towards universal web parsebanks. In *Proceedings of the International Conference on Dependency Linguistics (Depling'15)*, pages 211–220. Uppsala University.

Thomas Mueller, Helmut Schmid, and Hinrich Schütze. 2013. Efficient higher-order CRFs for morphological tagging. In *Proceedings of the 2013 Conference on Empirical Methods in Natural Language Processing*, pages 322–332. Association for Computational Linguistics.

Franz Josef Och and Hermann Ney. 2003. A systematic comparison of various statistical alignment models. *Computational Linguistics*, 29(1):19–52.

Franz Josef Och. 2003. Minimum error rate training in statistical machine translation. In *Proceedings of ACL*, pages 160–167.

Robert Östling. 2015. *Bayesian Models for Multilingual Word Alignment*. Ph.D. thesis, Stockholm University. software at https://github.com/robertostling/efmaral.

Tommi A. Pirinen. 2015. Omorfi —free and open source morphological lexical database for Finnish. In *Proceedings of the 20th Nordic Conference of Computational Linguistics (NODALIDA 2015)*, pages 313–315.

Sampo Pyysalo, Jenna Kanerva, Anna Missilä, Veronika Laippala, and Filip Ginter. 2015. Universal dependencies for Finnish. In *Proceedings of NoDaLiDa 2015*, pages 163–172. NEALT.

Andreas Stolcke. 2002. SRILM – an extensible language modelling toolkit. In *ICSLN'02: Proceedings of the international conference on spoken language processing*, pages 901–904.

Sara Stymne, Maria Holmqvist, and Lars Ahrenberg. 2008. Effects of morphological analysis in translation between German and English. In *Proceedings of the Third Workshop on Statistical Machine Translation (WMT'08)*, pages 135–138, Columbus, Ohio, USA.

Jörg Tiedemann, Filip Ginter, and Jenna Kanerva. 2015a. Morphological segmentation and OPUS for Finnish-English machine translation. In *Proceedings of the Tenth Workshop on Statistical Machine Translation*, pages 177–183, Lisbon, Portugal, September. Association for Computational Linguistics.

Jörg Tiedemann, Filip Ginter, and Jenna Kanerva. 2015b. Morphological segmentation and OPUS for Finnish-English machine translation. In *WMT'15: Proceedings of the Tenth Workshop on Statistical Machine Translation*, pages 177–183.

Jörg Tiedemann. 2012. Parallel data, tools and interfaces in OPUS. In *Proceedings of the Eighth International Conference on Language Resources and Evaluation (LREC-2012)*, pages 2214–2218, Istanbul, Turkey, May. European Language Resources Association (ELRA).

Jörg Tiedemann. 2015. Baseline models for pronoun prediction and pronoun-aware translation. In *Proceedings of the Second Workshop on Discourse in Machine Translation*, pages 108–114, Lisbon, Portugal, September. Association for Computational Linguistics.

Jörg Tiedemann. 2016. Finding alternative translations in a large corpus of movie subtitles. In *Proceedings of the 10th International Conference on Language Resources and Evaluation (LREC-2016)*, Portorož, Slovenia.

Kristina Toutanova, Hisami Suzuki, and Achim Ruopp. 2008. Applying Morphology Generation Models to Machine Translation. In *ACL'08: Proceedings of the 46th Annual Meeting of the Association for Computational Linguistics: Human Language Technologies*, pages 514–522. Association for Computational Linguistics.

Edinburgh's Statistical Machine Translation Systems for WMT16

Philip Williams[1], Rico Sennrich[1], Maria Năacabdecirdejde[1],
Matthias Huck[2], Barry Haddow[1], Ondřej Bojar[3]
[1]School of Informatics, University of Edinburgh
[2]Center for Information and Language Processing, LMU Munich
[3]Institute of Formal and Applied Linguistics, Charles University in Prague
`pwillia4@inf.ed.ac.uk` `rico.sennrich@ed.ac.uk` `M.Nadejde@sms.ed.ac.uk`
`mhuck@cis.lmu.de` `bhaddow@inf.ed.ac.uk` `bojar@ufal.mff.cuni.cz`

Abstract

This paper describes the University of Edinburgh's phrase-based and syntax-based submissions to the shared translation tasks of the ACL 2016 First Conference on Machine Translation (WMT16). We submitted five phrase-based and five syntax-based systems for the news task, plus one phrase-based system for the biomedical task.

1 Introduction

Edinburgh's submissions to the WMT 2016 news translation task fall into two distinct groups: neural translation systems and statistical translation systems. In this paper, we describe the statistical systems, which includes a mix of phrase-based and syntax-based approaches. We also include a brief description of our phrase-based submission to the WMT16 biomedical translation task. Our neural systems are described separately in Sennrich et al. (2016a).

In most cases, our statistical systems build on last year's, incorporating recent modelling refinements and adding this year's new training data. For Romanian—a new language this year—we paid particular attention to language-specific processing of diacritics. For English→Czech, we experimented with a string-to-tree system, first using Treex[1] (formerly TectoMT; Popel and Žabokrtský, 2010) to produce Czech dependency parses, then converting them to constituency representation and extracting GHKM rules.

In the next two sections, we describe the phrase-based systems, first describing the core setup in Section 2 and then describing system-specific extensions and experimental results for each individual language pair in Section 3. We describe the

core syntax-based setup and experiments in Sections 4 and 5.

2 Phrase-based System Overview

2.1 Preprocessing

The training data was preprocessed using scripts from the Moses toolkit. We first normalized the data using the `normalize-punctuation.perl` script, then performed tokenization (using the `-a` option), and then truecasing. We did not perform any corpus filtering other than the standard Moses method, which removes sentence pairs with extreme length ratios, and sentences longer than 80 tokens.

2.2 Word Alignment

For word alignment we used `fast_align` (Dyer et al., 2013)—except for German↔English, where we used MGIZA++ (Gao and Vogel, 2008)—followed by the standard `grow-diag-final-and` symmetrization heuristic.

2.3 Language Models

Our default approach to language modelling was to train individual models on each monolingual corpus (except CommonCrawl) and then linearly-interpolate them to produce a single model. For some systems, we added separate neural or CommonCrawl LMs. Here we outline the various approaches and then in Section 3 we describe the combination used for each language pair.

Interpolated LMs For individual monolingual corpora, we first used lmplz (Heafield et al., 2013) to train count-based 5-gram language models with modified Kneser-Ney smoothing (Chen and Goodman, 1998). We then used the SRILM toolkit (Stolcke, 2002) to linearly interpolate the models

---

[1]`http://ufal.mff.cuni.cz/treex`

Proceedings of the First Conference on Machine Translation, Volume 2: Shared Task Papers, pages 399–410,
Berlin, Germany, August 11-12, 2016. ©2016 Association for Computational Linguistics

using weights tuned to minimize perplexity on the development set.

CommonCrawl LMs Our CommonCrawl language models were trained in the same way as the individual corpus-specific standard models, but were not linearly-interpolated with other LMs. Instead, the log probabilities of CommonCrawl LMs were added as separate features of the systems' linear models.

Neural LMs For some of our phrase-based systems we experimented with feed-forward neural network language models, both trained on target n-grams only, and on "joint" or "bilingual" n-grams (Devlin et al., 2014; Le et al., 2012). For training these models we used the NPLM toolkit (Vaswani et al., 2013), for which we have now implemented *gradient clipping* to address numerical issues often encountered during training.

2.4 Baseline Features

We follow the standard approach to SMT of scoring translation hypotheses using a weighted linear combination of features. The core features of our model are a 5-gram LM score (i.e. log probability), phrase translation and lexical translation scores, word and phrase penalties, and a linear distortion score. The phrase translation probabilities are smoothed with Good-Turing smoothing (Foster et al., 2006). We used the hierarchical lexicalized reordering model (Galley and Manning, 2008) with 4 possible orientations (monotone, swap, discontinuous left and discontinuous right) in both left-to-right and right-to-left direction. We also used the operation sequence model (OSM) (Durrani et al., 2013) with 4 count based supportive features. We further employed domain indicator features (marking which training corpus each phrase pair was found in), binary phrase count indicator features, sparse phrase length features, and sparse source word deletion, target word insertion, and word translation features (limited to the top K words in each language, typically with $K = 50$).

2.5 Tuning

Since our feature set (generally around 500 to 1000 features) was too large for MERT, we used k-best batch MIRA for tuning (Cherry and Foster, 2012). To speed up tuning we applied threshold pruning to the phrase table, based on the direct translation model probability.

2.6 Decoding

In decoding we applied cube pruning (Huang and Chiang, 2007) with a stack size of 5000 (reduced to 1000 for tuning), Minimum Bayes Risk decoding (Kumar and Byrne, 2004), a maximum phrase length of 5, a distortion limit of 6, 100-best translation options and the no-reordering-over-punctuation heuristic (Koehn and Haddow, 2009).

3 Phrase-based Experiments

3.1 Finnish→English

Similar to last year (Haddow et al., 2015), we built an unconstrained system for Finnish→English using data extracted from OPUS (Tiedemann, 2012). Our parallel training set was the same as we used previously, but the language model training set was extended with the addition of the news2015 monolingual corpus and the large WMT16 English CommonCrawl corpus. We used newsdev2015 for tuning, and newsdev2015 for testing during system development.

One clear problem that we noted with our submission from last year was the large number of OOVs, which were then copied directly into the English output. This is undoubtedly due to the agglutinative nature of Finnish, and probably was the cause of our system being poorly judged by human evaluators, despite having a high BLEU score. To address this, we split the Finnish input into subword units at both train and test time. In particular, we applied *byte pair encoding (BPE)* to split the Finnish source into smaller units, greatly reducing the vocabulary size. BPE is a technique which has been recently used to good effect in neural machine translation (Sennrich et al., 2016b), where the models cannot handle large vocbaularies. It is actually a merging algorithm, originally designed for compression, and works by starting with a maximally split version of the training corpus (i.e. split to characters) and iteratively merging common clusters. The merging continues for a specified number of iterations, and the merges are collected up to form the BPE model. At test time, the recorded merges are applied to the test corpus, with the result that there are no OOVs in the test data. For the experiments here, we used 100,000 BPE merges to create the model.

Applying BPE to Finnish→English was clearly effective at addressing the unknown word problem, and in many cases the resulting translations are quite understandable, e.g.

source yös Intian on sanottu olevan kiinnostunut puolustusyhteistyösopimuksesta Japanin kanssa.

base India is also said to be interested in puolus-tusyhteistyösopimuksesta with Japan.

bpe India is also said to be interested in defence cooperation agreement with Japan.

reference India is also reportedly hoping for a deal on defence collaboration between the two nations.

However applying BPE to Finnish can also result in some rather odd translations when it overzealously splits:

source Balotelli oli vielä kaukana huippu-vireestään.

base Balotelli was still far from huippuvireestään.

bpe Baloo, Hotel was still far from the peak of its vitality.

reference Balotelli is still far from his top tune.

We built four language models: an interpolated count-based 5-gram language model with all corpora, apart from the WMT16 CommonCrawl; separate count-based language models with WMT16 CommonCrawl and news2015; and a neural LM on news2015. A performance comparison across different language model combinations, and with and without BPE is shown in Table 1.

system	BLEU	
	fi-en	ro-en
only interpolated LM	22.9	34.2
+ CommonCrawl LM	23.2	35.0
+ CC LM & news2015 (count)	**23.4**	34.9
+ CC LM & news2015 (neural)	23.4	**35.2**
+ all	23.4	35.0
without BPE	22.2	–
without diacritic removal	–	32.2

Table 1: Comparison of different language model combinations and preprocessing regimes for Finnish→English and for Romanian→English. The submitted system is shown in bold. The preprocessing variant uses the same language model combination as the submitted system. Cased BLEU scores are on newstest2016.

3.2 Romanian→English

We trained our Romanian→English system using all data available for the constrained task. For system development, we split the newsdev2016 set into two parts randomly (so as to balance the "born English" and "born Romanian" portions), using one for tuning and one for testing. For building the final system, and for the contrastive experiments, we used the whole of newsdev2016 for tuning, and newstest2016 for testing.

In early experiments we noted that both the training and the development data were inconsistent in their use of diacritics leading to problems with OOVs and sparse statistics. To address this we stripped off all diacritics from the Romanian texts and the result was a significant increase in performance in our development setup. We also experimented with different language model combinations during development, with our submitted system using three different language model features: a neural LM trained on just news2015 monolingual, an n-gram language model trained on the WMT16 English CommonCrawl corpus, and a linear interpolation of language models trained on all other WMT16 English corpora.

In Table 1 we show how system performance varies under different language model combination and preprocessing conditions.

3.3 English→Romanian

For English→Romanian, we used all the data in the constrained track, including the CommonCrawl language model data, and as with the Romanian→English system, we used newsdev2016 for the final tuning run.

The inconsistent use of diacritics in Romanian text also affected the English→Romanian system, however removing altogether would be problematic as we would then need a method for restoring them for the final system. So the only extra preprocessing we performed on the Romanian was to ensure that "t-comma" and "s-comma" were written correctly, with a comma rather than a cedilla.

Our final system used two different count-based 5-gram language models (one trained on all data, including the WMT16 Romanian CommonCrawl corpus, without pruning, and one trained on news2015 monolingual only), a neural language model trained on news2015 monolingual, and a bilingual language model trained on the parallel data, with source window of 15 and target window of 1. In Table 2 we show ablation experiments where we remove each of these language models.

system	BLEU
submitted	26.8
+ prune all	26.2
- all	25.6
- news2015	26.4
- neural LM	26.6
- bilingual LM	26.5

Table 2: Effect of each of the language models used in the English→Romanian system. The experiments are not cumulative, so we first try pruning the "all" language model, then go back to the unpruned version and remove each LM in turn, observing the effect. The submitted system used all four LMs, and the scores shown are uncased BLEU scores on newstest2016.

3.4 English→German

For the English→German phrase-based system, we exploited several translation factors in addition to word surface forms, in particular: Och clusters (with 50 classes) and part-of-speech tags (Ratnaparkhi, 1996) on the English side, as well as Och clusters (50 classes), morphological tags, and part-of-speech tags on the German side (Schmid, 2000). Recent experiments for our IWSLT 2015 phrase-based system have reconfirmed that English→German translation quality can benefit from these factors when supplementary models over factored representations are used (Huck and Birch, 2015). For WMT16, we utilized the factors in the translation model, in operation sequence models, and in language models (for linearly interpolated 7-gram LMs over Och clusters and morphological tags).

Sparse source word deletion, target word insertion, and word translation features were integrated over the top 200 word surface forms and over selected factors (source and target Och clusters, source part-of-speech tags and target morphological tags). An unpruned 5-gram LM over words that was trained on all German data except the CommonCrawl monolingual corpus was supplemented by a separate pruned LM trained on the CommonCrawl data that had been provided as permissible data for the "constrained" track. Rather than applying a simple linear distortion score, we opted for sparse distortion features as described by Green et al. (2010), which we reimplemented in Moses. We activated sparse distortion features with a feature template based on jump distance, source part-of-speech tags, and target morpholog-

ical tags.

The feature weights for our final system were tuned with hypergraph MIRA (i.e. batch MIRA over lattices representing the decoding search space) on a concatenation of newssyscomb2009 and newstest2008–2012.

3.5 German→English

For phrase-based translation from German, we applied syntactic pre-reordering (Collins et al., 2005) and compound splitting (Koehn and Knight, 2003) in a preprocessing step on the source side. The operation sequence model for the German→English phrase-based system was unpruned. We integrated three language models: an unpruned LM over all English data except the CommonCrawl monolingual corpus; a pruned LM over CommonCrawl; and a pruned LM over the monolingual News Crawl 2015 corpus. In addition to lexical smoothing with the standard lexicon models, we utilized a source-to-target IBM Model 1 (Brown et al., 1993) for sentence-level lexical scoring in a similar manner as described by Huck et al. (2011) for hierarchical systems. We tuned on the concatenation of newssyscomb2009 and newstest2008–2012.

Unlike last year's system (Haddow et al., 2015)—and different from the inverse translation direction (English→German)—we refrained from using any factors and instead set up a system that operates over surface form word representations only. In relation to last year's system, we were able to maintain high translation quality as measured in BLEU despite the abandonment of factors. However, we suspect that human judgment scores may suffer a bit from the abandonment of a factored model. We decided to drop the factored representations in favour of gains in decoding efficiency.

We furthermore did not employ any sparse features (sparse phrase length, source word deletion, target word insertion, or word translation features) in the German→English system since we did not observe any clear gains in preliminary experiments, and sparse features slow down tuning and decoding.

English→German and German→English translation results with our phrase-based systems are given in Table 3.

3.6 Spanish→English Biomedical

For our submission to the Spanish→English biomedical task, we created a parallel corpus using

system	de-en				en-de			
	2013	2014	2015	2016	2013	2014	2015	2016
last year's phrase-based	27.2	28.8	29.3	33.8	20.8	21.1	22.8	28.3
this year's phrase-based	27.8	30.0	29.9	35.1	21.5	21.9	23.7	28.4

Table 3: Experimental results with phrase-based systems for German→English and English→German. We report case-sensitive BLEU scores on each of the newstest2013–2016 test sets.

all relevant data from WMT13, as well as the extra biomedical data provided by the task organisers, and the EMEA corpus from OPUS (Tiedemann, 2012). In total we had around 16M sentences of parallel data. Our monolingual corpus was made up of three parts: all the English monolingual medical data from WMT14 medical, WMT16 biomedical and EMEA (11M sentences); all the English LDC GigaWord data (180M sentences); and all the English general domain data from WMT16 (240M sentences). We used the monolingual data to build three different language models which were then linearly interpolated. System tuning was with the SCIELO development data provided for the biomedical task.

4 Syntax-based System Overview

For all syntax-based systems, we used a string-to-tree model based on a synchronous context-free grammar (SCFG) with linguistically-motivated labels on the target side.

4.1 Preprocessing

Except for English-Czech, which we describe separately in Section 5.1, preprocessing was similar to the phrase-based systems (Section 2.3). To parse the target-side of the training data, we used the Berkeley parser (Petrov et al., 2006; Petrov and Klein, 2007) for English, and the ParZu dependency parser (Sennrich et al., 2013) for German. Except where stated otherwise, we right-binarized the trees after parsing to increase rule coverage.

4.2 Word Alignment

As in the phrase-based models, we used `fast_align` for word alignment and the `grow-diag-final-and` heuristic for symmetrization.

4.3 Language Models

As in the phrase-based systems (Section 2.3), we used linearly-interpolated language models as standard, with some systems adding Common-

Crawl and neural LMs. We detail the system-specific combinations in Section 5.

4.4 Rule Extraction

SCFG rules were extracted from the word-aligned parallel data using the Moses implementation (Williams and Koehn, 2012) of the GHKM algorithm (Galley et al., 2004, 2006).

Minimal GHKM rules were composed into larger rules subject to restrictions on the size of the resulting tree fragment. We used the settings shown in Table 4, which were chosen empirically during the development of 2013's systems (Nadejde et al., 2013).

parameter	unbinarized	binarized
rule depth	5	7
node count	20	30
rule size	5	7

Table 4: Parameter settings for rule composition. The parameters were relaxed for systems that used binarization to allow for the increase in tree node density.

Further to the restrictions on rule composition, fully non-lexical unary rules were eliminated using the method described in Chung et al. (2011) and rules with scope greater than 3 (Hopkins and Langmead, 2010) were pruned from the translation grammar. Scope pruning makes parsing tractable without the need for grammar binarization.

4.5 Baseline Features

Our core set of string-to-tree feature functions is unchanged from previous years. It includes the n-gram language model's log probability for the target string, the target word count, the rule count, and several pre-computed rule-specific scores. The rule-specific scores were: the direct and indirect translation probabilities; the direct and indirect lexical weights (Koehn et al., 2003); the monolingual PCFG probability of the tree fragment from which the rule was extracted; and a rule rareness penalty.

4.6 Decoding

Decoding for the string-to-tree models is based on Sennrich's (2014) recursive variant of the CYK+ parsing algorithm combined with LM integration via cube pruning (Chiang, 2007).

4.7 Tuning

The feature weights for the English→Czech and Finnish→English systems were tuned using the Moses implementation of MERT (Och, 2003). For the remaining systems we used k-best MIRA (Cherry and Foster, 2012) due to the use of sparse features.

We used randomly-chosen subsets of the previous years' test data to speed up decoding.

5 Syntax-based Experiments

5.1 English→Czech

For English→Czech, we used Treex to preprocess and parse the Czech-side of the training data. Treex uses the MST parser (McDonald et al., 2005), which produces dependency graphs with non-projective arcs. In order to extract SCFG rules, we first applied the following conversion process: i) the dependency graphs were projectivized using the Malt Parser, which implements the method described in Nivre and Nilsson (2005) (we used the 'Head' encoding scheme); ii) the projective dependency graphs were converted to CFG trees. In addition, we reduced the complex positional tags to simple POS tags by discarding the morphological attributes. The CFG trees were not binarized.

We also experimented with unification-based agreement and case government constraints (Williams and Koehn, 2011; Williams, 2014). Specifically, our constraints were designed to enforce: i) case, gender, and number agreement between nouns and pre-nominal adjectival modifiers; ii) number and person agreement between subjects and verbs; iii) case agreement between prepositions and nouns; iv) use of nominative case for subject nouns. For every Czech word in the training data, we obtained a set of morphological analyses using MorphoDiTa (Straková et al., 2014). From these analyses, we constructed a lexicon of feature structures. For constraint extraction, we used handwritten rules along the lines of those described in Williams (2014).

In preliminary experiments we used a smaller training set, comprising 2 million sentence pairs sampled from OPUS and monolingual data from last year's WMT translation task. We used two test sets from the HimL project and the Khresmoi test set. Results with and without constraints are shown in Table 5. We used hard constraints and reused the baseline weights (re-tuning did not appear to give additional gains).

system	BLEU		
	HimL1	HimL2	Khresmoi
baseline	23.3	18.6	20.4
+ constraints	23.6	18.8	20.7

Table 5: Translation results on the development system for English→Czech with unification-based constraints. Cased BLEU scores are shown. They are averaged over three tuning runs (note that baseline weights are reused in the experiments with constraints).

Although the gains in BLEU were small, previous analysis for German showed that BLEU lacks sensitivity to grammatical improvements when compared to human evaluators (Williams, 2014).

We trained the final system on all of the provided training and monolingual data. In addition to the interpolated LM, we used a model trained on the CommonCrawl data. Results are shown in Table 6.

system	BLEU	
	2015	2016
baseline	17.3	20.1
+ constraints	17.5	20.2
+ CC LM	17.9	20.9

Table 6: Translation results on the final system for English→Czech with unification-based constraints. Cased BLEU scores are shown. Note that baseline weights are reused in the experiments with constraints.

5.1.1 Manual Analysis

We carried out a small manual analysis of the submitted system with and without unification-based constraints (the CC LM was used in both cases). In order to remove the effect of tuning variance, we used the same model weights in both cases (the weights were learned on the version without constraints). The BLEU scores of the two systems were 20.9 (with constraints) and 20.7 (without constraints). A large majority of the outputs (81% of the 2999 sentences in the newstest2016) are identical.

Looking at a sample of 100 sentences with some differences, we classified differring areas to see in what aspects the outputs of the two systems differ. In total, there were 104 such areas (some sentences had more than one area of interest).

Table 7 summarizes the overall evaluation of these areas (the annotation was not blind, we knew which system was which). The majority of the areas were of an equal quality, in fact equally bad overall, so neither of the compared systems delivered an acceptable translation.

Much Better	Better	Equal	Worse	Crazy Reordering
4	41	44	12	3

Table 7: Manual evaluation of translations as proposed by the English→Czech system with unification constraints vs. the same system without constraints.

In 4 cases, the system with constraints delivered much better translation, and three of those were overall improvement of the sentence structure.

In 41 cases, the area was better for various reasons. Most frequently (16 cases), this was indeed the agreement within noun and prepositional phrases (adjective matching in case the preposition etc.). In 9 additional cases, the NP or PP was better translated but in other aspects than morphological case, number of gender. For instance the baseline system translated the phrase "between the departments of individual hospitals" as "between the individual departments of the hospitals" (in morphologically well-formed Czech). Beyond better NPs and PPs, the constraints have also helped overall sentence or clause structure (5 cases), lexical choice (4 cases) and verbs and their belongings (2 cases).

In 15 cases, the constraints forced the system to select a worse translation, damaging sentence structure, lexical choice, spuriously introducing negation etc. We highlight 3 of these cases, where the system with constraints accidentally moved words far away from their correct location ("Crazy Reordering" in Table 7). This suggests that due to sparse data, the application of constraints should

system	BLEU dev	test
last year's system	24.0	29.3
+particle verb restructuring	24.4	30.2
+News 2015 training data	24.5	30.6

Table 8: Translation results of English→German string-to-tree translation system on dev (newstest2015) and test (newstest2016).

be better balanced with respect to other parts of the model. In constrast to German, targetting Czech usually does not need long-distance reordering and doing it risks more serious translation errors than sticking to the English word order.

Since the hard unification constraints effectively only avoid some of the possible translations (i.e. reduce the search space), we conclude that having to obey mere agreement constraints helps to select a hypothesis better in a surprisingly larger span of words, improving overall sentence structure on average.

5.2 English→German

This year's string-to-tree submission for English→German is similar to last year's system (Williams et al., 2015). In addition to the baseline feature functions, it contains count-based 5-gram Neural Network language model (NPLM) (Vaswani et al., 2013), a relational dependency language model (RDLM) (Sennrich, 2015), and soft source-syntactic constraints (Huck et al., 2014). The parameters of the model are tuned towards the linear interpolation of BLEU and the syntactic metric HWCM (Liu and Gildea, 2005; Sennrich, 2015). Trees are transformed through binarization and a hierarchical representation of morphologically complex words (Sennrich and Haddow, 2015).

For the soft source-syntactic constraints, we annotate the source text with the Stanford Neural Network dependency parser (Chen and Manning, 2014), along with heuristic projectivization (Nivre and Nilsson, 2005).

Results are shown in Table 8. We report results of last year's system (Williams et al., 2015), which was ranked (joint) first at WMT 15. Our improvements this year stem from particle verb restructuring (Sennrich and Haddow, 2015), and the use of the new monolingual News Crawl 2015 corpus for the Kneser-Ney language model.[2]

5.3 Finnish→English

Our Finnish→English syntax-based system was similar to last year's (Williams et al., 2015). The main difference from the basic setup of Section 4 is that we preprocessed the Finnish data to segment words into morphemes. We also added a CommonCrawl language model in addition to the interpolated LM.

For segmentation, we used Morfessor 2.0 with default settings, first training a segmentation model, then using it to segment all words in the source-side training and test data. Morfessor takes a set of word types as input and we found that it was important for translation quality to use a large training vocabulary. Table 9 gives mean BLEU scores for this setup, averaged over three MERT runs. Our baseline is the standard string-to-tree setup (i.e. without segmentation and without the CommonCrawl LM). For segmentation, we experimented with varying amounts of training data, initially using the Finnish side of the provided parallel corpora, then adding the monolingual Finnish data (apart from CommonCrawl), and finally adding 10% of the CommonCrawl vocabulary (we extracted the full vocabulary from CommonCrawl and then randomly sampled 10%). We found that using larger amounts of training data was prohibitively slow.

system	BLEU	
	2015	2016
baseline	16.0	18.2
+ Morfessor (all parallel)	16.8	19.1
+ Morfessor (non-CC mono)	17.6	20.1
+ Morfessor (10% CC)	17.9	20.1
+ CC LM	18.0	20.3

Table 9: Comparison of different preprocessing and language model regimes for Finnish→English (syntax-based). Cased BLEU scores are given for the newstest2015 and newstest2016 test sets, averaged over three tuning runs.

5.4 German→English

For German→English we built a string-to-tree system with a similar setup to last year's (Williams et al., 2015). In addition we used sparse features to determine the non-terminal labels for un-

---

system	BLEU	
	dev	test
baseline (phrase-structure)	28.6	33.5
+ NER before split	28.8	33.8
+ CommonCrawl LM*	29.4	34.4
contrastive (dependency)		
+ NER before split	28.1	33.0

Table 10: Translation results of German→English string-to-tree translation system on dev (newstest2015) and test (newstest2016). *submitted system.

known words similar to the English→German systems described by Williams et al. (2014) and Sennrich et al. (2015). We also tagged named entities to avoid over-splitting of compounds. For example the script provided with Moses for compound splitting will split *Florstadt nach Bad Salzhausen* into *flor Stadt nach Bad Salz hausen*. This is then wrongly translated by the baseline system as *Flor after bath salt station*. We applied a 3–class named entity tagger (Finkel et al., 2005; Faruqui and Padó, 2010) on the German side of the corpus prior to splitting and removed the annotations afterwards. We also trained a contrastive system with target–side dependency relations instead of PTB–style phrase-structures. The English side of the parallel corpora was annotated with the Stanford Neural Network dependency parser (Chen and Manning, 2014), along with heuristic projectivization (Nivre and Nilsson, 2005) and head-binarization (Sennrich and Haddow, 2015). We report the cased BLEU scores for different setups of our system in Table 10.

5.5 Romanian→English

For Romanian→English we built a string-to-tree system similar to the German→English system. However we did not use compound splitting and we allowed glue rules. Similar to the phrase-based setup we used half of the newsdev2016 for tuning and the other half as development set. We normalized the corpora by removing all diacritics from the Romanian side. We report the cased BLEU scores for different setups of our system in Table 11.

6 Conclusion

The Edinburgh team built a total of 11 phrase-based and syntax-based translation systems us-

system	BLEU	
	dev	test
baseline (phrase-structure)	33.9	32.9
+ UNK NT labels	34.2	33.0
+ CommonCrawl LM*	35.2	33.6
contrastive (dependency)		
+ UNK NT labels	33.7	32.3

Table 11: Translation results of Romanian→English string-to-tree translation system on dev (half of newsdev2016) and test (newstest2016). *submitted system.

ing the open source Moses toolkit. Our Finnish→English and Romanian→English systems ranked first according to cased BLEU on the newstest2016 evaluation set.[3]

Acknowledgments

We are grateful to Martin Popel for assistance with Treex. This project has received funding from the European Union's Horizon 2020 research and innovation programme under grant agreements 645452 (QT21), 644333 (TraMOOC) and 644402 (HimL).

References

Peter F. Brown, Stephen A. Della Pietra, Vincent J. Della Pietra, and Robert L. Mercer. 1993. The Mathematics of Statistical Machine Translation: Parameter Estimation. *Computational Linguistics* 19(2):263–311.

Danqi Chen and Christopher Manning. 2014. A Fast and Accurate Dependency Parser using Neural Networks. In *Proceedings of the 2014 Conference on Empirical Methods in Natural Language Processing (EMNLP)*. Association for Computational Linguistics, Doha, Qatar, pages 740–750.

Stanley F. Chen and Joshua Goodman. 1998. An empirical study of smoothing techniques for language modeling. Technical report, Harvard University.

Colin Cherry and George Foster. 2012. Batch Tuning Strategies for Statistical Machine Translation. In *Proceedings of the 2012 Conference of the North American Chapter of the Association*

for Computational Linguistics: Human Language Technologies. Montréal, Canada, pages 427–436.

David Chiang. 2007. Hierarchical phrase-based translation. *Comput. Linguist.* 33(2):201–228.

Tagyoung Chung, Licheng Fang, and Daniel Gildea. 2011. Issues Concerning Decoding with Synchronous Context-free Grammar. In *Proceedings of the 49th Annual Meeting of the Association for Computational Linguistics: Human Language Technologies*. Portland, Oregon, USA, pages 413–417.

Michael Collins, Philipp Koehn, and Ivona Kucerova. 2005. Clause Restructuring for Statistical Machine Translation. In *Proceedings of the 43rd Annual Meeting of the Association for Computational Linguistics (ACL'05)*. Ann Arbor, MI, USA, pages 531–540.

Jacob Devlin, Rabih Zbib, Zhongqiang Huang, Thomas Lamar, Richard Schwartz, and John Makhoul. 2014. Fast and Robust Neural Network Joint Models for Statistical Machine Translation. In *Proceedings of the 52nd Annual Meeting of the Association for Computational Linguistics (Volume 1: Long Papers)*. Baltimore, MD, USA, pages 1370–1380.

Nadir Durrani, Alexander Fraser, Helmut Schmid, Hieu Hoang, and Philipp Koehn. 2013. Can Markov Models Over Minimal Translation Units Help Phrase-Based SMT? In *Proceedings of the 51st Annual Meeting of the Association for Computational Linguistics (Volume 2: Short Papers)*. Sofia, Bulgaria, pages 399–405.

Chris Dyer, Victor Chahuneau, and Noah A. Smith. 2013. A Simple, Fast, and Effective Reparameterization of IBM Model 2. In *Proceedings of the 2013 Conference of the North American Chapter of the Association for Computational Linguistics: Human Language Technologies*. Atlanta, GA, USA, pages 644–648.

Manaal Faruqui and Sebastian Padó. 2010. Training and evaluating a german named entity recognizer with semantic generalization. In *Proceedings of KONVENS 2010*. Saarbrücken, Germany.

Jenny Rose Finkel, Trond Grenager, and Christopher Manning. 2005. Incorporating non-local information into information extraction systems by gibbs sampling. In *Proceedings of the 43rd*

---

[3] http://matrix.statmt.org/?mode=all&test_set[id]=23

Annual Meeting on Association for Computational Linguistics. pages 363–370.

George Foster, Roland Kuhn, and Howard Johnson. 2006. Phrasetable Smoothing for Statistical Machine Translation. In *Proceedings of the Conference on Empirical Methods for Natural Language Processing (EMNLP)*. Sydney, Australia, pages 53–61.

Michel Galley, Jonathan Graehl, Kevin Knight, Daniel Marcu, Steve DeNeefe, Wei Wang, and Ignacio Thayer. 2006. Scalable inference and training of context-rich syntactic translation models. In *ACL-44: Proceedings of the 21st International Conference on Computational Linguistics and the 44th annual meeting of the Association for Computational Linguistics*. Morristown, NJ, USA, pages 961–968.

Michel Galley, Mark Hopkins, Kevin Knight, and Daniel Marcu. 2004. What's in a Translation Rule? In *HLT-NAACL '04*.

Michel Galley and Christopher D. Manning. 2008. A Simple and Effective Hierarchical Phrase Reordering Model. In *Proceedings of the 2008 Conference on Empirical Methods in Natural Language Processing*. Honolulu, HI, USA, pages 848–856.

Qin Gao and Stephan Vogel. 2008. Parallel implementations of word alignment tool. In *Software Engineering, Testing, and Quality Assurance for Natural Language Processing*. Stroudsburg, PA, USA, SETQA-NLP '08, pages 49–57.

Spence Green, Michel Galley, and Christopher D. Manning. 2010. Improved Models of Distortion Cost for Statistical Machine Translation. In *Human Language Technologies: The 2010 Annual Conference of the North American Chapter of the Association for Computational Linguistics*. Los Angeles, California, pages 867–875.

Barry Haddow, Matthias Huck, Alexandra Birch, Nikolay Bogoychev, and Philipp Koehn. 2015. The Edinburgh/JHU Phrase-based Machine Translation Systems for WMT 2015. In *Proceedings of the Tenth Workshop on Statistical Machine Translation*. Association for Computational Linguistics, Lisbon, Portugal, pages 126–133.

Kenneth Heafield, Ivan Pouzyrevsky, Jonathan H. Clark, and Philipp Koehn. 2013. Scalable modified Kneser-Ney language model estimation.

In *Proceedings of the 51st Annual Meeting of the Association for Computational Linguistics*. Sofia, Bulgaria, pages 690–696.

Mark Hopkins and Greg Langmead. 2010. SCFG decoding without binarization. In *Proceedings of the 2010 Conference on Empirical Methods in Natural Language Processing*. Cambridge, MA, pages 646–655.

Liang Huang and David Chiang. 2007. Forest Rescoring: Faster Decoding with Integrated Language Models. In *Proceedings of the 45th Annual Meeting of the Association of Computational Linguistics*. Prague, Czech Republic, pages 144–151.

Matthias Huck and Alexandra Birch. 2015. The Edinburgh Machine Translation Systems for IWSLT 2015. In *Proceedings of the International Workshop on Spoken Language Translation*. Da Nang, Vietnam, pages 31–38.

Matthias Huck, Hieu Hoang, and Philipp Koehn. 2014. Preference Grammars and Soft Syntactic Constraints for GHKM Syntax-based Statistical Machine Translation. In *Proceedings of SSST-8, Eighth Workshop on Syntax, Semantics and Structure in Statistical Translation*. Association for Computational Linguistics, Doha, Qatar, pages 148–156.

Matthias Huck, Saab Mansour, Simon Wiesler, and Hermann Ney. 2011. Lexicon Models for Hierarchical Phrase-Based Machine Translation. In *Proceedings of the International Workshop on Spoken Language Translation*. San Francisco, CA, USA, pages 191–198.

Philipp Koehn and Barry Haddow. 2009. Edinburgh's Submission to all Tracks of the WMT 2009 Shared Task with Reordering and Speed Improvements to Moses. In *Proceedings of the Fourth Workshop on Statistical Machine Translation*. Athens, Greece, pages 160–164.

Philipp Koehn and Kevin Knight. 2003. Empirical Methods for Compound Splitting. In *Proceedings of the 10th Conference of the European Chapter of the Association for Computational Linguistics (EACL)*. Budapest, Hungary, pages 187–194.

Philipp Koehn, Franz Josef Och, and Daniel Marcu. 2003. Statistical phrase-based translation. In *NAACL '03: Proceedings of the 2003 Conference of the North American Chapter of the Association for Computational Linguistics on Human Language Technology*. Morristown, NJ, USA, pages 48–54.

Shankar Kumar and William Byrne. 2004. Minimum Bayes-Risk Decoding for Statistical Machine Translation. In *HLT-NAACL 2004: Main Proceedings*. Boston, MA, USA, pages 169–176.

Hai Son Le, Alexandre Allauzen, and François Yvon. 2012. Continuous Space Translation Models with Neural Networks. In *Human Language Technologies: Conference of the North American Chapter of the Association of Computational Linguistics, Proceedings, June 3-8, 2012, Montréal, Canada*. pages 39–48.

Ding Liu and Daniel Gildea. 2005. Syntactic Features for Evaluation of Machine Translation. In *Proceedings of the ACL Workshop on Intrinsic and Extrinsic Evaluation Measures for Machine Translation and/or Summarization*. Ann Arbor, Michigan, pages 25–32.

Ryan McDonald, Fernando Pereira, Kiril Ribarov, and Jan Hajic. 2005. Non-projective dependency parsing using spanning tree algorithms. In *Proceedings of Human Language Technology Conference and Conference on Empirical Methods in Natural Language Processing*.

Maria Nadejde, Philip Williams, and Philipp Koehn. 2013. Edinburgh's Syntax-Based Machine Translation Systems. In *Proceedings of the Eighth Workshop on Statistical Machine Translation*. Sofia, Bulgaria, pages 170–176.

Joakim Nivre and Jens Nilsson. 2005. Pseudo-Projective Dependency Parsing. In *Proceedings of the 43rd Annual Meeting of the Association for Computational Linguistics (ACL'05)*. Association for Computational Linguistics, Ann Arbor, Michigan, pages 99–106.

Franz Josef Och. 2003. Minimum error rate training in statistical machine translation. In *Proceedings of the 41st Annual Meeting on Association for Computational Linguistics - Volume 1*. Morristown, NJ, USA, ACL '03, pages 160–167.

Slav Petrov, Leon Barrett, Romain Thibaux, and Dan Klein. 2006. Learning accurate, compact, and interpretable tree annotation. In *Proceedings of the 21st International Conference on Computational Linguistics and the 44th annual meeting of the Association for Computational Linguistics*. ACL-44, pages 433–440.

Slav Petrov and Dan Klein. 2007. Improved Inference for Unlexicalized Parsing. In *Human Language Technologies 2007: The Conference of the North American Chapter of the Association for Computational Linguistics; Proceedings of the Main Conference*. Rochester, New York, pages 404–411.

Martin Popel and Zdeněk Žabokrtský. 2010. TectoMT: Modular NLP framework. In Hrafn Loftsson, Eirikur Rögnvaldsson, and Sigrun Helgadottir, editors, *Lecture Notes in Artificial Intelligence, Proceedings of the 7th International Conference on Advances in Natural Language Processing (IceTAL 2010)*. Iceland Centre for Language Technology (ICLT), Springer, Berlin / Heidelberg, volume 6233 of *Lecture Notes in Computer Science*, pages 293–304.

Adwait Ratnaparkhi. 1996. A Maximum Entropy Part-Of-Speech Tagger. In *Proceedings of the Conference on Empirical Methods in Natural Language Processing*. Philadelphia, PA, USA.

Helmut Schmid. 2000. LoPar: Design and Implementation. Bericht des Sonderforschungsbereiches "Sprachtheoretische Grundlagen für die Computerlinguistik" 149, Institute for Computational Linguistics, University of Stuttgart.

Rico Sennrich. 2014. A CYK+ Variant for SCFG Decoding Without a Dot Chart. In *Proceedings of SSST-8, Eighth Workshop on Syntax, Semantics and Structure in Statistical Translation*. Doha, Qatar, pages 94–102.

Rico Sennrich. 2015. Modelling and Optimizing on Syntactic N-Grams for Statistical Machine Translation. *Transactions of the Association for Computational Linguistics* 3:169–182.

Rico Sennrich and Barry Haddow. 2015. A Joint Dependency Model of Morphological and Syntactic Structure for Statistical Machine Translation. In *Proceedings of the 2015 Conference on Empirical Methods in Natural Language Processing*. Association for Computational Linguistics, Lisbon, Portugal, pages 2081–2087.

Rico Sennrich, Barry Haddow, and Alexandra Birch. 2016a. Edinburgh Neural Machine Translation Systems for WMT 16. In *Proceedings of the First Conference on Machine Translation (WMT16)*. Berlin, Germany.

Rico Sennrich, Barry Haddow, and Alexandra Birch. 2016b. Neural Machine Translation of Rare Words with Subword Units. In *Proceedings of the 54th Annual Meeting of the Association for Computational Linguistics (ACL 2016)*. Berlin, Germany.

Rico Sennrich, Martin Volk, and Gerold Schneider. 2013. Exploiting Synergies Between Open Resources for German Dependency Parsing, POS-tagging, and Morphological Analysis. In *Proceedings of the International Conference Recent Advances in Natural Language Processing 2013*. Hissar, Bulgaria, pages 601–609.

Rico Sennrich, Philip Williams, and Matthias Huck. 2015. A tree does not make a well-formed sentence: Improving syntactic string-to-tree statistical machine translation with more linguistic knowledge. *Computer Speech & Language* 32(1):27–45.

Andreas Stolcke. 2002. SRILM – an Extensible Language Modeling Toolkit. In *Proc. of the Int. Conf. on Spoken Language Processing (ICSLP)*. Denver, CO, USA, volume 3.

Jana Straková, Milan Straka, and Jan Hajič. 2014. Open-Source Tools for Morphology, Lemmatization, POS Tagging and Named Entity Recognition. In *Proceedings of 52nd Annual Meeting of the Association for Computational Linguistics: System Demonstrations*. Association for Computational Linguistics, pages 13–18.

Jörg Tiedemann. 2012. Parallel Data, Tools and Interfaces in OPUS. In Nicoletta Calzolari (Conference Chair), Khalid Choukri, Thierry Declerck, Mehmet Ugur Dogan, Bente Maegaard, Joseph Mariani, Jan Odijk, and Stelios Piperidis, editors, *Proceedings of the Eight International Conference on Language Resources and Evaluation (LREC'12)*. European Language Resources Association (ELRA), Istanbul, Turkey.

Ashish Vaswani, Yinggong Zhao, Victoria Fossum, and David Chiang. 2013. Decoding with Large-Scale Neural Language Models Improves Translation. In *Proceedings of the 2013 Conference on Empirical Methods in Natural Language Processing, EMNLP 2013*. Seattle, Washington, USA, pages 1387–1392.

Philip Williams. 2014. *Unification-based Constraints for Statistical Machine Translation*. Ph.D. thesis, University of Edinburgh.

Philip Williams and Philipp Koehn. 2011. Agreement constraints for statistical machine translation into german. In *Proceedings of the Sixth Workshop on Statistical Machine Translation*. Association for Computational Linguistics, Edinburgh, Scotland, pages 217–226.

Philip Williams and Philipp Koehn. 2012. GHKM Rule Extraction and Scope-3 Parsing in Moses. In *Proceedings of the Seventh Workshop on Statistical Machine Translation*. Montréal, Canada, pages 388–394.

Philip Williams, Rico Sennrich, Maria Nadejde, Matthias Huck, Eva Hasler, and Philipp Koehn. 2014. Edinburgh's Syntax-Based Systems at WMT 2014. In *Proceedings of the Ninth Workshop on Statistical Machine Translation*. Baltimore, Maryland, USA, pages 207–214.

Philip Williams, Rico Sennrich, Maria Nadejde, Matthias Huck, and Philipp Koehn. 2015. Edinburgh's Syntax-Based Systems at WMT 2015. In *Proceedings of the Tenth Workshop on Statistical Machine Translation*. Association for Computational Linguistics, Lisbon, Portugal, pages 199–209.

PJAIT Systems for the WMT 2016

Krzysztof Wołk
Multimedia Department
Polish-Japanese Academy of
Information Technology,
Koszykowa 86,
02-008 Warsaw
kwolk@pja.edu.pl

Krzysztof Marasek
Multimedia Department
Polish-Japanese Academy of
Information Technology,
Koszykowa 86,
02-008 Warsaw
kmarasek@pja.edu.pl

Abstract

In this paper, we attempt to improve Statistical Machine Translation (SMT) systems between Czech and English. To accomplish this, we performed translation model training, created adaptations of training settings for each language pair, and obtained comparable corpora for our SMT systems. Innovative tools and data adaptation techniques were employed. Only the official parallel text corpora and monolingual models for the WMT 2016 evaluation campaign were used to train language models, and to develop, tune, and test the system. We explored the use of domain adaptation techniques, symmetrized word alignment models, the unsupervised transliteration models and the KenLM language modeling tool. To evaluate the effects of different preparations on translation results, we conducted experiments and used the BLEU, NIST and TER metrics. Our results indicate that our approach produced a positive impact on SMT quality.

1 Introduction

Statistical Machine Translation (SMT) must deal with a number of problems to achieve high quality. These problems include the need to align parallel texts in language pairs and cleaning harvested parallel corpora to remove errors. This is especially true for real-world corpora developed from text harvested from the vast data available on the Internet. Out-Of-Vocabulary (OOV) words must also be handled, as they are inevitable in real-world texts (Wolk and Marasek, 2014a).

The lack of enough parallel corpora is another significant challenge for SMT. Since the approach is statistical in nature, a significant amount of quality language pair data is needed to improve translation accuracy. In addition, very general translation systems that work in a general text domain have accuracy problems in specific domains. SMT systems are more accurate on corpora from a domain that is not too wide. This exacerbates the data problem, calling for the enhancement of parallel corpora for particular text domains (Wolk and Marasek, 2014b).

This paper describes SMT research that addresses these problems, particularly domain adaptation within the limits of permissible data for the WMT 2016 campaign. To accomplish this, we performed model training, created adaptations of training settings and data for each language pair.

Innovative tools and data adaptation techniques were employed. We explored the use of domain adaptation techniques, symmetrized word alignment models, the unsupervised transliteration models, and the KenLM language modeling tool (Heafield, 2011). To evaluate the effects of different preparations on translation results, we conducted experiments and evaluated the results using standard SMT metrics (Koehn et al., 2007).

The languages translated during this research were: Czech, and English, in both directions. Czech is found in the Slavic branch of that language family. English falls in the Western group (The Technology Development Group, 2013-2014)

This paper is structured as follows: Section 2 explains the data preparation. Section 3 presents

Proceedings of the First Conference on Machine Translation, Volume 2: Shared Task Papers, pages 411–414,
Berlin, Germany, August 11-12, 2016. ©2016 Association for Computational Linguistics

experiment setup and the results. Lastly in Section 4 we summarize the work.

2 Data Preparation

This section describes our techniques for data preparation for our SMT systems. We give particular emphasis to preparation of the language data and models and our domain adaptation approach.

2.1 Data pre-processing

Two languages were involved in this research: Czech and English. The text was encoded in UTF-8 format, separated into sentences, and provided in pairs of languages.

Pre-processing, both automatic and manual, of this training data was required. There were a variety of errors found in this data, including spelling errors, unusual nesting of text, text duplication, and parallel text issues. Approximately 2% of the text in the training set contained spelling errors, and approximately 4% of the text had insertion errors. A tool described in (Wolk and Marasek, 2014b) was used to correct these errors. Previous studies have found that such cleaning increases the BLEU score for SMT by a factor of 1.5–2 (Wolk and Marasek, 2014a).

SyMGiza++, a tool that supports the creation of symmetric word alignment models, was used to extract parallel phrases from the data. This tool enables alignment models that support many-to-one and one-to-many alignments in both directions between two language pairs. SyMGiza++ is also designed to leverage the power of multiple processors through advanced threading management, making it very fast. Its alignment process uses four different models during training to progressively refine alignment results. This approach has yielded impressive results in Junczys-Dowmunt and Szał (2012).

Out-Of-Vocabulary (OOV) words pose another significant challenge to SMT systems. If not addressed, unknown words appear, untranslated, in the output, lowering the translation quality. To address OOV words, we used implemented in the Moses toolkit Unsupervised Transliteration Model (UTM). UTM is an unsupervised, language-independent approach for learning OOV words (Moses statistical machine translation, 2015). We used the post-decoding transliteration option with this tool. UTM uses a transliteration phrase translation table to evaluate and score multiple possible transliterations (Durrani et al., 2014).

The KenLM tool was applied to the language model to train and binarize it. This library enables highly efficient queries to language models, saving both memory and computation time. The lexical values of phrases are used to condition the reordering probabilities of phrases. We used KenLM with lexical reordering set to hier-msd-bidirectional-fe. This setting uses a hierarchical model that considers three orientation types based on both source and target phrases: monotone (M), swap (S), and discontinuous (D). Probabilities of possible phrase orders are examined by the bidirectional reordering model (Costa-Jussa and Fonollosa, 2010; Moses statistical machine translation, 2013).

2.2 Domain Adaptation

The news data sets have a rather a wide domain, but rather not as wide-ranging in topic as the variety of WMT permissible texts. Since SMT systems work best in a defined domain, this presents another considerable challenge. If not addressed, this would lead to lower translation accuracy.

The quality of domain adaptation depends heavily on training data used to optimize the language and translation models in an SMT system. Selection and extraction of domain-specific training data from a large, general corpus addresses this issue (Axelrod, He and Gao, 2011). This process uses a parallel, general domain corpus and a general domain monolingual corpus in the target language. The result is a pseudo in-domain sub-corpus.

As described by Wang et al. in (2014), there are generally three processing stages in data selection for domain adaptation. First, sentence pairs from the parallel, general domain corpus are scored for relevance to the target domain. Second, resampling is performed to select the best-scoring sentence pairs to retain in the pseudo-do in-domain sub-corpus. Those two steps can also be applied to the general domain monolingual corpus to select sentences for use in a language model. After collecting a substantial amount of sentence pairs (for the translation model) or sentences (for the language model), those models are trained on the sub-corpus that represents the target domain (Wang et al., 2014).

Similarity measurement is required to select sentences for the pseudo in-domain sub-corpus. There are three state-of-the-art approaches for similarity measurement. The cosine tf-idf criterion looks for word overlap in determining similarity. This technique is specifically helpful in reducing the number of OOV words, but it is sensitive to noise in the data. A perplexity-based criterion considers the n-gram word order in addition to collocation. Lastly, edit distance simultaneously considers word order, position, and overlap. It is the strictest of the three approaches. In their study (Wang et al., 2014), Wang et al. found that a combination of these approaches provided the best performance in domain adaptation for Chinese-English corpora (Wang et al., 2014)

In accordance with Wang et al. (2014)'s approach, we use a combination of the criteria at both the corpora and language models. The three similarity metrics are used to select different pseudo in-domain sub-corpora. The sub-corpora are then joined during resampling based on a combination of the three metrics. Similarly, the three metrics are combined for domain adaptation during translation. We empirically found acceptance rates that allowed us only to harvest 20% of most domain-similar data (Wang et al., 2014).

3   Experimental Results

Various versions of our SMT systems were evaluated via experimentation. In preparation for experiments, we processed the corpora. This involved tokenization, cleaning, factorization, conversion to lower case, splitting, and final cleaning after splitting. Language models were developed and tuned using the training data.

The Experiment Management System (Koehn et al., 2007) from the open source Moses SMT toolkit was used to conduct the experiments. Training of a 6-gram language model was accomplished our resulting systems using the KenLM Modeling Toolkit instead of 5-gram SRILM (Stolcke, 2002) with an interpolated version of Kneser-Key discounting (interpolate – unk –kndiscount) that was used in our baseline systems. Word and phrase alignment was performed using SyMGIZA++ (Junczys-Dowmunt and Szał, 2012) instead of GIZA++. KenLM was also used, as described earlier, to binarize the language models. The OOV's were handled by using Unsupervised Transliteration Model (Durrani, 2014).

The results are shown in Table 1. Each language pair was translated in both directions. "BASE" in the tables represents the baseline SMT system. "EXT" indicates results for the baseline system, using the baseline settings but extended with additional permissible data (limited to parallel Europarl v7, Common Crawl,

News Commentary, CzEng and monolingual News Crawl 07-15) with data adaptation. "BEST" indicates the results when the new SMT settings were applied and using all permissible data after data adaptation.

Three well-known metrics were used for scoring the results: Bilingual Evaluation Understudy (BLEU), the US National Institute of Standards and Technology (NIST) metric and Translation Error Rate (TER).

The results show that the systems performed well on all data sets in comparison to the baseline SMT systems. Application of the new settings and use of all permissible data improved performance even more.

LANG	SYSTEM	BLEU	NIST	TER
CS-EN	BASE	25.99	5.51	64.35
	EXT	27.92	6.04	62.58
	BEST	29.31	6.97	60.45
EN-CS	BASE	22.20	5.36	67.60
	EXT	24.62	5.57	64.25
	BEST	26.14	5.74	62.02

Table 1: Progressive Results, 2014 Test Data

4   Summary

We have improved SMT for CS-EN in 2 directions in News Translation task, using only data permissible for the WMT 2016 evaluation campaign. We cleaned, prepared, and tokenized the training data. Symmetric word alignment models were used to align the corpora. UTM was used to handle OOV words. A language model was created, binarized, and tuned. We performed domain adaptation of language data using a combination of similarity metrics.

The results show a positive impact of our approach on SMT quality across the choose language pair.

Reference

Amittai Axelrod, Xiaodong He and Jianfeng Gao.. 2011. Domain adaptation via pseudo in-domain data selection. In: Proceedings of the Conference on Empirical Methods in Natural Language Processing (EMNLP '11), p. 355–362

Marta R. Costa-Jussa and Jose R. Fonollosa. 2010. Using linear interpolation and weighted reordering hypotheses in the Moses system, Barcelona, Spain

Nadir Durrani, et al. 2014. Integrating an unsupervised transliteration model into statistical machine translation. In: EACL 2014, p. 148.

Marcin Junczys-Dowmunt and Arkadiusz Szał. 2012. SyMGiza++: symmetrized word alignment models for statistical machine translation. In: Security and Intelligent Information Systems. Springer Berlin Heidelberg, p. 379-390.

Kenneth Heafield. 2011. KenLM: Faster and smaller language model queries, In: Proc. of Sixth Workshop on Statistical Machine Translation, Association for Computational Linguistics

Philipp Koehn et al. 2007. Moses: Open Source Toolkit for Statistical Machine Translation, In: Proceedings of the ACL 2007 Demo and Poster Sessions, Prague, pp. 177–180

Moses statistical machine translation, "OOVs." Last revised February 13, 2015. Retrieved September 27, 2015 from: http://www.statmt.org/moses/?n=Advanced.OOVs #ntoc2

Moses statistical machine translation, "Build reordering model." Last revised July 28, 2013. Retrieved October 10, 2015 from: http://www.statmt.org/moses/?n=FactoredTraining. Build ReorderingModel

The Technology Development Group. 2014. Czech. Last revised March 21, 2014. Retrieved September 27, 2015 from: aboutworldlanguages.com/Czech

The Technology Development Group. 2014. English. Last revised October 14, 2013. Retrieved Septeber 27, 2015 from: aboutworldlanguages.com/english

The Technology Development Group. 2014. French. Last revised March 21, 2014. Retrieved September 27, 2015 from: aboutworldlanguages.com/french

The Technology Development Group. 2014. German. Last revised March 21, 2014. Retrieved September 27, 2015 from: aboutworldlanguages.com/german

The Technology Development Group. 2014. Vietnamese. Last revised March 21, 2014. Retrieved September 27, 2015 from: aboutworldlanguages.com/vietnamese

Andreas Stolcke. 2002. SRILM - An Extensible Laguage Modeling Toolkit., INTERSPEECH, 2002.

Longyue Wang, Derek F. Wong, Lidia S. Chao, Yi Lu, and Junwen Xing. 2014. A Systematic Coparison of Data Selection Criteria for SMT Domain Adaptation., The Scientific World Journal, vol. 2014, doi:10.1155/2014/745485

Krzysztof Wołk, Krzysztof Marasek. 2014a. Polish - English Speech Statistical Machine Translation Systems for the IWSLT 2014, In: Proceedings of International Workshop on Spoken Language Translation, Lake Tahoe, California, USA, pp. 143-148.

Krzysztof Wołk, Krzysztof Marasek. 2014b. A Sentence Meaning Based Alignment Method for Parallel Text Corpora Preparation. In: New Perspectives in Information Systems and Technologies, Volume 1. Springer International Publishing, 2014. p. 229-237.

Krzysztof Wołk and Krzysztof Marasek. 2015. Tuned and GPU-accelerated Parallel Data Mining from Comparable Corpora, In: Lecture Notes in Artificial Intelligence, p. 32 – 40

DFKI's system for WMT16 IT-domain task, including analysis of systematic errors

Eleftherios Avramidis, Aljoscha Burchardt, Vivien Macketanz and Ankit Srivastava
German Research Center for Artificial intelligence (DFKI)
Language Technology Lab, Berlin
`firstname.lastname@dfki.de`

Abstract

We are presenting a hybrid MT approach in the WMT2016 Shared Translation Task for the IT-Domain. Our work consists of several translation components based on rule-based and statistical approaches that feed into an informed selection mechanism. Additions to last year's submission include a WSD component, a syntactically-enhanced component and several improvements to the rule-based component, relevant to the particular domain. We also present detailed human evaluation on the output of all translation components, focusing on particular systematic errors.

1 Introduction

We are presenting extensions on our hybrid MT approach from the WMT 2015 translation task in the generic-domain (Avramidis et al., 2015). The system combines several SMT and RBMT components that feed into an informed selection mechanism. For WMT 2016, several new system components have been submitted to the IT-task that are described in more detail in this paper.

In our work, detailed evaluation of translation quality using a wide variety of methods from automatic scores to human error annotation is an active part of the MT development process. Already in previous work (Popović et al., 2014), we have argued for an approach to MT research and development (R&D) that makes a more direct use of the knowledge and expertise of language professionals.

One of the reasons is that it is difficult to build hybrid architectures (that take advantage of the fact that different engines make different errors) solely based on the rough feedback provided by automatic scores. As scores like BLEU (Pap-

ineni et al., 2002) are not suitable for comparison across different types of engines like Statistical Machine Translation (SMT) and Rule-based Machine Translation (RBMT), we have included human feedback by a language professional in the development of the components reported in this paper.

To this end, we complement our system development with specific manual analysis. We have identified and manually inspected phenomena in the given domain that frequently lead to errors in our engines.

We are using the insights gained from this detailed analysis to guide further improvements of our engines and selection mechanism, some of which are detailed below. Therefore, the components developed follow the direction of addressing some of the most observed systematic issues. Nevertheless, the systems submitted to this task are only a stage in the continuous development effort.

The short paper is structured as follows: Section 2 includes a description of the individual components and the hybridization mechanism, section 3 presents a detailed manual evaluation focusing on systematic errors, whereas conclusions and ideas for further work are given in section 4.

2 System components

We hereby present the systems that appear in our submissions and our hybrid system:

2.1 Phrase-based SMT baseline

The baseline system consists of a basic phrase-based SMT model, trained with the state-of-the-art settings on both the generic and technical data. The translation table was trained on a concatenation of generic and technical data, filtering out the sentences longer than 80 words. Batch 1 was used as a tuning set for MERT (Och, 2003).

One language model (monolingual) of order 5 was trained on the target side from both the

Proceedings of the First Conference on Machine Translation, Volume 2: Shared Task Papers, pages 415–422,
Berlin, Germany, August 11-12, 2016. ©2016 Association for Computational Linguistics

corpus	entries	words
Chromium browser	6.3K	55.1K
Drupal	4.7K	57.4K
Libreoffice help	46.8K	1.1M
Libreoffice UI	35.6K	143.7K
Ubuntu Saucy	182.9K	1.6M
Europarl (mono)	2.2M	54.0M
News (mono)	89M	1.7B
Commoncrawl (parallel)	2.4M	53.6M
Europarl (parallel)	1.9M	50.1M
MultiUN (parallel)	167.6K	5.8M
News Crawl (parallel)	201.3K	5.1M

Table 1: Size of corpora used for SMT.

technical (IT-domain) and Europarl corpora, plus one language model was trained on the target-language news corpus from the years 2007 to 2013 (Callison-Burch et al., 2007). All language models were interpolated on the tuning set (Schwenk and Koehn, 2008). The size of the training data is shown in Table 1.

The text has been tokenized and truecased (Koehn et al., 2008) prior to the training and the decoding, and de-tokenized and de-truecased afterwards. A few regular expressions were added to the tokenizer, so that URLs are not tokenized before being translated. Normalization of punctuation was also included, mainly in order to fix several issues with variable typography on quotes.

The phrase-based SMT system was trained with Moses (Koehn, 2010) using EMS (Koehn, 2010), whereas the language models were trained with SRILM (Stolcke, 2002) and queried with KenLM (Heafield, 2011).

All statistical systems presented below are extensions of this system, also based on the same data and settings, unless stated otherwise.

2.2 SMT with Word Sense Disambiguation

The word-sense-disambiguated SMT system is a factored phrase-based statistical system with two decoding paths, one basic and one alternative. In the basic path, all nouns of the source language (English) have been annotated with a WSD system (Weissenborn et al., 2015) that assigns BabelNet senses to nouns and has recently shown improvements over state-of-the-art results on several corpora. The sense labels are estimated based on the disambiguation analysis on the sentence level by

	system variants	BLEU	METEOR
1.	SMT baseline	31.06	55.8
2.	sense → word	25.52	50.4
3.*	sense → word, word → word (alt)	29.89	54.8
4.	word → word, sense → word (alt)	29.88	54.3

Table 2: Automatic scores for factored SMT variants with WSD. (*) indicates the version included in the selection mechanism.

choosing the best ranked sense out of the ones provided by the WSD system. Each produced WSD label replaces the respective base word form of the noun. In the alternative path, non-annotated input is used. The alternative path allows for decoding phrases when there are no WSD labels or the decoder cannot form a translation with a good probability.

Due to the high computational demands of the WSD annotation, this model was trained on less data than the respective phrase-based models, using the first 1.1M sentences of Europarl and ommiting the entire Commoncrawl. We experimented with four different settings concerning the translation path. These settings with the corresponding automatic scores are depicted in Table 2, which includes the results on the development set 2. On this set, WSD does not show a positive effect over the baseline in terms of automatic scores.

2.3 Syntax-enhanced SMT

Motivated by the importance of grammar in the translation between English and German, we developed a syntax-enhanced SMT system. The process is similar to that of our baseline, but this version includes syntax-aware phrase extraction. Phrase pairs in the baseline SMT system were augmented with linguistically-motivated phrase pairs. These phrases were extracted by generating constituency and dependency parse trees for both the source and target languages, followed by node-aligning the parallel parse trees using a statistical tree aligner (Zhechev, 2009). The syntax-aware phrase extraction algorithm obtains surface-level chunks (syntax-aware) from the aligned subtrees (Srivastava and Way, 2009).

Intermediate experiments were conducted by using either constituency parsing or dependency parsing and it was discovered that despite containing phrase pairs unique to each parsing model (around 28%), no statistically significant difference was observed in the MT system performance. We therefore present the version that uses both of them by concatenating all phrase pairs in one table in an attempt to beenfit from multiple knowledge sources (Srivastava et al., 2009). Aditionally informed by the manual inspection in Section 3, we performed a pseudo-Named Entity Recognition (words and phrases tagged as nouns) in order to identify in-domain terminology and translate them separately in a post-decoding automatic post-editing framework.

For the constituency and dependency parsing we employed the Berkeley Parser (Petrov and Klein, 2007) and the Stanford Dependency Parser (Klein and Manning, 2003) respectively.

2.4 Rule-based component

The rule-based system Lucy (Alonso and Thurmair, 2003) is also part of our experiment, due to its state-of-the-art performance in the previous years. Additionally, manual inspection on the development set has shown that it provides better handling of complex grammatical phenomena particularly when translating into German, due to the fact that it operates based on transfer rules from the source to the target syntax tree.

This year's work on RBMT focuses on issues revealed through manual inspection of its performance on the development set:

- **Separate menu items**: The rule-based system was observed to be incapable of handling menu items properly, mostly when they were separated by the ">" symbol, as they often ended up as compounds. We identified the menu items by searching for consequent title-cased chunks before and after each separator. These items were translated separately from the rest of the sentence, to avoid them being bundled as compounds. The rule-based system was then forced to treat the pre-translated menu items as chunks that should not be translated.

- **Menu items by SMT**: Additionally, we used the method above to check whether menu items could be translated with the baseline SMT system instead of Lucy.

- **Unknown words by SMT**: Since Lucy is

flagging unknown words, we translated these individually with the baseline SMT system.

Finally, we experimented with normalization of the punctuation (which was previously included in the pre-processing steps of SMT but not in RBMT), addition of quotes on the menu items and some additional automatic source pre-processing in order to remove redundant phrases such as "where it says".

We ran exhaustive search with all possible combinations of the modification above and the most indicative automatic scores are shown in table 3. Although automatic scores have in the past shown low performance when evaluating RBMT systems, our proposed modifications have a lexical impact that can be adequately measured with n-gram based metrics. Our investigation and discussion is performed on Batch 2. The best combination of the suggested modifications achieves an overall improvement of 0.51 points BLEU and 0.68 points METEOR over the baseline. In particular:

- Adding quotes around menu items resulted in a significant drop of the automatic scores, so it was not used; this needs to be further evaluated, as references do not use quotes for menu items either. Nevertheless, quotes were not always useful due to an occasional erroneous identification of menu item boundaries.

- Separate translation of the menu items (sepMenus) gives a positive result of about 0.46 BLEU and 0.63 METEOR.

- Normalizing punctuation (normPunct) has a slightly positive effect when the menu items are translated separately by Lucy.

- Passing only RBMT's unknown words (unk) to SMT results in a loss of 0.4 BLEU.

- Translating the RBMT's menus with SMT (SMTmenus) also deteriorates the scores and

- translating both menu items and unknown words with SMT (unk+SMTmenus) has a positive effect against the baseline and it seems to be comparable with the best system without SMT (sepMenus+normPunct).

The phrase "where it says" appears in 7% of the sentences in Batch 2 and 2% of the sentences in Batch 1. Although the removal of "where it says" on the source sentence seems to slightly lower the

	BLEU	METEOR	manual
baseline	24.90	44.38	
quotes	24.00	44.29	
sepMenus	25.39	45.01	
sepMenus + normPunct	25.41	45.06	15.8%
sepMenus + normPunct - WhereItSays*	25.36	45.00	84.2%
SMTmenus	24.06	42.83	
unk	24.50	44.05	
unk + sepMenus	23.68	43.30	
unk + SMTmenus	25.41	44.95	
unk + SMTmenus - WhereItSays*	25.36	44.88	

Table 3: Improvements on the RBMT system. (*) indicates the submitted variations.

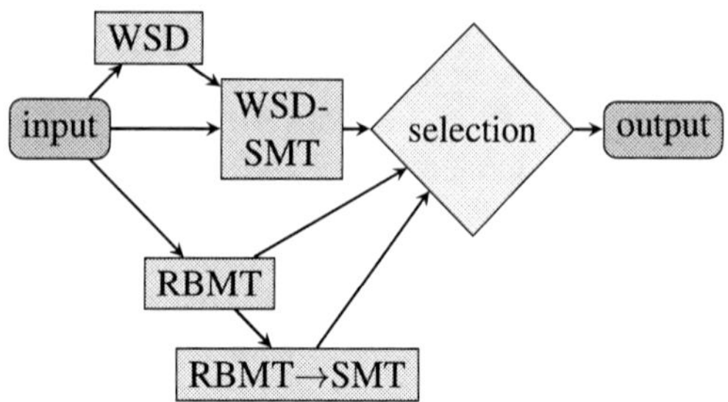

Figure 1: Architecture of the selection mechanism

automatic scores, the difference does not seem significant, and manual inspection raised the concern that this may be because of the way this phrase has been translated in the references. We therefore conducted manual sentence selection on 38 (out of the 69) sentences where this phrase appeared and in 84.2% of the cases its removal made the translation preferable. We therefore concluded in selecting this variation, despite the slightly lower scores.

2.5 Serial RBMT post-editing with SMT

As an alternative to automatic post-editing of the RBMT system, a serial RBMT+SMT system combination is used, as described in (Simard et al., 2007). For building it, the first stage is translation of the source language part of the training corpus by the RBMT system. In the second stage, a SMT system is trained using the RBMT translation output as a source language and the target language part as a target language. Later, the test set is first translated by the RBMT system, and the obtained translation is translated by the SMT system.

2.6 Selection mechanism

The selection mechanism aims to combine various systems, by selecting the best MT output for every sentence. The architecture of the system is illustrated in figure 1. The core of the selection mechanism is a ranker which reproduces ranking by aggregating pairwise decisions by a binary classifier (Avramidis, 2013). Such a classifier is trained on binary comparisons in order to select the best one out of two different MT outputs given one source sentence at a time. As training material, we used the test-sets of WMT evaluation task (2008-2014). The rank labels for the training are automatically generated, after ordering the given MT outputs based on their sentence-level METEOR (Lavie and Agarwal, 2007) against the references. We have previously experimented with training on ranking provided by users, but experiments showed that for this task, ranks made out of sentence-level METEOR maximize all automatic scores on our development set, including other document-level ones, such as BLEU.

We exhaustively tested the available feature sets with many machine learning methods and Support Vector Machines seemed to give the best performance. The binary classifiers were wrapped into rankers using the *soft pairwise recomposition* (Avramidis, 2013) to reduce ties between the systems. Due to technical reasons, the version of the selection mechanism that is submitted to this task is only a pilot version that includes WSD-SMT (section 2.2), baseline RBMT (section 2.4) and RBMT→SMT (section 2.5). When ties occurred, despite the soft recomposition, the system was selected based on a predefined system priority (WSD-SMT, RBMT, RBMT→SMT). The predefined order of the systems needs to be further confirmed as part of the future work.

3 Manual evaluation

Apart from the automatic evaluation scores, we include manual evaluation performed by a professional German linguist.

3.1 Manual evaluation methodology

The manual evaluation was performed in four phases:

- The annotator reads through the development set translated by all systems and identifies the phenomena where often errors occur.

- For each one of the prominent linguistic phenomena, the annotator selects 100 source segments including the respective phenomenon that is prone to MT errors.

- The total occurrences of each phenomenon in all source segments are counted (each phenomenon may occur more than once in a segment, and each segment may contain more than one sentences).

- Consequently, the annotator counts the times each phenomenon has been translated correctly. For a translation to be correct it does not have to be identical with the reference translation. This is repeated for the output of every MT system. The accuracy is calculated as the ratio of the correct translations of the phenomenon divided by the occurrences of the phenomenon in the source.

3.2 Manual evaluation results

The most prominent error categories were found to be **imperatives, compounds, quotation marks, menu item sequences** (separated by ">"), **missing verbs, phrasal verbs** and **terminology**. In these 7 categories, 657 source segments were chosen from development set Batch 2 to demonstrate the phenomena bound to the frequent errors[1]. Many segments contained multiple instances of the respective phenomena, resulting in 2104 instances of phenomena in overall. The results appear in table 4.

The two baseline systems **SMT** and **RBMT** seem to have complementary behavior regarding the investigated phenomena. SMT performs well on terminology, menu items and quotation marks, but seems to suffer on imperatives, missing verbs, phrasal verbs and generation of compounds. On the contrary, RBMT does relatively well with imperatives, compounds, verbs and phrasal verbs, whereas it has issues with menu items and is relatively worse with terminology.

The linear combination system **RBMT→SMT** manages to successfully combine the performance of the two systems regarding imperatives and maintains almost the same performance on verbs and terminology, whereas all other phenomena deteriorate, despite achieving higher automatic scores in overall.

The **SMT-syntax** and the **SMT-WSD** systems seem to have relatively lower performance in all categories.[2] Since the performance of the WSD analyzer has already been confirmed, the failure of the SMT-WSD system to achieve a good performance on terminology and high n-gram-based automatic scores may be an indication that the current data setting does not face ambiguity issues and the senses probably only add additional complexity.

The **selection mechanism** (which in its current version only included SMT-WSD, RBMT and RBMT→SMT) performs better with the terminology and the quotation marks, whereas it maintains the good performance of its components on verbs and menu items. Performance on phrasal verbs nevertheless suffers. Additionally it achieves the highest accuracy on the selected phenomena, with 2% less errors than its best component, the baseline RBMT system.

The two improved versions of the RBMT system appear to have solved the problems they were developed for, namely the compounded menu items and one of them also does better with the quotation marks. The performance on imperatives, verbs and terminology remains the same, but the deterioration on phrasal verbs is obvious. A postmortem analysis attributes this loss to a logical bug in the menu items detection, which often erroneously included title-cased verbs in the beginning of the sentence, preventing them from being translated as an active part of the sentence.

---

[1] Despite the goal of collecting 100 segments per category, it was possible to find only 57 segments with phrasal verbs within the development set Batch 2.

[2] A pre-processing bug prevented SMT-syntax from translating quotation marks.

	#	SMT	SMT-WSD	SMT-syntax	RBMT	RBMT →SMT	RBMT menus	RBMT SMTm	sel mech
imperatives	247	68%	65%	68%	**79%**	**83%**	**79%**	**79%**	77%
compounds	220	55%	41%	56%	87%	64%	**89%**	**86%**	78%
">" separators	148	**99%**	75%	97%	39%	66%	84%	80%	74%
quotation marks	431	97%	93%	0%	94%	86%	75%	95%	**98%**
verbs	504	85%	73%	81%	**93%**	**92%**	**93%**	**93%**	**92%**
phrasal verbs	89	22%	3%	7%	**69%**	51%	29%	29%	24%
terminology	465	**64%**	52%	52%	50%	**62%**	54%	53%	**60%**
average		76%	65%	52%	77%	77%	75%	**78%**	**79%**

Table 4: Translation accuracy on manually evaluated sentences focusing on particular phenomena. Test-sets consist of hand-picked source sentences of Batch 2 that include the respective phenomenon. Boldface indicates best systems on each phenomenon (row) with a 0.95 confidence level.

4   Discussion and further work

In our shared task submission we included:

(i) the SMT and RBMT baseline systems,

(ii) the syntax-enhanced system (DFKI-syntax),

(iii) the RBMT system with separate menu items, normalization of punctuation and removal of "where it says" (previously appearing as sepMenus+normPunct-WhereItSays, submitted as qtl-RBMT-menus),

(iv) the RBMT system with removal of "where it says", passing menu items and unknown words to SMT (previously appearing as unk+SMTmenus-WhereItSays, submitted as qtl-RBMT-SMTmenus) and

(v) the selection mechanism which includes the systems SMT-WSD, RBMT and RBMT→SMT.

The results of the official evaluation campaign for our systems appear in the table 5. RBMT-menus appears to be slightly better than all the other systems we developed, but the difference with the other RBMT systems is not statistically significant. Nevertheless, it is our only system that competes with another competitor system for the 2nd position. Additionally, it is worth noting the failure of BLEU to correlate with the human preferences, mainly for the systems that relate to RBMT, inline with past observations (Callison-Burch et al., 2006).

In future work, we intend to continue this line of development by including all the individual components in the selection mechanism. Additionally,

	rank	TrueSkill	BLEU
RBMT-SMTmenus	2-6	-0.062	25.4
RBMT baseline	3-6	-0.093	25.2
RMBT-menus	3-6	-0.098	25.2
SMT-syntax	7-8	-0.190	34.8
selection	9	-0.382	29.0
SMT baseline	10	-0.485	34.0

Table 5: Human ranks and automatic scores of our submitted systems on the tests, as a result of the official evaluation. Ranks are given in a range in order to account for confidence intervals.

we would focus on solving issues on the particular phenomena, by employing specialized methods. Finally, we should perform a more in-depth evaluation of the selection mechanism and study how the insights gained from the manual inspection of errors can be translated into features that improve the selection.

Acknowledgments

This work has received support from (a) the ECs FP7 (FP7/2007-2013) under grant agreement number 610516: "QTLeap: Quality Translation by Deep Language Engineering Approaches" and (b) the German Federal Ministry of Education and Research (BMBF), Unternehmen Region, instrument Wachstumskern-Potenzial number 03WKP45: "DKT: Digitale Kuratierungstechnologien."

References

Alonso, J. A. and Thurmair, G. (2003). The Comprendium Translator system. In *Proceedings of the Ninth Machine Translation Summit*. International Association for Machine Translation (IAMT).

Avramidis, E. (2013). Sentence-level ranking with quality estimation. *Machine Translation*, 27(Special issue on Quality Estimation):239–256.

Avramidis, E., Popovic, M., and Burchardt, A. (2015). DFKI's experimental hybrid MT system for WMT 2015. In *Proceedings of the Tenth Workshop on Statistical Machine Translation. Workshop on Statistical Machine Translation (WMT-2015), 10th, September 17-18, Lisbon, Portugal*, pages 66–73. Association for Computational Linguistics.

Callison-Burch, C., Fordyce, C., Koehn, P., Monz, C., and Schroeder, J. (2007). (Meta-) Evaluation of Machine Translation. In *Proceedings of the Second Workshop on Statistical Machine Translation*, pages 136–158, Prague, Czech Republic. Association for Computational Linguistics.

Callison-Burch, C., Osborne, M., and Koehn, P. (2006). Re-evaluating the Role of Bleu in Machine Translation Research. In *Proceedings of the 11th Conference of the European Chapter of the Association for Computational Linguistics*, pages 249–256, Trento, Italy.

Heafield, K. (2011). KenLM : Faster and Smaller Language Model Queries. In *Proceedings of the Sixth Workshop on Statistical Machine Translation*, number 2009, pages 187–197, Edinburgh, Scotland. Association for Computational Linguistics.

Klein, D. and Manning, C. D. (2003). Accurate Unlexicalized Parsing. In *Proceedings of the 41st Annual Meeting on Association for Computational Linguistics - Volume 1*, ACL '03, pages 423–430, Stroudsburg, PA, USA. Association for Computational Linguistics.

Koehn, P. (2010). An Experimental Management System. *The Prague Bulletin of Mathematical Linguistics*, 94(-1):87–96.

Koehn, P., Arun, A., and Hoang, H. (2008). Towards better Machine Translation Quality for the German-English Language Pairs. In *Proceedings of the Third Workshop on Statistical Machine Translation*, pages 139–142, Columbus, Ohio. Association for Computational Linguistics.

Lavie, A. and Agarwal, A. (2007). METEOR: An Automatic Metric for MT Evaluation with High Levels of Correlation with Human Judgments. In *Proceedings of the Second Workshop on Statistical Machine Translation*, pages 228–231, Prague, Czech Republic. Association for Computational Linguistics.

Och, F. J. (2003). Minimum error rate training in statistical machine translation. In *ACL '03: Proceedings of the 41st Annual Meeting on Association for Computational Linguistics*, pages 160–167, Morristown, NJ, USA. Association for Computational Linguistics.

Papineni, K., Roukos, S., Ward, T., and Zhu, W.-J. (2002). BLEU: a Method for Automatic Evaluation of Machine Translation. In *Proceedings of the 40th Annual Meeting of the Association for Computational Linguistics*, pages 311–318, Philadelphia, Pennsylvania, USA. Association for Computational Linguistics.

Petrov, S. and Klein, D. (2007). Improved inference for unlexicalized parsing. In *Proceedings of the 2007 Annual Conference of the North American Chapter of the Association for Computational Linguistics*, Rochester, New York. Association for Computational Linguistics.

Popović, M., Avramidis, E., Burchardt, A., Hunsicker, S., Schmeier, S., Tscherwinka, C., Vilar, D., and Uszkoreit, H. (2014). Involving language professionals in the evaluation of machine translation. *Language Resources and Evaluation*, 48(4):541–559.

Schwenk, H. and Koehn, P. (2008). Large and Diverse Language Models for Statistical Machine Translation. In *Proceedings of the Third International Joint Conference on Natural Language Processing: Volume-II*.

Simard, M., Goutte, C., and Isabelle, P. (2007). Statistical Phrase-based Post-editing. *Proceedings of the 2007 Annual Conference of the North American Chapter of the Association for Computational Linguistics*, (April):508–515.

Srivastava, A., Penkale, S., Groves, D., and Tinsley, J. (2009). Evaluating Syntax-Driven Approaches to Phrase Extraction for MT. In *Proceedings of the 3rd International Workshop on Example-based Machine Translation*, pages 19–28, Dublin, Ireland.

Srivastava, A. K. and Way, A. (2009). Using Percolated Dependencies for Phrase Extraction in SMT. In *Proceedings of the Machine Translation Summit XII*, pages 316–323, Ottawa, Canada.

Stolcke, A. (2002). SRILM an Extensible Language Modeling Toolkit. In *System*, volume 2, pages 901–904. ISCA.

Weissenborn, D., Hennig, L., Xu, F., and Uszkoreit, H. (2015). Multi-Objective Optimization for the Joint Disambiguation of Nouns and Named Entities. In *Proceedings of the 53rd Annual Meeting of the Association for Computational Linguistics and the 7th International Joint Conference on Natural Language Processing of the Asian Federation of Natural Language Processing*, pages 596–605, Beijing, China. Association for Computer Linguistics.

Zhechev, V. (2009). Unsupervised Generation of Paral-
lel Treebank through Sub-Tree Alignment. *Prague
Bulletin of Mathematical Linguistics, Special Issue:
Open Source Tools for MT*, \bf 91:89–98.

ILLC-UvA Adaptation System (Scorpio) at WMT'16 IT-DOMAIN Task

Hoang Cuong and **Stella Frank** and **Khalil Sima'an**
Institute for Logic, Language and Computation
University of Amsterdam
Science Park 107, 1098 XG Amsterdam, The Netherlands

Abstract

This paper describes *Scorpio*, the ILLC-UvA Adaptation System submitted to the IT-DOMAIN translation task at WMT 2016, which participated with the language pair of English-Dutch. This system consolidates the ideas in our previous work on latent variable models for adaptation, and demonstrates their effectiveness in a competitive setting.

1 Introduction

ILLC-UvA participated in the WMT 2016 Shared Task of Machine Translation for the Information Technology (IT) Domain. In this paper, we briefly describe our system, which was submitted for the language pair of English–Dutch. Our system uses simple latent domain variable models for adaptation proposed in Cuong and Sima'an (2014b) and Cuong and Sima'an (2014a). More specifically, we enhance a standard phrase-based baseline system (Koehn et al., 2007) with adapted translation models and language models.

We equip these models with a latent domain variable and adapt them to an in-domain task represented by a seed corpus. We do not adapt the reordering models as we find reordering adaptation does not help much for this language pair. Several additional adapted features proposed in Cuong and Sima'an (2015) and Cuong et al. (2016) are also deployed, including domain-specific and domain-invariant translation features.

Despite the simplicity of our adaptation models, our results show effective adaptation performance for the task. This system consolidates the ideas in our previous work of latent variable models for adaptation, and shows their effectiveness in a competitive setting.

2 Data

We use all the training data provided by the organizers. Table 1 summarizes the data.

English-Dutch			
In-Domain	Sents	**211K**	
	Words	$1.69M$	$1.65M$
General-Domain	Sents	**1.95M**	
	Words	$52.60M$	$52.95M$
Internal Dev	Sents	**1800**	
	Words	$41.35K$	$42.06K$
Internal Test	Sents	**200**	
	Words	$6.4K$	$6.3K$

Table 1: Data Preparation.

More specifically, we use the European Parliament (Europarl) parallel corpus (Koehn, 2005) as general-domain data. We use the corpora of IT-related terms from *Wikipedia* and *Localization PO* files as the in-domain data. For training Dutch language models we use the monolingual Dutch side of Europarl, together with in-domain data.

We split the provided development data (2K sentence pairs) into two different internal datasets:

- A dev set of 1800 sentence pairs used for system optimization.

- A test set of 200 sentence pairs used for evaluation.

Preprocessing

All the data is preprocessed before training. For preprocessing we remove all sentences that have

Proceedings of the First Conference on Machine Translation, Volume 2: Shared Task Papers, pages 423–427,
Berlin, Germany, August 11-12, 2016. ©2016 Association for Computational Linguistics

more than 80 tokens. The data is tokenized and lowercased using the standard Moses toolkit (tokenizer.perl and lowercase.perl). A recaser is also built for postprocessing the system output. Finally, the standard Moses detokenizer script is used to detokenize the output.

For the submission, we also apply a few additional rules that we believe would help recasing and detokenization, such as:[1]

- " *'s* " → " *'s* " (We remove spaces before *'s*.)

- "> a" → "> A", "> b" → "> B", etc. (We uppercase the first character after > .)

- If the target sentence contains the string "> " (which has a space) but the source sentence contains only ">" (which does not have a space), we replace all "> " with ">".

Despite those additional efforts, we found there is still (1): a huge difference in final performance between BLEU case-insensitive and BLEU case-sensitive; (2): a quite big difference between BLEU scores on the final test set and our (admittedly small) validation set. This suggests that there is still lots of room for improving our final translations with better de-tokenization. However, this was not the focus of our submission.

3 System Description

We first train a baseline with standard phrase-based system, using all the parallel data, i.e. the concatenation of in-domain and general-domain data. The system includes MOSES (Koehn et al., 2007) baseline feature functions, plus eight hierarchical lexicalized reordering model feature functions (Galley and Manning, 2008). The training data is first word-aligned using GIZA++ (Och and Ney, 2003) and then symmetrized with *grow(-diag)-final-and* (Koehn et al., 2003). We limit the phrase length to a maximum of seven words.

Somewhat surprisingly, we find that increasing the maximum number of words for phrases from *three* to *seven* significantly improves the baseline on the adaptation task. We believe this is quite important. It suggests that for validating domain adaptation methods over a phrase-based system,

---

[1]However, we are not sure whether these "heuristics" rules are correct or not, as there is no way to verify them.

the system itself should be built over phrases with a reasonable maximum length (e.g. seven words).

We use the phrase extraction component from Stanford Phrasal (Cer et al., 2010), instead of the phrase extraction component included in Moses. Our experience has been that this usually produces better translation accuracy, making the baseline stronger.

Note that we do not filter any phrases. All phrases generated from the word alignments are kept. In this way, instead of discarding phrases with small translation probabilities, we keep all of them and assign a fixed and small translation probability of 0.0001 in such cases.

To tune the system, we use the k-best batch MIRA (Cherry and Foster, 2012). Finally, we use MOSES as a decoder (Koehn et al., 2007).

Our Dutch language models are interpolated 4-grams with Kneser-Ney smoothing, estimated using KenLM (Heafield et al., 2013).

In the following, we denote features from the baseline system as **Concatenation**. To improve the baseline, we enhance the system with additional adaptation models that are trained by utilizing the in-domain data. The following sections will describe our methods in detail.

3.1 Biasing translation models

Given the general-domain corpus and the small in-domain corpus, we first bias the learning of translation models over the general-domain corpus, with guidance from the in-domain data that directly represents the task. We use simple latent domain variable model for adaptation proposed in (Cuong and Sima'an, 2014b; Cuong and Sima'an, 2014a). There are four translation models we aim to learn here, specifically two translation models and two lexical weightings. More technical detail can be found in (Cuong and Sima'an, 2014b; Cuong and Sima'an, 2014a).

Along with our biased translation models (**Weighted**), we also train translation models directly on the provided in-domain data (**In-domain**). Note that our biased translation models are sharp in terms of having low entropies in translation distributions. Meanwhile, the translation statistics we induce from the in-domain are even sharper. Meanwhile, the translation statistics we induce from the in-domain are even sharper. Our experience suggests the statistics induced from in-domain data still incrementally contributes to the adaptation.

We combine all three different types of translation models together. The combination is optimized over the (internal) development set using linear combination (Sennrich, 2012).

To have an idea what the combining weights look like, Table 2 presents results for four translation features, i.e. the translation models (TM) and lexical weights (LEX) in both directions (en-nl and nl-en).

Combining weights for translation features			
	Concat.	Weighted	In-Domain
TM en-nl	0.002	0.724	0.274
Lex en-nl	0.001	0.594	0.405
TM nl-en	0.002	0.755	0.243
Lex nl-en	0.001	0.573	0.426

Table 2: Combining weights

We see that most of the adaptation is credited to the models trained with biased weighting. The models trained on the in-domain data still partially contributes to the adaptation. On the other hand, the model trained on the simple concatenation of the data does not contribute much.

3.2 Biasing language models

Along with biasing the translation models, we find it useful to bias the language models as well. With similar simple latent domain variable models (but in this case, trained on target side data only), we learn the relevance of each sentence with respect to the target domain. We train 3-gram language models with relevance weights. To avoid overfitting, we find that it is necessary to apply an expected smoothing approach in training. We choose *expected Kneser-Ney smoothing* technique (Zhang and Chiang, 2014) as it is simple and achieves state-of-the-art performance on the language modeling problem.

Note that we also train a 3-gram language model directly on the provided in-domain data, as well as another one trained on the concatenation of in- and general- domain data. This results in three different language models, similar to the three translation models we trained above. They are treated as separate dense features for our system.

We provide the combining weights (after tuning) in Table 3, in order to demonstrate the relative importance of the different language models.

Tuning weights for language modeling features		
Concatenation	Weighted	In-Domain
0.0336	0.0397	0.009

Table 3: Optimized weights for language models

All language models incrementally contribute to the adaptation performance. The model that trains with biased weighting contribute most. Meanwhile, the model trained on the concatenation of all data also contributes significantly to the adaptation performance. The model trained on the in-domain data, however, contributes least, probably because its size is relatively small.

3.3 Biasing reordering models

We also try adapting reordering models with the same technique. This, however, does not lead to much improvement, at least for the language pair we deployed. We thus drop this direction.

3.4 Additional adaptation features

Following (Cuong and Sima'an, 2015), we find it useful to exploit the word-level feature derived from IBM model 1 score (Och et al., 2004). Note that adding word-level features from both translation sides does not help much, as observed by (Och et al., 2004). We thus add only one from a translation side. More technical detail can be found in Cuong and Sima'an (2015).

Finally, we found it useful to add domain-invariant translation features for SMT. Specifically, we push the system to make safer choices, preferring domain-invariant translations which work well across latent domains, over risky domain-specific alternatives. More technical detail can be found in Cuong et al. (2016). The improvement we achieve, however, is quite modest compared to what we achieve by utilizing the in-domain data. Nonetheless, we believe this is very natural, as the most effective adaptation method always comes from providing more in-domain data.

4 Results

Our baseline, as described earlier, is created from the concatenation of all parallel data provided by the organizer. The language models are also trained by concatenating all monolingual data provided by the organizer. The baseline has 17 translation and language modeling features in total. Meanwhile, our system has 23 features (17 + 6 adapted features).

Table 4 and 5 present translation results on the internal dev and test sets respectively, with BLEU (Papineni et al., 2002), METEOR (Denkowski and Lavie, 2011), TER (Snover et al., 2006) and finally BEER (Stanojević and Sima'an, 2014).

English-Dutch				
System	BLEU	METEOR	TER	BEER
Baseline	28.1	28.7	53.3	18.4
Scorpio	30.1	29.9	51.6	20.9

Table 4: Results on Dev set

English-Dutch				
System	BLEU	METEOR	TER	BEER
Baseline	34.5	32.9	45.3	24.7
Scorpio	36.8	34.5	43.1	28.7

Table 5: Results on Test set

Note that these results are case-insensitive, without the post-processing steps for detokenizing/recasing sentences as described above.

Despite the simplicity of the adaptation models, our experiments suggest efficient adaptation performance for the task. The adaptations consistently improve all measures by more than 1 point, occasionally much more.

5 Conclusion

We have described our ILLC-UvA adaptation system (Scorpio) at WMT'16 IT-DOMAIN Task. Relying on simple latent domain variable models proposed in our previous work (Cuong and Sima'an, 2014b; Cuong and Sima'an, 2014a), the system shows promising performance for the adaptation task.

Acknowledgements

We thank two anonymous reviewers for their constructive comments on earlier versions. The first author is supported by the EXPERT (EXPloiting Empirical appRoaches to Translation) Initial Training Network (ITN) of the European Union's Seventh Framework Programme. The second author is supported by funding from the European Union's Horizon 2020 research and innovation programme under grant agreement Nr. 645452. The third author is supported by VICI grant nr. 277-89-002 from the Netherlands Organization for Scientific Research (NWO).

References

Daniel Cer, Michel Galley, Daniel Jurafsky, and Christopher D. Manning. 2010. Phrasal: A toolkit for statistical machine translation with facilities for extraction and incorporation of arbitrary model features. In *NAACL HLT 2010 Demonstration Session*.

Colin Cherry and George Foster. 2012. Batch tuning strategies for statistical machine translation. In *NAACL HLT*.

Hoang Cuong and Khalil Sima'an. 2014a. Latent domain phrase-based models for adaptation. In *EMNLP*.

Hoang Cuong and Khalil Sima'an. 2014b. Latent domain translation models in mix-of-domains haystack. In *COLING*.

Hoang Cuong and Khalil Sima'an. 2015. Latent domain word alignment for heterogeneous corpora. In *Proceedings of NAACL-HLT*.

Hoang Cuong, Khalil Sima'an, and Ivan Titov. 2016. Adapting to all domains at once: Rewarding domain invariance in SMT. In *TACL*.

Michael Denkowski and Alon Lavie. 2011. Meteor 1.3: Automatic metric for reliable optimization and evaluation of machine translation systems. In *Proceedings of the Sixth Workshop on Statistical Machine Translation*, WMT '11. Association for Computational Linguistics.

Michel Galley and Christopher D. Manning. 2008. A simple and effective hierarchical phrase reordering model. In *EMNLP*.

Kenneth Heafield, Ivan Pouzyrevsky, Jonathan H. Clark, and Philipp Koehn. 2013. Scalable modified kneser-ney language model estimation. In *ACL (Short Papers)*.

Philipp Koehn, Franz Josef Och, and Daniel Marcu. 2003. Statistical phrase-based translation. In *NAACL*.

Philipp Koehn, Hieu Hoang, Alexandra Birch, Chris Callison-Burch, Marcello Federico, Nicola Bertoldi, Brooke Cowan, Wade Shen, Christine Moran, Richard Zens, Chris Dyer, Ondřej Bojar, Alexandra Constantin, and Evan Herbst. 2007. Moses: Open source toolkit for statistical machine translation. In *ACL (Interactive Poster and Demonstration Sessions)*.

Philipp Koehn. 2005. Europarl: A Parallel Corpus for Statistical Machine Translation. In *MTSummit*.

Franz Josef Och and Hermann Ney. 2003. A systematic comparison of various statistical alignment models. *Comput. Linguist.*, 29(1):19–51, March.

Franz Josef Och, Daniel Gildea, Sanjeev Khudanpur, Anoop Sarkar, Kenji Yamada, Alex Fraser, Shankar Kumar, Libin Shen, David Smith, Katherine Eng, Viren Jain, Zhen Jin, and Dragomir Radev. 2004. A smorgasbord of features for statistical machine translation. In *HLT-NAACL*.

Kishore Papineni, Salim Roukos, Todd Ward, and Wei-Jing Zhu. 2002. Bleu: A method for automatic evaluation of machine translation. In *ACL*.

Rico Sennrich. 2012. Perplexity minimization for translation model domain adaptation in statistical machine translation. In *EACL*.

Matthew Snover, Bonnie Dorr, R. Schwartz, L. Micciulla, and J. Makhoul. 2006. A study of translation edit rate with targeted human annotation. In *AMTA*.

Miloš Stanojević and Khalil Sima'an. 2014. Beer: Better evaluation as ranking. In *WMT*.

Hui Zhang and David Chiang. 2014. Kneser-Ney smoothing on expected counts. In *ACL*.

Data Selection for IT Texts using Paragraph Vector

Mirela-Stefania Duma and Wolfgang Menzel
University of Hamburg
Natural Language Systems Division
{mduma, menzel}@informatik.uni-hamburg.de

Abstract

This paper presents an overview of the system submitted by the University of Hamburg to the IT domain shared translation task as part of the ACL 2016 First Conference of Machine Translation (WMT 2016). We have chosen data selection as a domain adaptation method. The filtering of the general domain data makes use of paragraph vectors as a novel approach for scoring the sentences. Experiments were conducted for English-German under the constrained condition.

1   Introduction

The WMT 2016 shared task of translating IT documents focuses on translation of answers in a cross-lingual help-desk service. This paper describes the system submitted by the University of Hamburg to this task. We took part in the English-German translation track in which twelve systems (seven constrained and five unconstrained ones) from four different organizations participated. The challenges for this task came from the fact that the available in-domain data for the constrained condition is very small. Moreover, the in-domain differs considerably from any of the domains of the given general domain data.

We propose a method of data selection by filtering the general domain data applying a threshold on the similarity between vector representations for the sentences from the general domain and the in-domain. Sentences are described by paragraph vectors which are trained together with word vectors in order to predict the upcoming words within that paragraph (Le and Mikolov, 2014). Given a sentence from the general domain, our procedure identifies a set of candidate sentences that are most similar to the reference. If at least one of the re-

trieved sentences comes from the in-domain then the general domain sentence is considered similar to the in-domain, otherwise it is discarded. This binary decision has the advantage that only one MT system needs to be trained and the disadvantage that it gives only a fixed ratio of general domain data to be kept depending on the chosen threshold.

In order to overcome the disadvantage that the paragraph vector method has, we extend it from using a binary decision filtering to scoring and ranking all the sentences from the general domain from which a certain amount of training sentences can be selected. This extended version is a prerequisite for being able to train and compare multiple MT systems using different ratios of data to be kept.

We first summarize related work in data selection for Statistical Machine Translation (SMT) in Section 2, then describe Paragraph Vector that we used for our data selection method in Section 3. Section 4 presents the experimental settings of the submitted systems and section 5 contains an overview of their performance in the shared IT task.

2   Related work

A range of different methods for domain adaptation of models for statistical machine translation have been developed including mixture modeling, instance weighting, transductive learning, or data selection (Chen et al., 2013).

The data selection approach is the focus of this paper. In the state of the art, data selection is used at the corpus-level, where the selected data is joined together, or at the model-level, where several models are combined together in the translation phase (Wang et al., 2013a). The main workflow of the data selection method consists of the

Proceedings of the First Conference on Machine Translation, Volume 2: Shared Task Papers, pages 428–434,
Berlin, Germany, August 11-12, 2016. ©2016 Association for Computational Linguistics

following steps:

- scoring: a measure is used to determine how similar the sentences from the general domain are to the in-domain

- filtering: sentences from the general domain are selected, if their similarity score is greater than a predefined threshold.

- training: the selected sentences are used as additional training data to develop the language model, to weight the phrase pairs or for tuning purposes.

To compute the similarity score three approaches are commonly used: information retrieval inspired, perplexity-based and edit distance similarity inspired.

TF-IDF[1] term weighing as used in information retrieval was adopted by (Hildebrand et al., 2005) where each sentence from the source side of the bilingual training data constitutes one document (represented using *TF-IDF*) and each sentence from the test data is used as a query. The cosine distance similarity is used to compute the relevance of the queries to the documents. Lü et al. (2007) also uses the cosine to select sentences for offline and online training data optimization. Tamchyna et al. (2012) presents a method where sentences are extracted from the general domain by translating the source side of a test set and using it in computing the cosine similarity to the general domain.

In Mandal et al. (2008) and in Axelrod et al. (2011) language model perplexity was used to score sentences. Foster et al. (2010) used phrase pairs instead of sentences and learned weights for them using in-domain features based on word frequencies and perplexities. In Mansour et al. (2011), the cross-entropy score is used for language model filtering together with a translation model score that estimates the likelihood that a source and a target sentence are a translation of each other. Toral et al. (2015) introduced linguistic information such as lemmas, named entities and part-of-speech tags into the preprocessing of the data and then ranked the sentences by perplexity.

The edit distance which computes the minimum number of edits needed to transform a sentence from the general domain into a sentence from the

in-domain was used in Wang et al. (2013b). A combination of the three data selection approaches is presented in Wang et al. (2013a, 2013c).

We propose a new approach of filtering general domain sentences using paragraph vectors (Le and Mikolov, 2014) to determine sentence similarity in a high-dimensional vector space. To the knowledge of the authors, this is the first time Paragraph vector is applied to data selection for SMT.

3 Paragraph vector

In this section we describe Paragraph vector (Le and Mikolov, 2014) which stands at the core of the proposed data selection method. It has been successfully employed in sentiment detection and information retrieval tasks. Le and Mikolov (2014) propose an unsupervised framework that learns continuous distributed vector representations for phrases, sentences or documents.

The idea of learning paragraph vectors is similar to the approach used in learning word vectors (Mikolov et al., 2013): word vectors are used in predicting a word given its sentential context and paragraph vectors adopt the same idea to contexts sampled from a paragraph.

The model maps context words and a paragraph identifier to the word that is going to be predicted. The contexts have a fixed length and are sampled from a sliding window over the paragraph. The mapping is established by means of two matrices: one consisting of the trained paragraph vectors and the other consisting of word vectors. The paragraph vector is shared among all the contexts sampled from the same paragraph (but not among all paragraphs). The word vectors are shared between all the paragraphs. Paragraph and word vectors are combined during training and inference either by concatenation or by averaging. The paragraph and word vectors are trained on pairs consisting of the word to be predicted and a sampled context tagged by a paragraph identifier. (Le and Mikolov, 2014)

We use single sentences as paragraphs. The reason why we adopted Paragraph vector is because they reflect semantic relatedness, similar to word vectors. Moreover, we have chosen paragraph vectors for representing sentences as vectors because the approach does not require tuning, parsing or availability of labeled data. The implementation of paragraph vectors we used is Doc2vec from the *gensim* toolkit[2] (Řehůřek and Sojka, 2010).

---

[1]Term frequency - Inverse document frequency

[2]`https://radimrehurek.com/gensim/`

4 Experiments

For all the submitted systems, we used only the data distributed for the shared IT task. For the general domain training data we chose Commoncrawl[3] (made available by WMT) because it is a relatively large corpus and contains crawled data from a variety of domains including the IT domain. As in-domain training data we concatenated the corpora provided by the task. We tuned the systems with 2000 sentences from Batch1a and Batch2a provided by the shared task and evaluated them on Batch3a.

Our systems have been developed using the Moses phrase-based MT toolkit (Koehn et al., 2007) and the Experiment Management System (Koehn, 2010) that facilitates the preparation of scripts for experiments.

4.1 Data preprocessing

All the available data were tokenized, cleaned (i.e. restricted to a maximum sentence length of 80 words) and lowercased. The general domain data was filtered by removing the sentence pairs that do not pertain to the English-German language pair as well as sentences that contain non-alpha characters. In addition to that, punctuation was normalized using the *normalize-punctuation.perl* script. Approximately 25K sentences were removed because they were not considered English-German sentence pairs by the jlangdetect library[4] and further 650 sentences have been discharged because they contained non-alpha characters. Table 1 presents some data statistics for both domains after preprocessing:

Corpora	**Sentences**	**Tokens**	
		English	German
Commoncrawl	2.34M	50.33M	46.11M
IT	210K	1.48M	1.44M

Table 1: Corpora statistics after preprocessing

4.2 Experimental settings

We performed word alignment using GIZA++ (Och and Ney, 2003) with the default *grow-diag-final-and* alignment symmetrization method. For the language model (LM) estimation we trained

5-gram LMs using the SRILM toolkit (Stolcke, 2002) with Kneser-Ney discounting (Kneser and Ney, 1995) on the target side of the Commoncrawl and IT corpora. When LM interpolation was needed, the in-domain LM and the general domain LM were interpolated using weights tuned to minimize the perplexity on the tuning set. The same data was used for tuning the systems with MERT (Och, 2003).

For the BLEU-cased scores training recasing was performed using the default configuration from the EMS script: language model trained using KenLM (Heafield, 2011) and order 3. Due to time limitations, we did not try to further improve the recaser model.

4.3 Baselines

The baseline system $UHBS\_simple$ was trained on the concatenation of the in-domain data and the complete general domain data. The second baseline, $UHBS\_lmi$, only differed from $UHBS\_simple$ in its language model that was created by LM interpolation. The motivation for training a second, i.e. stronger baseline, is that we intended to compare the translation results of the system submitted to the competition ($UHDS\_doc2vec$) with the one produced by a competitive approach.

4.4 Data selection using Doc2vec

In this section the submitted system $UHDS\_doc2vec$ is described. The filtering procedure receives as input the bilingual in-domain corpus $\mathcal{I}n$, the bilingual general domain $\mathcal{G}en$, the number of most similar sentences $\mathcal{N}$ that should be retrieved given a threshold δ that will be described later. Our approach is monolingual as we used only the source side of the corpus data to select sentences from the general domain corpus. To train the paragraph vectors we concatenated $\mathcal{I}n$ and $\mathcal{G}en$ resulting in the data set $\mathcal{C}$. Training the doc2vec model required tagging every sentence from the source side of the concatenated corpus $\mathcal{C}_{source}$ with its corresponding line number in the corpus and building a vocabulary from the tagged $\mathcal{C}$. Therefore, a sentence that came from $\mathcal{I}n$ was tagged with a number from $[1, size_{In}]$ and a sentence that came from $\mathcal{G}en$ was tagged with a number from $[size_{In} + 1, size_{In} + size_{Gen}]$.

The doc2vec model was trained on the tagged $\mathcal{C}_{source}$. After obtaining the doc2vec model $\mathcal{M}$, the algorithm iterates through every sentence pair

models/doc2vec.html
[3]http://commoncrawl.org/
[4]https://github.com/melix/jlangdetect

Algorithm 1 Doc2vec Filtering

1: **procedure** FILTER($\mathcal{I}n, \mathcal{G}en, \mathcal{N}, \delta$)
2:      $\mathcal{C} \leftarrow \mathcal{I}n + \mathcal{G}en$
3:      **for each** sentence $s_i \in \mathcal{C}_{source}$ **do**
4:          tag s_i with the line number i
5:      build vocabulary from tagged $\mathcal{C}_{source}$
6:      train doc2vec model $\mathcal{M}$ using tagged $\mathcal{C}_{source}$
7:      **for each** sentence pair $(s_i, t_i) \in \mathcal{G}en$ **do**
8:          $\mathcal{R}_i = top(\mathcal{N}, mostSimilar(\mathcal{M}, s_i))$
9:          $Sim_{s_i} = \{(index, score) \in \mathcal{R}_i |\ index \in [1, size_C], score \in (0, 1)\}$
10:         **if** $\exists (index, score) \in Sim_{s_i} : (index < size_{In}, score > \delta)$ **then**
11:             add (s_i, t_i) to *FilteredCorpus*

Figure 1: Doc2vec filtering algorithm

from $\mathcal{G}en$. Given a sentence pair $(s_i, t_i) \in \mathcal{G}en$, the top $\mathcal{N}$ most similar vectors to s_i are retrieved in the form of a pair $(index, score)$ where $index$ gives the tag (i.e. the line number) of the selected similar sentence to s_i and $score$ specifies the similarity between s_i and s_{index}. The similarity is computed as the cosine between the two vectors.

The list of top $\mathcal{N}$ most similar sentences for each sentence from Gen is now filtered by comparing them to a prespecified threshold δ creating a reduced data set $FilteredCorpus$. A sentence pair (s_i, t_i) is included into $FilteredCorpus$ if at least one pair $(index, score)$ originates from the in-domain ($index < size_{In}$) and has a $score >$ δ. With a value setting of $\delta = 0.5$ we selected 47% of the sentences of Gen. Systematic experiments with other values of δ are planned for future work. Eventually, we trained the final system $UHDS\_doc2vec$ on a concatenation of the reduced general domain corpus $FilteredCorpus$ and the in-domain data $\mathcal{I}n$. Two separate language models were trained with the in-domain data In and the full general domain corpus Gen. They have been interpolated and the interpolated model has been used in both $UHBS\_lmi$ (strong baseline) and $UHDS\_doc2vec$ (the submission to the competition). In Figure 1 the pseudocode for filtering the general domain corpus is presented.

Doc2vec filtering selects in one step all the general domain sentences similar to the in-domain producing one $FilteredCorpus$. Eventually, each sentence from $\mathcal{G}en$ is either discarded or added to $FilteredCorpus$).

In order to be able to compare our method with other data selection approaches, we modified the binary decision from step 10 of the algorithm with a step that produces a score for each sentence $s_i \in \mathcal{G}en$ (Figure 2). Therefore, in addition to the submitted systems to the WMT competition, we also conducted experiments with the extended Doc2vec algorithm and with a perplexity-based metric which defines the state-of-the-art for data selection for MT (Axelrod et. al, 2011). We name SEF (Sentence Embedding Filtering) the method presented in Figure 2 and PPL (Perplexity) the state-of-the-art method.

In addition to the input parameters that the algorithm presented in Figure 1 uses, the adapted algorithm receives as input also a percentage $\mathcal{P}$ which gives the number of sentences to be selected from $\mathcal{G}en$. Given a sentence $s_i \in \mathcal{G}en$, the SEF method uses the similarity score between s_i and its $\mathcal{N}$ most similar sentences for producing a final score. Moreover, since the position in Sim_{s_i} matters, we multiply each intermediary score with the inverse position $(\mathcal{N} - j + 1)$. For example, if the most similar sentence to s_i is s_j placed on the first position in Sim_{s_i}, then their $score_{ij}$ is multiplied with the highest possible value $\mathcal{N}$. After scoring all the sentences from $\mathcal{G}en$, they are sorted by their score in descending order.

The comparison between SEF and PPL was evaluated on a range of percentages from 10 till 90, incrementing the ratio in steps of 10.

5   Results

In this section we present the evaluation scores obtained in the WMT competition for the three sub-

---

Algorithm 2 Doc2vec Filtering using percentage $\mathcal{P}$

1: **procedure** Filter-Percentage($\mathcal{I}n, \mathcal{G}en, \mathcal{N}, \delta, \mathcal{P}$)

2: $\quad \mathcal{C} \leftarrow \mathcal{I}n + \mathcal{G}en$

3: $\quad$ **for each** sentence $s_i \in \mathcal{C}_{source}$ **do**

4: $\quad\quad$ tag s_i with the line number i

5: $\quad$ build vocabulary from tagged $\mathcal{C}_{source}$

6: $\quad$ train doc2vec model $\mathcal{M}$ using tagged $\mathcal{C}_{source}$

7: $\quad$ **for each** sentence pair $(s_i, t_i) \in \mathcal{G}en$ **do**

8: $\quad\quad \mathcal{R}_i = top(\mathcal{N}, mostSimilar(\mathcal{M}, s_i))$

9: $\quad\quad Sim_{s_i} = \{(index, score) \in \mathcal{R}_i | \; index \in [1, size_C], score \in (0,1)\}$

10: $\quad\quad$ **for** $(index_j, score_j) \in Sim_{s_i}$ **do**

11: $\quad\quad\quad score_{i,j} = \begin{cases} score_{i,j} * (\mathcal{N} - j + 1)^2, & \text{if } index_j < size_{In} \text{ and } score_j > \delta \\ 0, & \text{otherwise} \end{cases}$

12: $\quad\quad score_i = \sum_{j=1}^{\mathcal{N}} score_{i,j}$

13: $\quad$ sort sentences $\in \mathcal{G}en$ by their score in descending order

14: $\quad$ **while** $i \leq \mathcal{P}$ **do**

15: $\quad\quad$ add (s_i, t_i) to $FilteredCorpus_{\mathcal{P}}$

Figure 2: Doc2vec filtering algorithm adapted to select a given percentage $\mathcal{P}$ of sentences

mitted systems. Moreover, we present the evaluation scores for the SEF and PPL methods and discuss the results. Table 2 presents the BLEU (Papineni et al., 2002), the BLEU-cased and the TER (Snover et al., 2006) scores for the submitted systems to WMT:

System	BLEU	BLEU-c	TER
$UHBS\_lmi$	37.21	35.29	0.545
$UHDS\_doc2vec$	37.14	35.04	0.528
$UHBS\_simple$	36.02	34.17	0.546

Table 2: Submitted systems results

According to their BLEU scores, the strong baseline, $UHBS\_lmi$, performs almost on a par with the filtered general domain system, $UHDS\_doc2vec$, but with respect to TER $UHDS\_doc2vec$ clearly outperforms the baseline. The results are encouraging, since our selection method filtered out more than 50% of the general domain data without a substantial loss of translation quality compared to the strong baseline.

The BLEU and TER scores for the SEF and PPL methods are given in Table 3. The maximum BLEU score has been achieved by SEF (37.12) selecting 70% of $\mathcal{G}en$. The PPL method achieved its maximum BLEU score at a 90% ratio of $\mathcal{G}en$ with a score of 36.75 that is close to the score already achieved at 30% filtering (36.71). With respect to that, the SEF method also has a close score to it at 30% filtering (36.65). The TER scores are all very close for most of the steps, with the lowest score achieved by the PPL method at 30% filtering (0.532). A very similar score has been gained by the SEF method when filtering to 50% (0.535). In comparison to the systems submitted to WMT, the best BLEU and TER scores have still been achieved by $UHDS\_doc2vec$ and $UHBS\_lmi$.

6 Conclusions

In this paper we presented the system the University of Hamburg submitted to the WMT shared task of translating IT texts. We introduced a new method of data selection for filtering the general domain data by searching for sentences that are similar to the in-domain. The novel contribution of our approach consists in using paragraph vectors to capture crucial meaning aspects of a sentence and deploy them to determine intersentential similarity. With less than 50% general domain data the system performs almost as good

Percentage $\mathcal{P}$ of Gen	BLEU		TER	
	$\mathcal{SEF}$	$\mathcal{PPL}$	$\mathcal{SEF}$	$\mathcal{PPL}$
10	35.37	36.28	0.549	0.537
20	36.25	36.36	0.549	0.539
30	36.65	36.71	0.539	**0.532**
40	35.94	36.69	0.546	0.535
50	36.97	36.39	**0.535**	0.541
60	37.08	36.57	0.535	0.536
70	**37.12**	36.29	0.536	0.542
80	37.09	36.45	0.538	0.541
90	36.43	**36.75**	0.546	0.546

Table 3: Evaluation results for $\mathcal{SEF}$ and $\mathcal{PPL}$

as the strong baseline in terms of BLEU.

We also presented an adaptation of the paragraph vector filtering method that is able to select any required percentage of the general domain data and we conducted experiments using a range of ratios for this method and a state-of-the-art method. The BLEU results indicated that the adapted paragraph vector method outperforms the state-of-the-art method.

These results make filtering using paragraph vector for scoring sentences particularly attractive for scenarios where a large pool of general domain data is available, but only a very small amount of in-domain data.

References

Amittai Axelrod, Xiaodong He and Jianfeng Gao. 2011. Domain Adaptation via Pseudo In-Domain Data Selection. *Proceedings of EMNLP 2011*.

Boxing Chen, Roland Kuhn and George Foster. 2013. Vector Space Model for Adaptation in Statistical Machine Translation *Proceedings of the 51st Annual Meeting of the Association for Computational Linguistics*, pages 1285-1293, Sofia, Bulgaria, August 4-9 2013.

George Foster, Cyril Goutte and Roland Kuhn. 2010. Discriminative instance weighting fordomain adaptation in statistical machine translation. *Proceedings of the 2010 Conference on Empirical Methods in Natural Language Processing*. Association for Computational Linguistics, Stroudsburg, PA,USA, pages 451-459.

Kenneth Heafield. 2011. KenLM: Faster and Smaller Language Model Queries. *Proceedings of Proceedings of the Sixth Workshop on Statistical Machine Translation*, Edinburgh, UK.

Almut Silja Hildebrand, Matthias Eck, Stephan Vogel, and Alex Waibel. 2005. Adaptation of the Translation Model for Statistical Machine Translation based on Information Retrieval. *Proceedings of EAMT 2005*.

Reinhard Kneser and Hermann Ney. 1995. Improved backing-off for N-gram language modeling. *Proceedings ICASSP*, pages 181-184.

Philipp Koehn, Hieu Hoang, Alexandra Birch, Chris Callison-Burch, Marcello Federico, Nicola Bertoldi, Brooke Cowan, Wade Shen, Christine Moran, Richard Zens, Chris Dyer, Ondřej Bojar, Alexandra Constantin and Evan Herbst. 2007. Moses: open source toolkit for statistical machine translation. *Proceedings of the 45th Annual Meeting of the ACL on Interactive Poster and Demonstration Sessions*. June 25-27, 2007, Prague, Czech Republic.

Philipp Koehn. 2010. An experimental management system. *The Prague Bulletin of Mathematical Linguistics*, 94.

Quoc Le and Tomas Mikolov. 2014. Distributed Representations of Sentences and Documents. *Proceedings of the 31st International Conference on Machine Learning*, volume 32, Beijing, China. JMLR: W&CP.

Yajuan Lü, Jin Huang and Qun Liu. 2007. Improving Statistical Machine Translation Performance by Training Data Selection and Optimization. *Prooceedings of EMNLP-CoNLL 2007*.

A. Mandal, D. Vergyri, W. Wang, J. Zheng, A. Stolcke, G. Tur, D. Hakkani-Tür, and N. F. Ayan. 2008. Efficient data selection for machine translation. *Proceedings IEEE Workshop on Spoken Language Technology*.

Saab Mansour, Joern Wuebker and Hermann Ney. 2011. Combining Translation and Language Model Scoring for Domain-Specific Data Filtering. *Proceedings of IWSLT*.

Tomas Mikolov, Kai Chen, Greg Corrado and Jeffrey Dean. 2013. Efficient Estimation of Word Representations in Vector Space. *arXiv preprint arXiv:1301.3781*.

Franz Josef Och. 2003. Minimum error rate training in statistical machine translation. *Proceedings of the 41st Annual Meeting on Association for Computational Linguistics*, pages 160-167, July 07-12, 2003, Sapporo, Japan.

Franz Josef Och and Hermann Ney. 2003. A Systematic Comparison of Various Statistical Alignment Models. *Computational Linguistics*, volume 29, number 1, pages 19-51.

Kishore Papineni, Salim Roukos, Todd Ward and Wei-Jing Zhu. 2002. BLEU: a method for automatic evaluation of machine translation. *Proceedings of the 40th Annual Meeting on Association for Computational Linguistics*, July 07-12, 2002, Philadelphia, Pennsylvania.

Radim Řehůřek and Petr Sojka. 2010. Software Framework for Topic Modelling with Large Corpora. *Proceedings of the LREC 2010 Workshop on New Challenges for NLP Frameworks*, pages 45-50.

Matthew Snover, Bonnie Dorr, Richard Schwartz, Linnea Micciulla, and John Makhoul. 2006. A study of translation edit rate with targeted human annotation. *Proceedings of the 7th Biennial Conference of the Association for Machine Translation in the Americas*, Cambridge, Massachusetts.

Andreas Stolcke. 2002. SRILM - an Extensible Language Modeling Toolkit. *International Conference on Spoken Language Processing*.

Aleš Tamchyna, Galuščáková Petra, Kamran Amir, Stanojević Miloš and Bojar Ondřej. 2012. Selecting Data for English-to-Czech Machine Translation. *Proceedings of the Seventh Workshop on Statistical Machine Translation*.

Antonio Toral, Pavel Pecina, Longyue Wang and Josef van Genabith. 2015. Linguistically-augmented perplexity-based data selection for language models. *Computer Speech & Language*, Volume 32, Issue 1, July 2015, pages 11-26.

Longyue Wang, Derek F. Wong, Lidia S. Chao, Yi Lu, and Junwen Xing. 2013a. A Systematic Comparison of Data Selection Criteria for SMT Domain Adaptation. *The Scientific World Journal*, vol. 2014.

Longyue Wang, Derek F. Wong, Lidia S. Chao, Junwen Xing and Yi Lu. 2013b. Edit Distance: A New Data Selection Criterion for Domain Adaptation in SMT. *Proceedings of Recent Advances in Natural Language Processing*.

Longyue Wang, Derek F. Wong, Lidia S. Chao, Yi Lu, and Junwen Xing. 2013c. iCPE: A Hybrid Data Selection Model for SMT Domain Adaptation. *Lecture Notes in Artificial Intelligence (LNAI) Springer series*. 12th CCL&1st NLP-NABD

SMT and Hybrid systems of the QTLeap project in the WMT16 IT-task

Rosa Del Gaudio

Higher Functions Sistemas Inteligentes, Lisbon, Portugal
`rosa.gaudio@pcmedic.pt`

Gorka Labaka, Eneko Agirre

University of the Basque Country, UPV/EHU, San Sebastian, Spain
`{gorka.labaka,e.agirre}@ehu.eus`

Petya Osenova, Kiril Simov

Linguistic Modelling Department, IICT-BAS, Sofia, Bulgaria
`{petya,kivs}@bultreebank.org`

Martin Popel

Charles University in Prague, Faculty of Mathematics and Physics, ÚFAL, Czechia
`popel@ufal.mff.cuni.cz`

Dieke Oele, Gertjan van Noord

Rijksuniversiteit Groningen, Groningen, The Netherlands
`{d.oele,g.j.van.noord}@rug.nl`

Luís Gomes, João Rodrigues, Steven Neale, João Silva,
Andreia Querido, Nuno Rendeiro, António Branco

Universidade de Lisboa, Departamento de Informática, Faculdade de Ciências
`luisgomes@gmail.com,{joao.rodrigues,steven.neale,jsilva,`
`andreia.querido,nuno.rendeiro,antonio.branco}@di.fc.ul.pt`

Abstract

This paper presents the description of 12 systems submitted to the WMT16 IT-task, covering six different languages, namely Basque, Bulgarian, Dutch, Czech, Portuguese and Spanish. All these systems were developed under the scope of the QTLeap project, presenting a common strategy. For each language two different systems were submitted, namely a phrase-based MT system built using Moses, and a system exploiting deep language engineering approaches, that in all the languages but Bulgarian was implemented using TectoMT. For 4 of the 6 languages, the TectoMT-based system performs better than the Moses-based one.

1 Introduction

The QTLeap[1] project focuses on the development of an articulated methodology for machine translation that explores deep language engineering approaches and sophisticated semantic datasets. The

underling hypothesis is that the deeper the level of representation, the better the translation becomes since deeper representations abstract away from surface aspects that are specific to a given language. At the limit, the representation of the meaning of a sentence, and of all its paraphrases, would be shared among all languages.

This purpose is supported by recent advances in terms of lexical processing. These advances have been made possible by enhanced techniques for referential and conceptual ambiguity resolution, and supported also by new types of datasets recently developed as linked open data.

The overall goal of the project is to produce quality translation between English (EN) and another language X by using deep linguistic information. All language pairs follow the same processing pipeline of analysis, transfer and synthesis (generation) and adopt the same hybrid MT approach of using both statistical as well as rule-based components in a tightly integrated way for the best possible results.

In this paper, we present the systems developed by the University of Basque Country for Basque

---

[1] `http://www.qtleap.eu`

435

Proceedings of the First Conference on Machine Translation, Volume 2: Shared Task Papers, pages 435–441,
Berlin, Germany, August 11-12, 2016. ©2016 Association for Computational Linguistics

and Spanish, Charles University in Prague for Czech, by University of Groningen for Dutch, by University of Lisbon for Portuguese and by IICT-BAS of the Bulgarian Academy of Sciences for Bulgarian.

For each language two different systems were submitted, corresponding to different phases of the project, namely a phrase-based MT system built using Moses (Koehn et al., 2007), and a system exploiting deep language engineering approaches, that in all the languages but Bulgarian was implemented using TectoMT (Žabokrtský and Popel, 2009). For Bulgarian, its second MT system is not based on TectoMT, but on exploiting deep factors in Moses. All 12 systems are constrained, that is trained only on the data provided by the WMT16 IT-task organizers.

We present briefly the Moses common setting and the TectoMT structure and then more detailed information for each language system are provided. In the last Section, results based on BLEU and TrueSkill are given and discussed.

2 Moses

All the systems submitted that were based on Moses have been trained on a phrase-based model by Giza++ or mGiza with "grow-diag-final-and" symmetrization and "msd-bidirectional-fe" reordering (Koehn et al., 2003). For the language pairs where big quantities of domain-specific monolingual data were available along with the generic domain data, separate language models (domain-specific and generic) were interpolated against our ICT domain-specific development set. For LM training and interpolation, the SRILM toolkit (Stolcke, 2002) was used. The method of truecasing has been adopted for several language pairs where it proved useful.

3 TectoMT

The deep translation is based on the TectoMT system, an open-source MT system based on the Treex platform for general natural-language processing. TectoMT uses a combination of rule-based and statistical (trained) modules (blocks in Treex terminology), with a statistical transfer based on HMTM (Hidden Markov Tree Model) at the level of a deep, so-called tectogrammatical, representation of sentence structure. The general TectoMT pipeline is language independent, and consists of analysis, deep transfer, and synthesis

steps.

The design of TectoMT is highly modular and consists of a language-universal core and language-specific additions and distinguishes two levels of syntactic description:

- Surface dependency syntax (a-layer) – surface dependency trees containing all the tokens in the sentence.

- Deep syntax (t-layer) – dependency trees that contain only content words (nouns, main verbs, adjectives, adverbs) as nodes. Each node has a deep lemma (t-lemma), a semantic function label (functor), a morpho-syntactic form label (formeme), and various grammatical attributes (grammatemes), such as number, gender, tense, or modality.

T-layer representations of the same sentence in different languages are closer to each other than the surface texts; in many cases, there is a 1:1 node correspondence among the t-layer trees. TectoMTs transfer exploits this by translating the tree isomorphically, i.e., node-by-node and assuming that the shape will not change in most cases (apart from a few exceptions handled by specific rules).

The translation is further factorized: t-lemmas, formemes, and grammatemes are translated using separate Translation Models (TM). The t-lemma and formeme TMs are an interpolation of maximum entropy discriminative models (MaxEnt) (Mareček et al., 2010) and simple conditional probability models. The MaxEnt models are in fact an ensemble of models, one for each individual source t-lemma/formeme. The combined translation models provide several translation options for each node along with their estimated probability. The best options are then selected using a Hidden Markov Tree Model (HMTM) with a target-language tree model (Žabokrtský and Popel, 2009).

For this specific task, where we need to work on a specific domain, an extended version of TectoMT was used allowing interpolation of multiple TMs (Rosa et al., 2015).

4 Basque

Both English-Basque submissions are trained on the same training corpora. That is, the PaCO2-eneu corpus for translation and language modeling, and the in-domain Batch1 corpus for domain adaptation and MERT training. Batch2 domain corpus was used for testing during development.

The Moses system, `EU-Moses`, uses factored models to allow lemma-based word-alignment. After word alignment, the rest of the training process is based on lowercased word-forms and standard parameters: Stanford CoreNLP (Manning et al., 2014) and Eustagger (Alegria et al., 2002) tools are used for tokenization and lemmatization, MGIZA for word alignment with the "grow-diag-final-and" symmetrization heuristic, a maximum length of 75 tokens per sentence and 5 tokens per phrase, translation probabilities in both directions, lexical weightings in both directions, a phrase length penalty, a "phrase-mslr-fe" lexicalized reordering model and a target language model. As for the language model, a 5-gram model was trained. The weights for the different components were adjusted to optimize BLEU using MERT tuning over the Batch1 development set, with an n-best list of size 100.

For the TectoMT system, `EU-Treex` existing tools were used in order to get the a-layer. Eustagger is a robust and wide coverage morphological analyzer and POS tagger. The dependency parser is based on the MATE-tools (Bjrkelund et al., 2010). Basque models have been trained using the Basque Dependency Treebank (BDT) corpus (Aduriz et al., 2003). Transformation from the a-level analysis into t-level is partially performed with language-independent blocks thanks to the support of Interset (Zeman, 2008).

The English-to-Basque TectoMT system uses the PaCo2 and the Batch1 corpora to train two separate translation models, and they are used to create an interpolated list of translation candidates. In addition to that, the terminological equivalences extracted from the localization PO files (VLC, LO and KDE) as well as the domain terms extracted from Wikipedia are used to identify domain terms before syntactical analysis and to ensure domain translation on transfer. Finally, an extra module to treat non linguistic elements (URLs, shell commands, ...) has been used, to identify the elements that should be maintained untranslated on the output.

5 Bulgarian

Bulgarian team participated with two systems implemented using Moses: `BG-Moses` — a system that is based on standard factored Moses with factors retrieved from POS tagged, lemmatized parallel corpora; and `BG-DeepMoses` — a system that also is based on standard factored Moses but the translation is done in two steps: (1) semantics-based translation of the source language text to a mixed source-target language text which is then (2) translated to the target language via Moses. The latter system builds on Simov et al. (2015).

As training data for both systems the following corpora were used: the Setimes parallel corpus, the Europarl parallel corpus and a corpus created on the basis of the documentation of LibreOffice. The corpora are linguistically processed with the IXA[2] pipeline for the English part and the BTB pipeline for the Bulgarian. The analyses include POS tagging, lemmatization and WSD, using the UKB system,[3] which provides graph-based methods for Word Sense Disambiguation and lexical similarity measurements.

For the `BG-Moses` system, the following factors have been constructed: WordForm|Lemma|POStag.

For the `BG-DeepMoses` system, we exploited also the information from word sense annotation in order to predict some translations from English to Bulgarian based on the WordNet synsets and their mappings to the Bulgarian WordNet. Thus, we replaced the English word form with a *representative lemma* in Bulgarian. The motivation for using representative lemmas in Bulgarian is as follows: we aim at unifying the various synsets with similar translations in the Bulgarian language. After the creation of this intermediate English/Bulgarian text, we trained Moses with the following factors: ENWordForm-BGLemma|Lemma|BGPOStag, where ENWordForm-BGLemma is an English word form when there is no appropriate Bulgarian one, or the Bulgarian lemma; BGPOStag is the appropriate Bulgarian tag representing grammatical features like number, tense, etc.

6 Czech

The Czech Moses system follows the CU-Bojar system (Bojar et al., 2013). A factored phrase-based model was trained based on truecased forms translated directly to the pair <truecased form, morphological tag>. There were three LMs for Czech:

---

[2]http://ixa2.si.ehu.es/ixa-pipes/
[3]http://ixa2.si.ehu.es/ukb/

- 8grams of morphological tags from the monolingual part of news and political corpora,

- 6grams of forms from the monolingual part of news and political corpora and

- 6grams from the Czech side of a bilingual Czech-English corpus CzEng.

The pre-processing of this SMT system has been harmonized with the pre-existing version of Tecto-MT: Tokenization and lemmatization is handled by Treex followed by further tokenization at any letter-digit-punctuation boundary. Additionally, casing is handled by a Czech-specific supervised truecasing method. The output of the lemmatizer is used, as names have lemmas capitalized, the casing of the lemma is cast to the token (lowercasing non-names at sentence beginnings, lowercasing also ALL CAPS if correctly lemmatized). Finally, the translation is done using case-sensitive tokens and finally the first letter in every sentence is only capitalized.

The TectoMT analysis pipeline is based on the annotation pipeline of the CzEng 1.0 corpus (Bojar et al., 2012) starting with a rule-based tokenizer and a statistical part-of-speech tagger (Straková et al., 2014) and dependency parser (McDonald et al., 2005; Novák and Žabokrtský, 2007). These steps result in a-layer trees, which are then converted to t-layer using a rule-based process.

The English-to-Czech transfer uses a combination of translation models and tree model reranking. The Czech synthesis pipeline has remained basically unchanged since the original TectoMT system (Žabokrtský et al., 2008).

7 Dutch

The Moses system for Dutch was trained on the third version of the Europarl corpus (Koehn, 2005) and the in-domain KDE4 Localization data (Tiedemann, 2012). Words are aligned with GIZA++ and tuning was done with MERT. The applied heuristics for the Dutch baselines were set to "grow-diag-final-and" alignment and "msd-bidirectional-fe" reordering. For the creation of the language models, IRSTLM was used to train a 5-gram language model with Kneser-Ney smoothing on the monolingual part of the training corpora.

For the TectoMT system, the analysis of Dutch input uses the Alpino system (Noord, 2006), a stochastic attribute value grammar. The transfer uses discriminative (context-sensitive) and dictionary translation models. In addition, a few rule-based modules are employed that handle changes in t-tree topology and Dutch grammatical gender.

The Dutch synthesis pipeline includes morphology initialization and agreements (subject-predicate and attribute-noun), insertion of prepositions and conjunctions based on formemes, and insertion of punctuation, possessive pronouns and Dutch pronominal adverbs. The t-tree resulting from the transfer phase is first converted into an Abstract Dependency Tree (ADT) using rule-based modules implemented in Treex. The ADT is then passed to the Alpino generator (de Kok and Noord, 2010), which handles the creation of the actual sentence including inflected word forms.

8 Spanish

The Moses system developed for the translation from English to Spanish, ES-Moses, uses standard parameters: tokenization and truecasing using tools available in Moses toolkit, MGIZA for word alignment with the "grow-diag-final-and" symmetrization heuristic, a maximum length of 80 tokens per sentence and 5 tokens per phrase, translation probabilities in both directions with Good–Turing discounting, lexical weightings in both directions, a phrase length penalty, an "msd-bidirectional-fe" lexicalized reordering model and a 5-gram target language model. The weights for the different components were adjusted to optimize BLEU using MERT tuning over the Batch1 development set, with an n-best list of size 100.

The English-to-Spanish TectoMT, ES-Treex, system uses the Europarl and the Batch1 corpora to train two separate translation models, and these were used to create an interpolated list of translation candidates. In addition to that, the terminological equivalences extracted from the localization PO files (VLC, LO and KDE) as well as the domain terms extracted from Wikipedia are used to identify domain terms before syntactic analysis and to ensure domain translation on transfer. Finally, an extra module to treat non linguistic elements (URLs, shell commands, ...) has been used to identify the elements that should be maintained untranslated on the output.

Both systems were trained using the same training corpora: the 7th version of the Europarl corpus was used for both translation and language modeling, and the in-domain batch1 corpus was used for domain adaptation and MERT training. The Batch2 domain-specific corpus was used for testing during development. We have not used all the available parallel corpora, because of the computational restrictions in analyzing all those corpora at the tectogrammatical level of the TectoMT system.

9 Portuguese

The Moses system for the translation from English to Portuguese, `PT-Moses`, was obtained by using the default parameters and tools regarding the training of a phrase-based model. For the pre-processing, a sentence length of 80 words was used and the tokenization was performed by the Moses tokenizer. No lemmatization or compound splitting was used and the casing was obtained with the Moses truecaser. For the training, a phrase-based model was used with a language model order of 5, with Kneser-Ney smoothing, which was interpolated using the SRILM tool. The word alignment was done with Giza++ on full forms and the final tuning was done using MERT. The Europarl corpus was used for the training data, both as monolingual data for training language models and as parallel data for training the phrase-table.

Regarding the English-to-Portuguese TectoMT system (Silva et al., 2015)(Rodrigues et al., 2016a), `PT-Treex`, in order to get the a-layer the Portuguese system resorted to LX-Suite (Branco and Silva, 2006), a set of pre-existing shallow processing tools for Portuguese that include a sentence segmenter, a tokenizer, a POS tagger, a morphological analyser and a dependency parser, all with state-of-the-art performance. Treex blocks were created to be called and interfaced with these tools.

After running the shallow processing tools, the dependency output of the parser is converted into Universal Dependencies (UD) (de Marneffe et al., 2014). These dependencies are then converted into the a-layer tree (a-tree) in a second step. Both steps are implemented as rule-based Treex blocks. Converting the a-tree into a t-layer tree (t-tree) is done through rule-based Treex blocks that manipulate the tree structure.

The transfer phase is handled by a tree-to-tree maximum entropy translation model (Mareček et al., 2010) working at the deep syntactic level of tectogrammatical trees. Two separate models were trained and interpolated, the first model with over 1.9 million sentences from Europarl (Koehn, 2005) and the second model composed of the Batch1, the Microsoft Terminology Collection and the LibreOffice localization data (Štajner et al., 2016). Each pair of parallel sentences, one in English and one in Portuguese, are analyzed by Treex up to the t-layer level, where each pair of trees are fed into the model.

The TectoMT synthesis (Rodrigues et al., 2016b) included other two lexical-semantics-related modules, the HideIT and gazetteers. The HideIT module handles entities that do not require translation such as URLs and shell commands. The gazetteers are specialized lexicons that handle the translation of named entities from the IT-domain such as menu items and button names.

Finally, synset IDs were used as additional contextual features in the lemma-to-lemma Discriminative Translation Models (Neale et al., 2016).

10 Results

Table 1 presents the results of automatic and manual evaluation, based on BLEU and TrueSkill[4] scores respectively. For 4 of the 6 languages, the TectoMT-based system performs better than the Moses-based one when considering both BLEU and TrueSkill scores. For Bulgarian, the `BG-DeepFMoses` performs worse than the `BG-FMoses` on both scores. For Dutch, the Moses system outperforms the TectoMT only when considering the BLUE score, but not the TrueSkill score.

Regarding Bulgarian, although `BG-Deep-FMoses` system performed worse than `BG-Moses`, the automatic conversion of the source text into near-target language text represents a promising direction for further improvement of the English-to-Bulgarian MT system. We assume that the current drop might be overcome by improving the WordNet information for Bulgarian, its mapping to the English WordNet as well as the processing pipelines. Also, we plan to train this system on more data and to exploit other bilingual dictionaries.

For the English→Dutch translation direction, the Moses system outperforms TectoMT in terms of BLEU score. The results of the manual evaluation, however, are in favor of the TectoMT sys-

---

[4]For details, see the overview paper in these proceedings.

	Moses		**TectoMT**		**Deep-Moses**	
Language	BLEU	TrueSkill	BLEU	TrueSkill	BLEU	TrueSkill
Basque	8.3	−1.570	10.3	1.570		
Bulgarian	16.6	5.262	-	-	15.3	−5.262
Czech	20.8	−0.616	21.5	0.130		
Dutch	21.9	−2.462	19.0	0.154		
Spanish	16.0	−1.926	24.2	−0.809		
Portuguese	13.7	−2.276	15.2	−1.063		

Table 1: Automatic and manual evaluation results.

tem. This difference may in part be caused by the fact that BLEU only scores exact word or phrase matches and the TectoMT output shows more lexical flexibility as compared to Moses. We get better results, in terms of BLEU-score, in the opposite translation direction which indicates that more effort should be put into this translation direction. Our focus here lies on the Dutch synthesis pipeline where we still need to fix some basic errors. Also we intend to implement more modules that are based on lexical semantics.

We also presented at the IT-task a third system for Czech, Dutch, Spanish and Portuguese, called Chimera that combines Moses and TectoMT (Rosa et al., 2016).

Acknowledgments

This work has been supported by the 7th Framework Programme of the EU grant QTLeap (No. 610516).

References

Itzair Aduriz, Mara Jess Aranzabe, Jose Mari Arriola, Aitziber Atutxa, Arantza Daz de Ilarraza, Aitzpea Garmendia, and Maite Oronoz. 2003. Construction of a Basque dependency treebank. In *Proceedings of the 2nd Workshop on Treebanks and Linguistic Theories*, pages 201–204.

Iñaki Alegria, Maria Jesus Aranzabe, Aitzol Ezeiza, Nerea Ezeiza, and Ruben Urizar. 2002. Robustness and customisation in an analyser/lemmatiser for basque. In *Proceedings of the 3rd International Conference on Language Resources and Evaluation (LREC). Customizing knowledge in NLP applications Workshop*.

Anders Bjrkelund, Bernd Bohnet, Love Hafdell, and Pierre Nugues. 2010. A high-performance syntactic and semantic dependency parser. In *Coling 2010: Demonstrations*, pages 33–36, Beijing, China, August. Coling 2010 Organizing Committee.

Ondřej Bojar, Zdeněk Žabokrtský, Ondřej Dušek, Petra Galuščáková, Martin Majliš, David Mareček, Jiří Maršík, Michal Novák, Martin Popel, and Aleš Tamchyna. 2012. The joy of parallelism with czeng 1.0. In Nicoletta Calzolari, editor, *Proceedings of the Eight International Conference on Language Resources and Evaluation (LREC'12)*, Istanbul, Turkey, May. European Language Resources Association (ELRA).

Ondřej Bojar, Rudolf Rosa, and Aleš Tamchyna. 2013. Chimera – three heads for English-to-Czech translation. In *Proceedings of the Eighth Workshop on Statistical Machine Translation*, pages 92–98, Sofia, Bulgaria, August. Association for Computational Linguistics.

António Branco and João Silva. 2006. A Suite of Shallow Processing Tools for Portuguese: LX-Suite. In *Proceedings of the 11th Conference of the European Chapter of the Association for Computational Linguistics (EACL)*.

Daniel de Kok and Gertjan Van Noord. 2010. A sentence generator for dutch. In *LOT Occasional Series*, pages 75–90.

Marie-Catherine de Marneffe, Natalia Silveira, Timothy Dozat, Katri Haverinen, Filip Ginter, Joakim Nivre, and Christopher Manning. 2014. Universal Stanford dependencies: A cross-linguistic typology. In *Proceedings of the 9th Language Resources and Evaluation Conference*.

Philipp Koehn, Franz Josef Och, and Daniel Marcu. 2003. Statistical phrase-based translation. In *Proceedings of the Conference of the North American Chapter of the Association for Computational Linguistics on Human Language Technology - Volume 1*, pages 48–54. Association for Computational Linguistics.

Philipp Koehn, Hieu Hoang, Alexandra Birch, Chris Callison-Burch, Marcello Federico, Nicola Bertoldi, Brooke Cowan, Wade Shen, Christine Moran, Richard Zens, Chris Dyer, Ondrej Bojar, Alexandra Constantin, and Evan Herbst. 2007. Moses: Open source toolkit for statistical machine translation. In *ACL*. The Association for Computer Linguistics.

Philipp Koehn. 2005. Europarl: A parallel corpus for statistical machine translation. In *Proceedings of the Tenth Machine Translation Summit*, pages 79–86.

Christopher D. Manning, Mihai Surdeanu, John Bauer, Jenny Finkel, Steven J. Bethard, and David Mc-Closky. 2014. The Stanford CoreNLP natural language processing toolkit. In *Association for Computational Linguistics (ACL) System Demonstrations*, pages 55–60.

David Mareček, Martin Popel, and Zdeněk Žabokrtský. 2010. Maximum entropy translation model in dependency-based MT framework. In *Proceedings of the Joint 5th Workshop on Statistical Machine Translation and MetricsMATR*, pages 201–206.

Ryan McDonald, Fernando Pereira, Kiril Ribarov, and Jan Haji. 2005. Non-projective dependency parsing using spanning tree algorithms. In *In Proceedings of Human Language Technology Conference and Conference on Empirical Methods in Natural Language Processing*, pages 523–530.

Steven Neale, Luis Gomes, Eneko Agirre, Oier Lopez de Lacalle, and António Branco. 2016. Word sense-aware machine translation: Including senses as contextual features for improved translation models. In *Proceedings of the 10th Language Resources and Evaluation Conference (LREC), European Language Resources Association*, Portorož, Slovenia. To appear.

Gertjan Van Noord. 2006. At last parsing is now operational. In *In TALN 2006, Verbum Ex Machina, Actes De La 13e Conference sur Le Traitement Automatique des Langues naturelles*, pages 20–42.

Václav Novák and Zdeněk Žabokrtský. 2007. Feature engineering in maximum spanning tree dependency parser. In Václav Matoušek and Pavel Mautner, editors, *Text, Speech and Dialogue: 10th International Conference, TSD 2007, Pilsen, Czech Republic, September 3-7, 2007. Proceedings*, pages 92–98, Berlin, Heidelberg. Springer Berlin Heidelberg.

João Rodrigues, Luıs Gomes, Steve Neale, Andreia Querido, Nuno Rendeiro, Sanja Štajner, João Silva, and António Branco. 2016a. Domain-specific hybrid machine translation from english to portuguese. In *Lecture Notes in Artificial Intelligence*. Springer. To appear.

João Rodrigues, Nuno Rendeiro, Andreia Querido, Sanja Štajner, and António Branco. 2016b. Bootstrapping a hybrid mt system to a new language pair. In *Proceedings of the 10th Language Resources and Evaluation Conference (LREC), European Language Resources Association*, Portorož, Slovenia. To appear.

Rudolf Rosa, Ondřej Dušek, Michal Novák, and Martin Popel. 2015. Translation model interpolation for domain adaptation in tectomt. In *Proceedings of the 1st Deep Machine Translation Workshop*, pages 89–96, Praha, Czechia. ÚFAL MFF UK.

Rudolf Rosa, Roman Sudarikov, Michal Nov4k, Martin Popel, and Ondřej Bojar. 2016. Dictionary-based domain adaptation of mt systems without retraining. In *Proceedings of the 1sh Conference of Machine Translation, WMT2016*, Berlin, Germany. To appear.

João Silva, João Rodrigues, Luıs Gomes, and António Branco. 2015. Bootstrapping a hybrid deep mt system. In *Proceedings of the ACL2015 Fourth Workshop on Hybrid Approaches to Translation*, pages 1–5.

Kiril Simov, Iliana Simova, Velislava Todorova, and Petya Osenova. 2015. Factored models for deep machine translation. In *Proceedings of the 1st Deep Machine Translation Workshop (DMTW 2015)*, pages 97–105.

Andreas Stolcke. 2002. SRILM - an Extensible Language Modeling Toolkit. In *Proceedings of the International Conference on Spoken Language Processing (ICSLP)*, pages 901–904.

Jana Straková, Milan Straka, and Jan Hajič. 2014. Open-source tools for morphology, lemmatization, pos tagging and named entity recognition. In *In Proceedings of 52nd Annual Meeting of the Association for Computational Linguistics: System Demonstrations*, page 1318, Baltimore, Maryland. Association for Computational Linguistics.

Jrg Tiedemann. 2012. Parallel Data, Tools and Interfaces in OPUS. In *Proceedings of the Eight International Conference on Language Resources and Evaluation (LREC'12)*. European Language Resources Association.

Sanja Štajner, Andreia Querido, Nuno Rendeiro, João Rodrigues, and António Branco. 2016. Use of domain-specific language resources in machine translation. In *Proceedings of the 10th Language Resources and Evaluation Conference (LREC), European Language Resources Association*, Portorož, Slovenia. To appear.

Zdeněk Žabokrtský and Martin Popel. 2009. Hidden Markov Tree Model in Dependency-based Machine Translation. In *Proceedings of the ACL-IJCNLP 2009 Conference Short Papers*, pages 145–148.

Zdeněk Žabokrtský, Jan Ptáček, and Petr Pajas. 2008. Tectomt: Highly modular mt system with tectogrammatics used as transfer layer. In *Proceedings of the Third Workshop on Statistical Machine Translation*, StatMT '08, pages 167–170, Stroudsburg, PA, USA. Association for Computational Linguistics.

Daniel Zeman. 2008. Reusable tagset conversion using tagset drivers. In Nicoletta Calzolari, editor, *Proceedings of the Sixth International Conference on Language Resources and Evaluation (LREC'08)*, Marrakech, Morocco, May. European Language Resources Association (ELRA). http://www.lrec-conf.org/proceedings/lrec2008/.

JU-USAAR: A Domain Adaptive MT System

Koushik Pahari[1], Alapan Kuila[2], Santanu Pal[3], Sudip Kumar Naskar[2],
Sivaji Bandyopadhyay[2], Josef van Genabith[3,4]
[1] Indian Institute of Engineering Science and Technology, Shibpur, India
[2]Jadavpur University, Kolkata, India
[3]Universität des Saarlandes, Saarbrücken, Germany
[4]German Research Center for Artificial Intelligence (DFKI), Germany
{pahari.koushik,alapan.cse}@gmail.com,
sudip.naskar@jdvu.ac.in, sivaji_cse_ju@yahoo.com
{santanu.pal, josef.vangenabith}@uni-saarland.de

Abstract

This paper presents the JU-USAAR English–German domain adaptive machine translation (MT) system submitted to the IT domain translation task organized in WMT-2016 . Our system brings improvements over the in-domain baseline system by incorporating out-domain knowledge. We applied two methodologies to accelerate the performance of our in-domain MT system: (i) additional training material extraction from out-domain data using data selection method, and (ii) language model and translation model adaptation through interpolation. Our primary submission obtained a BLEU score of 34.5 (14.5 absolute and 72.5% relative improvements over baseline) and a TER score of 54.0 (14.7 absolute and 21.4% relative improvements over baseline).

1 Introduction

Statistical Machine Translation (SMT) is the currently dominant MT technology. The underlying statistical models in SMT always tend to closely approximate the empirical distributions of the bilingual training data and monolingual target-language text. However, the performance of SMT systems quickly degrades when testing conditions deviate from training conditions. In order to achieve optimal performance, an SMT system should be trained on data from the same domain. Now-a-days domain adaptation has gained interest in SMT to cope with this performance drop. The basic aim of domain adaptation is to maintain the identity of the in-domain data while using the best of the out-domain data. However, large amount of additional out-domain data may bias the resultant distribution towards the out-domain. In practice,

it is often difficult to obtain sufficient amount of in-domain parallel data to train a system which can provide good performance in a specific domain. The performance of an in-domain model can be improved by selecting a subset from the out-domain data which is very similar to the in-domain data (Matsoukas et al., 2009; Moore and Lewis, 2010), or by re-weighting the probability distributions (Foster et al., 2006; Sennrich et al., 2013) in favor of the in-domain data.

In this task, the information technology (IT) domain English–German parallel corpus released in the WMT-2016 IT-domain shared task serves as the in-domain data and the Europarl, News and Common Crawl English–German parallel corpus released in the Translation Task are treated as out-domain data.

In this paper we describe the joint submission of Jadavpur University (JU) and Saarland University (USAAR) English–German machine translation (MT) system (JU-USAAR) to the shared task on IT domain translation organized in WMT-2016. In our approach we initially applied data selection method where we directly measured cross entropy for the source side of the text; successively we applied Moore and Lewis (2010) method of data selection and ranked the out-domain bilingual parallel data according to cross entropy difference. Finally, we built domain specific language models on both in-domain and selected out-domain target language monolingual corpus, linearly interpolate them choosing weights that minimize perplexity on a held out in-domain development set. In addition, we also interpolated the translation models trained on the in-domain and selected out-domain parallel corpora. However, instead of using bilingual cross-entropy difference, we applied bilingual cross-perplexity difference to model our data selection process.

442

Proceedings of the First Conference on Machine Translation, Volume 2: Shared Task Papers, pages 442–448,
Berlin, Germany, August 11-12, 2016. ©2016 Association for Computational Linguistics

2 Related Work

Koehn (2004; Koehn (2005) first proposed domain adaptation in SMT by integrating terminological lexicons in the translation model, as a result of which there was a significant reduction in word error rate (WER). Over the last decade, many researchers (Foster and Kuhn, 2007; Duh et al., 2010; Banerjee et al., 2011; Bisazza and Federico, 2012; Sennrich, 2012; Sennrich et al., 2013; Haddow and Koehn, 2012) investigated the problem of combining multi-domain datasets.

To construct a good domain-specific language model, sentences which are similar to the target domain should be included (Sethy et al., 2006) in the monolingual target language corupus on which the language model is trained. Lü et al. (2007) identified those sentences using the tf/idf method and they increased the count of such sentences.

Domain adaptation in MT have been explored in many different directions, ranging from adapating language models and translation models to alignment adaptation approach to improve domain-specific word alignment.

Koehn et al. (2007) used multiple decoding paths for combining multiple domain-specific translation tables in the state-of-the-art PB-SMT decoder MOSES. Banerjee et al. (2013) combined an in-domain model (translation and reordering model) with an out-of-domain model into MOSES and they derived log-linear features to distinguish between phrases of multiple domains by applying the data-source indicator features and showed modest improvement in translation quality.

Bach et al. (2008) suggested that sentences may be weighted by how much it matches with the target domain. A comparison among different domain adaptation methods for different subject matters in patent translation was carried out by (Ceauşfu et al., 2011) which led to a small gain over the baseline.

In order to select supplementary out-of- domain data relevant to the target domain, a variety of criteria have been explored ranging from information retrieval techniques to perplexity on in-domain datasets. Banerjee et al. (2011) proposed a prediction based data selection technique using an incremental translation model merging approach.

3 System Description

3.1 Data selection Approach

Among the different approaches proposed for data selection, the two most popular and successful methodologies are based on monolingual cross-entropy difference (Moore and Lewis, 2010) and bilingual cross-entropy difference (Axelrod et al., 2011). The data selection approach taken in the present work is also motivated by the bilingual cross-entropy difference (Axelrod et al., 2011) based data selection. However, instead of using bilingual cross-entropy difference, we applied bilingual cross-perplexity difference to model our data selection process. The difference in cross-entropy is computed on two language models (LM); the domain-specific LM is estimated from the entire in-domain corpus (lm_{in}) and the second LM (lm_o) is estimated from the out-domain corpus. Mathematically, the cross-entropy $H(P_{lm})$ of language model probability P_{lm} is defined as in Equation 1 considering a k-gram language model.

$$H(P_{lm}) = -\frac{1}{N} \sum_{i=1}^{N} \log P_{lm}(w_i|w_{i-k+1}...w_{i-1})$$

$$(1)$$

We calculated perplexity ($PP = 2^H$) of individual sentences of out-domain with respect to in-domain LM and out-domain LM for both source (sl) and target (tl) language.

The score, i.e., sum of the two cross-perplexity differences, for the jth sentence pair $[s_j - t_j]$ is calculated based on Equation 2.

$$score = |PP_{in_{sl}}(s_j) - PP_{o_{sl}}(s_j)|$$
$$+ |PP_{in_{tl}}(t_j) - PP_{o_{tl}}(t_j)| \quad (2)$$

Subsequently, sentence pairs $[s - t]$ from the out-domain corpus (o) are ranked based on this score.

3.2 Interpolation Approach

To combine multiple translation and language models, a common approach is to linearly interpolate them. The language model interpolation weights are automatically learnt by minimizing the perplexity on the development set. For interpolating the translation models, we use moses training pipeline which selects the interpolation weights that optimizes performance on the development set. These weights are subsequently used to combine the individual feature values for every phrase pair from two different phrase-tables (i.e., in-domain phrase table $p_{in}(e|f)$ and out-domain phrase table $p_o(e|f)$) using the formula in Equation 3 where f and e are source and target phrases respectively and the value of λ ranges between 0 and 1.

$$p(f|e) = \lambda \times p_{in}(f|e) + (1 - \lambda) \times p_o(f|e) \quad (3)$$

4 Experiments and Results

We first accumulate all the domain specific corpus and clean them. We also use out of domain data to accelerate the performance of the in-domain MT system. The following subsections describe the datasets used for the experiments, detailed experimental settings and systematic evaluation on both the development set and test set.

4.1 Datasets

In-domain Data: The detailed statistics of in-domain data is reported in Table 1. We considered all the data provided by the WMT-2016 organizers for the IT translation task. We combined all data and performed cleaning in two steps: (i) Cleaning-1: following the cleaning process described in (Pal et al., 2015), and (ii) Cleaning 2: using the Moses (Koehn et al., 2007) corpus cleaning scripts with minimum and maximum number of tokens set to 1 and 80 respectively. Additionally, 1000 sentences are used for development set ('Batch 1' in Table 3) and anther 1000 sentences are used for development test set ('Batch2' in Table 3).

Out-domain Data: We utilized all the parallel training data provided by the WMT-2016 shared task organizers for the English-German translation task. The out of domain training data includes Europarl, News Commentary and Common Crawl. this corpus is noisy and contains some non-German, as well as, non-English words and sentences. Therefore, we applied a language identifier (Shuyo, 2010) on both bilingual English–German parallel data and monolingual German corpora. We discarded those parallel sentences from the bilingual training data which were detected as belonging to some different languages by the language identifier. The same method was also applied to the monolingual data. Successively, the corpus cleaning process was carried out first by calculating the global mean ratio of the number of characters in a source sentence to that in the corresponding target sentence and then filtering out sentence pairs that exceed or fall below 20% of the global ratio (Tan and Pal, 2014). Tokenization and punctuation normalization were performed using Moses scripts. In the final step of cleaning, we filtered the parallel training data on maximum allowable sentence length of 80 and sentence length ratio of 1:2 (either direction). Approximately 36% sentences were removed from the total training data during the cleaning process. Table 2 shows the out-domain data statistics after filtering.

4.2 Experimental Settings

We used the standard log-linear PB-SMT model for our experiments. All the experiments were carried out using a maximum phrase length of 7 for the translation model and 5-gram language models. The other experimental settings involved word alignment model between EN–DE trained with Berkeley Aligner (Liang et al., 2006). The phrase-extraction heuristics of (Koehn et al., 2003) were used to build the phrase-based SMT systems. The reordering model was trained with the hierarchical, monotone, swap, left to right bidirectional (hier-mslr-bidirectional) (Galley and Manning, 2008) method and conditioned on both the source and target languages. The 5-gram language models were built using KenLM (Heafield, 2011). Phrase pairs that occur only once in the training data are assigned an unduly high probability mass (i.e., 1). To alleviate this shortcoming, we performed smoothing of the phrase table using the Good-Turing smoothing technique (Foster et al., 2006). System tuning was carried out using Minimum Error Rate Training (MERT) (Och, 2003) on a held out development set (Batch1 in Table 3) of size 1,000 sentences provided by the WMT-2016 task organizers. After the parameters were tuned, decoding was carried out on the held out development test set (Batch2 in Table 3) as well as test set released by the shared task organizers. We evaluated the systems using three well known automatic MT evaluation metrics: BLEU (Papineni et al., 2002), METEOR (Lavie and Agarwal, 2007) and TER (Snover et al., 2006). The evaluation results of our baseline systems trained on in-domain and out-domain data are reported in Table 3.

Data Source		Sentences	Tokens	
			EN	DE
Localization	-	157,414	860,169	814,863
IT Term	-	23,136	52,201	45,773
Technical documentation	Liboffice	95,997	794,498	760,444
	Drupal	4,682	41,081	41,081
	Ubuntu	6,320	120,274	113,792
	Chromium	6,306	38,278	37,631
	Undoc	167,627	5,105,968	4,949,335
Total	-	461,479	7,012,469	6,762,919
Cleaning-1	-	456,042	9,105,378	8,958,348
Cleaning-2	-	440,780	7,553,659	7,426,095

Table 1: In-domain data statistics, Cleaning-1: tokenization and cleaning (Pal et al., 2015) and Cleaning-2 is MOSES cleaner with minimum token is set to 1 and maximum 80

Data	Sentences	Tokens	
		EN	DE
Europarl and news	1,623,546	36,050,888	34,564,547
Common crawl	1,811,826	37,456,978	35,172,840
Total	3,435,372	73,507,866	69,737,387

Table 2: Out-domain cleaned data statistics

5 Result and Analysis

We have taken various attempts to enhance the quality of translation for the English–German IT domain translation task.

Figure 1 shows how data selection method helps to enhance the in-domain baseline system by incrementally adding a subset of data from the out-domain corpus as additional training material.

We applied bilingual cross-perplexity difference based method (cf. Section 3.1) to rank the out-domain sentences according to their proximity to the in-domain data from which we incrementally select top ranking sentence pairs and add them as additional training material to our in-domain training set. We trained the incremental in-domain PB-SMT models in an iterative manner for each incremental batch size of 100K top ranked additional parallel data from the remaining 'ranked' out-domain data. The iterative process is stopped when the learning curve falls down in two successive iterations. BLEU is considered as the objective function for the learning curve experiment. Finally, we selected 400K sentence pairs as additional training material from the entire out-domain data as it provided the optimum result in BLEU on the development test set. The rest of our experiments are carried out with this 400K additional training data. Therefore, our submitted JU-USAAR system is built on 440,780 in-domain training data, as well as 400K additional training data selected from the out-domain parallel corpus.

We made use of the out-domain data selected by the data selection method (Moore and Lewis, 2010; Axelrod et al., 2011) using simple merging as well as interpolation technique (Sennrich, 2012).

Linear interpolation with instant weighting (Sennrich, 2012) was used for interpolating the translation and language models.

Our baseline system was trained on the in-domain English–German parallel corpus containing 440,780 sentence pairs. As reported in Table 4, the baseline system obtained a BLEU score of 20 and TER of 68.7 on the test set. We developed two different systems.

System1: System1 is trained on 440,780 in-domain training data combined with additional 400K parallel sentences selected from the out-domain dataset. This system produced a BLEU score of 31.9 and a TER of 66.6 on the test set which are far better than the baseline scores.

System2: System2 uses exactly the same amount of training data as System1, however, in this case instead of simply merging the two datasets (440,780 in-domain and 400K selected out-domain sentence pairs) separate translation

Data		BLEU	METEOR	TER
Out-domain	Batch1	18.47	24.03	63.18
	Batch2	16.54	24.04	60.33
In-domain	Batch1	26.12	28.48	59.18
	Batch2	30.76	32.67	48.66

Table 3: Experiment result of Baseline system trained on in-domain and out-domain data respectively

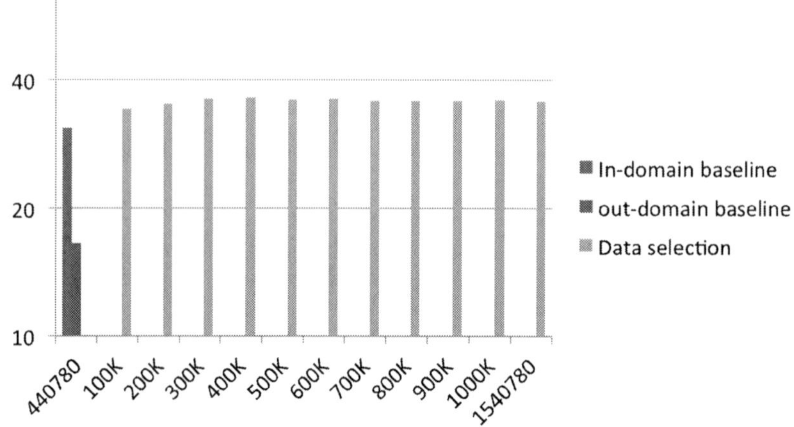

Figure 1: Learning curve experiments on BLEU by incremental data selection of 100K batch size from out-domain data

Systems	BLEU	BLEU (cased)	TER
Baseline	20.0	18.7	68.7
System1	31.9	29.4	66.6
System2	**34.5**	**33.7**	**54.0**

Table 4: Systematic evaluation on test set

models and language models are built on each dataset and they are interpolated based on instant weighting. Before decoding we forced the decoder to avoid translation of URLs. System2 resulted in 34.5 BLEU (14.5 absolute and 72.5% relative improvements over baseline) and 54.0 TER (14.7 absolute and 21.4% relative improvements over baseline) scores. System2 represents our primary submission.

6 Conclusions and Future Work

The JU-USAAR system employs two techniques for improving the performance of MT in the English–German translation task for the IT domain. We used bilingual cross-perplexity difference based data selection method and carried out learning curve experiments to identify additional "in-domain like" training material from the out-domain dataset. We made use of the selected additional training data using both simple merging and interpolation. Simple merging yielded in significant improvements over the baseline while linear interpolation of the translation and language models with instant weighting produced further improvements. Our primary submission (data selection and interpolation based model combination) resulted in 14.5 absolute and 72.5% relative improvements in BLEU and 14.7 absolute and 21.4% relative improvements in TER over the baseline system trained on just the in-domain dataset.

References

Amittai Axelrod, Xiaodong He, and Jianfeng Gao. 2011. Domain Adaptation via Pseudo In-domain Data Selection. In *Proceedings of the Conference on Empirical Methods in Natural Language Processing*, EMNLP '11, pages 355–362.

Nguyen Bach, Qin Gao, and Stephan Vogel. 2008. Improving word alignment with language model based confidence scores. In *Proceedings of the Third Workshop on Statistical Machine Translation*, pages 151–154, Columbus, Ohio, June. Association for Computational Linguistics.

Pratyush Banerjee, Sudip Kumar Naskar, Johann Roturier, Andy Way, and Josef van Genabith. 2011. Domain adaptation in statistical machine translation of user-forum data using component level mixture modelling. In *Proceedings of the 13th Machine Translation Summit (MT Summit XIII)*, pages 285–292. International Association for Machine Translation.

Pratyush Banerjee, Raphael Rubino, Johann Roturier, and Josef van Genabith. 2013. Quality estimation-guided data selection for domain adaptation of SMT. In *Machine Translation Summit XIV*, pages 101–108.

Arianna Bisazza and Marcello Federico. 2012. Cutting the long tail: Hybrid language models for translation style adaptation. In *Proceedings of the 13th Conference of the European Chapter of the Association for Computational Linguistics*, pages 439–448, Avignon, France, April. Association for Computational Linguistics.

Alexandru Ceauşfu, John Tinsley, Jian Zhang, and Andy Way. 2011. Experiments on domain adaptation for patent machine translation in the PLuTO project. In Mikel L. Forcada, Heidi Depraetere, and Vincent Vandeghinste, editors, *Proceedings of the 15th International Conference of the European Association for Machine Translation (EAMT)*, pages 21–28.

Kevin Duh, Katsuhito Sudoh, and Hajime Tsukada. 2010. Analysis of Translation Model Adaptation in Statistical Machine Translation. In *Proceedings of the seventh International Workshop on Spoken Language Translation (IWSLT)*, pages 243–250.

George Foster and Roland Kuhn. 2007. Mixture-model adaptation for smt. In *Proceedings of the Second Workshop on Statistical Machine Translation*, StatMT '07, pages 128–135. Association for Computational Linguistics.

George Foster, Roland Kuhn, and Howard Johnson. 2006. Phrasetable Smoothing for Statistical Machine Translation. In *Proceedings of the 2006 Conference on Empirical Methods in Natural Language Processing*, pages 53–61.

Michel Galley and Christopher D. Manning. 2008. A Simple and Effective Hierarchical Phrase Reordering Model. In *Proceedings of the Conference on Empirical Methods in Natural Language Processing*, pages 848–856.

Barry Haddow and Philipp Koehn. 2012. Analysing the Effect of Out-of-Domain Data on SMT Systems. In *Proceedings of the Seventh Workshop on Statistical Machine Translation*, pages 175–185, Montreal, Canada, June. Association for Computational Linguistics.

Kenneth Heafield. 2011. KenLM: Faster and Smaller Language Model Queries. In *Proceedings of the Sixth Workshop on Statistical Machine Translation*, pages 187–197.

Philipp Koehn, Franz Josef Och, and Daniel Marcu. 2003. Statistical Phrase-based Translation. In *Proceedings of the 2003 Conference of the North American Chapter of the Association for Computational Linguistics on Human Language Technology*, pages 48–54.

Philipp Koehn, Hieu Hoang, Alexandra Birch, Chris Callison-Burch, Marcello Federico, Nicola Bertoldi, Brooke Cowan, Wade Shen, Christine Moran, Richard Zens, Chris Dyer, Ondřej Bojar, Alexandra Constantin, and Evan Herbst. 2007. Moses: Open Source Toolkit for Statistical Machine Translation. In *Proceedings of the 45th Annual Meeting of the ACL on Interactive Poster and Demonstration Sessions*, pages 177–180.

Philipp Koehn. 2004. Statistical significance tests for machine translation evaluation.

Philipp Koehn. 2005. Europarl: A parallel corpus for statistical machine translation.

Alon Lavie and Abhaya Agarwal. 2007. Meteor: An Automatic Metric for MT Evaluation with High Levels of Correlation with Human Judgments. In *Proceedings of the Second Workshop on Statistical Machine Translation*, pages 228–231.

Percy Liang, Ben Taskar, and Dan Klein. 2006. Alignment by agreement. In *Proceedings of the Main Conference on Human Language Technology Conference of the North American Chapter of the Association of Computational Linguistics*, HLT-NAACL '06, pages 104–111, Stroudsburg, PA, USA. Association for Computational Linguistics.

Yajuan Lü, Jin Huang, and Qun Liu. 2007. Improving statistical machine translation performance by training data selection and optimization. In *Proceedings of the 2007 Joint Conference on Empirical Methods in Natural Language Processing and Computational Natural Language Learning (EMNLP-CoNLL)*, pages 343–350.

Spyros Matsoukas, Antti-Veikko I. Rosti, and Bing Zhang. 2009. Discriminative corpus weight estimation for machine translation. In *Proceedings of the 2009 Conference on Empirical Methods in Natural Language Processing: Volume 2 - Volume 2*, EMNLP '09, pages 708–717. Association for Computational Linguistics.

Robert C. Moore and William Lewis. 2010. Intelligent selection of language model training data. In *Proceedings of the ACL 2010 Conference Short Papers*, ACLShort '10, pages 220–224. Association for Computational Linguistics.

Franz Josef Och. 2003. Minimum Error Rate Training in Statistical Machine Translation. In *Proceedings of the 41st Annual Meeting on Association for Computational Linguistics - Volume 1*, pages 160–167.

Santanu Pal, Sudip Naskar, and Josef van Genabith. 2015. UdS-Sant: English–German Hybrid Machine Translation System. In *Proceedings of the Tenth Workshop on Statistical Machine Translation*, pages 152–157, Lisbon, Portugal, September. Association for Computational Linguistics.

Kishore Papineni, Salim Roukos, Todd Ward, and Wei-Jing Zhu. 2002. BLEU: A Method for Automatic Evaluation of Machine Translation. In *Proceedings of the 40th Annual Meeting on Association for Computational Linguistics*, ACL '02, pages 311–318.

Rico Sennrich, Holger Schwenk, and Walid Aransa. 2013. A Multi-Domain Translation Model Framework for Statistical Machine Translation. In *Proceedings of the 51st Annual Meeting of the Association for Computational Linguistics*, pages 832–840.

Rico Sennrich. 2012. Perplexity minimization for translation model domain adaptation in statistical machine translation. In *Proceedings of the 13th Conference of the European Chapter of the Association for Computational Linguistics*, pages 539–549, Avignon, France, April. Association for Computational Linguistics.

Abhinav Sethy, Panayiotis Georgiou, and Shrikanth Narayanan. 2006. Selecting relevant text subsets from web-data for building topic specific language models. In *Proceedings of the Human Language Technology Conference of the NAACL, Companion Volume: Short Papers*, pages 145–148, New York City, USA, June. Association for Computational Linguistics.

Nakatani Shuyo. 2010. Language Detection Library for Java.

Matthew Snover, Bonnie Dorr, Richard Schwartz, Linnea Micciulla, and John Makhoul. 2006. A study of Translation Edit Rate with Targeted Human Annotation. In *Proceedings of association for machine translation in the Americas*, pages 223–231.

Liling Tan and Santanu Pal. 2014. Manawi: Using Multi-word Expressions and Named Entities to Improve Machine Translation. In *Proceedings of Ninth Workshop on Statistical Machine Translation*.

Dictionary-based Domain Adaptation of MT Systems without Retraining

Rudolf Rosa, Roman Sudarikov, Michal Novák, Martin Popel, Ondřej Bojar
Charles University in Prague, Faculty of Mathematics and Physics
Institute of Formal and Applied Linguistics
Malostranské náměstí 25, Prague, Czech Republic
{rosa,sudarikov,mnovak,popel,bojar}@ufal.mff.cuni.cz

Abstract

We describe our submission to the IT-domain translation task of WMT 2016. We perform domain adaptation with dictionary data on already trained MT systems with no further retraining. We apply our approach to two conceptually different systems developed within the QTLeap project: TectoMT and Moses, as well as Chimera, their combination. In all settings, our method improves the translation quality. Moreover, the basic variant of our approach is applicable to any MT system, including a black-box one.

1 Introduction

In this paper, we describe our work on domain adaptation of machine translation systems, performed in close collaboration with numerous partners within the QTLeap project.[1] The project focuses on high-quality translation for the IT domain, and our systems were submitted to the IT-domain translation task of the First Conference on Machine Translation (WMT16).[2] The experiments relate to our previous work on domain adaptation (Rosa et al., 2015), in which we also surveyed and evaluated common domain adaptation techniques.

The aim of our work is to find a way to perform domain adaptation of an already trained MT system without having to retrain it, which may be a useful ability for reasons discussed in § 2. We focus on forced translation of domain-specific entities according to a bilingual lexicon, as described in § 3. We explore several methods based on preprocessing and postprocessing of the data

before and after processing them by the MT system, and provide both system-specific and system-independent approaches.

We employ the MT systems used and further developed by us and our partners within the QTLeap project, namely Moses (Koehn et al., 2007), TectoMT (Žabokrtský et al., 2008), and their combination Chimera (Bojar et al., 2013). We briefly describe the systems in § 4. In § 5, we evaluate our domain-adaptation methods (as well as the standard method of retraining the system with all available data) applied to these MT systems for translation from English to Czech (EN→CS), Spanish (EN→ES), Dutch (EN→NL), and Portuguese (EN→PT).

2 Motivation

A quite typical situation in domain adaptation of an MT system is as follows: there is an MT system trained on large general-domain data, and there is a small amount of parallel data from the target domain, often in the form of a dictionary rather than parallel sentences.

In such a case, the standard solution is to add the in-domain data to the general-domain data and retrain the MT system; or, if there is support from the system, to train a secondary in-domain translation model (phrase table) and add it to the system (which may require retuning the system). However, in this work, we investigate the options of performing domain adaptation of the system without having to train (or tune) anything.

There is a range of reasons why one would avoid retraining the system for the specific domain, some of which we list below.

Training costs The simplest reason is that the costs of retraining the system might be impractical or even prohibitive, be it costs in terms of computational power, money, or time. This issue may be-

---

[1] http://qtleap.eu
[2] http://www.statmt.org/wmt16/
it-translation-task.html

Proceedings of the First Conference on Machine Translation, Volume 2: Shared Task Papers, pages 449–455,
Berlin, Germany, August 11-12, 2016. ©2016 Association for Computational Linguistics

come even more pronounced with the modern neural MT systems, which can take weeks to train.[3]

Running costs In case there is a number of separate domains for which the MT system must be adapted, even the costs of operating a number of separate MT systems may become significant. This situation may occur e.g. in a translation company which uses a lot of domain-specific or even client-specific glossaries. Operating only one system with lightweight domain adaptation done in preprocessing and/or postprocessing might save a lot of costs.

Unsuitable data In some cases, the in-domain data itself may not be suitable for standard MT processing. Dictionary-like and/or small data cannot be used to reliably estimate translation probabilities, which may lead to the in-domain data having only a low influence on the MT system. These problems and possible solutions are also discussed by Daumé III (2009).

Black-box scenario This is a rather theoretical situation in the research area, but in practice it constitutes a real and common mode of operation. Both individual and business users often simply use a trained MT system as a "black box", without the ability or possibility to retrain it or directly modify it. Such users then have no other option than to resort to domain adaptation methods that rely only on preprocessing and postprocessing.

Dependence on non-retrainable tools Many MT systems consist of several components, some of which may require specific data for training, not available for the target domain, or they may even be rule-based and thus only adaptable through a certain amount of manual labor. A prominent example is the TectoMT system, which relies, among other, on morphological taggers and syntactic parsers to analyze the input sentences, which are typically trained on general-domain data (mostly news) and are rather hard to adapt to domains that differ significantly lexically or even structurally. However, even simple tools, such as the standard Moses tokenizer, may need to be adjusted to the target domain. In the IT domain specifically, we frequently observe structures such as URLs, file paths, computer commands, or chains of menu items, which are rather rare or even non-existent

in the general-domain texts, and thus can greatly confuse the analyzers; this is especially true for TectoMT, where such unexpected structures cause significant problems already to the morphological tagger and dependency parser, leading to quite unpredictable results in the subsequent linguistic processing. In such cases, a careful preprocessing may be able to adjust the input texts to better resemble general-domain texts, hiding "surprising" structures from the system.

3 Method

The general principle of our method is to force-translate some domain-specific expressions according to a gazetteer (a domain-specific bilingual lexicon), without modifying our MT system.

Based on an error analysis on the Batch2 part of the provided in-domain data, we target named entities from the IT domain that need to be translated or localized, such as menu items, button names, their sequences, and messages. These are expected to appear in a fixed form, which allows us to apply a technique of directly matching the expressions from a gazetteer in the surface source text and replacing them by their equivalents in the target language.[4] As our gazetteer, we use the dictionary available from the website of the task, constructed automatically mainly from localization files of various software products.

The crucial task is to identify the source expressions to be force-translated (§ 3.1). The technical implementation of the forced translation can then be either independent of the MT system (§ 3.2), or, if the system has support for forced translations, a system-specific method can be used (§ 3.3, § 3.4).

We implemented the methods in the Treex NLP framework of Popel and Žabokrtský (2010).[5]

3.1 Identification of domain-specific entities

This is the most complex stage of the whole process. Lexicon items are matched in the source tokenized text and the matched items, which can possibly span several neighboring tokens, are marked for forced translation.

In the initialization stage, the source-language part of the lexicon is loaded and structured in a word-based trie to reduce time complexity of the text search. In the current implementation, if an

---

[3]That said, if the training is done with online learning (or mini-batches) a simple domain-adaptation technique is to continue training on in-domain data, which is much faster.

[4]This means that only the base forms contained in the gazetteer are processed; expressions in a different form are not handled.

[5]http://ufal.mff.cuni.cz/treex

expression appears more than once in the source gazetteer list, only its first occurrence is stored, regardless what its translation is.[6]

The trie is then used to match the expressions from the gazetteer in the source text. As they might overlap, each matched expressions is assigned a score estimating the extent to which it is a named entity, using a heuristic scorer:

- +10 if it starts with a capital letter; -10 if not
- +10 if the corresponding gazetteer item starts with a capital letter; -50 if not
- +2 if it matches the gazetteer case-sensitively
- +1 if all its words start with a capital letter; -1 if not
- -50 if it spans the first word of the sentence; +1 if not
- -50 if its last word is "menu"
- -100 if it contains only non-alphabetical characters

The resulting score is then multiplied by the number of tokens in the matched expression.

The matches with positive score are ordered by the score and filtered to get non-overlapping matches, taking those with higher score first. Neighboring entities are then collapsed into one.[7]

The translation of each entity is then constructed as a concatenation of the translations of the source entities according to the lexicon, and the entity is marked in one of the ways described in the following sections.

3.2 XXX placeholders

A simple approach is to replace the matched entities by unique placeholders (such as "xxxitemaxxx", "xxxitembxxx"...), storing the corresponding translations into a text file together with their assigned placeholders.

The preprocessed text is then passed through the MT system; if sufficiently complex placeholders are constructed, it is safe to assume that they will constitute out-of-vocabulary items for the MT system and will pass through unchanged (that is, unless the system has a policy of dropping OOVs).

Finally, the translated text is postprocessed, replacing each placeholder with the corresponding translation from the text file.

This approach is independent of the MT system, and can even be used in a black-box scenario. However, introducing a large number of OOVs may negatively influence the performance of the MT system, as it forces it to use a very limited linear context around the placeholders.

3.3 Moses XML annotation

Moses supports XML markup for marking forced translations of some parts of the sentence.[8] For instance, in the sentence "Click the icon, then select Shut Down.", we can suggest to translate "Shut Down" into Czech as "Vypnout":

```
Click the icon, then select
<item translation="Vypnout"
   prob="0.8">Shut Down</item>.
```

The XML annotation feature is enabled in the decoder by using the `-xml-input` switch, instructing the decoder to do one of the following (based on the value of the switch):

- to treat the XML markup as part of the sentence (`pass-through`) – the default,
- to strip the XML markup (`ignore`),
- to make the suggested translation compete with phrase table choices (`inclusive` or `constraint`),
- or to use only the suggested translation, ignoring all phrases that overlap with the annotated span (`exclusive`).

We always used only one forced translation for each entity, and the `exclusive` setting. However, Moses supports listing a set of suggested translations together with translation probabilities, leaving it up to the decoder to choose the best translation in the given context. We leave this, together with experimenting with the `inclusive` setting, for future research.

3.4 TectoTM/Treex wild attributes

Unlike Moses, which operates on plaintext only, TectoMT uses a structured layered representation of the texts, which makes it easy to add a new annotation layer specifying the translations. The easiest is to use a set of general-purpose Treex attributes, called *wild attributes*.

The preprocessing consists of replacing each matched entity with a placeholder (we used the word "Menu" as a placeholder) and storing the translation into a wild attribute of the entity. This

---

[6] Therefore, the performance of gazetteer matching machinery depends on the ordering of the entries in the gazetteer.

[7] The entities are collapsed also when they are separated by a > symbol; the separators are retained in the forced translations. This measure is aimed at translation of menu items and button labels sequences, which frequently appear in the IT domain data.

[8] http://www.statmt.org/moses/?n=Advanced.Hybrid

is done just after tokenization of the source text, so that for subsequent analysis steps, such as linguistic taggers and parsers, the entity already appears as one token. Moreover, we assume that using a common word for the placeholder makes the sentence even more fluent and easy to process for the analyzers.

The specified translation is forced in the transfer step, in which the decoder checks for the wild attribute, and, if present, uses its contents to generate the translation of the token instead of its translation models.

3.5 Forced non-translations

For TectoMT, we use an additional preprocessing step, which we call *forced non-translations*: we enforce certain special structures, frequent in the IT domain, to remain untranslated (namely URLs, e-mail addresses, Windows and Unix paths and file names, and shell commands). In principle, this is the same thing as forced translations, but based on regular expressions rather than a dictionary, since we identify these entities based on structural rather than lexical cues.

Although preliminary experiments with TectoMT and Batch2 dataset indicated a significant potential of this step (up to +0.4 BLEU), further evaluation revealed that this is mostly specific to this particular setup, as Batch2 contains a large number of these structures, and TectoMT greatly benefits from the single-token placeholder analysis of these structures. The Moses tokenizer can be setup to tokenize URLs and e-mails as single tokens, and even in case of multi-token analysis the Moses decoder is not confused so much as the TectoMT analysis steps.

Therefore, we omit an analysis of performance of the forced non-translations from the evaluation section: we simply always apply it in the TectoMT system, but never in the Moses system.[9]

4 MT Systems

We use two systems, Moses (Koehn et al., 2007) and TectoMT (Žabokrtský et al., 2008), as well as their combination Chimera (Bojar et al., 2013); see also a more detailed description of the Moses and TectoMT systems within the QTLeap project by Gaudio et al. (2016) in these proceedings.

All of our systems are "constrained", i.e. trained and tuned using only the general-domain and IT-domain training data provided by the IT-translation task organizers. All the three systems domain-adapted: they are trained and tuned on the Batch1 and Batch2 parts of the in-domain training data, as described below. Thus, even without the domain adaptation through in-domain lexicons (which were also provided by the task organizers), the systems constitute strong baselines within the IT domain. Still, the lexicons were not used to train nor tune the systems.

4.1 Moses

Moses is a standard phrase-based statistical machine translation system.

We train Moses on general-domain training data and tune it on the Batch2 part from in-domain training data using MERT (Och, 2003).

We perform domain adaptation of Moses using either XXX placeholders or XML annotations. EN→CS uses factored translation (with part-of-speech tags as additional target-side factors), which is not compatible with the XML annotations, and thus only XXX placeholders are used for EN→CS.

We apply some rather standard pre- and post-processing steps (implemented as Treex blocks).
Preprocessing:

- segmentation into sentences[10]
- tokenization[11,12]
- normalization of quotes, dashes and contracted forms (for EN→CS)[13]
- entity escaping[14]
- truecasing (for EN→NL)[15]/lowercasing

Postprocessing:

- projection of case of identical words from source to target[16]
- sentence capitalization[17]

4.2 TectoMT

TectoMT is a hybrid MT system, combining statistical and rule-based Treex blocks to perform translation with transfer on the layer of tectogrammatical (deep) syntax.

---

[9]This holds even for the Chimera combination, i.e. this method is applied in its TectoMT component but not in the Moses component.

[10]`W2A::ResegmentSentences`
[11]`W2A::TokenizeMoses`
[12]`W2A::TokenizeMorphoDiTa` for EN→CS
[13]`W2W::NormalizeEnglishSentence`
[14]`W2A::EscapeMoses`
[15]`W2A::TruecaseMoses`
[16]`A2A::ProjectCase`
[17]`A2W::CapitalizeSentStart`

We use TectoMT's translation model interpolation (Rosa et al., 2015), uniformly interpolating a translation model trained on the out-of-domain training data with one trained on the Batch1 part of the in-domain training data. Unlike Moses, TectoMT does not support automatic tuning of parameters; however, some parameters were tuned manually using Batch2 from in-domain training data.

We only experiment with domain adaptation of TectoMT via Treex wild attributes (§ 3.4).

4.3 Chimera

Chimera is a system combination of TectoTM and Moses. The input text is first translated by TectoMT, thus creating an additional parallel corpus from the input and the output. This is used to construct a secondary phrase table for Moses, which is then applied to the input to produce the translations (Bojar et al., 2013).

In Chimera, we always use domain adaptation for the TectoMT component (via Treex wild attributes), and only experiment with switching it on or off for the Moses component.

In the experiments reported in this paper, we do not employ the Depfix component of Chimera (Rosa et al., 2012), as it has little relevance to the domain-adaptation problem and would thus clutter the results unnecessarily. However, Depfix is used in the EN→CS Chimera system submitted to the translation task.

4.4 WMT submissions

We submitted the following constrained systems to the IT domain translation task of WMT16:

Chimera with domain adaptation using XXX placeholders in the Moses component. For EN→CS, Depfix is also applied. Also denoted as Chimera-plus.

TectoMT with domain adaptation using Treex annotations. This is the 3rd pilot MT system in the QTLeap project (still in development).

Moses baseline vanilla Moses system, tuned on Batch1 only.[18] QTLeap pilot 0.

Chimera pure non-adapted Chimera system, without Depfix postprocessing. Only submitted for EN→CS.

---

[18]Unlike the Moses system used in the experiments reported in this paper, which is tuned on the Batch2 portion of the in-domain training data.

System	Annotations	→ES	→NL	→PT
Moses	(not adapted)	22.23	23.40	14.01
	XXX	23.61	24.89	15.47
	XML	**24.22**	**25.41**	**15.58**
Chimera	(not adapted)	26.01	21.82	13.11
	XXX	26.89	**23.52**	14.19
	XML	**27.40**	23.26	**14.21**

Table 1: BLEU evaluation of two forced translation styles for Moses: XXX placeholders and XML markup. For comparison, the non-adapted system is also included.

5 Results and Discussion

We use the WMT16 IT task test set (i.e. Batch3 from the QTLeap corpus[19]) to evaluate our experiments using (case-insensitive) BLEU (Papineni et al., 2002).

First, in Table 1, we compare the two annotation styles we can use for Moses. In general, the XML annotations perform better, in half of the cases leading to a result better by about +0.5 BLEU than that of the XXX placeholders while performing worse only once. Although the documentation in the Moses manual is not very detailed in this respect, we believe that the XML annotations are more palatable to the language model, which can then make meaningful decisions at the boundaries of the force-translated entities, while the XXX placeholders simply constitute out-of-vocabulary items for the language model and thus the context it can use is limited. We therefore stick to XML annotations in Moses in further experiments.[20] Still, even the results obtained using the XXX placeholders are competitive and clearly improve over the non-adapted baseline.

In Table 2, we compare the adapted and non-adapted systems. In all but one case,[21] the domain adapted system performs much better than the non-adapted baseline, with an average gain of +1.3 BLEU.

As for the the individual systems, Moses typ-

---

[19]http://metashare.metanet4u.eu/go2/
qtleapcorpus

[20]However, we used the XXX placeholders in the systems submitted to the WMT16 IT domain translation task, since the XML preprocessing was not implemented in time. Also, for EN→CS we still use the XXX because the XML placeholders are not compatible with the factored translation.

[21]For EN→CS Chimera, our domain adaptation improves case-sensitive BLEU, but worsens case-insensitive BLEU (23.47 vs. 23.36 in Table 2) and also human evaluation (rank 1–2 vs. 4–5 in Table 3). Two possible explanations are: a) the TectoMT component of Chimera is already domain-adapted with gazetteers, b) EN→CS Chimera uses XXX (but for the other languages in Table 2, Chimera uses XML).

System	Adapted	→CS	→ES	→NL	→PT
TectoMT	no	19.98	23.24	18.83	13.87
	yes	**21.89**	**24.31**	**19.89**	**15.51**
Moses	no	23.25	22.23	23.40	14.01
	yes	**23.71**	**24.22**	**25.41**	**15.58**
Chimera	no	**23.47**	26.01	21.82	13.11
	yes	23.36	**27.40**	**23.26**	**14.21**

Table 2: BLEU evaluation of the domain adaptation, using Treex annotations for TectoMT and XML annotations for Moses (except for EN→CS, which uses XXX annotations in Moses).

System	Adapted	→CS	→ES	→NL	→PT
TectoMT	yes	3	**1–2**	3	**1**
Moses	no	4–5	3	4	3
Chimera	no	**1–2**			
	yes	4–5	**1–2**	2	2
another		**1–2**		**1**	

Table 3: Human evaluation ranks of constrained systems in WMT2016 IT-domain task.

ically outperformed both TectoMT and Chimera. The only exception is EN→ES, where TectoMT is stronger than Moses, and the Chimera combination is even stronger than the individual systems.[22]

Table 3 shows results of the human evaluation based on TrueSkill scores (for details, see the overview paper in these proceedings). For EN→CS and EN→ES, there was not better constrained system than Chimera (for EN→CS the non-adapted one, see footnote 21). For EN→NL and EN→PT, Chimera was the second best system (for EN→PT, TectoMT was better than Chimera, in accordance with the BLEU results in Table 2).

Finally, in Table 4, we compare our domain adaptation of Moses (through preprocessing and XML annotations) with the standard approach, where a secondary in-domain phrase table was created from the provided in-domain bilingual lexicons (this experiment was only performed for EN→NL). As could be expected, the standard approach is more powerful, leading to a gain of +4 BLEU, while our approach achieves a +2 BLEU gain. Therefore, the standard approach should be used whenever possible. Still, the fact that our simple and light-weight domain adaptation techniques are able to get half of the achievable improvement is encouraging for scenarios where the standard approach is not applicable.

---

[22]TectoMT's quality depends not only on the size of training data but also on the taggers, parsers etc. used in the pipeline. Chimera profits from different distribution of errors types in TectoMT and Moses.

Adaptation	→NL
(not adapted)	23.40
XML annotations	25.41
In-domain phrase table	**27.48**

Table 4: BLEU evaluation of the Moses system on EN→NL, comparing the baseline non-adapted Moses, Moses adapted by forced translations annotated with XML markup, and Moses using a secondary in-domain phrase table.

6 Conclusion

Domain adaptation without retraining can be effectively performed through preprocessing and postprocessing, and achieves about half of the quality gain compared to the standard method (training an additional in-domain phrase table), as measured in BLEU improvement above the baseline non-adapted Moses system.

A system-specific forced translation mechanism, such as Moses XML markup, can perform better than simple placeholders. Still, even the placeholders are competitive and may be useful if the MT system in question does not support any mechanism for forcing specific translations.

Acknowledgments

This research was supported by the grants FP7-ICT-2013-10-610516 (QTLeap), GAUK 1572314, SVV 260 333, and using language resources distributed by the LINDAT/CLARIN project of the Ministry of Education, Youth and Sports of the Czech Republic (LM2015071). We thank the two anonymous reviewers for useful comments.

References

Ondřej Bojar, Rudolf Rosa, and Aleš Tamchyna. 2013. Chimera–three heads for English-to-Czech translation. In *Proceedings of the Eighth Workshop on Statistical Machine Translation*, pages 90–96.

Hal Daumé III. 2009. Frustratingly easy domain adaptation. *CoRR*, abs/0907.1815.

Rosa Gaudio, Petya Osenova, Kiril Simov, Gorka Labaka, and Dieke Oele. 2016. SMT and hybrid systems of the QTLeap project in the WTM16 IT-task. In *Proceedings of the 1st Conference on Machine Translation*, Stroudsburg, PA, USA. Association for Computational Linguistics.

Philipp Koehn, Hieu Hoang, Alexandra Birch, Chris Callison-Burch, Marcello Federico, Nicola Bertoldi,

Brooke Cowan, Wade Shen, Christine Moran, Richard Zens, Chris Dyer, Ondřej Bojar, Alexandra Constantin, and Evan Herbst. 2007. Moses: Open source toolkit for statistical machine translation. In *Proceedings of the 45th Annual Meeting of the ACL on Interactive Poster and Demonstration Sessions*, ACL '07, pages 177–180, Stroudsburg, PA, USA. Association for Computational Linguistics.

Franz Josef Och. 2003. Minimum error rate training in statistical machine translation. In *Proceedings of the 41st Annual Meeting on Association for Computational Linguistics - Volume 1*, ACL '03, pages 160–167, Stroudsburg, PA, USA. Association for Computational Linguistics.

Kishore Papineni, Salim Roukos, Todd Ward, and Wei-Jing Zhu. 2002. BLEU: A method for automatic evaluation of machine translation. In *Proceedings of the 40th Annual Meeting on Association for Computational Linguistics*, ACL '02, pages 311–318, Stroudsburg, PA, USA. Association for Computational Linguistics.

Martin Popel and Zdeněk Žabokrtský. 2010. TectoMT: Modular NLP framework. In *Proceedings of the 7th International Conference on Advances in Natural Language Processing*, IceTAL'10, pages 293–304, Berlin, Heidelberg. Springer-Verlag.

Rudolf Rosa, David Mareček, and Ondřej Dušek. 2012. DEPFIX: A system for automatic correction of Czech MT outputs. In *Proceedings of the Seventh Workshop on Statistical Machine Translation*, WMT '12, pages 362–368, Stroudsburg, PA, USA. Association for Computational Linguistics.

Rudolf Rosa, Ondřej Dušek, Michal Novák, and Martin Popel. 2015. Translation model interpolation for domain adaptation in TectoMT. In Jan Hajič and António Branco, editors, *Proceedings of the 1st Deep Machine Translation Workshop*, pages 89–96, Praha, Czechia. ÚFAL MFF UK.

Zdeněk Žabokrtský, Jan Ptáček, and Petr Pajas. 2008. TectoMT: Highly modular MT system with tectogrammatics used as transfer layer. In *Proceedings of the Third Workshop on Statistical Machine Translation*, StatMT '08, pages 167–170.

English-Portuguese Biomedical Translation Task Using a Genuine Phrase-Based Statistical Machine Translation Approach

José Aires[1,2]   Gabriel Pereira Lopes[1,2]   Luís Gomes[1,2]

[1] NOVA LINCS, Faculdade de Ciências e Tecnologia, Universidade Nova de Lisboa, Portugal
[2] ISTRION BOX, Translation and Revision, Lda, Portugal
`{jose.aires,gabriel.lopes,luis.gomes}@istrionbox.com`

Abstract

Our approach to produce translations for the ACL-2016 Biomedical Translation Task on the English-Portuguese language pair, in both directions, is described. Own preliminary tests results and final results, measured by the shared task organizers, are also presented.

1 Introduction

This paper shows how we obtained our results using our patented Machine Translation system (Lopes et al., 2015) to produce translations for the English-Portuguese language pair from the Biomedical Translation Task.

Our approach differs from common Statistical Machine Translation approaches like Moses (Koehn et al., 2007) in several aspects:

- phrases are not analyzed at their word level in any model;

- the language model depends on the target alternatives of given adjacent sources and does not try to avoid null scores to phrases that do not occur;

- the translation score is not log-linear, but instead a tuned weighted average between the translation model and the language model, and so no smoothing techniques are required;

- several models can be used with different relevances or weights; and

- instead of simply relying on statistics, we include human validation and correction on several stages of the system, namely for validating extracted term translations, to improve the quality of the source data used in the automatically produced translations.

As requested, the translation results were produced using the sentence-aligned training data described below (for the English-Portuguese language pair, in our case), provided by the shared task organizers:

- **medline-pubmed**: parallel corpora from medline;

- **scielo-gma-biological**: parallel biological documents from the Scielo database (Neves et al., 2016); and

- **scielo-gma-health**: parallel health documents from the Scielo database (Neves et al., 2016).

Table 1 shows the features of the English (en) and Portuguese (pt) languages of each provided corpora, namely their number of lines and words.

corpus	lines	words
medline-pubmed-en	74,645	917,307
medline-pubmed-pt	74,645	1,041,079
scielo-gma-biological-en	120,301	3,338,244
scielo-gma-biological-pt	120,301	3,736,817
scielo-gma-health-en	507,987	13,443,076
scielo-gma-health-pt	507,987	14,901,240

Table 1: Training corpora data after normalization.

The translation task then consisted in translating one document from English to Portuguese and another from Portuguese to English, for both the biological and the health domains, with the number of lines and words from those test documents shown in Table 2.

Besides the provided training data, we have also included our English and European Portuguese bilingual lexicon (described in §2.3.2), as well as our named entities database, for additional term coverage.

Proceedings of the First Conference on Machine Translation, Volume 2: Shared Task Papers, pages 456–462,
Berlin, Germany, August 11-12, 2016. ©2016 Association for Computational Linguistics

document	lines	words
biological_pt2en	4,029	119,410
biological_en2pt	4,333	111,038
health_pt2en	3,826	111,073
health_en2pt	3,858	96,240

Table 2: Test documents data after normalization.

The training corpora had to undergo several processing stages in order to support the production of the intended translations, as described in the following section.

2 Data Processing

In order to produce translations, our system (like any other Statistical Machine Translation system) requires a translation model and a language model to support the translation decoding stage. To calculate such models the available data had to go through several processing steps described in the following subsections.

Since each of the training corpus has been made available separately, we also opted to process each of them separately so that we were then able to use them with different weights, assigning more or less weight to models with higher or lower relevance, respectively. See extended explanation in §4.

2.1 Considerations about the provided data

It should be noted that we have detected a few flaws in the provided data, namely several sentences incorrectly considered as parallel, as well as the existence of many spelling errors, not only in the training data, but also in the testing documents.

We believe that many of the typos result from PDF extraction and/or OCR processes, which are never perfect, having found and corrected a total of 127,198 misspellings. Yet, it should be noted that some misspelling errors are easy to correct, but errors which still produce correct words require sentence analysis which was not carried out.

Some of the parallel problems are illustrated, for instance, by having the first Portuguese line from medline-pubmed *"ERRATA."* aligned with the first English line *"Inequalities in self-rated health: an analysis of the Brazilian and Portuguese populations."*, which should be *"ER-RATA."* instead.

Filtering wrong translation units as the one above, as well as translation units which the language was not Portuguese, reduced this corpora by almost 2,000 translation units.

Some errors were simply detected by chance, like first and last entries of medline-pubmed, while other errors were detected by looking at the untranslated terms in the initial testing §3 and realizing that some terms were misspellings, as well as spelling and vocabulary differences between European and Brazilian Portuguese.

corpus	lines	words
medline-pubmed-en	74,645	917,307
medline-pubmed-rev-en	72,651	898,051
medline-pubmed-pt	74,645	1,041,079
medline-pubmed-rev-pt	72,651	1,006,069

Table 3: medline-pubmed revision impact.

Table 3 shows the differences between the original version medline-pubmed and its revised version medline-pubmed-rev. The reduction in size towards the revised version is mainly due to the removal of non-parallel sentences.

However, efforts to correct such situations were only made over the mentioned medline-pubmed parallel document set, since the other sets were significantly larger, as shown in Table 1. Also, no corrections were applied to the testing documents because we assumed they were not supposed to be edited.

Yet, another "noise" element was the already mentioned difference in spelling and vocabulary between European Portuguese (which has been our main focus of attention throughout our research experience) and Brazilian Portuguese (the version of the provided biomedical data), which can also impact results negatively.

2.2 Text tokenization and normalization

Text tokenization ensures that words are properly separated by a single blank space, while normalization ensures that they are represented by a "standard" version. In English, this means that cases like *"wasn't"* or *"isn't"* are going to be replaced by *"was not"* and *"is not"*, respectively. In Portuguese, this means that cases like *"do"* (*of the*) or *"nas"* (*in the*) are going to be replaced by *"de o"* (*of the*) and *"em as"* (*in the*), respectively. These tokenization and normalization changes are reverted when presenting the final translation results.

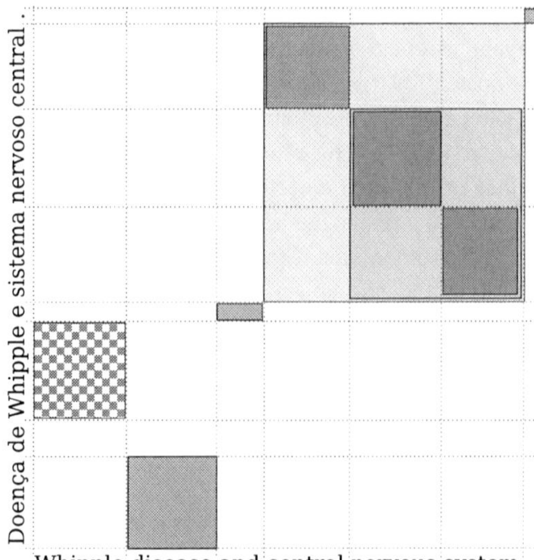

Figure 1: Example lexicon- and cognate-based alignment of a short sentence from the medline-pubmed corpus. Gray-filled rectangles represent word- and phrasal-matches from the lexicon while the checkerboard-filled rectangle shows a cognaticity-based match.

2.3 Phrase alignment

Phrase-level alignment was obtained with a modified version of the lexicon-based aligner proposed by Gomes (2009). The aligner matches bilingual phrase pairs provided in an input lexicon (described ahead in §2.3.2) and selects a maximal-coverage[1] subset of *coherent* alignments. While the original method imposed a monotonicity constraint, i.e. it selected a maximal-coverage chain of phrase alignments without allowing phrase reorderings, the new method applied has a more relaxed coherency criteria: it only requires that a source-language phrase is not simultaneously aligned with two distinct target-language phrases. Therefore, it allows phrase reordering as shown in the example in Figure 1.

2.3.1 Alignment as an optimization problem

Similar to the ILP (Integer Linear Programming) solution proposed by (DeNero and Klein, 2008), we treat the alignment problem as an optimization problem, but we employ a greedy optimization algorithm which allows us to align longer sentences with reasonable time and memory. The algorithm

constructs a solution (a set of coherent alignments) incrementally. It starts by settling alignments of longer phrases, which tend to be more reliable, and progresses towards shorter phrases or words, which are allowed to align only if they are coherent with previously settled alignments.

2.3.2 Input bilingual lexicon

Our EN-PT input lexicon has 931,568 manually validated translations (words and phrases). This lexicon has been compiled in a long term effort started in the context of project ISTRION[2]. The translations were extracted automatically from several corpora, including Europarl (Koehn and Monz, 2005), JRC-Acquis (Steinberger et al., 2006), OPUS EMEA (Tiedemann, 2009) and others, using a combination of complementary alignment and extraction methods: GIZA (Och and Ney, 2003), Anymalign (Lardilleux and Lepage, 2009), spelling similarity measure SpSim (Gomes and Lopes, 2011) combined with co-occurrence Dice measure, and others. The automatically extracted word and phrasal translations were automatically classified, prior to human validation, using an SVM classifier trained on previously validated translations as described by Mahesh et al. (2015). The automatic classification speeds up human validation because very few translations (less than 5%) are incorrectly classified, and only those need to be manually labeled as correct or incorrect.

We did not perform any extraction or validation of new translations from the corpus provided for this shared task. We did, however, complement our lexicon with cognate and homograph alignments using the SpSim (Gomes and Lopes, 2011) spelling similarity measure.

2.3.3 Lexicon coverage

Our lexicon covers 59.5% of the EN corpus tokens and 55.4% of the PT corpus tokens. There were 143,317 unique phrasal translations matched out of 931,568 in our lexicon. The cognaticity-based matching was responsible for aligning 8% of the EN corpus and 7.2% of the PT corpus[3]. The remainder 32.5% of the EN corpus and 37.4% of the PT corpus were left unaligned. These unaligned tokens are handled as gaps by the phrase table extraction algorithm described in (Aires et al., 2009).

---

[1]*Maximal-coverage* means that the selected phrase alignments cover as much text as possible from both sentences

[2]Project ISTRION was funded by the Portuguese Foundation for Science and Technology under contract PTDC/EIA-EIA/114521/2009

[3]cognaticity alignment was applied only to tokens not covered by the input lexicon

2.4 Language model training

The language model used is supported by the indexation of the texts in each language of the provided corpora. Such indexation will support determining the likelihood of the occurrence of phrases in the target language for the several adjacent translation fragments in decoding, a process based on the structures presented in (Aires et al., 2008).

2.5 Translation model training

The translation model depends on the alignment to determine phrase translation equivalents by establishing phrase relations between source and target languages, as well as to determine a degree of likelihood of those same relations, to be used in decoding to produce new translations, a process based on the methodology presented in (Aires et al., 2009).

2.6 Decoding

The decoding stage is the one that will finally produce the actual translations. First, an original text is fragmented into smaller pieces of text, which will then be used to retrieve their corresponding translations. The several combinations of the translations of those smaller pieces will represent many possible translations and the purpose of decoding is to find the most likely one, according to the provided scores from the language and the translation models. As mentioned before, separate models can be obtained from separate corpora and be assigned with different relevances or weights, according to their importance to the translation in question.

As such, and as explained in Lopes et al. (2015), decoding is carried out as a best path finding in a directed acyclic graph, where its edges are weighed by: the translation model score between source and target phrases; and the language model scores between adjacent target phrases. Each complete path will represent a possible translation in which the final score is a composition of the scores of the several edges that compose the given path. An additional penalty is introduced to provide lower scores to larger paths, which are known to produce worse results.

3 Initial Testing Preparation

Since no development data was supplied, we took the initiative to prepare some development sets in order to have an idea of the most promising set of parameters to be used in our system over the provided data to produce the intended translations. As such, several documents were removed from the original training data, composed by the medline-pubmed, biological and health sets, applying the training methods on the remaining documents and using the selected ones to translate and compare the translations against their originals by determining their BLEU (Papineni et al., 2002) scores. However, in order to get a clearer picture of the type of results that could be expected, some additional tests were carried out including the selected set of documents in the training data.

Our translation model supports: a conservative extraction approach, which is more restrictive, allowing fewer translation equivalents, having a lower recall but a higher precision; and a flexible extraction approach, which is more permissive, allowing a larger number of equivalents but at the cost of an increase of incorrect ones. We were interested in evaluating the impact of both approaches on results.

Table 4 shows the average results on both translation directions of those preliminary tests, consisting of the average BLEU scores for the conservative (cons.) and flexible (flex.) approaches, as well as the average times taken to translate the documents on either extraction approaches. Those results concern the following configurations:

- **full**: the documents used for testing were not removed from the training set (medline-pubmed, biological and health);

- **dev**: the documents used for testing were removed form the training set;

- **dev-europarl**: the same as dev, but including the europarl corpus; and

- **dev-europarl-low**: the same as dev-europarl, but assigned a lower relevance to the europarl corpus.

configuration	cons.	flex.	time
full	83.98	81.97	15.1 s
dev	51.72	55.46	3.5 s
dev-europarl	52.34	55.98	49.9 s
dev-europarl-low	52.54	56.21	46.8 s

Table 4: Initial testing results.

These preliminary tests have shown that the flexible extraction approach produced on average better translation results when the reference documents were not included in the test set, which is the normal testing situation, so we used the flexible approach.

The Europarl corpus[4], which is significantly larger (54,543,044 words in English and 60,375,477 words in Portuguese), was tested as a source of additional term coverage, which allowed a translation quality improvement lower than 1 BLEU point. However, given its significant increase in processing time because of its large size, a time increase around 14 times larger, we had to drop it from the submission tests due to deadline constraints. Additionally, these results show that assigning a lower relevance to a corpus from a totally different domain may have some positive impact on average results.

Once we have decided, from this initial testing preparation, which would be the most promising and interesting features to use in the final runs, we ran the training processes again to include the documents that have been left out, this way using the full data provided by the organizers for the runs to be submitted.

4 Submitted Results

Considering that the test documents to be translated, provided by the shared task organization, share their domain with the training data, we decided to propose for submission the three possible translation runs for each document according to the criteria described in each of the following subsections.

4.1 Run 1

This run uses the medline-pubmed, biological and health training corpora with the same relevance to translate every translation test document. These can be considered our simplest set of tests since the possible model relevance difference is not explored and no additional sources are included. In this case we achieved a total of 7228 unique untranslated terms[5].

4.2 Run 2

This run also uses the medline-pubmed, biological and health training corpora, but assigns a higher

relevance to the biological corpora to translate the biological test documents and then assigns a higher relevance to the health corpora to translate the health test documents. Because the changes introduced in this set of tests only concerned the relevance of the models, the total of 7228 unique untranslated terms did not change.

4.3 Run 3

This last run shares the same features as the previous run (assigning higher relevances to corresponding corpora) but this time our bilingual lexicon and named entities database was included for term coverage improvement, and an alignment based on cognates (Gomes and Lopes, 2011) is used.

About our bilingual lexicon, considering that it was built mainly from the European legislation, it was given a lower relevance because past experiences have shown us that, when the domain is not shared with the texts to be translated, it should not have the same relevance in order to reduce the probability of using inadequate terms for the intended translation domain or subject. Again, this is a situation that has also been confirmed and noted in Table 4 between dev-europarl and dev-europarl-low: reducing the relevance of europarl contributed to a slight score increase compared to when the relevance is the same.

As a side note, translating the tests took nearly 14 hours for each run[6]. Had we included europarl, judging by Table 4, we would have taken nearly 200 hours, which is more than a week, expecting to simply gain 0.75 BLEU points, on average, so we had no other option than leaving it out. Such increase in translation time is due to the substantial increase of translation equivalents available for decoding from such a large corpus.

The decision to carry out the alignment based on cognates was taken because after a first run of tests we realized that many of the untranslated terms referred to medical terms and diseases, which shared many letters between both languages and therefore had a high level of cognaticity.

All these changes allowed a significant reduction of the unique untranslated terms to a total of 4700, and for all the reasons in this subsection, we have considered this run as being our best.

---

[4]http://www.statmt.org/europarl/
[5]Terms can have one or more words

[6]On a 3.3GHz CPU with 32GB RAM and 4TB disk

5   Conclusions and Future Work

The scores of our submitted translations are shown in Table 5.

run	score
Istrionbox_run1_biological_en2pt	17.55
Istrionbox_run2_biological_en2pt	16.47
Istrionbox_run3_biological_en2pt	16.45
Average	**16.80**
Istrionbox_run1_biological_pt2en	20.88
Istrionbox_run2_biological_pt2en	20.17
Istrionbox_run3_biological_pt2en	20.14
Average	**20.40**
Istrionbox_run1_health_en2pt	19.01
Istrionbox_run2_health_en2pt	18.33
Istrionbox_run3_health_en2pt	18.37
Average	**18.57**
Istrionbox_run1_health_pt2en	21.50
Istrionbox_run2_health_pt2en	20.17
Istrionbox_run3_health_pt2en	20.62
Average	**20.76**

Table 5: Initial testing results.

The results obtained were clearly below what we had expected. And what is most disturbing is the negative impact of features we expected to improve results, an expectation backed by our own tests.

However, there are a few reasons we can think of for these values, namely the way the BLEU measure has been calculated (case sensitivity and synonyms penalty - translating "home" instead of "house" might be perfectly fine), the differences between European Portuguese and Brazilian Portuguese, and the presence of several spelling and alignment errors in the training data.

Nonetheless, we can still take several actions to improve our system: namely testing both parallel corpora, health and biology, with identical weights: using Europarl and eventually EMEA corpus; the refinement of our phrase translation extraction; the extraction of specific bilingual terminology, additionally to the use of cognaticity; subsentence realignment after the bilingual terminology extraction, and a more efficient implementation of the patterns (comparable to a hierarchical translation) application.

Acknowledgments

This work was supported by ISTRION BOX, Fundação para a Ciência e Tecnologia through research project ISTRION (contract PTDC/EIA-EIA/114521/2009), individual PhD grants SFRH/BD/48839/2008, SFRH/BD/65059/2009, SFRH/BD/64371/2009, and NOVA LINCS (ref. UID/CEC/04516/2013). We would also like to thank Hugo Delgado for his support.

References

J. Aires, G. P. Lopes, and J. F. da Silva. 2008. Efficient multi-word expressions extractor using suffix arrays and related structures. pages 1–8. CIKM-ACM.

J. Aires, G. P. Lopes, and L. Gomes. 2009. Phrase translation extraction from aligned parallel corpora using suffix arrays and related structures. In *Progress in Artificial Intelligence*, volume 5816 of *LNAI*, pages 587–597. Springer-Verlag Berlin Heidelberg.

J. DeNero and D. Klein. 2008. The complexity of phrase alignment problems. In *Proceedings of ACL-08: HLT, Short Papers*, pages 25–28, Columbus, Ohio, June. ACL.

L. Gomes and G. P. Lopes. 2011. Measuring spelling similarity for cognate identification. In *Progress in Artificial Intelligence*, volume 7026 of *LNAI*, pages 624–633, Lisbon, Portugal, October. Springer.

L. Gomes. 2009. Parallel texts alignment. Master's thesis, Faculdade de Ciências e Tecnologia, Universidade Nova de Lisboa, Monte de Caparica, Portugal.

P. Koehn and C. Monz. 2005. Shared task: Statistical machine translation between european languages. In *Proceedings of the ACL Workshop on Building and Using Parallel Texts*, pages 119–124. ACL.

P. Koehn, H. Hoang, A. Birch, C. Callison-Burch, M. Federico, N. Bertoldi, B. Cowan, W. Shen, C. Moran, R. Zens, C. Dyer, O. Bojar, A. Constantin, and E. Herbst. 2007. Moses: Open source toolkit for statistical machine translation. In *Proceedings of the 45th Annual Meeting of the ACL on Interactive Poster and Demonstration Sessions*, ACL '07, pages 177–180, Stroudsburg, PA, USA. ACL.

A.n Lardilleux and Y. Lepage. 2009. Sampling-based multilingual alignment. In *Proceedings of Recent Advances in Natural Language Processing*, pages 214–218, Borovets Bulgaria, 09.

G. P. Lopes, J. Aires, and L. Gomes. 2015. Statistical machine translation computer system and method. Submitted at National (Portugal) Level (INPI), 8. Provisional Patent Request No. 0151000065353.

K. Mahesh, L. Gomes, J. Aires, and G. P. Lopes. 2015. Selecting translation candidates for parallel corpora alignment. In *Progress in Artificial Intelligence*, volume 9273 of *LNAI*, pages 723–734, Coimbra, Portugal, September. Springer.

M. Neves, A. J. Yepes, and A. Névéol. 2016. The scielo corpus: a parallel corpus of scientific publications for biomedicine. In Nicoletta Calzolari (Conference Chair), Khalid Choukri, Thierry Declerck, Sara Goggi, Marko Grobelnik, Bente Maegaard, Joseph Mariani, Helene Mazo, Asuncion Moreno, Jan Odijk, and Stelios Piperidis, editors, *Proceedings of the Tenth International Conference on Language Resources and Evaluation (LREC 2016)*, Paris, France, may. European Language Resources Association (ELRA).

F. J. Och and H. Ney. 2003. A systematic comparison of various statistical alignment models. *Computational Linguistics*, 29(1):19–51.

K. Papineni, S. Roukos, T. Ward, and Wei-Jing Zhu. 2002. Bleu: A method for automatic evaluation of machine translation. In *Proceedings of the 40th Annual Meeting on ACL*, ACL '02, pages 311–318, Stroudsburg, PA, USA. ACL.

R. Steinberger, B. Pouliquen, A. Widiger, C. Ignat, T. Erjavec, D. Tufis, and D. Varga. 2006. The jrc-acquis: A multilingual aligned parallel corpus with 20+ languages. In *Proceedings of LREC'2006 pp. 2142-2147. Genoa, Italy, 24-26 May 2006*, Genoa, Italy, 5. ELRA.

J. Tiedemann. 2009. News from opus-a collection of multilingual parallel corpora with tools and interfaces. In *Recent advances in natural language processing*, volume 5, pages 237–248.

The TALP–UPC Spanish–English WMT Biomedical Task: Bilingual Embeddings and Char-based Neural Language Model Rescoring in a Phrase-based System

Marta R. Costa-jussà, Cristina España-Bonet, Pranava Madhyastha,
Carlos Escolano, José A. R. Fonollosa
TALP Research Center
Universitat Politècnica de Catalunya, Barcelona
{marta.ruiz,jose.fonollosa}@upc.edu, {cristinae,pranava}@cs.upc.edu,
carlos.escolano@est.fib.upc.edu

Abstract

This paper describes the TALP–UPC system in the Spanish–English WMT 2016 biomedical shared task. Our system is a standard phrase-based system enhanced with vocabulary expansion using bilingual word embeddings and a character-based neural language model with rescoring. The former focuses on resolving out-of-vocabulary words, while the latter enhances the fluency of the system. The two modules progressively improve the final translation as measured by a combination of several lexical metrics.

1 Introduction

Machine Translation (MT) has been evolving in recent years achieving successful translations as shown by international evaluations such as WMT[1] and increasing use of MT in commercial applications. However, specific domains like legal, biomedical, etc., still lag behind the state-of-the-art MT systems. This can mostly be attributed to the lack of available corpora. The new biomedical task from WMT 2016 especially helps in improving our understanding in this direction.

In this paper, we describe our participation in the WMT 2016 biomedical task. We participated with a phrase-based SMT system enhanced with bilingual word embeddings and a character-based neural language model. Section 2 presents some related work to our approach. Next, Section 3 introduces the theoretical aspects of the system components and Section 4 the experiments. Finally, we justify our choice for the final submission and draw the conclusions in Section 5.

2 Related Work

In this paper, we are interested in research in the area that target OOVs and approaches to re-rank n-best lists of translations.

Our work closely follows Vulic and Moens (2015) and Zhao et al. (2015) in spirit, where word vectors are used to induce bilingual lexicons of words or phrases. We go a step further and build lexicons from bilingual word embeddings to be later used within an SMT system.

There is also a rich body of recent literature that focuses on obtaining bilingual word embeddings using aligned corpora (Bhattarai, 2012; Gouws et al., 2015; Kočiský et al., 2014). We approach the problem differently and obtain embeddings separately on monolingual corpora and then use supervision in the form of a small sparse bilingual dictionary. This is similar to Mikolov et al. (2013b), who obtain monolingual embeddings for both the languages separately and then learn transformation for projecting the embeddings of words onto embeddings of the word translation pairs using a big bilingual dictionary.

On the other hand, there have been several language models used for rescoring in SMT. For example, neural feed-forward language models (Schwenk et al., 2006) have been used to rescore both n-gram-based and phrase-based systems. Mikolov (2012) re-ranks n-best lists with recurrent neural networks. Vaswani et al. (2013) combine feed-forward language models, with rectified linear units and noise-contrastive estimation. Luong et al. (2015) propose to use deeper neural models which improve re-ranking. In this paper, we are using Kim et al. (2016) a character-based language model to re-rank the output of the phrase-based system.

---

[1] http://www.statmt.org/wmt16

Proceedings of the First Conference on Machine Translation, Volume 2: Shared Task Papers, pages 463–468,
Berlin, Germany, August 11-12, 2016. ©2016 Association for Computational Linguistics

3　The Translation System

The TALP-UPC translation system is built on three different components. We describe their theoretical basis in the following subsections.

3.1　Phrase-based SMT

The standard phrase-based machine translation system (Koehn et al., 2003) focuses on finding the most probable target sentence given the source sentence. The phrase-based system has evolved from the noisy-channel to the log-linear model which combines a set of feature functions in the decoder, including the translation and language model, the reordering model and the lexical models. Although the phrase-based system is a commoditized technology used at the academic and commercial level, there are still many challenges to solve, such as OOVs.

3.2　Vocabulary Expansion using Bilingual Word-Embeddings

We look at this task as a bilinear prediction task as proposed by (Madhyastha et al., 2014). The proposed model makes use of word embeddings of both languages with no additional features. The basic function is formulated —the probability of a target word given a source word— as log-linear model and takes the following form:

$$\Pr(t|s; W) = \frac{\exp\{\phi_{\bar{s}}(s)^{\top} W \phi_{\bar{t}}(t)\}}{\sum_{t'} \exp\{\phi_{\bar{s}}(s)^{\top} W \phi_{\bar{t}}(t')\}} \quad (1)$$

Where $\phi(.)$ denotes the n-dimensional distributed representation of the words, and we assume we have both source ($\phi_{\bar{s}}$) embeddings and target ($\phi_{\bar{t}}$) embeddings.

Essentially, our problem reduces to: a) first getting the corresponding word embeddings of the vocabularies on both the languages on a significantly large monolingual corpus and b) estimating W given a relatively small dictionary. To learn W we use the source word to target word dictionaries as training supervision.

We learn W by minimizing the negative log-likelihood of the dictionary using a nuclear norm regularized objective as: $L(W) = -\sum_{s,t} \log(\Pr(t|s; W)) + \lambda\|W\|_*$. λ is the constant that controls the capacity of W. To find the optimum, we follow the previous work and use an optimization scheme based on Forward-Backward Splitting (FOBOS) (Singer and Duchi, 2009).

Table 1: Size of the parallel (top) and monolingual (bottom) corpora used to train the translation systems

Corpus	Segments	Words	Vocab
Biomedical	$1 \cdot 10^6$	$20 \cdot 10^6$	$0.3 \cdot 10^6$
Quest	$13 \cdot 10^6$	$340 \cdot 10^6$	$0.5 \cdot 10^6$
Bio-mono/en	$0.1 \cdot 10^6$	$2 \cdot 10^6$	$0.1 \cdot 10^6$
Bio-mono/es	$0.01 \cdot 10^6$	$0.1 \cdot 10^6$	$0.01 \cdot 10^6$
Wikipedia/en	$92 \cdot 10^6$	$1900 \cdot 10^6$	$2.0 \cdot 10^6$
Wikipedia/es	$20 \cdot 10^6$	$465 \cdot 10^6$	$0.8 \cdot 10^6$

3.3　Character-based Neural Language Model

Language models based on Recurrent Neural Networks are currently one of the best performing approaches in terms of perplexity (Mikolov et al., 2010). They are also a good re-ranking option in tasks such as speech recognition and machine translation. However, the standard lookup-based word embeddings are limited to a finite-size vocabulary for both computational and sparsity reasons. Moreover, the orthographic representation of the words is completely ignored. The standard learning process is blind to the presence of stems, prefixes, suffixes and any other kind of affixes in words.

As a solution to those drawbacks, new alternative character-based word embeddings have been recently proposed for tasks as language modeling (Kim et al., 2016; Ling et al., 2015), parsing (Ballesteros et al., 2015) or part-of-speech tagging (Ling et al., 2015; Santos and Zadrozny, 2014). For our system we selected the best character-based embedding architecture proposed by Kim et al. (Kim et al., 2016). The computation of the representation of each word starts with a character-based embedding layer that associates each word (sequence of characters) with a sequence of vectors. This sequence of vectors is then processed with a set of 1D convolution filters of different lengths (from 1 to 7 characters) followed with a max pooling layer and two additional highway layers. The output of the second highway layer provide us with the final vector representation of each source word that replaces the standard source word embedding in the recurrent neural network used for language modeling (Kim et al., 2016).

4 Experimental Framework

4.1 Data

Our main corpus is the compilation of the corpora assigned for the shared task, which was built using scientific publications gathered from the Scielo database. We focus on the Spanish–English language pair, for which the size of the corpora is summarised in Table 1. We further increase the vocabulary of the system by using standard parallel corpora for the Spanish–English language pair (i.e., UN corpora, Europarl corpora, News corpus, etc.[2]). This corpus appears as Quest in Table 1. For the monolingual corpus we use an English and Spanish Wikipedia dump[3].

The corpora has been pre-processed with a standard pipeline for both Spanish and English: tokenizing and keeping parallel sentences between 1 and 80 words. Additionally, for Spanish we used Freeling (Padró and Stanilovsky, 2012) to tokenize pronouns from verbs (i.e. *comenzándose* to *comenzando + se*), we also split prepositions and articles, i.e. *del* to *de + el* and *al* to *a + el*. This was done for similarity to English.

We divided the provided parallel corpus into training, development and test sets. Sentences from development and test set were taken randomly, proportionally to the amount of Medline and Scielo (biomedical and health) sources and only from unique parallel sentences.

Since the domain of the test set is the same as the domain of training corpus, the number of OOV words is small. Table 2 shows the total number and percentage of unknown words in our in-house development and test sets with respect to translation tables (see the following section). For comparison, we also include the figures for the two test sets made available for the final evaluation.

4.2 System Description

As introduced in the previous section, three different modules build our system: the SMT engine, the module to resolve OOVs and the module for re-reranking.

SMT Engine. Three different state-of-the-art phrase-based SMT translation systems are trained on the parallel corpora detailed in Table 1. For the purely in-domain system, we use only the biomedical data made available for the task (*STT* systems, small translation table). For more general systems, we also use the Quest data; we name these systems *BTT* (big translation table).

For the in-domain system, a 5-gram language model is estimated on the target side of the corpus using interpolated Kneser-Ney discounting with SRILM (Stolcke, 2002) (*SLM*, small language model). For the extended systems, we use all the monolingual corpora available and the target side of the large parallel corpus (*BLM*, big language model). Word alignment is done with GIZA++ (Och and Ney, 2003) and both phrase extraction and decoding are done with the Moses package (Koehn et al., 2007). The optimisation of the weights of the model is trained with MERT (Och, 2003) against the BLEU (Papineni et al., 2002) evaluation metric on devBio.

OOVs resolution. This module first obtains bilingual embeddings from the monolingual ones as explained in Section 3.2. For estimating monolingual word vector models, we use the CBOW algorithm as implemented in the Word2Vec package (Mikolov et al., 2013a) using a 5-token window. We obtain 300 dimension vectors for English and Spanish from the monolingual and the source side of the parallel corpora in Table 1. The bilingual counterpart has been estimated using 34,806 words from the *Apertium* bilingual dictionary[4] as seed lexicon divided for training and validation. Each bilingual pair has an associated probability given by Eq. 1. We keep the top-10 pairs for each out-of-vocabulary word in the test (development) set and include these new translation options at decoding time. Since we are only dealing with OOVs, the new options do not interact with the other phrase pairs in the translation table, but there is interaction with the language model.

Re-ranking. The 1000-best list of translations given by the SMT engine is re-ranked using the characted-based language model described in Section 3.3. It has 1D convolutional filters of width [1,2,3,4,5,6,7] and size [50, 100, 150, 200, 200, 200, 200] for a total of 1,100 filters with a tanh activation, 2 highway layers with a ReLU activation, and 2 LSTM with 650 hidden units. The network

---

[2]In particular, we use the parallel data given for the Quality Estimation task at WMT13, `http://statmt.org/~buck/wmt13qe/wmt13qe_t13_t2_MT_corpus.tgz`

[3]Dumps downloaded from `https://dumps.wikimedia.org` in January 2015.

[4]`http://repositori.upf.edu/handle/10230/17110`

Table 2: Figures –tokens and OOVs– on the development and test sets used in the experiments

		English			Spanish		
	Seg.	Tokens	OOV_{STT}	OOV_{BTT}	Tokens	OOV_{STT}	OOV_{BTT}
devBio	1000	18967	16 (0.08%)	2 (0.01%)	19931	14 (0.07%)	6 (0.03%)
testBio	1000	26105	31 (0.11%)	19 (0.07%)	27651	25 (0.09%)	9 (0.03%)
Biological	4344	115709	434 (0.37%)	333 (0.29%)	126008	415 (0.33%)	254 (0.20%)
Health	5111	125624	133 (0.10%)	98 (0.08%)	146368	160 (0.11%)	40 (0.03%)

has been trained on the monolingual part of the in-domain data (Biomedical corpus in Table 1).

4.3 Results

We evaluate the performance of each module when added to the three standard SMT systems built with different amount of training data (STTSLM, STTBLM, BTTBLM). In the following, we denote the module for OOV resolution with *oov* and the module for re-reraking with *reranked*. For the *total.reranked* system, we re-ranked the n-best lists for the thirteen systems with our neural language model. We conduct the evaluation automatically with a set of lexical metrics calculated with the Asiya toolkit[5] (Giménez and Màrquez, 2010). Table 3 reports the results for the English-to-Spanish translation systems and Table 4 for the Spanish-to-English ones.

The first thing to notice is that the best translation is obtained when only in-domain data are used to build the translation model. This is true in both directions. When going from Spanish into English, we obtain 0.45 BLEU points of improvement when adding the oov module to the in-domain system (STTSLM.oov) and an additional 0.15 with the re-ranking module (STTSLM.oov.reranked). Even if the number of OOV is only a 0.09% in this test set, the improvement with this module is consistent through all metrics. The main reason is that making available new translation options at decoding time allows the language model to modify the sentence as a whole, and the neighbouring words can be modified accordingly.

In the English-to-Spanish direction, the trends are less homogeneous through the set of metrics. For BLEU and METEOR (with the stemming variant, MTRst), the best system is still STTSLM.oov. However, with NIST and TER, the best system is STTBLM. In this case, enlarging the language model has a similar effect as injecting

new vocabulary through OOV translations. This is because only a 31% of the OOV belong to the biomedical domain, suggesting that in this case and for an in-domain test set, it is important to gain fluency on the general domain phrases. The effect of the re-ranking module is more evident in this direction: the more data one uses, the more distinct the final n-best list is and the more improvement one can obtain. For the in-domain system the re-ranking is not promoting a better translation, but for the general system the improvement is significant.

5 Conclusions

We have built thirteen translation systems per direction. The ones chosen for the final submission follow two criteria: i) they have a top performance according to BLEU and METEOR (the official metrics) and, ii) they allow us a coherent comparison among languages and methodologies. With this criteria, our primary submission both for the health and biological test sets is the strictly in-domain system with the OOV module (*STTSLM.oov*). For comparison, we also submitted our baseline as a second run: the same system without the OOV module (*STTSLM*). Finally, we submitted as third run a system with re-ranking of a 1000-best list. Due to time constraints, we could not submit the system that re-ranks all the n-best lists for the thirteen systems, *total.reranked*, but we used instead the two most promising options per direction.

According to the preliminary results of the shared task, the OOV module consistently improves the translations with respect to our baseline specially in the health subdomain as measured by BLEU. The effect is similar to the results in our in-house test set. On the other hand, the re-ranking module is also always better than the in-domain phrase-based baseline and, in this case, the performance on the competition test set is significantly better than the one in our test set, espe-

[5] http://nlp.cs.upc.edu/asiya

Table 3: Automatic evaluation of the in-house test set for the En2Es systems

	WER	PER	TER	BLEU	NIST	GTM-2	MTRst	MTRpa	RG-S*	ULC
BTTBLM.oov	48.45	29.82	44.27	43.84	8.81	36.30	61.58	62.87	49.85	66.03
BTTBLM.oov.reranked	47.58	**29.74**	43.56	44.43	8.90	36.97	62.01	63.25	50.43	67.16
BTTBLM	47.74	30.39	43.72	43.61	8.86	36.51	61.50	62.76	49.98	66.19
BTTBLM.reranked	47.64	29.91	43.52	44.24	8.89	36.90	61.88	63.14	50.29	66.95
STTBLM.oov	48.00	29.60	43.73	44.32	8.87	36.65	62.13	63.32	50.12	66.88
STTBLM.oov.reranked	47.22	29.85	43.11	44.57	8.96	37.21	62.22	63.42	50.44	67.57
STTBLM	**47.01**	29.93	**42.81**	44.51	**8.98**	37.36	62.28	63.47	50.49	67.75
STTBLM.reranked	47.10	29.91	42.96	44.65	8.97	37.40	62.31	63.46	**50.68**	67.78
STTSLM.oov	47.84	29.28	43.61	**44.99**	8.88	37.36	**62.33**	63.44	50.51	67.60
STTSLM.oov.reranked	47.41	29.82	43.25	44.52	8.94	37.29	62.25	63.36	**50.68**	67.54
STTSLM	47.29	29.84	43.16	44.64	8.96	**37.58**	62.27	63.42	50.56	67.71
STTSLM.reranked	47.40	29.93	43.24	44.39	8.94	37.36	62.21	63.30	50.56	67.44
total.reranked	47.06	29.82	43.03	44.75	**8.98**	37.56	**62.33**	**63.53**	50.66	**67.88**

Table 4: Automatic evaluation of the in-house test set for the Es2En systems

	WER	PER	TER	BLEU	NIST	GTM-2	MTRst	MTRpa	RG-S*	ULC
BTTBLM.oov	50.95	29.98	46.79	40.94	8.59	35.02	35.03	37.28	49.13	65.30
BTTBLM.oov.reranked	50.41	29.75	46.23	41.58	8.65	35.52	35.25	37.48	49.50	66.24
BTTBLM	50.21	29.33	45.98	41.97	8.68	35.88	35.44	37.65	50.01	66.97
BTTBLM.reranked	50.41	29.63	46.28	41.62	8.65	35.51	35.27	37.53	49.50	66.29
STTBLM.oov	50.75	29.95	46.68	40.82	8.61	34.83	35.05	37.12	49.15	65.27
STTBLM.oov.reranked	50.19	29.22	46.04	42.10	8.71	35.72	35.57	37.65	49.95	67.04
STTBLM	50.91	29.74	46.74	41.16	8.62	34.97	35.33	37.40	49.39	65.67
STTBLM.reranked	50.27	**29.08**	46.01	42.19	8.72	35.79	35.62	**37.66**	50.08	67.20
STTSLM.oov	**49.79**	29.45	**45.62**	42.16	**8.75**	35.94	35.57	37.60	**50.13**	67.31
STTSLM.oov.reranked	50.15	**29.08**	45.99	**42.30**	8.71	35.88	**35.65**	**37.66**	50.10	67.30
STTSLM	50.62	29.53	46.46	41.71	8.65	35.47	35.46	37.48	49.71	66.34
STTSLM.reranked	50.25	29.12	46.04	42.13	8.70	35.76	35.59	37.62	49.97	67.09
total.reranked	50.06	29.42	45.93	42.06	8.71	35.80	35.47	37.65	49.93	67.00

cially for English-to-Spanish. Run 3, the system that includes re-ranking with a char-based neural language model, is 2 points of BLEU over the average value among participants in the biological subdomain and 1 point of BLEU on the health subdomain.

Acknowledgements

This work is supported by the 7th Framework Program of the European Commission through the International Outgoing Fellowship Marie Curie Action (IMTraP-2011-29951) and also by the Spanish Ministerio de Economía y Competitividad and European Regional Development Fund, contract TEC2015-69266-P (MINECO/FEDER, UE).

References

Miguel Ballesteros, Chris Dyer, and Noah A. Smith. 2015. Improved transition-based parsing by modeling characters instead of words with lstms. In *Proceedings of the 2015 Conference on Empirical Methods in Natural Language Processing*, pages 349–359, Lisbon, Portugal, September.

Alexandre Klementiev Ivan Titov Binod Bhattarai. 2012. Inducing Crosslingual Distributed Representations of Words. In *Proceedings of COLING 2012*, pages 1459–1474, Mumbai, India, December.

Jesús Giménez and Lluís Màrquez. 2010. Asiya: an Open Toolkit for Automatic Machine Translation (Meta-)Evaluation. *The Prague Bulletin of Mathematical Linguistics*, 94:77–86.

Stephan Gouws, Yoshua Bengio, and Greg Corrado. 2015. BilBOWA: Fast Bilingual Distributed Representations without Word Alignments. In *Proceedings of the 32nd International Conference on Machine Learning, ICML 2015, Lille, France, 6-11 July 2015*, pages 748–756, July.

Yoon Kim, Yacine Jernite, David Sontag, and Alexander M. Rush. 2016. Character-aware neural language models. In *Proceedings of the 30th AAAI Conference on Artificial Intelligence (AAAI'16)*.

Tomáš Kočiskỳ, Karl Moritz Hermann, and Phil Blunsom. 2014. Learning bilingual word representations by marginalizing alignments. *arXiv preprint arXiv:1405.0947*.

Philipp Koehn, Franz Joseph Och, and Daniel Marcu. 2003. Statistical Phrase-Based Translation. In *Proc. of the 41th Annual Meeting of the Association for Computational Linguistics*.

Philipp Koehn, Hieu Hoang, Alexandra Birch Mayne, Christopher Callison-Burch, Marcello Federico, Nicola Bertoldi, Brooke Cowan, Wade Shen, Christine Moran, Richard Zens, Chris Dyer, Ondrej Bojar, Alexandra Constantin, and Evan Herbst. 2007. Moses: Open source toolkit for statistical machine translation. In *Annual Meeting of the Association for Computation Linguistics (ACL), Demonstration Session*, pages 177–180, June.

Wang Ling, Chris Dyer, Alan W Black, Isabel Trancoso, Ramon Fermandez, Silvio Amir, Luis Marujo, and Tiago Luis. 2015. Finding function in form: Compositional character models for open vocabulary word representation. In *Proceedings of the 2015 Conference on Empirical Methods in Natural Language Processing*, pages 1520–1530, Lisbon, Portugal, September.

Thang Luong, Michael Kayser, and Christopher D. Manning. 2015. Deep neural language models for machine translation. In *Proceedings of the Nineteenth Conference on Computational Natural Language Learning*, pages 305–309, Beijing, China, July.

Swaroop Pranava Madhyastha, Xavier Carreras, and Ariadna Quattoni. 2014. Learning task-specific bilexical embeddings. In *Proceedings of COLING 2014, the 25th International Conference on Computational Linguistics: Technical Papers*, pages 161–171.

Tomas Mikolov, Martin Karafiát, Lukás Burget, Jan Cernocký, and Sanjeev Khudanpur. 2010. Recurrent neural network based language model. In *INTERSPEECH 2010, 11th Annual Conference of the International Speech Communication Association, Makuhari, Chiba, Japan, September 26-30, 2010*, pages 1045–1048.

Tomas Mikolov, Kai Chen, Greg Corrado, and Jeffrey Dean. 2013a. Efficient Estimation of Word Representations in Vector Space. In *Proceedings of Workshop at ICLR*. http://code.google.com/p/word2vec.

Tomas Mikolov, Quoc V. Le, and Ilya Sutskever. 2013b. Exploiting Similarities among Languages for Machine Translation. abs/1309.4168.

Tomas Mikolov. 2012. *Statistical Language Models based on Neural Networks*. Ph.D. thesis, Brno University of Technology.

Franz Josef Och and Hermann Ney. 2003. A systematic comparison of various statistical alignment models. *Computational Linguistics*, 29(1):19–51.

Franz Josef Och. 2003. Minimum Error Rate Training in Statistical Machine Translation. In *Proceedings of the Association for Computational Linguistics*, pages 160–167, Sapporo, Japan, July 6-7.

Lluís Padró and Evgeny Stanilovsky. 2012. Freeling 3.0: Towards wider multilinguality. In *International Conference on language Resources and Evaluation*.

Kishore Papineni, Salim Roukos, Todd Ward, and Wei-Jing Zhu. 2002. BLEU: A Method for Automatic Evaluation of Machine Translation. In *Proceedings of the Association of Computational Linguistics*, pages 311–318.

Cicero D. Santos and Bianca Zadrozny. 2014. Learning character-level representations for part-of-speech tagging. In *Proceedings of the 31st International Conference on Machine Learning (ICML-14)*, pages 1818–1826.

Holger Schwenk, Marta R. Costa-Jussà, and José A. R. Fonollosa. 2006. Continuous space language models for the IWSLT 2006 task. In *2006 International Workshop on Spoken Language Translation, IWSLT 2006, Keihanna Science City, Kyoto, Japan, November 27-28, 2006*, pages 166–173.

Yoram Singer and John C Duchi. 2009. Efficient learning using forward-backward splitting. In *Advances in Neural Information Processing Systems*, pages 495–503.

Andreas Stolcke. 2002. SRILM - An Extensible Language Modeling Toolkit. In *Proceedings of the Seventh International Conference of Spoken Language Processing (ICSLP2002)*, pages 901–904, Denver, Colorado, USA.

Ashish Vaswani, Yinggong Zhao, Victoria Fossum, and David Chiang. 2013. Decoding with large-scale neural language models improves translation. In *Proceedings of the 2013 Conference on Empirical Methods in Natural Language Processing*, pages 1387–1392, Seattle, Washington, USA, October.

Ivan Vulic and Marie-Francine Moens. 2015. Bilingual Word Embeddings from Non-Parallel Document-Aligned Data Applied to Bilingual Lexicon Induction. In *Proceedings of the 53rd Annual Meeting of the Association for Computational Linguistics and the 7th International Joint Conference on Natural Language Processing of the Asian Federation of Natural Language Processing, ACL 2015*, pages 719–725, July.

Kai Zhao, Hany Hassan, and Michael Auli. 2015. Learning Translation Models from Monolingual Continuous Representations. In *The 2015 Conference of the North American Chapter of the Association for Computational Linguistics: Human Language Technologies, NAACL HLT 2015*, pages 1527–1536, June.

LIMSI's Contribution to the WMT'16 Biomedical Translation Task

Julia Ive[1,2], Aurélien Max[1], François Yvon[1]
LIMSI, CNRS, Univ Paris-Sud, Université Paris-Saclay, 91 403 Orsay, France,[1]
Cochrane France, INSERM U1153, 75181 Paris, France[2]
{firstname.lastname}@limsi.fr

Abstract

The article describes LIMSI's submission to the first WMT'16 shared biomedical translation task, focusing on the sole English-French translation direction. Our main submission is the output of a MOSES-based statistical machine translation (SMT) system, rescored with Structured OUtput Layer (SOUL) neural network models. We also present an attempt to circumvent syntactic complexity: our proposal combines the outputs of PB-SMT systems trained either to translate entire source sentences or specific syntactic constructs extracted from those sentences. The approach is implemented using Confusion Network (CN) decoding. The quality of the combined output is comparable to the quality of our main system.

1 Introduction

The paper provides the details of LIMSI's submission to the first shared biomedical translation task at WMT'16. For our main submission we built a phrase-based statistical machine translation (SMT) system using MOSES and attempted to improve the quality of its output by rescoring its n-best list with Structured OUtput Layer (SOUL) neural network models.

Our secondary submission was designed to mitigate the negative effects of syntactic complexity of sentences. This complexity creates a challenge for the phrase-based SMT (PBSMT) paradigm that only sees a sentence as a sequential structure. To overcome this problem, the output of PB-SMT systems can be combined with the output of "syntax-aware" MT systems (rule-based, syntax-based, etc. (Freitag et al., 2014b; Avramidis et al., 2015; Li et al., 2015)).

As the building of the latter type of systems can be costly, we propose a light-weight alternative that combines the outputs of several PBSMT systems trained for the translation of (a) entire sentences, and (b) separate continuous and discontinuous syntactic constructions extracted from those sentences. The combination is performed using confusion network (CN) decoding. The quantitative difference with the baseline is rather small, but our comparative analysis of this system allows us to better understand its potential and limitations.

2 Systems Overview

In all our experiments we used the MOSES implementation of the phrase-based approach to SMT (Koehn et al., 2007).

2.1 Additional Parallel Data

The translation of scientific abstracts in the biomedical domain is a task that is characterized by the availability of high-quality in-domain corpora. In all our experiments, we used the English-French Cochrane corpus of medical review abstracts, which resembles the shared task data (Ive et al., 2016).[1] This corpus was split in two parts: titles (COCHRANE-TITLES) and abstracts (COCHRANE-ABS). The same split was performed for the SCIELO corpus (SCIELO-TITLES and SCIELO-ABS, respectively). We will further refer to the union of all the provided task data and of the COCHRANE data as the IN-DOMAIN-DATA. Additionally, we used the data distributed for the WMT'14 medical task,[2] even though its relatedness to the SCIELO test data is lesser.

---

[1] http://www.translatecochrane.fr/corpus
[2] http://statmt.org/wmt14/medical-task

Proceedings of the First Conference on Machine Translation, Volume 2: Shared Task Papers, pages 469–476,
Berlin, Germany, August 11-12, 2016. ©2016 Association for Computational Linguistics

2.2 Additional Monolingual Data

As additional monolingual data we used the full French dataset provided by the organizers of the WMT'15 translation task.[3]

2.3 Preprocessing and Word Alignment

Tokenization and detokenization for both source (English) and target (French) texts were performed by our in-house text processing tools (Déchelotte et al., 2008). Additionally, the MEDLINE-TITLES corpus provided with the shared task was cleaned as follows: we excluded source sentences with generic comments instead of translations (e.g., "In Process Citation"). This reduced the count of the original corpus sentences by 3%. Details on the WMT'14 and WMT'15 data preprocessing schemes can be found in (Pécheux et al., 2014; Marie et al., 2015). The statistics regarding the preprocessed data are in Table 1. Word alignments were computed using `fast_align` (Dyer et al., 2013).

2.4 Language Models

We built an in-domain 6-gram language model (LM) (`In-domain-LM1`) combined with a 4-gram LM developed in the context of WMT'14 (`In-domain-LM2`); both are trained using the corresponding monolingual parts of the parallel data with modified Kneser-Ney smoothing (Kneser and Ney, 1995; Chen and Goodman, 1996), using the SRILM (Stolcke, 2002) and KENLM (Heafield, 2011) toolkits. We also used an out-of-domain 4-gram LM (`Out-of-domain-LM`), described in (Marie et al., 2015).

2.5 SOUL

We also made use of *Structured OUtput Layer* (SOUL) neural network Language and Translation models (Le et al., 2011; Le et al., 2012a) as these have been shown to systematically improve our systems in recent evaluations (Le et al., 2012b; Allauzen et al., 2013; Pécheux et al., 2014; Marie et al., 2015). The SOUL architecture can estimate LMs of higher n-gram order (e.g., $n = 10$ instead of $n = 4$) for large output vocabulary; SOUL is used to rescore n-best lists of the MOSES system.

[3]http://www.statmt.org/wmt15/
translation-task.html

2.6 Development and Test Sets

In the absence of official development data, we chose our development (LIMSIDEV) and internal test (LIMSITEST) data randomly out of the provided SCIELO-ABS and SCIELO-TITLES corpora. Each set contains 14% of the total count of SCIELO-TITLES sentences and 11% of the total count of SCIELO-ABS sentences.

Given the quantity of misspelled words in the data (e.g. "externai" for "external", "leveI" instead of "level", etc.), we tried to select datasets with an OOV rate not higher than the rate of the rest of the SCIELO corpus, as compared to the vocabulary of the IN-DOMAIN-DATA (SCIELO data excluded) and WMT'14 medical data (e.g., for SCIELO-ABS the OOV rate $\approx 2\%$).

LIMSIDEV and LIMSITEST were used to respectively tune and test our main PBSMT systems. LIMSITEST was further split into LIMSIDEV2 and LIMSITEST2 for SOUL and system combination optimizations. Statistics for these datasets are in Table 1.

2.7 Evaluation Metrics

BLEU scores (Papineni et al., 2002) are computed using the cased `multi-bleu.perl` script and our own tokenizer for reference translations .

3 Baseline System

3.1 Details of System Building

For our baseline system, all the available IN-DOMAIN-DATA were used to train the translation models consisting of the phrase table (PT) and the lexicalized reordering models (`msd-bidirectional-fe`). We used the WMT'14 medical task parallel data to train additional models. More specifically, these models were used as `back-off` models to search for n-grams (up to $n = 4$) with no translation in the main models. The three LMs described in Section 2.4 were used. This system was tuned with `kb-mira` (Cherry and Foster, 2012) using 300-best lists.

3.2 Experiments and Results

The results of our baseline system are in Table 2. For our experiments with neural network models we took the 10-gram SOUL models trained for the LIMSI participation to WMT'12 (Le et al., 2012b). SOUL models define *five* additional features: a monolingual target LM score and four

Corpus	# Lines	# Tok., en	# Tok., fr
SCIELO-ABS	≈ 8 K	≈ 200 K	≈ 280 K
SCIELO-TITLES	≈ 700	≈ 10 K	≈ 14 K
MEDLINE-TITLES	≈ 600 K	≈ 7 M	≈ 8 M
COCHRANE-ABS	≈ 140 K	≈ 3 M	≈ 5 M
COCHRANE-TITLES	≈ 8 K	≈ 90 K	≈ 130 K
IN-DOMAIN-DATA	≈800 K	≈ 10 M	≈ 13 M
COPPA	≈ 454 K	≈ 10 M	≈ 12 M
EMEA	≈ 324 K	≈ 6 M	≈ 7 M
PATTR-ABS	≈ 635 K	≈ 20 M	≈ 24 M
PATTR-CLAIMS	≈ 889 K	≈ 32 M	≈ 36 M
PATTR-TITLES	≈ 386 K	≈ 3 M	≈ 4 M
UMLS	≈ 2 M	≈ 8 M	≈ 8 M
WIKIPEDIA	≈8 K	≈ 17 K	≈ 19 K
WMT'14 medical task	≈6 M	≈ 160 M	≈ 190 M
WMT'15 translation task			≈ 2.2 B

Set	# Lines	# Tok., en	# Tok., fr
LIMSIDEV-TITLES	100	1360	1834
LIMSIDEV-ABS	900	24367	30560
LIMSIDEV	1000	25727	32394
LIMSIDEV2-TITLES	50	686	943
LIMSIDEV2-ABS	450	13116	16261
LIMSIDEV2	500	13802	17204
LIMSITEST2-TITLES	50	738	915
LIMSITEST2-ABS	450	12487	15276
LIMSITEST2	500	13225	16191
LIMSITEST	1000	27027	33395

Table 1: Corpora used for training (left); development and test (right)

translation model scores (Le et al., 2012a). The baseline 300-best list was reranked according to the combination of all baseline features and the SOUL features. Reranking allowed us to obtain an improvement of +1.17 BLEU over our baseline system. The system tends to perform better on the LIMSITEST2-TITLES part than on the LIMSITEST2-ABS part. In the rest of this article, we focus our efforts on improving the translation quality of abstracts only.

4 Using Phrase-Based Statistical Machine Translation to Circumvent Syntactic Complexity

Scientific medical texts are characterized by a large quantity of compound terms and complex sentences. Their translation can be especially challenging for PBSMT due to its intrinsic limitations which include, among others, the generation of translations by mere concatenation and the inability to resolve long-distance relations between sentence components. These limitations can be overcome in PBSMT by combining with the outputs of "syntax-aware" MT systems (rule-base MT (RBMT), syntax-based MT (SBMT)) (Costa-Jussà et al., 2012; Avramidis et al., 2015; Li et al., 2015). The combination of system outputs is often performed with the help of Confusion Network (CN) decoding as an effective means to recombine translation alternatives at the word level (Deng et al., 2015; Freitag et al., 2014a; Freitag et al., 2014b; Zhu et al., 2013).

Less costly solutions seek to better explore the potential of phrase-based architectures. For instance, Hewavitharana et al. (2007) propose to im-prove the PBSMT outputs by separately translating noun phrases (NPs) extracted from source sentences.

Inspired by this study, we propose to combine the baseline hypotheses with partial, local hypotheses by means of CN decoding. To obtain those partial hypotheses, we trained separate PBSMT systems to translate on the one hand the NPs (NP-SMT), often representing complex terms, and on the other hand, simplified variants of the source sentences where NPs are replaced by their syntactic head (NP-Reduced-SMT) (see Figure 1).

4.1 Methodology

A CN is a weighted directed acyclic graph where all the paths go through all the nodes (Mangu et al., 2000). There may be one or more arcs between two consecutive nodes. Arcs can here be considered as alternative translation choices for target words (including the empty NULL word).

Building a confusion network implies several decisions:

1. Choice of the main hypothesis (backbone) to guide the word order: This choice is crucial for the final translation quality (see e.g. (Hildebrand and Vogel, 2008)). In our case, we chose the 1-best baseline hypothesis as the backbone.

2. Choice of the word alignment strategy between the hypotheses: Alternative hypotheses are usually aligned to the backbone without taking their alignments with source tokens into account (Rosti et al., 2012; Rosti et al., 2008; Matusov et al., 2006). Following Du et al. (2009), we instead aligned hypotheses according to the source-target alignments produced by the decoder. Figure 2 illustrates the hypothesis alignment

system	LIMSITEST2	LIMSITEST2-TITLES	LIMSITEST2-ABS
MOSES	30.38	**49.42**	**29.20**
MOSES + SOUL	**31.55**	50.44	30.27

Table 2: Results (BLEU) for MOSES and MOSES + SOUL on the in-house test set

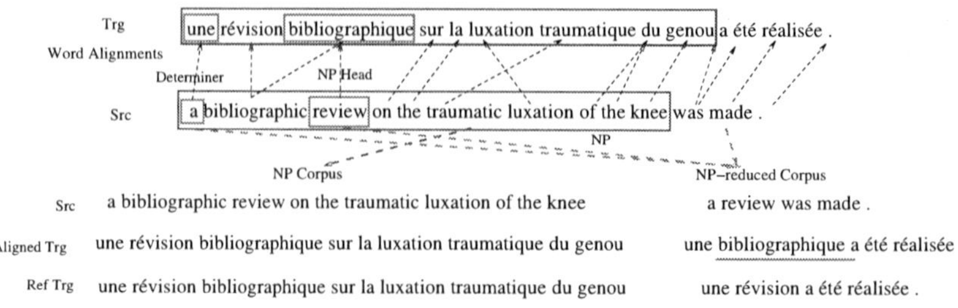

Figure 1: Extraction of NP and NP-reduced instances

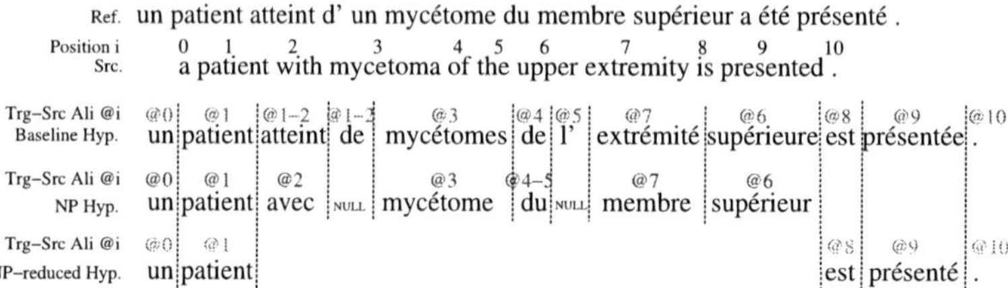

Figure 2: Source-based hypothesis alignment. @i denotes to the source index of a given target word.

procedure. We used source-target phrasal alignments produced by the decoder to assign un-aligned words to several positions (see e.g. "de" highlighted in yellow on Figure 2). It may also happen that a target phrase in a partial hypothesis is longer than the corresponding baseline translation; in this case the backbone is extended as needed with NULL arcs.

3. Arc scores. Each arc labelled u receives a score equal to the posterior unigram probability $P(u|\varepsilon)$ of the system generating u at this position. $P(u|\varepsilon)$ is computed as in (de Gispert et al., 2013):

$$P(u|\varepsilon) = \frac{\sum_{E \in \varepsilon_u} \exp(\alpha H(E, F))}{\sum_{E' \in \varepsilon} \exp(\alpha H(E', F))},$$

where ε is the space of translation hypotheses of a PBSMT system (a $10K$-best list was chosen), and $H(E, F)$ is the score assigned by the model to the sentence pair (E, F).

The posterior probabilities for the word (arcs) in NP-SMT and NP-Reduced-SMT hypotheses were rescaled to give more weigth to local translation variants.

4. Choice of the combined hypotheses. The CN-DECODING diversity was increased by combining 30-best hypotheses from each system (baseline, NP-Reduced-SMT and NP-SMT).

Each path is the CN is finally scored as follows:

$$S(E|F) = \alpha S_{post}(E) + \beta S_{LM}(E) + \gamma N_w(E),$$

where S_{post} is the path posterior probability, S_{LM} is the interpolated LM score (In-domain-LM1 and Out-of-domain-LM), and N_w is the path length (excluding NULL arcs).

All CN-DECODING experiments, including the feature weight optimization (BLEU maximization), were performed using the SRILM (Stolcke, 2002) toolkit.

4.2 Details of System Building

We used the SCIELO-ABS and COCHRANE-ABS corpora, as well as LIMSIDEV and LIMSITEST to create the NP-SMT and NP-Reduced-SMT training, development and test data. The NP-SMT source data contained the NPs extracted from the source side of all bitexts. The NP-Reduced-SMT target data contained the original source sentences with the NPs replaced by their heads (also preserving the associated article or possessive determiner) (Klein and Manning, 2003; Toutanova et al., 2003). The NP-SMT and NP-Reduced-SMT target data were created using the translations of the corresponding syntactic structures obtained from the fast_align source-target word alignments, where the non-aligned words were not considered. The `NP-SMT` training corpus was enriched with the titles and glossary corpora data (SCIELO-TITLES, COCHRANE-TITLES, MEDLINE-TITLES, PATTR-TITLES, UMLS, WIKIPEDIA).

These systems were built and tuned in a way similar to the baseline (see Figure 3). For each system, we prioritized `NP-SMT` or `NP-Reduced-SMT` model correspondingly, the other models being used as `back-off` models. LMs were built as explained in Section 2.4. We also used again the `Out-of-domain-LM`.

To evaluate these specialized systems, we compared the BLEU scores of the `NP-SMT` and `NP-Reduced-SMT` translations with artificial hypotheses derived from baseline hypotheses.

The results in Table 3 show small quality gains with our `NP-SMT` variant (+0.22 BLEU). Conversely, a slight decrease in quality (-0.35 BLEU) is observed for the `NP-Reduced-SMT` system. This is somewhat paradoxical, as we expected the simplified sentences to be easier to translate than the original sentences. This might be explained by the poor quality and frequent ungrammaticality of the `NP-Reduced-SMT` target side development and test sentences, the computation of which critically relies on word alignments.

system	BLEU
NP−SMT	**27.47**
NP−SMT + SOUL	28.46
base MOSES (NPs)	**27.25**
base MOSES + SOUL (NPs)	28.33
NP−Reduced−SMT	**22.81**
NP−Reduced−SMT + SOUL	23.53
base MOSES (NP-reduced)	**23.16**
base MOSES + SOUL (NP-reduced)	24.04

Table 3: `NP-SMT` and `NP-Reduced-SMT` performance for LIMSITEST2-ABS.

4.3 Experiments and Results

The resulting CN-DECODING 300-best lists were compared to the 300-best lists of the baseline system. On average, 11% of unique 1-grams from each CN-DECODING hypothesis search space are new (see Table 4), a significant proportion of novelty relative to our baseline system.

We also compared our approach to the MOSES `xml-mode` that enables to propose to the decoder alternative partial translations with their proba-

n-gram	%
1-gram	11
2-gram	28
3-gram	39
4-gram	48

Table 4: Average % of new unique n-gram per CN-DECODING hypothesis (using 300-best lists) LIMSITEST2-ABS.

bility. Using 30-best lists of `NP-SMT` translations reranked by SOUL, we marked the source sentences with possible NP translations which competed with PT choices (`inclusive` option). Each NP translation variant was assigned a probability proportional to the $\prod_{0<n\leq l_{np}} P(u_n|\varepsilon)$ of the 1-grams u_n composing it. CN-DECODING decoding was performed according to the configuration described in Section 4.1, with the 30-best `NP-SMT` list reranked by SOUL.

Results in Table 5 confirm that CN-DECODING is superior here to MOSES `xml-mode` (+2.06 BLEU for LIMSITEST2-ABS).

test set	MOSES base	MOSES + xml	CN-DECODING
LIMSIDEV2-ABS	32.38	29.59	32.84
LIMSITEST2-ABS	29.20	**26.79**	**28.85**

Table 5: Results (BLEU) for different strategies of NP injection.

For the remaining CN-DECODING experiments, the 30-best lists of each system are reranked by SOUL prior to system combination.

We noticed that the `NP-SMT` and `NP-Reduced-SMT` hypotheses tend to be shorter than the corresponding local translations in the baseline output. We tried to reduce the negative impact on quality and avoided aligning baseline words to `NULL` in the CN-DECODING alignment procedure. We assigned the rest of the `NULL` arcs a very low probability of $p(NULL) = 0.001$ (compared to the previously assigned average score of all the other arcs between two consecutive nodes).

In this condition, the quality of CN-DECODING output reranked by SOUL shows an insignificant gain over the baseline MOSES + SOUL (+0.18 BLEU for LIMSITEST2-ABS, see Tables 6, 2). It seems that the CN-DECODING procedure allowed our system to locally choose "good" translation variants, in spite of the quality decrease that we observed for `NP-Reduced-SMT` hypotheses (see

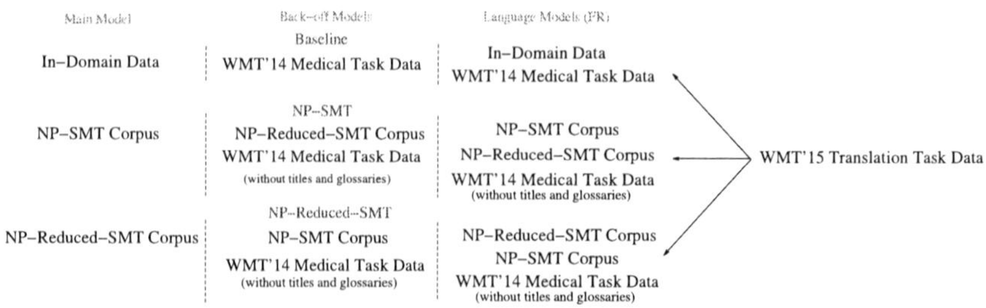

Figure 3: Data used in systems building

Table 3).

test set	LimsiTest2-Abs
CN-decoding	30.01
CN-decoding + Soul	**30.45**

Table 6: Results (BLEU) for CN-decoding experiments.

4.4 Observations and Further Improvements

Manual inspection of the CN-decoding output showed that the majority of the changes with respect to the baseline hypotheses concern introduction of synonyms, and only a few cases include the right choice of an article or of a grammatical form.

Our observations of the quality of the NP-SMT and NP-Reduced-SMT hypotheses suggest that the target development sets automatically created from source-target word alignments for those systems do not provide the right guidance for tuning, and also yield biased BLEU scores for these systems. More effort should be invested notably to compute better simplified versions of the original target sentences. Additionally, a more fine-grained procedure is required to estimate the quality of partial hypotheses before introducing them to CN-decoding.

5 Conclusions

This paper described LIMSI's submission to the shared WMT'16 biomedical translation task. We reported the results for the English-French translation direction. Our submitted system used Moses and neural network SOUL models in a post-processing step.

In our experiments, we developed an approach aimed at mitigating the syntactic complexity which is a characteristic of a medical scientific publications. Our solution exploits the potential of phrase-based Statistical Machine Transla-tion. We combined the output of the PBSMT system, trained to translate entire source sentences, with the outputs of specialized PBSMT systems, trained to translate syntactically defined subparts of the source sentence: complex noun phrases on the one hand, simplified sentences on the other hand. The combination was performed using confusion network decoding and showed small improvements over a strong baseline when the output of CN decoding is reranked using Soul. In our future work, we plan to improve the extraction procedure for the reduced systems, as well as to separately improve their performance. For the NP-SMT system, this could be achieve by digging additional resources such as comparable corpora.

Acknowledgments

The work of the first author is supported by a CIFRE grant from the French ANRT.

474

References

Alexandre Allauzen, Nicolas Pécheux, Quoc Khanh Do, Marco Dinarelli, Thomas Lavergne, Aurélien Max, Hai-Son Le, and François Yvon. 2013. LIMSI @ WMT13. In *Proceedings of WMT*, Sofia, Bulgaria.

Eleftherios Avramidis, Maja Popović, and Aljoscha Burchardt. 2015. DFKI's experimental hybrid MT system for WMT 2015. In *Proceedings of the Tenth Workshop on Statistical Machine Translation*, pages 66–73, Lisbon, Portugal, September.

Stanley F. Chen and Joshua T. Goodman. 1996. An empirical study of smoothing techniques for language modeling. In *Proceedings of ACL*, Santa Cruz, US.

Colin Cherry and George Foster. 2012. Batch tuning strategies for statistical machine translation. In *Proceedings of NAACL-HLT*, Montréal, Canada.

Marta Costa-Jussà, Mireia Farrús, José Mariño, and José Fonollosa. 2012. Study and comparison of rule-based and statistical catalan-spanish machine translation systems. *Computing and Informatics*, 31(2).

Adrià de Gispert, Graeme W. Blackwood, Gonzalo Iglesias, and William Byrne. 2013. N-gram posterior probability confidence measures for statistical machine translation: an empirical study. *Machine Translation*, 27(2):85–114.

Daniel Déchelotte, Gilles Adda, Alexandre Allauzen, Olivier Galibert, Jean-Luc Gauvain, Hélène Maynard, and François Yvon. 2008. LIMSI's statistical translation systems for WMT'08. In *Proceedings of NAACL-HTL Statistical Machine Translation Workshop*, Columbus, Ohio.

Dun Deng, Nianwen Xue, and Shiman Guo. 2015. Harmonizing word alignments and syntactic structures for extracting phrasal translation equivalents. In *Proceedings of the Ninth Workshop on Syntax, Semantics and Structure in Statistical Translation*, pages 1–9, Denver, Colorado, USA, June.

Jinhua Du, Yanjun Ma, and Andy Way. 2009. Source-side context-informed hypothesis alignment for combining outputs from machine translation systems. In *Proceedings of the Twelfth Machine Translation Summit (MT Summit XII)*. International Association for Machine Translation.

Chris Dyer, Victor Chahuneau, and Noah A. Smith. 2013. A simple, fast, and effective reparameterization of IBM model 2. In *Proceedings of NAACL*, Atlanta, Georgia.

Markus Freitag, Matthias Huck, and Hermann Ney. 2014a. Jane: Open source machine translation system combination. In *Proceedings of the Demonstrations at the 14th Conference of the European Chapter of the Association for Computational Linguistics*, pages 29–32, Gothenburg, Sweden, April.

Markus Freitag, Stephan Peitz, Joern Wuebker, Hermann Ney, Matthias Huck, Rico Sennrich, Nadir Durrani, Maria Nadejde, Philip Williams, Philipp Koehn, Teresa Herrmann, Eunah Cho, and Alex Waibel. 2014b. EU-BRIDGE MT: Combined machine translation. In *Proceedings of the Ninth Workshop on Statistical Machine Translation*, pages 105–113, Baltimore, Maryland, USA, June.

Kenneth Heafield. 2011. KenLM: Faster and Smaller Language Model Queries. In *Proceedings of WMT*, Edinburgh, Scotland.

Sanjika Hewavitharana, Alon Lavie, and Vogel Stephan. 2007. Experiments with a noun-phrase driven statistical machine translation system. In *Conference Proceedings: the 11th Machine Translation Summit*, pages 247–253, Copenhagen, Denmark, September.

Almut Silja Hildebrand and Stephan Vogel. 2008. Combination of machine translation systems via hypothesis selection from combined n-best lists. In *Proceedings of the Eighth Conference of the Association for Machine Translation in the Americas (AMTA)*, pages 254–261.

Julia Ive, Aurélien Max, François Yvon, and Philippe Ravaud. 2016. Diagnosing high-quality statistical machine translation using traces of post-edition operations. In *Proceedings of the LREC 2016 Workshop: Translation Evaluation: From Fragmented Tools and Data Sets to an Integrated Ecosystem*, Portorož, Slovenia, May.

Dan Klein and Christopher D. Manning. 2003. Accurate unlexicalized parsing. In *Proceedings of the 41st Annual Meeting of the Association for Computational Linguistics*, pages 423–430, Sapporo, Japan, July.

Reinhard Kneser and Herman Ney. 1995. Improved backing-off for m-gram language modeling. In *Proceedings of the International Conference on Acoustics, Speech, and Signal Processing, ICASSP'95*, pages 181–184, Detroit, MI.

Philipp Koehn, Hieu Hoang, Alexandra Birch, Chris Callison-Burch, Marcello Federico, Nicola Bertoldi, Brooke Cowan, Wade Shen, Christine Moran, Richard Zens, Chris Dyer, Ondrej Bojar, Alexandra Constantin, and Evan Herbst. 2007. Moses: Open source toolkit for statistical machine translation. In *Proceedings of the ACL Demo*, Prague, Czech Republic.

Hai-Son Le, Ilya Oparin, Alexandre Allauzen, Jean-Luc Gauvain, and François Yvon. 2011. Structured output layer neural network language model. In *Proceedings of ICASSP*, Prague, Czech Republic.

Hai-Son Le, Alexandre Allauzen, and François Yvon. 2012a. Continuous space translation models with neural networks. In *Proceedings of NAACL-HLT*, Montréal, Canada.

Hai-Son Le, Thomas Lavergne, Alexandre Allauzen, Marianna Apidianaki, Li Gong, Aurélien Max, Artem Sokolov, Guillaume Wisniewski, and François Yvon. 2012b. LIMSI @ WMT12. In *Proceedings of WMT*, Montréal, Canada.

Hongzheng Li, Kai Zhao, Yun Hu, Renfen Zhu, and Yaohong Jin. 2015. A hybrid system for chinese-english patent machine translation. In *Conference Proceedings: the 15th Machine Translation Summit*, pages 52–67, Miami, Florida, USA, November.

Lidia Mangu, Eric Brill, and Andreas Stolcke. 2000. Finding consensus in speech recognition: word error minimization and other applications of confusion networks. *Computer Speech & Language*, 14(4):373–400.

Benjamin Marie, Alexandre Allauzen, Franck Burlot, Quoc-Khanh Do, Julia Ive, Elena Knyazeva, Matthieu Labeau, Thomas Lavergne, Kevin Löser, Nicolas Pécheux, and François Yvon. 2015. LIMSI@WMT'15 : Translation task. In *Proceedings of the Tenth Workshop on Statistical Machine Translation*, pages 145–151, Lisbon, Portugal, September.

Evgeny Matusov, Nicola Ueffing, and Hermann Ney. 2006. Computing consensus translation for multiple machine translation systems using enhanced hypothesis alignment. In *Proceedings of the 11th Conference of the European Chapter of the Association for Computational Linguistics*, Trento, Italy, April.

Kishore Papineni, Salim Roukos, Todd Ward, and Wei-Jing Zhu. 2002. Bleu: a Method for Automatic Evaluation of Machine Translation. In *Proceedings of ACL*, Philadelphia, US.

Nicolas Pécheux, Li Gong, Quoc Khanh Do, Benjamin Marie, Yulia Ivanishcheva, Alexandre Allauzen, Thomas Lavergne, Jan Niehues, Aurélien Max, and François Yvon. 2014. LIMSI @ WMT14 Medical Translation Task. In *Proceedings of WMT*, Baltimore, Maryland.

Antti-Veikko I. Rosti, Bing Zhang, Spyros Matsoukas, and Richard Schwartz. 2008. Incremental hypothesis alignment for building confusion networks with application to machine translation system combination. In *Proceedings of the Third Workshop on Statistical Machine Translation*, pages 183–186, Columbus, Ohio, June.

Antti-Veikko Rosti, Xiaodong He, Damianos Karakos, Gregor Leusch, Yuan Cao, Markus Freitag, Spyros Matsoukas, Hermann Ney, Jason Smith, and Bing Zhang. 2012. Review of hypothesis alignment algorithms for mt system combination via confusion network decoding. In *Proceedings of the Seventh Workshop on Statistical Machine Translation*, pages 191–199, Montréal, Canada, June.

Andreas Stolcke. 2002. SRILM - an extensible language modeling toolkit. In *Proceedings of the International Conference on Spoken Language Processing (ICSLP)*, pages 901–904, Denver, Colorado, September.

Kristina Toutanova, Dan Klein, Christopher D. Manning, and Yoram Singer. 2003. Feature-rich part-of-speech tagging with a cyclic dependency network. In *Proceedings of the 2003 Human Language Technology Conference of the North American Chapter of the Association for Computational Linguistics*.

Junguo Zhu, Muyun Yang, Sheng Li, and Tiejun Zhao. 2013. Repairing incorrect translation with examples. In *Proceedings of the Sixth International Joint Conference on Natural Language Processing*, pages 967–971, Nagoya, Japan, October. Asian Federation of Natural Language Processing.

IXA Biomedical Translation System at WMT16 Biomedical Translation Task

Olatz Perez-de-Viñaspre and **Gorka Labaka**
IXA NLP Group
University of the Basque Country UPV/EHU
Donostia, Basque Country
`olatz.perezdevinaspre,gorka.labaka@ehu.eus`

Abstract

In this paper we present the system developed at the IXA NLP Group of the University of the Basque Country for the Biomedical Translation Task in the First Conference on Machine Translation (WMT16). For the adaptation of a statistical machine translation system to the biomedical domain, we developed three approaches based on a baseline system for English-Spanish and Spanish-English language pairs. The lack of terminology and the variation of the prominent sense of the words are the issues we have addressed on these approaches. The best of our systems reached the average of all the systems submitted in the challenge in most of the evaluation sets.

1 Introduction

In this paper we present the system developed at the IXA NLP Group from the University of the Basque Country for the Biomedical Translation Task in the First Conference on Machine Translation (WMT16). This is the first shared task organized for the biomedical domain inside WMT.

The Biomedical Translation Task consists of translating scientific abstracts in health and biological domains for languages such as English, Spanish, French and Portuguese. In our case, we developed a system for English-Spanish and Spanish-English pairs.

We present a system that takes a general Moses statistical machine translation system (Koehn et al., 2007) and adapts it to the biomedical domain. The adaptation of a MT system to a specific domain comes with two main issues: i) a bigger set of out-of-vocabulary (OOV) words and ii) the variation of the prominent sense of the words.

The integration of a bilingual biomedical terminology bank to the system can mitigate great part of the lack of terminology. In any case, this may not be enough and a transliteration[1] module may be helpful. In addition, morphological variability may be a problem in no-frequent lemmas, as plurals in English or genders and plurals in Spanish.

The remaining of the paper is as follows. We first present in section 2 the resources we used. We then describe in section 3 the approaches we developed for our system and in section 4 the BLEU results for our runs. Finally, conclusions are drawn.

2 Resources

In this section we describe the resources used to train the models that will be explained in section 3. There are two main resource types involved in this work: corpora and terminological resources.

2.1 Corpora

The corpora pertains to two different sub-domains: health and biology. Thus, the corpus extracted from Scielo is separated by the domain the abstracts pertains. In the case of the Medline corpus there is a unique corpus for both sub-domains.

Although the corpora is in general bilingual and aligned at sentence level, in some cases sentences from the parallel corpora were not available, as in the Medline corpus some English sentences were marked as "[Not Available]". We removed those sentences from the parallel corpus and we created a monolingual corpus of Spanish sentences to be used for language modeling.

The Scielo corpora gives the word alignments as well as sentence alignments. Thus, in table 2.1 we show the number of sentences and words that

---

[1] Although transliteration is commonly used between languages with different scripts, it may also be used to adapt the spelling differences of borrowings.

477

Proceedings of the First Conference on Machine Translation, Volume 2: Shared Task Papers, pages 477–482,
Berlin, Germany, August 11-12, 2016. ©2016 Association for Computational Linguistics

are aligned in the bilingual corpora for the Spanish and English pairs.

Corpus	Sentences	Words
Scielo - Biological	125,828	723,202
Scielo - Health	587,299	2,871,232
Medline	285,584	-

Table 1: Bilingual corpora

From this bilingual corpora, we excluded some sentences for development. On the one hand, we created a domain-balanced set of 2,945 sentences for tuning of the translation model as well as to interpolate the LM. This set was taken in a randomized and balanced way so we maintained the percentages of the original sets. That is, we took 361 sentences from the biological set, 1,726 sentences from the health set and 858 from the Medline set.

On the other hand, we excluded a separate set of each corpus (health, biological and Medline). In this case, we excluded 2,000 sentences from each of the subdomains, which have also been randomly selected.

In table 2.1 we show the number of sentences of the monolingual corpora. The corpora is composed by the corpus that organizers made available from the Scielo corpora, as well as the sentences we extracted from the Medline corpus that were not aligned.

Corpus	English	Spanish
Scielo - Biological	55,346	1,248
Scielo - Health	68,992	5,163
Medline	0	2,227

Table 2: Monolingual corpora

In addition to the in-domain corpora, we also included some other corpora available in other machine translation tasks inside the WMT challenge.

- Parallel Corpora:

  - Europarl[2] (Koehn, 2005): it is a corpus of parallel texts in 11 languages from the proceedings of the European Parliament. The version we used for this task has 2,218,201 English sentences and 2,123,835 Spanish sentences. For a direct alignment we excluded some of the sentences, obtaining 1,965,734 parallel sentences.

  - News commentary: this corpus consists in political and economic commentary crawled from the web site Project Syndicate[3]. It is composed of 247,966 sentences in English and 206,534 Spanish sentences. The parallel set has 174,441 sentences.

  - Common Crawl[4]: it is an open corpus of web crawl data. It has 1,845,286 parallel sentences for the English-Spanish language pair.

- Monolingual Corpora:

  - News Crawl (articles from 2007 to 2012): these 6 corpora (one per year) are articles extracted from various online news publications. In total, the English corpus has 68,521,621 sentences and the Spanish one 13,384,314.

2.2 Terminological Resources

SNOMED CT (*Systematized Nomenclature of Medicine – Clinical Terms*) (IHTSDO, 2014) is considered the most comprehensive, multilingual clinical health care terminology in the world. The use of a standard clinical terminology improves the quality of health care by enabling consistent representation of meaning in an electronic health record[5].

SNOMED CT provides the core terminology for electronic health records and contains more than 296,000 active concepts with their descriptions organized into hierarchies. (Humphreys et al., 1997) shows that SNOMED CT has an acceptable coverage of the terminology needed to record patient conditions. Concepts are defined by means of description logic axioms and are also used to group terms with the same meaning. Those descriptions are more generally considered as terms.

There are two types of descriptions in SNOMED CT: Fully Specified Names (FSN) and Synonyms. Fully Specified Names are the descriptions used to identify the concepts and they have a semantic tag in parenthesis that indicates its semantic type and, consequently, its hierarchy. Those are descriptions to unambiguously identify the concept, and they are not proper terms you can find in texts.

---

[2] http://www.statmt.org/europarl/

[3] https://www.project-syndicate.org/

[4] http://commoncrawl.org/

[5] http://www.ihtsdo.org/snomed-ct/whysnomedct/snomedfeatures/

Synonyms are the ones used in real texts, and SNOMED CT distinguishes between Preferred Terms and Acceptable Synonyms. As the name indicates, the Preferred Terms are the ones preferred and there is one defined for each concept in each language or dialect. In addition, there are as many Acceptable Synonyms as needed.

3 Systems

In this section we describe the systems we developed for the Biomedical Translation Task. First, we describe the baseline system. Then, we continue describing the three approaches we presented to the task, that deal with the most frequent issues of domain adaptation.

The baseline system has not been submitted for the Shared Task, and it is a reference system.

3.1 System 0: Baseline

To create our baseline system we trained a Moses statistical machine translation system on the corpora made available for the WMT Biomedical Translation Task, as well as and some general corpora publicly available on previous WMT tasks.

The system configuration is based on standard parameters: Tokenization, lowercasing and recasing using tools available in Moses toolkit, MGIZA for word alignment with the "grow-diag-final-and" symmetrization heuristic, a maximum length of 80 tokens per sentence and 5 tokens per phrase, translation probabilities in both directions with Good Turing discounting, lexical weightings in both directions, a phrase length penalty, a "msd-bidirectional-fe" lexicalized reordering model and a target language model. The weights for the different components were adjusted to optimize BLEU using Minimum Error Rate Training (MERT) with an n-best list of size 100.

For the Language Modeling we create a separate Language Model (LM) for each of the sub-corpora we have available and interpolated all of them with the balanced development set extracted from the bilingual in-domain corpora. We must highlight that we used the monolingual corpora as well as the target language part of the bilingual corpora.

As we had too many LMs, we grouped them in the following way to train a hierarchical interpolation. The main criterion to generate the interpolation groups has been the source/domain of the

corpora. That is, we grouped all the News corpora together, the Scielo Health bilingual and monolingual together, the Scielo Biological bilingual and monolingual as well, and in the case of Spanish we grouped also the Medline bilingual with the monolingual, and in the case of English we took the Medline bilingual on its own.

The same corpora used in the language model interpolation was used to optimize the weights of the different components of the statistical machine translation system. That is, the balanced development set explained in section 2.

3.2 System 1: SNOMED CT

The adaptation of a machine translation system to a specific domain has much to do with the specialized terminology that a general system lacks. This lack of terminology is related with the quantity of unknown words or out-of-vocabulary (OOV) words.

In this first approach we faced the lack of terminology by adding a widely recognized multilingual terminology bank to our translation system. More concretely, we included the terminological content of SNOMED CT's English and Spanish International Releases to the system as parallel corpus.

As mentioned in section 2, SNOMED has many synonyms to name a concept. In this case, we aligned all the synonyms from the source language to the Preferred Term of the target language. Thus we avoid the generation of ambiguity as we do not have resources to solve it and we take advantage of the choice made by SNOMED CT developers.

Similarly, we also used the target language Preferred Terms to train a language model that was interpolated with the previous ones.

3.3 System 2: Morphology Variability and Transliteration

In the first system, we reduced the number of OOV words by adding a terminology bank to the training corpora. Even with such a large amount of specialized terms, the number of OOV words may not be zero, as the terminology used in texts is even wider. So, we developed a module to extend the phrase tables.

We enlarged the generated phrase tables in two ways: morphology variability of the plural or feminine words to the canonical form (singular and masculine) and transliteration of the remaining words.

In regard to morphology variability, we implemented a script that checks whether the OOV word is a morphology variation of the canonical form of a term that appears in the phrase table. In the case of English words, the process is as simple as making singular the plural forms and look for the translation candidates of the singular form in the phrase table. In order to avoid inconsistencies, we extracted only the translation candidates which are also made up by a single word, and we convert them into plural.

In contrast, the Spanish morphology made the process more complex, as in addition to the number variability, we must also take into consideration the gender of the words, and even the combination of both (feminine and plural).

With respect to transliteration, (Callison-Burch et al., 2006) exposes that state-of-the-art systems usually apply two strategies to cope with OOV words, neither of them satisfactory. In the first strategy the unknown word is omitted and in the second one it is not translated. The first strategy is even excluded as solution in (Habash, 2008), because the author considers it a trick to score better precision in evaluation metrics. Nevertheless, the second approach can be a good strategy whenever the OOV word is a Named Entity, such as a proper name or an organization name. Otherwise some action is needed.

State-of-the-art shows many approaches for transliteration in machine translation, most of them based on statistical methods (Deselaers et al., 2009; Habash, 2008; Hermjakob et al., 2008; Rama and Gali, 2009).

In a previous work, we developed a system to automatically translate English medical neoclassical compounds such as "glaucoma" or "meningitis" into Basque (Perez-de Viñaspre and Oronoz, 2015). This translation system is based on affix translation and a transliteration module was also implemented. In this case, we adapted the transliteration module for the English-Spanish and Spanish-English pair for the neoclassical medical words as well as for the substances and pharmaceutical products.

The module was implemented using Foma, a free software tool to specify finite-state automata and transducers (Hulden, 2009).

3.4 System 3: Sub-domain Optimization

The organizers of the Shared Task gave two test sets for the evaluation of the systems. One of the sets corresponded to the health domain and the other to the biological domain.

Taking that into account, we optimized the System 2 to each of the sub-domains.

As explained in System 0, the optimization of the system may be done in two levels: interpolation of the Language Model and the tuning of the weights of the different statistical machine translation components in MERT.

In the interpolation of the LM we maintained the groups done for the previous systems and we changed the interpolation corpus. In this case we replaced the balanced development set with the sub-domain tuning development set of each sub-domain. That is, for the LM for health, we used the health tuning development set of health, and similarly for the biological LM, the set of biology.

Likewise, we replaced the same sets in the tuning of the whole statistical machine translation system.

4 Results

In this section we provide the results given by the organizers that measures the BLEU score of the systems submitted as the test sets are not publicly available yet. Each team was allowed to submit up to 3 runs per test file, in our case, 3 runs for the biological test sets from English to Spanish and vice versa, and 3 runs for each of the health test sets. We submitted the Systems 1, 2 and 3, and, therefore, the System 0 remained out of the evaluation.

Table 4 shows the BLEU results of the three systems we submitted for the four test sets. The results of the remaining systems have not been published yet, so we can not compare our systems to the others. In any case, we can compare them with the average of all the runs submitted for the language pair for each sub-domain.

System	Biological		Health	
	en-es	es-en	en-es	es-en
System 1	**31.57**	**30.66**	28.09	27.96
System 2	31.32	30.59	28.06	27.97
System 3	29.61	29.51	**28.13**	**28.12**
Average	31.34	30.17	28.3	27.79

Table 3: BLEU results of our systems.

The results obtained do not show any significant improvement of the different systems and in general we are close to the average. We obtained a small improvement from the average in three of the sets and we are very close to it in the fourth one (English to Spanish translation on the Health domain).

If we consider each System on its own, we can conclude that the System 2 does not give any advantage on what BLEU results regards as it decreases the results of the first system in most of the cases. In any case, we will need to check the manual evaluation that will be published in the overview paper to be sure about this conclusion.

In the case of the Biological sets, in both language pairs the best system seems to be the first one, as it outperformed the System 3 in one BLUE point and is above the average. On the contrary, the Health sets show that the last system improves a bit the results but nothing significant.

5   Conclusions

We present the IXA system for the Biomedical Translation Task from the WMT16 challenge which meets all the requirements established by the organizers. We implemented a system that translates biological and health science text from English to Spanish and Spanish to English.

We used all the corpora offered by the organizers as well as more corpora available for other tasks. In addition, we included a widely recognized multilingual terminology called SNOMED CT and a transliteration module that also solved the morphological variability of non-canonical words (plurals and feminines).

Our systems showed to be close to the average of all the submitted systems, and in three out of four of the cases even above the average. Overall we are pleased with the results even if we are surprised with the lack of improvement shown by the second system. We would like to try a new run training the optimization system based on the first system that only extends the OOV words with the terminology from SNOMED CT, so the optimization may be better on overall results.

The organizers will provide more details and additional results in the WMT'16 overview paper, such as manual evaluation of the runs submitted.

References

Chris Callison-Burch, Philipp Koehn, and Miles Osborne. 2006. Improved Statistical Machine Translation Using Paraphrases. In *Proceedings of the Main Conference on Human Language Technology Conference of the North American Chapter of the Association of Computational Linguistics*, HLT-NAACL '06, pages 17–24, Stroudsburg, PA, USA. Association for Computational Linguistics.

Thomas Deselaers, Saša Hasan, Oliver Bender, and Hermann Ney. 2009. A deep learning approach to machine transliteration. In *Proceedings of the Fourth Workshop on Statistical Machine Translation*, pages 233–241. Association for Computational Linguistics.

Nizar Habash. 2008. Four Techniques for Online Handling of Out-of-vocabulary Words in Arabic-English Statistical Machine Translation. In *Proceedings of the 46th Annual Meeting of the Association for Computational Linguistics on Human Language Technologies: Short Papers*, HLT-Short '08, pages 57–60, Stroudsburg, PA, USA. Association for Computational Linguistics.

Ulf Hermjakob, Kevin Knight, and Hal Daumé III. 2008. Name Translation in Statistical Machine Translation-Learning When to Transliterate. In *ACL*, pages 389–397.

M. Hulden. 2009. Foma: a Finite-State Compiler and Library. In *Proceedings of EACL 2009*, pages 29–32, Stroudsburg, PA, USA.

Betsy L Humphreys, Alexa T McCray, and May L Cheh. 1997. Evaluating the coverage of controlled health data terminologies: report on the results of the NLM/AHCPR large scale vocabulary test. *Journal of the American Medical Informatics Association*, 4(6):484–500.

International Health Terminology Standards Development Organisation IHTSDO. 2014. SNOMED CT Starter Guide. February 2014. Technical report, International Health Terminology Standards Development Organisation.

Philipp Koehn, Hieu Hoang, Alexandra Birch, Chris Callison-Burch, Marcello Federico, Nicola Bertoldi, Brooke Cowan, Wade Shen, Christine Moran, Richard Zens, et al. 2007. Moses: Open source toolkit for statistical machine translation. In *Proceedings of the 45th annual meeting of the ACL on interactive poster and demonstration sessions*, pages 177–180. Association for Computational Linguistics.

Philipp Koehn. 2005. Europarl: A parallel corpus for statistical machine translation. In *MT summit*, volume 5, pages 79–86.

Olatz Perez-de Viñaspre and Maite Oronoz. 2015. SNOMED CT in a language isolate: an algorithm for a semiautomatic translation. *BMC medical informatics and decision making*, 15(Suppl 2):S5.

Taraka Rama and Karthik Gali. 2009. Modeling Machine Transliteration As a Phrase Based Statistical Machine Translation Problem. In *Proceedings of the 2009 Named Entities Workshop: Shared Task on Transliteration*, NEWS '09, pages 124–127, Stroudsburg, PA, USA. Association for Computational Linguistics.

CobaltF: A Fluent Metric for MT Evaluation

Marina Fomicheva, Núria Bel
IULA, Universitat Pompeu Fabra
`firstname.lastname@upf.edu`

Lucia Specia
University of Sheffield, UK
`l.specia@sheffield.ac.uk`

Iria da Cunha
Univ. Nacional de Educación a Distancia
`iriad@flog.uned.es`

Anton Malinovskiy
Nuroa Internet S. L.
`amalinovskiy@gmail.com`

Abstract

The vast majority of Machine Translation (MT) evaluation approaches are based
on the idea that the closer the MT output is to a human reference translation,
the higher its quality. While translation
quality has two important aspects, adequacy and fluency, the existing reference-
based metrics are largely focused on the
former. In this work we combine our
metric UPF-Cobalt, originally presented at
the WMT15 Metrics Task, with a number
of features intended to capture translation
fluency. Experiments show that the integration of fluency-oriented features significantly improves the results, rivalling the
best-performing evaluation metrics on the
WMT15 data.

1 Introduction

Automatic evaluation plays an instrumental role
in the development of Machine Translation (MT)
systems. It is aimed at providing fast, inexpensive,
and objective numerical measurements of translation quality. As a cost-effective alternative to
manual evaluation, the main concern of automatic
evaluation metrics is to accurately approximate
human judgments.

The vast majority of evaluation metrics are
based on the idea that the closer the MT output
is to a human reference translation, the higher its
quality. The evaluation task, therefore, is typically
approached by measuring some kind of similarity between the MT (also called candidate translation) and a reference translation. The most
widely used evaluation metrics, such as BLEU
(Papineni et al., 2002), follow a simple strategy
of counting the number of matching words or
word sequences in the candidate and reference

translations. Despite its wide use and practical
utility, automatic evaluation based on a straightforward candidate-reference comparison has long
been criticized for its low correlation with human
judgments at sentence-level (Callison-Burch and
Osborne, 2006).

The core aspects of translation quality are fi-
delity to the source text (or adequacy, in MT par-
lance) and acceptability (also termed fluency) regarding the target language norms and conventions
(Toury, 2012). Depending on the purpose and intended use of the MT, manual evaluation can be
performed in a number of different ways. However, in any setting both adequacy and fluency
shape human perception of the overall translation
quality.

By contrast, automatic reference-based metrics
are largely focused on MT adequacy, as they do
not evaluate the appropriateness of the translation
in the context of the target language. Translation
fluency is thus assessed only indirectly, through
the comparison with the reference. However,
the difference from a particular human translation
does not imply that the MT output is disfluent
(Fomicheva et al., 2015a).

We propose to explicitly model translation fluency in reference-based MT evaluation. To this
end, we develop a number of features representing translation fluency and integrate them with our
reference-based metric UPF-Cobalt, which was
originally presented at WMT15 (Fomicheva et al.,
2015b). Along with the features based on the
target Language Model (LM) probability of the
MT output, which have been widely used in the
related fields of speech recognition (Uhrik and
Ward, 1997) and quality estimation (Specia et al.,
2009), we design a more detailed representation of
MT fluency that takes into account the number of
disfluent segments observed in the candidate translation. We test our approach with the data avail-

Proceedings of the First Conference on Machine Translation, Volume 2: Shared Task Papers, pages 483–490,
Berlin, Germany, August 11-12, 2016. ©2016 Association for Computational Linguistics

able from WMT15 Metrics Task and obtain very promising results, which rival the best-performing system submissions. We have also submitted the metric to the WMT16 Metrics Task.

2 Related Work

The recent advances in the field of MT evaluation have been largely directed to improving the informativeness and accuracy of candidate-reference comparison. Meteor (Denkowski and Lavie, 2014) allows for stem, synonym and paraphrase matches, thus addressing the problem of acceptable linguistic variation at lexical level. Other metrics measure syntactic (Liu and Gildea, 2005), semantic (Lo et al., 2012) or even discourse similarity (Guzmán et al., 2014) between candidate and reference translations. Further improvements have been recently achieved by combining these partial measurements using different strategies including machine learning techniques (Comelles et al., 2012; Giménez and Màrquez, 2010b; Guzmán et al., 2014; Yu et al., 2015). However, none of the above approaches explicitly addresses the fluency of the MT output.

Predicting MT quality with respect to the target language norms has been investigated in a different evaluation scenario, when human translations are not available as benchmark. This task, referred to as confidence or quality estimation, is aimed at MT systems in use and therefore has no access to reference translations (Specia et al., 2010).

Quality estimation can be performed at different levels of granularity. Sentence-level quality estimation (Specia et al., 2009; Blatz et al., 2004) is addressed as a supervised machine learning task using a variety of algorithms to induce models from examples of MT sentences annotated with quality labels. In the word-level variant of this task, each word in the MT output is to be judged as correct or incorrect (Luong et al., 2015; Bach et al., 2011), or labelled for a specific error type.

Research in the field of quality estimation is focused on the design of features and the selection of appropriate learning schemes to predict translation quality, using source sentences, MT outputs, internal MT system information and source and target language corpora. In particular, features that measure the probability of the MT output with respect to a target LM, thus capturing translation fluency, have demonstrated highly competitive performance in a variety of settings (Shah et al., 2013).

Both translation evaluation and quality estimation aim to evaluate MT quality. Surprisingly, there have been very few attempts at joining the insights from these two related tasks. A notable exception is the work by Specia and Giménez (2010), who explore the combination of a large set of quality estimation features extracted from the source sentence and the candidate translation, as well as the source-candidate alignment information, with a set of 52 MT evaluation metrics from the `Asiya Toolkit` (Giménez and Màrquez, 2010a). They report a significant improvement over the reference-based evaluation systems on the task of predicting human post-editing effort. We follow this line of research by focusing specifically on integrating fluency information into reference-based evaluation.

3 UPF-Cobalt Review

UPF-Cobalt[1] is an alignment-based evaluation metric. Following the strategy introduced by the well known Meteor (Denkowski and Lavie, 2014), UPF-Cobalt's score is based on the number of aligned words with different levels of lexical similarity. The most important feature of the metric is a syntactically informed context penalty aimed at penalizing the matches of similar words that play different roles in the candidate and reference sentences. The metric has achieved highly competitive results on the data from previous WMT tasks, showing that the context penalty allows to better discriminate between acceptable candidate-reference differences and the differences incurred by MT errors (Fomicheva et al., 2015b). Below we briefly review the main components of the metric. For a detailed description of the metric the reader is referred to (Fomicheva and Bel, 2016).

3.1 Alignment

The alignment module of UPF-Cobalt builds on an existing system – Monolingual Word Aligner (MWA), which has been shown to significantly outperform state-of-the-art results for monolingual alignment (Sultan et al., 2014). We increase the coverage of the aligner by comparing distributed word representations as an additional source of lexical similarity information,

---

[1]The metric is freely available for download at `https://github.com/amalinovskiy/ upf-cobalt`.

which allows to detect cases of quasi-synonyms (Fomicheva and Bel, 2016).

3.2 Scoring

UPF-Cobalt's sentence-level score is a weighted combination of precision and recall over the sum of the individual scores computed for each pair of aligned words. The word-level score for a pair of aligned words (t, r) in the candidate and reference translations is based on their lexical similarity ($LexSim$) and a context penalty which measures the difference in their syntactic contexts (CP):

$$score(t, r) = LexSim(t, r) - CP(t, r)$$

Lexical similarity is defined based on the type of lexical match (exact match, stem match, synonyms, etc.)[2] (Denkowski and Lavie, 2014). The crucial component of the metric is the context penalty, which is applied at word-level to identify the cases where the words are aligned (i.e. lexically similar) but play different roles in the candidate and reference translations and therefore should contribute less to the sentence-level score. Thus, for each pair of aligned words, the words that constitute their syntactic contexts are compared. The syntactic context of a word is defined as its head and dependent nodes in a dependency graph. The context penalty (CP) is computed as follows:

$$CP(t, r) = \frac{\sum_{1..i} w(C_i^*)}{\sum_{1..i} w(C_i)} \times ln\left(\sum_{1..i} w(C_i) + 1\right)$$

where w refers to the weights that reflect the relative importance of the dependency functions of the context words, C refers to the words that belong to the syntactic context of the word r and C_i^* refers to the context words that are **not** equivalent.[3] For the words to be equivalent two conditions are required to be met: a) they must be aligned and b) they must be found in the same or equivalent syntactic relation with the word r. The context penalty is calculated for both candidate and reference words. The metric computes an average between reference-side context penalty and candidate-side context penalty for each word

pair. The sentence-level average can be obtained in a straightforward way from the word-level values (we use it as a feature in the decomposed version of the metric below).

4 Approach

In this paper we learn an evaluation metric that combines a series of adequacy-oriented features extracted from the reference-based metric UPF-Cobalt with various features intended to focus on translation fluency. This section first describes the metric-based features used in our experiments and then the selection and design of our fluency-oriented features.

4.1 Adequacy-oriented Features

UPF-Cobalt incorporates in a single score various distinct MT characteristics (lexical choice, word order, grammar issues, such as wrong word forms or wrong choice of function words, etc.). We note that these components can be related, to a certain extent, to the aspects of translation quality being discussed in this paper. The syntactic context penalty of UPF-Cobalt is affected by the well-formedness of the MT output, and may reflect, although indirectly, grammaticality and fluency, whereas the proportion of aligned words depends on the correct lexical choice.

Using the components of the metric instead of the scores yields a more fine-grained representation of the MT output. We explore this idea in our experiments by designing a decomposed version of UPF-Cobalt. More specifically, we use 48 features (grouped below for space reasons):

- Percentage and number of aligned words in the candidate and reference translations
- Percentage and number of aligned words with different levels of lexical similarity in the candidate and reference translations
- Percentage and number of aligned function and content words in the candidate and reference translations
- Minimum, maximum and average context penalty
- Percentage and number of words with high context penalty[4]
- Number of words in the candidate and reference translations

---

[2]Specifically, the values for different types of lexical similarity are: same word forms - 1.0, lemmatizing or stemming - 0.9, WordNet synsets - 0.8, paraphrase database - 0.6 and distributional similarity - 0.5.

[3]The weights w are: argument/complement functions - 1.0, modifier functions - 0.8 and specifier/auxiliary functions - 0.2.

[4]These are words with the context penalty value higher than the average computed on the training set used in our experiments.

4.2 Fluency-oriented Features

We suggest that the fluency aspect of translation quality has been overlooked in the reference-based MT evaluation. Even though syntactically-informed metrics capture structural differences and are, therefore, assumed to account for grammatical errors, we note that the distinction between adequacy and fluency is not limited to grammatical issues and thus exists at all linguistic levels. For instance, at lexical level, the choice of a particular word or expression may be similar in meaning to the one present in the reference (adequacy), but awkward or even erroneous if considered in the context of the norms of the target language use. Conversely, due to the variability of linguistic expression, neither lexical nor syntactic differences from a particular human translation imply ill-formedness of the MT output.

Sentence fluency can be described in terms of the frequencies of the words with respect to a target LM. Here, in addition to the LM-based features that have been shown to perform well for sentence-level quality estimation (Shah et al., 2013), we introduce more complex features derived from word-level n-gram statistics. Besides the word-based representation, we rely on Part-of-Speech (PoS) tags. As suggested by (Felice and Specia, 2012), morphosyntactic information can be a good indicator of ill-formedness in MT outputs.

First, we select 16 simple sentence-level features from previous work (Felice and Specia, 2012; Specia et al., 2010), summarized below.

- Number of words in the candidate translation
- LM probability and perplexity of the candidate translation
- LM probability of the candidate translation with respect to an LM trained on a corpus of PoS tags of words
- Percentage and number of content/function words
- Percentage and number of verbs, nouns and adjectives

Essentially, these features average LM probabilities of the words to obtain a sentence-level measurement. While being indeed predictive of sentence-level translation fluency, they are not representative of the number and scale of the disfluent fragments contained in the MT sentence. Moreover, if an ill-formed translation contains various word combinations that have very high probability according to the LM, the overall sentence-level LM score may be misleading.

To overcome the above limitations, we use word-level n-gram frequency measurements and design various features to extend them to the sentence level in a more informative way. We rely on LM backoff behaviour, as defined in (Raybaud et al., 2011). LM backoff behaviour is a score assigned to the word according to how many times the target LM had to back-off in order to assign a probability to the word sequence. The intuition behind is that an n-gram not found in the LM can indicate a translation error. Specifically, the backoff behaviour value $b(w_i)$ for a word w_i in position i of a sentence is defined as:

$$b(w_i) = \begin{cases} 7, & \text{if } w_{i-2}, w_{i-1}, w_i \text{ exists in the model} \\ 6, & \text{if } w_{i-2}, w_{i-1} \text{and } w_{i-1}, w_i \text{ both exist} \\ & \quad \text{in the model} \\ 5, & \text{if only } w_{i-1}, w_i \text{ exists in the model} \\ 4, & \text{if only } w_{i-2}, w_{i-1} \text{and } w_i \text{ exist} \\ & \quad \text{separately in the model} \\ 3, & \text{if } w_{i-1} \text{and } w_i \text{ both exist} \\ & \quad \text{in the model} \\ 2, & \text{if only } w_i \text{ exists in the model} \\ 1, & \text{if } w_i \text{ is an out-of-vocabulary word} \end{cases}$$

We compute this score for each word in the MT output and then use the mean, median, mode, minimum and maximum of the backoff behaviour values as separate sentence-level features. Also, we calculate the percentage and number of words with low backoff behaviour values (< 5) to approximate the number of fluency errors in the MT output.

Furthermore, we introduce a separate feature that counts the words with a backoff behaviour value of 1, i.e. the number of out-of-vocabulary (OOV) words. OOV words are indicative of the cases when source words are left untranslated in the MT. Intuitively, this should be a strong indicator of low MT quality.

Finally, we note that UPF-Cobalt, not unlike the majority of reference-based metrics, lacks information regarding the MT words that are not aligned or matched to any reference word. Such fragments do not necessarily constitute an MT error, but may be due to acceptable linguistic variations. Collecting fluency information specifically for these fragments may help to distinguish acceptable variation from MT errors. If a candidate word or phrase is absent from the reference but is fluent in the target language, then the difference is possibly not indicative of an error and should be penalized less. Based on this observation, we introduce a separate set of features that compute the word-level measurements discussed above only for the words that are not aligned to the reference translation.

This results in 49 additional features, grouped here for space reasons:

- Summary statistics of the LM backoff behaviour (word and PoS-tag LM)
- Summary statistics of the LM backoff behaviour for non-aligned words only (word and PoS tag LM)
- Percentage and number of words with low backoff behaviour value (word and PoS tag LM)
- Percentage and number of non-aligned words with low backoff behaviour value (word and PoS tag LM)
- Percentage and number of OOV words
- Percentage and number of non-aligned OOV words

5 Experimental Setup

For our experiments, we use the data available from the WMT14 and WMT15 Metrics Tasks for into-English translation directions. The datasets consist of source texts, human reference translations and the outputs from the participating MT systems for different language pairs. During manual evaluation, for each source sentence the annotators are presented with its human translation and the outputs of a random sample of five MT systems, and asked to rank the MT outputs from best to worst (ties are allowed). Pairwise system comparisons are then obtained from this compact annotation. Details on the WMT data for each language pair are given in Table 1.

| | WMT14 | | | WMT15 | | |
LP	Rank	Sys	Src	Rank	Sys	Src
Cs-En	21,130	5	3,003	85,877	16	2,656
De-En	25,260	13	3,003	40,535	13	2,169
Fr-En	26,090	8	3,003	29,770	7	1,500
Ru-En	34,460	13	3,003	44,539	13	2,818
Hi-En	20,900	9	2,507	-	-	-
Fi-En	-	-	-	31,577	14	1,370

Table 1: Number of pairwise comparisons (Rank), translation systems (Sys) and source sentences (Src) per language pair for the WMT14 and WMT15 datasets

In our work we focus on sentence-level metrics' performance, which is assessed by converting metrics' scores to ranks and comparing them to the human judgements with Kendall rank correlation coefficient (τ). We use the WMT14 official Kendall's Tau implementation (Macháček and Bojar, 2014). Following the standard practice at WMT and to make our work comparable to the official metrics submitted to the task, we exclude ties in human judgments both for training and for testing our system.

Our model is a simple linear interpolation of the features presented in the previous sections. For tuning the weights, we use the learn-to-rank approach (Burges et al., 2005), which has been successfully applied in similar settings in previous work (Guzmán et al., 2014; Stanojevic and Sima'an, 2015). We use a standard implementation of Logistic Regression algorithm from the Python toolkit `scikit-learn`[5]. The model is trained on WMT14 dataset and tested on WMT15 dataset.

For the extraction of word-level backoff behaviour values and sentence-level fluency features, we use `Quest++`[6], an open source tool for quality estimation (Specia et al., 2015). We employ the LM used to build the baseline system for WMT15 Quality Estimation Task (Bojar et al., 2015).[7] This LM provided was trained on data from the WMT12 translation task (a combination of news and Europarl data) and thus matches the domain of the dataset we use in our experiments. PoS tagging was performed with TreeTagger (Schmid, 1999).

6 Experimental Results

Table 2 summarizes the results of our experiments. Group I presents the results achieved by UPF-Cobalt and its decomposed version described in Section 4.1. Contrary to our expectations, the performance is slightly degraded when using the metrics' components (UPF-Cobalt$_{comp}$). Our intuition is that this happens due to the sparseness of the features based on the counts of different types of lexical matches.

Group II reports the performance of the fluency features presented in Section 4.2. First of all, we note that these features on their own (FeaturesF)

[5]http://scikit-learn.org/
[6]https://github.com/ghpaetzold/questplusplus
[7]http://www.statmt.org/wmt15/quality-estimation-task.html.

487

	Metric	cs-en	de-en	fi-en	fr-en	ru-en	Avg τ
I	UPF-Cobalt	.457±.011	.427±.011	.437±.011	.386±.011	.402±.011	.422±.011
	UPF-Cobalt$_{comp}$	.442±.011	.418±.011	.428±.011	.387±.011	.388±.011	.413±.012
II	FeaturesF	.373±.011	.337±.011	.359±.011	.267±.011	.263±.011	.320±.011
	CobaltF$_{simple}$	.487±.011	.445±.011	.455±.011	.401±.011	.395±.011	.437±.012
	CobaltF$_{comp}$	.481±.011	.438±.011	.464±.011	.403±.011	.395±.011	.436±.011
	MetricsF	.502±.011	.457±.011	.450±.011	.413±.011	.410±.011	**.447±.011**
III	DPMFcomb	.495±.011	.482±.011	.445±.011	.395±.011	.418±.011	.447±.011
	BEER_Treepel	.471±.011	.447±.011	.438±.011	.389±.011	.403±.011	.429±.011
	RATATOUILLE	.472±.011	.441±.011	.421±.011	.398±.011	.393±.011	.425±.010
IV	BLEU	.391±.011	.360±.011	.308±.011	.358±.011	.329±.011	.349±.011
	Meteor	.439±.011	.422±.011	.406±.011	.380±.011	.386±.011	.407±.012

Table 2: Sentence-level evaluation results for WMT15 dataset in terms of Kendall rank correlation coefficient (τ)

achieve a reasonable correlation with human judgments, showing that fluency information is often sufficient to compare the quality of two candidate translations. Secondly, fluency features yield a significant improvement when used together with the metrics' score (CobaltF$_{simple}$) or with the components of the metric (CobaltF$_{comp}$). We further boost the performance by combining the scores of the metrics BLEU, Meteor and UPF-Cobalt with our fluency features (MetricsF).

The results demonstrate that fluency features provide useful information regarding the overall translation quality, which is not fully captured by the standard candidate-reference comparison. These features are discriminative when the relationship to the reference does not provide enough information to distinguish between the quality of two alternative candidate translations. For example, it may well be the case that both MT outputs are very different from human reference, but one constitutes a valid alternative translation, while the other is totally unacceptable.

Finally, Groups III and VI contain the results of the best-performing evaluation systems from the WMT15 Metrics Task, as well as the baseline BLEU metric (Papineni et al., 2002) and a strong competitor, Meteor (Denkowski and Lavie, 2014), which we reproduce here for the sake of comparison. DPMFComb (Yu et al., 2015) and RATATOUILLE (Marie and Apidianaki, 2015) use a learnt combination of the scores from different evaluation metrics, while BEER_Treepel (Stanojevic and Sima'an, 2015) combines word matching, word order and syntax-level features. We note that the number and complexity of the metrics used in the above approaches is quite high. For instance, DPMFComb is based on 72 separate evaluation systems, including the resource-heavy linguistic metrics from the `Asiya Toolkit` (Giménez and Màrquez, 2010a).

7 Conclusions

The performance of reference-based MT evaluation metrics is limited by the fact that dissimilarities from a particular human translation do not always indicate bad MT quality. In this paper we proposed to amend this issue by integrating translation fluency in the evaluation. This aspect determines how well a translated text conforms to the linguistic regularities of the target language and constitutes a strong predictor of the overall MT quality.

In addition to the LM-based features developed in the field of quality estimation, we designed a more fine-grained representation of translation fluency, which in combination with our reference-based evaluation metric UPF-Cobalt yields a highly competitive performance for the prediction of pairwise preference judgments. The results of our experiments thus confirm that the integration of features intended to address translation fluency improves reference-based MT evaluation.

In the future we plan to investigate the performance of fluency features for the modelling of other types of manual evaluation, such as absolute scoring.

Acknowledgments

This work was partially funded by TUNER (TIN2015-65308-C5-5-R) and MINECO/FEDER, UE. Marina Fomicheva was supported by funding from the FI-DGR grant program of the Generalitat de Catalunya. Iria da Cunha was supported by a Ramón y Cajal contract (RYC-2014-16935). Lucia Specia was supported by the QT21 project (H2020 No. 645452).

References

Nguyen Bach, Fei Huang, and Yaser Al-Onaizan. 2011. Goodness: A Method for Measuring Machine Translation Confidence. In *Proceedings of the 49th Annual Meeting of the Association for Computational Linguistics: Human Language Technologies-Volume 1*, pages 211–219. Association for Computational Linguistics (ACL).

John Blatz, Erin Fitzgerald, George Foster, Simona Gandrabur, Cyril Goutte, Alex Kulesza, Alberto Sanchis, and Nicola Ueffing. 2004. Confidence Estimation for Machine Translation. In *Proceedings of the 20th International Conference on Computational Linguistics*, pages 315–321. ACL.

Ondřej Bojar, Rajen Chatterjee, Christian Federmann, Barry Haddow, Matthias Huck, Chris Hokamp, Philipp Koehn, Varvara Logacheva, Christof Monz, Matteo Negri, Matt Post, Carolina Scarton, Lucia Specia, and Marco Turchi. 2015. Findings of the 2015 Workshop on Statistical Machine Translation. In *Proceedings of the Tenth Workshop on Statistical Machine Translation*, pages 1–46, Lisbon, Portugal, September. ACL.

Chris Burges, Tal Shaked, Erin Renshaw, Ari Lazier, Matt Deeds, Nicole Hamilton, and Greg Hullender. 2005. Learning to Rank Using Gradient Descent. In *Proceedings of the 22nd international conference on Machine learning*, pages 89–96. ACM.

Chris Callison-Burch and Miles Osborne. 2006. Re-evaluating the Role of BLEU in Machine Translation Research. In *In Proceedings of the European Association for Computational Linguistics (EACL)*, pages 249–256. ACL.

Elisabet Comelles, Jordi Atserias, Victoria Arranz, and Irene Castellón. 2012. VERTa: Linguistic Features in MT Evaluation. In *Proceedings of the International Conference on Language Resources and Evaluation (LREC)*, pages 3944–3950.

Michael Denkowski and Alon Lavie. 2014. Meteor Universal: Language Specific Translation Evaluation for any Target Language. In *Proceedings of the Ninth Workshop on Statistical Machine Translation*, pages 376–380.

Mariano Felice and Lucia Specia. 2012. Linguistic Features for Quality Estimation. In *Proceedings of the Seventh Workshop on Statistical Machine Translation*, pages 96–103. ACL.

Marina Fomicheva and Núria Bel. 2016. Using Contextual Information for Machine Translation Evaluation. In *Proceedings of the Tenth International Conference on Language Resources and Evaluation (LREC 2016)*, pages 2755–2761.

Marina Fomicheva, Núria Bel, and Iria da Cunha. 2015a. Neutralizing the Effect of Translation Shifts on Automatic Machine Translation Evaluation. In *Computational Linguistics and Intelligent Text Processing*, pages 596–607.

Marina Fomicheva, Núria Bel, Iria da Cunha, and Anton Malinovskiy. 2015b. UPF-Cobalt Submission to WMT15 Metrics Task. In *Proceedings of the Tenth Workshop on Statistical Machine Translation*, pages 373–379.

Jesús Giménez and Lluís Màrquez. 2010a. Asiya: An Open Toolkit for Automatic Machine Translation (Meta-)Evaluation. *The Prague Bulletin of Mathematical Linguistics*, (94):77–86.

Jesús Giménez and Lluís Màrquez. 2010b. Linguistic Measures for Automatic Machine Translation Evaluation. *Machine Translation*, 24(3):209–240.

Francisco Guzmán, Shafiq Joty, Lluís Màrquez, and Preslav Nakov. 2014. Using Discourse Structure Improves Machine Translation Evaluation. In *ACL (1)*, pages 687–698.

Ding Liu and Daniel Gildea. 2005. Syntactic Features for Evaluation of Machine Translation. In *Proceedings of the ACL Workshop on Intrinsic and Extrinsic Evaluation Measures for Machine Translation and/or Summarization*, pages 25–32.

Chi-Kiu Lo, Anand Karthik Tumuluru, and Dekai Wu. 2012. Fully Automatic Semantic MT Evaluation. In *Proceedings of the Seventh Workshop on Statistical Machine Translation*, pages 243–252. ACL.

Ngoc-Quang Luong, Laurent Besacier, and Benjamin Lecouteux. 2015. Towards Accurate Predictors of Word Quality for Machine Translation: Lessons Learned on French–English and English–Spanish Systems. *Data & Knowledge Engineering*, 96:32–42.

Matouš Macháček and Ondřej Bojar. 2014. Results of the WMT14 Metrics Shared Task. In *Proceedings of the Ninth Workshop on Statistical Machine Translation*, pages 293–301.

Benjamin Marie and Marianna Apidianaki. 2015. Alignment-based Sense Selection in METEOR and the RATATOUILLE Recipe. In *Proceedings of the Tenth Workshop on Statistical Machine Translation*, pages 385–391.

Kishore Papineni, Salim Roukos, Todd Ward, and Wei-Jing Zhu. 2002. BLEU: a Method for Automatic Evaluation of Machine Translation. In *Proceedings of the 40th Annual Meeting of the ACL*, pages 311–318. ACL.

Sylvain Raybaud, David Langlois, and Kamel Smaïli. 2011. this sentence is wrong. detecting errors in machine-translated sentences. *Machine Translation*, 25(1):1–34.

Helmut Schmid. 1999. Improvements in part-of-speech tagging with an application to german. In *Natural language processing using very large corpora*, pages 13–25. Springer.

Kashif Shah, Trevor Cohn, and Lucia Specia. 2013. An Investigation on the Effectiveness of Features for Translation Quality Estimation. In *Proceedings of the Machine Translation Summit*, volume 14, pages 167–174.

Lucia Specia and Jesús Giménez. 2010. Combining Confidence Estimation and Reference-based Metrics for Segment-level MT Evaluation. In *The Ninth Conference of the Association for Machine Translation in the Americas*.

Lucia Specia, Marco Turchi, Nicola Cancedda, Marc Dymetman, and Nello Cristianini. 2009. Estimating the Sentence-level Quality of Machine Translation Systems. In *13th Conference of the European Association for Machine Translation*, pages 28–37.

Lucia Specia, Dhwaj Raj, and Marco Turchi. 2010. Machine Translation Evaluation versus Quality Estimation. *Machine Translation*, 24(1):39–50.

Lucia Specia, Gustavo Paetzold, and Carolina Scarton. 2015. Multi-level Translation Quality Prediction with QuEst++. In *53rd Annual Meeting of the Association for Computational Linguistics and Seventh International Joint Conference on Natural Language Processing of the Asian Federation of Natural Language Processing: System Demonstrations*, pages 115–120.

Miloš Stanojevic and Khalil Sima'an. 2015. BEER 1.1: ILLC UvA Submission to Metrics and Tuning Task. In *Proceedings of the Tenth Workshop on Statistical Machine Translation*, pages 396–401.

Md Arafat Sultan, Steven Bethard, and Tamara Sumner. 2014. Back to Basics for Monolingual Alignment: Exploiting Word Similarity and Contextual Evidence. *Transactions of the ACL*, 2:219–230.

Gideon Toury. 2012. *Descriptive Translation Studies and beyond: Revised edition*, volume 100. John Benjamins Publishing.

C. Uhrik and W. Ward. 1997. Confidence Metrics Based on N-gram Language Model Backoff Behaviors. In *Proceedings of Fifth European Conference on Speech Communication and Technology*, pages 2771–2774.

Hui Yu, Qingsong Ma, Xiaofeng Wu, and Qun Liu. 2015. CASICT-DCU Participation in WMT2015 Metrics Task. In *Proceedings of the Tenth Workshop on Statistical Machine Translation*, pages 417–421.

DTED: Evaluation of Machine Translation Structure Using Dependency Parsing and Tree Edit Distance

Martin McCaffery
School of Computer Science
University of St Andrews
KY16 9SX, United Kingdom

Mark-Jan Nederhof
School of Computer Science
University of St Andrews
KY16 9SX, United Kingdom

Abstract

We present DTED, a submission to the WMT 2016 Metrics Task using structural information generated by dependency parsing and evaluated using tree edit distances. In this paper we apply this system to translations produced during WMT 2015, and compare our scores with human rankings from that year. We find moderate correlations, despite the human judgements being based on all aspects of the sentences while our metric is based only on word order.

1 Introduction

In the ever-growing field of translation metrics, a number of systems exist which attempt to provide an overall rating for a sentence. Most of these use one or more reference translations produced by a human as a gold standard. One of the earliest examples of such a metric may be BLEU (Papineni et al., 2002), using an adapted version of the well-known principle of Precision. More recently, NIST (Doddington, 2002) and Meteor (Lavie and Agarwal, 2007) have used n-gram analysis to provide similar heuristics, and many other techniques have been proposed (Dahlmeier et al., 2011; Gamon et al., 2005).

These metrics are useful when making high-level comparisons between several machine translation systems, but they offer very limited insight into the linguistic workings of the machine translation process. They can be used in automatic processes such as training systems through hill-climbing iterations, or as broad descriptions of a system's overall quality. It is however difficult to use this kind of score to gain more precise insights into a system's features; for example, different tasks may have different priorities for which er-

rors are least desirable. Deeper analysis might also be able to pinpoint specific areas of improvement within a system. With these and other goals in mind, granular metrics have been created to evaluate individual aspects of the translated output in isolation (Zeman et al., 2011; Popović, 2011).

When developing such granular metrics, the question of which linguistic aspects of translations to focus on is far from trivial. While there has been much related discussion in the professional and educational spheres of the factors which can affect understanding of a given translation, the academic sphere has been less prolific. Nonetheless, a widely-used taxonomy on the distinct problem types which can be observed has been produced by Vilar et al. (2006), while Birch et al. (2008) investigated those which most affect overall understanding of a translation.

One of the prime factors identified by Birch et al. (2008) was word order, and metrics have been produced since then which focus on this factor (Talbot et al., 2011; Birch et al., 2010). These metrics apply various techniques, but most are based on the concept of comparing individual substrings of a source and reference sentence. While these techniques allow lightweight algorithms to produce rough scores, they ignore how the structure of a sentence can dramatically affect the impact of a mistake in ordering. For example, the mistake in the hypothesis of sentence 1 of Table 1 is much less significant than that of sentence 2, despite the latter being closer in a 'flat' judgement.

In an attempt to mitigate these problems, though without the explicit goal of focusing on word order, some work has been done using structural evaluation of sentences through dependency parsing (Gaifman, 1965). These systems either focus on applying BLEU-style n-gram matching to a tree context (Liu and Gildea, 2005; Owczarzak et al., 2007) or focus on specific relationships between

491

	Reference	Hypothesis
1	I spoke to him there.	I spoke there to him.
2	She let it be and left.	She let it and be left.

Table 1: Example word order errors

and groupings of nodes in the trees and compare those features between hypothesis and reference trees to produce holistic judgements (Habash and Elkholy, 2008; Yu et al., 2014).

The approach of our system, named DTED (Dependency-based Tree Edit Distance), differs from existing word order literature by including dependency structures, but adds to the body of dependency-based work by focusing on node order rather than attempting to give an overall score. We work on complete dependency trees, rather than specific subsections, to produce an edit distance between the hypothesis and reference trees.

A tree edit distance is a count of the actions required to convert one ordered tree into another. In the manner of Levenshtein distances (Levenshtein, 1965) and Word Error Rate (Nießen et al., 2000), these actions are limited to Renaming, Deleting an existing node, or Inserting a new one. A number of variants on this model have been proposed, many attempting to improve the efficiency of the algorithm when applied in large-scale or high-throughput areas (Bille, 2005). The algorithm we have implemented is an extension of that proposed by Demaine et al. (2009), which is worst-case optimal, running in $O(n^3)$ time where n is the number of words in the shorter sentence.

Its output is thus a count of required modifications, which is in turn converted to a normalised score between 0 and 1. This is coupled with a weighting, indicating when aggregating scores to a system level what proportion of nodes were indicated as aligned by a preprocessing step. Our assumption is that the position of an aligned word is more reliable than an unaligned one, so when calculating corpus-wide scores we should disproportionately consider the information of those with many aligned words.

Our algorithm thus requires nothing more than the source and reference pairs, plus tools to calculate alignments and dependency trees for the chosen target language. We have used English, but the methodology would be easily applicable to any other target language for which these two components exist.

2 Related Work

2.1 Holistic metrics

Word Error Rate (Nießen et al., 2000) uses an approach closely linked to Levenshtein distances (Levenshtein, 1965), producing a straightforward count of the number of insertions, deletions and substitutions needed to convert the hypothesis into a given reference. The Position-Independent Error Rate (Tillmann et al., 1997) performs similar calculations without considering word ordering. More recently, Translation Error Rate (Snover et al., 2006) allows 'phrase shifting' of word groups together, while CDer (Leusch et al., 2006) places higher priority and level of detail on block movement calculations.

BLEU (Papineni et al., 2002) on the other hand has achieved success by directly comparing n-grams between the two sentences: it calculates a geometric mean of n-gram precisions and applies a penalty for short sentences.

A more recent and substantial metric, Meteor (Lavie and Agarwal, 2007), first applies the parameterised harmonic mean of the Precision and Recall (Rijsbergen, 1979), which measures the correctness of the individual word choices in the hypothesis sentence. It includes a second step, taking into account the ordering of those words. It does this by 'chunking' the sentences, finding the smallest number of groups of aligned words such that each contains words which are both adjacent and identical in both hypothesis and reference sentences. The ratio of the chunk count to the total number of aligned words represents the 'goodness' of the ordering, and is then multiplied with the original harmonic mean to produce a final score.

2.2 Unstructured word order systems

The standalone nature of the second phase of Meteor's pipeline means that we can use it in isolation and consider it an existing metric for word order. We have thus modified Meteor trivially to ignore the initial harmonic mean and produce only a fragmentation score; results for both this and the off-the-shelf system are reported in section 4.

Talbot et al. (2011) use a similar technique to Meteor-Frag, basing its results on the number of chunks of contiguous words aligned by a human annotator. Birch et al. (2010) provide a different approach to the problem, representing word order as mathematical permutations and counting individual disagreements in order, and transformations required to convert one sentence into another, in a number of ways. They ignore all features of a text other than word order of aligned nodes, to produce a mathematically pure model, but sacrifice some of the less vital – but still useful – information represented by unaligned nodes and inter-word semantic relationships.

Contrary to the above metrics' focus on word order in isolation, two tools have been designed to provide a simple approximation of several error categories at once. Both Addicter (Zeman et al., 2011) and Hjerson (Popović, 2011) use comparisons of aligned words to provide a quick analysis of missing, unexpected and moved nodes.

2.3 Dependency-structured systems

While the above metrics all apply to n-grams or other unstructured representations of data, a number of proposals exist of metrics which use dependency parsing to represent sentence structure. Liu and Gildea (2005) improved on the base concept behind BLEU to calculate headword chain precision for unlabelled dependency trees, while Owczarzak et al. (2007) extend this to use labelled dependencies.

Habash and Elkholy (2008) use a different approach to dependency trees, merging n-gram precision subscores calculated similarly to BLEU with 'span-extended structural bigram precision subscores', using two methods to compare similarities between surface (flat) distances for different pairs of adjacent nodes. Yu et al. (2014) use a different approach again, considering only the reference trees' structural elements and observing, for a variety of structural segments which they consider most relevant, whether the hypothesis sentences contain the same words as those segments in the same order.

3 Metric design

3.1 Phase 1: parsing

In order to best represent the structure of the sentences we follow past examples and parse them into dependency trees. Dependency parsing has become recognised as providing a good balance between deep semantic analysis and simplicity of parsing procedure. First devised by Gaifman (1965), it uses a simplified semantic role analysis to link words by their dependency relations, providing a bare-bones structural description of the

sentences, which can then be compared.

We used the dependency parsing framework provided by Python's NLTK toolkit (Bird, 2006). This in turn wraps around the Java-implemented Malt parser (Nivre, 2003).

3.2 Phase 2: tree edit

In order to produce a measure of the correctness of word order given the structural representations produced by dependency parsing, we now need to compare the structures. To do this, we use a tree edit distance algorithm, as originally put forward by Zhang and Shasha (1989). The principle behind a tree edit distance is to count the number of delete, insert and/or match (substitution) operations needed to turn one tree into another. In the version we use (Demaine et al., 2009), the 'insert' operation, whereby a node is created in one tree X to correspond to a node in tree Y, is simply represented by a 'delete' of the corresponding node in tree Y.

The most straightforward way of executing a tree edit distance is simply to give equal weighting to all operations on all nodes. This gives us a simple measure of the structural similarity of the two trees: two identical trees will have the minimum cost, namely one 'match' operation per node, while any sub-optimally placed nodes will need to be deleted and inserted elsewhere, costing 2 actions each. While other variants of DTED are available, this version - labelled 'Pure' in section 4 - has been used for both WMT2015 and WMT2016.

3.3 Phase 3: normalisation

The tree edit distance produced by the previous stage represents actions required to convert one tree into the other. We apply a simple formula to convert this count to a normalised score between 0 and 1: a more intuitive and comparable value when dealing with larger numbers of sentences. This is done slightly differently depending on the variant of DTED being used, but the score calculated by the Pure version for a given sentence pair s, with hypothesis of length n_H and reference of length n_R, is very simple. Having determined that $dist$ actions need to be performed across the trees, we say that:

$$score_s = 1 - \frac{dist}{n_H + n_R} \qquad (1)$$

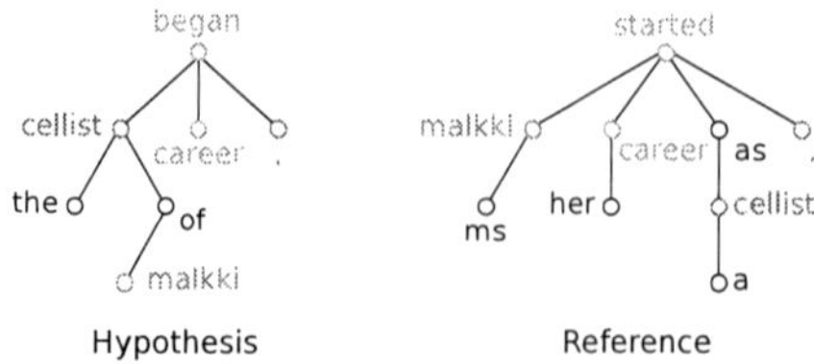

Figure 1: Sample parsed dependency trees. Matching colours show alignment between nodes.

	Reference	Hypothesis
Deleted	ms	cellist
	cellist	
	a	
Matched	began	started
	the	malkki
	of	career
	malkki	her
	.	.
	career	as

Table 2: Edit operations calculated by DTED for sentences shown in Figure 1.

3.4 Variants

While we have implemented a number of variants of DTED, for WMT 2015 and WMT 2016 we use only the 'Pure' version which processes only the structure of the sentences while ignoring other information such as word alignments. DTED has been run on two types of input. First, we have run each version on normal dependency trees, leveraging the full structural information available. For comparison, we have also run each on flattened trees from which the structural information has been removed. This is done in a preprocessing step by artificially forcing each node to be the only child of its predecessor. This version is intended to nullify the structural advantage given by the rest of the system, to provide a baseline for comparison.

With the 'pure' version of DTED, the modifications shown in Table 2 are calculated.

3.5 Result aggregation

Combining individual sentence scores to an overall system-level result is done in two ways. The straightforward way is to simply take an arithmetic mean of all sentence scores, indicated in table 4 as unweighted or *not W*. This gives a total score for corpus c containing N sentences as:

$$unweighted_c = \frac{\sum_s score_s}{N} \qquad (2)$$

Additionally, to investigate the importance of the aligned words in our sentence, we produce a version which assigns each sentence a weight equal to the proportion of nodes aligned in the sentence. With n_a aligned nodes and n_{na} unaligned nodes, the weight for sentence s for the Weighted version of DTED (*W* in table 4) is calculated as:

$$weight_s = \frac{n_a}{n_a + n_{na}} \qquad (3)$$

For an individual sentence the score and weight can be viewed separately, while overall values for a corpus are calculated as:

$$weighted_c = \frac{\sum_s (score_s \times weight_s)}{\sum_s weight_s} \qquad (4)$$

3.6 Example

Figure 1 shows dependency trees for the following sentences which occur in the WMT 2015 corpus. All pairs of words shared by both sentences are aligned, as are 'started' and 'began'.

Hyp: The cellist of Malkki began career.
Ref: Ms Malkki started her career as a cellist.

This comes to a total of 4 Delete operations and 6 Match operations, resulting in a total matching *dist* of 10. With the hypothesis tree containing $n_H = 7$ nodes and the reference containing $n_R = 9$, we can normalise this (as per equation 1) to:

$$score_s = 1 - \frac{10}{7+9} = 0.375$$

Finally, we may optionally consider a weighting for the sentence as per equation 3.

$$weight_s = \frac{10}{10+6} = 0.625$$

This weighting indicates that we consider our low rating of the sentence partially trustworthy relative to others in the corpus.

4 Results & Discussion

4.1 Setup & Evaluation

DTED has been run on sentences provided for the 2015 (Bojar et al., 2015) and 2016 Workshops on Statistical Machine Translation. The results

Metric	cs-en	de-en	fi-en	fr-en	ru-en	all
BLEU	**0.989**	0.836	0.920	0.970	0.643	0.622
WER	0.913	0.813	0.794	0.972	0.700	0.524
TER	0.929	0.822	0.846	0.975	0.712	0.563
PER	0.980	0.764	0.858	0.967	0.753	**0.670**
CDER	0.955	0.813	0.944	**0.981**	0.762	0.561
Meteor	0.984	**0.934**	**0.961**	0.968	**0.877**	0.647

Table 3: System-level correlations of holistic metrics with normalised human rankings

Metric	*Version*	*W*	*F*	cs-en	de-en	fi-en	fr-en	ru-en	all
Meteor	Frag	-	-	0.905	0.853	**0.941**	0.927	0.781	**0.615**
DTED	Pure	X	X	0.974	**0.877**	0.841	**0.993**	**0.824**	0.522
DTED	Pure	X	✓	0.964	0.542	0.867	0.729	0.431	0.461
DTED	Pure	✓	X	**0.975**	0.872	0.814	0.992	0.822	0.522
DTED	Pure	✓	✓	0.963	0.507	0.886	0.476	0.337	0.445

Table 4: System-level correlations of word order metrics with normalised human rankings

for 2015 data are provided in this paper, while for 2016 the reader is referred to the Findings of the 2016 Workshop on Machine Translation. For the latter, DTED uses unflattened trees, without weighting by aligned nodes. Sentences from all available into-English corpora were used, but only segments for which corresponding human judgements were available. The number of individual systems for each language pair, and the count of sentences within each, are given in table 5.

Human judgements during the Workshop were given as rankings between up to 5 systems, with ties allowed. We have normalised these ranks into scores out of 1: for example, a rank of 3 between five systems is converted to 0.5, reflecting that an equal number of systems were preferred to it as were considered less good, while a system ranked best would achieve a perfect score of 1.

It should be noted that while DTED is intended to evaluate word order in isolation, rankings at WMT were based on *all* features of the sentences. As no data of sufficient quantity and quality was available for human judgements specifically of word order, we have used the holistic data. As such, we do not expect cutting-edge correlational values for this data; instead, such comparisons are provided for two separate reasons.

First, as word order is clearly involved in some non-trivial way in human judgements, we can assume that holistic ranks contain an implicit word order component. A limited level of similarity between human judgements and DTED is thus to be expected, as they are at least partially measuring the same phenomenon. In addition, while the DTED algorithm is intended to measure word order alone, the structure and alignment of the trees we use may themselves depend on other factors. For example, a badly chosen word may occupy a different role in its sentence than the reference choice would, resulting in an unpredictable change in the actions needed to correct it.

Second, if we assume DTED's results to be successfully representative of a sentence's word order quality and human judgements to contain a word order component, the level of correlation can begin to quantify the significance of word order within the overall judgement. In the ideal theoretical case where DTED perfectly simulated human intuition on word order, such correlational coefficients would give direct insight into the significance of that intuition to overall quality judgements.

4.2 Ratings

We have performed analysis on two types of metric: holistic and word order specific. Table 3 compares human judgements to those produced by a number of well-known and widely used baseline metrics, while table 4 shows the same values for metrics designed specifically for word order. In both tables, the highest score for each corpus is highlighted.

Meteor's fragmentation-only subsystem (see section 2.2) is included in the latter table, while

	cs-en	de-en	fi-en	fr-en	ru-en	all
Num. systems	7	13	14	6	13	53
Total sentences	909	692	510	815	782	3708

Table 5: Sizes of corpora used for all empirical calculations, all produced during WMT 2015

the version of Meteor in the former is a standard off-the-shelf installation. For DTED, the W column indicates whether sentences were considered equally when aggregating, or were *Weighted* based on aligned word content as per section 3.5. Results run on *F*lattened trees (section 3.4) are indicated by the column F.

All scores except those for DTED and Meteor were calculated using implementations of the metrics provided with the well-known open-source system Moses (Koehn et al., 2007). In all cases, the numbers shown are Pearson correlation coefficients between the output of the given metric at the system level and the normalised human judgements provided at WMT 2015.

4.3 Discussion

The main trend we can see from tables 3 and 4 is that for the versions of DTED with the highest correlation values to human judgement, those values are similar to, if marginally lower than, the scores of the baseline metrics. To represent this trend, the unflattened version of DTED (irrespective of weighting) has an overall correlation almost exactly the same as the baseline metric WER which performed the most poorly.

While the correlations of DTED versions are thus fairly encouraging when compared to those of other metrics, they are also interesting when compared to each other. An almost universal trend is that when applied on flattened trees DTED was significantly less effective in predicting human judgements. This strongly indicates that we have succeeded in leveraging the structural information in the non-flattened dependency trees and used the information to good purpose in a similar way to a human.

It should be noted that weighting the sentences according to the proportion of aligned nodes provided a boost to correlations, albeit an extremely small one.

5 Conclusions & Future Work

DTED represents the first work we know of which uses tree edit distances to incorporate structure

into the evaluation of machine translation word order. Our results suggest that this approach, while not as holistically accurate as metrics designed for that purpose, nonetheless provides scores with non-trivial similarities to human ratings. This suggests that our metric does indeed measure a significant component of humans' intuition on sentence quality for English. While not a conclusion that can be drawn from the empirical results as such, we feel confident that our metric does primarily evaluate word order as opposed to other factors such as word choice. Taking these two assumptions together, we can say that a significant component of humans' sentence-quality intuition is based on the order of words.

Though the statement that word order accounts for a large part of humans' quality judgements is highly interesting, it would be worthwhile to investigate the relationship more directly. An obvious way to produce results more tailored to it would be to obtain human judgements based solely and explicitly on word order. Such judgements would also allow us to more appropriately evaluate the more alignment-focused versions of DTED: while in the experiments we have performed on WMT judgements these have done less well, this may simply be because these variants are intended to more precisely focus on word order. An increase in such precision will necessarily result in less broad scores and thus lower correlation with the broad-scope judgements available.

While tree edit distance leverages much of the information contained in structural representations of sentences, it fails to account for the distances through which nodes must be moved. We thus intend to consider models more akin to gradual movement than disparate operations, such as those related to the concept of inversion numbers (Conlon et al., 1999). A further avenue of investigation would be whether the structural and order-specific functionality of a tree edit distance could be approximated or reproduced by a more lightweight algorithm.

References

Philip Bille. 2005. A survey on tree edit distance and related problems. *Theoretical Computer Science*, 337(1-3):217–239, jun.

Alexandra Birch, Miles Osborne, and Philipp Koehn. 2008. Predicting success in machine translation. In *Proceedings of the Conference on Empirical Methods in Natural Language Processing*, pages 745–754.

Alexandra Birch, Miles Osborne, and Phil Blunsom. 2010. Metrics for MT evaluation: evaluating reordering. *Machine Translation*, 24(1):15–26, jan.

Steven Bird. 2006. NLTK: The Natural Language Toolkit. In *Proceedings of the COLING/ACL on Interactive presentation sessions (COLING-ACL '06)*, pages 69–72.

Ondej Bojar, Rajen Chatterjee, Christian Federmann, Barry Haddow, Matthias Huck, Chris Hokamp, Philipp Koehn, Varvara Logacheva, Christof Monz, Matteo Negri, Matt Post, Carolina Scarton, Lucia Specia, and Marco Turchi. 2015. Findings of the 2015 Workshop on Statistical Machine Translation. In *Proceedings of the 10th Workshop on Statistical Machine Translation*, pages 1–46, Lisboa, Portugal.

Margaret M Conlon, Maria Falidas, Mary Jane Forde, John W Kennedy, S McIlwaine, and Joseph Stern. 1999. Inversion numbers of graphs. *Graph Theory Notes of New York*, 37:42–48.

Daniel Dahlmeier, Chang Liu, and Hwee Tou Ng. 2011. TESLA at WMT 2011: Translation evaluation and tunable metric. In *Proceedings of the Sixth Workshop on Statistical Machine Translation*, pages 78–84.

Erik D. Demaine, Shay Mozes, Benjamin Rossman, and Oren Weimann. 2009. An optimal decomposition algorithm for tree edit distance. *ACM Transactions on Algorithms*, 6:1–19.

George Doddington. 2002. Automatic evaluation of machine translation quality using n-gram co-occurrence statistics. In *Proceedings of the Second International Conference on Human Language Technology Research*, pages 138–145.

Haim Gaifman. 1965. Dependency systems and phrase-structure systems. *Information and Control*, 8(3):304–337.

Michael Gamon, Anthony Aue, and Martine Smets. 2005. Sentence-level MT evaluation without reference translations: Beyond language modeling. In *Proceedings of the European Association for Machine Translation*, pages 103–111.

Nizar Habash and Ahmed Elkholy. 2008. SEPIA: Surface Span Extension to Syntactic Dependency Precision-based MT Evaluation. In *Proceedings of the NIST Metrics for Machine Translation Workshop at the Association for Machine Translation in the Americas Conference*, Waikiki, HI.

Philipp Koehn, Hieu Hoang, Alexandra Birch, Chris Callison-Burch, Marcello Federico, Nicola Bertoldi, Brooke Cowan, Wade Shen, Christine Moran, Richard Zens, Chris Dyer, Ondej Bojar, Alexandra Constantin, and Evan Herbst. 2007. Moses: Open source toolkit for statistical machine translation. In *Proceedings of the 45th Annual Meeting of the ACL on Interactive Poster and Demonstration Sessions*, pages 177–180. Association for Computational Linguistics.

Alon Lavie and Abhaya Agarwal. 2007. METEOR: An automatic metric for MT evaluation with high levels of correlation with human judgments. In *Proceedings of the Second Workshop on Statistical Machine Translation*, pages 228–231.

Gregor Leusch, Nicola Ueffing, and Hermann Ney. 2006. CDer: Efficient MT evaluation using block movements. In *Proceedings of EACL-2006 (11th Conference of the European Chapter of the Association for Computational Linguistics)*, pages 241–248.

Vladimir Iosifovich Levenshtein. 1965. Binary codes capable of correcting deletions, insertions, and reversals. *Soviet Physics Dokl.*, 10(1):707–710.

Ding Liu and Daniel Gildea. 2005. Syntactic features for evaluation of machine translation. In *Proceedings of the ACL Workshop on Intrinsic and Extrinsic Evaluation Measures for Machine Translation and/or Summarization*, pages 25–32.

Sonja Nießen, Franz-Josef Och, Gregor Leusch, and Hermann Ney. 2000. An evaluation tool for machine translation: fast evaluation for MT research. *LREC*, pages 0–6.

Joakim Nivre. 2003. An efficient algorithm for projective dependency parsing. *Proceedings of the 8th International Workshop on Parsing Technologies*, pages 149–160.

Karolina Owczarzak, Josef van Genabith, and Andy Way. 2007. Labelled dependencies in machine translation evaluation. In *Proceedings of the Second Workshop on Statistical Machine Translation*, pages 104–111.

Kishore Papineni, Salim Roukos, Todd Ward, and Wei-Jing Zhu. 2002. BLEU: a method for automatic evaluation of machine translation. In *Proceedings of the 40th Annual Meeting on Association for Computational Linguistics*, pages 311–318.

Maja Popović. 2011. Hjerson: An open source tool for automatic error classification of machine translation output. *The Prague Bulletin of Mathematical Linguistics*, 96:59–67.

C J Van Rijsbergen. 1979. *Information Retrieval*. Butterworth-Heinemann, Newton, MA, USA, 2nd edition.

Matthew Snover, Bonnie Dorr, College Park, Richard Schwartz, Linnea Micciulla, and John Makhoul. 2006. A Study of Translation Edit Rate with Targeted Human Annotation. In *Proceedings of the 7th Conference of the Association for Machine Translation in the Americas,*, number August, pages 223–231, Cambridge, Massachusetts.

David Talbot, Hideto Kazawa, Hiroshi Ichikawa, Jason Katz-Brown, Masakazu Seno, and Franz-Josef Och. 2011. A lightweight evaluation framework for machine translation reordering. In *Proceedings of the Sixth Workshop on Statistical Machine Translation*, pages 12–21. Association for Computational Linguistics.

C Tillmann, S Vogel, H Ney, A. Zubiaga, and H. Sawaf. 1997. Accelerated DP Based Search for Statistical Translation. *Fifth European Conference on Speech Communication and Technology*, pages 2667–2670.

David Vilar, Jia Xu, Luis Fernando D'Haro, and Hermann Ney. 2006. Error analysis of statistical machine translation output. In *Proceedings of the Conference on Language Resources and Evaluation*, pages 697–702, Genoa.

Hui Yu, Xiaofeng Wu, Jun Xie, Wenbin Jiang, Qun Liu, and Shouxun Lin. 2014. RED: A Reference Dependency Based MT Evaluation Metric. In *Proceedings of COLING 2014, the 25th International Conference on Computational Linguistics: Technical Papers*, pages 2042–2051.

Daniel Zeman, Mark Fishel, Jan Berka, and Ondej Bojar. 2011. Addicter: What is Wrong with My Translations? *The Prague Bulletin of Mathematical Linguistics*, (96):79–88.

Kaizhong Zhang and Dennis Shasha. 1989. Simple Fast Algorithms for the Editing Distance between Trees and Related Problems. *SIAM Journal on Computing*, 18(6):1245–1262.

CHRF deconstructed: β parameters and n-gram weights

Maja Popović
Humboldt University of Berlin
Berlin, Germany
`maja.popovic@hu-berlin.de`

Abstract

Character n-gram F-score (CHRF) is shown to correlate very well with human rankings of different machine translation outputs, especially for morphologically rich target languages. However, only two versions have been explored so far, namely CHRF1 (standard F-score, $\beta = 1$) and CHRF3 ($\beta = 3$), both with uniform n-gram weights. In this work, we investigated CHRF in more details, namely β parameters in range from 1/6 to 6, and we found out that CHRF2 is the most promising version. Then we investigated different n-gram weights for CHRF2 and found out that the uniform weights are the best option. Apart from this, CHRF scores were systematically compared with WORDF scores, and a preliminary experiment carried out on small amount of data with direct human scores indicates that the main advantage of CHRF is that it does not penalise too hard acceptable variations in high quality translations.

1 Introduction

Recent investigations (Popović, 2015; Stanojević et al., 2015) have shown that the character n-gram F-score (CHRF) represents a very promising evaluation metric for machine translation, especially for morphologically rich target languages – it is simple, it does not require any additional tools or information, it is language independent and tokenisation independent, and it correlates very well with human rankings. However, only two versions of this score have been investigated so far: standard F-score CHRF1 where $\beta = 1$, i.e. precision and recall have the same weight, as well as CHRF3, where recall has three times more weight.

In this work, we systematically investigate β parameters: standard version ($\beta = 1$), five β values favorising recall (2,3,4,5,6) and five β values favorising precision (1/2, 1/3, 1/4, 1/5 and 1/6). In addition, we also compare CHRFβ scores with WORDFβ scores.

The CHRFβ and WORDFβ scores are calculated for all available translation outputs from the WMT14 (Bojar et al., 2014) and WMT15 (Bojar et al., 2015) shared tasks and then compared with human rankings on segment level using Kendall's τ rank correlation coefficient.

The scores were analysed for all available target languages. i.e. English, French, German, Czech, Russian, Hindi and Finnish.

2 CHRF and WORDF scores

The general formula for n-gram based F-score is:

$$ngrF\beta = (1 + \beta^2)\frac{ngrP \cdot ngrR}{\beta^2 \cdot ngrP + ngrR} \qquad (1)$$

where $ngrP$ and $ngrR$ stand for n-gram precision and recall arithmetically averaged over all n-grams from $n = 1$ to N:

- $ngrP$
  n-gram precision: percentage of n-grams in the hypothesis which have a counterpart in the reference;

- $ngrR$
  n-gram recall: percentage of n-grams in the reference which are also present in the hypothesis.

and β is a parameter which assigns β times more weight to recall than to precision. If $\beta = 1$, they have the same weight; if $\beta = 4$, recall has four times more importance than precision; if $\beta = 1/4$,

Proceedings of the First Conference on Machine Translation, Volume 2: Shared Task Papers, pages 499–504,
Berlin, Germany, August 11-12, 2016. ©2016 Association for Computational Linguistics

precision has four times more importance than recall.

WORDF is then calculated on word n-grams and CHRF is calculated on character n-grams. Maximum n-gram length N for both metrics is investigated in previous work, and N=4 is shown to be optimal for WORDF (Popović, 2011), N=6 for CHRF (Popović, 2015).

3 Comparison of CHRFβ and WORDFβ scores

The CHRFβ and WORDFβ scores are calculated for the following β parameters: 1/6, 1/5, 1/4, 1/3, 1/2, 1, 2, 3, 4, 5 and 6. For each CHRFβ and WORDFβ score, the segment level τ correlation coefficients are calculated for each translation output. In total, 20 τ coefficients were obtained for each score – five English outputs from the WMT14 task and five from the WMT15, together with ten outputs in other languages, i.e. two French, two German, two Czech, two Russian, one Hindi and one Finnish. The obtained τ coefficients were then summarised into the following four values:

- *mean*
  τ averaged over all translation outputs;

- *diff*
  averaged difference between the τ of the particular metric and the τs of all other metrics investigated in this work;

- *rank>*
  percentage of translation outputs where the particular metric has better τ than the other metrics investigated in this work;

- *rank⩾*
  percentage of translation outputs where the particular metric has better or equal τ than the other metrics investigated in this work.

These values for each metric are presented in Table 1. In addition, the values are shown separately for translation into English (Table 2) and for translation out of English (Table 3).
Table 1 shows that:

- CHRF ranks better than WORDF;

- recall is more important than precision;

- the most promising metric is CHRF2;

metric	mean	diff	rank>	rank⩾
CHRF1/6	0.330	0.114	52.1	58.6
CHRF1/5	0.332	0.314	58.1	65.0
CHRF1/4	0.334	0.538	63.5	69.5
CHRF1/3	0.338	1.043	69.0	74.3
CHRF1/2	0.347	1.971	75.5	81.9
CHRF1	0.365	3.871	86.2	92.6
CHRF2	**0.370**	**4.400**	**86.7**	**93.6**
CHRF3	0.369	4.286	83.1	91.4
CHRF4	0.368	4.162	80.5	88.6
CHRF5	0.367	4.090	77.6	87.1
CHRF6	0.367	4.081	76.9	87.1
WORDF1/6	0.296	-3.443	6.2	16.6
WORDF1/5	0.296	-3.357	6.9	19.8
WORDF1/4	0.296	-3.348	9.5	21.9
WORDF1/3	0.298	-3.200	16.0	26.9
WORDF1/2	0.300	-2.924	21.9	30.7
WORDF1	0.306	-2.309	31.9	39.8
WORDF2	<u>0.309</u>	<u>-1.995</u>	<u>38.3</u>	<u>47.6</u>
WORDF3	0.308	-2.038	30.2	44.5
WORDF4	0.308	-2.076	28.1	43.1
WORDF5	0.308	-2.090	23.3	39.5
WORDF6	0.308	-2.090	23.8	40.0

Table 1: Overall average segment level (τ) correlation *mean* (column 1), *diff* (column 2), *rank>* (column 3) and *rank⩾* (column 4) for each CHRFβ score. Bold represents the overall best value and underline represents the best WORDFβ value. The most promising metric is CHRF2.

- $\beta = 2$ is the best option both for CHRF (bold) as well as for WORDF (underline).

Additional observations from Tables 2 and 3:

- for translation into English:
  - the most promising metrics are CHRF2 and CHRF1;
  - the best WORDFβ variant is WORDF2.

- for translation out of English:
  - the most promising metrics are CHRF2 and CHRF3
  - the best WORDFβ variants are WORDF2 and WORDF3

indicating that the recall is even more important for morphologically rich(er) languages.

Regardless to these slight differences between English and non-English texts, CHRF2 can be considered as the most promising variant generally.

metric	mean	diff	rank>	rank⩾
CHRF1/6	0.357	1.514	57.6	63.8
CHRF1/5	0.358	1.638	64.8	71.0
CHRF1/4	0.359	1.781	69.0	74.3
CHRF1/3	0.363	2.138	74.8	79.5
CHRF1/2	0.368	2.695	81.9	87.6
CHRF1	0.377	3.695	**91.0**	**98.1**
CHRF2	**0.378**	**3.710**	85.7	91.9
CHRF3	0.376	3.476	83.3	90.0
CHRF4	0.374	3.281	77.6	84.8
CHRF5	0.372	3.091	70.5	78.6
CHRF6	0.372	3.048	70.0	78.1
WORDF1/6	0.308	-3.605	6.2	13.8
WORDF1/5	0.309	-3.481	5.7	16.7
WORDF1/4	0.309	-3.538	10.5	20.5
WORDF1/3	0.311	-3.333	15.2	24.3
WORDF1/2	0.313	-3.076	18.1	24.8
WORDF1	0.320	-2.324	33.3	40.0
WORDF2	<u>0.323</u>	<u>-2.010</u>	<u>40.0</u>	<u>49.0</u>
WORDF3	0.322	-2.143	28.1	41.9
WORDF4	0.322	-2.157	28.1	41.4
WORDF5	0.322	-2.195	23.3	39.0
WORDF6	0.321	-2.205	22.9	38.1

Table 2: Translation into English: average segment level (τ) correlation *mean* (column 1), *diff* (column 2), *rank>* (column 3) and *rank⩾* (column 4) for each CHRFβ score. Bold represents the overall best value and underline represents the best WORDFβ value. The most promising metric is CHRF2.

metric	mean	diff	rank>	rank⩾
CHRF1/6	0.290	-1.381	46.0	52.9
CHRF1/5	0.292	-1.138	50.8	58.7
CHRF1/4	0.295	-0.767	57.7	64.6
CHRF1/3	0.302	- 0.138	63.0	68.8
CHRF1/2	0.314	1.186	68.8	74.1
CHRF1	0.342	4.067	82.0	87.8
CHRF2	**0.353**	**5.224**	**87.8**	**94.7**
CHRF3	**0.353**	**5.224**	83.1	93.7
CHRF4	0.352	5.148	83.1	91.5
CHRF5	**0.353**	**5.219**	83.1	93.7
CHRF6	**0.353**	**5.224**	83.6	93.8
WORDF1/6	0.271	-3.367	6.3	20.1
WORDF1/5	0.271	-3.281	8.4	23.8
WORDF1/4	0.272	-3.267	9.5	25.4
WORDF1/3	0.273	-3.152	16.9	28.6
WORDF1/2	0.276	-2.838	24.3	34.9
WORDF1	0.281	-2.319	29.6	38.1
WORDF2	0.284	-1.976	<u>36.5</u>	45.5
WORDF3	<u>0.285</u>	<u>-1.900</u>	34.4	<u>48.2</u>
WORDF4	<u>0.285</u>	-1.919	29.6	45.5
WORDF5	0.284	-1.929	24.3	40.2
WORDF6	<u>0.285</u>	-1.919	25.9	42.3

Table 3: Translation from English: average segment level (τ) correlation *mean* (column 1), *diff* (column 2), *rank>* (column 3) and *rank⩾* (column 4) for each CHRFβ score. Bold represents the overall best value and underline represents the best WORDFβ value. The most promising metric is CHRF2.

However, taking these differences into account together with the fact that for English, CHRF1 performed better than CHRF3 in the WMT15 metrics shared task, we decided to submit CHRF2 together with CHRF1 and CHRF3 in order to be able to draw more reliable conclusions.

3.1 Investigating n-gram weights for CHRF2

As already mentioned, all CHRFβ variants explored so far are based on the uniform distribution of n-gram weights. Nevertheless, one can assume that character n-grams of different lengths are not equally important – for example, it is conceivable that character 1-grams are not really important for assessment of translation quality. Therefore we carried out the following experiment on the best CHRF variant, namely CHRF2. First step was to examine τ coefficients independently for each n-gram. The results presented in Table ?? indicate

that the character 1-grams indeed have the lowest correlation whereas 2-grams and 3-grams have the highest.

Taking these indications into account, we investigated the following three combinations of n-gram weights:

- 0-1-1-1-1-1
  removing 1-grams and keeping uniform weights for the rest of n-grams;

- 1-2-2-2-2-2
  assigning doubled 1-gram weight to the rest of n-grams;

- 1-5-5-4-3-3
  distribution of n-gram weights according to individual n-gram correlations.

The τ coefficients for each n-gram weight distribution are shown in Table 4 – although some of

(a) individual n-grams

n-gram	τ
1-gram	0.280
2-gram	0.361
3-gram	0.367
4-gram	0.358
5-gram	0.347
6-gram	0.334

(b) different n-gram weight distributions

Kendall's τ	fr-en		de-en		cs-en		ru-en		hi-en	fi-en	avg.
011111	**.397**	.384	.320	.424	.266	.437	.317	.385	.396	.406	.373
122222	.395	**.385**	.325	**.425**	.270	.451	.318	.389	.405	.405	.377
155433	.396	**.385**	.327	**.425**	.274	.451	.319	.388	.403	**.407**	.377
uniform	.394	.381	**.331**	.424	**.275.**	**.451**	**.320**	**.394**	**.410**	.398	**.378**

Kendall's τ	en-fr		en-de		en-cs		en-ru		en-hi	en-fi	avg.
011111	.300	**.345**	.256	.382	.334	.441	**.460**	**.420**	.304	.359	.360
122222	.302	.338	.261	.388	**.336**	.445	.457	.418	.304	.366	.361
155433	**.303**	.342	.260	.387	**.336**	**.449**	.456	.419	.305	.366	.362
uniform	.302	.338	**.264**	**.393**	.334	.444	.453	.418	**.307**	**.375**	**.363**

Table 4: Analysis of n-grams: (a) average τ for individual n-grams (b) τ on WMT14 (left) and WMT15 (right) documents for different n-gram weight distributions.

the proposed distributions outperform the uniform one for some of the texts, especially for translation out of English, none of them is unquestionably better than the uniform distribution of weights.

Therefore, the uniform n-gram weights were used for the WMT16 metrics task.

4 CHRF and WORDF for good and bad translations

In order to try to better understand the differences between WORDF and CHRF scores, i.e. the advantages of the CHRF score, we carried out a preliminary experiment on three data sets for which the absolute (direct) human scores were available. The data sets are rather heterogeneous: they contain three different target languages, they were produced and evaluated independently, for different purposes, and the human scores were not defined in the same way. In addition, two of the three data sets are rather small. Therefore the described experiment is rather preliminary, however we believe that it represents a good starting point for further research regarding differences between word and character based metrics.

τ coefficients for comparing four systems using direct human scores

The starting point was testing τ coefficients for CHRF2 and WORDF2 on the English→Spanish data set described in (Specia et al., 2010) and the motivation was simply to explore the correlations obtained on direct human scores instead of relative rankings. The data set contains 4000 source segments and their reference translations, machine translation outputs of four SMT systems, as well as human estimations of required post-editing effort in the interval from 1 (requires complete retranslation) to 4 (fit for purpose). The distribution of segments with each of the four human ratings for each of the systems is shown in Table 5a and it can be seen that the fourth system is significantly worse than the other three, which are rather close.

The obtained τ coefficients (Table 5b, first column) were however puzzling – the τ coefficients are very close, the one for the WORDF2 is even slightly higher, which is a rather different result than all the results described in the previous sections and related work. On the other hand, taking into account that the number of systems is small, as well as that the performance of the fourth sys-

(a) Distribution of direct human scores

human score	1	2	3	4	mean
sys1	4.2	24.8	54.3	16.7	2.83
sys2	8.9	36.5	44.4	10.2	2.56
sys3	9.7	38.5	43.2	8.6	2.51
sys4	73.0	20.6	5.9	0.5	1.34

(b) τ correlations

τ	4 sys	3 sys
WORDF2	**0.615**	0.275
CHRF2	0.608	**0.313**

Table 5: English→Spanish data set with direct human scores: (a) percentage of the sentence level human scores for each of the four systems together with the average human score for each system – system 4 is significantly worse than the other three. (b) τ coefficients for all four systems (first column) and for the three similar systems (second column).

tem is clearly distinct than of the others, another experiment is carried out: the worst system is removed and only the remaining three similar systems are compared. For this set-up, the expected results were obtained (second column), i.e. the τ coefficients are higher for the CHRF2 score. This somewhat controversial finding lead to the following two hypotheses:

1. word-based metrics are good at distinguishing systems/segments of distinct quality but not so good at ranking similar systems/segments;

2. word-based metrics are good for evaluating low quality systems/segments but not so good for evaluating high quality systems/segments.

Standard deviations of automatic metrics for different direct human scores

In order to further examine the two hypotheses, the following experiment has been carried out: for each of the human ratings, standard deviation of the corresponding automatic scores is calculated. This experiment is carried out on the previously described data set as well as on two additional small[1] data sets:

- English→Irish SMT translations rated from 1 to 4 for the overall quality (1=bad, 4=good);

[1]about 200 segments

(a) English→Spanish

hum	WORDF2	CHRF2
1	10.4	11.5
2	12.8	12.1
3	15.8	14.2
4	21.7	17.3

(b) English→Irish

hum	WORDF2	CHRF2
1	7.7	7.0
2	8.1	9.6
3	6.3	4.3
4	24.3	14.0

(c) English→Serbian

hum	WORDF2	CHRF2
1	6.8	8.9
1.5	4.6	6.4
2	11.2	9.9
2.5	13.4	11.1
3	13.2	11.5
3.5	11.2	8.3
4	15.4	9.9
4.5	16.4	7.4
5	25.0	7.7

Table 6: Standard deviations of WORDF2 and CHRF2 for each value of direct human scores on three distinct datasets: (a) English→Spanish, estimated post-editing effort (b) English→Irish, overall quality (c) English→Serbian, average of adequacy and fluency.

- English→Serbian SMT translations rated from 1 to 5 in terms of adequacy and fluency (1=bad, 5=good) – the mean value of the two has been taken as the direct human score.

The obtained standard deviations in Table 6 show that for poorly rated sentences, the deviations of CHRF2 and WORDF2 are similar – both metrics assign relatively similar (low) scores. On the other hand, for the sentences with higher human rates, the deviations for CHRF2 are (much) lower. In addition, the higher the human rating is, the greater is the difference between the WORDF2 and CHRF2 deviations. These results confirm the hypothesis 2), namely that CHRF is better than WORDF mainly for segments/systems of higher translation quality. The most probable reason is that CHRF, contrary to the word-based metrics, does not penalise too hard acceptable morphosyntactic variations. The CHRF scores for good translations are therefore more concentrated in the higher range, whereas the WORDF scores are often too low. The results are also consistent with the hypothesis 1), however this one is confirmed only partially since the outlier is a low quality system – further work should include comparison of different low quality systems.

Nevertheless, as stated at the beginning of the section, it should be kept in mind that this is only a preliminary experiment in this direction, performed on very limited amount of data. Further experiments on large data sets, more systems and more languages should be carried out in order to get more reliable results and better insight into underlying phenomena.

5 Summary and outlook

The results presented in this work show that generally, the F-scores which are biased towards recall correlate better with human rankings than those biased towards precision. Particularly, it is shown that CHRF2 version of the CHRF score with uniform n-gram weights is the most promising for machine translation evaluation. Therefore this/these version has been submitted to the WMT16 metrics task, however together with CHRF1 and CHRF3 in order to explore differences between English and morphologically richer target languages more systematically.

In addition, it is shown that the CHRF score performs better than the WORDF score. Preliminary experiments on small data sets with available direct human scores show that for sentences of higher translation quality, standard deviations of WORDF is much larger than standard deviations of CHRF, indicating that the main advantage of the CHRF is that it does not penalise too strong different variants of acceptable translations. However, more systematic experiments on large data sets should be carried out in this direction. Furthermore, a broader investigation including different word and character based metric in addition to the two presented F-scores would be useful.

Apart from this, application of CHRF on more distinct languages such as Arabic, Chinese etc. should be explored.

Acknowledgments

This work emerged from research supported by TRaMOOC project (Translation for Massive Open Online Courses) partially funded by the European Commission under H2020-ICT-2014/H2020-ICT-2014-1 under grant agreement number 644333. Special thanks to Mihael Arčan and Sanja Štajner for providing additional small data sets with direct human scores.

References

Ondrej Bojar, Christian Buck, Christian Federmann, Barry Haddow, Philipp Koehn, Johannes Leveling, Christof Monz, Pavel Pecina, Matt Post, Herve Saint-Amand, Radu Soricut, Lucia Specia, and Aleš Tamchyna. 2014. Findings of the 2014 workshop on statistical machine translation. In *Proceedings of the 9th Workshop on Statistical Machine Translation (WMT-14)*, pages 12–58, Baltimore, Maryland, USA, June.

Ondřej Bojar, Rajen Chatterjee, Christian Federmann, Barry Haddow, Matthias Huck, Chris Hokamp, Philipp Koehn, Varvara Logacheva, Christof Monz, Matteo Negri, Matt Post, Carolina Scarton, Lucia Specia, and Marco Turchi. 2015. Findings of the 2015 workshop on statistical machine translation. In *Proceedings of the 10th Workshop on Statistical Machine Translation (WMT-15)*, pages 1–46, Lisbon, Portugal, September.

Maja Popović. 2011. Morphemes and POS tags for n-gram based evaluation metrics. In *Proceedings of the Sixth Workshop on Statistical Machine Translation (WMT 2011)*, pages 104–107, Edinburgh, Scotland, July.

Maja Popović. 2015. chrF: character n-gram F-score for automatic MT evaluation. In *Proceedings of the 10th Workshop on Statistical Machine Translation (WMT-15)*, pages 392–395, Lisbon, Portugal, September.

Lucia Specia, Nicola Cancedda, and Marc Dymetman. 2010. A dataset for assessing machine translation evaluation metrics. In *Seventh Conference on International Language Resources and Evaluation*, LREC, pages 3375–3378, Valletta, Malta.

Miloš Stanojević, Amir Kamran, Philipp Koehn, and Ondřej Bojar. 2015. Results of the WMT15 Metrics Shared Task. In *Proceedings of the 10th Workshop on Statistical Machine Translation (WMT-15)*, pages 256–273, Lisbon, Portugal, September.

CharacTER: Translation Edit Rate on Character Level

Weiyue Wang, Jan-Thorsten Peter, Hendrik Rosendahl, Hermann Ney
Human Language Technology and Pattern Recognition, Computer Science Department
RWTH Aachen University, 52056 Aachen, Germany
`<surname>@i6.informatik.rwth-aachen.de`

Abstract

Recently, the capability of character-level evaluation measures for machine translation output has been confirmed by several metrics. This work proposes translation edit rate on character level (CharacTER), which calculates the character level edit distance while performing the shift edit on word level. The novel metric shows high system-level correlation with human rankings, especially for morphologically rich languages. It outperforms the strong CHRF by up to 7% correlation on different metric tasks. In addition, we apply the hypothesis sentence length for normalizing the edit distance in CharacTER, which also provides significant improvements compared to using the reference sentence length.

1 Introduction

The approaches for automatic evaluation of machine translation facilitated the development of statistical machine translation. They provide objective evaluation criteria for the translation results, and avoid the tedious and expensive manual evaluation. Currently the most commonly applied evaluation measures are the *Bilingual Evaluation Understudy* (BLEU) (Papineni et al., 2002) and the *Translation Edit Rate* (TER) (Snover et al., 2006) evaluation indicators. Most of the researchers use BLEU and TER as the primary metrics for evaluating their translation hypotheses.

The aim of the machine translation evaluation is to properly and objectively reflect the achievements and the functionality of machine translation. Through the evaluation, the developers of machine translation systems can learn the problems of the system and keep improving them. The evaluation metric not only provides the most reliable basis for machine translation systems, but also can be applied as the optimizing criterion in the parameter tuning step like BLEU. Thus, a good evaluation metric should demonstrate accuracy, universality and applicability.

In order to evaluate the applicability of different evaluation metrics, the correlation with human judgement is calculated. Currently the most common techniques for calculating the correlation between human and automatic evaluations are the *Spearman's rank correlation coefficient* (Spearman, 1904) and the *Pearson product-moment correlation coefficient* (Pearson, 1895).

In the recent past, several groups have reported further evaluation metrics, such as BEER (Stanojević and Sima'an, 2014) and CHRF (Popović, 2015), which actually outperformed the classic BLEU and TER metrics on Spearman and Pearson correlation with human judgement. In this work, we propose a novel *translation edit rate on character level* (CharacTER), which achieves a better correlation on the system-level for four different morphologically rich languages compared to BEER and CHRF. In addition, we also found that if we apply the hypothesis sentence length instead of reference sentence length to normalize the edit distance, the correlations of TER and CharacTER are improved by up to 9% on different languages.

2 Related Work

The most related work is the widely applied TER metric (Snover et al., 2006), which evaluates the amount of necessary editing to adjust a hypothesis so that it is accurately equal to a reference translation. Compared to the *Word Error Rate* (WER), TER introduced a *shift* edit on top of the *Levenshtein distance*, since in many languages different sequence orders are allowed. A hypothesis with

Proceedings of the First Conference on Machine Translation, Volume 2: Shared Task Papers, pages 505–510,
Berlin, Germany, August 11-12, 2016. ©2016 Association for Computational Linguistics

another sequence order is not necessarily a bad translation. The TER is calculated by normalizing the total cost of edits over the entire sentence. The CharacTER inherits the word-level shift technique applied in TER and splits the shifted words into characters to calculate the edit distance.

This work is mainly motivated by (Popović, 2015), who proposed to apply character n-grams for automatic machine translation evaluation and achieved promising correlations. In this work, we will demonstrate that the TER on character level can also show a good performance, especially for morphologically rich languages, in which TER may miss matches due to various suffixes.

In addition to TER and CHRF, several other works are dedicated to the measurement of lexical similarity. These include, the commonly applied BLEU metric (Papineni et al., 2002), which calculates the geometric mean of the n-gram precision in a hypothesis based on a reference, and the METEOR metric (Lavie and Agarwal, 2007), which computes unigram overlaps between hypothesis and reference sequences considering stem matches and synonyms. The correlation of further evaluation metrics such as NIST (Doddington, 2002) and BEER (Stanojević and Sima'an, 2014) with human judgement are also presented in Section 4.

3 Character Level Edit Rate

Similar to TER, CharacTER is specified as the minimum number of character edits required to adjust a hypothesis, so that it absolutely matches the reference, normalized by the length of the hypothesis sentence (Equation 1). Note that here we apply the hypothesis instead of reference sentence length for normalization.

$$\text{CharacTER} = \frac{\text{shift cost} + \text{edit distance}}{\#\text{characters in the hypothesis sentence}} \quad (1)$$

3.1 Shift Edit

Unlike in speech or handwriting recognition, the *Character Error Rate* (CER) was not widely applied in machine translation. That is mainly because the shift edit is introduced for the translation metric, which is not necessary in speech recognition. In the calculation of TER, a greedy search is applied to discover the batch of shifts, by picking out the shift which most decreases the edit distance over and over again, until no more advantageous shifts exist. In other words, the shift edit is

based on searching matched phrases between hypothesis and reference. Since the alphabet size in each language is very limited compared to the vocabulary size, characters are more likely to match each other than words, and thus the shift edit on the character level may corrupt words into meaningless pieces (Figure 1).

Besides the misplacement, the computational time is another big issue for directly applying TER on the character level. On the word level, we go through the hypothesis and compare the current word with each word in the reference. If a matched word is found at a different position in the reference, the succeeding words of the current word will be iteratively compared, in order to discover the longest matched phrases. This procedure becomes expensive on character level. The much higher matching probability of characters compared to words will result in many computations. For instance, for the example sentence in Figure 1, the computational time of the CER is 44 times as much as that of the TER.

In order to counter these issues, we applied a heuristic to calculate the translation edit rate on character level. Instead of shifting characters, we adopt the shift edit on word level as for calculating the TER. Then the shifted hypothesis sequence is split into characters and the Levenshtein distance is computed. In this way the computational time only increases by about 10% in our experiments. Note that here we consider the spaces in each sentence as extra characters, unlike in CHRF, since the correlation scores (Table 1) confirm the utility of this variant. We applied two different shift or phrase matching criteria: Two words are considered to be matched if

1. they are exactly the same,

2. or the edit distance between them is below a threshold value.

The first variant is the same as the phrase matching criterion in TER. In the second variant, the aim of introducing the threshold is to capture word pairs with the same stem, like `code` and `codes`. For the example in Figure 1, if we set a distance threshold to be 1, the shifted hypothesis sentence will be:
```
saudis the denied this week
information published in the new
your times
```
where `saudis` and `the` changed their positions

```
ref : saudi arabia denied this week information published in the american new york
      times
hyp : this week the saudis denied information published in the new york times
TER : the saudis denied this week information published in the new york times
CER : saudittis denied nhis week formation published in the nehew york times
```

Figure 1: The hypothesis sentence after shift edit according to TER and CER technique. The characters marked with red color are the ones which are misplaced by the character level shift edit.

resulting in a smaller edit distance in this case. Based on the fact that the tolerance should be the same for long and short words, we applied absolute distances instead of ratios. For instance, if we use an error rate of 0.2 as the threshold value, words `eat` and `eats` are not considered to be matched, while words `translation` and `transition` will be matched. This issue can be fixed if we use an absolute edit distance equal to 1 as the threshold.

Another variant is the shift cost. In the calculation of TER, the shift of one entire phrase has a cost of 1, no matter how far this phrase moves. This penalty would be too mild for CharacTER, since the costs of insertions, deletions and substitutions become much larger on character level. Thus, we apply the average word length of the shifted phrase as the cost. For instance, the shift cost of phrase `the day before yesterday` will be $\frac{3+3+6+9}{4} = 5.25$. We also tried other possible costs, such as a fixed value or average word length of the whole data set. The experimental results are shown in Section 4.1.

3.2 Normalization

Both WER and TER techniques utilize a normalization over the reference sentence length by default, because the length of reference sentences stays unchanged, while different systems provide different translations with different hypothesis sentence lengths. In this case, the same edit distance of two hypotheses to the reference also indicates that they have the same TER, and the length of different translations is not taken into consideration. In this work we take advantage of other normalization alternatives.

First we used the hypothesis sentence length for the normalization. That means, with the same edit distance, the longer hypothesis results in a smaller error rate. For instance, let us consider the following reference and corresponding hypothesis sentences:

```
ref : this is actually an estimate
hyp₁: this is in fact an estimate
hyp₂: indeed this is an estimate
```

Compared to the reference sentence, the edit distances of both hyp_1 and hyp_2 are 2. Normalizing over the reference length results in TER $= \frac{2}{5} = 0.4$ for both hypotheses, whereas using the hypothesis length provides different results for them, equal to 0.33 and 0.4 respectively.

We also used other normalizer, such as the average, maximum or minimum length of reference and hypothesis sentence. We also calculated a CharacTER based on the entire data set, for which we sum up the edit distances of all sentences and also normalize the sum over the number of characters in the whole data set. According to our experimental results (Table 1) of the human correlation scores, normalizing using hypothesis length outperforms the other options, which is the case in all conducted experiments for both TER and our CharacTER. We suppose that human prefers the longer one, if two translations have equal quality. In addition, we note that in our translation experiments the default TER setup is heavily influenced by the hypothesis length: With the same BLEU score, a shorter translation normally achieves lower TER. The normalization over the hypothesis sentence length can effectively counter this issue.

4 Experiments

The evaluation metrics are correlated with human rankings by means of Spearman's rank correlation coefficient for the WMT13 task (Macháček and Bojar, 2013) and Pearson product-moment correlation coefficient for the WMT14 task (Macháček and Bojar, 2014) and WMT15 task (Stanojević et al., 2015) on the system level. Through the experiments we aim to investigate the following points:

- What is the most suitable threshold value to

identify the phrase matching?

- What shift cost should we apply?

- Which normalizer performs better?

- How does CharacTER perform compared to other metrics?

4.1 Comparison of different variants

First of all we would like to find out which is the best variant of the CharacTER. We conduct experiments on different shift costs and normalizers as described in Section 3, the correlation scores on different metric tasks are shown in Table 1. `basic setup` indicates the default setup of our metric, namely using the average length of the shifted words as the shift cost, considering only the exactly same words or phrases as matching and normalizing by length of each reference sentence. Other variants have the following meaning:

`w/o space` leaving out spaces in sentences

`threshold` the threshold edit distance to identify word matching

`shift` the shift cost of a phrase

`average` normalization over the average length of hypothesis and reference sentences

`max` normalization over the maximum length of hypothesis and reference sentences

`hyp` normalization over length of the hypothesis sentence

`whole` sum and normalization at the data set level instead of the sentence level

We also conducted experiments on other variants and variant combinations, such as other threshold values or shift costs. Only the variants with relative high correlation are presented in Table 1.

First of all, using the hypothesis sentence length as normalizer provides considerable improvements for both CharacTER and TER. Thus, we initiate to apply the hypothesis sentence length for normalizing not only our CharacTER but also the widely-used TER. Besides that, using an edit distance threshold also achieves significant improvements, while other configuration variants do not seem to be helpful. Thus on the following demonstrated experiments as well as on the shared metric task 2016, the configuration of CharacTER is organized as follows (the row with a cyan background in Table 1):

	WMT13		WMT14	
	en-*	*-en	en-*	*-en
TER	0.824	0.805	0.795	0.852
+ hyp	0.842	0.894	0.860	0.853
basic setup	0.857	0.832	0.833	0.868
+ w/o space	0.837	0.796	0.833	0.847
+ threshold 1	0.880	0.839	0.882	0.876
+ threshold 2	0.867	0.822	0.865	0.855
+ shift 1	0.836	0.813	0.820	0.847
+ shift 3	0.849	0.824	0.830	0.860
+ shift 5	0.839	0.818	0.836	0.866
+ average	0.917	0.913	0.871	0.928
+ max	0.908	0.918	0.849	0.918
+ hyp	0.925	0.928	0.908	0.930
+ whole	0.927	**0.931**	0.896	0.916
+ threshold 1	**0.934**	0.928	**0.916**	**0.938**

Table 1: Average correlations on WMT13 (Spearman) and WMT14 (Pearson) tasks for different variants of CharacTER. en-* indicates the average correlation for translations out of English, while *-en the translations into English. The best results in each direction are in bold.

- threshold value 1 to identify word matching

- average length of shifted words as shift cost

- hypothesis sentence length for normalization

- spaces in each sentence as extra characters

4.2 Comparison with other metrics

In this part the comparisons among different evaluation metrics are conducted. The correlations on different language pairs for the CharacTER metric along with the three mostly applied metrics BLEU, TER and METEOR, as well as the well-performing metrics for the corresponding tasks, are demonstrated in Table 2. The CharacTER metric performs quite well for out of English direction, especially on English→Russian, English→German and English→French tasks. On average we get up to 7% improvement compared to other strong metrics. It is noteworthy that on the WMT14 English→German task the CharacTER still provides a strong correlation, while other automatic metrics are negatively influenced by a large number of engaged systems of comparable quality. Additionally we list the best performing metrics in the WMT16 metrics task (Bojar et al., 2016) in Table 3. CharacTER surpasses other strong

WMT13	en-fr	en-de	en-es	en-cs	en-ru	avg.	fr-en	de-en	es-en	cs-en	ru-en	avg.
CharacTER	**0.944**	**0.926**	**0.916**	0.926	**0.957**	**0.934**	0.966	0.952	0.953	0.938	0.830	0.928
CHRF3[1]	0.914	0.919	0.758	0.895	0.820	0.861	0.984	**0.980**	**0.986**	**0.991**	**0.889**	**0.966**
SIMPBLEU[2]	0.924	0.925	0.830	0.867	0.710	0.851	0.978	0.936	0.923	0.909	0.798	0.909
BLEU	0.917	0.832	0.764	0.895	0.657	0.813	**0.989**	0.902	0.895	0.936	0.695	0.883
TER	0.912	0.854	0.753	0.860	0.538	0.783	0.951	0.833	0.825	0.800	0.581	0.798
METEOR	0.924	0.879	0.780	**0.937**	0.569	0.818	0.984	0.961	0.979	0.964	0.789	0.935

WMT14	en-fr	en-hi	en-cs	en-ru	avg.*	en-de	fr-en	de-en	hi-en	cs-en	ru-en	avg.
CharacTER	**0.957**	0.965	0.974	**0.933**	**0.958**	**0.757**	**0.976**	**0.957**	0.927	**0.986**	**0.844**	**0.938**
CHRF3	0.937	0.976	0.978	0.919	0.952	0.425	0.971	0.938	0.597	0.974	0.816	0.859
NIST[3]	0.941	**0.981**	**0.985**	0.927	**0.958**	0.200	0.955	0.811	0.784	0.983	0.800	0.867
BLEU	0.937	0.973	0.976	0.915	0.950	0.216	0.952	0.832	**0.956**	0.909	0.789	0.888
TER	0.954	0.829	0.978	0.931	0.923	0.324	0.952	0.775	0.618	0.976	0.809	0.826
METEOR	0.941	0.975	0.976	0.923	0.953	0.263	0.975	0.927	0.457	0.980	0.805	0.829

WMT15	en-fr	en-fi	en-de	en-cs	en-ru	avg.	fr-en	fi-en	de-en	cs-en	ru-en	avg.
CharacTER	0.942	0.854	**0.955**	0.970	**0.982**	**0.941**	**0.988**	0.888	**0.972**	0.960	0.884	0.939
CHRF3	0.932	**0.878**	0.848	**0.977**	0.946	0.916	0.979	0.903	0.956	0.968	0.898	0.941
BEER[4]	**0.961**	0.808	0.879	0.962	0.970	0.916	0.979	**0.965**	0.946	**0.983**	0.971	**0.969**
BLEU	0.948	0.602	0.573	0.936	0.841	0.780	0.975	0.929	0.865	0.957	0.851	0.915
TER	0.948	0.614	0.564	0.917	0.883	0.785	0.979	0.872	0.890	0.907	0.907	0.911
METEOR	0.959	0.760	0.650	0.953	0.892	0.843	0.982	0.950	0.953	**0.983**	**0.976**	**0.969**

Table 2: System-level correlations of automatic evaluation metrics and the official WMT human scores. The best results in each direction are in bold. We calculated the CharacTER and CHRF3 scores and cited the other scores from the WMT metric papers (Macháček and Bojar, 2013; Macháček and Bojar, 2014; Stanojević et al., 2015).

* English→German scores are not included in the averages of the WMT14 metrick task.

[1] CHRF3 (Popović, 2015)

[2] SIMPBLEU-RECALL (Song et al., 2013)

[3] NIST (Doddington, 2002)

[4] BEER (Stanojević and Sima'an, 2014)

WMT16	en-cs	en-de	en-fi	en-ro	en-ru	en-tr	cs-en	de-en	fi-en	ro-en	ru-en	tr-en
CharacTER	0.779	**0.915**	0.933	**0.959**	**0.954**	0.930	**0.997**	**0.985**	0.921	**0.970**	0.955	0.799
MPEDA	0.977	0.684	0.944	0.786	0.856	0.860	0.996	0.956	**0.967**	0.938	0.986	0.972
CHRF3	0.935	0.745	**0.974**	0.818	0.936	0.916	0.991	0.958	0.946	0.915	0.981	0.918
UoW.REVAL	-	-	-	-	-	-	0.993	0.949	0.958	0.919	**0.990**	0.977
BEER	0.972	0.732	0.940	0.947	0.906	**0.956**	0.996	0.949	0.964	0.908	0.986	**0.981**
WORDF3	**0.989**	0.768	0.901	0.931	0.836	0.714	0.991	0.898	0.786	0.909	0.955	0.803

Table 3: The preliminary results of the WMT16 metrics task: Absolute Pearson correlation of out-of-English and to-English system-level metric scores. All results are cited from (Bojar et al., 2016).

metrics on half of the language pairs. It performs especially well for English↔German and English↔Romanian. The results in Table 2 and 3 show that the CharacTER outperforms all other metrics on English→German by a large margin.

5 Conclusions

The experimental results showed in this paper exhibit that the translation edit rate on character level CharacTER represents a metric with high human correlations on the system-level, especially for the morphologically rich languages, which benefits from the character level information. We show the promising performance, while the concept is simple and straightforward. It is also noteworthy that the hypothesis sentence length is a better normalizer for both TER and CharacTER compared to the reference sentence length. As future work, we would like to apply CharacTER as optimization criterion and conduct more experiments on non-European languages such as Chinese and Arabic.

Acknowledgments

This paper has received funding from the European Union's Horizon 2020 research and innovation programme under grant agreement n° 645452 (QT21).

References

Ondřej Bojar, Yvette Graham, Amir Kamran, and Miloš Stanojević. 2016. Results of the WMT16 Metrics Shared Task. In *Proceedings of the First Conference on Statistical Machine Translation*, Berlin, Germany, August.

George Doddington. 2002. Automatic Evaluation of Machine Translation Quality Using N-gram Co-occurrence Statistics. In *Proceedings of the Second International Conference on Human Language Technology Research*, pages 128–132, San Diego, CA, USA, March.

Alon Lavie and Abhaya Agarwal. 2007. METEOR: An automatic metric for mt evaluation with high levels of correlation with human judgments. In *Proceedings of the ACL 2007 Workshop on Statistical Machine Translation*, pages 228–231, Prague, Czech Republic, June.

Matouš Macháček and Ondřej Bojar. 2013. Results of the WMT13 metrics shared task. In *Proceedings of the Eighth Workshop on Statistical Machine Translation*, pages 45–51, Sofia, Bulgaria, August.

Matouš Macháček and Ondřej Bojar. 2014. Results of the WMT14 metrics shared task. In *Proceedings of the Ninth Workshop on Statistical Machine Translation*, pages 293–301, Baltimore, MA, USA, June.

Kishore Papineni, Salim Roukos, Todd Ward, and Wei-Jing Zhu. 2002. BLEU: A Method for Automatic Evaluation of Machine Translation. In *Proceedings of the 40th Annual Meeting on Association for Computational Linguistics*, pages 311–318, Philadelphia, PA, USA, July.

Karl Pearson. 1895. Notes on Regression and Inheritance in the Case of Two Parents. In *Proceedings of the Royal Society of London*, volume 58, pages 240–242, London, UK, June.

Maja Popović. 2015. CHRF: Character n-gram F-Score for Automatic MT Evaluation. In *Proceedings of the Tenth Workshop on Statistical Machine Translation*, pages 392–395, Lisboa, Portugal, September.

Matthew Snover, Bonnie Dorr, Richard Schwartz, Linnea Micciulla, and John Makhoul. 2006. A study of translation edit rate with targeted human annotation. In *Proceedings of the Conference of the Association for Machine Translation in the Americas*, pages 223–231, Cambridge, MA, USA, August.

Xingyi Song, Trevor Cohn, and Lucia Specia. 2013. BLEU deconstructed: Designing a better MT evaluation metric. In *Proceedings of the 14th International Conference on Intelligent Text Processing and Computational Linguistics*, Samos, Greece, March.

Charles Spearman. 1904. The Proof and Measurement of Association between Two Things. *The American Journal of Psychology*, 15:72–101, January.

Miloš Stanojević and Khalil Sima'an. 2014. BEER: BEtter Evaluation as Ranking. In *Proceedings of the Ninth Workshop on Statistical Machine Translation*, pages 414–419, Baltimore, MA, USA, June.

Miloš Stanojević, Amir Kamran, Philipp Koehn, and Ondřej Bojar, 2015. *Results of the WMT15 Metrics Shared Task*. Association for Computational Linguistics.

Extract Domain-specific Paraphrase from Monolingual Corpus for Automatic Evaluation of Machine Translation

Lilin Zhang, Zhen Weng, Wenyan Xiao, Jianyi Wan, Zhiming Chen, Yiming Tan, Maoxi Li, Mingwen Wang

School of Computer Information Engineering, Jiangxi Normal University
```
{1006806747, 1091013334, 51852710, 1363955817}@qq.com,
{qqchenzhiming, tt_yymm, mosesli, mwwang}@jxnu.edu.cn
```


Abstract

Paraphrase can help match synonyms or match phrases with the same or similar meaning, thus it plays an important role in automatic evaluation of machine translation. The traditional approaches extract paraphrase in general domain from bilingual corpus. Because the WMT16 metrics task consists of three sub-tasks, namely news domain, medical domain, and IT domain, we propose to extract domain-specific paraphrase tables from monolingual corpus to replace the general paraphrase table. We utilize the M-L approach to filter the large scale general monolingual corpus into a domain-specific sub-corpus, and exploit Markov Network model to extract paraphrase tables from the sub-corpus. The experimental results on WMT15 Metrics task show that METEOR metric using the domain-specific paraphrase tables outperforms that using the paraphrase table in general domain extracted from the bilingual corpus.

1 Introduction

Machine translation (MT) automatic evaluation metrics, such as BLEU (Papineni et al., 2002), NIST (Doddington, 2002), METEOR (Banerjee et al., 2005), TER (Snover et al., 2006), MAXSIM (Chan et al., 2008) etc., evaluate the quality of the MT system output by calculating the similarity between the translation output and the human reference. Accurately matching words or phrases with the same or similar meaning is critical to the performance of the automatic evaluation metrics (Li et al., 2013; Li et al., 2016).

Recently, many works enhanced traditional metrics by adding paraphrase match. For instance, in the latest version of METEOR package (Denkowski and Lavie, 2014), the paraphrase match was added after the standard exact word match, stem match and synonym match. And the latest version of TER package (Bannard et al., 2005) relaxes the condition of word match or chunk shift by adding paraphrase match. Note that the paraphrase tables used in latest METEOR and TER metrics belong to the general domain and they are extracted from bilingual parallel corpus by the Pivot approach (Bannard et al., 2005). However, the WMT16 metrics task consists of sub-tasks on specific domains involving several different languages. Confronted with the changes, we propose a Monolingual Paraphrase Extraction method based on Domain Adaptation (MPEDA), and use the new domain-specific paraphrase table to replace the traditional paraphrase tables in the latest METEOR package.

2 Related Work

In statistical natural language processing, both the scale and the quality of the training data have a direct impact on the performance of statistical learning. Take statistical MT for an example, if the size of training data is larger and the more it covers n-gram appeared in the test set, the quality of the MT outputs will be better.

To expand the scale of the existing domain-specific corpus, Moore and Lewis (2010) trained models with general corpus and domain-specific corpus, and computed cross entropy of each sentence in the general corpus to extract a sub-corpus much larger than the existing domain-specific corpus. In this way, a large scale domain-specific training corpus for statistical MT was established. Along this approach, Amittai et al. (2011) proposed a bilingual parallel data selection approach based on cross entropy to improve the MT performance for spoken language translation. And Juri et al. (2015) filtered training data for automatic extraction of paraphrase by using Moore and Lewis' approach to extract paraphrases from the filtered training data via the Pivot approach.

Automatically extracting paraphrases from the large scale corpus is low cost. Barzilay and McKeown (2001) presented an unsupervised learning approach to extract paraphrases of

Proceedings of the First Conference on Machine Translation, Volume 2: Shared Task Papers, pages 511–517,
Berlin, Germany, August 11-12, 2016. ©2016 Association for Computational Linguistics

words and phrases from different English translations of the identical source language sentences. Bannard and Callison-Burch (2005) employed the word alignment technique of statistical MT to extract paraphrases from bilingual parallel corpus. Shinyama et al. (2002) used the named entity recognition features to extract paraphrases from monolingual comparable corpus. Barzilay and Lee (2003) used text strings alignment algorithm to learn paraphrases at sentence level from the unannotated comparable corpus. Yet, there are still great restrictions of the latter two monolingual paraphrase extraction methods. Therefore, we adopt the Markov-based method proposed by Weng et al. (2015) to extract paraphrases in specific domain from monolingual corpus because that it has no restrictions on monolingual corpus in the target language as it can extract paraphrase by constructing the Markov networks of words. Prior to the paraphrase extraction, we first filter large scale monolingual corpus into sub-corpus close to the domain of the human reference. Compared with general training corpus, the filtered sub-corpus is smaller and more related to the target domain, which results in the improvement on the quality of paraphrase table as well as the performance when the paraphrase table is applied in automatic evaluation metric.

3 MPEDA: Monolingual Paraphrase Extraction Based on Domain Adaptation

We extract domain-specific paraphrases from the monolingual corpus which are the most related to the test data. Our approach aims at accurately matching synonyms and phrases with the same or similar meaning in MT outputs and in human references with the help of the domain-specific paraphrase. We first filter a sub-corpus from a large general corpus by the extended M-L method, and then extract paraphrases based on Markov Network model and finally apply the paraphrase table to METEOR metric.

3.1 Extracting paraphrases based on word chunks

According to the Markov Network model, we first use the term co-occurrence in the text set to calculate the correlation among terms and construct a term Markov network where the correlation between two words in the network (edge weight) is computed by the joint conditional probability of two terms in the text set according

to Formula (1) - (3), in which conditional probability $P(t_i|t_j)$ and $P(t_j|t_i)$ are not equal.

$$R(t_i, t_j) = \frac{P(t_i \mid t_j) + P(t_j \mid t_i)}{2} \qquad (1)$$

$$P(t_i \mid t_j) = \frac{C(t_i, t_j)}{C(t_j)} \qquad (2)$$

$$P(t_j \mid t_i) = \frac{C(t_i, t_j)}{C(t_i)} \qquad (3)$$

In Formula (1) − (3), t_i and t_j stand for two terms, $C(t_i, t_j)$ is the number of documents that in the whole training data term t_i and term t_j co-occur in the same window, $C(t_i)$ and $C(t_j)$ denote the numbers of documents that term t_i and term t_j occur in the whole training data respectively, $R(t_i, t_j)$ denotes the correlation between term t_i and term t_j. The greater the R value, the higher the correlation between the two terms.

Extracting paraphrases from the constructed term Markov network is built on the following hypothesis: the more word chunks co-occurring between two terms, the more similar their semantic meanings are, and thus the two terms are a paraphrase pair. Therefore, we need to build an n-gram word chunk set for each term and then calculate the ratio between the number of co-occurring word chunks of two terms and the total number of word chunks with one term occurring. The ratio is considered as the possibility of the two terms constructing a paraphrase pair, which can be obtained by formula (4) - (6). Formula (6) is used to calculate the weight of n-gram word chunk.

$$pos(t_i, t_j) = \frac{W_3(t_i, t_j)}{\frac{1}{2}(W_3(t_i) + W_3(t_j))} \qquad (4)$$

$$W_3(t_i, t_j) = \sum_{k \neq i \wedge k \neq j \wedge t_k \in clique(t_i, t_j, t_k)} w_3(t_i, t_j, t_k) \qquad (5)$$

$$w_n\{t_1, t_2, \ldots t_n\} = \frac{\sum_{1 \leq i, j \leq n} R(t_i, t_j)}{\frac{1}{2} n(n-1)} \qquad (6)$$

In the above formulas, $pos(t_i, t_j)$ is the paraphrase probability of term t_i and term t_j, $W_3(t_i, t_j)$ is the sum of weights of all the 3-gram word chunks containing term t_i and term t_j, $W_3(t_i)$ is the sum of weights of all the 3-gram word chunks containing term t_i, $W_3(t_j)$ denotes the sum of weights of all the 3-gram word chunks containing term t_j, n denotes the number of nodes in word chunk, $R(t_i, t_j)$ denotes the correlation between term t_i and term t_j.

We use the terms co-occurrence to construct a term Markov network and extract phrases in the corpus as a node of Markov network. Figure 1 shows an example of *3*-gram word chunk, where t_1 stands for the term *"computer"*, t_2 stands for the term *"Internet"*, t_3 stands for the term *"calculating machine"*, t_4 stands for the term *"electronic"*. In this example, the *3*-gram word chunk set for each term is $S(C_3(t_1))=$ {{ t_1, t_2, t_3}, {t_1, t_3, t_4}}, $S(C_3(t_2))=$ { t_1, t_2, t_3}, $S(C_3(t_3)=$ {{ t_1, t_2, t_3}, {t_1, t_3, t_4}}, $S(C_3(t_4))=$ { t_1, t_3, t_4}. It can be observed that $S(C_3(t_1))=$ $S(C_3(t_3))=$ {{ t_1, t_2, t_3}, {t_1, t_3, t_4}}, hence, there is a high correlation between the two terms of t_1 and t_3 . Based on the hypothesis of this paper, we think term t_1, *"computer"*, and term t_3, *"calculating machine"*, in this example is a paraphrase pair.

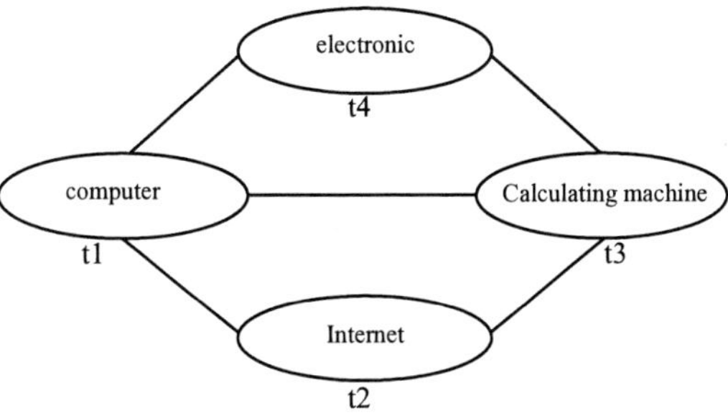

Figure 1: 3-gram word chunk

3.2 Corpus filtering

3.2.1 M-L corpus filtering

The corpus filtering method is built similar to the M-L method proposed by Moore and Lewis (2010). To extract a sub-corpus of target domain from the large general corpus, we first select a domain-specific corpus and a general large scale corpus. To improve the automatic MT metric, we use the human references of each sub-task in the metric tasks as the domain-specific corpus, and train the language model of the two corpora respectively, furthermore, we calculate the cross entropy of the two models. Finally, the similarity between the sentences and the human references is measured by calculating the difference of two cross entropy of the same sentence according to Formula (7). Generally, smaller value means the sentence is closer to the target domain.

$$\delta_{S_i} = H_{ref}(S_i) - H_{train}(S_i) \qquad (7)$$

In formula (7), S_i denotes the *i*-th sentence, H_{ref} denotes the cross entropy of the language model trained from the human references, while H_{train} denotes the cross entropy of the language model trained from the training data.

3.2.2 Document sets filtering

The Markov network-based automatic paraphrase extraction approach requires divide a general monolingual corpus into different document sets. Weng et al. (2015) divided the text of a fixed length into a document without considering the correlation among documents. Hence, we form the sentences in the corpus into cluster via *K*-means clustering algorithm, and then use the bag of word model to create a vector for each sentence in the corpus. Thus the distance between two sentences can be obtained by calculating the cosine value of the two vectors. Each cluster is viewed as a document. In the process of clustering, dividing documents via *K*-means algorithm can guarantee that the sentences in a document approximately belong to the same domain.

Then, the M-L method is used to extract the sub-sets of documents which are close to the target domain from the clustered general document sets. This signifies that it is the document not the sentence that is regarded as the smallest filtering unit in the process of corpus filtering. And we want to identify documents which are similar to our target domain by summing up the difference of cross entropy of each sentence in the document. However, when dividing the large-scale corpus into documents via *K*-means algorithm, the number of sentences in the documents varies, thus we calculate the mean after summing up the difference of cross entropy of each sentence to obtain the score of each document δ_{D_i} by Formula (8),

$$\delta_{D_i} = \frac{\sum_{j=1}^{n}(H_{ref}(S_j) - H_{train}(S_j))}{n} \qquad (8)$$

where δ_{D_i} is the score of the *i*-th document, $H_{ref}(S_j)$ is the cross entropy of the *j*-th sentence in the document D_i derived from the language model of the references, $H_{train}(S_j)$ is the cross entropy of the *j*-th sentence in the document D_i derived from the language model of the training data, n is the number of sentences in the document D_i. Then we sort δ_{D_i} in ascending order. The lower score implies the document is more like the human references.

4   Experiments

To test the quality of the domain-specific paraphrase extracted from monolingual corpus by the proposed approach, we conducted experiments on WMT15 Metrics task.

The METEOR-Universal metric (Denkowski and Lavie, 2014) using the paraphrase tables which were extracted from the bilingual parallel corpus was set as the baseline metric. We used the paraphrase tables in general domain extracted by the Markov Network model, and the domain-specific paraphrase tables extracted by our ap-proach substituted for the original paraphrased tables, respectively. The updated metrics are called as METEOR-Markov and METEOR-MPEDA. We compared the METEOR-MPEDA metric with the METEOR-Markov metric and METEOR-Universal metric to demonstrate the quality of the domain-specific paraphrase table extracted by our approach. Besides, we com-pared the METEOR-MPEDA with METEOR metric (Banerjee et al., 2005) which only uses the exact word match, stem match and synonym match.

Data	en-cs	en-de	en-fr	en-fi	en-ru	cs-en	de-en	fr-en	fi-en	ru-en
T-corpus	1000k	1920k	2007k	1926k	1074k	2218k	2218k	2218k	2218k	2218k
ref	2656	2169	1500	1370	2818	2656	2169	1500	1370	2818

Table 1. The statistics of the corpus

Data	en-cs	en-de	en-fr	en-fi	en-ru	cs-en	de-en	fr-en	fi-en	ru-en
D-corpus	28230	39684	39763	39921	28643	39684	39684	39684	39684	39684

Table 2. The number of documents in training data

4.1   Corpus

The training data and the human references we used in the experiment are all provided in WMT15 Translation task and Metrics task (Bojar et al., 2015), every training data has its corre-sponding references. Table 1 shows the number of sentences in the corpora. The row "*T-corpus*" denotes the training data, while the row "*ref*" denotes the references.

The training data was processed by text clus-tering. We used K-means clustering algorithm to gather the corpus sentences in different clusters, and then adopted the bag of word to create a vec-tor for each sentence. By computing the cosine value of the two vectors, we obtained the dis-tance between two sentences. Each cluster was viewed as a document. The i-th document in training data was named D_i, and the number of sentences in each document was different. Table 2 is the number of documents after training data clustering. The row "*D-corpus*" is the number of document used in the training data.

4.2   Experiments Settings

After dividing the training data into documents, we processed the corpus by the following proce-dure: tokenize the training data and the refer-ences; delete the punctuations; transform the cap-italized letters of words into lower case. Then, we employed 4-gram language model with *Kneser-Ney* discounting to train corresponding language models for training data and the refer-ences. The difference of cross entropy of each sentence in the training data language model was calculated. Then we summed up and normalized the difference of the cross entropy of the docu-ments' sentences. Thus every document in the training data received a score. The smaller the value is, the closer the document is to the refer-ence. Later, we arranged the values in an ascend-ing order, meanwhile, a threshold value was set, and the corpus beyond the threshold was aban-doned. In this way, we obtained a smaller sub-corpus with the approximately same domain with the training data. Finally, we gave different threshold value to the different sub-tasks, in oth-er words, we selected the top n documents after ordering.

We used the Markov network to build a term Markov network model in the sub-corpus, then we calculated the relation among words accord-ing to words co-occurrence, next, we extracted the word chunks in the Markov network, and computed the likelihood that two words are a paraphrase pair by comparing the two chunks' similarity. In this work, we extracted ten para-phrase tables for ten sub-tasks in six languages on WMT15.

4.3 Results

The Pearson Coefficient is used to compute the system-level correlation between automatic evaluation and human judgments as follows:

$$r = \frac{\sum_{i=1}^{n}(H_i - \bar{H})(M_i - \bar{M})}{\sqrt{\sum_{i=1}^{n}(H_i - \bar{H})^2}\sqrt{\sum_{i=1}^{n}(M_i - \bar{M})^2}} \quad (9)$$

where H_i and M_i are the i-th system scores of human judgment and that of the automatic evaluation metrics, respectively.

The system-level correlation for the three metrics is given in Table 3 and Table 4, from the tables, we found that the system-level correlation of METEOR-MPEDA metric is better than METEOR, METEOR-Universal and METEOR-Markov on average.

Furthermore, Kendall's τ coefficient was used to compute the correlation between automatic evaluation metrics and human judgments at segment -level as follows:

$$\tau = \frac{|\,Concordant\,| - |\,Discordant\,|}{|\,Concordant\,| + |\,Discordant\,|} \quad (10)$$

where *Concordant* denotes the set where the human judgment and the automatic evaluation metrics' score are concordant, while *Discordant* denotes the set where they are discordant.

The segment-level correlation is given in Table 5 and 6. It can be observed that the segment-level correlation of METEOR-MPEDA metric on evaluation translation into English tasks is better than METEOR, METEOR-Universal metric and METEOR-Markov metric on average. However, when evaluating translation out of English tasks, the performance of the METEOR-MPEDA metric is slightly lower than METEOR-Universal metric. It can be explained that when we have a large amount of bilingual parallel training data, the paraphrase table extracted from the bilingual corpus is better than that from monolingual corpus for automatic evaluation of MT.

Metrics	de-en	cs-en	fr-en	fi-en	ru-en	Average
METEOR	0.926	0.973	**0.979**	0.929	0.959	0.953
METEOR-Universal	0.953	**0.974**	**0.979**	0.934	0.964	0.961
METEOR-Markov	0.950	**0.974**	0.978	0.929	**0.965**	0.959
METEOR-MPEDA	**0.959**	**0.974**	**0.979**	**0.939**	0.963	**0.963**

Table 3. The system-level correlation of metrics on evaluation translation into English on WMT15 Metrics task

Metrics	en-de	en-cs	en-fr	en-fi	en-ru	Average
METEOR	0.680	0.957	0.951	0.713	0.864	0.833
METEOR-Universal	0.722	0.940	0.952	**0.724**	0.845	0.837
METEOR-Markov	0.705	**0.954**	0.949	0.712	0.845	0.833
METEOR-MPEDA	**0.735**	0.938	**0.955**	0.714	**0.851**	**0.839**

Table 4. The system-level correlation of metrics on evaluation translation out of English on WMT15 Metrics task

Metrics	de-en	cs-en	fr-en	fi-en	ru-en	Average
METEOR	0.389	0.406	0.375	0.385	0.358	0.378
METEOR-Universal	0.431	**0.437**	**0.386**	0.388	0.379	0.404
METEOR-Markov	0.421	0.429	**0.386**	0.393	0.367	0.400
METEOR-MPEDA	**0.431**	0.434	0.376	**0.404**	**0.383**	**0.406**

Table 5. The segment-level correlation of metrics on evaluation translation into English on WMT15 Metrics task

Metrics	en-de	en-cs	en-fr	en-fi	en-ru	Average
METEOR	0.319	0.389	0.335	0.251	0.373	0.333
METEOR-Universal	0.339	0.388	**0.342**	**0.274**	0.380	**0.345**
METEOR-Markov	0.332	**0.389**	0.339	0.251	**0.381**	0.338
METEOR-MPEDA	**0.342**	0.385	0.341	0.251	**0.381**	0.340

Table 6. The segment-level correlation of metrics on evaluation translation out of English on WMT15 Metrics task

5 Conclusion

In this paper, we describe the submissions of our metric for WMT16 Metrics task in detail. We propose an approach to extract domain-specific paraphrase table from monolingual corpus for automatic evaluation of MT, and use it to replace the original paraphrase table in METEOR metric to improve the correlation between human judgment and automatic evaluation metrics. The proposed approach is tested on the newswire domain. In future work, we will systematically apply it to different specific domains such as the medical domain, IT domain, etc.

Acknowledgments

This research has been funded by the Natural Science Foundation of China under Grant No.61203313, 61462044, 61462045, and 61562042, and supported by the Natural Science Foundation of Jiangxi Provincial Department of Science and Technology of China under Grant No 20151BAB207025, and also supported by the Natural Science Foundation of Jiangxi Educational Committee of China under Grant No. GJJ150352.

References

Amittai Axelrod, Xiaodong He and Jianfeng Gao, 2011. Domain Adaptation via Pseudo In-Domain Data Selection. Proceedings of the 2011 Conference on Empirical Methods in Natural Language Processing, pages 355-362, Edinburgh, Scotland, UK.

Satanjeev Banerjee and Alon Lavie, 2005. METEOR: An Automatic Metric for MT Evaluation with Improved Correlation with Human Judgments. Proceedings of the ACL Workshop on Intrinsic and Extrinsic Evaluation Measures for Machine Translation and/or Summarization, pages 65-72, Ann Arbor.

Colin Bannard and Chris Callison-Burch, 2005. Paraphrasing with Bilingual Parallel Corpora. Proceedings of the 43rd Annual Meeting of the Association for Computational Linguistics, pages 597-604, Ann Arbor, Michigan.

Regina Barzilay and Kathleen R. McKeown, 2001. Extracting Paraphrases from a Parallel Corpus. Proceedings of 39th Annual Meeting of the Association for Computational Linguistics, pages 50-57, Toulouse, France.

Regina Barzilay and Lillian Lee, 2003. Learning to Paraphrase: An Unsupervised Approach Using Multiple-Sequence Alignment. Proceedings of the 2003 Human Language Technology Conference of the North American Chapter of the Association for Computational Linguistics, pages 16-23.

Ondrej Bojar, Rajen Chatterjee, Christian Federmann, Barry Haddow, Matthias Huck, Chris Hokamp, Philipp Koehn, Varvara Logacheva, Christof Monz, Matteo Negri, Matt Post, Carolina Scarton, Lucia Specia and Marco Turchi, 2015. Findings of the 2015 Workshop on Statistical Machine Translation. Proceedings of the Tenth Workshop on Statistical Machine Translation, pages 1-46, Lisbon, Portugal.

Yee Seng Chan and Hwee Tou Ng, 2008. MAXSIM: A Maximum Similarity Metric for Machine Translation Evaluation. Proceedings of the 46th Annual Meeting of the Association for Computational Linguistics, pages 55-62, Columbus, Ohio.

Michael Denkowski and Alon Lavie, 2014. Meteor Universal: Language Specific Translation Evaluation for Any Target Language. Proceedings of the Ninth Workshop on Statistical Machine Translation, pages 376-380.

George Doddington, 2002. Automatic Evaluation of Machine Translation Quality Using N-gram Co-occurrence Statistics. Proceedings of the second international conference on Human Language Technology Research, pages 138-145, San Diego, California, CA, USA.

Maoxi Li, Aiwen Jiang and Mingwen Wang, 2013. Listwise Approach to Learning to Rank for Automatic Evaluation of Machine Translation. Proceedings of Machine Translation Summit XIV, pages 51-59, Nice, France.

Maoxi Li, Mingwen Wang, Hanxi Li, Fan Xu, 2016. Modeling Monolingual Character Alignment for Automatic Evaluation of Chinese Translation. ACM Transactions on Asian and Low-Resource Language Information Processing, 15(3), pages 1-16.

Robert C. Moore and William Lewis, 2010. Intelligent Selection of Language Model Training Data. Proceedings of the ACL 2010 Conference (Short Papers), pages 220-224, Uppsala, Sweden.

Kishore Papineni, Salim Roukos, Todd Ward and Wei-Jing Zhu, 2002. BLEU: a Method for Automatic Evaluation of Machine Translation. Proceedings of the 40th Annual Meeting on Association for Computational Linguistics, pages 311-318, Philadelphia, Pennsylvania.

Ellie Pavlick, Juri Ganitkevitch, Tsz Ping Chan, Xuchen Yao, Benjamin Van Durme and Chris Callison-Burch, 2015. Domain-Specific Paraphrase Extraction. Proceedings of the 53rd Annual Meeting of the Association for Computational Linguistics and the 7th International Joint Conference on Natural Language Processing, pages 57–62, Beijing, China.

Yusuke Shinyama, Satoshi Sekine and Kiyoshi Sudo, 2002. Automatic Paraphrase Acquisition from News Articles. Proceedings of the second international conference on Human Language Technology Research, pages 313-318.

Matthew Snover, Bonnie Dorr, Richard Schwartz, John Makhoul, Linnea Micciulla and Ralph Makhoul, 2006. A Study of Translation Edit Rate with Targeted Human Annotation. Proceedings of Association for Machine Translation in the Americas, pages 223-231, Cambridge.

Zhen Weng, Maoxi Li, Mingwen Wang, 2015. Enhance Automatic Evaluation of Machine Translation by Markov Network Based Paraphrases (in Chinese). Journal of Chinese Information Processing, 29(6), pages 136-142.

Particle Swarm Optimization Submission for WMT16 Tuning Task

Viktor Kocur
CTU in Prague
FNSPE
kocurvik@fjfi.cvut.cz

Ondřej Bojar
Charles University in Prague
MFF ÚFAL
bojar@ufal.mff.cuni.cz

Abstract

This paper describes our submission to the Tuning Task of WMT16. We replace the grid search implemented as part of standard minimum-error rate training (MERT) in the Moses toolkit with a search based on particle swarm optimization (PSO). An older variant of PSO has been previously successfully applied and we now test it in optimizing the Tuning Task model for English-to-Czech translation. We also adapt the method in some aspects to allow for even easier parallelization of the search.

1 Introduction

Common models of statistical machine translation (SMT) consist of multiple features which assign probabilities or scores to possible translations. These are then combined in a weighted sum to determine the best translation given by the model. Tuning within SMT refers to the process of finding the optimal weights for these features on a given tuning set. This paper describes our submission to WMT16 Tuning Task[1], a shared task where all the SMT model components and the tuning set are given and task participants are expected to provide only the weight settings. We took part only in English-to-Czech system tuning.

Our solution is based on the standard tuning method of Minimum Error-Rate Training (MERT, Och, 2003). The MERT algorithm described in Bertoldi et al. (2009) is the default tuning method in the Moses SMT toolkit (Koehn et al., 2007). The inner loop of the algorithm performs optimization on a space of weight vectors with a given

translation metric[2]. The standard optimization is a variant of grid search and in our work, we replace it with the Particle Swarm Optimization (PSO, Eberhart et al., 1995) algorithm.

Particle Swarm Optimization is a good candidate for an efficient implementation of the inner loop of MERT due to the nature of the optimization space. The so-called Traditional PSO (TPSO) has already been tested by Suzuki et al. (2011), with a success. Improved versions of the PSO algorithm, known as Standard PSO (SPSO), have been summarized in Clerc (2012).

In this paper, we test a modified version of the latest SPSO2011 algorithm within the Moses toolkit and compare its results and computational costs with the standard Moses implementation of MERT.

2 MERT

The basic goal of MERT is to find optimal weights for various numerical features of an SMT system. The weights are considered optimal if they minimize an automated error metric which compares the machine translation to a human translation for a certain tuning (development) set.

Formally, each feature provides a score (sometimes a probability) that a given sentence e in goal language is the translation of the foreign sentence f. Given a weight for each such feature, it is possible to combine the scores to a single figure and find the highest scoring translation. The best translation can then be obtained by the following formula:

$$e^* = \operatorname*{argmax}_{e} \sum_{i} \lambda_i \log\left(p_i(e|f)\right) = g_p(\lambda) \quad (1)$$

---

[1] http://www.statmt.org/wmt16/tuning-task/

[2] All our experiments optimize the default BLEU but other metrics could be directly tested as well.

Proceedings of the First Conference on Machine Translation, Volume 2: Shared Task Papers, pages 518–524,
Berlin, Germany, August 11-12, 2016. ©2016 Association for Computational Linguistics

The process of finding the best translation e^* is called decoding. The translations can vary significantly based on the values of the weights, therefore it is necessary to find the weights that would give the best result. This is achieved by minimizing the error of the machine translation against the human translation:

$$\lambda^* = \underset{\lambda}{\arg\min}\, err_f(g_p(\lambda), e_{human}) \qquad (2)$$

The error function can also be considered as a negative value of an automated scorer. The problem with this straight-forward approach is that decoding is computationally expensive. To reduce this cost, the decoder is not run for every considered weight setting. Instead, only some promising settings are tested in a loop (called the "outer loop"): given the current best weights, the decoder is asked to produce n best translation for each sentence of the tuning set. This enlarged set of candidates allows us to estimate translation scores for similar weight settings. An optimizer uses these estimates to propose a new vector of weights and the decoder then tests this proposal in another outer loop. The outer loop is stopped when no new weight setting is proposed by the optimizer or no new translations are found by the decoder. The run of the optimizer is called the "inner loop", although it need not be iterative in any sense. The optimizer tries to find the best weights so that the least erroneous translations appear as high as possible in the n-best lists of candidate translations.

Our algorithm replaces the inner loop of MERT. It is therefore important to describe the properties of the inner loop optimization task.

Due to finite number of translations accumulated in the n-best lists (across sentences as well as outer loop iterations), the error function changes only when the change in weights leads to a change in the order of the n-best list. This is represented by numerous plateaus in the error function with discontinuities on the edges of the plateaus. This prevents the use of simple gradient methods. We can define a local optimum not in a strict mathematical sense but as a plateau which has only higher or only lower plateaus at the edges. These local optima can then be numerous within the search space and trap any optimizing algorithm, thus preventing convergence to the global optimum which is desired.

Another problem is the relatively high dimensionality of the search space. The Tuning Task model has 21 features but adding sparse features, we can get to thousands of dimensions.

These properties of the search space make PSO an interesting candidate for the inner loop algorithm. PSO is stochastic so it doesn't require smoothness of the optimized function. It is also highly parallelizable and gains more power with more CPUs available, which is welcome since the optimization itself is quite expensive. The simplicity of PSO also leaves space for various improvements.

3 PSO Algorithm

The PSO algorithm was first described by Eberhart et al. (1995). PSO is an iterative optimization method inspired by the behavior of groups of animals such as flocks of birds or schools of fish. The space is searched by individual particles with their own positions and velocities. The particles can inform others of their current and previous positions and their properties.

3.1 TPSO

The original algorithm is defined quite generally. Let us formally introduce the procedure. The search space S is defined as

$$S = \bigotimes_{d=1}^{D}[min_d, max_d] \qquad (3)$$

where D is the dimension of the space and min_d and max_d are the minimal and maximal values for the d-th coordinate. We try to find a point in the space which maximizes a given function $f : S \mapsto \mathbb{R}$.

There are p particles and the i-th particle in the n-th iteration has the following D-dimensional vectors: position $\mathbf{x}_i^n$, velocity $\mathbf{v}_i^n$, and two vectors of maxima found so far: the best position $\mathbf{p}_i^n$ visited by the particle itself and the best known position $\mathbf{l}_i^n$ that the particle has learned about from others.

In TPSO algorithm, the $\mathbf{l}_i^n$ vector is always the globally best position visited by any particle so far.

The TPSO algorithm starts with simple initialization:

$$\mathbf{x}_i^0 = rand(S) \tag{4}$$

$$\mathbf{v}_i^0 = \frac{rand(S) - \mathbf{x}_i^0}{2} \tag{5}$$

$$\mathbf{p}_i^0 = \mathbf{x}_i^0 \tag{6}$$

$$\mathbf{l}_i^0 = \operatorname*{argmax}_j f(\mathbf{p}_j^0) \tag{7}$$

where the function $rand(S)$ generates a random vector from space S with uniform distribution.

The velocity for the next iteration is updated as follows:

$$\mathbf{v}_i^{t+1} = w\mathbf{v}_i^t + U(0,1)\phi_p\mathbf{p}_i^t + U(0,1)\phi_l\mathbf{l}_i^t \tag{8}$$

where $U(0,1)$ denotes a random number between 0 and 1 with uniform distribution. The parameters w, ϕ_p, $\phi_l \in (0,1)$ are set by the user and indicate a slowdown, and the respective weight for own vs. learned optimum.

All the following vectors are then updated:

$$\mathbf{x}_i^{t+1} = \mathbf{x}_i^t + \mathbf{v}_i^{t+1} \tag{9}$$

$$\mathbf{p}_i^{t+1} = \mathbf{x}_i^{t+1} \quad \text{if } f(\mathbf{x}_i^{t+1}) > f(\mathbf{p}_i^t) \tag{10}$$

$$\mathbf{l}_i^{t+1} = \operatorname*{argmax}_j (f(\mathbf{p}_j^{t+1})) \tag{11}$$

The process continues with the next iteration until all of the particles converge to proximity of a certain point. Other stopping criteria are also used.

3.2 Modified SPSO2011

We introduce a number of changes to the algorithm SPSO2011 described by Clerc (2012).

In SPSO2011 the global best position $\mathbf{l}_i^t$ is replaced by the best position the particle has received information about from other particles. In the original SPSO2011 this is done in a synchronized fashion: after every iteration, all particles send their best personal positions to m other particles. Every particle chooses the best position it has received in the current iteration and sets its $\mathbf{l}_i^t$ accordingly. This generalization of $\mathbf{l}_i^t$ is introduced in order to combat premature convergence to a local optimum.

To avoid waiting until all particles finish their computation, we introduce per-particle memory of "learned best positions" called the "neighbourhood set" (although its members do not have to be located in any close vicinity). This set of best positions is limited to k elements, each new addition over the limit k replaces the oldest information. To establish the "global" optimum $\mathbf{l}_i^t$, every particle consults only its set of learned best positions.

The algorithm starts with the initialization of particle vectors given by the equations (4-6). The $\mathbf{l}_i^0$ is initialized with the value of $\mathbf{p}_i^0$. The sets of learned best positions are initialized as empty.

Two constants affect computations given below: w is again the slowdown and c controls the "expansion" of examined neighbourhood of each particle. We set w and c to values that (as per Bonyadi and Michalewicz, 2014) ensure convergence:

$$w = \frac{1}{2ln(2)} \approx 0.721 \tag{12}$$

$$c = \frac{1}{2} + ln(2) \approx 1.193 \tag{13}$$

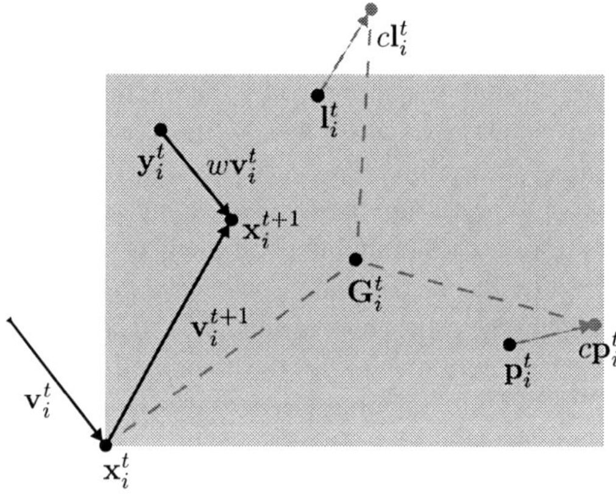

Figure 1: Construction of the particle position update. The grey area indicates $P(\mathbf{G}, \mathbf{x})$.

For the update of velocity, it is first necessary to calculate a "center of gravity" $\mathbf{G}_i^t$ of three points: the current position $\mathbf{x}_i^t$, a slightly "expanded" current best position $\mathbf{p}_i^t$ and a slightly expanded best position known by colleagues $\mathbf{l}_i^t$. The "expansion" of the positions is controlled by c and directed outwards from $\mathbf{x}_i^t$:

$$\mathbf{G}_i^t = \mathbf{x}_i^t + c \cdot \frac{\mathbf{p}_i^t + \mathbf{l}_i^t - 2\mathbf{x}_i^t}{3} \tag{14}$$

To introduce further randomness, $\mathbf{x}_i^t$ is relocated to a position $\mathbf{y}_i^t$ sampled from the uniform distribution in the area $P(\mathbf{G}_i^t, \mathbf{x}_i^t)$ formally defined as:

$$P(\mathbf{G}, \mathbf{x}) = \bigotimes_{d=1}^{D} \left[G_d - |G_d - x_d|, G_d + |G_d - x_d| \right] \tag{15}$$

Our $P(\mathbf{G}, \mathbf{x})$ is a hypercube centered in $\mathbf{G_i^t}$ and touching $\mathbf{x}_i^t$, see Figure 1 for an illustration. The original SPSO2011 used a d-dimensional ball with the center in $\mathbf{G}$ and radius $\|\mathbf{G} - \mathbf{x}\|$ to avoid the bias of searching towards points on axes. We are less concerned about this and opt for a simpler and faster calculation.

The new velocity is set to include the previous velocity (reduced by w) as well as the speedup caused by the random relocation:

$$\mathbf{v}_i^{t+1} = w\mathbf{v}_i^t + \mathbf{y}_i^t - \mathbf{x}_i^t \tag{16}$$

Finally, the particle position is updated:

$$\mathbf{x}_i^{t+1} = \mathbf{x}_i^t + \mathbf{v}_i^{t+1} = w\mathbf{v}_i^t + \mathbf{y}_i^t \tag{17}$$

The optimized function is evaluated at the new position $\mathbf{x}_i^{t+1}$ and the particle's best position is updated if a new optimum was found. In any case, the best position $\mathbf{p}_i^{t+1}$ together with its value is sent to m randomly selected particles (possibly including the current particle) to be included in their sets of learned best positions as described above. The particle then sets its $\mathbf{l}_i^{t+1}$ to best position from its own list of learned positions.

The next iteration continues with the updated vectors. Normally, the algorithm would terminate when all particles converge to a close proximity to each other, but it turns out that this often leads to premature stopping. There are many other approaches possible to this problem (Xinchao, 2010; Evers and Ben Ghalia, 2009), but we choose a simple restarting strategy: when the particle is sending out its new best position and value to m fellows, the manager responsible for this checks if this value was not reported in the previous call (from any other particle). If it was, then the current particle is instructed to restart itself by setting all of its vectors to random initial state.[3] The neighborhood set is left unchanged. The restart prevents multiple particles exploring the same area.

The drawback of restarts is that the stopping criterion is never met. In our first version, we ran

____

[3]The use of score and not position is possible due to the nature of the space in which a same score of two points very likely means that the points are equivalent.

the algorithm for a fixed number of position updates, specifically 32000. Later, we changed the algorithm to terminate after the manager has seen 3200 position updates without any update of the global best position. In the following section, we refer to the former as PSO without the termination condition (PSO) and the latter as PSO with the termination condition (PSO-T).

Properties of SPSO2011 have been investigated by Bonyadi and Michalewicz (2014). We use a slightly different algorithm, but our modifications should have an effect only on rotational invariance, which is not so much relevant for our purpose. Aside from the discussion on the values of w and c with respect to the convergence of all particles to the same point, Bonyadi and Michalewicz also mention that SPSO2011 is not guaranteed to converge to a local optimum. Since our search space is discontinuous with plateaus, the local convergence in the mathematical sense is not especially useful anyway.

4 Implementation

We implemented the algorithm described above with one parameter, the number of particles. We set the size of the neighborhood set, denoted k above, to 4 and the number of random particles receiving the information about a particle's best position so far (m) to 3.

The implementation of our version of the PSO algorithm is built within the standard Moses code. The algorithm itself creates a reasonable parallel structure with each thread representing a single particle.

We use similar object structure as the baseline MERT implementation. The points are represented by their own class which handles basic arithmetic and stream operations. The class carries not only the vector of the current position but also its associated score.

Multiple threads are maintained by the standard Moses thread pools (Haddow, 2012). Every thread ("Task" in Moses thread pools) corresponds to a particle and is responsible for calculating its search in the space using the class `PSOOptimizer`. There are no synchronous iterations, each particle proceeds at its own pace.

All optimizers have access to a global manager object of class `PSOManager`, see Figure 2 for an illustration. The manager provides methods for the optimizers to get the best vector $\mathbf{l}_i^t$ from the

Run	PSO-16	PSO-64	PSO-T-16	PSO-T-64	MERT-16
1	14.5474	15.6897	15.6133	15.6613	14.5470
2	17.3292	18.7340	18.7437	18.4464	18.8704
3	18.9261	18.9788	18.9711	18.9069	19.0625
4	19.0926	19.2060	19.0646	19.0785	19.0623
5	19.1599	19.2140	19.0968	19.0738	19.1992
6	19.2444	19.2319	-	19.0772	19.1751
7	19.2470	19.2383	-	-	19.0480
8	19.2613	19.2245	-	-	19.1359
12	-	-	-	-	19.1625

Table 1: The final best BLEU score after the runs of the inner loop for PSO without and with the termination condition with 16 and 64 threads respectively and standard Moses MERT implementation with 16 threads.

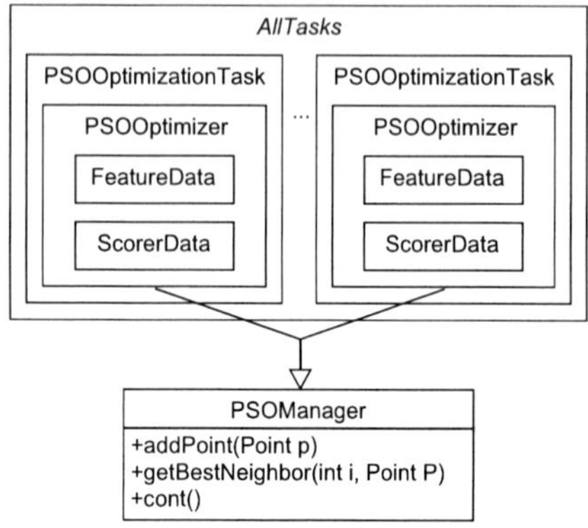

Figure 2: Base structure of our PSO algorithm

neighborhood set, to report its best position to the random m particles (`addPoint`) and to check if the optimization should still run (`cont`) or terminate. The method `addPoint` serves two other purposes: incrementing an internal counter of iterations and indicating through its return value whether the reporting particle should restart itself.

Every optimizer has its own `FeatureData` and `ScorerData`, which are used to determine the score of the investigated points. As of now, the data is loaded serially, so the more threads we have, the longer the initialization takes. In the baseline implementation of MERT, all the threads share the scoring data. This means that the data is loaded only once, but due to some unexpected locking, the baseline implementation never gains speedups higher than 1.5, even with 32 threads, see Table 2 below.

This structure allows an efficient use of multiple cores. Methods of the manager are fast compared to the calculations performed in the optimizers. The only locking occurs when threads are trying to add points; read access to the manager can be concurrent.

5 Results

We ran the tuning only for the English to Czech part of the tuning task. We filtered and binarized the model supplied by the organizers to achieve better performance and smaller memory costs.

For the computation, we used the services of Metacentrum VO. Due to the relatively high memory demands we used two SGI UV 2000 machines: one with 48x 6-core Intel Xeon E5-4617 2.9GHz and 6TB RAM and one with 48x 8-core Intel Xeon E5-4627v2 3.30GHz and 6TB RAM. We ran the tuning process on 16 and 64 CPUs, i.e. with 16 and 64 particles, respectively. We submitted the weights from the 16-CPU run. We also ran a test run using the standard Moses MERT implementation with 16 threads for a comparison.

Table 1 shows the best BLEU scores at the end of each inner loop (as projected from the n-best lists on the tuning set of sentences). Both methods provide similar results. Since the methods are stochastic, different runs will lead to different best positions (and different scores).

Comparison of our implementation with with the baseline MERT on a test set is not necessary. Both implementations try to maximize BLEU score, therefore any overtraining occurring in the baseline MERT occurs also in our implementation and vice versa.

Table 2 shows the average run times and reached scores for 8 runs of the baseline MERT and our PSO and PSO-T, starting with the same

Outer Loop	CPUs	Wall Clock [s]			Projected BLEU Reached		
		MERT	PSO	PSO-T	MERT	PSO	PSO-T
1	1	186.24±10.63	397.28±2.13	62.37±19.64	14.50±0.03	13.90±0.05	13.84±0.05
1	4	123.51±3.58	72.75±1.12	21.94±4.63	14.51±0.03	14.48±0.08	14.46±0.06
1	8	135.40±8.43	43.07±0.78	15.62±3.40	14.52±0.04	14.53±0.05	14.42±0.12
1	16	139.43±8.00	33.00±1.37	14.59±2.21	14.53±0.02	14.51±0.08	14.48±0.10
1	24	119.69±4.43	32.20±1.62	16.89±3.16	14.52±0.02	14.55±0.06	14.47±0.07
1	32	119.04±4.47	33.42±2.16	19.16±2.92	14.53±0.03	14.50±0.04	14.50±0.07
3	1	701.18±47.13	1062.38±1.88	117.64±0.47	18.93±0.04	18.08±0.00	18.08±0.00
3	4	373.69±28.37	189.86±0.64	57.28±23.61	18.90±0.00	18.82±0.12	18.81±0.07
3	8	430.88±24.82	111.50±0.53	37.92±8.68	18.95±0.05	18.89±0.09	18.87±0.06
3	16	462.77±18.78	80.54±5.39	29.62±4.34	18.94±0.04	18.94±0.07	18.90±0.05
3	24	392.66±13.39	74.08±3.64	31.67±3.47	18.94±0.04	18.93±0.05	18.86±0.05
3	32	399.93±27.68	82.83±3.82	37.70±4.52	18.91±0.01	18.90±0.05	18.87±0.06

Table 2: Average run times and reached scores. The ± are standard deviations.

n-best lists as accumulated in iteration 1 and 3 of the outer loop. Note that PSO and PSO-T use only as many particles as there are threads, so running them with just one thread leads to a degraded performace in terms of BLEU. With 4 or 8 threads, the three methods are on par in terms of tuning-set BLEU. Starting from 4 threads, both PSO and PSO-T terminate faster than the baseline MERT implementation. Moreover the baseline MERT proved unable to utilize multiple CPUs efficiently, whereas PSO gives us up to 14-fold speedup.

In general, the higher the ratio of the serial data loading to the search computation time, the worse the speedup. The search in PSO-T takes much shorter time so the overhead of serial data loading is more apparent and PSO-T seems parallelized badly and gives only quadruple speedup. The reduction of this overhead is highly desirable.

6 Conclusion

We presented our submission to the WMT16 Tuning Task, a variant of particle swarm optimization applied to minimum error-rate training in statistical machine translation. Our method is a drop-in replacement of the standard Moses MERT and has the benefit of easy parallelization. Preliminary experiments suggest that it indeed runs faster and delivers comparable weight settings.

The effects on the number of iterations of the MERT outer loop as well as on the test-set performance have still to be investigated.

Acknowledgments

This work has received funding from the European Union's Horizon 2020 research and innovation programme under grant agreement no. 645452 (QT21). This work has been using language resources stored and distributed by the LINDAT/CLARIN project of the Ministry of Education, Youth and Sports of the Czech Republic (project LM2015071). Computational resources were supplied by the Ministry of Education, Youth and Sports of the Czech Republic under the Projects CESNET (Project No. LM2015042) and CERIT-Scientific Cloud (Project No. LM2015085) provided within the program Projects of Large Research, Development and Innovations Infrastructures.

References

Nicola Bertoldi, Barry Haddow, and Jean-Baptiste Fouet. 2009. Improved minimum error rate training in moses. *The Prague Bulletin of Mathematical Linguistics* 91:7–16.

Mohammad Reza Bonyadi and Zbigniew Michalewicz. 2014. Spso 2011: Analysis of stability; local convergence; and rotation sensitivity. In *Proceedings of the 2014 conference on Genetic and evolutionary computation*. ACM, pages 9–16.

Maurice Clerc. 2012. Standard particle swarm optimisation .

Russ C Eberhart, James Kennedy, et al. 1995. A new optimizer using particle swarm theory. In *Proceedings of the sixth international symposium on micro machine and human science*. New York, NY, volume 1, pages 39–43.

George I Evers and Mounir Ben Ghalia. 2009. Regrouping particle swarm optimization: a new global optimization algorithm with improved performance consistency across benchmarks. In *Systems, Man and Cybernetics, 2009. SMC 2009. IEEE International Conference on*. IEEE, pages 3901–3908.

Barry Haddow. 2012. Adding Multi-Threaded Decoding to Moses. *Prague Bulletin of Mathematical Linguistics* 93:57–66.

Philipp Koehn, Hieu Hoang, Alexandra Birch, Chris Callison-Burch, Marcello Federico, Nicola Bertoldi, Brooke Cowan, Wade Shen, Christine Moran, Richard Zens, et al. 2007. Moses: Open source toolkit for statistical machine translation. In *Proceedings of the 45th annual meeting of the ACL on interactive poster and demonstration sessions*. Association for Computational Linguistics, pages 177–180.

Franz Josef Och. 2003. Minimum error rate training in statistical machine translation. In *Proceedings of the 41st Annual Meeting on Association for Computational Linguistics-Volume 1*. Association for Computational Linguistics, pages 160–167.

Jun Suzuki, Kevin Duh, and Masaaki Nagata. 2011. Distributed minimum error rate training of smt using particle swarm optimization. In *IJCNLP*. pages 649–657.

Zhao Xinchao. 2010. A perturbed particle swarm algorithm for numerical optimization. *Applied Soft Computing* 10(1):119–124.

Findings of the 2016 WMT Shared Task
on Cross-lingual Pronoun Prediction

Liane Guillou
LMU Munich
CIS
liane@cis.uni-muenchen.de

Christian Hardmeier
Uppsala University
Dept. of Linguistics & Philology
christian.hardmeier@lingfil.uu.se

Preslav Nakov
Qatar Computing Res. Inst.
HBKU
pnakov@qf.org.qa

Sara Stymne
Uppsala University
Dept. of Linguistics & Philology
sara.stymne@lingfil.uu.se

Jörg Tiedemann
University of Helsinki
Dept. of Modern Languages
jorg.tiedemann@helsinki.fi

Yannick Versley
LinkedIn
Dublin, Ireland
yversley@gmail.com

Mauro Cettolo
Fondazione Bruno Kessler
Trento, Italy
cettolo@fbk.eu

Bonnie Webber
ILCC, University of
Edinburgh, Scotland, UK
bonnie@inf.ed.ac.uk

Andrei Popescu-Belis
Idiap Research Institute
Martigny, Switzerland
apbelis@idiap.ch

Abstract

We describe the design, the evaluation setup, and the results of the 2016 WMT shared task on cross-lingual pronoun prediction. This is a classification task in which participants are asked to provide predictions on what pronoun class label should replace a placeholder value in the target-language text, provided in lemmatised and PoS-tagged form. We provided four subtasks, for the English–French and English–German language pairs, in both directions. Eleven teams participated in the shared task; nine for the English–French subtask, five for French–English, nine for English–German, and six for German–English. Most of the submissions outperformed two strong language-model-based baseline systems, with systems using deep recurrent neural networks outperforming those using other architectures for most language pairs.

1 Introduction

Pronoun translation poses a problem for current state-of-the-art Statistical Machine Translation (SMT) systems (Le Nagard and Koehn, 2010; Hardmeier and Federico, 2010; Novák, 2011; Guillou, 2012; Hardmeier, 2014).

anaphoric	I have an **umbrella**. **It** is red.
pleonastic	I have an umbrella. **It** is raining.
event	He lost his job. **It** came as a total surprise.

Figure 1: Examples of three different functions fulfilled by the English pronoun "it".

Problems arise for a number of reasons. In general, pronoun systems in natural language do not map well across languages, e.g., due to differences in gender, number, case, formality, or animacy/humanness, as well as due to differences in where pronouns may be used.

To this is added the problem of *functional ambiguity*, whereby pronouns with the same surface form may perform multiple functions (Guillou, 2016). For example, the English pronoun "it" may function as an anaphoric, pleonastic, or event reference pronoun. An *anaphoric* pronoun corefers with a noun phrase (NP). A *pleonastic* pronoun does not refer to anything, but it is required by syntax to fill the subject position. An *event reference* pronoun may refer to a verb phrase (VP), a clause, an entire sentence, or a longer passage of text. Examples of each of these pronoun functions are provided in Figure 1. It is clear that instances of the English pronoun "it" belonging to each of these functions would have different translation requirements in French and German.

Proceedings of the First Conference on Machine Translation, Volume 2: Shared Task Papers, pages 525–542,
Berlin, Germany, August 11-12, 2016. ©2016 Association for Computational Linguistics

The problem of pronouns in machine translation has long been studied. In particular, for SMT systems, the recent previous studies cited above have focused on the translation of anaphoric pronouns. In this case, a well-known constraint of languages with grammatical gender is that agreement must hold between an anaphoric pronoun and the NP with which it corefers, called its *antecedent*. The pronoun and its antecedent may occur in the same sentence (*intra-sentential anaphora*) or in different sentences (*inter-sentential anaphora*). Most SMT systems translate sentences in isolation, so inter-sentential anaphoric pronouns will be translated without knowledge of their antecedent and as such, pronoun-antecedent agreement cannot be guaranteed. The accurate translation of intra-sentential anaphoric pronouns may also cause problems as the pronoun and its antecedent may fall into different translation units (e.g., n-gram or syntactic tree fragment).

The above constraints start playing a role in pronoun translation in situations where several translation options are possible for a given source-language pronoun, a large number of options being likely to affect negatively the translation accuracy. In other words, pronoun types that exhibit significant *translation divergencies* are more likely to be erroneously translated by an SMT system that is not aware of the above constraints. For example, when translating the English pronoun "she" into French, there is one main option, "elle" (exceptions occur, though, e.g., in references to ships). However, several options exist for the translation of anaphoric "it": "il" (for an antecedent that is masculine in French) or "elle" (feminine), but also "cela", "ça" or sometimes "ce" (non-gendered demonstratives).

The challenges of correct pronoun translation gradually raised the interest in a shared task, which would allow the comparison of various proposals and the quantification of their claims to improve pronoun translation. However, evaluating pronoun translation comes with its own challenges, as reference-based evaluation cannot take into account the legitimate variations of translated pronouns, or their placement in the sentence. Building upon the experience from a 2015 shared task, the WMT 2016 shared task on pronoun prediction has been designed to test capacities for correct pronoun translation in a framework that allows for objective evaluation, as we now explain.

2 Task Description

The WMT 2016 shared task on cross-lingual pronoun prediction is a classification task in which participants are asked to provide predictions on what pronoun class label should replace a placeholder value (represented by the token REPLACE) in the target-language text. It requires no specific Machine Translation (MT) expertise and is interesting as a machine learning task in its own right. Within the context of SMT, one could think of the task of cross-lingual pronoun prediction as a component of an SMT system. This component may take the form of a decoder feature or it may be used to provide "corrected" pronoun translations in a post-editing scenario.

The design of the WMT 2016 shared task has been influenced by the design and the results of a 2015 shared task (Hardmeier et al., 2015) organised at the EMNLP workshop on Discourse in MT (DiscoMT). The first intuition about evaluating pronoun translation is to require participants to submit MT systems — possibly with specific strategies for pronoun translation — and to estimate the correctness of the pronouns they output. This estimation, however, cannot be performed with full reliability only by comparing pronouns across candidate and reference translations because this would miss the legitimate variation of certain pronouns, as well as variations in gender or number of the antecedent itself. Human judges are thus required for reliable evaluation, following the protocol described at the DiscoMT 2015 shared task on *pronoun-focused translation*. The high cost of this approach, which grows linearly with the number of submissions, prompted us to implement an alternative approach, also proposed in 2015 as *pronoun prediction* (Hardmeier et al., 2015). While the structure of the WMT 2016 task is similar to the shared task of the same name at DiscoMT 2015, there are two main differences, one conceptual and one regarding the language pairs, as specified hereafter.

In the WMT 2016 task, participants are asked to predict a target-language pronoun given a source-language pronoun in the context of a sentence. In addition to the source-language sentence, we provide a lemmatised and part-of-speech (PoS) tagged target-language human-authored translation of the source sentence, and automatic word alignments between the source-sentence words and the target-language lemmata.

In the translation, the words aligned to a subset of the source-language third-person subject pronouns are substituted by placeholders. The aim of the task is to predict, for each placeholder, the word that should replace it from a small, closed set of classes, using any type of information that can be extracted from the documents. In this way, the evaluation can be fully automatic, by comparing whether the class predicted by the system is identical to the reference one, assuming that the constraints of the lemmatised target text allow only one correct class (unlike the pronoun-focused translation task which makes no assumption about the target text).

Figure 2 shows an English–French example sentence from the development set. It contains two pronouns to be predicted, indicated by RE-PLACE tags in the target sentence. The first "it" corresponds to "ce" while the second "it" corresponds to "qui" (equivalent to English "which"), which belongs to the OTHER class, i.e., does not need to be predicted as is. This example illustrates some of the difficulties of the task: the two source sentences are merged into one target sentence, the second "it" becomes a relative pronoun instead of a subject one, and the second French verb has a rare intransitive usage.

The two main differences between the WMT 2016 and DiscoMT 2015 tasks are as follows. First, the WMT 2016 task introduces more language pairs with respect to the 2015 task. In addition to the English–French subtask (same pair as the DiscoMT 2015 task), we also provide subtasks for French–English, German–English and English–German. Second, the WMT 2016 task provides a lemmatised and PoS-tagged reference translation instead of the fully inflected text provided for the DiscoMT 2015 task. The use of this representation, whilst still artificial, could be considered to provide a more realistic SMT-like setting. SMT systems cannot be relied upon to generate correctly inflected surface form words, and so the lemmatised, PoS-tagged representation encourages greater reliance on other information from the source and target-language sentences.

The following sections describe the set of source-language pronouns and the target-language classes to be predicted, for each of the four subtasks. The subtasks are asymmetric in terms of the source-language pronouns and the prediction classes.

The selection of the source-language pronouns and their target-language prediction classes for each subtask is based on the variation that is to be expected when translating a given source-language pronoun, i.e., the translation divergencies of each pronoun type. For example, when translating the English pronoun "it" into French, a decision must be made as to the gender of the French pronoun, with "il" and "elle" both providing valid options. Alternatively, a non-gendered pronoun such as "cela" may be used instead. The translation of the English pronouns "he" and "she" into French, however, does not require such a decision. These may simply be mapped one-to-one, as "il" and "elle" respectively, in the vast majority of cases. The translation of "he" and "she" from English into French is therefore not considered an *interesting* problem and as such, these pronouns are excluded from the source-language set for the English–French subtask. In the opposite translation direction, the French pronoun "il" may be translated as "it" or "he", and "elle" as "it" or "she". As a decision must be taken as to the appropriate target-language translation of "il" and "elle", these are included in the set of source-language pronouns for French–English.

2.1 English–French

This subtask concentrates on the translation of subject-position "it" and "they" from English into French. The following prediction classes exist for this subtask (the class name, identical to the main lexical item, is highlighted in bold, but each class may include additional lexical items, indicated in plain font between quotes):

- **ce**: the French pronoun "ce" (sometimes with elided vowel as "c' " when preceding a word starting by a vowel) as in the expression "c'est" ("it is");
- **elle**: feminine singular subject pronoun;
- **elles**: feminine plural subject pronoun;
- **il**: masculine singular subject pronoun;
- **ils**: masculine plural subject pronoun;
- **cela**: demonstrative pronouns, including "cela", "ça", the misspelling "ca", and the rare elided form "ç' " when the verb following it starts with a vowel;
- **on**: indefinite pronoun;
- **OTHER**: some other word, or nothing at all, should be inserted.

ce OTHER   ce|PRON qui|PRON   It 's an idiotic debate . It has to stop .   REPLACE_0
être|VER un|DET débat|NOM idiot|ADJ REPLACE_6 devoir|VER stopper|VER .|.   0-0 1-1
2-2 3-4 4-3 6-5 7-6 8-6 9-7 10-8

Figure 2: English–French example sentence from the development set with two REPLACE tags to be replaced by "ce" and "qui" (OTHER class), respectively. The French reference translation, not shown to participants, merges the two source sentences into one: "C'est un débat idiot qui doit stopper."

2.2 French–English

This subtask concentrates on the translation of subject-position "elle", "elles", "il", and "ils" from French into English.[1] The following prediction classes exist for this subtask:

- **he**: masculine singular subject pronoun;
- **she**: feminine singular subject pronoun;
- **it**: non-gendered singular subject pronoun;
- **they**: non-gendered plural subject pronoun;
- **this**: demonstrative pronouns (singular), including both "this" and "that";
- **these**: demonstrative pronouns (plural), including both "these" and "those";
- **there**: existential "there";
- **OTHER**: some other word, or nothing at all, should be inserted.

2.3 English–German

This subtask concentrates on the translation of subject-position "it" and "they" from English into German. It uses the following prediction classes:

- **er**: masculine singular subject pronoun;
- **sie**: feminine singular, and non-gendered plural subject pronouns;
- **es**: neuter singular subject pronoun;
- **man**: indefinite pronoun;
- **OTHER**: some other word, or nothing at all, should be inserted.

2.4 German–English

This subtask concentrates on the translation of subject position "er", "sie" and "es" from German into English. The following prediction classes exist for this subtask:

- **he**: masculine singular subject pronoun;
- **she**: feminine singular subject pronoun;

- **it**: non-gendered singular subject pronoun;
- **they**: non-gendered plural subject pronoun;
- **you**: second person pronoun (with both generic or deictic uses);
- **this**: demonstrative pronouns (singular), including both "this" and "that";
- **these**: demonstrative pronouns (plural), including both "these" and "those";
- **there**: existential "there";
- **OTHER**: some other word, or nothing at all, should be inserted.

3 Datasets

3.1 Data Sources

The training dataset comprises Europarl, News and TED talks data. The development and test datasets consist of TED talks. Below we describe the TED talks, the Europarl and News data, the method used for selecting the test datasets, and the steps taken to pre-process the training, development, and test datasets.

3.1.1 TED Talks

TED is a non-profit organisation that "invites the world's most fascinating thinkers and doers [...] to give the talk of their lives". Its website[2] makes the audio and the video of TED talks available under the Creative Commons license. All talks are presented and captioned in English, and translated by volunteers world-wide into many languages.[3] In addition to the availability of (audio) recordings, transcriptions and translations, TED talks pose interesting research challenges from the perspective of both speech recognition and machine translation. Therefore, both research communities are making increased use of them in building benchmarks.

---

[1]We explain below in Section 3.3.3 how non-subject pronouns are filtered out from the data.

[2]http://www.ted.com/

[3]As is common in other MT shared tasks, we do not give particular significance to the fact that all talks are originally given in English, which means that French–English translation is in reality a back-translation.

TED talks address topics of general interest and are delivered to a live public audience whose responses are also audible on the recordings. The talks generally aim to be persuasive and to change the viewers' behaviour or beliefs. The genre of the TED talks is transcribed planned speech.

As shown in analysis presented by Guillou et al. (2014), TED talks differ from other text types with respect to pronoun usage. TED speakers frequently use first- and second-person pronouns (singular and plural): first-person to refer to themselves and their colleagues or to themselves and the audience, second-person to refer to the audience, the larger set of viewers, or people in general. TED speakers often use the pronoun "they" without a specific textual antecedent, in sentences such as "This is what they think." They also use deictic and third-person pronouns to refer to things in the spatio-temporal context shared by the speaker and the audience, such as props and slides. In general, pronouns are common, and anaphoric references are not always clearly defined.

For the WMT 2016 task, TED training and development sets come from the MT task of the 2015 IWSLT evaluation campaign (Cettolo et al., 2015). The test set from DiscoMT 2015 (Hardmeier et al., 2015) was also released for development purposes.

3.1.2 Europarl and News

For training purposes, in addition to TED talks, the Europarl[4] and News Commentary[5] corpora were made available. We used the alignments provided by OPUS, including the document boundaries from the original sources. For Europarl, we used version 7 of the data release and the News Commentary set refers to version 9. The data preparation is explained below.

3.2 Test Set Selection

We selected the test datasets for the shared task from talks added recently to the TED repository that satisfy the following requirements:

1. The talks have been transcribed (in English) and translated into both German and French.

2. They are not included in the training, development or test sets of the IWSLT evaluation campaigns, nor in the DiscoMT 2015 test set.

3. In total, they amount to a number of words suitable for evaluation purposes (some tens of thousands).

Once we found the talks satisfying these criteria, we automatically aligned them at the segment level. Then, we extracted a number of TED talks from the collection, following the criteria outlined in Section 3.2. Finally, we manually checked the sentence alignments of these selected TED talks in order to fix errors generated by either automatic or human processing. Table 1 shows some statistics about the test datasets prepared for each subtask.

subtask	segs	tokens	
		source	target
English–French	1,213	22,429	23,626
French–English	1,199	24,019	23,911
English–German	1,258	22,458	20,118
German–English	1,192	20,795	23,926

Table 1: Statistics about 2016 test datasets.

In total, we selected 16 TED talks for testing, which we split into two groups: 8 TED talks for the English to French/German direction, and 8 TED talks for the French/German to English direction. Another option would have been to create four separate groups of TED talks, one for each subtask. However, using a smaller set of documents reduced the manual effort in correcting the automatic sentence alignment of the documents.

The TED talks belonging to the test datasets are described in Tables 2 and 3. The English texts used for the English–French and English–German subtasks are the same. Differences in alignment of the sentences leads to different segmentation of the parallel texts for the different language pairs. Minor corrections to the sentence alignment and to the text itself, which were applied manually, resulted in small differences in token counts for the same English TED talk when paired with the French vs. the German translation.

The TED talks in the test datasets were selected to include more pronouns from the rare classes. For example, for the English to French/German dataset, we wished to include documents that contained more feminine pronouns in the French and in the German translations. For the German/French to English dataset, we wished to include documents with more demonstrative pronouns in the English translations. The group of documents for the translation from English to French/German was balanced to ensure that the preference for rare pronouns was satisfied for both target languages.

---

[4]http://www.statmt.org/europarl/

[5]http://opus.lingfil.uu.se/News-Commentary.php

ID	Speaker	Segs	Tokens		Segs	Tokens	
			English	French		English	German
1541	L. Kristine	124	2,883	3,224	124	2,883	2,614
1665	E. Schlangen	48	1,027	1,087	48	1,027	887
2155	J. Howard	174	3,943	3,794	184	3,972	3,321
2175	K. Gbla	220	3,474	3,592	249	3,475	3,110
2241	P. Ronald	161	2,870	3,104	172	2,882	2,672
2277	D. Hoffman	225	3,736	3,837	217	3,729	3,293
2289	M. McKenna	118	2,342	2,666	121	2,338	2,207
2321	Y. Morieux	143	2,154	2,322	143	2,152	2,014
	Total	1,213	22,429	23,626	1,258	22,458	20,118

Table 2: Test dataset documents: English to French/German.

ID	Speaker	Segs	Tokens		Segs	Tokens	
			French	English		German	English
2039	M. Gould Stewart	105	2,567	2,443	123	2,257	2,449
2140	E. Balcetis	127	2,725	2,541	132	2,206	2,509
2151	V. Myers	151	2,803	2,918	168	2,370	2,937
2182	R. Semler	235	4,297	4,530	261	3,848	4,548
2194	N. Burke Harris	93	2,592	2,380	105	1,977	2,369
2246	A. Davis	147	2,660	2,832	103	2,347	2,805
2252	E. Perel	162	3,369	3,220	163	3,162	3,226
2287	C. Kidd	179	3,006	3,047	137	2,628	3,083
	Total	1,199	24,019	23,911	1,192	20,795	23,926

Table 3: Test dataset documents: French/German to English.

3.3 Data Preparation

In order to extract pronoun examples, we first needed to align the data. We then extracted the pronoun examples based on the alignments. Finally, we filtered the examples in order to remove non-subjects. An innovation this year is the lemmatisation of the target data to remove the informative features coming from the inflections of the surrounding context. We used automatic lemmatisers and PoS taggers, and we further converted the PoS labels to 12 coarse universal PoS tags (Petrov et al., 2012). For all languages in our dataset, we used TreeTagger (Schmid, 1994) with its built-in lemmatiser. The tagsets were then converted to universal PoS tags using publicly available mappings,[6] except for French, for which no appropriate mapping was available. In French, we clipped the morphosyntactic information from the base word class, which is separated by a colon (':') in the tagset (e.g., *VER:futu*, *VER:impe* and all other verb tags would be reduced to *VER*, thus only keeping the verb tag, resulting in 15 tags. For German, we had to map pronominal adverbs to PROAV for the conversion to match the Tiger tagset used in the mapping to universal PoS tags.

---

[6]https://github.com/slavpetrov/universal-pos-tags

3.3.1 Alignment Optimisation

Since we extract examples based on word alignments, we need good alignment precision in order not to extract erroneous examples, and good recall in order not to overgenerate the OTHER class. For the DiscoMT 2015 shared task, we explored this issue for English–French and found that GIZA++ model 4 and HMM with grow-diag-final-and symmetrisation gave the best results. For pronoun–pronoun links, we had an F-score of 0.96, with perfect recall and precision of 0.93 (Hardmeier et al., 2015). This was slightly higher than for other links, which had an F-score of 0.92.

For German–English, we explored this issue this year since it is a new language pair. We used an aligned gold standard of 987 sentences from (Padó and Lapata, 2005), which has been extensively evaluated by Stymne et al. (2014). We used the same methodology as in 2015, and performed an evaluation on the subset of links between the pronouns we are interested in. We report precision and recall of links both for the pronoun subset and for all links, shown in Table 4. The alignment quality is considerably worse than for French–English both for all links and for pronouns, but again the results for pronouns is better than for all links in both precision and recall.

Alignment	Symmetrisation	All links		Pronouns	
		P	R	P	R
Model 4		.75	.79	.82	.88
fast-align	gdfa	.69	.73	.80	.81
		.80	.73	.87	.85
	gd	.81	.70	.89	.78
HMM	gdf	.73	.77	.77	.90
	∪	.71	.77	.76	.90
	∩	.92	.61	.92	.74

Table 4: Evaluation of German–English alignments for all links and pronouns using different alignment models and symmetrisation.

Across symmetrisation methods, HMM alignments give the best performance, especially for precision. The trade-off between precision and recall that holds for all links also applies to pronoun links. In the end, we decided to use HMM with intersection symmetrisation, since we believe that precision is more important than recall, in order not to add any false positive instances of the pronoun classes to our data. The lower recall will result in more examples from the OTHER class though. For English–French, we applied the same setup as last year using IBM Model 4 and the grow-diag-final-and symmetrisation heuristic. Similar to last year, we also perform backoff alignment with fast_align in cases that are filtered out before running GIZA++ because of length and length-ratio restrictions of the parallel data.

3.3.2 Example Selection

In order to select the acceptable target classes, we computed the frequencies of pronouns aligned to the ambiguous source-language pronouns based on the PoS-tagged training data. Using these statistics, we defined the sets of predicted labels for each language pair. Based on the counts, we also decided to merge small classes such as the demonstrative pronouns 'these' and 'those'.

Using these datasets, we identified examples based on the automatic word alignments. We include cases in which multiple words are aligned to the selected pronoun if one of them belongs to the set of accepted target pronouns. If this is not the case, we use the shortest word aligned to the pronoun as the placeholder token.

Unlike in 2015, we find a translation placeholder token for the unaligned pronouns using the following heuristic: we use alignment links of surrounding source-language words to determine the likely position for the placeholder token.

We expand the window in both directions until we find a link. We insert the placeholder before or after the linked token, depending on whether the aligned source-language token is in left or right context of the selected pronoun. If no link is found in the entire sentence (an infrequent case), we use a position similar to the position of the selected pronoun within the source-language sentence.

3.3.3 Subject Filtering

The main interest of both the 2015 and the 2016 shared tasks has been on subject pronouns, and the pronoun sets have been selected with this in mind. However, several pronouns are ambiguous for the subject/object distinction. For the source datasets, this applies to English "it" and German "es" and "sie". In 2015, we ignored this issue, but this year we added a filtering step for the cases where English or German was the source language. We used automatic filtering for all datasets, and in addition, some manual filtering for the test dataset.

For the automatic filtering, we parsed the data using Mate Tools to perform joint PoS-tagging and dependency parsing. For the ambiguous pronouns, we then removed all pronoun instances that were not labelled as subjects, i.e., had the dependency label *SBJ* for English or *SB* for German. For French–English, no filtering was performed since all source pronouns are unambiguous subject pronouns. Table 5 shows how the subject filtering affected the IWSLT15 training set. For all languages, there was a large reduction for the OTHER class. For German–English, there were also large reductions for several other classes. Evaluations carried out after the shared task showed that this was mainly due to the dependency label *EP*, which marks expletives, and which should not have been filtered away. This mainly affected translation from "es gibt" / "there is", and explains the large reduction of the *there* class for German–English.

For the test dataset, we manually checked all of the pronouns that remained after the automatic filtering, in order to remove any remaining non-subjects. This showed that the performance of the parser for subjects was good and only a small amount of non-subjects remained, one for English–French, two for English–German, and six for German–English. We also noticed some issues with the casing of German "Sie", and changed it in four cases. Due to time constraints, we did not check the removed pronouns before releasing the data, but only for evaluation purposes afterwards.

We checked all removed pronouns, 70 for English–German, 71 for English–French, and a sample of 70 pronouns for German–English, where many more pronouns were filtered away. For English as a source language, the filtering was very accurate, and there were only two instances for English–French and no instances for English–German where a subject pronoun had been removed erroneously. In both cases, the erroneous removal of the subject position pronoun was due to sentence segmentation issues. For German, though, 34 of the 70 removed pronouns were subjects. In 27 cases, they were labelled as expletives, as described above, which could easily be remedied. The remaining cases are indirect speech, relative clauses, or subordinate clauses, which appear to be more difficult for the parser than the English counterparts. Even so, the performance was acceptable also for German, with a much lower rate of non-subjects than before the filtering.

4 Baseline Systems

The baseline system for each language pair is based on an n-gram language model. The architecture is similar to that used for the DiscoMT 2015 cross-lingual pronoun prediction task, but the systems are trained on lemmatised, PoS-tagged data instead of raw, unprocessed text. Given that none of the systems submitted to the cross-lingual pronoun prediction task at DiscoMT 2015 were able to beat the baseline system, we deemed it suitable for re-use this year.

We provided baseline systems for each subtask. Each baseline is based on a 5-gram language model trained on word lemmata, constructed from news texts, parliament debates, and the TED talks of the training/development portions of the datasets. The additional monolingual news data comprises the shuffled news texts from WMT including the 2014 editions for German and English and the 2007–2013 editions for French. The German corpus contains a total of 46 million sentences with 814 million lemmatised tokens, English contains 28 million sentences and 632 million tokens, and French includes 30 million sentences with 741 million tokens.

The justification for using a baseline system based on a language model remains unchanged from the DiscoMT 2015 shared task. That is, the aim is to reproduce the most realistic scenario for a phrase-based SMT system.

The main assumption here is that the amount of information that can be extracted from the translation table is not sufficient or is inconclusive. As a result, the pronoun prediction would be influenced primarily by the language model.

The baseline system fills the REPLACE token gaps by using a fixed set of pronouns (those to be predicted) and a fixed set of non-pronouns (which includes the most frequent items aligned with a pronoun in the provided test set) as well as the NONE option (i.e., do not insert anything in the hypothesis). The baseline system may be optimised using a configurable NONE penalty that accounts for the fact that n-gram language models tend to assign higher probability to shorter strings than to longer ones.

Two official baseline scores are provided for each subtask. The first was computed with the NONE penalty set to an unoptimised default value of zero. The second was computed with the NONE penalty set to an optimised value, which is different for each subtask. The NONE penalty was optimised on the development set by a grid search procedure where we tried values between 0 and -4, with a step of 0.5.

5 Submitted Systems

Eleven teams participated in the shared task, but not all teams submitted systems for all subtasks. Some teams also submitted second, contrastive systems for some subtasks. Ten of the groups submitted system description papers, which are cited hereafter. For the eleventh submission, UU-CAP, no system description paper was submitted. Brief summaries of each submission, including UU-CAP, are presented in the following sections.

5.1 CUNI

Charles University participated in the English–German and German–English subtasks (Novák, 2016). Each CUNI system is a linear classifier trained using a logistic loss optimised using stochastic gradient descent, implemented in the Vowpal Wabbit toolkit.[7] In the primary submission, the training examples are weighed with respect to the distribution of the target pronouns in the training data, which aims at improving the prediction accuracy of less frequent pronouns. The contrastive submission does not weigh examples.

---

[7] `https://github.com/JohnLangford/vowpal_wabbit/wiki`

German–English			English–German			English–French		
word	before	after	word	before	after	word	before	after
he	8,939	8,932	er	2,217	2092	ce	17,472	16,415
she	3,664	3,541	sie	22,779	21041	elle	3,483	3,286
it	33,338	23,628	es	26,923	21207	elles	3,305	3,276
they	18,581	17,896	man	662	622	il	10,126	9,682
this	1,479	983	OTHER	32,197	21279	ils	17,234	17,145
these	250	172				cela	8,071	6,908
there	6,935	2,905				on	1,713	1,549
OTHER	30,751	18,102				OTHER	27,530	11,226

Table 5: Number of pronouns for the different classes in the IWSLT15 data before and after filtering.

Before extracting the examples as feature vectors, the data is linguistically preprocessed using the Treex framework (Popel and Žabokrtský, 2010). The source-language texts undergo a thorough analysis and are enriched with PoS tags, dependency syntax, as well as semantic roles and coreference for English. On the other hand, only grammatical genders are assigned to nouns in the target language texts. The system uses three types of features: the features based on the target-language model estimates provided by the baseline system, linguistic features concerning the source word aligned to the target pronoun, and approximations of the coreference and dependency relations in the target language.

Following the submission of the CUNI systems for English–German, an error was discovered in the merging of the classifier output into the test data file for submission. Fixing it yielded an improvement, with the contrastive system achieving recall of 51.74, and 54.37 for the primary system.

Except for the English wordlist with gender distributions by Bergsma and Lin (2006), only the shared task data was used in the CUNI systems.

5.2 IDIAP

The IDIAP systems (Luong and Popescu-Belis, 2016) focus on English–French using two types of target-side information: a target-side pronoun language model (PLM) and several heuristic grammar rules. The goal is to test how much a target-side only PLM can improve the translation of pronouns, without any knowledge of the source texts, i.e., by looking at target-side fluency only.

The rules are specifically constructed for predicting two cases: the French pronoun "on" and the untranslated pronouns. They detect the source and target patterns signalling the possible presence of such pronouns, which are not always correctly captured by SMT systems.

For predicting all of the other pronouns, the IDIAP system relied solely on the scores coming from the proposed PLM model. This target-side PLM model uses a large target-language training dataset to learn a probabilistic relation between each target pronoun and the distribution of the gender-number of its preceding nouns and pronouns. For prediction, given each source pronoun "it" or "they", the system uses the PLM to score all possible candidates and to select the one with the highest score.

In addition to the PoS-tagged lemmatised data that was provided for the shared task, the WIT[3] parallel corpus (Cettolo et al., 2012), provided as part of the training data at the DiscoMT 2015 workshop, was used to train the PLM model. Furthermore, a French PoS-tagger, Morfette (Chrupala et al., 2008), was employed for gender-number extraction.

5.3 LIMSI

The LIMSI systems (Bawden, 2016) for the English–French task are linguistically-driven statistical classification systems. The systems use random forests, with few, high-level features, relying on explicit coreference resolution and external linguistic resources and syntactic dependencies. The systems include several types of contextual features, including a single feature using context templates to target particularly discriminative contexts for the prediction of certain pronoun classes, in particular the OTHER class.

The difference between the primary and contrastive systems is small. In the primary system, the feature value 'number' is assigned by taking the number of the last referent in the English-side coreference chain. In the contrastive system, the value of 'number' was taken directly from the English pronoun that was aligned with the placeholder: plural for "they" and singular for "it".

A number of tools and resources are used in the LIMSI system. Stanford CoreNLP is used for PoS tagging, syntactic dependencies, and coreference resolution over the English text. The Mate Parser (Bohnet and Nivre, 2012), retrained on SPMRL 2014 data (Seddah et al., 2014) (dependency trees), and the Lefff (Sagot, 2010), a morphological and syntactic lexicon (used for information on noun gender and impersonal adjectives and verbs), are both used for French.

5.4 TurkuNLP

The architecture for the TURKUNLP system (Luotolahti et al., 2016) is based on token-level sequence classification around the target pronoun using stacked recurrent neural networks.

The system learns token-level embeddings for the source-language lemmata, target-language tokens, PoS tags, combination of words and PoS tags and separate embeddings for the source-language pronouns that are aligned with the target pronoun. The network is fed sequences of these embeddings within a certain window to the left and to the right of the target pronoun. The window size used by the system is 50 tokens or until the end of the sentence boundary.

All of these inputs are read by two layered gated recurrent unit neural networks, except for the embedding for the aligned pronoun. All outputs of the recurrent layers are concatenated to a single vector along with the embedding of the aligned pronoun. This vector is then used to make the pronoun prediction by a dense neural network layer.

The primary systems are trained to optimise macro-averaged recall and the contrastive systems are optimised without preference towards rare classes. The system is trained only on the shared task data and all parts of the data, in-domain and out-of-domain, are used for training the system.

5.5 UEDIN

The UEDIN systems (Wetzel, 2016) for English–French and English–German are Maximum Entropy (MaxEnt) classifiers with the following set of features: tokens and their PoS tags are extracted from a context window around source- and target-side pronouns. N-gram combinations of these features are included by concatenating adjacent tokens or PoS tags. Furthermore, the pleonastic use of a pronoun is detected with NADA (Bergsma and Yarowsky, 2011) on the source side.

A Language Model (LM) is used to predict the most likely target-side pronoun, and then it is included as a feature. Another feature extracts the closest target-side noun antecedent (and its gender for German) via source coreference chains and word alignments. Additionally, the systems learn to predict NULL-translations (i.e., pronouns that do not have an equivalent translation). Experiments with linear-chain Conditional Random Fields (CRFs) treating pronouns of the same coreference chain as a sequence are conducted as well. All models are trained on a subset of the provided training data that has well-defined document boundaries in order to allow for meaningful extraction of coreference chains.

The MaxEnt classifiers consistently outperform the CRF models. Feature ablation shows that the antecedent feature is useful for English–German, and predicting NULL-translations is useful for English–French. It also reveals that the LM feature hurts performance.

5.6 UHELSINKI

The UHELSINKI system (Tiedemann, 2016) implements a simple linear classifier based on LibSVM with its L2-loss SVC dual solver. The system applies local source-language and target-language context using the given tokens and PoS labels as features. Coreference resolution is not used, but additional selected items in the prior context are extracted to enrich the model. In particular, a small number of the nearest determiners, nouns and proper nouns are taken as possible antecedent candidates. The contribution of these features is limited even with the lemmatised target-language context that makes it harder to disambiguate pronoun translation decisions. The model performs reasonably well especially for the prediction of pronoun translations into English.

5.7 UKYOTO

The UKYOTO system (Dabre et al., 2016) is a simple Recurrent Neural Network system with an attention mechanism which encodes both the source sentence and the context of the pronoun to be predicted and then predicts the pronoun. The interesting thing about the approach is that it uses a simple language-independent Neural Network (NN) mechanism that performs well in almost all cases. Another interesting aspect is that good performance is achieved, even though only the IWSLT data is used.

This indicates that the NN mechanism is quite effective. The only side effect is that the neural network overfits on the training and on the development datasets. In the future, the authors plan to use coreference resolution and system combination, which should help improve the performance.

5.8 UUPPSALA

The main contribution of the UUPPSALA-PRIMARY system (Loáiciga et al., 2016) for English–French is a Maximum Entropy classifier used to determine whether an instance of the English pronoun "it" functions as an anaphoric, pleonastic, or event reference pronoun. The classifier is trained on a combination of *semantic*, based on lexical resources such as VerbNet (Schuler, 2005) and WordNet (Miller, 1995), and frequencies computed over the annotated Gigaword corpus (Napoles et al., 2012), *syntactic*, from the dependency parser in the Mate tools (Bohnet et al., 2013), and *contextual* features. The event classification results are modest, reaching only 54.2 F-score for the event class.

The translation model, into which the classifier is integrated, is a 6-gram language model computed over target lemmata using modified Kneser-Ney smoothing and the KenLM toolkit (Heafield, 2011). In addition to the pure target lemma context, it also has access to the identity of the source-language pronoun, used as a concatenated label to each REPLACE item. This provides information about the number marking of the pronouns in the source, and also allows for the incorporation of the output of the 'it'-label classifier. To predict classes for an unseen test set, a uniform unannotated RE-PLACE tag is used for all classes. The 'disambig' tool of the SRILM toolkit (Stolcke, 2002) is then used to recover the tag annotated with the correct solution. The combined system with the 'it'-labels performed slightly worse than the system without it (57.03 vs. 59.84 macro-averaged recall).

The same underlying translation model forms the contrastive system for English–French, and the primary system for all other subtasks.

5.9 UU-Cap

The UU-CAP approach for English–German uses Conditional Random Fields (CRFs). Pronoun prediction is formulated as a sequence labelling problem, where each word in a sequence is to be labelled as either one of the pronouns or '0' if it does not correspond to a pronoun placeholder.

This CRF approach has been applied only to German, but there are plans to extend it to other languages.

For German, CRF models are trained using a rich feature set derived from both German and English. The German features include the word sequence itself, the lemma and the PoS-sequence, as well as the gender of the surrounding words (10-gram). The English features include the English word to which the placeholder pronouns have been aligned, and the number and gender features of the surrounding English words (10-gram).

The CRF model was trained on the IWSLT15 corpus and used the TED talks for development. The rule-based morphological Analyser SMOR (Schmid et al., 2004) as well as its English spinoff EMOR (not published) were used to derive the gender and number of the German and English words.

5.10 UU-Hardmeier

The UU-HARDMEIER system (Hardmeier, 2016) is a system combination of two different models. One of them, based on earlier work (Hardmeier et al., 2013), is a feed-forward neural network that takes as input the source pronoun and the source context words, target lemmata and target PoS tags in a window of 3 words to the left and to the right of the pronoun. In addition, the network receives a list of potential antecedent candidates identified by the preprocessing part of a coreference resolution system. Anaphora resolution is treated as a latent variable by the model. This system is combined by linear interpolation with a specially trained 6-gram language model identical to the contrastive system of the UUPPSALA submission described above. The neural network component on its own was submitted as a contrastive system.

In the evaluation, the system combination of the two components achieved better scores than each component individually. This demonstrates that both components contribute complementary information that is valuable for the task. A rather disappointing result is that the neural network classifier completely fails to predict the rare pronoun classes in this evaluation, even though previous work suggested that this should be one of its strengths (Hardmeier et al., 2013). The reasons for this require further investigation.

5.11 UU-Stymne

The UU-STYMNE systems (Stymne, 2016) use linear SVM classifiers for all language pairs. A number of different features were explored, but anaphora is not explicitly modelled. The features used can be grouped in the following way: source pronouns, local context words/lemmata, preceding nouns, target PoS n-grams with two different PoS tag-sets, dependency heads of pronouns, target LM scores, alignments, and pronoun position. A joint tagger and dependency parser on the source text is used for some of the features. The primary system is a 2-step classifier where a binary classifier is first used to distinguish between the OTHER class and pronoun, then a multi-class classifier distinguishes between the pronoun classes. The secondary system is a standard 1-step classifier. The Mate Tools parser (Bohnet and Nivre, 2012) is used for joint PoS tagging and parsing for all languages.

Across language pairs, source pronouns, local context and dependency features performed best. The LM and preceding noun features hurt performance. For the binary distinction between OTHER and pronouns, target PoS n-grams performed well.

The submitted systems for German–English and French–English unfortunately contained a bug in the feature extraction that severely affected the scores. The system description paper also reports the much higher scores with the bug resolved.

6   Evaluation

While in 2015 we used macro-averaged F_1 as an official evaluation measure, this year we adopted *macro-averaged recall*, which was also recently adopted by some other competitions, e.g., by SemEval-2016 Task 4 (Nakov et al., 2016). Moreover, as in 2015, we also report *accuracy* as a secondary evaluation measure.

Macro-averaged recall ranges in $[0, 1]$, where a value of 1 is achieved by the perfect classifier,[8] and a value of 0 is achieved by the classifier that misclassifies all examples. The value of $1/C$, where C is the number of classes, is achieved by a trivial classifier that assigns the same class to all examples (regardless of which class is chosen), and is also the expected value of a random classifier.

---

[8]If the test data did not have any instances of some of the classes, we excluded these classes from the macro-averaging, i.e., we only macro-averaged over classes that are present in the gold standard.

The advantage of macro-averaged recall over accuracy is that it is more robust to class imbalance. For instance, the accuracy of the majority-class classifier may be much higher than $1/C$ if the test dataset is imbalanced. Thus, one cannot interpret the absolute value of accuracy (e.g., is 0.7 a good or a bad value?) without comparing it to a baseline that must be computed for each specific test dataset. In contrast, for macro-averaged recall, it is clear that a value of, e.g., 0.7, is well above the majority-class and the random baselines, which are both always $1/C$ (e.g., 0.5 with two classes, 0.33 with three classes, etc.). Standard F_1 and macro-averaged F_1 are also sensitive to class imbalance for the same reason; see Sebastiani (2015) for more detail.

7   Results

The results of the evaluation are shown in Tables 6-9, one for each subtask. The tables contain two scores: *macro-averaged recall* (the official shared task metric) and *accuracy*.

As described in Section 4, we provide two official baseline scores for each subtask. The first, computed with the NONE penalty set to a default value of zero, appears in the tables as *baseline0*. The second, computed with the NONE penalty set to an optimised value, appears in the tables in the format *baseline<penalty>*. The optimised penalty values are different for each subtask.

As we use macro-averaged recall as an official evaluation measure, its value for the majority class and for a random baseline are both $1/C$, and thus we do not show them in the tables. Specifically, the macro-average recall of the random baseline is 12.50 for English–French and French–English (8 classes each), 20.00 for English–German, and 11.11 for German–English.

German–English. Table 6 shows the results for German–English. We can see that all six participating teams outperform the baselines by a wide margin. The top systems, TURKUNLP, UKYOTO and UHELSINKI score between 73.91 and 69.76 in macro-averaged recall. This is very much above the performance of *baseline0* and *baseline-1.5*, which are in the low-mid 40s. It is also well above the majority/random baseline (not shown) at 11.11, which is outperformed by far by all systems. Note that the top-3 systems in terms of macro-averaged recall are also the top-3 in terms of accuracy, but in different order.

	Submission	Macro-Avg Recall	Accuracy
1	**TurkuNLP-primary**	**73.91**$_1$	75.36$_3$
2	**UKYOTO-primary**	**73.17**$_2$	80.33$_1$
	TurkuNLP-contrastive	72.60	80.54
3	**UHELSINKI-primary**	**69.76**$_3$	77.85$_2$
	UU-Stymne-contrastive	60.83	70.60
4	**CUNI-primary**	**60.42**$_4$	64.18$_6$
5	**UUPPSALA-primary**	**59.56**$_5$	73.71$_4$
6	**UU-Stymne-primary**	**59.28**$_6$	69.98$_5$
	CUNI-contrastive	56.83	65.22
	baseline-1.5	*44.52*	54.87
	baseline0	*42.15*	53.42

Table 6: **Results for German-English.** The first column shows the rank of the primary systems with respect to the official metric: macro-averaged recall. The second column contains the team's name and its submission type: primary vs. contrastive. The following columns show the results for each system, measured in terms of macro-averaged recall (official metric) and accuracy (unofficial, supplementary metric). The subindices show the rank of the primary systems with respect to the evaluation measure in the respective column. The random/majority baseline macro-averaged recall is 11.11.

English–German. The results for English–German are shown in Table 7. This direction was arguably harder as about half of the nine participating teams are below the optimised *baseline-2* (with a score of 47.86), and one system is even below *baseline0*. The clear winner is TURKUNLP, with a macro-averaged recall of 64.41 (they are also second in accuracy), ahead of UKYOTO with 52.50 and UU-STYMNE with 52.12 (third and fourth in accuracy, respectively). All of the systems outperform the majority/random baseline (at 20.00), though some by a smaller margin than for German–English.

French–English. The results for French–English are shown in Table 8. Four of the five participating teams had a macro-averaged recall score above 50.00, and outperformed the LM-based baselines at 38.38 and 42.96 for the tuned and the untuned version, respectively. All of the systems outperformed by far the majority/random baselines at 12.50. Once again, TURKUNLP is the clear winner with 72.03 (second in accuracy). It is followed by UKYOTO with 65.63 (first in accuracy), UHELSINKI with 62.98 (third in accuracy), and UUPPSALA with 62.65 (fourth in accuracy).

English–French. The results for English–French are shown in Table 9. Seven of the nine participating teams outperformed the two baselines (in fact, *baseline0* was outperformed by all but one team). All of the participants outperformed the majority/random baseline of 12.50. The top system is TURKUNLP once again, with macro-averaged recall of 65.70, which is barely better than the 65.35 score of UU-STYMNE (second in accuracy). The third-best result, 62.44, is that of UKYOTO (fourth in accuracy).

Overall, there is a clear winner, TURKUNLP, which won all four pairs/directions, in two of the cases by a large margin. Naturally, *baseline0* performs worse than the tuned LM baseline in all four cases. Accuracy scores do not align perfectly well with macro-averaged recall, but the top systems in macro-averaged recall are generally also among the top in terms of accuracy.

8 Discussion

This year, almost all participating teams managed to outperform the corresponding baselines in their respective subtasks. This applies not only to the majority/random baselines, which proved quite easy to beat, but also to the more sophisticated LM-based baseline with tuned parameters. This is in stark contrast with the DiscoMT 2015 task, where none of the participating systems was able to outperform the baseline.

In the following subsections, we discuss the success of the WMT 2016 task with respect to the challenges of the individual subtasks, and the design of the submitted systems. We also include a brief comparison with the DiscoMT 2015 task.

	Submission	Macro-Avg Recall	Accuracy
1	**TurkuNLP-primary**	**64.41**$_1$	71.54$_2$
	TurkuNLP-contrastive	58.39	72.85
2	**UKYOTO-primary**	**52.50**$_2$	71.28$_3$
3	**UU-Stymne-primary**	**52.12**$_3$	70.76$_4$
4	**UU-Hardmeier-primary**	**50.36**$_4$	74.67$_1$
	UU-Stymne-contrastive	48.92	68.93
5	**uedin-primary**	**48.72**$_5$	66.32$_6$
	baseline−2	*47.86*	*54.31*
	uedin-contrastive	47.75	64.75
6	**UUPPSALA-primary**	**47.43**$_6$	68.67$_5$
	UU-Hardmeier-contrastive	46.64	72.06
7	**UHELSINKI-primary**	**44.69**$_7$	65.80$_7$
8	**UU-Cap-primary**	**41.61**$_8$	63.71$_8$
	baseline0	*38.53*	*50.13*
	CUNI-contrastive	30.70	46.48
9	**CUNI-primary**	**28.26**$_9$	42.04$_9$

Table 7: **Results for English-German.** The first column shows the rank of the primary systems with respect to the official metric: macro-averaged recall. The second column contains the team's name and its submission type: primary vs. contrastive. The following columns show the results for each system, measured in terms of macro-averaged recall (official metric) and accuracy (unofficial, supplementary metric). The subindices show the rank of the primary systems with respect to the evaluation measure in the respective column. The random/majority baseline macro-averaged recall is 20.00.

8.1 Challenges

The subtasks each with different combinations of source-language pronouns and target-language prediction classes, provide different challenges. Judging by the results, the prediction of pronouns for English–French and English–German was more difficult than for the reverse directions. This is perhaps to be expected given the agreement problems associated with predicting the translation of ambiguous English third-person singular pronouns in languages with grammatical gender. However, that is not to say that this is the only problem that these translation directions present.

In the case of English–French translation, systems must accurately determine when to use gendered vs. non-gendered translations of anaphoric pronouns. This is in addition to the problems arising from functional ambiguity in the source language. Nevertheless, the English–French and English–German tasks received a greater number of submissions than the tasks for the reverse directions. This is perhaps due to the greater availability of tools and resources for English, than for French and German, coupled with a tendency to focus more on source-language processing.

8.2 Comparison with the DiscoMT 2015 Task

The DiscoMT and WMT tasks are not directly comparable. The WMT 2016 baseline, also an n-gram language model, is trained on lemmatised, PoS-tagged data, and therefore cannot predict plural pronoun forms. We might therefore consider the WMT 2016 baseline systems to be weaker than the DiscoMT 2015 baseline, which is trained on fully inflected data. However, the submitted systems also have to contend with the same problem of missing number information on target-language nouns and pronouns. The fact that the systems were able to beat the baseline validates the use of more complex features and methods than simply relying on local target-side context.

8.3 Submitted Systems

The submitted systems used recurrent neural networks (TURKUNLP and UKYOTO), linear models (CUNI), including SVMs (UU-STYMNE and UHELSINKI), Maximum Entropy classifiers (UEDIN), Conditional Random Fields (UU-CAP), random forests (LIMSI), pronoun-aware language models (IDIAP and UUPPSALA), and a system combination incorporating a classifier and language model (UU-HARDMEIER).

	Submission	Macro-Avg Recall	Accuracy
1	**TurkuNLP-primary**	**72.03**$_1$	80.79$_2$
	TurkuNLP-contrastive	66.54	85.06
2	**UKYOTO-primary**	**65.63**$_2$	82.93$_1$
3	**UHELSINKI-primary**	**62.98**$_3$	78.96$_3$
4	**UUPSALA-primary**	**62.65**$_4$	74.39$_4$
	baseline-1.5	*42.96*	53.66
	baseline0	*38.38*	52.44
5	**UU-Stymne-primary**	**36.44**$_5$	53.66$_5$
	UU-Stymne-contrastive	34.12	52.13

Table 8: **Results for French-English.** The first column shows the rank of the primary systems with respect to the official metric: macro-averaged recall. The second column contains the team's name and its submission type: primary vs. contrastive. The following columns show the results for each system, measured in terms of macro-averaged recall (official metric) and accuracy (unofficial, supplementary metric). The subindices show the rank of the primary systems with respect to the evaluation measure in the respective column. The random/majority baseline macro-averaged recall is 12.50.

Overall, the most successful systems used recurrent neural networks (TURKUNLP and UKYOTO). The TURKUNLP system, which was the best performing system for all four subtasks, is a deep recurrent neural network, optimised to place a greater emphasis on the rare pronoun classes instead of the most common ones. The authors claim that the English–French and English–German systems in particular benefit from this greater emphasis on rare pronoun classes. However, this is not the only reason for its high performance, as the contrastive system, which treats all pronoun classes equally, also performs well. The UKYOTO team, whose system ranked second in three of the subtasks, report that the system performs well for common pronoun classes but poorly on rare ones, suggesting room for future improvement.

Given the good performance of the two recurrent neural network systems, we might conclude that this architecture is a suitable choice for the cross-lingual pronoun prediction task. It is difficult to determine any further clear patterns in terms of architecture type and performance.

The systems used a wide variety of features, and can be split into two main groups: those that use only contextual information from the source and the target language (TURKUNLP, UKYOTO, UHELSINKI, and the UUPPSALA source-aware language models), and those that make additional use of external tools and resources (CUNI, IDIAP, LIMSI, UEDIN, the UUPPSALA primary system for English–French, UU-CAP, UU-HARDMEIER and UU-STYMNE).

Popular external tools include those for anaphora/coreference resolution (CUNI, LIMSI and UEDIN), pleonastic "it" detection (CUNI, UEDIN and UUPPSALA) and dependency parsing (CUNI, LIMSI, UUPPSALA and UU-STYMNE). Beyond the observation that recurrent NNs perform well, there seems to be no clear pattern as to whether using external tools and resources vs. context only works best. However, context-only methods are applicable to any language pair.

In terms of data, most systems were trained only on the datasets provided for the shared task. The CUNI system used a wordlist with gender distributions collected by Bergsma and Lin (2006), the IDIAP system used the WIT^3 corpus (Cettolo et al., 2012), and the 'it'-disambiguation classifier used in the UUPPSALA system was trained on annotated data from ParCor (Guillou et al., 2014) and the *DiscoMT2015* test set (Hardmeier et al., 2016).

9   Conclusions

We have described the design and the evaluation of the shared task on cross-lingual pronoun prediction at WMT 2016. The task is similar to the DiscoMT 2015 task, which focused on English–French translation. This year, we invited participants to submit systems for four subtasks: for the English–French and English–German language pairs, in both translation directions. Unlike the DiscoMT 2015 task, in which fully inflected target-language sentences were provided in the training and test data, we provided a lemmatised, PoS-tagged representation.

	Submission	Macro-Avg Recall	Accuracy
1	**TurkuNLP-primary**	**65.70**$_1$	70.51$_5$
2	**UU-Stymne-primary**	**65.35**$_2$	73.99$_2$
3	**UKYOTO-primary**	**62.44**$_3$	70.51$_4$
4	**uedin-primary**	**61.62**$_4$	71.31$_3$
	TurkuNLP-contrastive	61.46	72.39
	UU-Stymne-contrastive	60.69	71.05
5	**UU-Hardmeier-primary**	**60.63**$_5$	74.53$_1$
	UUPPSALA-contrastive	59.84	70.78
	uedin-contrastive	59.83	68.63
	limsi-contrastive	59.34	68.36
6	**limsi-primary**	**59.32**$_6$	68.36$_7$
7	**UHELSINKI-primary**	**57.50**$_7$	68.90$_6$
	baseline$-$1	*50.85*	*53.35*
	UU-Hardmeier-contrastive	50.80	71.31
8	**UUPPSALA-primary**	**48.92**$_8$	62.20$_8$
	baseline0	*46.98*	*52.01*
9	**Idiap-primary**	**36.36**$_9$	51.21$_9$
	Idiap-contrastive	30.44	42.09

Table 9: **Results for English-French.** The first column shows the rank of the primary systems with respect to the official metric: macro-averaged recall. The second column contains the team's name and its submission type: primary vs. contrastive. The following columns show the results for each system, measured in terms of macro-averaged recall (official metric) and accuracy (unofficial, supplementary metric). The subindices show the rank of the primary systems with respect to the evaluation measure in the respective column. The random/majority baseline macro-averaged recall is 12.50.

We built on the success of the DiscoMT 2015 shared task, attracting increased attention from the community in terms of the number of participants. We received submissions from eleven groups, with many teams submitting systems for several subtasks. This year, the majority of the systems outperformed the official shared task baselines. This is in stark contrast to last year, where none of the systems was able to beat the baseline, an n-gram language model. Several factors may have affected this including changes to the task itself, and improved methods. We hope that the success in the cross-lingual pronoun prediction task will soon translate into improvements in pronoun translation by complete MT pipelines.

10 Acknowledgements

The organisation of this task has received support from the following project: Discourse-Oriented Statistical Machine Translation funded by the Swedish Research Council (2012-916). The work of Chistian Hardmeier and Sara Stymne is part of the Swedish strategic research programme eSSENCE.

References

Rachel Bawden. 2016. Cross-lingual pronoun prediction with linguistically informed features. In *Proceedings of the First Conference on Machine Translation (WMT 2016)*, Berlin, Germany.

Shane Bergsma and Dekang Lin. 2006. Bootstrapping path-based pronoun resolution. In *Proceedings of the 21st International Conference on Computational Linguistics and 44th Annual Meeting of the Association for Computational Linguistics (ACL-COLING 2006)*, pages 33–40, Sydney, Australia.

Shane Bergsma and David Yarowsky. 2011. NADA: A robust system for non-referential pronoun detection. In *Proceedings of The 8th Discourse Anaphora and Anaphor Resolution Colloquium (DAARC 2011)*, pages 12–23, Faro, Portugal.

Bernd Bohnet and Joakim Nivre. 2012. A transition-based system for joint part-of-speech tagging and labeled non-projective dependency parsing. In *Proceedings of the 2012 Joint Conference on Empirical Methods in Natural Language Processing and Computational Natural Language Learning (EMNLP-CoNLL 2012)*, pages 1455–1465, Jeju Island, Korea.

Bernd Bohnet, Joakim Nivre, Igor Boguslavsky, Richárd Farkas, Filip Ginter, and Jan Hajič. 2013. Joint morphological and syntactic analysis for richly inflected languages. *Transactions of the Association for Computational Linguistics (TACL)*, 1:415–428.

Mauro Cettolo, Christian Girardi, and Marcello Federico. 2012. WIT^3: Web inventory of transcribed and translated talks. In *Proceedings of the 16th Conference of the European Association for Machine Translation (EAMT 2012)*, pages 261–268, Trento, Italy.

Mauro Cettolo, Jan Niehues, Sebastian Stuker, Luisa Bentivogli, Roldano Cattoni, and Marcello Federico. 2015. The IWSLT 2015 evaluation campaign. In *Proceedings of the International Workshop on Spoken Language Translation (IWSLT 2015)*, pages 2–14, Da Nang, Vietnam.

Grzegorz Chrupala, Georgiana Dinu, and Josef van Genabith. 2008. Learning morphology with Morfette. In *Proceedings of the 6th International Conference on Language Resources and Evaluation (LREC 2008)*, pages 2362–2367, Marrakech, Morocco.

Raj Dabre, Yevgeniy Puzikov, Fabien Cromieres, and Sadao Kurohashi. 2016. The Kyoto university cross-lingual pronoun translation system. In *Proceedings of the First Conference on Machine Translation (WMT 2016)*, Berlin, Germany.

Liane Guillou, Christian Hardmeier, Aaron Smith, Jörg Tiedemann, and Bonnie Webber. 2014. ParCor 1.0: A parallel pronoun-coreference corpus to support statistical MT. In *Proceedings of the 9th International Conference on Language Resources and Evaluation (LREC 2014)*, pages 3193–3198, Reykjavik, Iceland.

Liane Guillou. 2012. Improving pronoun translation for statistical machine translation. In *Proceedings of the Student Research Workshop at the 13th Conference of the European Chapter of the Association for Computational Linguistics (EACL 2012)*, pages 1–10, Avignon, France.

Liane Guillou. 2016. *Incorporating Pronoun Function into Statistical Machine Translation*. Ph.D. thesis, University of Edinburgh.

Christian Hardmeier and Marcello Federico. 2010. Modelling pronominal anaphora in statistical machine translation. In *Proceedings of the 7th International Workshop on Spoken Language Translation (IWSLT 2010)*, pages 283–289, Paris, France.

Christian Hardmeier, Jörg Tiedemann, and Joakim Nivre. 2013. Latent anaphora resolution for cross-lingual pronoun prediction. In *Proceedings of the 2013 Conference on Empirical Methods in Natural Language Processing (EMNLP 2013)*, pages 380–391, Seattle, Washington, USA.

Christian Hardmeier, Preslav Nakov, Sara Stymne, Jörg Tiedemann, Yannick Versley, and Mauro Cettolo. 2015. Pronoun-focused MT and cross-lingual pronoun prediction: Findings of the 2015 DiscoMT shared task on pronoun translation. In *Proceedings of the 2nd Workshop on Discourse in Machine Translation (DiscoMT 2015)*, pages 1–16, Lisbon, Portugal.

Christian Hardmeier, Jörg Tiedemann, Preslav Nakov, Sara Stymne, and Yannick Versely. 2016. DiscoMT 2015 shared task on pronoun translation. LINDAT/CLARIN digital library at Institute of Formal and Applied Linguistics, Charles University in Prague. `http://hdl.handle.net/11372/LRT-1611`.

Christian Hardmeier. 2014. *Discourse in Statistical Machine Translation*. Ph.D. thesis, University of Uppsala.

Christian Hardmeier. 2016. Pronoun prediction with latent anaphora resolution. In *Proceedings of the First Conference on Machine Translation (WMT 2016)*, Berlin, Germany.

Kenneth Heafield. 2011. KenLM: Faster and smaller language model queries. In *Proceedings of the Sixth Workshop on Statistical Machine Translation (WMT 2011)*, pages 187–197, Edinburgh, United Kingdom.

Ronan Le Nagard and Philipp Koehn. 2010. Aiding pronoun translation with co-reference resolution. In *Proceedings of the Joint Fifth Workshop on Statistical Machine Translation and MetricsMATR (WMT 2010)*, pages 252–261, Uppsala, Sweden.

Sharid Loáiciga, Liane Guillou, and Christian Hardmeier. 2016. It-disambiguation and source-aware language models for cross-lingual pronoun prediction. In *Proceedings of the First Conference on Machine Translation (WMT 2016)*, Berlin, Germany.

Ngoc Quang Luong and Andrei Popescu-Belis. 2016. Pronoun language model and grammatical heuristics for aiding pronoun prediction. In *Proceedings of the First Conference on Machine Translation (WMT 2016)*, Berlin, Germany.

Juhani Luotolahti, Jenna Kanerva, and Filip Ginter. 2016. Cross-lingual pronoun prediction with deep recurrent neural networks. In *Proceedings of the First Conference on Machine Translation (WMT 2016)*, Berlin, Germany.

George A. Miller. 1995. WordNet: A lexical database for English. *Communications of the ACM*, 38(11):39–41.

Preslav Nakov, Alan Ritter, Sara Rosenthal, Veselin Stoyanov, and Fabrizio Sebastiani. 2016. SemEval-2016 task 4: Sentiment analysis in Twitter. In *Proceedings of the 10th International Workshop on Semantic Evaluation (SemEval 2016)*, pages 1–18, San Diego, California, USA.

Courtney Napoles, Matthew Gormley, and Benjamin Van Durme. 2012. Annotated Gigaword. In *Proceedings of the Joint Workshop on Automatic Knowledge Base Construction and Web-scale Knowledge*

Extraction (AKBC-WEKEX 2012), pages 95–100, Montreal, Quebec, Canada.

Michal Novák. 2011. Utilization of anaphora in machine translation. In *Proceedings of Contributed Papers, Week of Doctoral Students 2011*, pages 155–160, Prague, Czech Republic.

Michal Novák. 2016. Pronoun prediction with linguistic features and example weighing. In *Proceedings of the First Conference on Machine Translation (WMT 2016)*, Berlin, Germany.

Sebastian Padó and Mirella Lapata. 2005. Cross-linguistic projection of role-semantic information. In *Proceedings of the Human Language Technology Conference and the conference on Empirical Methods in Natural Language Processing (EMNLP 2005)*, pages 859–866, Vancouver, British Columbia, Canada.

Slav Petrov, Dipanjan Das, and Ryan McDonald. 2012. A universal part-of-speech tagset. In *Proceedings of the Eight International Conference on Language Resources and Evaluation (LREC'12)*, pages 2089–2096, Istanbul, Turkey.

Martin Popel and Zdeněk Žabokrtský. 2010. TectoMT: Modular NLP framework. In *Lecture Notes in Artificial Intelligence, Proceedings of the 7th International Conference on Advances in Natural Language Processing (IceTAL 2010)*, volume 6233, Reykjavik, Iceland. Springer.

Benoît Sagot. 2010. The Lefff, a freely available and large-coverage morphological and syntactic lexicon for French. In *Proceedings of the 7th International Conference on Language Resources and Evaluation (LREC'10)*, pages 2744–2751, Valletta, Malta.

Helmut Schmid, Arne Fitschen, and Ulrich Heid. 2004. SMOR: A German computational morphology covering derivation, composition and inflection. In *Proceedings of the 4th International Conference on Language Resources and Evaluation (LREC'04)*, pages 1263–1266, Lisbon, Portugal.

Helmut Schmid. 1994. Probabilistic part-of-speech tagging using decision trees. In *Proceedings of International Conference on New Methods in Language Processing*, pages 44–49, Manchester, United Kingdom.

Karin Kipper Schuler. 2005. *Verbnet: A Broad-coverage, Comprehensive Verb Lexicon*. Ph.D. thesis, Philadelphia, Pennsylvania, USA.

Fabrizio Sebastiani. 2015. An axiomatically derived measure for the evaluation of classification algorithms. In *Proceedings of the 5th ACM International Conference on the Theory of Information Retrieval (ICTIR 2015)*, pages 11–20, Northampton, Massachusetts, USA.

Djamé Seddah, Sandra Kübler, and Reut Tsarfaty. 2014. Introducing the SPMRL 2014 shared task on parsing morphologically-rich languages. In *Proceedings of the First Joint Workshop on Statistical Parsing of Morphologically Rich Languages and Syntactic Analysis of Non-Canonical Languages (SPMRL-SANCL 2014)*, pages 103–109, Dublin, Ireland.

Andreas Stolcke. 2002. SRILM - an extensible language modeling toolkit. In *Proceedings of the Seventh International Conference on Spoken Language Processing (ICSLP 2002)*, volume 2, pages 901–904, Denver, Colorado, USA.

Sara Stymne, Jörg Tiedemann, and Joakim Nivre. 2014. Estimating word alignment quality for SMT reordering tasks. In *Proceedings of the Ninth Workshop on Statistical Machine Translation (WMT 2014)*, pages 275–286, Baltimore, Maryland, USA.

Sara Stymne. 2016. Feature exploration for cross-lingual pronoun prediction. In *Proceedings of the First Conference on Machine Translation (WMT 2016)*, Berlin, Germany.

Jörg Tiedemann. 2016. A linear baseline classifier for cross-lingual pronoun prediction. In *Proceedings of the First Conference on Machine Translation (WMT 2016)*, Berlin, Germany.

Dominikus Wetzel. 2016. Cross-lingual pronoun prediction for English, French and German with maximum entropy classification. In *Proceedings of the First Conference on Machine Translation (WMT 2016)*, Berlin, Germany.

A Shared Task on Multimodal Machine Translation and Crosslingual Image Description

Lucia Specia
Department of Computer Science, University of Sheffield, UK
`l.specia@sheffield.ac.uk`

Stella Frank, Khalil Sima'an and **Desmond Elliott**
ILLC, University of Amsterdam, The Netherlands
`{s.c.frank, k.simaan, d.elliott}@uva.nl`

Abstract

This paper introduces and summarises the findings of a new shared task at the intersection of Natural Language Processing and Computer Vision: the generation of image descriptions in a target language, given an image and/or one or more descriptions in a different (source) language. This challenge was organised along with the Conference on Machine Translation (WMT16), and called for system submissions for two task variants: (i) a translation task, in which a source language image description needs to be translated to a target language, (optionally) with additional cues from the corresponding image, and (ii) a description generation task, in which a target language description needs to be generated for an image, (optionally) with additional cues from source language descriptions of the same image. In this first edition of the shared task, 16 systems were submitted for the translation task and seven for the image description task, from a total of 10 teams.

1 Introduction

In recent years, significant research has been done to address problems that require joint modelling of language and vision. Examples of popular applications involving both Natural Language Processing (NLP) and Computer Vision (CV) include image description generation and video captioning (Bernardi et al., 2016), image retrieval based on textual and visual cues (Feng and Lapata, 2010), visual question answering (Yang et al., 2015), among many others (see (Ramisa et al., 2016) for more examples). With very few exceptions (Grubinger et al., 2006; Funaki and Nakayama, 2015;

Gao et al., 2015), these applications are inherently monolingual and existing work explore mostly English data. In an attempt to push this interdisciplinary field to incorporate a multilingual component, we propose the first shared task on two new applications: Multimodal Machine Translation and Crosslingual Image Description. Generally speaking, this shared task targets the generation of image descriptions in a target language, given an image and one or more descriptions in a different (source) language. More specifically, the task can be addressed from two perspectives:

1. Task 1: a **Multimodal Machine Translation** task, which takes a source language description and translates it into the target language, where this process can be supported by information from the image; see Figure 1, and

2. Task 2: a **Crosslingual Image Description** task, which takes an image and generates a description for it in the target language, where this process can be supported by the source language description; see Figure 2.

This shared task has the following main goals:

- To push existing work on multimodal language processing towards multilingual multimodal language processing.

- To investigate the effectiveness of information from images in machine translation.

- To investigate the effectiveness of crosslingual textual information in image description generation.

The challenge was organised in the framework of the well-established WMT series of shared tasks.[1] Participants were called to submit systems focusing on either or both of these task variants. The tasks differ in the training data and in

---

[1] `http://www.statmt.org/wmt16/`

Proceedings of the First Conference on Machine Translation, Volume 2: Shared Task Papers, pages 543–553,
Berlin, Germany, August 11-12, 2016. ©2016 Association for Computational Linguistics

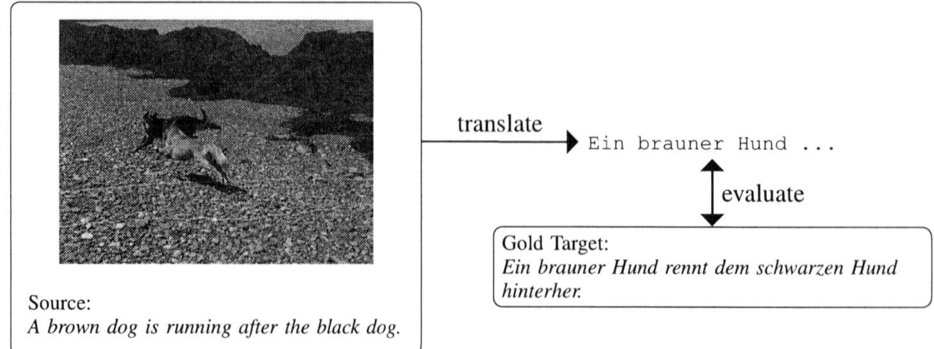

Figure 1: Multimodal Machine Translation (Task 1). English and translated German image descriptions are grounded to an image.

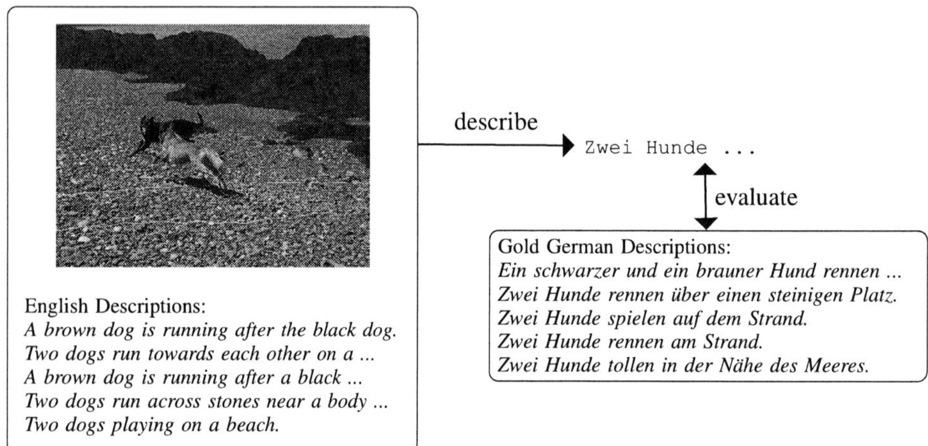

Figure 2: Multilingual Image Description (Task 2). The data consist of *independently* produced image descriptions in English and German.

	Sentences	Types	Tokens	Avg. length
Task 1: Translations				
English	31,014	11,420	357,172	11.9
German		19,397	333,833	11.1
Task 2: Descriptions				
English	155,070	22,815	1,841,159	12.3
German		46,138	1,434,998	9.6

Table 1: Corpus-level statistics about the translation and the description data over 31,014 images.

the way the target language descriptions are evaluated: against one translation of the corresponding source description (translation variant) or against five descriptions of the same image in the target language, created independently from the corresponding source description (image description variant). The data used for both tasks is an extended version of the Flickr30K dataset. Participants were also allowed to use external data and resources for unconstrained submissions.

Participants were encouraged to make use of both the sentences and the images as part of their submissions but they were not required to do so. The baseline systems for the translation task were a text-only Moses phrase-based statistical machine translation (SMT) model (Koehn et al., 2007) and the GroundedTranslation multilingual image description model (Elliott et al., 2015) (in particular, the MLM→LM variant). The baseline system for the description generation task was also the GroundedTranslation model.

In this paper we describe the data, image features and participants of the shared task (Sections 2 and 3), present its main findings (Section 4), and discuss interesting issues and directions for future research (Section 5).

2   Datasets and image features

We created a new dataset for the shared task by extending the Flickr30K dataset (Young et al., 2014) into another language. The **Multi30K** dataset (Elliott et al., 2016) contains two types of multilingual data: a corpus of English sentences *translated* into German (used for Task 1), and a corpus of *independently collected* English and German sentences (used for Task 2). For the translation corpus, one sentence (of five) was chosen for professional translation such that the final dataset is a combination of short, medium, and long length sentences. The second corpus consists of crowdsourced descriptions gathered from Crowdflower,[2] where each worker generated an independent description of the image. We used a translation of the original instructions used to gather the English sentences, in order to ensure as much similarity across the German and English descriptions as possible. Table 1 presents an overview of the data available for each task.

The images are publicly available[3] but to en-

courage participation we released two types of features extracted from the images. The use of such features was not mandatory, and participants could also extract image features from the original images in the Flickr30K dataset using their own algorithms. We released features extracted from the VGG-19 Convolutional Neural Network (CNN), as described in (Simonyan and Zisserman, 2015), from the FC_7 (relu7) and $CONV_{5,4}$ layers. We extracted these image features using Caffe RC2[4] with the `matlab_features_reference` code from NeuralTalk.[5]

3   Participants

Ten teams submitted a total of 23 systems for the two tasks. The teams are listed in Table 2. In what follows, we summarise the participating systems.

CMU (Task 1) The approach incorporates global and regional visual features with textual features from English (source) and German (target) to jointly train a Recurrent Neural Network (RNN). Visual features extracted from a region-based convolution neural network (RCNN) are designed to be appended in the head/tail of the textual feature or dissipated in parallel long short term memory (LSTM) threads to assist the LSTM reader in computing a representation. For rescoring, an additional bilingual dictionary is used to select the best sentence from candidates generated by five different models. The submission is thus unconstrained, with the German-English Dictionary from GLOSBE[6] used as additional resource.

CUNI (Tasks 1 and 2) The method is a system combination which implements the attentive neural Machine Translation (MT) (Bahdanau et al., 2014). The input of the decoder is a linear combination of the image features obtained from the penultimate layer of the VGG16 convolutional network (Simonyan and Zisserman, 2015) and two recurrent encoders coding the source sentence and its translation obtained from the Moses system. The Moses system uses the with additional language models based on coarse bitoken classes (Stewart et al., 2014).

---

[2]`http://www.crowdflower.com`
[3]`http://illinois.edu/fb/sec/229675`

[4]`http://github.com/BVLC/caffe/releases/tag/rc2`
[5]`http://github.com/karpathy/neuraltalk/tree/master/matlab_features_reference`
[6]`https://glosbe.com/en/de/`

ID	Participating team
CMU+NTU	Carnegie Melon University (Huang et al., 2016)
CUNI	Univerzita Karlova v Praze (Libovický et al., 2016)
DCU	Dublin City University (Hokamp and Calixto, 2016)
DCU-UVA	Dublin City University & Universiteit van Amsterdam (Calixto et al., 2016)
HUCL	Universität Heidelberg (Hitschler et al., 2016)
IBM-IITM-Montreal-NYU	IBM Research India, IIT Madras, Université de Montréal & New York University
LIUM	Laboratoire d'Informatique de l'Université du Maine (Caglayan et al., 2016)
SHEF	University of Sheffield (Shah et al., 2016)
UPC	Universitat Politècnica de Catalunya (Rodríguez Guasch and Costa-jussà, 2016)
UPC_b	Universitat Politècnica de Catalunya

Table 2: Participants in the WMT16 multimodal machine translation shared task.

DCU (Task 1) Both submissions from DCU are neural MT systems with an attention mechanism on the source-side representation (Bahdanau et al., 2014). The first submission is text-only, and the second submission includes the FC_7 image features in the target-side decoder initial state. The FC_7 features are passed through a 3-layer fully-connected feedforward network with Tanh non-linearities, and then summed with the final state of the source-side representation. This summed representation is passed through another feed-forward layer, and becomes the initial state for the decoder recurrent transition. The main novelty of our system is that we use a minimum-risk training objective to directly optimise the model for Meteor, instead of the word-level cross entropy loss function which is currently standard for NMT systems. This idea comes from (Shen et al., 2016), although our implementation is somewhat different than the idea outlined in that work. To optimise for expected Meteor, we take up to 100 samples from our model, compute an expectation over these samples, and use Stochastic Gradient Descent to directly optimise the model on this expected score.

DCU-UVA (Task 1) The approach integrates separate attention mechanisms over the source language and the $CONV_{5,4}$ visual features in a single decoder. The source language was represented using a bidirectional RNN with Gated Recurrent Units (GRU); the images were represented as 196x512 matrix from the pre-trained VGG-19 convolutional network. A separate, time-dependent context vector was constructed for the source sentence and the visual features, which were merged into a single multimodal context vector. This time-dependent multimodal context vector was input into the target language decoder, along with the previous hidden state and the previously emitted word. Throughout, 300D word embeddings, 1000D hidden states, and 1000D context vectors were used; the source and target languages were estimated over the entire vocabularies.

HUCL (Task 1) The submitted system for the constrained task extends a standard SMT pipeline by a re-ranking component that makes use of multimodal information. The `cdec` decoder (Dyer et al., 2010) was used to produce hypothesis lists, which were re-scored by comparison with similar image captions from the training corpus using the pivoting approach described in Hitschler et al. (2016), with some minor differences: Because all data for the shared task was parallel, a constrained model was built by employing a source side matching approach inspired by standard translation memories, instead of retrieving matching captions in the target language by pivoting on larger image-caption data as described by Hitschler et al. (2016), which would have resulted in an unconstrained model. That is, the submission resorted to textual similarity (as measured by the TF-IDF score (Spärck Jones, 1972)) on the source language side as well as visual similarity (as measured by the Euclidean distance between the feature values of the FC_7 layer of the

VGG16 deep convolutional model (Simonyan and Zisserman, 2015), supplied by the task organisers) for retrieval of matches. The retrieval model architecture was identical to that in Hitschler et al. (2016). Instead of TF-IDF, a modified version of BLEU (Papineni et al., 2002) was used in order to re-score hypotheses based on the target-language text of retrieved captions. Fixed settings were used for some parameters ($d = 90$, $b = 0.01$ and $k_m = 20$), while k_r and λ were optimised on the validation set (parameters as defined in (Hitschler et al., 2016)).

IBM-IITM-Montreal-NYU (Tasks 1 and 2)[7] The approach for Task 1 is similar to that of (Elliott et al., 2015) with two differences. First, instead of using a RNN based encoder for the source (English) sentence, a simple bag of words encoder is used. In other words, the representation of the source sentence is simply a sum of the representations of the words in it. These word representations are randomly initialised and then learned during training. Second, unlike (Elliott et al., 2015), the image and source sentence representation are fed at every timestep to the target RNN decoder. The approach for Task 2 is same as that for Task 1, except that now instead of having a single source sentence representation, the representations of all the five source sentences are concatenated. This is then further concatenated with the image representation and the result is fed at every timestep to the target decoder. The FC_7 features for images as provided by the task organisers are used and tuned during training. The source and target RNNs contain 512 hidden neurons and the word embeddings are also of size 512. The models for both the tasks are trained for 10 epochs. For the unconstrained setup, the MSCOCO dataset, which contains English captions for images, was explored. These English captions were translated into German using IBM's translation services and then these pseudo Image-English-German tuples were used as additional training data, together with the training data provided by the task organisers. These are referred to as pseudo tuples since the German captions were machine translated and not human generated.

LIUM (Tasks 1 and 2) All submissions from LIUM are constrained.

LIUM_1_MosesNMTRnnLMSent2Vec_C and LIUM_1_MosesNMTRnnLMSent2VecVGGFC7_C are phrase-based systems based on Moses (14 standard features plus operation sequence models. They include re-scoring with several models and more particularly with a continuous space language model (CSLM) and a neural MT system (see TextNMT system). The CSLMs can use image feature maps as auxiliary data, in order to provide some context to the probabilities. The LIUM_1_TextNMT_C and LIUM_2_TextNMT_C systems are monomodal (text-only) fully neural MT systems similar to the one proposed by DL4MT school.[8] They are made of a bidirectional recurrent encoder followed by a conditional Gated Recurrent Unit decoder which embeds an attention mechanism. The difference between the two systems is the training and development data, as provided by the organisers. Finally, the LIUMCVC_1_MultimodalNMT_C and LIUM-CVC_2_MultimodalNMT_C are an extension of the previous systems, where an additional input is given: the convolutional feature maps extracted with a very deep ResNet (up to 152 layers) from the images (He et al., 2015). The attention mechanism is shared across the two modalities (with softmax activations remaining distinct). The architecture of the decoder is the same as before. The difference between the two systems is again the training and development data.

SHEF (Task 1) Both submissions from the Sheffield team are constrained, each focusing on one language direction: SHEF_1_en-de-Moses-rerank_C cover the official task direction (English-German), while SHEF_1_de-en-Moses-rerank_C covers the opposite direction (German-English). Our proposed systems are standard phrase-based statistical MT systems based on the Moses decoder, trained on the provided data. We investigate how image features can be used to re-rank the n-best output of the SMT model, with the aim of improving performance by grounding the translations on images. Image features from a CNN are used to re-rank the n-best list along with standard Moses features. We also propose an alternative scheme for the German-to-English direction, where terms in the English image descriptions are matched with 1,000 WordNet synsets, and the probability of these synsets occurring in the image estimated using CNN predictions on the images.

---

[7] Systems submitted by Amrita Saha, Mitesh M. Khapra, Janarthanan Rajendran, Sarath Chandar, Kyunghyun Cho

[8] http://dl4mt.computing.dcu.ie/

The aggregated probabilities are then used to re-rank the n-best list, with the intuition that the best translations should contain these entities. Our submissions to re-rank the n-best translations with image vectors are able to marginally outperform the strong, text-only baseline Moses system for both directions.

UPC (Task 1) Bidirectional Recurrent Neural Networks (BiRNNs) have shown outstanding results on sequence-to-sequence learning tasks. This architecture becomes especially interesting for multimodal machine translation task, since BiRNNs can deal with images and text. On most translation systems the same word embedding is fed to both BiRNN units. In our submission, we enhance a baseline sequence-to-sequence system (Elliott et al., 2015) by using double embeddings. These embeddings are trained on the forward and backward directions of the input sequence. The system was trained, validated and tested using the task's dataset only.

UPC$_b$ (Task 2)[9] The two submissions from UPC$_b$ use the same method with different training data, one is constrained (UPC_2_MNMT_C), while the other is unconstrained (UPC_2_MNMT2_U). Captions are generated from two different directions. One caption is generated through translating the captions in the source language directly using the method proposed in (Bahdanau et al., 2014). The other one is generated based on the image feature using method proposed in (Vinyals et al., 2015). After that, an SVM-based model decides which one is better according to the sentence's score from a language model and the score from the model that generated the sentence. The only difference between the two submissions is that the unconstrained one used Task 1 dataset in the training of text translator.

Baseline - GroundedTranslation (Tasks 1 & 2) This method follows (Elliott et al., 2015):[10] A source language multimodal RNN model is initialised with a visual feature vector (i.e., a multimodal model for the source language). The final hidden state is then used to initialise a target

language model, which generates the target language description. The source language multimodal RNN language model was trained until the loss stopped falling on the validation data. The target model was initialised with the final hidden state transferred from the source model and trained until the loss stopped falling on the validation data. The source model and target models were parameterised with 300D word embeddings and 1000D GRU hidden states; the source model was initialised with the 4096D FC$_7$ visual feature vector; for Task 1, the target model was initialised with a 1000D source model feature vector; for Task 2 the feature vectors corresponding to each source language description were summed into a 1000D feature vector. For both tasks, we found the optimal combination of target model language generation timesteps and beam width size using grid search.

Baseline - Moses (Task 1) This baseline system uses text-only information. It is a standard phrase-based SMT system built using the Moses toolkit (Koehn et al., 2007). The models were trained using the extended version of Flickr30K parallel dataset provided for the task only ($29,000$ sentence pairs), and tuned with the official validation dataset ($1,014$ segment pairs). Default settings and features in Moses were used, with a 4-gram language model trained on the target side of the parallel data.

4 Results

Tables 3 and 4 present the official results for the Multimodal Machine Translation and Crosslingual Image Description tasks. We evaluated the submissions based on Meteor (Denkowski and Lavie, 2014) (primary), BLEU (Papineni et al., 2002) and TER (Snover et al., 2006) using `MultEval` (Clark et al., 2011)[11] with default parameters.

4.1 Task 1

Table 4 shows the final results for the Multimodal Machine Translation task on the official test set, where systems are ranked by their Meteor scores. Meteor, BLEU and TER were computed based on the single reference (human translation) provided for the test set. For Meteor, we replaced the default version by the latest version of the metric (Meteor Version 1.5). Both reference and system submissions were first normalised for punctuation.

---

[9]Systems submitted by Zhiwen Tang and Marta Ruiz Costa-jussà; code available: `https://github.com/Z-TANG/re-scorer`.

[10]`https://github.com/elliottd/Grounded Translation`

[11]`https://github.com/jhclark/multeval`

System submissions that preserved casing or had been tokenised were further processed for lower-casing and detokenisation.[12] For all of these pre-processing steps, we used Moses scripts.[13]

It is interesting to note that while the three evaluation metrics do not fully agree on the ranking of participating systems, their overall Pearson's correlation (English-German direction) is very high: 0.98 between Meteor and BLEU, and -0.97 between Meteor and TER.

The three winning submissions from the LIUM and SHEF teams are heavily based on the output of a standard phrase-based SMT system (Moses) built using only the shared task data. This is a remarkable result, given the size of the dataset: 29,000 parallel segments. They all use additional features to re-rank the k-best output of a text-only phrase-based system, including visual features, although these seem to play a minor role and lead to only marginally better results.

Submissions based on the output of a Moses translation model – like the main baseline (1_en-de-Moses_C) – have very similar Meteor scores. In fact, SHEF_1_en-de-Moses-rerank_C and CMU+NTU_1_MNMT+RERANK_U are not considered significantly different from this baseline Shah et al. (2016) provide some analysis on the differences between SHEF_1_en-de-Moses-rerank_C and 1_en-de-Moses_C. They show that the output of these systems differ in 260 out of the 1,000 segments. However, despite differences in the actual translations, the Meteor scores for many of these cases may be the same/close.

Disappointingly, truly multimodal systems, which in most cases use neural MT approaches (e.g. CUNI_1_MMS2S-1_C, DCU_1_min-risk-multimodal_C) do not fare as well as the text-only SMT systems (or those followed by multimodal-based translation rescoring), except when additional resources are used for rescoring translations (CMU_1_MNMT+RERANK_U).

Only two submissions made use of additional data (unconstrained submissions, _U) and in both cases it proved helpful in comparison with the constrained submissions by the same teams.

---

[12]We note that `MultEval` does not perform any normalisation of the segments. Scores with tokenised texts would be consistently higher.

[13]`https://github.com/moses-smt/mosesdecoder/blob/master/scripts/`

4.2 Task 2: Crosslingual Image Description

Table 4 presents the final results for the Crosslingual Image Description task. Meteor is the primary evaluation measure because it has been shown to have a much stronger correlation with human judgements than BLEU or TER for this task (Elliott and Keller, 2014). The data for this task was lowercased and had punctuation removed where necessary.

The strongest performing *constrained* submission (LIUM_2_TextNMT_C) does not use any visual features. Including multimodal features (i.e., LIUM_2_MultimodalNMT_C) results in a 2.8 Meteor drop in performance for that model type. The baseline system 2_GroundedTranslation_C outperformed all but these two systems. In general, there is a wide range of performances, and an intriguing discrepancy between Meteor and BLEU rankings. This discrepancy was much larger than the one observed in Task 1, where the overall ranking trend for all metrics is similar. We believe the difference between metrics in Task 2 is due to the different ways in which these metrics use multiple references (which are only available for Task 2). While Meteor (and TER) will match the single closest reference (the entire sentence) to the system output, BLEU allows n-grams from different references to be used for its n-gram matching.

Only two groups submitted *unconstrained* runs, marked in grey and with _U in Table 4. The IBM-IITM-Montreal-NYU_2_NeuralTranslation_U submission resulted in a small improvement over the IBM-IITM-Montreal-NYU_2_NeuralTranslation_C submission, but the UPC_2_MNMT_U resulted in a small decrease compared to the analogous constrained submission UPC_2_MNMT_C.

5 Discussion

Although the Multimodal Machine Translation and Crosslingual Description tasks are based on the same collection of images, there are a number of important differences in the textual data, outlined below, which lead to different patterns of results for both tasks.

The nature of the sentences The sentences in Task 1 are professional translations, whereas the sentences in Task 2 are independent descriptions. The differences between translations and descriptions may affect the performance of image de-

System ID	Meteor ↑	BLEU ↑	TER ↓
English-German			
•LIUM_1_MosesNMTRnnLMSent2Vec_C	53.2	34.2	48.7
•LIUM_1_MosesNMTRnnLMSent2VecVGGFC7_C	53.2	34.1	48.7
•*SHEF_1_en-de-Moses-rerank_C	52.6	32.8	49.8
1_en-de-Moses_C	52.5	32.5	50.2
*CMU_1_MNMT+RERANK_U	51.9	33.6	52.4
HUCL_1_RROLAPMBen2de_C	51.5	32.2	51.1
CMU_1_MNMT_C	50.8	35.1	49.2
DCU_1_min-risk-baseline_C	49.7	31.8	52.6
LIUM_1_TextNMT_C	49.2	32.5	51.6
DCU_1_min-risk-multimodal_C	48.4	32.5	49.8
CUNI_1_MMS2S-1_C	46.5	29.7	53.5
DCU-UVA_1_doubleattn_C	46.4	27.4	59.7
LIUMCVC_1_MultimodalNMT_C	45.0	27.8	57.3
DCU-UVA_1_imgattninit_C	44.1	26.5	60.1
IBM-IITM-Montreal-NYU_1_NeuralTranslation_U	39.1	21.8	61.9
UPC_1_SIMPLE-BIRNN-DEMB_C	37.7	22.1	60.4
IBM-IITM-Montreal-NYU_1_NeuralTranslation_C	31.1	16.0	69.4
1_GroundedTranslation_C	24.7	9.4	77.2
German-English			
•*SHEF_1_de-en-Moses-rerank_C	36.5	39.8	41.0
•1_de-en-Moses_C	36.2	38.1	40.8
HUCL_1_RROLAPMBde2en_C	35.1	37.0	42.4

Table 3: Official results for the WMT16 Multimodal Machine Translation task. The baseline results are underlined. Systems with grey background indicate use of resources that fall outside the constraints provided for the shared task. The winning submissions are indicated by a •. These are the top-scoring submission and those that are not significantly different (based on Meteor scores) according the approximate randomisation test (with p-value $<= 0.05$) provided by `MultEval`. Submissions marked with a * indicate those that are not significantly different from the main baseline (1_Moses_C) according to the same test.

scription models relative to the translation models. This can be seen by comparing the results of teams that submitted the same systems (but separately trained) to both tasks: LIUM, IBM-IITM-Montreal-NYU, and the Grounded-Translation baseline. The LIUM and IBM-IITM-Montreal-NYU submissions seem to benefit from training over translation data instead of the description data, as suggested by the higher Meteor scores achieved in Task 1 (1 reference) vs. Task 2 (5 references); the GroundedTranslation submissions exhibit the opposite effect (this may be explained by the fact that this submission is an image description model and not a translation model). We hypothesize that the differences in performance may originate from the possibility that (a) the description data is merely a *comparable* corpus instead of a *parallel* corpus leading to

noisier pairing of source-target pairs, and/or (b) in the description task the training data is less compatible with the test data than in the translation task. This demands further exploration.

The number of training examples Submissions for Task 1 are trained over 29,000 parallel instances (one sentence pair per image), whereas submissions for Task 2 are trained over 145,000 (five independent sentences per language per image). The number of training examples for each task further complicates the analysis of the difference in performance between the two tasks, as the larger-data scenario in Task 2 does not lead to a straightforward improvement in performance. The type and the quality of the parallel translation data – despite its small size – makes it relatively easy to train high-performing translation models, as we can see by comparing the absolute Meteor scores

	System ID	**Meteor** ↑	BLEU ↑	TER ↓	Visual Features?
English-German					
•	LIUM_2_TextNMT_C	35.1	23.8	62.1	—
	LIUM_2_MultimodalNMT_C	32.3	19.2	70.0	ResNet
	2_GroundedTranslation_C	31.2	15.8	76.4	FC_7
	IBM-IITM-Montreal-NYU_2_NeuralTranslation_U	29.5	9.7	89.0	FC_7
	IBM-IITM-Montreal-NYU_2_NeuralTranslation_C	29.1	17.8	60.0	FC_7
	CUNI_2_MMS2S-2_C	13.1	1.2	73.3	FC_7
	UPC_b_2_MNMT_C	12.1	1.5	63.1	FC_7
	UPC_b_2_MNMT_U	11.7	1.0	82.2	FC_7

Table 4: Official results for the WMT16 Crosslingual Image Description task. The baseline results are underlined. Systems with grey background indicate use of resources that fall outside the constraints provided for the shared task. The winning submission, indicated by a •, is significantly different from all other submissions based on Meteor scores. Submissions marked with a * are not significantly different compared to the baseline (2_GroundedTranslation_C).

in Tables 3 and 4. In fact, it is quite remarkable that both statistical and neural MT approaches performed so well with only 29,000 sentence pairs for training, particularly for English→German translation. In different text domains (e.g. Europarl, News), this language pair and direction is well known as a challenging case. The two languages are structurally distant and the target language – German – is morphologically richer than English, which poses a problem in machine translation particularly when not enough training instances are available with examples of the various morphological variants of target words. The fact that the performance for Task 1 was so high seems to indicate that the data for this task is much simpler and probably significantly more repetitive than data used in other shared tasks, for example, the News translation task at WMT (Bojar et al., 2015).

The amount of evaluation data Task 1 submissions are evaluated against one reference translation and Task 2 submissions are evaluated against five independent sentences. The larger number of references for Task 2 should make it easier for submissions to achieve high Meteor scores but this is not borne out in the results. One reason for this could be that each independently collected description had a free choice in what to describe and how to describe it (Elliott and Keller, 2014). This has led to collected descriptions that are not translations of their English counterparts. We could collect five professionally translated references for each image to study this issue. We would expect the absolute Meteor scores for Task 1 to increase

with more references (Dreyer and Marcu, 2012); however, we should also bear in mind that the image descriptions are quite simple and there is likely to be very high similarity among translations.

Further research is needed to determine whether having more parallel translation data or more references for evaluation will lead to better performance for both tasks. However, this data would be very expensive to collect. Collecting more independent descriptions would be significantly cheaper.

Use of visual information The use of visual information had very different effects in the two tasks. While for Task 1 this information only proved marginally useful in indirect ways (i.e. rescoring k-best translations), visual information featured prominently in submissions for Task 2: six submissions used the FC_7 features, one submission used features extracted from the ResNet-50 network, and one submission used no visual features. The submission with ResNet-50 features outperformed all submissions with FC_7 features, which is not surprising given the difference in object categorisation performance between the models (4.49% top-5 error on the ILSVRC validation data (Russakovsky et al., 2014) compared to 7.1% error). However, the submission without visual features achieved the best performance for Task 2.

In light of our aim of furthering multimodal research with multilingual multimodal data, this is a somewhat disappointing result. However, we believe that it only reinforces the call to develop more robust models that can integrate visual and linguistic features into a single model. Building more realistic and challenging datasets is also an interesting direction for future research.

Acknowledgments

SF was supported by European Union's Horizon 2020 research and innovation programme under grant agreement nr. 645452. DE and KS are supported by the NWO Vici grant nr. 277-89-002.

References

Dzmitry Bahdanau, Kyunghyun Cho, and Yoshua Bengio. 2014. Neural machine translation by jointly learning to align and translate. *CoRR*, abs/1409.0473.

Raffaella Bernardi, Ruket Cakici, Desmond Elliott, Aykut Erdem, Erkut Erdem, Nazli Ikizler-Cinbis, Frank Keller, Adrian Muscat, and Barbara Plank. 2016. Automatic description generation from images: A survey of models, datasets, and evaluation measures. *CoRR*, abs/1601.03896.

Ondřej Bojar, Rajen Chatterjee, Christian Federmann, Barry Haddow, Matthias Huck, Chris Hokamp, Philipp Koehn, Varvara Logacheva, Christof Monz, Matteo Negri, Matt Post, Carolina Scarton, Lucia Specia, and Marco Turchi. 2015. Findings of the 2015 workshop on statistical machine translation. In *Proceedings of the Tenth Workshop on Statistical Machine Translation*, pages 1–46, Lisbon, Portugal.

Ozan Caglayan, Walid Aransa, Yaxing Wang, Marc Masana, Mercedes García-Martínez, Fethi Bougares, Loïc Barrault, and Joost van de Weijer. 2016. Does multimodality help human and machine for translation and image captioning? In *Proceedings of the First Conference on Machine Translation*, Berlin, Germany.

Iacer Calixto, Desmond Elliott, and Stella Frank. 2016. Dcu-uva multimodal mt system report. In *Proceedings of the First Conference on Machine Translation*, Berlin, Germany.

Jonathan H. Clark, Chris Dyer, Alon Lavie, and Noah A. Smith. 2011. Better hypothesis testing for statistical machine translation: Controlling for optimizer instability. In *Proceedings of the 49th Annual Meeting of the Association for Computational Linguistics: Human Language Technologies: Short Papers - Volume 2*, pages 176–181, Portland, Oregon.

Michael Denkowski and Alon Lavie. 2014. Meteor universal: Language specific translation evaluation for any target language. In *Proceedings of the Ninth Workshop on Statistical Machine Translation*, pages 376–380, Baltimore, Maryland.

Markus Dreyer and Daniel Marcu. 2012. Hyter: Meaning-equivalent semantics for translation evaluation. In *Proceedings of the 2012 Conference of the North American Chapter of the Association for Computational Linguistics: Human Language Technologies*, pages 162–171, Montréal, Canada, June.

Chris Dyer, Adam Lopez, Juri Ganitkevitch, Johnathan Weese, Ferhan Ture, Phil Blunsom, Hendra Setiawan, Vladimir Eidelman, and Philip Resnik. 2010. cdec: A decoder, alignment, and learning framework for finite-state and context-free translation models. In *Proceedings of the 48th Annual Meeting of the Association for Computational Linguistics*, pages 7–12, Uppsala, Sweden.

Desmond Elliott and Frank Keller. 2014. Comparing Automatic Evaluation Measures for Image Description. In *Proceedings of the 52nd Annual Meeting of the Association for Computational Linguistics*, pages 452–457, Baltimore, Maryland.

Desmond Elliott, Stella Frank, and Eva Hasler. 2015. Multi-language image description with neural sequence models. *CoRR*, abs/1510.04709.

Desmond Elliott, Stella Frank, Khalil. Sima'an, and Lucia Specia. 2016. Multi30K: Multilingual English-German Image Descriptions. In *Proceedings of the 5th Workshop on Vision and Language*, Berlin, Germany.

Yansong Feng and Mirella Lapata. 2010. Topic models for image annotation and text illustration. In *Proceedings of Human Language Technologies: The 2010 Annual Conference of the North American Chapter of the Association for Computational Linguistics*, pages 831–839, Los Angeles, California.

Ruka Funaki and Hideki Nakayama. 2015. Image-mediated learning for zero-shot cross-lingual document retrieval. In *Proceedings of the Conference on Empirical Methods in Natural Language Processing*, pages 585–590, Lisbon, Portugal.

Haoyuan Gao, Junhua Mao, Jie Zhou, Zhiheng Huang, Lei Wang, and Wei Xu. 2015. Are you talking to a machine? dataset and methods for multilingual image question answering. *Advances in Neural Information Processing Systems*, pages 2287–2295.

Michael Grubinger, Paul D. Clough, Henning Muller, and Thomas Desealers. 2006. The IAPR TC-12 benchmark: A new evaluation resource for visual information systems. In *Proceedings of the Language Resources and Evaluation Conference*.

Kaiming He, Xiangyu Zhang, Shaoqing Ren, and Jian Sun. 2015. Deep residual learning for image recognition. *CoRR*, abs/1512.03385.

Julian Hitschler, Shigehiko Schamoni, and Stefan Riezler. 2016. Multimodal Pivots for Image Caption Translation. In *Proceedings of the 54th Annual Meeting of the Association for Computational Linguistics*, Berlin, Germany.

Chris Hokamp and Iacer Calixto. 2016. Multimodal neural machine translation using minimum risk training. `https://www.github.com/chrishokamp/multimodal_nmt`.

Po-Yao Huang, Frederick Liu, Sz-Rung Shiang, Jean Oh, and Chris Dyer. 2016. Attention-based multimodal neural machine translation. In *Proceedings of the First Conference on Machine Translation*, Berlin, Germany.

Philipp Koehn, Hieu Hoang, Alexandra Birch, Chris Callison-Burch, Marcello Federico, Nicola Bertoldi, Brooke Cowan, Wade Shen, Christine Moran, Richard Zens, et al. 2007. Moses: Open source toolkit for statistical machine translation. In *Proceedings of the 45th Annual meeting of Association for Computational Linguistics*, pages 177–180, Prague, Czech Republic.

Jindřich Libovický, Jindřich Helcl, Marek Tlustý, Ondřej Bojar, and Pavel Pecina. 2016. Cuni system for wmt16 automatic post-editing and multimodal translation tasks. In *Proceedings of the First Conference on Machine Translation*, Berlin, Germany.

Kishore Papineni, Salim Roukos, Todd Ard, and Wei-Jing Zhu. 2002. Bleu: a method for automatic evaluation of machine translation. In *Proceedings of the 40th Annual Meeting of the Association for Computational Linguistics*, pages 311–318, Philadelphia, Pennsylvania.

Arnau Ramisa, Fei Yan, Francesc Moreno-Noguer, and Krystian Mikolajczyk. 2016. Breakingnews: Article annotation by image and text processing. *CoRR*, abs/1603.07141.

Sergio Rodríguez Guasch and Marta R. Costa-jussà. 2016. Wmt 2016 multimodal translation system description based on bidirectional recurrent neural networks with double-embeddings. In *Proceedings of the First Conference on Machine Translation*, Berlin, Germany.

Olga Russakovsky, Jia Deng, Hao Su, Jonathan Krause, Sanjeev Satheesh, Sean Ma, Zhiheng Huang, Andrej Karpathy, Aditya Khosla, Michael S. Bernstein, Alexander C. Berg, and Fei-Fei Li. 2014. Imagenet large scale visual recognition challenge. *CoRR*, abs/1409.0575.

Kashif Shah, Josiah Wang, and Lucia Specia. 2016. Shef-multimodal: Grounding machine translation on images. In *Proceedings of the First Conference on Machine Translation*, Berlin, Germany.

Shiqi Shen, Yong Cheng, Zhongjun He, Wei He, Hua Wu, Maosong Sun, and Yang Liu. 2016. Minimum Risk Training for Neural Machine Translation. In *Proceedings of the 54th Annual Meeting of the Association for Computational Linguistics*, Berlin, Germany.

Karen Simonyan and Andrew Zisserman. 2015. Very deep convolutional networks for large-scale image recognition. In *Proceedings of the International Conference on Learning Representations*.

Matthew Snover, Bonnie Dorr, and Richard Schwartz. 2006. A study of translation edit rate with targeted human annotation. In *Proceedings of Association for Machine Translation in the Americas*, Cambridge, Massachusetts.

Karen Spärck Jones. 1972. A statistical interpretation of term specificity and its application in retrieval. *Journal of Documentation*, 28:11–21.

Darlene Stewart, Roland Kuhn, Eric Joanis, and George Foster. 2014. Coarse split and lump bilingual language models for richer source information in SMT. In *Proceedings of the Eleventh Conference of the Association for Machine Translation in the Americas*, pages 28–41, Vancouver, Canada.

Oriol Vinyals, Alexander Toshev, Samy Bengio, and Dumitru Erhan. 2015. Show and tell: A neural image caption generator. In *The IEEE Conference on Computer Vision and Pattern Recognition*.

Zichao Yang, Xiaodong He, Jianfeng Gao, Li Deng, and Alexander J. Smola. 2015. Stacked attention networks for image question answering. *CoRR*, abs/1511.02274.

Peter Young, Alice Lai, Micha Hodosh, and Julia Hockenmaier. 2014. From image descriptions to visual denotations: New similarity metrics for semantic inference over event descriptions. *Transactions of the Association for Computational Linguistics*, 2:67–78.

Findings of the WMT 2016 Bilingual Document Alignment Shared Task

Christian Buck
School of Informatics
University of Edinburgh
Scotland, European Union

Philipp Koehn
Johns Hopkins University
phi@jhu.edu
and
School of Informatics
University of Edinburgh
Scotland, European Union

Abstract

This paper presents the results of the WMT16 Bilingual Document Alignment Shared Task. Given crawls of web sites, we asked participants to align documents that are translations of each other. 11 research groups submitted 19 systems, with a top performance of 95.0%.

1 Introduction

Parallel corpora are especially important for training statistical machine translation systems, but so far the collection of such data within the academic research community has been ad hoc and limited in scale. To promote this research problem we organized a shared task on one of the core processing steps in acquiring parallel corpora from the web: aligning bilingual documents from crawled web sites.

The task is to identify pairs of English and French documents from a given collection of documents such that one document is the translation of the other. As possible pairs we consider all pairs of documents from the same webdomain for which the source side has been identified as (mostly) English and the target side as (mostly) French.

Lack of data in some cases has held back research. To give an example, there are significant research efforts on various Indic languages (Post et al., 2012; Joshi et al., 2013; Singh, 2013), but this work has been severely hampered, since it uses very small amounts of data. But even for the language pairs tackled in high profile evaluation campaigns, such as the ones organized around WMT, IWSLT, and even NIST, we use magnitudes of data less than what has been reported to be used in the large-scale efforts of Google or Microsoft. This diminishes the value of research findings: reported improvements for methods may not hold up once more data is used. Work in reduced data settings may also distract from efforts to tackle problems that do not go away with more data, but are inherent limitations of current models.

2 Related Work

Although the idea of crawling the web indiscriminately for parallel data goes back to the 20th century (Resnik, 1999), work in the academic community on extraction of parallel corpora from the web has so far mostly focused on large stashes of multilingual content in homogeneous form, such as the Canadian Hansards, Europarl (Koehn, 2005), the United Nations (Rafalovitch and Dale, 2009; Ziemski et al., 2015), or European Patents (Täger, 2011). A nice collection of the products of these efforts is the OPUS web site[1] (Skadiņš et al., 2014).

These efforts focused on individual web sites allow for writing specific rules for aligning documents as well as extracting and aligning content. Scaling these manual efforts to thousands or millions of web sites is not practical.

A typical processing pipeline breaks up parallel corpus extraction into five steps:

- Identifying web sites with bilingual content
- Crawling web sites
- Document alignment
- Sentence alignment
- Sentence pair filtering

For each of these steps, there has been varying amount of prior work and for some tools are readily available. Since there has been comparatively little work on document alignment, we picked this problem as the subject for the shared task this year, but other steps are valid candidates for future tasks.

---

[1] http://opus.lingfil.uu.se/

Proceedings of the First Conference on Machine Translation, Volume 2: Shared Task Papers, pages 554–563,
Berlin, Germany, August 11-12, 2016. ©2016 Association for Computational Linguistics

2.1 Web Crawling

Web crawling is a topic that has not received much attention from a specific natural language processing perspective. There are a number of challenges, such as identification of web sites with multilingual content, avoiding to crawl web pages with identical textual content, learning how often to recrawl web sites based on frequency of newly appearing content, avoiding crawling of large sites that have content in different languages that is not parallel, and so on.

We used for the preparation of this shared task the tool Httrack[2] which is a general web crawler that can be configured in various ways. Papavassiliou et al. (2013) present the focused crawler ILSP-FC[3] that integrates crawling more closely with subsequent processing steps like text normalization and deduplication.

2.2 Document Alignment

Document alignment can be defined as a matching task that takes a pair of documents and computes a score that reflects the likelihood that they are translations of each others. Common choices include edit-distance between linearized documents (Resnik and Smith, 2003), cosine distance of idf-weighted bigram vectors (Uszkoreit et al., 2010), and probability of a probabilistic DOM-tree alignment model (Shi et al., 2006).

2.3 Sentence Alignment

The topic of sentence alignment has received a lot of attention, dating back to the early 1990s with the influential Church and Gale algorithm that is language-independent and easy to implement. It relies on relative sentence lengths for alignment decisions and hence is not tolerant to noisy input.

Popular tools are Hunalign[4] (Varga et al., 2005), Gargantua[5] (Braune and Fraser, 2010), Bilingual Sentence Aligner (Moore, 2002) Bleualign[6] (Sennrich and Volk, 2010), and Champollion[7] (Ma, 2006). Shi and Zhou (2008) make use of the HTML structure to guide alignment. All of these use bilingual lexicons which may have to be provided upfront or are learned unsupervised.

It is not clear, which of these tools fares best with noisy parallel text that we can expect from web crawls, which may have spurious content and misleading boilerplate.

2.4 Filtering

A final stage of the processing pipeline filters out bad sentence pairs. These exist either because the original web site did not have any actual parallel data (garbage in, garbage out), or due to failures of earlier processing steps.

As Rarrick et al. (2011) point out, a key problem for parallel corpora extracted from the web is filtering out translations that have been created by machine translation. Venugopal et al. (2011) propose a method to watermark the output of machine translation systems to aid this distinction. Antonova and Misyurev (2011) report that rule-based machine translation output can be detected due to certain word choices, and machine translation output due to lack of reordering.

This year, a shared task on sentence pair filtering[8] was organized, albeit in the context of cleaning translation memories which tend to be cleaner that the data at the end of a pipeline that starts with web crawls.

2.5 Comprehensive Tools

For a few language pairs, there have been individual efforts to cast a wider net, such as the billion word French–English corpus collected by Callison-Burch et al. (2009), or a 200 million word Czech–English corpus collected by Bojar et al. (2010). Smith et al. (2013) present a set of fairly basic tools to extract parallel data from the publicly available web crawl CommonCrawl[9].

In all these cases, the corpus collection effort reinvented the wheel and wrote dedicated scripts to download web pages, extract text, and align sentences, with hardly any description of the methods used.

Our data preparation for the shared task builds partly on Bitextor[10], which is a comprehensive pipeline from corpus crawling to sentence pair cleaning (Esplà-Gomis, 2009).

---

[2] https://www.httrack.com/

[3] http://nlp.ilsp.gr/redmine/projects/ilsp-fc

[4] http://mokk.bme.hu/en/resources/hunalign/

[5] https://sourceforge.net/projects/gargantua/

[6] https://github.com/rsennrich/Bleualign

[7] https://sourceforge.net/projects/champollion/

[8] NLP4TM 2016: Shared task
http://rgcl.wlv.ac.uk/nlp4tm2016/shared-task/

[9] http://commoncrawl.org/

[10] https://sourceforge.net/p/bitextor/wiki/Home/

3 Training and Test Data

We made available crawls of web sites (defined as pages under the same webdomain) that have translated content. We also annotated some document pairs to provide supervised training data to the participants of the shared task.

3.1 Terminology

A quick note on terminology: Unfortunately, the notion of *domain* is ambiguous in NLP applications, and we use an unusual meaning of the word in this report. To avoid confusion we will instead use the term webdomain to refer to content from a specific website, e.g,"This page is from the `statmt.org` webdomain." We distinguish between webdomains using their Fully Qualified Domain Name (FQDN). Thus, `www.example.com` and `example.com` are considered to be different webdomains.

We will use *source* to denote English pages and *target* for French ones. This does not imply that translation was performed in that direction. In fact we cannot know if translation from one side to the other was performed at all, both sides could possibly be translations of a third language document.

The task was organized as part of the First Conference on Machine Translation (WMT), and all data can be downloaded from its web page[11].

3.2 Data Preparation

We crawled full web sites with the web site copyer **HTTrack**, from the homepage down, restricted to HTML content. Web sites differed significantly in their size, from a few hundred pages to almost 100,000.

In the test data we removed all duplicates from the crawl[12]. Duplicates are defined as web pages, whose text content is identical. Duplicates may differ in markup and URL. To extract the text we used a Python implementation of the HTML5 parser to extract text as a browser would see it. As the text is free of formatting, determining whitespace is important. While generally following the standard, e.g. inserting line breaks after block level elements[13], we found that inserting spaces around <span> tags helps tokenization as these are often visually separated using CSS.

We restricted the task to the alignment of French and English documents, so we filtered out all web pages that are not in these two languages. However, we did not expect that participants would develop language-specific approaches. To detect the language of a document we feed the extracted text into an automatic language detector [14]. We note that language detection is a noisy process and many pages contain mixed language context, for example English boilerplate but French content. We take the overall majority language per page as the document language.

We decided to have a large collection of web sites, to encourage methods that can cope with various types of web sites, such as differing in size, balance in the number of French and English pages, and so on.

Given the large number of correct document pairs, we did not even attempt to annotate all of them, but instead randomly selected a subset of pages and identified their corresponding translated page. We augmented this effort with aligned document pairs that are indicated at the web site **Linguee**[16], a searchable collection of parallel corpora, in which each retrieved sentence is annotated with its source web page.

The task then is to find these document pairs. Since this is essentially a recall measure, which can be gamed by returning all possible document pairs, we enforce a 1-1 rule, so that participants may align each web page only once.

3.3 Training Data

As training data we provide a set of 1,624 EN-FR pairs from 49 webdomains. The number of annotated document pairs per webdomain varies between 4 and over 200. All pairs are from within a single webdomain, possible matches between two different webdomains, e.g. `siemens.de` and `siemens.com`, are not considered in this task.

The full list of webdomains in the training data is listed in Table 1. Webdomains range in size from 33×29 pages (`schackportalen.nu`) to $24,325 \times 43,045$ pages (`www.nauticnews.com`).

3.4 Test Data

For testing, we provide 203 additional crawls of new webdomains, distinct from the ones in the training data in the same format. No aligned pairs

---

[11]`http://www.statmt.org/wmt16/bilingual-task.html`
[12]Because we provide the extracted texts of the training pages participants were able to do the same
[13]`https://developer.mozilla.org/en-US/docs/Web/HTML/Block-level_elements`

[14]Compact Language Detector 2 (CLD2)[15]
[16]`http://www.linguee.com/`

Website	Source Documents	Target Documents	Possible Pairs	Train Pairs
cineuropa.mobi	23 050	15 972	368 154 600	73
forcesavenir.qc.ca	3 592	3 982	14 303 344	8
galacticchannelings.com	4 231	1 283	5 428 373	9
golftrotter.com	377	361	136 097	8
ironmaidencommentary.com	6 028	635	3 827 780	41
kicktionary.de	2 752	888	2 443 776	29
kustu.com	1 544	1 511	2 332 984	13
manchesterproducts.com	15 621	9 651	150 758 271	10
minelinks.com	736	212	156 032	66
pawpeds.com	983	135	132 705	19
rehazenter.lu	201	317	63 717	16
tsb.gc.ca	5 885	5 828	34 297 780	236
virtualhospice.ca	43 500	22 327	971 224 500	46
www.acted.org	3 333	2 431	8 102 523	21
www.artsvivants.ca	5 487	1 368	7 506 216	12
www.bonnke.net	414	129	53 406	27
www.cyberspaceministry.org	1 534	958	1 469 572	29
www.dfo-mpo.gc.ca	25 277	19 087	482 462 099	97
www.ec.gc.ca	12 266	15 404	188 945 464	26
www.eu2005.lu	5 649	5 704	32 221 896	34
www.inst.at	3 203	543	1 739 229	62
www.krn.org	115	115	13 225	67
www.lameca.org	692	1 567	1 084 364	6
www.pawpeds.com	1 011	136	137 496	43
bugadacargnel.com	919	779	715 901	19
cbsc.ca	1 595	904	1 441 880	20
creationwiki.org	8 417	203	1 708 651	22
eu2007.de	3 201	2 488	7 964 088	11
eu.blizzard.com	10 493	6 640	69 673 520	10
iiz-dvv.de	1 160	894	1 037 040	67
santabarbara-online.com	1 151	1 099	1 264 949	11
schackportalen.nu	33	29	957	14
www.antennas.biz	812	327	265 524	30
www.bugadacargnel.com	919	779	715 901	7
www.cgfmanet.org	9 241	6 260	57 848 660	25
www.dakar.com	17 420	14 582	254 018 440	45
www.eohu.ca	2 277	2 136	4 863 672	4
www.eu2007.de	3 249	2 535	8 236 215	11
www.fao.org	11 931	5 004	59 702 724	6
www.luontoportti.com	3 645	1 796	6 546 420	30
www.nato.int	40 063	8 773	351 472 699	36
www.nauticnews.com	24 325	43 045	1 047 069 625	21
www.prohelvetia.ch	5 209	4 421	23 028 989	7
www.socialwatch.org	13 803	2 419	33 389 457	21
www.summerlea.ca	434	338	146 692	58
www.the-great-adventure.fr	2 038	2 460	5 013 480	18
www.ushmm.org	10 472	967	10 126 424	26
www.usw.ca	5 006	2 247	11 248 482	83
www.vinci.com	3 564	3 374	12 024 936	24
Total	348 858	225 043	4 246 520 775	1 624

Table 1: Training data statistics.

are provided for the any of these domains. We removed exact duplicates of pages, keeping only one instance. Otherwise, we processed the data in the same way as the training data.

3.5 Data Format

The training document pairs are specified as one pair per line:

```
Source_URL<TAB>Target_URL
```

For the crawled data we provide one file per webdomain in `.lett` format adapted from Bitextor. This is a plain text format with one line per page. Each line consists of 6 tab-separated values:

- Language ID (e.g. en)
- Mime type (always text/html)
- Encoding (always charset=utf-8)
- URL
- HTML in Base64 encoding
- Text in Base64 encoding

To facilitate use of the `.lett` files we provide a simple reader class in Python. We make sure that the language id is reliable, at least for the documents in the train and test pairs.

Text extraction was performed using an HTML5 parser. As the original HTML pages are available, participants are welcome to implement their own text extraction, for example to remove boilerplate.

Additionally, we have identified spans of French text in French documents for which we produced English translations using MT. We use a basic Moses statistical machine translation engine (Koehn et al., 2007) trained on Europarl and News Commentary with decoding settings geared towards speed (no lexicalized reordering model, no additional language model, cube pruning with pop limit 500).

These translations are not part of the lett files but provided separately. The format for the source segments and target segments is

```
URL<TAB>Text
```

where the same URL might occur multiple times if several lines/spans of French text were found. The URLs can be used to identify the corresponding documents in the .lett files.

3.6 Baseline Method

We provide a baseline systems that relies on the URL matching heuristic used by Smith et al. (2013). Here two URLs are considered a pair if both can be transformed into the same string through stripping of language identifiers. Strings indicating languages are found by splitting a large number of randomly sampled URLs into components and manually picking substrings that correlate with the detected language.

We further improve the approach by allowing matches where only one URL contains a strip-able language identifier, e.g. we match `x.com/index.htm` and `x.com/fr_index.htm`. If a URL has several matching candidates we pick the one that requires the fewest rewrites, i.e. we prefer the pair above over `x.com/en/index.htm` `x.com/fr_index.htm`.

The baseline achieves roughly 60% recall, compared to 95.0% of the best submission.

4 Evaluation

Our main evaluation metric is recall of the known pairs, i.e. what percentage of the aligned pages in the test set are found. We strictly enforce the rule that every page may only be aligned once, so that participants cannot just align everything. After a URL has been seen as part of a submitted pair, all later occurrences are ignored.

After we released the gold standard alignments, a number of participants pointed out that some predicted document pairs were unfairly counted as wrong, even if their content differed only insignificantly from the gold standard.

To give an example, the web pages
`www.taize.fr/fr_article10921.html?chooselang=1`
and
`www.taize.fr/fr_article10921.html`
are almost identical, but the first offers a checkbox to select a language, while the second does not. Since the text on the pages differs slightly, these were not detected as (exact) duplicates.

To address this problem, we also included a **soft scoring metric** which counts such near-matches as correct. We chose that to be a close duplicate, the edit distance between the text of two pages, normalized by the maximum of their lengths (in characters) must not exceed 5%.

If we observe a predicted pair (s, t) that is not in the gold set, but (s, t') is and $\mathrm{dist}(t, t') \leq 5\%$, then this pair is still counted as correct. The same applies for a close duplicate s' of s but not both as we still follow the 1-1 rule.

Acronym	Participant
ADAPT	ADAPT Research Center, Ireland (Lohar et al., 2016)
BADLUC	University of Montréal, Canada (Jakubina and Langlais, 2016)
DOCAL	Vicomtech (Azpeitia and Etchegoyhen, 2016)
ILSP/ARC	Athena Research and Innovation Center, Greece (Papavassiliou et al., 2016)
JIS	JIS College of Engineering, Kalyani, India (Mahata et al., 2016)
MEVED	Lexical Computing / Masaryk University, Slovakia (Medved et al., 2016)
NOVALINCS	Universidade Nova de Lisboa, Portugal (Gomes and Pereira Lopes, 2016)
UA PROMPSIT	University of Alicante / Prompsit: Bitextor, Spain (Esplà-Gomis et al., 2016)
UEDIN COSINE	University of Edinburgh, Scotland — Buck (Buck and Koehn, 2016)
UEDIN LSI	University of Edinburgh, Scotland — German (Germann, 2016)
UFAL	Charles University in Prague, Czech Republic (Le et al., 2016)
YSDA	Yandex School of Data Analysis, Russia (Shchukin et al., 2016)
YODA	Carnegie Mellon University (Dara and Lin, 2016)

Table 2: List of participants

5 Results

11 research groups participated in the shared task, some with multiple submissions. The list of participants is shown in Table 2, with a citation of their system descriptions, which are included in these conference proceedings.

Each participant submitted one or more collections of document pairs. We enforced the 1-1 rule on the collections, and scored them against the gold standard. Results are summarized in Table 3. Almost all systems outperformed the baseline by a wide margin. The best system is NOVALINCS-URL-COVERAGE with 2,281 correct pairs, 95.0% of the total.

Note that the submissions varied in the number of document pairs, but after enforcing the 1-1 rule, most submissions comprise about 200,000-300,000 document pairs.

Table 4 displays the results with soft scoring. Essentially, every system improved, mostly by around 3%. The top two performers swapped places, with YODA now having the best showing with 96.0%. We also experimented with a tighter threshold of 1% which gave almost identical results.

6 System Descriptions

NOVALINCS (Gomes and Pereira Lopes, 2016) submitted 3 systems that use a phrase table from a phrase-based statistical machine translation system to compute coverage scores, based on the ratio of phrase pairs covered by a document pair. In addition to the purely coverage-based system, NOVALINCS-COVERAGE (88.6%), they also submit a system that uses coverage-based matching as a preference over URL matching NOVALINCS-COVERAGE-URL (85.8%) and the converse system that prefers URL matching over coverage-based matching NOVALINCS-URL-COVERAGE (95.0%).

YODA (Dara and Lin, 2016) submitted one system (93.9%) that uses the machine translation of the French document, and finds the English corresponding document based on bigram and 5-gram matches, assisted by a heuristics based on document length ratio.

UEDIN1 (Buck and Koehn, 2016) submitted one system (89.1%) that uses cosine similarity between tf/idf weighted vectors, extracted by collecting n-grams from the English and machine translated French text. They compare many hyperparameters such as weighting schemes and two pair selection algorithms.

DOCAL (Azpeitia and Etchegoyhen, 2016) submitted one system (88.6%) that used word translation lexicons to compute document similarity scores based on bag-of-word representations. They expand a basic translation lexicon by adding all capitalized tokens, numbers, and longest common prefixes of known vocabulary items.

UEDIN2 (Germann, 2016) submitted 2 systems based on word vector space representations of documents using latent semantic indexing and URL matching, UEDIN LSI (85.8%) and UEDIN LSI (87.6%). In addition to a global cosine similarity score, a local similarity score is computed by re-centering the vector around the mean vector for a webdomain.

Name	Predicted pairs	Pairs after 1-1 rule	Found pairs	Recall %
ADAPT	61 094	61 094	644	26.8
ADAPT-v2	69 518	69 518	651	27.1
BadLuc	681 610	263 133	1 905	79.3
DOCAL	191 993	191 993	2 128	88.6
ILSP-ARC-pv42	291 749	287 860	2 040	84.9
JIS	323 929	28 903	48	2.0
Medved	155 891	155 891	1 907	79.4
NovaLincs-coverage-url	207 022	207 022	2 060	85.8
NovaLincs-coverage	235 763	235 763	2 129	88.6
NovaLincs-url-coverage	235 812	235 812	**2 281**	**95.0**
UA PROMPSIT bitextor 4.1	95 760	95 760	748	31.1
UA PROMPSIT bitextor 5.0	157 682	157 682	2 001	83.3
UEdin1 cosine	368 260	368 260	2 140	89.1
UEdin2 LSI	681 744	271 626	2 062	85.8
UEdin2 LSI-v2	367 948	367 948	2 105	87.6
UFAL-1	592 337	248 344	1 953	81.3
UFAL-2	574 433	178 038	1 901	79.1
UFAL-3	574 434	207 358	1 938	80.7
UFAL-4	1 080 962	268 105	2 023	84.2
YSDA	277 896	277 896	2 021	84.1
YODA	318 568	318 568	2 256	93.9
Baseline	148 537	148 537	1 436	59.8

Table 3: Official Results of the WMT16 Bilingual Document Alignment Shared Task.

Name	Pairs found	Δ	Recall	Δ	Rank	Δ
ADAPT	726	+82	30.2	+3.4	20	0
ADAPT-v2	733	+82	30.5	+3.4	19	0
BadLuc	2 062	+157	85.9	+6.5	13	+3
DOCAL	2 235	+107	93.1	+4.5	4	+1
ILSP-ARC-pv42	2 185	+145	91.0	+6.0	7	+2
JIS	48	0	2.0	0.0	21	0
Medved	1 986	+79	82.7	+3.3	15	0
NovaLincs-coverage-url	2 130	+70	88.7	+2.9	9	−1
NovaLincs-coverage	2 192	+63	91.3	+2.6	6	−2
NovaLincs-url-coverage	2 303	+22	95.9	+0.9	2	−1
UA PROMPSIT bitextor 4.1	775	+27	32.3	+1.1	18	0
UA PROMPSIT bitextor 5.0	2 117	+116	88.1	+4.8	10	+2
UEdin1 cosine	2 227	+87	92.7	+3.6	5	−2
UEdin2 LSI	2 146	+84	89.3	+3.5	8	−1
UEdin2 LSI-v2	2 281	+176	95.0	+7.3	3	+3
UFAL-1	2 060	+107	85.8	+4.5	14	−1
UFAL-2	1 954	+53	81.4	+2.2	17	0
UFAL-3	1 980	+42	82.4	+1.8	16	−2
UFAL-4	2 078	+55	86.5	+2.3	12	−2
YSDA	2 102	+81	87.5	+3.4	11	0
YODA	**2 307**	+51	**96.0**	+2.1	**1**	+1

Table 4: Soft Scoring Results of the WMT16 Bilingual Document Alignment Shared Task, allowing 5% edits between predicted and expected pairing.

ILSP/ARC (Papavassiliou et al., 2016) submitted one system (84.9%), which uses boilerplate removal, and carries out document alignment based on features such as links to documents in the same webdomain, URLs, digits, image filenames and HTML structure. Their paper also describes in detail the open source ILSP Focused Crawler.

YSDA (Shchukin et al., 2016) submitted one system (84.1%) that uses n-gram matches between the machine translation of the French document and the English document. They cluster French and English words into bilingual clusters of up to 90 words, starting with word pairs with high translation probability in both directions, and then adding words that translated well into existing words in a cluster.

UA PROMPSIT (Esplà-Gomis et al., 2016) submitted 2 systems based on Bitextor and describe improvements to the Bitextor toolkit. Their submissions contrast the old version of the tool, UA PROMPSIT BITEXTOR 4.1 (31.1%), with the recent release, UA PROMPSIT BITEXTOR 5.0 (83.3%). Improved document alignment quality is based on various new features: ratio of shared links, similarity of link URLs, ratio of shared images, binary feature indicating if the documents are linked, and similarity of URLs, in addition to the old features bag of words similarity using a translation dictionary and DOM structure similarity.

UFAL (Le et al., 2016) submitted 4 systems, each using a different method. UFAL-1 (81.3%) uses identical word matches by also considering their position in the text. UFAL-2 (79.1%) matches translations of French documents with English documents based on word occurrence probabilities. UFAL-3 (80.7%) adds Levenshtein distance on URLs to this method. UFAL-4 (84.2%) combines UFAL-1 and UFAL-3.

MEDVED (Medved et al., 2016) submitted one system (79.4%), which determines the top 100 keywords based on tf/idf scores for each document and uses word translation dictionaries to match them.

BADLUC (Jakubina and Langlais, 2016) submitted one system (79.3%) that uses the information retrieval tool Apache Lucene to create two indexes, on URLs and text content, and retrieves the most similar documents based on variants of td/idf scores. Both monolingual queries and bilingual queries based on a word translation dictionary are

performed.

ADAPT (Lohar et al., 2016) submitted one system (and a revision) that combines similarity metrics computed on ratio of number of sentences in documents, ratio of number of words in the documents, and matched named entities.

JIS (Mahata et al., 2016) submitted one system (2.0%), which uses text matching based on sentence alignment and word dictionaries. Their paper also described improvements over the original submission.

Acknowledgment

This shared task is partially supported by a Google Faculty Research Award. This work was also supported by the European Union's Horizon 2020 research and innovation programme under grant agreement 645487 (MMT).

References

Antonova, A. and Misyurev, A. (2011). Building a web-based parallel corpus and filtering out machine-translated text. In *Proceedings of the 4th Workshop on Building and Using Comparable Corpora: Comparable Corpora and the Web*, pages 136–144, Portland, Oregon. Association for Computational Linguistics.

Azpeitia, A. and Etchegoyhen, T. (2016). Docal - vicomtech's participation in the wmt16 shared task on bilingual document alignment. In *Proceedings of the First Conference on Machine Translation*.

Bojar, O., Liška, A., and Žabokrtský, Z. (2010). Evaluating utility of data sources in a large parallel Czech-English corpus CzEng 0.9. In *Proceedings of LREC2010*.

Braune, F. and Fraser, A. (2010). Improved unsupervised sentence alignment for symmetrical and asymmetrical parallel corpora. In *Coling 2010: Posters*, pages 81–89, Beijing, China. Coling 2010 Organizing Committee.

Buck, C. and Koehn, P. (2016). Quick and reliable document alignment via tf/idf-weighted cosine distance. In *Proceedings of the First Conference on Machine Translation*.

Callison-Burch, C., Koehn, P., Monz, C., and Schroeder, J. (2009). Findings of the 2009 Workshop on Statistical Machine Translation. In *Proceedings of the Fourth Workshop on Statistical Machine Translation*, pages 1–28,

Athens, Greece. Association for Computational Linguistics.

Dara, A. A. and Lin, Y.-C. (2016). Yoda system for wmt16 shared task: Bilingual document alignment. In *Proceedings of the First Conference on Machine Translation*.

Esplà-Gomis, M. (2009). Bitextor: a free/open-source software to harvest translation memories from multilingual websites. In *MT Summit Workshop on New Tools for Translators*. International Association for Machine Translation.

Esplà-Gomis, M., Forcada, M., Ortiz Rojas, S., and Ferrández-Tordera, J. (2016). Bitextor's participation in wmt'16: shared task on document alignment. In *Proceedings of the First Conference on Machine Translation*.

Germann, U. (2016). Bilingual document alignment with latent semantic indexing. In *Proceedings of the First Conference on Machine Translation*.

Gomes, L. and Pereira Lopes, G. (2016). First steps towards coverage-based document alignment. In *Proceedings of the First Conference on Machine Translation*.

Jakubina, L. and Langlais, P. (2016). Bad luc@wmt 2016: a bilingual document alignment platform based on lucene. In *Proceedings of the First Conference on Machine Translation*.

Joshi, A., Popat, K., Gautam, S., and Bhattacharyya, P. (2013). Making headlines in hindi: Automatic english to hindi news headline translation. In *The Companion Volume of the Proceedings of IJCNLP 2013: System Demonstrations*, pages 21–24, Nagoya, Japan. Asian Federation of Natural Language Processing.

Koehn, P. (2005). Europarl: A parallel corpus for statistical machine translation. In *Proceedings of the Tenth Machine Translation Summit (MT Summit X)*, Phuket, Thailand.

Koehn, P., Hoang, H., Birch, A., Callison-Burch, C., Federico, M., Bertoldi, N., Cowan, B., Shen, W., Moran, C., Zens, R., Dyer, C. J., Bojar, O., Constantin, A., and Herbst, E. (2007). Moses: Open source toolkit for statistical machine translation. In *Proceedings of the 45th Annual Meeting of the Association for Computational Linguistics Companion Volume Proceedings of the Demo and Poster Sessions*,

pages 177–180, Prague, Czech Republic. Association for Computational Linguistics.

Le, T., Vu, H. T., Oberländer, J., and Bojar, O. (2016). Using term position similarity and language modeling for bilingual document alignment. In *Proceedings of the First Conference on Machine Translation*.

Lohar, P., Afli, H., Liu, C.-H., and Way, A. (2016). The adapt bilingual document alignment system at wmt16. In *Proceedings of the First Conference on Machine Translation*.

Ma, X. (2006). Champollion: A robust parallel text sentence aligner. In *International Conference on Language Resources and Evaluation (LREC)*.

Mahata, S., Das, D., and Pal, S. (2016). Wmt2016: A hybrid approach to bilingual document alignment. In *Proceedings of the First Conference on Machine Translation*.

Medved, M., Jakubícek, M., and Kovár, V. (2016). English-french document alignment based on keywords and statistical translation. In *Proceedings of the First Conference on Machine Translation*.

Moore, R. C. (2002). Fast and accurate sentence alignment of bilingual corpora. In Richardson, S. D., editor, *Machine Translation: From Research to Real Users, 5th Conference of the Association for Machine Translation in the Americas, AMTA 2002 Tiburon, CA, USA, October 6-12, 2002, Proceedings*, volume 2499 of *Lecture Notes in Computer Science*. Springer.

Papavassiliou, V., Prokopidis, P., and Piperidis, S. (2016). The ilsp/arc submission to the wmt 2016 bilingual document alignment shared task. In *Proceedings of the First Conference on Machine Translation*.

Papavassiliou, V., Prokopidis, P., and Thurmair, G. (2013). A modular open-source focused crawler for mining monolingual and bilingual corpora from the web. In *Proceedings of the Sixth Workshop on Building and Using Comparable Corpora*, pages 43–51, Sofia, Bulgaria. Association for Computational Linguistics.

Post, M., Callison-Burch, C., and Osborne, M. (2012). Constructing parallel corpora for six indian languages via crowdsourcing. In *Proceedings of the Seventh Workshop on Statistical Machine Translation*, pages 154–162, Montreal, Canada. Association for Computational Linguistics.

Rafalovitch, A. and Dale, R. (2009). United Nations General Assembly resolutions: A six-language parallel corpus. In *Proceedings of the Twelfth Machine Translation Summit (MT Summit XII)*. International Association for Machine Translation.

Rarrick, S., Quirk, C., and Lewis, W. (2011). MT detection in web-scraped parallel corpora. In *Proceedings of the 13th Machine Translation Summit (MT Summit XIII)*, pages 422–430. International Association for Machine Translation.

Resnik, P. (1999). Mining the web for bilingual text. In *Proceedings of the 37th Annual Meeting of the Association of Computational Linguistics (ACL)*.

Resnik, P. and Smith, N. A. (2003). The web as a parallel corpus. *Computational Linguistics*, 29(3):349–380.

Sennrich, R. and Volk, M. (2010). MT-based sentence alignment for OCR-generated parallel texts. In *Proceedings of the Ninth Conference of the Association for Machine Translation in the Americas*.

Shchukin, V., Khristich, D., and Galinskaya, I. (2016). Word clustering approach to bilingual document alignment (wmt 2016 shared task). In *Proceedings of the First Conference on Machine Translation*.

Shi, L., Niu, C., Zhou, M., and Gao, J. (2006). A dom tree alignment model for mining parallel data from the web. In *Proceedings of the 21st International Conference on Computational Linguistics and the 44th annual meeting of the Association for Computational Linguistics*, pages 489–496.

Shi, L. and Zhou, M. (2008). Improved sentence alignment on parallel web pages using a stochastic tree alignment model. In *Proceedings of the 2008 Conference on Empirical Methods in Natural Language Processing*, pages 505–513, Honolulu, Hawaii. Association for Computational Linguistics.

Singh, T. D. (2013). Taste of two different flavours: Which manipuri script works better for english-manipuri language pair smt systems? In *Proceedings of the Seventh Workshop on Syntax, Semantics and Structure in Statistical Translation*, pages 11–18, Atlanta, Georgia. Association for Computational Linguistics.

Skadiņš, R., Tiedemann, J., Rozis, R., and Deksne, D. (2014). Billions of parallel words for free: Building and using the eu bookshop corpus. In *Proceedings of the International Conference on Language Resources and Evaluation (LREC)*.

Smith, J. R., Saint-Amand, H., Plamada, M., Koehn, P., Callison-Burch, C., and Lopez, A. (2013). Dirt cheap web-scale parallel text from the common crawl. In *Proceedings of the 51st Annual Meeting of the Association for Computational Linguistics (Volume 1: Long Papers)*, pages 1374–1383, Sofia, Bulgaria. Association for Computational Linguistics.

Täger, W. (2011). The sentence-aligned european patent corpus. In Forcada, M. L., Depraetere, H., and Vandeghinste, V., editors, *Proceedings of the 15th International Conference of the European Association for Machine Translation (EAMT)*, pages 177–184.

Uszkoreit, J., Ponte, J., Popat, A., and Dubiner, M. (2010). Large scale parallel document mining for machine translation. In *Proceedings of the 23rd International Conference on Computational Linguistics (Coling 2010)*, pages 1101–1109, Beijing, China. Coling 2010 Organizing Committee.

Varga, D., Halaácsy, P., Kornai, A., Nagy, V., Németh, L., and Trón, V. (2005). Parallel corpora for medium density languages. In *Proceedings of the RANLP 2005 Conference*, pages 590–596.

Venugopal, A., Uszkoreit, J., Talbot, D., Och, F., and Ganitkevitch, J. (2011). Watermarking the outputs of structured prediction with an application in statistical machine translation. In *Proceedings of the 2011 Conference on Empirical Methods in Natural Language Processing*, pages 1363–1372, Edinburgh, Scotland, UK. Association for Computational Linguistics.

Ziemski, M., Junczys-Dowmunt, M., and Pouliquen, B. (2015). The united nations parallel corpus v1.0. In *International Conference on Language Resources and Evaluation (LREC)*.

Cross-lingual Pronoun Prediction with Linguistically Informed Features

Rachel Bawden
LIMSI, CNRS, Univ. Paris-Sud, Université Paris-Saclay,
91405 Orsay cedex, France
`rachel.bawden@limsi.fr`

Abstract

We present the LIMSI's cross-lingual pronoun prediction system for the WMT 2016 shared task. We use high-level linguistic features with explicit coreference resolution and expletive detection and rely on dependency annotations and a morphological lexicon. We show that our few, carefully chosen features perform significantly better than several language model baselines and competitively compared to the other systems submitted.

1 Introduction

This paper describes the LIMSI's submission to the cross-lingual pronoun prediction shared task at WMT 2016 (Guillou et al., 2016) for the language direction English to French. The task involves classifying the subject pronouns *it* and *they* into the French pronoun classes *il*, *ils*, *elle*, *elles*, *ce*, *cela*, *on* and *OTHER* (which also includes the null pronoun). Target sentences are human translations, in which pronouns to be predicted are replaced by placeholders. An automatic word alignment is given between English and French sentences. Unlike the same version of the task for DiscoMT 2015 (Hardmeier et al., 2015), target sentences are supplied in lemmatised and part-of-speech (PoS) tagged format, without the original tokens.[1] The official metric for the task is the macro-averaged recall, which has the effect of giving more weight to rarer pronouns. Training data is news and speech-based and the development and test sets are speech transcriptions (Ted Talks).

Our system is based on a statistical feature-based classification approach. It is linguisti-cally motivated with carefully chosen, high-level features designed to tackle particular difficulties of the classification problem, including explicit anaphora resolution using coreference chains and the detection of expletive pronouns.

On top of a set of language model-based features, which form our baseline, we design a set of features to exploit linguistic annotations and resources for: (i) coreference resolution and expletive detection to guide the prediction of the pronoun classes *il*, *ils*, *elle* and *elles*, (ii) local context features based on syntactic dependencies, and (iii) the use of highly discriminative corpus-extracted contexts, in particular for the *OTHER* class.

2 Linguistic challenges of the task

There are a number of difficulties in the translation of the subject pronouns *it* and *they* into French. A major issue is that, in French, pronouns and nouns are marked for grammatical gender (masculine and feminine) and number (singular and plural), whilst in English, *it* and *they* are only marked for number. When French pronouns are anaphoric, (i.e. they refer to an entity that is present in the text or context), their gender and number is almost always determined by their referent.[2] Knowing which pronoun to use therefore relies on knowing to which noun the pronoun refers as well as the gender and number of the noun. Automatic tools exist for anaphora resolution, often also constructing coreference chains to link all mentions that refer to the same entity. PoS tags and morphological lexica can provide information about gender and number. This is of course a simplification,

---

[1] In many cases the morphology of the surrounding local context could supply the correct pronoun. Not a single submission scored higher than the language model baseline according to the official metric, the macro-averaged F-score.

[2] There are some exceptions, such as the singular, gender-neutral *they*. Another example is when the referential expression refers to a group of people, such as *équipe* 'team'. The anaphoric pronoun can be a plural *ils* 'they' rather than singular. Common in English, and although less accepted in French, there exist several examples of this in the task data.

Proceedings of the First Conference on Machine Translation, Volume 2: Shared Task Papers, pages 564–570,
Berlin, Germany, August 11-12, 2016. ©2016 Association for Computational Linguistics

and the situation is in reality much more complex, for example when the referent is two coordinated nouns or when the English pronoun is the *singular*, gender-neutral pronoun *they*. There is also the case of the indefinite pronoun *on*, which is used as a translation of the indefinite English pronoun *one, you*, and sometimes *they*.

An added difficulty is the fact that *it* is sometimes translated as the expletive (or impersonal) *il*, as in *il pleut* '**it** is raining'. These should not be confused with the anaphoric pronouns, and not all automatic coreference tools explicitly detect them. Dependency parsing can be particularly useful for detecting them via individual local features, such as looking at the verb on which the pronoun depends. There are also other possible translations of *it*, namely *ce* and the demonstrative pronoun *cela/ça*, which can sometimes be predicted from the context, but are often difficult to translate.

In the task data, the English pronoun is frequently aligned with a word that does not belong to the 7 main pronoun classes described above, or is simply not translated at all. In these cases, the target pronoun is said to belong to the class *OTHER*, a class that is frequent, heterogeneous and therefore likely to pose problems for prediction.

3   System overview

To resolve these difficulties, we choose to privilege the use of linguistic tools and resources to exploit a small number of linguistically motivated features rather than approach the problem by using a great number of weakly motivated features.

3.1   Tools and resources

We used various annotations for both English source sentences and French target sentences: PoS tagging and dependency parsing for both languages, coreference resolution for English and morphological analysis for French. English annotations were all produced using the Stanford Core-NLP toolkit (Manning et al., 2014). Standard, pre-trained parsing models could not be used on the lemma-based French sentences, and we therefore re-trained a parsing model solely based on lemmas and PoS-tags, using the Mate Graph-based transition parser (Bohnet and Nivre, 2012) and the French training data for the 2014 SPMRL shared task (Seddah et al., 2014). Some pre-processing was necessary to create a compatible tagset be-

tween the SPMRL data and the task training data.[3] We enriched the French annotations using a morphological and syntactic lexicon, the Le*fff* (Sagot, 2010), to include noun gender by mapping lemmas to their genders (allowing for ambiguity). We also used the lexicon to provide information about impersonal verbs and adjectives (Sec. 3.2.2).

3.2   Linguistic features

We use as our main baseline a set of language model features (Sec. 3.2.1), which also form the starting point of our system. We add to this three types of features: coreference resolution and expletive detection (Sec. 3.2.2), local, syntax-based features (Sec. 3.2.3) and a syntactic context template feature (Sec. 3.2.4).

3.2.1   Language model features

Using a language model provides a way of modelling local context using the words immediately surrounding the pronoun. In our case, it provides no information concerning number, since the French target sentences are lemmatised, and the feminine gender is also unlikely to be well predicted by the model in the case of anaphoric pronouns unless the referent is in a very local context.

We base our language model features on the pronoun class probabilities provided by the task organisers as part of the official language model baseline. These features are based on the probability of the most probable pronoun class as per the language model: (i) the most probable class, (ii-iv) the most probable class if its probability is superior to 90%, 80%, 50%, and (v) the concatenation of the two most probable classes.

3.2.2   Coreference features

We use two features to represent anaphora resolution, namely the gender (masculine, feminine or impersonal) and number (singular, plural or impersonal) of the pronoun's referent.

Standard anaphora resolution: To identify the referent of an anaphoric pronoun, we applied the Stanford coreference resolver (de Marneffe et al., 2015) to the English sentences, separated by document, and used the automatic alignments to identify the corresponding referent in French (see Figure 1). Gender is determined by that of the French referent (as provided by the Le*fff*). Since French

---

[3] We analysed the quality of the syntactic annotations, using the SPMRL test set and scorer, to give an unlabelled attachment score of 89.83%.

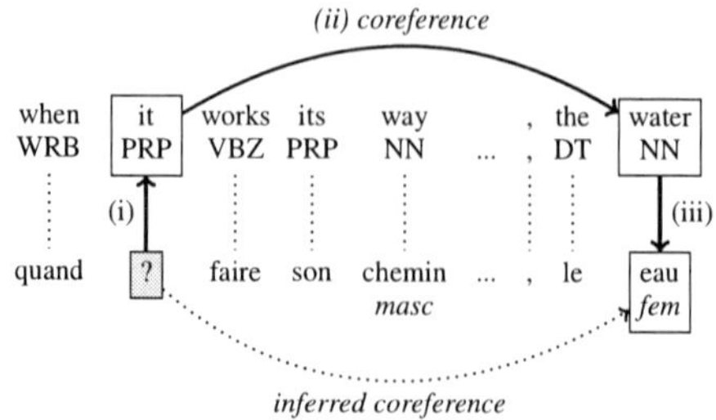

Figure 1: Use of coreference chains to determine gender and number of anaphoric pronouns.

sentences are lemmatised, number must be sought in the English sentence. We test two variants, in which number is determined by (i) the number of the English referent (which is integrated in the PoS tagset), as shown in Figure 1, and (ii) the number of the aligned English pronoun: singular for *it* and plural for *they*. Coreference chains can cross sentence boundaries, and mentions can span several words, in which case we took information associated with the mention's head.

The accuracy of our coreference features depends on the ability of the coreference tool to detect accurate and complete chains, the quality of the automatic alignments, the accuracy of the PoS tags to predict number and the coverage of the lexicon for French noun gender.

We evaluate the quality of the coreference tool on the development set by manually annotating the French pronouns and comparing the predicted and gold referents. Of 237 pronouns of the form *il*, *elle*, *ils* or *elles*, 194 were anaphoric with a textual referent. The correct coreferent was provided in only 52.6% of cases, the majority being for the masculine plural class *ils*. Moreover, 32% of these pronouns were linked only to other pronouns, therefore with no explicit referent (in particular for the feminine plural *elles*). The tool also often fails to predict impersonal pronouns, erroneously supplying coreference chains for 18 impersonal pronouns out of 25.

Back-off anaphora resolution: Given these insufficiencies of the coreference tool, we developed a back-off coreference method, in cases where it provides no gender and number. It consists of providing additional values for the two coreferences features by taking the nearest preceding noun phrase in the previous sentence as the pronoun's referent. Although likely to add a certain amount of noise, especially in cases where the pronoun is non-anaphoric, this method provides more data values.

Expletive pronoun detection: One case of non-anaphoric pronoun detection that can be dealt with directly is the case of the French impersonal pronoun *il*. We apply heuristic rules[4] to detect such impersonals on the French side, modifying the coreference feature values to *impersonal* when one is detected. We consider a pronoun to be an impersonal *il* when it is in an impersonal construction (containing an impersonal verb or adjective), information provided by a look-up in the Le*fff*. Certain cases of non-ambiguous impersonals such as *il **faut** le faire* 'it must be done' are easily dealt with. Ambiguous cases, where the adjective or verb can be used both personally and impersonally, can be disambiguated by the context, for example by the presence of a following *de* 'to' for verbs and adjectives or *que* 'that' for verbs.[5]

3.2.3 Local features

For the other pronouns, *ce*, *cela*, *on* and *OTHER*, the local context plays a crucial role. We include a number of local, syntax-guided context features, based on the syntactic governor, as provided by the dependency parse. The features include the form of the English aligned token (raw and lowercased), the form, PoS tag and lemma of the syntactic governor of the English aligned token and the PoS tag and lemma of the syntactic governor of the French pronoun. Finally, we include a boolean feature indicating whether or not the pronoun is found at the beginning of the sentence.

3.2.4 Context template feature

We also look at the target pronoun's wider and richer context, using relative and syntactic positions, to produce a single, strong feature, whose value is the class (if any) to which the pronoun's context indicates that it is particularly likely to be associated. In a preliminary step, we extracted all context templates from the training and development sets defined by storing the lemmas and PoS tags of the words at the following positions: (i) 2 following, (ii) 1 preceding and 2 following, (iii) 1

---

[4]Tools do exist for impersonal detection, however they are designed to process tokens and not lemmas.

[5]For example, *il est intéressant.* 'it/he is interesting' vs. *il est intéressant de...* 'it is interesting to...'

Position Relative to the pronoun					class	Num.	%
-1	+1	+2	+3	gov.			
	un	NOM			OTHER	1503	99
VER				NOM_{det}	OTHER	1003	97
la/le				VER_{subj}	on	478	96
,	être	ADJ	que		il	4131	98
PUN	être	ADJ	de		il	5239	95

Table 1: Examples of context templates with their associated class. We also give the percentage of occurrences of the template with the associated class and their frequency of co-occurrence.

preceding and 3 following, (iv) the governor, (v) the governor and the function, (vi) the governor and its governor, and (vii) the preceding token and the governor and its function.

See Table 1 for some examples of context template values, linked with a certain class, for which they are particularly well associated. This is indicated by the high frequency of occurrence of the <template, class> pair and the high percentage of occurrences of the template with the class, as observed in the training and development sets.

Relevance score used: Our aim was to select the pairs that were the most discriminative for the corresponding class and which were most frequent, in order to create an aggregated, reliable feature. We therefore ranked the pairs according to the following heuristic relevance score based on frequency counts in the corpora (Equation 1).

$$score(<\!c,y\!>) = \frac{occ(<\!c,y\!>)}{\sum\limits_{y' \in Y} occ(<\!c,y'\!>)} \sqrt{occ(<\!c,y\!>)} \quad (1)$$

where c is a given context, y a given class and Y is the set of possible classes.

The score is designed to be a reasonable compromise between the probability of the context being associated with the given class and their frequency of co-occurrence.[6] We select the 10,000 top-ranked pairs and further filter to only keep pairs where the context is associated with the class more than 95% of the time.[7] When the pronoun to be predicted is found within the context of one of

these templates, the feature value is the class associated with the context. A total of 5,003 templates were retained: 2,658 for *OTHER*, 1,987 for *il*, 347 for *ce*, 9 for *on* and 2 for *cela*.

The templates are particularly useful for detecting the *OTHER* class, which include empty instances (where the English pronoun is untranslated) and words other than the 7 target pronoun classes. For example, if followed by the determiner *un* and a noun, there is a strong association with the *OTHER* class (first example in Table 1). They can be especially useful in cases of alignment problems or anomalous predictions, and also for detecting certain collocations.

3.3 Classification setup

We use a random forest classifier, as implemented in Scikit-learn (Pedregosa et al., 2011). Our choice of machine learning algorithm is partly based on the ability of random forests to account for class imbalance and outliers, a necessary trait in the case of this task.[8] They also have the advantage of not being linear, and therefore of being able to find patterns in the data using a relatively small number of features, as is our aim here.[9] We split the task into separate classifiers for *it* and *they*; a preliminary comparative study suggested that this produces slightly better results than training a single classifier for all source pronouns.

4 Results

We provide the results of several variants of our system, in order to analyse the different components. We report scores for the two official baselines *baseline*$_{WMT-1}$ and *baseline*$_{WMT-2}$. We also provide two extra baselines: *baseline*$_{mostFreqPro}$, which predicts the most frequent class for each English pronoun (masc. sg. *il* for *it* and masc. pl. *ils* for *they*) and a second, *baseline*$_{LM}$, which uses as features the form of the English pronoun (*it* or *they*) and the language model features described in Sec. 3.2.1. All scores are produced using the official evaluation script and are reported "as is" using two significant decimal figures.

A minor implementation issue was found concerning the use of the context templates for the two submissions. We nevertheless include the results

---

[6]Although not normalised, the score, which is greater for a more relevant pair, has the advantage of being constant for a given probability and frequency count, and is therefore not dependent on the rarity of either the class or the context, unlike similar measures such as the log-likelihood ratio.

[7]We tested several values in preliminary experiments on the development set and found these values to be a good compromise between score optimisation and training time.

[8]Please refer to the Shared Task overview paper for the class distributions.

[9]We use Gini as the optimising criterion, 250 estimators, a maximum depth of 500 and a minimum number of leaf samples of 1. All other parameters are those provided by default.

System	Macro-avg. Recall (%)		Acc. (%)
	Dev	Test	Test
baseline$_{WMT-1}$	40.63	46.98	52.01
baseline$_{WMT-2}$	-	50.85	53.35
baseline$_{mostFreqPro}$	24.03	24.39	34.58
baseline$_{LM}$	48.63	55.21	65.95
*LIMSI$_1$	56.14	59.32	68.36
*LIMSI$_2$	55.08	59.34	68.36
LIMSI$_1$	55.65	60.94	69.44
LIMSI$_2$	54.82	59.37	68.36
LIMSI$_{1,NoLM}$	51.66	54.35	62.73
LIMSI$_{2,NoLM}$	50.87	54.94	63.54
LIMSI$_{1,SimpleCR}$	55.45	61.26	71.05
LIMSI$_{2,SimpleCR}$	**56.16**	60.58	70.51

Table 2: Comparative results of baseline systems, the LIMSI submissions and several variants.

of these two systems (marked with an asterisk), whose results do not however differ wildly from those of the corrected versions. The two different versions (labelled 1 and 2) correspond to the two different methods of providing the number value of the coreference features (see Sec. 3.2.2): the first method taking the number of the last referent identified by the coreference tool, and the second from the form of the aligned English pronoun.

We provide two additional variants for each version. *NoLM* variants do not use language model features, whereas *SimpleCR* variants only rely on the Stanford tool for coreference resolution, excluding our back-off method (see Sec. 3.2.2).

5 Discussion

The evaluation metric for the task (macro-averaged recall) is such that very sparse classes hold a huge weight in the final evaluation.[10] There are also vast differences in classification quality between the datasets, as illustrated by the systematic percentage point increase in score (up to 6 points) between the development and the test set. This highlights the fact that the heterogeneity of data should be taken into account when designing a system, and supports the idea of features based on external (and therefore static) linguistic resources rather than relying too much on the data itself. The result is that our best performing system during development is not always our best performing on the test set (see the results of LIMSI$_{1,SimpleCR}$ vs. LIMSI$_{2,SimpleCR}$).

---

[10]Correctly predicting a single extra *on* improves the overall score by more than 1%.

There is no significant difference between the two variants of the LIMSI system. However the first variant performs better on both development and test sets more often than the second.

Compared to the four baselines, the linguistically rich systems perform systematically better. The much lower scores of *baseline$_{LM}$* compared to *LIMSI$_1$* and *LIMSI$_2$* show that adding our linguistic features provides extra and different information from the language model features. A slightly disconcerting observation is that if we remove the language model features (*LIMSI$_{1,NoLM}$* and *LIMSI$_{2,NoLM}$*), the score compared to *baseline$_{LM}$* is up to 3 percentage points higher on the development set, but lower on the test set, suggesting that the information needed to predict the pronouns in the test set was probably mostly local, requiring less linguistic knowledge, another effect of the different natures of the sets and their small sizes.

The experiments with simple coreference give comparable scores on the development set and higher scores on the test set (up to 61.26% macro-averaged recall for *LIMSI$_{1,SimpleCR}$*). It is difficult to draw any conclusions about which method of gender and number induction is best, although our back-off method appears to be too noisy.

5.1 Finer analysis

The classification matrix for the results on the test set for LIMSI$_{2,SimpleCR}$ (the best performing model on the development set) is shown in Table 3. Unsurprisingly, the most problematic classes are *elle* and *elles*, for which the only means of correctly predicting the gender is to have access to the pronoun's textual referent and its gender. Although a majority of the feminine pronouns were classified as having the correct number, only 3 out of 25 occurrences of *elles* were assigned the correct class. The other two classes for which the system performed less well were *cela* (often confused with *il*) and *on* (confused with *ils* and *OTHER*). These were all the least frequent pronoun classes, which therefore have a large impact on the overall score because of the macro-averaged metric. The classes which were best predicted were *ce*, with a high precision of 91.53%, *OTHER* with a high recall of 88.24% and *ils* with a recall of 78.87%.

5.2 Oracle coreference resolver

One of the weaknesses of the system is, as expected, the prediction of the gender of the French pronoun, which is dependent on the quality of an

			Classified as									
	ce	elle	elles	il	ils	cela	on	other	SUM	P (%)	R (%)	F (%)
ce	**54**	1	0	11	0	0	0	2	68	91.53	79.41	85.04
elle	0	**13**	1	6	0	2	0	1	23	41.94	56.52	48.15
elles	1	2	**3**	1	13	1	0	4	25	23.08	12.00	15.79
il	2	7	0	**44**	1	2	1	4	61	61.97	72.13	66.67
ils	0	1	9	0	**56**	0	0	5	71	75.68	78.87	77.24
cela	0	5	0	7	0	**13**	1	5	31	72.22	41.94	53.06
on	0	0	0	0	2	0	**5**	2	9	55.56	55.56	55.56
OTHER	2	2	0	2	2	0	2	**75**	85	76.53	88.24	81.97
SUM	59	31	13	71	74	18	9	98				
Micro-averaged										70.51	70.51	70.51
Macro-averaged										62.31	**60.58**	60.43

Table 3: A decomposition of results for the system $\text{LIMSI}_{2,\text{SimpleCR}}$ on the test set.

external coreference tool. In order to assess the performance of our system independently of this specific tool, we imagine a scenario in which we have access to perfect impersonal detection and coreference resolution and can therefore correctly predict all instances of *il*, *ils*, *elle* and *elles*. This gives perfect recall for these four pronouns and enables us to assess the capacity of the system's other features to distinguish between the remaining pronouns, had coreference resolution been perfect.

We first automatically detect the impersonal pronoun *il* using the dedicated tool *ilimp* (Danlos, 2005). Since the tokenised French sentences were available for the French-to-English version of the same task, we directly applied the tool to raw training and development sentences. For the remaining personal pronouns, we take gender and number directly from the gold label, as if a coreference system had correctly predicted them.

The results (for the development set) when using oracle coreference resolution, with a macro-averaged recall of 85.31%, show that if the anaphoric pronouns are predicted with 100% precision and recall, there are still lacunas in the system, notably for the label *on*, for which the precision is 57.14% and the recall only 40%, due to 6 out of 10 occurrences being classified as *OTHER*. The other class with a low recall (although a high precision of 97.14%) is *cela*, for which 25 out of 63 occurrences were incorrectly classified as *OTHER*. This suggest that there is a positive bias towards the *OTHER* class, which is the third most frequent. We speculate that the overprediction of this class could be due to the context template feature, which was geared to predict the *OTHER* class. Having such a statistically strong feature, with contexts highly related to a certain class does not allow for exceptions to the rule.

This shows that there is room for improvement for the other pronouns, even with perfect coreference resolution. To improve the use of context templates, there are two options. Firstly, the thresholds for the inclusion of templates could be revised; they could either be increased to reinforce the feature's strength, or decreased to allow for more noise, enabling other features to counterbalance it in some cases. Secondly, more well-designed features that allow for a greater decomposition of decisions could be used, rather than relying on a single feature that does not allow any deviation from the rule.

6   Conclusion

We have presented a linguistic, feature-based pronoun prediction system, using explicit anaphora resolution and expletive detection. We have explored the use of dependencies for local context features and discriminative context templates to target particular difficulties of the task. Our results are well above the baseline, and our system was ranked sixth out of nine submissions. We see two possible improvements for the system, either relying on a more sophisticated, better performing language model (such as LSTMs), or, more interestingly, improving our linguistic features and the resources and tools that they are based on.

The approach is generalisable to other language pairs, provided that similar tools and resources are available for those languages. The features would have to be adjusted to take into account the different pronoun mappings of the two languages. For example, for the reverse direction, French to English, named entities and animacy features are crucial for mapping the French pronouns *il/elle* to *s/he* for gender-specific beings such as people and to *it* for objects.

References

Bernd Bohnet and Joakim Nivre. 2012. A Transition-Based System for Joint Part-of-Speech Tagging and Labeled Non-Projective Dependency Parsing. In *Proceedings of the 2012 Joint Conference on Empirical Methods in Natural Language Processing and Computational Natural Language Learning (EMNLP-CoNLL '12)*, pages 1455–1465, Jeju Island, Korea.

Laurence Danlos. 2005. Automatic recognition of French expletive pronoun occurrences. In *Proceedings of the 2nd International Joint Conference on Natural Language Processing (IJCNLP '05)*, pages 73–78, Jeju Island, Korea.

Marie-Catherine de Marneffe, Marta Recasens, and Christopher Potts. 2015. Modeling the Lifespan of Discourse Entities with Application to Coreference Resolution. *Journal of Artificial Intelligence Research*, 52:445–475.

Liane Guillou, Christian Hardmeier, Preslav Nakov, Sara Stymne, Jörg Tiedemann, Yannick Versley, Mauro Cettolo, Bonnie Webber, and Andrei Popescu-Belis. 2016. Findings of the 2016 WMT shared task on cross-lingual pronoun prediction. In *Proceedings of the 1st Conference on Machine Translation (WMT '16)*, Berlin, Germany.

Christian Hardmeier, Preslav Nakov, Sara Stymne, Jörg Tiedemann, Yannick Versley, and Mauro Cettolo. 2015. Pronoun-focused MT and cross-lingual pronoun prediction: Findings of the 2015 DiscoMT shared task on pronoun translation. In *Proceedings of the 2nd Workshop on Discourse in Machine Translation (DiscoMT '15)*, pages 1–16, Lisbon, Portugal. Association for Computational Linguistics.

Christopher D. Manning, Mihai Surdeanu, John Bauer, Jenny Finkel, Steven J. Bethard, and David McClosky. 2014. The Stanford CoreNLP Natural Language Processing Toolkit. In *Proceedings of the 52nd Annual Meeting of the Association for Computational Linguistics (ACL '14)*, pages 55–60, Baltimore, Maryland, USA.

Fabian Pedregosa, Gaël Varoquaux, Alexandre Gramfort, Vincent Michel, Bertrand Thirion, Olivier Grisel, Mathieu Blondel, Peter Prettenhofer, Ron Weiss, Vincent Dubourg, Jake Vanderplas, Alexandre Passos, David Cournapeau, Matthieu Brucher, Matthieu Perrot, and Édouard Duchesnay. 2011. Scikit-learn: Machine Learning in Python. *Journal of Machine Learning Research*, 12:2825–2830.

Benoît Sagot. 2010. The Le*fff*, a Freely Available and Large-coverage Morphological and Syntactic Lexicon for French. In *Proceedings of the 7th International Conference on Language Resources and Evaluation (LREC '10)*, pages 2744–2751, Valletta, Malta.

Djamé Seddah, Sandra Kübler, and Reut Tsarfaty. 2014. Introducing the SPMRL 2014 shared task on parsing morphologically-rich languages. In *Proceedings of the 1st Joint Workshop on Statistical Parsing of Morphologically Rich Languages and Syntactic Analysis of Non-Canonical Languages (SPMRL-SANCL '14)*, pages 103–109, Dublin, Ireland.

The Kyoto University Cross-Lingual Pronoun Translation System

Raj Dabre
Graduate School of Informatics
Kyoto University, Japan
`prajdabre@gmail.com`

Yevgeniy Puzikov
Graduate School of Informatics
Kyoto University, Japan
`puzikov@nlp.ist.i.kyoto-u.ac.jp`

Fabien Cromieres
JST, Japan
Kyoto University
`fabien@nlp.ist.i.kyoto-u.ac.jp`

Sadao Kurohashi
Graduate School of Informatics
Kyoto University, Japan
`kuro@i.kyoto-u.ac.jp`

Abstract

In this paper we describe our system we designed and implemented for the cross-lingual pronoun prediction task as a part of WMT 2016. The majority of the paper will be dedicated to the system whose outputs we submitted wherein we describe the simplified mathematical model, the details of the components and the working by means of an architecture diagram which also serves as a flowchart. We then discuss the results of the official scores and our observations on the same.

1 Introduction

The cross-lingual pronoun prediction task in WMT 2016 is a lot more challenging than its 2015 counterpart (Hardmeier et al., 2015) since one cannot rely on solely the target side sentence due to loss of grammatical gender, number and person which is a consequence of lemmatization. As such looking at the source side sentence is quite essential. Since Deep Neural Networks (NN) are becoming increasingly popular and being shown to be extremely effective when it comes to many NLP tasks we decided to go for a full NN approach to see how far it can go. We refer to the shared task overview paper (Guillou et al., 2016) for details of the task and the various other submitted systems.

2 Our System

Here we describe in detail our system and give brief overviews of its variants.

2.1 Motivation

As mentioned earlier, we chose a purely neural network approach since many recent works have shown that NNs are extremely effective when it comes to NLP tasks and can produce results that are able to beat the state of art systems by a reasonable margin. (Mikolov et al., 2010) showed that the word embeddings obtained using a simple feed-forward neural network give better results for word similarity tasks compared to those given by the embeddings obtained using GLOVE(Pennington et al., 2014). Furthermore, (Devlin et al., 2014) have shown that using a Neural Network based Lexical Translation Model can help boost the quality of Statistical Machine Translation. (Bahdanau et al., 2014) showed that it is possible to perform end to end MT whose quality surpasses that of Moses(Koehn et al., 2007) by using a combination of Recurrent Neural Networks (RNNs) and dictionary based unknown word substitution.

In particular we wanted to test the capabilities of Recurrent Neural Networks augmented with an Attention Based Mechanism for this task. They are easy to design, implement and test due to the availability of NN frameworks like Chainer[1], Torch[2], Tensorflow[3] etc. Since Chainer provides a lot of useful functionality and enables rapid prototyping we decided to use it to implement our system.

2.2 System Description

Refer to Figure-1 for a simple overview of our pronoun translation system which we describe in detail below.

Consider that the input sentence (IN) is : *Cabin restaurants , as they 're known in the trade , are venues for forced prostitution .*, the lemmatized output sentence (OUT) is : *le " restaurant cabane " , comme REPLACE_PRON la appeler dans ce commerce , être du lieu de prostitution forcé .* and the pronoun to be predicted in place of RE-PLACE_PRON is *on*. The following must be no-

---

1. http ://docs.chainer.org
2. https ://github.com/torch/distro
3. http ://tensorflow.org

571

Proceedings of the First Conference on Machine Translation, Volume 2: Shared Task Papers, pages 571–575,
Berlin, Germany, August 11-12, 2016. ©2016 Association for Computational Linguistics

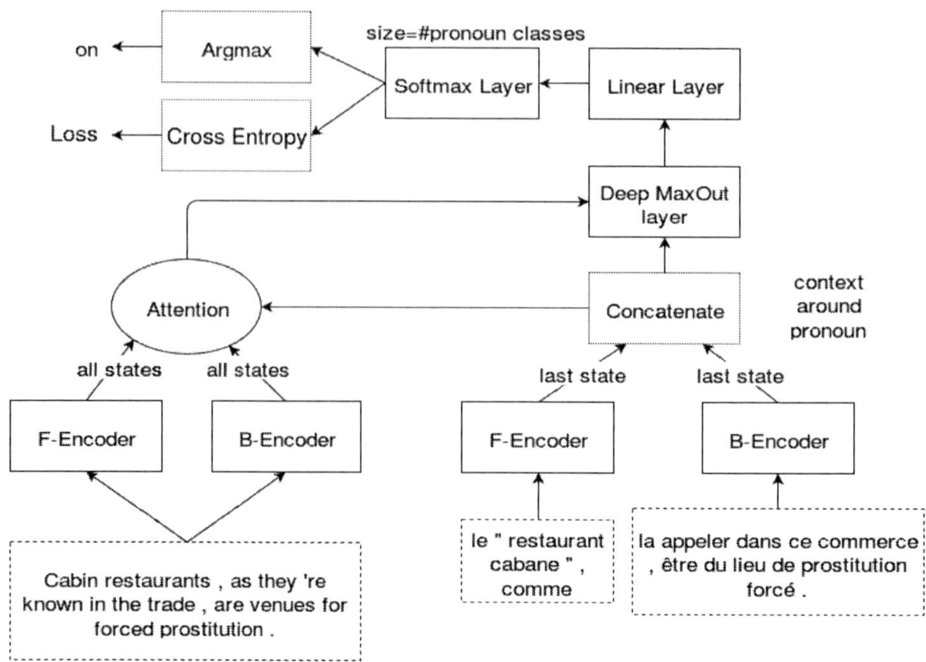

FIGURE 1 – The RNN Pronoun Translation System

ted :

— In the target sentence, *le " restaurant cabane " , comme* and *la appeler dans ce commerce , être du lieu de prostitution forcé .* represent the context before (left) and after (right) the pronoun respectively.

— In case the contexts contain other pronouns to be predicted then they are simply represented by a token called "PRON_PLACEHOLDER".

— If either of the contexts are empty (the pronoun is the first word of the sentence) we use a padding like "UNK" or "#".

— The memory cells used in the RNN encoders are GRUs and we do not consider stacked RNNs.

— The prefixes F and B represent forward (left to right) and backward (right to left) respectively and indicate the direction of the RNN encoding of the sentence. The encoders used for the source and target languages are separate.

— The size of the output of the Softmax layer is equal to the number of the pronoun classes in the target language.

— Unless mentioned otherwise, all the Neural network layers like Attention, Softmax, Linear and Deep Maxout are the same as the ones mentioned in (Bahdanau et al., 2014).

To predict the pronoun given the input sentence (IN) and the target side contexts (OUT-Left and OUT-Right) we perform the following steps :

1. FWD_ENC_SRC=F-Encoder(IN) and BWD_ENC_SRC=B-Encoder(IN). These are 2 sequences of RNN states with a forward and backward representation for each word.

2. FWD_ENC_TGT=Last(F-Encoder(OUT-Left)) and BWD_ENC_TGT=Last(B-Encoder(OUT-Right)). TGT_CONTEXT=Concatenate(FWD_ENC_TGT, BWD_ENC_TGT). We select the last states which represent left and right context. As mentioned before, the encoders for the source and target languages are separate and do not share parameters.

3. SRC_ATTENTION=Attention(FWD_ENC_SRC, BWD_ENC_SRC). This gives an attention vector which is a weighted average of the forward and backward RNN state sequences.

4. LOGITS=Linear(Maxout(SRC_ATTENTION, TGT_CONTEXT)).

These give the logits which represent the weights for each pronoun class.

5. LOSS=Softmax-Cross-Entropy(LOGITS) and PREDICTION=Argmax(LOGITS). The criterion for the prediction loss (on which backpropagation is done) is the Softmax Cross Entropy. The pronoun class which receives the maximum weight is output as the predicted class.

Apart from this, we do not do any post-editing of any sort. Thus the NN model tries to learn the following probability distribution :

$$P_\theta(REPLACE\_PRON|IN, OUT)$$

The optimization objective is simply to maximize the following likelihood function :

$$L_\theta = \prod_{\forall (PR,IN,OUT)\in T} P_\theta(PR|IN, OUT)$$

Where *PR* is the same as REPLACE_PRON, the pronoun to be predicted and T is the training set collecting all input, output and the label to be predicted. Note that OUT is decomposed as (OUT-Left,OUT-right).

2.3 Training and Testing

We only used the IWSLT corpus for each language pair for training and the corresponding TEDdev corpus as the development set. We refer to the shared task overview paper for the corpora details. We simply process the corpora to convert it into the format (as in figure-1) which our system accepts. No other kind of preprocessing or annotation in terms of anaphora resolution is performed. No external/extra corpus was used. Our objective was to see how far a pure Neural Network system could go. We use the following neural network parameters/vector dimensions.

— Vocabulary size : 600000 (which is enough to cover all words in the training data and more than 99.5% of the words in the development and test set)
— Source and target words embedding size : 100
— Source and target GRU cell output size : 200
— Attention Module Hidden layer size : 200
— Maxout output size : 150
— Minibatch size : 80 (80 pronouns predicted per batch)
— Weight decay : 0.000001 (for regularization)

— Optimization algorithm : ADAM (Kingma and Ba, 2014)

Additionally we tried with embedding and other layer sizes 5 times the above but they had very little effect. Moreover, the reduced dimensionality gave smaller models and allowed for faster training. As an early stopping criterion we evaluate our model every 50 iterations (4000 predictions) on the development set and save it only if its performance on the development set improves over the previous evaluation. We give the results of the evaluation of the test set pronoun translations for the various languages in the following section.

2.4 Results and Discussion

Refer to Table-1 for the official scores for all language pairs. The official score is the Macro Averaged R score. In general our system secured 2nd rank in 3 out of 4 language pairs with respect to R-score and 1st rank in 2/4 language pairs with respect to the Accuracy. Based on our preliminary evaluations our system performs well on the non-rare classes. Based on the confusion matrices obtained on the results, we noted that pronoun classes that rarely occurred in the training corpus (and equivalently in the development and text corpus) had very low classification accuracy and hence contributed to reduced R-scores. Another interesting observation is that although our accuracies were high, the R-score was not which is a further indicator that our system simply does not learn to classify the rare pronouns accurately.

If one takes a look at the language pairs then it is interesting to note that when German is the target language our system has the worst performance but is almost on par with the best system when it is the source language. We believe that since we use both the input and output sentences for the pronoun prediction and that German is a morphologically rich language our system is able to leverage the morphological richness through the attention mechanism. It is also evident that only using the target side sentence to predict the pronoun (like the baseline system does) will not be very helpful since the pronoun depends on information such as gender, number and person information (which is removed as a result of lemmatization) of the word that it refers to.

As a side note we would like to point out that we evaluated our system every 50 iterations and recorded the scores at each stage. In case of German-

Language Pair	R-score	Accuracy	Rank	Difference wrt Best System
German-English	73.17%	80.33%	2/6	-0.74%
English-German	52.50%	71.28%	2/9	-11.91%
French-English	65.63%	82.93%	2/5	-7.4%
English-French	62.44%	70.51%	3/9	-3.26%

TABLE 1 – The R-Scores and Accuracies on the test sets for all language pairs

English we observed that we had overfitted on the development set and during a previous iteration the R-score on the test set was 58.37%. This clearly indicates that if the development set is different from the test set then overfitting can have undesirable consequences. One way of avoiding overfitting is reducing the size of the NN (in terms of the sizes of layers and embeddings) which cannot be really verified in our case since it needs a grid search on all possible NN sizes which in turn needs a lot of time and/or a large number of GPUs which we lacked. However, as we have mentioned before, a five-fold reduction in parameter space did not hurt the performance and hence it would be interesting to find out the smallest model (in terms of number of parameters) that can still have high performance.

3 Conclusion

We have reported our Recurrent Neural Network based pronoun classification (or translation) system in sufficient detail along with the official scores. Overall we have secured second place in the competition inspite of a simple RNN system which uses a very small amount of data (IWSLT only) for training without any additional pre/post processing involving coreference resolution. In the future, we would like to work on leveraging larger corpora and coreference resolution so as to address the rare pronoun classes. We would also like to conduct a proper grid search so as to determine the best embedding and layer sizes. Finally we would like to investigate into ensemble systems where we train a bunch of RNN systems for the same language pair and then use a simple scheme like max-voting to overcome the problem of models that have overfitted on the development set and those that may have inferior performance possibly due to reasons such as model initialization.

Acknowledgments

The first two authors would like to thank MEXT (Japan Government) for the scholarship they receive. We would also like to thank John Richardson for a number of tips with respect to the neural network parameters we chose for our system. We also thank the organizers and the reviewers for their efforts and helpful reviews.

References

Dzmitry Bahdanau, Kyunghyun Cho, and Yoshua Bengio. 2014. Neural machine translation by jointly learning to align and translate. *CoRR*, abs/1409.0473.

Jacob Devlin, Rabih Zbib, Zhongqiang Huang, Thomas Lamar, Richard Schwartz, and John Makhoul. 2014. Fast and robust neural network joint models for statistical machine translation. In *Proceedings of the 52nd Annual Meeting of the Association for Computational Linguistics (Volume 1 : Long Papers)*, pages 1370–1380, Baltimore, Maryland, June. Association for Computational Linguistics.

Liane Guillou, Christian Hardmeier, Preslav Nakov, Sara Stymne, Jörg Tiedemann, Yannick Versley, Mauro Cettolo, Bonnie Webber, and Andrei Popescu-Belis. 2016. Findings of the 2016 WMT shared task on cross-lingual pronoun prediction. In *Proceedings of the First Conference on Machine Translation (WMT16)*, Berlin, Germany. Association for Computational Linguistics.

Christian Hardmeier, Preslav Nakov, Sara Stymne, Jörg Tiedemann, Yannick Versley, and Mauro Cettolo. 2015. Pronoun-focused mt and cross-lingual pronoun prediction : Findings of the 2015 discomt shared task on pronoun translation. In *Proceedings of the Second Workshop on Discourse in Machine Translation*, pages 1–16, Lisbon, Portugal, September. Association for Computational Linguistics.

Diederik Kingma and Jimmy Ba. 2014. Adam : A method for stochastic optimization. *arXiv preprint arXiv :1412.6980*.

Philipp Koehn, Hieu Hoang, Alexandra Birch, Chris Callison-Burch, Marcello Federico, Nicola Bertoldi, Brooke Cowan, Wade Shen, Christine Moran, Richard Zens, et al. 2007. Moses : Open source toolkit for statistical machine translation. In *Proceedings of the 45th annual meeting of the ACL on interactive poster and demonstration sessions*, pages 177–180. Association for Computational Linguistics.

Tomas Mikolov, Martin Karafiát, Lukás Burget, Jan Cernocký, and Sanjeev Khudanpur. 2010. Recurrent neural network based language model. In *INTERSPEECH 2010, 11th Annual Conference of the International Speech Communication Association*, pages 1045–1048.

Jeffrey Pennington, Richard Socher, and Christopher D. Manning. 2014. Glove : Global vectors for word representation. In *Empirical Methods in Natural Language Processing (EMNLP)*, pages 1532–1543.

Pronoun Prediction with Latent Anaphora Resolution

Christian Hardmeier
Uppsala University
Department of Linguistics and Philology
Box 635, 751 26 Uppsala, Sweden
`christian.hardmeier@lingfil.uu.se`

Abstract

This paper describes the UU-Hardmeier submissions to the WMT 2016 shared task on cross-lingual pronoun prediction. Our model is a system combination of two different approaches, one based on a neural network with latent anaphora resolution and the other one on an n-gram model with an additional dependency on the source pronoun. The combination of the two models results in an improvement over each individual system, but it appears that the contribution of the neural network is more likely due to its context modelling capacities than to the anaphora resolution subnetwork.

1 Introduction

The primary submission of the UU-Hardmeier system to the pronoun prediction shared task at WMT 2016 (Guillou et al., 2016) consists of two components. The first is a reimplementation of the pronoun prediction neural network proposed by Hardmeier et al. (2013). The other system component is based on a standard n-gram language model over the lemmas of the target side. Apart from implementation details, the main difference between this model and the official baseline provided by the shared task organisers is the integration of information about the pronoun found on the source side, which allows the model to recognise whether a given pronoun was singular or plural in the source.

2 Neural Network Component

The first component of our model is a modified reimplementation of the pronoun prediction network introduced by Hardmeier et al. (2013). The main differences between the model used in this work and the previous implementation are the following:

- A complete reimplementation of the neural network code based on Theano (The Theano Development Team, 2016) and Keras (Chollet, 2016).

- Substitution of the coreference preprocessing component by CORT (Martschat and Strube, 2015).

- Inclusion of target-language context lemma and part-of-speech features.

- (Accidental) omission of a hidden layer in the submitted systems.

- Substitution of the internal softmax layer (**V**) by a sigmoid layer.

The overall structure of the network is shown in figure 1. To create input data for the network, we first generate a set of antecedent candidates for a given pronoun by running the preprocessing pipeline of the coreference resolution system CORT (Martschat and Strube, 2015). Each training example for our network can have an arbitrary number of antecedent candidates. Next, we prepare four types of features. *Anaphor source context features* describe the source language (SL) pronoun (**P**) and its immediate context consisting of three words to its left (**L1** to **L3**) and three words to its right (**R1** to **R3**), encoded as one-hot vectors. *Anaphor target context features* cover a window of three TL lemmas and part-of-speech tags to the left and to the right of the pronoun, each encoded as a one-hot vector.

Antecedent features (**A**) describe an antecedent candidate. Candidates are represented by the TL words aligned to the syntactic head of the source language markable noun phrase, again represented as one-hot vectors. These vectors cannot be fed into the network directly because their number depends on the number of antecedent candidates and on the

Proceedings of the First Conference on Machine Translation, Volume 2: Shared Task Papers, pages 576–580,
Berlin, Germany, August 11-12, 2016. ©2016 Association for Computational Linguistics

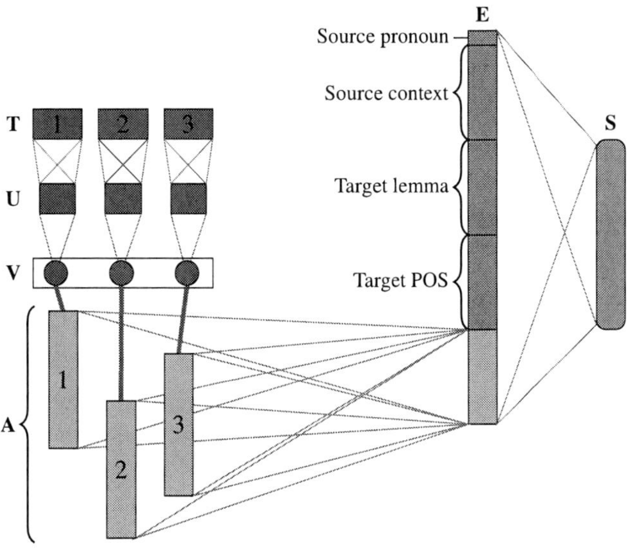

Figure 1: Neural network with latent anaphora resolution

number of TL words aligned to the head word of each antecedent. Instead, they are averaged to yield a single vector per antecedent candidate.

Finally, *anaphoric link vectors* (**T**) describe the relationship between an anaphor and a particular antecedent candidate. These vectors are generated by the feature extraction machinery in CORT and include a standard set of features for coreference resolution borrowed wholesale from the default configuration of the coreference resolution system, including a number of lexicalised feature templates that generate a large number of individual features. To increase the efficiency of the training process, all input feature sets are limited to a vocabulary consisting of the 1000 most frequent words per feature type.

In the forward propagation pass, the input word representations are mapped to a low-dimensional representation in an embedding layer (**E**). In this layer, the embedding weights for all the SL vectors (the pronoun and its 6 context words) are tied, so if two words are the same, they are mapped to the same lower-dimensional embedding regardless of their position relative to the pronoun. To process the information contained in the antecedents, the network first computes the link probability for each antecedent candidate. The anaphoric link features (**T**) are mapped to a hidden layer with logistic sigmoid units (**U**). The activations of the hidden units are then mapped to a single value, which functions as an element in an internal soft-

max layer over all antecedent candidates (**V**). This softmax layer assigns a probability $p_1 \ldots p_n$ to each antecedent candidate. The antecedent feature vectors **A** are projected to lower-dimensional embeddings, weighted with their corresponding link probabilities and summed. The weighted sum is then concatenated with the source language embeddings in the **E** layer. To improve the training of the antecedent-related network parts, whenever a training example is presented to the network, with a probability of 20 % all source and target context features are set to zero. The **E** layer is connected to a softmax output layer predicting the pronoun class as defined by the shared task specification.

In our setup, the dimensionality of the word embeddings is 30 for the source context words, target lemmas and antecedent features and 15 for the target POS features, resulting in a total embedding layer size of 482 (two source pronoun features, six 30-dimensional source context embeddings, six 30-dimensional target lemma embeddings, six 15-dimensional target POS embeddings and one 30-dimensional antecedent feature vector). The network is regularised with an ℓ_2 penalty that was set to 10^{-6} using grid search over a held-out development set. It is trained with the ADAGRAD algorithm with minibatches of size 16 and with cross-entropy as the training objective. The gradients are computed using backpropagation. Note that the number of weights in the network is the same for all training examples even though the number of antecedent

Source:	**It** 's got these fishing lures on the bottom .
Target lemmas:	**REPLACE_0** avoir ce leurre de pêche au-dessous .
Solution:	*ils*
LM training data:	It **REPLACE_ils** avoir ce leurre de pêche au-dessous .
LM test data:	It **REPLACE** avoir ce leurre de pêche au-dessous .

Figure 2: Data for the source-aware language model

candidates varies because all weights related to antecedent word features and anaphoric link features are shared between all antecedent candidates. The model is trained for 60 epochs on the training data in the IWSLT set; the other training data sets are not used.

3 Source-Aware Language Model

In the pronoun prediction task at DiscoMT 2015 (Hardmeier et al., 2015), it turned out that a simple n-gram model considering only the target-side local context of the word to be predicted outperformed all submissions to the shared task. These results suggest that it is important to include strong n-gram modelling capacities into any system. The neural network system described in the previous section does not necessarily have this, so we decided to address this problem with a system combination approach.

The official baseline of the current shared task is identical to that of the previous year, but the task is different in that the target language words are provided in lemmatised form only. Lemmatisation deprives the language model of important morphological information about the context words, in particular about their number. As a result, we observe much lower scores with the official baseline than in the 2015 shared task. Frequently, however, a look at the source pronoun would be entirely sufficient to supply the required information for the source language at least, and while the correspondence of number marking across languages is not perfect, the number of the pronoun in the source language is a strong hint.

Our source-aware language model is an n-gram model trained on an artificial corpus generated from the target lemmas of the parallel training (Figure 2). Before every REPLACE tag occurring in the data, we insert the source pronoun aligned to the tag (without lowercasing or any other processing). The alignment information attached to the REPLACE tag in the shared task data files is stripped off.

In the training data, we instead add the pronoun class to be predicted. The n-gram model used for this component is a 6-gram model with modified Kneser-Ney smoothing (Chen and Goodman, 1998) trained with the KenLM toolkit (Heafield, 2011) on the complete set of training data provided for the shared task.

To predict classes for an unseen test set, we first convert it to a format matching that of the training data, but with a uniform, unannotated RE-PLACE tag used for all classes. We then recover the tag annotated with the correct solution using the `disambig` tool of the SRILM language modelling toolkit (Stolcke et al., 2011). This tool runs the Viterbi algorithm to select the most probable mapping of each token from among a set of possible alternatives. The map used for this task trivially maps all tokens to themselves with the exception of the REPLACE tags, which are mapped to the set of annotated REPLACE tags found in the training data.

The source-aware language model described here is identical to the base model of the UUPP-SALA system (Loáiciga et al., 2016). Its output was submitted to the shared task as the UUPP-SALA primary submission for English–German, German–English and French–English and as the UUPPSALA contrastive submission for English–French.

4 System Combination

To combine the neural predictor with the source-aware language model, we linearly interpolated the probabilities assigned to each class by each model. The class finally predicted was the one that scored highest according to the interpolated probability distribution.

The neural network prediction probabilities are obtained trivially as the posterior distribution of the final softmax layer **S**. For the source-aware language model, we run SRILM's `disambig` tool with the `-posteriors` option, which causes it

578

English–French			
Class	NN	LM	NN+LM
ce	0.865	0.825	0.855
elle	–	0.483	0.325
elles	–	0.167	0.143
il	0.624	0.667	0.677
ils	0.787	0.747	0.810
cela	0.603	0.542	0.679
on	–	0.400	0.444
OTHER	0.873	0.889	0.905
Macro-F	0.469	0.590	0.605
Macro-R	0.508	0.598	0.606

English–German			
Class	NN	LM	NN+LM
er	–	0.091	–
sie	0.793	0.716	0.788
es	0.684	0.688	0.718
man	–	0.182	0.222
OTHER	0.756	0.729	0.800
Macro-F	0.447	0.481	0.506
Macro-R	0.466	0.474	0.504

NN: neural network (Section 2; contrastive submission)
LM: source-aware language model (Section 3)
NN+LM: interpolated model (Section 4; primary submission)

Table 1: F-scores per class and macro-averaged F-score and recall for component and combined systems

to output an approximate posterior distribution derived from information collected during the Viterbi decoding pass. For all classes i, the probability $p_{\text{NN}}(i)$ predicted by the neural network and the probability $p_{\text{LM}}(i)$ predicted by the source-aware language model were combined as follows:

$$p(i) = \lambda\, p_{\text{NN}}(i) + (1 - \lambda)\, p_{\text{LM}}(i) \qquad (1)$$

The single weight λ ($0 \leq \lambda \leq 1$) was determined by grid search on a linearly spaced grid of step size 0.1 to maximise the macro-averaged recall score for the *DiscoMT2015.test* corpus (for English–French) and the *TEDdev* corpus (for English–German). The weights used by the submitted systems are $\lambda = 0.5$ for English–French and $\lambda = 0.6$ for English–German. The fact that the optimal weight setting assigns close to equal weight to the two systems for both language pairs demonstrates that both systems have complementary information to contribute and both of them are useful to improve the overall result.

5   Results and Discussion

Table 1 shows the F-scores per class for each of the two component systems and for the system combination that we submitted as our primary system. The most important observation that we can make is the complete failure of the neural network model to predict the infrequent classes: *elle*, *elles* and *on* for English–French and *er* and *man* for English–German. This is highly disappointing since we hoped that the neural network, with its ability to see potential antecedents, would be in a better position to make accurate predictions for these classes.

Good performance for the French feminine plural class *elles* was a key motivating factor in our initial development of the pronoun prediction network (Hardmeier et al., 2013), but unfortunately we have repeatedly struggled to produce similarly good results with different data sets and tasks. In this shared task, we are forced to conclude that the effect of the neural network classifier is detrimental for the French feminine singular and plural classes and for the German masculine singular when combined with the source-aware language model.

In the system combination, we do observe improvements over the source-aware language model for all other classes, including the infrequent generic classes *on* and *man*. For the latter two classes, the neural network brings about an improvement in the combination even though it completely fails to predict the classes on its own.

In sum, the score patterns of our two component systems suggest that the value added in this task by the neural network stems from its better ability to distinguish between the various impersonal pronoun classes rather than, as we had hoped, from improved performance on anaphoric pronouns.

Acknowledgements

This work was supported by the Swedish Research Council under project 2012-916 *Discourse-Oriented Statistical Machine Translation*. The experiments were performed on resources provided by SNIC through the Uppsala Multidisciplinary Center for Advanced Computational Science (UPPMAX) under project SNIC2016/7-36.

References

Stanley F. Chen and Joshua Goodman. 1998. An empirical study of smoothing techniques for language modeling. Technical report, Computer Science Group, Harvard University, Cambridge (Mass.).

François Chollet. 2016. Keras. `https://github.com/fchollet/keras`.

Liane Guillou, Christian Hardmeier, Preslav Nakov, Sara Stymne, Jörg Tiedemann, Yannick Versley, Mauro Cettolo, Bonnie Webber, and Andrei Popescu-Belis. 2016. Findings of the 2016 WMT shared task on cross-lingual pronoun prediction. In *Proceedings of the First Conference on Machine Translation (WMT16)*. Association for Computational Linguistics, Berlin (Germany).

Christian Hardmeier, Preslav Nakov, Sara Stymne, Jörg Tiedemann, Yannick Versley, and Mauro Cettolo. 2015. Pronoun-focused MT and cross-lingual pronoun prediction: Findings of the 2015 DiscoMT shared task on pronoun translation. In *Proceedings of the 2nd Workshop on Discourse in Machine Translation (DiscoMT 2015)*. Lisbon (Portugal).

Christian Hardmeier, Jörg Tiedemann, and Joakim Nivre. 2013. Latent anaphora resolution for cross-lingual pronoun prediction. In *Proceedings of the 2013 Conference on Empirical Methods in Natural Language Processing*. Association for Computational Linguistics, Seattle (Washington, USA), pages 380–391.

Kenneth Heafield. 2011. KenLM: faster and smaller language model queries. In *Proceedings of the Sixth Workshop on Statistical Machine Translation*. Association for Computational Linguistics, Edinburgh (Scotland, UK), pages 187–197.

Sharid Loáiciga, Liane Guillou, and Christian Hardmeier. 2016. It-disambiguation and source-aware language models for cross-lingual pronoun prediction. In *Proceedings of the First Conference on Machine Translation (WMT16)*. Association for Computational Linguistics, Berlin (Germany).

Sebastian Martschat and Michael Strube. 2015. Latent structures for coreference resolution. *Transactions of the Association for Computational Linguistics* 3:405–418.

Andreas Stolcke, Jing Zheng, Wen Wang, and Victor Abrash. 2011. SRILM at sixteen: Update and outlook. In *Proceedings of the IEEE Automatic Speech Recognition and Understanding Workshop*. Waikoloa (Hawaii, USA).

The Theano Development Team. 2016. Theano: A Python framework for fast computation of mathematical expressions. *ArXiv e-prints* 1605.02688.

It-disambiguation and source-aware language models for cross-lingual pronoun prediction

Sharid Loáiciga
Département de Linguistique
University of Geneva
sharid.loaiciga@unige.ch

Liane Guillou
CIS
LMU Munich
liane@cis.uni-muenchen.de

Christian Hardmeier
Dept. of Linguistics & Philology
Uppsala University
christian.hardmeier@lingfil.uu.se

Abstract

We present our systems for the WMT 2016 shared task on cross-lingual pronoun prediction. The main contribution is a classifier used to determine whether an instance of the ambiguous English pronoun "it" functions as an anaphoric, pleonastic or event reference pronoun. For the English-to-French task the classifier is incorporated in an extended baseline, which takes the form of a source-aware language model. An implementation of the source-aware language model is also provided for each of the remaining language pairs.

1 Introduction

The WMT 2016 shared task on cross-lingual pronoun prediction focuses on the translation of the subject position pronouns "it" and "they" for several language pairs (Guillou et al., 2016). Both of these pronouns perform multiple functions in text, and disambiguation is required if they are to be translated correctly into other languages (Guillou, 2016). The pronoun "they" is typically used as an anaphoric pronoun, but may also be used generically, for example in "*They* say it always rains in Scotland". The pronoun "it" may be used as an anaphoric, pleonastic or event reference pronoun. Examples of these pronoun functions are provided in Figure 1.

anaphoric	I have a **bicycle**. **It** is red.
pleonastic	**It** is raining.
event	He lost his job. **It** came as a total surprise.

Figure 1: Examples of different pronoun functions

Anaphoric pronouns corefer with a noun phrase (i.e. the *antecedent*). *Pleonastic* pronouns, in contrast, do not refer to anything but are required to fill the subject position in many languages, including English, French and German. *Event reference* pronouns may refer to a verb, verb phrase, clause or even an entire sentence.

Different French pronouns are required when translating an instance of "it" depending on its function. For example, anaphoric "it" may be translated with the third-person singular pronouns "il" [masc.] and "elle" [fem.], or with an non-gendered demonstrative such as "cela". The French pronoun "ce" may function as both an event reference and a pleonastic pronoun, but "il" is used only as a pleonastic pronoun.

As revealed in an analysis of the systems submitted to the DiscoMT 2015 shared task on pronoun translation (Hardmeier et al., 2015a), the translation of pleonastic and event reference pronouns poses a particular problem for MT systems (Guillou and Hardmeier, 2016). Poor performance may be attributed to the inability of the systems to disambiguate the various possible functions of the pronoun "it". In the case of systems that incorporate coreference resolution and methods for identifying instances of pleonastic "it", inaccurate output may harm translation performance. No suitable tools exist for the detection of event reference pronouns in English.

To address the problem of disambiguating the function of "it", we propose a classifier that uses information from the current and previous sentences, as well as external tools, and indicates for each instance of "it" whether the pronoun function is anaphoric, pleonastic or event reference. The classifier was trained using data from the ParCor corpus (Guillou et al., 2014) and the *DiscoMT2015.test* dataset (Hardmeier et al., 2016). In both corpora, pronouns are labelled according to their function, following the ParCor annotation scheme. The classifier is incorporated

Proceedings of the First Conference on Machine Translation, Volume 2: Shared Task Papers, pages 581–588,
Berlin, Germany, August 11-12, 2016. ©2016 Association for Computational Linguistics

in an extended baseline system for the English-to-French task. The extended baseline takes the form of a n-gram language model that operates over target-language lemmas, but also has access to the identity of the source-language pronouns. Source-aware language models are also provided for the other tasks: English-to-German, German-to-English and French-to-English.

2 Previous Work

Work on pronoun translation, in which a complete machine translation pipeline is provided, has also considered different functions of the pronoun "it". Le Nagard and Koehn (2010) identify and exclude instances of pleonastic "it" in their English-to-French system. Guillou (2015) distinguishes between anaphoric vs. non-anaphoric pronouns in an English-to-French automatic post-editing system. Novák et al. (2013) consider the translation of three different uses of "it" in English-to-Czech translation: *referential it*, referring to a noun phrase, *anaphoric it*, referring to a verb phrase, and *pleonastic it*. These three categories correspond to those that we refer to as anaphoric, event reference and pleonastic, respectively.

Work by Navarretta (2004) and Dipper et al. (2011) has focused on resolving abstract anaphora in Danish and on the manual annotation of abstract anaphora in English and German. Abstract anaphora, in which pronouns refer to abstract entities such as facts or events, is referred to as event reference in this paper. The automatic detection of instances of pleonastic "it" has been addressed by NADA (Bergsma and Yarowsky, 2011), and also by the Stanford sieve-based coreference resolution system (Lee et al., 2011).

The cross-lingual pronoun prediction task formalised by Hardmeier (2014) was first introduced as a shared task at DiscoMT 2015 (Hardmeier et al., 2015a). The participants used a range of features in their classifiers, but this paper marks the first attempt to incorporate a component to disambiguate the various uses of "it".

3 Disambiguating "it"

3.1 Data

The ParCor corpus (Guillou et al., 2014) and *DiscoMT2015.test* dataset (Hardmeier et al., 2016) were used to train the classifier. Under the ParCor annotation scheme, which was used to annotate both corpora, pronouns are labelled according to their function. For all instances of "it" labelled as anaphoric, pleonastic or event reference, the sentence-internal position of the pronoun and the sentence itself are extracted[1]. The pronouns "this" and "that", when used as event reference pronouns, may in many cases be used interchangeably with the pronoun "it" (Guillou, 2016). Consider Ex. 1, in which the pronouns "this" and "it" may be used to express the same meaning.

(1)   John arrived late. [This/it] annoyed Mary.

To increase the number of training examples, instances of event reference "this" and "that" are replaced with "it" and added to the training data.

The data was divided into 1504 instances for training, and 501 each for the development and test sets. All sentences were shuffled before the corpus was divided, promoting a balanced distribution of the classes (Table 1).

Data Set	*it*-Event	Anaphoric	Pleonastic	Total
Training	504	779	221	1504
Dev	157	252	92	501
Test	169	270	62	501
Total	830	1301	375	2506

Table 1: Distribution of classes in the training data

All classifiers were trained using the Stanford Maximum Entropy package (Manning and Klein, 2003).

3.2 Features

To parse the corpus, we used the joint part-of-speech tagger and dependency parser of Bohnet et al. (2013) from the Mate toolkit. We used the pre-trained models for English that are available online[2]. In addition, the corpus was lemmatised using the TreeTagger lemmatiser (Schmid, 1994). Although other tools were used, we relied on the output of these two parsers to extract most of our features.

For each training example, we extract the following information:

1. Previous three tokens. This includes words and punctuation. It also includes the tokens in the previous sentence when the *it*- occupies the first position of the current sentence.

---

[1] A small number of instances of "it" are labelled as cataphoric or extra-textual in the corpora. These are excluded from the classifier training data.

[2] https://code.google.com/p/mate-tools/downloads/list

2. Next two tokens

3. Lemmas of the next two tokens

4. Head word. As the task is limited to subject *it* and *they*, most of the time the head word is a verb.

5. Whether the head word takes a 'that' complement (verbs only)

6. Tense of head word (verbs only). This is computed using the rules described in Loáiciga et al. (2014).

7. Presence of 'that' complement in previous sentence. A binary feature which follows Navarretta (2004)'s conclusion (for Danish) that a particular demonstrative pronoun (*dette*) is often used to refer to the last mentioned situation in the previous sentence, often expressed in a subordinated clause.

8. Predications head. This refers to the predicative complements of the verbs *be*, *appear*, *seem*, *look*, *sound*, *smell*, *taste*, *feel*, *become* and *get*.

9. Closest noun phrase (head) to the left

10. Closest noun phrase (head) to the right

11. Presence of a cleft construction. A binary feature which refers to constructions containing adjectives which trigger extraposed sentential subjects as in '*So it's difficult to attack malaria from inside malarious societies, [...]*.

12. Closest adjective to the right

13. VerbNet selectional restrictions of the verb. VerbNet (Kipper et al., 2008) specifies 36 types of argument that verbs can take. We limited ourselves to the values of 'abstract', 'concrete' and 'unknown'.

14. Lemma of the head word

15. Likelihood of head word taking an event subject (verbs only). An estimate of the likelihood of a verb taking a event subject was computed over the Annotated English Gigaword v.5 corpus (Napoles et al., 2012). We considered two cases where an event subject appears often and may be identified by exploiting the parse annotation of the Gigaword corpus. The first case is when the subject is a gerund and the second case is composed of "this" pronoun subjects.

16. NADA probability. The probability that the non-referential "it" detector, NADA (Bergsma and Yarowsky, 2011), assigns to the instance of "it".

We also experimented with other features and options. For features 2 and 3, a window of three tokens showed a degradation in performance. For features 9 and 10, we experimented with adding their WordNet type (WordNet (Princeton University, 2010) contains 26 types of nouns), but this had no effect. The feature combination of noun and adjectives to the left or right also had no effect.

3.3 Results

For development and comparison we built two different baselines. One is a 3-gram language model built using KenLM (Heafield, 2011) and trained over a modified version of the annotated corpus in which every *it* is concatenated with its type (e.g. *it_event*). For testing, the *it* position is filled with each of the three *it_label* and the language model is queried. This baseline functions in a very similar way to the share-task own baseline.

Table 2 presents the results of this baseline using 14-fold cross-validation and a single held-out test set (all test-set mentions refer to the same test set). The motivation for the choice of the number of folds is threefold. First, we wanted to respect document boundaries; second, we aimed for a fair proportion of the three classes in all folds; and, lastly, we tried to lessen the variance given the relatively small size of the corpus. The second baseline is a setting in which all instances of the test set are set to the majority class *it-anaphoric*.

A quick scan of Tables 2 and 3 anticipates one of the conclusions of this paper: predicting event reference pronouns is a complex problem. The 3-gram baseline appears to be biased towards the pleonastic class, as suggested by its high precision and very low recall for the event and anaphoric classes and the opposite situation for the pleonastic class. While our own classifier is more balanced, it achieves only moderate results with the event class. Compared to both of the baselines, it shows only a very small improvement.

14-fold cross-validation			
	Precision	Recall	F1
it- anaphoric	0.5985	0.2475	0.3502
it- pleonastic	0.1521	0.6213	0.2444
it- event	0.5275	0.2772	0.3633
Test-set			
	Precision	Recall	F1
it- anaphoric	0.7320	0.2629	0.3869
it- pleonastic	0.1387	0.6935	0.2312
it- event	0.5213	0.2899	0.3726
Test-set majority class			
	Precision	Recall	F1
it- anaphoric	0.5389	1	0.7004

Table 2: Baselines for the classification of the three types of *it*.

A manual inspection of the results shows that discriminating between anaphoric and event reference instances of *it* is indeed a very subtle process. Determining the presence or the lack of a specific (np-like) antecedent requires the understanding of the complete coreference chain. Take for instance the following example taken from a dialogue in the corpus:

> $_1$You're part of a generation that grew up with the Internet, and it seems as if you become offended at almost a visceral level when you see something done that you think will harm the Internet. $_2$Is there some truth to it? $_3$*It* is. $_4$I think it's very true. $_5$This is not a left or right issue. $_6$Our basic freedoms, and when I say our, I don't just mean Americans, I mean people around the world, *it*'s not a partisan issue .

In the example above the first italicised *it* is an event reference pronoun while the second is an anaphoric pronoun. With access to the whole coreference chain, one can see that the *it* in sentence 3 refers to the event expressed in the first sentence, therefore it is annotated as an event. This same entity is then referred to with the word *issue* in sentence 5, which in turn becomes the antecedent to the *it* in sentence 6. The classifier, however, labelled these two instances as anaphoric and event respectively.

It is worth noting that from the 2031 segments composing the annotated corpus, 349 (17%) contain co-occurrences of between 2 and 7 *it* pronouns within the same segment. We experimented including the previous *it-label*, when there are several within the same sentence, as an additional feature and obtained important gains in performance. It can be seen in the *w/ oracle feature* section of Table 3 that performance improves in almost all cases when this feature is used. The only exception is for the *it-pleonastic* class of the test set. We then tried to approximate this feature by using the relative position of the *it-label* to other *it-labels* within the same sentence (e.g., first, second, etc.). Contrary to the oracle feature, the approximated feature did not lead to any improvement. Modelling co-occurrences of pronouns seems like a promising step in future work.

Binary classification (event vs. non-event) consistently underperformed when compared to the three class set-up.

4 Source-Aware Language Model

The pronoun prediction part of our models is based on an n-gram model over target lemmas similar to the official shared task baseline. In addition to the pure target lemma context, our model also has access to the identity of the source language pronoun, which, in the absence of number inflection on the target words, provides valuable information about the number marking of the pronouns in the source and opens a way to inject the output of the pronoun type classifier into the system.

Our source-aware language model is an n-gram model trained on an artificial corpus generated from the target lemmas of the parallel training data (Figure 2). Before every REPLACE tag occurring in the data, we insert the source pronoun aligned to the tag (without lowercasing or any other processing). The alignment information attached to the REPLACE tag in the shared task data files is stripped off. In the training data, we instead add the pronoun class to be predicted. Note that all REPLACE tags are placeholders for one word translations guaranteed to correspond to a source pronoun *it* or *they* according to the shared-task data preparation (Hardmeier et al., 2015b; Guillou et al., 2016). The n-gram model used for this component is a 6-gram model with modified Kneser-Ney smoothing (Chen and Goodman, 1998) trained

	Dev				Test			
w/o oracle feature	Accuracy	Precision	Recall	F1	Accuracy	Precision	Recall	F1
it- anaphoric	0.703	0.685	0.758	0.719	0.707	0.716	0.756	0.735
it- pleonastic	0.884	0.758	0.543	0.633	0.936	0.750	0.726	0.738
it- event	0.715	0.545	0.541	0.543	0.703	0.564	0.521	0.542
w/ oracle feature	Accuracy	Precision	Recall	F1	Accuracy	Precision	Recall	F1
it- anaphoric	0.725	0.705	0.778	0.740	0.727	0.729	0.785	0.756
it- pleonastic	0.886	0.746	0.576	0.650	0.926	0.705	0.694	0.699
it- event	0.739	0.586	0.567	0.576	0.729	0.611	0.538	0.572

Table 3: Classification results of the three types of *it* on the development and test sets.

Source:	**It** 's got these fishing lures on the bottom .
Target lemmas:	**REPLACE_0** avoir ce leurre de pêche au-dessous .
Solution:	*ils*
LM training data:	It **REPLACE_ils** avoir ce leurre de pêche au-dessous .
LM test data:	It **REPLACE** avoir ce leurre de pêche au-dessous .

Figure 2: Data for the source-aware language model

with the KenLM toolkit (Heafield, 2011).

To predict classes for an unseen test set, we first convert it to a format matching that of the training data, but with a uniform, unannotated RE-PLACE tag used for all classes. We then recover the tag annotated with the correct solution using the `disambig` tool of the SRILM language modelling toolkit (Stolcke et al., 2011). This tool runs the Viterbi algorithm to select the most probable mapping of each token from among a set of possible alternatives. The map used for this task trivially maps all tokens to themselves with the exception of the REPLACE tags, which are mapped to the set of annotated REPLACE tags found in the training data.

The source-aware language model described here is identical to the language model component included in the UU-Hardmeier submission (Hardmeier, 2016).

5 English-French "it" Disambiguation System

We used the classifier described in Section 3 to annotate all instances of *it* from the source side of the data which were mapped to a REPLACE item according to the alignment provided. Afterwards, a new source-aware language model is trained in the manner described in Section 4. In this way, instead of the sentence *'It 's got these fishing lures on the bottom .'* presented in Figure 2, the system receives the labelled input *'It_anaphoric 's got*

these fishing lures on the bottom .' All the data provided for the shared-task was used in training this system.

6 Results and Analysis

Unfortunately, following the submission of our system we identified an error related to the feature extraction process. We relied on contextual information of the previous sentence for some of our features. However, due to the $1 : N$ alignments, the context information was sometimes inaccurate. The correction of this problem produced the results reported in the section titled *Submitted corrected* in Table 4. The macro-averaged recall obtained is 57.03%, which is considerably better than the result of the submitted system (48.92%), but still slightly lower than the score of 59.84% which was obtained by the unmodified system.

However, some pronouns present better scores using the *submitted corrected* system than the unmodified system. Precision, in particular, is higher (bolded scores in Table 4). This outcome is expected for the pronoun *cela*, which is the French neuter demonstrative pronoun frequently used for event reference. However, there are also gains in precision for *on*, *elles* and *ils*. In our opinion, this suggests that while not directly treating any of the other source-language pronouns (in the context of this shared-task, other source pronouns refers only to *they*), the disambiguation of *it* positively affects the translation of the other target-language

Submitted - w/o labels R: 59.84%

Pronoun	Precision	Recall	F1
ce	89.66	76.47	82.54
elle	40.00	60.87	48.28
elles	27.27	12.00	16.67
il	63.24	70.49	66.67
ils	67.82	83.10	74.68
cela	76.47	41.94	54.17
on	36.36	44.44	40.00
OTHER	88.37	89.41	88.89

Submitted - w/ labels R: 48.92%

Pronoun	Precision	Recall	F1
ce	70.11	89.71	78.71
elle	0.00	0.00	0.00
elles	20.00	16.00	17.78
il	70.97	36.07	47.83
ils	50.96	74.65	60.57
cela	48.65	58.06	52.94
on	42.86	33.33	37.50
OTHER	86.59	83.53	85.03

Submitted corrected - w/ labels R: 57.03%

Pronoun	Precision	Recall	F1
ce	89.09	72.06	79.67
elle	31.25	43.48	36.36
elles	**30.77**	16.00	21.05
il	54.43	70.49	61.43
ils	**69.41**	83.10	75.64
cela	**86.67**	41.94	56.52
on	**40.00**	44.44	42.11
OTHER	85.71	84.71	85.21

Table 4: Final system

Source:	**it_anaphoric** just takes a picture of objective reality as **it_anaphoric** is .
LM w/o labels:	il OTHER
LM w/labels:	elle OTHER
Baseline:	cela OTHER
Gold	**elle** prendre juste un image objectif de **la** réalité .

Figure 3: Examples of predictions of the final systems. The Gold translation is lemmatized.

particular, it can be difficult to determine the antecedent of an event reference pronoun. The identification of pleonastic realisations, on the other hand, is almost impossible in an n-gram context such as that provided by a language model. However, it is feasible in the three class setting, and at the same time helpful for the disambiguation of the event and anaphoric realisations.

While our results are modest, they point towards an improvement in the general quality of pronoun translation. Accurate disambiguation of the pronoun "it" has the potential to help NLP applications such as Machine Translation and Coreference Resolution.

In the near future, we will experiment with other classification algorithms suitable for small training sets. We also intend to experiment with features that incorporate semantic knowledge in the form of statistics computed over external resources, including the Gigaword corpus. Last, with the generated data from this shared-task, we plan to do bootstrap and experiment with self-training.

Acknowledgments

SL was supported by the Swiss National Science Foundation under grant no. P1GEP1_161877. CH and LG were supported by the Swedish Research Council under project 2012-916 *Discourse-Oriented Statistical Machine Translation*. Large-scale computations were performed on the Abel cluster, owned by the University of Oslo and the Norwegian metacenter for High Performance Computing (NOTUR), under project nn9106k.

pronouns. The pronoun *it*, after all, is used three times more frequently than *they* in the training data (Loáiciga and Wehrli, 2015).

Looking at the predictions, we confirmed that both source-aware language models produced identical results almost all of the time, with the system without the labels producing more correct predictions in total. However, there are some few examples where the system with the labels outperforms both the baseline and the un-labelled one. A contrastive example can be seen in Figure 3.

7 Conclusions and Future Work

Distinguishing between anaphoric and event reference realisations of "it" is a very complex task. In

586

References

Shane Bergsma and David Yarowsky. 2011. NADA: A robust system for non-referential pronoun detection. In Iris Hendrickx, Sobha Lalitha Devi, António Branco, and Ruslan Mitkov, editors, *Anaphora Processing and Applications: 8th Discourse Anaphora and Anaphor Resolution Colloquium (DAARC)*, Lecture Notes in Artificial Intelligence, pages 12–23. Springer, Faro, Portugal.

Bernd Bohnet, Joakim Nivre, Igor Boguslavsky, Richárd Farkas, Filip Ginter, and Jan Hajič. 2013. Joint morphological and syntactic analysis for richly inflected languages. *Transactions of the Association for Computational Linguistics*, 1:415–428.

Stanley F. Chen and Joshua Goodman. 1998. An empirical study of smoothing techniques for language modeling. Technical report, Computer Science Group, Harvard University, Cambridge (Mass.).

Stefanie Dipper, Christine Rieger, Melanie Seiss, and Heike Zinsmeister. 2011. Abstract anaphors in german and english. In Iris Hendrickx, Sobha Lalitha Devi, António Branco, and Ruslan Mitkov, editors, *Anaphora Processing and Applications: 8th Discourse Anaphora and Anaphor Resolution Colloquium (DAARC)*, Lecture Notes in Artificial Intelligence, pages 96–107. Springer, Faro, Portugal.

Liane Guillou and Christian Hardmeier. 2016. PROTEST: A test suite for evaluating pronouns in machine translation. In *Proceedings of the Eleventh Language Resources and Evaluation Conference (LREC'16)*, Portorož (Slovenia), May.

Liane Guillou, Christian Hardmeier, Aaron Smith, Jörg Tiedemann, and Bonnie Webber. 2014. ParCor 1.0: A parallel pronoun-coreference corpus to support statistical MT. In *Proceedings of the Tenth Language Resources and Evaluation Conference (LREC'14)*, pages 3191–3198, Reykjavík (Iceland).

Liane Guillou, Christian Hardmeier, Preslav Nakov, Sara Stymne, Jörg Tiedemann, Yannick Versley, Mauro Cettolo, Bonnie Webber, and Andrei Popescu-Belis. 2016. Findings of the 2016 WMT shared task on cross-lingual pronoun prediction. In *Proceedings of the First Conference on Machine Translation (WMT16)*, Berlin, Germany. Association for Computational Linguistics.

Liane Guillou. 2015. Automatic Post-Editing for the DiscoMT Pronoun Translation Task. In *Proceedings of the Second Workshop on Discourse in Machine Translation*, pages 65–71, Lisbon, Portugal. Association for Computational Linguistics.

Liane Guillou. 2016. *Incorporating Pronoun Function into Statistical Machine Translation*. Ph.D. thesis, University of Edinburgh.

Christian Hardmeier, Preslav Nakov, Sara Stymne, Jörg Tiedemann, Yannick Versley, and Mauro Cettolo. 2015a. Pronoun-focused MT and cross-lingual pronoun prediction: Findings of the 2015 DiscoMT shared task on pronoun translation. In *Proceedings of the 2nd Workshop on Discourse in Machine Translation (DiscoMT 2015)*, pages 1–16, Lisbon (Portugal).

Christian Hardmeier, Preslav Nakov, Sara Stymne, Jörg Tiedemann, Yannick Versley, and Mauro Cettolo. 2015b. Pronoun-focused MT and cross-lingual pronoun prediction: Findings of the 2015 DiscoMT shared task on pronoun translation. In *Proceedings of the Second Workshop on Discourse in Machine Translation*, DiscoMT 2015, Lisbon, Portugal.

Christian Hardmeier, Jörg Tiedemann, Preslav Nakov, Sara Stymne, and Yannick Versely. 2016. DiscoMT 2015 Shared Task on Pronoun Translation. LINDAT/CLARIN digital library at Institute of Formal and Applied Linguistics, Charles University in Prague. `http://hdl.handle.net/11372/LRT-1611`.

Christian Hardmeier. 2014. *Discourse in Statistical Machine Translation*. Ph.D. thesis, University of Uppsala.

Christian Hardmeier. 2016. Pronoun prediction with latent anaphora resolution. In *Proceedings of the First Conference on Machine Translation (WMT)*, Berlin (Germany).

Kenneth Heafield. 2011. KenLM: faster and smaller language model queries. In *Proceedings of the Sixth Workshop on Statistical Machine Translation*, pages 187–197, Edinburgh (Scotland, UK), July. Association for Computational Linguistics.

Karin Kipper, Anna Korhonen, Neville Ryant, and Martha Palmer. 2008. A large-scale classification of english verbs. *Language Resources and Evaluation Journal*, 42(1):21–40.

Ronan Le Nagard and Philipp Koehn. 2010. Aiding Pronoun Translation with Co-Reference Resolution. In *Proceedings of the Joint Fifth Workshop on Statistical Machine Translation and MetricsMATR*, pages 252–261, Uppsala, Sweden. Association for Computational Linguistics.

Heeyoung Lee, Yves Peirsman, Angel Chang, Nathanael Chambers, Mihai Surdeanu, and Dan Jurafsky. 2011. Stanford's Multi-Pass Sieve Coreference Resolution System at the CoNLL-2011 Shared Task. In *Proceedings of the Fifteenth Conference on Computational Natural Language Learning: Shared Task*, CONLL Shared Task '11, pages 28–34, Portland, Oregon. Association for Computational Linguistics.

Sharid Loáiciga and Éric Wehrli. 2015. Rule-based pronominal anaphora treatment for machine translation. In *Proceedings of the Second Workshop on Discourse in Machine Translation*, DiscoMT 2015, Lisbon, Portugal.

Sharid Loáiciga, Thomas Meyer, and Andrei Popescu-Belis. 2014. English-french verb phrase alignment in europarl for tense translation modeling. In *Proceedings of the 9th International Conference on Language Resources and Evaluation*, LREC'14, pages 674–681, Reykjavik, Iceland. European Language Resources Association (ELRA).

Christopher Manning and Dan Klein. 2003. Optimization, MaxEnt models, and conditional estimation without magic. In *Tutorial at HLT-NAACL and 41st ACL conferences*, Edmonton, Canada and Sapporo, Japan.

Courtney Napoles, Matthew Gormley, and Benjamin Van Durme. 2012. Annotated gigaword. In *Proceedings of the Joint Workshop on Automatic Knowledge Base Construction and Web-scale Knowledge Extraction*, AKBC-WEKEX, pages 95–100, Montreal, Canada. Association for Computational Linguistics.

Costanza Navarretta. 2004. Resolving individual and abstract anaphora in texts and dialogues. In *Proceedings of the 20th International Conference on Computational Linguistics*, COLING'04, pages 233–239, Geneva, Switzerland. Association for Computational Linguistics.

Michal Novák, Anna Nedoluzhko, and Zdeněek Žabokrtský. 2013. Translation of "it" in a deep syntax framework. In *Proceedings of the Workshop on Discourse in Machine Translation*, pages 51–59, Sofia, Bulgaria. Association for Computational Linguistics.

Princeton University. 2010. Wordnet.

Helmut Schmid. 1994. Probabilistic part-of-speech tagging using decision trees. In *Proceedings of International Conference on New Methods in Language Processing*, Manchester, UK.

Andreas Stolcke, Jing Zheng, Wen Wang, and Victor Abrash. 2011. SRILM at sixteen: Update and outlook. In *Proceedings of the IEEE Automatic Speech Recognition and Understanding Workshop*, Waikoloa (Hawaii, USA).

Pronoun Language Model and Grammatical Heuristics
for Aiding Pronoun Prediction

Ngoc Quang Luong and **Andrei Popescu-Belis**
Idiap Research Institute
Rue Marconi 19, CP 592
1920 Martigny, Switzerland
`{nluong,apbelis}@idiap.ch`

Abstract

The cross-lingual pronoun prediction task at WMT 2016 requires to restore the missing target pronouns from source text and target lemmatized and POS-tagged translations. We study the benefits for this task of a specific Pronoun Language Model (PLM), which captures the likelihood of a pronoun given the gender and number of the nouns or pronouns preceding it, on the target-side only. Experimenting with the English-to-French subtask, we select the best candidate pronoun by applying the PLM and additional heuristics based on French grammar rules to the target-side texts provided in the subtask. Although the PLM helps to outperform a random baseline, it still scores far lower than system using both source and target texts.

1   Introduction

The translation of pronouns has been recognized as a challenge since the early years of machine translation (MT), as pronoun systems do not map 1:1 across languages. Recently, specific strategies for translating pronouns have been proposed and evaluated, as reviewed by Hardmeier (2014, Section 2.3.1) and by Guillou (Guillou, 2016).

Following the DiscoMT 2015 shared task on pronoun-focused translation (Hardmeier et al., 2015), the goal of the 2016 WMT pronoun shared task (Guillou et al., 2016) is to compare systems that are able to predict the translation of a source pronoun among a small, closed set of target candidates. The task was proposed for four language pairs: English/German and English/French, in both directions. Besides the original source documents (transcripts of TED talks), participants were given the formatted target documents, where all words were lemmatized and POS-tagged, and all pronouns were hidden. Participants were required to restore (or predict) each translated pronoun, in a fully inflected form.

We participate in the subtask of English-to-French pronoun prediction, with the main goal of testing the merits of a simple target-only approach. In previous work, we found that this approach improved the translation of neuter English pronouns *it* and *they* into French, and outperformed the DiscoMT 2015 baseline by about 5% relative improvement on an automatic metric (Luong and Popescu-Belis, 2016). Our method uses only the fact that the antecedent of a pronoun is likely to be one of the noun phrases preceding it closely. Therefore, if a majority of these nouns exhibit the same gender and number, it is more likely that the correct French pronoun agrees in gender and number with them. We model this majority gender and number as a Pronoun Language Model (PLM, see Luong and Popescu-Belis (2016)). This knowledge-lean approach does not make any hypothesis on which of the nouns is the antecedent, though it is augmented, for the 2016 shared task, with language-dependent grammar heuristics to determine the right candidate for neuter French pronouns, which are less constrained in gender and number.

In what follows, after introducing briefly the method (Section 3), we explain how to represent these intuitions in a formal probabilistic model – the PLM – that is learned from French data (Section 4) and we describe the grammar heuristics to deal with neuter pronouns as well (Section 5). Then, we show how these two resources are used to determine the target pronoun as required by the 2016 shared task (Section 6) and we analyze our results for both development and test sets (Section 7), showing that the benefits of our system remain inferior to those of systems using both the

Proceedings of the First Conference on Machine Translation, Volume 2: Shared Task Papers, pages 589–595,
Berlin, Germany, August 11-12, 2016. ©2016 Association for Computational Linguistics

source and the target sides. But first, we present a brief state of the art in pronoun translation in order to compare our proposal with related work.

2   Related Work

Several previous studies have attempted to improve pronoun translation by integrating anaphora resolution with statistical MT. Le Nagard and Koehn (2010) trained an English-French translation model on an annotated corpus in which each occurrence of English pronouns *it* and *they* was annotated with the gender of its antecedent in the target side, but this could not outperform a baseline that was not aware of coreference links. Hardmeier and Federico (2010) integrated a word dependency model into an SMT decoder as an additional feature function, to keep track of source antecedent-anaphor pairs, which improved the performance of their English-German SMT system.

Following a similar strategy, in our previous work (Luong et al., 2015), we linearly combined the score obtained from a coreference resolution system with the score from the search graph of the Moses decoder, to determine whether an English-French SMT pronoun translation should be post-edited into the opposite gender (e.g. *il* $\rightarrow$ *elle*). Their system performed best among six participants on the pronoun-focused shared task at the 2015 DiscoMT workshop (Hardmeier et al., 2015), but still remained below the SMT baseline.

A considerable set of coreference features, used in a deep neural network architecture, was presented by Hardmeier (2014, Chapters 7–9), who observed significant improvements on TED talks and News Commentaries. Alternatively, to avoid extracting features from an anaphora resolution system, Callin et al. (2015) developed a classifier based on a feed-forward neural network, which considered mainly the preceding nouns, determiners and their part-of-speech as features. Their predictor worked particularly well on *ce* and *ils* pronouns, and had a macro F-score of 55.3% on the DiscoMT 2015 pronoun prediction task. Tiedemann (2015) built a cross-sentence n-gram language model over determiners and pronouns to bias the SMT model towards selecting correct pronouns. The goal of our paper, in the framework of pronoun-focused translation, is to test whether a target-side language model of nouns and pronouns can improve over a purely n-gram-based one.

3   Overview of the Method

The proposed method to predict target pronouns at the WMT 2016 task, for English-to-French, consists of two principal stages:

- We first apply several heuristics to determine if the predicted pronoun belongs to the ad-hoc cases (e.g. 'on', 'other') (see Section 5) and then predict its translation, as the PLM is not able to address them.

- If the anaphor is detected as not one of these above-mentioned cases, then we employ the PLM to score all possible candidates and select the one with the highest score (see Section 4).

In the next two sections, we discuss first in detail the construction of our pronoun language model, which has the strongest theoretical foundations, and then present the grammatical heuristics.

4   Pronoun Language Model

4.1   Overview of the PLM

The key intuition behind the idea of a Pronoun Language Model is that additional, probabilistic constrains on target pronouns can be obtained by examining the gender and number of the nouns preceding them, without any attempt to perform anaphora resolution, which is error-prone. For instance, considering the EN/FR translation divergency "*it* $\rightarrow$ *il/elle/...*", the higher the number of French masculine nouns preceding the pronoun, the higher the probability that the correct translation is *il* (masculine).

To this end, we first estimate from parallel data the probabilistic connection between the target-side distribution of gender and number features among the nouns preceding a pronoun and the actual translation of this pronoun into French (focusing on translations of *it* and *they* which exhibit strong EN/FR divergencies). Then, we use the above information to score all possible target candidates of each source pronoun *it* and *they* and select the one with highest score.

The above method is implemented as a pronoun-aware language model (PLM), which is trained as explained in the next subsection, and is then used for selecting pronoun candidate as explained in Section 6.

4.2 Learning the PLM

The data used for training the PLM is the target side (French) of the WIT^3 parallel corpus (Cettolo et al., 2012) distributed by the IWSLT workshops. This corpus is made of transcripts of TED talks, i.e. lectures that typically last 18 minutes, on various topics from science and the humanities with high relevance to society. The TED talks are given in English, then transcribed and translated by volunteers and TED editors. The French side contains 179,404 sentences, with a total of 3,880,369 words.

We process the data sequentially, word by word, from the beginning to the end. We keep track of the gender and number of the N most recent nouns and pronouns in a list, which is initialized as empty and is then updated when a new noun or pronoun is encountered. In these experiments, we set $N = 5$, i.e. we will examine up to four nouns or pronouns before a pronoun. This value is based on the intuition that the antecedent seldom occurs too far before the anaphor. To obtain the morphological tag of each word, specifically the gender and number of every noun and pronoun, we employ a French part-of-speech (POS) tagger, Morfette (Chrupala et al., 2008).

When a French pronoun is encountered, the sequence formed by the gender/number features of the N previous nouns or pronouns, acquired from the above list, and the pronoun itself is appended to a data file which will be used to train the PLM. If the lexical item can have multiple lexical functions, including pronoun – e.g. *le* or *la* can be object pronouns or determiners – then their POS assigned by Morfette is used to filter out the non-pronoun occurrences. We only process the French pronouns that are potential translations of the English *it* and *they*, namely the following list: *il, ils, elle, elles, le, la, lui, l', on, ce, ça, c', ç, ceci, celà, celui, celui-ci, celui-là, celle, celle-ci, celle-là, ceux, ceux-ci, ceux-là, celles, celles-ci, celles-là.*

In the next step, we apply the SRILM language modeling toolkit (Stolcke, 2002), with modified Kneser-Ney smoothing, to build a 5-gram language model over the training dataset collected above, which includes 179,058 of the aforementioned sequences. The sequences are given to SRILM as separate "sentences", i.e. two consecutive sequences are never joined and are considered independently of each other. The pronouns are always ending a sequence in the training data, but not necessarily in the n-grams generated by SRILM, as exemplified in Figure 1: the examples include n-grams that do not end with a pronoun, e.g. the fifth and the sixth ones. These will be needed for back-off search and are kept in the model used below.

```
-2.324736  masc.sing. masc.plur. elle
-1.543632  fem.sing.  fem.plur.  fem.sing.  elle
-0.890777  masc.sing. masc.sing. masc.sing. masc.sing. il
-1.001423  masc.sing. masc.plur. masc.plur. masc.plur. ils
-1.459787  masc.plur. masc.plur. masc.plur.
-1.398654  masc.sing. masc.plur. masc.sing. masc.sing.
```

Figure 1: Examples of PLM n-grams, starting with their log-probabilities, learned by SRILM.

4.3 Empirical Validation of the PLM

To test the intuition that a larger number of nouns and pronouns of a given gender and number increases the probability of a translation of *it* with the same gender and number, we examine in this section some parameters of the learned PLM. For instance, in Figure 2(a), first four bars, we represent how the log-probability of French masculine singular *il* varies with the number of masculine singular nouns or pronouns preceding it. We compute the average log-probability over all PLM n-grams containing exactly n time(s) (n from 1 to 4 for the bars from left to right) a masculine singular noun and finishing with *il*. The same operation can be done for other pronouns, such as *ce, ils, elle* or *elles*, as represented in the subsequent groups of bars in Figure 2(a), which all show the evolution of the probability to observe the respective pronoun after 1 or 2 or 3 or 4 masculine singular nouns (bars from left to right for each pronoun). The log-probability increases for *il* with the number of masculine singular (pro)nouns preceding it, and decreases for all the other pronouns, except for the neutral *ce*, for which it remains constant. A similar result in Figure 2(b) shows that the probability to observe *elle* after 1 or 2 or 3 or 4 feminine singular nouns increases with this number. Such results bring support to the idea of the PLM.

Similar observations can be made for the log-probability to observe one of the five pronouns listed above after 1 or 2 or 3 or 4 feminine singular nouns, as shown in Figure 2(b). Again, our proposal is supported by the fact that this probability increases for *elle* and decreases for all other pronouns.

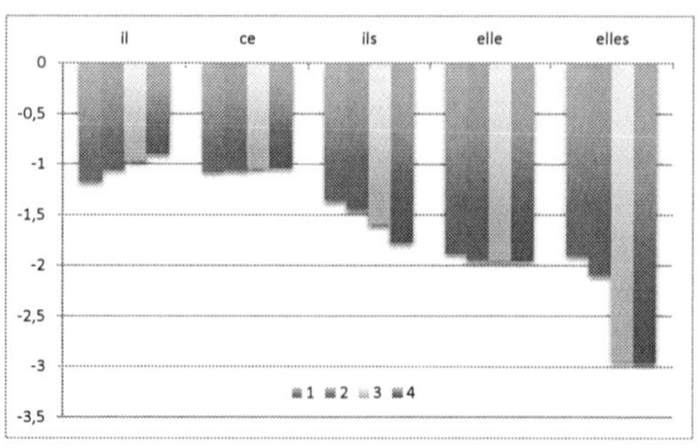

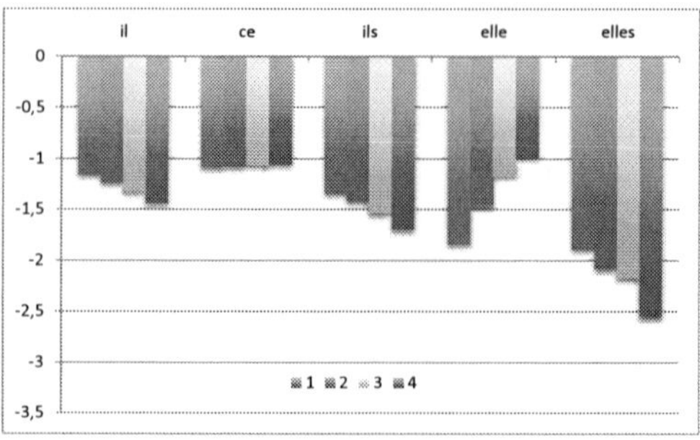

(a) masculine singular nouns   (b) feminine singular nouns

Figure 2: Log-probabilities to observe a given pronoun depending on the number of (pro)nouns of a given gender/number preceding it, either masculine singular in (a) or feminine singular in (b). In (a), the probability of *il* increases with the number of masculine singular (pro)nouns preceding it (four bars under *il*, 1 to 4 (pro)nouns from left to right), while the probabilities of all other pronouns decrease with this number. A similar result for *elle* with respect to the other pronouns is observed in (b), depending on the number of feminine singular (pro)nouns preceding *elle*.

Moreover, the log-probabilities for four combinations of features ({masculine, feminine} × {singular, plural}) and the twelve most frequent French pronouns which are translations of *it* and *they* are given in (Luong and Popescu-Belis, 2016). These results suggest that, for most third-person pronouns (*il*, *elle*, *ils*, *elles*, *le*, *la*) the average log-probability of the pronoun gradually increases when more and more nouns (or pronouns) of the same gender and number are found before it. By contrast, the log-probability decreases with the presence of more words of a different gender and number. However, such tendencies are not observed for the neuter indefinite pronoun *on*, the vowel-preceding object pronoun *l'*, or the indirect object pronoun *lui*.

Another important observation, which holds for all four possible combinations of gender and number values, is that the log-probability of the n-gram containing four nouns of the same gender and number as the pronoun (e.g. four masculine singular nouns followed by *il*) is always higher than those containing a different pronoun. Moreover, among the remaining pronouns, the PLM prioritizes the neuter ones (e.g. *ce*, *c'*, or *ca*) over those of the opposite gender or number, which is beneficial for pronoun selection by re-ranking hypotheses from an SMT decoder.

5 Grammar-Based Heuristics

Among the eight classes to predict (*il*, *elle*, *ils*, *elles*, *ce*, *cela*, *on*, *other*), the two classes *on* and *other* exhibit strong independence from the gender and number of the previous nouns and pronouns, hence they are unable to benefit from the PLM as much as the remaining ones. To detect their presence in the target sentence, we apply specific rules, based on their grammar constraints with the neighboring words.

5.1 Rule for Predicting *on*

In French, the pronoun *on* can be used in both personal and impersonal modes. The latter usage often occurs when translating an English sentence in passive voice, like in the following examples:

- *They were told to . . . → On leur a dit de . . .*

- *They are asked to . . . → On leur demande de . . .*

Nevertheless, in such cases, the French passive voice can just as well be used, respectively as: *"Il leur a été dit de . . ."* and *"Il leur est demandé de . . ."*, depending on the writing style, the latter variant being more formal. Our way to predict the presence of *on* in the target text is to examine the target word which follows the pronoun and which should not be the verb *être* (in English *to be*) in its lemmatized form. In fact, the pronoun *on*, if predicted, is not actually the translation of the source pronoun *they*, but has an impersonal function. However, in many cases of the task's training data, the placeholder appears before the actual translation, e.g. *"PLACE_HOLDER leur a dit..."*, therefore *on* is an appropriate candidate to consider. Algorithmically, the rule is formulated as follows:

```
if source = They + {are, were, 're, have been, 've been} +
   Verb (Past Participle) then
    if target = Pronoun + Verb (not être) then
        Pronoun == "on"
    end if
end if
```

In cases where the pronoun is not *on*, then it will be handled by the PLM.

5.2 Predicting Untranslated Pronouns

In English-French translation, the source pronoun might remain untranslated for instance to simplify the sentence or to avoid repeating a pronoun which was previously mentioned. For instance:

- Source: *But it takes time , it takes money .*

- Target: *Mais ça prend du temps et de l' argent.*

Although the PLM cannot address these usages, we attempt to predict the placeholder using the word following it. Specifically, if we encounter a noun, an adjective, a punctuation, a conjunction, a preposition or an adverb as the subsequent word of the placeholder, then it is very likely that the pronoun was skipped and the placeholder should be filled with an untranslated word, i.e. the *other* class.

6   Experimental Setting

We employ the TEDdev dataset from the 2015 shared task (Hardmeier et al., 2015), containing 1,664 sentences with reference translations, 563 *it* and *they* instances, as the development set to investigate the usefulness of the proposed PLM and rules. Firstly, the PLM is used independently for the prediction, and then it is incorporated with the grammar rules for detecting *on* and *other* classes.

Unlike the development set, the test set of the 2016 task (with 1,213 sentence pairs and 373 instances of *it* and *they*) comes in a lemmatized representation, which prevents participants from extracting explicitly the number of the target nouns and pronouns, though their gender is available. Hence, we only make use of the gender of the target word and the number of the source word aligned to it, using the alignment information provided.

7   Results and Analysis

The per-class micro-averaged Precision, Recall and F-score of two systems – the **PLM** alone and **PLM+rules** – are displayed in Table1: on the left-hand side for the development set and on the right-hand side for the test set.

The results on the development set demonstrate that while the PLM performs quite poorly when used alone, it is clearly improved by adding grammar rules, especially for *ils* (F = 81.37%), *ce* (F = 82.46%), and *other* (F = 55.17%). Hence, we selected **PLM+rules** as our primary submission, and kept **PLM** as the contrastive one.

The performance of our primary (**PLM+rules**) and contrastive (**PLM**) submissions, as well as the **Baseline** system for this sub-task on the test data are shown on the right side of Table 1. For the sake of completeness, we also report the official score used to rank systems, the macro-averaged Recall, on these systems in Table 2. Again, both systems perform best for *ils* and *ce*, in comparison to the remaining ones. In addition, making use of the rule for *other* class allows to boost significantly the prediction capability for this class, from zero to 57.60 F-score. Likewise, the rule for detecting *on* plays a positive role on the test data, although it brings a smaller improvement than that on the development data. Conversely, none of the two systems can output feminine plural subject pronoun *elles*, which is due to the fact that the score for *elles* is lower than that of *ils* on almost all gender-number combinations in our PLM.

Despite promising scores over certain classes, the macro-averaged recall scores (considered as the official criterion for performance assessment in the 2016 shared task) of our primary and contrastive submissions do not outperform the two baselines (36.36% and 30.44% respectively for our systems, vs. 50.85% and 46.98% for the two baselines). Furthermore, these results are markedly poorer than that of the first-ranked system (65.70%), suggesting that the target-side PLM and grammar rules, although useful, are shallow and inadequate when being used as the sole knowledge base for pronoun prediction. These results emphasize the necessity of using the source text, which is likely to contain essential features for predicting the translations of pronouns, and avoid relying on the target-side only, following a post-editing approach.

System	Pronoun	Development set			Test set		
		P (%)	**R (%)**	**F (%)**	**P (%)**	**R (%)**	**F (%)**
PLM+rules (Primary)	*il*	24.47	40.35	30.46	30.88	34.43	32.65
	elle	16.67	4.00	6.45	25.00	4.35	7.41
	ils	71.98	93.57	81.37	55.74	95.77	70.47
	elles	0.00	0.00	0.00	0.00	0.00	0.00
	ce	73.82	93.38	82.46	51.75	86.76	64.84
	cela	41.38	19.05	26.09	26.32	16.13	20.00
	on	36.36	40.00	38.10	100.00	11.11	20.00
	other	93.02	39.22	55.17	90.00	42.35	57.60
PLM (Contrastive)	*il*	14.05	59.65	22.74	25.93	34.43	29.58
	elle	13.04	12.00	12.50	14.29	4.35	6.67
	ils	59.52	17.86	27.47	51.49	97.18	67.32
	elles	0.00	0.00	0.00	0.00	0.00	0.00
	ce	38.71	15.89	22.54	49.18	88.24	63.16
	cela	17.39	6.35	9.30	26.09	19.35	22.22
	on	3.66	60.00	6.90	0.00	0.00	0.00
	other	0.00	0.00	0.00	0.00	0.00	0.00
Baseline	*il*	27.54	66.67	38.97	38.74	70.49	50.00
	elle	22.22	24.00	23.08	38.71	52.17	44.44
	ils	0.00	0.00	0.00	0.00	0.00	0.00
	elles	0.00	0.00	0.00	0.00	0.00	0.00
	ce	70.88	85.43	77.48	66.67	82.35	73.68
	cela	70.00	44.44	54.37	53.85	45.16	49.12
	on	8.11	30.00	12.77	21.88	77.78	34.15
	other	54.68	74.51	63.07	75.28	78.82	77.01

Table 1: The per-class micro-averaged Precision, Recall and F-score of **PLM+rules** (primary system), **PLM** (contrastive system) and **Baseline** on the development set and on the test set.

System	Dev. Set	Test set
PLM+Rules	41.20%	36.36%
PLM	38.66%	30.44%
Baseline	40.63%	50.85%

Table 2: The macro-averaged Recall of **PLM+rules**, **PLM** and **Baseline** on the development set and test set.

8 Conclusion and Perspectives

This paper addressed the English-French pronoun prediction task by using a Pronoun Language Model (PLM) complemented with some grammar heuristics. The PLM encodes the likelihood of each target pronoun given the sequence of gender/number values of preceding nouns and pronouns. Here, the PLM was employed to rank all possible candidate French pronouns. In two specific cases, namely for the passive or impersonal *on* and the elliptic target pronouns, the decisions were made by several specific heuristics. Although our system outperforms the baseline system on the development data, it shows a rather poor performance compared with other submissions on the test data. The presence of numerous cases where the preceding (pro)nouns are strongly divergent, and the complex usages of *on* and *other* classes in the test set, are likely the main reasons that make our approach unable to discriminate them, when used independently from decoder and source-side co-reference features.

In future work, we will integrate the PLM in the log-linear model of the decoder as a feature function. Besides, we will take into consideration the positional factor by putting more weight on the nouns and pronouns that are closer to the examined one, in comparison to more distant ones, when they share the same gender-number. Furthermore, we will also attempt to study and exploit linguistic characteristics to distinguish among neuter French pronouns.

Acknowledgments

We are grateful for their support to the Swiss National Science Foundation (SNSF) under the Sinergia MODERN project (www.idiap.ch/project/modern/, grant n. 147653) and to the European Union under the Horizon 2020 SUMMA project (www.summa-project.eu, grant n. 688139).

References

Jimmy Callin, Christian Hardmeier, and Jörg Tiedemann. 2015. Part-of-speech driven cross-lingual pronoun prediction with feed-forward neural networks. In *Proceedings of the Second Workshop on Discourse in Machine Translation (DiscoMT)*, pages 59–64, Lisbon, Portugal.

Mauro Cettolo, Christian Girardi, and Marcello Federico. 2012. WIT³: Web inventory of transcribed and translated talks. In *Proceedings of the 16th Conference of the European Association for Machine Translation (EAMT)*, pages 261–268, Trento, Italy.

Grzegorz Chrupala, Georgiana Dinu, and Josef van Genabith. 2008. Learning morphology with Morfette. In *Proceedings of the 6th International Conference on Language Resources and Evaluation (LREC)*, Marrakech, Morocco.

Liane Guillou, Christian Hardmeier, Preslav Nakov, Sara Stymne, Jörg Tiedemann, Yannick Versley, Mauro Cettolo, Bonnie Webber, and Andrei Popescu-Belis. 2016. Findings of the 2016 WMT shared task on cross-lingual pronoun prediction. In *Proceedings of the First Conference on Machine Translation (WMT16)*, Berlin, Germany. Association for Computational Linguistics.

Liane Guillou. 2016. *Incorporating Pronoun Function into Statistical Machine Translation*. PhD thesis, University of Edinburgh, UK.

Christian Hardmeier and Marcello Federico. 2010. Modelling pronominal anaphora in statistical machine translation. In *Proceedings of International Workshop on Spoken Language Translation (IWSLT)*, Paris, France.

Christian Hardmeier, Preslav Nakov, Sara Stymne, Jörg Tiedemann, Yannick Versley, and Mauro Cettolo. 2015. Pronoun-focused MT and cross-lingual pronoun prediction: Findings of the 2015 DiscoMT shared task on pronoun translation. In *Proceedings of the Second Workshop on Discourse in Machine Translation (DiscoMT)*, pages 1–16, Lisbon, Portugal.

Christian Hardmeier. 2014. *Discourse in Statistical Machine Translation*. PhD thesis, Uppsala University, Sweden.

Ronan Le Nagard and Philipp Koehn. 2010. Aiding pronoun translation with co-reference resolution. In *Proceedings of the Joint 5th Workshop on Statistical Machine Translation and Metrics (MATR)*, pages 258–267, Uppsala, Sweden.

Ngoc Quang Luong and Andrei Popescu-Belis. 2016. A contextual language model to improve machine translation of pronouns by re-ranking translation hypotheses. In *Proceedings of the 19th Conference of the European Association for Machine Translation (EAMT)*, pages 292–304, Riga, Latvia.

Ngoc Quang Luong, Lesly Miculicich Werlen, and Andrei Popescu-Belis. 2015. Pronoun translation and prediction with or without coreference links. In *Proceedings of the Second Workshop on Discourse in Machine Translation (DiscoMT)*, pages 94–100, Lisbon, Portugal.

Andreas Stolcke. 2002. SRILM – an extensible language modeling toolkit. In *Proceedings of the 7th International Conference on Spoken Language Processing (ICSLP)*, pages 901–904, Denver, CO, USA.

Jorg Tiedemann. 2015. Baseline models for pronoun prediction and pronoun-aware translation. In *Proceedings of the Second Workshop on Discourse in Machine Translation (DiscoMT)*, Lisbon, Portugal.

Cross-Lingual Pronoun Prediction with Deep Recurrent Neural Networks

Juhani Luotolahti[*,1] **Jenna Kanerva**[*,1,2] **and Filip Ginter**[1]
[1]Department of Information Technology, University of Turku, Finland
[2]University of Turku Graduate School (UTUGS), Turku, Finland
`mjluot@utu.fi  jmnybl@utu.fi  figint@utu.fi`

Abstract

In this paper we present our winning system in the WMT16 Shared Task on Cross-Lingual Pronoun Prediction, where the objective is to predict a missing target language pronoun based on the target and source sentences. Our system is a deep recurrent neural network, which reads both the source language and target language context with a softmax layer making the final prediction. Our system achieves the best macro recall on all four language pairs. The margin to the next best system ranges between less than 1pp and almost 12pp depending on the language pair.

1 Introduction

Automatic translation of pronouns across languages can be seen as an subtask of the full machine translation. In the pronoun translation task the special challenge is posed by anaphora resolution as well as differing gender marking in different languages. The WMT16 Shared Task on Cross-Language Pronoun Prediction strives to seek for methods to address this particular problem (Guillou et al., 2016).

This shared task includes two language pairs, English-French and English-German, and both translation directions, so in total four different source-target pairs must be considered. In the target language side selected set of pronouns are substituted with `replace`, and the task is then to predict the missing pronoun. Furthermore, the target side language is not given as running text, but instead in lemma plus part-of-speech tag format. This is to mimic the representation which many standard machine translation systems produce and to complicate the matter of standard

---

* Both authors contributed equally to this work.

*Source: That 's how **they** like to live .*
*Target: ce|PRON être|VER comme|ADV cela|PRON que|PRON **REPLACE_3** aimer|VER vivre|VER .|.*

Figure 1: An example sentence from the English to French training data, where the REPLACE_3 is a placeholder for the word to be predicted.

language modeling. An example of an English-French sentence pair is given in Figure 1. Furthermore, the training data as provided by the organizers of the the task includes automatically produced word-level alignments between the source and the target language.

In this paper we describe the pronoun prediction system of the Turku NLP Group. Our system is a deep recurrent neural network with word-level embeddings, two layers of Gated Recurrent Units (GRUs) and a softmax layer on top of it to make the final prediction. The network uses both source and target contexts to make the prediction, and no additional data or tools are used beside the data provided by the organizers. The system has the best macro recall score in the official evaluation on all four language pairs.

2 Related work

This shared task is a spiritual successor to an earlier cross-lingual pronoun prediction shared task (Hardmeier et al., 2015). The systems submitted to the earlier task provide us with a good view of the recent related work on the problem. The earlier task received altogether six system description papers. The organizers identify two main approaches used by the participants. Teams UEDIN (Wetzel et al., 2015) and MALTA (Pham and van der Plas, 2015) explicitly tried to resolve anaphoras in the text and using the information to

Proceedings of the First Conference on Machine Translation, Volume 2: Shared Task Papers, pages 596–601,
Berlin, Germany, August 11-12, 2016. ©2016 Association for Computational Linguistics

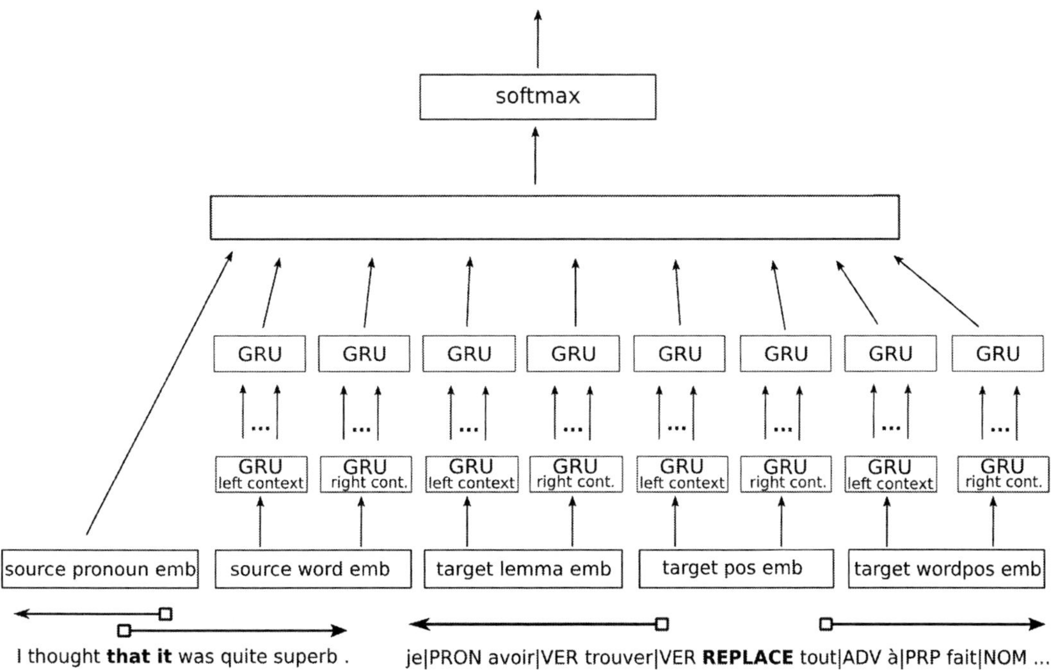

Figure 2: The architecture of our recurrent neural network system.

help predict the pronoun.

Other teams relied more on the context, for example UU-Tiedemann (Tiedemann, 2015) used a linear SVM with features from the context of the pronoun. IDIAP (Luong et al., 2015) went on to use a naive-bayes classifier with features from contextual noun-phrases. WHATELLES (Callin et al., 2015) used a neural network approach with features from preceding noun-phrases.

It is to be noted that the last year's task was won by a language model baseline, provided by the organizers. Our system fits the second category of systems, those relying on the context to predict the pronoun. None of the systems participating in the shared task seem to be using explicit sequence classification approaches.

3 Network

3.1 Architecture

Our system is a deep recurrent neural network model with learned token-level embeddings, two layers of Gated Recurrent Units (GRUs), a dense network layer with rectified linear unit (ReLU) activation, and a softmax layer. Our network architecture is described in Figure 2.

The first layer on the bottom of the Figure 2 illustrates how source and target contexts are read.

On the target side the context is read in the left and right direction starting from the `replace` token, and the `replace` token itself is not included in the context window. As the training data includes word-level alignments between the source and target language, we are able to identify the source language counterpart for the missing pronoun. This pronoun is used as a starting point for source context reading to both left and right direction the same way as in the target side. However, in the source side the aligned pronoun is always included in both context windows. If the `replace` token is aligned to multiple source side words (the pronoun to be translated can be considered as a multi-word expression), reading the right-side context always starts from the left-most alignment, and vice versa.

Starting from the input of the network, our system has five sets of 90-dimensional embedding matrices; embeddings for source language words, separate embeddings for the target language lemmas, part-of-speech tags and combination of lemmas and part-of-speech tags. In addition we have separate embeddings for source language pronouns aligned with the unknown target pronoun. Context windows are then sequences of indices for these different token-level embeddings, except the aligned source language pronoun, which is always just one index as the tokens are concatenated if the alignments refers to multiple source language words. Thus, the network has a total of nine inputs, two different directions for each set of context embeddings, and the aligned source language pronoun. As we do not use external data sources, these embeddings are randomly initialized.

Once the sequence of context words are turned into embeddings, they are given to the first layer of GRUs, which output is given as a sequence to the second layer of GRUs. The second GRU layer then reads the input sequence and outputs the last vector produced, i.e. a fixed-length representation of the input sequence. In all GRUs we use 90-dimensional internal representation.

All these eight products of the recurrent layers, are concatenated together with the embedding for the aligned source language pronoun and given to a 256-dimensional dense neural network layer, with ReLU activation function[1]. This vector is then fed to a layer with softmax activation and an output for each possible output pronoun to make the final prediction.

While our model relies on learned embeddings instead of predefined set of features, a process similar to feature engineering takes place while designing the system architecture. The design choices were made in a greedy manner and mostly the system was built additively, testing new features and adding the promising ones to the final system. Since not all design choice combinations were properly tested during the system development, we include a short evaluation of different settings in Section 4.1.

3.2 Training the system

Only the training data provided by the shared task organizers is used to train our system. The data is based on three different datasets, the Europarl dataset (Koehn, 2005), news commentary corpora (IWSLT15, NCv9), and the TED corpus[2]. We used the whole TED corpus only as development data, and thus our submitted systems are trained on the union of Europarl and news commentary texts, which are randomly shuffled on document level. The total size of training data for each source–target pair is approximately 2.4M sentences, having 590K–760K training examples depending on

the pair. The vocabulary sizes, when training with the full training data are listed in Table 1. The large number of aligned pronouns for French-English and English-French language pairs is because of the alignments for the pronoun were often multiple token in length.

In previous studies using only in-domain data has provided competitive performance (Tiedemann, 2015; Callin et al., 2015), and as Europarl can be seen as out-of-the-domain data, in Section 4 we compare the performance of our system when trained using only in-domain data.

Since the main metric in the official evaluation is macro recall, our primary submission is trained to optimize that. This is done by weighting the loss of the training examples relative to the frequencies of the classes, so that misclassifying a rare class is seen by the network as more serious mistake than misclassifying a common class. This scheme produces outputs with more emphasis on rare classes, rather than going after the most common ones. The contrastive submission is trained in the standard way, where each example is seen as equal.

In both our submissions exactly the same system architecture is used for all four language pairs, and no language-dependent optimization was carried out. However, the number of epochs used in training differs, and the prediction performance on the development set was used to decide the optimal number of epochs for each language pair.

The system was implemented in Keras (Chollet, 2015), and trained and developed on the CSC cluster[3] of NVidia Tesla 40KT GPUs. Only one GPU was used to train a single network. Depending on the settings of the network and training data size a single training epoch took 25 minutes to an hour, and all networks were trained in 9 hours. Usually the performance of the network peaked within the first 5 training epochs when evaluated on the development set, and most often reached performance very close to the maximum within three training epochs. All networks were evaluated on the development set after each training epoch, and the model with the highest macro recall was selected for evaluation.

The practical, time-wise, predictive performance of our system is reasonable and doesn't require the use of a GPU. Predicting a test set for an individual language pair takes on a 6-core Intel

---

[1] Dense layer with tanh activation was also tested, but ReLU turned out to give better results.

[2] http://www.ted.com

[3] www.csc.fi

	Target POS	Target Word	Target Word-POS	Source Word	Aligned Pronouns	Pronouns
de-en	15	170,484	181,531	539,980	9	9
en-de	15	446,645	454,175	198,244	6	5
fr-en	34	171,633	182,763	220,204	18,960	8
en-fr	39	158,755	179,299	199,774	7174	8

Table 1: The vocabulary sizes of the models

	De-En		En-De		Fr-En		En-Fr	
Architecture	Macro R	Micro F	Macro R	Micro F	Macro R	Micro F	Macro R	Micro F
primary	**73.91**	75.36	64.41	71.54	**72.03**	80.79	65.70	70.51
no stacking	65.63	75.98	61.84	73.37	68.84	77.74	70.00	74.26
only in-domain	59.18	75.36	50.72	66.06	57.80	74.09	58.09	65.15
short context	61.29	73.50	**65.66**	71.80	65.84	79.59	69.27	70.51
cross-sentence	60.76	70.81	46.91	49.61	60.46	78.05	61.33	69.17
contrastive	72.60	**80.54**	58.39	72.85	66.54	**85.06**	61.46	72.39
no stacking	65.35	79.30	59.71	**76.76**	61.23	81.71	**70.88**	**77.75**

Table 2: Macro recall and micro F-score for all our system combinations evaluated on the test set. In the **primary** section, the systems are trained to optimize macro recall, and in the **contrastive** section, the systems are optimized without preference towards rare classes. In **no stacking**, only one layer of GRUs is used. **Only in-domain** refers to a version where the Europarl data was not used in training, and **short-context** refers to a version in which the context window was set to 5. **Cross-sentence** refers to a version where the context was expanded also beyond the current sentence.

Xeon CPU 1m 55s, of which 9 seconds is used for prediction and the rest for loading model weights and building the network.

4 Results

In the official test evaluation results our primary system has the best score across all language pairs (see Table 3). In two language pairs, German–English and English–French, we have a modest improvement over the second best system. However, in the other two language pairs, the margin is substantial, 11.9pp for the English–German pair and 6.4pp for the French–English pair. When we look closer into class frequencies and system predictions, it can be seen that in these two pairs our system benefits especially much from predicting small classes relatively well.

In our primary submission, the system was optimized towards macro-averaged recall whereas in our contrastive submission standard training metrics were used. Therefore the prediction accuracy is better in our contrastive submission than it is in the primary submission by 1.3pp–5.2pp depending on the language pair, but at the same time macro recall decreases by 1.3pp–6.0pp. Yet, in the two language pairs with a wide margin to other teams, our contrastive system still achieves

better macro recall than any other system. For per-language scores for both our submissions, see rows *TurkuNLP* for primary and *TurkuNLP cont* for contrastive in Table 3.

4.1 Feature evaluation

We ran a small study of different system settings to evaluate our design choices. Results are shown in Table 2, where the performance is evaluated on the official test set. In the test set evaluation our primary system gives the highest score on two language pairs, but loses to another system setting in other two language pairs. Overall, the primary system still performs best on average when measured on macro recall.

As stated in Section 3.1, both our submissions are based on a version of the network with stacked GRU units. In preliminary studies, the stacked approach increased the prediction performance and this holds on the test set for all language pairs except English-French. While on average the stacked system performs 2.4pp better on macro recall, on the English-French pair the non-stacked model performs 4.3pp better.

Another important feature is the size of the context window. In previous work a rather small context was noted to work relatively well (Tiedemann,

System	Macro Recall			
	De–En	En–De	Fr–En	En-Fr
TurkuNLP	**73.91**	**64.41**	**72.03**	**65.70**
TurkuNLP cont	72.60	58.39	66.54	61.46
UKYOTO	73.17*	52.50*	65.63*	62.44
limsi				59.32
UHELSINKI	69.76	44.69	62.98	57.50
UU-Hardmeier		50.36		60.63
uedin		48.72		61.62
UUPSALA	59.56	47.43	62.65	48.92
UU-Stymne	59.28	52.12	36.44	65.35*
baseline–x	44.52	47.86	42.96	50.85
CUNI	60.42	28.26		
UU-Cap		41.61		
baseline–0	42.15	38.53	38.38	46.98
Idiap				36.36

Table 3: Scores for all primary systems and our contrastive system on the official test set evaluation sorted by the average score across language pairs. For each language pair the best score is bolded and the second best is marked with a star (our contrastive submission is not taken into account).

2015; Callin et al., 2015). However, in our submission systems the maximum size of the context was set to 50, and in our development experiments radically shorter context sizes hurt the prediction performance of our system. However, in test set evaluation both language pairs with English as the source language seem to benefit from shorter context, especially English-French pair which scores 3.6pp higher in macro recall than our primary system, but also loses to the version with longer context without stacking by 0.73pp in macro recall. Other language pairs benefit from larger context (see *short context* in Table 2).

In addition, we evaluate allowing the context window to extend beyond the current sentence boundary. The maximum context size is always 50, although when restricted to within one sentence, it naturally rarely reaches it. In our primary and contrastive submissions, the context was limited to include only the current sentence, and the results using the context beyond the sentence are in the row *cross-sentence* in Table 2. We can observe that no language pair seems to benefit from a larger context on the test set.

As mentioned earlier, the Europarl dataset can be considered as out-of-the-domain data. The *in-domain* row in Table 2 refers to an experiment where Europarl was discarded from the training data and thus the system was trained only on in-domain data. Naturally, the amount of training data is then much smaller, the data size drops from 2.4M sentences to approx. 400K sentences. This hurts the performance on all language pairs, indicating that our method benefits from a lot of training data and might be indicative of its ability to generalize to other domains.

5 Conclusion

In this paper we presented our system for the cross-lingual pronoun prediction shared task. Our system is based on recurrent neural networks and token-level embeddings of the source and target languages, and is trained without any external data. Our system fared well in the shared task, having the highest macro recall in all language pairs. Our results suggest sequence classification and recurrent neural networks to be an approach worthy of consideration when tackling the problem. It is also worth noting that our system is wholly language-agnostic and demonstrates that an approach with very little custom-built features can have a good performance on the task.

As the system is trained only using the official training data without any external tools, it would be interesting to test whether pre-trained token-level embeddings would increase its performance. Additionally, pre-training the network with monolingual data could be considered.

Our system is openly available at https://github.com/TurkuNLP/smt-pronouns.

Acknowledgments

This work was supported by the Kone Foundation. Computational resources were provided by CSC – IT Center for Science.

References

Jimmy Callin, Christian Hardmeier, and Jörg Tiedemann. 2015. Part-of-speech driven cross-lingual pronoun prediction with feed-forward neural networks. In *Proceedings of the Second Workshop on Discourse in Machine Translation*, pages 59–64. Association for Computational Linguistics.

Franois Chollet. 2015. Keras. `https://github.com/fchollet/keras`.

Liane Guillou, Christian Hardmeier, Preslav Nakov, Sara Stymne, Jörg Tiedemann, Yannick Versley, Mauro Cettolo, Bonnie Webber, and Andrei Popescu-Belis. 2016. Findings of the 2016 WMT shared task on cross-lingual pronoun prediction. In *Proceedings of the First Conference on Machine Translation (WMT16)*. Association for Computational Linguistics.

Christian Hardmeier, Preslav Nakov, Sara Stymne, Jörg Tiedemann, Yannick Versley, and Mauro Cettolo. 2015. Pronoun-focused MT and cross-lingual pronoun prediction: Findings of the 2015 DiscoMT shared task on pronoun translation. In *Proceedings of the Second Workshop on Discourse in Machine Translation*, pages 1–16. Association for Computational Linguistics.

Philipp Koehn. 2005. Europarl: A parallel corpus for statistical machine translation. In *MT summit*, volume 5, pages 79–86.

Ngoc-Quang Luong, Lesly Miculicich Werlen, and Andrei Popescu-Belis. 2015. Pronoun translation and prediction with or without coreference links. In *Proceedings of the Second Workshop on Discourse in Machine Translation*, pages 95–100. Association for Computational Linguistics.

Ngoc-Quan Pham and Lonneke van der Plas. 2015. Predicting pronouns across languages with continuous word spaces. In *Proceedings of the Second Workshop on Discourse in Machine Translation*, pages 101–107. Association for Computational Linguistics.

Jörg Tiedemann. 2015. Baseline models for pronoun prediction and pronoun-aware translation. In *Proceedings of the Second Workshop on Discourse in Machine Translation*, pages 108–114. Association for Computational Linguistics.

Dominikus Wetzel, Adam Lopez, and Bonnie Webber. 2015. A maximum entropy classifier for crosslingual pronoun prediction. In *Proceedings of the Second Workshop on Discourse in Machine Translation*, pages 115–121. Association for Computational Linguistics.

Pronoun Prediction with Linguistic Features and Example Weighing

Michal Novák
Charles University in Prague, Faculty of Mathematics and Physics
Institute of Formal and Applied Linguistics
Malostranské náměstí 25, CZ-11800 Prague 1
`mnovak@ufal.mff.cuni.cz`

Abstract

We present a system submitted to the WMT16 shared task in cross-lingual pronoun prediction, in particular, to the English-to-German and German-to-English sub-tasks. The system is based on a linear classifier making use of features both from the target language model and from linguistically analyzed source and target texts. Furthermore, we apply example weighing in classifier learning, which proved to be beneficial for recall in less frequent pronoun classes. Compared to other shared task participants, our best English-to-German system is able to rank just below the top performing submissions.

1 Introduction

Previous works concerning translation of pronouns[1] have shown that unlike other words, pronouns require a special treatment. Context and target language grammar influence pronoun translation much more profoundly than the translation of parts-of-speech carrying lexical information.

This paper presents a system for the WMT16 shared task of cross-lingual pronoun prediction (Guillou et al., 2016),[2] the task that looks at the problem of pronoun translation in a more simplified way. Here, the objective is to predict a target language pronoun from a set of possible candidates, given source text, lemmatized and part-of-speech-tagged target text, and automatic word alignment. We address specifically the sub-tasks of English-to-German and German-to-English pronoun prediction.

We take a machine learning approach to the problem and apply a linear classifier. Our approach combines features coming from the target language model with features extracted from the linguistically analyzed source and target texts. We also introduce training example weighing, which aims at improving the prediction accuracy of less populated target pronouns. All the source codes used to build the system are publicly available.[3]

According to the WMT16 pronoun translation shared task results (Guillou et al., 2016), our best German-to-English system ranks in the middle of the pack while our English-to-German systems seem to be the poorest. However, after the shared task submission deadline, we discovered an error in post-processing of the classifier predictions on the evaluation set for the English-to-German direction. After correcting this error, our system reaches the 2nd best result for this language direction.

The paper is structured as follows. After introducing the related work in Section 7, we describe three preprocessing components of our system that enrich the input data with additional information in Section 2. Section 3 then presents features extracted from the data whereas Section 4 gives more details about the method used to train the model. In Section 5, all our system configurations submitted to the shared tasks are evaluated. Finally, we examine the effect of individual features and example weighing in Section 6 before we conclude in Section 8.

2 Preprocessing components

The preprocessing stage combines three components, each of them enriching the input data with additional information: a target language model, an automatic linguistic analysis of the source sen-

---

[1] Summarized by Hardmeier (2014).

[2] `http://www.statmt.org/wmt16/pronoun-task.html`

[3] `https://github.com/ufal/wmt16-pronouns`

Proceedings of the First Conference on Machine Translation, Volume 2: Shared Task Papers, pages 602–608,
Berlin, Germany, August 11-12, 2016. ©2016 Association for Computational Linguistics

tences, and a basic automatic analysis of the target sentences.

2.1 Target language model

For language modeling, we employed the KenLM Language Model Toolkit (Heafield et al., 2013), an efficient implementation of large language models with modified Kneser-Ney smoothing (Kneser and Ney, 1995).

Lemmatized 5-gram models for English and German have been supplied as a baseline system by the organizers of the shared task. An integral part of the baseline system is a wrapper script[4] performing necessary preprocessing before the actual probability estimation. For instance, it selects words which may possibly belong to the OTHER class[5] and it enables setting a penalty for preferring an empty word.[6] We only adjusted the wrapper script so that it fits into our processing pipeline, making no modifications to the estimation machinery.

2.2 Source language analysis

In the input data supplied by the task organizers, source text is represented as plain tokenized sentences. We have processed the source texts with tools obtaining additional linguistic analysis. However, due to different availability of these tools for English and German, the depth of the analysis differs. We describe both analysis pipelines separately in the following:

English. English source texts have been analyzed up to the level of deep syntax using the Treex framework (Popel and Žabokrtský, 2010) incorporating several external tools. The processing pipeline consists of part-of-speech tagging with the Morče tool (Spoustová et al., 2007) dependency parsing conducted by the MST parser (McDonald et al., 2005), semantic role labeling (Bojar et al., 2016), and coreference resolution obtained as a combination of Treex coreference modules and the Bart 2 toolkit (Versley et al., 2008; Uryupina et al., 2012). Prior to the last step, all instances of the pronoun *it* are assigned a probability

---

[4]https://bitbucket.org/yannick/discomt_baseline/src

[5]The OTHER class comprise words, not necessarily pronouns, that appear often enough in the context typical for pronouns to be resolved but not enough to form their own class. Furthermore, it can be an empty word if the source pronoun has no target language counterpart.

[6]In all experiments, we used zero penalty.

of being anaphoric by the NADA tool (Bergsma and Yarowsky, 2011).

German. We utilized the MATE tools[7] (Björkelund et al., 2010) to perform part-of-speech tagging, morphological analysis (necessary to obtain grammatical categories such as gender or number), and transition-based dependency parsing (Bohnet and Nivre, 2012; Seeker and Kuhn, 2012).

2.3 Target language analysis

In the data supplied by the task organizers, the format of the target language sentences differs from the source language format. Not only are the target words to be predicted replaced by a placeholder, but all other tokens are also substituted with corresponding lemmas and coarse-grained part-of-speech tags.

For this reason, we needed to simplify the analysis of target texts. The parsers used for source texts do not accept the tagset used by the organizers. There are two possible solutions to fix this disagreement: either running a part-of-speech tagger producing tags that agree with the tagset required by the parser, or obtaining suitable part-of-speech tags by a transformation of the original tagset. However, both options are prone to errors. In the former option, the tags produced in this way would definitely be of low quality as only a lemmatized text is available. This would cause problems especially for German. The latter option brings another problem. The original tagsets (12 tags in both English and German) are more coarse-grained than the tagsets required by the parsers (44 and 53 tags in English and German, respectively), which makes the transformation in this direction difficult.

Due to these obstacles, we decided to abandon any additional linguistic processing except for the identification of noun genders. We consider gender and number information one of the most valuable inputs for correct pronoun translation. While the number information is hard to reconstruct from a lemmatized text with part-of-speech tags having no indication of grammatical number, gender can be reconstructed from a noun lemma itself quite satisfactorily. In each of the languages, we approached the task of obtaining gender for a given noun in a different way.

---

[7]https://code.google.com/archive/p/mate-tools/

English. The gender information was obtained using the data collected by Bergsma and Lin (2006).[8] They used paths in dependency trees to learn the likelihood of coreference between a pronoun and a noun candidate and then applied them in a bootstrapping fashion on larger data to obtain a noun gender and number distribution in different contexts.

For the sake of simplicity, we filtered their list only to single-word items. If we encounter a token with a noun tag assigned in the target sentence, its lemma is looked up in the list and assigned the most probable gender, if any is found. Otherwise, the neuter gender is assumed.

German. We run the MATE morphological analysis separately for every lemma labeled as a noun. If no gender information is obtained, the noun is assigned the neuter gender.

3 Feature extraction

Having both the source and the target texts enriched with additional linguistic information, we extract a set of instances that are later fed into into our classifier. An instance is extracted for every target-language pronoun (placeholder) to be classified represented by features that can be divided into several categories:

Target language model features. Using the KenLM with the wrapper supplied by the organizers, we obtain an estimated probability value for every candidate pronoun. From this, we produce features describing the actual probability values for each candidate word, quantized into 9 bins. Furthermore, features ranking the candidate words by their probabilities, quantized in three different ways, are extracted.

Source language features. The data supplied by the organizers also contain automatic word alignment between the source and the target sentences. Therefore, when extracting features for a given placeholder in the target language, we are able to do the same for its counterparts in the source language. Deeper linguistic analysis performed for the source language (see Section 2.2) allows us to extract richer features than for the target language.

For every source counterpart of a target pronoun placeholder, we extract its lemma, syntactic dependency function, the lemma of its parent in the dependency tree, and combinations of the previous features. As the analysis of English goes deeper than the surface syntax, we include the semantic function of the source counterpart. If the counterpart is an instance of the pronoun *it*, we add the anaphoricity probability estimated by the NADA detector, quantized in the same way as the probabilities coming from the KenLM model.

Target language features. The lemma of a parent verb of the target pronoun placeholder might also be a valuable feature. Even though we have not performed a syntactic analysis on the target text (see Section 2.3), we are still able to approximate it in several ways. The easiest option is to list all verb lemmas that appear in a relatively small context surrounding the placeholder (1, 3, or 5 words). Another approach is to project the parent dependency relation from the source sentence via word alignment. We also extract the part-of-speech tags of the parents collected in this way, since they might not be verbs due to possible errors.

Antecedent features. The gender of an anaphoric pronoun is often determined by the gender of its antecedent. Same as with syntactic trees, we have no information on coreference in the target text. Again, we approximate it in two ways. We project the coreference link via word alignment and use the gender of the projected antecedent. Note that this approach can be used only in the English-to-German direction due to missing coreference resolution for German. To extract similar information also for the opposite direction, we take advantage of the fact that the task is defined for subject pronouns only. A tendency of consecutive subjects to refer to the same entity inspired us to include the gender of the previous target language subject as a feature. The indicator whether a word is a subject is again projected via alignment from the source text.

4 Model

Pronoun prediction as specified by the organizers is a classification task. We address it by machine learning, building a linear model using the multiclass variant of the logistic loss and stochastic gradient descent optimization as implemented in the Vowpal Wabbit toolkit.[9] To train the model, we

---

[8]http://www.clsp.jhu.edu/~sbergsma/Gender/Data/

[9]Available at https://github.com/JohnLangford/vowpal_wabbit/wiki. Vowpal Wabbit has been chosen due

	Name	Setting	Dev		Eval	
			MACRO-R	ACC	MACRO-R	ACC
EN-to-DE	baseline	—	34.35	42.81	38.53	50.13
	CUNI-primary	weighted, passes: 5, L1: 3×10^{-7}	**45.63**	57.72	**54.37	*64.23
	CUNI-contrastive	unweighted, passes: 1, L1: 5×10^{-6}	42.54	63.51	*51.74	*71.80
DE-to-EN	baseline	—	36.08	50.47	42.15	53.42
	CUNI-primary	weighted, passes: 1, L1: 0	**56.47**	68.35	**60.42**	64.18
	CUNI-contrastive	unweighted, passes: 5, L1: 0	51.62	70.59	56.83	65.22

Table 1: Our Systems submitted to the shared task and their performance compared to the baseline system. The official measure of performance is macro-averaged recall (MACRO-R), while accuracy (ACC) serves as a contrastive measure. Scores labeled by the * symbol differ from the official results of the shared task (Guillou et al., 2016) as an error has been discovered after the task submission deadline.

run the learner over the training data with features described in Section 3, possibly in multiple passes and with various rates of L1 or L2 regularization.

Optimization with respect to the logistic loss function is a widely used approximation of the the accuracy measure. However, the official scoring metric set by the task organizers is the macro-averaged recall. Macro-averaging causes that improvements in recall for less frequent target pronouns have a stronger effect than improvements for more frequent pronouns. We address this issue by weighing the training data instances based on the target class. We weigh the classes in an inverse proportion to how frequently they appear in the training data. The less frequent a pronoun is, the heavier penalty is incurred if it is misclassified.

5 Submitted systems

We submitted four systems to the shared task – two systems to each of the two sub-tasks: English-to-German and German-to-English prediction. The systems trained on the weighted examples are considered as *primary* while the unweighted systems were submitted as *contrastive*.

Training examples have been extracted from all the data supplied for training by the organizers.[10] The same holds for the data designated for development and evaluation testing.

The best combination of learning parameters has been selected by a grid search with various parameter settings on the development data. Table 1 specifies the learning parameters used for all systems submitted. It also shows macro-averaged recall and accuracy measured on both the development and the evaluation set Moreover, it and compares the performance with the baseline system based on the KenLM target language model as supplied by the organizers (see Section 2.1).

Note that the scores of our English-to-German systems achieved on the evaluation set are much better than the scores presented in the official results of the shared task Guillou et al. (2016). An error that concerned merging of the classifier output into the test data file for submission, which was, however, discovered after the deadline for task submissions. According to the official results, our German-to-English primary system is ranked fourth among six participating primary systems. Our English-to-German primary system, ranked last among nine systems in the official results, would place as second if we took the correct scores.

6 Feature ablation and weighing analysis

In order to assess the effect of individual feature types, we carried out an additional experiment. For both translation directions we trained models on various subsets of the complete feature set. All the models have been trained in both weighted and unweighted scenarios.

The experiments were conducted with the following feature sets:

- `all`: the complete feature set as described in Section 3

- `-src`: the complete feature set, excluding source language features

---

to its fastest throughput among all machine learning tools known to us as well as due to the remarkable variety of options for learning, e.g. example weighing used in our experiments. However, there are still options that are worth to be examined in future experiments, for instance using other loss functions, e.g. a hinge loss which is equivalent to the SVM algorithm.

[10]http://data.statmt.org/wmt16/pronoun-task/

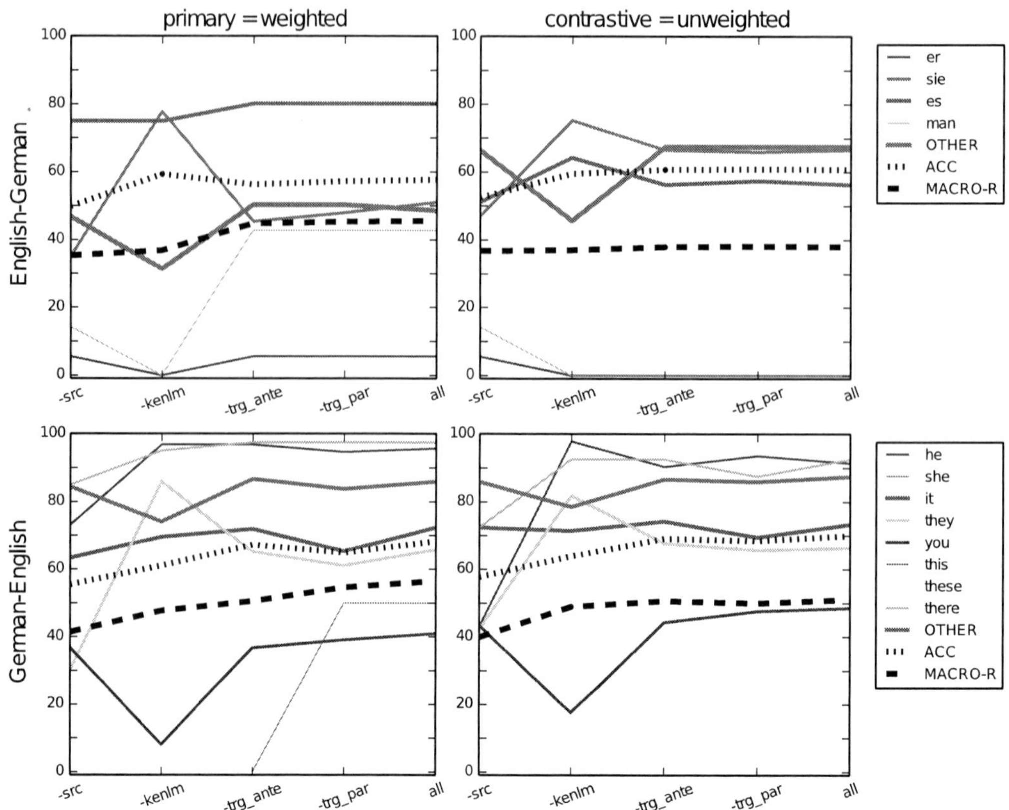

Figure 1: The impact of feature ablation on per-class recall (see Section 6 for details), macro-averaged recall (MACRO-R), and accuracy (ACC) in the four systems submitted to the shared task.

- `-kenlm`: the complete feature set, excluding KenLM features

- `-trg_ante`: the complete feature set, excluding features approximating the gender of the antecedent of the target pronoun

- `-trg_par`: the complete feature set, excluding features approximating the parent of the target pronoun

Figure 1 shows the performance of weighted and unweighted models for both translation directions if trained in all of the feature settings listed above. The performance is measured by recall on each of the target classes (solid color lines, whose widths illustrate the frequency of the class in the training data), as well as by micro-averaged recall, which equals to overall accuracy for this task (dotted line), and macro-averaged recall, which is the official measure in the shared task (dashed line).

The graphs show that the impact of individual feature categories on the macro-averaged recall is generally higher in the German-English direction

and for weighted models. For instance, leaving out the most valuable category of source language features decreases the performance level by just 1 percentage point for the English-German unweighted model while degrading the performance of the German-English model by 15 percentage points. The graphs also show that the KenLM features have the strongest effect on the final recall values for the individual pronoun classes. A positive effect of English coreference resolution to determining the correct gender of a German pronoun can be also observed. Adding antecedent features to English-to-German weighted system causes a small recall increase of the pronoun *sie* with almost no degradation to other classes.

The impact of instance weighing turns out to be more interesting. Focusing on scores for individual classes, one can observe that the pronouns that benefit from weighing the most are the less frequent ones, i.e., *man* and *er* in German, *there*, *he*, and *she* in English. On the other hand, the effect of weighing reduces performance in frequent classes, such as *OTHER*, German *sie*, and English *you*. The only exception is the German pronoun *es*, whose recall rises for weighted models even though it is one of the most frequent pronoun classes. Overall, instance weighting fulfills our expectations: although it causes a decrease in recall for frequent pronoun classes, it improves the official macro-averaged recall score.

7 Related work

A similar problem was addressed in the DiscoMT 2015 shared task on pronoun translation (Hardmeier et al., 2015) as a cross-lingual pronoun prediction subtask. It differed from the current task in one main aspect: the manually translated target text was available in its surface form as an input, i.e., it was neither machine-translated nor lemmatized and part-of-speech-tagged at least as it is in the WMT16 shared task. This aspect, far from a real-world machine translation scenario, probably caused that none of the participants was able to beat the baseline, the target language model.

Out of the DiscoMT 2015 shared task submissions, the system by Wetzel et al. (2015) is most similar to ours. On the source side (English in their case), they extract morphological information as well as coreference relations (they use Stanford CoreNLP (Lee et al., 2013) whereas we apply Bart 2 toolkit (Uryupina et al., 2012) for this task), and they detect the anaphoricity of the *it* pronoun using the NADA tool (Bergsma and Yarowsky, 2011). Another common feature is that both systems take advantage of the target language model. Wetzel et al. (2015)'s maximum entropy classifier Mallet (McCallum, 2002) uses the same logistic loss function as we do with the Vowpal Wabbit tool but the training data handling is different in these two tools. Mallet is a batch learner, optimizing over the whole data in a single step while Vowpal Wabbit optimizes incrementally after every example.

On the other hand, unlike us, Wetzel et al. (2015) do not use any syntactic information. The only syntax-based system in the DiscoMT 2015 shared task is the system of Loáiciga (2015). They make use of the Fips rule-based phrase-structure parser (Wehrli, 2007) whereas we acquire dependencies and syntactic functions using the MST parser (McDonald et al., 2005) and the MATE tools (Seeker and Kuhn, 2012) on the source side for English and German, respectively.

8 Conclusion

We presented our system submitted to the WMT16 shared task on cross-lingual pronoun prediction. It is based on Vowpal Wabbit and uses features from three sources: first, target language model (which served as the baseline in the shared task), second, the automatic linguistic analysis of the source text up to the levels of syntax and coreference, and third, a basic morphological analysis of the target text. Our systems were able to improve on the baseline in both language directions, with source language and target language model features having the largest impact on the results. Finally, we employ instance weighing, which proved to be a successful way to compensate for the differences between learning loss function and the official evaluation measure and to improve recall in infrequent pronoun classes.

Acknowledgments

This work has been supported by GAUK grant 338915 of the Charles University, Czech Science Foundation grant GA-16-05394S, the 7th Framework Programme of the EU grant QTLeap (No. 610516), and SVV project number 260 333. This work has been using language resources developed and/or stored and/or distributed by the LINDAT/CLARIN project No. LM2015071 of the Ministry of Education, Youth and Sports of the Czech Republic.

References

Shane Bergsma and Dekang Lin. 2006. Bootstrapping Path-Based Pronoun Resolution. In *Proceedings of the 21st International Conference on Computational Linguistics and 44th Annual Meeting of the Association for Computational Linguistics*, pages 33–40, Sydney, Australia. Association for Computational Linguistics.

Shane Bergsma and David Yarowsky. 2011. NADA: A Robust System for Non-referential Pronoun Detection. In *Proceedings of the 8th International Conference on Anaphora Processing and Applications*, pages 12–23, Berlin, Heidelberg. Springer-Verlag.

Anders Björkelund, Bernd Bohnet, Love Hafdell, and Pierre Nugues. 2010. A High-performance Syntactic and Semantic Dependency Parser. In *Proceedings of the 23rd International Conference on Computational Linguistics: Demonstrations*, pages 33–36, Stroudsburg, PA, USA. Association for Computational Linguistics.

Bernd Bohnet and Joakim Nivre. 2012. A Transition-based System for Joint Part-of-speech Tagging and Labeled Non-projective Dependency Parsing. In *Proceedings of the 2012 Joint Conference on Empirical Methods in Natural Language Processing and Computational Natural Language Learning*, pages 1455–1465, Stroudsburg, PA, USA. Association for Computational Linguistics.

Ondřej Bojar, Ondřej Dušek, Tom Kocmi, Jindřich Libovický, Michal Novák, Martin Popel, Roman Sudarikov, and Dušan Variš. 2016. CzEng 1.6: Enlarged Czech-English Parallel Corpus with Processing Tools Dockered. In *Text, Speech and Dialogue: 19th International Conference, TSD 2016, Brno, Czech Republic, September 12-16, 2016, Proceedings*. Springer Verlag. In press.

Liane Guillou, Christian Hardmeier, Preslav Nakov, Sara Stymne, Jörg Tiedemann, Yannick Versley, Mauro Cettolo, Bonnie Webber, and Andrei Popescu-Belis. 2016. Findings of the 2016 WMT shared task on cross-lingual pronoun prediction. In *Proceedings of the First Conference on Machine Translation (WMT16)*, Berlin, Germany. Association for Computational Linguistics.

Christian Hardmeier, Preslav Nakov, Sara Stymne, Jörg Tiedemann, Yannick Versley, and Mauro Cettolo. 2015. Pronoun-Focused MT and Cross-Lingual Pronoun Prediction: Findings of the 2015 DiscoMT Shared Task on Pronoun Translation. In *Proceedings of the Second Workshop on Discourse in Machine Translation*, pages 1–16, Lisbon, Portugal. Association for Computational Linguistics.

Christian Hardmeier. 2014. *Discourse in Statistical Machine Translation*. Ph.D. thesis, Uppsala University, Sweden.

Kenneth Heafield, Ivan Pouzyrevsky, Jonathan H. Clark, and Philipp Koehn. 2013. Scalable Modified Kneser-Ney Language Model Estimation. In *Proceedings of the 51st Annual Meeting of the Association for Computational Linguistics*, pages 690–696, Sofia, Bulgaria. Association for Computational Linguistics.

Reinhard Kneser and Hermann Ney. 1995. Improved backing-off for M-gram language modeling. In *International Conference on Acoustics, Speech, and Signal Processing*, volume 1, pages 181–184, Los Alamitos, CA, USA. IEEE Computer Society Press.

Heeyoung Lee, Angel Chang, Yves Peirsman, Nathanael Chambers, Mihai Surdeanu, and Dan Jurafsky. 2013. Deterministic Coreference Resolution Based on Entity-centric, Precision-ranked Rules. *Computational Linguistics*, 39(4):885–916.

Sharid Loáiciga. 2015. Predicting Pronoun Translation Using Syntactic, Morphological and Contextual Features from Parallel Data. In *Proceedings of the Second Workshop on Discourse in Machine Translation*, pages 78–85, Lisbon, Portugal, September. Association for Computational Linguistics.

Andrew Kachites McCallum. 2002. Mallet: A machine learning for language toolkit. http://mallet.cs.umass.edu.

Ryan McDonald, Fernando Pereira, Kiril Ribarov, and Jan Hajič. 2005. Non-projective Dependency Parsing Using Spanning Tree Algorithms. In *Proceedings of the Conference on Human Language Technology and Empirical Methods in Natural Language Processing*, pages 523–530, Stroudsburg, PA, USA. Association for Computational Linguistics.

Martin Popel and Zdeněk Žabokrtský. 2010. TectoMT: Modular NLP Framework. In *Proceedings of the 7th International Conference on Advances in Natural Language Processing*, pages 293–304, Berlin, Heidelberg. Springer-Verlag.

Wolfgang Seeker and Jonas Kuhn. 2012. Making Ellipses Explicit in Dependency Conversion for a German Treebank. In *Proceedings of the Eight International Conference on Language Resources and Evaluation*, Istanbul, Turkey. European Language Resources Association (ELRA).

Drahomíra Spoustová, Jan Hajič, Jan Votrubec, Pavel Krbec, and Pavel Květoň. 2007. The Best of Two Worlds: Cooperation of Statistical and Rule-based Taggers for Czech. In *Proceedings of the Workshop on Balto-Slavonic Natural Language Processing: Information Extraction and Enabling Technologies*, pages 67–74, Stroudsburg, PA, USA. Association for Computational Linguistics.

Olga Uryupina, Alessandro Moschitti, and Massimo Poesio. 2012. BART Goes Multilingual: The UniTN/Essex Submission to the CoNLL-2012 Shared Task. In *Joint Conference on EMNLP and CoNLL - Shared Task*, pages 122–128, Stroudsburg, PA, USA. Association for Computational Linguistics.

Yannick Versley, Simone Paolo Ponzetto, Massimo Poesio, Vladimir Eidelman, Alan Jern, Jason Smith, Xiaofeng Yang, and Alessandro Moschitti. 2008. BART: A Modular Toolkit for Coreference Resolution. In *Proceedings of the 46th Annual Meeting of the Association for Computational Linguistics on Human Language Technologies: Demo Session*, pages 9–12, Stroudsburg, PA, USA. Association for Computational Linguistics.

Eric Wehrli. 2007. Fips, a "Deep" Linguistic Multilingual Parser. In *Proceedings of the Workshop on Deep Linguistic Processing*, pages 120–127, Stroudsburg, PA, USA. Association for Computational Linguistics.

Dominikus Wetzel, Adam Lopez, and Bonnie Webber. 2015. A Maximum Entropy Classifier for Cross-Lingual Pronoun Prediction. In *Proceedings of the Second Workshop on Discourse in Machine Translation*, pages 115–121, Lisbon, Portugal. Association for Computational Linguistics.

Feature Exploration for Cross-Lingual Pronoun Prediction

Sara Stymne
Uppsala University
Department of Linguistics and Philology
`sara.stymne@lingfil.uu.se`

Abstract

We explore a large number of features for cross-lingual pronoun prediction for translation between English and German/French. We find that features related to German/French are more informative than features related to English, regardless of the translation direction. Our most useful features are local context, dependency head features, and source pronouns. We also find that it is sometimes more successful to employ a 2-step procedure that first makes a binary choice between pronouns and *other*, then classifies pronouns. For the pronoun/other distinction POS n-grams were very useful.

1 Introduction

This paper reports results for the UU-Stymne system on the WMT 2016 pronoun prediction shared task. The task entails classifying which among a set of target pronouns, or *other* is the correct translation of a given source pronoun. There are tasks for two language pairs, English and German/French, in both directions.

An example is shown in (1), where we need to predict which German pronoun should be the translation of *It*, which in this case should be *er* since it refers to the masculine word *Saal* (*room*) in the previous sentence. Had the antecedent instead been the neuter *Zimmer*, the correct pronoun would have been *es*. The target words are lemmatized with coarse POS-tags, to better mimic the SMT task, in contrast to previous versions of this task where full forms were used. For full details of the task and training data, see the task overview paper (Guillou et al., 2016).

(1) **It** 's smaller than this . REPLACE_0 sein|VERB
klein|ADJ als|CONJ dies|PRON hier|ADV .|.

We set out to establish the usefulness of a large number of features for this task in all translation directions, without any explicit use of anaphora resolution. We also investigate a 2-step classification procedure.

2 System

We followed Tiedemann (2015) by using linear SVMs implemented in LIBLINEAR (Fan et al., 2008). In all experiments we use L2-loss support vector classification with dual solvers and the 1-vs-rest strategy for multi-class classification. The regularization parameter C was optimized using grid search and cross-validation as implemented in LIBLINEAR. The results were quite stable for reasonable values of C, however, and in all cases we used values between 2^{-2} and 2^{-5}.

In most of our experiments we only used IWSLT training data, with 66K–92K pronoun examples, to train our classifier, since it contains TED talks like the dev and test sets. We perform final experiments where we investigate the usefulness of adding out-of-domain News data of similar size and much larger Europarl data. Due to space restrictions we will mainly give Macro-averaged Recall (Macro-R) scores, the official workshop metric, on the TED dev set. Macro-R gives the average recall for all classes and thus gives the same weight to rare classes as to common classes.

For some of our features we needed dependency trees and POS-tags for the source. We used Mate Tools to jointly tag and dependency parse (Bohnet and Nivre, 2012) the source text for sentences that contained pronoun examples. For all languages the output is a dependency parse tree and POS-tags, and for German and French it also gives morphological descriptions. For the target side we used the given POS-tags.

Proceedings of the First Conference on Machine Translation, Volume 2: Shared Task Papers, pages 609–615,
Berlin, Germany, August 11-12, 2016. ©2016 Association for Computational Linguistics

3   2-step classification

We had two approaches to classification, a standard classifier, which we will call 1-step, and a 2-step classifier. We noted that the *other* class often were quite different from the pronoun classes, since it is very diverse, and sometimes an artifact of alignment errors. This observation led us to design the 2-step system where we first trained a binary classifier to distinguish between *other* and all the pronoun classes grouped into one class. We then had a second classifier that only had to distinguish between the pronoun classes. For the training data we collected instances for the second classifier based on gold tags. At test time we used the results from the first classifier to feed the examples classified as pronouns to the second classifier.

4   Features

We explored a high number of features of different types, which will be described in this section. We did not explicitly attempt to model anaphora in any way, but tried to identify other types of features that could give indications of which pronoun translation to use. The main reasons why we decided not to use any anaphora software is that it is not readily available for all source languages, it is error prone, and it gave no clear improvements in the 2015 shared task. All our features are largely language independent; we did not design any specific features for a specific language pair.

The WMT 2016 shared task is a follow-up to the DiscoMT 2015 shared task on en-fr pronoun prediction. An important difference between these two tasks is that target full forms were given in 2015 and only lemma+POS in 2016. However, many of our features were inspired by the submissions to the 2015 shared task. For all feature groups below, we used special beginning and end of sentence markers when needed.

Source pronoun (SP)   The source pronoun to be translated was added as a feature. We believe that this is an important feature since it restricts the possible translations. Source pronouns has been used before for cross-lingual pronoun prediction (Hardmeier et al., 2013; Wetzel et al., 2015).

Local context (LCS, LCT)   For these features we considered the source words surrounding the source pronoun and the lemmas+POS-tags surrounding the target pronouns. We included up to 3 words before and 3 words after the pronouns. We tried both to use bag-of-words models for words before and after the pronoun, and to encode the position of each word. Local context features were the core of the best submitted system for the 2015 shared task (Tiedemann, 2015) and were also used in many other submissions.

Preceding nouns (NN)   The nouns preceding a pronoun are potential antecedents to the pronoun, and are therefore included. The target side of the shared task data included POS-tags, so there we used the four preceding nouns, including proper names, possibly going across sentence boundaries, but not crossing document boundaries. For the source side we had only parsed the sentences that contains pronouns. Because of this, we did not include cross sentence instances of source nouns, so we only included up to four previous nouns within the sentence, which meant that we often had 0 or just a few nouns on the source side. Since the source contains full forms, we also included some morphological information for these nouns, we added a feature for each POS-tag extended with morphology for number, and gender for proper names. Finally we added a feature indicating how many previous nouns there were in the sentence.

Preceding nouns or NPs have previously been used for this task with differing results. Callin et al. (2015) used up to four preceding nouns and determiners. Wetzel et al. (2015) also used preceding noun tokens, however they were identified by co-reference resolution. A difference from 2015 is that this year there are no determiners or other words on the target side that carries information such as gender, since it is lemmatized.

Target POS n-grams (POS)   To generalize from lemmas, we included target POS-tags. We used n-grams of POS-tags for words surrounding the pronoun position in the target language. Using the abbreviation b for words before the pronoun and a for words after, we included the following n-gram windows: 3b, 1b, 2b+2a, 1b+1a, 1a, 3a.

POS-tags were used in several 2015 systems (Callin et al., 2015; Loáiciga, 2015; Wetzel et al., 2015), with either positive results or no separate results shown in the paper. They all used single tags, though, not POS n-grams.

Target extended POS n-grams (EPOS)   The tag sets in the data are coarse-grained, with the 12 universal POS-tags (Petrov et al., 2012) for English and German, and a set of 15 POS-tags for French. To compensate somewhat for this, we also included n-grams using an extended tag set where we use the identity of the 100 most common lemmas in the training data in addition to the POS tags. As an example, *be-VERB-all* and *can-make-the* are two EPOS options for *VERB-VERB-DET*. We use the same n-gram windows as for standard POS n-grams.

As far as we know, no one has used this particular extension of POS-tags for this task. However, several teams successfully used fine-grained morphological target tags last year, for instance Pham and van der Plas (2015), which was not possible this year, given the lemma+POS representation.

Dependency head of pronouns (DEP)   For each source pronoun we identified its dependency head, based on the parse from Mate Tools. As features we used the head word and the label. In addition we used the POS-tag of the head for English, which distinguished between tenses and third person. For French and German we added morphological information about number and person to the POS-tag of the head. We also used indicator features for common verb suffixes that we thought were informative about tense, person and number: *s* and *d* for English, *en* and *t* for German and *e*, *nt* and *[^n]t* for French.

To find potential dependency heads in the target, we followed the alignment links from the word identified as dependency head in the source. For any aligned words that were POS-tagged as a verb, we included the lemma as a feature. We restricted this feature to verbs, since we believe they are most informative with regard to the pronoun, and to reduce noise from the automatic alignment.

The only work we are aware of that used syntactic feature for cross-lingual pronoun prediction is Loáiciga (2015), who parsed the target and used the dependency label of the pronoun, which only had a small impact on the results. This differed from our use since we used the dependency head, and parsed the source text and projected this information to the target through word alignments.

Target language model features (LM)   For this group we included language model scores from the baseline system provided by the shared task (Guillou et al., 2016). This system uses a target language LM to score the target pronouns and 11–22 other high-frequency words, and not using a

Null penalty	de-en	fr-en	en-de	en-fr
0	.361	.337	.344	.406
−2	.389	.388	.358	.411

Table 1: Macro-R for workshop baseline.

word, *NONE*. The language model we used was also provided for the shared task, a large 5-gram model trained using KenLM (Heafield, 2011) on the workshop data and monolingual News data (Guillou et al., 2016). There is a penalty for the *NONE* case, which we set to −2, which was the best value from the 2015 shared task (Hardmeier et al., 2015), and that we found to give good results for all language pairs, as shown in Table 1. Note that this LM used lemmatized data, which gave a much worse performance than the full form LM from 2015, which had .584 MACRO-F (Hardmeier et al., 2015), compared to .342 on lemmas.

The baseline system can output marginal probabilities for each pronoun or alternative word and *NONE*, giving all options larger than 0.001. We used these probabilities as feature values for each word. In addition we had features giving the highest scoring word, always and if it had a probability over 0.85; the highest probability for any pronoun, any other word, and other or *NONE*. We also had a feature for the number of options given, i.e. how many words that had a probability higher than 0.001. Target language model features were used by Wetzel et al. (2015) with mixed results.

Alignment, position, and length (APL)   We used a set of features related to position, sentence length and alignments, both on instance level and sentence level. We believe that this could both give some indication about pronouns, and about how close a translation the target is. We are not aware of these features being used for this task before.

The position of the pronoun in the sentence likely plays some importance to its identity. Thus we added as features the relative position of the source and target pronouns in the sentence, the difference in relative position, and three indicator features for the target and/or the source pronoun being in a sentence initial position.

We also included some features based on word alignments. For the pronouns we indicated how many words they were aligned to in the other language, which we believe can be useful especially for identifying non-pronoun translations, which are likely noisier than pronoun translations. In addition we added two features for the total number of alignments in the sentence, normalized by the length of the source and target sentence, respectively. On the sentence level, we also included the length ratio between the source and target sentence where the pronouns occurred.

5 Results

We performed most experiments for the 1-step classifier. For all experiments up to section 5.3 we use only IWSLT as training data. To start with we investigated whether it was best to use true-cased or lower-cased features. We did not try this individually for the different feature groups, instead we made this choice for all features for a language pair. Overall, for de-en true-casing leads to a clear improvement, which we believe is mainly caused by the *sie* pronoun, which is spelled with a capital *S* in the meaning *you* (polite), and with a lower-case *s* in the meaning *she* or *they*. For the other languages the difference is quite small, but we choose to use true-case when English is the target language, and lower-case otherwise.

5.1 Feature groups

To assess how useful each feature group is we first ran experiments using a single feature group at a time. Table 2 shows the results for individual features, all features combined and for features only from the source or target language. An interesting pattern is that features from German and French give better results than features from English, regardless of translation direction. Both for the grouped source and target features, and for local context with only source or target the best results for into English is when using source features, and from English using target features. For de-en using source features only is nearly as good as using all features. In French and German we have to distinguish between pronouns based on the gender of the antecedent, for which target features are clearly useful. English, though, does not have grammatical gender, and cannot benefit in this way from the target features.

The best individual feature group when used on its own is always local context, followed in most cases by dependency features. For en-fr we got relatively good results for EPOS and LM features. The extended EPOS-tags were clearly better than the coarse POS-tags. Using only nouns was clearly not useful, and performed even worse than APL, alignment, position and length, which

Group	de-en	fr-en	en-de	en-fr
All	.640	.597	.389	.583
+source	.636	.560	.345	.337
+target	.414	.368	.360	.494
+SP	.370	.371	.353	.244
+LC	.518	.561	.404	.560
+LCS	.514	.475	.339	.340
+LCT	.389	.365	.367	.456
+NN	.150	.155	.207	.161
+POS	.272	.278	.327	.300
+EPOS	.362	.353	.380	.450
+DEP	.449	.418	.369	.375
+LM	.382	.331	.338	.421
+APL	.178	.208	.276	.172

Table 2: Macro-R for individual feature groups and source and target features

Group	de-en	fr-en	en-de	en-fr
All	.640	.597	.389	.583
−SP	.536	.498	.358	.562
−LC	.639	.583	.375	.580
−LCS	.638	.592	.379	.577
−LCT	.638	.601	.389	.582
−NN	.643	.610	.375	.582
−POS	.640	.592	.386	.579
−EPOS	.649	.586	.400	.576
−DEP	.617	.589	.377	.580
−LM	.652	.674	.457	.599
−APL	.634	.595	.386	.580

Table 3: Feature ablation study. Macro-R with individual feature groups removed.

we did not expect to be very informative on its own. It is interesting to see that classification only by the source pronoun, a single feature, give similar results to many of the feature groups with a high number of features, which indicates its importance. While no individual group is close to the performance of all features, several feature groups are better than the baseline system.

Table 3 shows the results of an ablation study, where we removed one feature group at the time from the full set of features. Here we see that several features are not useful in combination with the other features, and improve the results when removed. The biggest improvement is seen when removing the LM features, even for en-fr where they had quite a good performance on their own. This is interesting since the LM is the most important knowledge source for pronoun translation in an SMT system. We believe that the lemmatized target has too little information for these features to be useful. It is always better to use the target context words directly in the classifier than to use the LM features derived from the target context. Removing the noun features improves results somewhat for into English. As expected, the source

Type	de-en	fr-en	en-de	en-fr
All, position	.640	.597	.389	.583
All, BOW	.654	.561	.396	.567
Best, position	.656	.609	.392	.581
Best, BOW	.656	.579	.397	.557
Window T	3+3	3+3	2+2	2+3
Window S	1+3	3+1	2+2	2+3

Table 4: Macro-R with different local context, and the best window sizes

pronouns are important also in combination with the other features, and gives the biggest score drop when removed. For most of the feature groups the score difference is quite small when removed.

5.2 Final feature sets

In the above experiments we used a local context window of 3 words before and 3 words after for both source and target context. In order to improve results we first tried all combinations of target windows, from 1 to 3 words, and with this window set, all source window sizes. We also tried using positions for the context words and compared to using bags-of-words for words before and after the pronoun. Table 4 shows the best windows. Changing the window sizes led to improvements for all language pairs, except en-fr, for which it, however, improved Macro-R from .563 to .573 on the DiscoMT15 test set. There is no clear pattern of which window size that is most useful across languages. For the best windows positional features were better or similar to bag-of-words features, whereas the results were conflicting with the full context window. These results were similar to Tiedemann (2015). We decided to use positional features with the best context windows.

Finally, we tried to remove combinations of the least useful feature groups, on the systems with optimized local context. Unfortunately, due to time constraints, we had not done the full ablation tests before submission time, and failed to notice the advantage of removing the LM and NN feature groups. We thus only tried to remove sets of other less promising features for the submitted systems. The results with removed features are shown in Table 5. For the final submitted systems we used the full feature sets for en-fr and fr-en, removed EPOS for en-de and removed alignment features for de-en. This led to an improvement for en-de but for de-en we have the same score as before. When trying to remove further feature groups we had large improvements for all language pairs ex-

System	de-en	fr-en	en-de	en-fr
Submitted	.656	.609	.411	.581
Final	.653	.675	.455	.619

Table 5: Macro-R for systems with removed sets of feature groups

Corpus	de-en	fr-en	en-de	en-fr	en-fr (D)
I	.656	**.609**	**.411**	.581	.572
IN	**.654**	.578	.379	.558	.581
IE	.627	.586	.377	.559	.582
INE	.632	.564	.395	.572	.581
INE−16	.630	.572	.377	**.557**	**.584**

Table 6: Macro-R with different combinations of training data with the feature set from the submitted system (I=IWSLT, N=News, E=Europarl), −16 means filtering away features occurring less than 16 times in the training data. (D) is for results on the DiscoMT15 set. The training data used in the submitted 1-step systems are marked in bold.

cept de-en when also removing the LM and NN feature groups. We call this system *Final*.

5.3 Training data

In this section we investigate the effect of adding more training data to IWSLT that was used in previous experiments. Table 6 shows the results. In most cases adding more training data led to considerably worse results on the TED dev set. For de-en, though, adding News gave similar Macro-R, and an improvement of accuracy from .853 to .873, which made us choose this option for our submitted system. For en-fr, on the DiscoMT15 dev set the results were better with more data.

With the large training data we have a very high number of features, between 263K and 563K for the different language pairs for the submitted feature sets. We tried two ways of reducing the number of features: by filtering features that occurred with a low frequency in the training data and by filtering features that had a low model score in the SVM training. When using only IWSLT data we saw little effect of either type of filtering. When training with all data we had some improvements by filtering, with the best results using frequencies. We tried many different values for filtering and overall we had good results by removing features occurring 16 times or less, but as shown in Table 6 results were mixed across language pairs and test data. Using this filtering reduced the number of features to between 31K and 55K, a reduction of around 90%. The final combination of training

System	Test set				Dev set			
	de-en	fr-en	en-de	en-fr	de-en	fr-en	en-de	en-fr
Submitted Primary (2-step)	.592	.364	.521	.654	.651	.606	.426	.592
Without bug	.702	.620	–	–				
Submitted Secondary (1-step)	.608	.341	.489	.607	.654	.609	.411	.557
Without bug	.715	.629	–	–				
Final 1-step (IWSLT)	.735	.615	.490	.616	.653	.675	.455	.619
Final 1-step (all training data)	.733	.685	.503	.613	.632	.622	.455	.608

Table 7: Macro-R for submitted system, and best systems trained after submission time,using IWSLT and all data for training.

data and filtering used for the submitted systems are shown in bold in Table 6.

5.4 2-step Classification

For the 2-step classification we needed to train two classifiers, one for the binary pronoun–*other* distinction and one for the distinction between the different target pronouns. For the first classifier we chose classifiers that gave high precision and reasonable recall on the *other* class from the 1-step classifiers. Across language pairs the best results we saw before submission was to either use only the POS or EPOS feature groups, or all features. In addition we tried using either IWSLT or all training data for this classifier. We had the best results using the following feature sets and data for the first binary classifier:

- de-en: all data, all features,
- fr-en: IWSLT, all features
- en-de: all data, POS
- en-fr: IWSLT, EPOS

Overall we tended to get better precision for the *other* class using (E)POS and better recall using all features. The fact that (E)POS-patterns gave a high precision, indicates that the *other* class tends to occur in different contexts than pronouns.

For the pronoun classifier we used the full feature set and only experimented with using either IWSLT or all data for training. We had the best results with all training data for en-fr and with IWSLT for the other language pairs, similar to the results for 1-step classification. The results for the 2-step classifier are shown in Table 7, labeled as primary. We choose to submit the 2-step classifier as our primary system since it performed best on the dev data for from English, and only slightly worse in the other direction. We believe that there is room for similar improvements with the 2-step classifier as with the 1-step classifier with more careful feature engineering. We leave this for future work.

5.5 Final results

Table 7 shows our submitted and final results on the TED dev set and on the WMT 2016 official test set. For the submitted system we unfortunately had a bug in the feature extraction for de-en and fr-en, which severely affected the scores, so for these systems we also show scores with the bug corrected. For the dev set we see that we could considerably improve the submitted scores by more careful feature engineering for all language pairs except de-en, but that we had worse or equal results for this feature set with large training data.

For the test set the primary 2-step system was better than the 1-step system only for translation from English. The final feature set helped mainly for de-en, which it did not on the dev set. For en-de and en-fr the final 1-step system did not beat the submitted 2-step system, as it did for the dev set. Adding more training data gave improvements or nearly equal scores for all language pairs. The discrepancy of the results between the dev and test sets could partly be explained by the different distribution of pronouns, especially for the rare classes that are important for Macro-R. It is also likely that our classifier has over-fitted somewhat to our dev data. In the workshop our best submitted system ended up in 2nd place for en-fr, which had the highest number of submissions.

6 Conclusion

We described the UU-Stymne system for the WMT shared task on cross-lingual pronoun prediction. We used linear SVMs with a high number of features, the most successful being local context, especially in German and French, source pronouns, and dependency heads. For the binary choice between pronoun and *other* we found part-of-speech patterns highly useful.

Acknowledgments

This work was supported by the Swedish strategic research programme eSSENCE.

References

Bernd Bohnet and Joakim Nivre. 2012. A transition-based system for joint part-of-speech tagging and labeled non-projective dependency parsing. In *Proceedings of the 2012 Joint Conference on Empirical Methods in Natural Language Processing and Computational Natural Language Learning*, pages 1455–1465, Jeju Island, Korea.

Jimmy Callin, Christian Hardmeier, and Jörg Tiedemann. 2015. Part-of-speech driven cross-lingual pronoun prediction with feed-forward neural networks. In *Proceedings of the Second Workshop on Discourse in Machine Translation*, pages 59–64, Lisbon, Portugal.

Rong-En Fan, Kai-Wei Chang, Cho-Jui Hsieh, Xiang-Rui Wang, and Chih-Jen Lin. 2008. LIBLINEAR: A library for large linear classification. *Journal of Machine Learning Research*, 9:1871–1874.

Liane Guillou, Christian Hardmeier, Preslav Nakov, Sara Stymne, Jörg Tiedemann, Yannick Versley, Mauro Cettolo, Bonnie Webber, and Andrei Popescu-Belis. 2016. Findings of the 2016 WMT shared task on cross-lingual pronoun prediction. In *Proceedings of the First Conference on Machine Translation (WMT16)*, Berlin, Germany.

Christian Hardmeier, Jörg Tiedemann, and Joakim Nivre. 2013. Latent anaphora resolution for cross-lingual pronoun prediction. In *Proceedings of the 2013 Conference on Empirical Methods in Natural Language Processing*, pages 380–391, Seattle, Washington, USA.

Christian Hardmeier, Preslav Nakov, Sara Stymne, Jörg Tiedemann, Yannick Versley, and Mauro Cettolo. 2015. Pronoun-focused MT and cross-lingual pronoun prediction: Findings of the 2015 DiscoMT shared task on pronoun translation. In *Proceedings of the Second Workshop on Discourse in Machine Translation*, pages 1–16, Lisbon, Portugal.

Kenneth Heafield. 2011. KenLM: Faster and smaller language model queries. In *Proceedings of the Sixth Workshop on Statistical Machine Translation*, pages 187–197, Edinburgh, Scotland.

Sharid Loáiciga. 2015. Predicting pronoun translation using syntactic, morphological and contextual features from parallel data. In *Proceedings of the Second Workshop on Discourse in Machine Translation*, pages 78–85, Lisbon, Portugal.

Slav Petrov, Dipanjan Das, and Ryan McDonald. 2012. A universal part-of-speech tagset. In *Proceedings of the 8th International Conference on Language Resources and Evaluation (LREC'12)*, Istanbul, Turkey.

Ngoc-Quan Pham and Lonneke van der Plas. 2015. Predicting pronouns across languages with continuous word spaces. In *Proceedings of the Second Workshop on Discourse in Machine Translation*, pages 101–107, Lisbon, Portugal.

Jörg Tiedemann. 2015. Baseline models for pronoun prediction and pronoun-aware translation. In *Proceedings of the Second Workshop on Discourse in Machine Translation*, pages 108–114, Lisbon, Portugal.

Dominikus Wetzel, Adam Lopez, and Bonnie Webber. 2015. A maximum entropy classifier for cross-lingual pronoun prediction. In *Proceedings of the Second Workshop on Discourse in Machine Translation*, pages 115–121, Lisbon, Portugal.

A Linear Baseline Classifier for Cross-Lingual Pronoun Prediction

Jörg Tiedemann
Department of Modern Languages
University of Helsinki

Abstract

This paper presents baseline models using linear classifiers for the pronoun translation task at WMT 2016. We explore various local context features and include history features of potential antecedents extracted by means of a simple PoS-matching strategy. The results show the difficulties of the task in general but also represent valuable baselines to compare other more-informed systems with. Our experiments reveal that the predictions of English correspondences for given ambiguous pronouns in French and German is easier than the other way around. This seems to verify that predictions, which need to follow more complex agreement constraints, require more reliable information about the referential links of the tokens to be inserted.

1 Introduction

This short system paper describes the baseline classifier we have submitted to the shared task on cross-lingual pronoun prediction at WMT 2016. The goal of the submission is to provide yet another baseline that is slightly more informed than the language model baseline provided by the organisers otherwise. In the following, we will briefly discuss the model and our feature engineering efforts. Thereafter, we discuss the results for each language pair and conclude.

2 The Model

Our model follows the setup of our submissions from last year to the same task at the workshop on discourse in machine translation (Tiedemann, 2015; Hardmeier et al., 2015). Again, we apply a linear SVM classifier out-of-the-box using liblinear (Fan et al., 2008) with its L2-loss SVC dual solver without any dedicated optimisation of regularisation parameters. This year, we did not experiment with alternative classifiers and rely on our positive experience from our previous experiments. Similar to our previous submission, we explore various context windows in source and target language and optimise the feature model in a brute-force manner on the provided development data.

The scenario is slightly different from the previous year. First of all, there is an additional language pair and the reverse direction for both language pairs is also explored. The four sub-tasks have different complexity as they cover different sets of target classes and different types of phenomena. However, we do not treat the language pairs differently and run our training procedures in a language-independent mode using the same kind of feature extraction for all of them. A difference is also that we can rely on the provided coarse-grained PoS labels in the target language as another source of information. However, we cannot make use of the inflectional information in the target language as the data sets are now lemmatised. This is a serious handicap for the system as the morphological features disambiguate the choice very well as we have seen last year.

We played with various variants of the feature model trying to systematically study the impact of certain extraction methods on classification performance. The following extraction parameters are explored:

- Source language context before the pronoun in question

- Source language context after the pronoun in question

Proceedings of the First Conference on Machine Translation, Volume 2: Shared Task Papers, pages 616–619,
Berlin, Germany, August 11-12, 2016. ©2016 Association for Computational Linguistics

	he	she	it	they	you	this	these	there	OTHER	
he	30	0	1	0	0	0	0	0	0	31
she	0	11	3	5	1	0	0	0	1	21
it	5	2	95	8	0	1	0	2	1	114
they	2	2	6	61	4	0	0	1	2	78
you	0	1	2	11	89	0	0	0	3	106
this	0	1	7	0	0	2	0	1	2	13
these	0	0	0	0	0	0	0	0	0	0
there	0	0	4	0	0	0	0	12	0	16
OTHER	1	0	8	7	12	0	0	0	76	104
-SUM-	38	17	126	92	106	3	0	16	85	

Table 1: The confusion matrix for German–English. Columns represent the predicted classes.

- Target language context before the placeholder token

- Target language context after the placeholder token

- Bag-of-word context versus context marked by relative position

- Lowercasing versus original casing

- Separate PoS and word features versus concatenated word/PoS features versus both types (separate and concatenated)

All of those features only explore local context which was quite successful in the previous year especially the local context in the target language. The new edition with lemmatised data, however, requires additional knowledge to make basic decisions that would otherwise work with local features. Last year, we included history features that list target language tokens aligned to preceding determiners and their local context as part of the potential antecedents that could determine pronoun choice based on gender and number agreement. The impact of these features was not very significant. However, with lemmatised data those features become more interesting.

We rely on the same procedure, simply including a fixed number of previous items without employing any kind of coreference resolution or deep linguistic analyses. However, this time we can rely on PoS labels to select the items we would like to include. Assuming that simple noun-phrases are common antecedents we define a pattern for matching PoS labels in prior context (determiners, nouns and proper nouns):

(DET | NOUN | NAM | NOM | PRON)

Furthermore, assuming that the nearest noun phrases have the highest likelihood to represent the referenced item, we extract the n closest words that match the pattern above. n is another parameter that we explore in tuning the model.

3　The Results

After running various combinations of parameters we ended up with settings that work best on the development data. First of all, lowercasing did not help but made things slightly worse. Adding relative position information to the context features also seems to work, so we always applied this method. Splitting tokens into separate features for lemma and PoS is also beneficial but additional keeping the concatenated variant has a positive effect.

We tested different sizes of the context window by varying the number of tokens before and after the source language pronoun and before and after the target language place-holder between zero and five in all combinations. Table 3 lists the final settings that gave the highest macro-averaged recall value on the development data.

We can see that the local context is rather small and the system does not seem to benefit from adding more data from surrounding context that is further away than 3-4 tokens. Note that we use position information for each token extracted from the context as discussed above. This worked slightly better than a bag-of-words approach that suffers less from data sparseness.

We also tried to optimise the number of antecedent candidate features coming from the history based on the PoS matching approach described earlier. We tried up to ten candidates but our models performed best with only a few of them in the feature model. In particular, we used four candidates for French–English and two candidates for all other language pairs. Using more confused the system and the performance on development data went down.

Finally, the official scores obtained using our

	ce	elle	elles	il	ils	cela	on	OTHER	
ce	57	1	0	5	2	1	0	2	68
elle	4	8	0	8	1	1	0	1	23
elles	1	1	2	0	20	1	0	0	25
il	1	11	0	40	2	5	2	0	61
ils	0	0	9	4	56	0	0	2	71
cela	0	4	0	9	0	14	0	4	31
on	0	0	2	0	2	0	5	0	9
OTHER	0	2	1	1	0	3	3	75	85
-SUM-	63	27	14	67	83	25	10	84	

Table 2: The confusion matrix for English–French. Columns represent the predicted classes.

	source		target	
language	before	after	before	after
Eng–Ger	1	0	4	4
Ger–Eng	1	4	3	4
Eng–Fre	1	3	1	3
Fre–Eng	3	1	3	4

Table 3: Final context windows used for each language pair.

	Macro-averaged			
language	precision	recall	F1	accuracy
Eng–Ger	60.43	44.69	45.24	65.80
Ger–Eng	75.05	69.76	70.02	77.85
Eng–Fre	57.11	57.50	56.99	68.90
Fre–Eng	70.54	62.98	63.72	78.96

Table 4: The official results of our submitted systems.

submitted systems are listed in 4. There is quite some variation in the quality of our classifiers. Especially English–German is quite poor, in particular in terms of macro-averaged recall, which is used as the official score of the campaign. The reason for this is not entirely clear but the confusion matrix presented below give some ideas about the situation.

3.1 English – German

The task for English–German includes only five target classes but seems (at least for our classifier) to be the hardest case. Our macro-averaged recall score is far below the other language pairs, which suggests that the model does not work well for small classes. The confusion matrix in Table 5 illustrates this as well. Recall for "er" and "man" is zero in both cases and this effects the official score significantly. The confusion between the more common classes "sie" and "es" with "OTHER" is also striking. The overall accuracy is also the worst among all language pairs considering that this sub-task has the lowest number of target classes involved.

	er	sie	es	man	OTHER	
er	0	3	10	0	2	15
sie	1	89	26	0	8	124
es	2	7	77	0	15	101
man	0	1	6	1	0	8
OTHER	1	26	23	0	85	135
-SUM-	4	126	142	1	110	

Table 5: The confusion matrix for English–German. Columns represent the predicted classes.

3.2 German – English

The results for German–English look much more promising. The overall accuracy is almost 78%, which is quite successful for a classification task with nine target classes. The confusion matrix in Table 1 shows the distribution of predicted labels and the model picks up the signals quite well for all classes. Even smaller classes like "she" and "there" work pretty well and we believe that the local context is again most informative for those decisions. The scores for "this" with its very few examples cause some problems for the macro-averaged recall score and "she" is also more frequently misclassified than bigger classes. Besides those issues, we are quite satisfied with the result for this language pair.

3.3 English – French

Similar to English–German, English–French also seems to be a harder case. The overall accuracy is in the same range as for English–German, slightly above, but now for eight classes, which is harder. The confusion matrix in Table 2 shows the frequent misclassifications for "elle" and "cela" and especially "elles", which is classified as "ils" in most of the cases. Even other classes show quite some confusion and the overall score is much below predicting pronoun translations in the other direction as we will see below.

	he	she	it	they	this	these	there	OTHER	
he	22	0	6	0	0	0	0	4	32
she	0	15	3	0	0	0	0	0	18
it	6	5	35	3	1	0	3	4	57
they	0	0	1	77	0	0	0	2	80
this	0	0	1	1	0	0	1	0	3
these	0	0	0	2	1	1	0	0	4
there	0	0	0	1	0	0	46	1	48
OTHER	4	1	5	10	1	0	2	63	86
-SUM-	32	21	51	94	3	1	52	74	

Table 6: The confusion matrix for French–English. Columns represent the predicted classes.

3.4 French – English

French–English is the best performing language pair in terms of overall accuracy. However, the macro-averaged scores are significantly below the scores for German–English; still a lot better than the predictions from English to the other two languages. The biggest problem appears in the small classes "this" and "these" but this effects the overall accuracy only little. Another class that seems more difficult is "it" with its around 64% F1 score and "he" is not much better. However, overall the model performs rather well for this language pair condering the limited information that is available to the classifier.

4 Conclusions

This paper presents baseline classifiers for the pronoun translation task at WMT 2016. Our linear classifier uses local context features and antecedent candidates from a simple PoS-based matching procedure. The results are satisfactory especially for the predictions of pronoun correspondences in English. This seems to be a simpler task than guessing the correct translations of the ambiguous English third-person pronouns into French and German with their grammatical gender and corresponding agreement problems. Our model shows that simple classifiers without further linguistic pre-processing can be used to obtain decent baseline scores in this difficult task. However, the prediction quality is still rather low and its use in machine translation or other cross-lingual applications remains to be seen.

References

Rong-En Fan, Kai-Wei Chang, Cho-Jui Hsieh, Xiang-Rui Wang, and Chih-Jen Lin. 2008. LIBLINEAR: A library for large linear classification. *Journal of Machine Learning Research*, 9:1871–1874.

Christian Hardmeier, Preslav Nakov, Sara Stymne, Jörg Tiedemann, Yannick Versley, and Mauro Cettolo. 2015. Pronoun-focused mt and cross-lingual pronoun prediction: Findings of the 2015 discomt shared task on pronoun translation. In *Proceedings of the Second Workshop on Discourse in Machine Translation*, pages 1–16, Lisbon, Portugal, September. Association for Computational Linguistics.

Jörg Tiedemann. 2015. Baseline models for pronoun prediction and pronoun-aware translation. In *Proceedings of the Second Workshop on Discourse in Machine Translation*, pages 108–114, Lisbon, Portugal, September. Association for Computational Linguistics.

Cross-lingual Pronoun Prediction for English, French and German with Maximum Entropy Classification

Dominikus Wetzel

School of Informatics

University of Edinburgh

10 Crichton Street, Edinburgh

d.wetzel@ed.ac.uk

Abstract

We present our submission to the cross-lingual pronoun prediction (CLPP) shared task for English-German and English-French at the First Conference on Machine Translation (WMT16). We trained a Maximum Entropy (MaxEnt) classifier based on features from Wetzel et al. (2015), that we adapted to the new task and applied to a new language pair. Additional features such as n-grams of the pronoun context and prediction of NULL-translations proved helpful to a varying degree. Experiments with a sequence classifier over pronoun sequences did not show any improvements. Our submission is among the top three systems for English-French (61.62% macro-averaged recall) and in the middle range for English-German (48.72%) out of nine submissions.

1 Introduction

Translation of pronouns is a non-trivial task due to ambiguities in the source language (event pronouns, referential and non-referential uses) and due to diverging usage of pronouns between two languages (e.g. morphological differences including gender and number, pro-drop languages, preference of passive construction with expletive *it*). In the recent past there has been work on analysing these differences and various approaches to tackle the problem exist (Hardmeier and Federico, 2010; Le Nagard and Koehn, 2010; Guillou, 2012; Weiner, 2014; Hardmeier et al., 2014; Guillou et al., 2014) including the submissions to the CLPP shared task (Hardmeier et al., 2015).

This shared task is organized again this year (Guillou et al., 2016). In addition to the English-French language pair, it introduces data sets for English-German, as well as the inverse translation directions from French and German into English. The task is to predict a target-side pronoun from a closed set of classes for each subject-position 3rd person pronoun in the source language.

One of the major differences to the shared task from last year is the target-side data. It comes in the form of lemmatized tokens with their Part-of-Speech (POS) tag, instead of the full word forms. This makes the task more challenging, since agreement features of words surrounding a pronoun are no longer available. For example all the determiners are mapped to one generic form irrespective of their gender or number. One can also argue that it makes the task more realistic, when considering Statistical Machine Translation (SMT) as the driving goal. SMT systems do not necessarily produce the correct target-side surface word forms and approaches to pronoun translation should not rely on error-free translations of the relevant context. This change therefore helps with handling more noisy or underspecified input.

In this paper we focus on learning to predict translations of pronouns from English into French and German. The set of source pronouns (i.e. *it* and *they*) is the same for both language pairs. For French, the closed target classes are: *ce, elle, elles, il, ils, cela, on,* OTHER and for German they are: *er, sie, es, man,* OTHER.

We use a MaxEnt classification model to learn pronoun predictions. This work is based on findings in (Wetzel et al., 2015). We incorporate source- and target-side bag-of-words context window features based on tokens and POS tags, a target-side pronoun antecedent feature and a target-side Language Model (LM) feature. Furthermore, we focus on predicting cases where the source pronoun does not have a corresponding translation and is therefore aligned to a special

Proceedings of the First Conference on Machine Translation, Volume 2: Shared Task Papers, pages 620–626,
Berlin, Germany, August 11-12, 2016. ©2016 Association for Computational Linguistics

NONE token. We conduct additional experiments in an attempt to exploit the sequential character of coreference chains that contain pronouns by using linear-chain Conditional Random Fields (CRFs).

2 Related Work

The CLPP shared task from last year (Hardmeier et al., 2015) had eight contributions and a very strong baseline. The official macro-averaged F1 metric ranked the baseline highest, however in terms of accuracy, a few of the submission managed to perform better.

Tiedemann (2015) explores models for CLPP with the focus on using only simple features. The major simplification is that no coreference resolution is performed. Experiments on using a sequence model for classification are reported, which makes predictions based on previous classification choices. However, only a degradation of performance was observed. One possible reason for that is that not every preceding classification choice corresponds to a mention of the same entity, and hence should only influence the current choice if it does. This distinction was not captured by (Tiedemann, 2015). We also explore the usefulness of a sequence classifier, however our sequences are more informed in that they follow automatically resolved source-side coreference chains.

Pham and van der Plas (2015) train a Multi-Layer Perceptron. Features consist of word-embeddings of local context words, averaged word vectors of target-side antecedents of a pronoun obtained via automatic coreference chains from the source projected to the target side via word-alignments and additional vectors containing morphological information. They use a subset of the types of our features, however integration is via word-embeddings and training is based on Neural Networks. They could not find any improvements when including target-side antecedents via source side coreference chains.

3 Features

In this section we motivate and describe the types of features we extract for learning the MaxEnt classifier and the CRF models. For a more detailed description of the features from last year, please refer to (Wetzel et al., 2015).

3.1 Context window

For each training instance, i.e. for each source pronoun for which we want a prediction, we extract a bag of words consisting of the ± 3 tokens around the source pronoun. Additionally, we extract the tokens in the ± 3 context window of the aligned target pronoun. The source-side feature consists of tokens in their full form, whereas the target-side feature uses the lemmatized tokens from the training data.

Additionally, we extract POS tags for these tokens. For the source side we automatically obtain POS tags with StanfordCoreNLP (Lee et al., 2013). For the target side the POS tags are provided as part of the training and test data.

A common strategy to improve linear classifiers is to include combinations of features so that the classifier can tune additional weights if predictive n-gram combinations provide useful information. Therefore, we experiment with combining the above context window features within each type. In addition to the unigram values, we extract n-gram values by concatenating adjacent tokens or POS tags.

All of the above features are extracted both from the source and the target side.

3.2 Pleonastic pronouns

Pleonastic pronouns are non-referential pronouns, i.e. they do not have an antecedent in the discourse. They behave differently compared to referential pronouns, e.g. grammatical agreement requirements do not exist. We use Nada (Bergsma and Yarowsky, 2011) to get an estimate if a particular pronoun is pleonastic and integrate this estimate directly as feature value into our classifier.

Furthermore, the Stanford deterministic coreference system (Lee et al., 2013), which we use in the feature described in Section 3.4, only has a very basic rule-based detection mechanism for pleonastic pronouns. Intuitively, Nada's estimates should therefore counterbalance erroneous handling in coreference resolution.

This feature is only applied on the source side.

3.3 Language Model prediction

LMs provide a probability of a sequence of words trained on large monolingual corpora and are used in SMT as a model to encourage fluency, i.e. producing typical target-language sentences. Wetzel et al. (2015) incorporated a LM feature based on the preceding 5-gram context of a target pronoun, by utilising the conditional probability $P(classLabel_5|w_1, w_2, w_3, w_4)$, where $classLabel$ is one of the class labels from the closed set of target classes, or the OTHER class, and w are the preceding words. This ignored any information following the pronoun, which could as well be indicative of the correct prediction. Therefore, we expand the feature to provide a rating for the entire sentence, i.e. $P(\langle s \rangle, w_1, ..., classLabel, ..., w_n, \langle /s \rangle)$, where n is the sentence length, and $\langle s \rangle$ and $\langle /s \rangle$ are sentence boundary markers.

The class label that produces the highest scoring sentence according to the LM is then used as a feature value in our classifier. To obtain such a prediction for the class labels that correspond to pronouns we can directly substitute the target-side pronoun placeholder with each class label when querying the LM.

The OTHER class requires special treatment, since it does not occur as such in the LM training data. We approximate the probability for this class in the same way as described in (Wetzel et al., 2015). We first collect frequencies of words that are tagged as OTHER from the training data. Then we query the LM with the top-n words as substitute for the placeholder. The highest scoring word within that group then competes as representative for OTHER against the probabilities of the rest of the class labels.

This feature is only applied on the target side.

3.4 Antecedent information

The antecedent feature proved useful in (Wetzel et al., 2015). Intuitively, if we know the closest target-side antecedent of a referential target-side pronoun, we have access to additional information such as grammatical gender and number. Both in German and French, the pronoun has to agree in gender and number with its antecedent. Furthermore, the fact whether we find an antecedent at all should be useful information as well, since it separates referential from non-referential cases.

We perform antecedent detection with the help of source-side coreference chains. We follow the source-side chain that contains the source pronoun of interest in reverse order (i.e. towards the beginning of the document) and check if the token that is aligned to the source-side mention head is a noun. If it is not, the search proceeds. The

Corpus	en-de	en-fr
NC9	63.72	25.12
IWSLT15	68.55	31.25
TEDdev	60.00	34.31

Table 1: Percentage of NONE within the OTHER class.

reason why we do not just search for the closest noun-antecedent on the source side and then take its projection is that nouns do not necessarily have to align to nouns, but could be aligned to NULL, pronouns, etc. We take the closest noun that we can find on the target side.

Since the target side only contains lemma information, where all gender- or number-specific information has been removed from nouns (or merged to the same token for e.g. determiners), we cannot apply a morphological tagger to give us this information. Therefore, we resort to a simpler method and look up the most frequent gender for a given lemma in a lexicon. We only experiment with this feature on the English-German task.

All of the above features are extracted from the target side (with the help of source-side annotation).

3.5 Predicting NONE

Source pronouns do not necessarily have a counterpart in the target language. These cases are recorded in the training data with NONE labels and occur very frequently (cf. Table 1). However, they are not part of the official set of class labels and mapped to the OTHER class for training and testing. If we know that a source pronoun does not have a translation, then this might be useful in an SMT scenario, where a feature function could score phrases higher that do not contain target-side pronouns. For CLPP our expectation is that it should help to improve prediction performance for the very heterogeneous OTHER class.

For training the classifiers we therefore first map all NONE cases from OTHER to NONE, train with the above features and map the final predictions back to OTHER before evaluation.

3.6 Pronoun prediction in a sequence

The MaxEnt classifier makes the assumption that the translation of the pronoun is only dependent on the source and target contexts and the antecedent

Sequence length	%
1	74.45
2	15.34
3	5.34
4	2.21
5	1.08

Table 2: Percentage of sequence lengths up to 5 in the English-German training data (IWSLT15 and NC9) for the ALLINONE setup.

Gender	Frequency
Masculine	20878
Feminine	21221
Neuter	12894
Total	54993

Table 3: Number of nouns with gender information in the raw Zmorge lexicon (zmorge-lexicon-20150315) for German.

it refers to (for referential pronouns). This ignores the fact that pronouns are part of a longer chain of co-referring expressions, among them other pronouns.

Therefore, we first prepare the training and test data such that all pronoun instances that belong to the same coreference chain form one training or testing sequence. We then train a linear-chain CRF with the same features as given above instead of a MaxEnt classifier to predict an optimal sequence of target pronouns, rather than making each prediction independently of the other pronouns. This way, typical patterns of pronoun sequences can be learnt, which might help with the prediction. Table 2 gives the distribution of sequence lengths.

4 Experiments

We first describe the experimental setup of our systems, then briefly describe the data we used and provide information about feature and parameter settings. Finally, we report our results on development and test data.

4.1 Systems

We use Mallet (McCallum, 2002) for training the MaxEnt classifiers and CRF models. For the MaxEnt classifier we use the default settings. For the CRF we train *three-quarter* order models (i.e. one weight for each ⟨feature, label⟩ pair, and one for each ⟨current label, previous label⟩ pair) and only allow label transitions that have been observed in the training data.

In all experiments, we have two setups. The POSTCOMBINED setup, where we split the training and test data for each source pronoun into separate sets, train separate classifiers and combine the predictions after classification. And the ALLINONE setup, where we do not split the data.

The systems marked with *initial* consist of the context window features, the pleonastic pronoun feature, the LM feature and the antecedent information (without gender information). We use *fGender* to refer to the gender feature, *3-gram window* to refer to the n-grams from the context window and *fNone* to refer to the NONE-prediction feature. Systems marked with *sequence* are the CRF models. We submit the best performing system according to the official macro-averaged recall measure on the development set for each language pair as primary test set submission.

The official BASELINE uses LM predictions similarly to our LM feature. Additionally, it attempts to find the optimal predictions for a sentence, if there are multiple pronouns that have to be predicted. It has a NULL penalty parameter that determines the influence of not predicting a pronoun at all. For a more detailed description, please refer to the shared task paper (Guillou et al., 2016).

4.2 Data

For training, we only extract information from the IWSLT15 and NewsCommentary (NC9) corpus. We do not employ the provided Europarl corpus, as it does not come with predefined document boundaries other than parliamentary sessions of a complete day. For development, we use the TEDdev set. For the final submission on the official test set we include TEDdev in the training data.

4.3 Features and parameters

For the LM feature, we take the provided trained models from the shared task, which are 5-gram modified Kneser-Ney LMs that work on lemmatized text. We use KenLM (Heafield, 2011) for obtaining probabilities. As proxy for the OTHER class we use the top 35 words for German, and the top 70 for French.

	Mac-R	Acc
BASELINE	34.35	42.81
ALLINONE-initial	39.24	56.14
+ fGender	40.00	57.37
+ fGender, 3-gram window	41.21	57.72
+ fGender, 3-gram win, fNone	40.86	58.77
ALLINONE-sequence-initial	35.67	54.91

Table 4: System performance in percent for English-German on the development data set.

	Mac-R	Acc
BASELINE	40.63	49.73
ALLINONE-initial	52.25	69.98
+ 3-gram window	54.68	73.36
+ 3-gram window, fNone	57.34	74.25
ALLINONE-sequence-initial	49.27	64.65

Table 5: System performance in percent for English-French on the development data set.

	en-de		en-fr	
	Mac-R	Acc	Mac-R	Acc
ALLINONE	48.72_5	66.32_6	61.62_4	71.31_3
POSTCOMBINED	47.75	64.75	59.83	68.63
BASELINE-1	n/a	n/a	50.85	53.35
BASELINE-2	47.86	54.31	n/a	n/a

Table 6: Official shared task results. Ranks of our primary submission are given in subscripts with a total of nine submissions for each language pair.

For gender detection of German antecedents we use the lexicon from Zmorge (Sennrich and Kunz, 2014). Gender distribution of nouns is given in Table 3. When a noun has multiple genders in the lexicon, we take the most frequent one for that noun.

The different parameters such as context window size were taken from our findings of the previous year (Wetzel et al., 2015). The n-grams of the context window are extracted for n=1..3 including beginning- and end-of-sentence markers if necessary.

4.4 Results

The results on the development set are given in Table 4 for English-German and in Table 5 for English-French. The final results including the ranks on the official test set of the shared task are given in Table 6.

The initial systems in each language-pair perform much better than the baseline, which is especially noticeable in English-French. Adding the gender feature to the English-German classifier shows some good improvements in performance, thereby confirming the usefulness of adding gender information.

The additional feature that predicts NONE as possible translation is helpful for the English-French pair. Results on English-German showed a decrease in performance with respect to macro-averaged recall. This decrease is surprising, especially considering the much larger frequency of NONE in the German data set (cf. Table 1).

5 Discussion

In general, performance is considerably lower for English-German compared to English-French, despite the former having a much smaller set of class

	er	sie	es	man	OTHER	Total
er	4/4	2/2	3/8	·	6/1	15
sie	3/2	73/100	11/15	3/·	34/7	124
es	2/·	9/4	61/85	2/·	27/12	101
man	·	·/1	2/4	1/1	5/2	8
OTHER	2/1	11/17	7/16	·	115/101	135
Total	11/7	95/124	84/128	6/1	187/123	383

	ce	elle	elles	il	ils	cela	on	OTHER	Total
ce	58/60	·	·	6/6	·/1	1/·	·	3/1	68
elle	2/2	10/9	2/·	5/8	·/1	2/3	·	2/·	23
elles	2/·	2/·	3/6	·	15/17	1/·	·/1	2/1	25
il	5/6	1/6	·	43/43	2/1	4/3	2/2	4/·	61
ils	·	·	9/7	·	54/63	·	·	8/1	71
cela	·	3/1	·	8/7	·	15/20	1/1	4/2	31
on	·	·	·	·/1	2/4	·	6/4	1/·	9
OTHER	1/3	1/·	·	4/7	1/·	1/1	·/2	77/72	85
Total	68/71	17/16	14/13	66/72	74/87	24/27	9/10	101/77	373

Table 7: Confusion matrices for the ALLINONE classifier on the English-German (top) and English-French (bottom) test set. Row labels are gold labels and column labels are labels as they were classified. Dots represent zeros. Numbers to the left represent our shared task submissions, numbers to the right are for the results when we removed the LM feature from these submissions.

	en-de		en-fr	
	Mac-R	Acc	Mac-R	Acc
ALLINONE	48.72	66.32	61.62	71.31
− fAntecedent	46.24	64.23	61.89	71.85
− fLM	55.76	75.98	63.03	74.26

Table 8: Feature ablation results on the test set when removing the antecedent or LM feature from our submitted systems.

labels to choose from. One reason for that might be that in the former setting, the OTHER class is even more heterogeneous than in French, and taking apart this class to the same degree as in the English-French data sets might be beneficial.

Performance between development and test sets varies greatly despite similar class label distributions (except for a much smaller amount of OTHER instances in the English-French test set). To a certain degree this is expected, however the big changes in performance suggest that there are other differences in the data sets which are worth exploring.

Training a MaxEnt classifier where we substitute our LM feature with predictions from the shared task baseline performed slightly worse. This suggests that a simpler LM feature is sufficient when included in the classifier, and that joint prediction of multiple target pronouns within one sentence is not necessary. However, we did not tune the NULL penalty of the baseline model.

The confusion matrix for English-German in Table 7 (top-left) shows that OTHER is over-predicted, which might explain the overall lower performance of the system compared to other participants. Furthermore, *es* and *sie* are confused by our classifier. For English-French in Table 7 (bottom-left) one can observe that the biggest confusion is between gender in plural pronouns (i.e. *elles* and *ils*). This might be because we did not include any explicit gender information as feature. As above, the OTHER class is also very confused over all cases.

Similarly to our findings from last year, the POSTCOMBINED setup scored consistently worse on the test sets (and only once slightly better on the development set). This provides evidence, that splitting the training data according to source pronouns is counterproductive. Furthermore, it might even be worse for the inverse prediction tasks, since there are a lot more source pronouns, hence making the available data even sparser.

The lemmatization of the French data merges singular and plural forms of *il* into one lemma, similarly for *elle*. The baseline which uses the LM trained on the lemmatized data is therefore never able to predict the plural forms of these two pronouns, resulting in zero precision and recall. This is confirmed by the corresponding confusion matrix. This might also have an indirect impact on the performance of our classifiers, since they use LM prediction as a feature.

Feature ablation experiments shown in Table 8 revealed that the antecedent feature is helpful for English-German, but not for English-French. One possible explanation for this might be that we do not have gender information of the antecedent in French and only adding the antecedent itself might not be sufficient.

Additional ablation experiments showed that the LM feature in fact hurts performance. Removing this feature gives a boost in performance, which brings our systems to the second place (first for accuracy) for English-German and to the third place (second for accuracy) for English-French. This contradicts findings from experiments we conducted for last year's shared task, where adding baseline predictions, which are very similar to our LM feature, greatly improved results. An explanation for this behaviour could be that the LM this year was trained on lemmatized text and therefore performs much worse than when trained on original data. Confusion matrices for these results are given in Table 7 (numbers to the right). For both language pairs we are now under-predicting OTHER, however gaining accuracy on the classes representing pronouns.

6   Conclusion

We experimented with MaxEnt classifiers for CLPP applied to English-German and English-French. Some of the features are only useful for one of the two language pairs. Adding LM predictions considerably worsened performance, which is contrary to experiments performed on last year's shared task. Modelling pronoun sequences with CRFs did not prove useful at all.

The greatly varying degree of performance between development and test sets relativizes any findings of the shared task, and it should be further investigated what the cause of that is.

Acknowledgments

This research has been funded through the European Union's Horizon 2020 research and innovation programme under grant agreement 644402 (HimL).

References

Shane Bergsma and David Yarowsky. 2011. NADA: A robust system for non-referential pronoun detection. In *Proceedings of the 8th Discourse Anaphora and Anaphor Resolution Colloquium (DAARC)*, pages 12–23, Faro, Portugal, October.

Liane Guillou, Christian Hardmeier, Aaron Smith, Jörg Tiedemann, and Bonnie Webber. 2014. Parcor 1.0: A parallel pronoun-coreference corpus to support statistical mt. In *Proceedings of the Ninth International Conference on Language Resources and Evaluation (LREC'14)*, Reykjavik, Iceland, May. European Language Resources Association (ELRA).

Liane Guillou, Christian Hardmeier, Preslav Nakov, Sara Stymne, Jörg Tiedemann, Yannick Versley, Mauro Cettolo, Bonnie Webber, and Andrei Popescu-Belis. 2016. Findings of the 2016 WMT shared task on cross-lingual pronoun prediction. In *Proceedings of the First Conference on Machine Translation (WMT16)*, Berlin, Germany. Association for Computational Linguistics.

Liane Guillou. 2012. Improving pronoun translation for statistical machine translation. In *Proceedings of the Student Research Workshop at the 13th Conference of the European Chapter of the Association for Computational Linguistics*, pages 1–10, Avignon, France, April. Association for Computational Linguistics.

Christian Hardmeier and Marcello Federico. 2010. Modelling Pronominal Anaphora in Statistical Machine Translation. In Marcello Federico, Ian Lane, Michael Paul, and François Yvon, editors, *Proceedings of the seventh International Workshop on Spoken Language Translation (IWSLT)*, pages 283–289.

Christian Hardmeier, Sara Stymne, Jörg Tiedemann, Aaron Smith, and Joakim Nivre. 2014. Anaphora models and reordering for phrase-based smt. In *Proceedings of the Ninth Workshop on Statistical Machine Translation*, pages 122–129, Baltimore, Maryland, USA, June. Association for Computational Linguistics.

Christian Hardmeier, Preslav Nakov, Sara Stymne, Jörg Tiedemann, Yannick Versley, and Mauro Cettolo. 2015. Pronoun-focused MT and cross-lingual pronoun prediction: Findings of the 2015 DiscoMT shared task on pronoun translation. In *Proceedings of the Second Workshop on Discourse in Machine Translation*, Lisbon, Portugal. http://www.idiap.ch/workshop/DiscoMT/shared-task.

Kenneth Heafield. 2011. KenLM: faster and smaller language model queries. In *Proceedings of the EMNLP 2011 Sixth Workshop on Statistical Machine Translation*, pages 187–197, Edinburgh, Scotland, United Kingdom, July.

Ronan Le Nagard and Philipp Koehn. 2010. Aiding pronoun translation with co-reference resolution. In *Proceedings of the Joint Fifth Workshop on Statistical Machine Translation and MetricsMATR*, pages 252–261, Uppsala, Sweden, July. Association for Computational Linguistics.

Heeyoung Lee, Angel Chang, Yves Peirsman, Nathanael Chambers, Mihai Surdeanu, and Dan Jurafsky. 2013. Deterministic coreference resolution based on entity-centric, precision-ranked rules. *Computational Linguistics*, 39(4):885–916.

Andrew Kachites McCallum. 2002. Mallet: A machine learning for language toolkit. http://mallet.cs.umass.edu.

Ngoc-Quan Pham and Lonneke van der Plas. 2015. Predicting pronouns across languages with continuous word spaces. In *Proceedings of the Second Workshop on Discourse in Machine Translation*, pages 101–107, Lisbon, Portugal, September. Association for Computational Linguistics.

Rico Sennrich and Beat Kunz. 2014. Zmorge: A german morphological lexicon extracted from wiktionary. In *Proceedings of the Ninth International Conference on Language Resources and Evaluation (LREC'14)*, Reykjavik, Iceland, may. European Language Resources Association (ELRA).

Jörg Tiedemann. 2015. Baseline models for pronoun prediction and pronoun-aware translation. In *Proceedings of the Second Workshop on Discourse in Machine Translation*, pages 108–114, Lisbon, Portugal, September. Association for Computational Linguistics.

Jochen Weiner. 2014. Pronominal anaphora in machine translation. Master's thesis, Karlsruhe Institute of Technology, January.

Dominikus Wetzel, Adam Lopez, and Bonnie Webber. 2015. A maximum entropy classifier for cross-lingual pronoun prediction. In *Proceedings of the Second Workshop on Discourse in Machine Translation*, pages 115–121, Lisbon, Portugal, September. Association for Computational Linguistics.

Does Multimodality Help Human and Machine for Translation and Image Captioning?

Ozan Caglayan[1,3], Walid Aransa[1], Yaxing Wang[2], Marc Masana[2],
Mercedes García-Martínez[1], Fethi Bougares[1], Loïc Barrault[1] and Joost van de Weijer[2]
[1] LIUM, University of Le Mans, [2] CVC, Universitat Autonoma de Barcelona,
[3] Galatasaray University
[1]`FirstName.LastName@lium.univ-lemans.fr`
[2]`{joost,mmasana,yaxing}@cvc.uab.es`
[3]`ocaglayan@gsu.edu.tr`

Abstract

This paper presents the systems developed by LIUM and CVC for the WMT16 Multimodal Machine Translation challenge. We explored various comparative methods, namely phrase-based systems and attentional recurrent neural networks models trained using monomodal or multimodal data. We also performed a human evaluation in order to estimate the usefulness of multimodal data for human machine translation and image description generation. Our systems obtained the best results for both tasks according to the automatic evaluation metrics BLEU and METEOR.

1 Introduction

Recently, deep learning has greatly impacted the natural language processing field as well as computer vision. Machine translation (MT) with deep neural networks (DNN), proposed by (Kalchbrenner and Blunsom, 2013; Sutskever et al., 2014) and (Bahdanau et al., 2014) competed successfully in the last year's WMT evaluation campaign (Bojar et al., 2015).

In the same trend, generating descriptions from images using DNNs has been proposed by (Elliott et al., 2015). Several attempts have been made to incorporate features from different modalities in order to help the automatic system to better model the task at hand (Elliott et al., 2015; Kiros et al., 2014b; Kiros et al., 2014a).

This paper describes the systems developed by LIUM and CVC who participated in the two proposed tasks for the WMT 2016 Multimodal Machine Translation evaluation campaign: Multimodal machine translation (Task 1) and multimodal image description (Task 2).

The remainder of this paper is structured in two parts: The first part (section 2) describes the architecture of the four systems (two monomodal and two multimodal) submitted for Task 1. The standard phrase-based SMT systems based on Moses are described in section 2.1 while the neural MT systems are described in section 2.2 (monomodal) and section 3.2 (multimodal). The second part (section 3) contains the description of the two systems submitted for Task 2: The first one is a monomodal neural MT system similar to the one presented in section 2.2, and the second one is a multimodal neural machine translation (MNMT) with shared attention mechanism.

In order to evaluate the feasibility of the multimodal approach, we also asked humans to perform the two tasks of this evaluation campaign. Results show that the additional English description sentences improved performance while the straightforward translation of the sentence without the image did not provide as good results. The results of these experiments are presented in section 4.

2 Multimodal Machine Translation

This task consists in translating an English sentence that describes an image into German, given the English sentence itself and the image that it describes.

2.1 Phrase-based System

Our baseline system for task 1 is developed following the standard phrase-based Moses pipeline as described in (Koehn et al., 2007), SRILM (Stolcke, 2002), KenLM (Heafield, 2011), and GIZA++ (Och and Ney, 2003). This system is trained using the data provided by the organizers and tuned using MERT (Och, 2003) to maximize BLEU (Papineni et al., 2002) and METEOR (Lavie and Agarwal, 2007) scores on the validation set.

Proceedings of the First Conference on Machine Translation, Volume 2: Shared Task Papers, pages 627–633,
Berlin, Germany, August 11-12, 2016. ©2016 Association for Computational Linguistics

We also used Continuous Space Language Model[1] (CSLM) (Schwenk, 2010) with the auxiliary features support as proposed by (Aransa et al., 2015). This CSLM architecture allows us to use sentence-level features for each line in the training data (i.e. all n-grams in the same sentence will have the same auxiliary features). By this means, better context specific LM estimations can be obtained.

We used four additional scores to rerank 1000-best outputs of our baseline system: The first two scores are obtained from two separate CSLM(s) trained on the target side (i.e. German) of the parallel training corpus and each one of the following auxiliary features:

- **VGG19-FC7 image features:** The auxiliary feature used in the first CSLM are the image features provided by the organizers which are extracted from the FC7 layer (relu7) of the VGG-19 network (Simonyan and Zisserman, 2014). This allows us to train a multimodal CSLM that uses additional context learned from the image features.

- **Source side sentence representation vectors:** We used the method described in (Le and Mikolov, 2014) to compute continuous space representation vector for each source (i.e. English) sentence that will be provided to the second CSLM as auxiliary feature. The idea behind this is to condition our target language model on the source side as additional context.

The two other scores used for n-best reranking are the log probability computed by our NMT system that will be described in the following section and the score obtained by a Recurrent Neural Network Language Model (RNNLM) (Mikolov et al., 2010). The weights of the original moses features and our additional features were optimized to maximize the BLEU score on the validation set.

2.2 Neural MT System

The fundamental model that we experimented[2] is an attention based encoder-decoder approach (Bahdanau et al., 2014) except some notable changes in the recurrent decoder called Conditional GRU.

---

[1]github.com/hschwenk/cslm-toolkit
[2]github.com/nyu-dl/dl4mt-tutorial

We define by X and Y, a source sentence of length N and a target sentence of length M respectively. Each source and target word is represented with an embedding vector of dimension E_X and E_Y respectively:

$$X = (x_1, x_2, ..., x_N), x_i \in \mathbb{R}^{E_X} \qquad (1)$$
$$Y = (y_1, y_2, ..., y_M), y_j \in \mathbb{R}^{E_Y} \qquad (2)$$

A bidirectional recurrent encoder reads an input sequence X in forwards and backwards to produce two sets of hidden states based on the current input and the previous hidden state. An annotation vector h_i for *each* position i is then obtained by concatenating the produced hidden states.

An attention mechanism, implemented as a simple fully-connected feed-forward neural network, accepts the hidden state h_t of the decoder's recurrent layer and one input annotation at a time, to produce the attention coefficients. A softmax activation is applied on those attention coefficients to obtain the attention weights used to generate weighted annotation vector for time t. The initial hidden state h_0 of the decoder is determined by a feed-forward layer receiving the mean annotation vector.

We use Gated Recurrent Unit (GRU) (Chung et al., 2014) activation function for both recurrent encoders and decoders.

2.2.1 Training

We picked the following hyperparameters for all NMT systems both for Task 1 and Task 2. All embedding and recurrent layers have a dimensionality of 620 and 1000 respectively. We used Adam as the stochastic optimizer with a mini-batch size of 32, Xavier weight initialization (Glorot and Bengio, 2010) and L2 regularization with $\lambda = 0.0001$ except the monomodal Task 1 system for which the choices were Adadelta, sampling from $\mathcal{N}(0, 0.01)$ and L2 regularization with $\lambda = 0.0005$ respectively.

The performance of the network is evaluated on the validation split using BLEU after each 1000 minibatch updates and the training is stopped if BLEU does not improve for 20 evaluation periods. The training times were 16 and 26 hours respectively for monomodal and multimodal systems on a Tesla K40 GPU.

Finally, we used a classical left to right beam-search with a beam size of 12 for sentence generation during test time.

2.3 Data

Phrase-based and NMT systems for Task 1 are trained using the dataset provided by the organizers and described in Table 1. This dataset consists of 29K parallel sentences (direct translations of image descriptions from English to German) for training, 1014 for validation and finally 1000 for the test set. We preprocessed the dataset using the punctuation normalization, tokenization and lowercasing scripts from Moses. In order to generalize better over the compound structs in German, we trained and applied a compound splitter[3] (Sennrich and Haddow, 2015) over the German vocabulary of training and validation sets. This reduces the target vocabulary from 18670 to 15820 unique tokens. During translation generation, the splitted compounds are stitched back together.

Side	Vocabulary	Words
English	10211	377K
German	15820	369K

Table 1: Training Data for Task 1.

2.4 Results and Analysis

The results of our phrase-based baseline and the four submitted systems are presented in Table 2. The **BL+4Features** system is the rescoring of the baseline 1000-best output using all the features described in 2.1 while **BL+3Features** is the same but excluding FC7 image features. Overall, we were able to improve test set scores by around 0.4 and 0.8 on METEOR and BLEU respectively over a strong phrase-based baseline using auxiliary features.

Regarding the NMT systems, the monomodal NMT achieved a comparative BLEU score of 32.50 on the test set compared to 33.45 of the phrase-based baseline. The multimodal NMT system that will be described in section 3.2, obtained relatively lower scores when trained using Task 1's data.

3 Multimodal Image Description Generation

The objective of Task 2 is to produce German descriptions of images given the image itself and one or more English descriptions as input.

[3]github.com/rsennrich/wmt2014-scripts

3.1 Visual Data Representation

To describe the image content we make use of Convolutional Neural Networks (CNN). In a breakthrough work, Krizhevsky et al. (Krizhevsky et al., 2012) convincingly show that CNNs yield a far superior image representation compared to previously used hand-crafted image features. Based on this success an intensified research effort started to further improve the representations based on CNNs. The work of Simonyan and Zisserman (Simonyan and Zisserman, 2014) improved the network by breaking up large convolutional features into multiple layers of small convolutional features, which allowed to train a much deeper network. The organizers provide these features to all participants. More precisely they provide the features from the fifth convolutional layer, and the features from the second fully connected layer of VGG-19. Recently, Residual Networks (ResNet) have been proposed (He et al., 2015). These networks learn residual functions which are constructed by adding skip layers (or projection layers) to the network. These skip layers prevent the vanishing gradient problem, and allow for much deeper networks (over hundred layers) to be trained.

To select the optimal layer for image representation we performed an image classification task on a subsection of images from SUN scenes (Xiao et al., 2010). We extract the features from the various layers of ResNet-50 and evaluate the classification performance (Figure 1). The results increase during the first layers but stabilize from Block-4 on. Based on these results and considering that a higher spatial resolution is better, we have selected layer 'res4fx' (end of Block-4, after ReLU) for the experiments on multimodal MT. We also compared the features from different networks on the task of image description generation with the system of Xu et al. (Xu et al., 2015). The results for generating English descriptions (Table 3) show a clear performance improvement from VGG-19 to ResNet-50, but comparable results are obtained when going to ResNet-152. Therefore, given the increase in computational cost, we have decided to use ResNet-50 features for our submission.

3.2 Multimodal NMT System

The multimodal NMT system is an extension of (Xu et al., 2015) and the monomodal NMT system described in Section 2.2.

System Description	Validation Set		Test Set	
	METEOR (norm)	BLEU	METEOR (norm)	BLEU
Phrase-based Baseline (BL)	53.71 (58.43)	35.61	52.83 (57.37)	33.45
BL+3Features	54.29 (58.99)	36.52	53.19 (57.76)	34.31
BL+4Features	54.40 (59.08)	36.63	53.18 (57.76)	34.28
Monomodal NMT	51.07 (54.87)	35.93	49.20 (53.10)	32.50
Multimodal NMT	44.55 (47.97)	28.06	45.04 (48.52)	27.82

Table 2: BLEU and METEOR scores on detokenized outputs of baseline and submitted Task 1 systems. The METEOR scores in parenthesis are computed with $-$norm parameter.

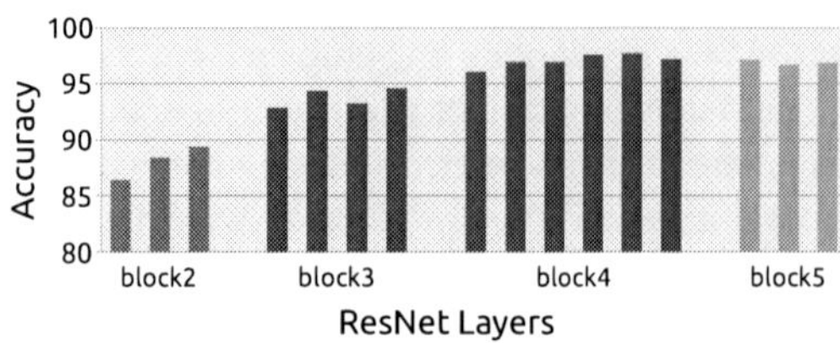

Figure 1: Classification accuracy on a subset of SUN scenes (Xiao et al., 2010) for ResNet-50: The colored groups represent the building blocks while the bars inside are the stacked blocks (He et al., 2015).

Network	BLEU-1	BLEU-2	BLEU-3	BLEU-4
VGG-19	58.2	31.4	18.5	11.3
ResNet-50	68.4	45.2	30.9	21.1
ResNet-152	68.3	44.9	30.7	21.1

Table 3: BLEU scores for various deep features on the image description generation task using the system of Xu et al. (Xu et al., 2015).

The model involves two GRU layers and an attention mechanism. The first GRU layer computes an intermediate representation s'_j as follows:

$$s'_j = (1 - z'_j) \odot \underline{s}'_j + z'_j \odot s_{j-1} \quad (3)$$
$$\underline{s}'_j = \tanh(W' E[y_{j-1}] + r'_j \odot (U' s_{j-1})) \quad (4)$$
$$r'_j = \sigma(W'_r E[y_{j-1}] + U'_r s_{j-1}) \quad (5)$$
$$z'_j = \sigma(W'_z E[y_{j-1}] + U'_z s_{j-1}) \quad (6)$$

where E is the target word embedding, $\underline{s}'_j$ is the hidden state, r'_j and z'_j are the reset and update gate activations. W', U'_r, W'_r, U'_r, W'_z and U'_z are the parameters to be learned.

A shared attention layer similar to (Firat et al., 2016) that consists of a fully-connected feed-forward network is used to compute a set of modality specific attention coefficients e^{mod}_{ij} at each timestep j:

$$e^{mod}_{ij} = U_{att} \tanh(W_{catt} h^{mod}_i + W_{att} s'_j) \quad (7)$$

The attention weight between source modality context i and target word j is computed by applying a softmax on e^{mod}_{ij}:

$$\alpha_{ij} = \frac{\exp(e^{txt}_{ij})}{\sum_{k=1}^{N} \exp(e^{txt}_{kj})} \quad (8)$$

$$\beta_{ij} = \frac{\exp(e^{img}_{ij})}{\sum_{k=1}^{196} \exp(e^{img}_{kj})} \quad (9)$$

The final multimodal context vector c_j is obtained as follows:

$$c_j = \tanh(\sum_{i=1}^{N} \alpha_{ij} h^{txt}_i + \sum_{i=1}^{196} \beta_{ij} h^{img}_i) \quad (10)$$

The second GRU generates s_j from the intermediate representation s'_j and the context vector c_j as follows:

$$s_j = (1 - z_j) \odot \underline{s}_j + z_j \odot s'_j \quad (11)$$
$$\underline{s}_j = \tanh(W c_j + r_j \odot (U s'_j)) \quad (12)$$
$$r_j = \sigma(W_r c_j + U_r s'_j) \quad (13)$$
$$z_j = \sigma(W_z c_j + U_z s'_j) \quad (14)$$

where $\underline{s}'_j$ is the hidden state, r_j and z_j are the reset and update gate activations. W, U_r, W_r, U_r, W_z and U_z are the parameters to be learned.

Finally, in order to compute the target word, the following formulations are applied:

$$o_j = L_o \tanh(E[y_{j-1}] + L_s s_j + L_c c_j) \quad (15)$$
$$P(y_j|y_{j-1}, s_j, c_j) = \text{Softmax}(o_j) \quad (16)$$

where L_o, L_s and L_c are trained parameters.

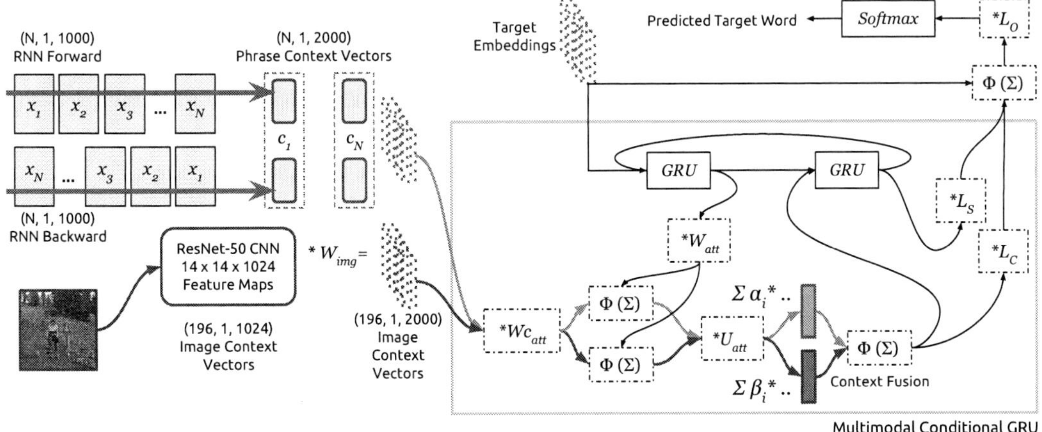

Figure 2: The architecture of the multimodal NMT system. The boxes with $*$ refers to a linear transformation while $\Phi(\Sigma)$ means a *tanh* applied over the sum of the inputs. The figure depicts a running instance of the network over a single example.

3.2.1 Generation

Since we are provided 5 source descriptions for each image in order to generate a single German description, we let the NMT generate a German description for each source and pick the one with the highest probability and preferably without an UNK token.

3.3 Data

The organizers provided an extended version of the Flickr30K Entities dataset (Elliott et al., 2016) which contains 5 *independently* crowd-sourced German descriptions for each image in addition to the 5 English descriptions originally found in the dataset. It is possible to use this dataset either by considering the cross product of 5 source and 5 target descriptions (a total of 25 description pairs for each image) or by only taking the 5 pairwise descriptions leading to 725K and 145K training pairs respectively. We decided to use the smaller subset of 145K sentences.

Side	Vocabulary	Words
English	16802	1.5M
German	10000	1.3M

Table 4: Training Data for Task 2.

The preprocessing is exactly the same as Task 1 except that we only kept sentence pairs with sentence lengths $\in [3, 50]$ and with a ratio of at most 3. This results in a final training dataset of 131K

sentences (Table 4). We picked the most frequent 10K German words and replaced the rest with an UNK token for the target side. Note that compound splitting was not done for this task.

3.4 Results and Analysis

System	Validation		Test	
	METEOR	BLEU	METEOR	BLEU
Monomodal	36.3	24.0	35.1	23.8
Multimodal	34.4	19.3	32.3	19.2

Table 5: BLEU and METEOR scores of our NMT based submissions for Task 2.

As we can see in Table 5, the multimodal system does not surpass monomodal NMT system. Several explanations can clarify this behavior. First, the architecture is not well suited for integrating image and text representations. This is possible as we did not explore all the possibilities to benefit from both modalities. Another explanation is that the image context contain too much irrelevant information which cannot be discriminated by the lone attention mechanism. This would need a deeper analysis of the attention weights in order to be answered.

4 Human multimodal translation and/or description

To evaluate the importance of the different modalities for the image description generation and translation task, we have performed an experiment

Method	BLEU-1	BLEU-2	BLEU-3	BLEU-4	METEOR
Image + sentences	54.30	35.95	23.28	15.06	39.16
Image only	51.26	34.74	22.63	15.01	38.06
Sentence only	39.37	23.27	13.73	8.40	32.98
Our system	60.61	44.35	31.65	21.95	33.59

Table 6: BLEU and METEOR scores for human translation/description generation experiments.

where we replace the computer algorithm with human participants. The two modalities are the five English description sentences, and the image. The output is a single description sentence in German. The experiment asks the participants for the following tasks:

- Given both the image and the English descriptions: *'Describe the image in one sentence in German. You can get help from the English sentences provided.'*

- Given only the image: *'Describe the image in one sentence in German.'*

- Given only one English sentence: *'Translate the English sentence into German.'*

The experiment was performed by 16 native German speakers proficient in English with age ranging from 23 to 54 (coming from Austria, Germany and Switzerland, of which 10 are female and 6 male). The experiment is performed on the first 80 sentences of the validation set. Participants performed 10 repetitions for each task, and not repeating the same image across tasks. The results of the experiments are presented in Table 6. For humans, the English description sentences help to obtain better performance. Removing the image altogether and providing only a single English description sentence results in a significant drop. We were surprised to observe such a drop, whereas we expected good translations to obtain competitive results. In addition, we have provided the results of our submission on the same subset of images; humans clearly obtain better performance using METEOR metrics, but our approach is clearly outperforming on the BLEU metrics. The participants were not trained on the train set before performing the tasks, which could be one of the reasons for the difference. Furthermore, given the lower performance of only translating one of the English description sentences on both metrics, it could possibly be caused by existing biases in the data set.

5 Conclusion and Discussion

We have presented the systems developed by LIUM and CVC for the WMT16 Multimodal Machine Translation challenge. Results show that integrating image features into a multimodal neural MT system with shared attention mechanism does not yet surpass the performance obtained with a monomodal system using only text input. However, our multimodal systems do improve upon an image captioning system (which was expected). The phrase-based system can benefit from rescoring with multimodal neural language model as well as rescoring with a neural MT system.

We have also presented the results of a human evaluation performing the same tasks as proposed in the challenge. The results are rather clear: image captioning can benefit from multimodality.

Acknowledgments

This work was supported by the Chist-ERA project M2CR[4]. We kindly thank KyungHyun Cho and Orhan Firat for providing the DL4MT tutorial as open source and Kelvin Xu for the arctic-captions[5] system.

References

Walid Aransa, Holger Schwenk, and Loic Barrault. 2015. Improving continuous space language models using auxiliary features. In *Proceedings of the 12th International Workshop on Spoken Language Translation*, pages 151–158, Da Nang, Vietnam, December.

Dzmitry Bahdanau, Kyunghyun Cho, and Yoshua Bengio. 2014. Neural machine translation by jointly learning to align and translate. *CoRR*, abs/1409.0473.

Ondřej Bojar, Rajen Chatterjee, Christian Federmann, Barry Haddow, Matthias Huck, Chris Hokamp, Philipp Koehn, Varvara Logacheva, Christof Monz, Matteo Negri, Matt Post, Carolina Scarton, Lucia Specia, and Marco Turchi. 2015. Findings of the 2015 workshop on statistical machine translation. In *Proceedings of the Tenth Workshop on Statistical Machine Translation*, pages 1–46, Lisbon, Portugal, September. Association for Computational Linguistics.

Junyoung Chung, Çaglar Gülçehre, KyungHyun Cho, and Yoshua Bengio. 2014. Empirical evaluation of gated recurrent neural networks on sequence modeling. *CoRR*, abs/1412.3555.

---

[4]m2cr.univ-lemans.fr
[5]github.com/kelvinxu/arctic-captions

Desmond Elliott, Stella Frank, and Eva Hasler. 2015. Multi-language image description with neural sequence models. *CoRR*, abs/1510.04709.

D. Elliott, S. Frank, K. Sima'an, and L. Specia. 2016. Multi30K: Multilingual English-German Image Descriptions. *CoRR*, abs/1605.00459.

Orhan Firat, Kyunghyun Cho, and Yoshua Bengio. 2016. Multi-way, multilingual neural machine translation with a shared attention mechanism. *arXiv preprint arXiv:1601.01073*.

Xavier Glorot and Yoshua Bengio. 2010. Understanding the difficulty of training deep feedforward neural networks. In *In Proceedings of the International Conference on Artificial Intelligence and Statistics (AISTATS'10). Society for Artificial Intelligence and Statistics*.

Kaiming He, Xiangyu Zhang, Shaoqing Ren, and Jian Sun. 2015. Deep residual learning for image recognition. *arXiv preprint arXiv:1512.03385*.

Kenneth Heafield. 2011. KenLM: faster and smaller language model queries. In *Proceedings of the EMNLP 2011 Sixth Workshop on Statistical Machine Translation*, pages 187–197, Edinburgh, Scotland, United Kingdom, July.

Nal Kalchbrenner and Phil Blunsom. 2013. Recurrent continuous translation models. Seattle, October. Association for Computational Linguistics.

Ryan Kiros, Ruslan Salakhutdinov, and Rich Zemel. 2014a. Multimodal neural language models. In Tony Jebara and Eric P. Xing, editors, *Proceedings of the 31st International Conference on Machine Learning (ICML-14)*, pages 595–603. JMLR Workshop and Conference Proceedings.

Ryan Kiros, Ruslan Salakhutdinov, and Richard S. Zemel. 2014b. Unifying visual-semantic embeddings with multimodal neural language models. *CoRR*, abs/1411.2539.

Philipp Koehn, Hieu Hoang, Alexandra Birch, Chris Callison-Burch, Marcello Federico, Nicola Bertoldi, Brooke Cowan, Wade Shen, Christine Moran, Richard Zens, Chris Dyer, Ondrej Bojar, Alexandra Constantin, and Evan Herbst. 2007. Moses: Open source toolkit for statistical machine translation. In *Meeting of the Association for Computational Linguistics*, pages 177–180.

Alex Krizhevsky, Ilya Sutskever, and Geoffrey E Hinton. 2012. Imagenet classification with deep convolutional neural networks. In *Advances in neural information processing systems*, pages 1097–1105.

Alon Lavie and Abhaya Agarwal. 2007. Meteor: an automatic metric for mt evaluation with high levels of correlation with human judgments. In *Proceedings of the Second Workshop on Statistical Machine Translation*, StatMT '07, pages 228–231, Stroudsburg, PA, USA. Association for Computational Linguistics.

Quoc V Le and Tomas Mikolov. 2014. Distributed representations of sentences and documents. *arXiv preprint arXiv:1405.4053*.

Tomas Mikolov, Martin Karafiát, Lukas Burget, Jan Cernocký, and Sanjeev Khudanpur. 2010. Recurrent neural network based language model. In *INTERSPEECH*, volume 2, page 3.

Franz Josef Och and Hermann Ney. 2003. A systematic comparison of various statistical alignment models. *Comput. Linguist.*, 29:19–51, March.

Franz Josef Och. 2003. Minimum error rate training in statistical machine translation. In *Proceedings of the 41st Annual Meeting on Association for Computational Linguistics - Volume 1*, ACL '03, pages 160–167, Stroudsburg, PA, USA. Association for Computational Linguistics.

Kishore Papineni, Salim Roukos, Todd Ward, and Wei-Jing Zhu. 2002. Bleu: a method for automatic evaluation of machine translation. In *Proceedings of the 40th Annual Meeting on Association for Computational Linguistics*, ACL '02, pages 311–318, Stroudsburg, PA, USA.

Holger Schwenk. 2010. Continuous space language models for statistical machine translation. In *The Prague Bulletin of Mathematical Linguistics, (93):137–146*.

Rico Sennrich and Barry Haddow. 2015. A joint dependency model of morphological and syntactic structure for statistical machine translation. In *Proceedings of the 2015 Conference on Empirical Methods in Natural Language Processing*, pages 114–121. Association for Computational Linguistics.

Karen Simonyan and Andrew Zisserman. 2014. Very deep convolutional networks for large-scale image recognition. *arXiv preprint arXiv:1409.1556*.

Andreas Stolcke. 2002. Srilm - an extensible language modeling toolkit. *Proceedings of the 7th International Conference on Spoken Language Processing (ICSLP 2002)*, pages 901–904.

Ilya Sutskever, Oriol Vinyals, and Quoc V. Le. 2014. Sequence to sequence learning with neural networks. *CoRR*, abs/1409.3215.

Jianxiong Xiao, James Hays, Krista A Ehinger, Aude Oliva, and Antonio Torralba. 2010. Sun database: Large-scale scene recognition from abbey to zoo. In *Computer vision and pattern recognition (CVPR), 2010 IEEE conference on*, pages 3485–3492. IEEE.

Kelvin Xu, Jimmy Ba, Ryan Kiros, Kyunghyun Cho, Aaron Courville, Ruslan Salakhudinov, Rich Zemel, and Yoshua Bengio. 2015. Show, attend and tell: Neural image caption generation with visual attention. In *Proceedings of The 32nd International Conference on Machine Learning*, pages 2048–2057.

DCU-UvA Multimodal MT System Report

Iacer Calixto
ADAPT Centre
School of Computing
Dublin City University
Dublin, Ireland
`iacer.calixto@adaptcentre.ie`

Desmond Elliott
ILLC
University of Amsterdam
Science Park 107
1098 XG Amsterdam
`d.elliott@uva.nl`

Stella Frank
ILLC
University of Amsterdam
Science Park 107
1098 XG Amsterdam
`s.c.frank@uva.nl`

Abstract

We present a doubly-attentive multimodal machine translation model. Our model learns to attend to source language and spatial-preserving $CONV_{5,4}$ visual features as separate attention mechanisms in a neural translation model. In image description translation experiments (Task 1), we find an improvement of 2.3 Meteor points compared to initialising the hidden state of the decoder with only the FC_7 features and 2.9 Meteor points compared to a text-only neural machine translation baseline, confirming the useful nature of attending to the $CONV_{5,4}$ features.

1 Introduction

Our system learns to translate image descriptions using both the source language descriptions and the images. We integrate an attention-based neural network for machine translation and image description in a unified model, in which two separate attention mechanisms operate over the language and visual modalities. We believe that this is a principled approach to learning which source words and which areas of the image to attend to when generating words in the target description.

We are inspired by recent successes in using attentive models in both neural machine translation (NMT) and neural image description. Originally, in non-attentive NMT models, the entire source sentence is encoded into a single vector which is in turn used by the decoder to generate a translation (Cho et al., 2014; Sutskever et al., 2014). In a similar vein, image description models can use a vector encoding the image as input for the description generation process (Vinyals et al., 2015; Mao et al., 2015, *inter-alia*).

Bahdanau et al. (2014) first proposed a NMT model with an attention mechanism over the source sentence. Their model is trained so that the decoder learns to attend to words in the source sentence when translating each token in the target sentence. Xu et al. (2015) introduced a similar attention-based neural image description model. In this case, the attention mechanism learns which parts of the image to attend to while generating words in the description.

When translating image descriptions, given both the source description and the source image (i.e., the setting for Task 1), we believe that both modalities can provide cues for generating the target language description. The source description provides the content for translation, but in cases where this may be ambiguous, the image features can provide contextual disambiguation. The system we propose is a first step towards integrating both modalities using attention mechanisms.

Previous work has demonstrated the plausibility of multilingual multimodal natural language processing. Elliott et al. (2015) showed how to generate descriptions of images in English and German by learning and transferring features between independent neural image description models. In comparison, our approach is a single end-to-end model over the source and target languages with attention mechanisms over both the source language and the visual features.

2 Model Description

We represent the source language with a bi-directional recurrent neural network (RNN) with a gated recurrent unit (GRU) that computes, for each word, forward and backward source annotation vectors $\overrightarrow{h_i}$ and $\overleftarrow{h_i}$. The final source annotation vector for a word h_i is the concatenation of both $[\overrightarrow{h_i}; \overleftarrow{h_i}]$.

Proceedings of the First Conference on Machine Translation, Volume 2: Shared Task Papers, pages 634–638,
Berlin, Germany, August 11-12, 2016. ©2016 Association for Computational Linguistics

We use the visual features released by the shared task organisers, extracted from the pre-trained VGG-19 convolutional neural network (CNN) (Simonyan and Zisserman, 2015).

The organisers release two types of visual features according to the layer they were extracted from: FC_7 features are extracted from the final fully-connected layer (FC_7), which encode information about the entire image in a 4096-dimensional feature vector; and $CONV_{5,4}$ features, extracted from the final convolutional layer ($CONV_{5,4}$), namely a 196 x 512 dimensional matrix where each row (i.e., a 512D vector) represents features from a specific spatial 'patch' and therefore encodes information about that specific 'patch' (i.e., area) of the image.

2.1 FC_7-initialised model

In this model, we use visual features extracted from the final fully-connected FC_7 layer from the pre-trained VGG-19 CNN. These features represent an abstract summary of the entire image and crucially are not spatially aware, unlike the $CONV_{5,4}$ features we use in the subsequent double-attention model. We integrate the FC_7 features into the initial state of the decoder.

We first affine-transform the 4096D FC_7 image feature vector i into the source language bidirectional RNN hidden states dimensionality, where the affine transformation parameters (W_I, b_I) are trained jointly with the model:

$$i_{\text{proj}} = i \cdot W_I + b_I. \qquad (1)$$

We then simply sum these projected image features i_{proj} with the first source language context vector h_1, obtained by the encoder bidirectional RNN, and use the resulting vector as input to a feed-forward neural network f_{init} used to initialise the decoder hidden state:

$$s_0 = f_{\text{init}}(h_1 + i_{\text{proj}}) \qquad (2)$$

2.2 Doubly-attentive model

The goal of the doubly-attentive model is to integrate separate attention mechanisms over the source language words and visual features in a single decoder. Similarly to the FC_7 model, we represent the source language using a bi-directional RNN with GRUs. We use visual features extracted from the $CONV_{5,4}$ layer of the VGG-19 CNN alongside the FC_7 features. The $CONV_{5,4}$ features consist of a 196 x 512 dimensional matrix,

where each row represents features from a specific spatial 'patch'. Analogous to how the attention mechanism for the source language can focus on specific words or phrases in the source description, the image attention mechanism can focus on specific parts of the image (Xu et al., 2015).

Our doubly-attentive decoder is conditioned on the source sentence and the image via the two separate attention mechanisms, as well as the previous hidden state of the decoder and the previously emitted word. Therefore, in computing the decoder hidden state s_t at time step t, the decoder has access to the following information:

- i_t – the image context vector for the current time step obtained via attention over the image representation;

- c_t – the source language context vector for the current time step obtained via attention over the source sentence representation;

- s_{t-1} – the decoder's previous hidden state;

- y_{t-1} – the target word emitted by the decoder in the previous time step.

Figure 1 illustrates the computation of the decoder hidden state s_t according to our *doubly-attentive* model.

2.3 Source sequence context vector

To compute the time-dependent source sentence context vector, we follow Bahdanau et al. (2014) and use a single-layer feed-forward network f^s_{score} for computing an *expected alignment* $e^s_{t,i}$ between each source annotation vector h_i — computed as the concatenation of forward and backward source annotation vectors $\overrightarrow{h_i}$ and $\overleftarrow{h_i}$ — and the target word to be emitted at the current time step t.

$$e^s_{t,i} = f^s_{\text{score}}(h_i, s_{t-1}, y_{t-1}), \qquad (3)$$

where f^s_{score} uses all source annotation vectors $\mathbf{h}$, the decoder's previous hidden state s_{t-1} and the previously emitted word y_{t-1} in computing the expected alignments for the target word at current time step t. In Equation 4, these alignments are then normalised and converted into probabilities.

$$\alpha_{t,i} = \frac{\exp\left(e^s_{t,i}\right)}{\sum_{j=1}^{N} \exp\left(e^s_{t,j}\right)}, \qquad (4)$$

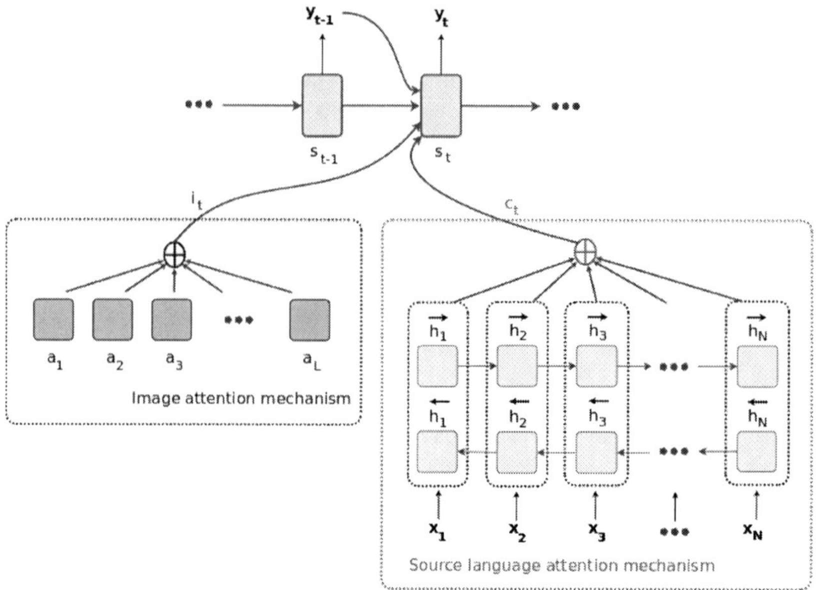

Figure 1: A doubly-attentive decoder learns to independently attend to image patches and source language words when generating translations.

where $\alpha_{t,i}$ are weights representing the attention over the source annotation vectors. The final time-dependent source context vector c_t is a weighted sum over the source annotation vectors, where each vector is weighted by the attention weight $\alpha_{t,i}$:

$$c_t = \sum_{i=1}^{N} \alpha_{t,i} h_i. \qquad (5)$$

2.4 Image context vector

The time-dependent image context vectors are based on the "soft" visual attention mechanism (Xu et al., 2015). As outlined above, the image annotation vectors are the features extracted from $\text{CONV}_{5,4}$ layer, resulting in 196 vectors (each corresponding to one of the 14×14 patches in the image) of 512 dimensions each. These annotation vectors are denoted a_l (with $l = 1 \ldots 196$) and are used analogously to the hidden states h_i of the source sentence encoder.

The expected alignments $e_{t,l}^i$ over the image features are computed by a single layer feed-forward network f_{score}^i:

$$e_{t,l}^i = f_{\text{score}}^i(a_l, s_{t-1}, y_{t-1}), \qquad (6)$$

where f_{score}^i uses all image annotation vectors a, the decoder previous hidden state s_{t-1} and the pre-

viously emitted word y_{t-1} in computing the expected image–target word alignments at current time step t. In Equation 7 these expected alignments are further normalised and converted into probabilities, as in the source context vector.

$$\alpha_{t,l}^i = \frac{\exp\left(e_{t,l}^i\right)}{\sum_{j=1}^{L} \exp\left(e_{t,j}^i\right)}, \qquad (7)$$

where $\alpha_{t,i}^i$ are the model's *image attention weights*. A time-dependent image context vector i_t is then computed by using these attention weights.

$$i_t = \sum_{l=1}^{N} \alpha_{t,l}^i a_l. \qquad (8)$$

Ideally, this image context vector i_t captures the image patches that are relevant to the current state of the decoder and for generating the next word.

3 Experiments

We report results for Task 1, which uses the translated data in the Multi30K corpus (Elliott et al., 2016). English and German descriptions in the Multi30K were normalised and tokenized, and compounds in German descriptions were further split in a pre-processing step[1].

---

[1] We use the scripts in the Moses SMT Toolkit to normalise, tokenize and split compounds (Koehn et al., 2007).

	Meteor
Moses	52.3
$CONV_{5,4}$-Multimodal NMT	46.4
FC_7-Multimodal NMT	44.1
Text-only Attention NMT	43.5
Elliott et al. (2015)	24.7

Table 1: Results for our models on Task 1. We find that attending over the source language and $CONV_{5,4}$ visual features is better than not using image features (text-only, attentive NMT model) and also just initialising an attention-based decoder with FC_7 features.

Throughout, we parameterise our models using 300D word embeddings, 1000D hidden states, and 1000D context vectors; the source and target languages are estimated over the entire vocabularies. Our non-recurrent matrices are initialised by sampling from a Gaussian distribution ($\mu = 0, \sigma = 0.01$), recurrent matrices are orthogonal and bias vectors are all initialised to zero. We apply dropout on the source language words (encoder) and before the readout operation (decoder) with probability of 0.3 and apply no other regularisation. We apply early stopping for model selection based on Meteor scores (Denkowski and Lavie, 2014), and if it has not increased for 20 epochs on a validation set, training is halted. The models are trained using the Adadelta optimizer (Zeiler, 2012) with an initial learning rate of 0.005.

In Table 1 we compare our models — $CONV_{5,4}$ and FC_7-Multimodal NMT — against a text-only, attention-based NMT baseline, the Moses translation baseline (Koehn et al., 2007) and the multilingual image description baseline (Elliott et al., 2015). First, it is clear that the Moses SMT baseline is very strong, given that it is only trained over the parallel text without any visual information. Our models are unable to match the performance of Moses, however, we do see a substantial increase of 20-22 Meteor points compared to the independent image description models (Elliott et al., 2015). The magnitude of the difference shows the importance of learning the source and target language representations in a single joint model.

We also observe improvements in Meteor when we compare our double-attentive $CONV_{5,4}$ model against the FC_7 initialised model (2.3 points) and against a text-only NMT model (2.9 points).

Our results indicate that incorporating image features in multimodal models helps, as compared to our text-only NMT baseline. Even though our neural models — both text-only and multimodal models — fall short of the SMT baseline performance, we believe that the use of neural architectures for this task is more principled, due to the ability to incorporate images and translations in one network that is trained end-to-end.

4 Conclusions and Future Work

We present a model which incorporates multiple multimodal attention mechanisms into a neural machine translation decoder. Source language and visual attention mechanisms have been well-studied in the recent literature, but our results indicate that multimodal attention appears to be more complex than simply combining two independent attention mechanisms. In particular, we hoped to find a greater improvement from adding visual features, relative to text-only models. However, the Multi30k dataset is relatively small, with a small vocabulary and simple syntactic structures (Elliott et al., 2016). Whereas SMT models can be trained effectively on such datasets, neural models usually perform best when a large amount of data is available. We believe that as the amount of data in multimodal translation datasets increase, neural models will become more competitive.

In future work we plan to study why the source language attention mechanism contributes more to the model than the visual attention. We believe that using the source language context vector c_t may help when computing the image context vector i_t. We also plan to investigate other attention mechanisms, for instance the "hard" attention as proposed by Xu et al. (2015). Soft attention may be too diffuse in this setting, especially over the large set of image context vectors.

Acknowledgements

This research is partially supported by Science Foundation Ireland through the CNGL Programme (Grant 12/CE/I2267) in the ADAPT Centre (www.adaptcentre.ie) at Dublin City University. DE was supported by the NWO Vici grant nr. 277-89-002. SF was supported by European Unions Horizon 2020 research and innovation programme under grant agreement nr. 645452.

References

Dzmitry Bahdanau, Kyunghyun Cho, and Yoshua Bengio. 2014. Neural machine translation by jointly learning to align and translate. *CoRR*, abs/1409.0473.

KyungHyun Cho, Bart van Merrienboer, Dzmitry Bahdanau, and Yoshua Bengio. 2014. On the properties of neural machine translation: Encoder-decoder approaches. *CoRR*, abs/1409.1259.

Michael Denkowski and Alon Lavie. 2014. Meteor universal: Language specific translation evaluation for any target language. In *Proceedings of the EACL 2014 Workshop on Statistical Machine Translation*.

Desmond Elliott, Stella Frank, and Eva Hasler. 2015. Multi-language image description with neural sequence models. *CoRR*, abs/1510.04709.

Desmond Elliott, Stella Frank, Khalil Sima'an, and Lucia Specia. 2016. Multi30k: Multilingual english-german image descriptions. *CoRR*, abs/1605.00459.

Philipp Koehn, Hieu Hoang, Alexandra Birch, Chris Callison-Burch, Marcello Federico, Nicola Bertoldi, Brooke Cowan, Wade Shen, Christine Moran, Richard Zens, et al. 2007. Moses: Open source toolkit for statistical machine translation. In *Proceedings of the 45th annual meeting of the ACL on interactive poster and demonstration sessions*, pages 177–180. Association for Computational Linguistics.

Junhua Mao, Wei Xu, Yi Yang, Jiang Wang, Zhiheng Huang, and Alan Yuille. 2015. Deep captioning with multimodal recurrent neural networks (m-RNN). In *ICLR*.

Karen Simonyan and Andrew Zisserman. 2015. Very deep convolutional networks for large-scale image recognition. In *ICLR*.

Ilya Sutskever, Oriol Vinyals, and Quoc V. V Le. 2014. Sequence to sequence learning with neural networks. In *Advances in Neural Information Processing Systems 27*, pages 3104–3112.

Oriol Vinyals, Alexander Toshev, Samy Bengio, and Dumitru Erhan. 2015. Show and tell: A neural image caption generator. In *The IEEE Conference on Computer Vision and Pattern Recognition (CVPR)*, June.

Kelvin Xu, Jimmy Ba, Ryan Kiros, Kyunghyun Cho, Aaron C. Courville, Ruslan Salakhutdinov, Richard S. Zemel, and Yoshua Bengio. 2015. Show, attend and tell: Neural image caption generation with visual attention. In *International Conference on Machine Learning*.

Matthew D. Zeiler. 2012. ADADELTA: an adaptive learning rate method. *CoRR*, abs/1212.5701.

Attention-based Multimodal Neural Machine Translation

Po-Yao Huang, Frederick Liu, Sz-Rung Shiang, Jean Oh[†], Chris Dyer

Language Technologies Institute, Robotics Institute[†]

Carnegie Mellon University

Pittsburgh, PA, USA

{poyaoh|fliul|sshiang|cdyer}@cs.cmu.edu, jeanoh@nrec.ri.cmu.edu[†]

Abstract

We present a novel neural machine translation (NMT) architecture associating visual and textual features for translation tasks with multiple modalities. Transformed global and regional visual features are concatenated with text to form attendable sequences which are dissipated over parallel long short-term memory (LSTM) threads to assist the encoder generating a representation for attention-based decoding. Experiments show that the proposed NMT outperform the text-only baseline.

1 Introduction

In fields of machine translation, neural network attracts lots of research attention recently that the encoder-decoder framework is widely used. Nevertheless, the main drawback of this neural machine translation (NMT) framework is that the decoder only depends on the last state of the encoder, which may deteriorate the performance when the sentence is long. To overcome this problem, attention based encoder-decoder framework as shown in Figure 1 is proposed. With the attention model, in each time step the decoder depends on both the previous LSTM hidden state and the context vector, which is the weighted sum of the hidden states in the encoder. With attention, the decoder can "refresh" it's memory to focus on source words that may help to translate the correct words rather than only seeing the last state of the sentences where the words in the sentence and the ordering of words are missing.

Most of the machine translation task only focus textual sentences of the source language and target language; however, in the real world, the sentences may contain information of what people see. Beyond the bilingual translation, in WMT 16' multimodal translation task, we would like to translate

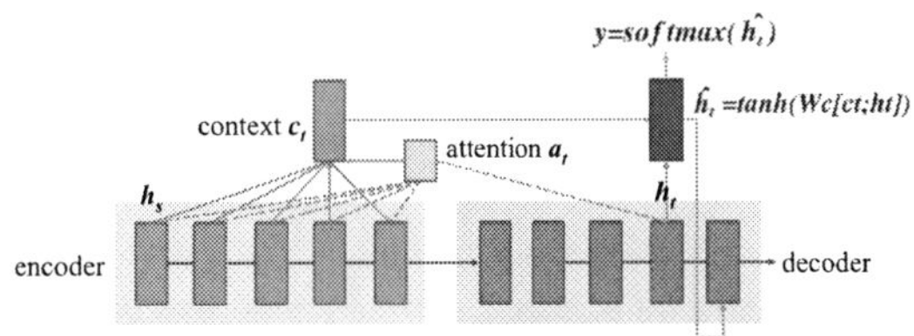

Figure 1: Attention-based neural machine translation framework using a context vector to focus on a subset of the encoding hidden states.

the image captions in English into German. With the additional information from images, we would further resolve the problem of ambiguity in languages. For example, the word "bank" may refer to the financial institution or the land of the river's edge. It would be confusing if we only look at the language itself. In this task, the image may help to disambiguate the meaning if it shows that there is a river and thus the "bank" means "river bank".

In this paper, we explore approaches to integrating multimodal information (text and image) into the attention-based encoder-decoder architecture. We transform and make the visual features as one of the steps in the encoder as text, and then make it possible to attend to both the text and the image while decoding. The image features we used are (visual) semantic features extracted from the entire images (global) as well as the regional bounding boxes proposed by the region-based convolutional neural networks (R-CNN) (Girshick et al., 2014). In the following section, we first describe the related works, and then we introduce the proposed multimodal attention-based NMT in Section 3, followed by re-scoring of the translation candidates in Section 4. Finally we demonstrate the experiments in Section 5.

2 Related Work

As the advances of deep learning, Neural Machine Translation (NMT) (Kalchbrenner and Blunsom,

639

2013; Jean et al., 2014) leveraging encode-decoder architecture attracts research attention. Under the NMT framework, less domain knowledge is required and large training corpora can compensate for it. However, encoder-decoder structure encodes the source sentence into one fixed-length vector, which may deteriorate the translation performance as the length of source sentences increasing. (Bahdanau et al., 2014) extended encoder-decoder structure that the decoder only focuses on parts of source sentence. (Luong et al., 2015) further proposed attention-based model that combine global, attending to all source words, and local, only focusing on a part of source words, attentional mechanism.

Rather than using the embedding of each modality independently, Some works (Hardoon et al., 2004; Andrew et al., 2013; Ngiam et al., 2011; Srivastava and Salakhutdinov, 2014) focus on learning joint space of different modalities. In machine translation fields, (Zhang et al., 2014; Su et al., 2015) learned phrase-level bilingual representation using recursive auto-encoder. Beyond textual embedding, (Kiros et al., 2014) proposed CNN-LSTM encoder to project two modalities into the same space. Based on the jointly learning of multiple modalities or languages, we find it possible to evaluate the quality of the translations that if the space of the translated sentence is similar to the source sentence or the image, it may imply that the translated sentence is good.

3 Attention-based Multimodal Machine Translation

Based on the encoder-decoder framework, the attention-based model aim to handle the missing order and source information problems in the basic encoder-decoder framework. At each time step t in the decoding phrase, the attention-based model attends to subsets of words in the source sentences that can form up the context which can help the decoder to predict the next word. This model infers a variable-length alignment weight vector $\mathbf{a_t}$ based on the current target state $\mathbf{h}_t$ and all source states $\mathbf{h}_s$. The context feature vector $\mathbf{c}_t = \mathbf{a}_t \cdot \mathbf{h}_s$ is the weighted sum of the source states $\mathbf{h}_s$ according to $\mathbf{a_t}$, which is defined as:

$$\mathbf{a}_t(s) = \frac{e^{score(\mathbf{h}_t, \mathbf{h}_s)}}{\sum'_s e^{score(\mathbf{h}_t, \mathbf{h}'_s)}} \quad (1)$$

The scoring function $score(\mathbf{h}_t, \mathbf{h}_s)$ can be re-ferred as a content-based measurement of the similarity between the currently translating target and the source words. We utilize a transformation matrix $\mathbf{W}_a$ which associates source and target hidden state to learn the general similarity measure by:

$$score(\mathbf{h}_t, \mathbf{h}_s) = \mathbf{h}_t \mathbf{W}_a \mathbf{h}_s \quad (2)$$

We produce an attentional hidden state $\hat{\mathbf{h}}_t$ by learning $\mathbf{W}_c$ of a single layer perceptron activated by $tanh$. The input is simply the concatenation of the target hidden state $\mathbf{h}_t$ and the source-side context vector $\mathbf{c}_t$:

$$\hat{\mathbf{h}}_t = tanh(\mathbf{W}_c[\mathbf{c}_t; \mathbf{h}_t]) \quad (3)$$

After generating the context feature vector and the attentional hidden state, the target word is predicted through the softmax layer with the attentional hidden state $\mathbf{h}_t$ vector by $p(y_t|\mathbf{x}) = softmax(\mathbf{W}_s \hat{\mathbf{h}}_t)$. The following we will introduce how we incorporate images features based on the attention models.

3.1 Model 1: LSTM with global visual feature

Visual features from convolution neural network (CNN) may provide additional information to textual features in machine translation with multiple modalities. As depicted in Figure 2, we propose to append visual features at the head/tail to the original text sequence in the encoding phase. Note that for simplicity, we omit the attention part in the following figures.

Global (i.e., whole image) visual feature are extracted from the last fully connected layer known as $fc7$, a 4096-dimensional semantic layer in the 19-layered VGG (Simonyan and Zisserman, 2014). With the dimension mismatch and the inherent difference in content between the visual and textual embedding, a transformation matrix $\mathbf{W}_{img}$ is proposed to learn the mapping. The encoder then encode both textual and visual feature sequences to generate the representation for decoding. In the decoding phase, the attention model weights all the possible hidden states in the encoding phase and produce the context vector $\mathbf{c}_t$ with Eq. 1 and Eq. 2 for NMT decoding.

3.2 Model 2: LSTM with multiple regional visual features

In addition to adding only one global visual feature, we extend the original NMT model by incorporating multiple regional features in the hope

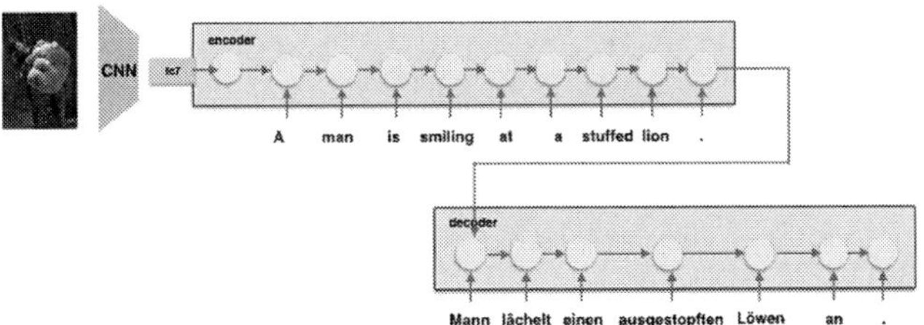

Figure 2: Model 1: Attention-based NMT with single additional global visual feature. Decoder may attend to both text and image steps of encoding. For clarity, the possible attention path is hidden here.

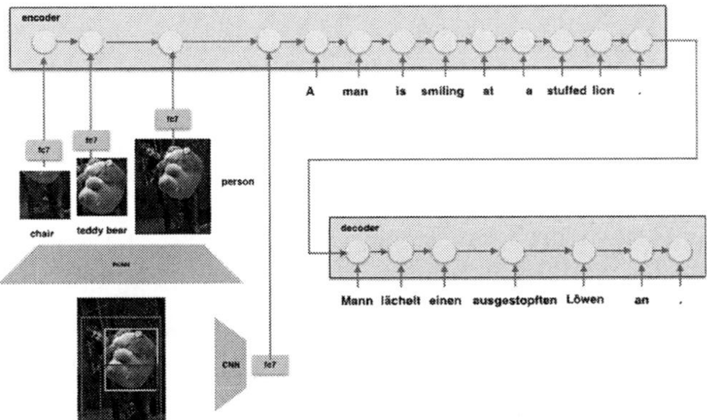

Figure 3: Model 2: Attention-based NMT with multiple additional regional visual features.

that those regional visual attributes would assist LSTM to generate better and more accurate representations. The illustration of the proposed model is depicted in 3. We will first explain how to determine multiple regions from one image and explain how these visual features are extracted and sorted.

Intuitively, objects in an image are most likely to appear in both source and target sentences. Therefore. we utilize the region proposal network (RPN) in the region-based convolutional neural network (Ren et al., 2015) (R-CNN) to identify objects and their bounding boxes in an image and then extract visual feature from those regions. In order to integrate these images to the original sequence in the LSTM model, we design a heuristic approach to sort those visual features. The regional features are fed in the ascending order of the size of the bounding boxes; followed by the original global visual feature and the text sequence. Visual features are sequentially fed in such order since important features are designed to be closer to the encoded representation. Heuristically, larger objects may be more noticeable and essential in an image described by both the source and target language contexts.

In the implementation, we choose top 4 regional objects plus the whole image and then extracted their $fc7$ with VGG-19 to form the visual sequence followed by the text sequence. If there are less than 4 objects recognized in the original image, zero vectors are padded instead for the batch process during training.

3.3 Model 3: Parallel LSTM threads

To further alleviate the assumption that regional objects share some pre-defined order, we further propose a parallel structure as shown in Figure 4. The encoder of NMT is composed of multiple encoding threads where all the LSTM parameters are shared. In each thread, a (regional) visual feature is followed by the text sequence. This parallel structure would associate the text to the most relevant objects in the encoding phase and distinguish them when computing attention during decoding. Intuitively, the text sequence follows a regional object would be interpreted as encoding the visual information with the textual description (i.e., encoding captions as well as visual features for that object). An encoder hidden state for attention can be interpreted as the "word" imprinted by the semantics features of some regional object. The decoder can therefore distinctively attend to

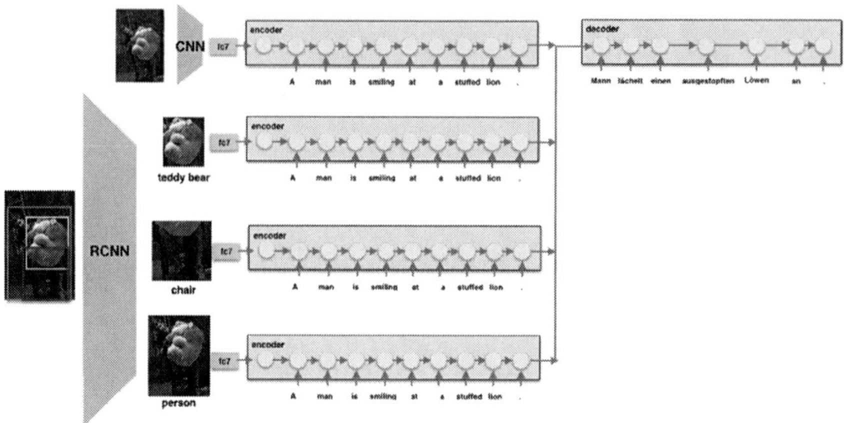

Figure 4: Model 3: Parallel LSTM threads with multiple additional regional visual features.

words that describe different visual objects in multiple threads.

In the encoding phase, parameters in LSTM are shared over threads. All possible hidden states over multiple threads are recorded for attention. At the end of encoding phase, the outputs of different encoding threads are fused together to generate the final embedding of the whole sentence as well as all the image objects. In the decoding phase, candidates of global attention are all the text hidden states over multiple threads. For example, at time t, the decoder may choose to attend to 'bear' at the second thread (which sees a teddy bear image at the beginning) as well as the 'bear' in the global image thread. At time $t + 1$, the decoder may switch to another thread and focus on "the man" with the person image.

For implementation simplicity for batch training, we limit the number of regional objects to 4 and add one global image thread. We also choose an average pooling in the encoder fusion process and back-propagate accordingly.

4 Re-scoring of Translation Candidates

In the neural machine translation, the easiest way to decode is to greedily get the words with highest probability step-by-step. To achieve better performance, ensemble of models are required. Translation candidates are generated from multiple models, and we aim to figure out which candidate should be the best one. The following we describe the approaches we investigated to re-score the translation candidates using monolingual and bilingual information.

4.1 Monolingual Re-scoring

To evaluate the quality of the translation, the most simple approach is to check whether the translated sentences are readable. To achieve this, using language model is an effective way to check whether the sentences fit into the model that trained on a large corpus. If the language model score is high, it implies that the sentence holds the high probability to be generated from the corpus. We trained a single layer LSTM with 300 hidden state to predicting the next word. Image caption datasets MSCOCO and IAPR TC-12 (overall 56,968 sentences) are used as training data.

4.1.1 Bilingual autoencoder

A good translation would also recognize the sentence in the source language. We utilize bilingual autoencoder (Ngiam et al., 2011) depicted as in Fig.5 to reconstruct source language given the source language. Bilingual autoencoder only uses single modality (here we used source language or target language) and re-constructs the both modalities. We project bilingual information into the joint space (the bottleneck layer); if the two target and source sentences have similar representation, the model is able to reconstruct both sentences. Moreover, if the similarity of values of bottleneck layer is high, it may indicate that the source sentence and the translated sentence are similar in concepts; therefore, the quality of the translation would be better. The inputs of the autoencoder are the last LSTM encoder states trained on monolingual image captions dataset. The dimension of the input layer is 256, and 200 for the middle, and 128 for the joint layer.

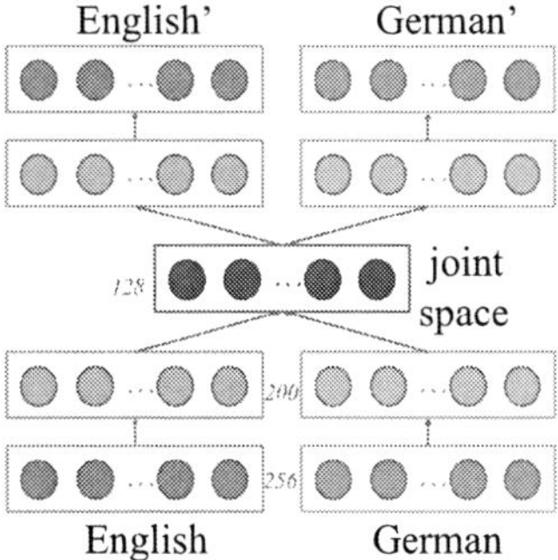

Figure 5: Bilingual auto-encoder to re-construct both English and German using only one of them.

4.2 Bilingual dictionary

In the WMT 16' multimodal task, captions are structured with simple grammars; therefore, only considering language model may be insufficient to distinguish good translations. In order to directly consider whether the concepts mentioned in the source sentences are all well-translated, we utilize the bilingual dictionary Glosbe[1], in which we use the words in one language extracting the corresponding words in the other language. We directly count the number of words in the source language that the synonyms in target language are also in the translated results as the re-ranking score.

5 Experiments

5.1 Experimental Setup

In the official WMT 2016 multimodal translation task dataset (Elliott et al., 2016), there are 29,000 parallel sentences from English to German for training, 1014 for validation and 1000 for testing. Each sentence describes an image from Flickr30k dataset (Young et al., 2014). We preprocessed all the descriptions into lower case with tokenization and German compound word splitting.

Global visual features (*fc7*) are extracted with VGG-19 (Simonyan and Zisserman, 2014). For regional visual features, the region proposal network in RCNN (Girshick et al., 2014) first recognizes bounding boxes of objects in an image and then we computed 4096-dimensional *fc7* features from these regions with VGG-19. The RPN of RCNN is pre-trained on ImageNet dataset [2] and then fine-tuned on MSCOCO dataset [3] with 80 ob-

[1] https://glosbe.com/en/de/
[2] http://image-net.org/
[3] http://mscoco.org/

Table 1: BLEU and METEOR of the proposed multimodal NMT

	BLEU	METEOR
Text baseline	34.5 (0.7)	51.8 (0.7)
m1:image at tail	34.8 (0.6)	51.6 (0.7)
m1:image at head	35.1 (0.8)	52.2 (0.7)
m2:5 sequential RCNNs	36.2 (0.8)	53.4 (0.6)
m3:5 parallel RCNNs	**36.5** (0.8)	**54.1** (0.7)

ject classes.

We use a single-layered LSTM with 256 cells and 128 batch size for training. The dimension of word embedding is 256. $\mathbf{W}_{img}$ is a 4096×256 matrix transforming visual features into the same embedding space as words. When training NMT, we follow (Luong et al., 2015) with similar settings: (a) we uniformly initialized all parameters between -0.1 and 0.1, (b) we trained the LSTM for 20 epochs using simple SGD, (c) the learning rate was initialized as 1.0, multiplied by 0.7 after 12 epochs, (d) dropout rate was 0.8. Note that the same dropout mask and NMT parameters are shared by all LSTM threads in model 3.

5.2 Results of Adding Visual Information

The quantitative performance of the proposed models can be seen in Table 1. We evaluate BLEU and METEOR scores with tokenization under the official settings of WMT 2016 multimodal machine translation challenge. The text-only baseline is the NMT implementation with global attention. Adding single global visual feature from an image at the head of a text sequence improves BLEU by 0.6% and METEOR by 0.4% respectively.

The results show that the additional visual information improves the translations in this dataset. However, the lukewarm improvement is not as significant as we expected. One possible explanation is that the information required for the multimodal translation task is mostly self-contained in the source text transcript. Adding global features from whole images do not provide extra supplementary information and thus results in a subtle improvement.

Detailed regional visual features provide extra attributes and information that may help the NMT translates better. In our experiment, the proposed model2 with multiple regional and one global visual features showed an improvement of 1.7% in BLEU and 1.6% in METEOR while model3 showed an improvement of 2.0% in BLEU and 2.3% in METEOR. The results correspond to our observation that most sentences would describe important objects which could be identified by R-CNN. The most commonly mentioned object is "person". It's likely that the additional attributes provided by the visual features about the person in an image help to encode more detailed context and thus benefit NMT decoding. Other high frequency objects are "car", "baseball", "cellphone", etc.

For the proposed LSTM with multiple regional visual features (model 2), the semantic features in $fc7$ of the regions-of-interest in an image provide additional regional visual information to form a better sentence representation. We also experimented other sorting methods including descending size, random, and categorical order to generate the visual sequences. However, ascending-ordered sequences achieve the best result.

For the proposed parallel LSTM architecture with regional visual features (model 3), the regional visual features further help the NMT decoder to attend more accurately and accordingly to focus on the right thread where the hidden states are twiddle by the local visual attributes. The best result of our models achieve 36.5% in BLEU and 54.1% in METEOR, which is comparable to the state-of-the-art Moses results in this challenge.

5.3 Results of Re-Scoring

The experimental results of re-scoring are shown in table 2, we compare our re-scoring methods based on the candidates generated by our best multimodal NMT modal (model 3). The second row is the results using LSTM monolingual language model with hidden size as 300. The reason why we can barely achieve improvement might be that the grammar in the caption task is much easier compared to other translation tasks such as dialog or News; therefore, the candidate sentences with low score of evaluation (BLEU or METEOR) may also looks like a sentence, but without relevance to the source sentence.

The third row shows the re-scoring results with the bi-lingual autoencoder. This approach results in drops in both BLEU and METEOR. The reason might be that the quality and quantity of our Bi-lingual corpus is insufficient for the purpose of learning a good autoencoder. Furthermore, we observe the test perplexity is higher than the training and validation perplexity, showing the over-fitting

Table 2: Results of re-scoring using monolingual LSTM, Bi-lingual auto-encoder, and dictionary based on multimodal NMT results.

	BLEU	METEOR
Original Model 3	**36.5** (0.8)	54.1 (0.7)
Language model	36.3 (0.8)	53.3 (0.6)
Bilingual autoencoder	35.9 (0.8)	53.4 (0.7)
Bilingual dictionary	35.7 (0.8)	**55.2** (0.6)

in language modeling and the effects of unknown words. It's clear that more investigation is required for designing a better bilingual autoencoder for re-scoring.

The last row shows the results using the bilingual dictionary. For each word in the source sentence and the target candidates, we retrieve the term and the translation in the other language, and count the number of matching. We can achieve much more improvement on METEOR compared to other methods. This is because that the quality of the translation of captions depends on how much we correctly translate the objects and their modifiers. The bad translation can still achieve fair performance without re-scoring because the sentence structure is similar to good translation. For example, a lot of sentences start with "A man" and both good and bad translation can also translate the sentences start with "Ein Mann". The bilingual dictionary is proved to be an efficient re-scoring approach to distinguish these cases.

6 Conclusions

We enhanced the attention-based neural machine translation by incorporating information in multiple modalities. We explored different encoder-decoder architectures including the LSTM with multiple sequential global/regional visual and textual features as states for attention and the parallel LSTM threads approach. Our best model achieved 2.0% improvement in BLEU score and 2.3% in METEOR using the visual features of an entire image and interesting regional objects within. For re-scoring translation candidates, we investigated monolingual LSTM language model, bilingual autoencoder, and bilingual dictionary re-scoring. We further achieved an additional 1.1% improvements in METEOR using a bilingual dictionary. Integration of more modalities such as audio would be a challenging but interesting next step.

Acknowledgments

This material is based in part on work supported by the National Science Foundation (NSF) under grant number IIS-1638429. Also, this work was conducted in part through collaborative participation in the Robotics Consortium sponsored by the U.S Army Research Laboratory under the Collaborative Technology Alliance Program, Cooperative Agreement W911NF-10-2-0016, and in part by ONR under MURI grant "Reasoning in Reduced Information Spaces" (no. N00014-09-1-1052). The views and conclusions contained in this document are those of the authors and should not be interpreted as representing the official policies, either expressed or implied, of the Army Research Laboratory of the U.S. Government. The U.S. Government is authorized to reproduce and distribute reprints for Government purposes notwithstanding any copyright notation herein.

References

Galen Andrew, Raman Arora, Karen Livescu, and Jeff Bilmes. 2013. Deep canonical correlation analysis. In *International Conference on Machine Learning (ICML)*, Atlanta, Georgia.

Dzmitry Bahdanau, Kyunghyun Cho, and Yoshua Bengio. 2014. Neural machine translation by jointly learning to align and translate. *CoRR*, abs/1409.0473.

D. Elliott, S. Frank, K. Sima'an, and L. Specia. 2016. Multi30K: Multilingual English-German Image Descriptions. *CoRR*, abs/1605.00459.

Ross Girshick, Jeff Donahue, Trevor Darrell, and Jitendra Malik. 2014. Rich feature hierarchies for accurate object detection and semantic segmentation. In *Computer Vision and Pattern Recognition*.

David R. Hardoon, Sandor R. Szedmak, and John R. Shawe-taylor. 2004. Canonical correlation analysis: An overview with application to learning methods. *Neural Comput.*, 16(12):2639–2664, December.

Sébastien Jean, Kyunghyun Cho, Roland Memisevic, and Yoshua Bengio. 2014. On using very large target vocabulary for neural machine translation. *CoRR*, abs/1412.2007.

Nal Kalchbrenner and Phil Blunsom. 2013. Recurrent continuous translation models. Seattle, October. Association for Computational Linguistics.

Ryan Kiros, Ruslan Salakhutdinov, and Richard S. Zemel. 2014. Unifying visual-semantic embeddings with multimodal neural language models. *CoRR*, abs/1411.2539.

Minh-Thang Luong, Hieu Pham, and Christopher D. Manning. 2015. Effective approaches to attention-based neural machine translation. *CoRR*, abs/1508.04025.

Jiquan Ngiam, Aditya Khosla, Mingyu Kim, Juhan Nam, Honglak Lee, and Andrew Y. Ng. 2011. Multimodal deep learning. In Lise Getoor and Tobias Scheffer, editors, *ICML*, pages 689–696. Omnipress.

Shaoqing Ren, Kaiming He, Ross Girshick, and Jian Sun. 2015. Faster R-CNN: Towards real-time object detection with region proposal networks. In *Advances in Neural Information Processing Systems (NIPS)*.

K. Simonyan and A. Zisserman. 2014. Very deep convolutional networks for large-scale image recognition. *CoRR*, abs/1409.1556.

Nitish Srivastava and Ruslan Salakhutdinov. 2014. Multimodal learning with deep boltzmann machines. *Journal of Machine Learning Research*, 15:2949–2980.

Jinsong Su, Deyi Xiong, Biao Zhang, Yang Liu, Junfeng Yao, and Min Zhang. 2015. Bilingual correspondence recursive autoencoder for statistical machine translation. In *Proceedings of the 2015 Conference on Empirical Methods in Natural Language Processing, EMNLP 2015, Lisbon, Portugal, September 17-21, 2015*, pages 1248–1258.

Peter Young, Alice Lai, Micah Hodosh, and Julia Hockenmaier. 2014. From image descriptions to visual denotations: New similarity metrics for semantic inference over event descriptions. *TACL*, 2:67–78.

Jiajun Zhang, Shujie Liu, Mu Li, Ming Zhou, and Chengqing Zong. 2014. Bilingually-constrained phrase embeddings for machine translation. In *Proceedings of the 52nd Annual Meeting of the Association for Computational Linguistics (Volume 1: Long Papers)*, pages 111–121, Baltimore, Maryland, June. Association for Computational Linguistics.

CUNI System for WMT16 Automatic Post-Editing and Multimodal Translation Tasks

Jindřich Libovický   Jindřich Helcl
Marek Tlustý   Ondřej Bojar   Pavel Pecina

Charles University in Prague
Malostranské náměstí 25, 112 00 Prague, Czech Republic
{libovicky,helcl,tlusty,bojar,pecina}@ufal.mff.cuni.cz

Abstract

Neural sequence to sequence learning recently became a very promising paradigm in machine translation, achieving competitive results with statistical phrase-based systems. In this system description paper, we attempt to utilize several recently published methods used for neural sequential learning in order to build systems for WMT 2016 shared tasks of Automatic Post-Editing and Multimodal Machine Translation.

1 Introduction

Neural sequence to sequence models are currently used for variety of tasks in Natural Language Processing including machine translation (Sutskever et al., 2014; Bahdanau et al., 2014), text summarization (Rush et al., 2015), natural language generation (Wen et al., 2015), and others. This was enabled by the capability of recurrent neural networks to model temporal structure in data, including the long-distance dependencies in case of gated networks (Hochreiter and Schmidhuber, 1997; Cho et al., 2014).

The deep learning models' ability to learn a dense representation of the input in the form of a real-valued vector recently allowed researchers to combine machine vision and natural language processing into tasks believed to be extremely difficult only few years ago. The distributed representations of words, sentences and images can be understood as a kind of common data type for language and images within the models. This is then used in tasks like automatic image captioning (Vinyals et al., 2015; Xu et al., 2015), visual question answering (Antol et al., 2015) or in attempts to ground lexical semantics in vision (Kiela and Clark, 2015).

In this system description paper, we bring a summary of the Recurrent Neural Network (RNN)-based system we have submitted to the automatic post-editing task and to the multimodal translation task. Section 2 describes the architecture of the networks we have used. Section 3 summarizes related work on the task of automatic post-editing of machine translation output and describes our submission to the Workshop of Machine Translation (WMT) competition. In a similar fashion, Section 4 refers to the task of multimodal translation. Conclusions and ideas for further work are given in Section 5.

2 Model Description

We use the neural translation model with attention (Bahdanau et al., 2014) and extend it to include multiple encoders, see Figure 1 for an illustration. Each input sentence enters the system simultaneously in several representations $\mathbf{x_i}$. An encoder used for the i-th representation $\mathbf{X_i} = (x_i^1, \ldots, x_i^k)$ of k words, each stored as a one-hot vector x_i^j, is a bidirectional RNN implementing a function

$$f(\mathbf{X}_i) = \mathbf{H}_i = (h_i^1, \ldots, h_i^k) \tag{1}$$

where the states h_i^j are concatenations of the outputs of the forward and backward networks after processing the j-th token in the respective order.

The initial state of the decoder is computed as a weighted combination of the encoders' final states.

The decoder is an RNN which receives an embedding of the previously produced word as an input in every time step together with the hidden state from the previous time step. The RNN's output is then used to compute the attention and the next word distribution.

The attention is computed over each encoder separately as described by Bahdanau et al. (2014). The attention vector a_i^m of the i-th encoder in the

Proceedings of the First Conference on Machine Translation, Volume 2: Shared Task Papers, pages 646–654,
Berlin, Germany, August 11-12, 2016. ©2016 Association for Computational Linguistics

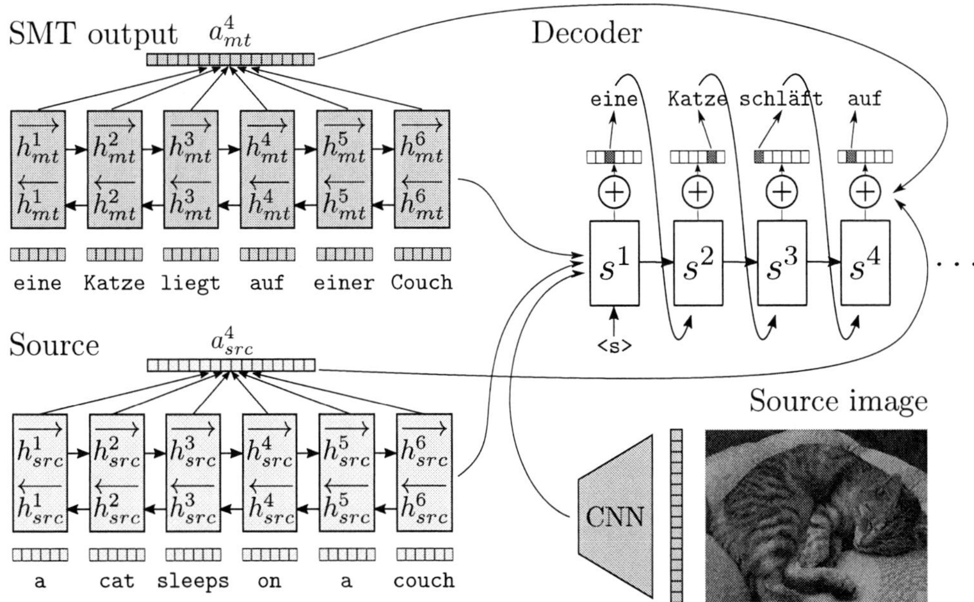

Figure 1: Multi-encoder architecture used for the multimodal translation.

m-th step of the decoder is

$$a_i^m = \sum_{h_i^k \text{ in } \mathbf{H}_i} h_i^k \alpha_i^{k,m} \qquad (2)$$

where the weights α_i^m is a distribution estimated as

$$\alpha_i^m = \text{softmax}\left(v^T \cdot \tanh(s^m + W_{\mathbf{H}_i}\mathbf{H}_i)\right) \quad (3)$$

with s^m being the hidden state of the decoder in time m. Vector v and matrix $W_{\mathbf{H}_i}$ are learned parameters for projecting the encoder states.

The probability of the decoder emitting the word y_m in the j-th step, denoted as $P\left(y_m|\mathbf{H}_1, \ldots, \mathbf{H}_n, \mathbf{Y}_{0..m-1}\right)$, is proportional to

$$\exp\left(W_o s^j + \sum_{i=1}^n W_{a_i} a_i^j\right) \qquad (4)$$

where $\mathbf{H}_i$ are hidden states from the i-th encoder and $\mathbf{Y}_{0..m-1}$ is the already decoded target sentence (represented as matrix, one-hot vector for each produced word). Matrices W_o and W_{a_i} are learned parameters; W_o determines the recurrent dependence on the decoder's state and W_{a_i} determine the dependence on the (attention-weighted) encoders' states.

For image captioning, we do not use the attention model because of its high computational demands and rely on the basic model by Vinyals et al. (2015) instead. We use Gated Recurrent Units (Cho et al., 2014) and apply the dropout of 0.5 on the inputs and the outputs of the recurrent layers (Zaremba et al., 2014) and L2 regularization of 10^{-8} on all parameters. The decoding is done using a beam search of width 10. Both the decoders and encoders have hidden states of 500 neurons, word embeddings have the dimension of 300. The model is optimized using the Adam optimizer (Kingma and Ba, 2014) with learning rate of 10^{-3}.

We experimented with recently published improvements of neural sequence to sequence learning: scheduled sampling (Bengio et al., 2015), noisy activation function (Gülçehre et al., 2016), linguistic coverage model (Tu et al., 2016). None of them were able to improve the systems' performance, so we do not include them in our submissions.

Since the target language for both the task was German, we also did language dependent pre- and post-processing of the text. For the training we split the contracted prepositions and articles (*am* $\leftrightarrow$ *an dem, zur* $\leftrightarrow$ *zu der, ...*) and separated some pronouns from their case ending (*keinem* $\leftrightarrow$ *kein -em, unserer* $\leftrightarrow$ *unser -er, ...*). We also tried splitting compound nouns into smaller units, but on the relatively small data sets we have worked with, it did not bring any improvement.

3 Automatic Post-Editing

The task of automatic post-editing (APE) aims at improving the quality of a machine translation system treated as black box. The input of an APE system is a pair of sentences – the original input sentence in the source language and the translation generated by the machine translation (MT) system. This scheme allows to use any MT system without any prior knowledge of the system itself. The goal of this task is to perform automatic corrections on the translated sentences and generate a better translation (using the source sentence as an additional source of information).

For the APE task, the organizers provided tokenized data from the IT domain (Turchi et al., 2016). The training data consist of 12,000 triplets of the source sentence, its automatic translation and a reference sentence. The reference sentences are manually post-edited automatic translations. Additional 1,000 sentences were provided for validation, and another 2,000 sentences for final evaluation. Throughout the paper, we report scores on the validation set; reference sentences for final evaluation were not released for obvious reasons.

The performance of the systems is measured using Translation Error Rate (Snover et al., 2006) from the manually post-edited sentences. We thus call the score HTER. This means that the goal of the task is more to simulate manual post-editing, rather than to reconstruct the original unknown reference sentence.

3.1 Related Work

In the previous year's competition (Bojar et al., 2015), most of the systems were based on the phrase-base statistical machine translation (SMT) in a monolingual setting (Simard et al., 2007).

There were also several rule-based post-editing systems benefiting from the fact that errors introduced by statistical and rule-based systems are of a different type (Rosa, 2014; Mohaghegh et al., 2013).

Although the use of neural sequential model is very straightforward in this case, to the best of our knowledge, there have not been experiments with RNNs for this task.

3.2 Experiments & Results

The input sentence is fed to our system in a form of multiple input sequences without explicitly telling which sentence is the source one and which one

method	HTER	BLEU
baseline	.2481	62.29
edit operations	.2438	**62.70**
edit operations+	**.2436**	62.62

Table 1: Results of experiments on the APE task on the validation data. The '+' sign indicates the additional regular-expression rules – the system that has been submitted.

is the MT output. It is up to the network to discover their best use when producing the (single) target sequence. The initial experiments showed that the network struggles to learn that one of the source sequences is almost correct (even if it shares the vocabulary and word embeddings with the expected target sequence). Instead, the network seemed to learn to paraphrase the input.

To make the network focus more on editing of the source sentence instead of preserving the meaning of the sentences, we represented the target sentence as a minimum-length sequence of edit operations needed to turn the machine-translated sentence into the reference post-edit. We extended the vocabulary by two special tokens *keep* and *delete* and then encoded the reference as a sequence of *keep*, *delete* and *insert* operations with the insert operation defined by the placing the word itself. See Figure 2 for an example.

After applying the generated edit operations on the machine-translated sentences in the test phase, we perform a few rule-based orthographic fixes for punctuation. The performance of the system is given in Table 1. The system was able to slightly improve upon the baseline (keeping the translation as it is) in both the HTER and BLEU score. The system was able to deal very well with the frequent error of keeping a word from the source in the translated sentence. Although neural sequential models usually learn the basic output structure very quickly, in this case it made a lot of errors in pairing parentheses correctly. We ascribe this to the edit-operation notation which obfuscated the basic orthographic patterns in the target sentences.

4 Multimodal Translation

The goal of the multimodal translation task is to generate an image caption in a target language (German) given the image itself and one or more captions in the source language (English).

Source	Choose Uncached Refresh from the Histogram panel menu.
MT	Wählen$_1$ Sie$_2$ Uncached$_3$ "$_4$ Aktualisieren$_5$ "$_6$ aus$_7$ dem$_8$ Menü$_9$ des$_{10}$ Histogrammbedienfeldes$_{11}$.$_{15}$
Reference	Wählen$_1$ Sie$_2$ "$_4$ Nicht$_{12}$ gespeicherte$_{13}$ aktualisieren$_{13}$ "$_6$ aus$_7$ dem$_8$ Menü$_9$ des$_{10}$ Histogrammbedienfeldes$_{11}$.$_{15}$
Edit ops.	*keep*$_1$ *keep*$_2$ *delete*$_3$ *keep*$_4$ Nicht$_{12}$ gespeicherte$_{13}$ aktualisieren$_{13}$ *delete*$_5$ *keep*$_6$ *keep*$_7$ *keep*$_8$ *keep*$_9$ *keep*$_{10}$ *keep*$_{11}$ **keep**$_{15}$

Figure 2: An example of the sequence of edit operations that our system should learn to produce when given the candidate MT translation. The colors and subscripts denote the alignment between the edit operations and the machine-translated and post-edited sentence.

Recent experiments of Elliott et al. (2015) showed that including the information from the images can help disambiguate the source-language captions.

The participants were provided with the Multi30k dataset (Elliott et al., 2016) which is an extension of the Flickr30k dataset (Plummer et al., 2015). In the original dataset, 31,014 images were taken from the users collections on the image hosting service Flickr. Each of the images were given five independent crowd-sourced captions in English. For the Multi30k dataset, one of the English captions for each image was translated into German and five other independent German captions were provided. The data are split into a training set of 29,000 images, a validation set of 1,014 images and a test set with 1,000 images.

The two ways in which the image annotation were collected also lead to two sub-tasks. The first one is called Multimodal Translation and its goal is to generate a translation of an image caption to the target language given the caption in source language and the image itself. The second task is the Cross-Lingual Image Captioning. In this setting, the system is provided five captions in the source language and it should generate one caption in target language given both source-language captions and the image itself. Both tasks are evaluated using the BLEU (Papineni et al., 2002) score and METEOR score (Denkowski and Lavie, 2011). The translation task is evaluated against a single reference sentence which is the direct human translation of the source sentence. The cross-lingual captioning task is evaluated against the five reference captions in the target language created independently of the source captions.

4.1 Related Work

The state-of-the-art image caption generators use a remarkable property of the Convolutional Neural Network (CNN) models originally designed for ImageNet classification to capture the semantic features of the images. Although the images in ImageNet (Deng et al., 2009; Russakovsky et al., 2015) always contain a single object to classify, the networks manage to learn a representation that is usable in many other cases including image captioning which usually concerns multiple objects in the image and also needs to describe complex actions and spacial and temporal relations within the image.

Prior to CNN models, image classification used to be based on finding some visual primitives in the image and transcribing automatically estimated relations between the primitives. Soon after Kiros et al. (2014) showed that the CNN features could be used in a neural language model, Vinyals et al. (2015) developed a model that used an RNN decoder known from neural MT for generating captions from the image features instead of the vector encoding the source sentence. Xu et al. (2015) later even improved the model by adapting the soft alignment model (Bahdanau et al., 2014) nowadays known as the attention model. Since then, these models have become a benchmark for works trying to improve neural sequence to sequence models (Bengio et al., 2015; Gülçehre et al., 2016; Ranzato et al., 2015).

4.2 Phrase-Based System

For the translation task, we trained Moses SMT (Koehn et al., 2007) with additional language models based on coarse bitoken classes. We follow the approach of Stewart et al. (2014): Based on the word alignment, each target word

system	Multimodal translation		Cross-lingual captioning	
	BLEU	METEOR	BLEU	METEOR
Moses baseline	32.2	54.4	11.3	33.8
MM baseline		27.2		32.6
tuned Moses	36.8	**57.4**	12.3	35.0
NMT	37.1	54.6	13.6	34.6
NMT + Moses	36.5	54.3	13.7	35.1
NMT + image	34.0	51.6	13.3	34.4
NMT + Moses + image	**37.3**	55.2	13.6	34.9
— " —, submitted	31.9	49.6	13.0	33.5
captioning only			9.1	25.3
5 en captions			22.7	38.5
5 en captions + image			**24.6**	**39.3**
— " —, submitted			14.0	31.6

Table 2: Results of experiments with the multimodal translation task on the validation data. At the time of the submission, the models were not tuned as well as our final models. The first six system are targeted for the translation task. They were trained against one reference – a German translation of one English caption. The last four systems are target to the cross-lingual captioning task. They were trained with 5 independent German captions (5 times bigger data).

is concatenated with its aligned source word into one bitoken (e.g."Katze-cat"). For unaligned target words, we create a bitoken with NULL as the source word (e.g. "wird-NULL"). Unaligned source words are dropped. For more than one-to-one alignments, we join all aligned word pairs into one bitoken (e.g. "hat-had+gehabt-had"). These word-level bitokens are afterwards clustered into coarse classes (Brown et al., 1992) and a standard n-gram language model is trained on these classes. Following the notation of Stewart et al. (2014), "400bi" indicates a LM trained on 400 bitoken classes, "200bi" stands for 200 bitoken classes, etc. Besides bitokens based on aligned words, we also use class-level bitokens. For example "(200,400)" means that we clustered source words into 200 classes and target words into 400 classes and only then used the alignment to extract bitokens of these coarser words. The last type is "100bi(200,400)", a combination of both independent clustering in the source and target "(200,400)" and the bitoken clustering "100bi".

Altogether, we tried 26 configurations combining various coarse language models. The best three were "200bi" (a single bitoken LM), "200bi&(1600,200)&100tgt" (three LMs, each with its own weight, where 100tgt means a language model over 100 word classes trained on the target side only) and "200bi&100tgt".

Manual inspection of these three best configurations reveals almost no differences; often the outputs are identical. Comparing to the baseline (a single word-based LM), it is evident that coarse models prefer to ensure agreement and are much more likely to allow for a different word or preposition choice to satisfy the agreement.

4.3 Neural System

For the multimodal translation task, we combine the RNN encoders with image features. The image features are extracted from the 4096-dimensional penultimate layer (*fc7*) of the VGG-16 Imagenet network Simonyan and Zisserman (2014) before applying non-linearity. We keep the weights of the convolutional network fixed during the training. We do not use attention over the image features, so the image information is fed to the network only via the initial state.

We also try a system combination and add an encoder for the phrase-based output. The SMT encoder shares the vocabulary and word embeddings with the decoder. For the combination with SMT output, we experimented with the CopyNet architecture (Gu et al., 2016) and with encoding the sequence the way as in the APE task (see Section 3.2). Since neither of these variations seems to have any effect on the performance, we report only the results of the simple encoder combina-

Source	A group of men are loading cotton onto a truck
Reference	Eine Gruppe von Männern lädt Baumwolle auf einen Lastwagen
Moses	eine Gruppe von Männern lädt <u>cotton</u> auf einen <u>Lkw</u>
2 Errors:	*untranslated "cotton" and capitalization of "LKW"*
MMMT	Eine Gruppe von Männern lädt <u>etwas</u> auf einem <u>Lkw</u>.
Gloss:	*A group of men are loading <u>something</u> onto a truck.*
CLC	Mehrere Personen stehen an einem LKW.
Gloss:	*More persons stand on a truck.*
Source	A man sleeping in a green room on a couch.
Reference	Ein Mann schläft in einem grünen Raum auf einem Sofa.
Moses	Ein Mann schläft in einem grünen Raum auf einem Sofa.
MMMT	Ein Mann schläft in einem grünen Raum auf einer Couch.
	No error, a correctly used synonym for "couch".
CLC	Eine Frau schläft auf einer Couch.
	A man ("Mann") is mistaken for a woman ("Frau").

Figure 3: Sample outputs of our multimodal translation (MMMT) system and cross-lingual captioning (CLC) system in comparison with phrase-based MT and the reference. The *MMMT* system refers to the 'NMT + Moses + image' row and *CLC* system to the '5 captions + image' row in Table 2.

tion.

Systems targeted for the multimodal translation task have a single English caption (and eventually its SMT and the image representation) on its input and produce a single sentence which is a translation of the original caption. Every input appears exactly once in the training data paired with exactly one target sentence. On the other hand, systems targeted for the cross-lingual captioning use all five reference sentences as a target, i.e. every input is present five times in the training data with five different target sentences, which are all independent captions in German. In case of the cross-lingual captioning, we use five parallel encoders sharing all weights combined with the image features in the initial state.

Results of the experiments with different input combinations are summarized in the next section.

4.4 Results

The results of both the tasks are given in Table 2. Our system significantly improved since the competition submission, therefore we report both the performance of the current system and of the submitted systems. Examples of the system output can be found in Figure 3.

The best performance has been achieved by the neural system that combined all available input both for the multimodal translation and cross-lingual captioning. Although, using the image as the only source of information led to poor results, adding the image information helped to improve

the performance in both tasks. This supports the hypothesis that for the translation of an image caption, knowing the image can add substantial piece of information.

The system for cross-lingual captioning tended to generate very short descriptions, which were usually true statements about the images, but the sentences were often too general or missing important information. We also needed to truncate the vocabulary which brought out-of-vocabulary tokens to the system output. Unlike the translation task where the vocabulary size was around 20,000 different forms for both languages, having 5 source and 5 reference sentences increased the vocabulary size more than twice.

Similarly to the automatic postediting task, we were not able to come up with a setting where the combination with the phrase-based system would improve over the very strong Moses system with bitoken-classes language model. We can therefore hypothesize that the weakest point of the models is the weighted combination of the inputs for the initial state of the decoder. The difficulty of learning relatively big combination weighting matrices which are used just once during the model execution (unlike the recurrent connections having approximately the same number of parameters) probably over-weighted the benefits of having more information on the input. In case of system combination, more careful exploration of explicit copy mechanism as CopyNet (Gu et al., 2016) may be useful.

5 Conclusion

We applied state-of-the art neural machine translation models to two WMT shared tasks. We showed that neural sequential models could be successfully applied to the APE task. We also showed that information from the image can significantly help while producing a translation of an image caption. Still, with the limited amount of data provided, the neural system performed comparably to a very well tuned SMT system.

There is still a big room for improvement of the performance using model ensembles or recently introduced techniques for neural sequence to sequence learning. An extensive hyper-parameter testing could be also helpful.

Acknowledgment

We would like to thank Tomáš Musil, Milan Straka and Ondřej Dušek for discussing the problem with us and countless tips they gave us during our work.

This work has received funding from the European Union's Horizon 2020 research and innovation programme under grant agreement no. 645 452 (QT21) and no. 644 753 (KConnect) and the Czech Science Foundation (grant n. P103/12/G084). Computational resources were provided by the CESNET LM2015042, provided under the programme "Projects of Large Research, Development, and Innovations Infrastructures."

References

Stanislaw Antol, Aishwarya Agrawal, Jiasen Lu, Margaret Mitchell, Dhruv Batra, C. Lawrence Zitnick, and Devi Parikh. 2015. VQA: Visual question answering. In *The IEEE International Conference on Computer Vision (ICCV)*. Santiago, Chile.

Dzmitry Bahdanau, Kyunghyun Cho, and Yoshua Bengio. 2014. Neural machine translation by jointly learning to align and translate. *CoRR* abs/1409.0473.

Samy Bengio, Oriol Vinyals, Navdeep Jaitly, and Noam M. Shazeer. 2015. Scheduled sampling for sequence prediction with recurrent neural networks. In *Advances in Neural Information Processing Systems, NIPS*.

Ondřej Bojar, Rajen Chatterjee, Christian Federmann, Barry Haddow, Matthias Huck, Chris Hokamp, Philipp Koehn, Varvara Logacheva, Christof Monz, Matteo Negri, Matt Post, Carolina Scarton, Lucia Specia, and Marco Turchi. 2015. Findings of the 2015 workshop on statistical machine translation. In *Proceedings of the Tenth Workshop on Statistical Machine Translation*. Association for Computational Linguistics, Lisbon, Portugal, pages 1–46.

Peter F. Brown, Peter V. de Souza, Robert L. Mercer, Vincent J. Della Pietra, and Jenifer C. Lai. 1992. Class-based n-gram models of natural language. *Computational Linguistics* 18(4):467–479.

Kyunghyun Cho, Bart van Merrienboer, Dzmitry Bahdanau, and Yoshua Bengio. 2014. On the properties of neural machine translation: Encoder–decoder approaches. In *Proceedings of SSST-8, Eighth Workshop on Syntax, Semantics and Structure in Statistical Translation*. Association for Computational Linguistics, Doha, Qatar, pages 103–111.

Jia Deng, Wei Dong, Richard Socher, Li-Jia Li, Kai Li, and Li Fei-Fei. 2009. Imagenet: A large-scale hierarchical image database. In *Computer Vision and Pattern Recognition, 2009. CVPR 2009. IEEE Conference on*. IEEE, pages 248–255.

Michael Denkowski and Alon Lavie. 2011. Meteor 1.3: Automatic metric for reliable optimization and evaluation of machine translation systems. In *Proceedings of the Sixth Workshop on Statistical Machine Translation*. Association for Computational Linguistics, Edinburgh, UK, pages 85–91.

D. Elliott, S. Frank, K. Sima'an, and L. Specia. 2016. Multi30K: Multilingual English-German Image Descriptions. *ArXiv e-prints* .

Desmond Elliott, Stella Frank, and Eva Hasler. 2015. Multi-language image description with neural sequence models. *CoRR* abs/1510.04709.

Jiatao Gu, Zhengdong Lu, Hang Li, and Victor O. K. Li. 2016. Incorporating copying mechanism in sequence-to-sequence learning. *CoRR* abs/1603.06393.

Çaglar Gülçehre, Marcin Moczulski, Misha Denil, and Yoshua Bengio. 2016. Noisy activation functions. *CoRR* abs/1603.00391.

Sepp Hochreiter and Jürgen Schmidhuber. 1997.

Long short-term memory. *Neural computation* 9(8):1735–1780.

Douwe Kiela and Stephen Clark. 2015. Multi- and cross-modal semantics beyond vision: Grounding in auditory perception. In *Proceedings of the 2015 Conference on Empirical Methods in Natural Language Processing, EMNLP 2015*. Lisbon, Portugal, pages 2461–2470.

Diederik P. Kingma and Jimmy Ba. 2014. Adam: A method for stochastic optimization. *CoRR* abs/1412.6980.

Ryan Kiros, Ruslan Salakhutdinov, and Rich Zemel. 2014. Multimodal neural language models. In *Proceedings of the 31st International Conference on Machine Learning (ICML-14)*. Beijing, China, pages 595–603.

Philipp Koehn, Hieu Hoang, Alexandra Birch, Chris Callison-Burch, Marcello Federico, Nicola Bertoldi, Brooke Cowan, Wade Shen, Christine Moran, Richard Zens, Chris Dyer, Ondrej Bojar, Alexandra Constantin, and Evan Herbst. 2007. Moses: Open source toolkit for statistical machine translation. In *Proceedings of the 45th Annual Meeting of the Association for Computational Linguistics Companion Volume Proceedings of the Demo and Poster Sessions*. Association for Computational Linguistics, Prague, Czech Republic, pages 177–180.

Mahsa Mohaghegh, Abdolhossein Sarrafzadeh, and Mehdi Mohammadi. 2013. A three-layer architecture for automatic post editing system using rule-based paradigm. In *Proceedings of the 4th Workshop on South and Southeast Asian Natural Language Processing*. Asian Federation of Natural Language Processing, Nagoya Congress Center, Nagoya, Japan, pages 17–24.

Kishore Papineni, Salim Roukos, Todd Ward, and Wei-Jing Zhu. 2002. BLEU: a method for automatic evaluation of machine translation. In *Proceedings of the 40th annual meeting on association for computational linguistics*. Association for Computational Linguistics, Philadelphia, PA, USA, pages 311–318.

Bryan A Plummer, Liwei Wang, Chris M Cervantes, Juan C Caicedo, Julia Hockenmaier, and Svetlana Lazebnik. 2015. Flickr30k entities: Collecting region-to-phrase correspondences for richer image-to-sentence models. In *Proceedings of the IEEE International Conference on Computer Vision*. pages 2641–2649.

Marc'Aurelio Ranzato, Sumit Chopra, Michael Auli, and Wojciech Zaremba. 2015. Sequence level training with recurrent neural networks. *CoRR* abs/1511.06732.

Rudolf Rosa. 2014. Depfix, a tool for automatic rule-based post-editing of SMT. *The Prague Bulletin of Mathematical Linguistics* 102:47–56.

Alexander M. Rush, Sumit Chopra, and Jason Weston. 2015. A neural attention model for abstractive sentence summarization. In *Proceedings of the 2015 Conference on Empirical Methods in Natural Language Processing*. Association for Computational Linguistics, Lisbon, Portugal, pages 379–389.

Olga Russakovsky, Jia Deng, Hao Su, Jonathan Krause, Sanjeev Satheesh, Sean Ma, Zhiheng Huang, Andrej Karpathy, Aditya Khosla, Michael Bernstein, et al. 2015. Imagenet large scale visual recognition challenge. *International Journal of Computer Vision* 115(3):211–252.

Michel Simard, Nicola Ueffing, Pierre Isabelle, and Roland Kuhn. 2007. Rule-based translation with statistical phrase-based post-editing. In *Proceedings of the Second Workshop on Statistical Machine Translation*. Association for Computational Linguistics, Prague, Czech Republic, pages 203–206.

Karen Simonyan and Andrew Zisserman. 2014. Very deep convolutional networks for large-scale image recognition. *CoRR* abs/1409.1556.

Matthew Snover, Bonnie Dorr, Richard Schwartz, Linnea Micciulla, and John Makhoul. 2006. A Study of Translation Edit Rate with Targeted Human Annotation. In *Proceedings AMTA*. pages 223–231.

Darlene Stewart, Roland Kuhn, Eric Joanis, and George Foster. 2014. Coarse split and lump bilingual language models for richer source information in SMT. In *Proceedings of the Eleventh Conference of the Association for Machine Translation in the Americas (AMTA)*. Vancouver, BC, Canada, volume 1, pages 28–41.

Ilya Sutskever, Oriol Vinyals, and Quoc V Le. 2014. Sequence to sequence learning with neural networks. In Z. Ghahramani, M. Welling, C. Cortes, N. D. Lawrence, and K. Q. Weinberger, editors, *Advances in Neural Information Processing Systems 27*, Curran Associates, Inc., pages 3104–3112.

Zhaopeng Tu, Zhengdong Lu, Yang Liu, Xiaohua Liu, and Hang Li. 2016. Coverage-based neural machine translation. *CoRR* abs/1601.04811.

Marco Turchi, Rajen Chatterjee, and Matteo Negri. 2016. WMT16 APE shared task data. LINDAT/CLARIN digital library at Institute of Formal and Applied Linguistics, Charles University in Prague.

Oriol Vinyals, Alexander Toshev, Samy Bengio, and Dumitru Erhan. 2015. Show and tell: A neural image caption generator. In *IEEE Conference on Computer Vision and Pattern Recognition, CVPR 2015, Boston, MA, USA, June 7-12, 2015*. pages 3156–3164.

Tsung-Hsien Wen, Milica Gasic, Nikola Mrkšić, Pei-Hao Su, David Vandyke, and Steve Young. 2015. Semantically conditioned lstm-based natural language generation for spoken dialogue systems. In *Proceedings of the 2015 Conference on Empirical Methods in Natural Language Processing*. Association for Computational Linguistics, Lisbon, Portugal, pages 1711–1721.

Kelvin Xu, Jimmy Ba, Ryan Kiros, Kyunghyun Cho, Aaron C. Courville, Ruslan Salakhutdinov, Richard S. Zemel, and Yoshua Bengio. 2015. Show, attend and tell: Neural image caption generation with visual attention. In *Proceedings of the 32nd International Conference on Machine Learning, ICML 2015*. Lille, France, pages 2048–2057.

Wojciech Zaremba, Ilya Sutskever, and Oriol Vinyals. 2014. Recurrent neural network regularization. *CoRR* abs/1409.2329.

WMT 2016 Multimodal Translation System Description based on Bidirectional Recurrent Neural Networks with Double-Embeddings

Sergio Rodríguez Guasch and Marta R. Costa-jussà

TALP Research Center

Universitat Politècnica de Catalunya, Barcelona

`sergio.rodriguez.guasch@est.fib.upc.edu,marta.ruiz@upc.edu`

Abstract

Bidirectional Recurrent Neural Networks (BiRNNs) have shown outstanding results on sequence-to-sequence learning tasks. This architecture becomes specially interesting for multimodal machine translation task, since BiRNNs can deal with images and text. On most translation systems the same word embedding is fed to both BiRNN units. In this paper, we present several experiments to enhance a baseline sequence-to-sequence system (Elliott et al., 2015), for example, by using double embeddings. These embeddings are trained on the forward and backward direction of the input sequence. Our system is trained, validated and tested on the Multi30K dataset (Elliott et al., 2016) in the context of the WMT 2016 Multimodal Translation Task. The obtained results show that the double-embedding approach performs significantly better than the traditional single-embedding one.

1 Introduction

Sequence-to-sequence learning is a new common approach to translation problems (Sutskever et al., 2014). The basic idea consists in mapping the input sentence into a vector of fixed dimensionality with a Recurrent Neural Network (RNN) and, then, do the reverse step to map the vector to the target sequence. From this new perspective, multimodal translation (Elliott et al., 2015) has become a feasible task. In particular, we are referring to the WMT 2016 multimodal task that consists in translating English sentences into German, given the English sentence itself and the image that it describes. This paper describes our participation in this task using a translation scheme based on Bidi-

rectional RNNs (BiRNNs) which allows to combine both information from image and text.

In this paper, we take as baseline system the one from (Elliott et al., 2015) and focus on experimenting with the word embedding system and encoding techniques.

The rest of the paper is organised as follows. Section 2 briefly describes related work on image captioning and machine translation. Section 3 gives details about the architecture of the multimodal translation system. Section 4 reports details on the experimental framework including the parameters of our model and the results obtained. Finally, Section 5 concludes and comments on further work.

2 Related work

Image captioning has gained interest in the community and deep learning has been applied in this area. The two most common caption-related problems are caption generation (Vinyals et al., 2014) and caption translation (Elliott et al., 2015).

Similarly, machine translation approaches based on neural networks (Sutskever et al., 2014; Cho et al., 2014) are competing with standard phrase-based systems (Koehn et al., 2003). Neural machine translation uses an encoder-decoder structure (Cho et al., 2014). The implementation of an attention-based mechanism (Bahdanau et al., 2015) has allowed to achieve state-of-the-art results. The community is actively investigating in this approach and there have been enhancements related to addressing unknown words (Luong et al., 2015), integrating language modeling (Gülçehre et al., 2015), using character information in addition to words (Costa-jussà and Fonollosa, 2016) or even combining different languages (Firat et al., 2016), among others.

Proceedings of the First Conference on Machine Translation, Volume 2: Shared Task Papers, pages 655–659,
Berlin, Germany, August 11-12, 2016. ©2016 Association for Computational Linguistics

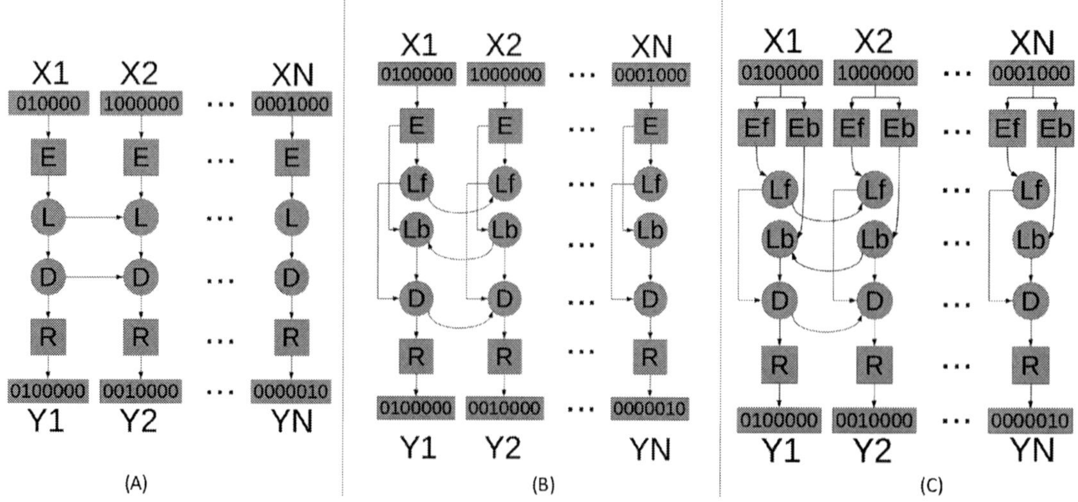

Figure 1: NMT architectures: (A) using unidirectional RNNs, (B) using BiRNNs, (C) adding double embedding.

3 System description

This section describes the main architectures that have been tested to build the final system.

3.1 Baseline approach

The baseline system is a RNN model over word sequences (Elliott et al., 2015), which can use visual and linguistic modalities. The core model is a RNN over word sequences, trained to predict the next word in the sequence, given the sequence so far. The input sequence is codified in *1-of-K* vector, which is embedded into a high-dimensional vector. Then, a unidirectional RNN is used. Finally, in the output layer, the softmax function is used to predict the next word. This model is extended to a multimodal language model, where sequence generation in addition to be conditioned on the previously seen words, are conditioned on image features. The translation model simply adds features from the source language model, following work from (Sutskever et al., 2014; Cho et al., 2014) and calling the source language model the *encoder* and the target language model the *decoder*.

3.2 Sequence-to-sequence approach and enhancements

Inspired by the architecture presented in (Sutskever et al., 2014), we train a system based on the many-to-many encoder-decoder architecture. It accepts a sequence $x_1, .., x_N$ as

input and returns a sequence $y_1, .., y_N$, where N is the maximum sequence length allowed.

The architectures that we have tested start in a unidirectional encoder-decoder, then we use a bidirectional encoder-decoder, a bidirectional encoder-decoder with double embeddings, and a final architecture that accepts a combination of input text and image. See Figure 1 (A), (B) and (C) and Figure 3.2 (D) for an schematic representation of these architectures.

Architecture (A) The model receives as input the codifications *1-of-K* of the source sequence $x_1...x_n$, then the word embedding is computed, obtaining a new representation $E(x_1)...E(x_n)$. This new sequence is processed by a RNN L, obtaining the vectors $L_1...L_n$. These vectors are processed by another RNN D, obtaining the sequence $D_1...D_n$, which is processed by a conventional neural network obtaining the target vectors which are normalised using $softmax$.

Architecture (B) The main difference is that we are using BiRNNs, processing the input sentence forward and backward. The BiRNN is implemented with LSTMs (Long Short Term Memories) for better long-term dependencies handling (Hochreiter and Schmidhuber, 1997; Chung et al., 2014). The BiRNN are represented by unit L, but in this case, one in each direction, generating two vectors Lf_i and Lb_i, corresponding to each input x_i.

Architecture (C) In addition to using BiRNNs, each input codification is processed by two different feed-forward neural networks E_f and E_b, generating two vectors $E_f(x_1)...E_f(x_n)$ and $E_b(x_1)...E_b(x_n)$ of size H, where H is a constant. At each timestep the pair of vectors are fed to the BiRNN Lf and Lb.

Architecture (D) Finally, the last architecture proposes to introduce an image. See Figure 3.2. This is the main advantage of using a machine translation system based on neural networks: we can use multimodal inputs. In this case, image and text. The model in this case has two inputs: the input text sequence $x_1...x_n$ and the image vector, which is the result of intermediate layers of a pre-trained convolutional neural network (Simonyan and Zisserman, 2014).

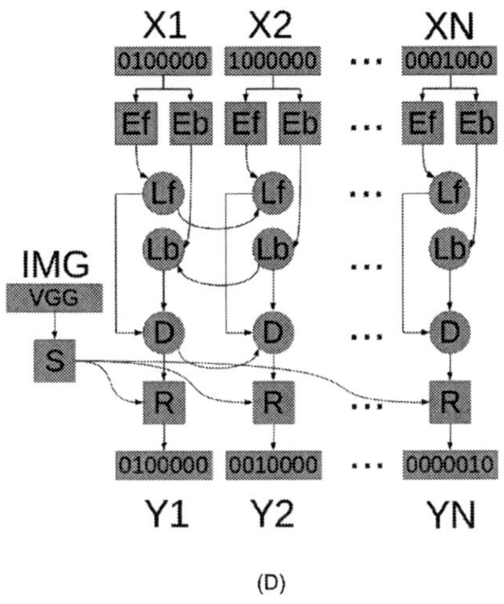

Figure 2: Diagram of NMT architecture (D) using image and text.

4 Experiments and results

4.1 Data

The system is developed, trained and tested with the Multi30K dataset provided by the WMT organization. On our experiments, all characters are converted to lower case. The chosen vocabulary consists on all the training source words and all the training target words that appear more than once. This choice is made to minimise the number of unknown tokens at the source sentences and to avoid an excessive model size and training time.

4.2 Model training

Each source sentence is encoded onto a $N \times V$ matrix M, where each row represents a *1-of-K* encoding of a word over a source vocabulary with V words. An unknown word is replaced by an special <U> token and a <E> token is appended at the end of the sequence. If the sequence length (including <E>) is less than N the remaining rows will be zeros. If the sequence is too long, then it is truncated in order to suit the input size restrictions. During the training phase, target sentences also have a <B> token before the first word. For a given example, the generated prediction is considered to be all the words generated between the <B> and <E> tokens. Unknown tokens are replaced by the second highest probability word.

Parameter	Description	Value
N	Maximum sequence length	45
V	Source vocabulary words	10364
T	Target vocabulary words	8012
H	Embedding size	512
DROP	Dropout rate	0.25
L2	L2 regularizer	10^{-8}

Table 1: Model parameters value

Dropout rate of 0.25 is applied to all non-recurrent units and a L2 regularization is applied to all weights and units.

Training is performed on batches of size 10000 and on mini-batches of size 128. The target metric is the categorical cross entropy and the used optimiser is Adam (Kingma and Ba, 2014). Results are validated at each epoch on the dataset validation split using the BLEU metric (Papineni et al., 2002), along with model perplexity.

BLEU scores during validation are also used as an early stop criteria in case the maximum score so-far is not surpassed on the following 10 epochs. In order to evaluate our system performance obtained results are compared against a single-embedding system trained under the same conditions and parameters. Their BLEU score monitorization can be observed in Figure 3 and the chosen parameter set is summarised in Table 1.

4.3 Results

Table 2 shows the BLEU and METEOR (Lavie and Denkowski, 2009) results for the main architectures described in section 3 for the official test set of the WMT 2016 Multimodal Translation

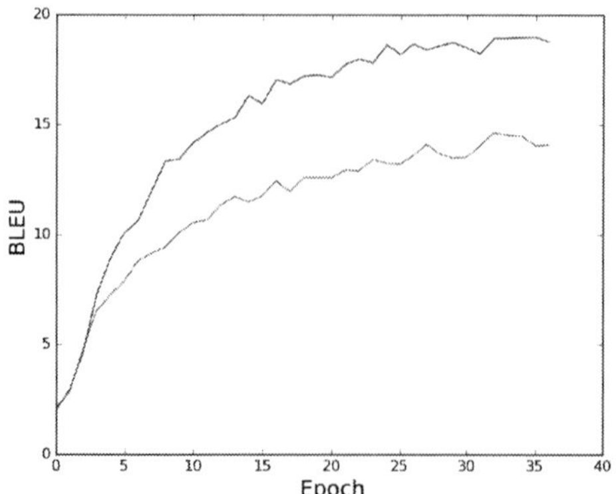

Figure 3: Evolution of BLEU scores (y-axis) on the validation split for the double-embedding system (top blue line) and the single-embedding one (bottom green line).

Task 1. Baseline results are kindly provided by the organisers, referred in the evaluation official results as *1_GroundedTranslation_C*.

We see that using BiRNNs improve vs RNNs, and double-embeddings improves over single-embeddings. Finally, adding the image information does not improve results. Therefore, the best architecture (C) is the one that participated in WMT 2016 Multimodal Translation Task. Official results ranked our system in the 14th position out of 16. We priorised participating with a pure multimodal extensible architecture. However, we know it would have improved our ranking just performing a simple technique as rescoring our system with a standard Moses (Koehn et al., 2007).

System	BLEU	METEOR
Baseline	9.41	24.71
Architecture (A)	19.16	34.23
Architecture (B)	20.89	35.97
Architecture (C)	**22.74**	**37.68**
Architecture (D)	17.74	32.39

Table 2: BLEU and METEOR Results. Official baseline *1_GroundedTranslation_C* kindly provided by the organisers.

The best architecture (C) (compared to using one embedding) is capable of solving problems like unknown words or chosing the appropriate word. Table 3 shows an example that shows the word fixation problem.

However, our generated translations have often many repeated words or end prematurely, mainly due to the differences in lengths and alignments between source and target sentences and the lack of feedback from previous timesteps. In any case, our system is still capable to generate readable translations and to replace unknown words with similar ones.

Source	a man sleeping in a green room on a couch
Generated	ein mann schlaft in einem grünen grünen auf einem sofa
Reference	ein mann schlaft in einem grünen raum auf einem sofa

Table 3: An example that shows the word fixation problem

Also, our system performance drastically decreases on long sentences, or on sentences where the length of the source and target sentences differ too much.

5 Conclusions

Our system is not competitive compared to standard phrase-based system (Koehn et al., 2003) or the auto-encoder neural machine translation system (Bahdanau et al., 2015) as shown by our ranking in the official evaluation (14 position out of 16). However, the architecture of our system makes it feasible to introduce image information. Maybe in a larger corpus we would get competitive results.

All software is freely available in github[1].

The main contribution of this paper is that we show that double embeddings (trained on forward and backward input sequence) provides a significant improvement over single embeddings.

As further work, we are considering experimenting towards replacing the word based encoder for a character-based embedding (Costa-jussà and Fonollosa, 2016), or to introduce attention-based decoders (Bahdanau et al., 2014). Due to the system's modularity, it is also possible to reuse intermediate outputs to train additional models. For example, it is possible to extract the BiRNN intermediate outputs and fed them to another decoder model, thus reducing training time.

---

[1] https://github.com/srgrr/Neural-Translation

Acknowledgements

This work is supported by the 7th Framework Program of the European Commission through the International Outgoing Fellowship Marie Curie Action (IMTraP-2011-29951) and also by the Spanish Ministerio de Economía y Competitividad and European Regional Development Fund, contract TEC2015-69266-P (MINECO/FEDER, UE).

References

Dzmitry Bahdanau, Kyunghyun Cho, and Yoshua Bengio. 2014. Neural machine translation by jointly learning to align and translate. *CoRR*, abs/1409.0473.

Dimitry Bahdanau, Kyunghyun Cho, and Yoshua Bengio. 2015. Neural machine translation by jointly learning to align and translate.

Kyunghyun Cho, Bart van Merrienboer, Çaglar Gülçehre, Fethi Bougares, Holger Schwenk, and Yoshua Bengio. 2014. Learning phrase representations using RNN encoder-decoder for statistical machine translation. *CoRR*, abs/1406.1078.

Junyoung Chung, Çaglar Gülçehre, KyungHyun Cho, and Yoshua Bengio. 2014. Empirical evaluation of gated recurrent neural networks on sequence modeling. *CoRR*, abs/1412.3555.

Marta R. Costa-jussà and José A. R. Fonollosa. 2016. Character-based neural machine translation. In *Proc. of the ACL*.

Desmond Elliott, Stella Frank, and Eva Hasler. 2015. Multi-language image description with neural sequence models. *CoRR*, abs/1510.04709.

Desmond Elliott, Stella Frank, Khalid Sima'an, and Lucia Specia. 2016. Multi30K: Multilingual English-German Image Descriptions. *CoRR*, abs/1605.00459.

Orhan Firat, KyungHyun Cho, and Yoshua Bengio. 2016. Multi-way, multilingual neural machine translation with a shared attention mechanism. *CoRR*, abs/1601.01073.

Çaglar Gülçehre, Orhan Firat, Kelvin Xu, Kyunghyun Cho, Loïc Barrault, Huei-Chi Lin, Fethi Bougares, Holger Schwenk, and Yoshua Bengio. 2015. On using monolingual corpora in neural machine translation. *CoRR*, abs/1503.03535.

Sepp Hochreiter and Jürgen Schmidhuber. 1997. Long short-term memory. *Neural Comput.*, 9(8):1735–1780, November.

Diederik P. Kingma and Jimmy Ba. 2014. Adam: A method for stochastic optimization. *CoRR*, abs/1412.6980.

Philipp Koehn, Franz Joseph Och, and Daniel Marcu. 2003. Statistical Phrase-Based Translation. In *Proceedings of the ACL*.

Philipp Koehn, Hieu Hoang, Alexandra Birch, Chris Callison-Burch, Marcello Federico, Nicolas Bertoldi, Brooke Cowan, Wade Shen, Christine Moran, Richard Zens, Chris Dyer, Ondrej Bojar, Alexandra Constantin, and Evan Herbst. 2007. Moses: Open Source Toolkit for Statistical Machine Translation. In *Proc. of the 45th Annual Meeting of the Association for Computational Linguistics*, pages 177–180.

Alon Lavie and Michael J. Denkowski. 2009. The meteor metric for automatic evaluation of machine translation. *Machine Translation*, 23(2-3):105–115, September.

Minh-Thang Luong, Ilya Sutskever, Quoc V. Le, Oriol Vinyals, and Wojciech Zaremba. 2015. Addressing the rare word problem in neural machine translation. In *Proceedings of the 53rd Annual Meeting of the Association for Computational Linguistics and the 7th International Joint Conference on Natural Language Processing of the Asian Federation of Natural Language Processing, ACL 2015, July 26-31, 2015, Beijing, China, Volume 1: Long Papers*, pages 11–19.

Kishore Papineni, Salim Roukos, Todd Ward, and Wei-Jing Zhu. 2002. Bleu: A method for automatic evaluation of machine translation. In *Proceedings of the 40th Annual Meeting on Association for Computational Linguistics*, ACL '02, pages 311–318.

Karen Simonyan and Andrew Zisserman. 2014. Very deep convolutional networks for large-scale image recognition. *CoRR*, abs/1409.1556.

Ilya Sutskever, Oriol Vinyals, and Quoc V. Le. 2014. Sequence to sequence learning with neural networks. *CoRR*, abs/1409.3215.

Oriol Vinyals, Alexander Toshev, Samy Bengio, and Dumitru Erhan. 2014. Show and tell: A neural image caption generator. *CoRR*, abs/1411.4555.

SHEF-Multimodal: Grounding Machine Translation on Images

Kashif Shah, Josiah Wang, Lucia Specia
University of Sheffield
211 Portobello Street, Sheffield, UK
{kashif.shah,j.k.wang,l.specia}
@sheffield.ac.uk

Abstract

This paper describes the University of Sheffield's submission for the WMT16 Multimodal Machine Translation shared task, where we participated in Task 1 to develop German-to-English and English-to-German statistical machine translation (SMT) systems in the domain of image descriptions. Our proposed systems are standard phrase-based SMT systems based on the Moses decoder, trained only on the provided data. We investigate how image features can be used to re-rank the n-best list produced by the SMT model, with the aim of improving performance by grounding the translations on images. Our submissions are able to outperform the strong, text-only baseline system for both directions.

1 Introduction

This paper describes the University of Sheffield's submission for a new WMT16 Multimodal Machine Translation shared task. The task is aimed at the generation of image descriptions in a target language, given an image and one or more descriptions in a different (source) language. We participated in Task 1, which takes a source language description and translates it into the target language, supported by information from images. We submitted systems for the translation between English and German in both directions.

Multimodal approaches for various applications related to language processing have been gaining wider attention from the research community in recent years. The main motivation is to investigate whether contextual information from various sources can be helpful in improving system performance. Multimodal approaches have been ex-

plored in various tasks such as image and video description, as well as question answering about images (see Section 4). However, not much work has been done to explore multimodality in the context of machine translation. Whilst a large number of approaches have been developed to improve translation quality, they concern solely textual information. The use of non-textual sources such as images and speech has been largely ignored partially because of the lack of datasets and resources. This shared task provides an interesting opportunity to investigate the effectiveness of information from images in improving the performance of machine translation systems.

The main objective of our proposed system is to explore how image features can be used to re-rank an n-best list of translations from a standard phrase-based Statistical Machine Translation (SMT) system. This is in contrast to existing work (Elliott et al., 2015) that uses image features jointly with image descriptions to train a Neural Network-based translation model. The dataset provided for this shared task contains short segments with simple grammar and repetitive vocabulary. Therefore, it is expected that a standard phrase-based SMT system can already produced reasonably good quality translations.

The intuition behind our approach is that image features may help further improve the translation of image descriptions, for example disambiguating words with multiple senses, when these alternatives are available in the n-best list produced by the SMT model. This approach also has the advantage over joint visual-textual alternatives in that the translation model itself is learnt independently from images, and thus does not require dataset-specific images at training time to generate candidate translations. In fact, images are only used at test time for n-best list re-ranking, and the visual classifier is pre-trained on a generic image dataset.

Proceedings of the First Conference on Machine Translation, Volume 2: Shared Task Papers, pages 660–665,
Berlin, Germany, August 11-12, 2016. ©2016 Association for Computational Linguistics

We use image features from a Convolutional Neural Network (CNN) along with standard Moses features to re-rank the n-best list. We also propose an alternative scheme for the German-to-English direction, where terms in the English image descriptions are matched against 1,000 WordNet synsets, and the probability of these synsets occurring in the image estimated using CNN predictions on the images. The aggregated probabilities are then used to re-rank the n-best list, with the intuition that the best translations will contain words representing these entities. Our submissions that re-rank the n-best translations with image vectors are able to marginally outperform the strong, text-only baseline system for both directions.

In Section 2 we describe the procedure to extract image features. In Section 3 we explain the experiments along with their results. We finally give a brief overview of related work in Section 4, before presenting some conclusion and future directions (Section 5).

2 Image features

Image features were extracted using the 16-layer version of VGGNet (VGG-16) (Simonyan and Zisserman, 2014), which is a Deep Convolutional Neural Network (CNN) pre-trained on 1,000 object categories of the classification/localisation task of the ImageNet Large Scale Visual Recognition Challenge (ILSVRC) (Russakovsky et al., 2015). More specifically, we used MatConvNet (Vedaldi and Lenc, 2015) to extract the final fully-connected layer (FC8) of VGG-16 after applying the softmax function. The 1,000-dimensional vector from this layer provides class posterior probability estimates for 1,000 object categories, each corresponding to a distinct WordNet concept (synset).

The 1,000 dimensional vector were used as features in our systems to re-rank the top-n output translations from the SMT model (Section 3.2). Each feature is an estimate of the probability that a given object category is depicted in the image. Note that the posterior probability estimates for VGGNet are not perfect (the top-5 error rate was 7.3% in the ILSVRC2014 challenge, where a prediction is considered correct if the correct category is within the top 5 guesses), and we expect such errors to propagate downstream to the translation task. Moreover, the classifiers are tuned

to the 1,000 categories of ILSVRC, and many categories may not be relevant to the Flickr30K dataset (Young et al., 2014) that is used for this task, and vice-versa, that is, many of the objects in the Flickr30K dataset may not exist in the ILSVRC dataset. This implies that the classification error in our dataset is probably much higher.

3 Experiments

3.1 Data

The data used for the shared task is a version of the Flickr30K dataset. For the translation task, the Flickr30K dataset was extended in the following way: for each image, one of the English descriptions was selected and manually translated into German by a professional translator. The resulting parallel data and corresponding images for training are divided into training, development and test sets. As training and development data, 29,000 and 1,014 triples were provided, respectively, each containing an English source sentence, its German human translation and corresponding image. As test data, set of 1,000 tuples containing an English description and its corresponding image was provided. More details about the shared task data can be found in (Elliott et al., 2016).

3.2 Training

Both our submissions are based on the Moses SMT toolkit (Koehn et al., 2007) to build phrase-based SMT models. They are constructed as follows: First, word alignments in both directions are calculated using GIZA++ (Och and Ney, 2000). The phrases and reordering tables are extracted using the default settings of the Moses toolkit. The parameters of Moses were tuned on the provided development set, using the MERT (Och, 2003) algorithm. 4-gram back-off language models were built using the target side of the parallel corpus. Training was performed using only the data provided by the task organisers, and so systems for both directions were built in the constrained setting.

We extracted the 100 best translations with our SMT model and re-ranked them using the image features described in Section 2, along with the standard Moses features. We used an off-the-shelf tool [1] to re-rank the n-best translations. More

---

[1] `https://github.com/moses-smt/`
`mosesdecoder/tree/master/scripts/`
`nbest-rescore`

specifically, we performed following steps:

- We ran our Moses decoder to generate 100-best lists for each translation in the development set.

- We extracted and added following image feature scores to the already existing feature values for each translation in the n-best list:

    - *prob*: Aggregated probability estimates of entities being depicted in the image and also being mentioned in the candidate translations. Here, we match terms occurring in the English candidate translations to the 1,000 synsets of ILSVRC, and estimate the probability of these synsets occurring in the image using the CNN predictions. In cases where more than one entity is matched, we average the probabilities of all matched synsets. The intuition is that the top translations should mention the entities depicted in the image, while lower ranked translations will have fewer entities mentioned, and thus a lower probability score overall. This feature is used only in the de-en direction since we only have access to the English version of WordNet.

    - *vec*: 1,000-dimensional FC8 vector from the CNN for both en-de and de-en directions. As mentioned in Section 2, each element in the vector corresponds to the posterior probability estimate of a WordNet synset, with the vector summing to 1 after applying the softmax function. Note that each element in the vector is considered as an independent score, with its weight learnt during re-ranking.

- We ran the optimiser K-best MIRA (Cherry and Foster, 2012) to learn new weights for all features in the n-best list. The optimiser creates a new config file that contains new weights for each feature. The choice of MIRA to learn new weights over MERT is based on the fact that MIRA is known to perform better than MERT for larger feature sets in terms of efficiency and performance.

- We used the original config file to generate 100-best lists for the test set.

Lang.	Train	Dev	Test	BLEU	Meteor
en-de	29000	1014	1000	0.383	0.576
de-en	29000	1014	1000	0.434	0.363

Table 1: Datasets size and results of a baseline system on the development set.

Lang.	Score	Re-Rank$_{prob}$	Re-Rank$_{vec}$
en-de	BLEU	-	0.386
	Meteor	-	0.580
de-en	BLEU	0.431	0.437
	Meteor	0.360	0.366

Table 2: Results on the development set after re-ranking.

Lang.	System	Meteor	Meteor-norm
en-de	Baseline	0.525	0.573
	Re-Rank$_{vec}$	0.526	0.574
de-en	Baseline	0.363	0.398
	Re-Rank$_{vec}$	0.365	0.401

Table 3: Results on the test set: Baseline Moses vs Re-ranking approach.

- We added the above mentioned image features to the test n-best list.

- Finally, we re-scored the 100-best list using the re-scoring weights file and extracted the top best translation for each source segment.

For our experiments, we used the same tuning set to train the re-ranker that was used to optimise the Moses decoder original features. We note that it could be better to use a distinct tuning set than the one on which the decoder weights were optimised.

3.3 Results

The results of our submissions for the German-English and English-German tasks are summarised in Tables 1, 2 and 3. Table 1 shows our baseline Moses systems (text-only) along with training, development and test data sizes. Table 2 presents our results with re-ranking on the development set. The system *Re-Rank$_{prob}$* uses the decoder features with additional aggregated probability estimates features, while the system

Re-Rank$_{vec}$ uses decoder features along with the 1,000-dimensional vector produced by VGGNet.

It can be observed that re-ranking with a 1,000-dimension image vector improves over the baseline for both directions, whereas posterior probability feature degrades the result. Note that although all (n-best) translation hypotheses for a given source description get the same image feature values (1,000 dimension image vector), the combination of the decoder features with these image vectors make the optimiser produce different discriminative weights, which may lead to better translation choices.

We submitted a system for each translation direction with vector features as the official submissions. It can be seen in Table 3 that our systems were able to improve over the baseline in the official metrics in both directions, although only marginally. Moreover, both systems are among the top three systems in the official ranking that outperform the strong Moses SMT baseline. The output of our systems is significantly different from that of the baseline: 260 out of the 1,000 segments differ between the baseline and the re-ranking approach. Figure 1 shows some examples of English-to-German translations for the test set from our proposed system using VGGNet FC8 features for re-ranking (Re-Rank$_{vec}$), in comparison to translations by the Moses baseline. In all cases, the translations produced by the two systems are different. In the first example, the Moses baseline translation, although not entirely correct, can be considered more accurate. In the second example, both translations are accurate, but that produced by the re-ranking approach matches exactly the reference. Finally, in the third example, the translation by the re-ranking approach is significantly better, and also much closer to the reference. An interesting observation is the fact that while the baseline system does not produce any translation that is exactly the same as the reference, the re-ranking approach produces 37 translations that are exactly the same as the reference translations. A better understanding on the differences between the baseline and re-ranking approaches would require more systematic human evaluation, which we plan to do in the future.

4 Related work

In computer vision, considerable progress has been made in the field of visual object recognition in recent years, especially since the CNN-based AlexNet (Krizhevsky et al., 2012) convincingly won the ILSVRC2012 challenge by a large margin compared to its closest rival. Progress in image classification ("what does this picture depict?") has since improved from strength to strength, from an error rate of 16.4% (correct label in top 5 guesses) by AlexNet down to 3.6% by ResNet (He et al., 2015) in the 2015 challenge. Despite the high success rate, there is still much work to be done in the object classification and localisation challenge ("what object category does this picture depict and where?") and the object detection challenge ("find all instances of this object category in all images, if any"), although the performance for these has also improved tremendously in recent years.

With the improved performance of object classifiers/detectors, there has also been increased interest in applying these classifiers/detectors to various downstream tasks, especially those that involve multiple modalities. For example, CNNs has been used in conjunction with Recurrent Neural Networks (RNN) (Mikolov et al., 2010) to generate image descriptions, e.g. (Karpathy and Fei-Fei, 2015; Donahue et al., 2015; Vinyals et al., 2015). Other multimodal tasks that have been explored include video description generation (Chen and Dolan, 2011; Yu and Siskind, 2013), visual question answering (Antol et al., 2015; Ren et al., 2015; Malinowski et al., 2015), multilingual image question answering (Gao et al., 2015), and multimodal translation of image descriptions (Elliott et al., 2015). Whilst the work of Elliott et al. (2015) focuses on learning multimodal image description translation in a joint fashion using CNNs and RNNs, our work uses a conventional phrase-based SMT decoder combined with features extracted from a CNN for re-ranking.

5 Conclusions

We presented the development of our SMT systems that incorporate image features for the first German-English and English-German WMT Multimodal Machine Translation shared task. In the official evaluation, the English-German system was ranked third according to the Meteor score, while the German-English system was ranked first, although there were only two other systems for this direction. Small but consistent improvements over than a strong text-only SMT baseline

EN	A young brunette woman eating and drinking something.
DE (Baseline)	Eine junge Frau mit braunen Haaren und isst und trinkt etwas .
DE (Re-Rank$_{vec}$)	Ein junger brünette Frau isst und trinkt etwas .
Reference	Eine junge brünette Frau isst und trinkt etwas.

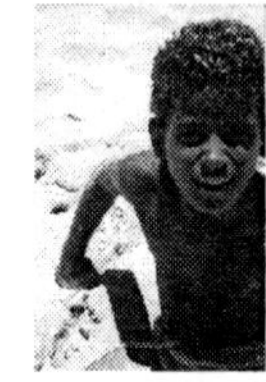

EN	A black boy is sitting in the sand.
DE (Baseline)	Ein dunkelhäutiger Junge sitzt im Sand .
DE (Re-Rank$_{vec}$)	Ein schwarzer Junge sitzt im Sand .
Reference	Ein schwarzer Junge sitzt im Sand.

EN	A man with a black vest holding a model airplane
DE (Baseline)	Ein Mann in einer schwarzen Weste und einem Modellflugzeug
DE (Re-Rank$_{vec}$)	Ein Mann mit einer schwarzen Weste hält einem Modellflugzeug
Reference	Ein Mann mit einer schwarzen Weste hält ein Modellflugzeug

Figure 1: Example English-to-German (EN–DE) output translations for Re-Rank$_{vec}$ on the test set, compared against the Moses baseline (before re-ranking).

system were found in both directions.

Our initial set of experiments can be improved in many directions. For instance, it would be interesting to explore incorporating image features directly into the decoding step and tuning the weights along with Moses parameters. It is also worth investigating other layers of image models instead of the final fully-connected layer to be used with textual features. Finally, increasing the size of n-best to re-rank translations could increase the chances of achieving better results by providing the re-ranker with more variety in terms of alternative translations.

Acknowledgments

This work was supported by the QT21 (H2020 No. 645452, Lucia Specia), Cracker (H2020 No. 645357, Kashif Shah) and the ERA-NET CHIST-ERA D2K 2011 VisualSense (ViSen) project (UK EPSRC Grant EP/K019082/1, Josiah Wang).

References

Stanislaw Antol, Aishwarya Agrawal, Jiasen Lu, Margaret Mitchell, Dhruv Batra, C. Lawrence Zitnick, and Devi Parikh. 2015. Vqa: Visual question answering. In *International Conference on Computer Vision (ICCV)*.

David L. Chen and William B. Dolan. 2011. Collecting highly parallel data for paraphrase evaluation. In *Proceedings of the 49th Annual Meeting of the Association for Computational Linguistics*, pages 190–200, Portland, Oregon, USA, June.

Colin Cherry and George Foster. 2012. Batch tuning strategies for statistical machine translation. In *Proceedings of the 2012 Conference of the North American Chapter of the Association for Computational Linguistics: Human Language Technologies*, NAACL HLT '12, pages 427–436, Stroudsburg, PA, USA. Association for Computational Linguistics.

Jeffrey Donahue, Lisa Anne Hendricks, Sergio Guadarrama, Marcus Rohrbach, Subhashini Venugopalan, Kate Saenko, and Trevor Darrell. 2015. Long-term recurrent convolutional networks for visual recognition and description. In *Proceedings of the IEEE Conference on Computer Vision & Pattern Recognition*.

Desmond Elliott, Stella Frank, and Eva Hasler. 2015. Multi-language image description with neural sequence models. *CoRR*, abs/1510.04709.

Desmond Elliott, Stella Frank, Khalil Sima'an, and Lucia Specia. 2016. Multi30K: Multilingual English-German Image Descriptions. *CoRR*, abs/1605.00459.

Haoyuan Gao, Junhua Mao, Jie Zhou, Zhiheng Huang, Lei Wang, and Wei Xu. 2015. Are you talking to a machine? dataset and methods for multilingual image question answering. In *Advances in Neural Information Processing Systems*, pages 2287–2295.

Kaiming He, Xiangyu Zhang, Shaoqing Ren, and Jian Sun. 2015. Deep residual learning for image recognition. *CoRR*, abs/1512.03385.

Andrej Karpathy and Li Fei-Fei. 2015. Deep visual-semantic alignments for generating image descriptions. In *Proceedings of the IEEE Conference on Computer Vision & Pattern Recognition*.

Philipp Koehn, Hieu Hoang, Alexandra Birch, Chris Callison-Burch, Marcello Federico, Nicola Bertoldi, Brooke Cowan, Wade Shen, Christine Moran, Richard Zens, et al. 2007. Moses: Open source toolkit for statistical machine translation. In *Proceedings of the 45th annual meeting of the ACL on interactive poster and demonstration sessions*, pages 177–180. Association for Computational Linguistics.

Alex Krizhevsky, Ilya Sutskever, and Geoffrey E. Hinton. 2012. Imagenet classification with deep convolutional neural networks. In F. Pereira, C. J. C. Burges, L. Bottou, and K. Q. Weinberger, editors, *Advances in Neural Information Processing Systems 25*, pages 1097–1105. Curran Associates, Inc.

Mateusz Malinowski, Marcus Rohrbach, and Mario Fritz. 2015. Ask your neurons: A neural-based approach to answering questions about images. In *2015 IEEE International Conference on Computer Vision, ICCV 2015, Santiago, Chile, December 7-13, 2015*.

Tomas Mikolov, Martin Karafit, Luks Burget, Jan Cernock, and Sanjeev Khudanpur. 2010. Recurrent neural network based language model. In Takao Kobayashi, Keikichi Hirose, and Satoshi Nakamura, editors, *INTERSPEECH*, pages 1045–1048. ISCA.

Franz Josef Och and Hermann Ney. 2000. Improved statistical alignment models. In *Proceedings of the Association for Computational Linguistics*, pages 440–447, Hongkong, China, October.

Franz Josef Och. 2003. Minimum error rate training in statistical machine translation. In *Proceedings of the 41st Annual Meeting on Association for Computational Linguistics-Volume 1*, pages 160–167. Association for Computational Linguistics.

Mengye Ren, Ryan Kiros, and Richard S. Zemel. 2015. Exploring models and data for image question answering. In *Advances in Neural Information Processing Systems 28: Annual Conference on Neural Information Processing Systems 2015, December 7-12, 2015, Montreal, Quebec, Canada*, pages 2953–2961.

Olga Russakovsky, Jia Deng, Hao Su, Jonathan Krause, Sanjeev Satheesh, Sean Ma, Zhiheng Huang, Andrej Karpathy, Aditya Khosla, Michael Bernstein, Alexander C. Berg, and Li Fei-Fei. 2015. ImageNet Large Scale Visual Recognition Challenge. *International Journal of Computer Vision (IJCV)*, 115(3):211–252.

Karen Simonyan and Andrew Zisserman. 2014. Very deep convolutional networks for large-scale image recognition. *CoRR*, abs/1409.1556.

Andrea Vedaldi and Karel Lenc. 2015. Matconvnet – convolutional neural networks for matlab. In *Proceeding of the ACM Int. Conf. on Multimedia*.

Oriol Vinyals, Alexander Toshev, Samy Bengio, and Dumitru Erhan. 2015. Show and tell: A neural image caption generator. In *Proceedings of the IEEE Conference on Computer Vision & Pattern Recognition*.

Peter Young, Alice Lai, Micah Hodosh, and Julia Hockenmaier. 2014. From image descriptions to visual denotations: New similarity metrics for semantic inference over event descriptions. *Transactions of the Association for Computational Linguistics*, 2:67–78, February.

Haonan Yu and Jeffrey Mark Siskind. 2013. Grounded language learning from video described with sentences. In *Proceedings of the Association for Computational Linguistics (ACL)*.

DOCAL - Vicomtech's Participation in the WMT16 Shared Task on Bilingual Document Alignment

Andoni Azpeitia and **Thierry Etchegoyhen**

Vicomtech-IK4

Mikeletegi Pasalekua, 57

Donostia / San Sebastian, Gipuzkoa, Spain

`{aazpeitia, tetchegoyhen}@vicomtech.org`

Abstract

This article presents the DOCAL system for document alignment, which took part in the WMT 2016 shared task on bilingual document alignment. The system is meant to offer a portable solution for varied document alignment scenarios, from parallel to comparable corpora, with minimal deployment effort. Its main goal is to provide an optimal balance between alignment precision and recall using minimal resources and adaptation across alignment scenarios. We describe and discuss the performance of the system in the recall-oriented shared task.

1 Introduction

Parallel corpora are essential to the development of data-driven approaches to translation such as statistical machine translation (Brown et al., 1990). As it feeds further processes in the creation of bitexts, multilingual document alignment plays an important role in building accurate resources.

This article presents the DOCAL system for document alignment, which took part in the WMT 2016 shared task on bilingual document alignment. The system is meant to offer a portable solution for varied document alignment scenarios, from parallel to comparable corpora.

The alignment of multilingual documents has been performed with a variety of techniques over the years, with alternatives targeting various scenarios, from parallel to weakly comparable corpora.

Simple approaches based on file name matching can provide fast document pairing, as they do not rely on any analysis of the content of documents. Unfortunately, these approaches rely on consistent file naming conventions, an assumption which is often defeated in practice (Tiedemann, 2011). This approach is thus often complemented with content-based alignment methods, as in (Chen et al., 2004), whose system includes a filename-based module and a semantic similarity component based on a vector space model with frequency-weighted term vectors.

The usefulness of document metadata for document alignment has been explored in depth by (Resnik and Smith, 2003), who exploit URL properties and structural tags to gather bilingual corpora from HTML pages on the Web. (Chen and Nie, 2000) is another example of an approach that exploits URL properties, along with document size and language identifiers. (Munteanu and Marcu, 2005) use date-aligned documents as input for their binary classification approach to comparable sentence alignment.

To address comparable corpora specifically, different types of content-based approaches have been proposed. (Fung and Cheung, 2004), for instance, present the first exploration of very non-parallel corpora using a document similarity measure based on bilingual lexical matching defined over mutual information scores on word pairs. (Patry and Langlais, 2005) present a feature-based method based on an Ada-Boost classifier that includes features such as length, entities, and punctuation, along with a filtering component to remove alignment duplicates. The BITS system is another alternative proposed by (Ma and Liberman, 1999) for bilingual text mining on the Web, measuring content similarity by counting the ratio of token translation pairs over the total number of tokens in the source document, where translation pairs are determined within fixed windows of text.

Other general methods include (Ion et al., 2011), who propose an approach based on expectation-maximization using bilingual lexi-

Proceedings of the First Conference on Machine Translation, Volume 2: Shared Task Papers, pages 666–671,
Berlin, Germany, August 11-12, 2016. ©2016 Association for Computational Linguistics

cons, and (Li and Gaussier, 2013), whose comparability metric measures the overall proportion of words for which a translation can be found in a comparable corpus using bilingual dictionaries.

The Jaccard coefficient (Jaccard, 1901), which is a core component of DOCAL, has been used for instance by (Paramita et al., 2013) whose comparable document similarity measure is partially based on this metric computed over a subset of sentence pairs in the documents.

DOCAL (Etchegoyhen and Azpeitia, 2016) is a simple method to measure multilingual document similarity, whose main goal is to provide an optimal balance between alignment precision and recall with minimal resources and adaptation across alignment scenarios. The next sections describe the system and its performance in the recall-oriented shared task.

2 DOCAL

The core of the DOCAL approach relies on expanded lexical translation sets, defined at the document level, and the Jaccard coefficient computed on those sets. Two token sets are thus extracted from each pair of documents, along with two corresponding sets containing lexical translations of the tokens. The translation sets are then augmented through set expansion operations, described below, and similarity is computed as the ratio of intersection over union on the original token sets and their corresponding translation sets.

Formally, the following components are generated for each document pair:

- d_i and d_j: tokenised documents in languages l_1 and l_2, respectively.

- S_i: set of tokens in d_i.

- S_j: set of tokens in d_j.

- T_{ij}: set of expanded lexical translations into l_2 for all tokens in S_i.

- T_{ji}: set of expanded lexical translations into l_1 for all tokens in S_j.

From these elements, the similarity score is computed as in Equation 1:

$$sim_{docal} = \frac{\frac{|T_{ij} \cap S_j|}{|T_{ij} \cup S_j|} + \frac{|T_{ji} \cap S_i|}{|T_{ji} \cup S_i|}}{2} \qquad (1)$$

In other words, the score is defined as the average of the document-level Jaccard similarity coefficients computed in both translation directions.

Lexical translations are extracted from seed parallel corpora, with translation probabilities computed according to IBM models (Brown et al., 1993).[1] For each token, the k-best translation options are selected among the alternatives ranked according to their lexical translation probability. The actual probability values are not used beyond the ranking they enable, i.e. all selected translations are equally considered in the computation of similarity. This is meant to abstract away from differences in lexical distributions between the seed corpora used to create translation tables and the data in the domain at hand, which is often of a different nature.

No filtering is performed on the token sets, leaving punctuation marks alongside functional and content words, and the text is preserved with its original capitalisation. Pre-processing is thus reduced to the minimal operation of tokenisation.

We now describe in turn the aforementioned set expansion operations, the retrieval of alignment candidates, and the available optimisations of the core method.

2.1 Set Expansion

Since lexical translation tables cannot be expected to cover a given domain satisfactorily, the translation sets are expanded with tokens that may be indicators of similarity, although absent from translation tables. First, all capitalised tokens are added to the sets if they are not found in the translation tables.[2] This simple operation, which we perform at set creation time, provides coverage for named entities, which can be viewed as important indicators of content similarity given their low relative frequency. The same process applies to numbers as well, which can also be strong indicators of similarity, in particular when they denote dates.

DOCAL includes an additional set expansion operation based on longest common prefixes (LCP), which are computed over the minimal sets of elements that may have a common stem, defined to be the following two set differences: $T'_{ij} = T_{ij} - S_j$

---

[1] We use GIZA++ (Och and Ney, 2003) to extract lexical translation tables.

[2] Checking for their presence in lexical translation tables allows one to distinguish between out-of-vocabulary tokens and entities with an existing translation, e.g. *Germany* translated into Spanish *Alemania*.

and $T'_{ji} = T_{ji} - S_i$. For each element in T'_{ij} (respectively T'_{ji}) and each element in S_j (respectively S_i), if a common prefix is found with an empirically set minimal length of n characters, the prefix is added to both sets. This specific expansion operation is not included by default in the actual usage of the system, as it increases the overall computational cost and its benefits are largely dependent on the specifics of the corpora and language pairs at hand.

2.2 Alignment Candidates

Alignments are computed from source to target documents, with the additional filtering described in Section 2.3.

In some document alignment scenarios, an alignment process based on the Cartesian product of the document sets might be the optimal approach, as the alignment space is guaranteed to be searched exhaustively. Since this approach has quadratic complexity, it is however computationally prohibitive if the volumes of documents reach a certain amount.

For scenarios where the volume of documents renders an exhaustive comparison unsustainable, a standard cross-linguistic information retrieval (CLIR) approach is provided. Target documents are first indexed using the Lucene search engine[3] and retrieved by building a query over the expanded translation sets created from each source document. This strategy drastically reduces the overall processing time and resource consumption, at the cost of missing some correct alignment pairs.[4]

2.3 Alignment Filtering

As the alignment process is executed from source to target documents, a given target document can be selected as the best alignment for more than one source document. This results in hidden correct alignments, often with scores that are marginally lower than the top alignment scores assigned by the similarity metric.

A simple solution to this issue consists in removing all alignments between a source document and a target if the latter is aligned to a different source document with a better similarity score. That is, we remove alignment tuples (d_i, d_j, sim_{ij}) between any two documents d_i and d_j if there exists a different tuple (d_k, d_j, sim_{kj}) such that $sim_{kj} > sim_{ij}$.

This process often produces large improvements, as it allows previously hidden correct alignments to surface, and is included by default in DOCAL.

3 WMT 2016 Bilingual Document Alignment Task

The WMT 2016 shared task on multilingual document alignment[5] consists in identifying pairs of English and French documents from a given collection of documents such that one document is the translation of the other. Candidate pairs were defined as all pairs of documents from the same web domain for which the source side has been identified as mostly English and the target side as mostly French.

Participants were to submit a list of possible pairings, with each source URL matched with at most one target URL and vice-versa. The evaluation metric was selected to be recall on the test set, i.e. the percentage of the test-set pairs that a participating system could find after enforcing the 1-1 alignment rule.

Our participation in the shared task was meant to check the effectiveness of DOCAL in a new large-scale document alignment task with no task-specific adaptation, in accordance with our stated aim at portability and ease of deployment across document alignment scenarios. Thus, the system was applied in its default configuration and the provided training datasets were not used beyond testing the processing tools provided for the task. Document metadata or URL properties were not exploited either, to strictly measure our content-based approach to document alignment.

In the next section, we describe the setup for our system, with results presented in Section 3.2.

3.1 System Setup

As mentioned above, DOCAL was applied in its default configuration. Lexical translation tables were created with GIZA++ on the JRC-Acquis Communautaire corpus.[6] For the English-French pair, the training corpus consisted in 708.896 aligned sentences. No experiments were made with different translation tables, larger or more varied, although

---

[3]https://lucene.apache.org.

[4]In experiments on different datasets, the loss of correct alignment pairs was minimal, at around 1% per test set.

[5]http://www.statmt.org/wmt16/bilingual-task.html.

[6]We used the latest available version of the corpus, as of November 2015, in the OPUS repository: http://opus.lingfil.uu.se/JRC-Acquis.php.

we view this research path as worth exploring in future work.

We set $k = 5$ to define the range of k-best lexical translations, as a compromise between larger sets with less reliable translation candidates and smaller sets which may miss translation alternatives. Note that this value could have been tuned on the provided training data, thus optimising the setting to this specific task. However, as previously mentioned, our goal was to evaluate the approach with portability in mind, where no particular adaptation is performed; we therefore used this default value for the k parameter.

Document content was tokenised using the scripts provided in the Moses toolkit (Koehn et al., 2007). For all but four web domains in the test set, the set of possible alignment pairs was computed using the Cartesian product of source-target documents, as this guaranteed an exhaustive search in the alignment space and the computation was deemed practical for up to 260 million possible pairings.[7] The remaining four domains featured potential pairs above the 300 million mark and the CLIR approach using Lucene was used in those cases.[8]

Finally, DOCAL was used with alignment filtering, as described in Section 2.3, and without the set expansion operation based on longest common prefixes described in Section 2.1.

3.2 Results and Discussion

Overall, DOCAL ranked in 5th place on the official test set, with 2128 pairs retrieved out of 2402 for a recall score of 88.59%. It is interesting to note that several systems, and in particular all four systems with better scores, have submitted a significantly larger number of pairs than DOCAL, which is indicative of underlying differences in terms of precision and f-measure. However, without knowing the correctness of the alignments outside the test set pairs, it is obviously not possible to determine whether these differences show better precision on the part of DOCAL or not.

While performing an error analysis of the cases where our system had retrieved the incorrect pair according to the test set, we found 100 cases where the test set contained what we consider to be incorrect alignments. That is, in all 100 cases, shown in Table 1,[9] the target pair found by DOCAL seems to us to be the correct one. In most of these cases, the French documents in the test set and the one retrieved by DOCAL were nearly identical, with only minor differences where the test set document was missing a small portion of information from the source document.[10]

These cases account for 4.16% of the test, and impact the final results, as shown in Table 2.[11] On the corrected test set, DOCAL reaches a score of 92.76%, significantly better than its result on the original test set.

It is of course entirely possible that other participating systems had actually retrieved the correct target documents as well in those cases, and that the final ranking of systems would thus be unaffected. Whether this is actually the case or not is unknown to us at the time of this writing.

4 Conclusion

Overall, we found the results obtained by DOCAL on the shared task to be satisfactory, in particular as a test case for the portability of the default method in a new large-scale alignment scenario.

The system was developed to seek an optimal balance between precision and recall, and has shown promising results along these lines in different scenarios involving both parallel and comparable corpora (Etchegoyhen and Azpeitia, 2016). In future tasks, it would be interesting to compare our approach to alternatives in terms of f-measure as well, to fully assess the usefulness of available methods for multilingual document alignment.

Acknowledgments

This work was partially funded by the Spanish Ministry of Economy and Competitiveness and the

---

[7]The documents were processed on a single server with 64G of RAM and 16 cores.

[8]The domains were: www.domainepechlaurier.com; www.desmarais-robitaille.com; italiasullarete.it; and: egodesign.ca.

[9]As many of the erroneous cases came from a single domain, namely www.lalettrediplomatique.fr, we indicate the URL structure once where replacing the place-holder X with one of the values in the last line forms the actual URL. Note also that we indicate ranges with a dash, e.g., X = 15-17 indicates that all values from 15 to 17 (included) lead to a URL that is in the set of identified errors.

[10]For instance, 94 of the cases came from the domain www.lalettrediplomatique.fr, where the English source document content contains a date which is accurately translated in the document retrieved by DOCAL, and incorrect in the target document in the test set.

[11]*wmt2016_corr* denotes the corrected version of the test set.

Source:	http://artfactories.net/Espace-Linga-Tere.html
Test set:	http://artfactories.net/-Republique-centrafricaine-.html
Correct:	http://artfactories.net/Espace-Linga-Tere-Bangui.html
Source:	http://www.ipu.org/hr-e/169/Co121.htm
Test set:	http://www.ipu.org/hr-f/168/Co121.htm
Correct:	http://www.ipu.org/hr-f/169/Co121.htm
Source:	http://www.lifegrid.fr/en/projets/projects/biomedicale-search.html
Test set:	http://www.lifegrid.fr/fr/projets/appel-a-projets-e-nnovergne-lifegrid-2006/recherche-biomedicale.html
Correct:	http://www.lifegrid.fr/fr/projets/31-recherche-biomedicale.html
Source:	http://www.nserc-crsng.gc.ca/Prizes-Prix/Excellence-Excellence/Profiles-Profils_eng.asp?ID=1008
Test set:	http://www.nserc-crsng.gc.ca/Prizes-Prix/Herzberg-Herzberg/Profiles-Profils_fra.asp?ID=1003
Correct:	http://www.nserc-crsng.gc.ca/Prizes-Prix/Excellence-Excellence/Profiles-Profils_fra.asp?ID=1008
Source:	http://www.rfimusique.com/musiqueen/articles/060/article_6465.asp
Test set:	http://www.rfimusique.com/musiquefr/articles/060/article_14625.asp
Correct:	http://www.rfimusique.com/musiquefr/articles/060/article_13250.asp
Source:	http://www.rfimusique.com/musiqueen/articles/129/article_8397.asp
Test set:	http://www.rfimusique.com/musiquefr/articles/128/article_18057.asp
Correct:	http://www.rfimusique.com/musiquefr/articles/129/article_18094.asp
Source:	http://www.lalettrediplomatique.fr/contribution.php?choixlang=2&id=10&idrub=**X**
Test set:	http://www.lalettrediplomatique.fr/contribution.php?id=10&idrub=**X**
Correct:	http://www.lalettrediplomatique.fr/contribution.php?choixlang=1&id=10&idrub=**X**
X =	5, 7, 11-12, 15-17, 23, 28-31, 35, 37-39, 43, 45-46, 50-52, 56-58, 61-65, 69, 83-84, 86, 89, 91-94, 96-100, 103-107, 109-111, 114-115, 119-120, 123-125, 127-130, 133-135, 137-141, 144, 146, 149-152, 155-156, 158, 160-163, 165-167, 169, 173, 175, 177, 194, 197

Table 1: Identified likely errors in the test set

TEST SETS	FOUND PAIRS	SUBMITTED PAIRS	PAIRS AFTER 1-1 RULE	RECALL
wmt2016	2.128	191.993	191.993	88.592839
wmt2016_corr	2.228	191.993	191.993	92.756037

Table 2: DOCAL results

Department of Economic Development and Competitiveness of the Basque Government through the AdapTA (RTC-2015-3627-7) and TRADIN (IG-2015/0000347) projects. We would like to thank MondragonLingua Translation & Communication for their support as coordinator of these projects, and the organisers of the shared task for their work and support.

References

Peter F Brown, John Cocke, Stephen A Della Pietra, Vincent J Della Pietra, Fredrick Jelinek, John D Lafferty, Robert L Mercer, and Paul S Roossin. 1990. A statistical approach to machine translation. *Computational linguistics*, 16(2):79–85.

Peter F Brown, Vincent J Della Pietra, Stephen A Della Pietra, and Robert L Mercer. 1993. The mathematics of statistical machine translation: Parameter estimation. *Computational linguistics*, 19(2):263–311.

Jiang Chen and Jian-Yun Nie. 2000. Parallel Web Text Mining for Cross-language IR. In *Content-Based Multimedia Information Access - Volume 1*, RIAO '00, pages 62–77, Paris, France, France. Centre des hautes tudes internationales d'informatique documentaire.

Jisong Chen, Rowena Chau, and Chung-Hsing Yeh. 2004. Discovering parallel text from the world wide web. In *Proceedings of the second workshop on Australasian information security, Data Mining and Web Intelligence, and Software Internationalisation-Volume 32*, pages 157–161. Australian Computer Society, Inc.

Thierry Etchegoyhen and Andoni Azpeitia. 2016. A Portable Method for Parallel and Comparable Document Alignment. *Baltic Journal of Modern Computing*, 4(2):243–255. *Special Issue: Proceedings of EAMT 2016*.

Pascale Fung and Percy Cheung. 2004. Mining Very Non-Parallel Corpora: Parallel Sentence and Lexicon Extraction via Bootstrapping and E.M. In *Proceedings of Empirical Methods in Natural Language Processing*, pages 57–63.

Radu Ion, Alexandru Ceauşu, and Elena Irimia. 2011. An expectation maximization algorithm for textual unit alignment. In *Proceedings of the 4th Workshop on Building and Using Comparable Corpora: Comparable Corpora and the Web*, pages 128–135. Association for Computational Linguistics.

Paul Jaccard. 1901. Distribution de la flore alpine dans le bassin des Dranses et dans quelques régions voisines. *Bulletin de la Société Vaudoise des Sciences Naturelles*, 37:241 – 272.

Philipp Koehn, Hieu Hoang, Alexandra Birch, Chris Callison-Burch, Marcello Federico, Nicola Bertoldi, Brooke Cowan, Wade Shen, Christine Moran, Richard Zens, et al. 2007. Moses: Open source toolkit for statistical machine translation. In *Proceedings of the 45th Annual Meeting of the ACL*, pages 177–180. Association for Computational Linguistics.

Bo Li and Eric Gaussier. 2013. Exploiting comparable corpora for lexicon extraction: Measuring and improving corpus quality. In *Building and Using Comparable Corpora*, pages 131–149. Springer.

Xiaoyi Ma and Mark Liberman. 1999. Bits: A method for bilingual text search over the web. In *Machine Translation Summit VII*, pages 538–542.

Dragos Stefan Munteanu and Daniel Marcu. 2005. Improving machine translation performance by exploiting non-parallel corpora. *Computational Linguistics*, 31(4):477–504.

Franz Josef Och and Hermann Ney. 2003. A systematic comparison of various statistical alignment models. *Computational linguistics*, 29(1):19–51.

Monica Lestari Paramita, David Guthrie, Evangelos Kanoulas, Rob Gaizauskas, Paul Clough, and Mark Sanderson. 2013. Methods for collection and evaluation of comparable documents. In *Building and Using Comparable Corpora*, pages 93–112. Springer.

Alexandre Patry and Philippe Langlais. 2005. Automatic identification of parallel documents with light or without linguistic resources. In *Proceedings of the 18th Canadian Society Conference on Advances in Artificial Intelligence*, AI'05, pages 354–365, Berlin, Heidelberg. Springer-Verlag.

Philip Resnik and Noah A Smith. 2003. The web as a parallel corpus. *Computational Linguistics*, 29(3):349–380.

Jörg Tiedemann. 2011. *Bitext Alignment*. Synthesis Lectures on Human Language Technologies. Morgan & Claypool Publishers.

Quick and Reliable Document Alignment via TF/IDF-weighted Cosine Distance

Christian Buck
University of Edinburgh
Edinburgh, Scotland
`christian.buck@ed.ac.uk`

Philipp Koehn
Center for Language and Speech Processing
Department of Computer Science
Johns Hopkins University, Baltimore, MD
`phi@jhu.edu`

Abstract

This work describes our submission to the WMT16 Bilingual Document Alignment task. We show that a very simple distance metric, namely Cosine distance of tf/idf weighted document vectors provides a quick and reliable way to align documents. We compare many possible variants for constructing the document vectors. We also introduce a greedy algorithm that runs quicker and performs better in practice than the optimal solution to bipartite graph matching. Our approach shows competitive performance and can be improved even further through combination with URL based pair matching.

1 Related Work

The process of finding bilingual data online has been investigated since the early days of the world wide web (Resnik, 1999). In this work we are concerned with the problem of finding pairs of documents, a problem that can be structured in the following steps:

1. **Candidate Generation** The naive approach of considering all possible pairs of websites is often not applicable on a web scale, even when limiting the scope to a single webdomain. To overcome computational complexity previous work has focused on (i) matching pairs of URLs (Resnik and Smith, 2003) by removing language identifiers such as `&lang=en` or `/fr/` from URLs, (ii) considering only documents that either link to each other or that share a *parent page* (Resnik, 1999) that links to them, (iii) following links on already aligned documents (Shi et al., 2006), (iv) querying a search engine for possible translations (Ruopp and Xia, 2008), and

(v) rephrasing the task as near-duplicate detection after translating all non-English content to English (Uszkoreit et al., 2010).

(Ture et al., 2011) map all document vectors into a target language space and use an approximation of cosine distance based on locally-sensitive hashing (LSH) together with a sliding window algorithm to efficiently collect similar pairs.

2. **Document alignment** After possible pairings have been generated any distance function that compares two documents can be used to remove unlikely candidates. Common choices include (i) edit-distance between linearized documents (Resnik and Smith, 2003) (ii) cosine distance of idf-weighted bigram vectors (Uszkoreit et al., 2010), and (iii) probability of a probabilistic DOM-tree alignment model (Shi et al., 2006).

2 Approach

In this work we deal mainly with the second problem, document alignment, and just allow all possible source/target pairings. Thus, the task can be formalized as such: We are given a set of possible pairings

$$C = \{(d_s, d_t) \mid d_s \in D_s, d_t \in D_t\}$$

where C is the set of candidates, $d_s \in D_s$ are source language documents and $d_t \in D_t$ are target language documents. The task is to find a subset of $C' = \{(d_{s,i}, d_{t,i}), \ldots\} \subset C$ such that $d_{s,i}$ is a translation of $d_{t,i}$ (and vice versa) and the number $|C'|$ of such pairings is maximized.

We consider all source/target pairings that come from the same webdomain so that $C = D_s \times D_t$. This yields a fully connected bipartite graph with

Proceedings of the First Conference on Machine Translation, Volume 2: Shared Task Papers, pages 672–678,
Berlin, Germany, August 11-12, 2016. ©2016 Association for Computational Linguistics

source and target pages being the partitions. By using a scoring function defined on edges the graph becomes weighted. We allow every page to occur not more than once in C', i.e. we do not allow $1{:}n$ or $m{:}1$ connections:

$$d_{s,i} = d_{s,j} \Leftrightarrow d_{t,i} = d_{t,j}$$
$$\forall\, (d_{s,i}, d_{t,i}), (d_{s,j}, d_{t,j}) \in C'$$

2.1 Selecting pairs

After computing a score for every edge of the bipartite graph, a matching of maximum weight can be found in $\mathcal{O}(\max(|D_s||D_t|)^3)$ by solving the assignment problem using the Kuhn-Munkres algorithm (Munkres, 1957). We expect every page of the non-dominant language to have a translated counterpart, thus $\min(|D_s|, |D_t|)$ pairs are generated.

In section 3.3, we compare the optimal assignment to a greedy solution by incrementally choosing the edge with the highest score and removing all other edges pointing to respective vertices. The greedy algorithm stops once no edges are left and produces the same number of pairs as the optimal solution but only requires $\mathcal{O}\left(|D_s||D_t| \times \log(|D_s||D_t|)\right)$ time to sort the score matrix.

3 Experiments

In total, the training dataset consists of 1624 document pairs from 49 web domains. The number of annotated aligned document pairs per web domain ranges from 4 to over 200.

Our experiments that led to the selection of the method used on the evaluation data are all based on a fixed and random split into train and development (dev) data: we split the data set into training (998 document pairs in 24 web domains) and test (626 document pairs in 25 web domains). The former is used for extensive experimentation, the latter to select the best approach for our shared task submission.

3.1 Performance considerations

Our approach requires us to produce a dense matrix of feature values which seems prohibitively expensive given the high number of possible pairings. In practice, even for the largest webdomains in our data, requiring the scoring of roughly 1B possible pairs, we are able to produce all values quickly enough that the run-time is dominated by I/O and preprocessing steps such as tokenization.

ngram size	$n = 1$	$n = 3$	$n = 5$
Number of unique n-grams			
Used for scoring	53k	1.2M	1.7M
Ignored because freq < 2	11k	351k	658k
Non-zero entries in (sparse) document matrix			
Source (English)	1.5M	5.7M	6.1M
Target (French)	0.4M	1.4M	1.4M
Time per processing step (single-threaded)			
Read tokenized corpus	117s	117s	117s
IDF estimation	15s	26s	30s
Document vectors	33s	86s	91s
Pairwise distances	8s	11s	20s

Table 1: Runtime details for generation of 971M pairwise cosine similarity features for n-grams of size $\{1, 3, 5\}$ on `virtualhospice.ca`. N-grams which occur fewer than 2 times are filtered from the corpus. Single-threaded execution on 2.66Ghz Xeon CPU.

As can be seen from Table 1, a total of 1.2M 3-grams types are used for scoring pages from `virtualhospice.ca` which holds 43.5k English and 22.3k French pages. Loading the corpus, estimating the idf weights, and populating the sparse document matrices with roughly 7M entries both take about 2 minutes. On the other hand, producing the $43.5k \times 22.3k = 971M$ pairwise distances only accounts for 11 seconds.

Speed and, more importantly, memory consumption can be further improved by pruning all n-grams that occur fewer times than a set threshold in the corpus. We find empirically that maintaining a very low minimum count cutoff somewhere below 10 is crucial for maintaining high recall, as shown in Figure 1.

3.2 TF-IDF weighting

In the literature (Manning et al., 2008) a number of different weighting schemes based on tf/idf have been proposed with the overall goal to assign lower scores to terms (or n-grams) that are less discriminatory for document comparison.

However, these approaches usually aim at document retrieval, i.e. finding relevant documents given a large (in comparison to the overall document size) number of search terms. In the setting of near duplicate detection, our *query* is a complete document and other weighting schemes may apply.

To empirically evaluate the fitness of different approaches we implement the following weighting schemes for term frequency (tf).

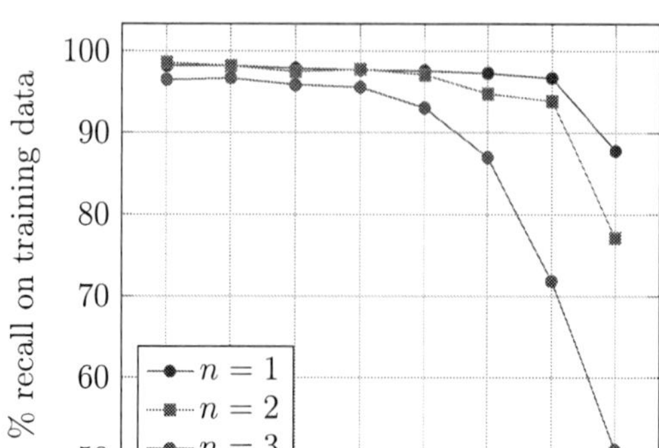

Greedy matching with MT

Figure 1: Recall on training set using varying minimum counts of n-grams in the corpus. N-grams seen fewer times than the threshold are ignored when building the document vectors.

In every case we define

$$\mathrm{tf}(w_1^n, d) = 0 \text{ if } w_1^n \notin d$$

and give the other case below:

$$\mathrm{tf}_1(w_1^n, d) = 1 \tag{1}$$

$$\mathrm{tf}_2(w_1^n, d) = \mathrm{freq}(w_1^n, d) \tag{2}$$

$$\mathrm{tf}_3(w_1^n, d) = 1 + log\left(\mathrm{freq}(w_1^n, d)\right) \tag{3}$$

$$\mathrm{tf}_4(w_1^n, d) = .4 + .6\frac{\mathrm{freq}(w_1^n, d)}{max_{w_1'^n} \mathrm{freq}(w_1'^n, d)} \tag{4}$$

$$\mathrm{tf}_5(w_1^n, d) = \frac{\mathrm{freq}(w_1^n, d)}{max_{(\bar{w}_1^n, \bar{d})} \mathrm{freq}(\bar{w}_1^n, \bar{d})} \tag{5}$$

$$\mathrm{tf}_6(w_1^n, d) = \sqrt{\mathrm{freq}(w_1^n, d)} \tag{6}$$

In the same way we implement weighting schemes for inverse document frequency $\mathrm{idf}(w_1^n, D_s, D_t) = idf(\cdot)$:

$$\mathrm{idf}_1(\cdot) = 1 \tag{7}$$

$$\mathrm{idf}_2(\cdot) = \frac{|D_s \cup D_t|}{1 + \mathrm{df}(w_1^n, D)} \tag{8}$$

$$\mathrm{idf}_3(\cdot) = log\left(1 + \frac{max_{\bar{w}_1^n} \mathrm{df}(\bar{w}_1^n, D)}{\mathrm{df}(w_1^n, D)}\right) \tag{9}$$

$$\mathrm{idf}_4(\cdot) = log\left(1 + \frac{|D_s \cup D_t|}{\mathrm{df}(w_1^n, D)}\right) \tag{10}$$

$$\mathrm{idf}_5(\cdot) = max\left(0, log\frac{|D_s \cup D_t| - \mathrm{df}(w_1^n, D)}{\mathrm{df}(w_1^n, D)}\right) \tag{11}$$

$$\mathrm{idf}_6(\cdot) = 1 + log\frac{|D_s \cup D_t|}{1 + \mathrm{df}(w_1^n, D)} \tag{12}$$

where $D = D_s \cup D_t$ and

$$\mathrm{df}(w_1^n, D) = |\{d \in D \mid w_1^n \in d\}|$$

Slight variations of the above definitions can be found in the wild, for example the search engine Apache Lucene[1] uses tf_6 and idf_6 but uses $1 + |D_s \cup D_t|$ in the numerator since version 6.

We evaluate the cross product of weighting schemes using the train and dev splits as described above. Looking at the results in Tables 2 and 3, a number of interesting observations can be made:

1. Performance differs between train and dev data, with results on the training portion of the data being several percents better. This indicates a skew in the data distribution which is surprising given that the web-domains were selected beforehand. We know from the training data that about $\frac{1}{4}$ of the known pairs, 236 of 998, are found in a single webdomain *tsb.gc.ca* which could explain the skew. However, the difference remains if that large webdomain is removed.

   Further investigation reveals that the underlying cause of poor performance on the dev set can be attributed to three webdomains that contain near duplicates, such as the same main content but interface elements in a different language.

2. When choosing the optimal length of scoring n-grams, shorter is better. Good recall can be achieved using 1-grams for the monolingual

---

case where no machine translated (MT) data is used and 1-grams or 2-grams for the case where all French data is translated to English beforehand.

3. In tf-idf weighting the inverse document frequency acts as an indicator of a term's importance. This is important in the case of information retrieval where query words differ in utility. In the duplicate detection setting idf weights play a less important role and a common choice such as idf_3 defined in Equation 9 can be used throughout.

4. Results produced by using only the untranslated text, a configuration that requires no bilingual resources and little computational resources, are better than we expected: only between 5% (for train) and 8% (for dev) below the recall achieved using machine translated texts. In this case we just ignore that two pages are written in different languages and only rely on untranslated parts such as boilerplate, names, and numbers to provide sufficient cues.

For our submission we used the machine translated text provided by the organizers and chose $n = 2$, tf_4 (Equation 4), and idf_3 (Equation 9).

3.3 Greedy vs. optimal solution

We found that producing the optimal solution for the assignment problem using the Kuhn-Munkres algorithm (Munkres, 1957) was slightly worse in almost all cases. We hypothesize that by maximizing the aggregate score for all selected pairs the low-scoring pairs for which no matching document exists are over-emphasized. To test this hypothesis we compare the scores of the selected pairs for both algorithms: For each webdomain we sort the selected pairs by their score and select, for each algorithm, the n top scoring pairs:

Let $s(d_s, d_t)$ be our scoring function, in this case we use Cosine similarity, and let

$$(d_{s,g_1}, d_{t,g_1}), \ldots, (d_{s,g_N}, d_{t,g_N})$$

be the document pairs selected by the greedy algorithm and, likewise,

$$(d_{s,o_1}, d_{t,o_1}), \ldots, (d_{s,o_N}, d_{t,o_N})$$

those selected by the optimal algorithm. Let these pairs be sorted by score such that

$$s(d_{s,g_i}, d_{t,g_i}) \geq s(d_{s,g_{i+1}}, d_{t,g_{i+1}}) \; \forall i$$

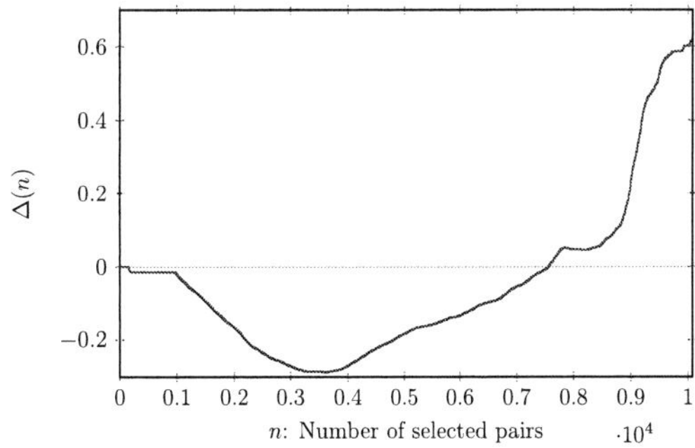

Figure 2: Difference in accumulated cosine distances between greedy and optimal algorithm. For more than the first half of the selected pairs, the greedy algorithm overall outperforms the optimal one, indicated by a negative $\Delta(n)$.

and

$$s(d_{s,o_i}, d_{t,o_i}) \geq s(d_{s,o_{i+1}}, d_{t,o_{i+1}}) \; \forall i$$

Let $\Delta(n)$ be the accumulated difference of scores for the first n pairs:

$$\Delta(n) = \sum_{i=1}^{n} s(d_{s,o_i}, d_{t,o_i}) - s(d_{s,g_i}, d_{t,g_i}) \quad (13)$$

Since the greedy algorithm is not necessarily optimal we know that $\Delta(N) \geq 0$. However, as can be seen from Figure 2, the greedy selection of the best scoring pairs outperforms the Kuhn-Munkres algorithm for the top-scoring half, confirming our assumption that lower scoring pairs are selected in order to find better scoring matches for the documents without a counterpart.

We note that even after selecting $10\,000$ pairs, the accumulated difference is comparatively small, hinting that very similar sets have been selected. Figure 3 shows the Jaccard Similarity between the top n pairs

$$P_g(n) = \{(d_{s,g_i}, d_{t,g_i}) | 1 \leq i \leq n\} \quad (14)$$
$$P_o(n) = \{(d_{s,o_i}, d_{t,o_i}) | 1 \leq i \leq n\} \quad (15)$$

for both algorithms. The Figure confirms that either approach selects virtually the same set of pairs for low numbers of n.

Thus, the globally optimal solution is not only expensive to compute but also very similar to the greedy selection and it outperforms the greedy algorithm mostly for pairs in the tail that are likely misaligned anyways, because no translated page exists. Hence, all our reported results use the greedy selection introduced in Section 2.1.

n		idf$_1$	idf$_2$	idf$_3$	idf$_4$	idf$_5$	idf$_6$	idf$_1$	idf$_2$	idf$_3$	idf$_4$	idf$_5$	idf$_6$
1	tf$_1$	90.4	93.5	93.9	93.9	93.9	93.4	86.1	86.1	86.3	86.1	86.3	85.9
	tf$_2$	65.5	83.7	80.6	81.7	81.2	83.5	69.5	80.8	80.7	80.8	81.0	80.7
	tf$_3$	86.8	91.3	92.0	92.1	91.8	91.4	83.4	85.0	84.8	84.8	84.3	85.1
	tf$_4$	88.7	**92.9**	**93.5**	**93.4**	**93.6**	92.9	86.6	**87.2**	**87.2**	**87.1**	**86.7**	**87.1**
	tf$_5$	65.5	83.7	80.6	81.7	81.2	83.5	69.3	80.8	80.7	80.8	81.0	80.7
	tf$_6$	65.6	83.7	80.5	81.6	81.2	83.5	68.8	80.2	80.4	81.0	80.8	80.2
2	tf$_1$	76.6	84.9	84.0	84.7	85.5	84.9	78.1	81.5	81.5	81.3	81.5	81.0
	tf$_2$	70.3	81.1	80.5	80.7	81.3	80.4	70.8	76.0	75.6	75.7	76.5	75.2
	tf$_3$	76.0	83.2	82.6	83.2	83.6	83.0	75.1	79.9	79.4	79.7	80.2	79.6
	tf$_4$	76.1	84.3	83.7	84.0	85.1	84.2	77.8	80.5	80.5	80.7	80.7	80.0
	tf$_5$	70.3	81.1	80.5	80.7	81.3	80.4	70.8	76.0	75.6	75.7	76.5	75.2
	tf$_6$	70.3	81.1	80.5	80.7	81.3	80.4	70.8	76.0	75.6	75.7	76.5	75.2
3	tf$_1$	65.7	72.2	71.7	72.3	72.6	72.0	64.9	65.3	65.3	65.8	65.2	65.2
	tf$_2$	62.7	70.5	70.0	70.3	70.6	70.1	61.2	63.6	63.3	63.7	63.4	63.6
	tf$_3$	65.3	71.8	71.4	71.6	72.0	71.2	62.9	64.5	64.9	64.9	64.2	65.0
	tf$_4$	65.1	71.9	71.7	71.9	72.5	71.7	63.4	65.8	66.0	66.0	65.7	66.0
	tf$_5$	62.7	70.5	70.0	70.3	70.6	70.1	61.2	63.6	63.3	63.7	63.4	63.6
	tf$_6$	62.7	70.5	70.0	70.3	70.6	70.1	61.3	63.6	63.3	63.7	63.4	63.6
4	tf$_1$	59.0	63.2	63.0	63.4	63.7	63.4	56.5	57.5	57.5	57.7	57.2	57.3
	tf$_2$	58.1	63.6	62.9	63.6	63.7	63.3	55.1	56.5	56.2	56.7	56.5	56.4
	tf$_3$	58.5	63.1	62.9	63.6	63.7	63.3	56.2	57.7	58.0	58.3	57.7	57.7
	tf$_4$	58.6	63.3	63.0	63.3	63.6	63.1	56.7	58.1	58.1	58.3	57.7	57.7
	tf$_5$	58.1	63.6	62.9	63.6	63.7	63.3	55.1	56.5	56.2	56.7	56.5	56.4
	tf$_6$	58.1	63.6	62.9	63.6	63.7	63.3	55.1	56.7	56.2	56.7	56.7	56.4

Table 2: Recall on train (left) and dev (right) split of the training data using different tf/idf weighting schemes and only *untranslated* text.

n		idf$_1$	idf$_2$	idf$_3$	idf$_4$	idf$_5$	idf$_6$	idf$_1$	idf$_2$	idf$_3$	idf$_4$	idf$_5$	idf$_6$
1	tf$_1$	97.7	97.9	97.9	97.9	97.9	97.9	89.8	89.8	89.8	86.7	89.8	89.8
	tf$_2$	93.1	94.8	94.8	94.8	91.0	94.8	88.2	89.9	89.9	89.9	87.5	89.9
	tf$_3$	97.9	97.7	97.7	97.8	97.7	97.8	89.8	90.4	90.4	90.4	90.6	90.4
	tf$_4$	97.9	**98.2**	**98.2**	**98.2**	**98.2**	98.2	89.6	89.1	89.1	89.1	89.1	89.1
	tf$_5$	93.2	94.9	94.9	94.9	91.1	94.9	88.2	89.9	89.8	89.9	87.5	89.9
	tf$_6$	93.4	94.9	95.1	94.9	91.1	95.1	88.5	89.9	89.5	89.5	86.9	90.3
2	tf$_1$	97.9	98.2	98.2	98.2	98.2	98.2	94.2	94.7	94.7	94.9	94.7	94.6
	tf$_2$	95.5	96.8	96.8	96.8	96.8	96.8	92.8	93.9	93.9	94.1	93.9	93.6
	tf$_3$	97.7	98.1	**98.2**	**98.2**	98.1	**98.3**	94.1	**95.4**	**95.4**	**95.4**	**95.4**	95.2
	tf$_4$	97.8	**98.2**	**98.2**	**98.2**	**98.2**	**98.3**	94.1	95.0	95.0	95.0	95.0	94.9
	tf$_5$	95.5	96.8	96.8	96.8	96.8	96.8	92.8	93.9	93.9	94.1	93.9	93.6
	tf$_6$	95.4	96.8	96.8	96.8	96.8	96.8	93.0	94.1	94.1	94.2	93.9	93.6
3	tf$_1$	96.6	96.9	96.9	96.8	96.9	96.9	94.1	93.5	93.5	93.5	93.5	93.5
	tf$_2$	95.3	96.1	96.1	96.1	96.1	96.1	92.3	93.5	93.5	93.3	93.5	93.5
	tf$_3$	96.2	96.5	96.5	96.5	96.5	96.5	93.6	93.6	93.6	93.6	93.6	93.6
	tf$_4$	96.5	96.7	96.7	96.7	96.7	96.7	93.8	93.5	93.5	93.5	93.5	93.5
	tf$_5$	95.4	96.1	96.1	96.1	96.1	96.1	92.3	93.5	93.5	93.3	93.5	93.5
	tf$_6$	95.2	96.1	96.1	96.1	96.1	96.1	92.7	93.5	93.5	93.5	93.5	93.6
4	tf$_1$	95.0	96.1	96.0	96.0	96.0	96.1	93.3	93.6	93.6	93.6	93.6	93.6
	tf$_2$	94.5	96.3	96.3	96.3	96.3	96.3	91.7	92.5	92.5	92.5	92.5	92.5
	tf$_3$	95.1	96.2	96.1	96.1	96.1	96.1	93.0	93.1	93.1	92.7	93.0	93.3
	tf$_4$	95.0	96.0	95.9	95.9	95.9	96.0	93.5	93.5	93.5	93.5	93.5	93.6
	tf$_5$	94.5	96.3	96.3	96.3	96.3	96.3	91.7	92.5	92.5	92.5	92.5	92.5
	tf$_6$	94.5	96.3	96.3	96.3	96.3	96.3	91.5	92.8	92.5	92.7	92.8	92.5

Table 3: Recall on train (left) and dev (right) split of the training data using different tf/idf weighting schemes to compare English and machine translated French text.

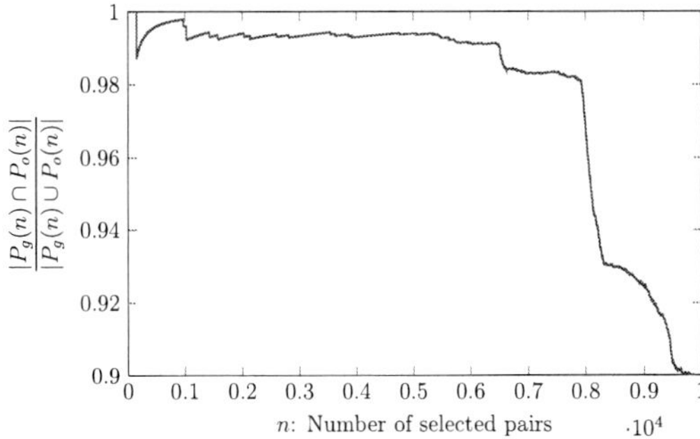

Figure 3: Jaccard Similarity between the top-n pairs selected by greedy and Kuhn-Munkres algorithm.

4 Results

The test data for the shared task consists of 203 crawled websites that are all distinct from the training set. No additional known pairs are provided for these webdomains, but the organizers offer translations of French text into English, as for the training data. As above, performance in evaluated via recall under the condition that every document can only be part of a single pair. The number of pages per domain varies wildly between 9 and almost 100k. In the latter case, 50k pairs need to be picked from roughly 2.5B possibilities. After some preprocessing such as tokenization we produce 368 260 pairs using greedy selection and cosine distance as explained above. For all webdomains this takes less than 4h on a single machine.

In total, 13 research teams contributed 21 submissions to the shared task. The official results can be found in Table 4. Our submission ranks on 3rd place. We would like to point out that, apart from selecting the best performing tf/idf weighting method, the training data is not used at all. Thus, besides a baseline machine translation system no additional resources are needed, which makes our approach widely applicable.

A baseline system based on matching URL patterns such as `site.com/home-fr/` and `site.com/home/en/` as used in previous work (Resnik and Smith, 2003; Smith et al., 2013) is provided by the organizers. We combine our approach and the Baseline by simply selecting all 148 537 baseline pairs first. While not on official submission, Table 4 shows that this combination outperforms all other systems.

Name	Recall %	Found
NovaLincs-url-coverage	94.96	2 281
YODA	93.92	2 256
UEdin1_cosine	**89.09**	**2 140**
NovaLincs-coverage	88.63	2 129
DOCAL	88.59	2 128
UEdin2_LSI-v2	87.64	2 105
UEdin2_LSI	85.85	2 062
NovaLincs-coverage-url	85.76	2 060
ILSP-ARC-pv42	84.93	2 040
UFAL-4	84.22	2 023
YSDA	84.14	2 021
UA_PROMPSIT_bitextor_5.0	83.31	2 001
UFAL-1	81.31	1 953
UFAL-3	80.68	1 938
Meved	79.39	1 907
Jakubina-Langlais	79.31	1 905
UFAL-2	79.14	1 901
UA_PROMPSIT_bitextor_4.1	31.14	748
ADAPT	27.10	651
ADAPT-v2	26.81	644
JIS	2.00	48
Baseline	59.78	1 436
Baseline + UEdin1_cosine[†]	**96.21**	**2 311**

Table 4: Official results on the shared task test data. Results described in this work are fat. Across all webdomains a total of 2402 known pairs were to be found. ([†]) indicates a non-official result that was produced post-submission.

5 Conclusion

We present a comparison of tf/idf weighting schemes for comparison of original and translated documents via cosine distance. We find that the right choice of term-frequence (tf) weighting is crucial in this setting, along with the inclusion of low-frequency words.

We compare a greedy selection algorithm to a computationally more expensive solution which yields a slightly better global solution. We can show that the former often outperforms the latter in practical settings where a tail of un-pairable document exits.

Our best results are based on machine translated documents. However, even when ignoring the fact that two documents are written, at least partially, in different languages, we are still able to discover a substantial number of parallel pages.

Results of the shared task show that our approach, which only uses the website's text, yields competitive results. Results improve further when our predictions are combined with pairs found via URL matching.

References

[Manning et al.2008] Christopher D. Manning, Prabhakar Raghavan, and Hinrich Schtze. 2008. *Introduction to Information Retrieval*. Cambridge University Press, New York.

[Munkres1957] James Munkres. 1957. Algorithms for the assignment and transportation problems. *Journal of the Society for Industrial and Applied Mathematics*, 5(1):32–38.

[Resnik and Smith2003] Philip Resnik and Noah A Smith. 2003. The web as a parallel corpus. *Computational Linguistics*, 29(3):349–380.

[Resnik1999] Philip Resnik. 1999. Mining the web for bilingual text. In *Proceedings of the 37th Annual Meeting of the Association for Computational Linguistics on Computational Linguistics*, ACL '99, pages 527–534, Stroudsburg, PA, USA. Association for Computational Linguistics.

[Ruopp and Xia2008] Achim Ruopp and Fei Xia. 2008. Finding parallel texts on the web using cross-language information retrieval. In *IJCNLP*, pages 18–25.

[Shi et al.2006] Lei Shi, Cheng Niu, Ming Zhou, and Jianfeng Gao. 2006. A dom tree alignment model for mining parallel data from the web. In *Proceedings of the 21st International Conference on Computational Linguistics and the 44th annual meeting of the Association for Computational Linguistics*, pages 489–496. Association for Computational Linguistics.

[Smith et al.2013] Jason Smith, Hervé Saint-Amand, Magdalena Plamada, Philipp Koehn, Chris Callison-Burch, and Adam Lopez. 2013. Dirt cheap web-scale parallel text from the common crawl. In *Proceedings of ACL*. Association for Computational Linguistics, August.

[Ture et al.2011] Ferhan Ture, Tamer Elsayed, and Jimmy Lin. 2011. No free lunch: Brute force vs. locality-sensitive hashing for cross-lingual pairwise similarity. In *Proceedings of the 34th international ACM SIGIR conference on Research and development in Information Retrieval*, pages 943–952. ACM.

[Uszkoreit et al.2010] Jakob Uszkoreit, Jay M Ponte, Ashok C Popat, and Moshe Dubiner. 2010. Large scale parallel document mining for machine translation. In *Proceedings of the 23rd International Conference on Computational Linguistics*, pages 1101–1109. Association for Computational Linguistics.

YODA System for WMT16 Shared Task: Bilingual Document Alignment

Aswarth Abhilash Dara and **Yiu-Chang Lin**
Language Technologies Institute
Carnegie Mellon University
5000 Forbes Ave, Pittsburgh, PA 15213, USA
{adara, yiuchanl}@cs.cmu.edu

Abstract

In this paper, we address the task of automatically aligning/detecting the bilingual documents that are translations of each other from a single web-domain as part of WMT 2016. [1] Given the large amounts of data available in each web-domain, a brute force approach like finding similarities between every possible pair is a computationally expensive operation. Therefore, we start with a simple approach on matching just the web page urls after some pre-processing to reduce the number of possible pairings to a small extent. This simple approach obtained a recall of 50% and the exact matches from this approach are removed from further consideration. We built on top of this using an n-gram based approach that uses the partial English translations of French web pages and achieved a recall of 93.71% on the training pairs provided. We also outline an IR-based approach that uses both content and the meta data of each web page url, thereby obtaining a recall of 56.31%. Our final submission to this shared task using n-gram based approach achieved a recall of 93.92%.

1 Introduction

Statistical Machine Translation systems rely a lot on the availability of parallel corpora and the automatic collection of such data so far has been ad hoc and limited in scale. In this paper, we would like to tackle the problem of aligning bilingual documents from crawled websites which is presented as one of the new shared tasks introduced at WMT 2016 i.e., the task of identifying pairs of English

and French documents from a given collection of documents such that one document is a translation of another. For each web-domain, we consider all the possible pairs for which the source side has been identified as English and the target side as French. 1,624 EN-FR pairs from 49 web-domains are provided as training data. The number of pairs per web-domain varies between 4 and over 200. All pairs are from within a single web-domain and possible matches between two different web-domains e.g. siemens.de and siemens.com are not considered in this task.

Mirrors of all the web pages in each domain which were crawled using httrack are provided. Each page has the following information: Language ID (e.g. en), Mime type (always text/html), Encoding (always charset=utf-8), URL, HTML in Base64 encoding and Text in Base64 encoding. Additionally, the English translations of French pages using MT for identified spans of text were produced by the organizers. However, it doesn't imply that we have full translations for each and every French web page. In other words, we only have partial translations for a random subset of French web pages.

Table 1 shows the various statistics of the training data set. Among 49 web-domains, *www.nauticnews.com* has the most possible pairings, 1,047,069,625, while *schackportalen.nu* has the least ones, 957. Each web-domain has roughly 87 million pairs on average.

The rest of the paper is organized as follows: Section 2 discusses the various challenges involved in this task. Section 3 gives an overview of the related work happened. The methodology and implementation details are provided in Section 4. Section 5 covers evaluation, results and analysis of the errors on the training data set given. Section 6 concludes the paper with possible future directions

---

[1] http://www.statmt.org/wmt16/bilingual-task.html

Proceedings of the First Conference on Machine Translation, Volume 2: Shared Task Papers, pages 679–684,
Berlin, Germany, August 11-12, 2016. ©2016 Association for Computational Linguistics

Web-Domain	Source Pages	Target Pages	Possible Pairings	Train Pairs Provided
www.nauticnews.com	24,325	43,045	1,047,069,625	21
schackportalen.nu	33	29	957	14
Average	7,119	4,592	86,663,689	33

Table 1: Various statistics on the training data. The first row shows the web-domain with most possible pairs and the second row shows the web-domain with the least possible pairs. The last row is the average statistics across 49 domains.

for this work.

2   Challenges

There are various challenges involved in dealing with the bilingual document alignment task and are as follows.

- The primary challenge is that the space of possible pairings is so huge that it is almost impossible to use any brute force approach for comparing every two documents from the source and target with any similarity metric. As shown in Table 1, the largest number of possible pairs come from a single domain in the training set is 1,047,069,625 whereas in the testing set, it comes from cinedoc.org which contains 2,444,607,480 pairs (around 2.4 billion pairs).

- Another challenge involves in obtaining the full translations on either source or target side (even if we restrict ourselves to first n-words in each page) is an expensive operation given the large amounts of processing data.

- Another approach in training the domain specific MT model for each of the 49 web-domains given only 1,624 training pairs is not encouraging because of the less availability of training data in each domain. Even if we train, it will not provide any advantage because the testing set web-domains are completely distinct from the training set.

- In addition to this, even if partial translations of the documents on target side are provided, making the most use of them is a crucial issue.

- Furthermore, documents vary in length and no positional information of these translations provided are available.

3   Related Work

In general, most statistical parallel corpus alignment works have focused on the sentence and vocabulary level. Kay and Röscheisen (1993) proposed to align texts with their translations that is based only on internal evidence. The idea of iterating the process of sentence level alignment with the results of vocabulary level alignment reinforce the certainty of both. More specifically, it exploits a partial alignment of the word level to induce a maximum likelihood alignment of the sentence level, which is in turn used in the next iteration, to refine the word level estimate. The algorithm appears to converge to the correct sentence alignment in only a few iterations.

Gale and Church (1991) focused their attention on robust statistics that tends to keep errors of commission low. They introduced a measurement of association between a pair of words based on a two by two contingency table and obtained bilingual vocabularies by presenting the co-occurrence statistics. Melamed (1999) used advanced bi-text mapping by formulating the problem in terms of pattern recognition where the success of a bi-text mapping algorithm lies in how well it performs in these three tasks: signal generation, noise filtering, and search. The proposed Smooth Injective Map Recognizer (SIMR) algorithm integrates innovative approaches to each of these tasks.

There are also works focusing on combining information from both sentence and vocabulary alignments (Moore, 2002), which combined Sentence length based methods and Word correspondence based methods for aligning sentences with their translations in a parallel bilingual corpus. It achieved a high accuracy at a modest computational cost, and required no knowledge of the languages or the corpus beyond division into words and sentences. Nazar (2011) presented a language independent algorithm for the alignment of parallel corpora at the document, sentence ad vocabulary levels. The process consists of the following phases: aligning documents with their corresponding translations, aligning sentences inside each pair of selected documents and finally, generating a bilingual vocabulary. For large scale document level alignment, Uszkoreit et al., (2010) proposed a distributed system that reliably mines parallel text from large corpora. In contrast to other approaches which require specific meta data, the system uses only the textual information. In this paper, we take inspiration from this approach and add some interesting heuristics on top of it to obtain a good recall.

Another family of work is to learn an intermediate document representation between documents from the source and target side where similar intermediate concepts are closely projected. There are various kinds of such deep learning models, for example, Deep Structured Semantic Models (Huang et al., 2013), Deep Boltzmann Machines (Salakhutdinov and Hinton, 2009), Stacked Denoising Autoencoder (Vincent et al., 2010), Encoder-Decoder (Cho et al., 2014) and Deep Canonical Component Analysis (Andrew et al., 2013). However, we have not tried any of these deep learning approaches as part of our experiments due to the limited availability of the training data.

4 Methodology

4.1 Baseline

The task organizers provided a baseline approach which uses only the meta data related to url of the web page like stripping the language identifiers etc. and reported the performance on the training data set. The code for the same is available on github.[2] Initially, we thought of building our models on top of this baseline, however the pairs they generate are not exact matches which serves as a main bottleneck in reducing the number of possible pairings.

4.2 Brute Force and URL Patterns Approach

For this task, the training data set consists of 1,624 English-French pairs from 49 web-domains. A straight forward approach is to simply model this as a binary classification problem where 1 indicates that two documents are translations of each other and 0 indicates that they are not. The 1,624 actual training set will become $1,624 \times$

$1,624$ pseudo training set that can be used to train a skewed classification model. The features can be from the baseline (meta data related to the urls), Machine Translation features (translating the source side and comparing with the possible candidates in the target side using MT evaluation metrics like BLEU (Papineni et al., 2002), METEOR (Lavie and Denkowski, 2009), TER (Snover et al., 2006) and also the features can be generated using standard metrics in document-similarity literature). However, due to the quadratic complexity of considering the similarity between every possible pair, we didn't pursue this approach. Also, lack intersection between the training and testing set web-domains add additional problems. Instead, we used a very simple baseline approach based on web page url matching to reduce the space of the number of possible pairings to be considered. We call this approach as URL Patterns.

For every source web page url, we first tokenize this url using the NLTK toolkit [3] and replace the word 'en' (if exists) with 'fr'. We reconstruct the url back and call it as a normalized url. Then, we search for this normalized url in the list of possible target urls and if it exists, we treat them as a possible pair and remove both of them for further consideration. This is a simple approach, however when we evaluated this approach on the training set given, we got around 50% recall. The following approaches are built on top of this simple approach.

4.3 Information Retrieval based Approach

The bilingual document alignment task could be viewed as an Information Retrieval problem where our goal is to retrieve the most relevant document on the source or target side given one from the other side. More specifically, for each French document, we extract queries from its provided English translation and search through all the English documents in the same domain. The one with the highest retrieval score is aligned to that French document. The IR framework implementation is done by the following steps with the use of Whoosh library.[4] First we built indices for every English web page. Second, for each French web page, the query generator extracts all possible trigrams from every sentence but remove those con-

---

[2]https://github.com/christianbuck/wmt16-document-alignment-task.git

[3]http://www.nltk.org/
[4]https://whoosh.readthedocs.io/en/latest/

taining punctuation, numbers or stop words. Finally, re-ranking is performed by comparing the degree of difference between the tokenized target url and the tokenized source urls. After the re-ranking, we pick the top-most result as the possible candidate and we treat this as the output for that source url.

4.4 N-gram based approach

In this approach, we used the partial English translations provided by task organizers for French web pages.[5] For this particular approach, without loss of generality, we consider French as the source and English as the target. The approach has been inspired from the approach mentioned in (Uszkoreit et al., 2010) and some of the best settings are borrowed with a different set of heuristics. As we are using partial English translations for French web pages and the target is in English, now we have both source and target sides in English language. Two types of indexes are built i.e., forward index and inverted index. Inverted index is built for both bi-grams and 5-grams where the key is either a bi-gram or a 5-gram and the posting list contains web page urls of both English and French web pages. A forward index is built where key is the web page url and the posting list contains the list of bi-grams [6] present in that web page url. This forward index is the one that is used for scoring the similarity between a source and target language web page pair.

The inverted index built based on 5-gram is used for generating the list of possible candidate pairs between both source and target side. Before the generation, we use some heuristics to remove some of the 5-grams that are to be considered. If the size of the posting list of any 5-gram is one, it means that this particular 5-gram is present in only one language and we can safely disregard them from consideration. We also remove the frequent 5-grams for consideration if the posting list of any 5-gram exceeds a certain threshold. Empirically, we found that threshold is 0.1. Similarly, using the inverted index for bi-grams, we propagate the document frequency of a bi-gram into the forward index thereby calculating the inverse document fre-

quency (idf) for this bi-gram. Now, in the forward index, for each web page, we have the list of bi-grams along with the *idf* of each bi-gram which can be used for scoring the cosine similarity between a pair of source and target web page. After this, for each 5-gram, we split the list into French and English web pages and form every possible pair as the candidates. The size of the possible candidate pairs obtained is still large and therefore we use another heuristic to reduce the computational space i.e., document length ratio. Given that the size of the English and French documents won't differ too much, we removed the candidate pairs if the ratio of the document length between the original French and English web pages is less than 0.5. [7] After applying all these, We noticed that the size of the possible candidates generated for all French web pages in each domain is around 1% of the all the possible pairings considered initially. This is a significant reduction in the number of possible pairings that are to be considered thus making the approach computationally feasible.

Finally, given a list of possible English web pages for each French web page, we compute the cosine similarity between the French web page and English web page. If we simply pick the maximum one for each French web page, then there exists a possibility that the English web page we pick may occur subsequently for some other French web page. However, there is a strict constraint enforced by the task organizers that each source web page can be aligned to only target web page and each target web page can get aligned only once. In order to enforce this constraint, we use a simple greedy approach where we first compute the cosine similarities between each French web page and list of possible candidates. Then, we pick the maximum scored pair out of all the possible pairs, and output it and remove it from further consideration. We repeat the same process until all the source side web pages are processed. We submitted our results on the testing data set using this approach to the shared task after conducting various experiments.

5 Evaluation and Results

The evaluation for this problem has been well defined in terms of recall as part of the shared task i.e., what percentage of the test-set pairs are found

---

[5]Since the translations of text spans are provided, we simply concatenate all partial text spans and translations in the same order provided for each web page before computing the n-grams.

[6]Empirically determined by experimenting with different n-grams on a subset of training data set provided.

[7]We empirically arrived at this threshold by experimenting with different values

Approach	Baseline	URL Patterns	IR-based	n-gram based
Recall	67.92	50.00	56.31	**93.71**

Table 2: Recall on the training set pairs using different approaches

on the predicted test pairs after enforcing the 1-1 rule (each source web page will be matched with at most one target web page and later occurrences of the source web pages are excluded from the evaluation). The performance of the model will be tuned on the training data set provided by the shared task organizers. The performance on the training data set (1624 pairs) is listed in Table 2.

As we observe in Table 2, the IR-based approach didn't work well and in fact it performed worse than the baseline provided by the task organizers. On the other hand, the n-gram based approach worked very well with a recall of 93.71%. We found that out of 49 web-domains, we got a recall of 100% in 31 web-domains. We have also performed an error analysis on the incorrect pairs to get a good understanding of the errors produced by the n-gram based approach. Based on our analysis, it has been found that relying mainly alone on the cosine similarity between a pair of possible candidate pairs is not itself alone, and have to do some re-ranking after computing the initial cosine similarity.

One of the interesting observations we made when looking at the errors is sometimes there exists no one-to-one correspondence between the source web page and target web page. This happens if a target web page is split into multiple target web pages and given only the availability of partial translations, aligning the source web page to maximum similar target web page requires some additional information. Since we only have the partial translations, there is no positional information of each n-gram which will be very useful in calculating the similarity metric. Most of these errors can be easily mitigated if we were provided the entire translation of each French web page instead of providing translations only for some text spans. However, obtaining the full translations for each and every web page is computationally intensive.

We submitted our results on the test set to this shared task using the best approach that is based on n-grams. Our system obtained a recall of 93.92%. It would be very interesting to see how these results change once the re-ranking phase is successfully implemented which serves as a promising future direction.

6 Conclusions and Future Directions

In this paper, we tackled the task of automatically aligning/detecting the bilingual (English and French) documents. With a simple approach of matching urls, we obtained around a recall of 50%. Using an n-gram based approach with interesting heuristics on top of it, we got a recall of around 93.71% and 93.92% on the training and testing data sets respectively.

The future directions for this work include systematically looking at where the errors occurred and increase the performance further. The re-ranking phase using word/document embeddings, structure of the the html document and a lot of other information serves as a straightforward extension to this paper. Another possible direction could be given a web page url as an input, how can we translate it effectively and if the translated url exists in the possible candidates, we can safely remove those pairs from further consideration. However, how to effectively tokenize and translate a web page url is still an interesting question to answer.

References

Galen Andrew, Raman Arora, Jeff Bilmes, and Karen Livescu. 2013. Deep canonical correlation analysis. In *Proceedings of the 30th International Conference on Machine Learning*, pages 1247–1255.

Kyunghyun Cho, Bart Van Merriënboer, Caglar Gulcehre, Dzmitry Bahdanau, Fethi Bougares, Holger Schwenk, and Yoshua Bengio. 2014. Learning phrase representations using rnn encoder-decoder for statistical machine translation. *arXiv preprint arXiv:1406.1078*.

Po-Sen Huang, Xiaodong He, Jianfeng Gao, Li Deng, Alex Acero, and Larry Heck. 2013. Learning deep structured semantic models for web search using clickthrough data. In *Proceedings of the 22nd ACM international conference on Conference on information & knowledge management*, pages 2333–2338. ACM.

Alon Lavie and Michael J. Denkowski. 2009. The meteor metric for automatic evaluation of machine translation. *Machine Translation*, 23(2-3):105–115, September.

Robert C Moore. 2002. *Fast and accurate sentence alignment of bilingual corpora*. Springer.

Kishore Papineni, Salim Roukos, Todd Ward, and Wei-Jing Zhu. 2002. Bleu: A method for automatic evaluation of machine translation. In *Proceedings of the 40th Annual Meeting on Association for Computational Linguistics*, ACL '02, pages 311–318, Stroudsburg, PA, USA. Association for Computational Linguistics.

Ruslan Salakhutdinov and Geoffrey E Hinton. 2009. Deep boltzmann machines. In *International conference on artificial intelligence and statistics*, pages 448–455.

Matthew Snover, Bonnie Dorr, Richard Schwartz, Linnea Micciulla, and John Makhoul. 2006. A study of translation edit rate with targeted human annotation. In *In Proceedings of Association for Machine Translation in the Americas*, pages 223–231.

Jakob Uszkoreit, Jay M Ponte, Ashok C Popat, and Moshe Dubiner. 2010. Large scale parallel document mining for machine translation. In *Proceedings of the 23rd International Conference on Computational Linguistics*, pages 1101–1109. Association for Computational Linguistics.

Pascal Vincent, Hugo Larochelle, Isabelle Lajoie, Yoshua Bengio, and Pierre-Antoine Manzagol. 2010. Stacked denoising autoencoders: Learning useful representations in a deep network with a local denoising criterion. *The Journal of Machine Learning Research*, 11:3371–3408.

Bitextor's participation in WMT'16: shared task on document alignment

Miquel Esplà-Gomis, Mikel L. Forcada
Departament de Llenguatges i Sistemes Informàtics
Universitat d'Alacant, E-03690 Sant Vicent del Raspeig, Spain
{mlf,mespla}@dlsi.ua.es

Sergio Ortiz-Rojas, Jorge Ferrández-Tordera
Prompsit Language Engineering,
Av. Universitat, s/n, Edifici Quorum III, E-03202 Elx, Spain
{sergio,jferrandez}@prompsit.com

Abstract

This paper describes the participation of Prompsit Language Engineering and the Universitat d'Alacant in the shared task on document alignment at the First Conference on Machine Translation (WMT 2016). Two systems have been submitted, corresponding to two different versions of the tool Bitextor: the last stable release, version 4.1, and the newest one, version 5.0. The paper describes the main features of each version of the tool and discusses the results obtained on the data sets published for the shared task.

1 Introduction

Parallel data harvesting has become a critical problem for many cross-lingual tasks in natural language processing. These data are the basis of many approaches, specially in the case of corpus-based machine translation (MT). One of the main sources of new parallel data is the Internet; in fact, many solutions have been proposed for exploiting specific websites by learning features of their structure. Some popular examples of corpora built by mining specific websites are the Europarl Corpus (Koehn, 2005), which exploits the European Parliament website, or the TED2013 corpus (Cettolo et al., 2012), that mines bitexts from the TED talks website,[1] a site that provides videos of public speeches and their transcriptions translated into several languages. Nevertheless, defining methodologies to surf the Web and identify parallel documents in any website is still an open problem. Some of the earliest tools developed for this purpose are STRAND (Resnik and Smith, 2003) and BITS (Ma and Liberman, 1999). These tools use similarities in the URLs and the content of the webpages to detect parallel documents in a given web domain.

Based on these principles, many later approaches have been proposed (Nie et al., 1999; Chen et al., 2004; Zhang et al., 2006; Désilets et al., 2008; San Vicente and Manterola, 2012; Papavassiliou et al., 2013); this paper describes the participation of Prompsit Language Engineering and the Universitat d'Alacant in the shared task on document alignment of WMT 2016, based on one of these tools: Bitextor (Esplà-Gomis and Forcada, 2010).

The rest of the paper is organised as follows: Section 2 describes the main features of Bitextor, highlighting the main differences between versions 4.1 and 5.0. Section 3 describes the steps taken to produce the submissions for the shared task on document alignment in WMT 2016, and discusses the results obtained. Finally, some concluding remarks are provided in Section 4.

2 Bitextor

Bitextor is a free/open-source tool for harvesting parallel data from multilingual websites; it is highly modular and is aimed at allowing users to easily obtain segment-aligned parallel corpora from the Internet. This section summarises the evolution of the tool from its earliest versions, paying special attention to versions 4.1 and 5.0, corresponding to the systems submitted to WMT 2016.

The first version of Bitextor was developed in 2006 as a monolithic library written in C++. The core component of Bitextor to find document and sentence-level alignments was an XHTML sentence aligner called TagAligner,[2] which heavily relied on the HTML structure of the documents to be compared. Some analysis on the performance of this tool versus other approaches was presented in (Sánchez-Villamil et al., 2006). The first version of Bitextor used TagAligner along with some strategies aimed at spotting language identifiers or names in document URLs.

---

[1] http://www.ted.com

[2] http://tag-aligner.sf.net

Proceedings of the First Conference on Machine Translation, Volume 2: Shared Task Papers, pages 685–691,
Berlin, Germany, August 11-12, 2016. ©2016 Association for Computational Linguistics

At some point, the monolithic nature of Bitextor and its dependence on unmaintained external libraries made it hard for users to install it and get it working. Addressing these issues led to a dramatic restructuring for version 4.0 in order to ease the maintenance and to improve the performance of the tool. Bitextor was fully re-implemented and deeply modularised with parallel processing in mind. The new version was mostly implemented in Python and Bash. Most of the external libraries were replaced: LangID[3] was adopted for language detection; XML/HTML normalisation, previously carried out by W3C HTML Tidy,[4] was done now with the more modern and powerful Apache Tika;[5] and the library Boilerpipe[6] was included in the pipeline to simplify the document structure by removing boilerplate material. As regards the strategies for document alignment, heuristics based on language identifiers in URLs were replaced by the use of bilingual lexicons for shallow indexing of documents. This method reduces the search space when looking for translation candidates for a given document. For a more reliable source of information, Bitextor kept relying on the use of XHTML structural comparison for document alignment.

2.1 Current version: Bitextor 4.1

The architecture of Bitextor in versions since 4.0 is based on a Unix-style pipeline, in which a collection of scripts are connected using text interfaces. This architecture favours the parallelisation of subtasks and eases the maintenance of the tool. Figure 1 represents this architecture, describing the main modules in Bitextor and how they interact. As can be seen, the user is required to provide one or more URLs of websites to be processed, the two languages (L_1 and L_2) for which the parallel corpus will be produced, and a bilingual lexicon in these two languages. The following list describes the modules in Bitextor and how this input data is processed to obtain a translation memory:

1. *Website crawling*: given the URL of a website, it is completely downloaded by means of the tool *HTTrack*,[7] keeping only HTML documents; this module does not produce text output, but downloads a mirror of a webpage.

2. *Webpage normalisation*: downloaded documents are preprocessed with *Apache Tika*[8] and *Boilerpipe*[9] (Kohlschütter et al., 2010) to normalise the HTML markup into XHTML and remove boilerplates. After normalisation, exact duplicates are discarded. This module outputs a list of tab-separated fields, in which every line corresponds to a file. Four fields are included in each line: the MIME type,[10] the character encoding, the local path to the file processed, and the content of the document after normalisation encoded in `base64`;[11] this format is henceforth called `ett`.

3. *Language identification*: this module receives as an input the list of processed documents in format `ett`; the language of each document is detected with *LangID* (Lui and Baldwin, 2012),[12] keeping only those documents in one of the target languages (L_1 or L_2). Before language identification, Apache Tika is used to convert the XHTML content of the document into plain text. The module outputs a list of files in `lett` format, which consists of the same fields than `ett` plus the language identifier of the document and the plain text extracted, encoded in `base64`.

4. *XHTML structure representation extraction*: this module receives a list of files in `lett` format and obtains a string that tries to represent the XHTML structure as follows: (i) every different XHTML tag is replaced by an arbitrary character, and (ii) the sequence W of words between two XHTML tags is represented with a reserved character, which is repeated $\log_2(|W|)$ times to account for the length of the text (in words) in the text block. The objective of this representation is to ease the comparison of the structure of the documents by reducing it to a string comparison. The new field is added to the `lett` input: the resulting format is the `lettr` format.

5. *Indexing of words in webpages*: this module receives a `lett` list of files and a bilingual lexicon and produces an `idx` index containing, for every word in the lexicon, the list of documents in which it occurs. The output of this module consists of a list of words, one

---

[3] `https://github.com/saffsd/langid.py`
[4] `http://tidy.sf.net`
[5] `https://tika.apache.org`
[6] `https://github.com/kohlschutter/boilerpipe`
[7] `http://www.httrack.com/`
[8] `http://tika.apache.org/`
[9] `http://code.google.com/p/boilerpipe/`
[10] `https://wikipedia.org/wiki/Media_type`
[11] `https://tools.ietf.org/html/rfc4648#section-4`
[12] `https://github.com/saffsd/langid.py`

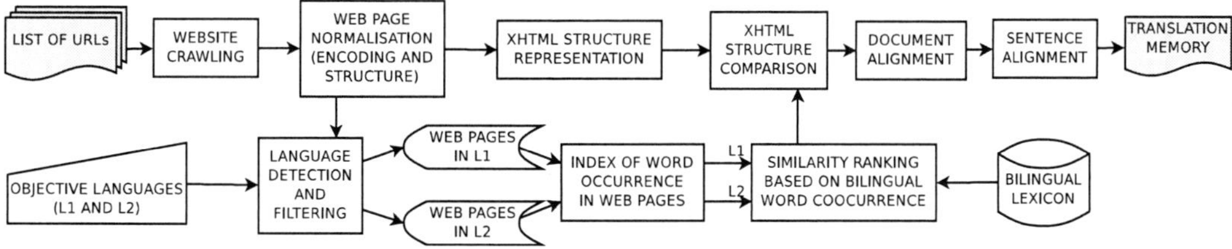

Figure 1: Architecture of Bitextor.

per line, and a numeric identifier for each of the documents in which the word appears; the first identifier corresponds to the line number of the first document in the `lett` list of documents, and the remaining identifiers are offsets to the previous line numbers, to reduce the size of the list. [13]

6. *Similarity ranking based on bilingual word coocurrence*: this module receives the `idx` word index and the `lett` document list and computes a bag-of-words overlapping metric for each pair of documents. This score is used to build a preliminary list of n-best candidates for each document.[14]

7. *N-best lists re-ranking*: the list of the n best candidates obtained for each document is re-ranked by using the similarity metric based on the Levenshtein edit distance between the representation of the XHTML structure of each pair of documents obtained in module 4; the `lettr` list of documents is used in this step.

8. *Document alignment*: Once re-ranked, the n-best lists for both languages are compared, and those documents that are mutually among the best candidates are aligned.[15]

9. *Sentence alignment*: aligned documents are finally aligned at the level of segments by using the tool *hunalign*[16] (Varga et al., 2007). The standard output after this step is a translation memory, but Bitextor can also be run to obtain just a list aligned documents. In this specific case, the list of document pairs obtained in the previous step is filtered by using the reliability score at the level of document pairs produced by hunalign to discard very unlikely document pairs.

Three main bottlenecks can be identified in this structure:

- crawling, given that this process is carried out by an external tool and it is only after the whole website is downloaded that the next step can start;

- obtaining the `lett` list of documents, since until the full list of documents is obtained it is impossible to compute the whole `idx` index of words; and

- n-best list candidates ranking, since documents cannot be aligned until the full ranking is obtained to check which documents are mutually best candidates.

The modules in between these bottlenecks are run in parallel; this allows Bitextor to obtain a high performance in machines with several processors.

2.2 What is new in Bitextor 5.0?

Version 5.0 of Bitextor has dramatically modified the way in which the tool performs two of the most important sub-tasks of its pipeline: crawling of websites and document alignment. This section is aimed at describing the main novelties as regards these modules. Note that the architecture shown in Figure 1 stays the same for Bitextor 5.0, despite the fact that the internal behaviour of the corresponding modules changes.

Web crawling. Until version 4.1, the tool HT-Track was used for downloading websites, and after this tool was done, the rest of the processing was carried out. Version 5.0 of Bitextor implements a new module for crawling websites based on the Python library `creepy`[17] which allows a better control of the crawling process, which can be interrupted at will to perform other processing. The two main advantages of this process are:

---

[13]For instance, if the word appears in documents 100, 105 and 180 the list would be `100:5:75`.

[14]The standard size of these n-best lists is 10.

[15]It is possible to specify how many documents in the re-ranked n-best list are taken into account: if only the first one is taken into account (the highest one after re-ranking), only mutual best-candidates are finally aligned.

[16]`http://mokk.bme.hu/resources/hunalign`

[17]`https://github.com/Aitjcize/creepy`

- *Better parallelisation of the processing*: with the new crawling module it is easier to control the way in which websites are crawled, allowing to specify the number of parallel threads that can be used. In addition, the need of storing a mirror of the original website locally disappears;[18] instead of this, the documents downloaded are directly stored in the `ett` format, which allows to start webpage normalisation before the whole website is downloaded.

- *Higher control of the crawling process*: the new module allows for a more controlled crawling process. For example, it is possible to avoid following links found in a document that is not written neither in L_1 nor L_2.

Document alignment. The modules of Bitextor involved in the identification of parallel documents in a given website have undergone important changes as well. As described in Section 2.1, previous versions of Bitextor used two sources of evidence to identify candidate pairs of documents: a bag-of-words overlapping metric and a similarity metric based on the structure of the documents, both using the distribution of the text and the XML/HTML structure. In Bitextor 4.1, the first source was used to reduce the search space and create a preliminary ranking of n-best candidates for every document, while the second one, more reliable, was used to re-rank this list. Bitextor version 5.0 keeps the initial strategy for reducing the search space by using the bag-of-words overlapping metric, but adds new sources of evidence and uses a logistic regression approach to combine them for re-ranking the n-best list of candidates. These new sources of information extracted for every candidate pair of documents are:

1. The Jaccard index of the URLs: when comparing documents D_1 and D_2, all the URLs in each document are extracted (using the HTML tag `href`) obtaining the sets U_1 and U_2, respectively; the Jaccard index is then computed as: $\dfrac{|\{U_1 \cap U_2\}|}{|\{U_1 \cup U_2\}|}$;

2. The similarity of URLs inside the document, represented by the Levenshtein distance (Wagner and Fischer, 1974) between the sequence of the URLs contained both in D_1 and D_2 at the character level;

3. The Jaccard index of the images shared: the URLs of the images in documents D_1 and D_2 are extracted (using the HTML tag `img`) obtaining the collections I_1 and I_2, respectively; the Jaccard index is then computed as: $\dfrac{|\{I_1 \cap I_2\}|}{|\{I_1 \cup I_2\}|}$;

4. Mutual links: a binary feature that is `true` if both documents are mutually linked, and `false` otherwise; and

5. Document URL distance: the Levenshtein distance (Wagner and Fischer, 1974) between the URLs corresponding to D_1 and D_2.

These new metrics, together with the two original ones (bag-of-words overlap and structure comparison), are used as features[19] in a logistic regression algorithm based on the use of a multilayer perceptron implemented with the Python library *keras*.[20] The logistic regression algorithm is trained to obtain a real number in $[0.0, 1.0]$ where 0.0 means that the documents are totally unrelated and 1.0 means that the documents are parallel. The score obtained by the logistic regressor allows to rank the candidates in the n-best list for every document. One of the main advantages of this approach, apart of being more empirical and less arbitrary than the previous heuristic approach is that it provides a similarity score at the level of document pairs, more reliable and easy to obtain than the one obtained from hunalign, and which does not require to align the documents at the level of segments.

3 Bitextor for document alignment in WMT 2016

This section describes the problem proposed by the organisers of the shared task in document alignment and the two systems submitted by Prompsit Language Engineering and the Universitat d'Alacant, the two main institutions supporting the tool Bitextor.

3.1 Data sets

The organisers of the shared task on document alignment provided a collection of `lett` files containing the collection of documents crawled from several multilingual websites. Two different data sets were provided: a training set consisting of a collection of 49 crawled websites with a total of

---

[18]This means that one of the bottlenecks specified in Section 2.1 is avoided in this version.

[19]All these metrics are normalised and take values in $[0.0, 1.0]$ except for *mutual link*, which is binary.
[20]`http://keras.io`

573,953 documents, and a test set consisting of a collection of 203 crawled websites, with a total of 1,204,239 documents. For the training set, a collection of gold document alignments was provided for a sub-set of the whole collection of documents.

The objective of the task is to build a collection of documents in English aligned to their translations in French.

3.2 Submitted systems

The only external resource required by Bitextor, a bilingual lexicon, was taken from the project's webpage.[21] The two versions of the tool used to produce the submissions were run with the standard parameters for document alignment, with the only exception of the parameter that specifies the amount of candidates to be taken into account in the n-best list: that was set to consider only the first one (see the description of the *document alignment* module in Section 2.1). As regards the submission based on Bitextor 4.1, its standard pipeline includes a filtering of the document pairs using the score provided by hunalign (see Section 2.1), while Bitextor 5.0 does not use any filtering at the document level.

Given that Bitextor 4.1 uses an heuristic approach, the training set was not used to build this system. However, Bitextor 5.0 does need[22] to train the logistic regressor used to rank the n-best translation candidates for a given document in a website; the training set was therefore used for this purpose in the following way:

1. the websites in the training set, which were already provided in the `lett` format, were processed up to the step in which the n-best lists are built and the features described in Section 2.2 were obtained for every candidate pair of documents, i.e. for the n pairs consisting of a document and each of its n-best candidates;

2. those document pairs for which neither of them was not found in the gold standard provided by the organisation were discarded;

3. for the remaining pairs of documents, those in the gold standard were considered as positive samples (for which the expected output of the logistic regressor is 1.0), while those aligning a document in the gold standard with a different document were considered as negative

samples (for which the expected output of the logistic regressor is 0.0).

Following this method, a collection of 30,815 training samples was obtained,[23] which was randomised to use 10% of the samples as development set, and the remaining 90% as training set.

3.3 Results

The results obtained with each version of Bitextor consisted of a collection of 95,760 pairs of documents in the case of Bitextor 4.1 and 157,682 in the case of Bitextor 5.0; that is, the new version detected about 60% more document pairs. The organisers of the task took a sample of 2,402 URL pairs as a gold standard for evaluating the recall of each system. On this evaluation framework, Bitextor 4.1 obtained a recall of about 31%, while Bitextor 5.0 obtained a recall of about 83%. After a careful revision of the results obtained, it is worth mentioning that some errors were detected in the gold standard, which led to considering as wrong some correct document pairs detected by Bitextor. After fixing them, Bitextor 5.0, the best performing version of the tool, obtained a recall of about 87.5%. In addition, some ambiguities were detected in the gold standard that had not been taken into account, such as URL aliases (having two alias that lead to the same document) or language variants (for example, having a document in British English and American English). After adding these ambiguous cases to the gold standard, the recall of Bitextor grew to almost 88%. Finally, it was possible to find websites translated into several languages for which some documents were not translated and are therefore written in the default language (English in most of the cases). This problem is discussed in Section 3.4.3 and, as explained in this section, after boilerplates removal, bitextor would keep only English text from these documents, producing a valid alignment. If we consider these alignments as valid, the recall would reach 89%.

Regarding the quality of the aligned document set obtained, Bitextor 4.1 reached a precision of about 85%, while in the case of Bitextor 5.0, the precision was higher than 90%. Taking into account the errors in the gold standard, this value grows to more than 95%.

These results confirm that the novelties in the new version of Bitextor provide a considerable improvement in the performance of the tool for docu-

---

[21]https://sf.net/projects/bitextor/files/lexicons/

[22]The new release published for Bitextor 5.0 includes a pre-trained regression model, so it does not need to be trained every time it is used.

[23]Since the standard size of the n-best lists is 10, about 10% of the samples were positive, while remaining samples were negative.

ment alignment. When compared to other systems participating in the task, Bitextor obtains a performance that falls in the middle of the ranking. However, taking into account the issues regarding the gold standard described in this section, Bitextor 5.0 would rank among the 5-top systems submitted in the current ranking.[24]

3.4 Error analysis

A deeper look into the data sets provided by the organisation of the shared task and the results obtained with Bitextor uncovered some of the most important problems faced when dealing with document alignment in an environment such as that of multilingual websites. The following are some of the main problems detected in the case of Bitextor.

3.4.1 Webpages not translated.

It is usual to find websites in which some pages are not translated in all the languages offered; this introduces noise into the task, since the tool may be looking for non-existing translations for some documents. If this happens only in a language (usually, the source language in which the original pages are written) it is not a big problem: untranslated webpages are just ignored. However, this issue has a relevant impact in the final accuracy when there are untranslated documents in both languages; in this case, the risk to end up aligning two documents for which no translation is available is higher. A good example of this situation in the test set is the website `http://academiedesprez.org`.

3.4.2 Webpages with little text.

This problem is usual in catalogues in which a template is used and only a few words or phrases (names, prices, measures, etc.) change in the different pages. This makes pages very similar and rises the probability of obtaining wrong alignments, which affect both precision and recall. An extreme example of this problem is the website `http://milltowndowntown.com` in the test set, that contains an extensive collection of pictures, each presented in a webpage without any text. For the purpose of building a corpus of parallel texts, it may be interesting to set a filter to discard those documents that do not contain a minimum amount of text to reduce the noise produced by this kind of webpages.

3.4.3 Repeated webpages.

In multilingual websites, it is usual to find that, when an article or a piece of news is not translated, it is shown in the *default* (original) language. As a result, it may happen that two webpages could be basically equivalent with the only exception of some menus or titles that are translated according to the template of the website.[25] In a real-world scenario, any of these "equivalent documents" would be a valid alignment and it would not be an error at all; however, given that the gold standard used for evaluation only provides a valid candidate for every document, this has an impact both in the precision and the recall of the tool. A good example of this problem is the website `https://pawpeds.com`. It is worth mentioning that, even though this issue affects the evaluation results, if the objective of document alignment is to produce a parallel corpus, aligning a document to any of its equivalent translations should not be considered an error at all.

4 Concluding remarks

This paper describes the systems submitted to the document alignment shared task at WMT 2016 by the team consisting of Prompsit Language Engineering and the Universitat d'Alacant. These submissions are based on Bitextor, a free/open-source tool for building parallel corpora from multilingual websites. For this shared task, two different versions of Bitextor were used to produce the two submissions: version 4.1 and 5.0. The results obtained show that the new version of Bitextor is able to identify a noticeably higher amount of parallel documents (about 60% more). In addition, the preliminary results obtained show that version 5.0 performs better than version 4.1 both as regards precision and recall in document classification.

Bitextor is distributed under version 3 of the GNU General Public Licence and can be downloaded from the project's website: `https://sf.net/projects/bitextor/ files/bitextor/`.

Acknowledgements: Supported by the European Commission through project PIAP-GA-2012-324414 (Abu-MaTran) and by the Spanish government through project TIN2015-69632-R (Effortune).

---

[24]It is worth noting that fixing these problems in the gold standard would possibly affect the rest of systems, and the whole ranking would need to be built again.

[25]This information is usually discarded when boilerplates are removed.

References

Mauro Cettolo, Christian Girardi, and Marcello Federico. 2012. Wit^3: Web inventory of transcribed and translated talks. In *Proceedings of the 16th Conference of the European Association for Machine Translation*, pages 261–268, Trento, Italy.

Jisong Chen, Rowena Chau, and Chung-Hsing Yeh. 2004. Discovering parallel text from the world wide web. In *Proceedings of the Second Workshop on Australasian Information Security, Data Mining and Web Intelligence, and Software Internationalisation*, volume 32, pages 157–161, Dunedin, New Zealand.

Alain Désilets, Benoit Farley, Marta Stojanovic, and Geneviève Patenaude. 2008. WeBiText: Building large heterogeneous translation memories from parallel web content. In *Proceedings of Translating and the Computer*, pages 27–28, London, UK.

Miquel Esplà-Gomis and Mikel L. Forcada. 2010. Combining content-based and URL-based heuristics to harvest aligned bitexts from multilingual sites with bitextor. *The Prague Bulletin of Mathematical Linguistics*, 93:77–86.

Philipp Koehn. 2005. Europarl: A parallel corpus for statistical machine translation. In *Proceedings of the X Machine Translation Summit*, pages 79–86, Phuket, Thailand.

Christian Kohlschütter, Peter Fankhauser, and Wolfgang Nejdl. 2010. Boilerplate detection using shallow text features. In *Proceedings of the third ACM international conference on Web search and data mining*, pages 441–450, New York, NY, USA.

Marco Lui and Timothy Baldwin. 2012. Langid.py: An off-the-shelf language identification tool. In *Proceedings of the ACL 2012 System Demonstrations*, pages 25–30, Jeju Island, Korea.

Xiaoyi Ma and Mark Liberman. 1999. BITS: A method for bilingual text search over the web. In *Machine Translation Summit VII*, pages 538–542, Singapore, Singapore.

Jian-Yun Nie, Michel Simard, Pierre Isabelle, and Richard Durand. 1999. Cross-language information retrieval based on parallel texts and automatic mining of parallel texts from the Web. In *Proceedings of the 22nd Annual International ACM SIGIR Conference on Research and Development in Information Retrieval*, pages 74–81, Berkeley, California, USA.

Vassilis Papavassiliou, Prokopis Prokopidis, and Gregor Thurmair. 2013. A modular open-source focused crawler for mining monolingual and bilingual corpora from the web. In *Proceedings of the Sixth Workshop on Building and Using Comparable Corpora*, pages 43–51, Sofia, Bulgaria.

Philip Resnik and Noah A. Smith. 2003. The Web as a parallel corpus. *Computational Linguistics*, 29(3):349–380.

Iñaki San Vicente and Iker Manterola. 2012. PaCo2: A fully automated tool for gathering parallel corpora from the web. In *Proceedings of the 8th International Conference on Language Resources and Evaluation*, pages 1–6, Istanbul, Turkey.

Enrique Sánchez-Villamil, Susana Santos-Antón, Sergio Ortiz-Rojas, and Mikel L Forcada. 2006. Evaluation of alignment methods for html parallel text. In *Advances in Natural Language Processing*, pages 280–290. Springer.

Dániel Varga, Péter Halácsy, András Kornai, Viktor Nagy, László Németh, and Viktor Trón. 2007. Parallel corpora for medium density languages. *Amsterdam Studies in the Theory and History of Linguistic Science, Series IV*, 292:247–258.

Robert A. Wagner and Michael J. Fischer. 1974. The string-to-string correction problem. *Journal of the Association for Computing Machinery*, 21(1):168–173.

Ying Zhang, Ke Wu, Jianfeng Gao, and Phil Vines. 2006. Automatic acquisition of Chinese–English parallel corpus from the web. In *Advances in Information Retrieval*, volume 3936, pages 420–431. Springer Berlin Heidelberg.

Bilingual Document Alignment with Latent Semantic Indexing

Ulrich Germann
School of Informatics
University of Edinburgh
ugermann@inf.ed.ac.uk

Abstract

We apply cross-lingual Latent Semantic Indexing to the Bilingual Document Alignment Task at WMT16. Reduced-rank singular value decomposition of a bilingual term-document matrix derived from known English/French page pairs in the training data allows us to map monolingual documents into a joint semantic space. Two variants of cosine similarity between the vectors that place each document into the joint semantic space are combined with a measure of string similarity between corresponding URLs to produce 1:1 alignments of English/French web pages in a variety of domains. The system achieves a recall of ca. 88% if no in-domain data is used for building the latent semantic model, and 93% if such data is included.

Analysing the system's errors on the training data, we argue that evaluating aligner performance based on exact URL matches under-estimates their true performance and propose an alternative that is able to account for duplicates and near-duplicates in the underlying data.

1   Introduction

Identifying document pairs that are mutual translations of one another in large multilingual document collections is an important processing step in harvesting parallel bilingual data from web crawls. The *Shared Task on Bilingual Document Alignment* at the *First Conference on Machine Translation (WMT16)* provides a common framework to investigate and compare approaches to solving this problem: given a collection of web site crawls, and a list of known matches, identify additional document pairs in the collection.

This paper explores the use of cross-lingual Latent Semantic Indexing (Berry and Young, 1995) in combination with a URL matching scheme for this task.

2   Latent Semantic Indexing

2.1   Singular Value Decomposition

Latent Semantic Indexing (LSI; Dumais et al., 1988; Deerwester et al., 1990) is a well-known indexing technique in information retrieval. It relies on reduced-rank singular value decomposition to map a high-dimensional *term-document matrix* into a "semantic" space of much lower dimensionality.

The term-document matrix is set up by counting word occurrence in documents. Each row in the matrix corresponds to a term in the vocabulary, each column to a document. The individual values in the matrix are weighted term counts of the respective term in the respective document. For this work, we use log-normalised term counts (tf – term frequency) weighted by term specificity as measured by the inverse document frequency (idf; Spärck-Jones, 1972[1]):

$$w_{t;d} = \mathsf{tf} \cdot \mathsf{idf} \tag{1}$$
$$\text{with}\quad \mathsf{tf} = 1 + \log \mathrm{count}_d(t) \tag{2}$$
$$\mathsf{idf} = \log \frac{|\mathcal{C}|}{\mathrm{count}_{\mathcal{C}}(d : t \in d)} \tag{3}$$

where t is a term from the vocabulary $\mathcal{V}$ and d a document from the document collection $\mathcal{C}$.

Singular value decomposition (SVD; cf., for example, Manning and Schütze, 1999) is then used to factorise this term-document matrix M with $m = |\mathcal{V}|$ rows and $n = |\mathcal{C}|$ columns into three matrices $\mathsf{T}_{m \times k}, \mathsf{S}_{k \times k}$, and $\mathsf{D}_{n \times k}$ (with with $k = \min(m, n)$), such that $\mathsf{T}\,\mathsf{S}\,\mathsf{D}^{\mathsf{T}} = \mathsf{M}$.

The column vectors of T and D are orthonormal bases of a k-dimensional vector space; S is a diagonal matrix with the Eigenvalues of M in descending order. In other words, dimensions in which the data differs the most come first, dimensions in which the data differs little come last. By truncating each of the SVD output matrices to the

---

[1]The technique was proposed by Spärck-Jones; the term idf was coined later.

Proceedings of the First Conference on Machine Translation, Volume 2: Shared Task Papers, pages 692–696,
Berlin, Germany, August 11-12, 2016. ©2016 Association for Computational Linguistics

respective first $r \ll k$ columns, we obtain a low-rank representation that approximates the original term-document Matrix: $\mathsf{T}'_{m \times r}\mathsf{S}'_{r \times r}(\mathsf{D}'_{n \times r})^{\mathsf{T}} \approx \mathsf{M}$. (Note, by the way, that $D'\mathsf{S}'D'^{\mathsf{T}}$ is the cosine similarity matrix in the new low-dimensional vector space.)

2.2 Document fold-in

To map a new document into this vector space, we compute the corresponding new row to be added to D' as $d_q = \mathsf{M}_q^{\mathsf{T}}\mathsf{T}'\mathsf{S}'^{-1}$, where M_q is an additional column in M that contains the weighted counts of terms in the respective document.

3 Alignment of multilingual web pages via cross-lingual LSI

3.1 Introduction

Web pages as delivered by web servers are a mix of data: HTML markup, which structures the document and pulls in additional resources such as cascading style sheets, JavaScript libraries, images, and video; scripts executable in the web browser that influence and extend its interactive behaviour and functionality; embedded images and videos, and, finally, text visible to the human user. Visible text comprises *boilerplate* and *payload*. Boilerplate text is text that appears repeatedly across a web site in the form of menus, page headers and footers, etc. While usually highly distinctive of a specific web site, boilerplate contributes little to being able to distinguish individual web pages on a specific site. Web site readers will usually not pay much attention to boilerplate text except when navigating the web site; it is nothing that they will actively read in order to satisfy information needs other than how to navigate the web site. Payload text, on the other hand, is text that users visit the specific page for.

While document structure, embedded links, etc. can provide valuable clues for the alignment of web pages, this work focuses on the text extracted from the original HTML, as provided by the workshop organisers as part of the data set.

3.2 Approach

The central idea in our approach is to use cross-lingual LSI to map monolingual documents into a joint vector space and use similarity between the corresponding embedding vectors to perform bipartite alignment of pairs of documents in different languages.

To obtain a cross-lingual model of latent semantics, we first set up a bilingual term-document matrix M using parallel documents, keeping the vocabularies of the two languages separate, so that identical word forms in the two languages correspond to different rows in M. Rank-reduced SVD is then performed on this bilingual matrix to map

the terms of the two languages into a common semantic space with 1,000 dimensions.[2] Via fold-in, all monolingual documents from the collection that have been labelled by the language recogniser as being in one or the other of the language in question are also be mapped into this common space.

We then use *Competitive Linking* (Melamed, 1997) to obtain a bipartite alignment of documents: first, we rank all possible bipartite alignment hypotheses by score. Processing the list of hypotheses in descending order, we keep all hypotheses that do not overlap or conflict with higher-ranking hypotheses and discard the others. (In fact, competitive linking is what the official evaluation procedure for this shared task does; for the purpose of participation in the Shared Task, it is sufficient to produce a ranked list).

3.3 Term Weighting

As mentioned above, text extracted from a web page consists of boilerplate and payload text. To reduce the influence of the former and boost the impact of the latter on the document vectors, we compute idf separately for each domain in the set (rather than globally across all domains). Thus, terms that occur frequently across a particular web site will receive a low specificity score (i.e., idf) on pages from that web site, yet may receive a high score if they appear elsewhere.

3.4 Scoring functions

In our experiments, we explored and combined the following scoring functions:

3.4.1 Cosine Similarity (cos)

This is the classical measure of similarity in LSI-based Information Retrieval. It computes the cosine of the angle between the two vectors that embed two candidate documents in the joint semantic vector space.

3.4.2 "Local" cosine similarity (lcos)

The intuition behind the local cosine similarity measure is this: since we perform SVD on a bilingual term-document matrix that consists of document column vectors for documents from a large collection of web sites, web pages from each specific web site will still appear quite similar if the web site is dedicated to a particular topic area (which the vast majority of web sites are). Similarity scores will thus be dominated by the general domain of the web site rather than the differences between individual pages within a given web site. The local cosine similarity measure tries to mediate this phenomenon by shifting the origin of the vector space to the centre of the sub-space in which the pages of

---

[2]We used the open-source software package *redsvd* (randomised SVD; Okanohara, 2010) to perform the singular value decomposition.

a particular web site reside before computing cosine similarity. In practice this is accomplished by subtracting the mean embedding vector for the domain in question from each individual embedding vector for pages in that domain. Note that we are only comparing pages that belong to the same web site within the context of the shared task.

3.4.3 URL similarity (url)

The data provided for the Shared Task contains many duplicates and near-duplicates of web pages. Duplicates occur when multiple URLs lead to exactly the same content (e.g. `www.domain.com` and `www.domain.com/index.html`); near-duplicates are often the result of dynamically created content, such as results of database look-up (e.g., calendars, stock price trackers), embedded page counts, or different boilerplate due to different language settings delivering the same payload (e.g., an English article delivered under two different country-specific user interfaces using different boilerplate text). Not knowing how the reference set for evaluation within the Share Task was constructed, we conjectured that the gold standard used for evaluation might be biased towards URL matches.

Hence, we devised the following match score for pairs of URLs.

1. All URLs within a domain are tokenised into blocks of either all letters or all numbers relying on POSIX UTF-8 character classes; punctuation is discarded.

2. For a given pair of candidate URLs, we determine via the Needleman-Wunsch algorithm (Needleman and Wunsch, 1970) the cumulative score of the longest match sequence between the token sequences corresponding to the two URLs. The match score for each individual token pair $\langle t_1, t_2 \rangle$ in the alignment is computed as follows:

   - $\text{score}(t_1, t_2) = 0$ if $t_1 \neq t_2$ and at least one of them is a number
   - $\text{score}(t_1, t_2) = \frac{1}{\text{cnt}(t_1)^2}$ if $t_1 = t_2$, where $\text{cnt}(t)$ is the position-independent count of token t in all the URLs in the collection. The match weighting based on relative frequency in the domain serves to discount very frequently occurring URL components, (such as *http* or *www*) and boost components that are rare in the URLs for this domain, such as, for example, article IDs.
   - $\text{score}(t_1, t_2) = \frac{2*\text{lcss}(t_1, t_2)}{\text{len}(t_1)+\text{len}(t_2)} \cdot \frac{1}{\text{cnt}(t_1)\cdot\text{cnt}(t_2)}$ if t_1 and t_2 both are sequences of letters, where $\text{lcss}(t_1, t_2)$ is the length of the longest common letter sub-sequence between t_1 and t_2. The idea behind this

soft match score is to reward cognates over candidate pairs that have no semblance of one another whatsoever. For example, the lcss score component for the pair $\langle London, Londres \rangle$ would be ca. 0.62 ($\frac{2*4}{\text{len}(\text{"London"})+\text{len}(\text{"Londres"})}$), whereas the pair $\langle London, Paris \rangle$ would receive a match score of 0, each of the scores yet to be weighted by $\frac{1}{\text{cnt}(t_1)\cdot\text{cnt}(t_2)}$. This soft matching score serves to accommodate web sites that base their URLs on, for example, the headlines of articles or posts.

4 Evaluation

4.1 Recall on training and test data

To rank alignment hypotheses, we investigated all uniform linear combinations of the three individual scoring functions. Table 1 shows the results for the training set, and, in the last row, the performance of the best feature combination on the test set. In the first set of experiments on the training set, whose results are shown in the left half of the table, we used the list of known matches in the training data both for seeding cross-lingual LSI and evaluation. These numbers give us a sense how well monolingual documents are mapped into the joint semantic space by LSI and document fold-in. The first column of the recall numbers ("strict") follows the official evaluation procedure, counting only exact URL matches as correct. The following columns show the performance if a more lenient notion of "matching documents" is applied. This more lenient measures computes the similarity between the expected and a proposed target document for a given source document (and vice versa) as follows:

$$\text{score}(\text{text}_1, \text{text}_2) = \frac{2 \cdot \text{lcss}(\text{text}_1, \text{text}_2)}{|\text{text}_1| + |\text{text}_2|} \quad (4)$$

The length of the longest common sub-sequence (lcss) is here measured in terms of space-separated tokens as they occur in the text. No more sophisticated tokenisation is performed. The content-based evaluation measure counts a proposed match as correct if the similarity between a proposed target (or source) document and the expected document is greater or equal to the threshold indicated in the column header.

The right half of the table shows the results for the same evaluation performed on the basis of original bilingual term-document matrices that *exclude* all known matches from the domain in question, relying only on known matches from other web domains. This leads to fewer vocabulary matches, as terms specific to the web site in question may not be included in the model. As expected, we see a drop in performance, but we are still able to recover

Table 1: Recall on the training and test data with known in-domain document pairs included in / excluded from the initial term-document matrix.

performance on the training data

| | | | included | | | | | excluded | | | | |
features used			strict[a]	1.00[b]	0.99[b]	0.95[b]	0.90[b]	strict[a]	1.00[b]	0.99[b]	0.95[b]	0.90[b]
cosine (cos)			86.7	93.4	95.4	96.7	97.6	82.5	88.9	91.3	92.9	93.7
"local" cos. (lcos)			86.7	92.8	94.7	95.8	96.9	83.3	88.9	91.4	92.8	93.6
URL similarity (url)			83.6	87.8	88.1	88.2	88.2	83.6	87.8	88.1	88.2	88.2
cos	lcos		87.2	93.7	95.6	96.6	97.5	83.3	89.7	92.1	93.6	94.4
cos		url	90.6	94.7	95.6	96.4	97.1	86.3	90.6	91.4	92.7	93.5
	lcos	url	91.3	95.4	96.3	97.2	97.8	86.8	91.3	92.2	93.4	94.2
cos	lcos	url	92.8	96.7	97.6	98.5	99.1	88.0	92.5	93.4	94.7	95.5

performance on the test data

cos	lcos	url						87.6	87.6	94.1	95.5	96.0

[a] exact string match with the reference ULR pairs
[b] soft match based on document similarity with different similarity thresholds.

Table 2: Distribution of missed pairs over domains with a soft similarity threshold of .95. Domains with a single miss are aggregated under "other".

domain	missed pairs
www.lagardere.com	20
meatballwiki.org	12
www.toucherdubois.ca	8
www.rfimusique.com	8
www.taize.fr	6
www.lalettrediplomatique.fr	4
www.publictendering.com	3
www.iisd.ca	3
hrcouncil.ca	3
arabpressnetwork.org	3
www.technip.com	2
www.kinnarps.com	2
www.gameonly.com	2
www.eufic.org	2
other	17

about 92.5% (down from 96.7%) of the known matches, even when counting only full matches and matches with exact duplicates.

4.2 Error analysis

Table 2 shows the distribution of missed page pairs over the respective domains in the test data. As we can see, errors are concentrated in only a few of the 203 domains in the test set. We will briefly discuss the top five here. The errors in `www.lagardere.com` originate from mixed-language pages, typically pages with the boilerplate text for the user interface in one language and the actual content in the other. The missed pairs in `meatballwiki.org` can be attributed to *red herrings*: URL pairs that erroneously suggest a corre-

spondence between the two pairs in question. The web site `www.toucherdubois.ca` provides teaching resources (including images and lesson plans) for teaching students about "the sociocultural heritage of the people of Madawaska" in Canada and the US. Some of the pages consist of little text wrapped around image resources; lesson plans are often very similar in terms of the vocabulary used, thus confusing the LSA model. The missing pairs from `www.rfimusique.com` and `www.taize.fr` are pairs of pages with a low payload-to-boilerplate (or near-boilerplate) ratio, i.e., they are dominated by text that can be found on multiple pages, thus leading to document alignment errors.

5 Related work

One of the first systematic approaches to identifying parallel data on the web is the STRAND algorithm (Resnik, 1999). It is a pipeline process that first generates candidate pairs via a web search (or by link analysis if a complete download of a web site is available). It then performs language identification on the retrieved pages and analyses the HTML structure of candidate documents in order to filter out document pairs that are too dissimilar in their document structure. Resnik and Smith (2003) extend this approach by adding content-based analysis. They use probabilistic word translation lexicons to assess the probability that two pages are translations of each other.

Very similarly to the work presented in this paper, Saad et al. (2014) use LSI for identification of parallel and comparable corpora. In addition to the cross-lingual LSI approach taken here, they also investigate monolingual LSI after document translation. They conclude that cross-lingual LSI is competitive with monolingual LSI of automatically translated texts.

6 Conclusion

We have investigated the feasibility of using cross-lingual LSI for identifying parallel documents in large collections of text. Our results suggest that this is a viable approach to harvesting parallel data from web crawls. We achieve the best performance with a combination of classical cosine measure, "local" cosine measure, and URL matching.

The existence of duplicate and near-duplicate documents in the data raises the question whether it is reasonable to measure performance in terms of URL matches, or whether evaluation should be based on the distance between retrieved and expected documents.

Acknowledgements

This work was conducted within the scopes of the Innovation Action *MMT* and the Research and Innovation Action *SUMMA*, which have received funding from the European Union's Horizon 2020 research and innovation programme under grant agreements No 645487 and 688139, respectively.

References

Berry, Michael W. and Paul G. Young. 1995. "Using latent semantic indexing for multilanguage information retrieval." *Computers and the Humanities*, 29(6):413–429.

Deerwester, Scott, Susan T. Dumais, George W. Furnas, Thomas K. Landauer, and Richard Harshman. 1990. "Indexing by latent semantic analysis." *Journal of the American Society for Information Science*, 41(6):391–407.

Dumais, Susan T., George W. Furnas, Thomas K. Landauer, Scot Deerwester, and Richard Harshman. 1988. "Using latent semantic analysis to improve access to textual information." *Proceedings of the SIGCHI Conference on Human Factors in Computing Systems*, CHI '88, 281–285. New York, NY, USA.

Manning, Christopher D. and Hinrich Schütze. 1999. *Foundations of Statistical Natural Language Processing*. Cambridge, MA, USA: MIT Press.

Melamed, I. Dan. 1997. "A word-to-word model of translational equivalence." *Proceedings of the 35th Annual Meeting of the Association for Computational Linguistics*, 490–497. Madrid, Spain.

Needleman, Saul B. and Christian D. Wunsch. 1970. "A general method applicable to the search for similarities in the amino acid sequence of two proteins." *Journal of Molecular Biology*, 48(3):443–453.

Okanohara, Daisuke. 2010. "redsvd." `http://mloss.org/software/view/274/`.

Resnik, Philip. 1999. "Mining the web for bilingual text." *Proceedings of the 37th Annual Meeting of the Association for Computational Linguistics*, 527–534. College Park, Maryland, USA.

Resnik, Philip and Noah A. Smith. 2003. "The web as a parallel corpus." *Computational Linguistics*, 29(3):349–380.

Saad, Motaz, David Langlois, and Kamel Smaïli. 2014. "Cross-lingual semantic similarity measure for comparable articles." *Proceedings of the 9th International Conference on NLP, PolTAL 2014*, 105–115. Warsaw, Poland.

Spärck-Jones, Karen. 1972. "A statistical interpretation of term specificity and its application in retrieval." *Journal of Documentation*, 28(1):11–21.

First Steps Towards Coverage-Based Document Alignment

Luís Gomes[1,2]   Gabriel Pereira Lopes[1,2]

[1]NOVA LINCS, Faculdade de Ciências e Tecnologia, Universidade Nova de Lisboa, Portugal
[2]ISTRION BOX, Translation and Revision, Lda, Portugal
`{luis.gomes,gabriel.lopes}@istrionbox.com`

Abstract

In this paper we describe a method for selecting pairs of parallel documents (documents that are a translation of each other) from a large collection of documents obtained from the web. Our approach is based on a *coverage* score that reflects the number of distinct bilingual phrase pairs found in each pair of documents, normalized by the total number of unique phrases found in them. Since parallel documents tend to share more bilingual phrase pairs than non-parallel documents, our alignment algorithm selects pairs of documents with the maximum coverage score from all possible pairings involving either one of the two documents.

1 Introduction

In this paper we describe our algorithm for bilingual document alignment, which is based on a coverage scoring function that reflects the ratio of unique bilingual phrase pairs from a Moses phrase table (Koehn et al., 2007) that are found in each bilingual pair of documents[1].

Basically, we exploit the fact that (parallel) phrase pairs are more likely to co-occur in parallel documents than in non-parallel ones. This insight came to our mind when we learned about the MT-based approach proposed by Sennrich and Volk (2010) to the closely related sentence alignment problem, which is to align parallel sentences within a pair of parallel documents. The MT-based approach to sentence alignment uses the BLEU score between sentences of one document and machine translated sentences of the other, as an indicator of parallelism between sentences. By using a phrase table directly we circumvent the decoding process which inevitably makes translation

choices (and sometimes errors) that differ from the ones made by the human translators.

One may argue that using a decoder would have the advantage of avoiding "noisy" phrase pairs from the phrase table. However, we observed that most of the "noisy" phrase pairs in the phrase table *are not* completely unrelated. Instead, they sometimes miss a word or two on one of the sides, but are otherwise parallel to some extent. Nevertheless, since we employ uniform weighting for all phrase pairs (we treat them as binary features; either they are present in a document or not), the effect of noisy entries becomes diluted in a large number of features. For the most sceptical amongst us, please consider that even if the phrase table was created by a *random aligner*, the mere fact that the phrase pairs were sampled from parallel sentences, would cause parallel documents to statistically share more of such phrase pairs than non-parallel documents.

Our earlier successful application of coverage-based scores to the problem of sentence alignment (Gomes and Lopes, 2016) prompted us to develop a similar solution to the document alignment problem. The main characteristics of our approach are:

- it takes advantage of existing knowledge encoded in PBSMT phrase tables (we consider this to be our main characteristic, as it was our foremost goal to reuse existing knowledge);

- it identifies pairs of documents with various degrees of document parallelism ranging from barely comparable to parallel;

- it is language and domain[2] independent, as long as we can manage to create a phrase table for the pair of languages at hand from a relatively general-domain parallel corpus;

---

[1]hereafter we will avoid repeating the word *bilingual* whenever we mention pairs of documents or phrases

[2]here *domain* refers to text domain

Proceedings of the First Conference on Machine Translation, Volume 2: Shared Task Papers, pages 697–702,
Berlin, Germany, August 11-12, 2016. ©2016 Association for Computational Linguistics

- it is purely content based (although this is not an advantage for the present shared task and other scenarios where metadata is available);

- it is agnostic with respect to document format (again, this is not an advantage in the present task, because all documents are HTML pages and some tag-structure features could be helpful)

2 Alignment Method Description

Our alignment method has three major steps: a *preparation* step, which constructs a phrase→document indexing data structure, a *candidate generation* step, which generates bilingual pairs of putative parallel documents, and finally, a *candidate selection* step which selects the pairs with maximum coverage score among all *competing candidates* from the generated set (we will define precisely what are *competing candidates*).

Each of these steps is described ahead, in dedicated sub-sections, but first we will define the *coverage score* which is the key concept of the whole method.

2.1 Coverage Score

We define the *coverage score* of a bilingual pair of documents as the geometric mean between two *coverage ratios*, one for each document. The coverage ratio of an English[3] document E when paired with a candidate parallel French document F is given by equation 1:

$$C(E, F) = \frac{|E \cap F|}{|E|} \qquad (1)$$

Conversely, to compute the coverage ratio of a French document F when paired with a candidate English document E we simply swap E with F in the equation above.

More formally, the capital letters E and F represent the set of unique phrases present in each document (i.e. in this algorithm a document is represented by the set of unique phrases occurring in it). To compute the cross-lingual intersection of E and F we resort to the Moses phrase table which allows us to match phrases of both languages. Please note that some phrases are common to English and French, such as proper nouns,

---

[3]although we refer to English and French documents throughout the document, the algorithm is nonetheless language independent

numbers, URLs, postal addresses, etc. We also consider such phrases as belonging to the cross-lingual intersection of E and F when computing the coverage score, even if they are not in the phrase table.

The coverage score of a candidate pair of documents, is given by a non-parametric combination of the two coverage ratios ($C(E, F)$ and $C(F, E)$). We chose the geometric mean (equation 2b) instead of the arithmetic (equation 2a) or harmonic (equation 2c) means, because it sits in the middle ground between the other two in terms of response to unbalanced inputs (see equation 2d). In fact, the equalities between the three means (equation 2d) only hold if the inputs a and b have the same value.

$$A(a, b) = \frac{a + b}{2} \qquad (2a)$$

$$G(a, b) = \sqrt{ab} \qquad (2b)$$

$$H(a, b) = \frac{2ab}{a + b} \qquad (2c)$$

$$H(a, b) \leq G(a, b) \leq A(a, b) \qquad (2d)$$

To better understand our choice of the geometric mean, let us consider for example three pairs of coverage ratios for three hypothetical pairings of documents: (0.9, 0.1), (0.65, 0.35) and (0.5, 0.5). The arithmetic mean of each of these pairs is 0.5 (the same for all pairs) while the geometric mean is 0.3 for the first, 0.48 for the second and 0.5 for the third, which is the most balanced pair. Therefore, if we use the arithmetic mean, then we will not differentiate among these three cases, although the pair with more balanced coverage ratios is more likely to be parallel. From observation we learned that extremely unbalanced coverage ratios typically indicate that one of the documents is much longer than the other. Since longer documents tend to have more unique phrases than shorter ones, whenever we compute the coverage ratios for such a pairing, the shorter document will have a greater coverage ratio than the the longer document. More precisely, the numerator of equation 1 is the same for both paired documents, but the denominator will be larger for the document with more unique phrases. The harmonic mean is slightly more sensitive to unbalanced input values than the geometric mean, and for the three pairings in the previous example we would get 0.18, 0.46 and 0.5 (which are not too far from the respective geometric means). In future work we may experiment replacing the geometric with the harmonic mean, but we do not expect dramatic changes in the performance.

Replacing a and b in equation 2b by the equation 1 for both documents, we get the following equation for the coverage score:

$$S(E, F) = \left(\frac{|E \cap F|^2}{|E| \, |F|} \right)^{\frac{1}{2}} \qquad (3)$$

For reasons explained in § 2.4, we will not simplify this equation.

2.2 Preparation Step

The preparation step is responsible for creating two phrase→document indices, one for each language, which are used later in the *candidate generation* step. In our prototype, these indices are implemented as hash tables mapping phrases (strings) into lists of document Ids (integers). The time needed for creation of these indices is proportional to the size of the document set, while the memory required is proportional to the number of unique phrases (hash table keys) times the average document-frequency of phrases (each phrase is associated with a list of unique document Ids where it occurs at least once). The creation of the indices is as simple as follows:

- for each document of a given web domain:

  - extract all unique phrases up to 5 tokens (the same maximum phrase length as the phrase table)
  - insert each phrase in the hash table of the respective language (if not there already) and append the document Id to the list of document Ids associated with each phrase

One important implementation detail is that the tokenization algorithm employed for processing the documents must be exactly the same as the one used to process the corpus from where the phrase table was extracted. In our prototype we used the tokenizer from the Moses toolkit (Koehn et al., 2007), and a pre-computed English-French phrase table extracted from the Europarl corpus (Koehn, 2005). Both the tokenizer and the pre-computed

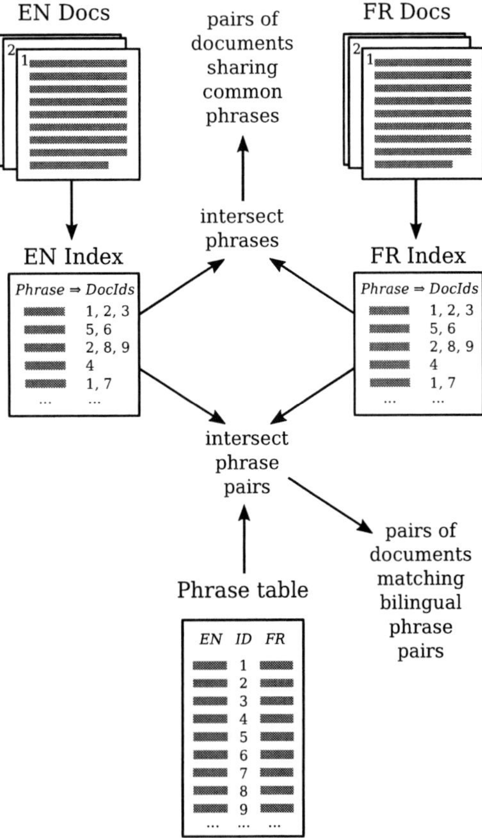

Figure 1: Overview of the candidate generation algorithm

phrase table were downloaded from the Moses website[4].

2.3 Candidate Generation Algorithm

The candidate generation algorithm is responsible for balancing the computation time required with the precision and recall of the aligner. If it generates too many candidates, then the aligner will take a long time to evaluate all generated candidates. If it generates too few candidates then there is an increased chance that some true parallel pairs are not among the generated candidates, and thus absent from the final aligner output.

For the smaller web domains, we may generate all possible pairings, thus ensuring that all true parallel pairs are passed into the selection step. However, in the general case, we need to prune the hypothesis space and generate only a subset of all possible pairs.

---

[4]http://www.statmt.org/moses/RELEASE-3.0/

Our heuristic for candidate generation is to define an average minimum number of candidates k to be generated for each document (we used k=100 in our experiments). Then, the global minimum number of candidates to be generated is computed by multiplying k by the average number of documents in both languages. For example, if there are 400 English documents and 600 French documents, and we set k=100, then the global minimum number of candidates to be generated is $k\frac{400+600}{2}$=50,000 which is much lower than the number of all possible pairings (400×600=240,000).

The algorithm generates candidate pairs incrementally, considering one bilingual pair of phrases at a time. It starts from the least frequent phrase pairs, which are also the most discriminant[5], and progresses towards the more frequent phrase pairs. For each bilingual phrase pair considered we generate all pairs of documents from the Cartesian product of the document Ids associated with each of the two phrases. Figure 1 shows an overview of the candidate generation algorithm and its interaction with the phrase indices and the phrase table.

As an example of this Cartesian product-based generation, if the English phrase "thank you" occurred in English documents 3 and 7 and the French phrase "merci" occurred in documents 2, 5 and 9, we would generate the following 6 candidate pairs: (3,2), (3,5), (3,9), (7,2), (7,5) and (7,9).

The candidate generation terminates when the required global minimum number of candidates has been generated.

2.4 Candidate Selection Algorithm

The candidate selection algorithm is responsible for selecting, among each group of *competing candidate pairs* (alternative hypotheses), the one with maximum coverage score.

We define *competing candidate pairs* of documents as pairs that share either of the two documents. For example, the pairs (E_1, F_1) and (E_1, F_2) are *competing pairs* since they share the English document E_1, but the pairs (E_1, F_1) and (E_2, F_2) are not. We assume that only one pair of all competing candidate pairs is indeed parallel, i.e. there is at most one parallel French document for each English document (and vice versa).

More formally, the selection algorithm selects

---

[5]A phrase pair that occurs in almost every document (such as the pair "the"↔"la") has very little discriminative power.

pairs of documents (E, F) that verify the following two inequalities, which warrant a maximum coverage among all competing pairs:

$$S(E, F) > S(E, \hat{F}) \quad \forall \hat{F} \neq F \quad (4a)$$
$$S(E, F) > S(\hat{E}, F) \quad \forall \hat{E} \neq E \quad (4b)$$

We call the selected (E, F) pairs as *maximal pairs*.

Please recall the coverage score equation $S(E, F)$ (equation 3), and its wrapping square root which we did not simplify away. Since the square root is a monotonically increasing function, and given that we are comparing coverage scores of competing pairings instead of looking at their absolute values, we may drop the square root from the equation and the comparisons across competing candidates will hold the same as before. Thus, we save a few computer clocks per candidate pair analysed.

3 Evaluation

The evaluation in this shared task is based on recall, i.e. the ratio of URL pairs from the testset that are correctly identified by the aligner. A one-to-one rule is enforced, which allows each English URL to be aligned with at most one French URL and vice versa.

Despite the merits of a pure content-based approach, which is applicable in scenarios where URLs and other metadata are not available, we acknowledge that for the present task we may obtain better results if we take advantage of all information available (page URL and HTML structure) besides the plain text content.

Therefore, besides evaluating our content-based method on its own, we submitted two additional *extended* sets of results obtained by trivial combinations of our content-based method with the metadata-based (URL-based) baseline method.

The first extended set, called *coverage/url*, gives priority to predictions of the coverage-based method, adding only URL-predicted pairs for URLs that were not aligned by the coverage-based method. Conversely, the second extended set, called *url/coverage*, gives priority to the predictions of the URL-based aligner.

The results obtained with our coverage-based aligner and the two trivial combinations with the baseline aligner for the development and test sets are summarized in Tables 1 and 2, respectively.

Method	Recall	# Predicted Pairs
baseline	67.92%	119979
coverage	72.78%	63207
coverage/url	89.53%	147857
url/coverage	90.52%	148278

Table 1: Evaluation results on the development set.

Method	Recall	# Predicted Pairs
baseline	53.03%	136086
coverage	85.76%	207022
coverage/url	88.63%	235763
url/coverage	94.96%	235812

Table 2: Evaluation results on the final test set.

The coverage-based aligner, alone, improves 5% over the baseline on the development set and 33% on the test set. But when combined with the baseline aligner, the recall is boosted up to 23% above the baseline on the development set and up to 42% on the test set. A possible explanation for the boosted recall is that since the methods rely on completely different feature sets, their predictions are to some degree complementary.

We would like to point out that the coverage-based aligner made substantially fewer predictions than the baseline (52.7%) in the development set, and still yielded higher recall (+4.86%). This allows us to speculate that the precision of the coverage-based alignment is likely to be higher than the precision of the baseline.

4 Future Work

This was our first look into the document alignment problem and a number of ideas for improving the current algorithm sprung up during the experiments. Next, we will briefly discuss ideas which we intend to explore in future work.

4.1 Improve Candidate Generation Strategy

The candidate generation algorithm presented in §2.3 is perhaps the weakest point of the whole method. We arrived at this conclusion when we noticed that many URL pairs from the development set were not being generated due to a too low frequency threshold, particularly for the largest domains. When we tried to counter this effect by increasing the threshold, then the algorithm

started to exhibit square asymptotic complexity, taking too long to align the larger domains. In the meantime, we discovered a better candidate generation strategy, but unfortunately, it was not possible to implement it on time for this shared task. The main difference is that instead of a global frequency threshold, we fix a minimum number of *competing candidates* to be compared with each document.

4.2 Better Integration With Metadata-based Features

As described earlier, we submitted two extra datasets resulting from trivial combinations of our aligner and baseline outputs. Due to lack of time, we didn't try more sophisticated forms of combining our content-based features with other kinds of feature, such as URL matching and HTML document structure as proposed in the Bitextor paper (Esplà-Gomis et al., 2010).

Since the trivial combinations achieved the best performance in the development set, we expect to improve the performance further still, if we combine content-, structure- and metadata-based features in a more principled manner.

One possibility for making use of URLs would be to consider the path component of URLs as a slash-delimited sentence, and match phrases from this sentence in the same way that we do for phrases in the text. Therefore, even if the URLs are not exactly identical (after stripping language-specific markers such as "lang=en"), they could still match partially.

4.3 Using Document Structure Information

Following the idea introduced by Bitextor (Esplà-Gomis et al., 2010), we could also compute document similarity based on HTML tag structure, given that many parallel webpages also have a parallel HTML structure. They propose a distance measure, based on edit-distance of a sequence of tags intermixed with text chunks (represented by their length). The computation of the distance measure takes $O(NM)$ time to compute, for a pair of documents with N and M tags respectively. This may be computationally expensive, particularly for large web domains, but we might resort to this measure only for documents with a very low coverage score and/or a very small distance to the second choices in the selection algorithm described in section 2.4.

5   Conclusion

The bilingual document alignment algorithm presented in this paper has several interesting properties, in our view: it is language and domain independent, it is able to align documents with varying degrees of parallelism (ranging from barely comparable documents to fully parallel ones), and it is purely content-based, which makes it applicable in a wider range of scenarios.

On its own, the performance of our aligner is above the baseline, but is not outstanding: 73% recall on the development set and 86% on the test set. But when combined with the URL-based predictions of the baseline aligner, we achieve 90% recall on the development set and 95% on the test-set. The performance boost of the combined systems may be explained by the complementary nature of the features employed by each method.

Finally, we believe that the *phrase-table-coverage* approach still has room for improvement, because this was our first look into the problem and we have several untried ideas for improving it.

Acknowledgements

This work was supported by ISTRION BOX, Translation and Revision, Lda, and the Portuguese Foundation for Science and Technology (FCT) through individual PhD grant (ref. SFRH/BD/65059/2009), research project ISTRION (ref. PTDC/EIA-EIA/114521/2009), and NOVA LINCS (ref. UID/CEC/04516/2013).

References

Miquel Esplà-Gomis, Felipe Sánchez-Martínez, and Mikel L. Forcada. 2010. Combining content-based and url-based heuristics to harvest aligned bitexts from multilingual sites with Bitextor. *The Prague Bulletin of Mathematical Lingustics*, 93:77–86.

Luís Gomes and Gabriel Pereira Lopes. 2016. First steps towards coverage-based sentence alignment. In *Proceedings of the Tenth International Conference on Language Resources and Evaluation (LREC 2016)*, Portorož, Slovenia. European Language Resources Association (ELRA).

Philipp Koehn, Hieu Hoang, Alexandra Birch, Chris Callison-Burch, Marcello Federico, Nicola Bertoldi, Brooke Cowan, Wade Shen, Christine Moran, Richard Zens, et al. 2007. Moses: Open source toolkit for statistical machine translation. In *Proceedings of the 45th annual meeting of the ACL on interactive poster and demonstration sessions*, pages 177–180. Association for Computational Linguistics.

Philipp Koehn. 2005. Europarl: A parallel corpus for statistical machine translation. In *MT summit*, volume 5.

Rico Sennrich and Martin Volk. 2010. Mt-based sentence alignment for ocr-generated parallel texts. In *The Ninth Conference of the Association for Machine Translation in the Americas (AMTA 2010), Denver, Colorado*.

$B_1A_3D_2$ LUC@WMT 2016: a Bilingual$_1$ Document$_2$ Alignment$_3$ Platform Based on Lucene

Laurent Jakubina
RALI - DIRO
Université de Montréal
jakubinl@iro.umontreal.ca

Philippe Langlais
RALI - DIRO
Université de Montréal
felipe@iro.umontreal.ca

Abstract

We participated in the Bilingual Document Alignment shared task of WMT 2016 with the intent of testing plain cross-lingual information retrieval platform built on top of the Apache `Lucene` framework. We devised a number of interesting variants, including one that only considers the URLs of the pages, and that offers — without any heuristic — surprisingly high performances. We finally submitted the output of a system that combines two informations (`text` and `url`) from documents and a post-treatment for an accuracy that reaches 92% on the development dataset distributed for the shared task.

1 Introduction

While many recent efforts within the machine translation community are geared toward exploiting bilingual comparable corpora — see (Munteanu and Marcu, 2005) for a pioneering work and (Sharoff et al., 2013) for an extensive review — there is comparatively much less work devoted to identifying parallel documents in a (potentially huge) collection. See (Uszkoreit et al., 2010; Smith et al., 2013) for two notable exceptions. This is due in large part to conventional wisdom that holds that comparable corpora can be found more easily and in larger quantity than parallel data. Still, we believe that parallel data should not be neglected and should even be preferred when available.

The Bilingual Document Alignment shared task of WMT 2016 is designed for precisely identifying parallel data in a (huge) collection of bilingual documents mined over the Web. The collection has been processed by the organizers in such a way that this is easy to test systems: the language of the documents is already detected, and we have access to the content of the Web pages. Although the organizers encouraged participants to test their own way of pre-processing data, we decided (for the sake of simplicity) to use the data as prepared.

We describe the overall architecture of the `BADLUC` framework as well as its components in Section 2. We explain in Section 3 the experiments we conducted and provide some analysis in Section 4. We conclude in Section 5.

2 BADLUC

We built variants of a Cross-Language Information Retrieval (CLIR) platform making use of the popular Apache framework `Lucene`.[1] We describe here the different components embedded in this platform.

We participated in this task by relying entirely on the pre-processing carried out by the organizers, that is, we used the text of the pages as it was extracted. Figure 1 shows an excerpt of the text extracted from a given URL. Sometimes, the conversion to text is noisy and deserves further work. While we could have used the machine translation provided as well, we decided to resort to a bilingual dictionary, mainly for the sake of simplicity: the resulting system is very light and can be deployed without retraining any component.

After some exploration with the platform, we settled for a configuration — named RALI — that we used for treating the official dataset of the shared task. RALI is a combination of variants that delivers good performance both in terms of processing time and accuracy. This system achieves 92.1% TOP@1 on the development dataset, a performance we consider satisfactory considering the simplicity of the approach.

---

[1] https://lucene.apache.org/core/

Proceedings of the First Conference on Machine Translation, Volume 2: Shared Task Papers, pages 703–709,
Berlin, Germany, August 11-12, 2016. ©2016 Association for Computational Linguistics

2.1 Indexes

We built two main indexes. One from the source and one from the target documents of the collection provided. This last was organized into web-domains (49 in the development set) but, to ease implementation, we built the indexes from all, and enforced a posteriori that only target documents of a given web-domain are returned. In each index, documents are indexed (and tokenized) into three `Lucene` fields, one based on the text itself (`text`), one based on its `url` and one with the size of the text content (in number of tokens).

`Lucene` provides a number of tokenizers, but we felt the need to develop our own in order to properly handle the cases where punctuations is glued to words, and other typical cases one finds in real data. One point worth mentioning is that our tokenizer splits `urls` into several tokens.[2] This way of handling `urls` leads us to a simple but efficient `url`-based baseline. See Figure 1 for an illustration of a few bag-of-word queries considered in BADLUC.

2.2 Query Instantiation

Each field of each (source) document can be treated as a bag-of-word query. We used the *More-LikeThis* query generator available in `Lucene`[3] to implement this. The generator uses a variant of *tf.idf* and allows for the adjustment of a number of meta-parameters mainly for finding an application-specific compromise between the retrieval speed and its accuracy. We investigated the following ones[4]:

- minimum frequency of a term in a document (tf) for it to be considered in a query,

- minimum ($mindf$) and maximum ($maxdf$) number of documents in the collection that should contain a candidate query term,

- minimum ($minwl$) and maximum ($maxwl$) word length of a term in a query,

- maximum number of terms in a query ($size$),

- only words absent from a specified stop-list are legitimate query terms ($stop$).

These meta-parameters allow to easily create specific-purpose queries on the fly. For instance, by setting $mindf$ and $maxdf$ to 1, we built a collection-wide hapax query, while setting $minwl$ and $maxwl$ to 1 allows to build queries containing only punctuations marks.

2.2.1 Mono and Bilingual Queries

We tested two main families of queries: monolingual (`mono`) and bilingual (`bili`). The former is a way of easily capturing the tendency of a document and its translation to share a number of specific entities such as named-entities, numbers, or `urls`, for which no translation is required. Obviously, we were not expecting a high accuracy with monolingual queries, but we thought it would provide us with a very simple baseline. Actually the performance of such an engine on a given collection might be a valid metric to report, as a measure of the *difficulty* of the collection.

Bilingual queries involve a translation procedure. We simply translate the terms of the query based on a bilingual lexicon. We could have used the machine translated text provided by the organizers, but we decided early on in our experiments to resort to a simple bilingual lexicon approach, to simplify deployment. As a matter of fact, in a previous work on identifying parallel material in Wikipedia (Rebout and Langlais, 2014), we observed the inadequacy of the features computed from a generic SMT engine. Arguably our lexicon might not be very good either to deal with the nature of data collected over the Web, but we felt that a *general* bilingual lexicon might be more robust in this situation.

There are two meta-parameters that control our translation procedure:

- *keep* when set to true (which we note K), will leave untranslated terms (that is, terms unknown from our lexicon) in the query.[5] Hopefully this will leave in named- and numerical-entities that are useful for distinguishing parallel documents (Patry and Langlais, 2011).

- *nbTrans* controls the number of translations to keep when there is more than one available for a given source term. We consider two possible values: `all` puts all available

---

[2]We split `urls` according to a list of 33 separators, among which: @,?,/,<,>,(,),+,!,%,~

[3]`https://lucene.apache.org/core/4_4_0/queries/index.html`

[4]The *MoreLikeThis* mechanism also allows to settle a boost factor per query term, but we did not play with it.

[5]At least terms that meet the *MoreLikeThis* meta-parameters.

`http://creationwiki.org/Earth`		
Earth - CreationWiki, the encyclopedia of creation science [...] 23.439281 0.409rad 26.044grad Physical characteristics Mass 5.9736 * 1024 kg [...] taking 23 hours, 56 minutes, and 4.091 seconds to line up relative to the stars (Sidereal day), and 24 hours plus or minus 20 seconds to line up relative to the sun [...] is closer to the sun at some times of the year than others; the Earth moves faster [...] Kepler's laws of planetary motion [...] Saturnine - Uranian - Neptunian [...]		
`text`	`mono`	*texttok:* hours neptunian 1024 tennessee 2008 closer 397 ...
	`bili`	*texttok:* hours neptunian 1024 penchant théorie visible intensité fois tennessee prononcée prénommé 2008 métrique note closer équateur ...
`url`	`mono`	*urltok:* earth creationwiki / org http . : ...
	`bili`	*urltok:* déblai masse tanière terre earth creationwiki / org http . : ...
`both`	`bili`	*texttok:* hours neptunian 1024 penchant théorie tennessee absorbant prononcée prénommé 2008 métrique 397 équateur ... *urltok:* déblai masse tanière terre earth creationwiki / org http . : ...

Figure 1: Excerpt of bag-of-word queries for `http://creationwiki.org/Earth`.

translations in the query, while `first` picks the first one listed in the bilingual lexicon.[6]

2.2.2 Queries on Both Fields

`Lucene` allows to combine queries made on different fields. We use this functionality in order to produce queries with terms to be searched in both fields (`text` and `url`) in a single pass. An explicit example of this query is illustrated at the bottom of Figure 1.

2.2.3 Length-based Filter

`Lucene` allows to write queries as filters. It is basically a query that is executed before the main one and that returns an initial list of target documents on which the main query is applied. We implemented one such filter (`size`), using the third indexed field, based on the observation that pairs of parallel documents should have similar lengths (counted in tokens). We assumed the size ratio of source/target documents follows a normal distribution whose variance defines a confidence interval in which the target document size should fall. Unfortunately we estimated the parameters of the normal distribution on all reference pairs of documents provided by the shared task. This could explain our unsatisfactory scores on the official test set of the shared task[7].

2.3 Post Processors

Query execution produces for each source document a ranked list of target documents. Since each query is carried out independently over the collection, we run the risk of having a given target document associated with more than one source document. As a solution, we tested a few post-processors that select exactly one candidate per source document:

hungarian the Hungarian Algorithm (Kuhn, 1955) is a well-known combinatorial optimization algorithm[8] that solves the assignment problem in polynomial time.

b-greedy a *batch* greedy solution which picks the best ranked candidate among all the source documents paired, removes the selected pairs and loops until all source documents get paired with exactly one document.

o-greedy an *online* version of the greedy procedure just described, where we select for each source document the top ranked candidate that has not been paired with a previous source document yet. Once selected, the target document is removed from the potential list of candidates for subsequent source documents.

On a task of identifying parallel documents in Wikipedia, (Rebout and Langlais, 2014) shows that both the `hungarian` and the `b-greedy` algorithms deliver good performance overall.

---

[6]There is no specific order in the multiple translations listed in our lexicon for a given term, but some lexicons might list more general translations first.

[7]We noticed this bias after the submission period.

[8]Implementation available here: `https://github.com/KevinStern/software-and-algorithms`

	Strategies		TOP (%)		
	Query	[MLT] + [Trans]	@1	@5	@100
		`text` variants			
default	`mono`	$[2, 5, \infty, 0, 25, \text{F}]$	6.4	15.8	49.5
default+tok		$[2, 5, \infty, 0, 25, \text{F}]$	35.4	57.0	83.9
		$[1, 1, \infty, 1, 200, \text{F}]$	48.3	78.2	94.7
		$[1, 1, \infty, 1, \infty, \text{T}]$	57.2	86.2	96.2
		$[1, 1, \infty, 1, 200, \text{T}]$	64.9	87.2	96.8
	`+size`	$[1, 1, \infty, 1, 200, \text{T}]$	76.2	92.1	97.3
	`+size`	$[1, 1, \infty, 1, \infty, \text{T}]$	76.6	92.6	97.2
stop words	`+size`	$[1, 1, \infty, 1, \infty, \text{F}]$	69.2	89.7	96.4
wl = 3	`+size`	$[1, 1, \infty, 3, \infty, \text{T}]$	75.1	92.0	97.1
hapax	`+size`	$[1, 1, 1, 1, \infty, \text{T}]$	49.5	49.8	49.8
	`bili`	$[1, 1, \infty, 1, \infty, \text{T}]$ + [K,`first`]	74.4	93.5	98.7
		$[1, 1, \infty, 1, \infty, \text{F}]$ + [K,`first`]	71.9	92.8	**98.8**
		$[1, 1, \infty, 1, \infty, \text{F}]$ + [K,`all`]	34.5	53.2	88.4
		$[1, 1, \infty, 1, \infty, \text{T}]$ + [K,`all`]	44.1	64.5	95.0
	`+size`	$[1, 1, \infty, 1, \infty, \text{F}]$ + [K,`all`]	81.2	**97.1**	98.3
	`+size`	$[1, 1, \infty, 1, \infty, \text{T}]$ + [¬K,`all`]	81.0	94.8	98.2
best-`text`	`+size`	$[1, 1, \infty, 1, \infty, \text{T}]$ + [K,`first`]	**83.3**	96.2	98.2
		`url` variants			
WMT 2016			67.9		
	`mono`	$[1, 1, \infty, 1, \infty, \text{F}]$	75.4	84.4	92.9
	`+size`	$[1, 1, \infty, 1, \infty, \text{F}]$	78.4	87.5	95.3
	`bili`	$[1, 1, \infty, 1, \infty, \text{F}]$ + [K,`all`]	77.0	86.6	93.5
	`+size`	$[1, 1, \infty, 1, \infty, \text{F}]$ + [K,`first`]	78.8	88.0	91.3
best-`url`	`+size`	$[1, 1, \infty, 1, \infty, \text{F}]$ + [K,`all`]	**80.1**	**88.6**	**95.6**
RALI	`bili-size`	best-`text`+best-`url`	**88.6**	**97.6**	98.3

Table 1: Performances of some selected variants we tested. The MLT meta-parameters are $[tf,$ $mindf, maxdf, minwl, maxwl, size, stop]$, while those specific to the translation process are $[keep,$ $nbTrans]$. See Section 2 for more.

3 Experiments

3.1 Protocol

We conducted these experiments on the `lett.train` webcrawl available on the WMT2016 shared task webpage.[9] This crawl consists of 49 webdomains of various sizes, and the language of each document has been identified.

The test set made available for participants to calibrate their systems contains 1624 English `url`s for which the target (French) parallel coun-terpart is known. It is noteworthy that the task does not evaluate the ability of a system to detect whether a given source `url` has its parallel counterpart in the collection, which would require to train a classifier. [10] Because of this, we always propose a target `url` for a source one; and we measure performance with accuracy at rank 1, 5 and 100. Accuracy at rank i (TOP@i) is computed as the percentage of source `url`s for which the reference `url` is identified in the top-i candidates.

On top of our tokenizer which is clearly bi-

[10]We have conducted the training of such a classifier in past experiments (Rebout and Langlais, 2014), with results we evaluated to be around 85%.

ased toward space-oriented language scripts, we use two language specific resources: a stop-word list for English which comprises 572 entries,[11] as well as an in-house English-French bilingual lexicon of 107 799 entries. Very roughly, our lexicon could help the translation of only half of the query terms, which is an issue we should look at in the future.

3.2 Results

We tested over a thousand configurations, varying the meta-parameters of the *MoreLikeThis* (MLT) query generator, as well as the components described in the previous section. Table 1 shows a selection of some of the variants we tested. A line in this table indicates the best MLT meta-parameters we found for the configuration specified.

First of all, and without much surprise, we are able to outperform the `url` baseline (line WMT 2016) proposed by the organizers and which relies on some rules for matching `urls` in both language. Our best variant (line best-`url`) relying only on `urls` significantly outperforms this baseline by 12 absolute points in TOP@1. This variant tokenizes the `url`, then translates its words.[12]

Focusing on variants that exploit the text of the documents, we achieve a decent result without involving translation at all: the best monolingual variant we tested performs at 76.6 TOP@1, which also outperforms the WMT baseline. It should be noted that the default `Lucene` configuration (line `default`) does not perform well at all. Clearly, some tuning is necessary. In particular, using our tokenizer instead of the default one (which separates words at spaces) drastically increases performance (line `default+tok`). See Figure 1 for the kind of noisy input a tokenizer needs to handle. Unquestionably, using translation increases performance. The best variant we tested (line best-`text`) picks only one translation per source word, and leaves in the query the terms without translation.

Another interesting fact is the positive impact of the length-based filter presented in Section 2.2.3. Not only does this filter improve performances (a gain of 2 to 40 absolute points in TOP@1 is observed depending on the configuration tested), it

also gives an appreciable speed up (2 to 10, depending on the variants).

Incidentally, we reproduced a proxy to systems that would only consider hapax words, somehow similarly to (Enright and Kondrak, 2007; Patry and Langlais, 2011). The best variant we obtained lagged far behind other variants exploiting all the available text. One reason for this bad result might simply be that only collection-wide hapax terms are considered here.

The impact of the post-processor can be observed in Table 2. With the exception of the `url` variants, applying a post-processor improves TOP@1, a finding that corroborates the observations made in (Rebout and Langlais, 2014). We do not observe a huge performance difference between the algorithms. For the final submission, we applied the `o-greedy` algorithm because the others could not handle the size of the data set[13].

	url	text	both
w/o	80.1	83.3	88.6
o-greedy	79.7	87.6	91.6
b-greedy	80.7	87.9	92.1
hungarian	80.4	87.9	**92.1**

Table 2: TOP@1 of the post-processors we tested.

4 Analysis

4.1 Sensitivity to Source Document Size

We explored how our variants behave as a function of (source) document length. Figure 2 reports the cumulative accuracy of selected variants as a function of document size. We observe (red curve) the tendency for the RALI variant (the one we submitted) to globally improve as source documents get larger. Comparing the two dotted green curves, we also see that the benefit of embedding translation increases with document size. It is not entirely clear why we observe an increase in performance of the `url` variants as document size increases, since only the `urls` are considered. There are not many documents with a very short size, therefore the very first point of each curve is likely not significant.

---

[11]We downloaded it from: `http://www.perseus.tufts.edu/hopper/stopwords`

[12]Keeping all translations is in this case preferable to keeping only one translation.

[13]Without deep modifications of the algorithms.

	Almost no text inside
src	`http://rehazenter.lu/en/medical/explorations_fonctionnelles/explorations_posture/laboratoire_de_biomecanique`
trg	`http://rehazenter.lu/fr/medical/explorations_fonctionnelles/explorations_posture/laboratoire_de_biomecanique`
src	`http://www.dakar.com/2009/DAK/RIDERS/us/equipage/57.html`
trg	`http://www.dakar.com/2009/DAK/RIDERS/fr/equipage/57.html`
	Reference problem
src	`http://www.nauticnews.com/en/2009/06/23/burger-boat-company-launches-151-03-fantail-motor-yacht-sycara-iv`
trg	`http://www.nauticnews.com/2009/07/13/ishares-cup-2009-a-bord-dholmatro`

Table 3: Examples of problematic pairs of `urls` found in the development set.

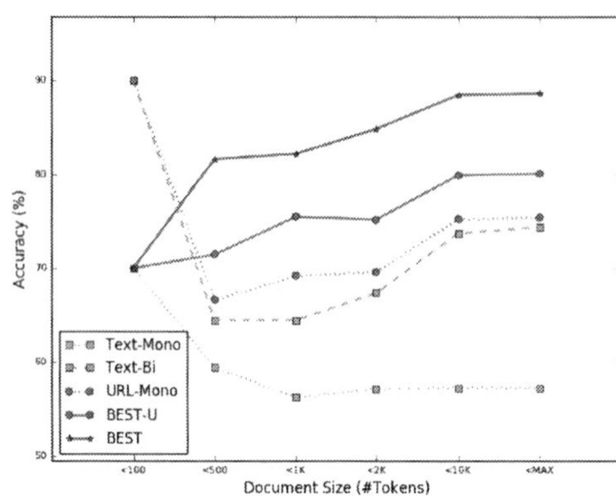

Figure 2: Accuracy (TOP@1) as a function of document size (counted in tokens).

4.2 Error Analysis

We conducted a small-scale analysis of the errors made by the RALI configuration. First of all, we observed frequent cases where a French page contains a fair amount of English material (which might explain part of the performance of monolingual variants). We also noticed that a given document has often several associated `urls`. In such a situation, our system will almost invariably pick the largest `url` (more tokens do match), which is not necessarily the case of the reference.

In the 1.7% cases of RALI could not identify the expected target document in the top-100 positions, we observed that many documents contained almost no text. Typical examples are provided in Table 3. In such cases, the `url`-based approach should be more efficient. This means that learning which variant to trust given a source document could be fruitful. We also observed inevitable reference errors (see the bottom line of Table 3 for an example). Last, we noticed that some documents are rather specific, and our lexicon does not help

much the translation process. This is the case for the document shown in Figure 1.

5 Conclusion

Our participation in the shared task has been carried out thanks to the `Lucene` framework. We devised a number of configurations by varying the parameters of the *MoreLikeThis* query mechanism, as well as by exploiting other built-in features. We notably found a simple yet efficient way of matching documents thanks to their `urls`, which outperforms the baseline provided by the organizers. We also observe that querying the target collection with queries built without translation already achieves a decent performance and that involving a translation mechanism as simple as using a bilingual lexicon gives a nice boost in performance. We also propose to filter target documents based on the length of the source document. This not only improves results, but also speeds up retrieval. Last, we measured that applying a post-processor (such as the Hungarian algorithm) further improves performance.

The best system we identified on the development set combines (in a single query) terms translated from the source document as well as terms from its `url`. A length-based filter is applied, as well as a post-processor (Hungarian algorithm). This system achieves a TOP@1 of 92.1, and a TOP@100 of 98.6, a respectable performance for such a simple system.

We are currently investigating whether better performance can be obtained by using machine translation instead of the lexicon-based translation approach used here.

Acknowledgments

This work has been founded by the *Fonds de Recherche du Québec en Nature et Technologie* (FRQNT).

References

Jessica Enright and Grzegorz Kondrak. 2007. A fast method for parallel document identification. In *Human Language Technologies 2007: The Conference of the North American Chapter of the Association for Computational Linguistics; Companion Volume, Short Papers*, pages 29–32.

H. W. Kuhn. 1955. The hungarian method for the assignment problem. *Naval Research Logistics Quarterly*, 2(1-2):83–97.

Dragos Stefan Munteanu and Daniel Marcu. 2005. Improving machine translation performance by exploiting non-parallel corpora. *Comput. Linguist.*, 31(4):477–504, December.

Alexandre Patry and Philippe Langlais. 2011. Identifying parallel documents from a large bilingual collection of texts: Application to parallel article extraction in wikipedia. In *Proceedings of the 4th Workshop on Building and Using Comparable Corpora: Comparable Corpora and the Web*, pages 87–95.

Lise Rebout and Philippe Langlais. 2014. An iterative approach for mining parallel sentences in a comparable corpus. In *LREC*, pages 648–655, Rekjavik, Iceland.

Serge Sharoff, Reinhard Rapp, and Pierre Zweigenbaum. 2013. Overviewing Important Aspects of the Last Twenty Years of Research in Comparable Corpora. In Serge Sharoff, Reinhard Rapp, Pierre Zweigenbaum, and Pascale Fung, editors, *Building and Using Comparable Corpora*, pages 1–17. Springer Berlin Heidelberg, January.

Jason R. Smith, Herve Saint-Amand, Magdalena Plamada, Philipp Koehn, Chris Callison-Burch, and Adam Lopez. 2013. Dirt cheap web-scale parallel text from the common crawl. In *Proceedings of the 51st Annual Meeting of the Association for Computational Linguistics*, pages 1374–1383.

Jakob Uszkoreit, Jay M. Ponte, Ashok C. Popat, and Moshe Dubiner. 2010. Large scale parallel document mining for machine translation. In *Proceedings of the 23rd International Conference on Computational Linguistics*, pages 1101–1109.

Using Term Position Similarity and Language Modeling for Bilingual Document Alignment

Thanh C. Le, Hoa Trong Vu, Jonathan Oberländer, Ondřej Bojar
Charles University in Prague
Faculty of Mathematics and Physics
Institute of Formal and Applied Linguistics
{thanhlct, hoavutrongvn, jonathan.oberlaender}@gmail.com
bojar@ufal.mff.cuni.cz

Abstract

The WMT Bilingual Document Alignment Task requires systems to assign source pages to their "translations", in a big space of possible pairs. We present four methods: The first one uses the term position similarity between candidate document pairs. The second method requires automatically translated versions of the target text, and matches them with the candidates. The third and fourth methods try to overcome some of the challenges presented by the nature of the corpus, by considering the string similarity of source URL and candidate URL, and combining the first two approaches.

1 Introduction

Parallel data play an essential role in training of statistical machine translation (MT) systems. While big collections have been already created, e.g. the corpus OPUS (Tiedemann, 2012), the World Wide Web remains a largely underexploited source. That is the motivation for the shared task "Bilingual Document Alignment" of the ACL 2016 workshop First Conference on Machine Translation (WMT16) which requires participants to align web page in one language to their translation counterparts in another language.

Given a large collection of documents, the first step in extracting parallel data is to organize the documents into heaps by the language they are written in. For two languages of interest, a brute-force approach would consider all pairs of documents from the two heaps. Since the number of possible pairings is too high, it is necessary to employ some broad and fast heuristics to filter out the obviously wrong pairs.

Some approaches to the task rely on document metadata (e.g. the similarity of document URLs or language tags within URLs), some emphasize more the actual content of the documents. Previous work (Rapp, 1999; Ma and Liberman, 1999) focused on document alignment by counting word co-occurrences between source and target documents in a fixed-size window. More recently, methods from cross-lingual information retrieval (CLIR) have been used (Snover et al., 2008; Abdul Rauf and Schwenk, 2011), ranking lists of target documents given a source document by a probabilistic model. Locality sensitive hashing has also been applied (Krstovski and Smith, 2011).

In this paper, we describe our attempt. The rest of the paper is organized as follows: In Section 2, we describe the methods we used in our four submitted systems. Section 3 describes our experimental setup and compares the results of the proposed methods. We conclude the paper and discuss possible future improvements in Section 4.

Proceedings of the First Conference on Machine Translation, Volume 2: Shared Task Papers, pages 710–716,
Berlin, Germany, August 11-12, 2016. ©2016 Association for Computational Linguistics

2 Methods

We submitted four different systems: UFAL-1 uses term position similarity (especially rare terms) between documents. UFAL-2 uses language modeling on automatically translated documents to perform the matching. UFAL-3 reorders the results of UFAL-2 to take into account the similarity in the URL structure, and UFAL-4 combines UFAL-3 and UFAL-1 to further improve the results.

2.1 Term position similarity (UFAL-1)

Two similar languages such as English and French can easily share a portion of their lexicons, especially proper names, some acronyms and numbers are likely to keep their forms after translation. If two documents are mutual translations, the sequence of positions of those terms should be correlated. Much past research (Ma and Liberman, 1999; Rapp, 1999) has exploited these features, using a fixed-size window and counting the co-occurrences in this range. This method, however, requires considerable tuning of parameters, and if two shared terms are located outside of the window, no credit will be added. In this work, we consider similarity which not only takes into account co-occurrences of terms but also their positions. This metric also assumes that co-occurrences of rare terms are more important than those of common terms. Experiments below show that our method performs much better than the fixed-window method.

Our term position similarity is defined as follows:

$$\rho(S, T) = \sum_{t \in S \cap T} \log(1 + \frac{\max(c)}{c_t}) \cdot$$

$$\cdot \sum_{i}^{N_t} \frac{l_S - |p_{S_t}^i - p_{T_t}^i|}{l_S} \quad (1)$$

Here S, T are the source and target documents, respectively, $S \cap T$ is the set containing all terms which occurs in both documents, $N_t = \min(|S_t|, |T_t|)$ where S_t, T_t is the number of occurrences of term t in the respective document. The length of the source document is denoted l_S. $p_{S_t}^i$ is the position of i-th occurrence of the term t in the source document and similarly for the target document ($p_{T_t}^i$). Finally, c_t is the total number occurrences of t in the data set and $\max(c)$ is

Figure 1: The noisy channel model for Bilingual Document Alignment

the total number of occurrences of the most frequent term in all the source documents. In sum, $\log(1 + \frac{\max(c)}{c_t})$ is a weight to promote the importance of rare terms and the inner sum $\sum_{i}^{N_t}$ measures the relative displacement of the term w in S compared to T.

To increase the number of terms contributing to the metric result, we employ a bilingual dictionary and translate all words from target document that do not appear in the source into their most frequent translation.

The submission using this method is called **UFAL-1**.

2.2 Language model-based approach (UFAL-2)

In contrast to the method in Section 2.1, the approach labeled UFAL-2 relies on automatic translation from one side to the other (either source-to-target or vice versa). With documents on both sides converted to one language, we then treat the task as a noisy channel problem, similarly to many works of information retrieval based on language modelling techniques (Ponte and Croft, 1998; Zhai and Lafferty, 2001; Xu et al., 2001).

Specifically, we assume that the observed output is the source page S, damaged by noisy transfer of some target page T. Through decoding, we want to find the target page T that most likely lead to the observed output S. The process is visualized in Figure 1. Therefore, like in the noisy channel model (Brill and Moore, 2000), to decode the input T, we estimate the probability of T given the output observation S, $P(T|S)$. Following Bayes' rule, the problem is characterized by Equation 2:

$$P(T|S) = \frac{P(S|T)P(T)}{P(S)} \quad (2)$$

(At this stage, it is no longer important, that T was the automatic translation of a French page into English and S was the original English source page.)

As our final aim is to find the best T that causes the output S, we can ignore the denominator $P(S)$ in Equation 2, since it is the same for every value of T. So we have the problem equation as follows:

$$T_{best} = \underset{T}{\operatorname{argmax}} \quad \underbrace{P(S|T)}_{generative\ model} \quad \overbrace{P(T)}^{prior} \quad (3)$$

Since estimating the generative model $P(S|T)$ in Equation 3 is intractable, we assume conditional independence of terms $t_i, t_j \in S$ given T:

$$P(S|T) = P(t_1, ..., t_{|S|}|T) \approx \prod_{i=1}^{|S|} P(t_i|T) \quad (4)$$

To slightly speed up the computation in Equation 4, we can group all occurrences of the same term together as in Equation 5. To avoid an underflow problem, we move the computation to log space, see Equation 6:

$$P(S|T) \approx \prod_{distinct\ t \in S} P(t|T)^{tf_S} \quad (5)$$

$$\log(P(S|T)) \approx \sum_{distinct\ t \in S} tf_S \log(P(t|T)) \quad (6)$$

where tf_S is the number of occurrences of the term t in S. The remaining problem is to estimate $P(t|T)$. Fortunately, this can be achieved simply using maximum likelihood estimation (Scholz, 1985) and it turns out to be the unigram language model (LM) as follows:

$$P(t|T) = \frac{tf_T}{|T|} \quad (7)$$

where tf_T is the number of occurrences of the term t in T. In order to avoid zero probabilities, a smoothing technique is necessary. We used Jelinek-Mercer smoothing (Jelinek, 1980). The estimation at document level in Equation 7 is smoothed with the estimation over the domain level, $P(t|D)$, where D is the set of all page translations available for webdomain D of page T. We additionally use add-one smoothing for $P(t|D)$ to make sure the model handles well also terms never seen in the webdomain data.

Back to prior in the problem equation (Equation 3), it may be used to integrate very useful information for each target French page. For example, a French page that has been selected to be a pair with another page should have a lower prior

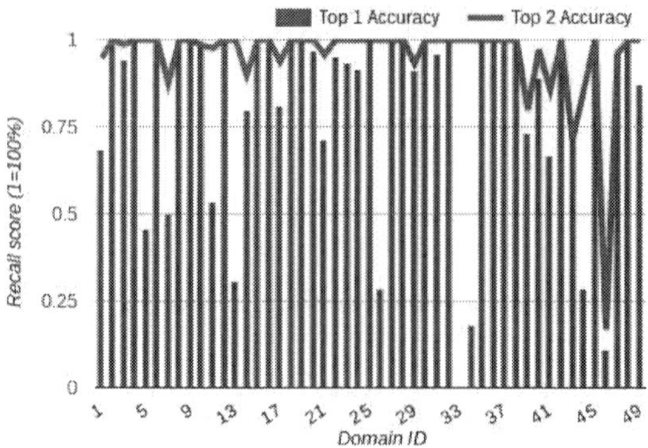

Figure 2: Performance of UFAL-2 on individual webdomains in the training set

for the next prediction. The prior may also reflect the difference in length of T and S, avoiding the alignment of pages differing too much. Here, for simplicity, we use uniform distribution as the prior. The final equation ranking target French pages T with respect to a given English source document S is thus:

$$T_{best} = \underset{T}{\operatorname{argmax}} \sum_{distinct\ t \in S} tf_S \log(\lambda P(t|T)$$
$$+ (1 - \lambda) P(t|D)) \quad (8)$$

where $P(t|D)$, as mentioned, is the probability of the term t occurring in the webdomain D and the parameter λ of Jelinek-Mercer smoothing is set to 0.5. We submit this method for evaluation under the label **UFAL-2**.

2.3 Optimizing for top-1 evaluation (UFAL-3)

We noticed that there were many cases where several documents contained the same (or almost the same) text, which therefore get scored (roughly) the same by each of UFAL-1 and UFAL-2. This issue will create noise that can harm us in the evaluation of the shared task, as can be seen in Figure 2: There is a significant difference between the top 1 and top 2 accuracy of our UFAL-2 system from Section 2.2, see e.g. the webdomains 5, 7, 13 (`kusu.com`), or 34 (`www.eu2007.de`). While both the 1st best and the 2nd best top predictions could be assumed correct since the two predicted pages are not distinguishable or only differ in unimportant details (e.g. Google Ads), the official scoring will be based on a single-best answer.[1]

A closer investigation reveals that the URLs that are marked correct in the training data are usually the ones most similar to the source URL. We therefore look at the top 10 candidates from the UFAL-2, and choose the candidate that is within some threshold of the top result and closest in Levenshtein distance from the source URL. The threshold value of **85** was obtained experimentally on the training data. The result after this refinement is submitted for the evaluation under the name **UFAL-3**.

2.4 Combining UFAL-3 and UFAL-1 into UFAL-4

We now have the outputs of two methods, UFAL-1 and UFAL-3 (as a replacement of UFAL-2), and we would like to combine them to one method. Since the result of UFAL-3 is very good (see Section 3.2), we decided to report UFAL-3 in most cases and resort to UFAL-1 only if we do not trust the proposal of UFAL-3.

To estimate the certainty of UFAL-3 prediction, we use Kullback-Leibler divergence (Kullback and Leibler, 1951) and measure how mismatching the predicted pair of documents is. To do so, we model the English source text and translation of the predicted candidate as multinomial distributions, and then compute the KL-divergence to see what their distance is. In particular, a higher KL-score presents a bigger distance between the pairs, in other words, they are less likely to be a correct pair.

Given the overall good performance of UFAL-3, there are not many negative examples to optimize the threshold for rejecting the predicted pair. We solve the issue by artificially creating new negative cases: we remove automatic translations of correct target French pages for two webdomains, rerun the predictions and then compute the KL-divergence for all predicted pairs. The result of 1624 pairs predicted is reported in Figure 3, in which the artificial negative examples are highlighted with a blue line.

Based on observations for the modified training data, we set the threshold to **0.35**. If the KL divergence for a pair of documents predicted by UFAL-3 exceeds this value, the pair is considered a wrong prediction. In that case, we use the method from

---

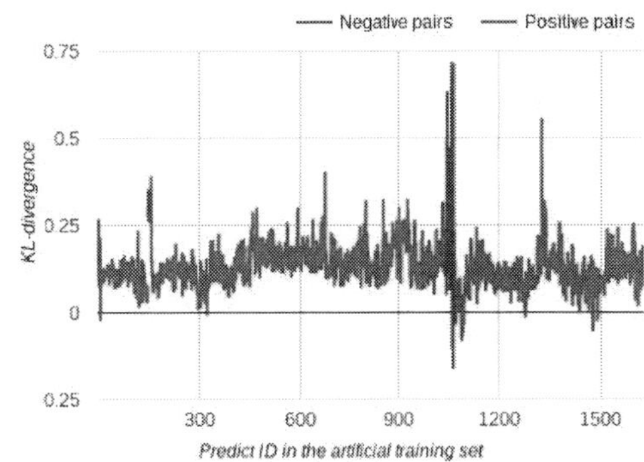

Figure 3: KL-divergence for all 1624 predicted pairs in the modified training set where two correct translations are removed.

Section 2.1 (UFAL-1) with the bilingual dictionary size of 5000 entries. Similar to the method from Section 2.3 (UFAL-3), we consider the top 2 candidates and choose the one with a lower Levenshtein distance. We call this combined method **UFAL-4** in the evaluation.

3 Experiments

3.1 Experimental setup

We used the data published with the Shared Task on Bilingual Document Alignment (WMT 2016), containing roughly 4200 million pairs, in which 1624 pairs have been labeled as mutual translations to serve as a development set.

Work on information extraction typically uses precision and recall of the extracted information as an evaluation measure. However, in this task, manually classifying all possible pairs is impossible, so the true recall cannot be established. The organizers thus decided to evaluate the methods on the recall *within the fixed set of document pairs*, the development set released prior submission deadline and the official test set disclosed only with the final results.

While the official scores are top-1 recall (i.e. the recall taking the single-best prediction for each input sentence), we also evaluate our systems at top 2 and top 5 outputs because, as discussed in Section 2.3, the there are many documents with the same content, but the development set of pairs mentions only one of them.

All documents are tokenized by splitting on white-space and passed to a filter which prunes all pairs having a ratio of the lengths in tokens of two

---

[1] We were told by the organizers later that the test set does not suffer from this problem of many very similar pages.

Dictionary size	Systems		
	Baseline	Fixed window	Term position
0	67.92	78.94	88.30
1000	67.92	80.6	88.36
5000	67.92	81.9	89.53 (UFAL-1)
10000	67.92	85.71	91.63
25000	67.92	88.73	94.27
50000	67.92	90.76	**96.06**

Table 1: Recall measures by baseline system, system using fixed-size window method and system using term position similarity

Method	Recall		
	Top 1	Top 2	Top 5
Baseline	67.92		
UFAL-1	89.53		
UFAL-2	88.40	97.40	98.30
UFAL-3	93.70		
UFAL-4	94.70		

Table 2: Result on the development set

documents bigger than 2. Afterwards, all documents are ranked by the discussed methods. The first 1, 2 or 5 ranked documents with score higher than a threshold are reported.

In the first experiment, we prepare three systems for comparison. We use the provided baseline system in the mentioned shared task which simply finds matching URLs by discarding language identifiers, such as en, fr. We also implement a fixed-size window method as described in Ma and Liberman (1999). We compare the fixed-size window method with our term position similarity in 6 tests with increasing size of the underlying bilingual dictionary. This dictionary is obtained by running IBM Model 2 implemented by Dyer et al. (2013) on the translations of the data set provided by the organizers. We extract the 50000 most frequent word alignments $fr - en$ having $P(en \mid fr) > 0.7$ and then randomly draw a subset of this dictionary for each test. The variant with 5000 entries is our submission called UFAL-1. If two documents have an identical score, the one having a shorter URL is preferred.

In the second experiment, we compare the term position similarity method (UFAL-1) with the language model-based approach (UFAL-2 and UFAL-3) and the combination method (UFAL-4). The term position similarity method uses a bilingual dictionary containing 5000 entries. Automatic translations for all target documents were provided by the organizers who used a baseline Moses setup trained on Europarl and the News Commentary corpus.

3.2 Experiment result

The results for first experiment are in Table 1. From these results, we can clearly see that term position similarity outperforms the fixed-size window method and surpasses the baseline system with around 20% even without a bilingual dictionary. By increasing size of the bilingual dictionary up to 50000 entries, we can boost up the term position similarity method by 8% to **96.06%**. However, there are still a number of avenues for improvement. First, as we found that our method encountered many errors on the webdomain www.luontoportti.com that contains extremely specialized words not covered by our dictionary, this makes a domain-based bilingual dictionary one of the most desirable potential improvements. Secondly, the term position similarity method is very sensitive to the case when a target document contains source language text, because it increases the co-occurrence rate between two documents. Any errors in language identification can thus adversely affect the final extracted parallel corpus.

We present the results of the second experiment in Table 2. The improved methods UFAL-3 and UFAL-4 show significant gains, achieving 93.7% and 94.7% in recall. We also clearly see the remarkable changes in recall for the top match vs. top two matches caused by the similar documents in the corpus, as discussed in Section 2.3.

Finally, we report the official scores in Table 3. The official test set consists of 2402 document pairs and methods are evaluated in terms of the percentage of these pairs that they reported ("Recall"). The shared task winner NovaLincs-url-coverage (denoted "NovaLics" in the table for short) reached 94.96%, our best method UFAL-4 ranked about in the middle of the methods with the recall of 84.22%. As we see in the remaining columns, UFAL-4 produces by far the highest number of document pairs (more that 1M). The official scoring script filters this list and keeps only the pairs where neither the source URL nor the target URL was previously reported ("After 1-1").

	Official	Pairs		Lenient
Method	Recall [%]	Reported	After 1-1	Recall
NovaLincs	94.96	235812	235812	?
UFAL-4	84.22	1080962	268105	92.67
UFAL-1	81.31	592337	248344	87.89
UFAL-3	80.68	574434	207358	89.97
UFAL-2	79.14	574433	178038	88.43

Table 3: The winner and our methods on the official test set.

After this style of deduplication, the number of pairs reduces to about 268k, slightly higher than the number of pairs reported by the winner.

The official test set results are in line with our observation on the development set: term position similarity (UFAL-1) performs well (although not as well as on the development set) and the two variations of the noisy-channel approach are slightly worse, with UFAL-3 (URL similarity) better than UFAL-2. The combination (UFAL-4) is the best of our methods.

We note that for systems like ours that produce all URL pairs they deem good enough, the 1-1 deduplication may be too strict. We thus also report a lenient form of the recall: whenever a pair of URLs from the test set appears (as an unordered pair) among the pairs produced by our method, we give a credit for it. As seen in the last column of Table 3, the noisy-channel methods seem better than term position similarity in this measure. Considering that UFAL-2 and UFAL-3 produced slightly fewer pairs than UFAL-1, it may seem that they are more precise. This however need not be the case; the set of pairs produced by the systems is again too large for manual validation so the true precision cannot be evaluated.

4 Conclusion and future work

In this paper, we presented four systems for the Bilingual Document Alignment shared task. These system all perform well on the provided development set (roughly 90% accuracy for top 1 recall) as well as on the official test set (above 80%; about in the middle of all the participating methods). One system, UFAL-1, uses term position similarity. The second system, UFAL-2, uses a probabilistic model inspired by language modelling and the noisy channel model. Two others systems, UFAL-3 and 4, are improvements of the two former ones, where UFAL-3 tries to overcome the fact that content is repeated in a web-based corpus and UFAL-4 is a more advanced combination of UFAL-3 and 1.

Several refinements of the proposed approaches are worth further investigation. In particular, a systematic method of creating a bilingual dictionary dedicated for each specific webdomain should increase the accuracy of the term position similarity method. For the language model approach, it might be valuable to use a more comprehensive generative model (e.g. bi/tri-gram language model). Adding a prior might also enhance model accuracy. Another potential for the LM-based approach is, instead of depending on translations of target pages, to apply a bilingual dictionary or a translation model directly for the generative process.

The method of UFAL-3 still misses some of the straightforward cases of URL mapping. For instance, it might be advisable to use a more specific variant of edit distance variant, e.g. to penalize changes in special characters like "/" or "?" compared to normal word characters.

Beyond our submissions to the shared task, we suggest that more attention should be paid to the evaluation method. The problem of repeated or very similar content on the web is omnipresent, so any attempt to handle it is likely to improve the reliability of top-1 recall measurements, improving the bilingual alignment task itself.

Acknowledgments

This work has received funding from the European Union's Horizon 2020 research and innovation programme under grant agreement no. 644402 (HimL).

Computational resources were supplied by the Ministry of Education, Youth and Sports of the Czech Republic under the Projects CESNET (Project No. LM2015042) and CERIT-Scientific Cloud (Project No. LM2015085) provided within the program Projects of Large Research, Development and Innovations Infrastructures.

References

Sadaf Abdul Rauf and Holger Schwenk. 2011. Parallel sentence generation from comparable corpora for improved smt. *Machine Translation* 25(4):341–375.

Eric Brill and Robert C Moore. 2000. An improved error model for noisy channel spelling correction. In *Proceedings of the 38th Annual Meeting on Association for Computational*

Linguistics. Association for Computational Linguistics, pages 286–293.

Chris Dyer, Victor Chahuneau, and Noah A Smith. 2013. A simple, fast, and effective reparameterization of ibm model 2. Association for Computational Linguistics.

Frederick Jelinek. 1980. Interpolated estimation of markov source parameters from sparse data. *Pattern recognition in practice* .

Kriste Krstovski and David A. Smith. 2011. A minimally supervised approach for detecting and ranking document translation pairs. In *Proceedings of the Sixth Workshop on Statistical Machine Translation*. Association for Computational Linguistics, Stroudsburg, PA, USA, WMT '11, pages 207–216.

Solomon Kullback and Richard A Leibler. 1951. On information and sufficiency. *The annals of mathematical statistics* 22(1):79–86.

Xiaoyi Ma and Mark Liberman. 1999. Bits: A method for bilingual text search over the web. In *Machine Translation Summit VII*. Citeseer, pages 538–542.

Jay M Ponte and W Bruce Croft. 1998. A language modeling approach to information retrieval. In *Proceedings of the 21st annual international ACM SIGIR conference on Research and development in information retrieval*. ACM, pages 275–281.

Reinhard Rapp. 1999. Automatic identification of word translations from unrelated english and german corpora. In *Proceedings of the 37th annual meeting of the Association for Computational Linguistics on Computational Linguistics*. Association for Computational Linguistics, pages 519–526.

FW Scholz. 1985. Maximum likelihood estimation. *Encyclopedia of Statistical Sciences* .

Matthew Snover, Bonnie Dorr, and Richard Schwartz. 2008. Language and translation model adaptation using comparable corpora. In *Proceedings of the Conference on Empirical Methods in Natural Language Processing*. Association for Computational Linguistics, pages 857–866.

Jörg Tiedemann. 2012. Parallel Data, Tools and Interfaces in OPUS. In Nicoletta Calzolari (Conference Chair), Khalid Choukri, Thierry Declerck, Mehmet Ugur Dogan, Bente Maegaard, Joseph Mariani, Jan Odijk, and Stelios Piperidis, editors, *Proceedings of the Eight International Conference on Language Resources and Evaluation (LREC'12)*. European Language Resources Association (ELRA), Istanbul, Turkey.

Jinxi Xu, Ralph Weischedel, and Chanh Nguyen. 2001. Evaluating a probabilistic model for cross-lingual information retrieval. In *Proceedings of the 24th annual international ACM SIGIR conference on Research and development in information retrieval*. ACM, pages 105–110.

Chengxiang Zhai and John Lafferty. 2001. A study of smoothing methods for language models applied to ad hoc information retrieval. In *Proceedings of the 24th annual international ACM SIGIR conference on Research and development in information retrieval*. ACM, pages 334–342.

The ADAPT Bilingual Document Alignment system at WMT16

Pintu Lohar, Haithem Afli, Chao-Hong Liu and Andy Way
ADAPT Centre
School of Computing
Dublin City University
Dublin, Ireland
{FirstName.LastName}@adaptcentre.ie

Abstract

Comparable corpora have been shown to be useful in several multilingual natural language processing (NLP) tasks. Many previous papers have focused on how to improve the extraction of parallel data from this kind of corpus on different levels. In this paper, we are interested in improving the quality of bilingual comparable corpora according to increased document alignment score. We describe our participation in the bilingual document alignment shared task of the First Conference on Machine Translation (WMT16). We propose a technique based on source-to-target sentence- and word-based scores and the fraction of matched source named entities. We performed our experiments on English-to-French document alignments for this bilingual task.

1 Introduction

Parallel corpora (or "bitexts"), comprising bilingual/multilingual texts extracted from parallel documents, are crucial resources for building SMT systems. Unfortunately, parallel documents are a scarce resource for many language pairs with the exception of English, French, Spanish, Arabic, Chinese and some European languages included in *Europarl*[1] (Koehn, 2005) and OPUS (Tiedemann, 2012).[2] Furthermore, these existing available corpora do not cover some special domains or sub-domains.

For the field of SMT, this can be problematic, because MT systems trained on data from a specific domain (e.g. parliamentary proceedings) perform poorly when applied to other domains, e.g.

sports news articles. As a result, the area of domain adaptation has been a hot topic in MT over the past few years.

One way to overcome this lack of data is to exploit comparable corpora which are much more easily available (Munteanu and Marcu, 2005). A comparable corpus is a collection of texts composed independently in their respective languages and combined on the basis of similarity of content. These are bilingual/multilingual documents that are comparable in content and form to various degrees and dimensions. Potential sources of textual comparable corpora are the output from multilingual news organizations such as Agence France Presse (AFP), Xinhua, Reuters, CNN, BBC, etc. These texts are widely available on the Web for many language pairs (Resnik and Smith, 2003). Another example is *Euronews*, which proposes news text in several languages clustered by domain (e.g. sports, finance, etc.). The degree of parallelism can vary considerably, from noisy parallel texts, to 'quasi parallel' texts (Fung and Cheung, 2004).

No matter what data we are dealing with, if we want to automatically create large amounts of parallel documents for SMT training, the ability to detect parallel sentences or sub-sentences contained in these kinds of comparable corpus is crucial. However, for some specific domains, such as news, the problem of document alignment can drastically reduce the quantity of the final parallel data extracted. For example, Afli et al. (2012) showed that they were able to extract only 20% of an expected 1.9M-token parallel sentence collection using their automatic parallel data extraction method. For this reason, they tried to improve this method by exploiting parallel *phrases* (i.e. not just parallel *sentences*) which increased the quantity of extracted data (Afli et al., 2013, 2016).

However, the precision of such automatic meth-

---

[1] http://www.statmt.org/europarl/
[2] http://opus.lingfil.uu.se/

Proceedings of the First Conference on Machine Translation, Volume 2: Shared Task Papers, pages 717–723,
Berlin, Germany, August 11-12, 2016. ©2016 Association for Computational Linguistics

ods is still much less than expected. We contend that the main problem comes from the document alignment of such comparable corpora. One of the challenges of our research is to build data and techniques for some under-resourced domains. We propose to investigate the improvement of alignment of bilingual comparable documents in order to solve this problem.

Accordingly, in this paper we describe an experimental framework designed to address a situation when we have large quantities of non-aligned parallel or comparable documents in different languages that we need to exploit. Our document alignment methods are based on a new scoring technique for parallel document detection based on the word-length and sentence-length ratio and named entity recognition (NER).

Apart from this, we also compared the total number of source and target named entities (NEs) so that they should not differ significantly which can play a major role in determining the comparability of two texts.

The remainder of the paper is structured as follows. The related work on parallel data extraction and comparability measures is briefly discussed in Section 2. In Section 3, we detail our proposed method and provide the results of our experiments on *WMT-2016* data in Section 4. In Section 5, we present the conclusion and directions for future work.

2 Related work

In the "Big Data" world that we now live in, it is widely believed that *there is no better data than more data* (e.g. Mayer-Schönberger and Cukier (2013)). In line with this idea, a considerable amount of work has taken place in the NLP community on discovering parallel sentences/fragments in a comparable corpus in order to augment existing parallel data collections. However, the extensive literature related to the problem of exploiting comparable corpora takes a somewhat different perspective than we do in this paper.

Typically, comparable corpora do not have any information regarding document-pair similarity. They are made of many documents in one language which do not have any corresponding translated document in the other language. Furthermore, when the documents are paired, they are not literal translations of each other. Thus, extracting parallel data from such corpora requires special algorithms. Many papers use the Web as a comparable corpus. An adaptive approach, proposed by Zhao and Vogel (2002), aims at mining parallel sentences from a bilingual comparable news collection collected from the Web. A maximum likelihood criterion was used by combining sentence-length models with lexicon-based models. The translation lexicon is iteratively updated using the mined parallel data to obtain better vocabulary coverage and translation probability estimation. Resnik and Smith (2003) propose a web-mining-based system called STRAND and show that their approach is able to find large numbers of similar document pairs. Yang and Li (2003) present an alignment method at different levels (title, word and character) based on dynamic programming (DP). The goal is to identify one-to-one title pairs in an English–Chinese corpus collected from the Web. They apply the longest common sub-sequence to find the most reliable Chinese translation of an English word. One of the main methods relies on cross-lingual information retrieval (CLIR), with different techniques for transferring the request into the target language (using a bilingual dictionary or a full SMT system). Utiyama and Isahara (2003) use CLIR techniques and DP to extract sentences from an English–Japanese comparable corpus. They identify similar article pairs, and having considered them as parallel texts, then align sentences using a sentence-pair similarity score and use DP to find the least-cost alignment over the document pair. Munteanu and Marcu (2005) use a bilingual lexicon to translate some of the words of the source sentence. These translations are then used to query the database to find matching translations using IR techniques. There have been only a few studies trying to investigate the formal quantification of how similar two comparable documents are. Li and Gaussier (2010) presented one of the first works on developing a comparability measure based on the expectation of finding translation word pairs in the corpus. Our approach follows this line of work based on a method developed by Sennrich and Volk (2010).

3 Aligning comparable documents

3.1 Processing the comparable documents

In this work, experiments are conducted on the test data[3] provided by the *WMT-2016* organizers, which comprised 203 web domains with more than 1 million documents in total. The data is provided in *.lett* format with following fields, 1) Language ID, 2) MIME type, 3) Encoding, 4) URL, 5) Complete content in Base64 encoding and 6) Main textual content in Base64 encoding. We extracted URLs and texts from this collection of data and converted them into *UTF-8* format.

3.2 Basic Idea

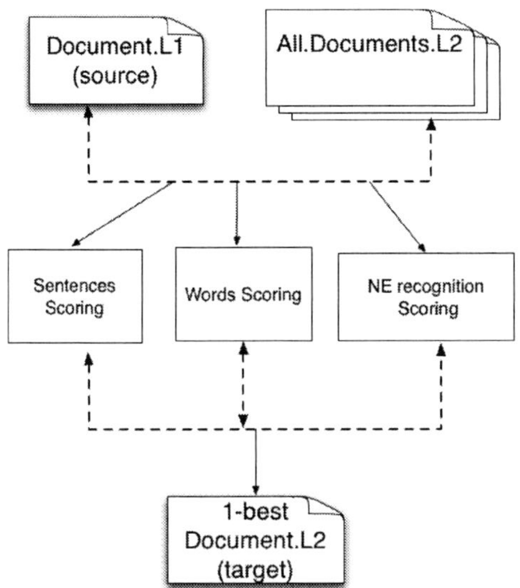

Figure 1: Architecture of comparable alignment system

In this work we propose an extension of the method described in Sennrich and Volk (2010). The basic system architecture is described in Figure 1. We begin by removing those documents that have very little contents in order to avoid all possible comparisons. Subsequently, we introduce three steps: sentence-based scoring, word-based scoring and NE-based scoring. Finally we used a combined weighted score of the three scores to select the target document with highest value.

3.3 Sentence-based scoring

Since there are a large number of source and target documents, there are billions of possible com-

parisons required to complete the calculations of finding possible document alignments. Therefore, we have to restrict the comparison calculations only to those source-target text pairs that have a close sentence-length ratio, otherwise they are less likely to be comparable texts. This is necessary since comparing each source with each target text would result in an undesirably large number of comparisons and thus a very long time to process all steps even for a single domain. Let us assume that S_s and S_t are the number of sentences in the source and target texts, respectively. We then follow a very simple formula to calculate source-target sentence-length ratio(R_{SL}), as in (1) :

$$R_{SL} = \frac{\min(S_s, S_t)}{\max(S_s, S_t)} \qquad (1)$$

We construct this equation in order to confine the value between 0 and 1 which implies that if either of the source or target text contains no sentences, R_{SL} will be 0, and 1 if they have the same number of sentences. Therefore, a value of 1 or even very close to it has a positive indication towards being comparable but this is not the only requirement, as there are many documents with the same (or very similar) number of sentences. For this reason, we consider word and NE-based scoring in Sections 3.4 and 3.5, respectively.

3.4 Word-based scoring

The reason behind this step is very similar to the step discussed in Section 3.3, but here it is based on word-length comparison. Let us assume that W_s and W_t are the number of words in the source and target texts, respectively. Hence our equation for calculating source-target word-length ratio (R_{WL}) is (2):

$$R_{WL} = \frac{\min(W_s, W_t)}{\max(W_s, W_t)} \qquad (2)$$

3.5 NE-based scoring

Having studies the comparable documents from a linguistic point of view, it appeared that looking for NEs present in both source and target texts might be a good way to select the 1-best target document. We extracted NEs from all the documents to be compared. Let us assume that the number of NEs in a source text and in a target text are NE_S and NE_T, respectively. Initially we calculate source-target NE-length ratio (R_{NL}) as in (3):

---

[3]http://www.statmt.org/wmt16/
bilingual-task.html

$$R_{NL} = \frac{\min(NE_S, NE_T)}{\max(NE_S, NE_T)} \qquad (3)$$

Then we calculated the ratio of the total number of source-target NE matches to the total number of source NEs, which we call R_{SNM}. Let us assume that the total number of NEs matched is M_{NE}. Considering this, R_{SNM} can be calculated as shown in (4):

$$R_{SNM} = \frac{M_{NE}}{NE_S} \qquad (4)$$

In many cases a text-pair in a comparison can have a huge difference between the number of NEs present in both documents. For example, if NE_S and NE_T are 5 and 50, respectively, and all of the source NEs match the target NEs, we might not necessarily want to link them. Accordingly, therefore, (3) is also taken into account, and we multiply R_{SNM} by R_{NL} to give our overall NE-based score(SC_{NE}) in (5) :

$$SC_{NE} = R_{SNM} * R_{NL} \qquad (5)$$

3.6 Combining all scores

We propose to re-rank our possible alignments based on adding sentence-, word- and NE-based scores and call this our alignment-score (SC_A), as in (6) :

$$SC_A = R_{SL} + R_{WL} + SC_{NE} \qquad (6)$$

Using equation (6), we calculate scores for each possible document pair and retain the 1-best pair with the maximum value.

4 Experimental results

4.1 Data and systems

In order to test our proposed techniques we conducted experiments on the provided development data and corresponding references. As discussed in Sections 3.4 and 3.5, we selected only those document pairs for comparison that have a sentence-length and word-length ratio of 1 (or very close to it).

It is usually seen that on average a French translation of an English document has 1.2 words for every English word in the original. In this work, since we are dealing with the comparable texts that are usually not proper translations of each other but contain similar information, we choose to set this ratio closer to 1.

In addition to this, we applied different weighted scores for the three features (i.e. sentence-based, word-based and NE-based scoring). The weights applied on the test data were extracted from our experiments on the development data. We held out the documents randomly selected from 10 web-domains in the training data. We assigned different sets of weights to the three features and conducted experiments on the development set using these weighted scores.

The Stanford Named Entity Recognizer[4] was used to detect NEs in our system.

4.2 Results

We assigned weights to the three features in five different combinations (termed as C_n, where n=1, 2 ...5) as shown in Table 1. The summation of these weights is always 1.

Feature	Weight assigned				
	C_1	C_2	C_3	C_4	C_5
R_{SL}	0.33	0.25	0.15	0.1	0
R_{WL}	0.33	0.25	0.15	0.1	0
SC_{NE}	0.33	0.5	0.7	0.8	1

Table 1: Weights assigned to different features with different combinations.

As can be seen in Table 1, C_1 represents the combination where all features are assigned an equal score. Subsequently, the weights of R_{SL} and R_{WL} are decreased but for SC_{NE} it is increased. C_5 indicates that the whole weight is assigned to SC_{NE} whereas R_{SL} and R_{WL} are not taken into account. Let us assume that the weights assigned to the sentence-based, word-based and NE-based features are λ_1, λ_2 and λ_3, respectively. Taking these weights into account, the overall alignment score of a document-pair is calculated as shown in equation (7):

$$SC_A = \lambda_1 R_{SL} + \lambda_2 R_{WL} + \lambda_3 SC_{NE} \qquad (7)$$

where, $\lambda_1 + \lambda_2 + \lambda_3 = 1$

The experimental results on the development data with different scoring combinations are given in Table 2.

Table 3 shows the detailed results using C_3 combinations. Prior to tuning the feature weights in the development phase, our published result on

---

[4] http://nlp.stanford.edu/software/ CRF-NER.shtml

720

Combination of Weights	References	System output	Recall
C_1	247	147	59.51
C_2	247	152	61.53
C_3	247	153	61.94
C_4	247	153	61.94
C_5	247	147	59.51

Table 2: Results of document alignment method used in our experiments.

Web-domain name	Ref.	Sys. o/p	Recall
bugadacargnel.com	19	9	47.36
cbsc.ca	20	12	60.0
cineuropa.mobi	73	58	79.45
creationwiki.org	22	4	18.18
eu2007.de	11	4	36.36
eu.blizzard.com	10	8	80.0
forcesavenir.qc.ca	8	3	37.5
galacticchannelings.com	9	1	11.11
golftrotter.com	8	8	100.0
iiz-dvv.de	67	45	67.16

Table 3: Detailed results of 10 web-domains of the development data.

System submitted	Rec.	Prec.	Num. found	1-1 pairs
ADAPT	27.10	0.93	651	69, 518
ADAPT-2	26.81	1.05	644	61, 094
arcpv42	84.92	0.7	2040	287, 860
ITRI-DCU	0.49	0.008	12	146, 566
DOCAL	88.59	1.1	2128	191, 993
Jakubina-Langlais	79.30	0.72	1905	263, 133
JIS	1.99	0.16	48	28, 903
Meved	79.39	1.22	1907	155, 891
NovaLincs	85.76	0.99	2060	207, 022
NovaLincs-2	88.63	0.9	2129	235, 763
NovaLincs-3	**94.96**	0.96	2281	235, 812
UA_bitextor_4.1	31.14	0.78	748	95, 760
UA_bitextor_5.0	83.30	**1.26**	2001	157, 682
UEdin1_cosine	89.09	0.58	2140	368, 260
UEdin2_LSI-v2	87.63	0.57	2105	367, 948
UEdin2_LSI	85.84	0.75	2062	271, 626
UFAL-1	81.30	0.78	1953	248, 344
UFAL-2	79.14	1.06	1901	178, 038
UFAL-3	80.68	0.93	1938	207, 358
UFAL-4	84.22	0.75	2023	268, 105
Yandex	84.13	0.72	2021	277, 896
YODA	93.92	0.7	2256	318, 568

Table 4: Published results with an extension of precision values.

Combination of weights	Rec.	Prec.	Num. found	1-1 pairs
C_3	29.1	1.1	699	63, 255

Table 5: Results obtained after applying tuned feature weights.

the test data was based on simple addition of the three features we used. The result is published on the basis of recall and contains 2,402 alignment pairs. We extended the published results with the precision values which is shown in Table 4.

Subsequently, we tuned the feature weights in the development phase and selected the weight combination C_3 to apply on the test data. Table 5 shows the results.

It can be observed from Table 5 that applying the tuned feature weights helps in increasing the recall value by up to 2% compared to our initial results ('ADAPT' in Table 4). The precision value is also slightly increased from 1.05% (in ADAPT-2) to 1.1%. However, in both Table 4 and Table 5, it is obvious that both of our systems produced much lower recall value than the top-ranked systems (e.g. NovaLincs, UEdin1_cosine etc.). In contrast, our precision is quite competitive to these systems and higher than most of the submitted systems.

Another very important observation is that our results on the development data are much better than on the test data. The main reason for this is

that we strictly pruned out many of the possible comparisons for the web-domains in the test set having a large number of texts in order to reduce the runtime of the whole process. It would have consumed a lot of time if we had considered all the documents (i.e. more than one million document pairs). Therefore, we removed those documents that contain only a few lines of text which resulted in discarding many possible alignments. In contrast, we applied a much softer pruning technique on the development data and produced much better recall values than that on the test data.

Finally, analysing the source of the problem of misalignments, we found that in our data we have many articles that deal with similar topics in different documents. Hence it may not always be helpful to rely mostly on NE-matching.

5 Conclusion

Despite the fact that phrase-based models of translation obtain state-of-the-art performance, sufficient amounts of good quality training data do not exist for many language pairs. Even for those language pairs where large amounts of data are available, these do not always occur in the required domain of application. Accordingly, many researchers have investigated the use of comparable corpora either to generate initial training data for SMT engines, or to supplement what data is already available.

In this paper, we seek to improve the quality of the multilingual comparable documents retrieved. In our approach, we actually quantify the amount of correct target-language documents retrieved. Here we propose a technique combining three features. The first one is based on matched source-to-target sentence scoring, the second on matched source-to-target sentence scoring and the third on NE-based scoring.

Analysing this result, in future work we would like to add more semantic features to our system and apply these techniques to other language pairs and data types. In addition to this, we would also like to automatically determine the weighted scores, for instance by using n-fold cross-validation. Our proposed method does not consider the difference between translation ratio of languages as we are dealing with different qualities of comparable corpora in this task, but we plan to investigate this problem with a specific corpus in different languages for our future work.

Acknowledgments

This research is supported by Science Foundation Ireland in the ADAPT Centre (Grant 13/RC/2106) (www.adaptcentre.ie) at Dublin City University.

References

Afli, H., Barrault, L., and Schwenk, H. (2012). Parallel texts extraction from multimodal comparable corpora. In *JapTAL*, volume 7614 of *Lecture Notes in Computer Science*, pages 40–51, Kanazawa, Japan.

Afli, H., Barrault, L., and Schwenk, H. (2013). Multimodal comparable corpora as resources for extracting parallel data: Parallel phrases extraction. In *International Joint Conference on Natural Language Processing*, pages 286–292, Nagoya, Japan.

Afli, H., Barrault, L., and Schwenk, H. (2016). Building and using multimodal comparable corpora for machine translation. *Natural Language Engineering*, 22(04):603 – 625.

Fung, P. and Cheung, P. (2004). Multi-level bootstrapping for extracting parallel sentences from a quasi-comparable corpus. In *Proceedings of the 20th international conference on Computational Linguistics*, COLING '04, pages 1051–1057, Geneva, Switzerland.

Koehn, P. (2005). Europarl: A parallel corpus for statistical machine translation. In *Proceedings of MT Summit*, volume 5, pages 79–86, Phuket, Thailand.

Li, B. and Gaussier, E. (2010). Improving corpus comparability for bilingual lexicon extraction from comparable corpora. In *Proceedings of the 23rd International Conference on Computational Linguistics (Coling 2010)*, pages 644–652, Beijing, China.

Mayer-Schönberger, V. and Cukier, K. (2013). *Big Data: A Revolution That Will Transform How We Live, Work, and Think*. Houghton Mifflin Harcourt.

Munteanu, D. S. and Marcu, D. (2005). Improving Machine Translation Performance by Exploiting Non-Parallel Corpora. *Computational Linguistics*, 31(4):477–504.

Resnik, P. and Smith, N. A. (2003). The web as a parallel corpus. *Comput. Linguist.*, 29:349–380.

Sennrich, R. and Volk, M. (2010). MT-based sentence alignment for OCR-generated parallel texts. In *Proceedings of The Ninth Conference of the Association for Machine Translation in the Americas (AMTA 2010)*, Denver, Colorado, USA.

Tiedemann, J. (2012). Parallel data, tools and interfaces in OPUS. In *Proceedings of the 8th International Conference on Language Resources and Evaluation (LREC'2012)*, pages 2214–2218, Istanbul, Turkey.

Utiyama, M. and Isahara, H. (2003). Reliable measures for aligning Japanese-English news articles and sentences. In *Proceedings of the*

41st Annual Meeting on Association for Computational Linguistics - Volume 1, ACL '03, pages 72–79, Sapporo, Japan.

Yang, C. C. and Li, K. W. (2003). Automatic construction of English/Chinese parallel corpora. *J. Am. Soc. Inf. Sci. Technol.*, 54:730–742.

Zhao, B. and Vogel, S. (2002). Adaptive parallel sentences mining from web bilingual news collection. In *Proceedings of the 2002 IEEE International Conference on Data Mining*, ICDM '02, pages 745–748, Washington, DC, USA. IEEE Computer Society.

WMT2016: A Hybrid Approach to Bilingual Document Alignment

Sainik Kumar Mahata[1], Dipankar Das[2], Santanu Pal[3]
[1]JIS College of Engineering, Kalyani, India
[2]Jadavpur University, Kolkata, India
[3]Universität des Saarlandes, Saarbrücken, Germany
`sainik.mahata@gmail.com,`
`ddas@cse.jdvu.ac.in, santanu.pal@uni-saarland.de`

Abstract

Large aligned corpora are required for any computer aided translation system to become effective. In this scenario, bilingual document alignment has gained utmost importance in recent days. We attempt a simple yet effective approach to align URLs (Uniform Resource Locator) within two documents in two languages as a part of WMT2016 Bilingual Document Alignment Shared Task. Our approach includes the processing of URLs and their embedded texts, which serves as the main matching criterion. In order to align the text initially, we have used Gale-Church algorithm, dictionary based translation and Cosine Similarity that in turn helps us to achieve better results in the alignment task.

1 Introduction

Bilingual document alignment has gained utmost importance these days [Brown et al.1991, Warwick et al.1990, Gale and Church1991, Kay and Röscheisen1993, Simard et al.1992, Kupiec1993,Matsumoto et al.1993,Dagan et al.1999, Church1993]. Research on calculating similarity of bilingual comparable corpora is attracting more attention [Vu et al.2009, Pal et al.2014, Tan and Pal2014]. Growth of monolingual data in different languages has made the task for aligning documents difficult [Jagarlamudi et al.2011]. What makes the problem more critical is the fact that one sentence in one language can correspond to many sentences in a different language [Wu1994]. For any translation system to work correctly and efficiently, it has to be fed with a large parallel corpora. Such corpora are very hard to find [Smith et al.2010] since it involves serious manual labour and cost. To eliminate the high cost,

computer aided sentence alignment of two different corpora has become very desirable. The presence of such computer aided aligned corpora aids in many Natural Language Processing (NLP) tasks such as Machine Translation, Word Sense Disambiguation as well as Cross Lingual Information Extraction [Patry and Langlais2005].

In our current task, we have worked on the data provided by WMT shared task[1], which had web crawls of 203 websites and were extracted in both English and French. The task was to extract 1-1 pairings of English and French URLs that has the same content but in respective languages. The data contained URLs followed by the text in each of the URLs. The task was to extract the text from both the English and French URLs and align them using our alignment algorithm. After alignment of the text, the URLs to which the text belongs to were also aligned. Our algorithm makes use of concepts given by [Gale and Church1991], translation of words using a dictionary created by Anymalign package [Lardilleux et al.2012] and the concept of Cosine Similarity. The following section will document the algorithm. Working of the algorithm will be shown in Section 2, followed by the results in Section 3.

2 Proposed System

2.1 Text and URL Extraction

The given *.lett* files are opened and the URL as well as the texts are extracted. The extracted text and URLs are given IDs so that it becomes easy to align the URLs after aligning the texts. The process is shown in Figure 1.

2.2 Text Selection using Algorithm proposed by Gale-Church

In their paper [Gale and Church1991], Gale and Church suggested that the source sentence and its

---

[1]http://www.statmt.org/wmt16/bilingual-task.html

Proceedings of the First Conference on Machine Translation, Volume 2: Shared Task Papers, pages 724–727,
Berlin, Germany, August 11-12, 2016. ©2016 Association for Computational Linguistics

```
en   text/html   charset=utf-8   http://academiedesprez.org/mailgb.php (1)    Message to Gilbert Blin (1)
en   text/html   charset=utf-8   http://academiedesprez.org/hamfelt/index.htm (2)    Message for / pour Gilbert Blin (2)
fr   text/html   charset=utf-8   http://academiedesprez.org/ (1) Académie Desprez (1)
en   text/html   charset=utf-8   http://academiedesprez.org/eng/dubos1eng.htm (3)    Message from / Message de : (3)
en   text/html   charset=utf-8   http://academiedesprez.org/eng/applications9009eng.htm (4)    Name / Nom (4)
en   text/html   charset=utf-8   http://academiedesprez.org/eng/communication1eng.htm (5)    Firstname / Prénom (5)
fr   text/html   charset=utf-8   http://academiedesprez.org/eng/musicales5eng.htm (6)    Présenté par Gilbert Blin (6)
```

Figure 1: Text and URL extraction

```
Message to Gilbert Blin A cadémie D esprez  Séjour de Lena Dahlström     17h Accueil à Paris Où ? Musée Cognacq-Jay  20h Dîner pour
Lena 10h Musée du Louvre Où ? Cinéma Saint-Lambert    Où ? Marc Anselmi   9h Château de Versailles      Où ? Maison Malbranche  21h
Dîner pour Lena 10h Musée de l'Armée     Où ? Musée Galliera Métro: Goncourt ou Belleville    Où ? Marché Saint-Pierre     Où ?
Maison Lesage  13 rue Grange Batelière 20h Dîner pour Lena Métro: Porte de Clignancourt    Conservatrice au Musée Galliera
Architecture théâtrale en France    Un Théâtre de Voltaire  Houdon, sculpteur des Lumières  La Danse de Mort     Salles, Scènes &
Salons 19h30Théâtre des Champs Elysées Descriptif prévisionnel du projet   Lauréat : Olivier Till  Olympie - 1762 (II-3).  Textes
descriptifs des costumes.    Dossier de Léna Dahlström   Phase 4 - Leyde Budget " costumes " Contrat avec le loueur Préparation
(essayages et repassage)    9- Fashion in Hair. Images de l'Album Ziesemis. 11- History of Theatre. Musical studies Des Orages
Poetry, declamation & music Le Carnaval de Venise   Présenté par Camille Tanguy Présenté par Gilbert Blin   Présenté par Rémy-
Michel Trotier    Présenté par Gilbert Blin  Séjour de Christer Nilsson  Bourse de Voyage "Servandoni"   Madame Danielle Durand,
Comédie-Française   Samedi 17 Novembre 2001 Dimanche 18 Novembre 2001    Où ? Musée Cognacq-Jay  02330 Condé en Brie Mardi 20
Novembre 2001  10h: les Grands Appartements    20h30 Concert: Trio Wanderer    Où ? Salle Gaveau   Mercredi 21 Novembre 2001
Accompagnateur : Magnus Johansson   Où ? Opéra Bastille Jeudi 22 Novembre 2001  12h30 Eglise Saint Sulpice  Vendredi 23 Novembre
2001    Où ? Palais Garnier Où ? Opéra Bastille Samedi 24 Novembre 2001 Métro: Porte de Clignancourt    Dimanche 25 Novembre 2001
    Qui était Servandoni ?  Fables de La Fontaine    14h Centre Culturel Suédois 11h Château de Vaux-le-Vicomte  10h Bibliothèque-
musée de l'Opéra   21h30 Théâtre du Lucernaire Le Barbier de Séville   9h Musée du Louvre  Déléguée à l'activité commerciale
Monsieur Patrice de Vogüé   Conservateur-archiviste de la Comédie-Française Discover the Armfelt grant: Who was Armfelt ?    Séjour
```

Figure 2: Text Selection according to size, using algorithm proposed by Gale and Church

translated sentence have the same length.

This idea forms the basis of our proposed system. We have found out the length of the source English sentence, that have been extracted from a URL pair, and have found matches in all the target French sentences, extracted from the same URL pair. This results in one-to-many relationship between the English and French sentences. The variance in this step is kept as 2, which means if the length of the French sentences exceeds or falls behind the length of the English sentence by a difference 2, when compared to the source English sentence, they are also included as a match with the English sentence. This step is shown in Figure 2, where the first sentence is the source English sentence and the corresponding French sentences are the ones with the same length, or length greater than or less than by a value of 2, as compared to the length of the source English sentence.

2.3 Dictionary creation using Anymalign Algorithm

WMT2016 provided us with a large English-French parallel corpus. We executed the Anymalign algorithm on this corpus to find out the word alignments. The alignments with a matching probability of more than or equal to 0.75 were kept as higher probability results in good translation. The rest of the alignments were discarded. This data served as our dictionary. The snapshot of the dictionary containing the source English words in the left column and the target French words in the

```
and et

Reply     Reply
English English
Equipement  Equipement
NauticNewsletter      NauticNewsletter
Congressional cup    Congressional Cup
Canada.ca    Canada.ca
welcome Accueil
&amp;       &
LBYC      LBYC
NauticNews   NauticNews
glossary    Glossaire
vessels bateaux
```

Figure 3: Dictionary creation using Anymalign algorithm

right column is shown in Figure 3.

2.4 Sentence matching using dictionary

For each of the words in the source English sentence, its corresponding translations are found out using the dictionary produced in the previous step. The words found were then matched with words in the various French sentences that we obtained using the concept provided by Gale and Church. The French sentences, with matched words equal to the length of the source English sentences or less by a factor of 2, were kept and the rest were discarded. This means that for an English sentence of 10 words, French translation for each of the English words were found out using the dictionary produced in the previous step.

If a French sentences with all the 10 words matching to the translated words was found, it was kept. Also, if there was a French sentence con-

Message to Gilbert Blin Présenté par Gilbert Blin   Présenté par Gilbert Blin   Coordination : Gilbert Blin Accompagnateur :
Gilbert Blin   Coordination : Gilbert Blin Accompagnateur : Gilbert Blin   Accompagnateur : Gilbert Blin   Camille Tanguy Gilbert
Blin Coordination : Gilbert Blin Accompagnateur : Gilbert Blin   Accompagnateur : Gilbert Blin   Lauréat : Gilbert Blin   Direction
: Gilbert Bezzina Présenté par Gilbert Blin   Présenté par Gilbert Blin   Coordination : Gilbert Blin Accompagnateur : Gilbert
Blin   Gilbert Blin Gilbert Blin   Gilbert Blin, directeur artistique et costumes: Gilbert Blin   et costumes: Gilbert Blin
Lubor Cukr Gilbert Blin Christophe Lécuyer Gilbert Blin Rémy-Michel Trotier Gilbert Blin

Figure 4: Sentence matching with the derived dictionary

Message to Gilbert Blin (1)   Présenté par Gilbert Blin (6)   (0.86)   Présenté par Gilbert Blin (6)   (0.86)   Coordination :
Gilbert Blin (12)   (0.54)   Accompagnateur : Gilbert Blin (19)   (0.59)   Coordination : Gilbert Blin Accompagnateur : Gilbert Blin
(21)   (0.48)   Accompagnateur : Gilbert Blin (19)   (0.59)

Figure 5: Exact Text Translation finding with Cosine Similarity

taining 10 words, but only 8 words words were matching to the translated words, it was also kept. French sentences with less number of matchings were discarded. This process is shown in Figure 4.

2.5 Exact Text Translation finding with Cosine Similarity

Out of the French sentences extracted in the previous step, Cosine Similarity is found out with respect to the source English sentence. The French sentence with the highest Cosine Similarity score is selected as the exact translation of the source English sentence. This process is shown in Figure 5.

2.5.1 Cosine Similarity

Cosine similarity is particularly used in positive space, where the outcome is neatly bounded in [0, 1]. The formula used in our approach is as follows.

$$
\begin{aligned}
Similarity = cos(\Theta) &= \frac{A.B}{\|A\|\,\|B\|} \\
&= \frac{\sum_{i=1}^{n} AiBi}{\sqrt{\sum_{i=1}^{n} Ai^2}\sqrt{\sum_{i=1}^{n} Bi^2}}
\end{aligned}
\tag{1}
$$

Where A and B are the source English sentence and the one of the target French sentences, respectively.

2.6 URL matching

The URL of the source English sentence is then matched the URL of the extracted French sentence with reference to the ID that was given in the first step. We can see from Figure 5 that the French sentences when compared to the source English sentence *"Message to Gilbert Blin"* have cosine similarity scores appended to it. From the above figure we see that *"Presnt par Gilbert Blin"*, has the highest cosine similarity score. So, this can

be treated as the exact translation of the source English sentence. We also see that an ID *"(1)"* is appended to the English sentence and an ID *"(6)"* is appended to the French sentence. From Figure 1, we can find out that, since the English sentence ID is *"(1)"*, it belongs to the webpage *"http://academiedesprez.org/mailgb.php"* and since the ID of the French sentence is *"(6)"*, it belongs to the webpage *"http://academiedesprez.org/eng/musicales5eng.htm"*. Thus, we can mark it as the exact alignment.

3 Evaluation

WMT 2016 provided us with a baseline system that finds 119979 extracted pairs after enforcing the 1-1 rule. Our proposed system when executed on the test data, found out 48 extracted pairs of URLs after enforcing the 1-1 rule. This gave our proposed system a percent recall value of 1.998335.

Systems	Extracted pairs
WMT2016 Baseline	119,979
Proposed System	48
Percent Recall	1.998335

Table 1: Evaluation of proposed system with baseline system provided by WMT2016.

4 Conclusion

The paper presents a hybrid approach to bilingual document alignment to the shared task proposed by WMT2016. We have developed an approach that uses the concept given by Gale and Church with respect to length of source-translated sentences, translation of words using a dictionary created by Anymalign and the concept of Cosine Similarity. Our approach was able to extract 48 pairs of URLs with a percent recall of 1.998335.

References

Peter F. Brown, Jennifer C. Lai, and Robert L. Mercer. 1991. Aligning sentences in parallel corpora. In *Proceedings of the 29th Annual Meeting on Association for Computational Linguistics*, ACL '91, pages 169–176, Stroudsburg, PA, USA. Association for Computational Linguistics.

Kenneth Ward Church. 1993. Char_align: A program for aligning parallel texts at the character level. In *In Proceedings of the 31st Annual Conference of the Association for Computational Linguistics*, pages 1–8.

I. Dagan, K. Church, and W. Gale, 1999. *Natural Language Processing Using Very Large Corpora*, chapter Robust Bilingual Word Alignment for Machine Aided Translation, pages 209–224. Springer Netherlands, Dordrecht.

William A. Gale and Kenneth W. Church. 1991. A program for aligning sentences in bilingual corpora. In *Proceedings of the 29th Annual Meeting on Association for Computational Linguistics*, ACL '91, pages 177–184, Stroudsburg, PA, USA. Association for Computational Linguistics.

Jagadeesh Jagarlamudi, Hal Daumé, III, and Raghavendra Udupa. 2011. From bilingual dictionaries to interlingual document representations. In *Proceedings of the 49th Annual Meeting of the Association for Computational Linguistics: Human Language Technologies: Short Papers - Volume 2*, HLT '11, pages 147–152, Stroudsburg, PA, USA. Association for Computational Linguistics.

Martin Kay and Martin Röscheisen. 1993. Text-translation alignment. *Comput. Linguist.*, 19(1):121–142, March.

Julian Kupiec. 1993. An algorithm for finding noun phrase correspondences in bilingual corpora. In *Proceedings of the 31st Annual Meeting on Association for Computational Linguistics*, ACL '93, pages 17–22, Stroudsburg, PA, USA. Association for Computational Linguistics.

Adrien Lardilleux, Franois Yvon, and Yves Lepage. 2012. Hierarchical sub-sentential alignment with Anymalign. pages 279–286, Trento, Italy.

Yuji Matsumoto, Hiroyuki Ishimoto, and Takehito Utsuro. 1993. Structural matching of parallel texts. In *Proceedings of the 31st Annual Meeting on Association for Computational Linguistics*, ACL '93, pages 23–30, Stroudsburg, PA, USA. Association for Computational Linguistics.

Santanu Pal, Partha Pakray, and Sudip Kumar Naskar. 2014. Automatic building and using parallel resources for smt from comparable corpora. *Proceedings of the 3rd Workshop on Hybrid Approaches to Translation (HyTra)@ EACL*, pages 48–57.

Alexandre Patry and Philippe Langlais, 2005. *Automatic Identification of Parallel Documents With Light or Without Linguistic Resources*, pages 354–365. Springer Berlin Heidelberg, Berlin, Heidelberg.

Michel Simard, George F. Foster, and Pierre Isabelle. 1992. Using cognates to align sentences in bilingual corpora. In *in Proceedings of the Fourth International Conference on Theoretical and Methodological Issues in Machine Translation*, pages 67–81.

Jason R. Smith, Chris Quirk, and Kristina Toutanova. 2010. Extracting parallel sentences from comparable corpora using document level alignment. In *Human Language Technologies: The 2010 Annual Conference of the North American Chapter of the Association for Computational Linguistics*, HLT '10, pages 403–411, Stroudsburg, PA, USA. Association for Computational Linguistics.

Liling Tan and Santanu Pal. 2014. Manawi: Using multi-word expressions and named entities to improve machine translation. *Proceedings of the Ninth Workshop on Statistical Machine Translation*, pages 201–206.

Thuy Vu, Ai Ti Aw, and Min Zhang. 2009. Feature-based method for document alignment in comparable news corpora. In *Proceedings of the 12th Conference of the European Chapter of the Association for Computational Linguistics*, EACL '09, pages 843–851, Stroudsburg, PA, USA. Association for Computational Linguistics.

Susan Warwick, Jan Hajič, and Graham Russell. 1990. Searching on tagged corpora: Linguistically motivated concordance analysis.

Dekai Wu. 1994. Aligning a parallel english-chinese corpus statistically with lexical criteria. In *Proceedings of the 32Nd Annual Meeting on Association for Computational Linguistics*, ACL '94, pages 80–87, Stroudsburg, PA, USA. Association for Computational Linguistics.

English-French Document Alignment
Based on Keywords and Statistical Translation

Marek Medveď'   **Miloš Jakubíček**   **Vojtech Kovář**

Lexical Computing CZ s.r.o.

&

Centre of Natural Language Processing, Faculty of Informatics, Masaryk University,
Botanická 68a 602 00 Brno

`firstname.lastname@sketchengine.co.uk`

Abstract

In this paper we present our approach to the Bilingual Document Alignment Task (WMT16), where the main goal was to reach the best recall on extracting aligned pages within the provided data.

Our approach consists of tree main parts: data preprocessing, keyword extraction and text pairs scoring based on keyword matching.

For text preprocessing we use the Tree-Tagger pipeline that contains the Unitok tool (Michelfeit et al., 2014) for tokenization and the TreeTagger morphological analyzer (Schmid, 1994).

After keywords extraction from the texts according TF-IDF scoring our system searches for comparable English-French pairs. Using a statistical dictionary created from a large English-French parallel corpus, the system is able to find comaparable documents.

At the end this procedure is combined with the baseline algorithm and best one-to-one pairing is selected. The result reaches 91.6% recall on provided training data.

After a deep error analysis (see section 5) the recall reached 97.4%.

1 Introduction

In this paper we describe our approach to solve the Bilingual Document Alignment Task (WMT16). It consists of tree main parts: data preprocessing, keyword extraction and text pairs scoring based on keyword matching.

According to these steps, the text is divided into three main sections. Section 2 describes the data preprocessing that was crucial for key-word extraction. In the next section we describe the key-word extraction process, and Section 4 describes scoring of comparable English-French pairs.

The final results on the training data are summarized in Section 5 where we also discuss errors of our system and problematic features of the provided data.

2 Preprocessing

The training and testing data were provided in the `.lett` format. Each `.lett` file consists of lines where each line contains these six parts:

- Language ID (e.g. "en")

- Mime type (always "text/html")

- Encoding (always "charset=utf-8")

- URL

- HTML in Base64 encoding

- Text in Base64 encoding

We pick up language id, URL and text as a input for our system. To obtain keywords for each text, our system converts plain text into a so-called vertical text, or word-per-line format. This format contains each word on a separate line together with morphological information, namely lemma (base form of the word) and morphological tag. For text tokenization we use the Unitok tool (Michelfeit et al., 2014) that splits sentences into tokens according to a predefined grammar. Unitok has a special grammar model for each language that was created using information extracted from large corpora. An example of Unitok output is the first column of Figure 1. The Unitok output is enhanced by a sentence boundaries recognizer (we use <s> and </s> for marking sentence boundaries).

After tokenization and sentence boundary detection, lemmatization and morphological analysis follows. For both we use TreeTagger

Proceedings of the First Conference on Machine Translation, Volume 2: Shared Task Papers, pages 728–732,
Berlin, Germany, August 11-12, 2016. ©2016 Association for Computational Linguistics

(Schmid, 1994) with language dependent models
(i.e. French model for French texts, English for
English texts). Figure 1 contains an example of a
morphologically analyzed sentence in the vertical
format.

Unitok and TreeTagger, together with sentence
boundary detection and few other small pre-
and post-processing scripts, form the TreeTagger
pipeline that is used in the Sketch Engine (Kilgarriff, 2014) corpus query and management system.

```
word          tag        lemma
<s>
A             DT         a
web           NN         web
page          NN         page
is            VBZ        be
a             DT         a
web           NN         web
document      NN         document
<g/>
.             SENT       .
</s>
```

Figure 1: TreeTagger morphological analysis

3 Keyword Extraction

In the previous section, we described the text pre-
processing needed for the next part of our system,
the keyword extraction.

The lemma (base form) information from the
morphological analysis was used for computing
"keyness", or specificity scores for each word in
the text. For this, we used three different variants
of the standard TF-IDF score (Equation 1, 2, 3)[1]
and a Simple math score[2] (Kilgarriff, 2009) used
in keywords extraction in Sketch Engine (Equation 4):

$$key_t = 1 * log\left(\frac{N}{n_t}\right) \qquad (1)$$

$$key_t = (1 + log(f_{t,d})) * log\left(\frac{N}{n_t}\right) \qquad (2)$$

$$key_t = \left(\frac{f_{t,d}}{f_d}\right) * log\left(\frac{N}{n_t}\right) \qquad (3)$$

---

[1]The difference between Equations 1,2 and 3 is in TF
weight score.

[2]Variant of statistic that choose keywords according rule:
'word W is N times as frequent in document/corpus X vs doc-
ument/corpus Y'.

$$key_t = \left(\frac{fpm_{t,d} + 1}{fpm_{t,ref} + 1}\right) \qquad (4)$$

Legend:

- N: number of documents in corpus

- n_t: number of documents containing a particular word (token) t

- $f_{t,d}$: frequency of token t in document d

- f_d: size (length) of document d

- $fpm_{t,d}$: frequency per million of token t in
  document d

- $fpm_{t,ref}$: frequency per million of token t in
  a reference corpus (large, representative sample of general language)

As reference corpora, the TenTen web corpora
in Sketch Engine for English and French were
used (Jakubíček et al., 2013), in particular enTen-
Ten 2013 and frTenTen 2012.

Sometimes the TF-IDF scoring can score some
of the most common words (like "the", "a", ...)
very high. These so-called stop-words do not have
any value when finding match between two texts,
as practically all of the texts will contain them.
Therefore, we created stop-word lists for English
and French (from enTenTen and frTenTen corpus)
that filter out these most frequent words so they
are never considered keywords.

As we will see, the Equation 3 gives the best
results on the training data, therefore we chose it
for the final evaluation.

4 Scoring

After obtaining the keyword list from each text,
the final step was to find matches between English
and French texts.

We used top 100 keywords from each text (this
number was estimated during the experiments).
Then we consulted a statistical dictionary which
contains 10 most probable French translations for
each English lemma (see below for more information about this dictionary).

We translated the English keywords into all of
their French variants, and intersected this list of
translations with the keyword lists etracted from
all of the French documents. The French document with the biggest intersection was selected as
the best candidate.

This procedure was combined with the baseline algorithm[3] based on finding language identification in the URLs of the documents – firstly, the baseline was applied, then (if no matching document was found) the matching by keywords was performed.

The data processing flow is on Figure 2.

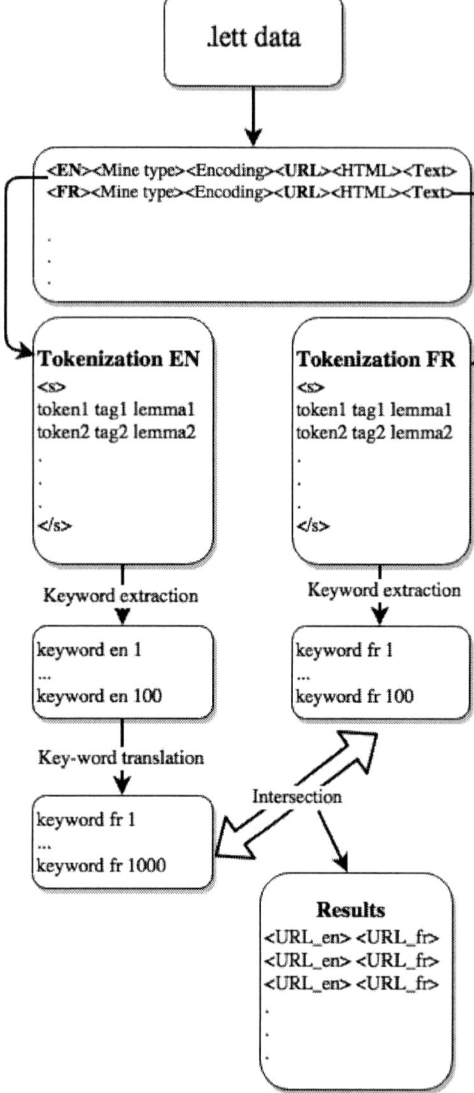

Figure 2: System data flow

4.1 Statistical translation dictionary

Sentence alignment in some of the available parallel corpora enables us to compute various statis-

tics over the number of aligned pairs, and to quantify the probability (or other metric) that word X translates to word Y, for each pair of words in the corpus. The procedure is similar to training a translation model in statistical machine translation (Och and Ney, 2003). Our implementation uses the logDice association score (Rychlý, 2008) which is the same measure that is used in scoring collocational strength in word sketches, the key feature of the Sketch Engine system. It depends on

- frequency of co-occurrence of the two words (e.g. "chat" and "cat") – the higher this frequency, the higher the resulting score; co-occurrence here means that the words occured in a pair of aligned sentences

- standalone frequencies of the two words – the higher these frequencies, the lower the resulting score

By computing these scores for all word pairs across the corpus, we are able to list the strongest "translation candidates" for each word, according to the score; for our purposes, we store 10 best candidates.

The procedure is computationally demanding – quadratic to the number of types (different words) in the corpus – and we exploit an algorithm for computing bi-grams to make it feasible even for very large corpora.

The statistical dictionary for this task was extracted from the English-French Europarl 7 corpus (Koehn, 2005).

5   Evaluation

The goal of this task was to find English-French URL pairs. Some training pairs were provided by authors of this task. Our procedure does not include any learning from the training data, therefore we can use them for quite a reliable evaluation. With regard to that data, our solution reached 91.6% recall, using the most successful TF-IDF equation 3; the results for the other equations are comparable and are summarized in Table 1.

If we did not include the baseline algorithm into the procedure, the recall was 82%.

After a detailed error analysis we found out that the provided data **contain duplicate web pages with different URLs**. This is an important problem – our error analysis shows that we have found

---

[3]The baseline algorithm iterates through all URLs and search for language identifiers inside URLs and then produces pairs of URLs that have the same language identifiers.

```
Expected  http://cineuropa.mobi/interview.aspx?lang=en&documentID=65143
          http://cineuropa.mobi/interview.aspx?lang=fr&documentID=65143
Found     http://cineuropa.mobi/interview.aspx?documentID=65143
          http://cineuropa.mobi/interview.aspx?lang=fr&documentID=65143

Expected  http://creationwiki.org/Noah%27s_ark
          http://creationwiki.org/fr/Arche_de_No%C3%A9
Found     http://creationwiki.org/Noah%27s_Ark
          http://creationwiki.org/fr/Arche_de_No%C3y%A9

Expected  http://pawpeds.com/pawacademy/health/pkd/
          http://pawpeds.com/pawacademy/health/pkd/index_fr.html
Found     http://pawpeds.com/pawacademy/health/pkd/index.html
          http://pawpeds.com/pawacademy/health/pkd/index_fr.html
```

Figure 3: Examples of false errors

Equation	Recall in %
1	89.2
2	89.5
3	**91.6**
4	88.7
Baseline	67.92

Table 1: Overall results according to "keyness" Equations

a correct document pair in many cases, but a document with a different URL (and identical text) was marked as correct in the data.

We went through the document pairs marked as errors of our algorithm and manually evaluated them for correctness. If we exclude the false errors (correct document pairs evaluated as incorrect), the recall is 97.4%. Some examples of these URL pairs are given in Figure 3 – as we can see, in many cases the duplicity is clear directly from the URL.

Unfortunately, we were unable to assess the number of duplicates in the data by the submission deadline. However, we believe it will be done, as the mentioned duplicates significantly reduce the soundness of such evaluation.

6 Conclusion

We have described a method for finding English-French web pages that are translations of each other. The method is based on statistical extraction of keywords and comparing them, using a translation dictionary. The results are promising, but detailed error analysis shows there are significant problems in the testing data, namely unmarked du-

plicate texts with different URLs.

Acknowledgments

This work has been partly supported by the Ministry of Education of CR within the LINDAT-Clarin project LM2015071 and by the Grant Agency of CR within the project 15-13277S. The research leading to these results has received funding from the Norwegian Financial Mechanism 2009–2014 and the Ministry of Education, Youth and Sports under Project Contract no. MSMT-28477/2014 within the HaBiT Project 7F14047.

References

Jan Michelfeit, Jan Pomikálek, Vít Suchomel. Text tokenisation using unitok. In: 8th Workshop on Recent Advances in Slavonic Natural Language Processing, Brno, Tribun EU, pp. 71-75, 2014

Helmut Schmid. Probabilistic part-of-speech tagging using decision trees. In: Proceedings of the international conference on new methods in language processing, pp. 44-49, 1994.

Adam Kilgarriff, Vít Baisa, Jan Bušta, Miloš Jakubíček, Vojtěch Kovář, Jan Michelfeit, Pavel Rychlý, Vít Suchomel. The Sketch Engine: ten years on. Lexicography, pp. 7-36, 2014

Adam Kilgarriff. Simple maths for keywords. In Proceedings of Corpus Linguistics Conference CL2009, Mahlberg, M., González-Díaz, V. & Smith, C. (eds.), University of Liverpool, UK, 2009.

Miloš Jakubíček, Adam Kilgarriff, Vojtěch Kovář, Pavel Rychlý, Vít Suchomel. The TenTen corpus family. The 7th International Corpus Linguistics Conference, Lancaster, 2013.

Franz Josef Och, Hermann Ney. A systematic comparison of various statistical alignment models, Computational Linguistics, volume 29, number 1, pp. 19-51, 2003.

Pavel Rychlý. A lexicographer-friendly association score. Proceedings of Recent Advances in Slavonic Natural Language Processing, RASLAN, pp. 6-9, 2008.

Philipp Koehn. Europarl: A parallel corpus for statistical machine translation, MT Summit, 2005.

The ILSP/ARC submission to the WMT 2016 Bilingual Document Alignment Shared Task

Vassilis Papavassiliou   **Prokopis Prokopidis**   **Stelios Piperidis**

Institute for Language and Speech Processing
Athena Research and Innovation Center
Athens, Greece
{vpapa, prokopis, spip}@ilsp.gr

Abstract

This paper describes ILSP-ARC-pv42, the Institute for Language and Speech Processing/Athena Research and Innovation Center submission for the WMT 2016 Bilingual Document Alignment shared task. We describe several document and collection-aware features that our system explored in the context of the task. On the test dataset, our submission achieved a recall of 84.93%, even though it does not make use of any language-specific resources like bilingual lexica or MT output. Instead, our system is based on shallow features (including links to documents in the same webdomain, URLs, digits, image filenames and HTML structure) that can be easily extracted from web documents. We also present examples to show that when de-duplication issues in the test dataset are properly addressed, our system reaches a significantly higher recall of 92.5%.

1 Introduction

There is a growing literature on using web-acquired data for constructing various types of language resources, including monolingual and parallel corpora. As shown in, among others, Pecina et al. (2014) and Rubino et al. (2015), such resources can be exploited in training generic or domain-specific machine translation systems. Nevertheless, compared to the acquisition of monolingual data from the web, construction of parallel resources is more challenging. Even though there are many multilingual websites with pairs of documents that are translations of each other, detection of such sites and identification of the document pairs is far from straightforward. Resnik and

Smith (2003) presented the STRAND system, in which they used a search engine to search for multilingual websites and examined the similarity of the HTML structures of the fetched webpages in order to identify pairs of potentially parallel pages. Esplà-Gomis and Forcada (2010) developed Bitextor, a system that combines language identification with shallow features. Barbosa et al. (2012) crawl the web and examine the HTML DOM tree of visited webpages with the purpose of detecting multilingual websites based on the collation of links that are very likely to point to in-site pages in different languages. Smith et al. (2013) used an extension of the STRAND algorithm to perform large-scale experiments of mining parallel documents from the Common Crawl[1] dataset.

This paper describes ILSP-ARC-pv42, the Institute for Language and Speech Processing/Athena Research Center submission for the WMT 2016 Bilingual Document Alignment shared task. The task consisted in identifying pairs of English and French documents from collections of documents corresponding to crawls of 203 webdomains.

2 System architecture

In this section, we describe the main processing steps in ILSP-ARC-pv42. Our system is based on the document alignment module of the ILSP Focused Crawler (Papavassiliou et al., 2013), an open-source tool[2] that integrates all necessary software[3] for the creation of high-precision parallel resources from the web in a language-independent fashion.

---

[1]http://commoncrawl.org/
[2]http://nlp.ilsp.gr/redmine/ilsp-fc/
[3]Including modules for metadata extraction, language identification, boilerplate removal, document clean-up, text classification and sentence alignment

Proceedings of the First Conference on Machine Translation, Volume 2: Shared Task Papers, pages 733–739,
Berlin, Germany, August 11-12, 2016. ©2016 Association for Computational Linguistics

2.1 Pre-processing shared task files

We pre-processed crawled data provided by the organizers as one file per webdomain in the `.lett` format adapted from Bitextor. This is a plain text format with one line per web document. Each line consists of 6 tab-separated values that include the (automatically detected) language ID ({en, fr}); the mime type (always text/html); the encoding (always charset=utf-8); the URL; the HTML content in Base64 encoding; and the text in Base64 encoding.

For each webdomain, we created a directory where we exported the contents of the 5th field of each entry in a *ll-file_id.html* file, where *ll* is the two letter language id ({en, fr}) provided in the lett files and *file_id* is an integer unique for each file of a webdomain. Using the URL information, we also store file-to-URL mappings in a separate file.

Apart from training and test data in this format, the organizers also identified spans of FR text for which they produced EN translations using a machine translation system. In an attempt to recreate real-life conditions where, at least for our team and for many language pairs, access to reliable MT output is not available, we did not use this information or any other type of language- or language-pair-dependent information in our system.

2.2 Boilerplate detection and exporting

Apart from its textual content, a typical webpage also contains boilerplate, i.e. "noisy" elements like navigation headers, advertisements, disclaimers etc., which are of only limited or no use for the production of good-quality language resources. We used a modified version of Boilerpipe[4] (Kohlschtter et al, 2010) to identify boilerplate in the `.html` files. Besides boileplate detection, we also identified structural information like *title*, *heading* and *list item* from each webpage. At this stage, text was also segmented into paragraphs on the basis of specific HTML tags like `<p>`, `</br>`, `<li>` etc.

For each `.html` file, we generated an `.xml` file where a `<body>` element contained the content of the document segmented into paragraphs. Apart from normalized text, each paragraph element was enriched with attributes providing more information about the process outcome. Specifically, paragraphs may contain the following at-

[4]`http://code.google.com/p/boilerpipe/`

tributes: i) *crawlinfo* with possible values *boilerplate*, meaning that the paragraph has been considered boilerplate; and ii) *type* with possible values: *title, heading* and *listitem*.

2.3 Document pair detection

Following exporting, a document pair detector, which constitutes the core module of our system, applies a set of complementary methods based on the content of the `.html` and the `.xml` files in order to identify translation pairs. The module does not exploit any language resources (e.g. lexica or output of MT engines). Instead it is based on shallow features including links to documents in the same webdomain, URLs, digits, image filenames and HTML structure.

We trivially avoid pairing files that are in the same language. We then examine all links in the `.html` files and we extract those that contain the `hreflang` attribute. Since "hreflang specifies the language and optional geographic restrictions for a document"[5], we use this strong indicator to pair documents, which we subsequently exclude from examination by other downstream methods[6]. We also examine links that match a set of patterns for the identification of translation links (e.g. link elements with the attribute `lang`) and we exploit them in the same way.

Next, we focus on URLs that include language indicators and examine if there are pairs of URLs that match pairs of specific patterns such as */lang1/* and */lang2/*, *_lang1* and *_lang2*, *=lang1* and *=lang2*, where *lang1* and *lang2* are alternative representations of the targeted languages (e.g. en, eng, english, fr, fra, french, francais, etc. in the context of this shared task). Some additional patterns are lang=*i*, langid=*i* and lingua=*i*, where $i \in \{0, .., 5\}$.

It is worth mentioning that in the past we have complemented the use of the above indicators with examination of features like document length in terms of tokens/paragraphs, in order to decide on document pairness. This was in accordance with our main interest in using the pair detector for the generation of high-quality resources that can be used in improving MT systems. However, in the context of this recall-evaluated shared task, the

[5]`https://en.wikipedia.org/wiki/Hreflang`

[6]We use this approach for all methods: documents that have been paired by one method are excluded from further examination.

system bases its decision on these indicators without any further checks.

Then, each `.xml` file is parsed and the following features are extracted: i) the document *language*[7]; ii) the *depth* of the original source page, (e.g. for `http://domain.org/d1/d2/d3/page.html`, depth is 4); iii) the *number of paragraphs*; iv) the *length* (in terms of tokens) of the main content, i.e. non-boilerplate text; v) the sequence of digits in the main content; and vi) the *fingerprint* of the main content, which is a sequence of integers that represent the structural information of the page, with boilerplate content ignored. For instance, in a fingerprint of $[-2, 28, 145, -4, 9, -3, 48, 740]$ for a document of 6 paragraphs, negative numbers -2, -3 and -4 denote that the *type* attributes of the 1st, 3rd and 4th <p> elements have *title*, *heading* and *listitem* values, respectively; and positive integers are the lengths of the 6 paragraphs in characters.

At this stage, webpages with a depth difference > 1 are not examined as candidate translations of each other, on the assumption that it is unlikely that translations can be found at very distant levels of the web site tree.

We next extract the filenames of the images from the HTML source and each document is represented as a list of images[8]. Our assumption at this stage is that two documents that contain the same or a similar set of images are good candidates for pairing. Since it is very likely that some images appear in many webpages, we count the occurrence frequency of each image and we discard "common", i.e. relatively frequent, images (e.g. social media icons, logos etc.) from these lists.

In order to classify images into "critical" or "common" (see Figure 1) we need to calculate a threshold. In principle, one should expect that low/high frequencies correspond to "critical"/"common" images. We employ a non-parametric approach for estimating the probability density function (Alpaydin, 2010) of the image frequencies using the following formula:

$$\hat{p}(x) = \frac{1}{Mh} \sum_{t=1}^{M} K\left(\frac{x - x^t}{h}\right)$$

where the random variable x defines the positions (i.e. images frequencies) at which the $\hat{p}(x)$ will be estimated, M is the amount of images, x^t denotes the values of data samples in the region of width h around the variable x, and $K(\cdot)$ is the normal kernel that defines the influence of values x^t in the estimation of $\hat{p}(x)$. The optimal value for h, i.e. the optimal bandwidth of the kernel smoothing window, was calculated as described in Bowman and Azzalini (1997).

Figure 2 serves as an illustration of the normalized histogram of image frequencies in an example webdomain (that was not part of the shared task datasets) and the estimated probability density function. One can identify a main lobe in the low values, around which "critical" images are clustered. Thus, the threshold is chosen to be equal to the minimum just after this lobe. The underlying assumption is that if a webpage in *l1* contains image(s), then the webpage with its translation in *l2* will contain a similar set of images. In case this assumption is not valid for a multilingual webdomain (i.e. if there are only images that appear in all pages, e.g. template icons), then all images will wrongly be assumed to be "critical". To eliminate this problem, we also discard as "common" all images that appear in more than 10% of the total `.html` files of each webdomain.

Following this step, each document is examined against all others on the basis of: a) the Jaccardian similarity coefficient of their image lists b) the reciprocal of edit distance of the sequences of digits in their main content c) the ratio of their number of paragraphs and d) the ratio of the number of tokens in non-boilerplate text. Two documents are considered parallel if (c), (d) and either or both of (a) and (b) are above predefined thresholds.

Additional document pairs are detected by examining structure similarity. Since the `.xml` files contain information about both (non-boilerplate) content *and* structure (i.e. titles, headings, list items), we use this representation instead of examining the similarity on the actual HTML source. A 3-dimensional feature vector is constructed for each candidate pair of parallel documents. The first element in this vector is the ratio of their fingerprint lengths, the second is the ratio of their paragraph size, and the third is the ratio of the edit distance of the fingerprints of the two documents to the maximum fingerprint length. Classification of a pair as parallel is performed using a

---

[7]In the case of the shared task, we replace the output of a language detection module with the language id provided by the organizers.

[8]Henceforth, we use the term "image" to mean "image filenames". We do not make use of any image features other than their filenames.

Figure 1: Critical (white) and common (red) images in two documents from the `www.jerome-alquie.com.lett` webdomain.

soft-margin polynomial Support Vector Machine trained with the positive and negative examples collected in the context of previous experiments (Pecina et al., 2012).

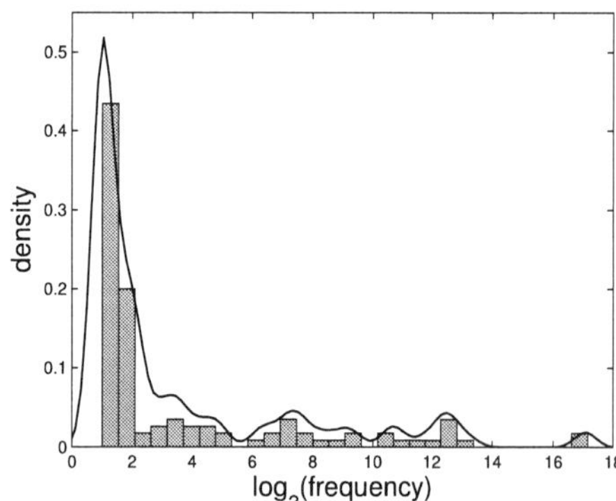

Figure 2: The normalized histogram and the estimated pdf of image frequencies in an example webdomain

As a final step, we mapped each *ll-file_id.html* to its URL and we produced a final set of 291,749 proposed pairs for all webdomains of the test data.

3 Evaluation Results

Before submitting our proposed pairs on the shared task test data, we also evaluated our system on the training data. The latter consisted of a set of 1,624 EN-FR pairs extracted by the organizers from 49 webdomains. The number of pairs per webdomain in the training set varied between 4 and over 230. The simple baseline provided by the organizers is based on URL matching. The baseline implementation iterates through all URLs and strips language identifiers such as */english/* from URLs. It then produces pairs of URLs that have the same stripped representation. Overall, the baseline proposes 143,851 candidate pairs, which are reduced to 119,979 pairs after enforcing the 1-1 rule, which requires that each source URL may be matched with at most one target url and vice-versa. Should a URL occur repeatedly, later occurrences are ignored. The baseline identifies 1,103 true positives, thus reaching a recall of 67.92%. Our system proposed 160,727 EN-FR pairs from which 1,460 are included in the EN-FR training set pairs, corresponding to a 89.90% recall on the training dataset.

Following our submission of predicted pairs on the shared task test data, the organizers evaluated it against a set of 2,402 EN-FR pairs from the 203 webdomains comprising the test data. The number of pairs per webdomain in the test data varies between 1 and 357, while the number of EN and FR webpages of each webdomain varies between 5 and circa 99K.

Our system proposed 291,749 pairs that were reduced to 287,860 after enforcing the 1:1 rule. These additional pairs were created because, for certain domains, EN or FR webpages contained translation links pointing to multiple webpages identified by the organizers as FR or EN documents, respectively. Our system identified 2,040 EN-FR pairs out of the 2,402 provided test pairs at a 84.93% recall and was ranked 9th among the 21 submitted systems by the 13 participant groups.

We counted the number of true positive pairs identified via each method, in order to examine each method's contribution. The top contributing method with 987 (48.38%) of the correctly detected pairs was the one exploiting URL patterns. Methods based on the existence of common images and/or similar digit sequences contributed 791 pairs (38.77%) while the in-webdomain links and HTML structure generated 180 (8.82%) and 82 (4.02%) pairs, respectively.

We also examined manually all document pairs missed in our submission in order to gather useful insights that could help us improve our system. A first conclusion is that a major issue in evaluating bilingual document alignment in terms of recall concerns (near) duplicates. We observed that we were scored as missing 182 pairs because the EN and/or FR documents participating in each of these pairs were aligned by our system with documents that contained the same content but originated from different URLs. For example, 50 and 103 test pairs from the `www.taize.fr` (see Figure 3) and the `www.lalettrediplomatique.fr` webdomains (where extra attribute-value strings in URLs like `choixlang=1`, `&bouton=1`, `&bouton=2`, etc. do not "influence" the content of the FR webpages) were considered fails due to this issue in the test data. Additional examples of perfectly valid pairs for extracting valuable content for downstream MT applications, which a) have been proposed by our system b) are equivalent to test pairs but c) have not been scored as true positives, are presented in Table 1. In particular, the `www.lagardere.com` and the `www.zigiz.com` webdomains (rows 7 and 8)

contribute 11 and 6 missed pairs, respectively. If we consider all these pairs as valid for extracting data in order to train MT systems, our system reaches a recall of 92.5%.

The majority of the remaining $(2402 - 2040 - 182 =)$ 180 of our misses concerned pairs where for a page A, the method based on structure similarity proposed a wrong document pair with page B. For instance, in the `http://www.toucherdubois.ca` webdomain, information (concerning learning scenarios and teaching resources) is presented in a specific format/template leading to errors during the examination of the structure fingerprint. Other misses were due to the length of the documents since it is very identify pairs of very short documents without using any lexical information.

4   Conclusions

In this paper we described the ILSP/ARC submission for the WMT 2016 Bilingual Document Alignment shared task. We provided details on the document and collection-aware features that our system explores. On the test set, our system reached a recall of 84.93% according to the official scoring. In the evaluation section of the paper we presented examples in order to show that the recall of our system is significantly higher once de-duplication issues in the test data are addressed.

Acknowledgments

This work was supported by the Abu-MaTran (FP7-People-IAPP, Grant 324414) project and the European Language Resource Coordination effort, CEF Programme. We would like to thank the organizers for preparing the task and answering questions.

References

Ethem Alpaydin. 2010. *Introduction to Machine Learning*. The MIT Press, 2nd edition.

Luciano Barbosa, Vivek Kumar Rangarajan, Sridhar, Mahsa Yarmohammadi, and Srinivas Bangalore. 2012. Harvesting parallel text in multiple languages with limited supervision. In *COLING*, pages 201–214.

Adrian W. Bowman and Adelchi Azzalini. 1997. *Applied smoothing techniques for data analysis: the kernel approach with S-Plus illustrations*, volume 18. Oxford University Press.

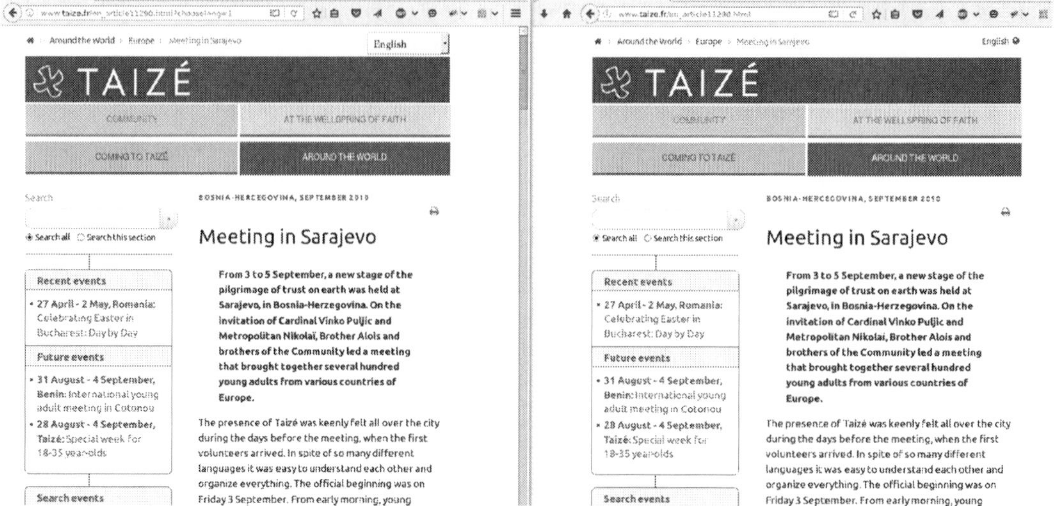

Figure 3: Duplicate EN webpages from `www.taize.fr`. Proposed pairs including `http://www.taize.fr/en_article11290.html?chooselang=1` (left) – `http://www.taize.fr/fr_article11286.html?chooselang=1` were not considered equivalent to test pairs including `http://www.taize.fr/en_article11290.html` (right) – `http://www.taize.fr/fr_article11286.html` even though the extra `?chooselang=1` attribute-value string in the URLs does not influence the textual content that can be extracted from proposed pairs.

Miquel Esplà-Gomis and Mikel L. Forcada. 2010. Combining content-based and url-based heuristics to harvest aligned bitexts from multilingual sites with bitextor. *The Prague Bulletin of Mathemathical Linguistics*, 93:77–86.

Vassilis Papavassiliou, Prokopis Prokopidis, and Gregor Thurmair. 2013. A modular open-source focused crawler for mining monolingual and bilingual corpora from the web. In *Proceedings of the Sixth Workshop on Building and Using Comparable Corpora*, pages 43–51, Sofia, Bulgaria. Association for Computational Linguistics.

Pavel Pecina, Antonio Toral, Vassilis Papavassiliou, Prokopis Prokopidis, and Josef van Genabith. 2012. Domain adaptation of statistical machine translation using web-crawled resources: a case study. In *Proceedings of the 16th Annual Conference of EAMT*, pages 145–152, Trento, Italy.

Pavel Pecina, Antonio Toral, Vassilis Papavassiliou, Prokopis Prokopidis, Aleš Tamchyna, Andy Way, and Josef Genabith. 2014. Domain adaptation of statistical machine translation with domain-focused web crawling. *Language Resources and Evaluation*, 49(1):147–193.

Philip Resnik and Noah A. Smith. 2003. The Web as a parallel corpus. *Computational Linguistics*, 29:349–380.

Raphael Rubino, Tommi Pirinen, Miquel Esplà-Gomis, Nikola Ljubešić, Sergio Ortiz Rojas, Vassilis Papavassiliou, Prokopis Prokopidis, and Antonio Toral. 2015. Abu-matran at wmt 2015 translation task: Morphological segmentation and web crawling. In *Proceedings of the Tenth Workshop on Statistical Machine Translation*, pages 184–191, Lisbon, Portugal, September. Association for Computational Linguistics.

Jason R. Smith, Herve Saint-Amand, Magdalena Plamada, Philipp Koehn, Chris Callison-Burch, and Adam Lopez. 2013. Dirt cheap web-scale parallel text from the common crawl. In *Proceedings of the 51st ACL*, pages 1374–1383, Sofia, Bulgaria.

id	type	EN URL	FR URL
1	T	http://www.lucistrust.org/it/service_activities/world_goodwill/world_view_archive/world_view_the_trained_observer	http://www.lucistrust.org/fr/service_activities/world_goodwill/world_view_archive/world_view_the_trained_observer
	S	http://www.lucistrust.org/en/service_activities/world_goodwill/world_view_archive/world_view_the_trained_observer	http://www.lucistrust.org/fr/service_activities/world_goodwill/world_view_archive/world_view_the_trained_observer
2	T	http://www.eufic.org/article/cs/page/BARCHIVE/expid/basics-child-adolescent-nutrition/	http://www.eufic.org/article/fr/page/BARCHIVE/expid/basics-alimentation-enfants-adolescents/
	S	http://www.eufic.org/article/en/page/BARCHIVE/expid/basics-child-adolescent-nutrition/	http://www.eufic.org/article/fr/page/BARCHIVE/expid/basics-alimentation-enfants-adolescents/
3	T	http://www.phytoclick.com/index.html?lang=en&pID=172	http://www.phytoclick.com/conditions-generales-de-vente/index.htm
	S	http://www.phytoclick.com/index.html?lang=en&pID=172&bID=151	http://www.phytoclick.com/index.html?pID=172&bID=151
4	T	http://www.eurovia.org/spip.php?article330	http://www.eurovia.org/spip.php?article329
	S	http://www.eurovia.org/spip.php?article330&lang=fr	http://www.eurovia.org/spip.php?article329&lang=es
5	T	http://www.haro.com/en/cork/all_about_cork/general.php	http://www.haro.com/fr/liege/tout_sur_le_liege/general.php
	S	http://www.haro.com/us/cork/all_about_cork/general.php	http://www.haro.com/fr/liege/tout_sur_le_liege/general.php
6	T	http://www.kinnarps.com/en/International/InteriorSolutions/KinnarpsBenefits/Ergonomics/Light/	http://www.kinnarps.com/fr/ch/Solutions-d-amenagement/Les-avantages-Kinnarps/Ergonomie/Lumiere/
	S	http://www.kinnarps.com/en/uk/InteriorSolutions/Ergonomics/Ergonomics/Light/	http://www.kinnarps.com/fr/ch/Solutions-d-amenagement/Les-avantages-Kinnarps/Ergonomie/Lumiere/
7	T	http://www.lagardere.com/press-room/press-releases/press-releases-363.html&idpress=1268	http://www.lagardere.com/centre-presse/communiques-de-presse/communiques-de-presse-122.html&idpress=3168
	S (11)	http://www.lagardere.com/press-room/press-releases/press-releases-363.html&idpress=1268	http://www.lagardere.com/press-room/press-releases/press-releases-363.html&idpress=3168
8	T	http://www.zigiz.com/en-EN/help/about_zigiz/help_parent_actievoorwaarden.html	http://www.zigiz.com/fr-FR/aide/about_zigiz/help_parent_actievoorwaarden.html
	S (6)	http://www.zigiz.com/en-EN/help/about_zigiz/help_parent_actievoorwaarden.html	http://www.zigiz.com/fr-FR/aide/help_parent_faq/help_allpaymentmethods.html
9	T	http://www.oras.com/en/professional/products/Pages/ProductVariant.aspx?productcode=6527A	http://www.oras.com/be/professional/products/Pages/ProductVariant.aspx?productcode=6527A
	S	http://www.oras.com/en/professional/products/Pages/ProductVariant.aspx?productcode=6527A	http://www.oras.com/fr/professional/products/Pages/ProductVariant.aspx?productcode=6527A
10	T	http://www.ipu.org/hr-e/169/Co121.htm	http://www.ipu.org/hr-f/168/Co121.htm
	S	http://www.ipu.org/hr-e/169/Co121.htm	http://www.ipu.org/hr-f/169/Co121.htm
11	T	http://www.nserc-crsng.gc.ca/Prizes-Prix/Excellence-Excellence/Profiles-Profils_eng.asp?ID=1008	http://www.nserc-crsng.gc.ca/Prizes-Prix/Herzberg-Herzberg/Profiles-Profils_fra.asp?ID=1003
	S	http://www.nserc-crsng.gc.ca/Prizes-Prix/Excellence-Excellence/Profiles-Profils_eng.asp?ID=1008	http://www.nserc-crsng.gc.ca/Prizes-Prix/Excellence-Excellence/Profiles-Profils_fra.asp?ID=1008
12	T	http://www.lalettrediplomatique.fr/contribution.php?choixlang=2&id=9&idrub=12	http://www.lalettrediplomatique.fr/contribution.php?id=9&idrub=12
	S	http://www.lalettrediplomatique.fr/contribution.php?choixlang=2&id=9&idrub=12	http://www.lalettrediplomatique.fr/contribution.php?choixlang=1&id=9&idrub=12
13	T	http://www.ledindon.com/en/anti-stress/index.php	http://www.ledindon.com/anti-stress/index.php
	S	http://www.ledindon.com/en/anti-stress/index.php?s=2	http://www.ledindon.com/anti-stress/index.php?s=2
14	T	http://www.lupusae.com/en/a_r2.htm	http://www.lupusae.com/en/a_f_r2.htm
	S	http://www.lupusae.com/cn/c_a_r2.htm	http://www.lupusae.com/en/a_f_r2.htm

Table 1: Examples of missed test pairs (T) and equivalent pairs proposed by our system (S). Numbers in parentheses next to (S) refer to the number of equivalent pairs proposed by our system for a specific webdomain. The URLs are those extracted from the .lett files.

Word Clustering Approach to Bilingual Document Alignment (WMT 2016 Shared Task)

Vadim Shchukin[1,2]   **Dmitry Khristich**[2]   **Irina Galinskaya**[2]

[1]Yandex School of Data Analysis,

[2]Yandex

`{rj42,khristich,galinskaya}@yandex-team.ru`

Abstract

Our participation in Bilingual Document Alignment shared task at WMT16 focuses on building a language-independent, scalable system for aligning documents based on content as opposed to using webpage meta information. The resulting system is capable of producing scored n-best lists of candidate pages and can therefore be adapted to tasks where either precision or recall is maximized. We conduct a series of experiments that show the effectiveness of the system without any specific tuning.

1   Introduction

Training statistical machine translation systems involves using two kinds of textual data: mono- and bilingual. While mining monolingual data is rather straightforward, determining pairs of parallel documents is a rather complicated task for a variety of reasons.

First of all, the largest source of text documents — the World Wide Web — has most of its parallel data in an unstructured form, meaning that it is often impossible to determine parallel pairs using meta info only. While a set of documents within a particular webdomain may be structured, the structure itself varies between domains and is therefore hard to exploit. This lack of stucture in the Web forces a mining system to compare every source language document to every target language document from the corpus, thus leading to quadratic complexity and making such straightforward algorithms not applicable to mining parallel data from large web corpora containing billions of documents.

Existing parallel data mining approaches deal with these problems in different ways.

Methods focused on meta info such as document URL (Resnik and Smith, 2003), publication dates or document structure, may work well on small structured corpora but suffer from sparsity and unreliability of meta info in the Web. One of the advantages of such methods is a lesser computational complexity — simple URL matching, for example, can be performed in linear time and doesn't even require to store HTML bodies as it only operates on URLs.

Another approach is to analyze document contents only, making zero assumptions about the document structure or meta info. This approach is more versatile but at the same time more resourse-demanding and tends to suffer from bad scalability. Applying it to big Web corpora requires implementation of special techniques that reduce the quadratic complexity of a naive algorithm to something manageable, preferrably making the number of document comparisons linear.

2   Previous work

Our approach is based on two papers working with different aspects of content-based document alignment. The first of them (Uszkoreit et al., 2010) aims at reducing the amount of pairwise comparisons of documents, while the other (Fukushima et al., 2006) speeds up the comparisons themselves. We describe both methods below.

2.1   Shingles and near-duplicate detection

Uszkoreit et al. (2010) describe a large scale parallel data mining method.

First, the system transforms a given multilingual input corpus into a monolingual one by translating every document into English using a baseline statistical machine translation system.

After that, candidates of parallel document pairs are extracted by applying a near-duplicate detection algorithm to the translated corpus. This re-

740

Proceedings of the First Conference on Machine Translation, Volume 2: Shared Task Papers, pages 740–744,
Berlin, Germany, August 11-12, 2016. ©2016 Association for Computational Linguistics

quires two different sets of n-grams (shingles) to be extracted from each document:

- **Matching n-grams** are used to construct the candidate sets, meaning that the system only considers pairs of documents that have at least one common matching n-gram. The key trick here is that we discard every matching n-gram whose frequency exceeds some fixed threshold. If the order of matching n-grams is sufficiently large, this operation prunes only a small fraction of the matching n-grams, and most importantly makes the number of pairwise document comparisons linear.

- **Scoring n-grams** are used only in the computation of a score for a given pair of documents. Every scoring n-gram is assigned a score equal to its inverse global document frequency in the input corpus. As the score of an n-gram is inversely proportional to its frequency, scoring n-grams with very high frequencies may be safely pruned, increasing performance. The score of a pair of documents is computed as cosine similarity of two corresponding vectors in the vector space of scoring n-grams.

In the next stage, candidate sets are built using matching n-grams, then pairs of documents from every set are scored using scoring n-grams, producing scored n-best lists for every document.

In the final stage, pairs are symmetrized, leaving only those where each document is a part of the other's n-best list.

The described method scales well as all steps can be parallelized, has linear computational complexity and provides high quality on big unstructured collections of documents. However, its quality is dependent on the quality of the baseline machine translation system and using a high quality baseline usually makes the first step — translation of every document in corpus — a very computationally complex task.

2.2 Word clustering

Fukushima et al. (2006) present an approach to the task of judging whether a pair of texts is parallel or not. The proposed algorithm scores a pair of documents based on the number of word pairs from the documents that are mutual translations of each other.

In the first step, the algorithm maps every noun from both languages to a special 'semantic ID' (non-nouns are ignored). The goal is to assign the same ID to every pair of words that are translations of each other.

To assign semantic IDs, the algorithm builds a word graph using a bilingual dictionary: nodes represent words and edges connect pairs of words that are translations of each other. Then, a threshold on the size of a connected component is selected and every component larger than the threshold is recursively divided into two smaller parts with an equal number of nodes. The process continues until every component is smaller than the threshold.

Graph partitioning is performed using a simple greedy algorithm. For a given connected component, it divides nodes into two equal groups such that the number of edges between the groups is minimized.

After the partitioning is complete, every component is assigned a unique semantic ID.

In the next step, every document from the corpus is preprocessed, converting each word to its corresponding semantic ID. The converted representations are then used to compare pairs of documents.

The method is reported to significantly speed up the document comparison without losing accuracy.

One of the disadvantages of this method is that it treats all edges of the word graph equally, while in reality some of the translations are more probable, and therefore more valuable than the others.

3 Our approach

The outline of our method is as follows. First, we run a bilingual word clustering algorithm similar to the one described in Section 2.2. Then, we preprocess the bilingual input corpus converting each word to its cluster ID. This operation produces a 'monolingual' corpus in a 'language' of cluster IDs which we then use as input data for the near-duplicate detection algorithm described in Section 2.1, thus skipping the computationally expensive step of machine-translating the entire input corpus.

Our approach to the bilingual word clustering problem is described in detail below.

3.1 Weighted word clustering

To form word clusters, we require a phrasetable of the corresponding translation direction as input data. This phrasetable can be built from the parallel data mined using some simple baseline method like URL mathching or, alternatively, the previous iteration of our algorithm.

In the first stage, we filter the phrasetable keeping only phrases where both source and destination parts consist of a single word. The result is used to form a graph with words as nodes and phrases as edges. Previously, Fukushima et al. (2006) used a dictionary as input and built an unweighted word graph. Our approach is to make a weighted graph using statistics from the phrasetable, namely phrase observation counts:

- $N_{src}(f)$ — the count of the source phrase f,

- $N_{tgt}(e)$ — the count of the target phrase e,

- $N(f, e)$ — the co-occurence count of the source phrase f and the target phrase e.

The resulting graph will most likely have one giant connected component containing most of the graph's vertices. Therefore, to form meaningful word clusters some of the edges have to be removed. We propose to use a variation of layered graph clustering algorithm (Algorithm 1).

It is an iterative process that takes some graph G as input and examines all connected components one by one. If the current component satisfies some fixed clustering criterion, a new word cluster is formed, assigned a unique ID and the component is removed from the graph. Otherwise, it takes a fraction of the edges of the current graph that have the worst weights, removes them, and runs recursively on the new graph. The process continues until the graph is empty.

Removing a constant fraction of edges during every step makes the complexity of the algorithm linear: $\Theta(E)$, where E is the number of the edges in the graph, i.e. the number of single word phrases in the input phrase table.

Whether the algorithm is capable of producing word clusters that have as many related (and as few unrelated) words as possible, depends on the choice of the weighting function and the connected component criterion. The weighting function that worked well during our experiments on various data, is as follows:

$$weight(f, e) = \frac{N^2(f, e)}{N_{src}(f) \cdot N_{tgt}(e)} \quad (1)$$

As for the connected component criterion — we chose the one that simply checks that the component has less than S nodes. S can be tuned on the training set.

Algorithm 1 Weighted Word Clustering

Input: graph G, cluster size threshold S, fraction of weak edges to remove F
Output: set of word clusters C

1: **function** CLUSTER(G, S, F)
2: $\quad$ $C \leftarrow \varnothing$
3: $\quad$ **for each** connected component $c \subseteq G$ **do**
4: $\quad\quad$ **if** $|c| \leq S$ **then**
5: $\quad\quad\quad$ $C \leftarrow C \cup \{c\}$
6: $\quad\quad$ **else**
7: $\quad\quad\quad$ remove $F\%$ of weak edges from c
8: $\quad\quad\quad$ $C \leftarrow C \cup$ CLUSTER(c, S, F)
9: $\quad$ **return** C

As we mentioned earlier, during the next step, the generated cluster IDs are used to substitute all the words in the input corpus.

Intuitively, this captures more information from the original corpus than the actual machine translation used in (Uszkoreit et al., 2010), because the result of the described transformation — a sequence of cluster IDs — represents many possible translations of every source document into target language and vice versa.

Besides, replacing machine translation with our method significantly improves overall performance of the system. First of all, the process is less demanding memory-wise as it doesn't require loading of phrase tables, language models, etc.; instead, only the cluster dictionary is used which is small ($<$100Mb of plain text in total for both languages even when using a phrase table built on a huge Web corpus). Second, it is also much faster as it basically consists of a single hashtable lookup per input word.

4 Data sets

The training data provided by WMT16 organizers consists of a set of 1,624 EN-FR URL pairs from 49 webdomains and all the pages crawled from the same domains. The crawled data for each page consists of the URL, language ID, mime type, encoding, HTML and text, of which our system only used URLs, language IDs and texts. The organizers also identified spans of French text and produced English translations using MT which we also didn't use.

As will be explained further, we did not perform any specific parameter tuning and only used training data for quality analysis and to ensure that no mistakes were made.

For testing, 203 additional crawls of new webdomains were provided, distinct from the ones in the training data in the same format. The final evaluation was performed using a subset of 2402 URL pairs from the test data.

5 System details

Our system could use the provided training data in two ways. First, we could mine parallel data from it using some baseline algorithm to build the input phrase table used in the word clustering algorithm. Instead, we used an in-house phrasetable built from a large Web corpus. Second, it could be used to fine-tune parameters such as upper threshold on word cluster size, but our experiments on multiple data sets for different language pairs showed that, once these parameters are set to some adequate values, tuning them does not have a big impact on the result, effectively making the system language- and domain-independent.

The chosen parameter values are:

- maximum size of a word cluster = 90,

- order of matching n-grams = 5,

- order of scoring n-grams = 3,

- upper threshold on matching n-gram frequency = 2000.

6 Results and analysis

Simple evaluation on the training data achieves a recall of 81.47 (Here and below, test data results are almost identical to train; for exact values on test, please refer to the tables). However, analysis of the results on the training set uncovered a number of problems in the data that made this result an underestimation. Some of these problems are:

- incorrect language detection,

- empty pages or pages with crawling errors,

- duplicate and near-duplicate pages.

While the first two kinds of errors mostly don't affect our system's performance as long as there

	train		test	
position	count	recall	count	recall
1	1482	91.26	2233	92.96
2	96	97.17	110	97.54
3	18	98.28	8	97.88
4	3	98.46	4	98.04
5	1	98.52	5	98.25
6	0	98.52	1	98.29
7	2	98.65	0	98.29
8	1	98.71	0	98.29
9	0	98.71	1	98.33
10	0	98.71	0	98.33
none	21		40	
total	1624		2402	

Table 1: Reference document positions and n-best recall on the train and test data sets.

are no such errors in test set pairs, the third problem turns out to be quite serious.

Some duplicate pages have exactly the same text content and only differ in some insignificant parameter in the URL, some are redirects, others only differ in a couple lines of boilerplate text (e.g., 'page viewed X times'), etc. Naturally, such sets of duplicates and near-duplicates negatively affect results of systems based on content analysis.

Also worth noting is the 1-1 rule enforced by the competition, which doesn't count pairs that include any of the URLs from the pairs accepted previously. This restriction significantly lowers the recall if the data contains near-duplicates of the pages from the reference pairs (which is almost always the case when working with crawled webpages). Evaluating our system on training data without the 1-1 rule yields a recall of 91.26.

To provide further analysis, we set our system to output n-best lists of size 10 for every source document. Table 1 shows the distribution of the positions of the reference documents in the generated n-best lists. As you can see, considering 3 best condidates per source document yields a recall of 98.28 while 10-best recall is 98.71.

We further investigate 121 source documents whose references were scored 2nd to 10th. For these source documents we examine the intersection of the best scored candidate and the reference document (see Figure 1).

The results show a big amount of full duplicates (100% intersection) and near-duplicates (high val-

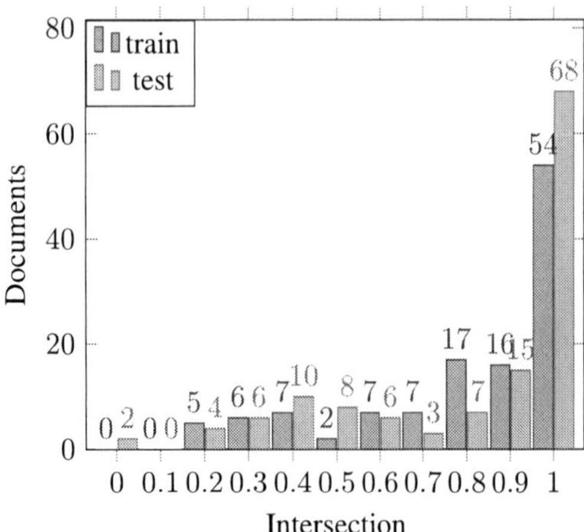

Figure 1: Intersection of the top-1 and the reference document in 10-best lists where reference document is on the 2nd - 10th place.

metric	train	test
1-1 rule recall	81.47	84.14
1-best recall	91.26	92.96
3-best recall	98.28	97.88
10-best recall	98.71	98.33
>80% similarity recall	96.61	96.71

Table 2: Quality on the training set using different metrics.

ues of intersection) in the generated n-best lists. This also brings us to a conclusion that most of the time the best scored candidate is not completely worthless but in fact can be used to mine parallel sentences from as it is very similar to the reference.

Considering top-1 scored documents that are not references but have 80% or more intersection with the reference 'correct' (which seems very reasonable), will achieve a recall of 96.61.

The most notable results for the training and test set are summarized in table 2.

7 Summary

We presented an effective, scalable and versatile approach to mining parallel data from big corpora of any nature. The method is based on textual content analysis and doesn't make any assumptions about the structure of the input data. Assuming the required input phrase table already exists, the system can work without any additional training data. Additionally, the parameters of the algorithm do not require any specific tuning, making it language- and domain-independent. We demonstrated that the system works well and achieves high values of recall on the provided data.

References

Ken'ichi Fukushima, Kenjiro Taura, and Takashi Chikayama. 2006. A fast and accurate method for detecting English-Japanese parallel texts. In *Proceedings of the Workshop on Multilingual Language Resources and Interoperability*, MLRI '06, pages 60–67, Stroudsburg, PA, USA. Association for Computational Linguistics.

Philip Resnik and Noah A. Smith. 2003. The web as a parallel corpus. *Computational Linguistics*, 29(3):349–380, September.

Jakob Uszkoreit, Jay M. Ponte, Ashok C. Popat, and Moshe Dubiner. 2010. Large scale parallel document mining for machine translation. In *Proceedings of the 23rd International Conference on Computational Linguistics*, COLING '10, pages 1101–1109, Stroudsburg, PA, USA. Association for Computational Linguistics.

The FBK Participation in the WMT 2016
Automatic Post-editing Shared Task

Rajen Chatterjee[1,2], José G. C. de Souza[2], Matteo Negri[2], Marco Turchi[2]
[1]University of Trento, Italy
[2]Fondazione Bruno Kessler, Italy
`{chatterjee, desouza, negri, turchi}@fbk.eu`

Abstract

In this paper, we present a novel approach to combine the two variants of phrase-based APE (*monolingual* and *context-aware*) by a factored machine translation model that is able to leverage benefits from both. Our factored APE models include part-of-speech-tag and class-based neural language models (LM) along with statistical word-based LM to improve the fluency of the post-edits. These models are built upon a data augmentation technique which helps to mitigate the problem of over-correction in phrase-based APE systems. Our primary APE system further incorporates a quality estimation (QE) model, which aims to select the best translation between the MT output and the automatic post-edit. According to the shared task results, our primary and contrastive (which does not include the QE module) submissions have similar performance and achieved significant improvement of 3.31% TER and 4.25% BLEU (relative) over the baseline MT system on the English-German evaluation set.

1 Introduction

Translation from and to multiple languages is a growing need of this era. Especially in a multilingual continent like Europe this poses a challenge to the language service providers (LSPs) that need to quickly deliver high quality translations. To cope with the increasing demand, the LSPs have shifted human translation from a completely manual process to a semi-automated one, with the help of computer-assisted translation (CAT) tools. CAT tools are indeed becoming a standard and ubiquitous tool for LSPs, which have to daily face the trade-off between quality and productivity, under the pressure of a growing demand. Machines, however, are not yet perfect: machine translation (MT), in particular, is often prone to systematic errors that human post-editing (PE) has to fix before publication. This process of translation results in the generation of parallel data consisting of MT output on one side and its corrected version on the other side. This data can be leveraged to develop Automatic Post-Editing (APE) systems capable not only to spot recurring MT errors, but also to correct them (in a broad sense, ranging from fixing typos to adapting terminology to a specific domain or even modeling the personal style of an individual translator). These capabilities become crucial especially when the MT system used to produce the translation suggestions is a "black-box" whose inner workings are not accessible and can not be tuned or re-trained (a frequent condition for small LSPs).

A recent study on APE by Chatterjee et al. (2015b) over six language pairs have reported consistent improvement (7.3% to 14.7% TER reduction) in the quality of machine translated text across all language pairs. They performed the experiments using the state-of-the-art statistical phrase-based machine translation technique with two variants, which are discussed briefly in Section 2. Based on the observed complementarity between the two variants and the room for mutual improvement, in Section 3 we present a factored APE model capable to leverage the two methods. In Section 4 we describe how to create different representations of the data in order to train each of the variants (monolingual, context-aware) and the factored models. Different configurations of our experiments and their corresponding results are discussed in Section 5. The results of our submissions in the shared task are reported in Section 6, followed by concluding remarks in Section 7.

Proceedings of the First Conference on Machine Translation, Volume 2: Shared Task Papers, pages 745–750,
Berlin, Germany, August 11-12, 2016. ©2016 Association for Computational Linguistics

2 Statistical APE Approaches

Most of the current statistical APE systems follow the phrase-based machine translation approach. They mainly differ in the way the data is represented in the parallel corpus. Unlike MT systems where the parallel corpus is made up of source and target language texts, APE systems use either i) MT text or ii) MT text with source annotations on the source side, and post-edits on the target side of the parallel corpus. The former variant (to use only MT text on the source side) was proposed by Simard et al. (2007), also known as *monolingual* translation, and the latter variant was proposed by Béchara et al. (2011), which is known as *context-aware* translation. The *monolingual* translation approach is more robust, it better generalizes the post-editing rules, and is less prone to word alignment errors which eventually impact on the quality of the post-editing rules. However, since the post-editing rules are learned from (*mt, pe*) (*mt*: machine translated; *pe*: post-edited) pairs, it loses connection with the source sentence, which implies that information lost or distorted in the machine translation process are impossible to recover by the APE system. This issue was addressed by the *context-aware* variant that annotates each word in the machine translated text by the corresponding source word (obtained from word alignment information between the *mt* and *source* text) to form a joint representation (*mt#source*) that represents the new source side of the parallel corpus (as shown in Table 1).

Source	See Paint on 3D models .
MT output	Siehe Bemalen von 3D-Modellen .
Joint Representation	Siehe#See Bemalen#Paint_on von#on 3D-Modellen#3D_models .

Table 1: An example of joint representation used in *context-aware* translation.

APE systems trained with the *context-aware* variant are more precise because they have the power to disambiguate when a *mt* word is a correct translation and when it should be post-edited, by having knowledge of the source context. How-ever, this variant faces two potential problems. First, preserving the source context results in multiple representations of the same *mt* word (each *mt* word can be aligned to multiple *source* words), causing a high increase of the vocabulary size, and, consequently, higher data sparseness that will eventually reduce the reliability of the word alignments and, consequently, of the post-editing rules. Second, the joint representation (*mt#source*) may be affected by the word alignment errors which may mislead the learning of translation options. Moreover, a technical problem with this representation occurs during tuning of the system. Since the input is a joint representation, the OOVs (*mt#source*) penalize the tuning metric even if the *mt* in *mt#source* is a correct translation thereby affecting the tuning process. To address these issues and to leverage the complementarity of the two alternative APE approaches, we propose a more elegant approach that combines them into a factored model as described in the following section.

3 Factored APE model

The factored machine translation model was proposed by Koehn and Hoang (2007). It enables a straightforward integration of additional annotation (called factors) at the word-level. These factors can be linguistic markup or automatically generated word classes. To build our factored APE systems, we pre-process the training data to obtain the factored representation. A fragment of our parallel corpus with factored representation is shown in Table 2. The source side of the parallel corpus has 2 factors (*mt_word* and *source_word*, similar to the joint representation), and the target side contains 3 factors (*pe_word*, *pos-tag*, and *class-id*). In this representation we can define:

- A word alignment mapping between *mt_word<->pe_word*. This helps to mitigate the problem of word alignment of *context-aware* APE approach;

- A translation mapping between *mt_word<->pe_word* (*monolingual* translation), and *mt_word|source_word<->pe_word* (*context-aware* translation). This allows us to leverage both the models during decoding;

- A generation mapping between *pe_word<->pos-tag*, and *pe_word<->class-id*. This allows us to improve the fluency of the trans-

<table>
<tr><td colspan="2" align="center">Parallel Corpus</td></tr>
<tr><td align="center">Source (<code>mt_word|source_word</code>)</td><td align="center">Target (<code>pe_word|pos-tag|class-id</code>)</td></tr>
<tr><td><code>Siehe|See Bemalen|Paint_on von|on 3D-
Modellen|3D_models .|.</code></td><td><code>Siehe|ADV|104 "|$(|373 Bemalen|NN|40 von|
APPR|382 3D-Modellen|NN|137 .|$.|451
"|$(|373</code></td></tr>
<tr><td><code>Bildrate|Framerate des|of_the Videos|video
MP4|MP4 .|.</code></td><td><code>Bildrate|NN|339 des|ART|407 MP4-Videos|NN
|41 .|$.|451</code></td></tr>
</table>

Table 2: Example of parallel corpus with factored representation.

lations by scoring them with both part-of-speech tag and class-based language models.

Source factors: The factor on the source side of the parallel corpus is obtained following the approach to obtain the joint representation (as described in Section 2) for *context-aware* APE, the only difference is that instead of joint representation (*mt#source*) we now have factored representation (*mt|source*) suitable to train factored models.

Target factors: We introduce two target factors to measure fluency of the translations at syntactic and semantic levels, i) POS-tag ($\sim$50 tags) obtained using the TreeTagger (Schmid, 1995), and ii) word-class id ($\sim$500 classes) obtained using $mkcls$[1] tool, which clusters words based on bigram contextual similarity. These factors are used to learn generation models ($P(pos\text{-}tag|pe)$ and $P(class\text{-}id|pe)$) to generate corresponding target factors for the test sentence, which are scored by their respective LMs during decoding.

4 Data set and Experimental setup

As defined in the shared task, the training data (English-German) consist of 12K triplets of source (*src*), MT output (*mt*), and human post-edits (*pe*). We split the development data (consisting of 1K triplets) released in this shared task into 400 and 600 triplets (selected randomly) to tune and evaluate our APE systems. We use the *pe* from the training data to build a 5-gram word-based statistical language model using the KENLM toolkit (Heafield, 2011), and 8-gram POS-tag and class-based language model using both KENLM (statistical) and the NPLM (neural) (Vaswani et al., 2013) toolkit. To build the joint representation (*mt#src*) and to obtain source factors (*mt|src*), we use the word alignment model trained on *src* and

---

[1] `https://github.com/clab/mkcls`

mt pairs of the training data by using MGIZA++ (Gao and Vogel, 2008).

To develop the APE systems we use the phrase-based statistical machine translation toolkit MOSES (Koehn et al., 2007) with alignment heuristic set to *"grow-diag-final-and"*, and reordering heuristic to *"msd-bidirectional-fe"*. For building the word alignment models we use MGIZA++ (Gao and Vogel, 2008). For tuning the feature weights we use MERT (Och, 2003) optimizing TER (Snover et al., 2006).

We run case-sensitive evaluation with TER, which is based on edit distance, and BLEU (Papineni et al., 2002), which is based on modified n-gram precision. In addition to the standard evaluation metrics, we also measure precision of our APE system using sentence level TER score as defined in Chatterjee et al. (2015a)

$$\text{Precision} = \frac{\text{Number of Improved Sentences}}{\text{Number of Modified Sentences}}$$

where the "Number of Improved Sentences" consists in all the APE outputs that have lower TER than the corresponding MT output and the "Number of Modified Sentences" consists in all the APE outputs that have TER scores different from the TER of the corresponding MT output.

5 Experiments and Results

Baseline: For internal evaluation we consider the MT system as one of the baselines (an APE system outputting the input sentence), and the two variants of phrase-based APE as described in Section 2. The *monolingual* variant is labeled as APE-1 and the *context-aware* as APE-2. The baseline results reported in Table 4 show that the naive *monolingual* APE system already outperforms the MT baseline by 1.5 BLEU score. However, the low precision of the APE systems indicate that they are prone to over-correction and modifies word-

	POS-tag LM			Class-based LM			POS-tag & Class-based LM		
Approach	TER	BLEU	Precision	TER	BLEU	Precision	TER	BLEU	Precision
Statistical	24.20	64.29	63.88	24.28	65.08	67.27	24.22	65.12	70.25
Neural	24.06	65.27	71.85	24.07	65.04	68.92	**24.07**	**65.31**	**72.72**

Table 3: Performance of the Factored APE-2 for various LMs (statistical word-based LM is present in all the experiments by default).

s/phrases which are already correct in the MT output.

Baselines	TER	BLEU	Precision
MT system	24.80	63.07	-
APE-1	**24.73**	**64.55**	**55.55**
APE-2	24.68	64.01	54.01

Table 4: Performance of the APE baselines.

Addressing over-correction: In order to avoid the problem of over-correction (making unnecessary corrections), the APE system should learn to preserve the chunks of the input which are already correct. To this aim, we augmented the parallel corpus with the post-editions (12K) available in the training data. So now our training corpus consist of 12K *mt-pe* or *mt#src-pe* pairs (to learn post-editing rules) and an additional 12K *pe-pe* or *pe#src-pe* pairs (to preserve correct input chunks). Replicating the baseline APE systems with the augmented data showed significant improvements with all the evaluation metrics as reported in Table 5. For this reason, we use the augmented parallel data in all the further experiments. Among the two variants we noticed that the APE-2 gets maximum benefit with an absolute precision improvement of 16.40% (from 54.01% to 70.41%).

	TER	BLEU	Precision
APE-1	24.46	64.74	63.27
APE-2	**24.08**	**64.88**	**70.41**

Table 5: Performance of the APE system with data augmentation technique.

Factored APE models: Both the APE variants have their own strengths and weaknesses as discussed in Section 2. To leverage their complementarity, we use factored translation approach as described in Section 3. Before combining the two variants, we decided to replicate the *context-aware* variant in the factored architecture (since it achieved the best performance as reported in Table 5) with the integration of different target LMs. Along with the 5-gram statistical word-based LM,

we study the effect on the performance of the APE system of using an additional 8-gram statistical as well as a neural POS-tag and a class-based LMs. The results are reported in Table 3. It is evident that the neural LM performs better than the statistical ones, and the combination of both POS-tag and class-based neural LM has slightly better precision than the individual neural LMs.

We hence decided to use the neural POS-tag and the class-based LMs along with statistical word-based LM for both the variants (*monolingual* and *context-aware*) in the factored architecture. The translation models of both the variants are used together during decoding with the help of the multiple decoding feature available in the MOSES toolkit (Koehn et al., 2007). The results of this combined factored APE system for various tuning strategies (i) MERT to optimize TER, ii) MERT to optimize BLEU, and iii) MIRA to optimize BLEU are shown in Table 6. Although the TER is almost the same for different tuning strategies, but slight improvement is observed with MIRA in terms of BLEU score.

Optimization	TER	BLEU	Precision
MERT-TER	24.03	65.03	69.71
MERT-BLEU	24.07	65.47	65.67
MIRA-BLEU **(Contrastive)**	**24.04**	**65.56**	**67.47**

Table 6: Performance of the combined factored model for various tuning configurations.

Factored APE model with quality estimation: To improve the performance of our APE system, we build a sentence-level quality estimation model (Mehdad et al., 2012; Turchi et al., 2014; C. de Souza et al., 2015) to decide whether to select the MT output or our factored APE output (MIRA-BLEU configuration from Table 6). To train the QE model we first extract 79 system-independent features that comprise three different aspects of the QE problem, namely: fluency (e.g. language model perplexity of the whole translation sentence), complexity (e.g. average token length of the source sentence) and adequacy (e.g. ratio between the number of nouns in the source and translation sentences). These features, obtained with the QuEst feature extractor implementation (Specia et al., 2013) are used to train a regression model that predicts the actual post-editing effort as measured by the TER between the MT-generated translation or the factored APE output and a human post-edited version. The regression model was trained using the extremly randomized trees (Geurts et al., 2006) implementation of scikit-learn library (Pedregosa et al., 2011). This method reached competitive results in sentence-level QE share-tasks in previous years (C. de Souza et al., 2013; C. de Souza et al., 2014). To select the final translation we check if the predicted score of MT output is lower[2] than the predicted score of the APE output by at least k points (threshold). We performed experiments with different threshold values, as reported in Table 7. Using QE with threshold of 5 performs slightly better than the one without QE, so our primary submission is the factored model with QE, whereas, the contrastive one is without QE.

Threshold	TER	BLEU	Precision
1	24.18	65.09	72.13
2	24.15	65.34	70.88
3	24.09	65.51	68.15
4	24.02	65.59	68.94
5 (Primary)	**23.99**	**65.65**	**67.83**
6	24.01	65.64	67.98
Contrastive (w/o QE)	24.04	65.56	67.47
Baseline (MT)	24.80	63.07	-

Table 7: Performance of the APE system with quality estimation for various thresholds.

6 Results of our submissions

The shared task evaluation was on 2,000 unseen samples consisting of *source* and *mt* pairs from the same domain of the training data. Our primary submission is a factored APE system which i) is trained with data augmentation technique, ii) leverages the two statistical phrase-based variants (*monolingual*, and *context-aware*), iii) uses a neural POS-tag and class-based LMs along with the statistical word-based LM, and iv) uses a quality estimation model. Our contrastive submission is similar to primary but without quality estimation.

According to the shared task results (reported in Table 8) both of our submissions achieves similar performance (with minimal difference in TER) with significant improvement of 3.31% TER and 4.25% BLEU (relative) over the baseline MT system. We also observe that the use of quality estimation in our primary submission did not yield the expected improvements.

	TER	BLEU
Baseline (MT)	24.76	62.11
Baseline (APE)	24.64	63.47
Primary	**23.94**	**64.75**
Contrastive	**23.92**	**64.75**

Table 8: Results of the shared task for our submissions

7 Conclusion

In this system description paper, we discussed the potential strength and weakness of the two phrase-based APE variants (*monolingual* and *context-aware*) and showed that their complementarity can be leveraged by combining them in a factored APE model. Factored models made it possible to integrate several target LMs and study their effect on the performance of the APE systems. From our experiments on LMs, we learn that i) using both the POS-tag, and the class-based LM in the APE system is better than using them in isolation, ii) building these LMs using neural approach is much better than statistical ones, and iii) the best LM combination achieves 0.4 BLEU improvement (from 64.88 to 65.31) over the APE system which do not use these LMs. We also showed that the problem of over-correction in phrase-based APE can be mitigated by our data augmentation technique which showed significant improvement of 0.6 TER, 0.8 BLEU, and 16.40% precision, for *context-aware* variant, over APE system which do not use data augmentation. Performance of our primary and contrastive submissions to the shared task were similar with a significant improvement of 3.31% TER and 4.25% BLEU (relative) over the baseline MT system. However, having a layer of quality estimation in our primary submission did not yield expected improvement.

8 Acknowledgements

This work has been partially supported by the EC-funded H2020 project QT21 (grant agreement no. 645452).

---

[2]Lower is better since we are predicting TER scores

References

Hanna Béchara, Yanjun Ma, and Josef van Genabith. 2011. Statistical post-editing for a statistical mt system. In *Proceedings of the XIII MT Summit*, pages 308–315.

José G. C. de Souza, Christian Buck, Marco Turchi, and Matteo Negri. 2013. FBK-UEdin participation to the WMT13 Quality Estimation shared-task. In *Proceedings of the Eighth Workshop on Statistical Machine Translation*, pages 352–358.

José G. C. de Souza, Jesús González-Rubio, Christian Buck, Marco Turchi, and Matteo Negri. 2014. FBK-UPV-UEdin participation in the WMT14 Quality Estimation shared-task. In *Proceedings of the Ninth Workshop on Statistical Machine Translation*, Baltimore, MD, USA, June.

José G. C. de Souza, Matteo Negri, Elisa Ricci, and Marco Turchi. 2015. Online Multitask Learning for Machine Translation Quality Estimation. In *Proceedings of the 53rd Annual Meeting of the Association for Computational Linguistics and the 7th International Joint Conference on Natural Language Processing (Volume 1: Long Papers)*, pages 219–228, Beijing, China, July.

Rajen Chatterjee, Marco Turchi, and Matteo Negri. 2015a. The fbk participation in the wmt15 automatic post-editing shared task. In *Proceedings of the Tenth Workshop on Statistical Machine Translation*, pages 210–215.

Rajen Chatterjee, Marion Weller, Matteo Negri, and Marco Turchi. 2015b. Exploring the Planet of the APEs: a Comparative Study of State-of-the-art Methods for MT Automatic Post-Editing. In *Proceedings of the 53rd Annual Meeting of the Association for Computational Linguistics*, Beijing, China.

Qin Gao and Stephan Vogel. 2008. Parallel implementations of word alignment tool. In *Software Engineering, Testing, and Quality Assurance for Natural Language Processing*, pages 49–57.

Pierre Geurts, Damien Ernst, and Louis Wehenkel. 2006. Extremely randomized trees. *Machine Learning*, 63(1):3–42, April.

Kenneth Heafield. 2011. Kenlm: Faster and smaller language model queries. In *Proceedings of the Sixth Workshop on Statistical Machine Translation*, pages 187–197.

Philipp Koehn and Hieu Hoang. 2007. Factored translation models. In *Proceedings of EMNLP-CoNLL*, pages 868–876.

Philipp Koehn, Hieu Hoang, Alexandra Birch, Chris Callison-Burch, Marcello Federico, Nicola Bertoldi, Brooke Cowan, Wade Shen, Christine Moran, Richard Zens, et al. 2007. Moses: Open source toolkit for statistical machine translation. In *Proceedings of the 45th annual meeting of the ACL on interactive poster and demonstration sessions*, pages 177–180.

Yashar Mehdad, Matteo Negri, and Marcello Federico. 2012. Match without a Referee: Evaluating MT Adequacy without Reference Translations. In *Proceedings of the Machine Translation Workshop (WMT2012)*, pages 171–180, Montréal, Canada.

Franz Josef Och. 2003. Minimum error rate training in statistical machine translation. In *Proceedings of the 41st Annual Meeting on Association for Computational Linguistics-Volume 1*, pages 160–167.

Kishore Papineni, Salim Roukos, Todd Ward, and Wei-Jing Zhu. 2002. Bleu: a method for automatic evaluation of machine translation. In *Proceedings of the 40th annual meeting on association for computational linguistics*, pages 311–318.

Fabian Pedregosa, Gaël Varoquaux, Alexandre Gramfort, Vincent Michel, Bertrand Thirion, Olivier Grisel, Mathieu Blondel, Peter Prettenhofer, Ron Weiss, Vincent Dubourg, Jake Vanderplas, Alexandre Passos, David Cournapeau, Mathieu Brucher, Mathieu Perrot, and Édouard Duchesnay. 2011. Scikit-learn : Machine Learning in Python. *Journal of Machine Learning Research*, 12:2825–2830.

Helmut Schmid. 1995. Improvements in part-of-speech tagging with an application to german. In *Proceedings of the Association for Computational Linguistics SIGDAT-Workshop*.

Michel Simard, Cyril Goutte, and Pierre Isabelle. 2007. Statistical Phrase-Based Post-Editing. In *Proceedings of the Annual Conference of the North American Chapter of the Association for Computational Linguistics (NAACL HLT)*, pages 508–515, Rochester, New York.

Matthew Snover, Bonnie Dorr, Richard Schwartz, Linnea Micciulla, and John Makhoul. 2006. A study of translation edit rate with targeted human annotation. In *Proceedings of association for machine translation in the Americas*, pages 223–231.

Lucia Specia, Kashif Shah, José G. C. de Souza, and Trevor Cohn. 2013. QuEstA translation quality estimation framework. In *Proceedings of the 51st Annual Meeting of the Association for Computational Linguistics*, pages 79–84.

Marco Turchi, Antonios Anastasopoulos, José G. C. de Souza, and Matteo Negri. 2014. Adaptive Quality Estimation for Machine Translation. In *Proceedings of the 52nd Annual Meeting of the Association for Computational Linguistics*, ACL '14.

Ashish Vaswani, Yinggong Zhao, Victoria Fossum, and David Chiang. 2013. Decoding with large-scale neural language models improves translation. In *Proceedings of the Empirical Methods in Natural Language Processing*, pages 1387–1392.

Log-linear Combinations of Monolingual and Bilingual
Neural Machine Translation Models for Automatic Post-Editing

Marcin Junczys-Dowmunt and **Roman Grundkiewicz**
Adam Mickiewicz University in Poznań
ul. Umultowska 87, 61-614 Poznań, Poland
`{junczys,romang}@amu.edu.pl`

Abstract

This paper describes the submission of the AMU (Adam Mickiewicz University) team to the Automatic Post-Editing (APE) task of WMT 2016. We explore the application of neural translation models to the APE problem and achieve good results by treating different models as components in a log-linear model, allowing for multiple inputs (the MT-output and the source) that are decoded to the same target language (post-edited translations). A simple string-matching penalty integrated within the log-linear model is used to control for higher faithfulness with regard to the raw machine translation output. To overcome the problem of too little training data, we generate large amounts of artificial data. Our submission improves over the uncorrected baseline on the unseen test set by -3.2% TER and +5.5% BLEU and outperforms any other system submitted to the shared-task by a large margin.

1 Introduction

This paper describes the submission of the AMU (Adam Mickiewicz University) team to the Automatic Post-Editing (APE) task of WMT 2016. Following the APE shared task from WMT 2015 (Bojar et al., 2015), the aim is to test methods for correcting errors produced by an unknown machine translation system in a black-box scenario. The organizers provide training data with human post-edits, evaluation is carried out part-automatically using TER (Snover et al., 2006) and BLEU (Papineni et al., 2002), and part-manually.

We explore the application of neural translation models to the APE task and investigate a number of aspects that seem to lead to good results:

- Creation of artificial post-edition data that can be used to train the neural models;

- Log-linear combination of monolingual and bilingual models in an ensemble-like manner;

- Addition of task-specific features in a log-linear model that allow to control for faithfulness of the automatic post-editing output with regard to the input, otherwise a weakness of neural translation models.

According to the automatic evaluation metrics used for the task, our system is ranked first among all submission to the shared task.

2 Related work

2.1 Post-Editing

State-of-the-art APE systems follow a monolingual approach firstly proposed by Simard et al. (2007) who trained a phrase-based SMT system on machine translation output and its post-edited versions. Béchara et al. (2011) proposed a "source-context aware" variant of this approach: automatically created word alignments are used to create a new source language which consists of joined MT-output and source token pairs. The inclusion of source-language information in that form is shown to be useful to improve the automatic post-editing results (Béchara et al., 2012; Chatterjee et al., 2015b). The quality of the word alignments plays an important role for this methods, as shown for instance by Pal et al. (2015).

A number of techniques have been developed to improve PB-SMT-based APE systems, e.g. approaches relying on phrase-table filtering techniques and specialized features. Chatterjee et al. (2015a) propose a pipeline where the best language model and pruned phrase table are selected through task-specific dense features. The goal was to overcome data sparsity issues.

Proceedings of the First Conference on Machine Translation, Volume 2: Shared Task Papers, pages 751–758,
Berlin, Germany, August 11-12, 2016. ©2016 Association for Computational Linguistics

The authors of the Abu-MaTran system (no publication, see Bojar et al. (2015)) incorporate sentence-level classifiers in a post-processing step which choose between the given MT output or an automatic post-edition coming from a PB-SMT APE system. Their most promising approach consists of a word-level recurrent neural network sequence-to-sequence classifier that marks each word of a sentence as *good* or *bad*. The output with the lower number of *bad* words is then chosen as the final post-editing answer. We believe this work to be among the first to apply (recurrent) neural networks to the task of automatic post-editing.

Other popular approaches rely on rule-based components (Wisniewski et al., 2015; Béchara et al., 2012) which we do not discuss here.

2.2 Neural machine translation

We restrict our description to the recently popular encoder-decoder models, based on recurrent neural networks (RNN).

An LSTM-based encoder-decoder model was introduced by Sutskever et al. (2014). Here the source sentence is encoded into a single continuous vector, the final state of the source LSTM-RNN. Once the end-of-sentence marker has been encoded, the network generates a translation by sampling the most probable translations from the target LSTM-RNN which keeps its state based on previous words and the source sentence state.

Bahdanau et al. (2015) extended this simple concept with bidirectional source RNNs (Cho et al., 2014) and the so-called soft-attention model. The novelty of this approach and its improved performance compared to Sutskever et al. (2014) came from the reduced reliance on the source sentence embedding which had to convey all information required for translation in a single state. Instead, attention models learn to look at particular word states at any position within the source sentence. This makes it also easier for these models to learn when to make copies, an important aspect for APE. We refer the reader to Bahdanau et al. (2015) for a detailed description of the discussed models. At the time of writing, no APE systems relying on neural translation models seem to have been published.[1]

---

[1] An accepted ACL 2016 paper is scheduled to appear: Santanu Pal, Sudip Kumar Naskar, Mihaela Vela and Josef van Genabith. A Neural Network based Approach to Automated Post-Editing. Proceedings of the 54th Annual Meet-

3 Data and data preparation

3.1 Used corpora

It was explicitly permitted to use additional data while preparing systems for the APE shared task. We made use of the following resources:

1. The official training and development data provided by the APE shared task organizers, consisting of 12,000 training triplets[2] and 1,000 development set triplets. In this paper we report our results for the 1,000 sentences of development data, and selected results on the unseen test data as provided by the task organizers.

2. The domain-specific English-German bilingual training data admissible during the WMT-16 shared task on IT-domain translation;

3. All other parallel English-German bilingual data admissible during the WMT-16 news translation task;

4. The German monolingual Common Crawl corpus admissible for the WMT-16 news translation and IT translation tasks.

3.2 Pre- and post-processing

The provided triplets have already been tokenized, the tokenization scheme seems to correspond to the Moses (Koehn et al., 2007) tokenizer without escaped special characters, so we re-apply escaping. All other data is tokenized with the Moses tokenizer with standard settings per language. We truecase the data with the Moses truecaser.

To deal with the limited ability of neural translation models to handle out-of-vocabulary words we split tokens into subword units, following Sennrich et al. (2015b).

Subword units were learned using a modified version of the byte pair encoding (BPE) compression algorithm (Gage, 1994). Sennrich et al. (2015b) modified the algorithm to work on character level instead of on bytes. The most frequent pairs of characters are iteratively replaced by a new character sequence created by merging the pairs of existent sequences. Frequent words

---

ings of the Association for Computational Linguistics, August 2016.

[2] A triplet consists of the English source sentence, a German machine translation output, and the German manually post-edited correction of that output.

are thus represented by single symbols and infrequent ones are divided into smaller units. The final size of the vocabulary is equal to the sum of merge operations and the number of initial characters. This method effectively reduces the number of unknown words to zero, as characters are always available as the smallest fall-back units. Sennrich et al. (2015b) showed that this method can deal with German compound nouns (relieving us from applying special methods to handle these) as well as transliterations for Russian-English.

This seems particularly useful in the case of APE, where we do not wish the neural models to "hallucinate" output when encountering unknown tokens. A faithful transliteration is more desirable. We chose vocabularies of 40,000 units per language. For German MT output and post-edited sentences we used the same set of subword units.

4   Artificial post-editing data

The provided post-editing data is orders of magnitude too small to train our neural models, and even with the in-domain training data from the IT translation task, we quickly see overfitting effects for a first English-German translation system. Inspired by Sennrich et al. (2015a) — who use back-translated monolingual data to enrich bilingual training corpora — we decided to create artificial training triplets.

4.1   Bootstrapping monolingual data

We applied cross-entropy filtering (Moore and Lewis, 2010) to the German Common Crawl corpus performing the following steps:

- We filtered the corpus for "well-formed" lines which start with a capital Unicode letter character and end in an end-of-sentence punctuation mark. We require the line to contain at least 30 Unicode letters.

- The corpus has been preprocessed as described above, including subword units, which may have a positive effect on cross-entropy filtering as they allow to score unknown words.

- Next, we built an in-domain trigram language model (Heafield et al., 2013) from the German post-editing training data and the German IT-task data, and a similarly sized out-of-domain language model from the Common Crawl data.

- We calculated cross-entropy scores for the first one billion lines of the corpus according to the two language models;

- We sorted the corpus by increasing cross-entropy and kept the first 10 million entries for round-trip translation and the top 100 million entries for language modeling.

4.2   Round-trip translation

For the next step, two phrase-based translation models, English-German and German-English, were created using the admissible parallel training data from the IT task. Word-alignments were computed with fast-align (Dyer et al., 2013), the dynamic-suffix array (Germann, 2015) holds the translation model. The top 10% bootstrapped monolingual data was used for language modeling in case of the English-German model, for the German-English translation system the language model was built only from the target side of the parallel in-domain corpora.[3]

The top 1% of the bootstrapped data have first been translated from German to English and next backwards from English to German. The intermediate English translations were preserved. In order to translate these 10 million sentences quickly (twice), we applied small stack-sizes and cube-pruning-pop-limits of around 100, completing the round-trip translation in about 24 hours.

This procedure left us with 10 million artificial post-editing triplets, where the source German data is treated as post-edited data, the German→English translated data is the English source, the round-trip translation results are the new uncorrected MT-output.

4.3   Filtering for TER

We hope that a round-trip translation process produces literal translations that may be more-or-less similar to post-edited triplets, where the distance between MT-output and post-edited text is generally smaller than between MT-output and human-produced translations of the same source. Having that much data available, we could continue our filtering process by trying to mimic the TER-statistics of the provided APE training corpus. While TER scores do only take into account the two German language parts of the triplet, it

---

[3]These models were not meant to be state-of-the-art quality systems. Our main objective was to create them within a few hours.

Data set	Sentences	NumWd	WdSh	NumEr	TER
training set	12,000	17.89	0.72	4.69	26.22
development set	1,000	19.76	0.71	4.90	24.81
round-trip.full	9,960,000	13.50	0.58	5,72	42.02
round-trip.n10	4,335,715	15.86	0.66	5.93	36.63
round-trip.n1	531,839	20.92	0.55	5.20	25.28

Table 1: Statistics of full and filtered data sets: number of sentences, average number of words, word shifts, errors, and TER score.

seems reasonable that filtering for better German-German pairs automatically results in a higher quality of the intermediate English part.

To achieve this, we represented each triplet in the APE training data as a vector of elementary TER statistics computed for the MT-output and the post-edited correction, such as the sentence length, the frequency of edit operations, and the sentence-level TER score. We do the same for the to-be-filtered artificial triplet corpus. The similarity measure is the inverse Euclidean distance over these vector representations.

In a first step, outliers which diverge from any maximum or minimum value of the reference vectors by more than 10% were removed. For example, we filtered triplets with post-edited sentences that were 10% longer than the longest post-edited sentence in the reference.

In the second step, for each triplet from the reference set we select n nearest neighbors. Candidates that have been chosen for one reference set triplet were excluded for the following triplets. If more than the 100 triplets had to be traversed to satisfy the exclusion criterion, less than n or even 0 candidates were selected. Two subsets have been created, one for $n = 1$ and one for $n = 10$. Table 1 sets the characteristics of the obtained corpora in relation to the provided training and development data. The smaller set (round-trip.n1) follows the TER statistics of the provided training and development data quite closely, but consists only of 5% of the artificial triplets. The larger set (round-trip.n10) consists of roughly 43% of the data, but has weaker TER scores.

5   Experiments

Following the post-editing-by-machine-translation paradigm, we explore the application of soft-attention neural translation models to post-editing. Analogous to the two dominating approaches de-

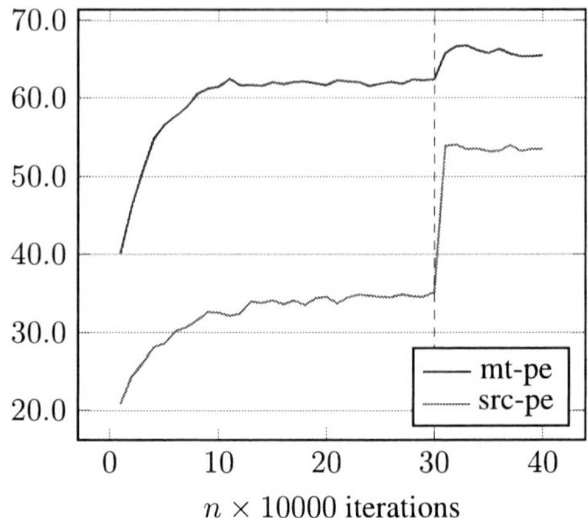

Figure 1: Training progress for mt-pe and src-pe models according to development set; dashed vertical line marks change from training set round-trip.n10 to fine-tuning with round-trip.n1.

scribed in Section 2.1, we investigate methods that are purely monolingual as well as a simple method to include source language information in a more natural way than it has been done for phrase-based machine translation.

The neural machine translation systems explored in this work are attentional encoder-decoder models (Bahdanau et al., 2015), which have been trained with Nematus[4]. We used mini-batches of size 80, a maximum sentence length of 50, word embeddings of size 500, and hidden layers of size 1024. Models were trained with Adadelta (Zeiler, 2012), reshuffling the corpus between epochs. As mentioned before tokens were split into subword units, 40,000 per language. For decoding, we used AmuNMT[5], our C++/CUDA decoder for NMT models trained with Nematus with a beam size of 12 and length normalization.

---

[4]https://github.com/rsennrich/nematus
[5]https://github.com/emjotde/amunmt

System	TER	BLEU
Baseline (mt)	25.14	62.92
mt→pe	23.37	66.71
mt→pe×4	23.23	66.88
src→pe	32.31	53.89
src→pe×4	31.42	55.41
mt→pe×4 / src→pe×4[*]	22.38	68.07
mt→pe×4 / src→pe×4 / pep[*]	**21.46**	**68.94**

Table 2: Results on provided development set. Best-performing models have been chosen based on this development set. Systems marked with [*] have weights tuned on the same development set.

5.1 MT-output to post-editing

We started training the monolingual MT-PE model with the MT and PE data from the larger artificial triplet corpus (round-trip.n10). The model has been trained for 4 days, saving a model every $10,000$ mini-batches. Quick convergence can be observed for the monolingual task and we switched to fine-tuning after the 300,000-th iteration with a mix of the provided training data and the smaller round-trip.n1 corpus. The original post-editing data was oversampled 20 times and concatenated with round-trip.n1.

This resulted in the performance jump shown in Figure 1 (mt→pe, blue). Training were continued for another 100,000 iterations and stopped when overfitting effects became apparent. Training directly with the smaller training data without the initial training on round-trip.n10 lead to even earlier overfitting.

Entry mt→pe in Table 2 contains the results of the single-best model on the development set which outperforms the baseline significantly. Models for ensembling are selected among the periodically saved parameter dumps of one training run. An ensemble mt→pe×4 consisting of the four best models shows only modest improvements over the single model. The same development set has been used to select the best-performing models, results may therefore be slightly skewed.

5.2 Source to post-editing

We proceed similarly for the English-German NMT training. When fine-tuning with the smaller corpus with oversampled post-editing data, we also add all in-domain parallel training data from the IT-task, roughly 200,000 sentences. Fine-tuning results in a much larger jump than in the monolingual case, but the overall performance of the NMT system is still weaker than the uncorrected MT-baseline.

As for the monolingual case, we evaluate the single-best model (src→pe) and an ensemble (src→pe×4) of the four best models of a training run. The src→pe×4 system is not able to beat the MT baseline, but the ensemble is significantly better than the single model.

5.3 Log-linear combinations and tuning

AmuNMT can be configured to accept different inputs to different members of a model ensemble as long as the target language vocabulary is the same. We can therefore build a decoder that takes both, German MT output and the English source sentence, as parallel input, and produces post-edited German as output. Since once the input sentence has been provided to a NMT model it essentially turns into a language model, this can be achieved without much effort. In theory an unlimited number of inputs can be combined in this way without the need of specialized multi-input training procedures (Zoph and Knight, 2016).[6]

In NMT ensembles, homogeneous models are typically weighted equally. Here we combine different models and equal weighting does not work. Instead, we treat each ensemble component as a feature in a traditional log-linear model and perform weighting as parameter tuning with Batch-Mira (Cherry and Foster, 2012). AmuNMT can produce Moses-compatible n-best lists and we devised an iterative optimization process similar to the one available in Moses. We tune the weights on the development set towards lower TER scores; two iterations seem to be enough. When ensembling one mt→pe model and one src→pe model, the assigned weights correspond roughly to 0.8 and 0.2 respectively. The linear combination of all eight models (mt→pe×4 / src→pe×4) improves quality by 0.9 TER and 1.2 BLEU, however, weights were tuned on the same data.

5.4 Enforcing faithfulness

We extend AmuNMT with a simple Post-Editing Penalty (PEP). To ensure that the system is fairly

---

[6]Which are still worth investigating for APE and likely to yield better results.

conservative — i.e. the correction process does not introduce too much new material — every word in the system's output that was not seen in its input incurs a penalty of -1.

During decoding this is implemented efficiently as a matrix of dimensions batch size × target vocabulary size where all columns that match source words are assigned 0 values, all other words −1. This feature can then be used as if it was another ensemble model and tuned with the same procedure as described above.

PEP introduces a precision-like bias into the decoding process and is a simple means to enforce a certain faithfulness with regard to the input via string matching. This is not easily accomplished within the encoder-decoder framework which abstracts away from any string representations. A recall-like variant (penalize for missing input words in the output) cannot be realized at decode-time as it is not known which words have been omitted until the very end of the decoding process. This could only work as a final re-ranking criterion, which we did not explore in this paper. The bag-of-words approach grants the NMT model the greatest freedom with regard to reordering and fluency for which these models seem to be naturally well-suited.

As before, we tune the combination on the development set. The resulting system (mt→pe×4 / src→pe×4 / pep) can again improve post-editing quality. We see a total improvement of -3.7% TER and +6.0% BLEU over the given MT baseline on the development set. The log-linear combination of different features improves over the purely monolingual ensemble by -1.8% TER and +2.1% BLEU.

6 Final results and conclusions

We submitted the output of the last system (mt→pe×4 / src→pe×4 / pep) as our final proposition for the APE shared task, and mt→pe×4 as a contrastive system. Table 3 contains the results on the unseen test set for our two systems (in bold) and the best system of any other submitting team as reported by the task organizers (for more details and manually judged results — which were not yet available at the time of writing — see the shared task overview paper). Results are sorted by TER from best to worse. For our best system, we see improvements of -3.2% TER and +5.5% BLEU over the unprocessed baseline 1 (uncor-

System	TER	BLEU
mt→pe×4 / src→pe×4 / pep	**21.52**	**67.65**
mt→pe×4 (contrastive)	**23.06**	**66.09**
FBK	23.92	64.75
USAAR	24.14	64.10
CUNI	24.31	63.32
Standard Moses (baseline 2)	24.64	63.47
Uncorrected MT (baseline 1)	24.76	62.11
DCU	26.79	58.60
JUSAAR	26.92	59.44

Table 3: Results on unseen test set in comparison to other shared task submissions as reported by the task organizers. For submissions by other teams we include only their best result.

rected MT), and -1.5% TER and +1.5% BLEU over our contrastive system. The organizers also provide results for a standard phrase-based Moses set-up (baseline 2) that can hardly beat baseline 1 (-0.1% TER, +1.4% BLEU). Both our systems outperform the next-best submission by large margins. In the light of these last results, our system seems to be quite successful.

We could demonstrate the following:

- Neural machine translation models can be successfully applied to APE;

- Artificial APE triplets help against early overfitting and make it possible to overcome the problem of too little training data;

- Log-linear combinations of neural machine translation models with different input languages can be used as a method of combining MT-output and source data for APE to positive effects;

- Task specific features can be easily integrated into the log-linear models and can control the faithfulness of the APE results.

Future work should include the investigation of integrated multi-source approaches like (Zoph and Knight, 2016) and better schemes of dealing with overfitting. We also plan to apply our methods to the data of last year's APE task.

7 Acknowledgements

This work is partially funded by the National Science Centre, Poland (Grant No. 2014/15/N/ST6/02330).

References

Dzmitry Bahdanau, Kyunghyun Cho, and Yoshua Bengio. 2015. Neural machine translation by jointly learning to align and translate. In *Proceedings of the International Conference on Learning Representations*, San Diego, CA.

Hanna Béchara, Yanjun Ma, and Josef van Genabith. 2011. Statistical post-editing for a statistical MT system. In *Proceedings of the 13th Machine Translation Summit*, pages 308–315, Xiamen, China.

Hanna Béchara, Raphaël Rubino, Yifan He, Yanjun Ma, and Josef van Genabith. 2012. An evaluation of statistical post-editing systems applied to RBMT and SMT systems. In *Proceedings of COLING 2012*, pages 215–230, Mumbai, India.

Ondřej Bojar, Rajen Chatterjee, Christian Federmann, Barry Haddow, Matthias Huck, Chris Hokamp, Philipp Koehn, Varvara Logacheva, Christof Monz, Matteo Negri, Matt Post, Carolina Scarton, Lucia Specia, and Marco Turchi. 2015. Findings of the 2015 Workshop on Statistical Machine Translation. In *Proceedings of the Tenth Workshop on Statistical Machine Translation*, pages 1–46, Lisbon, Portugal. Association for Computational Linguistics.

Rajen Chatterjee, Marco Turchi, and Matteo Negri. 2015a. The FBK participation in the WMT15 automatic post-editing shared task. In *Proceedings of the Tenth Workshop on Statistical Machine Translation*, pages 210–215, Lisbon, Portugal. Association for Computational Linguistics.

Rajen Chatterjee, Marion Weller, Matteo Negri, and Marco Turchi. 2015b. Exploring the planet of the APEs: a comparative study of state-of-the-art methods for MT automatic post-editing. In *Proceedings of the 53rd Annual Meeting of the Association for Computational Linguistics and the 7th International Joint Conference on Natural Language Processing*, pages 156–161, Beijing, China. Association for Computational Linguistics.

Colin Cherry and George Foster. 2012. Batch tuning strategies for statistical machine translation. In *Proceedings of the 2012 Conference of the North American Chapter of the Association for Computational Linguistics: Human Language Technologies*, pages 428–436, Stroudsburg, PA, USA. Association for Computational Linguistics.

Kyunghyun Cho, Bart van Merrienboer, Caglar Gulcehre, Dzmitry Bahdanau, Fethi Bougares, Holger Schwenk, and Yoshua Bengio. 2014. Learning phrase representations using RNN encoder–decoder for statistical machine translation. In *Proceedings of the 2014 Conference on Empirical Methods in Natural Language Processing*, pages 1724–1734, Doha, Qatar. Association for Computational Linguistics.

Chris Dyer, Victor Chahuneau, and Noah A. Smith. 2013. A simple, fast, and effective reparameterization of IBM model 2. In *Proceedings of the 2013 Conference of the North American Chapter of the Association for Computational Linguistics: Human Language Technologies*, pages 644–648, Atlanta, Georgia. Association for Computational Linguistics.

Philip Gage. 1994. A new algorithm for data compression. *The C Users Journal*, (2):23–38.

Ulrich Germann. 2015. Sampling phrase tables for the Moses statistical machine translation system. *Prague Bulletin of Mathematical Linguistics*, (1):39–50.

Kenneth Heafield, Ivan Pouzyrevsky, Jonathan H. Clark, and Philipp Koehn. 2013. Scalable modified Kneser-Ney language model estimation. In *Proceedings of the 51st Annual Meeting of the Association for Computational Linguistics*, pages 690–696, Sofia, Bulgaria.

Philipp Koehn, Hieu Hoang, Alexandra Birch, Chris Callison-Burch, Marcello Federico, Nicola Bertoldi, Brooke Cowan, Wade Shen, Christine Moran, Richard Zens, et al. 2007. Moses: Open source toolkit for statistical machine translation. In *Proceedings of the 45th Annual Meeting of the Association for Computational Linguistics*, pages 177–180. Association for Computational Linguistics.

Robert C. Moore and William Lewis. 2010. Intelligent selection of language model training data. In *Proceedings of the 48th Annual Meeting of the Association for Computational Linguistics*, pages 220–224, Stroudsburg, PA, USA. Association for Computational Linguistics.

Santanu Pal, Mihaela Vela, Sudip Kumar Naskar, and Josef van Genabith. 2015. USAAR-SAPE: An English–Spanish statistical automatic post-editing system. In *Proceedings of the Tenth Workshop on Statistical Machine Translation*, pages 216–221, Lisbon, Portugal. Association for Computational Linguistics.

Kishore Papineni, Salim Roukos, Todd Ward, and Wei-Jing Zhu. 2002. BLEU: A method for automatic evaluation of machine translation. In *Proceedings of the 40th Annual Meeting on Association for Computational Linguistics*, ACL '02, pages 311–318, Stroudsburg, PA, USA. Association for Computational Linguistics.

Rico Sennrich, Barry Haddow, and Alexandra Birch. 2015a. Improving neural machine translation models with monolingual data. *arXiv preprint arXiv:1511.06709*.

Rico Sennrich, Barry Haddow, and Alexandra Birch. 2015b. Neural machine translation of rare words with subword units. *arXiv preprint arXiv:1508.07909*.

Michel Simard, Cyril Goutte, and Pierre Isabelle. 2007. Statistical phrase-based post-editing. In *Proceedings of the Conference of the North American*

Chapter of the Association for Computational Linguistics, pages 508–515, Rochester, New York. Association for Computational Linguistics.

Matthew Snover, Bonnie Dorr, Richard Schwartz, Linnea Micciulla, and John Makhoul. 2006. A study of translation edit rate with targeted human annotation. In *Proceedings of Association for Machine Translation in the Americas*, pages 223–231, Cambridge, Massachusetts.

Ilya Sutskever, Oriol Vinyals, and Quoc V Le. 2014. Sequence to sequence learning with neural networks. In *Advances in Neural Information Processing Systems 27: 28th Annual Conference on Neural Information Processing Systems 2014*, pages 3104–3112, Montreal, Canada.

Guillaume Wisniewski, Nicolas Pécheux, and François Yvon. 2015. Why predicting post-edition is so hard? failure analysis of LIMSI submission to the APE shared task. In *Proceedings of the Tenth Workshop on Statistical Machine Translation*, pages 222–227, Lisbon, Portugal. Association for Computational Linguistics.

Matthew D. Zeiler. 2012. ADADELTA: an adaptive learning rate method. *arXiv preprint arXiv:1212.5701*.

Barret Zoph and Kevin Knight. 2016. Multi-source neural translation. *arXiv preprint arXiv:1601.00710*.

USAAR: An Operation Sequential Model for Automatic Statistical Post-Editing

Santanu Pal[1], Marcos Zampieri[1,2], Josef van Genabith[1,2]
[1]Saarland University, Saarbrücken, Germany
[2]German Research Center for Artificial Intelligence (DFKI), Germany
{santanu.pal, marcos.zampieri, josef.vangenabith}@uni-saarland.de

Abstract

This paper presents an automatic post-editing (APE) method to improve the translation quality produced by an English–German (EN–DE) statistical machine translation (SMT) system. Our system is based on Operation Sequential Model (OSM) combined with phrased-based statistical MT (PB-SMT) system. The system is trained on monolingual settings between MT outputs (TL_{MT}) produced by a black-box MT system and their corresponding post-edited version (TL_{PE}). Our system achieves considerable improvement over TL_{MT} on a held-out development set. The reported system achieves 64.10 BLEU (1.99 absolute points and 3.2% relative improvement in BLEU over raw MT output) and 24.14 TER and a TER score of 24.14 (0.66 absolute points and 0.25% relative improvement in TER over raw MT output) in the official test set.

1 Introduction

Translations produced by machine translation (MT) systems have improved substantially over the past few decades. This is particularly noticeable for some language pairs (e.g. English to German and English to French) and for domain specific language (e.g. technical documentation). Texts produced by MT systems are now widely used in the translation and localization industry. MT output is post-edited by professional translators and it has become an important part of the translation workflow. A number of studies confirm that post-editing MT output improves translators' performance in terms of productivity and it may also impact translation quality and consis-

tency (Guerberof, 2009; Plitt and Masselot, 2010; Zampieri and Vela, 2014).

With this respect the ultimate goal of MT systems is to provide output that can be post-edited with the least effort as possible by human translators. One of the strategies to improve MT output is to apply automatic post-editing (APE) methods (Knight and Chander, 1994; Simard et al., 2007a; Simard et al., 2007b). APE methods work under the assumption that some errors in MT systems are recurrent and they can be corrected automatically in a post-processing stage thus providing output that is more adequate to be post-edited. APE methods are applied before human post-editing increasing translators' productivity.

This paper presents a new approach to APE which was submitted by the USAAR team to the Automatic Post-editing (APE) shared task at WMT-2016. Our system combines two models: monolingual phrase-based and operation sequential model with an edit distance based word alignment between an English-German (EN-DE) Machine translation output and the corresponding human post-edited version of German Translation (Turchi et al., 2016).

Usually APE tasks focus on fluency errors produced by the MT system. The most frequent ones are incorrect lexical choices, incorrect word ordering, the insertion of a word, the deletion of a word. For the WMT2016 APE task, in order to automatically post-editing, we adopt operation sequential model (OSM) for SMT to build our Statistical APE (SAPE) System. We inspired from the work of Durrani et al. (2011) and Durrani et al. (2015). Since, in OSM model, the translation and reordering operations are coupled in a single generative story: the reordering decisions may depend on preceding translation decisions and translation decisions may depend on preceding reordering decisions. The model provides a natural re-

Proceedings of the First Conference on Machine Translation, Volume 2: Shared Task Papers, pages 759–763,
Berlin, Germany, August 11-12, 2016. ©2016 Association for Computational Linguistics

ordering mechanism and deal with both local and long-distance re-orderings consistently.

The remainder of the paper is organized as follows. Section 2 describes our proposed system, in particular PB-SMT coupled OSM model. In Section 3, we outline the data used for experiments and complete experimental setup. Section 4 presents the results of the automatic evaluation, followed by conclusion and future work in Section 5.

2 USAAR APE System

Our APE system is based on operational N-gram sequential model which integrates translation and reordering operations into the phrase-based APE system. Traditional PB-SMT (Koehn et al., 2003) provides a powerful translation mechanism which can directly be modelled to a phrase-based SAPE (PB-SAPE) system (Simard et al., 2007a; Simard et al., 2007b; Pal et al., 2015) using target language MT output (TL_{MT}) and their corresponding post-edited version (TL_{PE}) as a parallel training corpus. Unlike PB-SMT, PB-SAPE also follows similar kind of drawbacks such as dependency across phrases, handling discontinuous phrases etc. Our OSM-APE system is based on phrase based N-gram APE model, however reordering approach is essentially different, it considers all possible orderings of phrases instead of pre-calculated orientations. The model represents the post-edited translation process as a linear sequence of operations such as lexical generation of post-edited translation and their orderings. The translation and reordering decisions are conditioned on n previous translation and reordering decisions. The model also can able to consistently modelled both local and long-range reorderings. Traditional OSM based MT model consists of three sequence of operations:

- Generates a sequence of source and/or target words.

- For reordering operations, inserts gaps as explicit target positions

- Forward and backward jump operations

The sequence operation is based on n-gram model. The probability of a nth operation depends on the $n-1$ preceding operations. The generation of post-edited output (pe) from a given MT sentence (mt), the decoder provides a sequence of hypothesis H: $h_1,...,h_n$ and the APE model estimates the probability $p(mt, pe)$ given in Equation 1, from a sequence of I operations O ($o_1, ...o_I$) for m amount [1] of context has been used.

$$p(mt, pe) \approx \prod_{i=1}^{I} p(o_i | o_{i-m+1}...o_{i-1}) \quad (1)$$

The decoder searches best translation in Equation 2 from the model using language model $p_{lm}(pe)$

$$pe^* = argmax_{pe} \frac{p(mt, pe)}{p_{pr}(pe)} \times p_{lm}(pe) \quad (2)$$

$p_{pr}(pe) \approx \prod_{i=1}^{I} p(w_i | w_{i-m+1}...w_{i-1})$, is the prior probability that marginalize the joint probability $p(mt, pe)$. The model is then represented in a log-linear approach (Och and Ney, 2003) (in Equation 3) that makes it useful to incorporate standard features along with several novel features that improve the accuracy.

$$pe^* = argmax_{pe} \sum_{i=1}^{I} \lambda_i h_i(mt, pe) \quad (3)$$

where λ_i is the weight associated with the feature $h_i(mt, pe)$: $p(mt, pe)$, $p_{pr}(pe)$ and $p_{lm}(pe)$. Apart from this 8 additional features has been included in the log-linear model:

1. Length penalty: Length of the pe in words

2. Deletion penalty

3. Gap bonus: Total number of gap inserted to produce PE sentence

4. Open gap penalty : Number of open gaps, this penalty controls how quickly gap was closed.

5. Distortion: Distance based reordering which is similar to PB-SMT.

6. Gap distance penalty: The gap between mt and pe sentences generated during the generation process.

7. Lexical features: $mt–pe$ and $pe–mt$ lexical translation probability (Koehn et al., 2003).

---

[1] We use a 6-gram model trained on SRILM-Toolkit (Stolcke, 2002)

3   Experiment

The effectiveness of the present work is demonstrated by using the standard log-linear PB-SMT model for our phrase based SAPE (PB-SAPE) model. The MT outputs are provided by WMT-2016 APE task (c.f Table 1) are considered as baseline system translation. For building our SAPE system, we experimented with various maximum phrase lengths for the translation model and n–gram settings for the language model. We found that using a maximum phrase length of 10 for the translation model and a 6-gram language model produces the best results in terms of BLEU (Papineni et al., 2002) scores for our SAPE model.

The other experimental settings were concerned with word alignment model between TL_{MT} and TL_{PE} are trained on three different aligners: Berkeley Aligner (Liang et al., 2006), METEOR aligner (Lavie and Agarwal, 2007) and TER (Snover et al., 2006). The phrase-extraction (Koehn et al., 2003) and hierarchical phrase-extraction (Chiang, 2005) are used to build our PB-SAPE and hierarchical phrase-based statistical (HPB-SAPE) system respectively. The re-ordering model was trained with the hierarchical, monotone, swap, left to right bidirectional (hiermslr-bidirectional) method (Galley and Manning, 2008) and conditioned on both source and target language. The 5-gram target language model was trained using KenLM (Heafield, 2011). Phrase pairs that occur only once in the training data are assigned an unduly high probability mass (i.e. 1). To compensate this shortcoming, we performed smoothing of the phrase table using the Good-Turing smoothing technique (Foster et al., 2006). System tuning was carried out using Minimum Error Rate Training (MERT) (Och, 2003) optimized with k-best MIRA (Cherry and Foster, 2012) on a held out development set of size 500 sentences randomly extracted from training data. Therefore, all model has been build on 11,500 parallel TL_{MT}–TL_{PE} sentences. After the parameters were tuned, decoding was carried out on the held out development test set ('Dev' in Table 1) as well as test set.

Table 1 presents the statistics of the training, development and test sets released for the English–German APE Task organized in WMT-2016. These data sets did not require any preprocessing in terms of encoding or alignment.

	SEN	Tokens		
		EN	DE-MT	DE-PE
Train	12,000	201,505	210,573	214,720
Dev	1,000	17,827	19,355	19,763
Test	2,000	31,477	34,332	–

Table 1: Statistics of the the WMT-2016 APE Shared Task Data Set. SEN: Sentences, EN: English and DE: German

4   Results

We set various APE system settings for our experiments. We start our experiment with the provide TL_{MT} output, considering as baseline.

In the set of experiments are reported in Table 2, first, three word alignment (one statistical based aligner i.e., Berkeley aligner (Liang et al., 2006) and two edit distance based aligners i.e., METEOR aligner (Lavie and Agarwal, 2007) and TER aligner (Snover et al., 2006)) models are integrated separately within both the PB-SAPE as well as the HPB-SAPE systems. As a result, there are three different PB-SAPE (Experiment 2, 3 and 4 in Table 2) and HPB-SAPE (Experiment 5, 6 and 7 in Table 2) systems.

It is evident from Table 2 that the METEOR aligner is performed better than other two aligners. Therefore, our OSM coupled PB-SAPE model ('OSM' in Table 2) used METEOR based alignment. The experiment result shows that compare to other systems in Table 2, our OSM based model performed better in terms of two evaluation metric BLEU (Papineni et al., 2002) and TER. Evaluation result also shows that both PB-SAPE and HPB-SAPE system performed better over baseline system on development set data. The submitted primary system (OSM in Table 2) achieves 3.06% relative (1.99 absolute BLEU points) improvement over baseline[2] . The system also shows similar improvements is terms of TER evaluation measure.

According to the test set evaluation, our system achieves similar improvements as appeared in development set data. Table 3 shows that, there are two types of baseline systems: (i) *Baseline1* – based on raw MT output and (ii) *Baseline2* – based on Statistical APE (Simard et al., 2007b) (a phrase-based system (Koehn et al., 2007) build

---

[2]In Table 2, the raw MT output of development set data is considered as MT output of the baseline system.

System		Exp.	BLEU	MET	TER
Baseline	WMT MT-PE	1	65.02	47.79	24.42
PB-SAPE	Berkeley Aligner	2	65.89	48.23	24.51
	METEOR Aligner	3	65.97	48.34	24.36
	TER Aligner	4	65.14	47.85	24.96
HPB-SAPE	Berkeley Aligner	5	66.09	48.31	24.56
	METEOR Aligner	6	66.55	48.58	24.51
	TER Aligner	7	65.19	47.91	24.97
OSM	METEOR Aligner	8	67.01	48.80	24.04

Table 2: Systematic Evaluation on the WMT-2016 APE Shared Task Development Set

using MOSES[3] with default settings). There are two different systems called *OSM_Primary* and *OSM_Constrastive* have been submitted to the WMT-2016 APE shared task. The difference between the two submissions is that the *OSM_Primary* system is tuned with all phrase-based setting parameters including OSM parameters while *OSM_Constrastive* is also tuned with similar parameters but excluding OSM parameters. The tuning process of the OSM parameters is conducted with MERT and optimized with MIRA. Our primary submission obtained a BLEU score of 64.10 (1.99 absolute points and 3.2% relative improvement in BLEU) and a TER score of 24.14 (0.66 absolute points and 0.25% relative improvement in TER) over *Baseline1* system. If we consider *Baseline2* system, our primary submission achieved 0.63 absolute points and 0.99% relative improvement in BLEU and 0.50 absolute points and 0.20% relative improvement in TER.

System	BLEU	TER
Baseline1	62.11	24.76
Baseline2	63.47	24.64
OSM_Primary	**64.10**	**24.14**
OSM_Constrastive	64.00	**24.14**

Table 3: Evaluation on the WMT-2016 APE Shared Task Test Set

5 Conclusion and Future Work

This paper presents the USAAR system submitted in the English–German APE task at WMT-2016. The system demonstrates the crucial role METEOR-based alignment and OSM based SAPE can play in SAPE tasks. The use of statistical aligners in PB-SAPE/HPB-SAPE pipeline successfully improve the APE system, however performances with respect to the translations provided by the baseline are not promising. This is the reason behind use of edit distance-based word alignment into the pipeline. The reason for using OSM model is that, the model tightly couples translation and reordering. Apart from that, the OSM model also considers all possible reorderings instead perform search only on a limited number of pre-calculated orderings. The proposed system, OSM-based SAPE approach, was successful in improving over the PB-SAPE as well as HPB-SAPE performance.

The WMT-2016 APE shared task was a great opportunity to test APE methods that can be later applied in real-word post-editing and computer-aided translation (CAT) tools. We are currently working on implementing the APE methods described in this paper to CATaLog, a recently-developed CAT tool that provides translators with suggestions originated from MT and from translation memories (TM) (Nayek et al., 2015; Pal et al., 2016). In so doing, we aim to provide better suggestions for post-editing and we would like to investigate how this impacts human post-editing performance by carrying out user studies.

Acknowledgments

We would like to thank the WMT-2016 APE shared task organizers for this interesting shared task and for prompt replies to all our inquiries.

The research leading to these results has received funding from the EU FP7 Project EXPERT - the People Programme (Marie Curie Actions), under REA grant agreement no. 317471.

References

Colin Cherry and George Foster. 2012. Batch Tuning Strategies for Statistical Machine Translation. In *In Proceedings NAACL-HLT*.

---

[3] http://www.statmt.org/moses/

David Chiang. 2005. A Hierarchical Phrase-based Model for Statistical Machine Translation. In *Proceedings of ACL*.

Nadir Durrani, Helmut Schmid, and Alexander Fraser. 2011. A joint sequence translation model with integrated reordering. In *Proceedings of ACL*.

Nadir Durrani, Helmut Schmid, Alexander M. Fraser, Philipp Koehn, and Hinrich Schtze. 2015. The operation sequence model - combining n-gram-based and phrase-based statistical machine translation. *Computational Linguistics*, 41:185–214.

George Foster, Roland Kuhn, and Howard Johnson. 2006. Phrasetable Smoothing for Statistical Machine Translation. In *Proceedings of EMNLP*.

Michel Galley and Christopher D. Manning. 2008. A Simple and Effective Hierarchical Phrase Reordering Model. In *Proceedings of EMNLP*.

Ana Guerberof. 2009. Productivity and quality in the post-editing of outputs from translation memories and machine translation. *Localisation Focus*, 7(1):133–140.

Kenneth Heafield. 2011. KenLM: Faster and Smaller Language Model Queries. In *Proceedings of WMT*.

Kevin Knight and Ishwar Chander. 1994. Automated Post-Editing of Documents. In *Proceedings of AAAI*.

Philipp Koehn, Franz Josef Och, and Daniel Marcu. 2003. Statistical Phrase-based Translation. In *Proceedings of NAACL-HLT*.

Philipp Koehn, Hieu Hoang, Alexandra Birch, Chris Callison-Burch, Marcello Federico, Nicola Bertoldi, Brooke Cowan, Wade Shen, Christine Moran, Richard Zens, Chris Dyer, Ondřej Bojar, Alexandra Constantin, and Evan Herbst. 2007. Moses: Open Source Toolkit for Statistical Machine Translation. In *Proceedings of ACL*.

Alon Lavie and Abhaya Agarwal. 2007. METEOR: An Automatic Metric for MT Evaluation with High Levels of Correlation with Human Judgments. In *Proceedings of WMT*.

Percy Liang, Ben Taskar, and Dan Klein. 2006. Alignment by Agreement. In *Proceedings of NAACL-HLT*.

Tapas Nayek, Sudip Kumar Naskar, Santanu Pal, Marcos Zampieri, Mihaela Vela, and Josef van Genabith. 2015. CATaLog: New approaches to tm and post editing interfaces. In *Proceedings of the NLP4TM Workshop*.

Franz Josef Och and Hermann Ney. 2003. A Systematic Comparison of Various Statistical Alignment Models. *Computational Linguistics*, 29(1):19–51.

Franz Josef Och. 2003. Minimum Error Rate Training in Statistical Machine Translation. In *Proceedings of ACL*.

Santanu Pal, Mihaela Vela, Sudip Kumar Naskar, and Josef van Genabith. 2015. USAAR-SAPE: An English–Spanish Statistical Automatic Post-Editing System. In *Proceedings of WMT*, September.

Santanu Pal, Marcos Zampieri, Sudip Kumar Naskar, Mihaela Vela, and Josef van Genabith. 2016. CATaLog Online: Porting a Post-editing Tool to the Web. In *Proceedings of LREC*.

Kishore Papineni, Salim Roukos, Todd Ward, and Wei-Jing Zhu. 2002. BLEU: A Method for Automatic Evaluation of Machine Translation. In *Proceedings of ACL*.

Mirko Plitt and François Masselot. 2010. A productivity test of statistical machine translation post-editing in a typical localisation context. *The Prague Bulletin of Mathematical Linguistics*, 93:7–16.

Michel Simard, Cyril Goutte, and Pierre Isabelle. 2007a. Statistical Phrase-based Post-Editing. In *In Proceedings of NAACL-HLT*.

Michel Simard, Nicola Ueffing, Pierre Isabelle, and Roland Kuhn. 2007b. Rule-Based Translation with Statistical Phrase-Based Post-Editing. In *Proceedings of WMT*.

Matthew Snover, Bonnie Dorr, Richard Schwartz, Linnea Micciulla, and John Makhoul. 2006. A Study of Translation Edit Rate with Targeted Human Annotation. In *Proceedings of AMTA*.

Andreas Stolcke. 2002. Srilm – an extensible language modeling toolkit. In *IN Proceedings of ICSLP*.

Marco Turchi, Rajen Chatterjee, and Matteo Negri. 2016. WMT16 APE shared task data. LINDAT/CLARIN digital library at Institute of Formal and Applied Linguistics, Charles University in Prague.

Marcos Zampieri and Mihaela Vela. 2014. Quantifying the Influence of MT Output in the Translators Performance: A Case Study in Technical Translation. In *Proceedings of the HaCaT Workshop*.

Bilingual Embeddings and Word Alignments
for Translation Quality Estimation

Amal Abdelsalam*, **Ondřej Bojar****, **Samhaa El-Beltagy***
*Nile University in Egypt, Center of Informatics Science, Text Mining Research Group
am.mahmoud@nu.edu.eg, samhaa@computer.org
**Charles University in Prague, Faculty of Mathematics and Physics, Institute of Formal and Applied Linguistics
bojar@ufal.mff.cuni.cz

Abstract

This paper describes our submission UFAL_MULTIVEC to the WMT16 Quality Estimation Shared Task, for English-German sentence-level post-editing effort prediction and ranking. Our approach exploits the power of bilingual distributed representations, word alignments and also manual post-edits to boost the performance of the baseline QuEst++ set of features. Our model outperforms the baseline, as well as the winning system in WMT15, Referential Translation Machines (RTM), in both scoring and ranking sub-tasks.

1 Introduction

Recently, the task of quality estimation (QE) for machine translation (MT) output attracted interest among researchers in the machine translation community. QE systems play an important role in improving post-editing efficiency (in terms of the time and effort) in different ways, e.g. by filtering out low quality translations to avoid spending time post-editing them, or by providing end-users with an estimate on how good or bad the translation is.

In 2012, WMT established the first sentence-level quality estimation shared task (Callison-Burch et al., 2012). Since then, new sub-tasks, language pairs and datasets in different domains were introduced every year (Bojar et al., 2013, 2014, 2015). In contrast to automatic evaluation (the "metrics task"), QE task aims to develop systems that provide predictions on the quality of machine translated text without access to reference translations (Blatz et al., 2004; Specia et al., 2009).

Sentence-level QE is the most popular track in the WMT QE shared task, due to its presence in all editions of the task since the beginning. Many features have been explored by participating systems, including lexical, syntactic, semantic, embedding-based features (Shah et al., 2015), as well as features dependent on any details the particular MT systems may provide (Soricut et al., 2012; Camargo de Souza et al., 2013). In our model, we try to exploit the power of bilingual distributed representations combined with word alignment information to boost the performance of translation quality estimation. For this purpose, we use the implementation provided by the Multivec tool (Bérard et al., 2016) for the bilingual distributed representation model, described by Luong et al. (2015) and the GIZA++ word alignment model (Och and Ney, 2003).

The rest of this paper is organized as follows. In Sections 2 and 3, we give an overview of the bilingual distributional model and word alignment for our purposes. Section 4 gives a detailed description of our feature set, including the features derived from manual post-edits of other sentences. Section 5 describes the datasets and resources we used to build our model. Section 6 discusses the experiments conducted and the official results. The final Section 7 concludes the paper.

2 Bilingual Distributed Representations

Word embeddings have shown a great potential in tackling various NLP tasks recently, including multilingual tasks. However, there is a major problem with using word embeddings in a multilingual setting because models are trained independently for each of the languages and the resulting

764

Proceedings of the First Conference on Machine Translation, Volume 2: Shared Task Papers, pages 764–771,
Berlin, Germany, August 11-12, 2016. ©2016 Association for Computational Linguistics

representations can use the vector space very differently. Therefore, measuring similarity between words in different languages will be difficult because even similar words would likely have very different representations. Much research work has been conducted to address this problem. According to Luong et al. (2015), the approaches developed to learn bilingual models fall into three categories:

Bilingual Mapping , where word representations are trained for each language independently and a linear mapping is then learned to transform representations from one language to another (Mikolov et al., 2013a).

Monolingual Adaptation relies on pre-trained embeddings of the source language when learning target representations. A bilingual constraint (such as unsupervised word alignments derived from a parallel corpus; Zou et al., 2013) ensures that semantically similar words across languages end up with embeddings similar in the learned vector space.

Bilingual Training aims to jointly learn representations for both languages using a parallel corpus. There were attempts to jointly learn representations without relying on word alignments (Gouws et al., 2014; Hermann and Blunsom, 2014; Chandar A P et al., 2014) but the BiSkip model introduced by Luong et al. (2015) clearly benefits from word alignments and outperforms other approaches in bilingual tasks such as cross-lingual document classification.

In our submission, we use the BiSkip bilingual model, belonging to the Bilingual Training category, to measure the similarity between the source and target sentences using their compositional vector representations, where the term *compositional* indicates that the vector for the sentence is a simple sum of the vectors of all words.

BiSkip model adapts Mikolov et al. (2013b) skipgram model for the bilingual case. The joint representations are learnt using Algorithm 1 to the following objective:

$$\alpha(Mono_1 + Mono_2) + \beta Bi \qquad (1)$$

where $Mono_1$ and $Mono_2$ are the monolingual representations of each language, Bi is used tie the two monolingual spaces, and the hyperparameters α and β are used to balance the influence of the monolingual components over the bilingual one.

Data: Word-Aligned Parallel Corpus
Output: BiSkip Vector Representation
for *source-target sentence pair* **do**
    for $a(w_s,w_t) \in$ *set of alignment links* **do**
        Predict neighbors of w_s;
        Predict neighbors of w_t;
        Use w_s to predict neighbors of w_t;
        Use w_t to predict neighbors of w_s ;
    end
end

Algorithm 1: BiSkip learning algorithm by Luong et al. (2015)

3   Word Alignments

For cross-lingual semantic similarity, a word alignment model is an important component. According to the evaluation of the semantic textual similarity task in SemEval 2015, the best performing systems in both the English and Spanish subtasks relied mainly on word alignment techniques (Sultan et al., 2015; Hänig et al., 2015). Inspired by these results, we add features based on word alignment to the QE system.

According to Specia et al. (2015), alignment-based features are used for word-level QE only and there is no alignment-based features included in the baseline feature set for sentence-level QE.

We use GIZA++ (Och and Ney, 2003) to obtain the alignments. By default, GIZA++ alignments are not symmetric. We symmetrize them by taking the intersection of the two directions, leading to high-precision alignments. For pre-processing, we lowercase and stem words (naively taking just the first four letters) on both sides of the input.

Some of our features rely on the alignments of our training data (the ITcorpus and the training part of the QEcorpus, see Section 5 below) and some need alignments between the source and the evaluated translation candidates (the development and test part of the QEcorpus). We thus use two sets of alignments:

Run-1 obtained by aligning only the ITcorpus.

Run-2 obtained by aligning the ITcorpus concatenated with the QEcorpus.

4 Features

This section describes the different types of features we use in our QE system. We extend the set of baseline features (Section 4.1) with features based on bilingual embeddings (Section 4.2), word alignment (Section 4.3) and also n-grams seen in a collection of manually post-edited texts (Section 4.4).

4.1 QuEst++ Baseline Features

A set of 17 system-independent features was developed by Specia et al. (2013) to set the baseline system for QE tasks. The features set is extracted using QuEst++[1] (Specia et al., 2015), an open source implementation of the baseline for quality estimation for different granularities (sentence, word, and document level QE).

QuEst++ extracts features from either or both the source and target sides (i.e. the source sentence and the candidate translation), and also language model features relying on large monolingual data.

4.2 Bilingual Embedding Features (BE)

In our submission, we use three features derived from bilingual embeddings:

SentSim simply takes the value of cosine similarity between the source and target sentences in the bilingual compositional vector space.

WordSim uses the bilingual vector model and also word-alignment links. We take the average value of cosine similarity between source words and their aligned counterparts in the target sentence. The alignment links between the source and target are established automatically. Specifically, we use Run-2 alignments as defined in Section 3.

NounSim is similar to WordSim, but instead of taking all alignment links, we compute the average cosine similarity of only the links where the source (English) word is a noun. The POS tags were produced by Stanford POS Tagger (Toutanova et al., 2003).

4.3 Alignment-Based Features

We propose several features based on automatic word alignments as obtained in Section 3.

4.3.1 Alignment Quality Score

We assume that a good translation aligns well word-by-word with the source. While this need not be the case for human translations, it usually holds for machine-translated text. To assess the translation quality of a segment, we thus take an alignment quality score.

In our submission, alignment quality scores are inspired by components of the conditional probability $P(t_1...t_l|s_1...s_m, a_1...a_m)$, where s_i denotes the source words, t_j denotes the target words and a_i are the alignment links for each source word to the target (unambiguous, due to the intersection). We define the score as:

$$\text{score} = \sum_{i=1}^{m} P(t_j|s_{i_{a_i}}) \qquad (2)$$

$$P(t_j|s_{i_{a_i}}) = \frac{c(s_i, t_j)}{c(s_i)} \qquad (3)$$

The score is a simple sum of lexical translation probabilities (longer sentences with more aligned words thus get a higher score) and the lexical translation probabilities $P(t|s)$ are estimated from the count $c(s, t)$ how often the source s and target t words were aligned in our word-aligned corpus.

The formulas resemble IBM Model 1 (Brown et al., 1993), but the counts used to compute our probability estimates are based on the whole sequence of GIZA++ models and after the heuristic symmetrization.

Run-1 alignment (see Section 3) is used in this step to avoid unreliable alignments that could be produced from aligning the poor machine translation examples in the QE datasets.

4.3.2 POS Alignment Features

Two more alignment-based features were introduced to estimate translation quality of each source-target sentence pair with the help of their POS tags. In our experiments, we restrict the range of POS tags used to produce our features to only nouns, verbs, adverbs, and adjectives. The POS tags for both English and German come again from Stanford POS Tagger.

The two introduced features are:

Number of correctly matched tags represents the number of source words that are aligned to target words with the same POS tag.

---

[1] http://www.quest.dcs.shef.ac.uk/

Number of wrongly matched tags represents the number of source words that are aligned to target words with a different POS tag.

Since the alignments are needed for the source and candidate translation, they come from Run-2.

4.4 Post-Edited N-grams

As mentioned earlier, in quality estimation, there is no access to reference translation. However, the QE task organizers provided the participants with training data (called "QEcorpus" in Section 5) consisting of 12k training segments and 1k development segments machine-translated and manually post-edited. To benefit from this valuable resource, we introduce another set of features representing the most frequent bigrams in translation text that were changed through the post-editing.

The list of bigrams was extracted on the basis of GIZA++ alignment, preprocessing tokens and symmetrizing the two directions the same way as in Section 3. We extract all word-aligned bigrams occurring more than 10 times in the training and development 13k sentences, greatly reducing the number of bigrams to a few dozens of most general ones. Each of the bigrams serves as an independent boolean feature in the model.

Although lowercasing seems to be more helpful during the alignment, we avoid it during the actual bigram extraction since case changes are mostly rightful and important post-edits when translating into German. On the other hand, the order in which the words and their alignments are occurred in the text is checked to be reserved (e.g. bigrams with the second target word positioned before the first target word are excluded).

Table 1 summarizes the number of extracted bigrams. Lowercased n-grams would be more general so more would survive the thresholding, but we opt to use the cased n-grams.

Lowercasing	Extracted Bigrams	Thresholded ($>$10)
On	71294	80
Off	73313	74

Table 1: Extracted Bigrams Numbers

Having that the 1k development segments are used to extract the N-grams features, we report the performance of the N-grams features on the 2k testing segments only.

5 Data

Our experiments use the following corpora:

QEcorpus (our name) denotes the English-German corpus released by the WMT16 QE task organizers. It is the first time when this language pair appears in the segment-level QE. QEcorpus consist of 15k source sentences in the IT domain, divided into 12k training, 1k development and 2k testing segments. Source sentences are provided with their machine translations, post-editions and HTER (Snover et al., 2006) as post-editing effort scores.

ITcorpus denotes the parallel English-German domain-specific resources made available for the WMT IT-Domain Translation Task[2]. ITcorpus consist of 452546 parallel sentences assembled from different resources, see Table 2.

Data Source	Sent. Pairs
Cross-lingual help-desk service	2000
IT related terms from Wikipedia	23134
Technical Documentation (Libre-Office, Chromium, Ubuntu)	427412

Table 2: ITcorpus sources

ComparableNews is a pair of monolingual corpora, namely the English and German versions of the News Crawl monolingual corpus (only the year 2015) compiled from various online news publications for the WMT News Translation Task[3]. The corpus consists of 3.2 GB of English text with 27.2 million sentences and 5.5 GB of German text with 51.3 million sentences. The vocabulary size for this corpus is 1,774,792 English and 5,817,655 German words (excluding numbers and punctuation).

As pre-processing, the corpus used in each setup is first cleaned from hyperlinks and then tokenized using Moses tokenizer[4].

---

[2]http://www.statmt.org/wmt16/
it-translation-task.html
[3]http://www.statmt.org/wmt16/
translation-task.html
[4]http://www.statmt.org/moses/

Features	Pearson's r	MAE	RMSE	Spearman's ρ
Baseline (QuEst++)	0.350	14.515	19.332	0.395
Baseline + AlignQualityScore	0.365	14.434	19.216	0.407
Baseline + POSAlignment	0.349	14.560	19.347	0.388
Baseline + BE_SentSim	0.353	14.487	19.303	0.399
Baseline + BE_WordSim	0.349	14.518	19.337	0.395
Baseline + BE_NounSim	0.353	14.487	19.311	0.399
All Features	**0.374**	**14.362**	**19.144**	**0.412**

Table 3: Evaluation of the introduced features using WMT16 Sentence-Level QE Development set

Features	Pearson's r	MAE	RMSE	Spearman's ρ
Baseline (QuEst++)	0.347	13.755	17.835	0.387
Baseline + AlignQualityScore	0.367	13.634	17.683	0.403
Baseline + POSAlignments	0.347	13.767	17.838	0.385
Baseline + BE_SentSim	0.348	13.756	17.828	0.387
Baseline + BE_WordSim	0.348	13.753	17.831	0.387
Baseline + BE_NounSim	0.346	13.780	17.857	0.385
Baseline + Ngrams	0.366	13.663	17.705	0.402
All Features	**0.377**	**13.603**	**17.642**	**0.410**

Table 4: Evaluation of the introduced features using WMT16 Sentence-Level QE Test set

6   Experiments

In our submission, we use the Python wrapper for BiSkip provided in the MultiVec tool[5] (Bérard et al., 2016). To train the model, we use the ITcorpus with the default configuration of the tool. The model was trained using a learning rate α set to 0.05 and *sample* (a threshold on words' frequency) set to 0.001.

As a prediction model, we use the Linear Regression model to predict the post-editing effort need for each translation. In our experiments, we tried different combinations of the introduced features. Best results are obtained by training the model using all the features.

Tables 3 and 4 list the results of examined feature combinations on the development and test parts of QEcorpus, respectively. (The golden truth of the test part was made available only after the outputs submission deadline.) The models are evaluated in terms of Mean Absolute Error (MAE), Root Mean Squared Error (RMSE), and Pearson's correlation (Pearson's r) for post-editing effort prediction, and Spearman's rank correlation coefficient (Spearman's ρ) for the ranking task.

Results show that adding the alignment quality score to the set of baseline features gives the best performance compared to the other introduced features on the test set.

When added alone, features based on POS tags or bilingual embeddings do not help and sometimes even slightly degrade the performance, but apparently, they are useful in the combination.

Our submission to the task corresponds to the line "All Features" in Table 4.

Additionally, we experimented with replacing the parallel ITcorpus with only the comparable (but larger) ComparableNews when extracting bilingual embeddings. As documented in Table 5, the size of the monolingual data is apparently more important for the quality of the alignments. MultiVec, given two corpora, extracts the word alignments automatically, and obviously, it is going to fail most of the time when given a non-parallel corpus. Nevertheless, the few random alignments are probably sufficient to blend the source and target subspaces of the vector representation of words, because the setup with all BE features trained on ComparableNews instead of ITcorpus works better.

BE source	Pearson's r	MAE	RMSE
ITcorpus	0.377	13.603	17.642
ComparableNews	0.386	13.552	17.552

Table 5: Results of All Features with bilingual embeddings trained on ITcorpus or ComparableNews

[5] https://github.com/eske/multivec

6.1 Official Results

The official results of the WMT16 Sentence-Level QE task use Pearson's correlation as the primary evaluation metric for Scoring sub-task and Spearman's rank correlation as the primary evaluation metric for Ranking sub-task.

According to the official evaluation, our model is ranked 7th (out of 14) and 6th (out of 11) in the scoring and ranking sub-tasks respectively. As illustrated in Tables 6 and 7, our model outperforms the baseline system as well as the Referential Translation Machine model (RTM), the best performing system in WMT15 (Bicici et al., 2015), in both scoring and ranking sub-tasks on WMT16 IT-domain datasets.

7 Conclusion

In this paper, we described our submission to the WMT16 Quality Estimation Shared Task for English-German sentence-level post editing effort prediction and ranking. We introduced a new set of system independent features using bilingual distributed representations, word alignments and also frequent n-grams appearing in manually post-edited texts. Combined with baseline features, our features show an improvement in the performance of post-editing effort prediction in QE task.

An interesting observation is that the bilingual embeddings perform better when trained on a larger but only comparable corpus than on an in-domain parallel corpus. The bilingual embeddings are not trained specifically for the QE prediction and their contribution is thus arguably limited.

In the future, we plan to investigate more variants to the core learning model as well as training the embeddings for the specific task.

8 Acknowledgement

This work has received funding from the European Union's Horizon 2020 research and innovation programme under grant agreement no. 645452 (QT21).

References

Alexandre Bérard, Christophe Servan, Olivier Pietquin, and Laurent Besacier. 2016. Multi-Vec: a Multilingual and Multilevel Representation Learning Toolkit for NLP. In *The 10th edition of the Language Resources and Evaluation Conference (LREC 2016)*.

Ergun Bicici, Qun Liu, and Andy Way. 2015. Referential Translation Machines for Predicting Translation Quality and Related Statistics. In *Proceedings of the Tenth Workshop on Statistical Machine Translation*. Association for Computational Linguistics, Lisbon, Portugal, pages 304–308.

John Blatz, Erin Fitzgerald, George Foster, Simona Gandrabur, Cyril Goutte, Alex Kulesza, Alberto Sanchis, and Nicola Ueffing. 2004. Confidence Estimation for Machine Translation. In *Proceedings of the 20th international conference on Computational Linguistics*. Association for Computational Linguistics, page 315.

Ondřej Bojar, Christian Buck, Chris Callison-Burch, Christian Federmann, Barry Haddow, Philipp Koehn, Christof Monz, Matt Post, Radu Soricut, and Lucia Specia. 2013. Findings of the 2013 Workshop on Statistical Machine Translation. In *Proceedings of the Eighth Workshop on Statistical Machine Translation*. Association for Computational Linguistics, Sofia, Bulgaria, pages 1–44.

Ondřej Bojar, Christian Buck, Christian Federmann, Barry Haddow, Philipp Koehn, Johannes Leveling, Christof Monz, Pavel Pecina, Matt Post, Herve Saint-Amand, Radu Soricut, Lucia Specia, and Aleš Tamchyna. 2014. Findings of the 2014 Workshop on Statistical Machine Translation. In *Proceedings of the Ninth Workshop on Statistical Machine Translation*. Association for Computational Linguistics, Baltimore, Maryland, USA, pages 12–58.

Ondřej Bojar, Rajen Chatterjee, Christian Federmann, Barry Haddow, Matthias Huck, Chris Hokamp, Philipp Koehn, Varvara Logacheva, Christof Monz, Matteo Negri, Matt Post, Carolina Scarton, Lucia Specia, and Marco Turchi. 2015. Findings of the 2015 Workshop on Statistical Machine Translation. In *Proceedings of the Tenth Workshop on Statistical Machine Translation*. Association for Computational Linguistics, Lisbon, Portugal, pages 1–46.

Peter F Brown, Vincent J Della Pietra, Stephen A Della Pietra, and Robert L Mercer. 1993. The mathematics of statistical machine translation: Parameter estimation. *Computational linguistics* 19(2):263–311.

Chris Callison-Burch, Philipp Koehn, Christof

System	Pearson's r	MAE	RMSE
YSDA/SNTX+BLEU+SVM	0.525	12.30	16.41
POSTECH/SENT-RNN-QV2	0.460	13.58	18.60
SHEF/SVM-NN-both-emb-QuEst	0.451	12.88	17.03
POSTECH/SENT-RNN-QV3	0.447	13.52	18.38
SHEF/SVM-NN-both-emb	0.430	12.97	17.33
UGENT/SVM2	0.412	19.57	24.11
Our Model	**0.377**	**13.60**	**17.64**
RTM/RTM-FS-SVR	0.376	13.46	17.81
UU/UU-SVM	0.370	13.43	18.15
UGENT/SVM1	0.363	20.01	24.63
RTM/RTM-SVR	0.358	13.59	18.06
BASELINE	0.351	13.53	18.39
SHEF/SimpleNets-SRC	0.320	13.92	18.23
SHEF/SimpleNets-TGT	0.283	14.35	18.22

Table 6: Official results for WMT16 Sentence-Level QE Scoring sub-task

System	Spearman's rho	DeltaAvg
POSTECH/SENT-RNN-QV2	0.483	7.663
SHEF/SVM-NN-both-emb-QuEst	0.474	8.129
POSTECH/SENT-RNN-QV3	0.466	7.527
SHEF/SVM-NN-both-emb	0.452	7.886
UGENT/SVM2	0.418	7.615
Our Model	**0.410**	**7.114**
UU/UU-SVM	0.405	6.519
RTM/RTM-FS-SVR	0.400	6.655
BASELINE	0.390	6.298
RTM/RTM-SVR	0.384	6.379
UGENT/SVM1	0.375	7.008

Table 7: Official results for WMT16 Sentence-Level QE Ranking sub-task

Monz, Matt Post, Radu Soricut, and Lucia Specia. 2012. Findings of the 2012 Workshop on Statistical Machine Translation. In *Proceedings of the Seventh Workshop on Statistical Machine Translation*. Association for Computational Linguistics, Montréal, Canada, pages 10–51.

José Guilherme Camargo de Souza, Christian Buck, Marco Turchi, and Matteo Negri. 2013. FBK-UEdin Participation to the WMT13 Quality Estimation Shared Task. In *Proceedings of the Eighth Workshop on Statistical Machine Translation*. Association for Computational Linguistics, Sofia, Bulgaria, pages 352–358.

Sarath Chandar A P, Stanislas Lauly, Hugo Larochelle, Mitesh Khapra, Balaraman Ravindran, Vikas C Raykar, and Amrita Saha. 2014. An Autoencoder Approach to Learning Bilingual Word Representations. In Z. Ghahramani, M. Welling, C. Cortes, N. D. Lawrence, and K. Q. Weinberger, editors, *Advances in Neural Information Processing Systems 27*, Curran Associates, Inc., pages 1853–1861.

Stephan Gouws, Yoshua Bengio, and Greg Corrado. 2014. BiLBOWA: Fast Bilingual Distributed Representations without Word Alignments. *arXiv preprint arXiv:1410.2455* .

Christian Hänig, Robert Remus, and Xose de la Puente. 2015. ExB Themis: Extensive Feature Extraction from Word Alignments for Semantic Textual Similarity. In *Proceedings of the 9th International Workshop on Semantic Evaluation (SemEval 2015)*. Association for Computational Linguistics, Denver, Colorado, pages 264–268.

Karl Moritz Hermann and Phil Blunsom. 2014.

Multilingual Models for Compositional Distributed Semantics. *CoRR* abs/1404.4641.

Thang Luong, Hieu Pham, and Christopher D Manning. 2015. Bilingual word Representations with Monolingual Quality in Mind. In *Proceedings of the 1st Workshop on Vector Space Modeling for Natural Language Processing*. pages 151–159.

Tomas Mikolov, Quoc V Le, and Ilya Sutskever. 2013a. Exploiting Similarities among Languages for Machine Translation. *arXiv preprint arXiv:1309.4168* .

Tomas Mikolov, Ilya Sutskever, Kai Chen, Greg S Corrado, and Jeff Dean. 2013b. Distributed representations of words and phrases and their compositionality. In C. J. C. Burges, L. Bottou, M. Welling, Z. Ghahramani, and K. Q. Weinberger, editors, *Advances in Neural Information Processing Systems 26*, Curran Associates, Inc., pages 3111–3119.

Franz Josef Och and Hermann Ney. 2003. A Systematic Comparison of Various Statistical Alignment Models. *Computational Linguistics* 29(1):19–51.

Kashif Shah, Varvara Logacheva, Gustavo Paetzold, Frédéric Blain, Daniel Beck, Fethi Bougares, and Lucia Specia. 2015. SHEF-NN: Translation Quality Estimation with Neural Networks. In *Proceedings of the Tenth Workshop on Statistical Machine Translation*. Association for Computational Linguistics, Lisbon, Portugal, pages 342–347.

Matthew Snover, Bonnie Dorr, Richard Schwartz, Linnea Micciulla, and John Makhoul. 2006. A Study of Translation Edit Rate with Targeted Human Annotation. In *Proceedings AMTA*. pages 223–231.

Radu Soricut, Nguyen Bach, and Ziyuan Wang. 2012. The SDL Language Weaver Systems in the WMT12 Quality Estimation Shared Task. In *Proceedings of the Seventh Workshop on Statistical Machine Translation*. Association for Computational Linguistics, Montréal, Canada, pages 145–151.

Lucia Specia, G Paetzold, and Carolina Scarton. 2015. Multi-level Translation Quality Prediction with QuEst++. In *53rd Annual Meeting of the Association for Computational Linguistics and Seventh International Joint Conference on Natural Language Processing of the Asian Federation of Natural Language Processing: System Demonstrations*. pages 115–120.

Lucia Specia, Kashif Shah, José GC De Souza, and Trevor Cohn. 2013. QuEst - A Translation Quality Estimation Framework. In *ACL (Conference System Demonstrations)*. Citeseer, pages 79–84.

Lucia Specia, Marco Turchi, Nicola Cancedda, Marc Dymetman, and Nello Cristianini. 2009. Estimating the Sentence-Level Quality of Machine Translation Systems. In *13th Annual Conference of the European Association for Machine Translation*. Barcelona, Spain, EAMT, pages 28–37.

Md Arafat Sultan, Steven Bethard, and Tamara Sumner. 2015. DLS@CU: Sentence Similarity from Word Alignment and Semantic Vector Composition. In *Proceedings of the 9th International Workshop on Semantic Evaluation (SemEval 2015)*. Association for Computational Linguistics, Denver, Colorado, pages 148–153.

Kristina Toutanova, Dan Klein, Christopher D Manning, and Yoram Singer. 2003. Feature-Rich Part-of-Speech Tagging with a Cyclic Dependency Network. In *Proceedings of the 2003 Conference of the North American Chapter of the Association for Computational Linguistics on Human Language Technology-Volume 1*. Association for Computational Linguistics, pages 173–180.

Will Y Zou, Richard Socher, Daniel M Cer, and Christopher D Manning. 2013. Bilingual Word Embeddings for Phrase-Based Machine Translation. In *EMNLP*. pages 1393–1398.

SHEF-MIME: Word-level Quality Estimation Using Imitation Learning

Daniel Beck   **Andreas Vlachos**   **Gustavo H. Paetzold**   **Lucia Specia**
Department of Computer Science
University of Sheffield, UK
{debeck1,a.vlachos,gpaetzold1,l.specia}@sheffield.ac.uk

Abstract

We describe University of Sheffield's submission to the word-level Quality Estimation shared task. Our system is based on imitation learning, an approach to structured prediction which relies on a classifier trained on data generated appropriately to ameliorate error propagation. Compared to other structure prediction approaches such as conditional random fields, it allows the use of arbitrary information from previous tag predictions and the use of non-decomposable loss functions over the structure. We explore these two aspects in our submission while using the baseline features provided by the shared task organisers. Our system outperformed the conditional random field baseline while using the same feature set.

1   Introduction

Quality estimation (QE) models aim at predicting the quality of machine translated (MT) text (Blatz et al., 2004; Specia et al., 2009). This prediction can be at several levels, including word-, sentence- and document-level. In this paper we focus on our submission to the word-level QE WMT 2016 shared task, where the goal is to assign quality labels to each word of the output of an MT system.

Word-level QE is traditionally treated as a structured prediction problem, similar to part-of-speech (POS) tagging. The baseline model used in the shared task employs a Conditional Random Field (CRF) (Lafferty et al., 2001) with a set of baseline features. Our system uses a linear classification model trained with imitation learning (Daumé III et al., 2009; Ross et al., 2011). Compared to the baseline approach that uses a CRF, imitation learning has two benefits:

- We can directly use the proposed evaluation metric as the loss to be minimised during training;
- It allows using richer information from previous label predictions in the sentence.

Our primary goal with our submissions was to examine if the above benefits would result in better accuracy than that for the CRF. For this reason, we did not perform any feature engineering: we made use instead of the same features as the baseline model. Both our submissions outperformed the baseline, showing that there is still room for improvements in terms of modelling, beyond feature engineering.

2   Imitation Learning

A naive, but simple way to perform word-level QE (and any word tagging problem) is to use an off-the-shelf classifier to tag each word extracting features based on the sentence. These usually include features derived from the word being tagged and its context. The main difference between this approach and structure prediction methods is that it treats each tag prediction as independent from each other, ignoring the structure behind the full tag sequence for the sentence.

If we treat the observed sentence as a *sequence* of words (from left to right) then we can modify the above approach to perform a sequence of *actions*, which in this case are tag predictions. This setting allows us to incorporate structural information in the classifier by using features based on previous tag predictions. For instance, let us assume that we are trying to predict the tag t_i for word w_i. A simple classifier can use features derived from w_i and also any other words in the sentence. By framing this as a sequence, it can also use features extracted from the previously predicted tags $t_{\{1:i-1\}}$.

Proceedings of the First Conference on Machine Translation, Volume 2: Shared Task Papers, pages 772–776,
Berlin, Germany, August 11-12, 2016. ©2016 Association for Computational Linguistics

This approach to incorporating structural information suffers from an important problem: during training it assumes the features based on previous tags come from a perfectly predicted sequence (the gold standard). However, during testing this sequence will be built by the classifier, thus likely to contain errors. This mismatch between training and test time features is likely to hurt the overall performance since the classifier is not trained to *recover* from its errors, resulting in error propagation.

Imitation learning (also referred to as search-based structure prediction) is a general class of methods that attempt to solve this problem. The main idea is to first train the classifier using the gold standard tags, and then generate examples by using the trained classifier to re-predict the training set and update the classifier using these new examples. The example generation and classification training is usually repeated. The key point in this procedure is that because the examples are generated in the training set we are able to query the gold standard for the correct tags. So, if the classifier makes a wrong prediction at word w_i we can teach it to recover from this error at word w_{i+1} by simply checking the gold standard for the right tag.

In the imitation learning literature the sequence of predictions is referred to as *trajectory*, which is obtained by running a *policy* on the input. Three kinds of policy are commonly considered:

- *expert policy*, which returns the correct prediction according to the gold standard and thus can only be used during training,
- *learned policy*, which queries the trained classifier for its prediction,
- and *stochastic mixture* between *expert* and *learned*.

The most commonly used imitation learning algorithm, DAGGER (Ross et al., 2011), initially uses the expert policy to train a classifier and subsequently uses a stochastic mixture policy to generate examples based on a 0/1 loss on the current tag prediction with respect to the expert policy (which returns the correct tag according to the gold standard). This idea can be extended by, instead of taking the 0/1 loss, applying the same stochastic policy until the end of the sentence and calculating a loss over the entire tag sequence with respect to the gold standard. This generates a *cost-sensitive* classification training example and

---

Algorithm 1 V-DAGGER algorithm

Input training instances $\mathcal{S}$, expert policy π^*, loss function ℓ, learning rate β, cost-sensitive classifier CSC, learning iterations N

Output learned policy π_N

1: CSC instances $E = \emptyset$
2: **for** $i = 1$ to N **do**
3:      $p = (1 - \beta)^{i-1}$
4:      current policy $\pi = p\pi^* + (1 - p)\pi_i$
5:      **for** $s \in \mathcal{S}$ **do**
6:          ▷ assuming T is the length of s
7:          predict $\pi(s) = \hat{y}_{1:T}$
8:          **for** $\hat{y}_t \in \pi(s)$ **do**
9:              get observ. features $\phi_t^o = f(s)$
10:             get struct. features $\phi_t^s = f(\hat{y}_{1:t-1})$
11:             concat features $\phi_t = \phi_t^o || \phi_t^s$
12:             **for all** possible actions y_t^j **do**
13:             ▷ predict subsequent actions
14:             $y'_{t+1:T} = \pi(s; \hat{y}_{1:t-1}, y_t^j)$
15:             ▷ assess cost
16:             $c_t^j = \ell(\hat{y}_{1:t-1}, y_t^j, y'_{t+1:T})$
17:          **end for**
18:          $E = E \cup (\phi_t, c_t)$
19:          **end for**
20:      **end for**
21:      learn $\pi_i = CSC(E)$
22: **end for**

---

allows the algorithm to use arbitrary, potentially non-decomposable losses during training. This is the approach used by Vlachos and Clark (2014) and which is employed in our submission (henceforth called V-DAGGER). Its main advantage is that it allows us to use a loss based on the final shared task evaluation metric. The latter is the F-measure on 'OK' labels times F-measure on 'BAD' labels, which we turn into a loss by subtracting it from 1.

Algorithm 1, which is replicated from (Vlachos and Clark, 2014), details V-DAGGER. At line 4 the algorithm selects a policy to predict the tags (line 7). In the first iteration it is just the expert policy, but from the second iteration onwards it becomes a stochastic mixture of the expert and learned policies. The cost-sensitive instances are generated by iterating over each word in the instance (line 8), extracting features from the instance itself (line 9) and the previously predicted tags (line 10) and estimating a cost for each possible tag (lines 12-17). These instances are then used to train a cost-sensitive classifier, which becomes the new learned policy (line 21). The whole procedure is repeated until a desired iteration budget N is reached.

The feature extraction step at lines 9 and 10 can be made in a single step. We chose to split it between *observed* and *structural* features to emphasise the difference between our method and the CRF baseline. While CRFs in theory can employ any kind of structural features, they are usually restricted to consider only the previous tag for efficiency (1st order Markov assumption).

3 Experimental Settings

The shared task dataset consists of 15k sentences translated from English to German using an MT system and post-edited by professional translators. The post-edited version of each sentence is used to obtain quality tags for each word in the MT output. In this shared task version, two tags are employed: an 'OK' tag means the word is correct and a 'BAD' tag corresponds to a word that needs a post-editing action (either deletion, substitution or the insertion of a new word). The official split corresponds to 12k, 1k and 2k for training, development and test sets.

Model Following (Vlachos and Clark, 2014), we use AROW (Crammer et al., 2009) for cost-sensitive classification learning. The loss function is based on the official shared task evaluation metric: $\ell = 1 - [F(\text{OK}) \times F(\text{BAD})]$, where F is the tag F-measure at the sentence level.

We experimented with two values for the learning rate β and we submitted the best model found for each value. The first value is 0.3, which is the same used by Vlachos and Clark (2014). The second one is 1.0, which essentially means we use the expert policy only in the first iteration, switching to using the learned policy afterwards.

For each setting we run up to 10 iterations of imitation learning on the training set and evaluate the score on the dev set after each iteration. We select our model in each learning rate setting by choosing the one which performs the best on the dev set. For $\beta = 1.0$ this was achieved after 10 iterations, but for $\beta = 0.3$ the best model was the one obtained after the 6th iteration.

Observed features The features based on the observed instance are the same 22 used in the baseline provided by the task organisers. Given a word w_i in the MT output, these features are defined below:

- Word and context features:
  - w_i (the word itself)
  - w_{i-1}
  - w_{i+1}
  - w_i^{src} (the aligned word in the source)
  - w_{i-1}^{src}
  - w_{i+1}^{src}
- Sentence features:
  - Number of tokens in the source sentence
  - Number of tokens in the target sentence
  - Source/target token count ratio
- Binary indicators:
  - w_i is a stopword
  - w_i is a punctuation mark
  - w_i is a proper noun
  - w_i is a digit
- Language model features:
  - Size of largest n-gram with frequency $>$ 0 starting with w_i
  - Size of largest n-gram with frequency $>$ 0 ending with w_i
  - Size of largest n-gram with frequency $>$ 0 starting with w_i^{src}
  - Size of largest n-gram with frequency $>$ 0 ending with w_i^{src}
  - Backoff behavior starting from w_i
  - Backoff behavior starting from w_{i-1}
  - Backoff behavior starting from w_{i+1}
- POS tag features:
  - The POS tag of w_i
  - The POS tag of w_i^{src}

The language model backoff behavior features were calculated following the approach in (Raybaud et al., 2011).

Structural features As explained in Section 2, a key advantage of imitation learning is the ability to use arbitrary information from previous predictions. Our submission explores this by defining a set of features based on this information. Taking t_i as the tag to be predicted for the current word, these features are defined in the following way:

- Previous tags:
  - t_{i-1}
  - t_{i-2}
  - t_{i-3}
- Previous tag n-grams:
  - $t_{i-2}||t_{i-1}$ (tag bigram)
  - $t_{i-3}||t_{i-2}||t_{i-1}$ (tag trigram)
- Total number of 'BAD' tags in $t_{1:t-1}$

Results   Table 1 shows the official shared task results for the baseline and our systems, in terms of F1-MULT, the official evaluation metric, and also F1 for each of the classes. We report two versions for our submissions: the official one, which had an implementation bug[1] and a new version after the bug fix.

Both official submissions outperformed the baseline, which is an encouraging result considering that we used the same set of features as the baseline. The submission which employed $\beta = 1$ performed the best between the two. This is in line with the observations of Ross et al. (2011) in similar sequential tagging tasks. This setting allows the classifier to move away from using the expert policy as soon as the first classifier is trained.

	F1-BAD	F1-OK	F1-MULT
Baseline (CRF)	0.3682	0.8800	0.3240
Official submission			
$N = 6, \beta = 0.3$	0.3909	0.8450	0.3303
$N = 10, \beta = 1.0$	0.4029	0.8392	0.3380
Fixed version			
$N = 9, \beta = 0.3$	0.3996	0.8435	0.3370
$N = 9, \beta = 1.0$	0.4072	0.8415	0.3426

Table 1: Official shared task results.

Analysis   To obtain further insights about the benefits of imitation learning for this task we performed additional experiments with different settings. In Table 2 we compare our systems with a system trained using a single round of training (called *exact imitation*), which corresponds to using the same classifier trained only on the gold standard tags. We can see that imitation learning improves over this setting substantially.

Table 2 also shows results obtained using the original DAGGER algorithm, which uses a single 0/1-loss per tag. While DAGGER improves results over the exact imitation setting, it is outperformed by V-DAGGER. This is due to the ability of V-DAGGER to incorporate the task loss into its training procedure[2].

In Figure 1 we compare how the F1-MULT scores evolve through the imitation learning iterations for both DAGGER and V-DAGGER. Even though the performance of V-DAGGER fluctuates

---

[1] The structural feature t_{i-1} was not computed properly.

[2] Formally, our loss is not exactly the same as the official shared task evaluation metric since the former is measured at the sentence level and the latter at the corpus level. Nevertheless, the loss in V-DAGGER is much closer to the official metric than the 0/1-loss used by DAGGER.

	F1-BAD	F1-OK	F1-MULT
Exact imitation	0.2503	0.8855	0.2217
DAGGER			
$N = 10, \beta = 0.3$	0.3322	0.8483	0.2818
$N = 4, \beta = 1.0$	0.3307	0.8758	0.2897
V-DAGGER			
$N = 9, \beta = 0.3$	0.3996	0.8435	0.3370
$N = 9, \beta = 1.0$	0.4072	0.8415	0.3426

Table 2: Comparison between our systems (V-DAGGER), exact imitation and DAGGER on the test data.

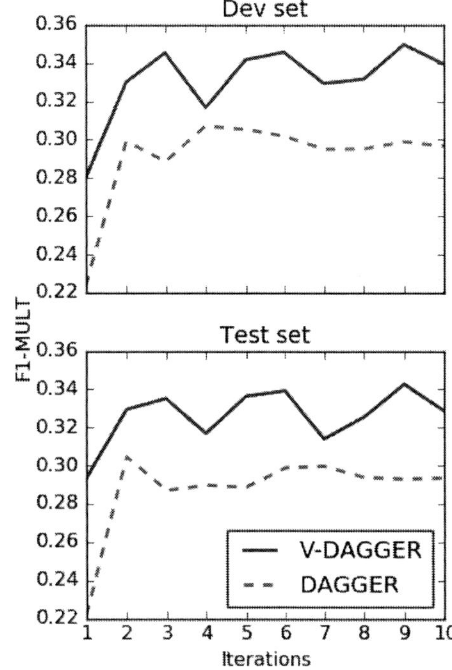

Figure 1: Metric curves for DAGGER and V-DAGGER over the official development and test sets. Both settings use $\beta = 1.0$.

more than that of DAGGER, it is consistently better for both development and test sets.

Finally, we also compare our systems with simpler versions using a smaller set of structural features. The findings, presented in Table 3, show an interesting trend. The systems do not seem to benefit from the additional structural information available in imitation learning and even a system with no information at all ("None" in Table 3) outperforms the baseline. We speculate that this is because the task only deals with a linear chain of binary labels, which makes the structure much less informative compared to the observed features.

	F1-BAD	F1-OK	F1-MULT
$\beta = 0.3$			
None	0.3948	0.8536	0.3370
t_{i-1}	0.3873	0.8393	0.3251
$t_{i-1} + t_{i-2}\|t_{i-1}$	0.3991	0.8439	0.3368
All	0.3996	0.8435	0.3370
$\beta = 1.0$			
None	0.3979	0.8530	0.3394
t_{i-1}	0.4089	0.8436	0.3449
$t_{i-1} + t_{i-2}\|t_{i-1}$	0.4094	0.8429	0.3451
All	0.4072	0.8415	0.3426

Table 3: Comparison between V-DAGGER systems using different structural feature sets. All models use the full set of observed features.

4 Conclusions

We presented the first attempt to use imitation learning for the word-level QE task. One of the main strengths of our model is its ability to employ non-decomposable loss functions during the training procedure. As our analysis shows, this was a key reason behind the positive results of our submissions with respect to the baseline system, since it allowed us to define a loss function using the official shared task evaluation metric. The proposed method also allows the use of arbitrary information from the predicted structure, although its impact was much less noticeable for this task.

The framework presented in this paper could be enhanced by going beyond the QE task and applying actions in subsequent tasks, such as automatic post-editing. Since this framework allows for arbitrary loss functions it could be trained by optimising MT metrics like BLEU or TER. The challenge in this case is how to derive expert policies: unlike simple word tagging, multiple action sequences could result in the same post-edited sentence.

Acknowledgements

This work was supported by CNPq (project SwB 237999/2012-9, Daniel Beck), the QT21 project (H2020 No. 645452, Lucia Specia) and the EPSRC grant Diligent (EP/M005429/1, Andreas Vlachos).

References

John Blatz, Erin Fitzgerald, and George Foster. 2004. Confidence estimation for machine translation. In *Proceedings of the 20th Conference on Computational Linguistics*, pages 315–321.

Koby Crammer, Alex Kulesza, and Mark Dredze. 2009. Adaptive Regularization of Weight Vectors. In *Advances in Neural Information Processing Systems*, pages 1–9.

Hal Daumé III, John Langford, and Daniel Marcu. 2009. Search-based structured prediction.

John D. Lafferty, Andrew McCallum, and Fernando C. N. Pereira. 2001. Conditional random fields: Probabilistic models for segmenting and labeling sequence data. In *Proceedings of the Eighteenth International Conference on Machine Learning*, ICML '01, pages 282–289, San Francisco, CA, USA. Morgan Kaufmann Publishers Inc.

Sylvain Raybaud, David Langlois, and Kamel Smali. 2011. This sentence is wrong. Detecting errors in machine-translated sentences. *Machine Translation*, (1).

Stéphane Ross, Geoffrey J. Gordon, and J. Andrew Bagnell. 2011. A Reduction of Imitation Learning and Structured Prediction to No-Regret Online Learning. In *Proceedings of AISTATS*, volume 15, pages 627–635.

Lucia Specia, Nicola Cancedda, Marc Dymetman, Marco Turchi, and Nello Cristianini. 2009. Estimating the sentence-level quality of machine translation systems. In *Proceedings of EAMT*, pages 28–35.

Andreas Vlachos and Stephen Clark. 2014. A New Corpus for Context-Dependent Semantic Parsing. *Transactions of the Association for Computational Linguistics*, 2:547–559.

Referential Translation Machines for Predicting Translation Performance

Ergun Biçici

ergunbicici@yahoo.com
bicici.github.com

Abstract

Referential translation machines (RTMs) pioneer a language independent approach for predicting translation performance and to all similarity tasks with top performance in both bilingual and monolingual settings and remove the need to access any task or domain specific information or resource. RTMs achieve to become 1st in document-level, 4th system at sentence-level according to mean absolute error, and 4th in phrase-level prediction of translation quality in quality estimation task.

1 Referential Translation Machines

Prediction of translation performance can help in estimating the effort required for correcting the translations during post-editing by human translators if needed. Referential translation machines achieve top performance in automatic and accurate prediction of machine translation performance independent of the language or domain of the prediction task. Each referential translation machine (RTM) model is a data translation prediction model between the instances in the training set and the test set and translation acts are indicators of the data transformation and translation. RTMs are powerful enough to be applicable in different domains and tasks while achieving top performance in both monolingual (Biçici and Way, 2015) and bilingual settings (Biçici et al., 2015b).

Figure 1 depicts RTMs and explains the model building process (Biçici, 2016). RTMs use ParFDA (Biçici et al., 2015a) for selecting instances and interpretants, data close to the task instances for building prediction models and machine translation performance prediction system (MTPPS) (Biçici and Way, 2015) for generating features. We improve our RTM models (Biçici et

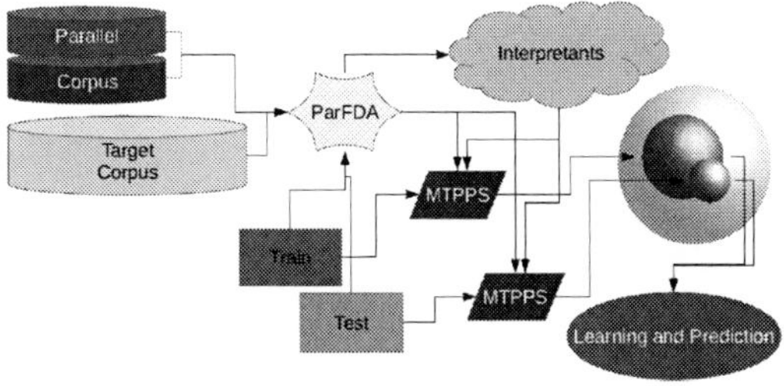

Figure 1: RTM depiction: ParFDA selects interpretants close to the training and test data using parallel corpus in bilingual settings and monolingual corpus in the target language or just the monolingual target corpus in monolingual settings; an MTPPS uses interpretants and training data to generate training features and another uses interpretants and test data to generate test features in the same feature space; learning and prediction takes place taking these features as input.

al., 2015b) with numeric expression identification using regular expressions and replace them with a label (Biçici, 2016).

2 RTM in the Quality Estimation Task

We develop RTM models for all of the four subtasks of the quality estimation task (QET) in WMT16 (Bojar et al., 2016) (QET16), which include English to Spanish (en-es), English to German (en-de), and German to English (de-en) translation directions. The subtasks are: sentence-level prediction (Task 1), word-level prediction (Task 2), phrase-level prediction (Task 2p), and document-level prediction (Task 3). Task 1 is about predicting HTER (human-targeted translation edit rate) (Snover et al., 2006) scores of sentence translations, Task 2 is about binary classification of word-level quality, Task 2p is about binary classification of phrase-level quality, and

Proceedings of the First Conference on Machine Translation, Volume 2: Shared Task Papers, pages 777–781,
Berlin, Germany, August 11-12, 2016. ©2016 Association for Computational Linguistics

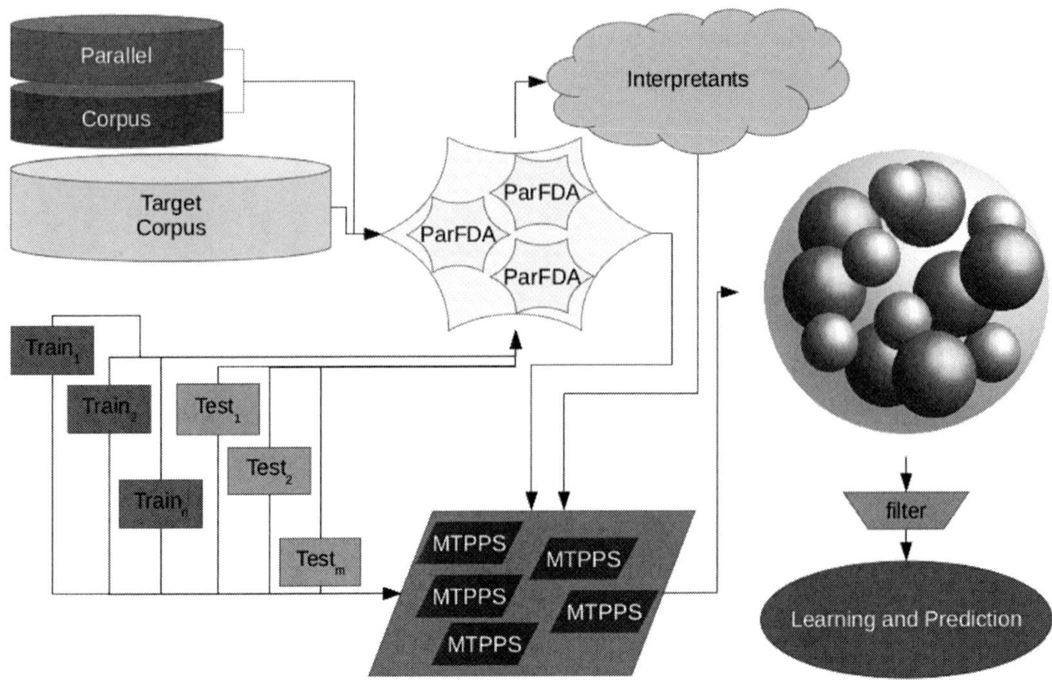

Figure 2: RTM depiction for Task 3 where document-level translation performance is predicted. Separate MTPPS instances are run for each train and test document to obtain corresponding feature representations, which are filtered and processed before learning and prediction.

| Task | Train | Test | RTM Interpretants | |
			Training	LM
Task 1 (en-de)	13000	3000	400K	10M
Task 2 (en-de)	13000	2000	500K	10M
Task 3 (en-es)	146	62	1M	10M

Table 1: Number of instances in different tasks and the number of sentences used as interpretants by the RTM models.

Task 3 is about predicting weighted HTER scores of document translations.

Language model (LM) are built using KENLM (Heafield et al., 2013). We tokenize and truecase all of the corpora using code released with Moses (Koehn et al., 2007) [1]. Table 1 lists the number of sentences in the training and test sets for each task. We also list the size of the interpretants used by the corresponding RTM models (K for thousand, M for million). We use the same number of interpretants for training as last year in Task 1. We increase the number of instances used for the LM to 10M. This

[1]https://github.com/moses-smt/
mosesdecoder/tree/master/scripts

year, we did not include features from backward LM in MTPPS and we used numeric expression identification in Task 1 and Task 3.

2.1 RTM Prediction Models

We present results using support vector regression (SVR) with RBF (radial basis functions) kernel (Smola and Schölkopf, 2004) and extremely randomized trees (TREE) (Geurts et al., 2006) for sentence and document translation prediction tasks. We also use them after a feature subset selection (FS) with recursive feature elimination (RFE) (Guyon et al., 2002) or a dimensionality reduction and mapping step using partial least squares (PLS) (Specia et al., 2009), or PLS after FS (FS+PLS). We use Global Linear Models (GLM) (Collins, 2002) with dynamic learning (GLMd) (Biçici et al., 2015b) for word-level translation performance prediction. GLMd uses weights in a range $[a, b]$ to update the learning rate dynamically according to the error rate as shown in Figure 3.

Figure 2 depicts how RTMs are used to build predictors for Task 3, where we run a separate MTPPS instance for each train or test document

Task	Translation	Model	r	MAE	RAE	MAER	MRAER
Task 1	en-de	SVR	0.39	0.1449	0.874	0.7653	0.824
	en-de	FS SVR	0.4	0.1453	0.877	0.7704	0.826
Task 3	en-es	FS+PLS TREE	0.55	0.3058	0.823	0.4394	0.815
	en-es	FS SVR	0.33	0.3383	0.91	0.4308	0.8

Table 2: Training performance of the top 2 individual RTM models prepared for different tasks.

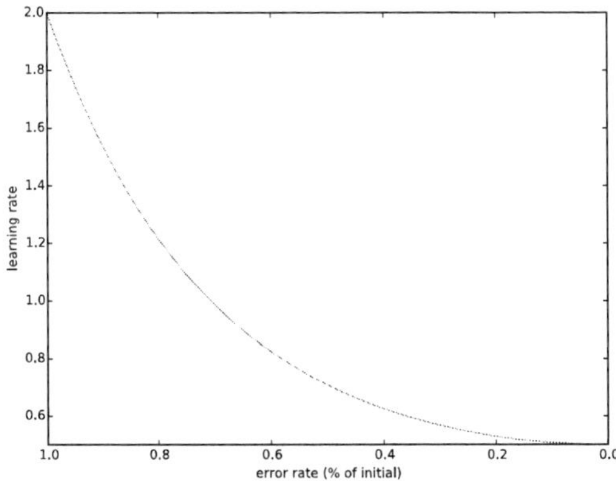

Figure 3: Learning rate curve.

Model	# splits	% error	weight range
GLMd	4	0.0688	$[0.5, 2]$
GLMd	5	0.0757	$[0.5, 2]$

Table 3: RTM Task 2 training results where GLMd parallelized over 4 splits is referred as GLMd s4 and GLMd with 5 splits as GLMd s5.

and obtain corresponding features (depicted with a green or salmon colored sphere). We obtain an RTM representation vector instance from each of these by using only the document-level features from MTPPS and the min, max, and average of the sentence-level features.

2.2 Training Results

We use mean absolute error (MAE), relative absolute error (RAE), root mean squared error (RMSE), Pearson's correlation (r_P), and Spearman's correlation (r_S) as well as relative MAE (MAER) and relative RAE (MRAER) to evaluate (Biçici and Way, 2015). MAER and MRAER consider both the predictor's error and the fluctuations of the target scores at the instance level. RTM test performance on various tasks sorted according to MRAER can help identify which tasks and subtasks may require more work. DeltaAvg (Callison-Burch et al., 2012) calculates

the average quality difference between the top $n - 1$ quartiles and the overall quality for the test set. Table 2 presents the training results for Task 1 and Task 3. Table 3 presents Task 2 training results obtained after the challenge.

2.3 Test Results

The results on the test set are listed in Table 4 [2] and Table 5. Ranks are out of 9, 8, 6, and 5 system submissions in Task 1, Task 2, Task 2p, and Task 3 respectively. RTMs with FS SVR is able to achieve the 6th rank in Task 1 according to r_P and 4th according to MAE. The top MAE is 12.3 where RTM obtains 9% more MAE. RTMs with FS+PLS TREE is able to achieve the 1st rank in Task 3.

2.4 Target Optimized Results

Table 6 lists the RTM results optimizing the target evaluation metric, r, obtained after the challenge. The results show that numerical expression identification did not improve the test results for QET Task 1 but we have observed improvements in semantic textual similarity in English (Biçici, 2016).

2.5 Comparison with Previous Results

We compare the difficulty of tasks according to MRAER levels achieved. In Table 7, we list the RTM test results for tasks and subtasks that predict HTER or METEOR from QET16, QET15 (Biçici et al., 2015b), QET14 (Biçici and Way, 2014), and QET13 (Biçici, 2013). Compared with QET15 Task 1 performance, MAER improved in QET16 and obtained the top MAER performance in sentence-level prediction. Compared with QET15 Task 2 performance, both F_1 OK and F_1 BAD improved even though the training error tripled. wF_1 calculation in QET16 is different than the calculation used in QET15.

---

[2] We calculate r_S using `scipy.stats`.

Task	Model	DeltaAvg	r_P	r_S	RMSE	MAE	RAE	MAER	MRAER	Rank
Task 1	en-de SVR	6.38	0.3581	0.3841	18.06	13.59	0.8992	0.7509	0.8567	7
	en-de FS SVR	6.66	0.3764	0.4003	17.81	13.46	0.8905	0.7537	0.8388	6
Task 3	en-es FS+PLS TREE	0.12	0.3562	0.46	0.3437	0.2533	0.8996	0.3285	0.8505	1
	en-es FS SVR	0.12	0.2929	0.3546	0.3529	0.2676	0.9505	0.333	0.9018	2

Table 4: Test performance of the top 2 individual RTM models prepared for different tasks.

	Model	wF_1	F_1 OK	F_1 BAD	Rank
Word	GLMd s4	0.2725	**0.8884**	0.3068	9
	GLMd s5	0.3081	0.8820	0.3494	$\sim$8
Phrase	GLMd s4	0.3070	**0.8145**	0.3770	5
	GLMd s5	0.3274	**0.8016**	0.4084	4

Table 5: RTM Task 2 results on the test set. wF_1 is the average weighted F_1 score. **bold** results obtain top performance.

3 Conclusion

Referential translation machines achieve top performance in automatic, accurate, and language independent prediction of translation performance. RTMs pioneer a language independent approach for predicting translation performance and to all similarity tasks and remove the need to access any task or domain specific information or resource.

Acknowledgments

We thank the reviewers for providing constructive comments.

References

Ergun Biçici and Andy Way. 2014. Referential translation machines for predicting translation quality. In *Proceedings of the Ninth Workshop on Statistical Machine Translation*, Baltimore, USA, 6. Association for Computational Linguistics.

Ergun Biçici and Andy Way. 2015. Referential translation machines for predicting semantic similarity. *Language Resources and Evaluation*, pages 1–27.

Ergun Biçici, Qun Liu, and Andy Way. 2015a. ParFDA for fast deployment of accurate statistical machine translation systems, benchmarks, and statistics. In *Proceedings of the EMNLP 2015 Tenth Workshop on Statistical Machine Translation*, Lisbon, Portugal, 9. Association for Computational Linguistics.

Ergun Biçici, Qun Liu, and Andy Way. 2015b. Referential translation machines for predicting translation quality and related statistics. In *Proceedings of the EMNLP 2015 Tenth Workshop on Statistical Machine Translation*, Lisbon, Portugal, 9. Association for Computational Linguistics.

Ergun Biçici. 2013. Referential translation machines for quality estimation. In *Proceedings of the Eighth Workshop on Statistical Machine Translation*, Sofia, Bulgaria, 8. Association for Computational Linguistics.

Ergun Biçici. 2016. RTM at SemEval-2016 task 1: Predicting semantic similarity with referential translation machines and related statistics. In *SemEval-2016: Semantic Evaluation Exercises - International Workshop on Semantic Evaluation*, San Diego, USA, 6.

Ondrej Bojar, Christian Buck, Rajan Chatterjee, Christian Federmann, Liane Guillou, Barry Haddow, Matthias Huck, Antonio Jimeno Yepes, Aurélie Névéol, Mariana Neves, Pavel Pacina, Martin Poppel, Philipp Koehn, Christof Monz, Matteo Negri, Matt Post, Lucia Specia, Karin Verspoor, Jörg Tiedemann, and Marco Turchi. 2016. Proc. of the 2016 conference on statistical machine translation. In *Proc. of the First Conference on Statistical Machine Translation (WMT16)*, Berlin, Germany, August.

Chris Callison-Burch, Philipp Koehn, Christof Monz, Matt Post, Radu Soricut, and Lucia Specia. 2012. Findings of the 2012 workshop on statistical machine translation. In *Proc. of the Seventh Workshop on Statistical Machine Translation*, pages 10–51, Montréal, Canada, June.

Michael Collins. 2002. Discriminative training methods for hidden markov models: theory and experiments with perceptron algorithms. In *Proc. of the ACL-02 conference on Empirical methods in natural language processing - Volume 10*, EMNLP '02, pages 1–8, Stroudsburg, PA, USA.

Pierre Geurts, Damien Ernst, and Louis Wehenkel. 2006. Extremely randomized trees. *Machine Learning*, 63(1):3–42.

Isabelle Guyon, Jason Weston, Stephen Barnhill, and Vladimir Vapnik. 2002. Gene selection for cancer classification using support vector machines. *Machine Learning*, 46(1-3):389–422.

Kenneth Heafield, Ivan Pouzyrevsky, Jonathan H. Clark, and Philipp Koehn. 2013. Scalable modified Kneser-Ney language model estimation. In *Proceedings of the 51st Annual Meeting of the Associa-*

Model	r	MAE	RAE	MAER	MRAER
FS-SVR	0.37	0.135	0.893	0.7471	0.846
+numeric PLS-SVR	0.37	0.1358	0.898	0.7572	0.865

Table 6: RTM top predictor testing results for Task 1 optimized for r.

Task	Translation Model		r	MAE	RAE	MAER	MRAER
QET16 Task 1 HTER	en-de	FS SVR	0.3764	13.4589	0.8905	0.7537	0.8388
QET16 Task 3 HTER	en-es	FS+PLS TREE	0.3562	0.2533	0.8996	0.3285	0.8505
QET15 Task 1 HTER	en-es	FS+PLS SVR	0.349	0.1335	0.903	0.8284	0.8353
QET15 Task 3 METEOR	en-de	FS SVR	0.6668	0.0728	0.7279	0.3249	0.6467
	de-en	FS+PLS SVR	0.6373	0.0494	0.7482	0.2996	0.68
QET14 Task 1.2 HTER	en-es	SVR	0.5499	0.134	0.8532	0.7727	0.8758
QET13 Task 1.1 HTER	en-es	PLS-SVR	0.5596	0.1326	0.8849	2.3738	1.6428

Table 7: Test performance of the top RTM results when predicting HTER or METEOR.

tion for Computational Linguistics, pages 690–696, Sofia, Bulgaria, August.

Philipp Koehn, Hieu Hoang, Alexandra Birch, Chris Callison-Burch, Marcello Federico, Nicola Bertoldi, Brooke Cowan, Wade Shen, Christine Moran, Richard Zens, Chris Dyer, Ondrej Bojar, Alexandra Constantin, and Evan Herbst. 2007. Moses: Open source toolkit for statistical machine translation. In *Proceedings of the 45th Annual Meeting of the Association for Computational Linguistics Companion Volume Proceedings of the Demo and Poster Sessions*, pages 177–180. Association for Computational Linguistics.

Alex J. Smola and Bernhard Schölkopf. 2004. A tutorial on support vector regression. *Statistics and Computing*, 14(3):199–222, August.

Matthew Snover, Bonnie Dorr, Richard Schwartz, Linnea Micciulla, and John Makhoul. 2006. A Study of Translation Edit Rate with Targeted Human Annotation. In *Proc. of Association for Machine Translation in the Americas,*.

Lucia Specia, Nicola Cancedda, Marc Dymetman, Marco Turchi, and Nello Cristianini. 2009. Estimating the sentence-level quality of machine translation systems. In *Proc. of the 13th Annual Conference of the European Association for Machine Translation (EAMT)*, pages 28–35, Barcelona, Spain, May.

UAlacant word-level and phrase-level machine translation quality estimation systems at WMT 2016

Miquel Esplà-Gomis   Felipe Sánchez-Martínez   Mikel L. Forcada
Departament de Llenguatges i Sistemes Informàtics
Universitat d'Alacant, E-03690 Sant Vicent del Raspeig, Spain
{mespla,fsanchez,mlf}@dlsi.ua.es

Abstract

This paper describes the Universitat d'Alacant submissions (labeled as UAlacant) to the machine translation quality estimation (MTQE) shared task at WMT 2016, where we have participated in the word-level and phrase-level MTQE sub-tasks. Our systems use external sources of bilingual information as a *black box* to spot sub-segment correspondences between the source segment and the translation hypothesis. For our submissions, two sources of bilingual information have been used: machine translation (Lucy LT KWIK Translator and Google Translate) and the bilingual concordancer Reverso Context. Building upon the word-level approach implemented for WMT 2015, a method for phrase-based MTQE is proposed which builds on the probabilities obtained for word-level MTQE. For each sub-task we have submitted two systems: one using the features produced exclusively based on on-line sources of bilingual information, and one combining them with the baseline features provided by the organisers of the task.

1 Introduction

Machine translation quality estimation (MTQE) (Blatz et al., 2004; Specia et al., 2010; Specia and Soricut, 2013) has aroused the interest of both the scientific community and translation companies on account of its noticeable advantages: it can be used to help professional translators in post-editing, to estimate the translation productivity for different translation technologies, or even for budgeting translation projects. In this context, the WMT 2016 MTQE shared task becomes one of the best scenarios in which different approaches to MTQE can be evaluated and compared for different granularities: segment-level (sub-task 1), phrase-level and word-level (sub-task 2), and document-level (sub-task 3).

For the second consecutive year, the submissions of the UAlacant team tackle the word-level MTQE sub-task, but this year they also cover phrase-level MTQE. This year, the shared task featured a dataset obtained by translating segments in English into German using MT, for which it is needed to identify which words and phrases are inadequately translated. In the case of words, this means detecting which words need to be deleted or replaced, while in the case of phrases this means detecting which phrases contain words translated inadequately, but also if there are missing words, or the order of the words in the phrase is not correct. The systems participating in the task are required to apply the labels BAD and OK, either to words or phrases. In this paper we describe the approach behind the submissions of the Universitat d'Alacant team to these sub-tasks. For our word-level submissions we have applied the approach proposed by Esplà-Gomis et al. (2015), where we used black-box bilingual on-line resources. The new task tackles MTQE for translating English into German. For this task we have combined two on-line-available MT systems,[1] Lucy LT KWIK Translator[2] and Google Translate,[3] and the bilingual concordancer Reverso

---

[1] In the original approach by Esplà-Gomis et al. (2015) Apertium was one of these MT systems, but this year it was replaced since it does not provide a translation system for the languages of the current year's task.
[2] http://www.lucysoftware.com/english/machine-translation/kwik-translator
[3] http://translate.google.com

Proceedings of the First Conference on Machine Translation, Volume 2: Shared Task Papers, pages 782–786,
Berlin, Germany, August 11-12, 2016. ©2016 Association for Computational Linguistics

Context[4] to spot sub-segment correspondences between a sentence S in the source language (SL) and a given translation hypothesis T in the target language (TL). As described by Esplà-Gomis et al. (2015), a collection of features is obtained from these correspondences and then used by a binary classifier to determine the final word-level MTQE labels. We have repeated the approach proposed in WMT 2015 for word-level sub-tasks, and have proposed a new one for phrase-level MTQE that builds upon the system trained for word-level MTQE.

The rest of the paper is organised as follows. Section 2 describes the approach used to produce our submissions. Section 3 describes the experimental setting and the results obtained. The paper ends with some concluding remarks.

2   Sources of bilingual information for machine translation quality estimation at the word and phrase levels

The method used to produce the word-level MTQE submissions is the same than that used by the UAlacant team in the last edition of the shared task of MTQE at WMT 2015 (Esplà-Gomis et al., 2015), which uses binary classification based on a collection of information. As in the previous edition of the shared task, we have used online sources of bilingual information to identify sub-segment alignments between the original SL segment S and a given translation hypothesis T in the TL. These sub-segment alignments are identified by: (i) splitting segments S and T in all possible overlapping sub-segments up to a given length L; (ii) using the sources of bilingual information to translate each sub-segment into the other language, i.e. SL sub-segments into TL, and vice versa; and (iii) attempting to match the translated sub-segments either in T or S.

The rest of the section briefly describes the features used for building the submissions both for word-level and phrase-level sub-tasks in the MTQE shared task of WMT 2016.

2.1   Word-level machine translation quality estimation

A complete description of the features used for word-level MTQE can be found in Section 2 of the paper by Esplà-Gomis et al. (2015). We provide here a general description of the type of features used. Esplà-Gomis et al. (2015) describe two types of features: positive and negative ones, i.e. features that would indicate that the current translation is OK, and features that would indicate that it is BAD.

Positive features use those sub-segment pairs (σ, τ) obtained by means of the external sources of bilingual information such that σ matches the source segment S and τ matches the translation hypothesis T. These features provide positive evidence for words in T matching τ. An additional positive feature is defined, which measures the confidence of the sub-segment pairs by using the translation frequency in those sources of bilingual information capable of providing several translation alternatives, such as bilingual concordancers or probabilistic lexicons.

On the other hand, negative features are built from those sub-segment pairs (σ, τ) for which σ fully matches S, but τ matches T only partially. These sub-segment pairs provide negative evidence for those words in T that do not match τ.

2.2   Phrase-level machine translation quality estimation

While the word-level MTQE task has been going on during the last three editions of WMT, this is the first time that this shared task tackles phrase-level MTQE. This problem, as proposed by the organisers of the task, may miss some kinds of errors that are plausible in a phrase, such as missing words (insertions). According to the instructions provided, the organisers describe the problem as follows: *"if a phrase has at least one 'BAD' word, all its labels are replaced with 'BAD'"*; in other words, the problem of phrase-level MTQE just extends the errors found in a given word to the words happening in the same phrase, but does not add new problems related to the new granularity.

The approach proposed for this task builds on the word-level MTQE method described in Section 2.1. In the case of phrase-level MTQE, a binary classifier is also used to classify a phrase either as OK or BAD. This classifier uses the probability of belonging to the class BAD of every word in a phrase as a feature, which is provided by the classifier trained for the task at the word-level. These features are combined with two more binary features, which are aimed at capturing the information provided by the external sources of bilingual information at the level of phrases. Basically, these features take value `true` when the phrase of the translation

---

hypothesis being evaluated is confirmed by one or more sources of bilingual information, i.e. if the TL phrase exactly corresponds to a sub-segment in the SL segment. Having two different features allows to capture this information for each translation direction, i.e. if the TL phrase is the result of translating a phrase in the SL, or if the translation of the TL phrase appears as a sub-segment in the SL segment.

Given that phrases have variable lengths (from 1 to 7 words in the data set provided by the organisation), we decided to train specific classifiers for each phrase length using as many features as words in the phrase (plus the two features at the phrase level described above). Alternatively, it would have been possible to experiment with an approach able to deal with sparse features.

3 Submissions to the WMT 2016 shared task on MTQE

This section describes the details of the systems submitted to the MTQE shared task at WMT 2016. This year, the task consisted in estimating the quality of a collection of segments in German that had been obtained through machine translation from English. The organisers provided three datasets:

- *training set*: a collection of 12,000 segments in English (S) and their corresponding machine translations in German (T); for every word/phrase in T, a label was provided: BAD for the words/phrases to be post-edited, and OK for those to be kept unedited;

- *development set*: 1,000 pairs of segments (S, T) with the corresponding MTQE labels, which can be used to optimise the binary classifier trained by using the training set;

- *test set*: 2,000 pairs of segments (S, T) for which the MTQE labels have to be estimated with the binary classifier built on the training and the development sets.

The same data set was used both for word-level and phrase-level MTQE sub-tasks, with the only difference that, for the latter, the limits of the phrases which make up the full translated segments T were provided. In addition, for every sub-task, a collection of baseline features was provided for each word or phrase in T, respectively, in the different datasets. For word-level quality estimation, this collection consists of 22 baseline features, such as

the number of occurrences of the word, or part-of-speech information.[5] For phrase-level quality estimation, this collection consists of 72 baseline features, such as the phrase length or its perplexity.[6]

Using these data, four systems have been submitted to the shared task on MTQE at WMT 2016: two for word-level MTQE and two more for phrase-level MTQE. All the systems are based on the binary classifier described bellow in Section 3.1, but using different collections of features. Of the two systems submitted to each sub-task: one was built using only the features described in Section 2, and the other combined them with the baseline features provided by the organisation. Section 3.2 describes the results obtained with each of these approaches by using the following metrics:

- The precision P^c, i.e. the fraction of instances correctly labelled among all the instances labelled as c, where c is the class assigned (either OK or BAD);

- The recall R^c, i.e. the fraction of instances correctly labelled as c among all the instances that should have been labelled as c;

- The F_1^c score, which is defined as

$$F_1^c = \frac{2P^c R^c}{P^c + R^c};$$

and

- The product of F_1^{OK} and F_1^{BAD} scores, which is the main metric used by the organisers of the task for comparing all the submissions made.

3.1 Binary classifier

A *multilayer perceptron* (Duda et al., 2000, Section 6) was used for classification, as implemented in Weka 3.7 (Hall et al., 2009). Following the approach by Esplà-Gomis et al. (2015), the perceptron was built with a single hidden layer containing the same number of nodes as the number of features; this was the best performing architecture in the preliminary experiments.[7] The training sets

---

[5] The list of features can be found in the file `features_list` in the package `http://www.quest.dcs.shef.ac.uk/wmt16_files_qe/task2_en-de_test.tar.gz`

[6] The list of features can be found in the file `features_list` in the package `http://www.quest.dcs.shef.ac.uk/wmt16_files_qe/task2p_en-de_test.tar.gz`

[7] The rest of parameters of the classifiers were also kept as in the approach by Esplà-Gomis et al. (2015).

provided by the organisation were used to train the binary classifiers, both for word and phrase levels, while the development sets were used as validation sets on which the training error was computed, in order to minimise the risk of overfitting. The binary classifiers for the sub-task on phrase-level MTQE was trained to optimise the main comparison metric: $F_1^{\mathrm{BAD}} \cdot F_1^{\mathrm{OK}}$, while the classifier for word-level MTQE was trained to optimise the F_1^{BAD} metric, which was the main comparison metric in WMT 2015.[8]

Given that the binary classifier used for the phrase-level sub-task depends on the output of the binary classifier for word-level MTQE, the training process was incremental, training first the word-level MTQE binary classifiers and then the phrase-level ones. It is worth mentioning that the binary classifiers for phrase-level MTQE use the probabilities provided by the best performing system for word-level MTQE: the one that combines the features obtained from on-line sources of bilingual information with the baseline features. However, the phrase-level baseline features are only used in one of the systems submitted.

3.2 Results

Table 1 shows the results obtained by the systems submitted to the shared task on MTQE, both at the level of words and at the level of phrases. The table also includes the results obtained with a binary classifier trained only on the baseline features (baseline), in order to estimate the contribution of the features described in this work on the performance of the system. Incidentally, and in spite of the changes in languages and machine translation systems, the results obtained for word-level MTQE are very similar to those obtained by Esplà-Gomis et al. (2015) for the translation from English into Spanish.

As can also be seen in Table 1, the classifiers using only the baseline features outperform those using only features based on sources of bilingual information, both at the word level and at the phrase level. The difference between both feature families is specially relevant in the case of the phrase-level MTQE. However, the most interesting results

are those obtained when combining both feature families. As a result of this combination, an improvement of 5% in F_1^{BAD} and more than 8% in F_1^{OK} with respect to the baseline is obtained for word-level MTQE. In the case of phrase-based MTQE, this improvement is more unbalanced: 1% for F_1^{BAD}, and more than 10% in F_1^{OK}. Therefore, it is possible to conclude that both the baseline features and those obtained from sources of bilingual information are reasonably independent and, therefore, combining them leads to much more successful systems for the two granularities evaluated.

4   Concluding remarks

In this paper we have described the submissions of the Universitat d'Alacant (called UAlacant) team to the sub-task 2 in the MTQE shared task at WMT 2016, which covers the problems of word-level and phrase-level MTQE. Our submissions used on-line available sources of bilingual information in order to obtain features about the translation hypotheses at different granularities. The approach employed is aimed at being system-independent, since it only uses resources produced by external systems, which makes the addition of new sources of bilingual information straightforward. In fact, one of the sources of bilingual information used in the previous edition of the shared task, Apertium, has been replaced by a new one: Lucy LT. The results obtained confirm the conclusion by Esplà-Gomis et al. (2015) that combining the baseline features with those obtained from external sources of bilingual information provide a noticeable improvement, in this case, not only for word-level MTQE, but also for phrase-level MTQE.

Some future work may be interesting, specially as regards the approach to phrase-level MTQE. As already mentioned, it would be interesting to use binary classifiers that support sparse features, in order to be able to directly train a single binary classifier capable to deal with phrases of any length. This would make it possible to put together all the data available, avoiding splitting it into smaller training sets for different classifiers, and therefore allowing to have larger training data set. On the other hand, it may also be interesting to try to use the features defined for word-level MTQE to train the phrase-level MTQE classifier, instead of defining two levels of classification. The main disadvantage of this approach would be the large amount of features, that would make training more expensive.

---

[8]This optimisation metric was chosen by mistake, following the implementation by Esplà-Gomis et al. (2015); however, when repeating the experiments with the correct optimisation, it was possible to confirm that the difference between the results of the submission and those obtained with the right optimisation metric was not significant.

Granularity	System	P^{BAD}	R^{BAD}	F_1^{BAD}	P^{OK}	R^{OK}	F_1^{OK}	$F_1^{\text{OK}} \times F_1^{\text{BAD}}$
word-level	baseline	29.3%	66.4%	40.6%	88.5%	61.6%	72.6%	29.5%
	SBI	28.9%	68.1%	40.6%	88.7%	59.9%	71.5%	29.0%
	SBI+baseline	35.9%	62.4%	45.6%	89.1%	73.4%	80.5%	36.7%
phrase-level	baseline	33.0%	88.7%	48.2%	83.5%	24.2%	37.5%	18.1%
	SBI	30.6%	80.3%	45.9%	82.2%	38.7%	21.3%	9.8%
	SBI+baseline	35.6%	80.3%	49.3%	82.2%	38.7%	52.6%	26.0%

Table 1: Precision (P), recall (R), and F_1 score obtained for the four systems submitted to the shared task on MTQE at WMT 2016. Two of them are based exclusively on the use of *sources of bilingual information* (SBI, see Section 2), and two more combine these SBI with the baseline features provided by the organisers of the task (SBI+baseline). The table also includes the results obtained when training the same binary classifier exclusively on the baseline features (baseline).

Acknowledgements

Work partially funded by the European Commission through project PIAP-GA-2012-324414 (Abu-MaTran) and by the Spanish government through project TIN2015-69632-R (Effortune). We specially thank Reverso-Softissimo and Prompsit Language Engineering for providing the access to the Reverso Context concordancer, the University Research Program for Google Translate that granted us access to the Google Translate service, and Anna Civil from Lucy Software for providing access to the Lucy LT machine translation system.

References

J. Blatz, E. Fitzgerald, G. Foster, S. Gandrabur, C. Goutte, A. Kulesza, A. Sanchis, and N. Ueffing. 2004. Confidence estimation for machine translation. In *Proceedings of the 20th International Conference on Computational Linguistics*, COLING '04, pages 315–321.

R. O. Duda, P. E. Hart, and D. G. Stork. 2000. *Pattern Classification*. John Wiley and Sons Inc., 2nd edition.

Miquel Esplà-Gomis, Felipe Sánchez-Martínez, and Mikel Forcada. 2015. UAlacant word-level machine translation quality estimation system at WMT 2015. In *Proceedings of the Tenth Workshop on Statistical Machine Translation*, pages 309–315, Lisbon, Portugal, September. Association for Computational Linguistics.

M. Hall, E. Frank, G. Holmes, B. Pfahringer, P. Reutemann, and I.H. Witten. 2009. The WEKA Data Mining Software: an Update. *SIGKDD Explorations*, 11(1):10–18.

L. Specia and R. Soricut. 2013. Quality estimation for machine translation: preface. *Machine Translation*, 27(3-4):167–170.

L. Specia, D. Raj, and M. Turchi. 2010. Machine translation evaluation versus quality estimation. *Machine Translation*, 24(1):39–50.

Recurrent Neural Network based Translation Quality Estimation

Hyun Kim
Creative IT Engineering,
Pohang University of Science and
Technology (POSTECH),
Pohang, Republic of Korea
`hkim.postech@gmail.com`

Jong-Hyeok Lee
Computer Science and Engineering,
Pohang University of Science and
Technology (POSTECH),
Pohang, Republic of Korea
`jhlee@postech.ac.kr`

Abstract

This paper describes the recurrent neural network based model for translation quality estimation. Recurrent neural network based quality estimation model consists of two parts. The first part using two bidirectional recurrent neural networks generates the quality information about whether each word in translation is properly translated. The second part using another recurrent neural network predicts the final quality of translation. We apply this model to sentence, word and phrase level of WMT16 Quality Estimation Shared Task. Our results achieve the excellent performance especially in sentence and phrase-level QE.

1 Introduction

We introduce the recurrent neural network based quality estimation (QE) model for predicting the sentence, word and phrase-level translation qualities, without relying on manual efforts to find QE related features.

Existing QE researches have been usually focused on finding desirable QE related features to use machine learning algorithms. Recently, however, there have been efforts to apply neural networks to QE and these neural approaches have shown potential for QE. Shah et al. (2015) use continuous space language model features for sentence-level QE and word embedding features for word-level QE, in combination with other features produced by QuEst++ (Specia et al., 2015). Kreutzer et al. (2015) apply neural networks using pre-trained alignments and word lookup-table to word-level QE, which achieve the excellent performance by using the combination of baseline features at word level. However, these are not 'pure' neural approaches for QE.

Kim and Lee (2016) apply neural machine translation (NMT) models, based on recurrent neural network, to sentence-level QE. This is the first try of using NMT models for the translation quality estimation. This recurrent neural network based quality estimation model is a pure neural approach for QE and achieves a competitive performance in sentence-level QE (English-Spanish).

In this paper, we extend the recurrent neural network based quality estimation model to word and phrase level. Also, we apply this model to sentence, word and phrase-level QE shared task (English-German) of WMT16.

2 Recurrent Neural Network based Quality Estimation Model

Recurrent neural network (RNN) based quality estimation model (Kim and Lee, 2016) consists of two parts: two bidirectional RNNs on the source and target sentences in the first part and another RNN for predicting the quality in the second part.

In the first part (Figure 1), modified RNN-based NMT model generates *quality vectors*, which indicate a sequence of vectors about target words' translation qualities. Each quality vector for each target word has, as not a number unit but a vector unit, the quality information about whether each target word is properly translated from source sentence. Each quality vector is generated by decomposing the probability of each target word from the modified NMT model.[1] Kim and Lee (2016) modify the NMT model to 1) use source and target

---

[1] Existing NMT models (Cho et al., 2014; Bahdanau et al., 2015) use RNNs on source and target sentences to predict the probability of target word.

Proceedings of the First Conference on Machine Translation, Volume 2: Shared Task Papers, pages 787–792,
Berlin, Germany, August 11-12, 2016. ©2016 Association for Computational Linguistics

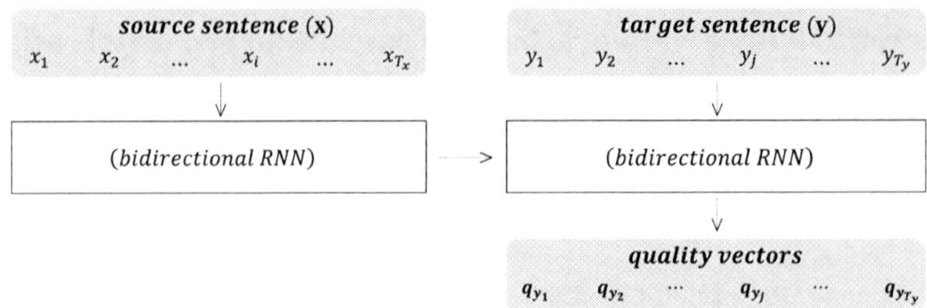

Figure 1: First part of recurrent neural network based quality estimation model for generating quality vectors (Kim and Lee, 2016)

sentences as inputs,[2] 2) apply bidirectional RNNs both on source and target sentences, which enable to fully utilize the bidirectional quality information, and 3) generate quality vectors for target words as outputs.

In the second part (Figure 2, 3 and 4), the final quality of translation at various level (sentence-level/word-level/phrase-level) is predicted by using the quality vectors as inputs. Kim and Lee (2016) apply RNN based model to sentence-level QE and we extend this model to word and phrase-level QE. In subsection 2.1, 2.2 and 2.3, we describe the RNN based[3] (second part) sentence, word and phrase-level QE models.[4]

The cause of these separated parts of the QE model comes from the insufficiency of QE datasets to train the whole QE model. Thus, the QE model is divided into two parts, and then different training data are used to train each of the separated parts: large-scale parallel corpora such as Europarl for training the first part and QE datasets, provided in Quality Estimation Shared Task of WMT, for training the second part.

2.1 RNN based Sentence-level QE Model

In RNN based sentence-level QE model (Figure 2), HTER (human-targeted translation edit rate) (Snover et al., 2006) in [0,1] for target sentence is predicted by using a logistic sigmoid func-

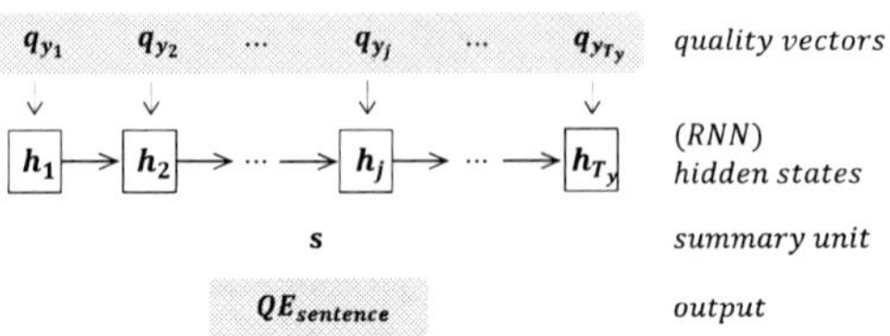

Figure 2: Recurrent neural network based sentence-level QE model (SENT/RNN) (Kim and Lee, 2016)

tion such that

$$QE_{sentence}(\mathbf{y}, \mathbf{x})$$
$$= QE'_{sentence}(q_{y_1}, \dots, q_{y_{T_\mathbf{y}}}) \qquad (1)$$
$$= \sigma(W_s \mathbf{s}).$$

W_s is the weight matrix of sigmoid function[5] at sentence-level QE. $\mathbf{s}$ is a summary unit of the sequential quality vectors and is fixed to the last hidden state[6] $h_{T_\mathbf{y}}$ of RNN. The hidden state h_j is computed by

$$h_j = f(q_{y_j}, h_{j-1}) \qquad (2)$$

where f is the activation function of RNN (Kim and Lee, 2016).

2.2 RNN based Word-level QE Model

In RNN based word-level QE model (Figure 3), we apply bidirectional RNN based binary classification (OK/BAD) using quality vectors as inputs. Through the bidirectional RNN, bidirectional hidden states $\{\vec{h}_j, \overleftarrow{h}_j\}$ for each target word y_j are

---

[2] In MT/NMT, only source sentence is used as a input. In QE, however, both source and target sentences can be used as inputs.

[3] In all activation functions of RNN, the gated hidden unit (Cho et al., 2014) is used to learn long-term dependencies.

[4] We, also, apply feedforward neural network (FNN) to the second part of QE model (see Appendix A). However, to reflect the dependencies between quality vectors and to fully utilize QE related information from QE datasets, we focus on the RNN based model.

[5] Bias terms are visually omitted in all equations.

[6] In RNN, the last hidden state is used as the summary of inputs.

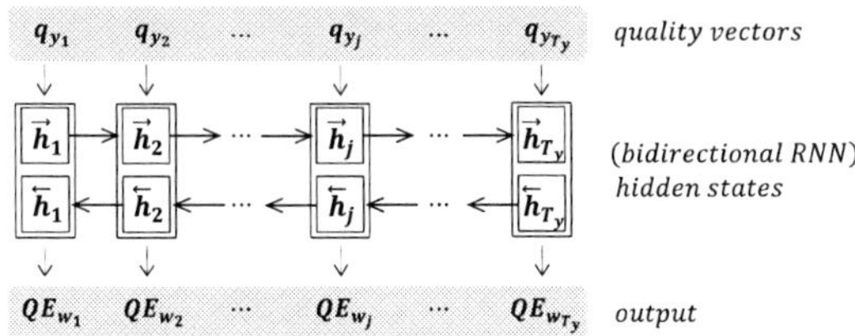

Figure 3: Recurrent neural network based word-level QE model (WORD/RNN)

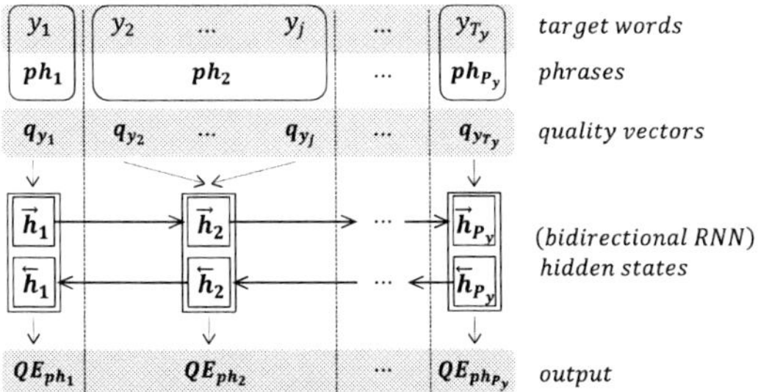

Figure 4: Recurrent neural network based phrase-level QE model (PHR/RNN)

made such that[7]

$$\vec{h}_j = f'(q_{y_j}, \vec{h}_{j-1})$$
$$\overleftarrow{h}_j = g'(q_{y_j}, \overleftarrow{h}_{j+1}) .$$
(3)

The forward hidden state $\vec{h}_j$ indicates summary information about the forward translation quality of target word y_j, reflecting qualities of preceding target words $\{y_1, ..., y_{j-1}\}$. And the backward hidden state $\overleftarrow{h}_j$ indicates summary information about the backward translation quality of target word y_j, reflecting qualities of following target words[8] $\{y_{j+1}, ..., y_{T_y}\}$. We use the concatenated hidden state $h_j^w (= [\vec{h}_j; \overleftarrow{h}_j])$ to predict the word-level quality for target word y_j such that

$$\begin{aligned} &\mathrm{QE}_{word}(\, y_j,\, \mathbf{x}\,) \\ &= \mathrm{QE}'_{word}(\, q_{y_j}) \\ &= \begin{cases} \mathrm{OK} & , \quad \text{if } \sigma(\, W_w\, h_j^w\,) \geq 0.5 \\ \mathrm{BAD}, & \quad \text{if } \sigma(\, W_w\, h_j^w\,) < 0.5 \,. \end{cases} \end{aligned}$$
(4)

W_w is the weight matrix of sigmoid function at word-level QE.

---

[7] $f'(g')$ is the activation function of the forward(backward) RNN at word-level QE.
[8] $T_{\mathbf{y}}$ is the length of target sentence.

2.3   RNN based Phrase-level QE Model

RNN based phrase-level QE model is the extended version of RNN based word-level QE model (in subsection 2.2). In RNN based phrase-level QE model (Figure 4), we also apply bidirectional RNN based binary classification. We use the simply averaged quality vector q_{ph_j} to predict the phrase-level quality of the phrase[9] ph_j, composed of the corresponding target words $\{y_k, y_{k+1}, ...\}$, such that

$$\begin{aligned} &\mathrm{QE}_{phrase}(\, ph_j,\, \mathbf{x}\,) \\ &= \mathrm{QE}'_{phrase}(\, q_{y_k}, q_{y_{k+1}}, ... \,) \\ &= \mathrm{QE}''_{phrase}(\, q_{ph_j}) \\ &= \begin{cases} \mathrm{OK} & , \quad \text{if } \sigma(\, W_{ph}\, h_j^{ph}\,) \geq 0.5 \\ \mathrm{BAD}, & \quad \text{if } \sigma(\, W_{ph}\, h_j^{ph}\,) < 0.5 \,. \end{cases} \end{aligned}$$
(5)

W_{ph} is the weight matrix of sigmoid function at phrase-level QE. $h_j^{ph} (= [\vec{h}_j; \overleftarrow{h}_j])$ is the concatenated hidden state for phrase ph_j of bidirectional RNN where[10]

$$\vec{h}_j = f''(q_{ph_j}, \vec{h}_{j-1})$$
$$\overleftarrow{h}_j = g''(q_{ph_j}, \overleftarrow{h}_{j+1}) .$$
(6)

3   Results

RNN based QE models were evaluated on the WMT16 Quality Estimation Shared Task[11] at sentence, word and phrase level of English-German. Because whole QE models are separated into two parts, each part of the QE models is trained separately by using different training data. To train the first part of the QE models, English-German parallel corpus of Europarl v7 (Koehn, 2005) were used. To train the second part of the QE models, WMT16 QE datasets of English-German (Specia et al., 2016) were used.

To denote the each method, the following naming format is used: $[level]/[model]$-QV$[num]$. $[level]$ is the QE granularity level: SENT (sentence level), WORD (word level) and PHR (phrase level). $[model]$ is the type of model used in the second part: RNN (of subsection 2.1, 2.2 and 2.3)

---

[9] $1 \leq j \leq P_{\mathbf{y}}$ where $P_{\mathbf{y}}$ is the number of phrases in target sentence and $P_{\mathbf{y}} \leq T_{\mathbf{y}}$.
[10] $f''(g'')$ is the activation function of the forward(backward) RNN at phrase-level QE.
[11] http://www.statmt.org/wmt16/quality-estimation-task.html

Task 1. Test	Pearson's r ↑	MAE ↓	RMSE ↓	Rank
SENT/RNN-QV2	0.4600	0.1358	0.1860	2
SENT/RNN-QV3	0.4475	0.1352	0.1838	4
SENT/FNN-QV2	0.3588	0.1517	0.2001	
SENT/FNN-QV3	0.3549	0.1529	0.2006	
BASELINE	0.3510	0.1353	0.1839	

Table 1: Results on **test set** for the **scoring** variant of WMT16 **sentence-level** QE (Task 1).

Task 1. Test	Spearman's ρ ↑	DeltaAvg ↑	Rank
SENT/RNN-QV2	0.4826	0.0766	1
SENT/RNN-QV3	0.4660	0.0753	3
SENT/FNN-QV3	0.3910	0.0589	
SENT/FNN-QV2	0.3905	0.0593	
BASELINE	0.3900	0.0630	

Table 2: Results on **test set** for the **ranking** variant of WMT16 **sentence-level** QE (Task 1).

and FNN (of subsection A.1, A.2 and A.3). At QV[num], [num] is the number of iterations while the first part is trained by using large-scale parallel corpora to make quality vectors (QV).

3.1 Results of Sentence-level QE (Task 1)

Pearson's correlation (r), mean absolute error (MAE), and root mean squared error (RMSE) are used to evaluate the scoring variant of sentence-level QE. And Spearman's rank correlation (ρ) and DeltaAvg are used to evaluate the ranking variant of sentence-level QE.

Table 1 and 2 (Table B.1 and B.2) present the results of the QE models on test (development) set for the scoring and ranking variants of the WMT16 sentence-level QE shared task (Task 1). In all aspects of evaluation at sentence-level QE, the RNN based QE model (SENT/RNN) showed the better performance than the FNN based QE model (SENT/FNN). Our two methods (SENT/RNN-QV2 and SENT/RNN-QV3), participated in WMT16 sentence-level QE shared task, achieved top rank: each 2nd and 4th at the scoring variant and each 1st and 3rd at the ranking variant.

3.2 Results of Word-level and Phrase-level QE (Task 2)

The multiplication of F1-scores for the 'OK' and 'BAD' classes and F1-score for the 'BAD' class are used to evaluate the word-level and phrase-level QE.

Table 3 and 4 (Table B.3 and B.4) respectively present the results on test (development) set of the WMT16 word-level and phrase-level QE shared task (Task 2). In all aspects of evaluation at word-level and phrase-level QE, the RNN based QE

Task 2. Test Word-level	Multiplication of F1-OK and F1-BAD ↑	F1-Bad ↑	F1-OK ↑	Rank
WORD/RNN-QV3	0.3803	0.4475	0.8498	5
WORD/RNN-QV2	0.3759	0.4538	0.8284	6
WORD/FNN-QV3	0.3273	0.3800	0.8615	
WORD/FNN-QV2	0.3241	0.3932	0.8242	
BASELINE	0.3240	0.3682	0.8800	

Table 3: Results on **test set** of WMT16 **word-level** QE (Task 2).

Task 2. Test Phase-level	Multiplication of F1-OK and F1-BAD ↑	F1-Bad ↑	F1-OK ↑	Rank
PHR/RNN-QV3	0.3781	0.4950	0.7639	2
PHR/RNN-QV2	0.3693	0.4785	0.7718	3
PHR/FNN-QV3	0.3505	0.4722	0.7423	
PHR/FNN-QV2	0.3353	0.4413	0.7599	
BASELINE	0.3211	0.4014	0.8001	

Table 4: Results on **test set** of WMT16 **phrase-level** QE (Task 2).

models (WORD/RNN and PHR/RNN) showed the better performance than the FNN based QE models (WORD/FNN and PHR/FNN). Our two methods (WORD/RNN-QV3 and WORD/RNN-QV2), participated in WMT16 word-level QE shared task, achieved each 5th and 6th rank. Our two methods (PHR/RNN-QV3 and PHR/RNN-QV2), participated in WMT16 phrase-level QE shared task, achieved top rank: each 2nd and 3rd.

4 Conclusion

This paper described recurrent neural network based quality estimation models of sentence, word and phrase level. We extended the (existing sentence-level) recurrent neural network based quality estimation model to word and phrase level. And we applied these models to sentence, word and phrase-level QE shared task of WMT16. These recurrent neural network based quality estimation models are pure neural approaches for QE and achieved excellent performance especially in sentence and phrase-level QE.

Acknowledgments

This research was partly supported by the "ICT R&D Program" of MSIP/IITP (R7119-16-1001, Core technology development of the real-time simultaneous speech translation based on knowledge enhancement) and "ICT Consilience Creative Program" of MSIP/IITP (R0346-16-1007)

References

Dzmitry Bahdanau, Kyunghyun Cho, and Yoshua Bengio. 2015. Neural machine translation by jointly learning to align and translate. In *ICLR 2015*.

Kyunghyun Cho, Bart van Merrienboer, Caglar Gulcehre, Dzmitry Bahdanau, Fethi Bougares, Holger Schwenk, and Yoshua Bengio. 2014. Learning phrase representations using rnn encoder–decoder for statistical machine translation. In *Proceedings of the 2014 Conference on Empirical Methods in Natural Language Processing (EMNLP)*, pages 1724–1734. Association for Computational Linguistics.

Hyun Kim and Jong-Hyeok Lee. 2016. A recurrent neural networks approach for estimating the quality of machine translation output. In *Proceedings of the 2016 Conference of the North American Chapter of the Association for Computational Linguistics: Human Language Technologies*, pages 494–498. Association for Computational Linguistics.

Philipp Koehn. 2005. Europarl: A parallel corpus for statistical machine translation. In *MT summit*, volume 5, pages 79–86. Citeseer.

Julia Kreutzer, Shigehiko Schamoni, and Stefan Riezler. 2015. Quality estimation from scratch (quetch): Deep learning for word-level translation quality estimation. In *Proceedings of the Tenth Workshop on Statistical Machine Translation*, pages 316–322. Association for Computational Linguistics.

Kashif Shah, Varvara Logacheva, Gustavo Paetzold, Frédéric Blain, Daniel Beck, Fethi Bougares, and Lucia Specia. 2015. Shef-nn: Translation quality estimation with neural networks. In *Proceedings of the Tenth Workshop on Statistical Machine Translation*, pages 342–347. Association for Computational Linguistics, September.

Matthew Snover, Bonnie Dorr, Richard Schwartz, Linnea Micciulla, and John Makhoul. 2006. A study of translation edit rate with targeted human annotation. In *Proceedings of association for machine translation in the Americas*, pages 223–231.

Lucia Specia, Gustavo Paetzold, and Carolina Scarton. 2015. Multi-level translation quality prediction with quest++. In *Proceedings of ACL-IJCNLP 2015 System Demonstrations*, pages 115–120. Association for Computational Linguistics and The Asian Federation of Natural Language Processing.

Lucia Specia, Varvara Logacheva, and Carolina Scarton. 2016. WMT16 quality estimation shared task training and development data. LINDAT/CLARIN digital library at Institute of Formal and Applied Linguistics, Charles University in Prague.

Appendix

A Feedforward Neural Network (FNN) based Quality Estimation Model

In this section, we describe the FNN based (second part) QE models of sentence, word and phrase level, for comparison with RNN based (second part) QE models. Quality vectors, generated from the same RNN based first part QE model, are used as inputs.

A.1 FNN based Sentence-level QE Model

In FNN based sentence-level QE model (Figure A.1), we also use a logistic sigmoid function of (1). But in FNN based model we make each hidden state h_j by only using each quality vector q_{y_j} for target word y_j. And for s, which is a summary unit of the whole quality vectors, we simply average all hidden states $\{h_1, ..., h_{T_{\mathbf{y}}}\}$.

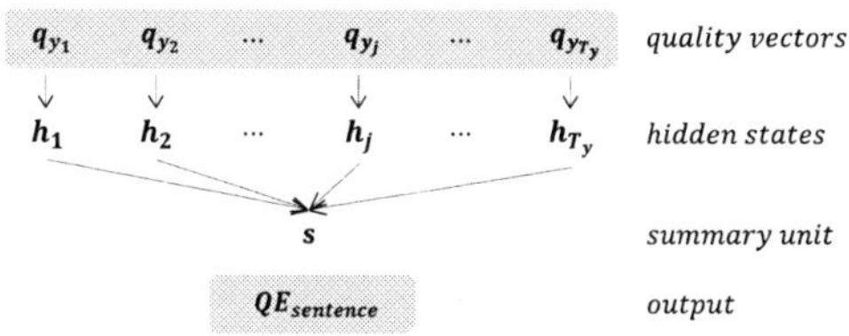

Figure A.1: Feedforward neural network based sentence-level QE model (SENT/FNN)

A.2 FNN based Word-level QE Model

In FNN based word-level QE model (Figure A.2), we apply FNN based binary classification (OK/BAD) using quality vectors as input. By only using each quality vector q_{y_j} for target word y_j, each hidden state $h_j (= h_j^w)$ is made. We predict the word-level QE by (4).

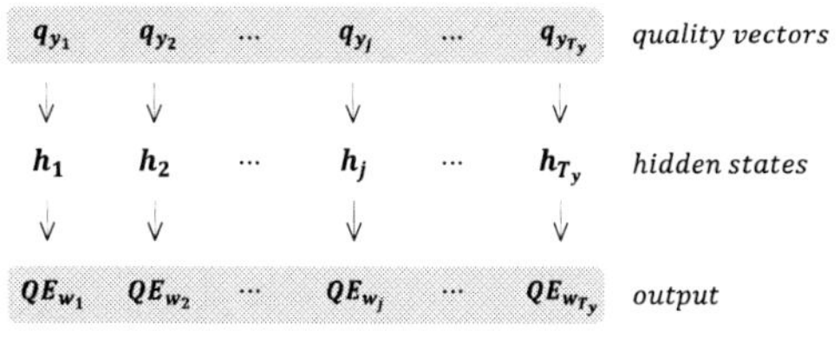

Figure A.2: Feedforward neural network based word-level QE model (WORD/FNN)

A.3 FNN based Phrase-level QE Model

In FNN based phrase-level QE model (Figure A.3), we also apply FNN based binary classification (OK/BAD). By only using the averaged quality vector q_{ph_j} for the phrase ph_j, composed of the corresponding target words $\{y_k, y_{k+1}, ...\}$, the hidden state $h_j(= h_j^{ph})$ is made. We predict the phrase-level QE by (5).

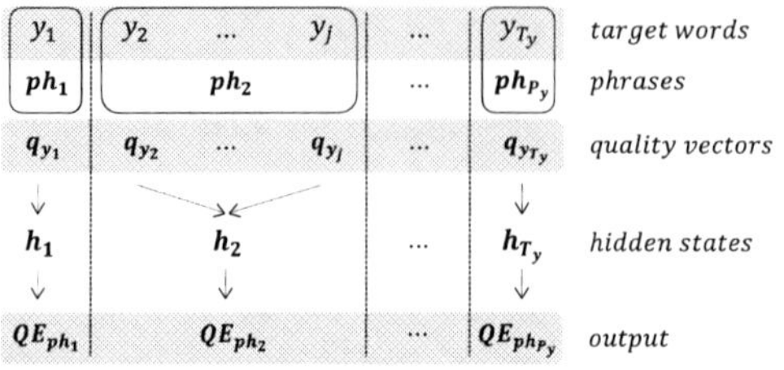

Figure A.3: Feedforward neural network based phrase-level QE model (PHR/FNN)

B Results on Development Set of WMT16 QE Shared Task

Task 1. Dev	Pearson's r ↑	MAE ↓	RMSE ↓
SENT/RNN-QV2	0.4661	0.1340	0.1921
SENT/RNN-QV3	0.4658	0.1341	0.1896
SENT/FNN-QV3	0.3915	0.1539	0.2007
SENT/FNN-QV2	0.3904	0.1560	0.2015

Table B.1: Results on **development set** for the **scoring** variant of WMT16 **sentence-level** QE (Task 1).

Task 1. Dev	Spearman's ρ ↑	DeltaAvg ↑
SENT/RNN-QV3	0.5222	0.0882
SENT/RNN-QV2	0.5154	0.0892
SENT/FNN-QV3	0.4370	0.0697
SENT/FNN-QV2	0.4227	0.0693

Table B.2: Results on **development set** for the **ranking** variant of WMT16 **sentence-level** QE (Task 1).

Task 2. Dev. Word-level	Multiplication of F1-OK and F1-BAD ↑	F1-Bad ↑	F1-OK ↑
WORD/RNN-QV3	0.3880	0.4567	0.8496
WORD/RNN-QV2	0.3838	0.4617	0.8313
WORD/FNN-QV3	0.3227	0.3812	0.8597
WORD/FNN-QV2	0.3171	0.3878	0.8178

Table B.3: Results on **development set** of WMT16 **word-level** QE (Task 2).

Task 2. Dev. Phase-level	Multiplication of F1-OK and F1-BAD ↑	F1-Bad ↑	F1-OK ↑
PHR/RNN-QV2	0.3831	0.4955	0.7731
PHR/RNN-QV3	0.3770	0.4975	0.7578
PHR/FNN-QV3	0.3526	0.4755	0.7416
PHR/FNN-QV2	0.3391	0.4447	0.7626

Table B.4: Results on **development set** of WMT16 **phrase-level** QE (Task 2).

YSDA Participation in the WMT'16 Quality Estimation Shared Task

Anna Kozlova[1,2]   **Mariya Shmatova**[2]   **Anton Frolov**[2]
{voron13e02,mashashma,anton-fr}@yandex-team.ru
[1]Yandex School of Data Analysis, 11/2 Timura Frunze St., Moscow 119021, Russia
[2]Yandex, 16 Leo Tolstoy St., Moscow 119021, Russia

Abstract

This paper describes Yandex School of Data Analysis (YSDA) submission for WMT2016 Shared Task on Quality Estimation (QE) / Task 1: Sentence-level prediction of post-editing effort. We solve the problem of quality estimation by using a machine learning approach, where we try to learn a regressor from feature space to HTER score. By enriching the baseline features with the syntactical features and additional translation system based features, we achieve Pearson correlation of 0.525 on the test set.

1 Introduction

The WMT'16 QE has included the sentence level sub-task. The goal is to predict the amount of effort required to post-edit machine-translated sentences. For this task the organizers provide a parallel corpus of English-German sentences obtained via some machine translation system, as well as corresponding manually post-edited reference sentences. The amount of post-editing is measured by edit-distance rate HTER (Snover et al., 2006) between the system's translation and the reference translation. HTER scores were computed by TER[1] software.

Our system extracts numerical features from sentences and uses a machine learning approach to predict HTER score. In addition to the baseline features we include syntactic features.

We also found that HTER scores have a long tailed distribution. More than 60% of examples have HTER score less than 30, at the same time the maximum value (on provided data) is 150, but there are only few sentences getting such high score. This observation led us to an idea first to

predict BLEU (which is currently the most popular metric for evaluation in MT (Papineni et al., 2002).

The paper is structured as follows: Section 2 describes analysis of provided data, Section 3 contains machine learning setup and features details, Section 4 summarizes and discusses the results.

2 Data analysis

The main goal of this task is to predict HTER score given source sentence and corresponding translation. The corpus contains HTER scores greater than 100 (in this task we use HTER * 100%, so the values should be in the range from 0 to 100). Organizers advised to clip scores at 100.

To analyze the data set we plotted the distribution of HTER (based on capped train data) (see Figure 1 and distribution statistics in Table 1).

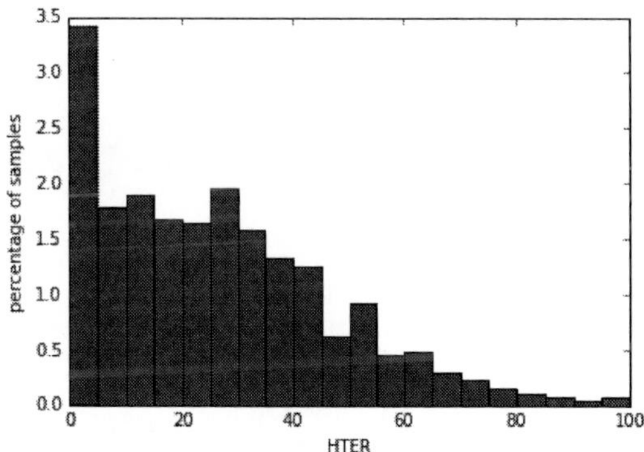

Figure 1: HTER distribution for train data

	HTER	BLEU
mean	25.79	0.61
std	20.59	0.24
min	0.0	0.07
25%	9.10	0.42
50%	23.08	0.60
75%	38.46	0.80
max	100.0	1.0

Table 1: Statistics of HTER and BLEU for train data

---

[1]http://www.cs.umd.edu/~snover/tercom/

Proceedings of the First Conference on Machine Translation, Volume 2: Shared Task Papers, pages 793–799,
Berlin, Germany, August 11-12, 2016. ©2016 Association for Computational Linguistics

The plot demonstrates that more than 3% of all examples have score equal to 0. This distribution has sample median of 23 and a long tail. Therefore, the problem is to predict this tail by a few number of examples.

Motivated by this statistics we computed BLEU score, using translation and post-edited variant as a reference. We found that HTER and BLEU have a high Pearson correlation (-0.8423), while BLEU distribution is much easier to predict. Comparison of distributions can be found in Table 1.

According to our experiments, modified 2-gram precision (Papineni et al., 2002) has the best Pearson correlation with HTER (-0.943). For this reason we decided also to use modified 2-gram precision to simplify prediction problem.

3 Model description

This section describes the regression algorithm used to predict HTER score and features details.

3.1 Algorithms

We use SVR with RBF-kernel from scikit-learn toolkit[2] for both regressors (BLEU and modified 2-gram precision), where C and γ were found by grid search on cross-validation. Then we use linear kernel SVR to combine predictions from the previous stage to predict target HTER.

3.2 Features

Along with the provided baseline features (Section 3.2.1), we extracted our own features:

- syntactically motivated features (Section 3.2.2)

- web-scaled language model features (Section 3.2.3)

- pseudo-reference and back-translation features (Section 3.2.4)

- miscellaneous features (Section 3.2.5)

- combinations of described above features (Section 3.2.6)

3.2.1 Baseline features

The next 17 baseline features were provided by organizers (Bojar et al., 2015):

1. number of tokens in the source sentence

2. number of tokens in the target sentence

3. average source token length

4. LM probability of source sentence

5. LM probability of target sentence

6. number of occurrences of the target word within the target hypothesis (averaged for all words in the hypothesis - type/token ratio)

7. average number of translations per source word in the sentence (as given by IBM 1 table thresholded such that prob(t|s) > 0.2)

8. average number of translations per source word in the sentence (as given by IBM 1 table thresholded such that prob(t|s) > 0.01) weighted by the inverse frequency of each word in the source corpus

9. percentage of unigrams in quartile 1 of frequency (lower frequency words) in a corpus of the source language (SMT training corpus)

10. percentage of unigrams in quartile 4 of frequency (higher frequency words) in a corpus of the source language

11. percentage of bigrams in quartile 1 of frequency of source words in a corpus of the source language

12. percentage of bigrams in quartile 4 of frequency of source words in a corpus of the source language

13. percentage of trigrams in quartile 1 of frequency of source words in a corpus of the source language

14. percentage of trigrams in quartile 4 of frequency of source words in a corpus of the source language

15. percentage of unigrams in the source sentence seen in a corpus (SMT training corpus)

16. number of punctuation marks in the source sentence

17. number of punctuation marks in the target sentence

3.2.2 Syntactically motivated features

We decided to use morphosyntactical information, that can be extracted from source and translation sentences.

To collect this information we used an implementation of dependency parser described in (Zhang and Nivre, 2011), trained for English and German.

---

[2] http://scikit-learn.org/

The intuition is the more syntactically complex the source sentence is, the more corrections during post-editing are needed.

Firstly, the features based on syntactic tree structure for source and translation were extracted:

- tree width, i.e. how many dependencies the root has

- maximum tree depth, i.e. maximum number of dependency levels in the tree

- average depth of the tree

- proportion of internal nodes in the tree

Secondly, the information obtained from POS-tags and dependency roles (for both: source and translation) was used:

- number of verbs

- number of verbs with dependent subjects

- number of nouns

- number of subjects

- whether the sentence begins with a verb (indicator feature)

- number of conjunctions

- whether the German polite imperative is used as a translation for the simple English imperative ('Fügen Sie' for 'Add').

Thirdly, source-side syntactic features were extracted:

- number of relative clauses (the more relative clauses the sentence has, the poorer the translation is likely to be)

- number of attributive clauses

Due to the parser's imperfection, it is also useful to inform the machine learning algorithm how confident we are that the sentence is parsed correctly. We use parsing scores for source and translation as additional features, as well as their difference, bearing the following observation in mind: it is more difficult to parse poorly translated sentence and a large difference is likely to be an indicator that more corrections will be required during post-editing.

3.2.3 Additional resources

It is well known that the performance of SMT systems heavily relies on the quality of their language models. We used in-house web-scale language models containing hundreds of millions ngrams to make the following features:

- Web LM probability for source and translation

- Web LM probability for translation with splitted compounds

- Web LM probability for translation without punctuation

- percentage of rare words in translated sentence – for each word we calculate Web LM probability and count percentage of words with weights lower than certain threshold. Threshold was chosen empirically by assumption, that terms, compounds, foreign and other rare words have lower probability. About 30% of all unique words in train set were marked as rare.

3.2.4 Pseudo-references and back-translations

Another set of features was obtained by using translations from additional online translation system[3]. For our purposes we generated two types of translations:

- pseudo-references for source sentence

- back-translations (Shigenobu, 2007) for machine translation

For both types of translation we calculated following features:

- BLEU

- modified 1-gram precision

- modified 2-gram precision

- modified 3-gram precision

- modified 4-gram precision

- brevity penalty

3.2.5 Miscellaneous features

We propose to use some information, which can be obtained from plain text:

---

[3]http://translate.yandex.com/

- number of quotation marks – an odd number of quotations in the translation often indicates incorrect translation

- number of words ending with hyphen – a possible indicator of sentence complexity and, sometimes, errors ("Pinsel- Popupmenü" should be "Pinsel-Popupmenü" or "Überschriften- und eine Liste" should be "Überschrift und einer Liste")

- whether the sentence contains an url address

- number of untranslated words

Some features were based on data provided for the QE sub-task 2 "Word and phrase-level QE" – word-level alignments between source and translation sentences:

- mean number of alignments for each source word

- maximum number of alignments for each source word

- number of unaligned words in translation

3.2.6 Feature combinations

Also we decided to use additional features, which were combined from ones described earlier. For example, if source part had 2 quotations, and translation has 3, we decided to indicate it somehow. For these reason we added differences between following features:

- number of punctuation marks in source and translation sentences

- number of quotations in source and translation sentences

- LM probabilities of source and translation sentences

- Web LM probabilities of source and translation sentences

- Web LM probabilities of translation before and after compounds splitting

- Web LM probabilities of source sentence and translation with splitted compounds

- Web LM probabilities of source sentence and translation without punctuation

- number of words in source and translation sentences

4 Experiments and Results

4.1 Preprocessing

Taking into consideration domain specifics of the data, i.e. large amount of URLs, file names, as well as presence of compounds in German, we make a simple preprocessing by applying the following rules:

- replace URLs and file names with a single dummy token

- split German compounds with compound splitting algorithm similar to (Koehn and Knight, 2003)

- remove redundant punctuation from provided machine translations

4.2 Feature selection

We applied the following popular feature selection algorithms to detect weak features:

- removing features with low variance

- univariate feature selection

Due to this analysis, two baseline features were removed: "percentage of unigrams in quartile 1 of frequency (lower frequency words) in a corpus of the source language (SMT training corpus)" and "percentage of trigrams in quartile 1 of frequency of source words in a corpus of the source language".

4.3 Feature scaling

Since features have different nature, feature normalization is needed. Every feature was scaled with the following transformation $x = \frac{x - mean(x)}{std(x)}$, where $mean$ is the feature's mean value and std is its standard deviation. Mean and std for each feature were extracted from train set. After this procedure every feature has zero mean and a standard deviation of 1.

4.4 Evaluation

There are three metrics for this task: Pearson correlation (primary metric), MSE, and RMSE. The main disadvantage of using MSE and RSME here is a long tail of target values: if the model fails to predict a high score, an absolute error for this prediction will be large as well.

Features set	Pearson correlation	MAE	RMSE
Baseline	0.387	13.83	18.98
Baseline + Syntax	0.438	13.50	18.51
Baseline + Syntax + Web LM	0.469	13.30	18.24
Baseline + Syntax + Web LM + Pseudo references	0.519	12.75	17.71
Baseline + Syntax + Web LM + Pseudo references + Miscellaneous + Combinations	**0.530**	**12.60**	**17.35**

Table 2: Results on dev set

Features set	Pearson correlation	MAE	RMSE
Baseline	0.370	13.43	18.05
Baseline + Syntax	0.445	12.95	17.44
Baseline + Syntax + Web LM	0.489	12.72	17.01
Baseline + Syntax + Web LM + Pseudo references	**0.530**	**12.28**	16.51
Baseline + Syntax + Web LM + Pseudo references + Miscellaneous + Combinations	0.525	12.30	**16.41**

Table 3: Results on test set

4.5 Results

Results on dev and test sets can be found in Tables 2 and 3 respectively. All experiments have the same preprocessing setup. Since BLEU ranges from 0 to 1, we clip predicted values to fit into this interval. Predicted HTER is also clipped to fit into [0, 100] interval.

Feature set names are as follows:

1. *Baseline* features contains provided 17 features. For the next experiments we used 15 baseline features, which remained after feature selection.

2. *Syntax* features use syntactical information about sentences (Section 3.2.2).

3. *Web LM* features are additional resource features (Section 3.2.3).

4. *Pseudo references* features use information from pseudo-references and back-translations (Section 3.2.4).

5. *Miscellaneous + Combinations* features include miscellaneous information from sentences and features combinations (Section 3.2.5, Section 3.2.6).

So the experiments described above led to significant improvement of classifier's quality. The most noticeable increase was achieved by implementing syntactically motivated features. This result is related to the fact that sentences with complex syntactical structure are difficult to translate. Moreover, syntax of poorly translated sentences is harder to parse, leading to less confident parsing scores.

Adding features based on pseudo-references also improves the quality of our model. Those cases, where translations differ from pseudo-references, are likely to be complex for MT. Back-translation features were also helpful for checking out whether the original meaning was lost during translation.

It is worth noting, that optimal features for the test set and the dev set differ. The best model has been chosen according to the dev set, so some adjustment to this set could occur. Despite it there are only 1000 sentences in the dev set and this could be insufficient for obtaining adequate estimation.

4.6 Feature importances

After model training we calculated the most informative features using Random Forest (Breiman, 2001) algorithms:

- modified 2-gram precision for pseudo-reference (*Pseudo references*)

- percentage of trigrams in quartile 4 of frequency of source words in a corpus of the source language (*Baseline*)

- LM probability of source sentence (*Baseline*)

- difference between syntactical parser scores of source and machine translation (*Syntax*)

- BLEU for pseudo-reference (*Pseudo references*)

- percentage of bigrams in quartile 4 of frequency of source words in a corpus of the source language (*Baseline*)

- BLEU for back-translation (*Pseudo references*)

- difference between LM probability of source and translation (*Combinations*)

- Web LM probability of machine translation (*Web LM*)

- average number of translations per source word in the sentence (as given by IBM 1 table thresholded such that prob(t|s) > 0.2) (*Baseline*)

4.7 Discussion

While analyzing results we found some MT-sentences, that receive small scores from our algorithm (predicted HTER – pHTER) and at the same time have large HTER scores.

There are cases, where the editor attempts to broaden the context rather than to minimize the number of corrections. For example, while the original translation is valid and no corrections are needed, it is completely rewritten by the editor:

SRC: Complete the dialog box .

MT: Füllen Sie das Dialogfeld .

PE: Nehmen Sie im Dialogfeld die erforderlichen Einstellungen vor .

HTER: 66.667

pHTER: 7.899

It can be seen here, that our regressor predicts small edit distance, while edit distance between MT and PE is over 50 (that means the translation is incorrect).

There is also inconsistency in the way German compounds are treated. In some cases a compound in machine translation is replaced with a combination of two words in post-edited sentence, while in others it remains joined. For example, in one case *"Kanälebedienfeld"* is replaced with *"Bedienfeld Kanäle"*, but in another – it stays the same. And the difference between HTER score and predicted score in second case is larger, respectively. There are also opposite cases, when words are joined into a single German compound in post-edited sentence.

Similar observation holds for sentences with if-clauses, where they are swapped with main clauses: in some cases post-edited sentence contains swapped clauses, but in others the original order is kept.

It was noticed, that there is no regularity in post-editings. This can lead to greater difference between original and predicted HTER scores as well as cause noise during machine learning. It can also be critical while training set is not very large and peculiarities mentioned above can affect algorithm adversely.

5 Conclusions and future work

In this paper YSDA submission for WMT16 Shared Task on Quality Estimation (QE) / Task 1: Sentence-level prediction of post-editing effort, is discussed. This work is based on the idea that the more complex the sentence is the more difficult it is to translate. For this purpose, the information, provided by syntactic parsing, was used. This allowed to estimate the quality of machine translated sentences as well as complexity of source sentences. We also decided to replace the target metric for the regressor (HTER to BLEU) to obtain a more robust machine learning solution. Further work will address the implementation of our model for other language pairs. It would be interesting to study how this approach works for distant language pairs (i.e. English-Turkish). We also plan to work on syntactically motivated features in order to extract more complex, as well as more informative, features from parsed data.

6 Acknowledgements

We thank Irina Galinskaya and Alexey Baytin for their help and detailed feedback.

References

Ondřej Bojar, Rajen Chatterjee, Christian Federmann, Barry Haddow, Matthias Huck, Chris Hokamp, Philipp Koehn, Varvara Logacheva, Christof Monz, Matteo Negri, Matt Post, Carolina Scarton, Lucia Specia, and Marco Turchi. 2015. Findings of the 2015 workshop on statistical machine translation. In *Proceedings of the Tenth Workshop on Statistical Machine Translation*, pages 1–46, Lisbon, Portugal, September. Association for Computational Linguistics.

Leo Breiman. 2001. Random forests. *Machine learning*, 45(1):5–32.

Philipp Koehn and Kevin Knight. 2003. Empirical methods for compound splitting. In *Proceedings of the tenth conference on European chapter of the Association for Computational Linguistics-Volume 1*, pages 187–193. Association for Computational Linguistics.

Kishore Papineni, Salim Roukos, Todd Ward, and Wei-Jing Zhu. 2002. BLEU: a method for automatic evaluation of machine translation. In *Proceedings of the 40th annual meeting on association for computational linguistics*, pages 311–318. Association for Computational Linguistics.

Tomohiro Shigenobu. 2007. Evaluation and usability of back translation for intercultural communication. In *Usability and Internationalization. Global and Local User Interfaces*, pages 259–265. Springer.

Matthew Snover, Bonnie Dorr, Richard Schwartz, Linnea Micciulla, and John Makhoul. 2006. A study of translation edit rate with targeted human annotation. In *Proceedings of association for machine translation in the Americas*.

Yue Zhang and Joakim Nivre. 2011. Transition-based dependency parsing with rich non-local features. In *Proceedings of the 49th Annual Meeting of the Association for Computational Linguistics: Human Language Technologies: short papers-Volume 2*, pages 188–193. Association for Computational Linguistics.

USFD's Phrase-level Quality Estimation Systems

Varvara Logacheva, Frédéric Blain and **Lucia Specia**
Department of Computer Science
University of Sheffield, UK
{v.logacheva, f.blain, l.specia}@sheffield.ac.uk

Abstract

We describe the submissions of the University of Sheffield (USFD) for the phrase-level Quality Estimation (QE) shared task of WMT16. We test two different approaches for phrase-level QE: (i) we enrich the provided set of baseline features with information about the context of the phrases, and (ii) we exploit predictions at other granularity levels (word and sentence). These approaches perform closely in terms of multiplication of F_1-scores (primary evaluation metric), but are considerably different in terms of the F_1-scores for individual classes.

1 Introduction

Quality Estimation (QE) of Machine Translation (MT) is the task of determining the quality of an automatically translated text without comparing it to a reference translation. This task has received more attention recently because of the widespread use of MT systems and the need to evaluate their performance on the fly. The problem has been modelled to estimate the quality of translations at the word, sentence and document levels (Bojar et al., 2015). Word-level QE can be particularly useful for post-editing of machine-translated texts: if we know the erroneous words in a sentence, we can highlight them to attract post-editor's attention, which should improve both productivity and final translation quality. However, the choice of words in an automatically translated sentence is motivated by the context, so MT errors are also context-dependent. Moreover, as it has been shown in (Blain et al., 2011), errors in multiple adjacent words can be caused by a single incorrect decision — e.g. an incorrect lexical choice can result in errors in all its syntactic de-

pendants. The task of estimating quality at the phrase level aims to address these limitations of word-level models for improved prediction performance.

The first effort to estimate the quality of translated n-grams (instead of individual words) was described in (Gandrabur and Foster, 2003), but there the multi-word nature of predictions was motivated by the architecture of the MT system used in the experiment: an interactive MT system which did not translate entire sentences, but rather predicted the next n word translations in a sentence. An approach was designed to estimate the confidence of the MT system about the prediction and was aimed at improving translation prediction quality.

The phrase-level QE in its current formulation – estimation of the quality of phrases in a pre-translated sentence using external features of these phrases – was first addressed in the work of Logacheva and Specia (2015), where the authors segmented automatically translated sentences into phrases, labelled these phrases based on word-level labels and trained several phrase-level QE models using different feature sets and machine learning algorithms. The baseline phrase-level QE system used in this shared task was based on the results in (Logacheva and Specia, 2015).

This year's Conference on Statistical Machine Translation (WMT16) includes a shared task on phrase-level QE (QE Task 2p) for the first time. This task uses the same training and test data as the one used for the word-level QE task (QE Task 2): the set of English sentences, their automatic translations into German and their manual post-editions performed by professional translators. The data belongs to the IT domain. The training set contains 12,000 sentences, development and test sets — 1,000 and 2,000 sentences, respectively. For model training and evaluation, the words are la-

Proceedings of the First Conference on Machine Translation, Volume 2: Shared Task Papers, pages 800–805,
Berlin, Germany, August 11-12, 2016. ©2016 Association for Computational Linguistics

belled as "BAD" or "OK" based on labelling generated with the TERcom tool[1]: if an edit operation (substitution or insertion) was applied to a word, it is labelled as "BAD"; contrarily, if the word was left unchanged, it is considered "OK". For the phrase-level task, the data was segmented also into phrases. The segmentation was given by the decoder that produced the automatic translations. The segments are labelled at the phrase level using the word-level labels: a phrase is labelled as "OK" if it contains only words labelled as "OK"; if one or more words in a phrase are "BAD"', the phrase is "BAD" itself. The predictions are done at the phrase level, but evaluated at the word level: for the evaluation phrase-level labels are unrolled back to their word-level versions (i.e. if a three-word phrase is labelled as "BAD", it is equivalent to three "BAD" word-level labels).

The baseline phrase-level features provided by the organisers of the task are *black-box* features that were originally used for sentence-level quality estimation and extracted using the QuEst toolkit[2] (Specia et al., 2015). While this feature set considers many aspects of sentence quality (mostly the ones that do not depend on internal MT system information and do not require language-specific resources), it has an important limitation when applied to phrases. Namely, it does not take into account the context of the phrase, i.e. words and phrases in the sentence, either before or after the phrase of interest. In order to advance upon the baseline results, we enhanced the baseline feature set with contextual information for phrases.

Another approach we experimented with is the use of predictions made by QE models at other levels of granularity: word level and sentence level. The motivation here is twofold. On the one hand, we use a wider range of features which are unavailable at the phrase level. On the other hand, the use of word-level and sentence-level predictions can help mitigate the uncertainty of phrase-level scores: there, a phrase is labelled as "BAD" if it has any number of "BAD" words, so "BAD" phrases can be of very different quality. We believe that information on the quality of individual words and the overall quality of a sentence can be complementary for phrase-level quality prediction.

The rest of the paper is organised as follows. We describe our context-based QE strategy in Section 2. In Section 3 we explain our approach to build phrase-level QE models using predictions of other levels. Section 4 reports the final results, while Section 5 outlines directions for future work.

2 Context-based model

The feature set used for the baseline system in the shared task considers various aspects of a phrase. It has features that allow to evaluate the likelihood of its source and target parts individually (e.g. probabilities of its source and target phrases as given by monolingual language models), and also the correspondences between the parts (e.g. the ratio of numbers of punctuation marks and words of particular parts of speech in the source and target sides of the phrase). However, this feature set does not take into account the words surrounding an individual phrase. This is explained by the fact that the feature set was originally designed for QE systems which evaluate the quality of automatic translations at the sentence level. Sentences in an automatically translated text are generally produced independently from each other, given that most MT systems cannot take extra-sentential context into account. Therefore, context features are rarely used for sentence-level QE.

2.1 Features

In order to improve the representation of phrases, we use a number of additional features (CONTEXT) that depend on phrases to the left and right of the phrase of interest, as well as the phrase itself. The intuition behind these features is that they evaluate how well a phrase fits its context. Here we list the new features and the values they can take:

- **out-of-vocabulary words (binary)** — we check if the source phrase has words which do not occur in a source corpus. The feature has value **1** if at least one of source words is out-of-vocabulary and **0** otherwise;

- **source/target left context (string)** — last word of the previous source/target phrase;

- **source/target right context (string)** — first word of the next source/target phrase;

- **highest order of n-gram that includes the first target word (0 to 5)** — we take the n-gram at the border between the current and previous phrase and generate the combination of the first target word in the phrase and 1 to 4 words that precede it in the sentence. Let us denote the first word from the phrase $\mathbf{w}_{first}$ and the 4-grams from the previous phrase $p_{-4}p_{-3}p_{-2}p_{-1}$. If the entire 5-gram $p_{-4}p_{-3}p_{-2}p_{-1}\mathbf{w}_{first}$ exists in the target LM, the feature value is 5. If it is not in the LM, n-grams of lower order (from $p_{-3}p_{-2}p_{-1}\mathbf{w}_{first}$ to unigram w_{first}) are checked, and the feature value is the order of the longest n-gram found in the LM;

- **highest order of n-gram that includes the last target word (0 to 5)** — feature that considers the n-gram $\mathbf{w}_{last}p_1p_2p_3p_4$ (where $\mathbf{w}_{last}$ is the last target word of the current phrase and $p_1p_2p_3p_4$ is the opening 4-gram of the next feature) analogously to the previous feature;

- **backoff behaviour of first/last n-gram (0 to 1)** — backoff behaviour of n-grams $p_{-2}p_{-1}\mathbf{w}_{first}$ and $\mathbf{w}_{last}p_1p_2$, computed as described in (Raybaud et al., 2011).

- **named entities in the source/target (binary)** — we check if the source and target phrases have tokens which start with capital letters;

- **part of speech of the source/target left/right context (string)** — we check parts of speech of words that precede or follow the phrase in the sentence.

Some of these features (e.g. highest n-gram order, backoff behaviour, contexts) are used because they have been shown useful for word-level QE (Luong et al., 2013), others are included because we believe they can be relevant for understanding the quality of phrases.

We compare the performance of the baseline feature set with the feature set extended with context information. The QE models are trained using CRFSuite toolkit (Okazaki, 2007). We chose to train a Conditional Random Fields (CRF) model because it has shown high performance in word-level QE (Luong et al., 2013) as well as phrase-level QE (Logacheva and Specia, 2015) tasks. CRFSuite provides five optimisation algorithms: L-BFGS with L1/L2 regularization (lbfgs), SGD with L2-regularization (l2sgd), Averaged Perceptron (ap), Passive Aggressive (pa), and Adaptive

	Feature set	
	Baseline	Extended
lbfgs	0.270	0.332
l2sgd	0.238	**0.358**
ap	0.316	0.355
pa	**0.329**	**0.357**
arow	0.292	0.315

Table 1: F_1-multiplied scores of models trained on baseline and extended feature sets using different optimisation algorithms for CRFSuite.

Regularization of Weights (arow). Since these algorithms could perform differently in our task, we tested all of them on both baseline and extended feature sets, using the development set.

Table 1 shows the performance of our CRF models trained with different algorithms. We can see that the extended feature set clearly outperforms the baseline for all algorithms. Passive-Aggressive scored higher for the baseline feature set and is also one of the best-performing algorithms on the extended feature set. Therefore, we used the Passive-Aggressive algorithm for our subsequent experiments and the final submission.

2.2 Data filtering

Many datasets for word-level QE suffer from the uneven distribution of labels: the "BAD" words occur much less often than those labelled as "OK". This characteristic stems from the nature of the word-level QE task: we need to identify erroneous words in an automatically translated text, but the state-of-the-art MT systems allow producing texts of high enough quality, where only a few words are incorrect. Since for the shared task data the phrase-level labels were generated from word-level labels, we run into the same problem at the phrase level. Here the discrepancy is not so large: the "BAD" labels make for 25% of all labels in the training dataset for the phrase-level task. However, we believe it is still useful to reduce this discrepancy.

Previous experiments with word-level QE showed that the distribution of labels can be smoothed by filtering out sentences with little or no errors (Logacheva et al., 2015). Admittedly, if a sentence has no "BAD" words it lacks information about one of the classes of the problem, and thus it is less informative. We thus applied the same strategy to phrase-level QE: we ranked the

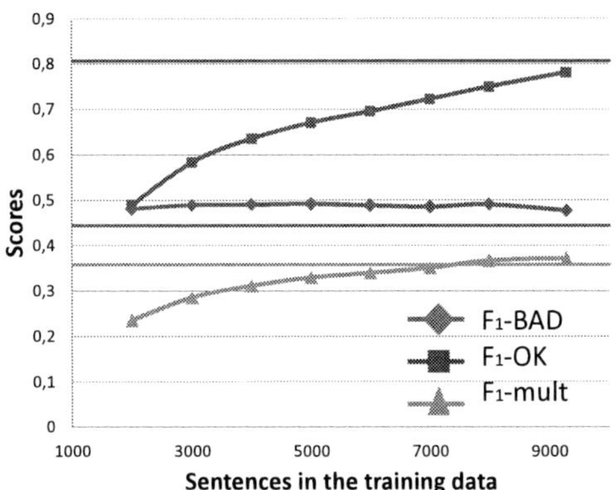

Figure 1: Performance of the phrase-level QE model with different numbers of training sentences.

training sentences by their HTER score (ratio of "BAD" words in a sentence) so that the worst sentences are closer to the top of the list, and trained our phrase-level QE model using only N top sentences from the training data (i.e. only sentences with larger number of errors).

Figure 1 shows how the scores of our phrase-level models change as we add more training data. We examine F_1-scores for both "BAD" and "OK" classes as well as their multiplication, which is the primary metric for the task (denoted as **F_1-mult**). The flat lines denote the scores of a model that uses the entire dataset (12,000 sentences): red for F_1-OK, blue for F_1-OK, green for F_1-mult. It is clear that F_1-BAD benefits from filtering out sentences with less errors. The models with reduced data never reach the F_1-OK score of the ones which use the full dataset, but their higher F_1-BAD scores result in overall improvements in performance. The F_1-mult score reaches its maximum when the training set contains only sentences with errors (9,280 out of 12,000 sentences), although F_1-BAD score is slightly lower in this case than with a lower number of sentences. Since F_1-mult is our main metric, we use this version of the filtered dataset for the final submission.

3   Prediction-based model

Following the approach in (Specia et al., 2015), which makes use of word-level predictions at sentence level, we describe here the first attempt to using both word-level and sentence-level predictions for phrase-level QE (W&SLP4PT).

Phrase-level labels by definition depend on the quality of individual words comprising the phrase: each phrase-level label in the training data is the generalisation of word-level labels within the considered phrase. However, we argue that the quality of a phrase can also be influenced by overall quality of the sentence.

We used the following set of features based on predictions of different levels of granularity and on the phrase segmentation itself:

- **Sentence-level prediction** features:

    1. sentence score — quality prediction score assigned for the current sentence. Same feature value for all phrases in a sentence.

- **Phrase segmentation** features:

    2. phrase ratio — ratio of the length of the current phrase to the length of the sentence;

    3. phrase length — number of words in the current phrase.

- **Word-level prediction** features:

    4/5. number of words predicted as "OK"/"BAD" in the current phrase;

    6/7. number of words predicted as "OK"/"BAD" in the sentence.

Similarly to the context-based model described in Section 2, we trained our prediction-based model with the CRFSuite toolkit and the Passive-Aggressive algorithm. The phrase segmentation features are extracted from the data itself and do not need any additional information. The sentence-level score is produced by the SHEF-LIUM-NN system, a sentence-level QE system with neural network features as described in (Shah et al., 2016). The word-level prediction features are produced by the SHEF-MIME QE system (Beck et al., 2016), which uses imitation learning to predict translation quality at the word level.

4   Results

We submitted two phrase-level QE systems: the first one uses the set of baseline features enhanced with context features, the second one uses the features based on predictions made by word-level and

	F_1-BAD	F_1-OK	F_1-mult
W&SLP4PT	0.486	0.757	**0.368**
CONTEXT	0.470	0.777	**0.365**
BASELINE	0.401	0.800	0.321

Table 2: Performance of our official submissions on the test set.

sentence-level QE models, plus the phrase segmentation features. The performance of our official submissions on the test set is given in Table 2.

For the prediction-based model, we used word-level predictions from the MIME system with β=0.3. While (Beck et al., 2016) reports better performance with $\beta = 1$, we obtained slightly lower performance both on F_1-mult = 0.367 and F_1-OK = 0.739. Only F_1-BAD was better = 0.497.

Even though the two systems are very different in terms of the features they use, their performance is very similar. The prediction-based model is slightly better in terms of F_1-BAD, whereas the context-based model predicts "OK" labels more accurately. Both systems outperform the baseline.

In terms of the F_1-multiplied metric, our prediction-based and context-based systems ranked 4th and 5th (out of 10 systems) in the shared task, respectively.

4.1 Model combination

Since both our models outperform the baseline system, we also combined them after the official submission to check whether further improvements could be obtained. Surprisingly, we got the exact same prediction performance as our prediction-based model. This is because two features of our prediction-based model – the number of words predicted as "BAD"/"OK" in the current phrase – have a strong bias and do most of the job by themselves[3]. The reason of this behaviour lies in the way both the training and test data have been tagged for the phrase-level task. The labelling was adapted from the word-level labels by assigning the "BAD" tag to any phrase that contains at least one "BAD" word. Consequently, during the training against gold standards labels, our model learns to tag as "BAD" any phrase that contains at least

---

[3]We get the exact same scores either combining the prediction-based features with the baseline features, both the baseline and context features, or considering the number of predicted "BAD" words in the current phrase as the only feature of our model.

	F_1-BAD	F_1-OK	F_1-mult
W&SLP4PT	0.389	0.727	0.283
+baseline	0.454	0.767	0.349
+context	0.473	0.772	**0.366**
BASELINE	0.401	0.800	0.321

Table 3: Performance for combinations of models on the test set.

on "BAD" word in a systematic way.

After removing the features 4 and 5 from the feature set, we retrained our prediction-based model and its new performance is given in the first row of Table 3. On its own, it performs worse than the baseline, but by successively adding the baseline and context features to it (without any data filtering), it performs as well as our official submissions in terms of F_1-BAD and F_1-multi, and gets higher F_1-OK.

5 Conclusion and future work

We presented two different approaches to phrase-level QE: one extends the baseline feature set with context information, another combines the scores of different levels of granularity to model the quality of phrases. Both performed similarly, although the prediction-based strategy is more "pessimistic" regarding the training data. Both outperformed the baseline.

In future work, we further experiments to gather a better understanding of these approaches. First, additional feature engineering can be performed: we did not check the usefulness of individual context features, nor of the additional features used in the prediction-based model. Secondly, the correspondences between labels of different granularities can be further examined: for example, it is interesting to see how the use of sentence-level and word-level predictions can influence the prediction of phrase-level scores.

Acknowledgements

This work was supported by the EXPERT (EU FP7 Marie Curie ITN No. 317471, Varvara Logacheva) and the QT21 (H2020 No. 645452, Lucia Specia, Frédéric Blain) projects.

References

Daniel Beck, Andreas Vlachos, Gustavo H. Paetzold, and Lucia Specia. 2016. SHEF-MIME: Word-level Quality Estimation Using Imitation Learning.

In *Proceedings of the First Conference on Machine Translation*, Berlin, Germany.

Frédéric Blain, Jean Senellart, Holger Schwenk, Mirko Plitt, and Johann Roturier. 2011. Qualitative Analysis of Post-Editing for High Quality Machine Translation. In *Proceedings of the MT Summit XIII*, pages 164–171, Xiamen, China.

Ondřej Bojar, Rajen Chatterjee, Christian Federmann, Barry Haddow, Matthias Huck, Chris Hokamp, Philipp Koehn, Varvara Logacheva, Christof Monz, Matteo Negri, Matt Post, Carolina Scarton, Lucia Specia, and Marco Turchi. 2015. Findings of the 2015 workshop on statistical machine translation. In *Proceedings of the Tenth Workshop on Statistical Machine Translation*, pages 1–46, Lisbon, Portugal.

Simona Gandrabur and George Foster. 2003. Confidence estimation for translation prediction. In *Proceedings of Seventh Conference on Natural Language Learning*, pages 95–102, Edmonton, Canada.

Varvara Logacheva and Lucia Specia. 2015. Phrase-level quality estimation for machine translation. In *Proceedings of the 2015 International Workshop on Spoken Language Translation*, Da Nang, Vietnam.

Varvara Logacheva, Chris Hokamp, and Lucia Specia. 2015. Data enhancement and selection strategies for the word-level quality estimation. In *Proceedings of the Tenth Workshop on Statistical Machine Translation*, pages 330–335, Lisbon, Portugal.

Ngoc Quang Luong, Benjamin Lecouteux, and Laurent Besacier. 2013. LIG system for WMT13 QE task: Investigating the usefulness of features in word confidence estimation for MT. In *Proceedings of the Eighth Workshop on Statistical Machine Translation*, pages 386–391, Sofia, Bulgaria.

Naoaki Okazaki. 2007. Crfsuite: a fast implementation of conditional random fields (CRFs). Available at `http://www.chokkan.org/software/crfsuite/`.

Sylvain Raybaud, David Langlois, and Kamel Smaïli. 2011. This sentence is wrong. Detecting errors in machine-translated sentences. *Machine Translation*, 25(1):1–34.

Kashif Shah, Fethi Bougares, Loic Barrault, and Lucia Specia. 2016. Shef-lium-nn: Sentence level quality estimation with neural network. In *Proceedings of the First Conference on Machine Translation*, Berlin, Germany.

Lucia Specia, G Paetzold, and Carolina Scarton. 2015. Multi-level translation quality prediction with quest++. In *Proceedings of the 53rd Annual Meeting of the Association for Computational Linguistics and Seventh International Joint Conference on Natural Language Processing of the Asian Federation of Natural Language Processing: System Demonstrations*, pages 115–120.

Unbabel's Participation
in the WMT16 Word-Level Translation Quality Estimation Shared Task

André F. T. Martins
Unbabel & Instituto de Telecomunicações
Lisbon, Portugal
andre.martins@unbabel.com

Ramón Astudillo
Unbabel & L2F/INESC-ID
Lisbon, Portugal
ramon@unbabel.com

Chris Hokamp
Dublin City University
Dublin, Ireland
chokamp@computing.dcu.ie

Fabio N. Kepler
L2F/INESC-ID, Lisbon, Portugal
University of Pampa, Alegrete, Brazil
fabio@kepler.pro.br

Abstract

This paper presents the contribution of the Unbabel team to the WMT 2016 Shared Task on Word-Level Translation Quality Estimation. We describe our two submitted systems: (i) UNBABEL-LINEAR, a feature-rich sequential linear model with syntactic features, and (ii) UNBABEL-ENSEMBLE, a stacked combination of the linear system with three different deep neural networks, mixing feedforward, convolutional, and recurrent layers. Our systems achieved $F_1^{\mathrm{OK}} \times F_1^{\mathrm{BAD}}$ scores of 46.29% and 49.52%, respectively, which were the two highest scores in the challenge.

1 Introduction

Quality estimation is the task of evaluating a translation system's quality without access to reference translations (Specia et al., 2013; Bojar et al., 2015). This paper describes the contribution of the Unbabel team to the Shared Task on Word-Level Quality Estimation (QE Task 2) at the 2016 Conference on Statistical Machine Translation (WMT 2016). The task aims to predict the word-level quality of English-to-German machine translated text, by assigning a label of OK or BAD to each word in the translation.

Our system's architecture is inspired by the recent QUETCH+ system (Kreutzer et al., 2015), which achieved top performance in the WMT 2015 Word Level QE task (Bojar et al., 2015). QUETCH+ predicts the labels of individual words by combining a linear feature-based classifier with a feedforward neural network (called QUETCH,

for QUality Estimation from scraTCH). The linear classifier is based upon Luong et al. (2014) and uses the baseline features provided in the shared task. The QUETCH neural network is a multi-layer perceptron, which takes as input the embeddings of the target words and the aligned source words, along with their context, and outputs a binary label for the target word. The combination is done by stacking the scores of the neural network and the linear classifier as additional features in another linear classifier.

Our main contributions are the following:

- We replaced the word-level linear classifier in QUETCH+ by a sentence-level first-order sequential model. Our model incorporates rich features for label unigrams and bigrams, detailed in §2.1–2.2.

- We included syntactic features that look at second-order dependencies between target words. This is explained in §2.3.

- We implemented three different neural systems, one extension of the original QUETCH model and two recurrent models with different depth. These are detailed in §3.1–3.3.

- We ensembled multiple versions of each neural system for different data shuffles and initializations as additional features for the linear system, via a stacking architecture. This is detailed in §4.

The following external resources were used: part-of-speech tags and extra syntactic dependency information were obtained with Turbo-Tagger and TurboParser (Martins et al., 2013),[1]

---

[1] Publicly available on http://www.cs.cmu.edu/~ark/TurboParser/.

Proceedings of the First Conference on Machine Translation, Volume 2: Shared Task Papers, pages 806–811,
Berlin, Germany, August 11-12, 2016. ©2016 Association for Computational Linguistics

trained on the Penn Treebank (for English) and on the version of the German TIGER corpus used in the SPMRL shared task (Seddah et al., 2014). For the neural models, we used pre-trained word embeddings from Polyglot (Al-Rfou et al., 2013) and embeddings obtained from a trained neural MT system (Bahdanau et al., 2014).

2 Linear Sequential Model

Our starting point is a discriminative feature-based linear sequential model. The input is a tuple $x := \langle s, t, \mathcal{A} \rangle$, where $s = s_1 \ldots s_M$ is the source sentence, $t = t_1 \ldots t_N$ is the translated sentence, and $\mathcal{A} \subseteq \{(m, n) \mid 1 \leq m \leq M, \ 1 \leq n \leq N\}$ is a set of word alignments. The goal is to predict a label sequence $\widehat{y} = y_1, \ldots, y_N$, where each $y_i \in \{\text{BAD}, \text{OK}\}$. This is done as follows:

$$\widehat{y} = \arg\max_{y} \tag{1}$$

$$\sum_{i=1}^{N} w \cdot f_u(x, y_i) + \sum_{i=1}^{N+1} w \cdot f_b(x, y_i, y_{i-1}),$$

where w is a vector of weights, $f_u(x, y_i)$ are unigram features (depending only on a single output label), $f_b(x, y_i, y_{i-1})$ are bigram features (depending on consecutive output labels), and y_0 and y_{N+1} are special start/stop symbols.

A detailed description of the features used in our submitted systems is provided below. The weights for these features are learned by running 50 epochs of the max-loss MIRA algorithm (Crammer et al., 2006) with $C = 0.001$. The cost function takes into account mismatches between predicted and gold labels, with a higher cost on false positives ($c_{FP} = 0.8$) and a lower cost on false negatives ($c_{FN} = 0.2$), to compensate for the fact that there are fewer BAD labels than OK labels in the data. These values were tuned on the development set.

2.1 Unigram Features

We used the following unigram features, taken from the baseline features provided by the organizers (with some slight changes that are detailed below). Each of the features below is conjoined with the target label at each position.

- BIAS. A bias feature.

- WORD, LEFTWORD, RIGHTWORD. Lexical features for the target word in the current, previous, and next positions.

- SOURCEWORD, SOURCELEFTWORD, SOURCERIGHTWORD. Lexical features for the source word aligned to the current target word, and their left/right neighboring words in the source sentence; these will all be NULL if the target word is unaligned. If there are multiple aligned source words, they are all concatenated into a single SOURCEWORD feature, and the contextual features are with respect to the leftmost and rightmost aligned source words, respectively.[2]

- LARGESTNGRAMLEFT/RIGHT, SOURCELARGESTNGRAMLEFT/RIGHT. The language model features provided by the shared task organizers, containing the length of the largest n-gram on each direction observed in the target and source language models.[3]

- POSTAG, SOURCEPOSTAG. Part-of-speech tag of the current target word, and of the source-aligned word, both predicted by TurboTagger (Martins et al., 2013). The latter will be NULL if the target word is unaligned, and a concatenation of POS tags if there are multiple aligned source words.[4]

Following Kreutzer et al. (2015), we conjoined some of the baseline features above as follows.

- WORD+LEFTWORD, WORD+RIGHTWORD. Bilexical features including the target word in the current position, conjoined with the previous/next target word.

- WORD+SOURCEWORD, POSTAG+SOURCEPOSTAG. Features conjoining the source and target word/POS tag.

2.2 Bigram Features

We constructed rich bigram features which conjoin the label pair (for each pair of consecutive target words) with two copies of the features in §2.1: one copy for the first word in the pair, and another for the second word in the pair. Furthermore, we also introduced the following trilexical features:

- WORDPAIR+LEFTWORD, WORDPAIR+RIGHTWORD. Trilexical features

---

[2]This is slightly different from the baseline feature provided by the organizers of the shared task, which consider the single source word aligned with the highest confidence.

[3]We did not use the provided backoff language model features.

[4]This differs from the features provided by the organizers in two ways: the POS tagger is different; and the SOURCEPOSTAG can have multiple tags for many-to-one alignments.

including the two target words in the current position, conjoined with the target word in the previous and next positions, respectively.

To understand the importance of these enriched feature sets, we also tried a "simple bigram" model using only a single indicator feature for the label pair.

2.3 Syntactic Features

A major novelty in our quality estimation system is the usage of syntactic features, which are useful to detect grammatically incorrect constructions. We used the following syntactic features based on dependencies predicted by TurboParser (Martins et al., 2013). With the exception of the first one, all the syntactic features below were used for unigrams only.

- DEPREL, WORD+DEPREL. The dependency relation between the current target word and its parent, as well as its conjunction with the target word itself.

- HEADWORD/POSTAG+WORD/POSTAG. Conjunction of the word/POS tag of the current target word with the one of its syntactic head.

- LEFTSIBWORD/POSTAG+WORD/POSTAG, RIGHTSIBWORD/POSTAG+WORD/POSTAG. Same, but for the closest sibling in the left/right.

- GRANDWORD/POSTAG+HEADWORD/POSTAG +WORD/POSTAG. Up to bilexical features involving the grandparent, head, and current target word/POS tag, including backed off versions of these features.

2.4 Performance of the Linear System

To help understand the contribution of each group of features in §2.1–2.3, we evaluated the performance of different variants of the UNBABEL-LINEAR system on the development set.

The results are shown in Table 1. As expected, the use of bigrams improves the simple unigram model, which is similar to the baseline model provided by the organizers. We can also see that the rich bigram features have a great impact in the scores (about 2.6 points above a sequential model with a single indicator bigram feature), and that the syntactic features help even further, contributing another 2.6 points. The net improvement exceeds 6.5 points over the unigram model.

Features	$F_1^{\text{GOOD}} \times F_1^{\text{BAD}}$
unigrams only	39.27
+simple bigram	40.65
+rich bigrams	43.31
+syntactic	45.94

Table 1: Performance on the dev-set of several configurations of the UNBABEL-LINEAR system. The model with simple bigrams has a single BIAS bigram feature, conjoined with the label pairs.

3 Neural Models

We next describe the three neural models implemented by our team. Five instances of each model were trained using different data shuffles, following the idea of Jean et al. (2015), and also using random initialization seeds (except for the model in §3.1). These instances were incorporated to the stacking architecture as different features, as will be described in §4. For reporting purposes, the instances of each model were also ensembled with two strategies: majority voting, where each instance contributes one vote, and averaged probability, where we average each instance's predicted probability of a word being BAD).

3.1 Feedforward Network

Our feedforward network is an adaptation of QUETCH (Kreutzer et al., 2015). The model classifies each word as OK/BAD by using each target language word and the corresponding aligned word from the source language as input. To increase the context available to the model, the words at the left and right of each target and source word are provided as well. Each of the 6 words is represented by a pre-trained word embedding, and all are concatenated into a single vector. There is a single hidden layer, which uses a hyperbolic tangent (`tanh`) non-linearity. The model is trained using stochastic gradient descent to maximize the log-likelihood. During training, the loss function is weighted to penalize BAD instances in order to compensate for the asymmetry in OK/BAD labels in the corpus.

All hyperparameters were tuned on the development set. The best performance was attained by using 64-dimensional Polyglot embeddings (Al-Rfou et al., 2013), updated during training, and a hidden layer size of 20. Words with no pre-trained embeddings were initialized to a vector of zeros and optimized during training. The BAD weight was set to 3. Despite its simplicity, this model provided a good performance when compared to neural models using no extra features.

In order to adapt to this year's shared task, several improvements were introduced to QUETCH. Similarly to the linear model, for many-to-one alignments we included all aligned words in the source (not just ones), with their corresponding size one contexts (see footnote 2). To obtain a fixed size vector, the average over the embeddings of each aligned word was used. A second improvement was the addition of a convolutional layer spanning 3 words after the hidden layer. This aimed to expand the local context used by QUETCH. Finally, a dropout of 20% after the concatenation of the embeddings was applied. Of the implemented improvements, dropout had the largest effect, whereas including all aligned words brought a small but consistent improvement.

When the five trained instances were ensembled by average probability, this rather simple approach led to a large improvement in performance, as shown in Table 2.

Model	$F_1^{\text{OK}} \times F_1^{\text{BAD}}$
Single Feed-forward Network (FFN)	41.74
5 FFN Ensemble (Majority Voting)	43.26
5 FFN Ensemble (Average Probability)	43.47

Table 2: Effect of intra-model ensembling of the feed-forward network reproducing QUETCH.

3.2 Bilingual, Bidirectional Recurrent Model

We also implemented a bidirectional model which takes target words and their aligned source words as inputs, and outputs a OK/BAD tag for each target word. The internal representations of the bidirectional model are then passed to a feedforward network where the first layer performs a maxout transformation with two pieces (Goodfellow et al., 2013). Dropout is applied before multiplication with the maxout layer's weights. The maxout layer is followed by two fully-connected layers with 100 and 50 hidden units, respectively. `tanh` is used as the non-linear function between layers. During development, we validated that this model improved performance over a vanilla feed-forward network using the WMT 2015 English-to-Spanish dataset.

Source and target word embeddings are initialized with embeddings from an English-German

neural machine translation (NMT) system (Bahdanau et al., 2014), trained with all data from the WMT 2015 English-to-German translation task (Bojar et al., 2015). The vocabulary size is 100,000 for both English and German, and words in the training data which do not occur in the NMT vocabulary are mapped to an "unknown" token. We experimented with tuning the embedding parameters during training, but found that leaving them static led to better performance.

Gated Recurrent Units (GRU) are used for the recurrent transitions (Chung et al., 2015). The size of the hidden layers is fixed at 500, and the embedding size is set to 200. Minibatch size is fixed at 40. Dropout is applied to all feedforward parameters of the models, but not to the parameters of the recurrent transitions. We tested the impact of ℓ_2 regularization, and our best performing system uses both dropout and ℓ_2 regularization.[5] All recurrent models are optimized using AdaDelta (Zeiler, 2012). The best model for each training run was selected using early-stopping according to the F_1-product score of the model on the development set. The intra-model ensembling results are shown in Table 3.

Model	$F_1^{\text{OK}} \times F_1^{\text{BAD}}$
Single Model (BBRM)	40.95
5 BBRN (Majority Voting)	41.52
5 BBRN (Average Probability)	41.31

Table 3: Effect of intra-model ensembling of the Bilingual, Bidirectional Recurrent Model.

3.3 Multi-Feature Convolutional Recurrent Network

Our second recurrent model uses both recurrent and convolutional components, along with POS tags obtained from TurboTagger for both target and aligned source words. As in §3.2, an entire sentence is fed at once to the network, which takes as input the target words and the aligned source words, both with their respective left and right contexts, and the POS tags for each target and source words, both with the two left and two right tags (i.e., we use a convolution with a window of size 3 for words and 5 for POS tags). The output is a sequence of OK/BAD tags for the target words.

The first network's layer are embeddings for all the aforementioned inputs: word embeddings are

---

[5]Peak performance was obtained with dropout probability set to 0.5, and ℓ_2 regularization coefficient $\alpha = 10^{-4}$.

initialized with Polyglot embeddings, as in §3.1, and tag embeddings of size 50 are initialized randomly. All are further trained along with the other network parameters. For each input timestep, all embeddings are concatenated and then passed to two consecutive feedforward hidden layers with 200 units. A bidirectional GRU layer with 200 units is then applied across all timesteps. The resulting representations are further passed to another feedforward network consisting of two layers of 200 units, followed by a softmax layer which classifies a target word as OK or BAD.

All activations besides softmax are rectified linear units (unlike the models in §3.1–§3.2, which use `tanh` activations), and a dropout of 20% is used in each layer. Optimization is carried out by RMSProp.[6] As in §3.2, early-stopping based on the F_1-product score over the development set was used for selecting the best model of each training run.

We verified empirically that shallower models performed worse, while the new POS tags and specially the middle bidirectional GRU gave a boost in score.

Model	$F_1^{\text{OK}} \times F_1^{\text{BAD}}$
Single Model (MFCRN)	44.33
5 MFCRN (Majority Voting)	46.58
5 MFCRN (Average Probability)	46.10

Table 4: Effect of intra-model ensembling of the multi-feature convolutional recurrent network model.

Table 4 shows the average performance of five trained instances and the ensembles performances of these instances as described in §3, which also led to large improvements as in the other models.

4 Stacking Architecture

As described in §3, each of the three neural models produced five trained instances, yielding 15 predictions in total for every word in the training, development and test datasets. For the three models, we used 10-fold jackknifing to obtain unbiased predictions for the training set. We then plugged these 15 predictions (as probability values) as additional features in the linear model described in §2. As unigram features, we used one real-valued feature for every model prediction at each position, conjoined with the label. As bigram features,

---

	$F_1^{\text{OK}} \times F_1^{\text{BAD}}$
Linear + 5 FFN	46.89
Linear + 5 BBLM	47.01
Linear + 5 MFCRN	48.58
Full Ensemble	49.25

Table 5: Performance of a stacked network ensembling each of the three deep models and the linear model, and of a full ensemble (UNBABEL-ENSEMBLE).

	F_1^{OK}	F_1^{BAD}	$F_1^{\text{OK}} \times F_1^{\text{BAD}}$
UNBABEL-LINEAR	87.48	52.92	46.29
UNBABEL-ENSEMBLE	88.45	55.99	49.52

Table 6: Performance of the submitted systems on the test set.

we used two real-valued features for every model prediction at the two positions, conjoined with the label pair.

The results obtained with this stacked architecture are shown in Table 5, where we compare with smaller ensembles that stack each individual deep model with the linear one (using only 5 extra features instead of 15). We can see that there is a clear benefit in combining all the deep models, which suggests that these systems complement each other by focusing on different quality aspects.

5 Final Results

Finally, we show in Table 6 the results obtained in the test set for our two submitted systems, UNBABEL-LINEAR and UNBABEL-ENSEMBLE. As expected, the ensemble system gave an additional boost (>3 points) over the linear model, which is consistent with the findings of the previous sections on the validation data.

6 Conclusions

We have presented a novel linear sequential model which uses the baseline task features along with a new set of syntactic features, leading to top performance on the word-level quality estimation task. Using this model as our baseline, we obtain further improvements by including a version of the feedforward QUETCH system, as well as two novel recurrent models, as stacked features in the sequential linear model. Our final ensemble achieved the best performance of all submitted systems.

Acknowledgments

This work was partially supported by the the the EXPERT project (EU Marie Curie ITN No. 317471), and by Fundação para a Ciência e Tecnologia (FCT), through contracts UID/EEA/50008/2013 and UID/CEC/50021/2013, the LearnBig project (PTDC/EEI-SII/7092/2014), and the GoLocal project (grant CMUPERI/TIC/0046/2014).

References

[Al-Rfou et al.2013] Rami Al-Rfou, Bryan Perozzi, and Steven Skiena. 2013. Polyglot: Distributed word representations for multilingual nlp. *arXiv preprint arXiv:1307.1662*.

[Bahdanau et al.2014] Dzmitry Bahdanau, Kyunghyun Cho, and Yoshua Bengio. 2014. Neural machine translation by jointly learning to align and translate. *CoRR*, abs/1409.0473.

[Bojar et al.2015] Ondrej Bojar, Rajan Chatterjee, Christian Federmann, Barry Haddow, Chris Hokamp, Matthias Huck, Varvara Logacheva, , Philipp Koehn, , Christof Monz, Matteo Negri, Pavel Pecina, Matt Post, Carolina Scarton, Lucia Specia, and Marco Turchi. 2015. Findings of the 2015 Workshop on Statistical Machine Translation. In *Tenth Workshop on Statistical Machine Translation*, WMT, Lisbon, Portugal.

[Chung et al.2015] Junyoung Chung, Çaglar Gülçehre, Kyunghyun Cho, and Yoshua Bengio. 2015. Gated feedback recurrent neural networks. In *Proceedings of the 32nd International Conference on Machine Learning, ICML 2015, Lille, France, 6-11 July 2015*, pages 2067–2075.

[Crammer et al.2006] K. Crammer, O. Dekel, J. Keshet, S. Shalev-Shwartz, and Y. Singer. 2006. Online Passive-Aggressive Algorithms. *Journal of Machine Learning Research*, 7:551–585.

[Goodfellow et al.2013] Ian J. Goodfellow, David Warde-Farley, Mehdi Mirza, Aaron C. Courville, and Yoshua Bengio. 2013. Maxout networks. *CoRR*, abs/1302.4389.

[Jean et al.2015] Sébastien Jean, Orhan Firat, Kyunghyun Cho, Roland Memisevic, and Yoshua Bengio. 2015. Montreal neural machine translation systems for wmt15. In *Proceedings of the Tenth Workshop on Statistical Machine Translation*, pages 134–140.

[Kreutzer et al.2015] Julia Kreutzer, Shigehiko Schamoni, and Stefan Riezler. 2015. Quality estimation from scratch (quetch): Deep learning for word-level translation quality estimation. In *Proceedings of the Tenth Workshop on Statistical Machine Translation*, pages 316–322.

[Luong et al.2014] Ngoc Quang Luong, Laurent Besacier, and Benjamin Lecouteux. 2014. Lig system for word level qe task at wmt14. In *Proceedings of the Ninth Workshop on Statistical Machine Translation*, pages 335–341, Baltimore, Maryland, USA, June. Association for Computational Linguistics.

[Martins et al.2013] André F. T Martins, Miguel B. Almeida, and Noah A. Smith. 2013. Turning on the turbo: Fast third-order non-projective turbo parsers. In *Proc. of the Annual Meeting of the Association for Computational Linguistics*.

[Seddah et al.2014] Djamé Seddah, Sandra Kübler, and Reut Tsarfaty. 2014. Introducing the SPMRL 2014 shared task on parsing morphologically-rich languages. In *Proceedings of the First Joint Workshop on Statistical Parsing of Morphologically Rich Languages and Syntactic Analysis of Non-Canonical Languages*, pages 103–109.

[Specia et al.2013] Lucia Specia, Kashif Shah, Jose G.C. de Souza, and Trevor Cohn. 2013. QuEst - a translation quality estimation framework. In *Proceedings of the 51st Annual Meeting of the Association for Computational Linguistics: System Demonstrations*, pages 79–84, Sofia, Bulgaria, August. Association for Computational Linguistics.

[Zeiler2012] Matthew D. Zeiler. 2012. Adadelta: An adaptive learning rate method. *CoRR*, abs/1212.5701.

SimpleNets: Machine Translation Quality Estimation with Resource-Light Neural Networks

Gustavo Henrique Paetzold and **Lucia Specia**
Department of Computer Science
University of Sheffield, UK
{ghpaetzold1,l.specia}@sheffield.ac.uk

Abstract

We introduce SimpleNets: a resource-light solution to the sentence-level Quality Estimation task of WMT16 that combines Recurrent Neural Networks, word embedding models, and the principle of compositionality. The SimpleNets systems explore the idea that the quality of a translation can be derived from the quality of its n-grams. This approach has been successfully employed in Text Simplification quality assessment in the past. Our experiments show that, surprisingly, our models can learn more about a translation's quality by focusing on the original sentence, rather than on the translation itself.

1 Introduction

The task of Machine Translation Quality Estimation (QE) has gained noticeable popularity in the last few years. The goal of QE is to predict the quality of translations produced by a certain Machine Translation (MT) system in the absence of reference translations. Reliable solutions for QE can be useful in various tasks, such as improving post-editing efficiency (Specia, 2011), selecting high quality translations (Soricut and Echihabi, 2010), translation re-ranking (Shah and Specia, 2014), and visual assistance for manual translation revision (Bach et al., 2011).

QE can be performed in various ways in order to suit different purposes. The most widely addressed form of this task is sentence-level QE. Most existing work addresses this task as a supervised learning problem, in which a set of training examples is used to learn a model that predicts the quality of unseen translations. As quality labels, previous work uses either real valued scores estimated by humans, which require for a given QE system to address the task as a regression problem, or likert scale discrete values, which allow for the task to be addressed as either a regression or a classification problem.

Sentence-level QE has been covered by shared tasks organised by WMT since 2012, with subsequent years covering also word and document-level tasks. Recent advances in Distributional Semantics have been showing promising results in the context of QE strategies for different prediction levels. An example of that are modern word embedding architectures, such as the CBOW and Skip-Gram models introduced by (Mikolov et al., 2013b), which have been used as features in some of the best ranking systems in the sentence and word-level QE shared tasks of WMT15 (Bojar et al., 2015). Word embeddings are not only versatile, but also cheap to produce, making for both reliable and cost-effective QE solutions.

Neural Networks have also been successfully employed in QE. The FBK-UPV-UEdin (Bojar et al., 2014) and HDCL (Bojar et al., 2015) systems are good examples of that. They achieved 1st and 2nd places in the word-level QE tasks of WMT14 and WMT15, respectively, outperforming strategies that resort to much more resource-heavy features. Another successful example are neural Language Models for sentence-level QE (Shah et al., 2015).

We were not able to find, however, any examples of sentence-level QE systems that combine word embedding models and Neural Networks. In this paper, we present our efforts in doing so. We introduce SimpleNets: the resource-light and language agnostic sentence-level QE systems submitted to WMT16 that exploit the principle of compositionality for QE. In the Sections that follow, we describe the sentence-level QE task of WMT16, introduce the approach used by the SimpleNets systems, and present the results obtained.

Proceedings of the First Conference on Machine Translation, Volume 2: Shared Task Papers, pages 812–818,
Berlin, Germany, August 11-12, 2016. ©2016 Association for Computational Linguistics

2 Task, Datasets and Evaluation

SimpleNets are two systems submitted to the sentence-level QE task of WMT16. In this task, participants were challenged to predict real-valued quality scores in 0,100 of sentences translated from English into German. The translations were produced by an in-house phrase-based Statistical Machine Translation system, and were then post-edited by professional translators. The real-valued quality scores are HTER (Snover et al., 2006) values that represent the post-editing effort spent on each given translation.

The task organisers provided three datasets:

- **Training:** Contains 12,000 translation instances accompanied by their respective post-edits and HTER values.

- **Development:** Contains 1,000 translation instances accompanied by their respective post-edits and HTER values.

- **Test:** Contains 2,000 translation instances only, without their respective post-edits or HTER values.

Each instance is composed by the original sentence in English along with its translation in German. HTER scores were capped to 100. The organisers also provided 17 baseline feature values extracted using QuEst++ (Specia et al., 2015) for each dataset.

3 The SimpleNets Approach

SimpleNets aim to provide a resource-light and language agnostic approach for sentence-level QE. Our main goal in conceiving SimpleNets was to create a reliable enough solution that could be cheaply and easily adapted to other language pairs, moving away from the use of extensive feature engineering.

The SimpleNets approach was first introduced by Paetzold and Specia (2016a) as a solution to the shared task on Quality Assessment for Text Simplification of QATS 2016[1], in which participants were asked to create systems that predict discrete quality labels for a set of automatically produced text simplifications. Labels could take three values: "Good", "Ok" and "Bad". Text Simplification differs from Machine Translation in the sense

[1] http://qats2016.github.io

that instead of attempting to transform a text written in a source language to an equivalent text written in a target language, it attempts to transform a text in a way that it becomes more easily readable and/or understandable by a certain target audience, while still retaining the text's grammaticality and meaning.

For the Quality Assessment for Text Simplification task of QATS 2016, SimpleNets used the approach illustrated in Figure 1. For training, it performed the following five steps:

1. **Decomposition:** Given a simplification and maximum n-gram size M, it obtains the n-grams with size $1 \leq n \leq M$ of both original and simplified sentences.

2. **Union:** It then creates a pool of n-grams by simply obtaining the union of n-grams from the original and simplified sentences.

3. **Attribution:** Exploiting an interpretation of the principle of compositionality, which states that the quality of a simplification can be determined by the quality of its n-grams, it assigns the quality label of the simplification instance itself to each and every n-gram in the pool.

4. **Structuring:** Using a trained word embeddings model, it transforms each n-gram into a training instance described by a matrix $M{\times}N$, where M is the previously mentioned maximum n-gram size, and N the size of the word embeddings used. Each of the M rows in matrix $M{\times}N$ represent a given word in the n-gram, and each of the N columns, its embedding values. If an n-gram is smaller than N, the matrix is padded with embedding values composed strictly of zeroes.

5. **Learning:** Training instances are then fed into a deep Long Short-Term Memory (LSTM) Recurrent Neural Network in mini-batches so that a quality prediction model can be learned.

Notice that this process yields a model that predicts the quality of individual n-grams rather than the quality of a simplification in their entirety, which is not what was required for the task. To address this, each simplification in the test set is first processed through Decomposition, Union and

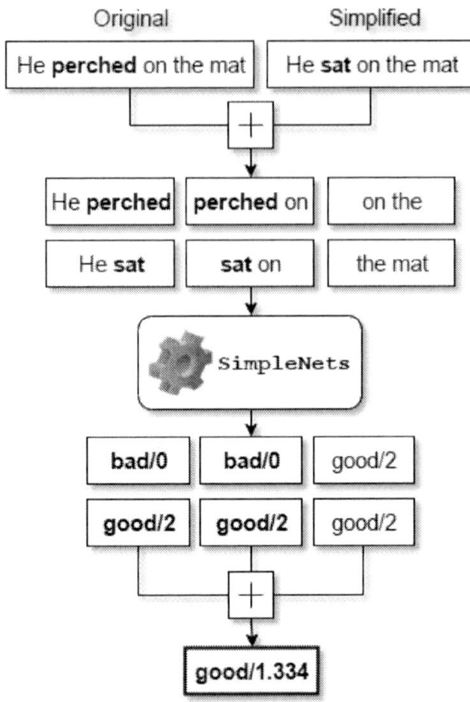

Figure 1: SimpleNets for Text Simplification

Structuring, but the complete quality prediction process has two complementary steps:

1. **Prediction:** The trained model is used to predict the quality of each n-gram of the simplification in question.

2. **Merging:** The quality of all n-grams in the simplification are merged using a certain policy, such as averaging.

After merging, a quality estimate for the simplification as a whole is produced. Although this approach has certain limitations, it addresses a very important challenge in using Recurrent Neural Networks for Text Simplification Quality Assessment: the small amount of training data available. With only 505 simplifications for training, it becomes very unlikely that a Recurrent Neural Network would be able to reliably learn a quality prediction model if it was presented with sentences in their entirety, such as how it has been done in Neural Translation and Text Generation (Schmidhuber, 2015). By splitting the sentences in the simplification in n-grams, the number of training instances available grows considerably, allowing for a better informed learning step. Addition-

ally, the length of the sequences used in the Recurrent Neural Network becomes shorter, which can help the network to generalise the knowledge available in the training set.

The results of the Quality Assessment for Text Simplification of QATS 2016 serve as evidence of the potential of this approach: SimpleNets ranked 1st in predicting the overall quality of simplifications. Nonetheless, the inherent differences between Machine Translation and Text Simplification make it impossible for the strategy described above to be directly applied to sentence-level QE without any adaptation. In the next Section, we describe how we adapt the SimpleNets approach for sentence-level QE.

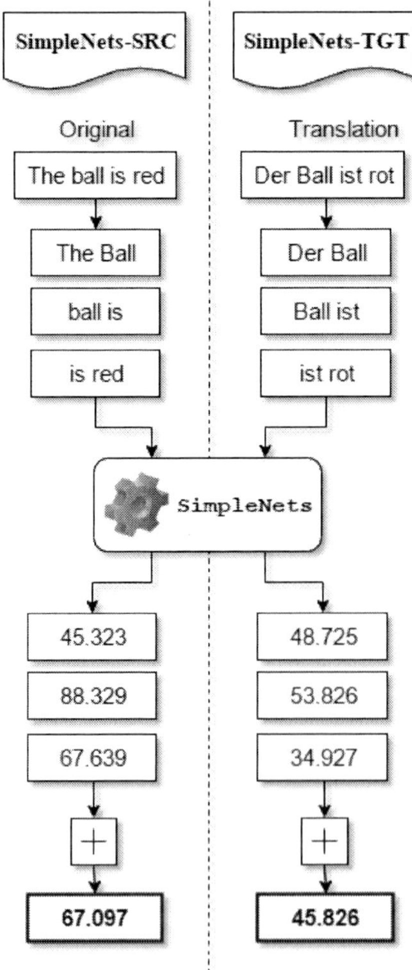

Figure 2: SimpleNets for Machine Translation

4 SimpleNets for Machine Translation

In order to use the SimpleNets strategy for sentence-level QE, we must address the biggest difference between Machine Translation and Text Simplification: while Text Simplification encompasses transformations within the constraints of a single language, Machine Translation has to handle two languages, which often have distinct vocabularies, grammar, etc. This difference prevents the application of the Union step from the process described in Section 3, since source (original) and target (translated) sentences are not in the same language, and hence cannot share the same word embeddings model during Structuring.

Another challenge in adapting SimpleNets for Machine Translation lies in the often found disparity in quality between the source sentence and its translation. Inspecting the datasets provided by the WMT16 organisers, we found that, unlike the source sentences, the majority of translations contain at least one noticeable error with respect to either grammar or coherence. This means that even if we used techniques such as the one employed by `bivec` (Luong et al., 2015), which allows for the training of bilingual word embeddings, the contrast between the quality of source and target sentences could confuse the SimpleNets approach, and hence compromise its capability of learning a reliable quality prediction model.

To overcome these challenges, we explore the hypothesis that SimpleNets can learn a better model for sentence-level QE by looking strictly at one of the sides of translations, rather than by trying to somehow combine the information from both the source and translated sentences. We train two variants of SimpleNets:

- **SimpleNets-TGT:** Explores the idea that the quality of a translation can be reliably determined based solely on the characteristics of the machine translated sentence itself, without the need to assess its relationship with the original sentence. This variant of SimpleNets aims to learn a model that is capable of quantifying the differences in quality of translated sentences.

- **SimpleNets-SRC:** Explores the idea that a translation's quality can be determined based solely on the original sentence itself, without any need to assess the intricacies of its translated version. This variant assumes that,

by focusing on the original sentences and the quality scores of their translations, SimpleNets can learn how to quantify just how likely the MT system in question will be of making a mistake while attempting to translate an unseen sentence. This is in line with work on QE that explores source features to measure the complexity of the source sentence (Specia et al., 2010).

Finally, we must also address the fact that, while the quality scores provided for the QATS 2016 shared task are discrete labels, the scores for the WMT16 task are real-valued. We solve this problem by simply replacing the multiple softmax activation nodes used in the QATS 2016 SimpleNets with a single dense node, and also by replacing the cross-entropy loss function with Mean Average Error.

The workflow followed by SimpleNets-TGT and SimpleNets-SRC is illustrated in Figure 2. In the Section that follow, we describe our experiments with these approaches.

5 Experimental Setup

To assess the efficacy of our SimpleNets, we train them over the training set provided by the organizers, which contain 12,000 instances. In order to select the architecture to be used by the LSTM networks of our SimpleNets, we resort to the technique used in (Paetzold and Specia, 2016a), in which each aspect of a Neural Network is determined through parameter optimisation over the development set. The optimisation metric used is Pearson correlation, since it is the main evaluation metric adopted by the WMT16 task. The aspects of the architecture considered and the values tested for each one of them are:

1. Number of hidden layers: 1 to 5 in steps of 1.

2. Hidden layer size: 100 to 500 in steps of 100.

3. Embeddings model: CBOW or Skip-Gram.

Even though SimpleNets-TGT and SimpleNets-SRC were optimised individually, the resulting architectures of the two approaches are surprisingly the same: three hidden layers with 200 nodes each, with CBOW embeddings.

The word embedding models used were trained with `word2vec` (Mikolov et al., 2013a). We use 300 word vector dimensions and train the

System	r	MAE	RMSE
YSDA/SNTX+BLEU+SVM	0.525	12.30	16.41
POSTECH/SENT-RNN-QV2	0.460	13.58	18.60
SHEF/SVM-NN-both-emb-QuEst	0.451	12.88	17.03
POSTECH/SENT-RNN-QV3	0.447	13.52	18.38
SHEF/SVM-NN-both-emb	0.430	12.97	17.33
UGENT/SVM2	0.412	19.57	24.11
UFAL/MULTIVEC	0.377	13.60	17.64
RTM/RTM-FS-SVR	0.376	13.46	17.81
UU/UU-SVM	0.370	13.43	18.15
UGENT/SVM1	0.363	20.01	24.63
RTM/RTM-SVR	0.358	13.59	18.06
BASELINE	0.351	13.53	18.39
SHEF/SimpleNets-SRC	0.320	13.92	18.23
SHEF/SimpleNets-TGT	0.283	14.35	18.22

Table 1: Sentence-level QE scores of systems submitted to the WMT16 task

models over a corpus of around 7 billion words comprised by SubIMDB (Paetzold and Specia, 2016b), UMBC webbase[2], News Crawl[3], SUB-TLEX (Brysbaert and New, 2009), Wikipedia and Simple Wikipedia (Kauchak, 2013).

For evaluation we use the task's official metrics, which are Pearson correlation (r), Mean Average Error and Root Mean Squared Error. We compare our SimpleNets with the baseline provided by the task organisers, as well as all other systems submitted. The baseline uses SVM regression with an RBF kernel and grid search for parameter optimisation.

6 Results

The task results illustrated in Table 1 reveal that SimpleNets are not as effective in sentence-level QE as they were for Text Simplification Quality Assessment. Although they outperform a few systems in terms of MAE and RMSE, when it comes to Pearson correlation, SimpleNets-SRC and SimpleNets-TGT feature at the bottom of the ranking.

What is even more surprising, however, is the difference between the performance of our SimpleNets systems. Intuitively, one would think that the n-grams of the translated sentence itself would be a more reliable indicator of a translation's quality, given that it only becomes possible for one to assess the grammaticality and meaning errors in a translation after inspecting the translated sentence itself. Interestingly, the performance scores suggest that the model employed by SimpleNets is more proficient in learning how difficult it will be for the source sentence to be translated.

The difference in performance between the SimpleNets variants became much more clear once we inspected the individual n-gram quality predictions made by them. Tables 2 and 3 show the n-grams in the development set with the highest and lowest HTER scores, as predicted by SimpleNets-TGT and SimpleNets-SRC, respectively, along the average gold HTER of the sentences in the development set which contain them. It can be noticed that the correlation between the highest scoring n-grams of SimpleNets-SRC and their average gold HTER seem to be much more pronounced than the one observed for the highest scoring n-grams of SimpleNets-TGT. The same phenomenon can be observed between the lowest scoring n-grams of the SimpleNets variants.

The Pearson correlation scores between predicted and average gold n-gram scores provide further insight on the limitations of SimpleNets in the context of sentence-level QE. While SimpleNets-TGT achieves a correlation score of 0.127, SimpleNets-SRC achieves a score of 0.151. Although SimpleNets-SRC does obtain a slightly higher Pearson score, both of them are low in comparison to other approaches, which ultimately suggests either that n-grams alone do not provide with enough information on the quality of a translation in order for a reliable Quality Estimation model to be learned, or that our method of assigning

[2]http://ebiquity.umbc.edu/resource/html/id/351
[3]http://www.statmt.org/wmt11/translation-task.html

Lowest			Highest		
N-gram	Pred.	Gold	N-gram	Pred.	Gold
das Dreieck ,	3.444	38.462	Zeile (ˆ	89.901	18.519
das Dreieck in	3.463	32.000	Vorteil dieser Methode	87.957	22.857
das Dreieck neben	3.519	11.111	Paket ist .	84.914	10.526
Dreieck , um	3.563	38.462	Lineares Licht verringert	84.042	29.412
ein Dreieck mit	3.648	76.923	einzelne Volltonfarben trennen	82.540	36.000

Table 2: N-grams with highest and lowest HTER scores, as predicted by SimpleNets-TGT

Lowest			Highest		
N-gram	Pred.	Gold	N-gram	Pred.	Gold
Backspace (Windows	2.539	10.000	gloss contour .	63.432	33.333
press Enter (	2.937	19.149	whale or white	63.432	46.154
or Option-click (	3.127	6.897	breakpoints , evaluating	63.092	57.576
Alt-click (Windows	3.128	6.897	halftone dot .	63.009	35.294
Command-D (Mac	3.397	22.857	lens focusing on	62.898	71.429

Table 3: N-grams with highest and lowest HTER scores, as predicted by SimpleNets-SRC

the translation's quality score to all n-grams during training prevents our models from learning to effectively differentiate between good and bad n-grams.

7 Final Remarks

In this paper we have described the SimpleNets systems for the sentence-level QE task of WMT16. SimpleNets aims to offer a resource-light solution to the task by exploiting Recurrent Neural Networks, word embedding models, and the principle of compositionality.

Two SimpleNets variants were described, SimpleNets-SRC and SimpleNets-TGT, which attempt to predict the quality of a translation based solely on the quality of the n-grams present in its source or target (translated) sides, respectively.

Although interesting and efficient, the SimpleNets systems have been shown not to perform well for the task at hand, featuring at the bottom of the task's final ranking. Nonetheless, our experiments have still provided with valuable insight on the impact of the source segment of a translation on the quality of its translation.

References

Nguyen Bach, Fei Huang, and Yaser Al-Onaizan. 2011. Goodness: a method for measuring MT confidence. In *Proceedings of the 49th ACL*, pages 211–219, Portland.

Ondrej Bojar, Christian Buck, Christian Federmann, Barry Haddow, Philipp Koehn, Johannes Leveling, Christof Monz, Pavel Pecina, Matt Post, Herve Saint-Amand, Radu Soricut, Lucia Specia, and Aleš Tamchyna. 2014. Findings of the 2014 workshop on statistical machine translation. In *Proceedings of the 9th WMT*, pages 12–58. Association for Computational Linguistics.

Ondřej Bojar, Rajen Chatterjee, Christian Federmann, Barry Haddow, Matthias Huck, Chris Hokamp, Philipp Koehn, Varvara Logacheva, Christof Monz, Matteo Negri, Matt Post, Carolina Scarton, Lucia Specia, and Marco Turchi. 2015. Findings of the 2015 workshop on statistical machine translation. In *Proceedings of the 10th WMT*, pages 1–46. Association for Computational Linguistics, September.

Marc Brysbaert and Boris New. 2009. Moving beyond kučera and francis: A critical evaluation of current word frequency norms and the introduction of a new and improved word frequency measure for american english. *Behavior research methods*, 41:977–990.

David Kauchak. 2013. Improving text simplification language modeling using unsimplified text data. In *Proceedings of the 51st ACL*, pages 1537–1546.

Minh-Thang Luong, Hieu Pham, and Christopher D. Manning. 2015. Bilingual word representations with monolingual quality in mind. In *Proceedings of the 2015 NAACL Workshop on Vector Space Modeling for NLP*, pages 151–159, Denver, United States.

Tomas Mikolov, Kai Chen, Greg Corrado, and Jeffrey Dean. 2013a. Efficient estimation of word representations in vector space. *arXiv preprint arXiv:1301.3781*.

Tomas Mikolov, Ilya Sutskever, Kai Chen, Greg S Corrado, and Jeff Dean. 2013b. Distributed representations of words and phrases and their compositionality. In *Advances in Neural Information Processing Systems 26*, pages 3111–3119.

Gustavo Henrique Paetzold and Lucia Specia. 2016a. Simplenets: Evaluating simplifiers with resource-light neural networks. In *Proceedings of the 1st QATS*, pages 42–46.

Gustavo Henrique Paetzold and Lucia Specia. 2016b. Unsupervised lexical simplification for non-native speakers. In *Proceedings of The 30th AAAI*.

Jürgen Schmidhuber. 2015. Deep learning in neural networks: An overview. *Neural Networks*, 61:85–117.

Kashif Shah and Lucia Specia. 2014. Quality estimation for translation selection. In *Proceedings of the 17th EAMT*.

Kashif Shah, Raymond W.M. Ng, Fethi Bougares, and Lucia Specia. 2015. Investigating continuous space language models for machine translation quality estimation. In *Proceedings of the 2015 EMNLP*, pages 1073–1078, Lisboa, Portugal.

Matthew Snover, Bonnie Dorr, Richard Schwartz, Linnea Micciulla, and John Makhoul. 2006. A study of translation edit rate with targeted human annotation. In *Proceedings of the 2006 AMTA*, pages 223–231.

Radu Soricut and Abdessamad Echihabi. 2010. Trustrank: Inducing trust in automatic translations via ranking. In *Proceedings of the 48th ACL*, pages 612–621.

Lucia Specia, Dhwaj Raj, and Marco Turchi. 2010. Machine translation evaluation versus quality estimation. *Machine Translation*, 24(1):39–50.

Lucia Specia, G Paetzold, and Carolina Scarton. 2015. Multi-level translation quality prediction with quest++. In *Proceedings of the 53rd ACL*, pages 115–120.

Lucia Specia. 2011. Exploiting objective annotations for measuring translation post-editing effort. In *Proceedings of the 15th EAMT*, pages 73–80.

Translation Quality Estimation using Recurrent Neural Network

Raj Nath Patel
CDAC Mumbai, India
`rajnathp@cdac.in`

Sasikumar M
CDAC Mumbai, India
`sasi@cdac.in`

Abstract

This paper describes our submission to the shared task on word/phrase level Quality Estimation (QE) in the First Conference on Statistical Machine Translation (WMT16). The objective of the shared task was to predict if the given word/phrase is a correct/incorrect (OK/BAD) translation in the given sentence. In this paper, we propose a novel approach for word level Quality Estimation using Recurrent Neural Network Language Model (RNN-LM) architecture. RNN-LMs have been found very effective in different Natural Language Processing (NLP) applications. RNN-LM is mainly used for vector space language modeling for different NLP problems. For this task, we modify the architecture of RNN-LM. The modified system predicts a label (OK/BAD) in the slot rather than predicting the word. The input to the system is a word sequence, similar to the standard RNN-LM. The approach is language independent and requires only the translated text for QE. To estimate the phrase level quality, we use the output of the word level QE system.

1 Introduction

Quality estimation is the process to predict the quality of translation without any reference translation (Blatz et al., 2004, Specia et al., 2009). Whereas, Machine Translation (MT) system evaluation does require references (human translation). QE could be done at word, phrase, sentence or document level. This paper describes the submission to the shared task on word and phrase level QE (Task 2) for English-German (en-de) MT.

The shared task has the trace of last five years' research in the field of QE (Callision-Burch et al., 2012; Bojar et al., 2013; Bojar et al., 2014; Bojar et al., 2015).

In recent years, RNN-LM has demonstrated exceptional performance in a variety of NLP applications (Mikolov et al., 2010; Mikolov et al., 2013a; Mikolov et al., 2013b; Socher et al., 2013a; Socher et al., 2013b). The RNN-LM represents each word as high-dimensional real-valued vectors, like the other continuous space language models such as feed forward neural network language models (Schwenk and Gauvain, 2002; Bengio et al., 2003; Morin and Bengio, 2005; Schwenk, 2007) and Hierarchical Log-Bi-linear language models (Minh and Hinton, 2009).

In this paper, we have used a modified version of RNN-LM, which accepts the word sequence (context window) as input and predicts label at the output for the middle word. For example, let us consider the following input/output sample:

English (MT input): Layer effects are retained by default .

German (MT output): " Effekte sind standardmig beibehalten .

German (Post-edited): Ebeneneffekte werden standardmig beibehalten .

Tags: BAD BAD BAD OK OK OK

Now if we have to predict the output tag (BAD) for the word "sind" in the MT output, our input sequence to the RNN-LM will be "Effekte sind standardmig" (if context window size is 3). Whereas, for standard RNN-LM model, "Effekte standardmig" would be the input to the network with "sind" as the output. We add padding at the start and end of the sentence according to the context window. The detailed description of the model and its implementation is given in section 3.

We have used the data provided by the or-

Proceedings of the First Conference on Machine Translation, Volume 2: Shared Task Papers, pages 819–824,
Berlin, Germany, August 11-12, 2016. ©2016 Association for Computational Linguistics

ganizers for the shared task on quality estimation (2016) which includes: (i) source sentence (ii) translated output (word/phrase level) (iii) word/phrase level tagging (OK/BAD) (iv) post edited translation (v) 22 baseline features (vi) word alignment. The goal of the task is to predict whether the given word/phrase is a correct/incorrect (OK/BAD) translation in the given sentence.

The remainder of the paper is organised as follows. Section 2 describes the related work. Section 3 presents RNN models we use, and its implementation. In section 4, we discuss the data distribution, our approaches, and results. Discussion of our methodology and different models is covered in section 5 followed by concluding remarks in section 6.

2 Related Work

For word level QE, supervised classification techniques are being used widely. Most of these approaches require manually designed features (Bojar et al., 2014), similar to the feature set provided by the organizers.

Logacheva et al. (2015) modeled the word level QE using the CRF++ tool with data selection and data bootstrapping in which data selection filters out the sentences having the smallest proportion of erroneous tokens and are assumed to be less useful for the task. The bootstrapping technique creates additional data instances and boosts the importance of BAD labels occurring in the training data. Shang et al. (2015) tried to solve the problem of label imbalance with creating sub-labels like OK_B (begin), OK_I (intermediate), OK_E (end). Shah et al. (2015) have used word embedding as an additional feature (+25 features) with SVM classifier. Bilingual Deep Neural Network (DNN) based model for word level QE was proposed by Kreutzer et al. (2015), in which word embedding was pre-trained and fine-tuned with other parameters of the network using stochastic gradient descent. de Souza et al. (2014) have used Bidirectional LSTM as a classifier for word level QE.

The architecture of RNN-LM has been used for Natural Language Understanding (NLU) (Yao et al., 2013; Yao et al., 2014) earlier. Our approach is quite similar to the Kreutzer et al. (2015), but we are using RNN instead of DNN. We have also tried to address the problem of label-imbalance, introducing sub-labels as suggested by Shang et

al. (2015).

3 RNN Models for QE

For this task, we exploited RNN's extensions, Long Short-Term Memory (LSTM) (Hochreiter and Schmidhuber, 1997) and Gated Recurrent Unit (GRU) (Cho et al., 2014). LSTM and GRU have shown to perform better at modeling the long-range dependencies in the data than the simple RNN. Simple RNN also suffers from the problem of exploding and vanishing gradient (Bengio et al., 1994). LSTM and GRU tackle this problem by introducing a gating mechanism. LSTM includes input, output and forget gates with a memory cell, whereas GRU has reset and update gates only (no memory cell). The detailed description of each model is given in the following subsections.

3.1 LSTM

Different researchers use slightly different LSTM variants (Graves, 2013; Yao et al., 2014; Jozefowicz et al., 2015). We implemented the version of LSTM described by the following set of equations:

$$i_t = sigm(W_{xi}x_t + W_{hi}h_{t-1} + b_i)$$
$$o_t = sigm(W_{xo}x_t + W_{ho}h_{t-1} + b_o)$$
$$f_t = sigm(W_{xf}x_t + W_{hf}h_{t-1} + b_f)$$
$$j_t = tanh(W_{xj}x_t + W_{hj}h_{t-1} + b_j)$$
$$c_t = c_{t-1} \odot f_t + i_t \odot j_t$$
$$h_t = tanh(c_t) \odot o_t$$

where $sigm$ is the logistic sigmoid function and $tanh$ is the hyperbolic tangent function to add non linearity in the network. $\odot$ is the element-wise multiplication of vectors. i, o, f are $input$, $output$, $forget$ gates respectively, j is the new memory content whereas c is the updated memory content. In these equations, W_* are the weight matrices and b_* are the bias vectors.

3.2 Deep LSTM

In this paper, we have used deep LSTM with two layers. Deep LSTM is created by stacking multiple LSTMs on the top of each other. We feed the output of the lower LSTM as the input to the upper LSTM. For example, if h_t is the output of the lower LSTM, we apply a matrix transform to form the input x_t for the upper LSTM. The matrix transformation allows having two consecutive LSTM layers of different sizes.

3.3 GRU

GRU is an architecture, which is quite similar to the LSTM. Chung et al. (2014) found that GRU outperforms LSTM on a suit of tasks. GRU is defined by the following set of equations:

$$r_t = sigm(W_{xr}x_t + W_{hr}h_{t-1} + b_r)$$
$$z_t = sigm(W_{xz}x_t + W_{hz}h_{t-1} + b_z)$$
$$\widetilde{h}_t = tanh(W_{xh}x_t + W_{hh}(r_t \odot h_{t-1}) + b_h)$$
$$h_t = z_t \odot h_{t-1} + (1 - z_t) \odot \widetilde{h}_t$$

In the above equations, W_* are the weight matrices and b_* are the bias vectors. r and z are known as the reset and update gate respectively. GRU does not use any separate memory cell as used in LSTM. However, gated mechanism controls the flow of information in the unit.

3.4 Implementation Details

We implemented all the models (LSTM, deep LSTM and GRU) with [1]THEANO framework (Bergstra et al., 2010; Bastien et al., 2012) as described above. For all the models in the paper, the size of a hidden layer is 100, the word embedding dimensionality is 100 and the context word window size is 5.

We initialized all the square weight matrices as random orthogonal matrices. All the bias vectors were initialized to zero. Other weight matrices were sampled from a Gaussian distribution with mean 0 and variance 0.01^2.

To update the model parameters, we have used Truncated Back-Propagation-Through-Time (T-BPTT) (Werbos, 1990) with stochastic gradient descent. We fixed the depth of BPTT to 7 for all the models. We used Ada-delta (Zeiler, 2012) to adapt the learning rate of each parameter automatically ($\epsilon = 10^{-6}$ and $\rho = 0.95$). We trained each model for 50 epochs.

4 Experiments and Results

In this section, we describe the experiments carried out for the shared task and present the experimental results.

4.1 Data distribution

We have used the corpus shared by the organizers for our experiments. The split for train-

[1]http://deeplearning.net/software/
theano/#download

ing/development/testing is detailed in table 1. Test1 split was used for evaluating the different experiments that we have carried out for the shared task. Evaluation scores displayed in the results section are against Test1 only. Organizers provided another set of test data (Test2), against which all the submitted systems were evaluated.

	#Sentences	#Tokens
Train	11000	184697
Dev	1000	17777
Test1	1000	16543
Test2	2000	34477

Table 1: Corpus distribusion.

4.2 Methodology

In the following subsections, we discuss our approaches for word/phrase level quality estimation.

4.2.1 Word Level QE

Our experiments are mainly focused on the word level QE. We have used the output of the word level QE system for the estimation of the phrase level quality.

As mentioned above, we have used the modified RNN-LM architecture for the experiments. Baseline (LSTM) system was developed by training word embedding from scratch with other parameters of the model. In another set of experiments, we have pre-trained the word embedding with *word2vec* (Mikolov et al., 2013b), and further tuned with the training of the model parameters. For pretraining, we have used an additional corpus (2M sentences approx.) from English-German Europarl data (Koehn, 2005).

For bilingual models, we restructured the source sentence (English) according to the target (German) using word alignment provided by the organizers. For many-to-one mapping in the alignment (English-German), we chose the first alignment only. The 'NULL' token was assigned to the words where were not aligned with any word on the target side. The input of the model is constructed by concatenating context words of source and target. For example, consider the source word sequence $s_1s_2s_3$, and the target word sequence $t_1t_2t_3$, then the input to the network will be $s_1s_2s_3t_1t_2t_3$.

In the training data, the distribution of the labels (OK/BAD) is skewed (OK to BAD ratio is approx. 4:1). To handle the issue, we tried one of the strategies proposed by Shang et al. (2015), in which we replace 'OK' label with sub-labels to balance the distribution. The sub-labels are OK_B, OK_I, OK_E, depending on the location of the token in the sentence.

4.2.2 Phrase Level QE

For phrase level QE, we have not trained any explicit system. As it was mentioned by the organizers that a phrase is tagged as 'BAD', if any word in the phrase is an incorrect translation. So, We have taken the output of the word level QE system and tagged the phrase as 'BAD', if any word in the phrase boundary is tagged 'BAD'. And other phrases (all words have the OK tag) are simply tagged as 'OK'.

Model/Test	F1 BAD	F1 OK
Baseline (LSTM)	35.60	82.93
LSTM_PT	37.27	83.25
LSTM_PT_SL	36.27	81.38
LSTM_BL	36.18	82.51
LSTM_BL_PT	38.53	83.80
LSTM_BL_PT_SL	39.17	83.20
DeepLSTM	35.86	80.35
DeepLSTM_PT	36.81	82.51
DeepLSTM_PT_SL	36.13	81.32
DeepLSTM_BL	37.41	81.92
DeepLSTM_BL_PT	38.38	81.41
DeepLSTM_BL_PT_SL	37.04	82.40
GRU	37.98	84.29
GRU_PT	39.42	84.81
GRU_PT_SL	**40.46**	**83.09**
GRU_BL	41.56	84.57
GRU_BL_PT	42.46	83.76
GRU_BL_PT_SL	42.92	83.62

Table 2: F1 scores of different experiments for Word level QE. (PT: Pretrain; BL: Bilingual; SL: Sublabels)

4.3 Results

To develop a baseline system for word and phrase level QE, organizers have used the baseline features (22 features) to train a Conditional Random Field (CRF) model with CRFSuite tool. The results of the experiments against Test2 are displayed in table 4 and 5.

We have evaluated our systems using the F1-score. As 'OK' class is dominant in the data and a naive system tagging all the words 'OK' will score high. Hence, F1-score of the 'BAD' class has been used as a primary metric for the system evaluation. We have used the separate set of test and development corpus as shown in table 1. The evaluation of all the experiments against Test1 corpus is displayed in table 2 for word level QE. Results for

Model/Test	F1 BAD	F1 OK
Baseline (LSTM)	43.46	75.41
LSTM_PT	45.41	75.67
LSTM_PT_SL	44.92	73.11
LSTM_BL	44.43	74.93
LSTM_BL_PT	45.75	77.17
LSTM_BL_PT_SL	46.96	75.73
DeepLSTM	43.83	71.98
DeepLSTM_PT	44.92	74.17
DeepLSTM_PT_SL	43.85	72.32
DeepLSTM_BL	45.65	73.81
DeepLSTM_BL_PT	46.50	72.68
DeepLSTM_BL_PT_SL	45.63	74.57
GRU	45.70	77.86
GRU_PT	46.49	80.00
GRU_PT_SL	**48.38**	**76.14**
GRU_BL	48.11	77.69
GRU_BL_PT	49.58	76.88
GRU_BL_PT_SL	49.61	77.20

Table 3: F1 scores of different experiments for Phrase level QE.

phrase level QE are shown in table 3.

From the result tables, it is evident that GRU outperforms LSTM as reported by Chung et al. (2014) for this task as well. Pre-training is helpful in all the models. Also, the introduction of sub-labels is able to handle the problem of label-imbalance up to some extent. The results of Bilingual models are better than monolingual models, as reported by Kreutzer et al. (2015).

4.4 Submission to the shared task

We have participated in the Task-2, which includes word and phrase level quality estimation. The submitted system setting was: $GRU + Pretrain + Sublabels$, which is **marked** in the result tables (2 and 3) as well. Table 4 and 5 detail the [2]results of the submission on Test2 corpus. The submission results were provided by the organizers.

	F1 BAD	F1 OK
Baseline (CRF)	36.82	88.00
Submitted system	41.92	84.21

Table 4: Results, word level submission.

	F1 BAD	F1 OK
Baseline (CRF)	40.14	80.01
Submitted system	50.31	75.50

Table 5: Results, phrase level submission.

---

[2]http://www.quest.dcs.shef.ac.uk/
wmt16_files_qe/wmt16_task2_results.pdf

5 Discussion

The approach is language independent and it uses only context words' vector for predicting the tag for a word. In the other words, we check if any word fits (grammatically) in the given slot of words or not. We could use language specific features to enhance the classification accuracy, though. Experiments with bilingual models are similar to the concept of adding more features to any machine learning algorithm. In monolingual models, we use only target (German) words' vector as feature whereas, in bilingual models, we use source (English) words' vector also. A challenge which machine learning practitioners often face is, how to deal with skewed classes in classification problems. The distribution of classes (OK/BAD) is skewed in our case as well. To handle the issue, we tried to balance the distribution of classes by introducing the sub-labels.

LSTM and GRU are quite similar models, except the gating mechanism. It is hard to say which model will perform better in what conditions or in general (Chung et al., 2014). In this paper and in general as well, this restricts us to conduct only the empirical comparison between the LSTM and the GRU units. Deep models generally perform better than the shallow models, which is opposite for this task where LSTM outperforms Deep LSTM. The reason could be the insufficient data for training the deep models.

6 Conclusion and Future Work

We have developed a language independent word/phrase level Quality Estimation system using RNN. We have used RNN-LM architecture, with LSTM, deep LSTM, and GRU. We showed that these models benefit from pretraining and the introduction of sub-labels. Also, models with bilingual features outperform the monolingual models.

We can extend the work for sentence and document level quality estimation. Improving the word level quality estimation with data selection and bootstrapping (Logacheva et al., 2015), more effective ways to handle label-imbalance, training bigger models, using language specific feature, other variations of LSTM architecture etc., are the other possibilities.

References

Frederic Bastien, Pascal Lamblin, Razvan Pascanu, James Bergstra, Ian Goodfellow, Arnaud Bergeron, Nicolas Bouchard, David Warde-Farley, and Yoshua Bengio. 2012. Theano: new features and speed improvements. In *NIPS 2012 deep learning workshop*.

Yoshua Bengio, Patrice Simard, and Paolo Frasconi. 1994. Learning long-term dependencies with gradient descent is difficult. In *IEEE Transactions on Neural Networks*, pages 157–166.

Yoshua Bengio, Rejean Ducharme, Pascal Vincent, and Christian Jauvin. 2003. A neural probabilistic language model. In *Journal of Machine Learning Reseach*, volume 3.

James Bergstra, Olivier Breuleux, Frederic Bastien, Pascal Lamblin, Razvan Pascanu, Guillaume Desjardins, Joseph Turian, David Warde-Farley, and Yoshua Bengio. 2010. Theano: a CPU and GPU math expression compiler. In *Proceedings of the Python for scientific computing conference (SciPy)*, volume 4.

John Blatz, Erin Fitzgerald, George Fostera, Simona Gandrabur, Cyril Goutte, Alex Kulesza, Alberto Sanchis, and Nicola Ueffing. 2004. Confidence Estimation for Machine Translation. In *COLING 2014*, pages 315–321. Geneva, Switzerland.

Ondrej Bojar, Christian Buck, Chris Callison-Burch, Christian Federmann, Barry Haddow, Philipp Koehn, Christof Monz, Matt Post, Radu Soricut, and Lucia Specia. 2013. Findings of the 2013 workshop on statistical machine translation. In *WMT13*, pages 1–44. Sofia, Bulgaria.

Ondrej Bojar, Christian Buck, Christian Federman, Barry Haddow, Philipp Koehn, Johannes Leveling, Christof Monz, Pavel Pecina, Matt Post, Herve Saint-Amand, Radu Soricut, Lucia Specia, and Ales Tamchyna. 2014. Findings of the 2014 workshop on statistical machine translation. In *WMT14*, pages 12–58. Baltimore, MD.

Ondej Bojar, Rajen Chatterjee, Christian Federmann, Barry Haddow, Matthias Huck, Chris Hokamp, Philipp Koehn, Varvara Logacheva, Christof Monz, Matteo Negri, Matt Post, Carolina Scarton, Lucia Specia, and Marco Turchi. 2015. Findings of the 2015 workshop on statistical machine translation. In *WMT15*, pages 1–47. Lisbon, Portugal.

Chris Callison-Burch, Philipp Koehn, Christof Monz, Matt Post, Radu Soricut, and Lucia Specia. 2012. Findings of the 2012 workshop on statistical machine translation. In *WMT12*, pages 10–51. Montreal, Canada.

Kyunghyun Cho, Bart Van Merrinboer, Caglar Gulcehre, Dzmitry Bahdanau, Fethi Bougares, Holger Schwenk, and Yoshua Bengio. 2014. Learning phrase representations using RNN encoder-decoder for statistical machine translation. In *Proceedings of the Conference on Empirical Methods in Natural Language Processing (EMNLP)*. Doha, Qatar.

Junyoung Chung, Caglar Gulcehre, KyungHyun Cho, and Yoshua Bengio. 2014. Empirical evaluation of gated recurrent neural networks on sequence modeling. In *arXiv:1412.3555 [cs.NE]*.

Jose GC de Souza, U. Politecnica de Valencia, Christian Buck, Marco Turchi, and Matteo Negri. 2014. FBK-UPV-UEdin participation in the WMT14 Quality Estimation shared-task. In *WMT14*, pages 322–328.

Alex Graves. 2013. Generating sequences with recurrent neural networks. In *arXiv:1308.0850 [cs.NE]*.

Sepp Hochreiter and Jurgen Schmidhuber. 1997. Long short-term memory. In *Neural computation*, pages 1735–1780.

Rafal Jozefowicz, Wojciech Zaremba, and Ilya Sutskever. 2015. An empirical exploration of recurrent network architectures. In *Proceedings of the 32nd International Conference on Machine Learning*, pages 2342–2350.

Philipp Koehn. 2005. Europarl: A parallel corpus for statistical machine translation. In *MT summit*, volume 5, pages 79–86.

Julia Kreutzer, Shigehiko Schamoni, and Stefan Riezler. 2015. QUality Estimation from ScraTCH (QUETCH): Deep Learning for Word-level Translation Quality Estimation. In *WMT15*, pages 316–322. Lisboa, Portugal.

Varvara Logacheva, Chris Hokamp, and Lucia Specia. 2015. Data enhancement and selection strategies for the word-level Quality Estimation. In *WMT15*, pages 330–335. Lisboa, Portugal.

Tomas Mikolov, Martin Karafiat, Lukas Burget, Jan Cernocky, and Sanjeev Khudanpur. 2010. Recurrent neural network based language model. In *Proceedings of Interspeech*, volume 2. Makuhari, Chiba, Japan.

Tomas Mikolov, Quoc V Le, and Ilya Sutskever. 2013a. Exploiting Similarities among Languages for Machine Translation. In *CoRR*, pages 1–10.

Tomas Mikolov, Ilya Sutskever, Kai Chen, Greg S Corrado, and Jeff Dean. 2013b. Distributed representations of words and phrases and their compositionality. In *Advances in Neural Information Processing Systems*, pages 3111–3119.

Andriy Mnih and Geoffrey E. Hinton. 2009. A scalable hierarchical distributed language model. In *Advances in neural information processing systems*, pages 1081–1088.

Frederic Morin and Yoshua Bengio. 2005. Hierarchical Probabilistic Neural Network Language Model. In *Aistats*, volume 5, pages 246–252.

Holger Schwenk and Jean-Luc Gauvain. 2002. Connectionist language modeling for large vocabulary continuous speech recognition. In *ICASSP. IEEE*, volume 1, pages I–765.

Holger Schwenk. 2007. Continuous space language models. In *Computer Speech and Language*, volume 21, pages 492–518.

Kashif Shah, Varvara Logacheva, G. Paetzold, Frederic Blain, Daniel Beck, Fethi Bougares, and Lucia Specia. 2015. SHEF-NN: Translation Quality Estimation with Neural Networks. In *WMT15*, pages 342–347. Lisboa, Portugal.

Liugang Shang, Dongfeng Cai, and Duo Ji. 2015. Strategy-Based Technology for Estimating MT Quality. In *WMT15*, pages 248–352. Lisboa, Portugal.

Richard Socher, John Bauer, Christopher D. Manning, , and Andrew Y. Ng. 2013a. Parsing With Compositional Vector Grammars. In *Proceedings of the ACL 2013*, pages 455–465.

Richard Socher, Alex Perelygin, , and Jy Wu. 2013b. Recursive deep models for semantic compositionality over a sentiment treebank. In *Proceedings of EMNLP*, pages 1631–1642.

Lucia Specia, Marco Turchi, Nicola Cancedda, Marc Dymetman, and Nello Cristianini. 2009. Estimating the Sentence-Level Quality of Machine Translation Systems. In *EACL 2009*, pages 28–37. Barcelona, Spain.

Paul J. Werbos. 1990. Backpropagation through time: what it does and how to do it. In *IEEE*, volume 78, pages 550–1560.

Kaisheng Yao, Geoffrey Zweig, Mei-Yuh Hwang, Yangyang Shi, and Dong Yu. 2013. Recurrent neural networks for language understanding. In *INTERSPEECH*, pages 2524–2528.

Kaisheng Yao, Baolin Peng, Yu Zhang, Dong Yu, Geoffrey Zweig, and Yangyang Shi. 2014. Spoken language understanding using long short-term memory neural networks. In *Spoken Language Technology Workshop (SLT), IEEE*, pages 189–194.

Matthew D. Zeiler. 2012. ADADELTA: an adaptive learning rate method. In *arXiv:1212.5701 [cs.LG]*.

The UU Submission to the Machine Translation Quality Estimation Task

Oscar Sagemo, Sara Stymne
Uppsala University
Department of Linguistics and Philology
`Oscar.Sagemo1914@student.uu.se, sara.stymne@lingfil.uu.se`

Abstract

This paper outlines the UU-SVM system for Task 1 of the WMT16 Shared Task in Quality Estimation. Our system uses Support Vector Machine Regression to investigate the impact of a series of features aiming to convey translation quality. We propose novel features measuring reordering and noun translation errors. We show that we can outperform the baseline when we combine it with a subset of our new features.

1 Introduction

In this paper, we describe Uppsala University's submission to the WMT16 shared task in Quality Estimation (QE). Machine Translation Quality Estimation is the task of assessing the quality of a machine translated unit at runtime, without using reference translations. The different units considered for the 2016 shared task in quality estimation are words, phrases and sentences. We participated in task 1, which focuses on sentence-level QE.

Most modern approaches set the task as a regression problem - attempting to accurately predict a continuous quality label through representing translations with feature vectors. The performance of such approaches rely on determining and extracting features that correlate strongly with the proposed quality label and the impact of a wide variety of features. Different types of systems, including system-dependent (glass-box) or system-independent (black-box), linguistically or statistically motivated features, have been explored (Blatz et al., 2004; Quirk, 2004; Specia et al., 2009). The quality label proposed for the sentence-level task is Human-targeted Translation Edit Rate (HTER) (Snover et al., 2006), which

sets the focus on predicting the post-editing effort needed to correct the translation.

As no information from the MT system used to translate the data was provided, only black-box features can be considered. Furthermore, since the dataset only consists of one translation direction, English-German, language-specific features can be exploited. Our submission proposes novel features attempting to capture some common noun translation errors from English to German as well as measuring the amount of reordering done by the SMT system. These features are combined with more generic linguistically motivated black-box features that improved the prediction accuracy.

2 Features and resources

In this section we will describe the dataset we used and the baseline system. We also give a detailed description of our suggested features.

2.1 Dataset

The dataset for task 1 spans a total of 15,000 English-German translations from the IT domain. Each entry consists of a source segment, its machine translation, a post-edition of the translation and an edit distance score (HTER) derived from the post-edited version. The dataset was split into 12,000 segments as training data, 1,000 for development and 2,000 for testing. The translations were produced by a single in-house MT system from which no system-dependent information was made available for the sentence-level task. These translations were post-edited by professional translators and the HTER was computed using TER(default settings: tokenised, case insensitive, exact matching only, but with scores capped to 100).

In addition to the dataset, we were provided with a set of resources consisting of a language

Proceedings of the First Conference on Machine Translation, Volume 2: Shared Task Papers, pages 825–830,
Berlin, Germany, August 11-12, 2016. ©2016 Association for Computational Linguistics

model (LM), an ngram-counts list of raw ngram occurrences as well as a lexical translation table.

2.2 Baseline system

In order to establish a common ground for measurement, we were provided with a robust baseline system trained with 17 features[1]. The same baseline system has been used for all previous shared tasks in QE and has proven to be well performing across multiple language pairs and text domains (Bojar et al., 2015). The features quantify the complexity of the source sentence and the fluency of the target sentence, by utilizing corpus frequencies, LM probabilites and token counts. We use these 17 baseline features (b17) as the foundation of our system and measure our performance in relation to the baseline system.

2.3 Proposed features

In addition to the provided resources, further tools were used to extract the features: A modified version of the QuEst++ framework, (Specia et al., 2015) with processors and features added and modified where needed, used to extract the baseline features and a majority of our features. Fast_align (Dyer et al., 2013) was used to generate word alignment files. We used Berkeley Parser (Petrov et al., 2006), trained with the included grammars for English and German, to extract phrase structure-based features. We also used SRILM (Stolcke, 2002) to train a Part-Of-Speech (POS) Language Model over the training dataset as well as to compute all LM-based segment probabilities and perplexities. Lastly, we used Tree-Tagger (Schmid, 1994) trained with the included models for English and German to obtain all POS-related features.

We aimed to obtain consistent features capturing sources of and results of difficulties for SMT systems by quantifying noun translation errors, reordering measures, grammatical correspondence and structural integrity. The following features were considered and tested for inclusion in the feature set for the submission:

Noun Translation Errors In our previous work on English–German SMT (Stymne et al., 2013), we have noted that the translation of noun compounds is problematic. It is common for English compounds, that are written as separate words, to be rendered as separate words or genitive constructions in German, instead of the idiomatic compound. Compounds tend to be common in technical domains, such as IT.

The language-specific scenario in the task setting allowed us to specifically model these issues. We implemented two features attempting to capture these errors in the direction English-German.

- Ratio of Noun groups between source and target

- Ratio of Genitive constructions between source and target

Due to the fact that split compound nouns is a common translation error for German machine translations, we implemented a feature to look for sequences of nouns in target text. The feature looks for any noun group in both source and target and is computed as the ratio of noun groups, where noun groups are defined as the number of occurrences of sequences of two or more nouns.

Another common compound translation is genitive constructions, which can be over-produced in German. We designed a feature that looks for possible genitive constructions in source and target, and is computed as the ratio of genitive constructions, defined as follows:

German: Any noun or proper noun preceded by a noun and the genitive article *des/der*.

English: Any noun or proper noun preceded by a noun and the possesive clitic *'s* or the possessive preposition *of*.

Note that these patterns could also match other constructions since "of" can have other uses and "der" is also used for masculine nominative and feminine dative.

Reordering measures Reordering is problematic for MT in general, and for English–German especially for the placement of verbs, which differ between these languages. We explored three metrics that measure the amount of reordering done by the MT system, to investigate a correlation between SMT reordering and edit operations. All metrics are based on alignments between individual words.

- Crossing score: the number of crossings in alignments between source and target

- Kendall Tau distance between alignments in source and target

---

[1]http://www.quest.dcs.shef.ac.uk/ quest_files/features_blackbox_baseline_ 17

- Squared Kendall Tau distance between alignments in source and target

Crossing score was suggested by Genzel (2010) for SMT reordering and Tau was suggested by Birch and Osborne (2011) for use in a standard metric with a reference translation. To our knowledge we are the first to use these measures for quality estimation. The features are computed over the crossing link pairs in a word alignment file, where the number of crossing links considers crossings of all lengths and the Squared Kendall Tau Distance (SKTD) is defined as shown in Eq. 1.

$$\mathrm{SKTD} = 1 - \sqrt{\frac{|\text{crossing link pairs}|}{|\text{link pairs}|}} \quad (1)$$

Grammatical correspondence We explored several features quantifying grammatical discrepancy, mainly measured in terms of occurences of syntactic phrases or POS tags in accordance with the work of Felice and Specia (2012).

- Ratio of percentage of verb phrases between source and target

- Ratio of percentage of noun phrases between source and target

- Ratio of percentage of nouns between source and target

- Ratio of percentage of pronouns between source and target

- Ratio of percentage of verbs between source and target

- Ratio of percentage of tokens consisting of alphabetic symbols between source and target

Different means of parameterising the relationship between syntactic and POS constituents were explored, we tested the absolute difference, the ratio of occurences as well as the ratio of percentage. We concluded that the ratio of percentage was the preferred metric.

Structural integrity We also investigated features measuring well-formedness as conveyed by syntactic parse trees in line with Avramidis (2012) as well as POS language models

- Source PCFG average confidence of all possible parses in the parser n-best list

- Target PCFG average confidence of all possible parses in the parser n-best list

- Source PCFG log probability

- Target PCFG log probability

- LM log perplexity of POS of the target

- LM log probability of POS of the target

We experimented with different sizes of n-best lists and found that small sizes (1-3) were preferred due to difficulties in coming up with more parse trees for several of the input sentences.

2.4 Learning

As per the baseline system methodology, we use SVM regression (Chang and Lin, 2011) with a Radial Basis Function (RBF) kernel and a grid search algorithm for parameter optimisation, implemented in QuEst++.

3 Experiments

Initial experiments consisted of concatenating features with the baseline set, in order to sort out the features that had a positive impact on performance and disregard the ones that had a negative impact. As per the QuEst++ framework, performance was measured in terms of Mean Average Error (MAE) and Root Mean Square Error (RMSE) which are defined in Eqs. 2 and 3, where x_i , ... , x_n are the values predicted by the SVM model and y_i , ... , y_n are the values provided by the organisers.

$$\mathrm{MAE} = \frac{1}{n} \sum_{i}^{n} |x_i - y_i| \quad (2)$$

$$\mathrm{RMSE} = \sqrt{\frac{1}{n} \sum_{i}^{n} x_i - y_i^2} \quad (3)$$

Positive Impact A majority of the proposed features proved to have a negative impact on the performance metrics through our experiments, leaving only 5/16 features with a positive impact:

	MAE	RMSE
baseline (b17)	13.826	19.507
b17 + Noun Group Ratio	13.759	19.503
b17 + Source PCFG	13.812	19.515
b17 + Target PCFG	13.819	19.534
b17 + Tau	13.801	19.460
b17 + Verb ratio	13.799	19.604
Combined	13.723	19.552

Table 1: Performance in terms of MAE and RMSE for the indiviual features in the Positive Impact set

Feature combinations	MAE	RMSE
baseline	13.826	19.507
+ Source PCFG	13.812	19.515
+ Target PCFG	13.805	19.560
+ Verb ratio	13.795	19.627
+ Tau	13.757	19.522
+ Noun Group Ratio	13.723	19.552

Table 2: Performance in terms of MAE and RMSE for the combined features resulting in the submitted system

- Noun group ratio

- Kendall Tau distance

- Source PCFG log probability

- Target PCFG log probability

- Ratio of percentage of verbs

We present their individual performance when added to the baseline features in Table 1 and when added in combination in Table 2. All these features have an individual positive impact on MAE, whereas only noun group ratio and Tau perform well on RMSE. Furthermore, the noun group ratio and Kendall Tau Distance showed promising results both individually and in combination with our other new features. The verb ratio feature, however, increased RMSE individually but was included in our final system despite this due to its contribution to MAE when combined, as MAE carries a heavier weight in evaluation. Due to time constraints, we did not investigate the relationship between the RMSE and MAE further.

The performance of the novel features in the noun translation errors and reordering measure groups in Table 3. For the reordering features, that are all different ways of measuring the amount of

	MAE	RMSE
baseline (b17)	13.826	19.507
b17 + Crossings	13.834	19.480
b17 + SKTD	13.836	19.468
b17 + Tau	13.801	19.460
b17 + Noun Group Ratio	13.759	19.503
b17 + Genitive constructions	13.840	19.539

Table 3: Performance in terms of MAE and RMSE for the indiviual features describing noun translation errors and reordering

reordering based on word alignments, we notice that only Tau give a positive impact. Our feature for genitive constructions did not give good results.

The surprisingly small amount of positive features may be a result of a disagreement between the proposed features and the data. The features mainly rely on linguistic analyses while the data, being exclusively from the IT-Domain, is inherently irregular. POS- and syntactic phrase-features appears to be particularly unreliable which may be due to the nature of the domain, where series of constituents of uncommon character are frequent, e.g:

Choose File > Save As , and choose
Photoshop DCS 1.0 or Photoshop DCS
2.0 from the Format menu .

$\downarrow$

Wählen Sie ” Bearbeiten ” ”
Voreinstellungen ” (Windows) bzw. ”
Bridge CS4 ” > ” Voreinstellungen ” (
Mac OS) und klicken Sie auf ”
Miniaturen . ”

This appears to especially affect syntactic parsers trained on out-of-domain PCFGs as phrase comparisons were error prone and the parser often had difficulties generating more than 3 trees per sentence. Nevertheless, the probabilities of the parse trees for both source and target slightly increased the performance of the model.

In order to improve the performance of syntactic and POS-related features, a first step would be to use parsers and taggers trained with or adapted to similar in-domain data, as the IT-domain notably differs from the conventional treebanks and corpora commonly used in the field. Furthermore, we think it would be worthwhile to explore the effect of employing dependency parsers rather than constituency-based parsers for measuring structural integrity and grammatical correspondence.

The amount of reordering done as measured in this paper can suffice to indicate irregularities in reordering through the learning methods. However, simply relying on counting crossings in 1-1 alignments, could inflict noise. All our measures for reordering only measures the difference in word order in a language independent way. For a specific language pair like English–German it would be useful to be able to measure known word order divergences like verb placement, through more carefully designed and targeted measures. A better solution could be adapt the feature to fit the expected reordering for specific translation directions and to quantify it based on infringements of word-order expectations.

4 Conclusion

We trained regression models using a combination of the baseline features and a series of features intended to convey translation quality. We also proposed novel features modeling noun translation errors and reordering amount. A majority of the proposed features were discarded through our experiments with the development data, yet the final feature set was sufficient to surpass the baseline. Of the final features, the noun group ratio showed particularly promising results, as seen in Table 1.

Results were submitted for both the scoring and ranking subtasks of the sentence-level task. The system was, however, intended and optimized for the scoring task. Therefore the ranks were simply defined as the ascending order of the scores with no separate optimization. When computing our model for the final test set, the training scores were capped to an upper bound of 100 and the predicted scores were capped to a lower bound of 0.

In the future we would like to investigate an expanded set of translation errors as well as adapt the concept of reordering measures as features to expected reordering in specific translation directions.

Acknowledgments

This work forms part of the Swedish strategic research programme eSSENCE.

References

Eleftherios Avramidis. 2012. Quality estimation for machine translation output using linguistic analysis and decoding features. In *Proceedings of the seventh workshop on statistical machine translation*, pages 84–90. Association for Computational Linguistics.

Alexandra Birch and Miles Osborne. 2011. Reordering metrics for mt. In *Proceedings of the 49th Annual Meeting of the Association for Computational Linguistics: Human Language Technologies-Volume 1*, pages 1027–1035. Association for Computational Linguistics.

John Blatz, Erin Fitzgerald, George Foster, Simona Gandrabur, Cyril Goutte, Alex Kulesza, Alberto Sanchis, and Nicola Ueffing. 2004. Confidence estimation for machine translation. In *Proceedings of the 20th international conference on Computational Linguistics*, page 315. Association for Computational Linguistics.

Ondřej Bojar, Rajen Chatterjee, Christian Federmann, Barry Haddow, Matthias Huck, Chris Hokamp, Philipp Koehn, Varvara Logacheva, Christof Monz, Matteo Negri, Matt Post, Carolina Scarton, Lucia Specia, and Marco Turchi. 2015. Findings of the 2015 workshop on statistical machine translation. In *Proceedings of the Tenth Workshop on Statistical Machine Translation*, pages 1–46, Lisbon, Portugal, September. Association for Computational Linguistics.

Chih-Chung Chang and Chih-Jen Lin. 2011. Libsvm: a library for support vector machines. *ACM Transactions on Intelligent Systems and Technology (TIST)*, 2(3):27.

Chris Dyer, Victor Chahuneau, and Noah A Smith. 2013. A simple, fast, and effective reparameterization of ibm model 2. In *Proceedings of the Conference of the North American Chapter of the Association for Computational Linguistics: Human Language Technologies*, pages 644–649. Association for Computational Linguistics.

Mariano Felice and Lucia Specia. 2012. Linguistic features for quality estimation. In *Proceedings of the Seventh Workshop on Statistical Machine Translation*, pages 96–103. Association for Computational Linguistics.

Dmitriy Genzel. 2010. Automatically learning source-side reordering rules for large scale machine translation. In *Proceedings of the 23rd international conference on computational linguistics*, pages 376–384. Association for Computational Linguistics.

Slav Petrov, Leon Barrett, Romain Thibaux, and Dan Klein. 2006. Learning accurate, compact, and interpretable tree annotation. In *Proceedings of the 21st International Conference on Computational Linguistics and the 44th annual meeting of the Association for Computational Linguistics*, pages 433–440. Association for Computational Linguistics.

Christopher Quirk. 2004. Training a sentence-level machine translation confidence measure. In *Proceedings of the Fourth International Conference on*

Language Resources and Evaluation (LREC), pages 825–828, Lisbon, Portugal.

Helmut Schmid. 1994. Probabilistic part-of-speech tagging using decision trees. In *Proceedings of the International Conference on New Methods in Language Processing*, pages 44–49, Manchester, UK.

Matthew Snover, Bonnie Dorr, Richard Schwartz, Linnea Micciulla, and John Makhoul. 2006. A study of translation edit rate with targeted human annotation. In *Proceedings of association for machine translation in the Americas*, pages 223–231.

Lucia Specia, Marco Turchi, Nicola Cancedda, Marc Dymetman, and Nello Cristianini. 2009. Estimating the sentence-level quality of machine translation systems. In *13th Conference of the European Association for Machine Translation*, pages 28–37, Barcelona, Spain.

Lucia Specia, Gustavo Paetzold, and Carolina Scarton. 2015. Multi-level translation quality prediction with quest++. In *Proceedings of ACL-IJCNLP 2015 System Demonstrations*, pages 115–120, Beijing, China, July. Association for Computational Linguistics and The Asian Federation of Natural Language Processing.

Andreas Stolcke. 2002. SRILM - an extensible language modeling toolkit. In *Proceedings of the Seventh International Conference on Spoken Language Processing*, Denver, Colorado, USA.

Sara Stymne, Nicola Cancedda, and Lars Ahrenberg. 2013. Generation of compound words for statistical machine translation into compounding languages. *Computational Linguistics*, 39(4):1067–1108.

Word embeddings and discourse information for Machine Translation Quality Estimation

Carolina Scarton, Daniel Beck, Kashif Shah, Karin Sim Smith and **Lucia Specia**
Department of Computer Science
University of Sheffield, UK
{c.scarton,debeck1,kashif.shah,kmsimsmith1,l.specia}
@sheffield.ac.uk

Abstract

In this paper we present the results of the University of Sheffield (SHEF) submissions for the WMT16 shared task on document-level Quality Estimation (Task 3). Our submission explore discourse and document-aware information and word embeddings as features, with Support Vector Regression and Gaussian Process used to train the Quality Estimation models. The use of word embeddings (combined with baseline features) and a Gaussian Process model with two kernels led to the winning submission in the shared task.

1 Introduction

The task of Quality Estimation (QE) of Machine Translation (MT) consists in predicting the quality of unseen data using Machine Learning (ML) models trained on labelled data points. Such a scenario does not require reference translations and only uses information from source and target documents. Therefore, QE is different from traditional automatic evaluation metrics (such as BLEU (Papineni et al., 2002)).

Sentence-level and word-level QE have been widely explored along the years (Callison-Burch et al., 2012; Bojar et al., 2013; Bojar et al., 2014; Bojar et al., 2015). On the other hand, document-level QE has only recently started to be addressed, with the first shared task organised last year (Bojar et al., 2015). Document-level QE is the task of predicting the quality of an entire document and is useful for *gisting* applications (mainly in cases where the user does not speak the source language) and fully automated uses of MT where post-editing is not an option.

Predicting the quality of documents is challenging: problems on all linguistic levels need be taken into account, including document-wide issues. Moreover, defining quality labels for documents is a complex task on itself, as pointed by Scarton et al. (2015b).

Little previous research has addressed this problem. Soricut and Echihabi (2010) explore pseudo-references and document-aware features for document-level ranking, using BLEU as quality label. Scarton and Specia (2014) apply pseudo-references, document-aware and discourse-aware features for document-level quality prediction, using BLEU and TER as quality scores. Last year, a paragraph-level QE shared task was organised for the first time at WMT (Bojar et al., 2015), using METEOR as quality label. Scarton (2015) explore discourse information for paragraph-level prediction. They also perform exhaustive search and find out that using only three features from the official baseline set leads to results comparable to those of the full baseline system. Biçici et al. (2015) apply referential translation machines for paragraph-level QE and obtain the best overall results in the shared task. Finally, Scarton (2015), Scarton and Specia (2015) and Scarton et al. (2015b) analyse the task of document-level QE from the perspective of defining reliable labels. They also investigate the correlation of discourse phenomena and document-lvel translation quality.

In this paper, we focus on feature engineering and the use of different ML techniques for document-level QE in the context of the WMT16 QE shared task (Task 3). We submitted two systems:

- GRAPH-BASE: counts on pronouns, connectives, Rhetorical Structure Theory (RST) and Elementary Discourse Units (EDUs) information (similar to (Scarton et al., 2015a)), plus scores from an entity graph-based model for the target documents (Sim Smith et al.,

831

Proceedings of the First Conference on Machine Translation, Volume 2: Shared Task Papers, pages 831–837,
Berlin, Germany, August 11-12, 2016. ©2016 Association for Computational Linguistics

2016) were used as features. This system was trained with the Support Vector Regression (SVR) algorithm. Discourse features were combined with the official baseline features.

- EMB-BASE-GP: word embeddings from the source documents combined with the official baseline features were used to train a Gaussian Process (GP)[1] with two-kernels: one for word embeddings and one for baseline features.

In addition to the official results of our submitted systems, we experiment with other feature combinations, such as scores from graph-based entity grid coherence models extracted from source documents and word embeddings generated for target documents. In Section 2 we describe the models used in our experiments and in Section 3 we present our results.

2 Systems Description

Our submissions for the shared task explore different approaches in terms of features and modelling. We describe them in detail in what follows.

2.1 Discourse-aware system

Pronouns, Connectives, EDUs and RST features (called hereafter PCER). Following (Scarton et al., 2015a), we use information from the Charniak parser (Charniak, 2000), the Discourse Parser from Joty et al. (2013), and the Discourse Connectives Tagger from Pitler and Nenkova (2009) as features for our discourse-aware model (these features could only be extracted for English, and thus for the source documents):

- Number of pronouns;

- Number of connectives (total number and number of connectives per class);

- Number of EDU breaks;

- Number of *Nucleus* and *Satellite* relations in the RST tree;

- Number of subtrees and height of the RST tree.[2]

Latent Semantic Analysis (LSA) cohesion features (called hereafter LSA). As done in Scarton and Specia (2014), we extract the following LSA features for both source and target documents:

- Average LSA Spearman rho correlation of adjacent sentences;

- Average LSA cosine distance of adjacent sentences;

- Average LSA Spearman rho correlation of all sentences;

- Average LSA cosine distance of all sentences.

Entity graph-based features (called hereafter GRAPH-source and GRAPH-target). We use an Entity Graph Model (Sim Smith et al., 2016), which is based on the bipartite graph of Guinaudeau and Strube (2013) and tracks the occurrence of entities throughout the document, including between non-adjacent sentences. Entities are taken as all nouns occurring in the document, as recommended by (Elsner, 2011). For our experiments, a POS tagger[3] is used to identify nouns. A local coherence score is calculated directly, without any training, and represents the distribution of entities in the document. This is based on the theory that coherent texts contain salient entities. Both the sentences and entities are represented as nodes, with edges connecting the entities to the sentences they occur in. The final model score reflects the total weight of all the edges leaving a sentence, which indicates how connected such a sentence is.

We use *weighted projections* (Guinaudeau and Strube, 2013). These take the number of shared entities into account, rating the projections higher for more shared entities. We calculate the coherence score of the source documents and of the target documents and incorporate these as features.

Model We combine the described features with the official baseline ones provided by the shared task organisers and use them in an SVR with RBF kernel and hyperparameters optimised via grid search (the same as the official shared task baseline system). We use the SVR implementation available in the scikit-learn toolkit (Pedregosa et al., 2011).[4]

---

[1] https://sheffieldml.github.io/GPy/
[2] These features are new with respect to (Scarton et al., 2015a).

[3] http://nlp.stanford.edu/software/tagger.shtml
[4] http://scikit-learn.org

2.2 Embeddings-based system

Embedding features (called hereafter EMB-source and EMB-target). The word embeddings used in our experiments are learned with the *word2vec* tool[5] (Mikolov et al., 2013b). The tool produces word embeddings using the Distributed Skip-Gram or Continuous Bag-of-Words (CBOW) models. The models are trained using large amounts of monolingual data with a neural network architecture that aims at predicting the neighbours of a given word. Unlike standard neural network-based language models for predicting the next word given the context of preceding words, a CBOW model predicts the word in the middle given the representation of the surrounding words, while the Skip-Gram model learns word embedding representations that can be used to predict a word's context in the same sentence. As suggested by the authors, CBOW is faster and more adequate for larger datasets, so we use this model in our experiments.

The data used to train the models for English is Google's billion-word corpus[6] with the vocabulary size of 527K. The Spanish data is a combination of Europarl, News-commentary and News-crawled corpora from WMT, totalling 614M words with vocabulary size of 557K. We train 500-dimensional representations with CBOW for all words in the vocabulary of both languages. We consider a 10-word context window to either side of the target word, sub-sampling option to 1e-05, and estimate the probability of a target word with the negative sampling method, drawing 10 samples from the noise distribution.

We then extract document embeddings by averaging the word embeddings in the document (for training and test sets) from these models and use these as features. These distributed numerical representations of words as features aim at locating each word as a point in a 500-dimensional space. Given that the word embeddings were trained using a large corpus, it is expected that similar words are mapped to close points in the 500-dimensional space. Therefore, the averaged word embeddings are expected to encode information about the cohesion of the document, since it encompasses information about word usage.

Model For this submission we employ a GP over the document embeddings and the baseline features. While we did try with SVR, preliminary results using cross-validation on the training set showed better results for the GP-based model.[7] Another reason for this decision is that GP easily allows the use of kernel combinations while keeping hyperparameter optimisation efficient. We explore this idea in our submission by using a sum of two isotropic[8] kernels, one for the baseline features and another one for the embeddings.

To select the best kernel combination we perform a 10-fold cross validation scheme on the training set and select the combination which performs the best in terms of Pearson's correlation score. We also consider doing model selection by picking the model with highest likelihood on the training data, similar to the scheme used in (Preoțiuc-Pietro and Cohn, 2013). However, this resulted in a worse model when compared to the cross validation scheme. We speculate that the resulting models overfit the training data, due to its small size.

The best combination, which we use in our submission, employs two Rational Quadratic (RatQuad) kernels (Rasmussen and Williams, 2006).[9] After fixing this combination, the hyperparameters are optimised by maximising the model likelihood on the full training data.

3 Experiments and Results

Apart from word embedding features, which use external corpora for training the embeddings, our systems only use the data provided by the task organisers.

Task Our participation is in Task 3 (document-level QE) in both scoring and ranking variants. Pearson r is the official primary evaluation metric for scoring, while Spearman rho is the official primary metric for ranking.

---

[7] We also experimented with a GP for training QE models using discourse-aware features, but the results were worse than with the SVR model.

[8] An alternative would be to employ Automatic Relevance Determination (ARD), a feature weighting scheme common in GPs and other Bayesian models. However, This would add a large number of hyperparameters in our case (one per feature/dimension), making the model difficult to optimise and prone to overfitting.

[9] Besides RatQuad, we also experimented with RBF, Exponential and Matern32 kernels. RatQuad showed the best results.

---

[5] https://code.google.com/p/word2vec/
[6] https://github.com/ciprian-chelba/1-billion-word-language-modeling-benchmark

Data The data of Task 3 consists of 208 documents for English-Spanish language pair, extracted from the WMT08-13 translation shared task datasets. The machine translation for each source document was randomly picked from the set of all systems that participated in the translation task. The documents were evaluated by following the two-stage post-editing method described in (Scarton et al., 2015a). In the first stage, sentences are post-edited out of context, whilst in the second stage the post-edited sentences are placed in context and any remaining mistakes are corrected. The quality scores are, then, a variation of Human-targeted Translation Edit Rate (HTER) (Snover et al., 2006) that combines results from both post-editing stages.

Baseline We use the 17 QUEST++ baseline features to train our baseline systems (Specia et al., 2015). We build a baseline system with SVR and another with GP, in order to compare our systems with comparable models.[10]

Models using discourse features and SVR The features sets we experimented with are:

- baseline + PCER + LSA + GRAPH-target + GRAPH-source;

- baseline + PCER + LSA + GRAPH-target.[11]

Our models using discourse information were trained with SVR as described in Section 2.1.

Models using word embeddings and GP The features sets we experimented with are:

- baseline + EMB-source + EMB-target;

- baseline + EMB-source;[12]

- EMB-source;

Our models using word embeddings were trained using GP as described in Section 2.2.

Model selection The best models for our submissions are selected by applying 10-fold cross-validation in the training set and choosing the model with the highest averaged Pearson r correlation. The ranks for the ranking task variant are defined by ordering the predicted values best to worst.

---

[10]For the GP model we used RatQuad kernel.

[11]Feature combination used in our GRAPH-BASE submission.

[12]Feature combination used in our BASE-EMB-GP submission.

3.1 Results

Table 1 shows the results for our experiments with discourse-aware features and SVR for the scoring sub-task. We report results of our 10-fold cross-validation method over the training and the results on the official test set. Results in the first column (10-fold) show that both discourse feature combination lead to improvements over the baseline. However, when testing on the test set, the models do not outperform the baseline. More investigation with additional data would be necessary to draw any conclusions on the reasons behind this difference.

Results for ranking using discourse-aware features are shown in Table 2. These results are reported only for the test set. Since the ranks were obtained by using the predicted scores, we could not generate rankings when testing models in the 10-fold cross-validation experiments. For this task variant, once again the discourse-aware features do not outperform the baseline features.

Tables 3 and 4 show results for scoring and ranking, respectively, for the models using word embeddings and GP. These models outperform a baseline which was also trained with GP for all cases in our 10-fold cross-validation experiment. However, when we evaluate our models on the test set, only the combination of baseline + EMB-source or EMB-source alone are better than the baseline. In fact, our result for baseline + EMB-source in the test set is the winner of the scoring sub-task, outperforming the official baseline (0.286 in Pearson r).

For ranking (calculated only for the test set), the feature sets show a similar behaviour: the model using EMB-target does not perform better than the baseline. On the other hand, EMB-source and baseline + EMB-source outperform the baseline, with the later scoring second in the official results of the shared task. It is worth mentioning that EMB-source alone is able to outperform the baseline in both sub-tasks. This is an interesting finding since word embeddings are relatively easy to acquire and only require large raw corpora as external resources.

4 Conclusions

In this paper we presented the results of our models submitted to the WMT16 QE shared task - Task 3: document-level QE. We discussed two different models: one using discourse features and SVR and

	10-fold	test set
baseline	0.357	**0.286**
baseline + PCER + LSA + GRAPH-target + GRAPH-source	0.423	0.284
baseline + PCER + LSA + GRAPH-target	0.424	0.256

Table 1: Pearson r correlation scores of models built with discourse-aware features and SVR.

	test set
baseline	0.354
baseline + PCER + LSA + GRAPH-target + GRAPH-source	0.282
baseline + PCER + LSA + GRAPH-target	0.285

Table 2: Spearman rho correlation scores of models built with discourse-aware features and SVR.

	10-fold	test set
baseline	0.340	0.266
baseline + EMB-source + EMB-target	0.479	0.232
baseline + EMB-source	0.493	**0.391**
EMB-source	0.481	0.319

Table 3: Pearson r correlation scores of models built with word embeddings and GP.

	test set
baseline	0.345
baseline + EMB-source + EMB-target	0.279
baseline + EMB-source	**0.393**
EMB-source	0.355

Table 4: Spearman rho correlation scores of models built with word-embeddings features and GP.

another using word-embeddings and GP.

Our results showed that using word-embeddings combined with baseline features and training a GP model with two kernels (one for the baseline features and another for the word-embeddings) achieved the most promising results, having ranked top of the scoring task variant. However, only word embeddings from the source documents were useful (word embeddings from the target documents produced worse results than the baseline). The differences between the data used to extract the embeddings for source and target can be the reason for such a result. Our hypothesis is that using bigger and more relevant data for the target language could lead to better results. Another possible reason for the low performance of target embeddings is the dimension of the vectors. Mikolov et al. (2013a) use different dimensions for source and target in order to achieve the best results. Therefore, in future work we will experiment with different dimensions. Finally, an important finding is that by using only word embeddings as features

we could build a model that outperforms the baseline. Nevertheless, more investigation on the topic needs to be done in order to draw concrete conclusions.

Finally, the use of discourse-aware features did not lead to improvements over the baseline on the official test sets. Our hypothesis was that discourse information would help distinguish translations with different quality levels. However, given the tools available, most discourse-aware features (e.g. RST counts) could only be extracted for English, i.e., the source documents (perfect text). We intend to further test these features in datasets where the target language (translations) is English.

Acknowledgments

This work was supported by EXPERT (EU Marie Curie ITN No. 317471, Carolina Scarton), QT21 (H2020 No. 645452, Lucia Specia) and Cracker (H2020 No. 645357, Kashif Shah) projects and CNPq (project SwB 237999/2012-9, Daniel Beck).

References

Ergun Biçici, Qun Liu, and Andy Way. 2015. Referential Translation Machines for Predicting Translation Quality and Related Statistics. In *Proceedings of the Tenth Workshop on Statistical Machine Translation*, pages 304–308, Lisbon, Portugal.

Ondřej Bojar, Christian Buck, Chris Callison-Burch, Christian Federmann, Barry Haddow, Philipp Koehn, Christof Monz, Matt Post, Radu Soricut, and Lucia Specia. 2013. Findings of the 2013 Workshop on Statistical Machine Translation. In *The Eighth Workshop on Statistical Machine Translation*, pages 1–44, Sofia, Bulgaria.

Ondřej Bojar, Christian Buck, Christian Federman, Barry Haddow, Philipp Koehn, Johannes Leveling, Christof Monz, Pavel Pecina, Matt Post, Herve Saint-Amand, Radu Soricut, Lucia Specia, and Ales Tamchyna. 2014. Findings of the 2014 workshop on statistical machine translation. In *Proceedings of the Ninth Workshop on Statistical Machine Translation*, pages 12–58, Baltimore, MD.

Ondřej Bojar, Rajen Chatterjee, Christian Federmann, Barry Haddow, Matthias Huck, Chris Hokamp, Philipp Koehn, Varvara Logacheva, Christof Monz, Matteo Negri, Matt Post, Carolina Scarton, Lucia Specia, and Marco Turchi. 2015. Findings of the 2015 workshop on statistical machine translation. In *Proceedings of the Tenth Workshop on Statistical Machine Translation*, pages 1–46, Lisbon, Portugal.

Chris Callison-Burch, Philipp Koehn, Christof Monz, Matt Post, Radu Soricut, and Lucia Specia. 2012. Findings of the 2012 workshop on statistical machine translation. In *Proceedings of the Seventh Workshop on Statistical Machine Translation*, pages 10–51, Montreal, Canada.

Eugene Charniak. 2000. A maximum-entropy-inspired parser. In *Proceedings of the 1st North American Chapter of the Association for Computational Linguistics (NAACL 2000)*, pages 132–139, Seattle, Washington.

Micha Elsner. 2011. *Generalizing Local Coherence Modeling*. Ph.D. thesis, Department of Computer Science, Brown University, Providence, Rhode Island.

Camille Guinaudeau and Michael Strube. 2013. Graph-based local coherence modeling. In *Proceedings of ACL*, pages 93–103.

Shafiq Joty, Giuseppe Carenini, Raymond T. Ng, and Yashar Mehdad. 2013. Combining intra- and multi-sentential rhetorical parsing for document-level discourse analysis. In *Proceedings of the 51st Annual Meeting of the Association for Computational Linguistics (ACL 2013)*, pages 486–496, Sofia, Bulgaria.

Tomas Mikolov, Quoc V. Le, and Ilya Sutskever. 2013a. Exploiting similarities among languages for machine translation. *arXiv preprint arXiv:1309.4168*.

Tomas Mikolov, Wen-tau Yih, and Geoffrey Zweig. 2013b. Linguistic regularities in continuous space word representations. In *Proceedings of NAACL 2013*.

Kishore Papineni, Salim Roukos, Todd Ward, and Weijing Zhu. 2002. BLEU: a Method for Automatic Evaluation of Machine Translation. In *The 40th Annual Meeting of the Association for Computational Linguistics*, pages 311–318, Philadelphia, PA.

Fabian Pedregosa, Gael Varoquaux, Alexandre Gramfort, Vincent Michel, Bertrand Thirion, Olivier Grisel, Mathieu Blondel, Peter Prettenhofer, Ron Weiss, Vincent Dubourg, Jake Vanderplas, Alexandre Passos, David Cournapeau, Matthieu Brucher, Matthieu Perrot, and Edouard Duchesnay. 2011. Scikit-learn: Machine learning in Python. *Journal of Machine Learning Research*, 12:2825–2830.

Emily Pitler and Ani Nenkova. 2009. Using Syntax to Disambiguate Explicit Discourse Connectives in Text. In *The Joint conference of the 47th Annual Meeting of the Association for Computational Linguistics and the Fourth International Joint Conference on Natural Language Processing of the Asian Federation of Natural Language Processing*, pages 13–16, Suntec, Singapore.

Daniel Preoţiuc-Pietro and Trevor Cohn. 2013. A temporal model of text periodicities using gaussian processes. In *2013 Conference on Empirical Methods in Natural Language Processing*, pages 977–988, Seattle, WA.

Carl E. Rasmussen and Christopher K. I. Williams. 2006. *Gaussian Processes for Machine Learning*. MIT Press, Cambridge, Massachusetts.

Carolina Scarton and Lucia Specia. 2014. Document-level translation quality estimation: exploring discourse and pseudo-references. In *The 17th Annual Conference of the European Association for Machine Translation*, pages 101–108, Dubrovnik, Croatia.

Carolina Scarton and Lucia Specia. 2015. A quantitative analysis of discourse phenomena in machine translation. *Discours - Revue de linguistique, psycholinguistique et informatique*, (16).

Carolina Scarton, Liling Tan, and Lucia Specia. 2015a. USHEF and USAAR-USHEF participation in the WMT15 QE shared task. In *Proceedings of the Tenth Workshop on Statistical Machine Translation*, pages 336–341, Lisbon, Portugal.

Carolina Scarton, Marcos Zampieri, Mihaela Vela, Josef van Genabith, and Lucia Specia. 2015b. Searching for Context: a Study on Document-Level Labels for Translation Quality Estimation. In *The*

18th Annual Conference of the European Association for Machine Translation, pages 121–128, Antalya, Turkey.

Carolina Scarton. 2015. Discourse and document-level information for evaluating language output tasks. In *The 2015 Conference of the North American Chapter of the Association for Computational Linguistics: Student Research Workshop*, pages 118–125, Denver, Colorado.

Karin Sim Smith, Wilker Aziz, and Lucia Specia. 2016. Cohere: A toolkit for local coherence. In *10th International Conference on Language Resources and Evaluation*, Portorož, Slovenia. To appear.

Matthew Snover, Bonnie Dorr, Richard Schwartz, Linnea Micciulla, and John Makhoul. 2006. A Study of Translation Edit Rate with Targeted Human Annotation. In *The Seventh biennial conference of the Association for Machine Translation in the Americas*, AMTA 2006, pages 223–231, Cambridge, MA.

Radu Soricut and Abdessamad Echihabi. 2010. TrustRank: Inducing Trust in Automatic Translations via Ranking. In *The 48th Annual Meeting of the Association for Computational Linguistics*, pages 612–621, Uppsala, Sweden.

Lucia Specia, Gustavo Paetzold, and Carolina Scarton. 2015. Multi-level Translation Quality Prediction with QuEst++. In *The 53rd Annual Meeting of the Association for Computational Linguistics and Seventh International Joint Conference on Natural Language Processing of the Asian Federation of Natural Language Processing: System Demonstrations*, Beijing, China.

SHEF-LIUM-NN: Sentence-level Quality Estimation with Neural Network Features

Kashif Shah[§], Fethi Bougares[†], Loïc Barrault[†] Lucia Specia[§]
§Department of Computer Science, University of Sheffield, UK
{kashif.shah,l.specia}@sheffield.ac.uk

†LIUM, University of Le Mans, France
{fethi.bougares,loïc.barrault}@lium.univ-lemans.fr

Abstract

This paper describes our systems for Task 1 of the WMT16 Shared Task on Quality Estimation. Our submissions use (i) a continuous space language model (CSLM) to extract sentence embeddings and cross-entropy scores, (ii) a neural network machine translation (NMT) model, (iii) a set of QuEst features, and (iv) a combination of features produced by QuEst and with CSLM and NMT. Our primary submission achieved third place in the scoring task and second place in the ranking task. Another interesting finding is the good performance obtained from using as features only CSLM sentence embeddings, which are learned in an unsupervised fashion without any additional handcrafted features.

1 Introduction

Quality Estimation (QE) aims at measuring the quality of the output of Machine Translation (MT) systems without reference translations. Generally, QE is addressed with various features indicating fluency, adequacy and complexity of the source and translation texts. Such features are used along with Machine Learning methods in order to learn prediction models.

Features play a key role in QE. A wide range of features from the source segments and their translations, often processed using external resources and tools, have been proposed. These go from simple, language-independent features, to advanced, linguistically motivated features. They include features that rely on information from the MT system that generated the translations, and features that are oblivious to the way translations were produced. This leads to a potential bottle-

neck: feature engineering can be time consuming, particularly because the impact of features vary across datasets and language pairs. Also, most features in the literature are extracted from segment pairs in isolation, ignoring contextual clues from other segments in the text. The focus of our contributions this year is to explore a new set of features which are language-independent, require minimal resources, and can be extracted in unsupervised ways with the use of neural networks.

Word embeddings have shown their potential in modelling long distance dependencies in data, including syntactic and semantic information. For instance, neural network language models (Bengio et al., 2003) have been successfully explored in many problems including Automatic Speech Recognition (Schwenk and Gauvain, 2005; Schwenk, 2007) and Machine Translation (Schwenk, 2012).

In this paper, we extend our previous work (Shah et al., 2015a; Shah et al., 2015b) to investigate the use of sentence embeddings extracted from a neural network language model along with cross entropy scores as features for QE. We also investigate the use of a neural machine translation model to extract the log likelihood of sentences as QE features. The features extracted from such resources are used in isolation or combined with hand-crafted features from QuEst to learn prediction models.

2 Continuous Space Language Model Features

Neural networks model non-linear relationships between the input features and target outputs. They often outperform other techniques in complex machine learning tasks. The inputs to the neural network language model used here (called Continuous Space Language Model (CSLM)) are

Proceedings of the First Conference on Machine Translation, Volume 2: Shared Task Papers, pages 838–842,
Berlin, Germany, August 11-12, 2016. ©2016 Association for Computational Linguistics

the h_j context words of the prediction: $h_j = w_{j-n+1}, ..., w_{j-2}, w_{j-1}$, and the outputs are the posterior probabilities of all words of the vocabulary: $P(w_j|h_j) \ \forall i \in [1, N]$ where N is the vocabulary size. A CSLM encodes inputs using the so called one-hot coding, i.e., the ith word in the vocabulary is coded by setting all elements to 0 except the ith element. Due to the large size of the output layer (vocabulary size), the computational complexity of a basic neural network language model is very high. Schwenk (2012) proposed an implementation of the neural network with efficient algorithms to reduce the computational complexity and speed up the processing using a subset of the entire vocabulary called *short list*.

As compared to shallow neural networks, deep neural networks can use more hidden layers and have been shown to perform better (Schwenk et al., 2014). In all CSLM experiments described in this paper, we use 40-gram deep neural networks with four hidden layers: a first layer for the word projection (320 units for each context word) and three hidden layers of 1024 units for the probability estimation. At the output layer, we use a *softmax* activation function applied to a *short list* of the 32k most frequent words. The probabilities of the out of the *short list* words are obtained using a standard back-off n-gram language model. The training of the neural network is done by the standard back-propagation algorithm and outputs are the posterior probabilities. The parameters of the models are optimised on a held out development set. Our CSLM models were trained with the CSLM toolkit [1] and used to extract the following features:

- source sentence cross-entropy

- source sentence embeddings

- translation output cross-entropy

- translation output embeddings.

Table 1, reports detailed statistics on the monolingual data used to train the back-off LM and CSLM. The training dataset consists of WMT16 translation task monolingual corpora with the Moore-Lewis data selection method (Moore and Lewis, 2010) to select the CSLM training data with respect to the task's development set. The

CSLM models are tuned using the WMT16 Quality Estimation development corpus.

Lang.	Train	Dev	4-g LM px	CSLM px
en	84G	17.8 k	61.30	50.69
de	79G	19.7 k	64.99	54.45

Table 1: Training and dev datasets size (in number of tokens) and models perplexity (px).

3 Neural Machine Translation Features

In addition to the monolingual features learned using the neural network language model, we experiment with bilingual features derived from a neural machine translation system (NMT). Our NMT system is developed based on a framework inspired from the dl4mt-material project[2]. The system is an end-to-end sequence to sequence model tuned to minimise the negative log-likelihood using a stochastic gradient descent. In our experiments we trained two NMT systems (EN $\leftrightarrow$ DE) with an attention mechanism similar to the one described in (Bahdanau et al., 2014).

Let X and Y be a source sentence of length T_x and a target sentence of length T_y respectively:

$$X = (x_1, x_2, ..., x_{T_x}) \qquad (1)$$
$$Y = (y_1, y_2, ..., y_{T_y}) \qquad (2)$$

Each source and target word is represented with a randomly initialised embedding vector of size E_s and E_t respectively. A bidirectional recurrent encoder reads an input sequence X in forward and backward directions to produce two sets of hidden states. At the end of the encoding step, we obtain a bidirectional annotation vector h_t for each source position by concatenating the forward and backward annotations:

$$h_t = \begin{bmatrix} \vec{h_t} \\ \overleftarrow{h_t} \end{bmatrix} \qquad (3)$$

A Gated Recurrent Unit (GRU) (Chung et al., 2014) is used for the encoder and decoder. They have 1000 hidden units each, leading to an annotation vector $h_t \in \mathbb{R}^{2000}$.

The attention mechanism, implemented as a simple fully-connected feed-forward neural network, accepts the hidden state h_t of the decoder's recurrent layer and one input annotation at a time,

---

[1] http://www-lium.univ-lemans.fr/cslm/

[2] github.com/kyunghyuncho/dl4mt-material

to produce the attention coefficients. A softmax activation is applied on those attention coefficients to obtain the attention weights used to generate the weighted annotation vector for time t.

Both NMT systems are trained with WMT16 Quality Estimation English-German datasets (we used post-editions on the German side) and tuned on the official development set. Table 2 reports the statistics of NMT training data and BLEU scores on the QE development set.

Trans. Direction	Train	Dev	BLEU
DE-to-EN	21k-20k	17.8 k	35.38
EN-to-DE	20k-21k	19.7 k	37.51

Table 2: Training and development datasets sizes (number of tokens) and development set BLEU scores.

4 Experiments

In what follows we present our experiments on the WMT16 QE Task 1 with CSLM and NMT features.

4.1 Dataset

Task 1's English-German dataset consists respectively of a training set and development set with $12,000$ and $1,000$ source segments, their machine translations, the post-editions of the latter, and the edit distance scores between the MT and its post-edited version (HTER). The test set consists of $2,000$ English-German source-MT pairs. Each of the translations was post-edited by professional translators, and HTER labels were computed using the TER tool (settings: tokenised, case insensitive, exact matching only, with scores capped to 1).

4.2 Features

We extracted the following features:

- **QuEst**: 79 black-box features using the QuEst framework (Specia et al., 2013; Shah et al., 2013a) as described in Shah et al. (2013b). The full set of features can be found on `http://www.quest.dcs.shef.ac.uk/quest_files/features_blackbox`.

- **CSLM$_{ce}$**: A cross-entropy feature for each source and target sentence using CSLM as described in Section 2.

- **NMT$_{ll}$**: A log likelihood feature for each source and target sentence using NMT as described in Section 3.

- **CSLM$_{emb}$**: Sentence features extracted by taking the mean of 320-dimension word vectors trained using CSLM for both source and target. We also experimented with taking the min or the max of the embeddings, but empirically it was found that the mean performs better. Therefore, all our results are reported using the mean of word embeddings.

4.3 Learning algorithm

We use the Support Vector Machines implementation in the `scikit-learn` toolkit (Pedregosa et al., 2011) to perform regression (SVR) on each feature set with either RBF kernels and parameters optimised using grid search.

To evaluate the prediction models we use all evaluation metrics in the task: Pearson's correlation r, Mean Absolute Error (MAE), Root Mean Squared Error (RMSE), Spearman's correlation ρ and Delta Average (DeltaAvg).

4.4 Results

We trained various models with different feature sets and algorithms and evaluated the performance of these models on the official development set. The results are shown in Table 3. Based on these findings, as official submissions for Task 1, we submitted two systems:

- SHEF-SVM-CSLM$_{ce}$-NMT$_{ll}$-CSLM$_{both-emb}$

- SHEF-SVM-QuEst-CSLM$_{ce}$-NMT$_{ll}$-CSLM$_{both-emb}$

These systems contain all of our CSLM and NMT features either with or without QuEst: 719 and 644 features in total, respectively. We named them SVM-NN-both-emb and SVM-NN-both-emb-QuEst in the official submissions. The official results are shown in Table 4. Our systems show promising performance across all of the metrics used for evaluation in both scoring and ranking task variants. Our best system was ranked:

- Third place in the scoring task variant according to Pearson r (official scoring metric), and second place according MAE and RMSE.

- Second place in the ranking task variant according to Spearman ρ (official ranking metric) and first place according to DeltaAvg.

System.	# of Feats.	MAE	RMSE	Pearson r
Baseline (SVM)	17	13.97	19.65	0.359
SHEF-SVM-QuEst	79	13.94	19.71	0.386
SHEF-SVM-QuEst-CSLM$_{ce}$-NMT$_{ll}$	83	14.27	19.92	0.460
SHEF-SVM-CSLM$_{src-emb}$	320	13.97	18.87	0.416
SHEF-SVM-CSLM$_{tgt-emb}$	320	13.70	18.60	0.422
SHEF-SVM-CSLM$_{both-emb}$	640	13.74	18.10	0.425
SHEF-SVM-CSLM$_{ce}$-NMT$_{ll}$-CSLM$_{both-emb}$	644	13.48	17.94	**0.500**
SHEF-SVM-QuEst-CSLM$_{ce}$-NMT$_{ll}$-CSLM$_{tgt-emb}$	383	13.49	17.99	0.500
SHEF-SVM-QuEst-CSLM$_{ce}$-NMT$_{ll}$-CSLM$_{both-emb}$	719	13.46	17.92	**0.501**

Table 3: Results on the development set of Task 1. Systems in bold are used as official submissions.

System.	MAE	RMSE	Pearson r	DeltaAvg	Spearman ρ
Baseline	13.53	18.39	0.351	62.981	0.390
SVM-NN-both-emb	12.97[3]	17.33[3]	0.430[5]	78.86[1]	0.452[2]
SVM-NN-both-emb-QuEst	12.88[2]	17.03[2]	0.451[3]	81.30[1]	0.474[2]

Table 4: Official results on the test set of Task 1. The superscript shows the overall ranking of the system against various official evaluation metrics.

Some of the interesting findings are:

- The mean of word embeddings extracted for each sentence performs much better than the max or min.

- Sentence features extracted from CSLM embeddings bring the largest improvements.

- Target embeddings produce better predictions than source embeddings, which is in-line with our previous findings (Shah et al., 2015b).

- CSLM cross entropy and NMT log likelihood features bring further improvements on top of embedding features.

- QuEst features bring improvements whenever added to either CSLM embeddings or cross entropy and NMT likelihood features.

- Neural Network features alone perform very well. This is a very encouraging finding since for many language pairs it can be difficult to find appropriate resources to extract hand-crafted features.

5 Conclusions

In this paper we have explored novel features for translation Quality Estimation which are obtained with the use of Neural Networks. When added to QuEst standard feature sets for the WMT16 QE Task 1, the CSLM sentence embedding features along with cross entropy and NMT likelihood led to large improvements in prediction. Moreover, CSLM and NMT features alone performed very well. Combining all CSLM and NMT features with the ones produced by QuEst improved the performance and led to very competitive systems according to the task's official results.

In the future work, we plan to explore bilingual embeddings extracted from our NMT models. Compared to the CSLM embeddings, NMT models generate embeddings (with the bidirectional Neural Network as presented in Section 3) of the whole sentence with a focus on the current word. In addition, we plan to train a Neural Network model to directly predict the QE scores.

Acknowledgements

This work was supported by the QT21 (H2020 No. 645452, Lucia Specia), Cracker (H2020 No. 645357, Kashif Shah) and the Chist-ERA M2CR[3] (Fethi Bougares and Loïc Barrault) projects.

References

Dzmitry Bahdanau, Kyunghyun Cho, and Yoshua Bengio. 2014. Neural machine translation by jointly learning to align and translate. *CoRR*, abs/1409.0473.

---

[3]m2cr.univ-lemans.fr

Yoshua Bengio, Réjean Ducharme, Pascal Vincent, and Christian Janvin. 2003. A neural probabilistic language model. *The Journal of Machine Learning Research*.

Junyoung Chung, Çaglar Gülçehre, KyungHyun Cho, and Yoshua Bengio. 2014. Empirical evaluation of gated recurrent neural networks on sequence modeling. *CoRR*, abs/1412.3555.

Robert C Moore and William Lewis. 2010. Intelligent selection of language model training data. In *Proceedings of the 48th ACL*.

F. Pedregosa, G. Varoquaux, A. Gramfort, V. Michel, B. Thirion, O. Grisel, M. Blondel, P. Prettenhofer, R. Weiss, V. Dubourg, J. Vanderplas, A. Passos, D. Cournapeau, M. Brucher, M. Perrot, and E. Duchesnay. 2011. Scikit-learn: Machine learning in Python. *Journal of Machine Learning Research*.

Holger Schwenk and Jean-Luc Gauvain. 2005. Training neural network language models on very large corpora. In *Proceedings of the Conference on Human Language Technology and Empirical Methods in Natural Language Processing*.

Holger Schwenk, Fethi Bougares, and Loic Barrault. 2014. Efficient training strategies for deep neural network language models. *Proceedings of NIPS*.

Holger Schwenk. 2007. Continuous space language models. *Computer Speech & Language*.

Holger Schwenk. 2012. Continuous space translation models for phrase-based statistical machine translation. In *Proceedings of COLING*.

Kashif Shah, Eleftherios Avramidis, Ergun Biçicic, and Lucia Specia. 2013a. Quest - design, implementation and extensions of a framework for machine translation quality estimation. *Prague Bull. Math. Linguistics*.

Kashif Shah, Trevor Cohn, and Lucia Specia. 2013b. An investigation on the effectiveness of features for translation quality estimation. In *Proceedings of the Machine Translation Summit*.

Kashif Shah, Varvara Logacheva, Gustavo Paetzold, Frédéric Blain, Daniel Beck, Fethi Bougares, and Lucia Specia. 2015a. Shef-nn: Translation quality estimation with neural networks. In *Tenth Workshop on Statistical Machine Translation*, pages 338–343, Lisboa, Portugal.

Kashif Shah, Raymond W.M. Ng, Fethi Bougares, and Lucia Specia. 2015b. Investigating continuous space language models for machine translation quality estimation. In *Conference on Empirical Methods in Natural Language Processing*, EMNLP, Lisboa, Portugal.

Lucia Specia, Kashif Shah, José G. C. de Souza, and Trevor Cohn. 2013. QuEst - A translation quality estimation framework. In *Proceedings of 51st ACL*.

UGENT-LT3 SCATE Submission for WMT16 Shared Task on Quality Estimation

Arda Tezcan   **Véronique Hoste**   **Lieve Macken**

LT3, Language and Translation Technology Team
Department of Translation, Interpreting and Communication
Ghent University
Groot-Brittannielaan 45, 9000 Ghent, Belgium
`{arda.tezcan, veronique.hoste, lieve.macken}@ugent.be`

Abstract

This paper describes the submission of the UGENT-LT3 SCATE system to the WMT16 Shared Task on Quality Estimation (QE), viz. English-German word and sentence-level QE. Based on the observation that the data set is homogeneous (all sentences belong to the IT domain), we performed bilingual terminology extraction and added features derived from the resulting term list to the well-performing features of the word-level QE task of last year. For sentence-level QE, we analyzed the importance of the features and based on those insights extended the feature set of last year. We also experimented with different learning methods and ensembles. We present our observations from the different experiments we conducted and our submissions for both tasks.

1 Introduction

Machine Translation (MT) Quality Estimation (QE) is the task of providing a quality indicator for unseen automatically translated sentences without relying on reference translations (Gandrabur and Foster, 2003; Blatz et al., 2004). The WMT16 QE shared task proposes three evaluation tasks: (1) scoring and ranking sentences according to predicted post-editing effort given a source sentence and its translation; predicting the individual (2a) words and (2b) phrases (segmented by the Statistical Machine Translation (SMT) decoder) that require post-editing; and (3) predicting the quality at document level. In this paper, we describe the UGENT-LT3 SCATE submissions to task 1 (sentence-level QE) and task 2a (word-level QE). By conceiving the QE as a supervised Machine Learning (ML) problem for both tasks, we ex-

tended the features that we extracted for our last year's submission (Tezcan et al., 2015), which try to capture the accuracy and fluency errors in MT output. While accuracy is concerned with how much of the meaning expressed in the source is also expressed in the target text, fluency is concerned with to what extent the translation is well-formed. This distinction between accuracy and fluency was suggested to break down human translation quality judgments into separate and smaller units (White, 1995) and is well known in quality assessment schemes for MT (White, 1995; Secară, 2005; Lommel et al., 2014). Similarly, we use the same distinction to break down the QE task into separate units. In addition to the features that try to capture accuracy and fluency errors, given the specialized domain of this year's data set (IT), for word-level QE, we extracted features that try to capture terminological problems. For both tasks, we experimented with different learning methods. For word-level QE we also built ensemble systems that are based on majority voting and bagging (random forests), in which multiple decision trees are constructed using bootstrapped training sets and the predictions of these trees are averaged.

The rest of this paper is organized as follows. Section 2 and Section 3 give an overview of the shared task on word-level QE and sentence-level QE respectively and describe the extracted features, the additional language resources that were used for feature extraction, the learning methods and the experiments that were conducted. Section 4 concludes by discussing the results and observations that were made.

2 Word-level Quality Estimation

Similar to the previous year, the word-level QE task in WMT16 is conceived as a binary classification task. The goal is to label translation er-

Proceedings of the First Conference on Machine Translation, Volume 2: Shared Task Papers, pages 843–850,
Berlin, Germany, August 11-12, 2016. ©2016 Association for Computational Linguistics

rors at word level by marking words either as OK or BAD. In WMT16, submissions are evaluated in terms of classification performance via the multiplication of F1-scores for the OK and BAD classes against the original labels due to the fact that the F1-score for the BAD class, which has been used as a primary metric in previous years, is biased towards 'pessimistic' labeling. In contrast, the multiplication of F1-OK and F1-BAD has two components and is more balanced.

The organizers provided a data set of English source sentences with the corresponding German MT output, generated by a statistical MT system and the post-edited MT output. This data set consists of a training set of 12,000 sentences, a development set of 1,000 sentences and a test set of 2,000 sentences. As in previous years, the MT output in the training and development data are automatically annotated for errors with binary word-level labels by using the alignments provided by the TER tool (Snover et al., 2006). The distribution of the binary labels and the average sentence length for the training and development sets (in number of tokens) are given in Table 1.

	# Words	OK	BAD	Length
Train	210958	78.5%	21.5%	17.57
Dev	19487	80.5%	19.5%	19.48

Table 1: Number of words, distribution of the binary labels and the average sentence length, on the training and development set.

2.1 Features and Language Resources

To characterize each target word of the MT output, in addition to the provided baseline features, which were described in the WMT15 QE shared task (Bojar et al., 2015), we extracted the features[1] we used for our last year's submission, for which detailed descriptions can be found in Tezcan et al. (2015).

Technical texts, like in the IT domain, express concepts in a concise and consistent form and leave little room for data redundancy. This is often achieved with the use a specialized terminology (Rinaldi et al., 2004). As a result, in professional translation services, correct and consistent handling of terminology becomes an important in-

dicator of translation quality (Pinnis, 2015). Given that the data set for the QE-tasks in WMT16 is in the IT domain, we designed three binary features based on the use of terminology, which indicate whether:

- the target word (tw) is part of a term in our bilingual term list;

- the source alignment (sw) of the tw is part of a term in our bilingual term list, given the alignments in the baseline feature set;

- the left or right context word of the sw is part of a term in our bilingual term list, given the alignments in the baseline feature set.

To be able to define these features, we used the bilingual terminology extraction tool TExSIS (Macken et al., 2013) to automatically extract a bilingual term list from the training corpus. Besides additional statistics, TExSIS output provides a frequency ratio for each extracted bilingual term pair, which corresponds to the source/target term frequency in the given data set. We filtered out the bilingual terms with a frequency ratio of less than 0.8 to focus only on the most reliable term pairs. The resulting bilingual term list includes 4198 entries. Examples of the extracted terms are provided in Table 2.

Source Term (EN)	Target Term (DE)
dialog box	Dialogfeld
SWF file	SWF-Datei
pop-up note	Popup-Notiz
export	exportieren
exported image	exportierten Bilds
cross-references	Querverweise

Table 2: Examples of bilingual terminology automatically extracted by TExSIS.

Based on this bilingual term list, we marked all entries, starting with the longest term found, in the training, development and test sets and extracted the three binary features mentioned before for each target word in the MT output.

Even though we only used the training set for extracting features relating to terminology, we used additional language resources for the other additional features we extracted (see Tezcan et al. 2015 for more details). These features are based on a surface Language Model (LM) and a Part-of-speech (PoS) LM of the target language, and a

---

[1] All features that are described in Tezcan et al. (2015) except the features based on named entities and simplified Part-of-Speech (PoS) tags.

Phrase Table consisting of phrase alignments and translation probabilities between the source and target languages. As bilingual data, we used the provided training set, the Autodesk Post-Editing Data[2] and a collection of corpora from OPUS (Tiedemann, 2012) in the IT domain. The number of sentence pairs collected from each corpus is presented in Table 3.

Corpus	# Segments	# Words (EN-DE)	
WMT16	12000	201505	228549
Autodesk	124486	1411351	1382342
Gnome	28439	201634	183958
KDE4	224035	1745841	1671591
PHP	39707	228549	228434
Ubuntu	12992	70136	66348
TOTAL	441659	3859016	3747393

Table 3: Additional language resources that were used to extract features and the number of segments in each data set.

We used the Moses Toolkit (Koehn et al., 2007) to obtain phrase alignments from the collected data. The phrase alignments were pruned to exclude entries with a direct alignment probability $P(t|s) < 0.01$. We built the LM and PoS LM on the target side of the collected bilingual data. The following preprocessing steps have been applied on the data prior to building the LM and the phrase table: normalization of digits, tokenization and lowercasing. The surface form LM has been built using KenLM (Heafield, 2011). For building the PoS LM, we used TreeTagger (Schmid, 1995) to obtain the PoS tags on the target (DE) data and IRSTLM (Federico et al., 2008) for building the LM. As smoothing technique we used Witten-Bell as the modified Kneser-Ney smoothing, which is used by KenLM, is not well defined when there are no singletons (Chen and Goodman, 1996) and leads to modeling issues on the PoS data. The resulting LMs and phrase table were stored in databases and indexed to speed up lookup operations.

2.2 Learning Methods

By combining different learning methods into ensemble systems based on majority voting, we were able to increase the word-level QE performance of individual systems in the past (Tezcan et al., 2015). This has motivated us to experiment with different learning methods and ensembles. In our experiments we used 6 different learning methods: Logistic Regression (LR), Perceptron (PE), Random Forest (RF) and Linear Support Vector Classification (SVC) using the Scikit-learn module in Python (Pedregosa et al., 2011), Conditional Random Fields (CRFs) using the CRF++ Toolkit (Kudo, 2005) and Memory-Based Learning (MBL) using TiMBL (Daelemans et al., 2004). For the algorithms that did not accept categorical features in the Scikit-learn module (such as LR and RF), one-hot encoding was applied to transform the feature sets prior to training.

2.3 Experiments

We carried out experiments with the six ML methods and combinations of three different feature sets, namely the baseline features (b), the SCATE features we used for WMT15 (s) and the new features we extracted, which identify words that appear in the bilingual term list (t). We applied hyper-parameter optimization for the ML algorithms (when applicable) using 10-fold cross validation on the training set and tested the classification performance on the development set. All the features were scaled to the [0, 1] range prior to training. The classification performance of different algorithms and feature sets, with respect to F1 scores for the BAD class, the OK class and the multiplication of the two (MLT), are provided in Table 4.

		LR	PE	**RF**	SVC	CRF	MBL
	BAD	0.33	0.37	0.23	0.24	0.30	0.29
b	OK	0.87	0.81	0.90	0.88	0.89	0.88
	MLT	0.29	0.30	0.20	0.21	0.26	0.25
	BAD	0.41	0.40	0.45	0.42	0.38	0.38
$b+s$	OK	0.83	0.83	0.85	0.83	0.80	0.80
	MLT	0.34	**0.33**	0.38	**0.35**	0.30	0.30
	BAD	0.45	0.37	0.45	0.43	0.44	0.39
$b+s$ $+t$	OK	0.83	0.85	0.86	0.82	0.82	0.81
	MLT	**0.37**	0.31	**0.39**	0.35	**0.36**	**0.32**

Table 4: The performance of different ML algorithms and feature sets on the development set. The plus sign '+' indicates the combined feature sets.

Under the hypothesis that different learners make different types of errors, we first analyzed the amount of disagreement by comparing the output of each system using the overall best feature

---

[2]https://autodesk.app.box.com/v/autodesk-postediting

set '*b+s+t*'.

	CRF	LR	PE	SVC	RF
MBL	21%	19%	29%	20%	21%
CRF		5%	19%	3%	19%
LR			21%	4%	18%
PE				19%	30%
SVC					18%

Table 5: The disagreement ratios between the predicted labels by different algorithms (feature set '*b+s+t*').

Based on the disagreement ratios between the different ML systems given in Table 5, we built two ensemble systems by combining individual ML systems with high disagreement ratios (low correlation) that vote for the final output, which is defined by the majority vote. The two ensemble systems and their performances on word-level QE are provided in Table 6. In this table, we provide the MLT scores for these two ensemble systems. For the second system, which combines an even number of algorithms, we consider the both possible output types (OK or BAD) in case of ties.

	MLT
MBL+PE+RF	0.35
MBL+PE+RF+LR (Ties OK)	0.35
MBL+PE+RF+LR (Ties BAD)	**0.37**

Table 6: The MLT scores for the two ensemble systems. The plus sign '+' indicates the combined algorithms.

Based on the results we obtained from these experiments, we selected the following systems for the submission of this year's shared task on word-level QE:

- *RF*: The RF system, which uses the '*b+s+t*' feature set (best scoring system)

- *ENS*: The ensemble system indicated as: MBL+PE+RF+LR (Ties BAD)

These two systems obtained MLT scores on the test set of respectively 0.41 and 0.38 and were ranked third and fourth on the word-level QE task.

3 Sentence-level Quality Estimation

The aim of sentence-level QE is to predict Human mediated Translation Edit Rate (HTER) (Snover

et al., 2006) scores that are obtained by comparing the MT output to its post-edited version. The ranking variant of this task is defined as ranking the MT output (per segment) from best to worst.

3.1 Features and Language Resources

In our experiments we initially used two feature sets: The baseline features (17) and the additional features (17) we used for our last year's submission. These additional features rely on the surface LM, PoS LM and the phrase table as well as the output of the best word-level QE system (RF) for each MT output. Detailed descriptions of these features can be found in Tezcan et al. (2015). Based on the observations we made during our experiments (see Section 3.3 for details) we designed two extra features that use additional information from the surface LM.

3.2 Learning Methods

We experimented with Support Vector Machines (SVMs), Linear Regression (LR) and Random Forests (RF) using the Scikit-learn module in Python to build regression models.

3.3 Experiments

In the first round of our experiments, we used two feature sets, namely the baseline features (*b*) and the additional features (*a*) that are described in Tezcan et al. (2015). We applied hyper-parameter optimization for the ML algorithms (when applicable) using 10-fold cross validation on the training set and tested the regression performance on the development set. The performance of the different ML algorithms and the different feature sets, with respect to Pearson's correlation (r), Mean Absolute Error (MAE) and Root Mean Squared Error (RMSE) are provided in Table 7.

		SVM	RF	LR
b	r	0.38	0.34	0.36
	MAE	13.87	14.66	14.29
	RMSE	19.52	19.43	19.29
b+a	r	0.42	0.39	0.42
	MAE	21.55	22.89	21.52
	RMSE	26.30	27.62	25.86

Table 7: The performance of different ML algorithms and feature sets on the development set. The plus sign '+' indicates the combined feature sets.

We analyzed the RF system to rank the features for their informativeness using the Scikit-learn module, which implements *gini importance* as described in Breiman et al. (1984). Gini importance, whose values are positive and sum to 1, provides information about the sum of impurity decrease for each variable, over all nodes in all decision trees. Based on this analysis, we list the top five features and corresponding importance scores in Table 8.

	Feature	Score
1	% of 5-grams that appear in the LM at least once (a)	**0.73**
2	% of words that are marked as BAD by the best WL QE system (a)	0.08
3	LM probability of the source sentence (b)	0.01
4	Average source token length (b)	0.01
5	% of 4-grams that appear in the LM at least once (a)	0.01

Table 8: The top five features for the RF system, with respect to gini importance scores, which uses the $b+a$ feature set. Each feature is marked in brackets with the feature set that it comes from.

Considering the fact that the surface LM features were found to be extremely informative by the RF system (especially the % of 5-grams that appear in the LM at least once), we extended this feature set with n-grams of size 6 and 7 and named them as *lm6* and *lm7*[3]. We provide the performances of the different systems using the extended feature sets in Table 9.

		SVM	RF	LR
$b+a$	r	**0.42**	0.39	**0.42**
$+lm6$	MAE	21.55	22.89	21.45
	RMSE	26.30	27.62	25.74
$b+a$	r	**0.42**	0.39	**0.42**
$+lm6$	MAE	**21.46**	22.93	21.48
$+lm7$	RMSE	26.21	27.66	25.80

Table 9: The performance of different ML algorithms and feature sets on the development set. The plus sign '+' indicates the combined feature sets.

The effectiveness of using the word-level QE

predictions as features for sentence-level QE systems has been shown in previous years (de Souza et al., 2014; Tezcan et al., 2015). Moreover, a single feature based on the word-level predictions was able to perform better than the baseline features in previous year's shared task on QE (Tezcan et al., 2015). To confirm these results on a new language pair and domain, we performed a final experiment. In table 10, we can see the differences in the performances of the different systems using features sets that include and exclude the word-level feature (wl) (% of words that are marked as BAD by the best WL QE system).

		SVM	RF	LR
	r	0.41	0.39	0.39
wl	MAE	18.24	19.33	19.79
	RMSE	23.07	23.97	25.37
a-wl+b	r	37.58	36.00	37.53
+lm6	MAE	21.47	22.75	27.17
+lm7	RMSE	26.03	27.17	25.40

Table 10: The performance of different ML algorithms and feature sets on the development set. While the plus sign '+' indicates inclusion, the minus sign '-' indicates the exclusion of a particular feature(s).

Based on the results we obtained from these experiments, for the scoring variant of the sentence-level QE task, we selected the following systems:

- *SVM1*: The SVM system, which uses the *a-wl+b+lm6+lm7* feature set

- *SVM2*: The SVM system, which uses the *a+b+lm6+lm7* feature set (best scoring system)

For the ranking variant of the sentence-level QE task, we used the output of these two systems to rank the sentences from best to worst. These two systems obtained *r* scores on the test set of respectively 0.36 and 0.41 and were ranked ninth and sixth on the sentence-level QE task.

4 Results and Discussion

For the word-level QE task, in addition to the baseline features, we extracted additional features based on accuracy and fluency of translations and features that utilize an automatically extracted bilingual terminology list. The results showed that

---

[3]No extension has been made to the features obtained from the PoS LMs.

all additional features were found to be informative by all the six ML algorithms we experimented with. Additionally, the best scores for five of these systems were obtained by including the features that are based on the bilingual terminology list. For the shared task, we worked with a small automatically extracted term list, but we assume that either a manually verified term list or a (larger) client-specific term list will further improve QE system performance, especially for the technical domain. Random forest, an ensemble of decision trees, was the best performing algorithm on the word-level QE, which utilized all the extracted features.

For sentence-level QE, we used different ML algorithms to train systems using the feature sets from our last year's submission. We extended this feature set based on a feature importance analysis we performed on the random forest system and added two new features (% of 6- and 7-grams that appear in the LM at least once). Including these features however showed only minor improvements on regression performance. This observation can be attributed to the high correlation between the features that all use the *n-gram* information on the target language, for different values of *n*.

Another interesting observation can be made for all three ML algorithms with respect to the baseline (*b*) and the merged feature sets (*b+a*). While the additional features improved the Pearson's correlation in all systems, they reduced the performance in terms of MAE and RMSE. To analyze this difference further, we plotted the errors made by the SVM system, using the two different feature sets, as shown in Figure 1.

The linear trend lines, provided in Figure 1, show that the slope of the equation *SVM(b+a) TL* (-0.67) is a better fit to the gold standard HTER scores ($y = 0$) than the slope of the equation *SVM(b) TL* (-0.82), which can explain the better correlation obtained with the *b+a* feature set, compared to *b*. On the other hand, the intercept of the equation *SVM(b+a) TL* (34) is further from the origin than the intercept of the equation *SVM(b) TL* (17), which can explain the lower MAE and RMSE scores obtained by the feature set *b*. A further analysis of the descriptive statistics for the HTER predictions coming from both systems and the gold standard HTER scores can be seen in Table 11.

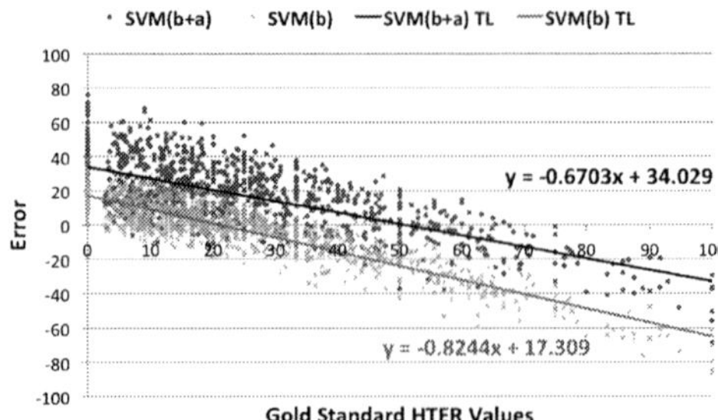

Figure 1: Errors made by the two SVM systems using the two different feature sets, sorted along the x-axis by their gold standard HTER scores. The equations for the linear trend lines (TL) for each data set are additionally provided.

	Mean	Std. Dev.	Max.
SVM(b)	21.82	9.28	48.22
SVM(b+a)	42.49	16.18	77.79
Gold Std.	25.69	20.37	100

Table 11: The mean, standard deviation and maximum values for each data set consisting of predicted and gold standard HTER scores.

Combining the information presented in Figure 1 and Table 11, we can see that the *SVM(b)* system has a smaller error margin on the lower end of the scale with respect to the HTER scores. This greatly influences the MAE and RMSE scores, given the fact that the gold standard HTER scores are skewed towards the lower end of the scale, centered around a mean of 25.69. In fact, the trend line *SVM(b) TL* corresponds to a smaller error margin between the gold standard HTER scores of 0 to 34.34 than the trend line *SVM(a+b) TL*[4]. The error margin for the former equation becomes greater than the latter starting from the HTER score of 34.34 (up to 100). The higher error margin on the high end of the scale can also be explained by the max. HTER predictions of the *SVM(b)* system (48.22). The additional features that are used in the *SVM(a+b)* system enable it to predict higher HTER values (max. 77.79), which seems to contribute to the higher correlation scores. Finally, we confirmed our observations from last year by showing that a sentence-level QE system, which uses a single feature based

---

[4]Based on Figure 1, solving the following equation for x gives us the gold standard HTER score, to which both equations are equidistant: $0 = -0.67x + 34 - 0.82x + 17$

on the word-level predictions of the best system, was able to beat the system trained on the baseline feature set. The performances of the sentence-level QE systems were further improved by combining this single feature with the baseline and the additional feature sets.

Acknowledgments

This research has been carried out in the framework of the SCATE[5] project funded by the Flemish government agency IWT.

References

John Blatz, Erin Fitzgerald, George Foster, Simona Gandrabur, Cyril Goutte, Alex Kulesza, Alberto Sanchis, and Nicola Ueffing. 2004. Confidence estimation for machine translation. In *Proceedings of the 20th international conference on Computational Linguistics*, page 315. Association for Computational Linguistics.

Ondrej Bojar, Rajen Chatterjeeand Christian Federmannand Barry Haddowand Matthias Huckand Chris Hokampand Philipp Koehnand Varvara Logachevaand Christof Monzand Matteo Negriand Matt Postand Carolina Scartonand Lucia Specia, and Marco Turchi. 2015. Findings of the 2015 workshop on statistical machine translation. In *Proceedings of the Tenth Workshop on Statistical Machine Translation*, pages 1–46.

Leo Breiman, Jerome Friedman, Charles J Stone, and Richard A Olshen. 1984. *Classification and regression trees*. CRC press.

Stanley F Chen and Joshua Goodman. 1996. An empirical study of smoothing techniques for language modeling. In *Proceedings of the 34th annual meeting on Association for Computational Linguistics*, pages 310–318. Association for Computational Linguistics.

Walter Daelemans, Jakub Zavrel, Kurt van der Sloot, and Antal Van den Bosch. 2004. Timbl: Tilburg memory-based learner. *Tilburg University*.

José GC de Souza, U Politecnica de Valencia, Christian Buck, Marco Turchi, and Matteo Negri. 2014. Fbk-upv-uedin participation in the wmt14 quality estimation shared-task. In *Proceedings of the Ninth Workshop on Statistical Machine Translation*, pages 322–328.

Marcello Federico, Nicola Bertoldi, and Mauro Cettolo. 2008. Irstlm: an open source toolkit for handling large scale language models. In *Interspeech*, pages 1618–1621.

Simona Gandrabur and George Foster. 2003. Confidence estimation for translation prediction. In *Proceedings of the seventh conference on Natural language learning at HLT-NAACL 2003-Volume 4*, pages 95–102. Association for Computational Linguistics.

Kenneth Heafield. 2011. Kenlm: Faster and smaller language model queries. In *Proceedings of the Sixth Workshop on Statistical Machine Translation*, pages 187–197. Association for Computational Linguistics.

Philipp Koehn, Hieu Hoang, Alexandra Birch, Chris Callison-Burch, Marcello Federico, Nicola Bertoldi, Brooke Cowan, Wade Shen, Christine Moran, Richard Zens, et al. 2007. Moses: Open source toolkit for statistical machine translation. In *Proceedings of the 45th annual meeting of the ACL on interactive poster and demonstration sessions*, pages 177–180. Association for Computational Linguistics.

Taku Kudo. 2005. Crf++: Yet another crf toolkit. *Software available at http://crfpp. sourceforge. net*.

Arle Lommel, Aljoscha Burchardt, Maja Popovic, Kim Harris, Eleftherios Avramidis, and Hans Uszkoreit. 2014. Using a new analytic measure for the annotation and analysis of mt errors on real data. *EAMT-2014*, pages 165–172.

Lieve Macken, Els Lefever, and Veronique Hoste. 2013. Texsis: bilingual terminology extraction from parallel corpora using chunk-based alignment. *Terminology*, 19(1):1–30.

Fabian Pedregosa, Gaël Varoquaux, Alexandre Gramfort, Vincent Michel, Bertrand Thirion, Olivier Grisel, Mathieu Blondel, Peter Prettenhofer, Ron Weiss, Vincent Dubourg, et al. 2011. Scikit-learn: Machine learning in python. *The Journal of Machine Learning Research*, 12:2825–2830.

Marcis Pinnis. 2015. Dynamic terminology integration methods in statistical machine translation. In *Proceedings of the Eighteenth Annual Conference of the European Association for Machine Translation (EAMT 2015)*.

Fabio Rinaldi, Michael Hess, James Dowdall, Diego Mollá Aliod, and Rolf Schwitter. 2004. Question answering in terminology-rich technical domains. In *New directions in question answering*, pages 71–86.

Helmut Schmid. 1995. Improvements in part-of-speech tagging with an application to german. In *In Proceedings of the ACL SIGDAT-Workshop*. Citeseer.

Alina Secară. 2005. Translation evaluation–a state of the art survey. In *Proceedings of the eCoLoRe/MeLLANGE Workshop, Leeds*, pages 39–44. Citeseer.

---

[5]http://www.ccl.kuleuven.be/scate

Matthew Snover, Bonnie Dorr, Richard Schwartz, Linnea Micciulla, and John Makhoul. 2006. A study of translation edit rate with targeted human annotation. In *Proceedings of association for machine translation in the Americas*, pages 223–231.

Arda Tezcan, Véronique Hoste, Bart Desmet, and Lieve Macken. 2015. Ugent-lt3 scate system for machine translation quality estimation. In *Tenth Workshop on Statistical Machine Translation*.

Jörg Tiedemann. 2012. Parallel data, tools and interfaces in opus. In *LREC*, pages 2214–2218.

John S White. 1995. Approaches to black box mt evaluation. In *Proceedings of Machine Translation Summit V*, page 10.